DICTIONARY

OF

THE UNITED STATES CONGRESS.

DICTIONARY

OF

THE UNITED STATES CONGRESS,

COMPILED AS

A MANUAL OF REFERENCE

FOR THE

LEGISLATOR AND STATESMAN.

BY

CHARLES LANMAN,

LATE LIBRARIAN HOUSE OF REPRESENTATIVES.

GOVERNMENT PRINTING OFFICE.

1864.

By resolutions of the Senate and House of Representatives of the United States, passed at the First Session of the Thirty-eighth Congress, fifteen hundred and fifty copies were ordered to be printed for the use of each of those bodies respectively; the copyright for those numbers having been duly assigned.

PREFACE.

Political laws, wisely framed, have made the United States powerful and wealthy to a degree unexampled in modern times; and I have thought that a book of facts, recording the public services of our National law-makers, from the foundation of the Government, would be a deserved tribute to them, and, at the same time, be generally useful. The record has been made in each case as correct and concise as possible. Of many men more might have been written, but that was not deemed expedient in a work of this kind; and where not enough has been said, the fault must be attributed to the indifference of the persons mostly interested, or to the neglect of their friends. Not being a politician, it has given me but little trouble to be impartial. My intention has been to express no opinions of living men, and but seldom to echo public opinion in regard to the dead. My leading object has been to prepare a kind of labor-saving machine, for the benefit of all who feel an interest in the political history and future prosperity of the Republic; and, in the Appendix, I have endeavored to bring together, from the Government archives, a mass of Legislative and Executive information, calculated to be of service to Members of Congress, while engaged in their public duties, and especially in their examination of the Public Documents.

Washington, January, 1864.

CONTENTS.

	PAGE
Senators and Representatives, with Biographical Data,	9–413
Successive Sessions of Congress, ...	417
Speakers of the House of Representatives, ...	419
Presidents of the Senate, ...	419
Secretaries of the Senate, ...	421
Clerks of the House of Representatives, ...	421
Chaplains to Congress, ...	422
Successive Administrations, ...	423
Presidential Electors, ...	427
The Supreme Court, ...	474
Ministers to Foreign Countries, ...	478
The Declaration of Independence, ...	499
Members of the Continental Congress, ...	505
Presidents of the Continental Congress, ...	509
Sessions of the Continental Congress, ...	509
The Constitution of the United States, ...	510
Organization of the Executive Departments, ...	522
The States and Territories of the American Union, . .	530
Origin of the Names of States, ...	536
Progress of Population in the United States, . . .	537
Population and Ratio of Representation, ...	538
The State and Territorial Governors, ...	540
Right of Suffrage in the Several States, ...	549
Qualifications for Governors, Senators, and Representatives, ...	552

BIOGRAPHICAL SKETCHES.

Abbott, Amos.—Born at Andover, Massachusetts, September 10, 1786. He was educated at a district school, but spent the most of his life as a trader and merchant. During the years 1835, 1836, and 1842, he was a Representative in the Massachusetts Legislature; and from 1840 to 1842 a member of the State Senate. He represented his native State in Congress from 1843 to 1849, and was a member of the Committees on the Militia, and on Manufactures.

Abbott, Joel.—Was born in Fairfield, Connecticut, emigrated to Georgia, and was elected a Representative in Congress, from Wilkes County, in that State, from 1817 to 1825, serving as a member of the Committees on Commerce and the Slave-Trade. Died November 19, 1826.

Abbott, Nehemiah.—Born in Sidney, Maine, March 29, 1806. He is a lawyer by profession; was a member of the House of Representatives, in the Maine Legislature, in 1842 and 1843, and was elected to the Thirty-fifth Congress, serving as a member of the Committee on Revolutionary Pensions.

Abercrombie, James.—He was born in Georgia, and, removing to Alabama, was a Representative in Congress, from that State, from 1851 to 1855.

Adair, John.—He was born in 1758; was a Senator of the United States, from Kentucky, during the years 1805 and 1806; commanded the Kentucky troops at the battle of New Orleans, under General Jackson; and was appointed a general in the army. He was elected a Representative in Congress, from Kentucky, from 1831 to 1833, and was a member of the Committee on Military Affairs. He died at Harrodsburg, May 19, 1840.

Adams, Benjamin.—Born at Worcester, Massachusetts; was a member of the Legislature, as Representative, from 1809 to 1814, and as Senator, in 1814 and 1815; and from 1822 to 1825; and was a Representative in Congress from his native State, from 1816 to 1821, and was a member of the Committees on Revolutionary Pensions and Public Expenditures. He died at Uxbridge, Massachusetts, in April, 1837.

Adams, Charles F.—Born in Boston, August 18, 1807; spent the most of his boyhood in St. Petersburg and London, whilst his father was Minister to Russia and England; he graduated at Harvard University in 1825; studied law, and was admitted to the bar in 1828; served three years in the Lower House, and two years in the Upper House of the Massachusetts Legislature; in 1848 he was the candidate for Vice-President on the ticket with Mr. Van Buren; and he was elected a Representative from Massachusetts to the Thirty-sixth Congress, serving as Chairman of the Committee on Manufactures. He was at one time the editor of a paper called the "Boston Whig," has been a contributor to the North American Review, was the editor of the well-known Adams Letters, and is the author of the standard Biography of John Adams. Re-elected to the Thirty-seventh Congress, but was appointed by President Lincoln Minister to England in 1861. In 1864 the degree of LL.D. was conferred upon him by Harvard University.

Adams, Green.—Born in Barboursville, Knox County, Kentucky, August 20, 1812; was bred a farmer, but read law and adopted that profession; in 1832 and 1833 he was Deputy Sheriff of Knox County; in 1839, he was elected to the State Legislature, and re-elected; he was a Representative in Congress, from Kentucky, from 1847 to 1849, and was a member of the Committee on Engraving. He was also a Presidential Elector in 1844 and 1856, and a Judge of the Circuit Court of Kentucky from 1851 to 1856. In 1859 he was elected a Representative from Kentucky to the Thirty-sixth Congress, serving on the Committee on Post-offices and Post-roads. In 1861 he was appointed by President Lincoln Sixth Auditor of the Treasury.

Adams, John.—Born at Braintree, Massachusetts, October 30, 1735; graduated at Harvard University in 1755; instructed a class of scholars in Latin and Greek for a subsistence; studied law, and having been admitted to the bar, settled at Quincy to practise his profession. As a member of the Old Congress, he was among the foremost in recommending an independent Government. In 1777, he was chosen Commissioner to the Court of Versailles. On his return he was chosen a member of the Convention called to prepare a form of government for Massachusetts. In September, 1779, he was appointed Minister Plenipotentiary to negotiate a peace, and had authority to form a commercial treaty with Great Britain. In June, 1780, he was appointed Ambassador to Holland; and, in 1782, he went to Paris to engage in the negotiation for peace, having previously obtained assurance that Great Britain would recognize the independence of the United States. After serving on two or three commissions to form treaties of amity and commerce with foreign powers, in 1785 he was appointed first Minister to London; and, in 1788, having been absent nine years, he returned to America. In March, 1789, the new Constitution of the United States went into operation, and he became the first Vice-President, which office he held during the whole of Washington's administration. On the resignation of Washington, he became, March 4, 1797, President of the United States. This was the termination of his public functions; and he spent the remainder of his days upon his farm in Quincy, occupying himself with agriculture, and obtaining amusement from the literature and politics of the day. He died on the fourth of July, 1826, with the same words on his lips which, fifty years before, on that day, he had uttered on the floor of Congress: "Independence forever!" His principal publications are, "Letters on the American Revolution," "Defence of the American Constitution," an "Essay on Canon and Federal Laws," a series of letters under the signature of Novanglus, and Discourses on Davila. It was as Vice-President that he had a seat in the Senate.

Adams, John.—He was a Representative in Congress, from Greene County, New York, from 1833 to 1835, and was a member of the Committee on Invalid Pensions. He died at Catskill, New York, September 28, 1854.

Adams, John Quincy.—Born in Braintree, now Quincy, Mass., July 11, 1767. When ten years of age, he accompanied his father to France; and when fifteen, was private secretary to the American Minister in Russia. He was graduated at Harvard University in 1787; studied law in Newburyport, and settled in Boston. From 1794 to 1801 he was American Minister to Holland, England, Sweden, and Prussia. He was a Senator in Congress from 1803 to 1808; Professor of Rhetoric in Harvard University, with limited duties, from 1806 to 1808; was appointed, in 1809, Minister to Russia; assisted in negotiating the Treaty of Ghent, in 1814; and assisted, also, as Minister, at the Convention of Commerce with Great Britain, in 1815. He was Secretary of State under President Monroe; and was chosen President of the United States in 1825, serving one term. In 1831 he was elected a Representative in Congress, and continued in that position until his death, which occurred in the Speaker's room, two days after falling from his seat in the House of Representatives, February 23, 1848. His last words were: "This is the end of earth; I am content." He published "Letters on Silesia," "Lectures on Rhetoric and Oratory," and various "Poems," besides many occasional letters and speeches. His unpublished writings, it is said, would make many volumes.

Adams, Parmenio.—He was born in Hartford, Connecticut, and was a Representative in Congress from Batavia, Genesee County, New York, from 1823 to 1827.

Adams, Robert H.—He was a Senator in Congress, by appointment, from Mississippi, from January to May, in 1830, and died on the second day of July following.

Adams, Stephen.—He was a native of Franklin County, Pennsylvania, and had been a member of the Senate of that State. Removing to Mississippi, he took an active part in public affairs; was a member of the State Legislature, and a Representative in Congress, from 1845 to 1847; he was elected Judge of the Circuit Court, and from 1852 to 1857 was a Senator in Congress from Mississippi. He removed to Tennessee with the intention of practising law at Memphis, where he died, May 11, 1857.

Addams, William.—He was born in Lancaster County, Pennsylvania; was a Representative in Congress from Pennsylvania from 1825 to 1829, and served on a Committee for the Deaf and Dumb Institutions of New York and Ohio.

Adgate, Asa.—He was a Representative in the Legislature of New York from Clinton County, from 1798 to 1799, and elected Representative in Congress from Essex County, in that State, from 1815 to 1817, and was again a member of the Legislature in 1823.

Adrain, Garnett B.—Born in the city of New York December 20, 1816. He graduated at Rutgers College, New Jersey, in 1833; studied law, and was admitted to the bar in 1837; and was a Representative in the Thirty-fifth Congress from New Jersey, serving as Chairman of the Committee on Engraving. He was also elected a member of the Thirty-sixth Congress, serving as Chairman of the Committee on Engraving. In January, 1861, he offered the resolution of thanks to Major Robert Anderson for his defence of Fort Sumter. Since he left Congress he has been devoted to his profession.

Ahl, John A.—He was born in Stansbury, Franklin County, Pennsylvània, in August, 1815; received a good English education; studied medicine with his father, and graduated at the "Washington Medical College" of Baltimore. He abandoned his profession in 1850, and turned his attention to various kinds of manufactures, and was elected a Representative from Pennsylvania to the Thirty-fifth Congress, serving as a member of the Committee on Manufactures.

Aiken, William.—He was born in Charleston, South Carolina, in 1806; graduated at the South Carolina College in 1825; was a member of the State Legislature in 1838, 1840, and 1842; was Governor of South Carolina in 1844; and a Representative in Congress from that State from 1851 to 1857. He was considered one of the most successful rice planters in his native State.

Albertson, Nathaniel.—He was born in Virginia, and was elected a Representative in Congress from the First Congressional District of Indiana, from 1849 to 1851, and was a member of the Committee on Public Lands.

Albright, Charles J.—He was born in Pennsylvania, and was elected from the State of Ohio a Representative to the Thirty-fourth Congress.

Aldrich, Cyrus.—Born in Smithfield, Rhode Island, in June, 1808; received a common school education; has followed the various occupations of a sailor, a boatman, a farmer, a contractor on public works, and a mail contractor; was a member of the Illinois Legislature; also a Register of Deeds and Register of the Land Office at Dixon in that State for four years; and, having removed to Minnesota, was a member of the Constitutional Convention of that State; member of the County Board of Hampshire County in that State; and was elected a Representative from Minnesota to the Thirty-sixth Congress, serving as a member of the Committee on Agriculture. Re-elected to the Thirty-seventh Congress, and was Chairman of the Committee on Indian

Affairs. After leaving Congress he was appointed by President Lincoln a commissioner to settle claims against the Sioux Indians.

Alexander, Adam R.—He was born in Washington County, Virginia, and was elected a Representative in Congress from Madison County, Tennessee, from 1823 to 1827, and served as a member of the Committee on Post-offices and Post-roads.

Alexander, Evan.--Born in North Carolina; was a member of the Legislature for two years; and a Representative in Congress from North Carolina, from 1805 to 1809. Died October 28, 1809.

Alexander, Henry P.—He was born in New York, and was a Representative in Congress from Herkimer County, in that State, from 1849 to 1851, and was a member of the Committee on Expenditures in the State Department.

Alexander, James, Jr.—He was born in Maryland; was a resident of St. Clairsville, Belmont County, Ohio, and elected a Representative in Congress from the Eleventh District in that State, from 1837 to 1839, and was a member of the Committee on Public Expenditures. Died August 6, 1846.

Alexander, John.—He was elected a Representative in Congress from Ohio, May 4, 1813, serving till 1817.

Alexander, Mark.—He was born in Mecklenburg County, Virginia, and elected a Representative in Congress from that State, from 1819 to 1833, and served on the Committees on Revolutionary Pensions, Ways and Means, and Expenditures in the State Department, and the District of Columbia.

Alexander, Nathaniel.--Graduated at Princeton College in 1776, and, after studying medicine, entered the army. At the close of the war he resided at the High Hills of Santee, pursuing his profession, and afterwards at Mecklenburg. While he held a seat in Congress, from 1803 to 1805, the Legislature elected him Governor for 1806. He died at Salisbury, March 8, 1808, aged fifty-two. In all his public stations he is said to have discharged his duty with ability and firmness.

Alford, Julius C.—He was born in Georgia, and was elected a Representative in Congress from Troup County, in that State, from 1839 to 1842, and served as a member of the Committee on Indian Affairs.

Allen, Charles.—He was born in Worcester, Massachusetts, August 9, 1797, and was a Representative in Congress from that State from 1849 to 1853, and a member of the Committee on the District of Columbia. He was also a member of the State Legislature in 1829, 1833, 1834, 1838 and 1840; and a State Senator in 1835, 1838 and 1839; Judge of the Court of Common Pleas from 1842 to 1844; Chief Justice of the Superior Court from 1858 to 1859; member of the State Constitutional Conventions of 1848, 1853 and 1859; and a commissioner to negotiate the Webster Treaty in 1842. He was also a delegate to the Peace Congress of 1861.

Allen, Chilton.—He was born in Albemarle County, Virginia, April 6, 1786, and settled in Kentucky as a wheelwright. He educated himself for the legal profession; from Clark County was elected in 1811 to the Legislature of Kentucky for several terms; and he was a Representative in Congress from that State from 1831 to 1837, officiating as Chairman of the Committee of Territories, and a member of the Committee on Foreign Affairs. In 1838 he was President of the Board of Internal Improvement; and in 1842 he was again returned to the State Legislature, which was the last public position he occupied. He died at Winchester, September 3, 1858. He was a man of ability and of rare virtues.

Allen, Elisha H.—Born in New Salem, Massachusetts, January 28, 1804; was bred a lawyer; served in the Legislature of Maine from 1836 to 1841, and in 1846; in 1838 as Speaker; and was elected a Representative in Congress from Maine, from 1841 to 1843, serving as a member of the Committee on Manufactures. In 1847 he removed to Boston, and was elected to the Massachusetts Legislature in 1849; after which he was appointed Consul to Honolulu, and has since that time been connected with the Government of the Sandwich Islands. In 1856 he visited the United States as Envoy; and in 1857 was Chief Justice and Chancellor of the Sandwich Islands, serving until 1864.

Allen, Heman.—He was born in 1776; was a resident, if not a native, of Milton, Vermont; adopted the profession of law, in which he became distinguished; and was a Representative in Congress from Vermont, from 1827 to 1829, and again from 1833 to 1839, serving as an active member of the Committee on Claims. He subsequently settled in Burlington, Vermont, where he died December 11, 1844.

Allen, Heman.—He was born in 1779, and a resident of Colchester, Vermont; he graduated at Dartmouth College in 1795, and adopted the profession of law. He was Sheriff of Chittenden County in 1808 and 1809; from 1811 to 1814 he was Chief Justice of the Chittenden County Court; from 1812 to 1817 he was an active member of the State Legislature; was appointed quartermaster of militia, with the title of brigadier; and was a trustee of the University of Vermont. He was first elected a Representative in Congress from Vermont in 1817, but resigned in 1818 to accept from President Monroe the appointment of United States Marshal for the District of Vermont. In 1823 he received from the same President the appointment of Minister to Chili, which he resigned in 1828; in 1830 he was appointed President of the United States Branch Bank, at Burlington, which he held until the expiration of its charter, after which he settled in the town of Highgate, Vermont, where he died of heart disease, April 9, 1852.

Allen, James C.—He was born in Shelby County, Kentucky, January 28, 1823; received a good common school education, studied law, and was admitted to the bar in Indiana in 1843; in 1846 was elected, for two years, Prosecuting Attorney in the Seventh Judicial District of Indiana; and, having removed to Illinois in 1848, was elected a member, in 1850 and 1851, of the State Legislature, and was chosen a Representative in Congress from Illinois, from 1853 to 1855, and re-elected to the Thirty-fourth Congress. He was chosen Clerk of the House of Representatives for the Thirty-fifth Congress, and in 1862 he was re-elected to the Thirty-eighth Congress as a Representative, serving on the Committees of Indian Affairs and Unfinished Business.

Allen, John.—Born in Great Barrington, Massachusetts, in 1763; was a lawyer by profession, and a member of the State Council of Connecticut for several years; was a Representative from that State during the last Congress which was held in Philadelphia, from 1797 to 1799. He died at Litchfield, Connecticut, July 31, 1812.

Allen, John J.—He was born in Virginia, was a resident of Harrison County, and was elected a Representative in Congress, from Virginia, from 1833 to 1835, and served as a member of the Committee on the District of Columbia. He subsequently held the office of Chief Justice of the Supreme Court of Virginia.

Allen, John W.—Born in Litchfield, Connecticut, in 1802; settled in Cleveland, Ohio, in 1825, and was a member of the Senate of that State from 1835 to 1837, also Mayor of Cleveland; and was elected a Representative in Congress from 1837 to 1841, serving as a member of the Committee on the Militia and Military Affairs.

Allen, Joseph.—He was born in Boston; was a merchant in Leicester, and benefactor of the Academy there; twice Elector for President; was a Clerk of the County Court and a State Councillor; and a Representative in Congress, from Massachusetts, from 1811 to 1813. He died at Worcester, September 2, 1827, aged seventy-eight years.

Allen, Judson.—He was born in Connecticut, and removing to New York was elected a Representative in Congress, from that State, from 1839 to 1841, and was a member of the Committee on Mileage.

Allen, Nathaniel.—He was born in Dutchess County, New York; served in the Assembly of that State in 1812, and was a Representative in Congress, from 1819 to 1821, and a member of the Committee on Manufactures.

Allen, Philip.—He was born in

Providence, Rhode Island, September 1, 1785; graduated at Brown University in 1803; was elected to the State Legislature in 1819, 1820, and 1821; devoted much attention to the business of manufacturing; was Governor of Rhode Island during the years 1851, 1852, and 1853; and was elected a Senator in Congress, from his native State, from March 3, 1853, serving as a member of the Committees on Commerce and on Naval Affairs.

Allen, Robert.—Born in Augusta County, Virginia. He was a colonel in the army under General Jackson, a Representative in Congress, from Tennessee, from 1819 to 1827, serving as a member of the Committees on Commerce, the Library, and Revolutionary Claims. He died at Carthage, Tennessee, August 19, 1844, aged sixty-seven years.

Allen, Robert.—Born in Woodstock, Shenandoah County, Virginia, July 30, 1794. He was educated at Dickinson and Washington colleges, having left the latter institution on a furlough of three months, for the purpose of joining a volunteer military force in 1813, but returned and graduated. He studied law, and practised in his native place. He held for a time the office of Prosecutor for the Commonwealth; served five years in the Senate of Virginia, and was a Representative in Congress, from that State, from 1827 to 1833, serving on the Committee for the District of Columbia.

Allen, Samuel C.—Born in Franklin County, Massachusetts; graduated at Dartmouth College in 1794; was a Representative in the Massachusetts Legislature from 1806 to 1810; a State Senator from 1812 to 1815, and in 1831; and a member of the Executive Council in 1829 and 1830; was a Representative in Congress, from Massachusetts, from 1817 to 1829, officiating as Chairman of the Committee on Accounts. He died at Northfield, February 8, 1842, aged seventy years.

Allen, William.—He was born in Ohio, adopted the profession of law, and was a Representative in Congress, from Ross County, Ohio, from 1833 to 1835, serving as a member of the Committee on Indian Affairs; was elected a Senator in Congress, from 1837 to 1849, serving as a member of several important committees in the Senate, during his first term.

Allen, William.—Born in Butler County, Ohio, August 13, 1827; received a good English education, and taught school for a time; studied law, and was admitted to the bar in 1849; in 1850 he was elected a County Prosecuting Attorney, and re-elected in 1852; and in 1858 was elected a Representative, from Ohio, to the Thirty-sixth Congress, serving on the Committee on Accounts. Re-elected to the Thirty-seventh Congress, serving as Chairman of Committee on Interior Department. Was a delegate to the Chicago Convention in 1864.

Allen, William J.—He was born in Tennessee in 1828; removed with his father to Illinois in 1829; studied law, and was admitted to the bar in 1848; in 1854 he was elected to the Illinois Legislature; in 1855 was appointed United States Attorney for the District of Illinois, which he resigned in 1860, and was then elected Judge of the Circuit Court. In 1862 he was elected a Representative, from Illinois, to the Thirty-seventh Congress, for the unexpired term of John S. Logan, resigned, and was re-elected to the Thirty-eighth Congress, serving on the Committee of Claims.

Allen, Willis.—He was born in Tennessee, and was a Representative in Congress, from Illinois, from 1851 to 1855.

Alley, John B.—Born in Lynn, Massachusetts, January 7, 1817; received a good common school education; was apprenticed to a shoemaker, and received his freedom when nineteen years of age, after which he devoted himself to trading; he subsequently entered largely into the shoe and leather business, which he has since followed; he served several years in the City Councils of Lynn; was a member of the Governor's Council in 1851; a member of the Massachusetts Senate in 1852; of the State Constitutional Convention held in 1853, and in 1858 was elected a Representative from Massachusetts to the Thirty-sixth Congress, serving on the Committee on Post-offices and Post-roads. Re-elected to the Thirty-seventh and also to the Thirty-eighth Congress, serving as Chairman of the Committee on Post-offices and Post-roads.

Allison, James.—He was elected a Representative in Congress, from Beaver County, Pennsylvania, from 1823 to 1825.

Allison, John.—He was born in Pennsylvania, and was a Representative in Congress, from that State, from 1851 to 1853, and was re-elected to the Thirty-fourth Congress.

Allison, Robert.—He was born in Pennsylvania, and was a Representative in Congress, from Pennsylvania, from 1831 to 1833.

Allison, William B.—He was born in the Township of Perry, Wayne County, Ohio, March 2, 1829; spent the most of his boyhood on a farm; was educated chiefly at Alleghany College, Pennsylvania, and at the Western Reserve College, Ohio; studied law, came to the bar in 1851, and practised the profession in Ohio until 1857, when he settled in Dubuque, Iowa. He was a delegate to the Chicago Convention of 1860; in 1861 he was a member of the Governor's staff, and rendered essential service in raising troops for the war; and in 1862 he was elected a Representative from Iowa to the Thirty-eighth Congress, serving on the Committees on Public Lands, and Roads and Canals.

Alston, Lemuel J.—He was a Representative in Congress, from South Carolina, from 1807 to 1811.

Alston, William J.—He was born in Georgia, and removing to Alabama, was a Representative in Congress, from that State, from 1849 to 1851, and was a member of the Committee on Post-offices and Post-roads.

Alston, Willis.—Born in Halifax County, North Carolina. He appeared in public life as early as 1794, serving in the State Legislature for several years, and was a Representative in Congress, from 1799 to 1803. Died, April 10, 1837.

Alston, Willis, Jr.—Born in North Carolina, and was a Representative in Congress, from that State, from 1803 to 1815, and from 1825 to 1831. During the war of 1812 he was Chairman of the Committee of Ways and Means.

Alvord, C.—He was a native of Massachusetts; received a liberal education; adopted the profession of law; served one term in each branch of the State Legislature; and was elected a Representative from Massachusetts to the Twenty-sixth Congress, but died before taking his seat, in the latter part of 1839.

Ames, Fisher.—He was born in Dedham, Massachusetts, April 9, 1756, and died July 4, 1808. He entered Harvard University at the age of twelve years, and graduated with honor; and having studied law, commenced the practice of his profession, in his native town, in 1781. He was acknowledged to be the most eloquent debater in the House of Representatives, and was the author of the "Address" of that body, to Washington, on his retirement from the Presidency. He was a prominent member of the Massachusetts Convention for ratifying the Constitution, in 1788, and after retiring from political life, having served in Congress for eight years, he was elected President of Harvard University, but declined the honor. He was an industrious writer as well as a great orator; and his collected writings, with a memoir, were published in 1809.

Ames, Oakes.—He was born in Easton, Bristol County, Massachusetts, January 10, 1804; has ever been a manufacturer by profession; was a member, for two years, of the Executive Council of the State, and in 1862 he was elected a Representative from Massachusetts to the Thirty-eighth Congress, serving on the Committees on Revolutionary Claims, and Manufactures.

Ancona, Sydenham E.—He was born in Warwick, Lancaster County, Pennsylvania, November 20, 1824, and was elected in 1860 a Representative from Pennsylvania to the Thirty-seventh Congress, serving on the Committees on the Militia and on Manufactures. In 1862 he was re-elected to the Thirty-eighth Congress, serving as a member of the Committees on Manufactures, and on the Militia.

Anderson, Alexander.—He was a Senator in Congress, from the Knoxville District, Tennessee, during the years 1840 and 1841, a part of a term, and served as a member of the Committee on the Militia.

Anderson, Hugh J.—Born in 1801, in Maine, and was Clerk of the Waldo County Courts from 1827 to 1837, and a Representative in Congress, from Maine, from 1837 to 1841, and a member of the Committee on Naval Affairs. He was a lawyer by profession; Governor of Maine from 1844 to 1847; and Commissioner of Customs in Washington, from 1853 to 1858.

Anderson, Isaac.—He was a Representative in Congress, from Pennsylvania, from 1803 to 1807.

Anderson, John.—He was born in Cumberland, Maine; was a graduate of Bowdoin College in 1813; studied law and admitted to the bar in 1816; a member of the Maine Senate in 1824, and was elected a Representative in Congress, from Cumberland County, Maine, from 1825 to 1833, serving as a member of the Committees on Elections and Naval Affairs. He was also Mayor of Portland in 1833 and 1842; United States District Attorney from 1833 to 1837; and Collector of Customs at Portland from 1837 to 1841, and from 1843 to 1848. He died August 21, 1853, aged sixty-one years.

Anderson, Joseph.—He was born near Philadelphia, Pennsylvania, November 5, 1757; enjoyed what was called at the time a good education; studied law; was appointed an ensign in the New Jersey line in 1775; was promoted to an adjutancy; as a captain, fought at the battle of Monmouth; he also went, in 1779, with Sullivan against the Six Nations; in 1780 he was at Valley Forge; in 1781 at the siege of York; and after the war he retired with the rank of brevet-major. He practised law in Delaware for seven years. In 1791 was appointed by Washington Judge of the territory south of the Ohio River; remained in that position until the first Constitution of Tennessee was formed, which he aided in forming in convention; and he was an influential member of the United States Senate, from Tennessee, from 1797 to 1815, serving at all times upon important committees, and acting on two occasions as President *pro tempore* of the Senate. He was appointed in 1815 First Comptroller of the Treasury, where he remained until 1836. He died in Washington, April 17, 1837.

Anderson, Joseph H.—He was born in New York, and was elected a Representative in Congress from that State from 1843 to 1847, and was Chairman of the Committee on Agriculture, and a member of the Committee on Expenditures in the Treasury Department.

Anderson, Josiah M.—He was born in Tennessee, and was elected a Representative in Congress from the Third District in that State, from 1849 to 1852, and was a member of the Committee on Private Land Claims. He was also a Delegate to the Peace Congress of 1861.

Anderson, J. P.—He was born in Tennessee, and was elected a Delegate to the Thirty-fourth Congress from the Territory of Washington.

Anderson, Lucien.—Was born in Mayfield, Kentucky, in June, 1824; received a good English education; adopted the profession of law; and served for two terms as a member of the Kentucky Legislature. In 1863 he was elected a Representative from Kentucky to the Thirty-eighth Congress, serving as a member of the Committee on the District of Columbia. During the month of November, 1863, he was taken prisoner by a party of "Confederates," and retained in custody until just before the meeting of Congress, when he was exchanged. He was a Delegate to the Baltimore Convention of 1864, and a Presidential Elector in 1853.

Anderson, Richard C., Jr.—Born in Jefferson County, Kentucky; was elected a Representative in Congress from Kentucky, from 1817 to 1821, and was Chairman of the Committee on Public Lands during the Sixteenth Congress. In 1823 he was appointed Minister Plenipotentiary to Colombia, and in 1826 Envoy Extraordinary to Panama; but died November 6, 1826.

Anderson, Samuel.—Born in 1774, in Pennsylvania. He served repeatedly in the Legislature of that State; was Speaker of its House in 1848 and 1849; and elected a Representative in Congress, from 1827 to 1829, and was a member of the Committee on the Boundary-Line of Missouri. He died in Chester, Pennsylvania, January 17, 1850.

Anderson, Simeon H.—Born in Garrard County, Kentucky, March 2, 1832; studied law and practised with success; served frequently in the Kentucky Legislature; was elected a Representative in Congress from the Fifth Congressional District of Kentucky, from 1839 to 1841, and served as a member of the Committee on Post-offices and Post-roads. He died at his residence near Lancaster, Kentucky, August 11, 1840, before the expiration of his term of service. He had the reputation of being a remarkably industrious, useful, and amiable man.

Anderson, Thomas S.—Born in Greene County, Kentucky, December 8, 1808. He was self-educated, and removed to Missouri in 1830, where he commenced the practice of law at twenty-one years of age. He was elected to the Legislature of that State in 1840; was a Presidential Elector in 1844, 1848, 1852, and 1856; and a member of the Convention for remodelling the State Constitution in 1845, and was elected a Representative to the Thirty-fifth Congress, serving as a member of the Committee on Invalid Pensions. He was reelected to the Thirty-sixth Congress, serving on the Committee on Private Land Claims.

Anderson, William.—Born in Chester County, Pennsylvania, in 1763, and served throughout the Revolutionary War with credit, taking a prominent part at the siege of Yorktown. After the war he returned to Delaware County, Pennsylvania, and was a Representative in Congress, from that State, from 1809 to 1815, and from 1817 to 1819. He was afterwards a Judge of Delaware County Court, and a Custom-house officer at Chester, in that county, where he died, December 13, 1829.

Anderson, William C.—Born in Lancaster, Garrard County, Kentucky, December 6, 1826; educated at the College of Danville; adopted the profession of law; served in the Kentucky Legislature in 1851 and 1853; was a Presidential Elector in 1856; and in 1859 was elected a Representative, from Kentucky, to the Thirty-sixth Congress, serving as a member of the Committee on the District of Columbia. Died at Frankfort, Kentucky, December 23, 1861.

Andrews, Charles.—Born in Paris, Maine, in 1814; studied law, and was admitted to the bar in 1837; was a member of the State Legislature from 1839 to 1843, a portion of the time Speaker of the House; and a Representative in Congress, from Maine, from 1851 to the time of his death, which occurred in Paris, April 30, 1852.

Andrews, George R.—He was born in New York, and was a Representative in Congress, from the Fourteenth Congressional District in that State, from 1849 to 1851, and was a member of the Committee on Elections.

Andrews, John T.—He was born in New York, and was elected a Representative in Congress, from that State, from 1837 to 1839, serving as a member of the Committee on Expenditures in the State Department.

Andrews, Landaff W.—Born in Fleming County, Kentucky, February 12, 1803; graduated at Transylvania University in 1824; and commenced the practice of law in 1826, in which profession he has since been actively engaged. He was a member of the Kentucky Legislature in 1834, and in 1838 was elected a Representative in Congress, serving from 1839 to 1843, and acted on the Committees on Revolutionary Pensions and Accounts. He was also a member of the Kentucky Senate.

Andrews, Samuel G.—He was born in Derby, New Haven County, Connecticut, October 16, 1799; received an academical education, and removed with his father to Rochester, New York, in 1816. He was occupied chiefly in mercantile and manufacturing pursuits; was for several years Mayor of Rochester; was a member of the New York Legislature in 1831 and 1832, from Monroe County, New York; Clerk of the Monroe County Court; Secretary of the

State Senate of New York for four years; Clerk of the Court of Dernier Resort for four years; and was Postmaster of Rochester. He was elected a Representative, from New York, to the Thirty-fifth Congress, serving as a member of the Committee on Roads and Canals. Died in Rochester, New York, in 1863.

Andrews, Sherlock J.—Born in Wallingford, Connecticut, in 1801; graduated at Union College; settled in Cleveland, Ohio, in 1825, and practised law; was Judge of the Superior Court of that State, and elected a Representative in Congress, from 1841 to 1843, and was a member of the Committee on Commerce.

Angel, William G.—He was a native of Newshoreham, Rhode Island; was elected a Representative in Congress, from Burlington, Otsego County, New York, from 1825 to 1827, and again from 1829 to 1833, and was a member of the Committees on Indian Affairs, and on Territories.

Anthony, Henry B.—He was born in Coventry, Rhode Island, April 1, 1815, of Quaker ancestry; graduated at Brown University in 1833; and in 1838 he assumed the editorial charge of the Providence Journal, which he retained until called to a seat in the United States Senate. He was elected Governor of Rhode Island in 1849, re-elected in 1850, and declined a re-election; was elected a Senator in Congress, from Rhode Island, for the term commencing in 1859, serving as Chairman of the Committee on Printing; and in 1864 was re-elected for the long term, ending in 1871.

Anthony, Joseph B.—Born in Pennsylvania; was elected a Representative in Congress, from that State, from 1833 to 1837, serving as a member of the Committees on Territories and Military Affairs. He died at Williamsport, Pennsylvania, January 17, 1851.

Appleton, John.—Born in Beverly, Massachusetts, February 11, 1815; graduated at Bowdoin College, Maine, in 1834; was admitted to practise law at Portland, Maine, in 1837. In the winter of 1838–39 he became editor of a Democratic newspaper in that city (The Eastern Argus), and continued to be its editor for the next four or five years, during a part of which time he was also Register of Probate for the County of Cumberland. In 1845 he accepted an invitation from Mr. Bancroft, the Secretary of the Navy, to become Chief Clerk of the Navy Department; subsequently he succeeded Mr. Trist as Chief Clerk of the State Department, which was then presided over by Mr. Buchanan. In 1848 he was appointed, by President Polk, Chargé d'Affaires of the United States to Bolivia. On his return from that mission, which he resigned after the election of General Taylor, he resumed the practice of law at Portland, in partnership with Nathan Clifford, now one of the judges of the Supreme Court of the United States; but soon afterwards, in September, 1850, he was elected, from the Portland District, a member of the Thirty-second Congress. In 1855 he joined Mr. Buchanan, at London, as Secretary of Legation, but returned home in time for the Presidential canvass of 1856. In 1857, having been obliged from ill health to decline the position to which he had been invited, of editor of the "Washington Union," he was appointed, by President Buchanan, Assistant Secretary of State. In May, 1860, he was appointed Minister to Russia. He died, in Portland, Maine, August 22, 1864.

Appleton, Nathan.—Born at New Ipswich, New Hampshire, October 6, 1779. He entered Dartmouth College in 1794, but left his studies there, after being invited by his brother to join him in the mercantile business in Boston. He became interested in the cotton manufacture, and in 1821 was one of the three original founders of Lowell. He was at different periods a member of the Legislature of Massachusetts, and from 1831 to 1833, and again in 1842, was elected a Representative of that State in Congress; but soon resigned his seat, and has since taken no part in public affairs. He has published pamphlets and essays on Currency, Banking, and the Tariff. He died in Boston, July 14, 1861.

Appleton, William.—Born in Brookfield, Massachusetts, November, 1786, and was educated for mercantile pursuits, in which he has been engaged extensively and successfully for more than fifty years. He has taken a prominent part in various public enterprises and benevolent objects; given much attention to banking and financial operations, and was for some years, and until the close of the institution, President of the Branch Bank of the United States in Boston. In 1850 he was elected a Representative in Congress, from Massachusetts, and re-elected in 1852. He was also elected to the Thirty-seventh Congress, but died in February, 1862, in Boston.

Archer, John.—He was born in Harford County, Maryland, in 1741, and graduated at Nassau Hall in 1760. He studied divinity, but on account of a throat affection, turned his attention to medicine, and went through a course of study at the Philadelphia Medical College, having received the first medical diploma ever issued in the New World. At the commencement of the Revolution, he had command of a military company; was a member of the State Legislature; and after the war he practised his profession; he was a Representative in Congress from Maryland, from 1801 to 1807; and died in 1810. As a medical man he commanded great influence, and several discoveries were made by him, which have been adopted by the profession.

Archer, Stephenson.—He was born in Harford County, Maryland, and elected a Representative in Congress, from that State, from 1811 to 1817, when he was appointed Judge of Mississippi Territory. He was chosen a Representative in Congress again, from 1819 to 1821, and was a member of the Committee on Foreign Affairs.

Archer, William S.—Born in Amelia County, Virginia, March 5, 1789. He came of a Welsh family, a number of whom acquitted themselves with honor in the revolutionary war. He obtained the rudiments of his education at the best grammar schools of the day; graduated at the College of William and Mary; and studied law. In 1812 he was elected to the State Legislature, where he served, excepting one year, until 1819. In 1820 he was elected a Representative in Congress from Virginia, where he remained until 1835, taking an active part in all matters of national importance, and exerting a paramount influence, especially as Chairman of the Committee on Foreign Relations, and member of the Committee on the Missouri Compromise. In 1841 he was elected to the United States Senate, where he remained until 1847, having, from the start, been placed at the head of the Committee on Foreign Relations in that body. By his public acts, he commanded the respect of the country; and by the charms of his private character, won the friendship of many of the leading men of his day. On his retirement from public life, he devoted himself to the improvement of his paternal estate; and died March 28, 1855, of neuralgia, with which he had been afflicted for twenty years.

Armstrong, James.—A native of Pennsylvania; distinguished himself in the Indian wars, and was consulted by the proprietors of Pennsylvania on all matters connected with Indian affairs. In 1776, Congress promoted him from the rank of colonel to that of brigadier-general, and he assisted in the defence of Fort Moultrie, and in the battle of Germantown; in 1777 he resigned his commission in consequence of dissatisfaction as to rank. He was subsequently elected a Representative to Congress from Pennsylvania, serving from 1793 to 1795, and sustained a number of other honorable offices. He died at Carlisle, Penna., March 9, 1795, a few days after the expiration of his term in Congress.

Armstrong, John.—He was a native of Pennsylvania, and served as an officer during the revolutionary war. At the close of the war, in order to obtain redress for the grievances sustained by the officers of the army, he prepared the celebrated "Newburgh Letters," and they produced a deep sensation. After the war he returned to Pennsylvania, where he was made adjutant-general of the State; and to him was intrusted the direction of the last Pennsylvania war against the Connecticut settlers of Wyoming. Returning to New York, he was sent to the Senate of the United States, serving from 1800 to 1804, when he resigned. On the return of Chancellor Livingston from the French embassy, he was commissioned Minister in his place in 1804. Returning to his own country, he was called to the War Department by President

Madison. During the campaign of 1813, he visited the northern frontier. His flight from Washington, with Mr. Madison and his cabinet, at the sacking of 1814, gave the *coup de grâce* to his official career as Secretary of War. It was charged that the capital was lost by reason of his neglect to provide the means of defence. He was dismissed from office, and the duties of the War Department devolved upon Mr. Monroe, then Secretary of State. From that time he lived in retirement upon his estate at Red Hook, but passed a few years in Maryland. He published a brief history of the last war with England. He died at Red Hook, New York, April 1, 1843, aged eighty-four years.

Armstrong, William.—He was born in Lisburn, Antrim County, Ireland, December 23, 1782. He came to this country in 1792; had a limited education; studied law in Winchester, Virginia; devoted himself to mercantile pursuits. In 1813 he was appointed by President Madison Collector for the Sixth District of Virginia; in 1818 and 1819 he was a member of the Virginia House of Delegates; in 1822 and 1823, a member of the Board of Public Works; and in 1820 and 1824 he was a Presidential Elector; for many years a Justice of the Peace; one year High Sheriff of Hampshire County; and he was a Representative in Congress from 1825 to 1833. Since that time he has lived in retirement in the pleasant valley of the South Branch of the Potomac.

Arnold, Benedict.—He was a member of the Assembly of New York, from Amsterdam, Montgomery County, in 1816 and 1817, and was a Representative in Congress, from that State, from 1829 to 1831.

Arnold, Isaac N.—Born in Hardwicke, Otsego County, New York, in November, 1815; while engaged in acquiring an education he taught school, studied law, and came to the bar in 1835; in 1836 he removed to Chicago, Illinois; in 1837 he was First Clerk of the City of Chicago; in 1843 he was elected to the Illinois Legislature, and took an active part in the canal improvements; in 1844 he was Presidential Elector; was for a time attorney for the Illinois and Michigan Canal; and in 1860 he was elected a Representative, from Illinois, to the Thirty-seventh Congress, serving as chairman of the Select Committee on the Defences and Fortifications of the Great Lakes and Rivers. In 1862 he was elected for another term to the Thirty-eighth Congress, serving on the Committee of Manufactures, and as Chairman of that on Roads and Canals.

Arnold, Lemuel H.—Born in St. Johnsbury, Vermont, January 29, 1792, and removed to Rhode Island at an early age. He graduated at Dartmouth College, in 1811; was educated for the bar, but turned his attention to mercantile pursuits. In 1831, he was elected Governor of Rhode Island, and re-elected in 1832; he was a member of the Governor's Council during the Dorr rebellion in 1842; was a Representative in Congress, from 1845 to 1847; and died in Kingston, Rhode Island, June 27, 1852.

Arnold, Samuel.—He was born in Haddam, Middlesex County, Connecticut, June 1, 1806; received his education at Plainfield Academy, in Connecticut, and Westfield Academy, in Massachusetts; has devoted the most of his life to agricultural pursuits, and to various interests of commerce; having also for many years carried on one of the most extensive stone quarries in the Union. He was, also, for a number of years, President of the Bank of East Haddam. He served his native county, in the Legislature, during the years 1839, 1842, 1844, and 1851, and was elected to the Thirty-fifth Congress, as a Representative from Connecticut, serving as a member of the Committee on Claims.

Arnold, Samuel G.—Born in Providence, Rhode Island, April 12, 1821; graduated at Brown University in 1841; having taken a year from the course to travel in Europe and the East; spent two years in a counting-house in Providence, and again visited Europe; spent two years at the Harvard Law School, and having graduated, came to the bar in 1845; but instead of practising, again visited Europe, and also South America. In 1852 he was elected Lieutenant-Governor of Rhode Island; in 1859 and 1860, he published the History of the State of Rhode Island, a work upon which he had long been engaged; in 1861 he was a Delegate to the Peace Convention, and again chosen Lieutenant-Governor of the State; and on the breaking out of the Rebellion, he took the field, for a few weeks, in command of a battery of artillery, as aide-de-camp to Governor Sprague. In 1862, he was again elected Lieutenant-Governor of Rhode Island, and was soon afterwards chosen Senator in Congress from Rhode Island, for the unexpired term of J. F. Simmons, resigned, serving on the Committees on Commerce and Claims.

Arnold, Thomas D.—He was elected a Representative in Congress, from Knox County, Tennessee, from 1831 to 1833, and for a second term, from 1841 to 1843, representing Greenville County; he was a member of the Committees on Elections and Claims.

Arrington, Archibald.—He was born in North Carolina, and represented that State in Congress, from 1841 to 1845, after which he retired to private life. He was a member of the Committee on Expenditures in the War Department.

Ash, Michael W.—He was born in Pennsylvania, and was a Representative in Congress, from that State, from 1835 to 1837, serving as a member of the Committee on Naval Affairs.

Ashe, John Baptiste.—He was a Representative in Congress, from 1790 to 1793; was elected Governor of the State of North Carolina, in 1801; and died November 27, 1802. He was a Delegate to the Continental Congress in 1787 and 1788.

Ashe, John B.—He was elected a Representative in Congress, from Tennessee, from 1843 to 1845, representing the Tenth District, and serving as a member of the Committees on Invalid Pensions, and Expenditures in the State and Treasury Departments.

Ashe, William S.—Born in Wilmington, North Carolina; a lawyer by profession; served in the State Legislature in 1846, and was re-elected in 1848; he was a Representative in Congress, from 1849 to 1853, serving on the Committee on Expenditures in the State Department.

Ashley, Chester.—Born at Westfield, Massachusetts, June 1, 1790, but was removed in infancy to Hudson, New York, where he resided until he reached the age of twenty-seven. He then went to Illinois, and after practising law in that State for two years, removed to the Territory of Arkansas, and established himself in Little Rock, then a mere landing. He was chosen a Senator in Congress, in 1847, and was Chairman of the Judiciary Committee in that body. He served until his death, which occurred in Washington City, April 29, 1848.

Ashley, Henry.—He was born in Cheshire, New Hampshire, and was elected a Representative in Congress, from Delaware and Greene counties, New York, from 1825 to 1827.

Ashley, James M.—Born in Virginia in 1824; was self-educated; became an adventurer at the age of fifteen, at one time acting as clerk on the store boats of the Ohio and Mississippi, and then doing service in a printing office. He studied law, and was admitted to the bar of Ohio in 1849; but, instead of practising his profession, he went into the business of boat-building, and was connected with the press. He subsequently settled at Toledo, and went into the wholesale drug business, and was elected a Representative from Ohio, to the Thirty-sixth Congress, serving as a member of the Committee on Territories. Re-elected to the Thirty-seventh Congress, and made Chairman of the Committee on Territories, and also re-elected to the Thirty-eighth Congress, serving on the Committee of Claims, and as Chairman of the Committee on Territories.

Ashley, William H.—Born in Powhatan County, Virginia, and emigrated to Missouri, then Upper Louisiana, in 1808, and settled near the Lead Mines. In 1822, he projected the scheme of the "Mountain Expedition," by uniting the Indian trade in the Rocky Mountains with the hunting and trapping business. He enlisted about three hundred hardy men in the business, and, after various successes and reverses, having sustained numerous losses by Indian robbery and river disasters, he and his associates realized a handsome fortune. He was the first Lieutenant-

Governor of Missouri, after it became a State, and a Representative in Congress, from 1831 to 1837. He died near Boonville, Missouri, March 26, 1838.

Ashmore, John D.—Born in Greenville District, South Carolina, August 7, 1819; served as a merchant's clerk for several years, and then taught school until he became of age; studied law, but instead of following that profession, turned his attention to agriculture; when quite young, filled various offices in the State Militia; was a member of the South Carolina Legislature in 1848, 1850, and 1852; in 1853, he was elected Comptroller-General of the State for two years, and re-elected for a second term; and he was subsequently elected a Representative from South Carolina to the Thirty-sixth Congress. Resigned in December, 1860.

Ashmun, Eli Pease.—He was a distinguished lawyer, and for several years a member of the House of Representatives and Senate of Massachusetts; and was elected, in 1816, to succeed General Varnum as Senator from that State, in Congress; this office he resigned in 1818. He died at Northampton, Massachusetts, May 10, 1819, aged forty-eight.

Ashmun, George.—Born in Brandford, Massachusetts, December 25, 1804; graduated at Yale College in 1823; studied law and settled in Springfield in 1828. He served in the State Legislature during the years 1833, 1835, 1836, 1838, and 1841, officiating as Speaker of the House in the latter year. He was a Representative in Congress from 1845 to 1851, and was a member of the Committees on the Judiciary, Indian Affairs, and on Rules. Since that time he has been devoted to the practice of his profession. In 1860 he was elected President of the Chicago Convention, convened to nominate a President and Vice-President.

Atchison, David R.—He was born in Frogtown, Fayette County, Kentucky, August 11, 1807; was educated for the bar; and removed to Missouri in 1830. He was elected to the Legislature of that State in 1834 and 1838. In 1841 he was appointed Judge of the Platte County Circuit Court; and during the year 1843, was appointed a Senator in Congress, to which position he was twice elected, serving until 1855, frequently at the head of important committees, and for several sessions as President *pro tempore* of the Senate. He was subsequently devoted to agricultural pursuits.

Atherton, Charles G.—He was born in Hillsborough County, New Hampshire, July 4, 1804; graduated at Cambridge in 1822; studied law, but engaged in politics when quite young; he was for many years in the Legislature of New Hampshire, and for three years Speaker of the House; he was a Representative in Congress, from 1837 to 1843; a Senator in Congress, from 1843 to 1849; and, in November, 1852, he was re-elected a Senator to fill a vacancy, and died of apoplexy in Manchester, New Hampshire, November 15, 1853. He was Chairman, in the Senate, of the Committee on Finance.

Atherton, Charles H.—He was born in Amherst, New Hampshire, August 14, 1773, and graduated at Harvard College in 1794. He held the office of Register of Probate, from 1798 to 1807; was a Representative in Congress, from 1815 to 1817; and stood at the head of the bar in Hillsborough County for many years. He died in Amherst, January 8, 1853.

Atkins, John D. C.—He was born in Henry County, Tennessee, on the 4th of June, 1825; graduated at the University of East Tennessee in 1846; was elected to the lower branch of the Legislature in 1849 and 1851; was elected to the State Senate in 1855; was a Presidential Elector in 1856; and was elected a Representative in Congress, from Tennessee, in 1857, and was a member of the Committee on Post-offices and Post-roads.

Atkinson, Archibald.—Born in Isle of Wight County, Virginia, September 13, 1792. He left school at the age of eighteen, and entered the office of the Clerk of the County Court, and performed the duties of copyist, devoting his leisure time to the study of law, which he completed at the Law School of William and Mary College. In 1813 he joined the troops at Norfolk, as ensign of a volunteer company, which was attached to the 29th Regiment, and was at the battle of Craney Island. Upon leaving the army he commenced the practice of law in Smithfield, and was a member of the General Assembly from 1815 to 1817, and also of the House of Delegates and State Senate for several years. In 1843 he was elected a Representative in Congress, from Virginia, and served until 1848, and was a member of the Committees on Naval Affairs and Commerce. He was Prosecuting Attorney for his county twenty years; Mayor of Smithfield, and a magistrate.

Austin, Archibald.—He was a Representative in Congress, from Virginia, from 1817 to 1819.

Averett, Thomas H.—He was born in Virginia; was a resident of Halifax County, and elected a Representative in Congress, from the Third District in that State, from 1849 to 1853, and was a member of the Committees on Invalid Pensions, and on Revisal, and Unfinished Business.

Avery, Daniel.—He was elected a Representative in Congress, from Hamilton County, New York, from 1811 to 1815, and from Cayuga County, from 1816 to 1817.

Avery, William T.—Born in Maury County, Tennessee, November 11, 1819, and was very early in life thrown upon his own resources for education and support; he is a lawyer by profession; and was elected to the Legislature of Tennessee in 1843. He held several creditable positions in his native State, and was chosen a Representative to the Thirty-fifth Congress, serving as a member of the Committees on Expenditures in the State Department, and on Private Land Claims; re-elected to the Thirty-sixth Congress, serving on the Committee on Private Land Claims.

Aycrigg, John B.—He was born in New York, and was elected a Representative in Congress, from New Jersey, from 1837 to 1839, and again from 1841 to 1843, and was a member of the Committee on Expenditures in the Treasury Department, and the Joint Committee on the Library, and on Invalid Pensions. He was a candidate for election to the Twenty-sixth Congress, and although he came with the "Broad Seal" of New Jersey, he was not admitted.

Babbitt, Elijah.—Born in Providence, Rhode Island, in 1796; received a common school and academic education, in the States of New York and Pennsylvania; studied law in the latter State, and was admitted to the bar in 1824; was Prosecuting Attorney for the State in 1833; served in the State Legislature in 1836 and 1837; was a State Senator in 1844 and 1845; and was elected a Representative, from Pennsylvania, to the Thirty-sixth Congress, serving as a member of the Committee on Revolutionary Pensions. Re-elected to the Thirty-seventh Congress.

Babcock, Alfred.—He was a Representative in Congress, from New York, from 1841 to 1843.

Babcock, Leander.—He was born in New York, and was a Representative in Congress, from that State, from 1851 to 1853.

Babcock, William.—He was a Representative in Congress, from New York, from 1831 to 1833.

Bacon, Ezekiel.—He was born in Stockbridge, Massachusetts, in 1776; graduated at Yale College in 1804; the son of John Bacon; was a member of the State Legislature in 1805 and 1806; Chief Justice of the Court of Common Pleas for the Western District of Massachusetts, in 1813; First Comptroller of the United States Treasury from 1813 to 1815; and a Representative in Congress, from Massachusetts, from 1807 to 1813.

Bacon, John.—He was born in Canterbury, Connecticut, in 1737; graduated at the College of New Jersey in 1765; studied theology, and, after preaching for a time in Maryland, removed to Massachusetts, and settled in Boston. Owing to some difficulties with his congregation, he relinquished the ministry, and subsequently held the positions of magistrate, Representative in the State Legislature, Presiding Judge of the Court of Common Pleas, a member and President of the State Senate, and that of Representative in Congress, from Massachusetts, from 1801 to 1803. He died in Berkshire County, October 25, 1820.

Badger, George E.—Born in the

town of Newbern, North Carolina, in 1795. He graduated at Yale College in 1813; studied and practised law; and was elected to the Legislature in 1816. In 1820, he was elected a Judge of the Supreme Court, which he resigned in 1825; he was appointed Secretary of the Navy by President Harrison in 1841; and was elected a Senator in Congress in 1846, and re-elected in 1848 for a term of six years, serving on the Committees on Military and Naval Affairs. Of late years he has been wholly devoted to the practice of his profession, visiting Washington occasionally to argue cases in the Supreme Court of the United States.

Badger, Luther.—Born in Partridgefield, Berkshire County, Massachusetts, April 10, 1785, but his father removed to Broome County, New York, in 1786. Having made sufficient acquaintance in the common branches of an English education, he entered Hamilton College at the age of nineteen, and spent two years there. In 1807 he commenced the study of law, and was admitted to the bar in 1812, and continued to practise his profession until 1824, when he was elected a Representative to the Nineteenth Congress. He had been engaged in military services in his State, and in 1819 was appointed, by Governor Clinton, Judge-Advocate for the 27th Brigade of Infantry of New York State, which office he held for eight years. In 1832 he resumed the practice of law, and in 1840 was appointed Examiner in Chancery and Commissioner of United States Loans, which office he held for three years. From 1846 to 1849 he was United States District Attorney for New York.

Baer, George.—He was a Representative in Congress, from Maryland, from 1797 to 1801, and again from 1815 to 1817.

Bagby, Arthur P.—He was born in Virginia in 1794; was liberally educated; adopted the profession of law, and settled in Alabama in 1818; was elected a member of the Legislature in 1820 and 1822, and was Speaker of the House; was Governor of Alabama from 1837 to 1843; and a Senator in Congress, from that State, from 1842 to 1849. His last public position was that of Minister to Russia, to which he was appointed in 1848. He died of yellow fever at Mobile, September 21, 1858.

Bailey, David J.—He was born in Georgia, and was a Representative in Congress, from that State, from 1851 to 1855.

Bailey, Goldsmith F.—Born in Westmoreland, New Hampshire, July 17, 1823; finished his schooling at the age of sixteen; became a printer and edited a country paper; studied law and was admitted to the bar in 1848; in 1856 he was elected to the Legislature of Massachusetts; in 1858 and 1860 to the Senate of the State; and was elected a Representative from Massachusetts to the Thirty-seventh Congress. His health was impaired when he took his seat in Congress, and he died at Fitchburg, Massachusetts, May 8, 1862.

Bailey, Jeremiah.—He was born at Little Compton, Rhode Island; graduated at Brown University, and studied law. He was a member of the Maine Legislature from 1811 to 1814; a Judge of Probate from 1814 to 1835; and a Representative in Congress, from Lincoln County, Maine, from 1835 to 1837, serving on the Committees on Agriculture and Expenditures in the Post-office Department. He was also Collector of Customs at Wiscasset, from 1849 to 1853; and died in July of that year.

Bailey, John.—He was born in Norfolk County, Massachusetts; was a member of the Massachusetts Legislature from 1815 to 1818; a clerk in the Department of State for a year; a State Senator in 1831 and 1834; and a Representative in Congress, for Massachusetts, from 1823 to 1831, serving on the Committees on Public Expenditures and Expenditures in the State Department; and died at Dorchester, Massachusetts, June 26, 1835.

Bailey, Theodorus.—He was born in 1752; was a Representative in Congress, from New York, from 1793 to 1797, and again from 1799 to 1803; and a Senator in Congress, from 1803 to 1804, when he resigned and was appointed Postmaster of New York City. He died September 6, 1828.

Baily, Joseph.—He was born on the Brandywine battle-ground, Chester County, Pennsylvania, March 18, 1810 ; received a limited education through his own exertions, on account of the moderate circumstances of his father, and was early apprenticed to a mechanical branch of business, which was his first step to eminent success. From 1839 to 1845 he represented his native county in both branches of the Legislature, and from 1850 to 1854 represented Perry County, in the State Senate. In 1854 he was Treasurer of the State of Pennsylvania, and in 1860 was elected a Representative from Pennsylvania to the Thirty-seventh Congress, serving on the committees on Agriculture and Printing. He was also re-elected to the Thirty-eighth Congress, and served on the same Committees.

Baker, Caleb.—He was born in Providence, Rhode Island ; served four years in the New York Assembly ; and was a Representative in Congress, from that State, from 1819 to 1821.

Baker, David J.—He was a Senator in Congress, from Illinois, from 1830 to 1831.

Baker, Edward D.—Was born in England, brought to this country when a child, and was early left an orphan in Philadelphia. His father was a weaver, and when a boy, he worked at that business himself. He obtained an education under many difficulties; first studied for the ministry, but soon turned his attention to the law, becoming famous as an advocate in Illinois, to which State he emigrated in his nineteenth year. After serving in the Illinois Legislature for two years ; he resigned, and in 1846, went to Mexico as a colonel of volunteers, acquitting himself with credit at Cerro Gordo. He was a Representative in Congress, from Illinois, from 1849 to 1851 ; after which, he took an active part in the building of the Panama Railroad ; in 1852, he settled in San Francisco, devoting himself to his profession ; he subsequently removed to Oregon, which State he represented as a Senator in Congress, taking his seat in March, 1861. At the outbreak of the Rebellion, in 1861, he raised a body of men in Philadelphia, called the California Regiment, and while gallantly leading them in battle at Leesburg, Virginia, against a superior force, he was shot from his horse and killed, October 21, 1861.

Baker, Ezra.—He was a Representative in Congress, from New Jersey, from 1815 to 1817.

Baker, John.—He was a Representative in Congress, from Virginia, from 1811 to 1813. He was a lawyer, and died in Shepherdstown, Virginia, August 18, 1823.

Baker, Osmyn.—He was born in Amherst, Massachusetts, May 18, 1800 ; graduated at Yale College in 1822 ; adopted the profession of law ; and was a Representative in Congress, from his native State, from 1839 to 1845. He was also a member of the Massachusetts Legislature in 1833 and 1834 ; State Councillor in 1853 and 1854.

Baker, Stephen.—He was born in the city of New York, August 12, 1819 ; at an early age engaged in mercantile pursuits, from which he retired in 1849, to a country seat in Dutchess County, New York ; and was elected a Representative from New York to the Thirty-seventh Congress, serving on the Committees on Roads and Canals, and on Patents.

Baldwin, Abraham.—Was a native of Connecticut, and a graduate of Yale College in 1772, and from 1775 to 1779 he was a tutor in that institution. Having studied law, he settled in Savannah, Georgia, and soon after his arrival there he was chosen a member of the Legislature. He originated the plan of the University of Georgia, drew up the charter, and persuaded the Assembly to adopt it, and was for some time its President. He was a member of the Continental Congress from 1785 to 1788, and a member of the Convention which framed the Constitution of the United States. From 1789 to 1799 he was a Representative in Congress, and from 1799 to 1807 he was a member of the United States Senate, part of the time President *pro tem.* of the Senate. He died March 4, 1807, aged fifty-three years.

Baldwin, Augustus C.—Was born in Salina, New York, December

24, 1817; received a common school education, and having lost his father when young, became dependent upon his own efforts for support; in 1837 he emigrated to Michigan and settled in Oakland County; studied law, and at the same time taught school, and came to the bar in 1842. In 1844 and 1846 he was elected to the Legislature of Michigan; in 1853 and 1854 was Prosecuting Attorney for his adopted county; was a Delegate to the Charleston and Baltimore Conventions of 1860; and in 1862 he was elected a Representative, from Michigan, to the Thirty-eighth Congress, serving on the Committees on Agriculture and Expenditures in the Interior Department. Was a Delegate to the Chicago Convention in 1864.

Baldwin, Henry.—He was born in New Haven, Connecticut, in 1779; graduated at Yale College in 1797; and was a Representative in Congress, from Pennsylvania, from 1817 to 1822. He was a distinguished lawyer, and was for many years Associate Judge of the Supreme Court of the United States. He died in Philadelphia, April 21, 1844.

Baldwin, John.—He was born in Windham, Connecticut; and was a Representative in Congress, from that State, from 1825 to 1829, serving on one standing and one select committee.

Baldwin, John D.—Was born in North Stonington, Connecticut, September 28, 1810; was educated in Yale College, receiving the degree of A.M.; read law, but never practised; went through a course of theological studies, devoted himself to literary pursuits, and published a volume of verses. In 1842 he became associated with the press, first in Hartford, and then in Boston, and was editor of the Daily Commonwealth, a writer for the Advertiser, and subsequently became the proprietor of the Worcester Spy. In 1862 he was elected a Representative, from Massachusetts, to the Thirty-eighth Congress, serving on the Committees of Expenditures, on Public Buildings, and on Printing.

Baldwin, Roger Sherman.—Born at New Haven, Connecticut, January 4, 1793; graduated at Yale College in 1811; studied law at Litchfield Law School; was admitted to the bar in 1814, and established himself in practice at New Haven, where he has since continued to reside. In 1837 he was elected to the State Senate, re-elected in 1838, and chosen President *pro tem.* of that body. In 1840 and 1841 he was a Representative in the General Assembly, and in the latter year was associated with J. Q. Adams in the argument before the Supreme Court of the United States, in the case of the Africans of the Amistad. In 1844 and 1845 he was Governor of the State, and in 1847 was elected to the United States Senate by the Legislature of Connecticut, serving until 1851. He subsequently engaged in his professional duties. He was also a member of the Peace Congress of 1861, and died in New Haven, February 19, 1863.

Baldwin, Simeon.—Born at Norwich, Connecticut, December 14, 1761; graduated at Yale College in 1781. In 1783 he was appointed tutor at the College, and continued in that station until 1786, when he was admitted to the bar in New Haven, and commenced the practice of law. From 1790 to 1803 he was Clerk of the District and Circuit Courts of the United States; was a Representative in Congress, from 1803 to 1805, and declined a re-election. In 1806 he was appointed, by the Legislature, Associate Judge of the Superior Court and of the Supreme Court of Errors, and held the office until 1817. In 1822 was chosen by the General Assembly one of the Commissioners to locate the Farmington Canal, and was made President of that Board. In 1826 was elected Mayor of New Haven. In 1830 he resigned his office as Commissioner. He died in New Haven, May 26, 1851.

Ball, Edward.—He was born in Virginia, and was a Representative in Congress, from Ohio, from 1853 to 1855, and was re-elected to the Thirty-fourth Congress.

Ball, William Lee.—Born in Lancaster County, Virginia, and was a Representative in Congress, from that State, from 1817 to 1824. Died in Washington, February 28, 1824, aged forty-five years.

Banks, John.—Was born in Juniata County, Pennsylvania, in 1793; studied law, and came to the bar in

1819, and settled in the western part of the State; was a Representative in Congress, from Pennsylvania, from 1831 to 1836, when he resigned to accept the appointment of President Judge of the Third Judicial District of the State; in 1841 was the Whig candidate for Governor, but failed to be elected; and in 1847 he resigned the judgeship and became the State Treasurer. He was subsequently engaged in the practice of his profession, and died at Reading, on the 3d of April, 1864.

Banks, Linn.—Born in Virginia, and was for twenty successive years Speaker of the House of Delegates of that State, and a Representative in Congress, from Virginia, from 1838 to 1842, and was a member of the Committee on Claims. He was found drowned in a stream in Madison County, Virginia, February 24, 1842.

Banks, Nathaniel P.—Born in Waltham, Massachusetts, January 30, 1816, of poor but respectable parents, operatives in a factory. He had no advantages but those afforded by the common school, but he became a lover of books at an early day, and that love has been a source of gratification to him all his life. His first venture before the public was in the capacity of newspaper editor in his native town, and he followed the same pursuit at Lowell. He studied law, but did not practise to any great extent, and in 1848 he was elected to the Legislature of Massachusetts, serving in both houses, and officiating for a time as Speaker. He was chosen President of the Convention held in 1853, for revising the Constitution of Massachusetts, and was soon afterwards elected a Representative in Congress, serving from 1853 to 1857, when he was elected Governor of Massachusetts, by a majority of 24,000. During his second term in Congress, he was elected Speaker, and, as a presiding officer, won a reputation for impartiality, as it is said that not one of his decisions was ever overruled by the House. He was elected Governor of Massachusetts for a second term, in 1858, and for a third term in 1859. During the Rebellion of 1861–64, he served in the Union army as a major-general of volunteers.

Barber, Levi.—He was born in Litchfield County, Connecticut, and was a Representative in Congress, from Ohio, from 1817 to 1819, and again from 1821 to 1823.

Barber, Noyes.—He was born in Groton, Connecticut, April 28, 1781; was in early life a merchant, but a lawyer by profession; and was a Representative in Congress, from his native State, from 1821 to 1835. He died at Groton, January 3, 1845. He was a man of ability, and while in Congress accomplished much good for his native State, where he was universally respected as a man and a statesman.

Barbour, James.—A native of Virginia; was Speaker of the House of Delegates, and Governor of that State; and a Senator in Congress, from 1815 to 1825, officiating as President *pro tem.* of the Senate, as Chairman of the Committees on Foreign Relations and the District of Columbia, and serving on other important committees. He was appointed Secretary of War in 1825, and Minister to England in 1828. He died in Orange County, Virginia, June 8, 1842, aged sixty-six years.

Barbour, John S.—Born in Culpeper County, Virginia, in 1810, and died in Culpeper County, Virginia, January 12, 1855. He was in early life a member of the State Legislature; was from 1823 to 1833 a member of Congress from Virginia; again in the State Legislature in 1833–34; and member of the Constitutional Convention in 1829–30. He was a gentleman of much ability, and exercised considerable influence in the public affairs of his State.

Barbour, Lucien.—He was born in Canton, Connecticut, March 4, 1811; graduated at Amherst College in 1837, having, while receiving his own education, been a teacher himself; he removed to Indiana, studied law, and settled in the practice at Indianapolis. He was appointed, by President Polk, United States District Attorney; acted a number of times as arbitrator between the State of Indiana and private corporations; in 1852 was appointed a Commissioner to prepare a code of practice for the State; and was a Representative in the Thirty-fourth Congress; since which time he has been devoted to his profession.

Barbour, Philip P.—Born in

1779; was educated for the law, in the practice of which he was successful; he was a member of Congress, from Virginia, from 1814 to 1825; Speaker of the House of Representatives in 1821; in 1825 he was appointed Judge of the Eastern District of Virginia; was again in Congress from 1827 to 1830, officiating as Chairman of the Judiciary Committee; and in 1836 was appointed by President Jackson an Associate Judge of the Supreme Court of the United States. He died in Washington City, of ossification of the heart, February 25, 1841.

Barclay, David.—He was born in Pennsylvania, and was a Representative in Congress, from his native State, from 1855 to 1857.

Bard, David.—He was a graduate of Princeton College in 1773, and a Representative in Congress, from Pennsylvania, from 1795 to 1799, and again from 1803 to 1815.

Barker, David.—He was a lawyer by profession, and was a Representative in Congress, from New Hampshire, from 1827 to 1829, and died in Rochester, New Hampshire, April 1, 1834, aged thirty-seven years.

Barker, Joseph.—He commenced his classical studies at Harvard University, and graduated at Yale College in 1771; and was a Representative in Congress, from Massachusetts, from 1805 to 1809. He died in 1815.

Barkesdale, William.—Born in Rutherford County, Tennessee, August 21, 1821, and pursued a partial course of studies at the Nashville University. He is a lawyer by profession; held a commission in the staff of the 2d Mississippi Regiment, in the Mexican war, in 1847; was a member of the Mississippi Convention called in 1851 to discuss the Compromise measures of 1850; and was elected Representative, from Mississippi, in the Thirty-third, Thirty-fourth, Thirty-fifth, and Thirty-sixth Congresses; serving as a member of the Committee on Foreign Affairs. Joined the Great Rebellion in 1861.

Barlow, Stephen.—He was a Representative in Congress, from Pennsylvania, from 1827 to 1829, and was a member of the Committee on Agriculture.

Barnard, D. D.—He was born in Berkshire County, Massachusetts; graduated at Williams College in 1818; studied law, and was admitted to the bar, in New York, in 1821; in 1826 was elected District Attorney for the County of Monroe, New York; and was a Representative in Congress, from New York, from 1827 to 1829, and again from 1839 to 1845. In 1850 he was appointed Minister to Prussia. He has devoted much attention to literary pursuits, and the degree of LL.D. was conferred upon him by the colleges of Geneva and New York. Of late years he devoted himself to the publication of a work called "A Journal of Education." Died at Albany in April, 1861.

Barnard, Isaac D.—He was a Senator in Congress, from Pennsylvania, from 1827 to 1831, and died at West Chester, Pennsylvania, February, 1834.

Barnett, William.—He was elected a Representative in Congress, from Georgia, from 1812 to 1815, when he was appointed one of the Commissioners to run the Creek boundary line.

Barney, John.—He was a son of Commodore Joshua Barney, and a member of Congress, from Maryland, from 1825 to 1827. He died in Washington, District of Columbia, January 26, 1857, aged seventy-two years. He was known in Washington society for many years as an agreeable gentleman; and he left behind him an unfinished record of "Personal Recollections of Men and Things," both in this country and Europe.

Barnitz, Charles A.—He was a Representative in Congress, from Pennsylvania, from 1833 to 1835, and died at York, in that State, in March, 1850.

Barnwell, Robert.—He was a Representative in Congress, from South Carolina, from 1791 to 1793.

Barnwell, R. W.—He was born in South Carolina; graduated at Harvard University in 1821; studied law and was a Representative in Congress, from South Carolina, from 1829 to 1833; was President of the South Carolina College from 1835 to 1843, and was a Senator in Congress in 1850. In December, 1860, he was appointed one of the Commissioners to visit Washington in behalf of South Carolina, and served as a member of the "Confederate" Congress.

Barr, Thomas J.—Born in New York City in 1812; commenced life by devoting himself to a variety of pursuits; from 1835 to 1842 he held the position of a landlord in New Jersey; in 1849 and 1850 he was an Assistant Alderman in the City Councils of New York; in 1853 he was elected a member of the State Senate; and he was elected a Representative in Congress, from New York, taking his seat during the second session of the Thirty-fifth Congress, and re-elected to the Thirty-sixth Congress, serving as a member of the Committee on Expenses in the State Department.

Barrere, Nelson.—He was a Representative in Congress, from Ohio, from 1851 to 1853.

Barrett, J. Richard.—Born in Kentucky, and removing to Missouri, was elected a Representative from that State to the Thirty-sixth Congress, serving as a member of the Committee on Public Lands.

Barringer, Daniel L.—Born in Mecklenburg County, North Carolina, October 1, 1788; had a good classical education; studied law, and practised with success in Wake County; served in the Legislature of North Carolina in 1813, and again from 1819 to 1822; and was a Representative in Congress, from 1826 to 1835. He subsequently removed to Tennessee, and was elected Speaker of the House of Representatives of that State. He died October 16, 1852.

Barringer, Daniel Moreau.—Was born in Cabarras County, North Carolina, and graduated at the University of North Carolina in 1826; he selected the law as a profession, having commenced to practise in 1829. In that year he was elected a member of the State Legislature, in which position he continued for a number of years. In 1835 he was a member of a Convention to amend the State Constitution. He was a Representative in Congress, from 1843 to 1849, when he was appointed by President Taylor Minister to Spain, and continued in that mission by President Fillmore. On resigning his position as Minister, after serving four years, he travelled extensively in Europe, and, on his return home, was elected to the State Legislature, and in 1855, having declined a re-election, retired to private life, devoting himself to literary studies and pursuits. He was also elected a Delegate to the Peace Congress of 1861.

Barrow, Alexander.—Born in Nashville, Tennessee, in 1801, where, after completing his education, he was admitted to the bar; he soon after removed to Louisiana, gave up the practice of law, and turned his attention to planting. He served a number of years in the Legislature of Louisiana, and was a Senator in Congress from 1841 to 1847. Died December 29, 1846.

Barrow, Washington.—He is a native of Tennessee; a lawyer by education and profession; was a Representative in Congress, from that State, from 1847 to 1849, serving on the Committee for the District of Columbia; and in 1841 was appointed American Chargé d'Affaires to Portugal.

Barry, William S.—He was born in Mississippi, and was a Representative in Congress, from that State, from 1853 to 1855.

Barry, William T.—He was born in Fairfax County, Virginia, March 18, 1780; and was a Senator in Congress, from Kentucky, from 1814 to 1816, having previously served in the State Legislature as Speaker, and during the years 1810 and 1811, been a Representative in Congress from the same State. He was also a member of President Jackson's cabinet, as Postmaster-General (the first, as such, admitted to that honor), and at the time of his death, which occurred in Liverpool, England, August 30, 1835, he was Minister Plenipotentiary of the United States to Spain.

Barstow, Gamaliel H. — He served three years in the Assembly of New York, four years in the State Senate, and was a Representative in Congress, from that State, from 1831 to 1833.

Barstow, Gideon.—A native of Massachusetts; was a member of both branches of the Legislature of that State, and a Representative in Congress, from 1821 to 1823. He died in St. Augustine, Florida, where he had gone for his health, March 26, 1852, aged sixty-nine years.

Bartlett, Bailey.—He was Sheriff of Essex County, Massachusetts, for many years, and a Representative in Congress, from Massachusetts, from 1797 to 1801.

Bartlett, Ichabod.—He was born in Salisbury, Hillsborough County, New Hampshire, in 1786; graduated at Dartmouth College in 1808; studied law, and settled in Portsmouth, where he was eminently successful in his profession, and was a Representative in Congress, from 1823 to 1829, serving on the Committee on Naval Affairs. He was also frequently in the State Legislature, and a member of the Convention to revise the State Constitution. He died in Portsmouth, October 19, 1853.

Bartlett, Josiah.—Born in New Hampshire in 1768, and died at Stratham, in that State, April 14, 1838. He was a physician of extensive practice, and a Representative in Congress, from New Hampshire, from 1811 to 1813. His father, bearing the same name, was a man of note, and the first Governor of New Hampshire after the adoption of the Federal Constitution.

Bartlett, Thomas, Jr.—He was born in Vermont; adopted the profession of law; and was a Representative in Congress, from that State, from 1851 to 1853. He served three years in the State Legislature, both houses; was County Attorney in 1839 and 1841; and President of the State Constitutional Convention of 1850.

Bartley, Mordecai.—He was born in Fayette County, Pennsylvania, and was a Representative in Congress, from Ohio, from 1823 to 1831, and Governor of Ohio, from 1844 to 1846.

Barton, David.—He was one of the first emigrants to the Territory of Missouri; President of the Convention which met to form a State Constitution, in 1820; was a Senator in Congress, from Missouri, from 1821 to 1831, and a man of distinguished talents. Died near Boonville, Missouri, September 28, 1837.

Barton, Richard W.—He was born in Virginia, and was a Representative in Congress, from that State, from 1841 to 1843. He also served in the State Legislature, and was the first President of the Valley Agricultural Society. Died in Frederick County, Virginia, March 15, 1859.

Barton, Samuel.—He was born in New York, served three years in the Assembly of that State, and was a Representative in Congress, from 1835 to 1837.

Basset, Richard.—He was a member from Delaware of the Convention which formed the Constitution, and a Senator in Congress, from its adoption until 1793. He was also a Justice of the Federal Supreme Court; Governor of Delaware, from 1798 to 1801; and died in September, 1815.

Bassett, Burwell.—He was born in New Kent County, Virginia, and was a Representative in Congress, from that State, from 1805 to 1813, from 1815 to 1819, and from 1821 to 1831.

Bateman, Ephraim.—He was born in Cumberland, New Jersey; was a Senator in Congress, from that State, from 1826 to 1829; and was a member of the Committees on Agriculture and Enrolled Bills; having previously been a Representative in Congress, from 1815 to 1823; serving on the Committees on the Post-office and Accounts. Died January 21, 1829.

Bates, Edward.—Was born September 4, 1793, at Belmont, Goochland County, Virginia. His education was commenced by his father, and succeeded by several years of academic instruction, mostly at Charlotte Hall, Maryland, and finished by an accomplished private tutor. In early youth he declined a midshipman's warrant, and served in 1813, at Norfolk, in the Virginia Militia, from February to October. In 1814 he migrated to St. Louis, there studied law, and began to practise in 1816. In 1818 he was appointed Prosecuting Attorney for that Circuit; in 1820 was a delegate to the State Constitutional Convention, and was the same year appointed Attorney-General of the new State of Missouri. He resigned that office in 1822, and was elected to the lower branch of the State Legislature. In 1824 he was appointed by President Monroe United States Attorney for the Missouri District; in 1826 resigned, and was elected a Representative in Congress from Missouri, serving from 1827 to 1829. In 1830 he was elected to the State Senate, and in 1834 again to the lower house of the Legislature. In 1835, being enfeebled by sedentary labor, he moved to the country, and practised law for seven years, travelling much on horseback around the prairies. In 1842 he returned to St. Louis; and in 1850 he was appointed by President Fillmore Secretary of War, but declined the office. In 1853 was elected Judge of the St. Louis Land Court, which office he resigned in 1856. During that year he presided at the Whig Convention of Baltimore, and in 1858 received from Harvard University the degree of LL.D. In 1861 was appointed Attorney-General in President Lincoln's Cabinet.

Bates, Isaac C.—Born at Granville, Massachusetts, in 1780, and graduated at Yale College in 1802. He studied law and attained a high position as an advocate. He was frequently in the State Legislature and a member of the Executive Council; was a Representative in Congress, from 1827 to 1833, and a Senator in Congress, from 1841 to 1845; and was Chairman of the Committee on Pensions. He died in Washington City, March 16, 1845.

Bates, James.—He was bred a physician; for some years connected with the Insane Hospital at Augusta; and was a Representative in Congress, from Somerset County, Maine, from 1831 to 1833, and a member of the Committee on Expenditures in the Post-office Department.

Bates, James W.—He was born in Goochland County, Virginia, and was a Delegate to Congress, from the Territory of Arkansas, from 1820 to 1823.

Bates, Martin W.—He was born in Salisbury, Litchfield County, Connecticut, February 24, 1787; he received a good English education, and became a lawyer by profession; having first studied medicine. He removed to Delaware, and was several times elected to the Legislature of that State; and in 1850 was a member of the Constitutional Convention of the State of Delaware. He took his seat in the Thirty-fifth Congress, as a Senator from Delaware, serving on the Committees on Pensions and Revolutionary Pensions.

Baxter, Portus.—Was born in Brownington, Orleans County, Vermont; received a liberal education, adopted the occupation of a merchant, and was elected a Representative from Vermont to the Thirty-seventh Congress, serving on the Committee on Elections; re-elected to the Thirty-eighth Congress, and served on the same Committee, and also on that of Expenditures in the Navy Department. In 1857 he was a Presidential Elector.

Bay, William V. N.—He was born in New York, and having become a citizen of Missouri, was elected a Representative in Congress, from 1849 to 1851.

Bayard, James A.—He was born in Pennsylvania, in 1767. After studying law at Philadelphia, he commenced the practice in Delaware. In 1796 he was elected a Representative in Congress, serving from 1797 to 1801; when he was appointed Minister to France. In 1804 he was elected to the United States Senate, of which body he continued a member, till he was appointed by President Madison, in 1813, a Commissioner to negotiate a peace with Great Britain. The absence of the Emperor from St. Petersburg preventing the transaction of any business, he proceeded to Holland. He lent his able assistance in the negotiation of the treaty of peace at Ghent. At Paris, he was apprised of his appointment as Envoy to the Court of St. Petersburg; this he declined. He tendered, however, his co-operation in forming a commercial treaty with Great Britain; but an alarming illness compelled him to return to the United States. He arrived in June, and died August 6, 1815.

Bayard, James A.—He has been a Senator in Congress, from Delaware, ever since 1851, and was Chairman of the Committee on the Judiciary, and a member of the Committees on the Library and on Public Grounds. In 1863 he was re-elected for his third term, but resigned in January, 1864.

Bayard, Richard H.—He was born in Delaware, graduated at Princeton College in 1814, and was a Senator in Congress, from Delaware, from 1836 to 1839, and again from 1841 to 1845. He was subsequently appointed American Minister to Belgium.

Baylies, Francis.—Born in Bristol County, Massachusetts, in 1784; was Register of Probate in Bristol County, Massachusetts, from 1812 to 1820; a member of the State Legislature, from 1827 to 1832, and also in 1835; was a Representative in Congress, from Massachusetts, from 1821 to 1827, and in 1832 was appointed Chargé d'Affaires to Buenos Ayres, and died October 28, 1852. He was the author of "A History of the Plymouth Colony."

Baylies, William.—He graduated at Harvard College in 1760; was a member of the Provincial Congress in 1775; often a member of the Massachusetts State Council; and a Representative in Congress, from Massachusetts, from 1805 to 1809. He died at Dighton, Massachusetts, June 17, 1826, aged eighty-two years.

Baylies, William.—He was born in Massachusetts in 1777, educated a lawyer, and held many public offices, having been in the State Legislature in 1830 and 1831. He was a Representative in Congress from Massachusetts, from 1813 to 1817, and from 1833 to 1835, serving as a member of the Committee on Revolutionary Claims.

Bayley, Thomas.—He was born in Somerset County, Maryland, and was a Representative in Congress, from that State, from 1817 to 1823.

Baylor, R. E. B.—He was a Representative in Congress, from Alabama, from 1829 to 1831.

Bayly, Thomas Henry.—Born in Accomac County, Virginia, in 1810; graduated at the University of Virginia, and came to the bar in 1830. At the age of twenty-six, he was chosen a member of the General Assembly of Virginia, and was re-elected for five years in succession. While a member of the Legislature, he was elected by that body a Brigadier-General of the militia of Eastern Virginia. He resigned his seat, and was elected Judge of the Circuit Superior Court of Law. In 1844 he resigned his seat on the bench, and was elected to the House of Representatives from the Accomac District, and continued, by successive elections, a member of the House for twelve years, until the time of his death; during the Thirty-first Congress officiating as Chairman of the Committee of Ways and Means. He lived and died on the same spot where his ancestors from England landed in 1666, and where they established the family home. He commanded the same brigade which his grandfather had commanded; and he held the same seat in the General Assembly of his State and in the House of Representatives, which his father had occupied before him. He died June 22, 1856, aged forty-five years.

Bayly, Thomas M.—Born in Virginia in 1775; entered public life in 1798, and continued therein until 1830; served in both branches of the State Legislature, and was a member of the State Constitutional Convention of 1830; having been a Representative in Congress, from Virginia, from 1813 to 1815. It was said of him that he never lost an election. Died in Accomac County in 1834.

Beale, Charles L.—Born in Canaan, Columbia County, New York, March 5, 1824; was prepared for college by a private tutor, and graduated at Union College in 1844; studied law at Kinderhook, and was admitted to the bar in 1849; was for several years a member of the Republican State Central Committee of New York; and in 1858 was elected a Representative to the Thirty-sixth Congress, from New York, serving as a member of the Committee on Public Buildings and Grounds.

Beale, James M. H.—He was born in Virginia, and was a Representative in Congress, from that State, from 1833 to 1837, and for two other terms, from 1849 to 1853.

Beale, R. L. T.—Born at Hickory Hill, Westmoreland County, Virginia, May 22, 1819; his education was obtained chiefly at Northumberland Academy, spending a short time at Dickinson College, Pennsylvania. In 1836 he commenced the study of law, and graduated at the University of Virginia, as a student of that profession, in 1838, and was licensed to practise in 1839. In 1847 he was elected a Representative in Congress, and was a member of the Committee on the Militia; he declined a re-election at the expiration of his term. In 1850 he was a member of the Reform Convention of Virginia, and in 1857 was elected to the State Senate.

Beall, Rezin.—He was an officer in Wayne's army, with Harrison and Van Rensselaer; occupied various public stations in Ohio, and was a member of Congress, from that State, from 1813 to 1815, and died at Wooster, Ohio, February 20, 1843, aged seventy-three years.

Beaman, Fernando C.—He was born in Chester, Windsor County, Vermont, June 28, 1814; removed with his father to New York when a boy, and left an orphan at the age of fifteen; received a good English education at the Franklin County Academy; studied law in Rochester; removed to Michigan in 1838, and commenced the practice of his profession; was for six years Prosecuting Attorney for Lenawe County; was Judge of Probate for four years, and in 1860 was elected a Representative, from Michigan, to the Thirty-seventh Congress, serving on the Committee on Roads and Canals; re-elected to the Thirty-eighth Congress, and served on the same Committee, and also on that on Territories.

Bean, Benning M.—He was born in New Hampshire; he occupied a seat in the Legislature for five years, and was President of the Senate in 1832; was a State Councillor in 1829; was a Representative in Congress, from 1833 to 1837, serving as a member of the Committee on Agriculture.

Beardsley, Samuel.—He was born in Otsego County, New York; studied and adopted the profession of law; settled at Rome, Oneida County, and was District Attorney of the same; also held the post of Attorney-General of the State; was a Representative in Congress, from Oneida County, New York, from 1831 to 1836, and was Chairman of the Committee on the Judiciary. He also held the offices of State Senator in 1823, and Asssistant Justice and Chief Justice of the Supreme Court of the State, and the Federal appointment of United States District Attorney for New York. Died at Utica, New York, May 6, 1860.

Beatty, John.—He graduated at Princeton College in 1769, and studied medicine; was a Representative in Congress, from New Jersey, from 1793 to 1795, having been a Delegate to the Continental Congress, from 1783 to 1785. He died at Trenton, April 30, 1826, aged seventy-seven years.

Beatty, Martin.—He was a Representative in Congress, from Kentucky, from 1833 to 1835.

Beatty, William.—He was born in Ireland, and was a Representative in Congress, from Pennsylvania, from 1837 to 1841.

Beaumont, Andrew.—He was born in Pennsylvania, and was a Representative in Congress, from that State, from 1833 to 1837, and died at Wilkesbarre, Pennsylvania, October 30, 1853.

Becker, George L.—He was a Representative in Congress, from Minnesota; elected to the Thirty-fifth Congress.

Bedinger, George M.—He was an officer in the revolutionary war, having served as Adjutant in the expedition against Chillicothe, in 1779, and as a Major at the battle of Blue Licks, in 1782; he was one of the earliest emigrants into the State of Kentucky; was a member of the Kentucky Legislature in 1792, and a Representative in Congress, from 1803 to 1807. He spent the close of his life in retirement, and died at an advanced age.

Bedinger, Henry.—He was born in Virginia; received a classical education; adopted the profession of law; and was a Representative in Congress, from Virginia, from 1845 to 1849, where he was distinguished for his eloquence as a debater. In 1853 he was appointed Chargé d'Affaires to Denmark, and returned home in the autumn of 1858.

A few weeks after his return he partook of a complimentary dinner tendered to him by his fellow-citizens of all parties. He died of pneumonia, at Shepherdstown, Virginia, November 26, 1858. During his residence in Denmark, he was successful in bringing about the treaty abolishing the Sound Dues.

Beecher, Philemon.—Born in New Haven, Connecticut; he was an able lawyer, and one of the early settlers of Ohio, to which he emigrated from Connecticut. He was a Representative in Congress, from Ohio, from 1817 to 1821, serving as a member of the Committee on the Judiciary, and re-elected from 1823 to 1829. He died at Lancaster, Ohio, November 30, 1839, aged sixty-four years.

Beekman, Thomas.—He was a Representative in Congress, from New York, from 1829 to 1831.

Beeson, Henry W.—He was born in Pennsylvania, and was a Representative in Congress, from that State, from 1841 to 1843.

Belcher, Hiram.—Born in Augusta, Maine; educated at Hallowell Academy; studied law and admitted to the bar in 1812; was for four or five years a member of the Maine Legislature; and was a Representative in Congress, from that State, from 1847 to 1849. Died May 7, 1857, aged sixty-seven years.

Belcher, Nathan.—Born in Griswold, Connecticut, June 23, 1813; graduated at Amherst College in 1832; studied law with Samuel Ingham, of Essex, and at the Cambridge Law School; was admitted to the bar in 1836, and practised at Clinton, Connecticut, until 1841, when he removed to New London, relinquished the practice of law, and engaged in manufacturing. He was a member of the House of Representatives of Connecticut in 1846 and 1847, and of the State Senate in 1850, and a Representative in Congress, from 1853 to 1855.

Belden, George O.—He was a Representative in Congress, from New York, from 1827 to 1829.

Bell, Hiram.—He was born in Vermont, and was a Representative in Congress, from Ohio, from 1852 to 1853.

Bell, James.—Born November 13, 1804, in Francistown, Hillsborough County, New Hampshire; graduated at Bowdoin College in 1822; studied law, and completed his course at Litchfield; was admitted to the bar in 1825, and commenced to practise at Gilmanton; removed to Exeter, and thence to Gilford; and for many years held a distinguished rank in his profession. In 1846 he was elected to the Legislature, and was a member of the Constitutional Convention of the State in 1850. He was elected United States Senator, in June, 1855, for six years; and died in Laconia, New Hampshire, May 26, 1857, whither he had gone from Washington to recruit his health.

Bell, James M.—He was born in Ohio, and was a Representative in Congress, from that State, from 1833 to 1835.

Bell, John.—He was born near Nashville, Tennessee, February 15, 1797. He commenced his studies at Cumberland College, now the Nashville University, and graduated at the latter in 1814; he studied law, and was admitted to the bar in 1816. In 1817 he was elected to the State Senate; declined a re-election, and devoted the next ten years of his life wholly to his profession; in 1827 he was elected a Representative in Congress, and continued to be re-elected until 1841, officiating during one term as Speaker; in 1841 he accepted a seat in President Harrison's cabinet as Secretary of War, which post he resigned in five months after the accession of President Tyler; in 1847 he accepted a seat in the House of Representatives of Tennessee, but before the close of the year he was elected to the United States Senate, and was re-elected in 1852, serving, from time to time, as chairman of important committees until the close of the Thirty-fifth Congress. In May, 1860, he received from the Union party the nomination for President of the United States, but was defeated.

Bell, John.—He was a Representative in Congress, from Ohio, from 1850 to 1851.

Bell, Joshua F.—He was born in

Kentucky, and elected a Representative in Congress, from that State, from 1845 to 1847, serving as a member of the Committee on Invalid Pensions, and declined a re-election. He is a lawyer, and distinguished in the West as an orator. He was also a member of the Peace Convention of 1861.

Bell, Peter H.—He was born in Virginia, and was a Representative in Congress, from Texas, from 1853 to 1857. He was also Governor of that State from 1849 to 1853, and subsequently Judge of the Supreme Court of that State.

Bell, Samuel.—Born in 1769, and died at Chester, New Hampshire, December 23, 1850. He was a graduate of Dartmouth College in 1793; a Judge of the Supreme Court of New Hampshire, from 1816 to 1819; Governor of the State, from 1819 to 1823; and a Senator in Congress, from 1823 to 1835, serving as a member of the Committees on Foreign Affairs and Claims, and officiating as Chairman of the latter during the Twenty-third Congress.

Bellinger, Joseph.—He was a Representative in Congress, from South Carolina, from 1817 to 1819.

Belser, James E.—He was born in South Carolina, and was a Representative in Congress, from Alabama, from 1845 to 1847. Died at Montgomery, Alabama, January 16, 1859.

Benjamin, Judah P.—Was a Presidential Elector in 1849; he is a lawyer by profession; and was elected a Senator in Congress, from Louisiana, to serve from 1853 to 1859, serving as Chairman of the Committee on Private Land Claims, and as a member of the Committees on the Judiciary and on Commerce. In 1859 was re-elected for a term of six years. He is of Hebrew descent. He became identified with the Rebellion of 1861, and was Attorney-General of the so-called "Southern Confederacy."

Bennet, Benjamin.—Born in 1762; was a Baptist minister, and a Representative in Congress, from New Jersey, from 1815 to 1819. He died at Middletown, New Jersey, October 8, 1840.

Bennet, Henry.—He was born in New Lisbon, Otsego County, New York, September 29, 1808; studied law, and was admitted to the bar in 1832; and having been elected to Congress as a Representative from that State in 1848, has continued to be re-elected until the present time, so that at the end of the Thirty-fifth Congress he will have served in that capacity continuously, the period of ten years. During the Thirty-fourth Congress he was Chairman of the Committee on Public Lands, and reported a number of important bills for the benefit of the Western States, and during the Thirty-fifth Congress he served as a member of the same committee.

Bennett, Hiram P.—Was born in Carthage, Maine, September 2, 1826; received a common school education in Ohio; in 1852 he was elected to a Judgeship in Western Iowa; moved to Nebraska Territory in 1854, and was at once elected a member of the Territorial Council; in 1858 he was re-elected to the Nebraska Legislature, and made Speaker of the House; removed to Colorado Territory in 1859, and was chosen a Delegate therefrom to the Thirty-seventh Congress; and in 1862 was re-elected to the Thirty-eighth Congress.

Bennett, H. S.—Born in Williamson County, Tennessee, March 7, 1807; received a limited education; studied law, and began to practise in 1830, when he removed to Mississippi, where he held the office of Circuit Judge for eight years, and of which State he was a Representative in Congress during the Thirty-fourth Congress. Of late years he has been devoted to planting.

Benson, Egbert.—He was eminent as a statesman and jurist, and died at Jamaica, New York, in August, 1833, in the eighty-seventh year of his age. He was a Representative in Congress, from New York, from 1789 to 1793, taking an active part in its deliberations. He had previously served as a delegate in the Continental Congress from 1784 to 1788. He was a graduate of Columbia College in 1765, and received literary honors from Harvard University in 1808, and from Dartmouth in 1811.

Benson, Samuel P.—He was born in the town of Winthrop, Maine; graduated at Bowdoin College in 1825; adopted the profession of law; was a member of the State Legislature in 1834 and 1836; Secretary of State in 1838 and 1841; and was elected a Representative in Congress, from Maine, in 1853, and was re-elected to the Thirty-fourth Congress, when he served as Chairman of the Committee on Naval Affairs. He was at one time one of the overseers of Bowdoin College.

Benton, Charles S.—He was born in Maine, and was a Representative in Congress, from New York, from 1843 to 1849.

Benton, Samuel.—He was a Representative in Congress, from South Carolina, from 1793 to 1798.

Benton, Thomas Hart.—He was born in Hillsborough, North Carolina, March 14, 1782, and educated at Chapel Hill College. He left that institution without receiving a degree, and forthwith commenced the study of law in William and Mary College, Virginia, under Mr. St. George Tucker. In 1810 he entered the United States Army, but soon resigned his commission of lieutenant-colonel, and in 1811 was at Nashville, Tennessee, where he commenced the practice of the law. He soon afterwards emigrated to St. Louis, Missouri, where he connected himself with the press as the editor of a newspaper, the Missouri Argus. In 1820 he was elected a member of the United States Senate, serving as chairman of many important committees, and remained in that body till the session of 1851, at which time he failed of re-election. As Missouri was not admitted into the Union till August 10, 1821, more than a year of Mr. Benton's first term of service expired before he took his seat. He occupied himself during this interval before taking his seat in Congress in acquiring a knowledge of the language and literature of Spain. Immediately after he appeared in the Senate he took a prominent part in the deliberations of that body, and rapidly rose to eminence and distinction. Few public measures were discussed between the years 1821 and 1851 that he did not participate in largely, and the influence he wielded was always felt and confessed by the country. He was one of the chief props and supporters of the administrations of Presidents Jackson and Van Buren. The people of Missouri long clung to him as their apostle and leader, and it required persevering effort to defeat him. But he had served them during the entire period of thirty years without interruption, and others, who aspired to honors he enjoyed, became impatient for an opportunity to supplant him. His defeat was the consequence. Colonel Benton was distinguished for his learning, iron will, practical mind, and strong memory. As a public speaker he was not interesting or calculated to produce an effect on the passions of an audience, but his speeches were read with avidity, always producing a decided influence. He was elected a Representative in the Thirty-third Congress for the District of St. Louis, and on his retirement from public life devoted himself to the preparation of a valuable register of the debates in Congress, upon which he labored until his death, which occurred in Washington, on the 10th of April, 1858, of cancer in the stomach.

Bergen, John T.—He was a Representative in Congress, from New York, from 1831 to 1833.

Bernhisel, John M.—Born in Cumberland County, Pennsylvania, June 23, 1799; graduated in the Medical Department of Pennsylvania University; engaged in the practice of medicine; and was elected a Delegate to the Thirty-fifth Congress, from the Territory of Utah. Re-elected to the Thirty-sixth and Thirty-seventh Congresses.

Berrien, John McP.—Born in New Jersey, August 23, 1781, but when a child removed with his father to Georgia. He graduated at Princeton in his fifteenth year, and was admitted to the bar in 1799. In 1809 he was elected Solicitor-General, and the next year Judge of the Eastern Circuit. During the war of 1812 he had command of a regiment of volunteer cavalry. He served in the State Legislature for several years. In 1824 he was elected to the United States Senate, where he remained until 1829, when he took a seat in the cabinet of President Jackson as Attorney-General. For a while afterwards he held various positions of responsibility in Georgia, and in 1840 was again elected to the United States Senate for six years, taking an active part in all leading measures, and officiating most of the time as Chairman of the Judiciary Committee. In 1845 he was elected one of the Judges of the Supreme Court of Georgia, and in 1847 was once more elected to the United States Senate, resigning his seat in May, 1852. On his return to Georgia, he still continued, in various ways, to promote the public good, and he died at Savannah, January 1, 1856, universally lamented. He was undoubtedly one of the best, most distinguished, and high-minded statesmen of the country.

Bethune, Laughlin.—A native of North Carolina, for several years a Senator in the State Legislature, and from 1831 to 1833 a Representative in Congress, from Cumberland County, serving as a member of the Committee on Elections.

Betton, Silas.—He graduated at Dartmouth College in 1787; was a Representative in Congress, from New Hampshire, from 1803 to 1807; held the office of Sheriff of Rockingham County for several years; and died at Salem, New Hampshire, in 1822, aged fifty-eight years.

Betts, Samuel R.—He was a Representative in Congress, from New York, from 1815 to 1817.

Betts, Thaddeus.—He was born in Norwalk, Connecticut; graduated at Yale College in 1807, and acquired great distinction as a lawyer. He was at one time Lieutenant-Governor of Connecticut, and an influential member of the United States Senate, from 1839 to the date of his death, April 7, 1840. He was greatly respected for his talents and character.

Bibb, George M.—He was born in Virginia in 1772; graduated at Princeton College in 1792; studied law and settled in Kentucky. He was a Justice and twice Chief Justice of the Court of Appeals of Kentucky; was in the State Senate two years; held the position of Chancellor of the Court of Chancery; was Secretary of the Treasury under President Tyler; afterwards practised his profession in the City of Washington, and acted as an assistant in the office of the Attorney-General of the United States. His services in Congress were rendered as a Senator, from 1811 to 1814, and again from 1829 to 1835. He died in Georgetown, D. C., April 14, 1859. One of his marked peculiarities was a fondness for fishing, which he practised with enthusiasm.

Bibb, William W.—Died at his residence, in Fort Jackson, Alabama, July 9, 1820, aged thirty-nine years. He was a Representative in Congress, from Georgia, from 1806 to 1814, and a Senator in Congress, from 1813 to 1816; and was appointed in 1817 Governor of the Territory of Alabama. He was elected first Governor, under the Constitution of that State, in 1819. He was originally educated for the medical profession.

Bibighaus, Thomas M.—Born in Pennsylvania in 1816; and was a Representative in Congress, from that State, from 1851 to the time of his death, which occurred in Lebanon, Pennsylvania, June 18, 1853.

Bicknell, Bennet.—He was born in Mansfield, Connecticut, in 1803; and was a Representative in Congress, from New York, from 1837 to 1839; having been in the Assembly of the State in 1812, and a State Senator from 1815 to 1818. Died at Morrisville, Madison County, in 1863.

Biddle, Charles John.—Born in Philadelphia in 1819; studied law and came to the bar in 1840; served as a Captain of Voltigeurs, United States Army, in the war with Mexico, and was in the actions of Contreras, Churubusco, Molino del Rey, Chapultepec, and the taking of the City of Mexico, having been breveted a Major for gallant and meritorious services. After the Mexican war he resumed the practice of his profession in Philadelphia. In 1861 he was appointed a Colonel in the Pennsylvania Reserve Volunteer Corps, and while in the field in Virginia he was elected a Representative, from Pennsylvania, to the Thirty-seventh Congress, to fill the vacancy caused by the resignation of E. Joy Morris. Before quitting the field he was tendered the commission of Brigadier-General, but declined it, preferring to serve his constituents in a civil capacity.

Biddle, John.—He was born in Philadelphia; was an officer in the war of 1812, acquitting himself with bravery; held the position of Paymaster in the Army; also that of Indian Agent; and was a Delegate to Congress, from the Territory of Michigan, from 1829 to 1831, when he was appointed Register of the Land Office, at Detroit, Michigan. For some years before his death, he had been travelling in Europe, and died at the White Sulphur Springs, Virginia, August 25th, 1859, aged about seventy years.

Biddle, Richard.—He was a brother of Nicholas Biddle, and a Representative in Congress, from Western Pennsylvania, from 1837 to 1841, and died at Pittsburg, July 7, 1847. Was the author of a Life of Sebastian Cabot.

Bidlack, Benjamin A.—He was born in Pennsylvania, and was a Representative in Congress, from Pennsylvania, from 1841 to 1845; and died at Bogota, New Granada, February 29, 1849, to which country he had been appointed Chargé d'Affaires, immediately after leaving Congress.

Bidwell, Barnabas.—He graduated at Yale College in 1785; received the degree of LL.D. from that institution; and was a Representative in Congress, from Massachusetts, from 1805 to 1807; from 1801 to 1805 he was a member of the Massachusetts Legislature, and Attorney-General for the State from 1807 to 1810. He died in 1833.

Bigelow, Abijah.—Born in Westminster, Worcester County, Massachusetts, December 5, 1775. He graduated at Dartmouth College in 1795; studied law and was admitted to practice in 1798; was town clerk of Leominster for five years; served two years as a member of the General Court of Massachusetts; and was a Representative in Congress, from 1810 to 1815. In 1838 he was appointed a Master in Chancery for Worcester County; from 1817 to 1833, he was Clerk of the County Court of Worcester; at one time treasurer and trustee of Leicester Academy; and has held the minor office of Justice of the Peace for about fifty years.

Bigelow, Lewis.—Born in Worcester County, Massachusetts, in 1783; was a Representative in Congress, from his native State, from 1821 to 1823; was the author of the "Digest of the first twelve volumes of Massachusetts Reports;" and, removing to Peoria, Illinois, became Clerk of the County Court there, and died in October, 1838.

Biggs, Asa.—Born in Williamstown, Martin County, North Carolina, February 4, 1811. He was educated at an academy, served as a merchant's clerk, studied law, and was admitted to the bar in 1831. In 1835 he was elected a member of the Constitutional Convention of that State; in 1840, 1842 and 1844, he was elected to the State Legislature; he was chosen a member of the Twenty-ninth Congress; in 1850 he was one of three Commissioners appointed to revise the statutes of the State; in 1854 he went a second time into the State Senate; and he was elected a Senator in Congress, in 1854, for six years, but resigned May 3, 1858, for the appointment of Judge of the United States District Court of North Carolina, conferred upon him by President Buchanan. He was a member of the Committees on Finance and on Private Land Claims.

Bigler, William.—Born at Shermansburg, Cumberland County, Pennsylvania, in December, 1814. He received a moderate school education, and instead of a college, graduated in a printing-office; by his own personal efforts, he established, and for several years carried on, entirely unaided, the Clearfield Democrat; disposing of his paper, he devoted himself for a time to mercantile pursuits and politics; in 1841 he was elected to the State Convention, and was a member of the State Senate, part of the time Speaker, up to 1847; in 1851 he was elected Governor of Pennsylvania; subsequently became President of the Philadelphia and Erie Railroad Company; and in 1855 was elected a Senator in Congress, serving on the Committees on Commerce, Post-offices and Post-roads, and Engrossed Bills. Was a delegate to the Chicago Convention in 1864.

Billinghurst, Charles.—He was born in Brighton, Monroe County, New York, July 27, 1818; adopted the profession of law, and after practising a few years, removed to Wisconsin in

1847, and was a member of the first Legislature of that State in 1848; was a Presidential Elector in 1852; and was elected a Representative to the Thirty-fourth Congress, from Wisconsin, and was re-elected to the Thirty-fifth Congress, serving as a member of the Judiciary Committee, and was also re-elected to the Thirty-sixth Congress.

Bines, Thomas.—He was a Representative in Congress, from New Jersey, from 1814 to 1815, and again from 1819 to 1820.

Bingham, John A.—He was born in Pennsylvania in 1815; received an academical education; spent two years in a printing-office; entered Franklin College, in Ohio, but his health prevented him from graduating; he studied law in Ohio, and was admitted to the bar in 1840; from 1845 to 1849 he was Attorney for the State in Tuscarawas County; and in 1854 he was elected a Representative in the Thirty-fourth Congress, and re-elected to the Thirty-fifth Congress. During his first term, he was a member of the Committee on Elections, and made a report on the Illinois contested cases, which was adopted by the House, and served as a member of the Committee on Expenditures in the State Department. He was also re-elected to the Thirty-sixth Congress, serving on the Judiciary Committee; re-elected to the Thirty-seventh Congress; and in 1864, was appointed a Judge-Advocate in the Army. In August of the same year, he was appointed Solicitor of the Court of Claims.

Bingham, Kinsley S.—He was born at Camillus, Onondaga County, New York, December 16, 1808; received a fair academic education; taught school for a time at Bennington, Vermont; spent three years in the office of a lawyer as clerk; emigrated to Michigan in 1833, and settled upon a farm; he was elected to the Michigan Legislature in 1835, and was five years a member of that body; three years elected Speaker; he was a Representative in Congress, from Michigan, from 1849 to 1851, and served on the Committee on Commerce; and was elected Governor of Michigan in 1854 and 1856. He has also held in other years the offices of Postmaster, Supervisor, Prosecuting Attorney, Judge of Probate, and Brigadier-General of Militia. In 1859, he was elected a Senator in Congress, from Michigan. Died at Oak Grove, Livingston County, Michigan, October 5, 1861.

Bingham, William.—He graduated at the College of Philadelphia in 1768, and he was agent for this country at Martinique during the Revolution. In 1786 he was a Delegate to the Continental Congress from Pennsylvania, and was elected a Senator in Congress in 1795, serving until 1801, and as President *pro tem.* of the Senate during the Fourth Congress. He died at Bath, England, February 7, 1804, aged fifty-two years.

Binney, Horace.—He was born in Philadelphia, Pennsylvania, January 4, 1780; graduated at Harvard University in 1797; and was educated a lawyer. He was a Director of the old United States Bank, and one of the trustees to whom its affairs were intrusted when it was wound up. He was a member of the Pennsylvania Legislature in 1806–7, and declined a re-election; and a Representative in Congress, from Pennsylvania, from 1833 to 1835; and was a member of the Committee on Ways and Means, and again declined a re-election. In 1827 the degree of LL.D. was conferred upon him by Harvard University.

Bird, John.—A native of Litchfield, Connecticut; afterwards settled in Troy, New York; and was early distinguished at the bar of that State, and in the Legislature. He was a Representative in Congress from 1799 to 1801.

Birdsall, Ausburn.—He was born in New York, and was a Representative in Congress, from that State, from 1847 to 1849.

Birdsall, James.—He was a Representative in Congress, from New York, from 1815 to 1817, and a member of the Assembly of that State in 1837.

Birdsall, Samuel.—He was a Representative in Congress, from New York, from 1837 to 1839.

Birdseye, Victory.—He was a Representative in Congress, from New York, from 1815 to 1817, and again from 1841 to 1843; a Delegate to the State Constitutional Convention of 1821; and a State Senator in 1828 and 1829, as well as a member of the Assembly for three years.

Birne, Andrew.—He was a native of Ireland, and on becoming a citizen of Virginia, was elected a Representative in Congress from 1837 to 1841.

Bishop, James.—He was born in New Brunswick, New Jersey, and was a Representative in Congress, from that State, from 1855 to 1857; he was bred a merchant, and has served in the Legisture of his native State.

Bishop, Phanuel.—He was a Representative in Congress, from Massachusetts, from 1799 to 1807. From 1787 to 1791 he was a member of the State Senate; and in 1792, 1793, 1797 and 1798 a Representative in the State Legislature.

Bishop, William D. — He was born in Bloomfield, New Jersey, September 14, 1827; graduated at Yale College in 1849; studied law as a profession, but soon engaged almost exclusively in railroad business, having for several years been President of the Naugatuck Railroad Company. He was elected a Representative to the Thirty-fifth Congress, from Connecticut, and was chairman of the Committee on Manufactures. In May, 1859, he was appointed by President Buchanan Commissioner of Patents, but resigned in January, 1860.

Bissell, William H.—Born in Hartwick, Otsego County, New York, April 25, 1811. He was self-educated, attending school in the summer, and teaching school in the winter; he studied medicine, and graduated in 1834 at the Medical College in Philadelphia; he removed to Illinois, and after practising his profession until 1840, was elected to the State Legislature; he studied law, and was admitted to the bar of Illinois; after practising with success, he was, in 1844, elected a Prosecuting Attorney; he served with distinction in the Mexican war, and especially at Buena Vista, as captain of the 2d Regiment Illinois Volunteers; he was a Representative in Congress, from Illinois, from 1849 to 1855; and in 1856 he was elected Governor of Illinois for four years, to the duties of which office he devoted his undivided attention. Died at Springfield, Illinois, March 18, 1860.

Black, Edward J. — Born in Beaufort, South Carolina, in 1806. He never attended college, but read law, and was admitted to the bar of Augusta, Georgia, in 1827. He commenced his public life by going into the State Legislature, where he served for several years, and was elected a Representative in Congress, from Georgia, in 1838, remaining there until 1845. He died in Barnwell District, South Carolina, whither he had gone for change of scene, in 1849.

Black, James.—He was born in Pennsylvania, and was a Representative in Congress, from that State, from 1843 to 1847.

Black, James A.—He was born in South Carolina, and was a Representative in Congress, from that State, from 1843 to 1847. Died in Washington, April 5, 1848.

Black, John.—He was at one time a resident of Louisiana, but removing to Mississippi, was elected a Senator in Congress, from 1832 to 1838, officiating as Chairman of the Committee on Private Land Claims during the first term. He died in Winchester, Virginia, August 29, 1854.

Blackledge, William.—Presumed to have been the father of the following. He was for several years a member of the General Assembly of North Carolina, and served that State as Representative in Congress, from 1803 to 1809, and from 1811 to 1813. Died at Spring Hill, Lenoir County, North Carolina, October 19, 1828.

Blackledge, William S.—He was born in Pitt County, North Carolina; was a member of the General Assembly of North Carolina; and he was elected to Congress, from that State, for the term, from 1821 to 1823. Died in Newbern, North Carolina, March 21, 1857, aged sixty-four.

Blackmar, Esbon.—He was a native of New York, and a Representative in Congress, from that State, from 1848 to 1849; he also served two years in the State Assembly, from Wayne County.

Blackwell, Julius W.—He was born in Virginia, and was a Representative in Congress, from Tennessee, from 1839 to 1841, and again from 1843 to 1845.

Blaine, James Gillespie.—He was born in Washington County, Pennsylvania, in 1830; graduated at Washington College in 1847; adopted the profession of editor, and, having removed to Maine, edited the Kennebec Journal and Portland Advertiser for several years. He served four years in the Maine Legislature, two of which as Speaker of the House; and in 1862 he was elected a Representative from Maine to the Thirty-eighth Congress, serving as a member of the Committee on the Post-office and Post-roads.

Blair, Barnard.—He was a native of New York, and a Representative in Congress, from that State, from 1841 to 1843, serving as a member of the Committee on Elections.

Blair, Francis P., Jr.—Born in Lexington, Kentucky, February 19, 1821, graduated at Princeton College, adopted the profession of law, was a member of the Missouri Legislature in 1852 and 1854, and elected a Representative from Missouri to the Thirty-fifth Congress, serving on the Committee on Private Land Claims. Re-elected to the Thirty-seventh Congress, and was Chairman of the Committee on Military Affairs. He was also a Colonel of volunteers in 1861, and in 1862 he was appointed a Major-General in the army, and was subsequently re-elected to the Thirty-eighth Congress. During the first session of that Congress, he resigned his seat in the House to resume his position in the army, but by the action of the House, subsequently, the seat was assigned to his contestant, Samuel Knox.

Blair, Jacob B.—Was born in Parkersburg, Wood County, Virginia, April 11, 1821, studied and adopted the profession of law, was Prosecuting Attorney for Ritchie County for several years, and was elected a Representative from Virginia to the Thirty-seventh Congress, serving on the Committee on Public Buildings and Grounds. In 1863 he was elected a Representative from West Virginia to the Thirty-eighth Congress, serving on the Committees on Public Expenditures, and Public Buildings and Grounds.

Blair, James.—He was born in Lancaster, South Carolina, and was a Representative in Congress, from South Carolina, from 1821 to 1822, and from 1829 to 1834. He died at Washington, by his own hand, March 27, 1834.

Blair, John.—He was born in Washington County, Tennessee, and was a Representative in Congress, from Tennessee, from 1823 to 1837, and was a member of the Committee on Military Affairs. Before entering Congress, he served in both branches of the State Legislature, and died at Jonesborough, Tennessee, in July, 1863.

Blair, Samuel S.—He was born in Pennsylvania, and elected a Representative from that State, to the Thirty-sixth Congress, serving as a member of the Committee on Private Land Claims. Re-elected to the Thirty-seventh Congress, and was placed at the head of that committee, serving also on several other committees.

Blaisdell, Daniel.—He was a State Councillor from 1803 to 1808, and a Representative in Congress, from New Hampshire, from 1808 to 1811. Died in 1832, aged seventy-three years.

Blake, Harrison G.—Born in New Fane, Windham County, Vermont, March 17, 1818; received a common school education, and removed to Ohio in 1830. Whilst engaged as a merchant's clerk he studied law, and after devoting much of his life to mercantile pursuits he adopted the profession of law. He has served four years in the Ohio Legislature, and was President of the State Senate in 1848–49; and he was elected a Representative, from Ohio, to the Thirty-sixth Congress, serving as a member of the Committee on Accounts. Re-elected to the Thirty-seventh Congress, serving on the Committee on the Post-office.

Blake, John.—He was a native of New York, and a Representative in Congress, from that State, from 1805 to

1809, and was a member of the Assembly of that State in 1819.

Blake, Thomas H.—He was born in Calvert County, Maryland, June, 1792, and spent his boyhood in Washington City. He served at the battle of Bladensburg in 1814; was an early emigrant to the State of Kentucky, and afterwards to Indiana while a Territory; upon the formation of the State government, he settled at Terre Haute; there practised law, and served on the bench of the Circuit Court, and was District Attorney; and subsequently engaged in mercantile pursuits. He was, for many years, a member of the State Legislature, and a Representative in Congress, from Indiana, from 1827 to 1829. Under President Tyler's administration, he was Commissioner of the General Land Office, and, upon his resignation, was appointed President of the Wabash and Erie Canal Company. He held this office at the time of his death, having just returned from England, where, as the financial agent of his State, he had made satisfactory arrangements with its public creditors. He died at Cincinnati, while on his return from Washington, November 28, 1849.

Blanchard, John.—Born in the County of Caledonia, Vermont, September 30, 1787. He spent his boyhood on a farm; prepared himself for college, and graduated at Dartmouth in 1812; removed to Pennsylvania, and taught school; read law, and was admitted to practice; and was a Representative in Congress, from Pennsylvania, from 1845 to 1849. He died in Columbia, Lancaster County, March 8, 1849.

Bland, Theodoric.—Was a native of Virginia; he was bred a physician, but upon the commencement of the American war he quitted the practice for the army, and rose to the rank of Colonel, and had the command of a regiment of dragoons. In 1779, he had command of the troops at Albemarle Barracks, and continued in that station till elected to a seat in Congress in 1780. He served in that body three years. He was then chosen a member of the Virginia Legislature. He was a Representative in the first Congress under the Constitution, having voted for its adoption. He died at New York, June 1, 1790, while attending a session of Congress, aged forty-eight. He was the first member of Congress whose death was announced in that body.

Bledsoe, Jesse.—He was at one time a distinguished advocate and jurist of Kentucky, and a Senator in Congress, from that State, from 1813 to 1815; he was also Professor of Law in the University of Transylvania, and Chief Justice of the Supreme Court of Kentucky. He died at Nacogdoches, Texas, June 30, 1837.

Bleecker, Hermanus.—He was born at Albany, New York, in 1779, and died there, July 19, 1849. He was a member of Congress, from 1811 to 1813, and, by President Van Buren, was appointed, in 1839, Chargé d'Affaires at the Hague.

Bliss, George.—Was born in Jericho, Chittenden County, Vermont, January 1, 1813; received an academical education; went to Ohio in his twentieth year, and spent one year in Granville College; studied law and came to the bar in 1841; in 1850 he was appointed President Judge of the Eighth Judicial District of Ohio, serving one year, or until the State Constitution was changed; in 1852 was elected a Representative from Ohio, to the Thirty-third Congress, and in 1862 he was re-elected to the Thirty-eighth Congress, serving on the Committee on the Judiciary.

Bliss, Philemon.—Born in Canton, Connecticut, July 28, 1814; educated at Fairfield Academy, Oneida Institute, and Hamilton College, New York; is a lawyer by profession; removed to Ohio, and was elected President Judge of the Fourteenth Circuit Court, and, in 1854, a Representative to the Thirty-fourth Congress, and re-elected to the Thirty-fifth Congress. He is a member of the Committee on Manufactures.

Bloodworth, Timothy.—He was born in North Carolina, and was a Representative in Congress, from North Carolina, in 1790 and 1791, and a Senator of the United States, from 1795 to 1801. He died August 24, 1814.

Bloomfield, Joseph.—Born in the town of Woodbridge, Middlesex County, New Jersey; studied law until 1775, when he became an active friend of the Revolution; was afterwards Attorney-General for New Jersey; Governor of that State from 1801 to 1812; was appointed a Brigadier-General by President Madison; and was a Representative in Congress, from New Jersey, from 1817 to 1821. As Chairman of the Committee on Revolutionary Pensions he reported the bill granting pensions to soldiers of the Revolutionary army. He resided in Burlington, New Jersey, many years before his death.

Blount, Thomas.—He was born in North Carolina; was a General of militia in that State; and a Representative from the same, in the Twelfth Congress. Died in Washington, February 9, 1812.

Blount, William.—He was a Delegate to the Continental Congress in 1782, 1783, 1786, and 1787, from North Carolina; and was Governor of the territory south of the Ohio, having been appointed to that office in 1790. In 1796, he was chosen President of the Convention of Tennessee. He was elected, the same year, by that State, to a seat in the United States Senate, but was expelled in 1797, for having, as it was alleged, instigated the Creeks and Cherokees to assist the British in conquering the Spanish territories near the United States. While his impeachment was being tried in the United States Senate he was elected a member of the State Senate and made President thereof. He died at Knoxville, March 10, 1810, aged fifty-six years.

Blount, William G.—He was a Representative in Congress, from Tennessee, from 1815 to 1819. Died May 21, 1827.

Blow, Henry T.—Born in Southampton County, Virginia, July 15, 1817; removed to Missouri in 1830, and graduated at the St. Louis University; devoted himself to the drug and lead business; served four years in the State Senate; in 1861 he was appointed by President Lincoln Minister to Venezuela, which he resigned in less than a year, and in 1862 he was elected a Representative from Missouri to the Thirty-eighth Congress, serving on the Committee of Ways and Means. He was also a Delegate to the Baltimore Convention of 1864.

Boardman, Elijah.—Born in New Milford, Connecticut, March 7, 1760, and became a successful merchant. He was frequently a member of the Legislature, member of the Council, and a Senator in Congress, from 1821 to 1823. He died in Boardman, Ohio, October 8, 1823.

Boardman, William W.—He was born in New Milford, Connecticut, October 10, 1794; graduated at Yale College in 1812; studied law at Litchfield and Cambridge, and practised with success; was at one time Judge of Probate; for several years in the State Legislature, and Speaker of the House; and a Representative in Congress, from Connecticut, from 1841 to 1843.

Bockee, Abraham.—He was born in New York, and was a Representative in Congress, from that State, from 1829 to 1831, and again from 1833 to 1837; he subsequently served four years in the Senate and one year in the Assembly of the State of New York.

Bocock, Thomas S.—He was born in Buckingham County, Virginia, in 1815; graduated at Hampden Sidney College; adopted the profession of law; was Commonwealth Attorney for the County of Appomattox, in 1845 and 1846; for several sessions a member of the Virginia House of Delegates; and has been a Representative in Congress, from 1847 to the present time, serving, for some years, as Chairman of the Committee on Naval Affairs. Took part in the Rebellion of 1861 as a member of the "Confederate" Congress.

Boden, Alexander.—He was born in Carlisle, Pennsylvania, and was a Representative in Congress, from that State, from 1817 to 1821.

Bodle, Charles.—He was a Representative in Congress, from New York, from 1833 to 1835, and died in New York City, in 1836.

Bokee, David A.—He was born in New York, October 6, 1805; was a Representative in Congress, from New York, from 1849 to 1851, serving on the Committee on Indian Affairs; and his last public position was that of Naval Officer of the port of New York, under President Fillmore. He died in Washington, March 16, 1860; he was on a visit to that city and was found dead in his room.

Bond, Shadrack.—He was elected a Delegate to Congress, from the Territory of Illinois, from 1811 to 1815; and was the first Governor under the State Constitution. In 1814 was appointed Receiver of Public Moneys in Kaskaskia, Illinois. He died at Kaskaskia, April 13, 1832.

Bond, William Key.—He was born in St. Mary's County, Maryland; emigrated to Ohio in 1812; studied law and settled in the practice of the profession at Chillicothe, and subsequently at Cincinnati; was at one time a Colonel of militia; and a Representative in Congress, from Ohio, from 1835 to 1841. Died at Cincinnati, February 17, 1864.

Bonham, Milledge L.—He was born in South Carolina; graduated at the College of that State, in 1834; is a lawyer by profession; and was elected a Representative to the Thirty-fifth Congress, from his native State, serving as a member of the Committee on Military Affairs. He was re-elected to the Thirty-sixth Congress, but resigned in December, 1860. He was a Major-General of militia, and served in Mexico at the head of a batallion of South Carolina troops. Served as a Major-General in the Rebel army in 1861.

Boody, Azariah.—Born in New York, and was elected a Representative from that State to the Thirty-third Congress, but resigned in October, 1853.

Boone, Ratliff.—He was born in Franklin County, North Carolina, in 1781, and was a Representative in Congress, from Indiana, from 1825 to 1827, and again, from 1829 to 1839, officiating as Chairman of the Committee on Public Lands, during the Twenty-fourth Congress. He died in Louisiana, November 20, 1844.

Booth, Walter.—Born in Woodbridge, New Haven County, Connecticut, December 8, 1791, and after receiving a good school education in New Haven, he settled in the town of Meriden, where he still resides. He was for several years a merchant and manufacturer, and for eighteen years President of the Meriden Bank; he has been a member of the General Assembly and State Senate; and in 1834, was Associate Judge of the County Court. He was Major-General of militia, and elected a member of the Thirty-first Congress, serving on the Committee of Public Expenditures. He has since been engaged in agricultural pursuits.

Borden, Nathaniel B.—He was born in Fall River, Massachusetts, April 15, 1801, and was a Representative in Congress, from the Fall River District, in that State, from 1835 to 1839, and again, from 1841 to 1843, and was a member of the Committees on Elections and on Territories. He was also a member of the State Legislature in 1831, 1834, and 1851, and a State Senator from 1845 to 1848.

Borland, Charles.—He was born in Orange County, New York, and was a member of the New York Assembly in 1820; a Representative in Congress, from that State, from 1821 to 1823; and was again elected to the Assembly in 1836.

Borland, Solon.—He was born in Virginia; was educated in North Carolina; served in the war with Mexico as a volunteer; was a Senator in Congress, from Arkansas, from 1848 to 1853, and was appointed, by President Pierce, Minister to Central America. He also received, from President Pierce, the appointment of Governor of the Territory of New Mexico, but declined. He took part in the Rebellion of 1861 as a Brigadier-General. Died in Texas early in 1864.

Borst, Peter J.—He was a Representative in Congress, from the County of Schoharie, New York, from 1829 to 1831, and was a member of the Committee on Expenditures in the Post-office Department. Died at Middleburg, New York, November 14, 1848.

Boss, John L.—He was a Representative in Congress, from Rhode Island, from 1815 to 1819.

Bossier, Peter E.—He was descended from an old French family of

Louisiana, and after serving ten years in the State Senate, he was elected a member of the Twenty-eighth Congress, and died in Washington before the expiration of his term, April 24, 1844.

Boteler, Alexander R.—Born in Shepherdstown, Jefferson County, Virginia, May 16, 1815. After going through an academic course of studies in his native town, he entered Princeton College, and graduated in 1835, and since that time has been chiefly devoted to rural and literary pursuits. In 1852 and 1856, he was on the Electoral tickets, Whig and American; and in 1859 he was elected a Representative, from Virginia, to the Thirty-sixth Congress, serving on the Committee on Military Affairs. Resigned on the breaking out of the Rebellion in 1861.

Botts, John M.—Born in Dumfries, Prince William County, Virginia, September 16, 1802, but removed with his father to Fredericksburg, and subsequently to Richmond. In 1811 he lost his parents, at the conflagration of the Richmond theatre, and was sent to a boarding-school. At eighteen he was admitted to the bar, practised for six years, and then retired to a farm in Henrico County. He served in the Legislature, from 1833 to 1839, when he was elected a Representative in Congress, from Virginia, and occupied that position until 1843; was re-elected to the Thirtieth Congress, and was Chairman of the Committee on Military Affairs. He afterwards resumed the practice of his profession in Richmond, where he now resides, having, since 1851, declined all nominations for public office in his State.

Bouck, Joseph.—He was born in New York, and was a Representative in Congress, from that State, from 1831 to 1833, serving on the Committee on Imprisonment for Debt.

Boude, Thomas.—He was a Representative in Congress, from Pennsylvania, from 1801 to 1803.

Boudinot, Elias.—Was born in Philadelphia, May 2, 1740. He studied the law and became eminent in that profession. At an early period of the Revolutionary War, he was appointed by Congress Commissary-General of prisoners. In the year 1777, he was chosen a member of Congress, and in 1782 was made President of that body. After the adoption of the Constitution, he entered the House of Representatives, where he continued for six years. He then succeeded Rittenhouse as Director of the Mint of the United States, an office which he resigned in the course of a few years, and lived from that time at Burlington, New Jersey. He devoted himself earnestly to biblical literature, and being possessed of an ample fortune, made munificent donations to various charitable and theological institutions. The American Bible Society, of which he became President, was particularly an object of his bounty. He died at Burlington, New Jersey, October 24, 1821.

Bouldin, James W.—He was a Representative in Congress, from Virginia, from 1833 to 1839.

Bouldin, Thomas T.—He was born in Virginia; spent his youth in farming; adopted the profession of law, and reached a high judicial position; was a member of Congress, from Virginia, from 1829 to 1833, and died in the Capitol, at Washington, February 11, 1833. On the day preceding his death, he was censured by a colleague for omitting to call the attention of the House to the death of his predecessor, John Randolph; and he had risen to reply, when he was seized with paralysis, sank down into a chair, and died immediately. Before entering Congress, he had been a lawyer of high rank, and an able and upright judge, and highly respected for his talents and integrity.

Bouligny, Dominique.—He was born in Louisiana; was a lawyer by profession; was a Senator in Congress, from that State, from 1824 to 1829; and died in 1833.

Bouligny, John Edmond.—He was born in New Orleans, February 5, 1824, and was of Creole descent; received a good education; held several offices of trust in his native city; and was elected a Representative, from Louisiana, to the Thirty-sixth Congress. Of the representatives of twelve millions of people, he was the only one who refused to abandon his State to the leaders of the secession movement, and he continued in Congress until the close of his term. He died in Washington, of consumption, February 20, 1864. Dominique Bouligny, formerly a Senator from Louisiana, was his uncle.

Bourne, Benjamin.—He was a native of Bristol, Rhode Island, and was born about the year 1755, and educated at Harvard College, where he graduated in 1775. He was conspicuous for talents and learning, and spent a large part of his life in public and honorable employments. He was a Representative in Congress, from Rhode Island, from 1790 to 1796, when he resigned, and was appointed Judge of the United States District Court of Rhode Island. He died September 17, 1808.

Bourne, Shearjasub.—He was a graduate of Harvard College in 1764; was Chief Justice of the Court of Common Pleas for Suffolk County, Massachusetts; and a Representative in Congress, from 1791 to 1795. He died in 1806.

Boutwell, George S.—He was born in Brookline, Norfolk County, Massachusetts, January 28, 1818. When a boy he had some experience in farming; was in the mercantile business as apprentice, clerk, and proprietor for twenty years; studied law, and came to the bar in 1836; served seven years in the Massachusetts Legislature, between the years 1842 and 1850; was a member of the Massachusetts Constitutional Convention of 1853, and also of the Peace Congress of 1861; was a Bank Commissioner in 1849 and 1850; was Governor of Massachusetts in 1851 and 1852; Secretary of the Massachusetts Board of Education for eleven years; member for six years of the Board of Overseers of Harvard College; and Commissioner of Internal Revenue from July, 1862, to March, 1863. In 1862 he was elected a Representative, from Massachusetts, to the Thirty-eighth Congress, serving on the Judiciary Committee. He was also a Delegate to the Baltimore Convention of 1864.

Bovee, Matthew J.—He was born in New York, and was a Representative in Congress, from that State, from 1835 to 1837, serving on the Committee on Expenditures in the War Department.

Bowden, Lemuel J.—Was born in the North Neck of Virginia in 1812; graduated at William and Mary College; was a lawyer by profession; served three sessions in the Virginia Legislature; was a member of the Convention for amending the State Constitution in 1849; also of the Convention for the same purpose in 1851; suffered much, in his estate, from the Rebel armies, during the early part of the Rebellion. While our troops were at Williamsburg, he did much for the comfort of our officers and men; and in 1863 he was elected a Senator in Congress, from Virginia, but died in Washington City, January 2, 1864. In the Senate he served on the Committees on Pensions and Post-office and Post-roads.

Bowdon, Franklin W.—Born in Alabama, and was a Representative in Congress, from 1846 to 1851, from his native State. In 1852 he removed to Texas, and engaged in the practice of the law. He died at Henderson, Texas, June 6, 1857.

Bowen, John H.—He was a Representative in Congress, from Tennessee, from 1813 to 1815.

Bower, Gustavus B.—He was born in Virginia, and was a Representative in Congress, from Missouri, from 1843 to 1845.

Bowers, John M.—He was a Representative in Congress, from New York, from 1813 to 1814.

Bowie, Richard I.—He was born in Georgetown, District of Columbia, June 23, 1807. He received a classical education, and was admitted to the bar in his nineteenth year, and, subsequently, to practice in the Supreme Court of the United States. In 1836 and 1837 he was elected to the Legislature of Maryland; in 1840 he was a Delegate to the Harrisburg Convention, called to nominate a President; and he was a Representative in Congress, from 1849 to 1853. It is claimed by his friends that he made the first speech in the House of Representatives on the Compromise measures of 1850.

Bowie, Thomas F.—Born at Queen Ann, Prince George's County, Maryland, April 7, 1808; graduated, in

1837, at Union College, New York; adopted the profession of law; served as Deputy Attorney-General for Prince George's County sixteen years; served three terms in the Legislature of Maryland, and was elected a Representative, from Maryland, in the Thirty-fourth and Thirty-fifth Congresses. He was a member of the Committee on the District of Columbia.

Bowie, Walter.—He was a Representative in Congress, from Maryland, from 1802 to 1805.

Bowlin, James B.—Born in Spottsylvania County, Virginia, in 1804. He was reared a mechanic, but obtained a common school education; and, after studying law, was admitted to the bar, in Greenbrier County, in 1827. In 1833 he removed to St. Louis, Missouri; in 1834 was appointed Chief Clerk of the State House of Representatives, and in 1835 was elected a member of the Legislature. In 1837 he was made District Attorney for St. Louis; soon after attorney for the Bank of St. Louis; in 1839 he was elected Judge of the Criminal Court; and was a Representative in Congress, from 1843 to 1851. In 1858 he was appointed, by President Buchanan, Commissioner to Paraguay.

Bowne, Obadiah.—He was born in New York, and was a Representative in Congress, from that State, from 1851 to 1853.

Bowne, Samuel S.—He was a member of the New York Assembly in 1834, and a Representative in Congress, from that State, from 1841 to 1843.

Boyce, William W.—Born in Charleston, South Carolina, October 24, 1819, and was educated at the South Carolina College and Virginia University. He is a lawyer by profession; was a member of the Legislature of South Carolina in 1842, and was a Representative in Congress, from 1853 to December, 1860, when he resigned. He took part in the Rebellion as a member of the "Confederate" Congress. His tastes are of a literary character, and he is said to be a hard student. When reelected to the Thirty-sixth Congress, he served as a member of the Committee on Elections, and at the time of his leaving Congress, he was a member of the famous Committee of Thirty-three.

Boyd, Adam.—He was a Representative in Congress, from New Jersey, from 1803 to 1805, and again from 1808 to 1813. He was an active supporter of the Revolution, and a man of strong natural ability. He died in Hackensack, New Jersey, at an advanced age.

Boyd, Alexander.—He was a Representative in Congress, from New York, from 1813 to 1815.

Boyd, John H.—He was born in New York, and was a Representative in Congress, from that State, from 1851 to 1853. He was a member, in 1840, of the State Assembly, from Washington County.

Boyd, Linn.—Was born in Nashville, Tennessee, November 22, 1800. His early advantages were limited, but on arriving at man's estate he removed to Kentucky, entered into politics, and in 1827 was elected to the Legislature of that State, from Calloway County, serving three sessions, and in 1831 was re-elected for another session, from Trigg County. He was a Representative in Congress, from Kentucky, from 1835 to 1837, from 1839 to 1847, and again from 1847 to 1855. He was Chairman of the Committee on Territories during the Thirty-first Congress; and during his last term in Congress occupied the chair of Speaker of the House of Representatives. He also served one term as Lieutenant-Governor of Kentucky. During his career in Congress he labored faithfully and constantly for his constituents, and retired to private life with a high reputation. Died in Paducah, Kentucky, December 16, 1859.

Boyd, Sempronius H.—He was born in Williamson County, Tennessee, May 28, 1828; received a good English education; adopted the profession of law; in 1861 raised a regiment for the war and became its commander, the same having acquired reputation as "the Lyon legion;" and in 1862 he was elected a Representative, from Missouri, to the Thirty-eighth Congress, serving on the Committee on Indian Affairs, and as Chairman of the Committee on Unfinished Business.

Boyden, Nathaniel. — Born in Franklin Township, Massachusetts, August 16, 1796; he graduated at Union College, New York, in 1820; in 1821 removed to North Carolina; there he taught school, studied law, and was elected a number of times to the State Legislature. He was in Congress as a Representative, from 1847 to 1849, and was a member of the Committee on Expenditures in the Navy Department; he declined a re-election, for the purpose of devoting his whole attention to the practice of his profession.

Boyle, John. — He was born in Kentucky, liberally educated, and a lawyer by profession. He was a Judge of the Supreme Court of Kentucky, also Chief Justice of the State; and a Representative in Congress, from 1803 to 1809, when he was appointed Governor of Illinois Territory. He was a distinguished and successful lawyer, and able judge, and died in Kentucky, January 28, 1834. During the eight years immediately preceding his death, he was Judge of the United States District Court for Kentucky, having been appointed by President Adams.

Brabson, Reese B.—Born in Tennessee, and elected a Representative, from that State, to the Thirty-sixth Congress, serving as a member of the Committee on Invalid Pensions. Died in Tennessee, in September, 1863.

Brace, Jonathan.—He was born in Harrington, Connecticut, November 12, 1754, and died at Hartford, Connecticut, August 26, 1837. He was a graduate of Yale College in 1779, and was elected a Judge of Próbate, Chief Judge of the Hartford County Court, and a Representative in Congress, from 1798 to 1800. He was also frequently in the State Legislature, at one time State's Attorney for Hartford County, and for nine years Mayor of Hartford.

Bradbury, George. — Was born in Portland, then called Falmouth, Massachusetts, in 1770. He graduated at Harvard College in 1789, and immediately commenced the study of law. He established himself in the practice at Portland. From 1806 to 1810 he was a member of the State Legislature, and also in 1811 and 1812. In 1812 he was chosen to represent the Cumberland District in Congress, as successor to William Widgery, whose vote on, and support of war measures, rendered him unpopular with his constituents. Mr. Bradbury received the approbation of a second election in 1814. After this service he returned to his profession, which he pursued to the time of his death, which took place in Portland, November 7, 1823, having been Associate Clerk of a court in Portland from 1817 to 1820, and a State Senator in 1822.

Bradbury, James W.—He was born in Maine, in 1805; graduated at Bowdoin College in 1825; adopted the profession of law; was a County Attorney from 1834 to 1838; a Presidential Elector in 1844; and was a Senator in Congress, from Maine, from 1847 to 1853, serving as Chairman of the Committee on Printing.

Bradbury, Theophilus. — Was born in that portion of Newbury, now Newburyport, in 1739. Having graduated at Harvard University at the age of eighteen, he then studied law, and practised in Falmouth, Maine, until 1779, when he returned to his native town. After filling several local offices, he was chosen to represent the Essex District in Congress, from 1795 to 1797. About six years before his death, which occurred September 6, 1803, he was appointed a Judge of the Supreme Court of Massachusetts.

Bradford, William.—Was born at Plymton, Massachusetts, November 4, 1729. He studied medicine, and established himself in practice at Warren, Rhode Island, but afterwards removed to Bristol. He then turned his attention to the law, and became one of the most distinguished civilians of the State. He took an active part in the cause of his country during the Revolution, and afterwards held many important stations. He was Lieutenant-Governor of the State, and a member of the United States Senate, from 1793 to 1797, when he resigned. He was President *pro tem.* of the Senate during a part of the Fifth Congress. He died July 6, 1808.

Bradley, Stephen R. — He was born in Connecticut, and graduated at Yale College in 1775. He was a General of militia, the intimate friend of General Ethan Allen, and the aid of General

Wooster when that officer fell in a skirmish with the enemy. He was a lawyer by profession, and the first Senator from Vermont in the Congress of the United States, serving from 1791 to 1795, and from 1801 to 1813; a man of eminent ability, but of eccentric habits; and died in New Hampshire, December 16, 1830, aged seventy-six years. During a part of the Seventh and Tenth Congresses he officiated as President *pro tem.* of the Senate.

Bradley, William C.—Born at Westminster, Vermont, March 23, 1782. He entered Yale College, and was compelled to leave when a freshman, in 1796, and yet in 1817, the Corporation of the Institution surprised him with the degree of M.A. He studied law with his father, Stephen R. Bradley, and was admitted to the bar in 1802. The public positions held by him are as follows: From 1800 to 1803, Secretary of Commissioners of Bankruptcy; from 1804 to 1811, State's Attorney for Windham County, and part of this period Clerk of Westminster; in 1806–7, Representative in the State Legislature; in 1812, member of the State Council; a Representative in Congress from 1813 to 1815; from 1817 to 1822, agent of the United States under the Treaty of Ghent; again in Congress, from 1823 to 1827; in 1850 again in the State Legislature; in 1856 a Presidential Elector; in 1857 a member of the State Constitutional Convention; and in 1858 took formal leave of the bar, at which he had practised for fifty-four years, conferring honor upon his native State and winning a spotless reputation as a man. He was also Presidential Elector in 1857.

Bradshaw, Samuel C.—He was born in Plumstead Township, Bucks County, Pennsylvania, June 10, 1809; received a common school education; studied medicine, and graduated at the Pennsylvania Medical College in 1833; and was a Representative, from his native State, to the Thirty-fourth Congress.

Brady, Jasper E.—He was born in New Jersey, and was a Representative in Congress, from Pennsylvania, from 1847 to 1849. He subsequently settled in the practice of law at Pittsburg, Pennsylvania.

Bragg, John.—He was born in North Carolina, and was a Representative in Congress, from Alabama, from 1851 to 1853.

Bragg, Thomas.—Born in Warrenton, Warren County, North Carolina, November 9, 1810; was chiefly educated at the Military Academy at Middletown, Connecticut; studied law and commenced practice in 1831; in 1842 was elected to the Assembly of his State; in 1853 was a Presidential Elector; was Governor of North Carolina for two terms, from 1855 to 1859; and was elected a Senator in Congress for the term commencing in 1859, serving on the Committees on Public Lands and Claims. Expelled from the Senate in July, 1861, having previously taken part in the Rebellion.

Brainard, S.—He was a Senator in Congress, from Vermont, during the session of 1854–5.

Branch, John.—Born in Halifax County, North Carolina, November 4, 1782; graduated at the University of North Carolina in 1801; studied and practised law; in 1811 was elected a State Senator; re-elected every year until 1817; was then elected Governor of the State; again entered the State Senate in 1822; served in the United States Senate from 1823 to 1829; and was in the latter year appointed Secretary of the Navy by President Jackson. On his return home from Washington, in 1831, he was elected to a seat in Congress as Representative; in 1834 was again elected to the State Senate; in 1835 elected a member of the Convention to revise the State Constitution; and in 1843 was appointed Governor of the Territory of Florida; after which he retired to private life, to enjoy in peace the love and respect of his many friends. Died at Enfield, North Carolina, January 4, 1863.

Branch, Lawrence O. B.—Born in North Carolina in 1820; graduated at Princeton College in 1838; is a lawyer by profession; and was elected a Representative, from North Carolina, to the Thirty-fourth, and re-elected to the Thirty-fifth and Thirty-sixth Congresses, serving as a member of the Committees on Territories, and on Foreign Affairs. He took part in the

Great Rebellion as a General, and was killed at the battle of Antietam, in September, 1862.

Brandegee, Augustus.—He was born in New London, Connecticut, July 15, 1828; graduated at Yale College in 1849, and at the Yale Law School in 1851; adopted the profession of law; was elected in 1854, 1858, 1859, and 1861 a member of the Connecticut Legislature, having been chosen Speaker in the latter year; in 1860 he was a Presidential Elector, and was elected a Representative, from Connecticut, to the Thirty-eighth Congress, serving as a member of the Committees on Naval Affairs, and Expenditures on Public Buildings, and also as Chairman of a special Committee on the Air-line Railroad from Washington to New York. He was also a Delegate to the Baltimore Convention of 1864.

Brayton, William D.—He was born in Warwick, Kent County, Rhode Island, November 6, 1815. He was educated at Brown University, and ill health preventing him from following a sedentary profession, he entered into active mercantile pursuits; he held the position for some time of Town Clerk; was elected in 1841 to the State Assembly, serving two terms; after serving for two years in the Town Councils, part of the time as president, he was in 1848 elected to the State Senate; again elected to the State Assembly in 1851; elected a second time to the Senate in 1855; was Presidential Elector in 1856; and was elected a member of the Thirty-fifth and Thirty-sixth Congresses, serving on the Committee on Patents, and as Chairman of the Committee on Expenditures on the Public Buildings.

Breck, Daniel.—He was born near Boston, Massachusetts, in 1788; graduated at Dartmouth College in 1812; he studied law, and removing to Kentucky in 1814, soon after commenced the practice of his profession there; his first public position in Kentucky was that of Judge of a county court; in 1824 he was elected to the State Legislature, and re-elected five years; from 1835 until 1843 he was President of the Branch Bank of Kentucky, at Richmond; in 1840 he was a Presidential Elector; in 1843 he was appointed Judge of the Supreme Court of Kentucky; and he was a Representative in Congress, from 1849 to 1851, and was a member of the Committee on Manufactures. The degree of LL.D. was conferred upon him, by the Transylvania University, in 1843, and he has attained the title of Colonel in the militia service. After leaving Congress, he resumed the office of bank president.

Breck, Samuel.—He was born in Boston, July 17, 1771; was a Representative in Congress, from Pennsylvania, from 1823 to 1825, and died in Philadelphia, September 1, 1862.

Breckinridge, James.—He was a Representative in Congress, from Virginia, from 1809 to 1817.

Breckinridge, James D.—He was born in Jefferson County, Kentucky, and was a Representative in Congress, from that State, from 1821 to 1823. He died at Louisville, May, 1849.

Breckinridge, John.—Was a Virginian by birth, and the author and advocate of the celebrated "Resolutions of 1798–99" in the Legislature of that State. Emigrating to Kentucky, he was elected United States Senator in 1801, and was appointed Attorney-General of the United States, by President Jefferson, in January, 1805, holding the office until January, 1806. One of his sons, Robert C. Breckinridge, is a distinguished Presbyterian divine; another, John Cabell Breckinridge, was an eminent lawyer, and the father of Vice-President Breckinridge. He died at Lexington, Kentucky, December 14, 1806.

Breckinridge, John C.—He was born near Lexington, Kentucky, January 16, 1821; was educated at Centre College, Kentucky; spent a few months at Princeton; studied law at the Transylvania Institute, and was admitted to the bar at Lexington. He emigrated to Burlington, Iowa, where he remained for a time, but returned to Lexington, where he has since resided, and when not engaged in public duties has practised his profession with success. He served as a Major of infantry during the war with Mexico, and while in that country, distinguished himself as the counsel of Major-General Pillow during the famous court-martial. On his return from Mexico, he was elected to the State Legislature; and was a Representative in Congress, from the Ashland District, from 1851 to 1855. During his administration, President Pierce tendered to him the mission to Spain, but family affairs compelled him to decline the honor. He was elected Vice-President of the United States in 1856, on the ticket with James Buchanan, and entered upon the duties of his office in March, 1857, as President of the United States Senate. In 1861 he went into the Senate as the successor of Mr. Crittenden. In 1860 he was nominated by the Southern Democratic party, as their candidate for President, but defeated. He took part in the Great Rebellion of 1861 as a General.

Breese, Sidney.—He was born in Whitesborough, Oneida County, New York, July 15, 1800. He attended Hamilton College, but graduated at Union College. He removed to Illinois, and after due preparation, and before becoming of age, was admitted to the bar. His first public position was that of Captain of militia, after which he became Assistant Secretary of State under Secretary Kane, and was appointed Postmaster of Kaskaskia. In 1822 he was appointed State Attorney, which office he held until 1827, when he was appointed Attorney of the United States for Illinois. In 1829 he published a volume of Decisions of the Supreme Court, which now bears his name, and was the first octavo volume published in the State; he served in the Black Hawk war as a Lieutenant of volunteers. In 1835 he was elected a Circuit Judge. He was a Senator in Congress, from Illinois, from 1843 to 1849, and officiated as Chairman of the Committee on Public Lands; he was a Regent of the Smithsonian Institute during President Polk's administration. In 1850 he went into the Illinois Legislature, and was elected Speaker. He was one of the originators of the Illinois Central Railroad. In 1855 he was again placed upon the Circuit Court bench, and having been made Chief Judge, still holds the position.

Brengle, Francis.—He was born in Maryland, and was a Representative in Congress, from that State, from 1843 to 1845. Died December 10, 1846.

Brent, Richard.—He was a Representative in Congress, from Virginia, from 1795 to 1799, and again from 1801 to 1803; and a Senator in Congress from 1809 to 1814. He died December 30, 1814.

Brent, William L.—He was born in Charles County, Maryland, and was a Representative in Congress, from Louisiana, from 1823 to 1829. Died in July, 1848.

Brenton, Samuel.—He was a native of Gallatin County, Kentucky; was a minister of the Gospel from the age of twenty until 1848, when, stricken by paralysis, he resigned, and was appointed Register of the Fort Wayne Land Office. He was elected to Congress in 1851, and again in 1855. He was also President of the Fort Wayne College. He died March 29, 1857, aged forty-eight years.

Brevard, James.—He was born in Iredell County, North Carolina, and was a Representative in Congress, from South Carolina, from 1819 to 1821.

Brewster, David P.—He was born in New York, and was a Representative in Congress, from that State, from 1839 to 1843.

Bridges, George W.—Was born in McMinn County, Tennessee, October 9, 1825; was educated at the East Tennessee University; adopted the profession of law; was Attorney-General of the State in 1849 and in 1854, holding the office for eleven years; held the positions of Bank Attorney and Railroad Director; was a Presidential Elector in 1860; was elected a Representative in Congress, from Tennessee, in 1861, to serve in the Thirty-seventh Congress; but having been arrested by the Confederates during the Rebellion, did not take his seat until towards the close of the last session.

Bridges, Samuel A.—He was born in Colchester, Connecticut, January 27, 1802; received an academic education, and graduated at Williamstown College in 1826; studied law, and was admitted to the bar in 1829. In 1830 he removed to Pennsylvania; was for seven years Deputy Attorney-General of the State for Lehigh County; and he was a Representative in Congress, from Pennsylvania, from 1848 to 1849, and from 1853 to 1855.

Briggs, George.—He was born in Fulton County, New York, in 1805, but removed to Vermont in 1813, to the Legislature of which State he was elected in 1837. In 1838 he settled in the City of New York, and for many years devoted himself to the hardware business, by which he amassed a fortune. He represented the City of New York in Congress, from 1849 to 1853, and in 1858 was elected to the Thirty-sixth Congress, serving as Chairman of the Committee on Revolutionary Claims.

Briggs, George N.—He was born in Adams or Andover, Berkshire County, Massachusetts, April 12, 1796; commenced life by learning the trade of a hatter; spent one year in an academy; studied law, and was admitted to the bar in 1818; was a Representative in Congress, from 1831 to 1843, officiating during the Twenty-seventh Congress as Chairman of the Committee on the Post-office; and from 1844 to 1851 was Governor of Massachusetts. From 1853 to 1859 he also held the position of Judge of the Court of Common Pleas; having been a member of the State Constitutional Convention of 1853, and Register of Deeds from 1824 to 1831. Died in 1861.

Brigham, Elijah.—He was a native of Northborough, Massachusetts; a graduate of Dartmouth College in 1778; studied law at Harvard; was a merchant by occupation; held many positions of trust and responsibility; and was a Representative in Congress, from Massachusetts, from 1811 to 1816. He died in Washington City, of croup, April 22, 1816, aged sixty-six years.

Bright, Jesse D.—Born at Norwich, Chenango County, New York, December 18, 1812; received an academic education, and studied law as a profession. He was Circuit Judge of Indiana, State Senator, Marshal of the United States for the District of Indiana, and Lieutenant-Governor of that State. He was a United States Senator from 1845 to 1857, and President of the Senate during several sessions. He was elected for an additional term in 1857, and was Chairman of the Committee on Public Buildings and Grounds, and a member of the Committees on Finance and the Pacific Railroad. Expelled for disloyalty in February, 1862.

Brinkerhoff, Henry R.—He was born in Adams County, Pennsylvania, in 1788, and emigrated at an early period to New York. During the last war with England, he served in command of a volunteer company, and distinguished himself at the battle of Queenstown. In 1837 he removed to Ohio, and was elected to Congress, as Representative from that State, in 1843, but died before the expiration of his term, in Huron County, Ohio, April 30, 1844.

Brinkerhoff, Jacob.—He was born in New York, and was a Representative in Congress, from Ohio, from 1843 to 1847.

Bristow, F. M.—Born near Nicholasville, Jessamine County, Kentucky, August 11, 1804; received a good English education; studied law, but divided his time between that profession and farming; in 1831 and 1833 he was elected to the Kentucky Legislature; in 1846 to the State Senate; in 1849 was a member of the State Constitutional Convention; in 1853 was elected a Representative in Congress for the unexpired term of Presley Ewing; and in 1859 was elected a Representative, from Kentucky, to the Thirty-sixth Congress, serving on the Committee on Agriculture. Died at Elkton, Kentucky, June 10, 1864.

Broadhead, John C.—He was a Representative in Congress, from New York, from 1831 to 1833, and again from 1837 to 1839.

Brockenbrough, William H.—Born in 1813; he originally went to Florida for the benefit of his health, which, during his residence there, was a continual depression upon his physical and mental energies. He, however, held no undistinguished position as a citizen, having been, under the Territorial government, a Senator from the Western District, and at one time President of the Senate, also United States District Attorney, and a Representative in Congress from 1845 to 1847. He died in Tallahassee, Florida, June, 1850, of pulmonary consumption.

Brockway, John H.—Born in Ellington, Connecticut; graduated at Yale College in 1820; he commenced active life by teaching the academy at East Windsor Hill; he studied law, and has been devoted to the practice of the profession ever since. He has frequently served in the two Houses of the State Legislature, and was a Representative in Congress from 1839 to 1843.

Broderick, David C.—Born in the District of Columbia, of Irish parentage, in December, 1818; when a boy of five years, removed to New York City with his father; during his youth he was apprenticed to the trade of a stonecutter, which was the trade of his father; was for many years foreman of a fire engine company in New York, during which period he was an active politician; removed to California in 1849, and engaged in the business of smelting and assaying gold; was a member of the Convention which drafted the Constitution of that State; served two years in the California Senate, and was President of that body in 1851; and he was elected a Senator in Congress in 1856 for the long term, taking his seat during the second session of the Thirty-fourth Congress. Died in San Francisco, California, September 16, 1859, from a wound received in a duel fought with David S. Terry, Chief Justice of the Supreme Court of that State, on the 13th of the same month. He was the first member of the United States Senate ever killed in a duel; and it is said that some of the marble pillars in the old Senate Chamber, where he had a seat, were cut by his own father.

Brodhead, John.—He was a minister of the Methodist Episcopal Church for forty-four years, and a Representative in Congress, from New Hampshire, from 1829 to 1833. He died at New Market, New Hampshire, April 7, 1838, aged sixty-seven years.

Brodhead, Richard.—He was a native of Pike County, Pennsylvania; was a Representative in Congress from 1843 to 1849, and a Senator of the United States from 1851 to 1857, from Pennsylvania. Died at Easton, Pennsylvania, September 17, 1863.

Bronson, David.—Born in Suffield, Connecticut; graduated at Dartmouth College in 1819; studied law and admitted to the bar in 1823; was a member of the Legislature, as Representative, in 1832 and 1834, and as Senator in 1846; and was a Representative in Congress, from Norridgewock, Maine, from 1841 to 1843, and served as a member of the Committee on Public Lands. From 1850 to 1853, he was Collector of Customs at Bath, Maine; and from 1854 to 1857, was Judge of Probate for Sagadahock County. Died in Talbot County, Maryland, in November, 1863.

Bronson, Isaac H.—Born in Rutland, New York, October 16, 1802, and died at Pilatka, Florida, August 13, 1855. He was educated for the bar, and admitted to practice in 1822; and was a Representative in Congress, from New York, from 1837 to 1839, officiating as Chairman of the Committee on Territories, when he was appointed one of the Territorial Judges of Florida, and from that time until his death, he served continually on the bench,—at the time of his death being District Judge of the United States for Northern Florida.

Brooke, Walter.—He was a Senator in Congress, from Mississippi, from 1852 to 1853.

Brooks, David.—Was born in 1736; entered the army in 1776 as a Lieutenant in the Pennsylvania line; was captured at Fort Washington, and remained a prisoner for two years. Upon being exchanged, he was promoted Assistant Clothier-General at head-quarters,—an office of responsibility, which he so filled as to secure the friendship of Washington. After the close of the war, he removed to New York, and afterwards settled in Dutchess County, representing each locality in the State Legislature. He was a Representative in Congress from May, 1797, to July, 1797; a Commissioner for making the first treaty with the Seneca Indians (signed where the city of Utica now stands), and subsequently first Judge of Dutchess County for sixteen years. He died at his home, where he was universally esteemed, in August, 1838.

Brooks, James.—He was born in Portland, Maine, November 10, 1810. When only eleven years old he became a clerk in a store; when sixteen was a school-teacher, and at the age of nearly twenty-one, he graduated at the Waterville College. He has been an extensive traveller, both in this country and Europe, and has published a large number of letters descriptive of his tours. In 1835 he was elected to the Legislature of Maine; in 1836 he established the New York Daily Express, of which he has since been the chief editor and proprietor; in 1847 he was elected a member of the New York Legislature, and from 1849 to 1853 he was a Representative in Congress, from the city of New York, serving on the Committee of Public Lands; re-elected to the Thirty-eighth Congress, serving as a member of the Committee on Post-offices and Post-roads.

Brooks, Micah.—He was born in Cheshire, Connecticut, in 1775; was educated by his father, with whom he removed to Western New York, and where he taught school. He settled on a farm, but was a Justice of the Peace in 1806, and for twenty years thereafter he was a County Judge. He was a member of the New York Assembly in 1808 and 1809; was a Representative in Congress, from New York, from 1815 to 1817; a member of the State Constitutional Convention of 1821; and a Presidential Elector in 1824. He died in Livingston County, New York, July 7, 1857.

Brooks, Preston S.—He was born in Edgefield District, South Carolina, in August, 1819; graduated at the South Carolina College in 1839; studied law; was admitted to the bar in 1843, and was a State Representative in 1844. In 1846 he raised a company of volunteers, was made Captain, and served in the Palmetto Regiment during most of the Mexican war. After the war he devoted himself to planting. He was elected to Congress in 1853, and again in 1855. In 1856 he made a personal assault upon Charles Sumner, in the United States Senate Chamber, which event caused much excitement throughout the country. The attack was caused by words uttered in debate by Senator Sumner against Senator Butler, who was Mr. Brooks's relative. Mr. Brooks died in Washington, District of Columbia, January 27, 1857, of acute inflammation of the throat, leaving behind him many warm personal friends.

Broom, Jacob.—He was born in Baltimore, Maryland, July 25, 1808; received a classical education; on removing to Pennsylvania, was appointed, in 1840, Deputy Auditor of that State; in 1849 he was elected Clerk of the Orphan's Court for the City and County of Philadelphia; and was elected a Representative, from that State, to the Thirty-fourth Congress.

Broomall, John M.—Was born in Upper Chichester, Delaware County, Pennsylvania, January 19, 1816; received a common school education; studied law, and has been devoted to that profession; has served in the Legislature of the State, and in 1862 was elected a Representative, from Pennsylvania, to the Thirty-eighth Congress, and was a member of the Committees on Accounts, and Public Expenditures.

Broome, James M.—He was a Representative in Congress, from Delaware, from 1805 to 1807.

Brown, Aaron V.—Born in Brunswick County, Virginia, August 15, 1795. He graduated at Chapel Hill University in 1814, and in 1815 removed with his parents to Tennessee, where he devoted himself to the study of law; and when admitted to practice, became a partner of the late James K. Polk, in Giles County, serving in the mean time for a number of years in the Legislature of Tennessee. In 1839 he was elected a member of Congress, and re-elected in 1841 and 1843. On his retirement from Congress, in 1845, he was elected Governor of Tennessee; and he was at all times considered one of the most faithful and industrious leaders of the Democratic party in Tennessee. His last position was that of Postmaster-General in the cabinet of President Buchanan. Among the measures which marked his administration of our postal affairs may be mentioned the establishment of a new and shorter oceanic communication to California, by Tehuantepec, of the great overland mail from

Memphis and St. Louis to San Francisco, and another, across the continent, by the way of Salt Lake. His speeches, Congressional and political, were published at Nashville, in 1854, in a handsome volume of seven hundred pages. He died in Washington, March 8th, 1859.

Brown, Albert G.—He was born in Chester District, South Carolina, May 31, 1813; taken to Mississippi when a boy; adopted the law as a profession; was a member of the State Legislature from 1835 to 1839; and was a Representative in Congress, from Mississippi, in 1840 and 1841. He was also a Judge of the Circuit Superior Court, in 1852 and 1853; Governor of Mississippi, from 1844 to 1848; was again elected a Representative in Congress, from 1848 to 1854; was elected a United States Senator, from 1854 to 1858; and re-elected for six years, commencing March 4, 1859, but resigned in February, 1861, to join the Great Rebellion. He was Chairman of the Committee on the District of Columbia, in the Thirty-fifth Congress, and a member of the Committee on Indian Affairs, and that of Enrolled Bills. His collected speeches were published in one volume in 1859.

Brown, Anson.—He was born in New York, and was a Representative in Congress, from that State, during the years 1839 and 1840, and died at Ballston, New York, June 21, 1840, much respected for his character and acquirements.

Brown, Bedford.—Born in Caswell County, North Carolina, in 1795; was elected to the House of Commons, of that State, in 1815, in which capacity he served many years; and was a Senator in Congress, from that State, from 1829 to 1841, officiating as Chairman of the Committee on Agriculture during several sessions. He was subsequently elected to the General Assembly, and at the end of his term retired to private life.

Brown, Benjamin.—He was a Representative in Congress, from Massachusetts, from 1815 to 1817, having served in the State Legislature in 1809, 1811, and 1812.

Brown, B. Gratz.—He was born in Kentucky; graduated at Yale College; settled in Missouri, and served a number of years in the Legislature; from 1850 to 1857 was editor of the St. Louis Democrat; and in 1860 he was elected a Senator in Congress, from Missouri, for the term ending in 1867, serving on the Committees on Military Affairs and on Indians.

Brown, Charles.—He was born in Pennsylvania, and was a Representative in Congress, from that State, from 1841 to 1843, and again from 1847 to 1849. He subsequently held the office of Collector of the Port of Philadelphia.

Brown, Elias.—He was a Representative in Congress, from Maryland, from 1829 to 1831.

Brown, Ethan A.—He was Governor of Ohio, from 1818 to 1822, and from 1822 to 1825 a Senator in Congress, from that State, serving as a member of the Judiciary Committee.

Brown, George H.—He was born in New Jersey; graduated at Princeton College in 1828; adopted the profession of law; was a member of the Convention which formed the State Constitution of 1844; and was a Representative in Congress, from New Jersey, from 1851 to 1853.

Brown, James.—He was born in Virginia, October, 1766; studied law; settled first in Mississippi, at Natchez; and was appointed, by President Jefferson, Secretary of the Territory of Louisiana, after its acquisition. This led him to New Orleans, which became his home. He was appointed United States Attorney for the District of Louisiana, and rose to a high rank at the bar. He was chosen to the United States Senate, and served from 1812 to 1817, and again from 1819 to 1824, officiating as Chairman of the Committee on Foreign Relations, and was appointed Minister Plenipotentiary to France. He remained five years abroad, and subsequently settled in Philadelphia, where he died of apoplexy, April 7, 1835.

Brown, James S.—He was born in Hampden, Maine, February 1, 1824; removed to Cincinnati, Ohio, in 1840, where he studied law, and in 1844 took up his permanent residence in Milwaukee, Wisconsin. In 1846 he was chosen

Prosecuting Attorney for Milwaukee County; in 1848 was elected Attorney-General of the State; in 1861 was Mayor of Milwaukee; and in 1862 he was elected a Representative from Wisconsin to the Thirty-eighth Congress, serving on the Committee of Elections.

Brown, Jeremiah.—He was born in Pennsylvania in 1776; served in the Legislature of that State, as a member of one or two State Conventions; was the first Associate Judge, elected by the people, and was a Representative in Congress, from Pennsylvania, from 1841 to 1845. Died at Lancaster, March 2, 1848.

Brown, John.—He was a Representative in Congress, from Rhode Island, from 1799 to 1801.

Brown, John.—He was a Representative in Congress, from Maryland, from 1809 to 1810.

Brown, John.—He was born in Mifflin County, Pennsylvania, and was a Representative in Congress, from Pennsylvania, from 1821 to 1825.

Brown, John W.—He was born in Scotland, and was a Representative in Congress, from Orange County, New York, from 1833 to 1837, and was a member of the Committees on Invalid Pensions, Territories, and Expenditures on Public Buildings.

Brown, Milton.—He was born in Ohio, and on taking up his residence in Tennessee, was elected a Representative in Congress, from that State, from 1841 to 1847.

Brown, Robert.—He was a Representative in Congress, from Pennsylvania, from 1798 to 1815.

Brown, Titus.—He was born in Cheshire, New Hampshire; was a member of the Legislature of New Hampshire, from 1820 to 1825; was elected a Representative in Congress, from New Hampshire, from 1825 to 1829, serving as a member of the Committee on the Memorial of the Legislature of Tennessee. In 1842 he was elected to the State Senate and made President, and he also held the offices of Solicitor of Hillsborough County, from 1823 to 1825, and from 1829 to 1834, and Railroad Commissioner. Died at Francistown, New Hampshire, January 31, 1849, aged sixty-three years.

Brown, William.—He was born in Frederick County, Virginia, and was a Representative in Congress, from Kentucky, from 1819 to 1823.

Brown, William G.—He was born in Preston County, Virginia, September 25, 1801; received a good English education; studied law, and was admitted to the bar in 1823; in 1832 he was elected to the Legislature of Virginia, and served in that capacity again from 1840 to 1843. He was a Representative in Congress, from Virginia, from 1845 to 1849; in 1850 he was a member of the Virginia State Convention; in 1860 a delegate to the Charleston Convention, and also to that held in Baltimore; he was also a delegate to the Virginia Convention of 1861, and opposed the action of the secessionists; and on his return home he was elected a Representative to the Thirty-seventh Congress, serving on the Committees on Manufactures and the Militia; and in 1863 he was re-elected to the Thirty-eighth Congress as a Representative from West Virginia, and served on the Committee of Claims.

Brown, William J.—He was born in Kentucky, in 1805. He emigrated to Indiana in 1821, and was at one time Secretary of State for Indiana, and a member of the State Legislature; a Representative in Congress, from 1843 to 1845, and again from 1849 to 1851; he was also Assistant Postmaster-General, under President Polk; editor of the Indiana Sentinel; State Librarian of Indiana; and, at the time of his death, Special Agent of the Post-Office Department for Indiana and Illinois. He died near Indianapolis, March 18, 1857.

Browne, George H.—Was born in Gloucester, Rhode Island, in 1818; was left an orphan at an early age, but managing to obtain a common school education by his own exertions, graduated at Brown University in 1840. He studied law, but soon entering into politics, was elected to both the Charter and Suffrage Legislatures of his State in 1842; was admitted to the bar in 1844; was again elected to the Rhode Island

Legislature, and re-elected until 1852; during that year he was appointed by President Pierce United States Attorney for Rhode Island; was reappointed by President Buchanan, which office he held until elected a Representative from Rhode Island to the Thirty-seventh Congress, serving on the Committee of Elections. He was also a delegate to the Charleston and Baltimore Conventions, and to the Peace Congress of 1861.

Browne, John.—He was a Representative in Congress, from Virginia, from 1789 to 1793.

Browne, John.—He was born in 1757, and died at Frankfort, Kentucky, August 28, 1837. He was a Senator in Congress, from 1792 to 1805, and during the first session of the Eighth Congress officiated as President *pro tem.* of the Senate.

Bruce, Phineas.—He was a graduate of Yale College in 1786; was a member of the Massachusetts Legislature in 1792, 1793, 1796, and 1800, and elected a Representative in Congress, from Massachusetts, from 1803 to 1805.

Brush, Henry.—He was born in Dutchess County, New York, and was a Representative in Congress, from Ohio, from 1819 to 1821.

Bruyn, Andrew D. W.—Born in New York, and was elected a Representative in Congress, from that State, from 1837 to 1838, and died at Ithaca, in July, 1838.

Bryan, Guy M.—Was born in Missouri, June 12, 1821; received a liberal education and studied law; bore a part in the military campaign of Texas in 1836; in 1846 he went to the Rio Grande, under General Taylor; in 1847 was elected to the Texas Legislature, and served in the House and Senate seven years; and was elected a Representative, from Texas, to the Thirty-fifth Congress, serving on the Committee on Agriculture.

Bryan, Henry H.—Born in Martin County, North Carolina, and was a Representative in Congress, from Tennessee, from 1819 to 1823, and was a member of the Committee on Private Land Claims. He died in Montgomery County, of that State, in May, 1835.

Bryan, John H.—He was born in Newbern County, North Carolina, in 1798; and graduated at the University of North Carolina in 1815. He was a lawyer by profession; served a number of years in the State Legislature; and was a member of Congress, from North Carolina, from 1825 to 1827.

Bryan, Joseph.—He was elected a Representative in Congress, from Georgia, from 1803 to 1806.

Bryan, Joseph H.—He was a Representative in Congress, from North Carolina, from 1815 to 1819.

Bryan, Nathan.—Born in Jones County, North Carolina, and in 1791 represented that county in the House of Commons. He was a member of Congress, from 1795 to 1798, and died at Philadelphia, June 4, during the latter year. He was a prominent man among the Baptists, and a most exemplary Christian.

Buchanan, Andrew.—He was born in Pennsylvania, and was a Representative in Congress, from that State, from 1835 to 1839.

Buchanan, James.—Born in Franklin County, Pennsylvania, April 23, 1791. After a regular course of classical education he studied and practised law in Lancaster, Pennsylvania. In 1814 he was elected to the State Legislature of Pennsylvania, and re-elected the next year. In 1821 he entered Congress as a Representative from the Lancaster District, where he continued until 1831, when he declined a re-election. In 1832 he was appointed Minister to Russia by President Jackson, and on his return from that mission in 1834, he was elected by the Pennsylvania Legislature to the Senate of the United States, to fill the unexpired term of William Wilkins, who had resigned. He was re-elected in 1837, and again in 1843. In 1845 he resigned his seat in the Senate, and became Secretary of State, and the head of the cabinet of President Polk. At the close of that eventful administration, he retired to private life at his residence of "Wheatland," near Lancaster; but he was summoned again to the public service in 1853, when he accepted the appointment from President Pierce, of Minister of the United States to the Court of St. James. Having resigned his office, he returned home in 1856, and in the summer of that year received the Democratic nomination for President of the United States. In the following November he was elected to that position, and in March, 1857, he entered upon its duties.

Bucher, John C.—He was for many years a Judge of the Circuit Court of Pennsylvania; a Representative in Congress, from that State, from 1831 to 1833; and died in Harrisburg, Pennsylvania, October 26, 1851.

Buck, Daniel.—He was a lawyer by profession, and one of the earliest settlers in Vermont, and was a Representative in Congress, from that State, from 1795 to 1797, and died in 1817. He was the father of the Hon. Daniel A. A. Buck.

Buck, Daniel Azro A.—He was born in Vermont in 1789; graduated at Middlebury College in 1807, and also at the West Point Military Academy in 1808, when he entered the army. He resigned his commission in 1811; was reappointed, as a Captain in the army, in 1813, but finally left the military profession in 1815. He then established himself as a lawyer at Chelsea, Vermont, and was for fourteen years a member of the State Legislature, officiating about half of that time as Speaker of the Lower House. He filled the office of State Attorney for Orange County for six years; was a Representative in Congress, from Vermont, from 1823 to 1825, and again from 1827 to 1829; and was subsequently connected with the Indian Bureau of the War Department in Washington, where he died December 24, 1841.

Buckalew, Charles R.—Was born in Bloomsburg, Columbia County, Pa., in 1821; adopted the profession of law; served six years as a member of the Senate; was appointed by President Buchanan Minister to Ecuador; was Chairman of the Democratic Central Committee of Pennsylvania in 1857; and was appointed a Senator in Congress, from Pennsylvania, in 1863, for the term ending in 1869, serving on the Committees on the Post-office and on Indian Affairs.

Buckner, Alexander.—He emigrated from Indiana to Missouri in 1818; was a member of the Convention which formed the Constitution of that State; served several years in the State Legislature; and was a Senator in Congress, from Missouri, from 1831 to 1833, and died in May, 1833. His term would have expired in 1837. He was a member of the Committees on Pensions and on Engrossed Bills.

Buckner, Aylett.—He was born in Kentucky, and was a Representative in Congress, from that State, from 1847 to 1849.

Buckner, Richard A.—Born in Fauquier County, Virginia, 1763; was a Representative in Congress, from Kentucky, from 1823 to 1829, and died at his residence in Greensburg, Kentucky, December 8, 1847.

Buel, Alexander H.—Born in Fairfield, Herkimer County, New York; received a limited education; was a prominent and successful merchant; and a Representative in Congress, from New York, from 1850 until the time of his death, which occurred in Washington City, January 30, 1853.

Buel, Alexander W.—Born in Rutland County, Vermont, in 1813; graduated at the Vermont University in 1831; taught school for several years in Vermont and New York, during which period he prepared himself for the practice of the law. In 1834 he took up his residence in Michigan; in 1836 was Attorney for the City of Detroit; in 1837 was elected to the State Legislature; in 1843 and 1844 was Prosecuting Attorney for Wayne County; in 1847 was again elected to the Legislature; and from 1849 to 1851 was a Representative in Congress, from Michigan, and was a member of the Committee on Foreign Affairs.

Buffington, Joseph.—He was born in Pennsylvania, and was a Representative, in Congress, from that State, from 1843 to 1847.

Buffinton, James.—Born in Fall River, Massachusetts, March 16, 1817; educated at the Friends College, Providence; served for a time in a factory at Fall River; studied medicine, and went upon a whaling voyage; afterwards became a merchant by occupation; was Mayor of the City of Fall River during the years 1854 and 1855; and was elected a Representative from Massachusetts to the Thirty-fourth and Thirty-fifth Congresses, serving as a member of the Committee on Military Affairs. He was also re-elected to the Thirty-sixth Congress, serving as a member of the Committee on Military Affairs. Re-elected to the Thirty-seventh Congress, serving as Chairman of the Committee on Accounts.

Buffum, Joseph, Jr.—He was born in Fitchburg, Massachusetts; graduated at Dartmouth College in 1806; and was a Representative in Congress, from New Hampshire, from 1819 to 1821, and a member of the Committees on Expenditures in the Navy Department, and on Public Buildings.

Bugg, Robert M.—He was born in Tennessee, and was a Representative in Congress, from Tennessee, from 1853 to 1855.

Bull, John.—He was a Representative in Congress, from Missouri, from 1833 to 1835.

Bullard, Henry Adams.—Born in Groton, Massachusetts, September 9, 1788; was educated at Harvard University, and graduated in 1807. He was a lawyer by profession, but his knowledge of the modern languages brought him in contact with General Toledo, in Philadelphia, who was organizing an expedition to revolutionize New Mexico. He joined him as his aid and military secretary, and spent the winter of 1812 with him at Nashville, and accompanied him into New Mexico in the spring. They were defeated in a pitched battle by the royal troops at San Antonio, and suffered severe hardships, but he managed to reach Natchitoches, and there remained and commenced the practice of his profession. In 1822 he was elected to a seat on the District Court Bench, and performed its duties for several years. In 1831 was chosen a Representative in Congress, and served till 1834; he was then elevated to the Supreme Bench of Louisiana, and filled the office until 1846, with the exception of a few months in 1839, when he acted as Secretary of State. He then removed to New Orleans. In 1847 was appointed Professor of the Civil Law in the Law School of Louisiana, and delivered two courses of lectures. In 1850 he was elected to the Legislature, and a few weeks after was chosen to fill a vacancy in Congress, occasioned by the resignation of C. M. Conrad, and served again in the House of Representatives one year. On his return journey homeward he was prostrated by fatigue and exposure; he lingered three weeks, and died in New Orleans, April 17, 1851.

Bulloch, William B.—Born in Georgia in 1776; was a lawyer by profession, being a prominent member of the bar as early as 1800. In 1809 he was Mayor of Savannah, and subsequently Collector of that port. He was United States Senator in 1813; and in 1816 was chosen President of the Bank of Georgia, of which he was one of the founders, and held the office twenty-seven years. He died in Savannah, Georgia, March 6, 1852.

Bullock, Stephen.—Born in Massachusetts; was a member of the Convention which formed the Constitution of that State; frequently served in the State Legislature; and was a Representative in Congress, from Massachusetts, from 1797 to 1799. He subsequently became Judge of the Common Pleas for Bristol County, and served in the State Senate and as a member of the Executive Council of Massachusetts. He died in Massachusetts, aged eighty-one years.

Bullock, Wingfield. — He was elected a Representative in Congress, from Kentucky, during the years 1820 and 1821. Died October 13, 1821, before taking his seat.

Bunch, Samuel.—Was born in 1786. He commanded a regiment in the Indian war, under General Andrew Jackson, and in the charge of the battle of the Horseshoe, was the first or second man over the breastworks of the enemy. He was a Representative in Congress, from Tennessee, from 1833 to 1837; and died in Granger County, Tennessee, September 5, 1849.

Bunner, Rudolph.—He was a Representative in Congress, from New York, from 1827 to 1829, and died at

Otsego, July 23, 1837, aged fifty-eight years.

Bunt, Richard.—He was a native of Virginia, and a Senator in Congress, from that State, from 1809 to January 2, 1815, when he died.

Burch, John Chilton.—Born in Boone County, Missouri, February 1, 1826; received a liberal education and studied law; held the position of Military Secretary to the Governor of Missouri; in 1850 he emigrated to California, and turned his attention to mining; in 1853 he was elected District Attorney for his county, and commenced the practice of law; in 1856 was returned to the Assembly, and in 1857 to the State Senate, where he remained until 1859, when he was elected a Representative, from California, to the Thirty-sixth Congress, serving as a member of the Committee on Agriculture.

Burd, George.—He was a Representative in Congress, from Pennsylvania, from 1831 to 1835, and died at Bedford, Pennsylvania, January 13, 1844, aged fifty years.

Burges, Tristam.—Born in Plymouth County, Massachusetts, February 26, 1770, and died in Rhode Island, October 13, 1853. He graduated at the Rhode Island College; studied law and taught school at the same time; commenced the practice of his profession in Providence, and acquired great influence and distinction as an advocate; in 1811 was elected Chief Justice of Rhode Island; occupied the Chair of Oratory in Brown University; and was a Representative in Congress, from 1825 to 1835. He acquired great reputation by a parliamentary contest with John Randolph, and left behind him many interesting pamphlets on political and literary subjects. His characteristics as a debater, were withering sarcasm, combined with fervid eloquence and rare reasoning power.

Burgess, Dempsy. — He was a member of the Provincial Congress of North Carolina; a Lieutenant-colonel of the militia; and a Representative in Congress, from 1795 to 1798.

Burke, Edanus.—He was born in Galway, Ireland, and came to America at the beginning of the Revolution. In 1778 he was appointed a Judge of the Supreme Court of South Carolina, and was a Representative in Congress, from 1789 to 1791. He was an earnest Republican, and died at Charleston, March 30, 1802, aged fifty-nine years.

Burke, Edmund.—Born in Westminster, Vermont, January 23, 1809; was educated by private tutors; studied law, and was admitted to the bar in 1829; and removed to New Hampshire in 1833, where he established, in Sullivan County, the New Hampshire Argus, which he edited a number of years. He was a Representative in Congress, from New Hampshire, from 1839 to 1845, and was Chairman of the Committee on the Library, and a member of the Committees on Commerce and Claims; and, by President Polk, was appointed Commissioner of Patents in Washington.

Burleigh, William. — He was born in Rockingham, New Hampshire, bred a lawyer, and was a Representative in Congress, from South Berwick, York County, Maine, for two terms, from 1823 to 1827, and was a member of the Committee on Expenditures in the State Department. Died in July, 1827.

Burlingame, Anson.—Born in New Berlin, Chenango County, New York, November 14, 1822. His youth was spent on the Western frontiers, at one time acting with surveying parties and at another participating in the making of Indian treaties, far beyond the confines of civilization. He laid the foundation of his education at the Branch University of Michigan, but removing to Massachusetts, he entered Harvard University, where he received a degree in 1846. He studied law and practised in Boston. In 1852 he was elected to the State Senate, and in 1853 was a member of the Convention for revising the Constitution of Massachusetts. He was elected a Representative in the Thirty-fourth Congress; was re-elected to the Thirty-fifth, serving as a member of the Committee on Foreign Affairs. He was also re-elected to the Thirty-sixth Congress, serving on the same committee. In 1861 he was appointed by President Lincoln Minister to Austria, and subsequently to China.

Burnell, Barker.—He was a native of Nantucket. When only twenty-two years of age he was chosen a member of the House of Representatives in his native Commonwealth. A few years later, he passed into the Senatorial body, where, in spite of his youth, he became a leading member. He sat also in the Convention which framed the present Constitution of Massachusetts; took an active part in the Harrisburg Convention of 1840, and served as a Representative in Congress, from 1841 to 1843. He died in Washington, District of Columbia, June 4, 1843, aged forty-five years.

Burnett, Jacob.—Was born in Newark, New Jersey, on the 22d of February, 1770. He was a graduate of Princeton College in 1791; was admitted to the bar by the Supreme Court of New Jersey in 1796, and removed to Cincinnati immediately thereafter, where he continued to reside until his death. During the first twenty years of that residence, he devoted himself to the practice of his profession, and was ranked among the most distinguished members of the bar. When the second grade of the Territorial government was established, in 1799, he was appointed, by President Adams, a member of the Legislative Council, which appointment he held till the establishment of the State government of Ohio, in the winter of 1802-3. He was a member of the State Legislature during the war of 1812, and took an active part in sustaining the measures proposed in that body, to aid the General Government in maintaining the contest. In 1821 he was appointed one of the Judges of the Supreme Court of Ohio, which commission he resigned in December, 1828, and was immediately after elected to the Senate of the United States, to fill the vacancy occasioned by the resignation of his friend General Harrison, serving until 1831. In the same year he was chosen, by the Legislature of the State of Kentucky, one of the commissioners to settle the matters in controversy between that State and the Commonwealth of Virginia, in regard to the complaints of the latter against the statute of limitation. He was the first President of the Astronomical Society of Cincinnati, and still continued, in 1852, an active member of that institution. He was, for many years, the President of the Colonization Society of Hamilton County, President of the Board of Trustees of the Medical College of Ohio, and President of the Board of Trustees of the Cincinnati College, and, upon the nomination by Lafayette, had been elected a member of the French Academy. In 1847 he published a volume entitled "Notes on the Early Settlement of the Northwestern Territory," which is considered as containing much interesting information, especially as to Ohio, the progress of which he witnessed from a Territory. He died at Cincinnati in 1853.

Burnett, Henry C.—Born in Essex County, Virginia, October 5, 1825; studied law as a profession, and practised in Kentucky; was Clerk of the Circuit Court of Trigg County, in that State, from 1851 to 1853, and a Representative in the Thirty-fourth and Thirty-fifth Congresses. He was Chairman, during the first session of the Thirty-fifth Congress, of the Committee of Inquiry in regard to the sale of Fort Snelling, and a member of the Committee on the District of Columbia. Re-elected to the Thirty-sixth Congress, and also to the Thirty-seventh, but was expelled for treasonable conduct, in December, 1861.

Burnham, Alfred A.—Born in Windham, Windham County, Connecticut, March 8, 1819; prepared himself for college, at the Suffield Literary Institution; taught school for a while, and spent one year at Washington College, which he left for want of means; studied law, and was admitted to the bar in 1843; was elected to the Connecticut Legislature in 1844 and 1845; was Clerk of the State Senate in 1846; and was subsequently appointed Judge of Probate for the District of Danbury. In 1850 he was again elected to the State Legislature; in 1857 Lieutenant-Governor of Connecticut; in 1858 again elected to the Legislature and made Speaker; and in 1859 was elected a Representative, from Connecticut, to the Thirty-sixth Congress, serving as a member of the Committee on Patents. Re-elected to the Thirty-seventh Congress, serving on the Committee on Foreign Affairs.

Burns, Joseph.—Born in Waynesborough, Augusta County, Virginia,

March 11, 1800; was educated at the Ohio Union Schools; was by trade a hatter and then a farmer; has filled various County and State offices; and was elected, from the State of Ohio, a Representative in the Thirty-fifth Congress. He was a member of the Committees on Expenditures in the Post-office Department and on Invalid Pensions.

Burns, Robert.—He was born in New Hampshire; served three years in the State Legislature as Senator and Representative, and was a Representative in Congress, from New Hampshire, from 1833 to 1837.

Burnside, Thomas.—Was an Associate Judge of the Supreme Court of Pennsylvania, and was a Representative in Congress, from that State, from 1815 to 1819. He died at Germantown, Pennsylvania, March 25, 1827.

Burr, Aaron.—He was born in Newark, New Jersey, February 6, 1756. He graduated at Princeton College in 1772, at the age of sixteen; in 1775, in his twentieth year, he joined the American army under Washington, at Cambridge; accompanied General Arnold as a private soldier in his expedition against Quebec; after his arrival there, he acted as an aide-de-camp to General Montgomery; and on his return, in 1776, General Washington invited him to join his family at headquarters. Some circumstances soon took place, by which he forever lost the confidence of Washington; and the hostility of the former to the latter, from that time, was undisguised and unmitigated. In 1777, he was appointed Lieutenant-Colonel, and distinguished himself as an able and brave officer; but in March, 1779, he was, on account of the state of his health, compelled to resign his office, and retire from military life. He then devoted himself to the study of law; commenced practice at Albany, in 1782, but soon removed to the city of New York; he became distinguished in his profession; was appointed Attorney-General of New York in 1789; from 1791 to 1797 he was a member of the United States Senate, and bore a conspicuous part as a leader of the Democratic or Republican party. At the election of President of the United States for the fourth Presidential term, Thomas Jefferson and Aaron Burr had each seventy-three votes, and the choice was decided by Congress, on the thirty-sixth ballot, in favor of Jefferson for President, and Burr for Vice-President. On the 12th of July, 1804, Colonel Burr gave Alexander Hamilton, long his professional rival and political opponent, a mortal wound in a duel. He soon after conceived the project of his enterprise in the Western country of the United States; for which he was at length apprehended and brought to Richmond, in August, 1807, on a charge of treason; and after a long trial, was acquitted. He afterwards returned to the city of New York, practised law to some extent, but passed the remainder of his life in comparative obscurity and neglect. He was of small stature, yet he had a lofty mien, a military air, a remarkably brilliant eye, and a striking appearance. He possessed distinguished talents and many accomplishments. He died on Staten Island, New York, September 14, 1836.

Burrill, James.—He was born in Providence, Rhode Island, April 25, 1772; graduated at Brown University, in 1788; studied law, devoted himself to its practice, and was Attorney-General of the State of Rhode Island, from 1797 to 1813; was a member and Speaker of the Assembly in 1814; and was Chief Justice of the State in 1816. He was elected to the United States Senate in 1816, and served as a member of the Committees on the Judiciary, on Commerce, on Manufactures, and on Accounts. He died at Washington, before the expiration of his term, December 25, 1820. He was considered an able scholar and a wise judge.

Burroughs, Silas M.—He was born in New York; served four years in the Legislature of that State, and was elected a Representative to the Thirty-fifth Congress, from New York, and was a member of the Committee on Indian Affairs. He was re-elected to the Thirty-sixth Congress, and died at Medina, New York, June 3, 1860.

Burrows, Daniel.—He was born in Groton, Connecticut, and was a Representative in Congress, from Connecticut, from 1821 to 1823.

Burrows, Lorenzo.—He was born in Connecticut, and was a Representative in Congress, from New York, from 1849 to 1853.

Burt, Armistead.—He was born in South Carolina, received a liberal education, adopted the profession of law, and was a Representative in Congress, from South Carolina, from 1843 to 1853. During a part of the Thirtieth Congress he officiated as Speaker of the House of Representatives.

Burton, Hutchins G.—He was born in Granville County, North Carolina; studied law; in 1810 represented Mecklenburg in the State Legislature, and, in 1816, the County of Halifax; was for several years Attorney-General of the State. He served as a Representative in Congress, from 1819 to 1824, and was a member of the Committee on the Judiciary and Military Affairs; he was then elected Governor of North Carolina. He died in Iredell County, April 21, 1836.

Burwell, William B.—He was a Representative in Congress, from Virginia, from 1806 to 1821. Died February 16, 1821, in Washington City, before the expiration of his term.

Busby, George H.—He was born in Darstown, Northumberland County, Pennsylvania, July 10, 1794. In 1810 he removed with his father to Ohio, where he acquired a knowledge of the cabinet-making business and devoted himself to farming. In 1824 he was appointed Clerk of the Court of Common Pleas and of the Supreme Court, and subsequently a Recorder of Deeds in the County of Marion; and he was a Representative in Congress, from 1851 to 1853, from Ohio.

Butler, Andrew Pickens.—He was born in Edgefield District, South Carolina, November 19, 1796. He graduated at South Carolina College in 1817, studied law and came to the bar in 1818, became a member of the Legislature when quite a young man, and was appointed, in 1835, one of the Judges of the General Sessions of Common Pleas, which office he held until 1847, when he was appointed by the executive to fill the vacancy in the United States Senate, caused by the death of Mr. McDuffie. He was subsequently elected and re-elected to the same position, and was in this office at the time of his death, which occurred at his home, May 25, 1857. He was a statesman of distinguished ability and much influence, possessed an uncommon degree of both mental and physical ability, and in every particular was a high-toned gentleman. He was popular in the Senate, and left behind him many deeply attached friends.

Butler, Chester.—Born in Wilkesbarre, Luzerne County, Pennsylvania, in March, 1798; graduated at Princeton College in 1817; read law at the Litchfield School, and was admitted to the bar in 1820. He was a Representative in Congress, from Pennsylvania, from 1845 to 1850, and was a member of the Committee on Revolutionary Claims. He died in Philadelphia October 5, 1850.

Butler, Ezra.—He was a Representative in Congress, from Vermont, from 1813 to 1815, and Governor of that State during the years 1826 and 1827. He died at Waterbury, Vermont, July 19, 1838.

Butler, Josiah.—Born in Rockingham County, New Hampshire, in 1780, and died at Deerfield, October 29, 1854. He graduated at Harvard University in 1803; studied law in Virginia, and practised it in his native State. He was repeatedly elected to the State Legislature; was a county Sheriff, and a Clerk of the courts. He was elected a Representative in Congress, in 1817, and served in that capacity until 1823, officiating as Chairman of the Committee on Agriculture during the Seventeenth Congress. He was then appointed Judge of the Superior Court of New Hampshire, which he held until the office was abolished.

Butler, Pierce.—He came of the family of the Dukes of Ormond, in Ireland. Before the Revolution he was a Major in a British regiment in Boston, but afterwards attached himself to the republican institutions of America. In 1787 he was a Delegate, from South Carolina, to the old Congress; in 1788, a member of the Convention which framed the Constitution of the United States, and, under it, was one of the first Senators from South Carolina, and remained in Congress till 1796. On the death of J. E. Calhoun, in 1802, he became again a Senator, but resigned in 1804. He was opposed to some of the measures of Washington's administration, but approved of the war of 1812. He died at Philadelphia, February 15, 1822, aged seventy-seven.

Butler, Samson H.—He was born in South Carolina, and was a Representative in Congress, from that State, from 1840 to 1843.

Butler, Thomas.—He was born in Carlisle, Pennsylvania, and was a Representative in Congress, from Louisiana, from 1818 to 1821. Died August 14, 1847.

Butler, Thomas B.—He was born in Wethersfield, Connecticut, in 1807; was educated a lawyer; served in the Connecticut Legislature; and was a Representative in Congress, from Connecticut, from 1849 to 1851.

Butler, William.—He was the father of the late Senator, A. P. Butler, and graduated at the College of South Carolina, as a student of medicine; served as an officer and surgeon both in the army and navy of the United States; and was a Representative in Congress, from South Carolina, from 1801 to 1811. He died December 8, 1821.

Butler, William.—He was a native of South Carolina; graduated at the South Carolina College in 1810; and a Representative in Congress, from South Carolina, from 1841 to 1843. He was the brother of the late Senator, A. P. Butler, and his wife was the sister of the late Commodore O. H. Perry.

Butler, William O.—He was born in Jessamine County, Kentucky, in 1793, and came of a family honorably identified with the Revolution. He was liberally educated, and when the war of 1812 broke out, he enlisted as a soldier; was an ensign under General Winchester, at the battle of the River Raisin; and under General Jackson, in the South, he attained the rank of Captain, and was made a Colonel in 1817. After spending many years in retirement, he was elected a Representative in Congress, from Kentucky, in 1839, and re-elected in 1841; and during the war with Mexico he obtained such distinction, that he was promoted to the position of Major-General in the regular army; a sword was voted to him by Congress, March 2, 1847; and when General Scott was recalled from the City of Mexico, General Butler was left chief in command, and announced the ratification of the treaty of peace, May 29, 1848. In 1848 he was the Democratic candidate for Vice-President, on the ticket with Lewis Cass for President. He was appointed, by President Pierce, Governor of Nebraska Territory, but declined the appointment. He is the author of many fugitive pieces of poetry, several of which possess uncommon merit, and one, entitled "The Boat Horn," has attained great popularity. In 1861 he was a member of the Peace Congress held in Washington.

Butman, Samuel. — He was a member of the Maine Legislature in 1822, 1826, and 1827, and a Representative in Congress, from Penobscot County, Maine, from 1827 to 1831, and was a member of the Committee on Internal Improvements. In 1846 he was a County Commissioner, and in 1853 was re-elected to the Legislature, and made President of the Senate.

Butterfield, Martin. — He was elected a Representative, from New York, to the Thirty-sixth Congress, serving as Chairman of the Committee on Agriculture.

Bynam, Jesse A.—Born in Halifax County, North Carolina. He was educated at Union College, New York; served a number of years in the State Legislature; and was a member of Congress, from 1833 to 1841. While in Congress he fought a duel with Daniel Jenifer, which terminated harmlessly; and at the close of his last term he removed to Louisiana.

Cabell, Edward C.—Born in Richmond, Virginia, in 1817; graduated at the University of Virginia; and in 1837 removed to the Territory of Florida, where he settled as a cotton planter. He represented the State of Florida in Congress, from 1847 to 1853.

Cabell, Samuel J.—In the beginning of the war of the Revolution he was at William and Mary College, and left there to join the first armed corps raised in Virginia, and soon attained the rank of Lieutenant-Colonel in the Continental Army, serving with honor in all the campaigns, till the fall of Charleston, May 12, 1780, when he became a prisoner, and the close of the war restored him to liberty. For many years he was a member of the Virginia Assembly, and a Representative in Congress, from 1795 to 1803. He died in Nelson County, Virginia, September 4, 1818, aged sixty-one years.

Cable, Joseph.—He was born in Ohio, and was a Representative in Congress, from that State, from 1849 to 1853.

Cabot, George.—Born in Salem, Massachusetts, and employed the early part of his life in foreign commerce. Before he was twenty-six years old, he was elected a member of the Provincial Congress, from Massachusetts, where he advocated those principles of political economy for which he was afterwards distinguished; he was a member of the Convention which formed the Constitution of that State, and also of that which ratified the Constitution of the United States, to promote which he made the most strenuous exertions. From 1791 to 1796 he served in the United States Senate, and was one of the most distinguished members of that body; a confidential friend of Washington and Hamilton, to the latter of whom he rendered most important assistance in forming his financial system. In 1808 he was a member of the Council of Massachusetts, and in 1814 a delegate to the Hartford Convention, and was made President of that body. He, after that period, retired from public life, and died at Boston, April 18, 1823, aged seventy-two.

Cadwalader, John. — He was born in Pennsylvania, and was a Representative, from that State, to the Thirty-fourth Congress.

Cadwallader, Lambert.—He was born in Trenton, New Jersey. He commanded a regiment early in the Revolution, and was a Representative in Congress, from Pennsylvania, from 1789 to 1791, and again from 1793 to 1795. He died in Trenton, September 12, 1823, aged eighty-two years.

Cady, Daniel.—He was born in Chatham, Columbia County, New York, April 29, 1773; was bred a shoemaker; studied law, admitted to the bar in 1795, and practised with success; and was a Representative in Congress, from New York, from 1815 to 1817, having previously served five years in the State Legislature. In 1846 he was elected a Judge of the Supreme Court of New York, which he resigned in 1856; and he was a Presidential Elector in 1856, when he presided over the College. In April, 1859, without a moment's warning, he became totally blind. Died in Johnstown, New York, October 31, 1859.

Cady, John W.—He was a member of the New York Assembly in 1822, and a Representative in Congress, from that State, from 1823 to 1825.

Cage, Harry.—He was a Representative in Congress, from Mississippi, from 1833 to 1835.

Cahoon, William.—He was a Representative in Congress, from Vermont, from 1829 to 1833. From 1815 to 1820 he was also a State Councillor; County Judge for nine years; Lieutenant-Governor of Vermont in 1820 and 1821; and for seven years a member of the State Legislature.

Caldwell, George A.—He was born in Kentucky, and was a Representative in Congress, from that State, from 1843 to 1845, and again from 1849 to 1851.

Caldwell, Greene W.—Born in Gaston County, North Carolina, April 13, 1811. He studied medicine, and practised with success, but subsequently devoted himself to the law. He served a number of years in the State Legislature, and was a member of Congress, from 1841 to 1843. He was subsequently appointed Superintendent of the United States Mint, at Charlotte, which position he resigned. He participated in the war with Mexico as volunteer Captain of a company of dragoons.

Caldwell, James.—He was a Representative in Congress, from Ohio, from 1813 to 1817.

Caldwell, Joseph P.—Born in Iredell County, North Carolina, in 1808.

He was educated at Bethany Academy; studied law; and entered public life in 1838, as a member of the State Legislature, where he served a number of years, and was a Representative in Congress, from 1849 to 1853.

Caldwell, Patrick C.—He was a native of South Carolina, and a Representative in Congress, from that State, from 1841 to 1843, serving on the Committee on Manufactures.

Calhoun, John.—He was born in Kentucky, and was a Representative in Congress, from that State, from 1835 to 1839.

Calhoun, John C.—Born in Abbeville District, S. C., March 18, 1782. He was of an Irish family. His father, Patrick Calhoun, was born in Ireland, and at an early age came to Pennsylvania, thence went to the western part of Virginia, and after Braddock's defeat, moved to South Carolina in 1756. At the age of thirteen, he was put under the charge of his brother-in-law, Dr. Waddel, in Columbia County, Georgia. He entered Yale College in 1802, and graduated with distinction; studied law at Litchfield, Connecticut; and in 1807 was admitted to the bar of South Carolina. The next year he entered the Legislature of that State, where he served for two sessions with ability and distinction, and in 1811 was elected to Congress, where he continued until 1817, when he became Secretary of War under President Monroe, and conducted the affairs of that department with energy and ability for seven years. In 1825 he was elected Vice-President, and in 1831, upon General Hayne's leaving the Senate to become Governor of South Carolina, Mr. Calhoun resigned the Vice-Presidency, and was elected a member of the United States Senate by the Legislature of South Carolina. After the expiration of his senatorial term, he went voluntarily into retirement. Upon the death of Mr. Upshur, in 1843, he assumed the conduct of the State Department, which he held until the close of President Tyler's administration. In 1845 he was again elected Senator, which office he held until his decease. From 1811, when he entered Congress, until his death, he was rarely absent from Washington, and during the most of that period he was in the public service of his State and country. He entered Congress at a time of unusual excitement, preceding the declaration of war of 1812, and had great influence in favor of that measure. In the difficulties and embarrassments upon the termination of war, and the transition to a peace establishment, he took a responsible part. As a presiding officer of the Senate he was punctual, methodical, and accurate, and had a high regard for the dignity of the body, which he endeavored to preserve and maintain. His connection with nullification, his views of the tariff, his opinions in regard to slavery, and the many and exciting questions arising from it, are well known. He shaped the course and moulded the opinions of the people of his own State, and of some other Southern States, upon all these subjects. Amid all the strifes of party politics, there always existed between him and his political opponents a great degree of personal kindness. He died in Washington City, March 31, 1850, leaving behind him the reputation of one of the greatest and the purest of American statesmen. His collected writings and speeches have been published in several octavo volumes, edited by his son, and accompanied with a biography.

Calhoun, John E.—Born in 1749, and graduated at Princeton College in 1774. He afterwards studied law, in which profession he became distinguished. After being for many years in the State Legislature of South Carolina, he was a Senator in Congress from 1801 to 1802. He was a decided republican, and supporter of Mr. Jefferson. He was one of the committee who were instructed to report a modification of the judiciary system of the United States. He died in Pendleton District, November 3, 1802.

Calhoun, Joseph.—He was a Representative in Congress, from South Carolina, from 1807 to 1811.

Calhoun, William B.—He was born in Boston, Massachusetts, December 29, 1796; graduated at Yale College in 1814; bred to the law; and was a Representative in Congress, from his native State, from 1835 to 1843. He was also a member of the State Legislature from 1825 to 1835, and Speaker for two years; President of the State Senate in 1846 and 1847; Secretary of State from 1848 to 1851; Bank Commissioner from 1853 to 1855; Presidential Elector in 1844; and Mayor of Springfield in 1859.

Call, Jacob.—He was a Representative in Congress, from Indiana, from 1824 to 1825.

Call, Richard K.—He was born in Kentucky; and having taken an interest in military affairs, became aide-de-camp to General Jackson in 1818, and was promoted to a Captain soon afterwards, and subsequently was appointed Brigadier-General of the Florida militia. He was a member of the Legislative Council of Florida in 1822; a Delegate to Congress from 1823 to 1825; Receiver of Public Money for the Land-office; and he held the position of Governor of Florida from 1836 to 1844.

Calvert, Charles B.—He was born in Prince George County, Maryland, August 24, 1808; received his earliest education in Philadelphia, but graduated at the University of Virginia in 1827. His whole life has been devoted, on a large scale, to the pursuits of agriculture. He was for many years President of the Maryland Agricultural Society; also of the Prince George County Society; and Vice-President of the United States Agricultural Society. He has devoted special attention to the raising of superior breeds of cattle, every variety of which he has tried on his extensive farms. He was elected to the Legislature of Maryland in 1839, 1843, and 1844; and was elected a Representative, from Maryland, to the Thirty-seventh Congress, serving on the Committees on the District of Columbia and on Agriculture. Died at Riverside, Maryland, May 14, 1864.

Calvin, Samuel.—Born in Washingtonville, Columbia County, Pennsylvania, July 30, 1811. At the age of sixteen, after the death of his father, he was thrown upon his own resources, and became a school teacher, with the view of supporting his father's family, and obtaining the means for a classical education; he accomplished this object; subsequently studied law, and was admitted to the bar in 1836, and practised in Hollidaysburg, Pennsylvania. In 1848 he was elected a member of the Thirty-first Congress, and in 1850 declined a re-election.

Cambreling, Churchill C.—He was born in Washington, North Carolina, in 1786, and received an academical education at Newbern, in that State. He had a special fondness for field sports, but did not let them interfere with his duties as a clerk in a Carolina store, where he was engaged for two years. He removed to New York City in 1802, which has since that time been his home, excepting the year 1806, when he was a counting-house clerk in Providence, Rhode Island. He engaged at an early day in mercantile pursuits with John Jacob Astor, and travelled extensively over the world. He was a Representative in Congress, from New York, from 1821 to 1839, and officiated as Chairman of the Committees of Commerce, Ways and Means, and of Foreign Affairs. His reports and political pamphlets were at one time very numerous, one of the former, on Commerce and Navigation, having gone through several editions and been republished in London. While travelling in Europe in 1839, he received the appointment of Minister to Russia, and on his return to the United States he retired to private life. Died at West Neck, Long Island, April 30, 1862.

Cameron, Simon.—He was born in Lancaster County, Pennsylvania, in 1799, and was left an orphan when only nine years of age. He educated himself, while pursuing the employment of a printer in newspaper offices at Harrisburg and in Washington City, and when twenty-two years of age edited and published a Democratic journal at the former city, having previously had charge of a paper, the Pennsylvania Intelligencer, at Doylestown, Pennsylvania. In 1832 he established the Middletown Bank of Pennsylvania, and devoted much of his attention to the railroad interests of his native State, and before entering Congress he was the Cashier of a bank, President of two railroad companies, and Adjutant-General of Pennsylvania. He was first elected a Senator in Congress in 1845, where he served until 1849, and he was re-elected to the same position in 1857, for the term ending in 1863. He was spoken of in 1860 as one of the candidates for the Presidency, and in 1861 became Secretary of War under President Lincoln. He resigned that position, and was appointed Minister to Russia in 1861. He was also a Delegate to the Baltimore Convention of 1864.

Campbell, Alexander.—He was a Senator in Congress, from Ohio, from 1809 to 1813.

Campbell, Brookins.—He was born in Washington County, Tennessee, in 1808; was for many years a member of the State Legislature, and in 1845 was unanimously elected Speaker; he was an officer in the Quartermaster's Department in the war with Mexico, and a member of Congress, from 1852 to the time of his death, which occurred in Washington, District of Columbia, December 24, 1853.

Campbell, George W.—He was born in Tennessee in 1768; received a good education; was a Representative in Congress, from Tennessee, from 1803 to 1809, serving during the last two years of his term as Chairman of the Committee of Ways and Means; was Judge of the United States District Court; was elected Senator of the United States in 1811, but resigned on being appointed Secretary of the Treasury in 1814. He resumed his seat in the Senate the following year, and served till 1818, when he was appointed Minister to Russia, where he remained until 1821. He died at Nashville, Tennessee, February 17, 1848.

Campbell, James H.—He was born in Williamsport, Lycoming County, Pennsylvania, February 8, 1820; graduated at the Carlisle Law School; was admitted to the bar in 1841; was a member in 1844 of the Whig Baltimore Convention; and was a Representative in Congress, from Pennsylvania, from 1855 to 1857, and again from 1859 to 1861, serving on the Committee on Elections. Re-elected to the Thirty-seventh Congress, serving as Chairman of the Committee on the Pacific Railroad. In 1864 he was appointed by President Lincoln Minister Resident to Sweden.

Campbell, John.—He was a Representative in Congress, from Maryland, from 1801 to 1811; also Judge of the Orphans' Court in Charles County, where he died June 23, 1828, aged sixty-three years.

Campbell, John.—He was born in South Carolina; graduated at the South Carolina College in 1819; and was a Representative in Congress, from that State, from 1829 to 1831, and again from 1837 to 1845. Died at his residence in Marlborough District, South Carolina, May 19, 1845.

Campbell, John.—He was a Representative in Congress, from Kentucky, from 1837 to 1843.

Campbell, John H.—He was born in Pennsylvania, and was a Representative in Congress, from that State, from 1845 to 1847.

Campbell, John P.—He was born in Kentucky, and was a Representative, from that State, to the Thirty-fourth Congress.

Campbell, John W.—He was born in Augusta County, Virginia, and was a Representative in Congress, from Ohio, from 1817 to 1827. Died September 24, 1833.

Campbell, Lewis D.—Born in Franklin, Warren County, Ohio, August 9, 1811. He received a limited education; was attached at an early day to the Cincinnati Gazette, as printer and assistant editor; subsequently had the entire control of another political paper; and having studied law was admitted to practice. He was elected a member of Congress, from Ohio, in 1848, and has been re-elected to each successive Congress, down to the Thirty-fifth, when his seat was contested, and the House of Representatives decided against his claim. During the Thirty-third Congress he was Chairman of the Committee of Ways and Means.

Campbell, Robert B.—He was born in South Carolina; graduated at the South Carolina College in 1809; and was a Representative in Congress, from 1823 to 1825, and again from 1835 to 1837. He was subsequently appointed, by President Fillmore, American Consul at Havana, Cuba.

Campbell, Samuel.—He was born in Mansfield, Connecticut, and was a

Representative in Congress, from New York, from 1821 to 1823, having previously served five years in the Assembly of that State.

Campbell, Thomas F.—He was a native of South Carolina, and was a Representative in Congress, from that State, from 1834 to 1835.

Campbell, Thomas J.—He was a native of Tennessee, and a member of Congress, from that State, from 1841 to 1843, and twice Clerk of the House of Representatives. During the years 1813 and 1814 he was an Assistant Inspector-General of militia. He died in Washington, District of Columbia, April 13, 1850.

Campbell, Thompson.—He was born in Pennsylvania, and was a Representative in Congress, from Illinois, from 1851 to 1853.

Campbell, William B.—Was born in Tennessee, and when a young man served in Florida as Captain in the mounted volunteers. He was a member of the State Legislature; was a Representative in Congress, from 1837 to 1843; went to Mexico as Colonel commanding the First Regiment Tennessee Volunteers, distinguishing himself at Cerro Gordo and at Monterey; was unanimously elected Circuit Court Judge; and was Governor of Tennessee from 1851 to 1853.

Campbell, William W.—Born in Cherry Valley, New York, June 10, 1806; graduated at Union College in 1827, and studied law with Judge Kent, of New York, and in 1831 he commenced the practice of his profession in that city, having previously written and published a history of the Border War of New York. He was a Representative in Congress, from 1845 to 1847, and then spent a year in Europe. On his return, he was appointed a Justice of the Superior Court of New York City, and served seven years, and was subsequently elected a Judge of the Supreme Court of the State, which position he now holds.

Canby, Richard S.—He was born in Ohio, and was a Representative in Congress, from that State, from 1847 to 1849.

Cannon, Newton.—He was born in Guilford County, North Carolina, and was a Representative in Congress, from Tennessee, from 1814 to 1817, and again from 1819 to 1823, and was also appointed by President Monroe, in 1819, one of two Commissioners to treat with the Chickasaws. He was also Governor of Tennessee from 1835 to 1839. Died September 29, 1842.

Caperton, Hugh.—He was born in Virginia in 1780; was a farmer by occupation; a member, for many years, of the State Legislature; and a Representative in Congress, from the Greenbrier region of Virginia, from 1813 to 1815. He died in Monroe County, Virginia, February 9, 1847.

Carey, George.—He was a native of Charles County, Maryland, but removed to Georgia, and died in Upson County in 1844. He was a Representative in Congress, from Georgia, from 1823 to 1827.

Carey, John.—Born in Monongahela County, Virginia, April 5, 1792; removed with his parents to the Northwest Territory, in 1798; from that period until 1812 he labored with his father in the tanning business; in 1814 he assisted in building the first stone house in Columbus; after which he devoted himself to the various employments of carpentering, milling in its various branches, and farming; in 1825 he was elected an Associate Judge, which office he held for seven years; he was elected to the Ohio Legislature in 1828, 1836, and 1843; and was elected a Representative, from Ohio, to the Thirty-sixth Congress, serving on the Committee on Agriculture.

Carlile, John S.—Born in Winchester, Frederick County, Virginia, December 16, 1817. He was educated by his mother until fourteen years of age, and then went into a country store as salesman and clerk, and at the age of seventeen commenced business for himself. At the same time he read law, and was admitted to the bar in 1840, and settled in Beverly, Randolph County, in 1842, to practise. He was elected to the State Senate in 1847, and served till 1851. In 1850 he was a member of the Constitutional Convention of Virginia, and in 1855 was elected a Representative in Congress, serving one term. In 1861 he was elected a Representative, from Virginia, to the Thirty-seventh Congress, and was soon afterwards transferred to the Senate, serving on the Committees on Public Lands and Territories. His term expires in 1865.

Carlton, Peter.—He was a Representative in Congress, from New Hampshire, from 1807 to 1809.

Carmichael, R. B.—He was a native of Maryland, and a Representative in Congress, from that State, from 1833 to 1835.

Carnes, Thomas P.—He was born and educated in Maryland; studied law, and settled in Georgia. He was there successively Solicitor-General, Attorney-General, and Judge of the Supreme Court; and was a Representative in Congress, from 1793 to 1795. He died at Milledgeville, May 8, 1822.

Carpenter, Davis.—He was born in Walpole, Cheshire County, New Hampshire, December 25, 1799; received an academical education; studied medicine, and took the degree of M.D. at Middlebury College, Vermont, in 1824; he removed to the State of New York in 1825, and there attained the position of Colonel of a rifle corps; and was a Representative in Congress, from New York, from 1853 to 1855, in place of A. Boody, resigned. He was subsequently devoted to his profession and to surveying.

Carpenter, Levi D.—He was a Representative in Congress, from New York, from 1843 to 1845.

Carr, Francis.—He was a member of the Massachusetts Legislature, from 1806 to 1811, and was a Representative in Congress, from Massachusetts, from 1811 to 1813. Died in October, 1821, aged sixty-nine years.

Carr, James.—He served three years in the Massachusetts Legislature, from Bangor, and was a Representative in Congress, from Massachusetts, from 1815 to 1817.

Carr, John.—He was a Representative in Congress, from Indiana, from 1831 to 1837, and again from 1839 to 1841, and died in Clarke County, Indiana, January 20, 1845.

Carroll, Charles, of Carrollton.—He was born in Annapolis, Maryland, on the 20th of September, 1737; was descended from a respectable Irish family; was of the Roman Catholic religion, and inherited a very large estate. He was sent at an early age to St. Omer to be educated, and afterwards removed to Rheims. After having studied civil law in France, he went to London, and pursued the study of common law at the Temple; and returned to America at the age of twenty-seven. He soon became known as an advocate for liberty, and was one of the ablest political writers of Maryland. In 1776 he was elected a Delegate to the old Congress, and subscribed his name to the Declaration of Independence, and at the time of his death was the last surviving signer of that document. In 1778 he left Congress, and devoted himself to the councils of his native State; in 1789 he was elected a Senator to the new Congress, and in 1810 he quitted public life, and passed the remainder of his days in tranquillity, beloved and revered by his friends and neighbors, and honored by his country. He was ever considered a model of regularity in conduct and sedateness in judgment. He died in Baltimore, November 14, 1832.

Carroll, Charles H.—He was a Representative in Congress, from New York, from 1843 to 1847, a member of the Assembly of the State in 1836, and a State Senator in 1837.

Carroll, Daniel.—He was a Representative in Congress, from Maryland, from 1789 to 1791, and was that year appointed Commissioner for Surveying the District of Columbia.

Carroll, James.—He was born in Maryland, and was a Representative in Congress, from that State, from 1839 to 1841.

Carson, Samuel P.—Born at Pleasant Garden, Burke County, North Carolina. He was for several years a member of the State Legislature, and a Representative in Congress, from 1825 to 1833. He killed Doctor Robert B. Vance in a duel, in 1827; and at the close of his services in Congress, removed to Arkansas, where he died in November, 1840.

Carter, John.—Born on Black River, Sumter District, South Carolina, September 10, 1792; and graduated at South Carolina College, Columbia. He was a lawyer by profession; and a Representative in Congress, from South Carolina, from 1822 to 1829, when he declined a re-election. His residence was Camden, but he removed to Georgetown, District of Columbia, in 1836, where he remained until his death, which occurred June 20, 1850.

Carter, Luther C.—Born in Bethel, Oxford County, Maine, February 25, 1805; received an academic education; settled in New York City, and devoted himself to mercantile pursuits with success; was a member for some years of the Board of Education in that city; and having retired from business, he settled on a farm on Long Island; and was elected a Representative from New York, to the Thirty-sixth Congress, serving as Chairman of the Committee on the District of Columbia.

Carter, Timothy J.—He was educated for the legal profession; was Secretary of the Maine Senate, in 1833; County Attorney from 1833 to 1837; and he was a Representative in Congress, from Maine, from 1837 to the date of his death, which occurred at Washington, March 14, 1838.

Carter, William B.—Born in Tennessee, in 1812; was a member of the House and Senate in the State Legislature; President of the Constitutional Convention; and from 1835 to 1841 a Representative in Congress, from his native State. He died in Carter County, Tennessee, April 17, 1848.

Cartter, David R.—He was born in New York, and was a Representative in Congress, from Ohio, from 1849 to 1853.

Caruthers, Robert L.—Was born in Smith County, Tennessee, July 31, 1800; obtained the rudiments of an English education by his own unaided exertions; from 1816 to 1818 he was clerk in a store; subsequently improved his education at Woodward Academy and Greenville College; studied law and came to the bar in 1823; served one year as Clerk in the Legislature of Tennessee. Returning to his native county, was appointed Clerk of the Chancery Court there; edited a paper for one year; settled in Wilson County, in 1826, and was soon afterwards elected State's Attorney, holding the office five years; in 1834 he was elected a Brigadier-General of militia; was a member of the Tennessee Legislature in 1835; was a Presidential Elector in 1845, declining to run for Governor; was a Representative in Congress, from Tennessee, from 1841 to 1843, declining a reelection; in 1852 was called to a seat on the Supreme Bench of Tennessee, still holding the position; and was a Delegate to the Peace Convention of 1861.

Caruthers, Samuel.—Born in Madison County, Missouri, October 13, 1820; was educated at Clinton College, Tennessee; is a lawyer by profession; and was elected a member of the House of Representatives, in Congress, in 1853, which position he still occupies.

Cary, George B.—A member of Congress from the Petersburg District, Virginia, in 1842 and 1843. He died in Southampton County, Virginia, March 5, 1850.

Cary, Jeremiah E.—Born in Coventry, Rhode Island, April 30, 1803; commenced active life in the State of New York, by working on a farm and in the tannery of an uncle; he received a good common school education, which he paid for by his own exertions as a teacher; he studied law, and was admitted to the bar in 1829; was elected to Congress, from Cherry Valley County, in 1842, and, after his term as a Representative, removed to the city of New York, where he has since been engaged with success in the practice of his profession, and holding many important local offices connected with the cause of education.

Cary, Shepard.—He was a merchant and farmer; was a member of the Maine Legislature in 1832, 1833, from 1839 to 1842, in 1843, 1848, 1849, and from 1850 to 1854. He was a Representative in Congress, from Maine, from 1844 to 1845, and served as a member of the Committee on Claims. In 1836 he was a Presidential Elector.

Case, Charles.—Born at Austinburg, Ashtabula County, Ohio, December 21, 1817; a lawyer by profession, and a Representative in the Thirty-fifth Congress, from Indiana. He was a member of the Committee on Invalid Pensions. He was also re-elected to the Thirty-sixth Congress, serving on the Committee on Territories.

Case, Walter.—He was born in Dutchess County, New York, and was a Representative in Congress, from that State, from 1819 to 1821.

Casey, Joseph.—He was born in Maryland, and was a Representative in Congress, from Pennsylvania, from 1849 to 1851. In 1863 he was appointed, by President Lincoln, a Judge of the Court of Claims.

Casey, Levi.—He was a Representative in Congress, from South Carolina, from 1803 to 1807. Died February 1, 1807.

Casey, Samuel L.—He was elected a Representative, from Kentucky, to the Thirty-seventh Congress, and was subsequently appointed, by President Lincoln, a Commissioner to look after certain national interests in the Southwestern States.

Casey, Zadock.—He was born in Georgia, and on removing to Illinois, was a Representative in Congress, from that State, from 1833 to 1843, and also held the office of Lieutenant-Governor of the State. Died at Caseyville, Illinois, in 1862, aged sixty-six years.

Caskie, John S.—He was born in Virginia, and was first elected a Representative to Congress, from his native State, in 1851, and has been elected to each successive Congress, serving at the present time as a member of the Committee on the Judiciary.

Cass, Lewis.—Born in Exeter, New Hampshire, October 9, 1782. Having received a limited education at his native place, at the early age of seventeen he crossed the Alleghany Mountains on foot, to seek a home in the "great West," then an almost unexplored wilderness. Settled at Marietta, Ohio; he studied law, and was successful. Elected at twenty-five to the Legislature of Ohio, he originated the bill which arrested the proceedings of Aaron Burr, and, as stated by Mr. Jefferson, was the first blow given to what is known as Burr's conspiracy. In 1807 he was appointed, by Mr. Jefferson, Marshal of the State, and held the office till the latter part of 1811, when he volunteered to repel Indian aggressions on the frontier. He was elected Colonel of the Third Regiment of Ohio volunteers, and entered the military service of the United States at the commencement of the war of 1812. Having by a difficult march reached Detroit, he urged the immediate invasion of Canada, and was the author of the proclamation of that event. He was the first to land in arms on the enemy's shore, and, with a small detachment of troops, fought and won the first battle, that of the Tarontoe. At the subsequent capitulation of Detroit, he was absent, on important service, and regretted that his command and himself had been included in that capitulation. Liberated on parole, he repaired to the seat of government to report the causes of the disaster, and the failure of the campaign. He was immediately appointed a Colonel in the regular army, and, soon after, promoted to the rank of Brigadier-General; having, in the mean time, been elected Major-General of the Ohio volunteers. On being exchanged and released from parole, he again repaired to the frontier, and joined the army for the recovery of Michigan. Being at that time without a command, he served and distinguished himself, as a volunteer aide-de-camp to General Harrison, at the battle of the Thames. He was appointed, by President Madison, in October, 1813, Governor of Michigan. His position combined, with the ordinary duties of chief magistrate of a civilized community, the immediate management and control, as superintendent, of the relations with the numerous and powerful Indian tribes in that region of country. He conducted with success the affairs of the Territory under embarrassing circumstances. Under his sway peace was preserved between the whites and the treacherous and disaffected Indians, law and order established, and the Territory rapidly advanced in population, resources, and prosperity. He held this position till July, 1831, when he was, by President Jackson, made Secretary of War. In the latter part of 1836, President Jackson appointed him Minister to France, where he remained until 1842, when he requested his recall, and returned to this country. In January, 1845, he was elected, by the Legislature of Michigan, to the Senate of the United States; which place he resigned on his nomination, in May, 1848, as a candidate for the Presidency, by the political party to which he belonged. After the election of his opponent (General Taylor) to that office, the Legislature of his State, in 1849, re-elected him to the Senate for the unexpired portion of his original term of six years. When Mr. Buchanan became President, he invited General Cass to the head of the Department of State, which position he resigned in December, 1860. He has devoted some attention to literary pursuits, and his writings, speeches, and State papers would make several volumes.

Cassedy, George.—He was born in Bergen County, New Jersey, and was a Representative in Congress, from New Jersey, from 1821 to 1827, and died in Hackensack, New Jersey, December 31, 1842, aged fifty-eight years.

Cathcart, Charles W.—He was born in the Island of Madeira, in 1809; went to sea in early life and studied mechanics; removed to Indiana in 1831; was for several years a United States Surveyor; served in the State Legislature; and he was elected a Representative in Congress, from Indiana, from 1845 to 1849, and was a Senator in Congress, from 1852 to 1853, by appointment. Of late years he has been devoted to farming.

Catlin, George S.—Born in Harwington, Litchfield, County, Connecticut, in 1809; received a common school and academic education; studied law, and was admitted to the bar in 1830; and was a Representative in Congress, from 1843 to 1845. 'He was also a number of years in the State Legislature, State's Attorney, and Judge of the Windham County Court. He died in December, 1851.

Causin, John M. S.—He was born in Maryland; was a lawyer by profession; served several terms in the Legislature; and was a Representative in Congress, from his native State, from 1843 to 1845. Died at Cairo, Illinois, January 30, 1861.

Cavanaugh, J. M.—He was a Representative in the Thirty-fifth Congress, from Minnesota.

Chaffee, Calvin C.—Born in Westminster, Vermont, August 28, 1811. He early devoted himself to the study of medicine; graduated at Middlebury College; and on becoming a citizen of Massachusetts, he was elected a Representative in Congress, from that State, to the Thirty-fourth and Thirty-fifth Congresses, serving as a member of the Committee on Invalid Pensions. In 1859 he was appointed Librarian of the House of Representatives, which office he held until 1861.

Chalmers, Joseph W.—He was a Senator in Congress, from Mississippi, from 1845 to 1847.

Chamberlain, Ebenezer M.—He was born in Maine, and was a Representative in Congress, from Indiana, from 1853 to 1855.

Chamberlain, Jacob P.—He was born in Massachusetts, and was a Representative, from New York, to the Thirty-seventh Congress, serving on the Committee on Agriculture.

Chamberlain, John C.—He graduated at Harvard University in 1793; practised law at Alstead, New Hampshire; and was a Representative in Congress, from that State, from 1809 to 1811. He died at Utica, New York, December 8, 1834, aged sixty-two years.

Chamberlain, William.—He was a Representative in Congress, from Vermont, from 1803 to 1805, and again from 1809 to 1811. He was a State Councillor from 1796 to 1803; served five years in the State Legislature; was Lieutenant-Governor of Vermont from 1813 to 1815; and Chief Justice of the Randolph County Court from 1801 to 1803, and in 1814.

Chambers, David.—He was born in Allentown, Northampton County, Pennsylvania, in 1780. He was educated by his father, who was a school teacher; and in 1794 was employed as a confidential express to carry despatches from General Henry Lee to President Washington, during the Whiskey Insurrection; in 1796 he was placed in the office of the Aurora newspaper, to learn the printer's trade; and after spending the sixteen subsequent years on a farm in Virginia, he removed to Zanesville, Ohio, where he conducted a newspaper, and was elected State printer. When the seat of government was removed to Columbus, he was appointed Secretary of the Senate; during the years 1812 and 1813 he was aide-de-camp to General Cass; and was a Representative in Congress, from Ohio, from 1821 to 1823. He subsequently served a number of years in the State Legislature of Ohio; was Speaker in 1844, and was a member of the Constitutional Convention of 1851; having also been elected Mayor of Zanesville, Recorder, and Clerk of the Court of Common Pleas. Of late years he has been wholly devoted to agricultural pursuits. Died at Zanesville, Ohio, August 8, 1864.

Chambers, Ezekiel F.—Born in Kent County, Maryland, February 28, 1788; graduated at Washington College when seventeen years of age; studied law, and was admitted to the bar in 1808; he performed some military service in 1812, and subsequently attained the rank of Brigadier-General; in 1822 he was elected to the State Senate against his will; he took an active part in 1825 in arranging a system of legislation for the recovery of slaves; he was a Senator in Congress, from Maryland, from 1826 to 1835; in 1834 he was appointed Chief Judge of the Second Judicial District and a Judge of the Court of Appeals, which offices he held until 1851, when the Judiciary became elective; having been in 1850 an active member of the Convention which changed the State Constitution. He was offered, in 1852, by President Fillmore, the post of Secretary of the Navy, in the place of Secretary Graham, who resigned; but his health compelled him to decline the honor. In 1833 Yale College conferred upon him the degree of Doctor of Laws, and in 1852 he received the same honor from the Delaware College.

Chambers, George.—Born in Chambersburg, Pennsylvania, in 1786; graduated at Princeton College in 1804; studied law, and was admitted to the bar in 1807, and practised extensively in the Franklin County Courts. He was a Representative in Congress from 1833 to 1837, and was then elected a delegate to the Pennsylvania Constitutional Convention. In 1851 he was appointed by the Governor, with the unanimous consent of the Senate, a Justice of the Supreme Court of the State, which office he held until the expiration of its tenure under the constitution. Since that time he has lived in retirement, discharging many trusts and offices in promotion of religion and education, in the town of his birth, which bears his father's name.

Chambers, Henry.—He was a Senator in Congress from 1825 to 1826, from Alabama, and died January 25, 1826.

Chambers, John.—Born in New Jersey in 1779; emigrated to Kentucky when thirteen years of age; studied law, and practised the profession with success; was an aide-de-camp to General Harrison at the battle of the Thames; was appointed Governor of the Territory of Iowa by President Harrison, manifesting great ability and prudence in his intercourse with the Indians; and by President Taylor he was appointed a Commissioner to make a treaty with the Sioux Indians. He was a member of Congress, from Kentucky, from 1827 to 1829, and again from 1835 to 1839. He died near Paris, Kentucky, September 21, 1852.

Champion, Epaphroditus.—He was a Representative in Congress, from Connecticut, from 1807 to 1817; a man greatly respected for his public and private character; and died at East Haddam, Connecticut, November 22, 1835, aged seventy-eight years.

Champlin, Christopher G.—He was a native of Newport, Rhode Island; graduated at Harvard University in 1786; was a member of Congress from 1797 to 1801, and a Senator of the United States from 1809 to 1811. At the time of his death, which occurred March 18, 1840, in the seventy-fourth year of his age, he was President of the Rhode Island Bank.

Chandler, John.—Was a native of Maine when a part of Massachusetts, representing it in the State Senate from 1803 to 1805, and in Congress from 1805 to 1808, and for three years was Sheriff of Kennebeck County. In 1812 he was appointed Brigadier-General, and took an active part in the Canadian campaign, having his horse shot under him at the battle of Stony Creek, where he was wounded and taken prisoner. He was elected to the United States Senate in 1820, being one of the first two Senators from Maine after its separation from Massachusetts, serving two terms, until 1829. In 1829 he was appointed Collector of the port of Portland, serving until 1837; and he died at Augusta, September, 1841.

Chandler, Joseph R.—He was born in Massachusetts; was liberally educated, and studied law; edited a newspaper in Philadelphia for many years; was a Representative in Congress, from Pennsylvania, from 1849 to 1855; and was appointed Minister to Naples by President Buchanan in 1858.

Chandler, Thomas.—He was a State Senator in 1827, and a Representative in Congress, from New Hampshire, from 1829 to 1833.

Chandler, Zachariah.—Born in Bedford, New Hampshire, December 10, 1813; received an academical education; was bred a merchant; was Mayor of Detroit, Michigan in 1851; defeated candidate for Governor of Michigan in 1852; and is a Senator in Congress from Michigan, having succeeded Senator Cass in that capacity, and taking his seat in the Thirty-fifth Congress. He has served as a member of the Committee on the District of Columbia, and Chairman of the Committee on Commerce. He was re-elected to the Senate in 1863, for the term ending in 1869.

Chaney, John.—He was born in Maryland, and was a Representative in Congress, from Ohio, from 1833 to 1839.

Chanler, John Winthrop.—Born in the city of New York, in 1826; was a member of the New York Assembly, in 1859 and 1860, and declined a renomination; and in 1862 he was elected a Representative, from New York, to the Thirty-eighth Congress, serving on the Committee on Patents.

Chapin, Graham H.—He was born in Connecticut; graduated at Yale College in 1817; and was a Representative in Congress, from New York, from 1835 to 1837, and died in 1843.

Chapman, Augustus A.—He was born in Virginia, and was a Representative in Congress, from that State, from 1843 to 1847.

Chapman, Bird B.—He was born in Connecticut, and, on removing to Nebraska, was elected a Delegate, from that Territory, to the Thirty-fourth Congress.

Chapman, Charles.—Born at Newtown, Fairfield County, Connecticut, June 21, 1799; received a classical education; he is a lawyer by profession; was three times a member of the House of Representatives of the State; he was United States Attorney during the administration of Mr. Tyler, and a Representative in the Thirty-second Congress, from Connecticut.

Chapman, Henry.—He was born in Pennsylvania, and elected a Representative to the Thirty-fifth Congress, from his native State, serving as a member of the Committee on the Judiciary.

Chapman, John.—He was a Representative in Congress, from Pennsylvania, from 1797 to 1799.

Chapman, John G.—He was born in Charles County, Maryland, July 5, 1798, and died December 10, 1856. He laid the foundation of his education at Yale College, which he left during his senior term, on account of his health, and afterwards refused a diploma which was tendered to him by the faculty. He studied law with William Wirt, and, after practising for some time, turned his attention to politics, and between the years 1824 and 1844, he was almost constantly in the Legislature of Maryland. In 1845 he was elected a Representative in Congress, and again re-elected in 1847, serving on important committees, and doing much good for his constituents and the public at large. He was chosen President of the Convention which framed the present Constitution of Maryland; and his last public act was to preside as Chairman of the National Whig Convention, which met in Baltimore, in 1856, to nominate Millard Fillmore for the Presidency. He was an eloquent speaker, filled all his public trusts with fidelity, and died lamented by a large number of warm personal friends.

Chapman, Reuben.—He was born in Virginia, and was a Representative in Congress, from Alabama, from 1835 to 1847; also Governor of that State, from 1847 to 1849.

Chappell, A. H.—He was born in Georgia, and was a Representative, from that State, to the Twenty-eighth Congress.

Chappell, John J.—Born in Fairfield District, South Carolina, January 19, 1782; received a common school education; studied law and was admitted to the bar in 1804; was a Solicitor of Equity, Colonel of militia, a Trustee of the State College in 1809, and a Bank Director; and a Representative in Congress, from South Carolina, from 1813 to 1817.

Charlton, Robert M.—He was a Judge, and a Senator in Congress, from Georgia, in 1852 and 1853. He died in Savannah, January 18, 1854.

Chase, Dudley.—Was born in Cornish, Sullivan County, New Hampshire, December 30, 1771. He received an academic education, and graduated at Dartmouth College, in 1791. Having been admitted to the bar, he commenced practice in Vermont, and, from 1803 to 1811, he was State's Attorney for Orange County. He was a member of the Constitutional Conventions of 1814 and 1822. He was a Representative, from Randolph, to the Legislature of Vermont, in 1805, and the seven succeeding years, during five of which he was Speaker of the House of Representatives, and was again elected Representative, from the same town, in 1823 and 1824. He was elected United States Senator, from Vermont, from 1813 to 1819, but he resigned his seat in 1817. He was chosen Chief Justice of the Supreme Court of Vermont, in 1817, holding the same office, by annual re-elections, until 1821. He then returned to his profession of the law for a few years, and in 1824 he was again chosen United States Senator, from 1825 to 1831, inclusive, when he retired wholly from public life, and devoted his attention to farming and gardening, of which he was excessively fond. He was a brother of the late Philander Chase, Bishop of Illinois; and died at Randolph, Vermont, February 23, 1846.

Chase, George W.—He was born in New York, and was a Representative in Congress, from that State, from 1853 to 1855.

Chase, Lucien B.—He was born in Vermont, and was a Representative in Congress, from Tennessee, from 1845 to 1847, and for a second term, ending in 1849. He is the author of a work entitled "History of President Polk's Administration."

Chase, Salmon P.—He was born in Cornish, New Hampshire, January 13, 1808. His education began at home, and was continued at the schools and academies of New Hampshire and Central Ohio, and completed at the Cincinnati College, and at Dartmouth, in New Hampshire, graduating in 1826. He studied law, in Washington City, with William Wirt, and has practised his profession in Cincinnati, Ohio, for many years. His first public position was that of School Examiner, in Cincinnati, in 1839; in 1840 he was a City Councilman; in 1845 he projected what was called a Liberty Convention; was a member of the Free-soil Convention held at Buffalo in 1848; and was a Senator in Congress, from Ohio, from 1849 to 1855; and elected Governor of Ohio, in 1855, and re-elected in 1857. In 1860 he was again chosen a Senator in Congress, but on the day after he took his seat, he was appointed Secretary of the Treasury in President Lincoln's Cabinet; having been a member also, of the Peace Congress of 1861.

Chase, Samuel.—He was born in New York, and was a Representative in Congress, from New York, from 1827 to 1829.

Chastain, Edward W.—He was born in South Carolina, and was a Representative in Congress, from Georgia, from 1851 to 1855.

Cheatham, Richard.—He was a Representative in Congress, from Tennessee, from 1837 to 1839. Died in September, 1845.

Chestnut, James.—Born near Camden, South Carolina, in 1815; graduated at Princeton College; from 1842 to 1852 was a member of the State Legislature; from 1854 to 1858 he was a member of the State Senate; he was appointed to a seat in the United States Senate, taking his seat during the second session of the Thirty-fifth Congress, and was subsequently elected to that position, but resigned in December, 1860. He became identified with the Rebellion of 1861, as a member of the so-called Confederate Congress.

Chetwood, William.—Born in New Jersey in 1769; graduated at Princeton College in 1792; and admitted to the bar in 1798. During the Whiskey Insurrection he attended Major-General Lee, as aide-de-camp; at one time served in the State Council of New Jersey, and was elected to Congress, to fill a vacancy, during the administration of President. Jackson. He was an able lawyer, practised his profession until his seventieth year, and died December 18, 1857.

Cheves, Langdon.—He was born in Abbeville District, South Carolina, September 17, 1776; was admitted to the bar in 1801; elected to the State Legislature in 1808; and afterwards Attorney-General of the State. He was a Representative in Congress, from 1811 to 1816, and was Speaker during the second session of the Thirteenth Congress. He was also a Commissioner of Claims under the treaty of Ghent; Judge of the Court of Common Pleas, from 1816 to 1819, and for a time President of the United States Bank. Resigning this trust, he returned to Carolina, and withdrew from public life. He died June 26, 1857.

Childs, Thomas, Jr.—He was born in New York, and was a Representative, from that State, during the Thirty-fourth Congress.

Childs, Timothy.—He was born in Massachusetts; was a member of the Assembly of New York in 1828 and 1833; and was a Representative in Congress, from that State, from 1829 to 1831, from 1835 to 1839, and again from 1841 to 1843. Died at Santa Cruz in November, 1847.

Chilton, Samuel.—He was born in Virginia, and was a Representative in Congress, from that State, from 1843 to 1845.

Chilton, Thomas.—He was a native of Kentucky, and a Representative in Congress, from that State, from 1827 to 1831, and for a second term, from 1833 to 1835.

Chinn, Joseph W.—He was a Representative in Congress, from Virginia, from 1831 to 1835, and died at Richmond, December 5, 1840.

Chinn, Thomas W.—He was born in Kentucky, and, removing to Louisiana, was elected a Representative in Congress, from 1839 to 1841.

Chipman, Daniel.—Born in 1765, in Salisbury, Connecticut; graduated at Dartmouth in 1788; was a lawyer by profession, and practised at Ripton, Vermont. He was for many years in the Legislature, and was frequently Speaker of the House of Representatives of his State, and a member of the last State Constitutional Convention; he was the first reporter of the decisions of the Supreme Court, and author of an able work on Law Contracts for the Sale of Specific Articles, which is highly esteemed by the profession. He was a member of Congress, from 1814 to 1817, and died in Ripton, April 23, 1850.

Chipman, John S.—He was born in Vermont, and was a Representative in Congress, from Michigan, from 1845 to 1847.

Chipman, Nathaniel.—Born in Salisbury, Connecticut, November 15, 1752; graduated at Yale College in 1777; and settled as a lawyer in Tinmouth, Vermont, and was Professor of Law for twenty-eight years in Middlebury College. In 1786 he was elected a Judge of the Supreme Court; in 1789 he was chosen Chief Justice; and in 1791 was appointed Judge of the United

States District Court. He was subsequently again elected Chief Justice, and from 1797 to 1802 he was a member of the United States Senate, serving until 1803. In 1793 he published "Sketches of the Principles of Government," and "Reports and Dissertations." He died at Tinmouth, February 15, 1843.

Chipman, William W.—He was a Delegate to Congress, from the Territory of Iowa, from 1839 to 1841.

Chittenden, Martin.—He was born in 1769, in Salisbury, Connecticut. He was a member of Congress, from Vermont, from 1803 to 1813, and Governor of Vermont in 1813 and 1814. He was a graduate of Dartmouth College in 1789, and died in 1840.

Chittenden, T. C.—He was born in Massachusetts, and having removed to New York, was elected a Representative, from that State, to the Twenty-seventh Congress.

Choate, Rufus.—Was born at Ipswich, Massachusetts, October 1, 1799. He graduated at Dartmouth College in 1819, and was afterwards chosen a tutor in that institution, but having selected the law for his profession, he entered the Law School at Cambridge, and after spending a few months there, went to Washington and studied with William Wirt. He completed his legal studies at an office in Salem, and commenced the practice of his profession in the town of Danvers, in 1824. In 1825 he was elected a Representative to the Massachusetts Legislature, and in 1827 he was in the Senate of the same State. He took a prominent part in the debates, and won much reputation by his energy and sagacity. In 1832 he was elected a member of Congress from the Essex District, but declined a re-election in 1834, and removed to Boston, to devote himself to his profession. Here he took an eminent position at the bar, and soon came into an extensive practice. In 1841, on the retirement of Mr. Webster from the Senate, Mr. Choate was elected to fill the vacancy, and at the close of his term, he gave himself up wholly to his profession. He was a Regent of the Smithsonian Institution, but resigned the position. He was greatly distinguished for his eloquence, but his style of speaking was peculiar; his judgment in the management of causes was considered consummate. His published orations and arguments are quite numerous, and all of a high order. He died at Halifax, Nova Scotia, while on his way to Europe for his health, July 12, 1859.

Chrisman, James S.—He was born in Kentucky, and was a Representative in Congress, from that State, from 1853 to 1855.

Christie, Gabriel.—He was a Representative in Congress, from Maryland, from 1793 to 1797, and from 1799 to 1801.

Christie, Henry.—He was a Representative in Congress, from Kentucky, from 1809 to 1811.

Churchwell, William M.—He was born in Tennessee, and was a Representative in Congress, from that State, from 1852 to 1855.

Cilley, Bradbury.—He was a Representative in Congress, from New Hampshire, from 1813 to 1817.

Cilley, Jonathan.—He was born in Nottingham, New Hampshire, July 2, 1802; graduated at Bowdoin College in 1825; adopted the profession of law, and admitted to the bar in 1829; was at one time Speaker of the House of Representatives of Maine, of which he was a member from 1832 to 1837; and a member of Congress, from 1837 to the time of his death. He was killed, at the third fire, in a duel fought with William J. Graves, at Bladensburg, Maryland, February 24, 1838, with rifles, at eighty yards distance.

Cilley, Joseph.—He was born in New Hampshire, and was a Senator in Congress, from that State, from 1846 to 1847.

Claggett, Clifton.—He was born in Rockingham County, New Hampshire; was Judge of Probate of Hillsborough County, from 1823 to 1827; Judge of the Superior Court one or two years; was a Representative in Congress, from that State, from 1803 to

1805, and again from 1817 to 1821; and died in 1829, aged fifty-six years.

Claiborne, John.—He was a Representative in Congress, from Virginia, from 1805 to 1808. Died during the latter year.

Claiborne, John F. H.—Was a native of Natchez, Mississippi; educated and licensed as a lawyer in Virginia; was a Representative in the Legislature of Mississippi during three sessions, and a Representative in Congress, from 1835 to 1838; has since conducted the Natchez Fur Trader and also the Louisiana Courier, leading journals of the South, and was editor of an agricultural journal published in New Orleans. He held the office of United States Timber Agent, for the Districts of Louisiana and Mississippi, to which he was appointed by President Pierce. He wrote an historical work relating to the Southwest.

Claiborne, Nathaniel H.—He was born in Sussex County, Virginia; served many years in the Legislature of that State; was also a member of the Executive Council; and was a Representative in Congress, from that State, from 1825 to 1837. Died in Franklin County, Virginia, August 15, 1859, aged eighty-three years.

Claiborne, Thomas.—He was a Representative in Congress, from Virginia, from 1793 to 1799, and again from 1801 to 1805.

Claiborne, Thomas.—He was a Representative in Congress, from Tennessee, from 1817 to 1819.

Claiborne, William C. C.—He studied law, and settled in Tennessee, of which State he assisted in forming the Constitution, and afterwards represented it in Congress, from 1797 to 1801. In 1801 he was appointed Governor of the Mississippi Territory, and in 1804 of Louisiana; and to that office he was also chosen by the people, after the adoption of its Constitution, from 1812 to 1816. He was then elected a Senator of the United States, but died before he took his seat, at New Orleans, November 23, 1817.

Clapp, Asa W. H.—He was born in Maine, and was a Representative in Congress, from that State, from 1847 to 1849.

Clark, Abraham.—Born near Elizabethtown, New Jersey, February 15, 1726. He was a self-made man, and because of his habit of giving legal advice gratuitously, he was called the "Poor Man's Counsellor." He was Sheriff, and Clerk of the Colonial Assembly, one of the Delegates to the Continental Congress, and a signer of the Declaration of Independence; and, after the adoption of the Constitution, was a Representative in Congress, from 1791 to 1794. He died September 15, 1794, of stroke of the sun.

Clark, Ambrose W.—He was born near Cooperstown, Otsego County, New York, February 19, 1810; received a common school education; was employed in a printing office at Cooperstown until he became of age; published for five years the Otsego Republican; established and published for eight years, in Lewis County, the Northern Journal; and also published for sixteen years the Northern New York Journal, in Watertown, Jefferson County. In 1859 he was elected a Representative, from New York, to the Thirty-seventh Congress, serving on the Committee on Printing. He was re-elected to the Thirty-eighth Congress in 1862, and was Chairman of the Committee on Printing, and a member of the Committee on Accounts.

Clark, Archibald S.—He was a member of the New York Senate for four years, beginning with 1813, and was a Representative in Congress, from New York, from 1816 to 1817. He held the several positions of Clerk, Surrogate and Judge of Saratoga County. Died at Clarence, New York, December 4, 1821, aged forty-three years.

Clark, Beverly S.—He was born in Virginia, and was a Representative in Congress, from Kentucky, from 1847 to 1849.

Clark, Christopher.—He was a Representative in Congress, from Virginia, from 1804 to 1806.

Clark, Daniel.—He was born in Stratham, Rockingham County, New Hampshire, October 24, 1809; graduated at Dartmouth College in 1834; studied law, and came to the bar in 1837; was a member of the New Hampshire Legislature in the years 1842, 1843, 1846, 1854, and 1855; in 1857 he was elected a Senator in Congress, from New Hampshire, and in 1861 was re-elected for the term ending in 1867, serving as Chairman of the Committee on Claims, and as a member of other important committees. During the first session of the Thirty-eighth Congress he was chosen President *pro tem.* of the Senate.

Clark, Ezra, Jr.—He was born in Vermont, and having removed to Connecticut, was elected a Representative to the Thirty-fourth Congress, and re-elected to the Thirty-fifth Congress, serving as a member of the Committee on Elections.

Clark, Franklin.—He was born in Maine; a merchant by occupation; and was a Representative in Congress, from that State, from 1847 to 1849. Before entering Congress he served in the State Legislature, and was a member of the Executive Council in 1855.

Clark, Horace F.—He was born in Southbury, New Haven County, Connecticut; graduated at Williams College, Massachusetts; adopted the law as a profession; and was elected a member of the Thirty-fifth Congress, from New York, serving as a member of the Committee on the Judiciary. He has also been re-elected to the Thirty-sixth Congress, serving as a member of the Committee on Indian Affairs.

Clark, James.—He was born in Bedford County, Virginia, and was a Representative in Congress, from Kentucky, from 1813 to 1816, and again from 1825 to 1831, and was Governor of the State in 1836. He died at Frankfort, Kentucky, August 27, 1839.

Clark, James W.—Born in Bertie County, North Carolina; graduated at Princeton College in 1796; was for several years in the House of Commons; a Presidential Elector in 1812; three years a member of the State Senate; and a Representative in Congress, from 1815 to 1817. He was in 1828 appointed Chief Clerk of the Navy Department, and died in the sixty-fifth year of his age.

Clark, John B.—Born in Madison County, Kentucky, April 17, 1802. A lawyer by profession; removed to Missouri, and was appointed Clerk of Howard County Court, in 1824, serving till 1834. In 1832 commanded a regiment of mounted militia during the Black Hawk war, and made Major-General of militia in 1848; elected to the Legislature during the session of 1850–51; was chosen, by the State, as commanding officer to expel the Mormons from Missouri, and was a member of the Thirty-fifth Congress, serving on the Committee on Territories. He was re-elected to the Thirty-sixth Congress, serving on the Committee on Territories. Re-elected to the Thirty-seventh Congress, but took part in the Rebellion of 1861 as a Colonel, having been expelled from the House in July, 1861.

Clark, Lincoln.—He was born in Massachusetts, and, on removing to Iowa was elected a Representative in Congress, from that State, from 1851 to 1853.

Clark, Lot.—He was born in New York; was a Representative in Congress, from 1823 to 1825, when he was appointed Postmaster at Norwich, New York; and was a member of the New York Assembly in 1846.

Clark, M. S.—He was a Representative in Congress, from Pennsylvania, during the years 1820 and 1821.

Clark, Robert.—He was born in Washington County, New York; was a member of the Assembly of that State, from 1812 to 1815; a Representative in Congress, from 1819 to 1821; and a Delegate to the State Constitutional Convention held in the latter year.

Clark, Samuel.—He was born in New York, and was a Representative in Congress, from New York, from 1833 to 1835; on removing to Michigan, was elected a Representative in Congress, from that State, from 1853 to 1855.

Clark, William.—He was for some time prior to 1828, State Treasurer of Pennsylvania. In 1828 was appointed Treasurer of the United States, and held the office for one year. From 1833 to 1837 he was a member of the House of Representatives in Congress. He died in Dauphin County, Pennsylvania, April 28, 1851.

Clarke, Bayard.—Born in New York City, March 17, 1815; educated at Geneva College, and studied law. In 1836 he was Attaché and Secretary to General Cass's Embassy to France, and continued in that position four years. He then took a course of study at the Royal School of Cavalry, in France, and afterwards served in the Second Regiment of Dragoons, through the Florida war. He resigned in 1843, and settled at Westchester, New York, which District he represented in the Thirty-fourth Congress.

Clarke, Charles E.—He was born in New York, and was a Representative in Congress, from that State, from 1849 to 1851. In 1839 and 1840 he was a member of the New York Assembly, from Jefferson County.

Clarke, Daniel.—He was a Delegate to Congress, from the Territory of Orleans or Louisiana, from 1806 to 1809.

Clarke, Freeman.—He was born in Troy, New York, March 22, 1809; commenced active life as a merchant, but for twenty-seven years was engaged in the banking business, first as Cashier of the Bank of Orleans, at Albion, and subsequently as President of several banks in Rochester. He also held the offices of Vice-President and Treasurer of one or more savings banks and of several important railroad companies. In 1856 he was a Presidential Elector, and was elected a Representative, from New York, to the Thirty-eighth Congress, and was a member of the Committees on Manufactures, and Invalid Pensions.

Clarke, Henry S.—Born in Beaufort County, North Carolina. He studied law; went into the State Legislature in 1834; was Solicitor for the State in 1842; and a Representative in Congress, from North Carolina, from 1845 to 1847.

Clarke, John C.—He was born in Connecticut; served in the Assembly of New York in 1826; and was a Representative in Congress, from that State, from 1827 to 1829, and again from 1837 to 1843.

Clarke, John H.—He was a Senator in Congress, from Rhode Island, from 1847 to 1853.

Clarke, Staley N.—He was a Representative in Congress, from New York, from 1841 to 1843.

Clawson, Isaiah D.—He was born in Woodstown, New Jersey, March 30, 1822; graduated at Princeton College in 1840; studied medicine in the University of Pennsylvania, taking his degree in 1843; was a member of the New Jersey Assembly in 1853; and was elected a Representative from that State to the Thirty-fourth Congress, and re-elected to the Thirty-fifth Congress, serving as a member of the Committee on Revolutionary Claims.

Clay, Brutus J.—He was born in Madison County, Kentucky, July 1, 1808; was educated at Danville College, Kentucky, and settled in Bourbon County as a farmer in 1837. In 1840 he served in the State Legislature; was subsequently elected President of the Bourbon County Agricultural Society, which position he still holds. In 1853 he was elected President of the State Agricultural Society, was re-elected for four years, and then declined a re-election; was again elected to the Legislature in 1860; and was elected a Representative, from Kentucky, to the Thirty-eighth Congress, serving as Chairman of the Committee on Agriculture, and as a member on that of Revolutionary Pensions. Ever since his boyhood he has been devoted to agriculture, and especially to the raising of choice breeds of cattle.

Clay, Clement C.—He was born in Halifax County, Virginia, December 17, 1789; graduated at the University of East Tennessee; studied law, and was admitted to the bar in 1809; and removed to Huntsville, Alabama, in 1811, where he has resided ever since. During the Creek war, he saw some service as a soldier. He practised his profession until 1817, when he was elected a member of the Territorial Council of Alabama; in 1819 he was chosen one of the Judges of the Circuit

Court; in 1820 was chosen Chief Justice of that Court, and resigned in 1823; in 1828 he was elected to the State Legislature, and was made Speaker; he was a Representative in Congress, from Alabama, from 1827 to 1835; in 1835 he was elected Governor of Alabama, serving two years; and in 1837 he was elected a Senator in Congress for the term ending in 1842.

Clay, Clement C., Jr.—He was born in Madison, Alabama, about the year 1819; graduated at the University of Alabama, and spent two years at the University of Virginia; studied law, and commenced the practice at Huntsville, Alabama, in 1840; served in the Legislature of Alabama in 1842, 1844, and 1845; and was elected by the Legislature, in 1846, Judge of the Madison County Court, serving two years, when he resigned. In 1853 he was elected a Senator in Congress, from Alabama, and in 1857 was re-elected for the term of six years, receiving every vote in the Legislature. He left the Senate in February, 1861, and took part in the Rebellion of that year.

Clay, Henry.—Born in Hanover County, Virginia, April 12, 1777. Having received a common school education, he became at an early age a copyist in the office of the Clerk of the Court of Chancery, at Richmond. At nineteen he commenced the study of law, and shortly afterwards removed to Lexington, Kentucky, where he was admitted to the bar in 1799, and soon obtained extensive practice. He began his political career, by taking an active part in the election of delegates to frame a new Constitution for the State of Kentucky. In 1803 he was elected to the Legislature by the citizens of Fayette County; and in 1806 he was appointed to the United States Senate for the remainder of the term of General Adair, who had resigned. In 1807 he was again elected a member of the General Assembly of Kentucky, and was chosen Speaker. In the following year occurred his duel with Humphrey Marshall. In 1809 he was again elected to the United States Senate for the unexpired term of Mr. Thurston, resigned. In 1811 he was elected a member of the House of Representatives, and was chosen Speaker, on the first day of his appearance in that body, and was five times re-elected to this office. During this session, his eloquence aroused the country to resist the aggressions of Great Britain, and awakened a national spirit. In 1814, he was appointed one of the Commissioners to negotiate a treaty of peace at Ghent. Returning from this mission, he was re-elected to Congress, and in 1818 he spoke in favor of recognizing the independence of the South American Republics. In the same year, he put forth his strength in behalf of a national system of internal improvements. A monument of stone, inscribed with his name, was erected on the Cumberland Road, to commemorate his services in behalf of that improvement. In the session of 1819–20, he exerted himself for the establishment of protection to American industry, and this was followed by services in adjusting the Missouri Compromise. After the settlement of these questions, he withdrew from Congress, in order to attend to his private affairs. In 1823 he returned to Congress, and was re-elected Speaker; and at this session he exerted himself in support of the independence of Greece. Under John Quincy Adams, he filled the office of Secretary of State; the attack upon Mr. Adams's administration, and especially upon the Secretary of State, by John Randolph, led to a hostile meeting between him and Mr. Clay, which terminated without bloodshed. In 1829 he returned to Kentucky; and in 1831 was elected to the United States Senate, where he commenced his labors in favor of the Tariff; in the same month of his reappearance in the Senate, he was unanimously nominated for President of the United States. In 1836 he was re-elected to the Senate, where he remained until 1842, when he resigned, and took his final leave, as he supposed, of that body. In 1839 he was again nominated for the Presidency, but General Harrison was selected as the candidate. He also received the nomination, in 1844, for President, and was defeated in this election by Mr. Polk. He remained in retirement in Kentucky, until 1849, when he was re-elected to the Senate of the United States. Here he devoted all his energies to the measures known as the Compromise Acts. His efforts during this session impaired his strength, and he went for his health to Havana and New Orleans, but with no permanent advantage; he returned to Washington, but was unable to participate in the active duties of the Senate, and resigned his seat, to take effect upon the 6th of September, 1852. He died in Washington City, June 29, 1852. He was interested in the success of the Colonization Society, and was for a long time one of its most efficient officers, and also its President. His Life and Letters, and also his Speeches, were published in several volumes by the late Calvin Colton.

Clay, James B.—Born in Washington City, November 9, 1817. He received his classical education at Transylvania University, in Kentucky, and at the age of fifteen went to Boston, where he spent two years in a counting-house. From Boston he emigrated to St. Louis, Missouri, then a city of only eight thousand, and settled upon a farm; and when twenty-one years of age, he returned to Kentucky. After spending two years in the manufacturing business, he graduated at the Law School of Lexington, and practised law as the partner of his father, the Honorable Henry Clay, until 1849; and during that year President Taylor appointed him Chargé d'Affaires to Lisbon; and having returned home by order of the Government, he was mentioned by name in President Fillmore's Message of 1850. In 1851 he again took up his residence in Missouri, but returned to Kentucky in 1853, when he became the proprietor of Ashland. He was elected to Congress in 1857, serving one term, and on the Committee on Foreign Relations. He was also a member of the Peace Convention of 1861. held in Washington. Died in Montreal, January 26, 1864.

Clay, Joseph.—He graduated at Princeton College in 1784; was a Representative in Congress, from Pennsylvania, from 1803 to 1808; and died in 1811.

Clay, Matthew.—He was a Representative in Congress, from Virginia, from 1797 to 1813.

Clayton, Augustin S.—Born in Fredericksburg, Virginia, November 27, 1783, and died at his residence, in Athens, Georgia, June 21, 1839. He was educated at the University of Georgia; read law, and practised it with eminent success; served in the State Legislature; was appointed Judge of the Superior Court; and was a Representative in Congress, from 1831 to 1835. He was for many years skeptical on the subject of the Christian religion, but at the time of his death was a sincere believer, and a member of the Methodist Episcopal Church. He acquired some distinction as a politician, and the political pamphlet called "Crockett's Life of Van Buren," is said to have been the production of his pen.

Clayton, John M.—Born in Sussex County, Delaware, July 24, 1796; graduated at Yale College in 1815; was bred to the bar, having studied law in the office of John Clayton, and for a time in the Law School at Litchfield, Connecticut. He commenced practice in 1818, and soon attained eminence in his profession. He was, in 1824, elected to the State Legislature, and subsequently Secretary of State of Delaware; and in 1829 was chosen a Senator in Congress. He was re-elected in 1835, and resigned in December, 1836. In January, 1837, was appointed Chief Justice of Delaware, which office he resigned in 1839. He was again elected to the Federal Senate in 1845, and was a Senator until 1849, when he became Secretary of State under President Taylor, which position he occupied until the death of Taylor, in July, 1850. During this period he negotiated the famous Clayton-Bulwer Treaty. He was for the third time elected to the Senate, and took his seat March, 1851, and died a Senator, November 9, 1856. During his last term in the Senate, he vindicated, with marked ability, the principles of the treaty which he inaugurated. At the bar he was a learned lawyer and an eloquent advocate; and during his whole public career acquitted himself uprightly, with dignity and recognized ability. He had two sons, both of whom preceded him to the grave.

Clayton, Joshua.—He was the Governor of Delaware from 1793 to 1796, and was chosen a Senator of the United States in 1798, and died the following year.

Clayton, Thomas.—He was a Representative in Congress, from Delaware, from 1813 to 1817, and United States Senator from 1823 to 1826, and again from 1837 to 1847. He had been at different periods a member of the Delaware Legislature, Chief Justice of the Court of Common Pleas, and of the Superior Court. He died in Newcastle, Delaware, August 21, 1854, aged seventy-six years.

Cleaveland, J. F.—He was a Representative in Congress, from Georgia, from 1836 to 1839, but subsequently removed to Charleston, where he became a merchant, and died May 19, 1841.

Clemens, Jeremiah.—He was born in Huntsville, Alabama, December 28, 1814, and was educated at La Grange College, and the University of Alabama. He studied law at the University of Transylvania, in Kentucky, and was admitted to the bar in 1834. In 1838 he was appointed United States Attorney for the Northern District of Alabama; in 1839, 1840, and 1841 he was elected to the State Legislature; in 1842 raised a company of volunteer troops, and went to Texas, having been appointed Lieutenant-Colonel, and subsequently to the same office in the regular army; in 1843 and 1844 he was again elected to the Legislature; in 1844 served as a Presidential Elector; in 1848 was appointed Governor of the Civil and Military Department of Purchase in Mexico, which position he held until the close of the war; and he was a Senator in Congress, from Alabama, from 1849 to 1853. He was also a Presidential Elector in 1856. As an author Mr. Clemens has published two novels, entitled "Bernard Lile," and "Mustang Gray," the first in 1853 and the last in 1857. He was subsequently an editor.

Clemens, Sherrard.—Born at Wheeling, Virginia, April 28, 1826; graduated at Washington College, Pennsylvania; a lawyer by profession; and during political campaigns has held several confidential positions in his native State; and was elected a member of Congress, from December, 1852, to March, 1853, and elected to the Thirty-fifth Congress, serving on the Committees on Manufactures and Revolutionary Pensions. In 1859 he was wounded in a duel fought with Mr. Wise, and was prevented from attending the second session of the Thirty-fifth Congress. He was re-elected to the Thirty-sixth Congress, serving on the Committee on Commerce.

Clements, Andrew J.—Born in Jackson County, Tennessee, in 1832; received a common school education; studied medicine, and graduated at the University of Tennessee in 1858, after which he practised his profession; and in 1861 was elected a Representative, from Tennessee, to the Thirty-seventh Congress.

Clendenen, David.—He was a Representative in Congress, from Ohio, from 1815 to 1817.

Cleveland, Chauncey F.—Born in Hampton, Connecticut, in 1799; was educated in the common schools of that vicinity; studied law, and was admitted to the bar in 1819; he was in the Connecticut Legislature in 1826, 1827, 1828, 1829, 1832, 1835, 1836, 1838, 1847, and 1848, and twice elected Speaker. He was appointed Attorney for the State in 1832; and was Governor of Connecticut in 1842 and 1843. He was a Representative in Congress, from 1849 to 1853, and also a member of the Peace Congress of 1861.

Clifford, Nathan.—He was born in Rumney, Grafton County, New Hampshire, August 18, 1803. He fitted for college at the Haverhill Academy, and completed his education at the Hampton Literary Institution. He studied law, and, after being admitted to the bar, removed to Maine in 1827. He was elected to the Legislature, from York County, in 1830, and re-elected for three years, during the last two occupying the post of Speaker. In 1834 he was appointed Attorney-General for the State of Maine, which office he held four years; and he was a Representative in Congress, from 1839 to 1843. In 1846 he was appointed, by President Polk, Attorney-General of the United States, which office he held until March, 1847, when he was appointed Commissioner to Mexico. When peace was declared between this country and Mexico, he was appointed Minister to that Republic. On his return to the United States he settled in Portland, devoting himself to his profession; and in 1858 was appointed, by President Buchanan, an Associate Justice of the Supreme Court of the United States.

Clinch, Duncan L.—Was a General in the United States Army; and from 1843 to 1845 a Representative in Congress from Georgia. He was a brave soldier and noble-hearted man. Died at Macon, Georgia, October 28, 1849.

Clingman, Thomas L.—Born in Huntsville, Surry County, North Carolina. He commenced his classical studies under private instructors, and afterwards entered Chapel Hill University as a sophomore, where he graduated. After leaving Chapel Hill he studied law, and in a short time mastered the elementary principles of legal jurisprudence; but just as he was about to enter upon the practice of his profession, he was elected to the House of Commons of the State. On his retirement from the Legislature in 1836, he removed to Ashville, in Buncombe County, where he still resides. He was soon after elected by a large vote to a seat in the State Senate of North Carolina. In 1843 he was elected to Congress, and with the exception of one term, he has been a member, until recently, of the House of Representatives ever since his first election, a period of about thirteen years. On entering the Thirty-fifth Congress, he was appointed Chairman of the Committee on Foreign Affairs, and on the resignation of Senator Biggs, he was appointed a Senator in Congress, and in November, 1858, his appointment was confirmed by an election by the Legislature. Though so long identified with politics, he has not neglected the pursuits of literature and science, having made himself acquainted with the soil, climate, and manifold capabilities of his section of North Carolina; and from time to time has given to the world the result of his observations upon these subjects. He has made contributions to the sciences of geology and mineralogy, and brought to light many facts connected with the mountains of North Carolina, one of the highest peaks of which it was his fortune to explore and measure, and which now bears his name. He took part in the Rebellion of 1861 as a Colonel, having been expelled from the Senate in July, 1861.

Clinton, De Witt.—Born at Little Britain, in Orange County, New York, March 2, 1769. He graduated at Columbia College, with the highest honors, in 1786. He studied law, but never engaged much in its practice. He was elected to the Senate of New York in 1799. In July, 1802, he fought a duel with Mr. Swartwout, arising from political controversy concerning Mr. Burr. He was a Senator of the United States from 1802 to 1803, and was chosen Mayor of New York in 1803, holding this office until 1815, excepting the years 1807 and 1810. While he was Mayor, he was also for several years a State Senator, and the Lieutenant-Governor. Under his auspices, also, the Historical Society of New York and the Academy of Fine Arts were incorporated, the New York City Hall was founded, the Orphan Asylum established, and the city fortified. He took a great interest, as early as 1817, in, and did more than any other man in behalf of, the Erie Canal, and that great work was finished during his administration as Governor, in 1825. In 1812 he consented to become the candidate of the Peace party for the Presidency of the United States. In 1823 and 1824 he was President of the Board of Canal Commissioners, and during the latter year was elected Governor of the State, and in 1826 was re-elected to the same office; he afterwards declined the embassy to England, offered to him by President Adams. He died at Albany, February 11, 1828.

Clinton, George.—Born in Ulster County, New York, July 26, 1739, and died at Washington City, April 20, 1812. He commenced life by sailing in a privateer; served as a Lieutenant in the expedition against Fort Frontenac; he afterwards studied law; was a member of the Colonial Assembly, and also of the Provincial Congress in 1775; he was appointed a Brigadier-General in 1777; was Governor of New York for eighteen years; from 1795 to 1800 he lived in retirement; was again chosen Governor in 1804; and having been elected Vice-President of the United States during the last year, he retained the office until his death, consequently officiating as President of the Senate a period of eight years.

Clinton, George, Jr.—He was born in New York; was a member of the New York Assembly in 1801 and 1802; and a Representative in Congress, from that State, from 1804 to 1809.

Clinton, James G.—He was born in New York, and was a Representative in Congress, from New York, from 1841 to 1845.

Clopton, David.—Born in Georgia in 1820, and elected a Representative, from Alabama, to the Thirty-sixth Congress, serving as a member of the Committee on Public Expenditures. Resigned in February, 1861, to take part in the Rebellion of that year.

Clopton, John.—He was a Representative in Congress, from Virginia, from 1795 to 1799, and again from 1801 to 1816. Died September 11, 1816.

Clowney, W. K.—He was born in South Carolina; graduated at the South Carolina College in 1818; adopted the profession of law; was Commissioner in Equity of South Carolina; and was a Representative in Congress, from that State, from 1833 to 1835, and again from 1837 to 1839.

Clymer, George.—He was born in Philadelphia in 1739, and was a patriot of the Revolution. He engaged in mercantile pursuits, and early espoused the cause of his country. In 1773 he resolutely opposed the sale of tea sent out by the British Government, and not a pound was sold in Philadelphia. In 1775 he was one of the first Continental Treasurers. In 1776 he was a member of Congress, and signed the Declaration of Independence. In 1774 his furniture was destroyed by the enemy. In 1780 he co-operated with Robert Morris in the establishment of a bank for the relief of the country. He was a member of the old Congress in 1780, and a Representative, under the Constitution, from 1789 to 1791. In 1791 he was placed at the head of the Excise Department in Pennsylvania. In 1796 he was sent to Georgia to negotiate a treaty with the Creek and Cherokee Indians. He was afterwards President of the Philadelphia Bank and of the Academy of Fine Arts. He died at Morrisville, Bucks County, January 23, 1813.

Cobb, Amasa.—Born in Crawford County, Illinois, September 27, 1823; received a common school education; emigrated to Wisconsin Territory in 1842; spent five years in the lead mining business, and served in the Mexican war as a private soldier, during which time he occasionally read law, and at the end of the war he began to practice the legal profession. In 1850 he was elected a District Attorney, and served four years; in 1854 was elected to the State Senate, and served two years; in 1855 he was appointed Adjutant-General of the State, and again in 1857; was elected to the State Legislature in 1860; re-elected in 1861, and chosen Speaker; in 1862 he served in the volunteer service as Colonel of the Fifth Wisconsin regiment, and was elected a Representative, from Wisconsin, to the Thirty-eighth Congress, and was a member of the Committee on the Militia, and Chairman of the Joint Committee on Enrolled Bills.

Cobb, David.—He graduated at Princeton College in 1783; was a Representative in Congress, from Massachusetts, from 1793 to 1795; and was also a member of the State Legislature. He died April 17, 1830.

Cobb, George T.—He was born in New Jersey, and elected a Representative, from that State, to the Thirty-seventh Congress, serving on the Committee on Invalid Pensions.

Cobb, Howell.—The uncle of Secretary Cobb, and for whom he was named, was born in Granville, North Carolina, and was a Representative in Congress, from Georgia, from 1807 to 1812. During the last war with England he served with credit as a Captain in the army, and after peace was declared he settled upon a plantation, and devoted his whole attention to agriculture. He died about the year 1820.

Cobb, Howell.—He was born at Cherry Hill, in Jefferson County, Georgia, September 7, 1815. When a child, his father removed to Athens, Georgia, where he has since resided. He graduated at Franklin College in 1834; he studied law, and was admitted to the bar in 1836; in 1837 he received the appointment of Solicitor-General of the Western Circuit, which he held four years; and he was elected a Representative in Congress in 1842, having been re-elected in 1844, 1846, and 1848, and during his latter term he was elected Speaker. On his retirement from Congress, he was chosen Governor of Georgia; in 1855 he was again elected to Congress; and on the accession of Mr. Buchanan to the Presidency, Governor Cobb went into his Cabinet as Secretary of the Treasury. He took a prominent part in the Rebellion of 1861, and was a member of the so-called Confederate Congress, and a Brigadier-General.

Cobb, Thomas W.—He was born in Columbia County, Georgia, in 1784, and attained a high position as a lawyer. He was a Representative in Congress, from Georgia, from 1817 to 1821, and again from 1823 to 1824; and he was a Senator in Congress from 1824 to 1828. He was subsequently chosen a Judge of the Superior Court, and died at Greensborough, February 1, 1830. He was the author of many political Essays.

Cobb, Williamson R. W.—He was born in Ray County, Tennessee, in 1807, and in 1809 his father removed to Madison County, Alabama, with the prosperity of which State his name has been identified for many years. He received a good common school education, and then turned his attention to farming. From this pursuit he was called, in 1845, to a seat in the State Legislature, where he remained two years. In 1847 he was elected a Representative in Congress, from Alabama, in which capacity he served his adopted State, by successive re-elections, down to 1860. During eight years of his Congressional career, he has officiated as Chairman of the Committee on Unfinished Business, and the balance of the time as Chairman of the Committee on Public Lands. The credit is awarded to him of having engineered through Congress the Bounty Land Bill of 1850, and the Graduation Bill of 1854.

Coburn, Stephen.—He was born in Maine, and in January, 1861, was elected a Representative, from that State, to the Thirty-sixth Congress, for the unexpired term of Israel Washburn, Jr., resigned.

Cochran, James.—He was a Major of militia, and represented the State of New York in Congress, from 1797 to 1799. He died at Oswego, New York, November 7, 1848, aged seventy-nine years. He was at one time Post-master of Oswego.

Cochrane, Clark B.—Born in New Boston, New Hampshire, May 31, 1815; graduated at Union College, Schenectady, New York; a lawyer by profession; member of the New York Legislature in 1843 and 1844; and a Representative in the Thirty-fifth Congress, from New York, serving on the Committee on Expenditures in the War Department. He was also re-elected to the Thirty-sixth Congress, serving as a member of the Committee on Private Land Claims. He was also a Delegate to the Baltimore Convention of 1864.

Cochrane, John.—Born at Palatine, Montgomery County, New York; studied at Union College and graduated at Hamilton College, New York; is a lawyer by profession; was Surveyor of the port of New York for four years, and elected to the Thirty-fifth Congress, acting as Chairman of the Committee on Commerce. He was also re-elected to the Thirty-sixth Congress, serving as a member of the Committee on Commerce. Also served as a General of volunteers in the Union army in 1861-2. In 1864 he was nominated for the office of Vice-President of the United States, on the ticket with J. C. Fremont.

Cocke, John.—He was born in Brunswick County, Virginia, in 1772; in early life he emigrated to Tennessee, adopted the profession of law, and became a member of the first Legislature of the State, in 1796; he was Speaker of the House for many years, and also a member of the Senate. From 1819 to 1827 he was a Representative in Congress, from his adopted State. He died in Grundy County, Tennessee, February 16, 1854.

Cocke, William.—He was born in Virginia, participated in the military, civil, legislative, and judicial services of that State; and on removing to Tennessee, became a General of militia; served in the State Legislature in 1813; became one of the Judges of the Circuit Court; and was a Senator in Congress, from Tennessee, from 1796 to 1797, and again from 1799 to 1805; and was appointed in 1814, by President Madison, Indian Agent for the Chickasaw nation.

Cocke, William M.—He was born in Tennessee, and was a Representative in Congress, from that State, from 1845 to 1847, and for a second term, ending in 1849.

Cockerell, Joseph R.—He was born in Virginia, and, having removed to Ohio, was elected a Representative to the Thirty-fifth Congress, and was a member of the Committees on Public Expenditures and Expenses in the War Department.

Cockran, James.—A Representative in Congress, from North Carolina, from 1809 to 1813.

Coffee, John.—He was a member of Congress, from Georgia, from 1833 to 1837, and died in Telfair County, of that State, September 25, 1836.

Coffin, Charles G.—He was a Representative in Congress, from Ohio, from 1838 to 1839.

Coffin, Peleg.—He was born September, 1756, and was a Representative in Congress, from Massachusetts, from 1793 to 1795. He served a number of years in the State Senate, and was State Treasurer from 1797 to 1802. Died March 6, 1805.

Coffroth, A. H.—Born in Somerset, Somerset County, Pennsylvania, May 18, 1828; was self-educated; read law and commenced the practice in 1851; was a delegate to the Charleston Convention in 1860, and was elected a Representative, from Pennsylvania, to the Thirty-eighth Congress, and served on the Committees on Revolutionary Pensions, and on Expenditures in the Interior Department.

Coit, Joshua.—Born in New London, Connecticut, October 7, 1758; graduated at Harvard University in 1776; he studied law and settled in New London in 1779; and he was a Representative in Congress, from 1793 to 1798. He also served a number of years in the Legislature of Connecticut. Died in New London, September 5, 1798, of yellow fever.

Coke, Richard.—He was a lawyer by profession, and possessed talents of a high order, and an energy seldom equalled. He was a Representative in Congress, from Virginia, from 1829 to 1833, and for many years a prominent member of the bar. He died in Abingdon, Virginia, March 30, 1851.

Colcock, William F.—He was born in South Carolina; graduated at the South Carolina College in 1823; adopted the profession of law; was a member of the State Legislature, and Speaker of the House; and was a Representative in Congress, from South Carolina, from 1849 to 1853.

Colden, Cadwallader D.—He was for many years a prominent member of the New York bar; served also in the Legislature of that State; held the post of District Attorney of the United States for many years; was at one time Mayor of New York; and a member of Congress, from 1821 to 1823. He was an early and intimate friend of Robert Fulton, and wrote his biography; he was highly respected for his talents and virtues, and died in Jersey City, New Jersey, February 7, 1834, aged sixty-five years.

Cole, Cornelius.—Born in Lodi, New York, September 17, 1822; bred to the business of a farmer; graduated at the Wesleyan University in Connecticut; adopted the profession of law; emigrated to California in 1849, and mined for gold one year; subsequently prosecuted his profession in San Francisco and Sacramento; was District Attorney at the latter place for two years; and in 1863 he was elected a Representative, from California, to the Thirty-eighth Congress, serving on the Committee on Post-offices and Post-roads. From 1856 to 1860 he was a member of the National Republican Committee; and during the Presidential campaign of 1860 was the editor of a newspaper in California.

Cole, George E.—Was born in Oneida County, New York, December 23, 1826; went to Iowa in 1849; crossed the plains to California in 1850, and went to Oregon the same year; was a member of the Oregon Legislature in 1851, 1852, and 1853; during the years 1859 and 1860 he was Clerk of the United States District Court for Oregon; removed to Washington Territory in 1861; and in 1863 he was elected a Delegate from Washington Territory to the Thirty-eighth Congress.

Cole, Orsamus.—He was born in New York, and was a Representative in Congress, from Wisconsin, from 1849 to 1851.

Coleman, Nicholas D.—He was a Representative in Congress, from Kentucky, from 1829 to 1831, and was in that year appointed Postmaster at Maysville, Kentucky.

Coles, Isaac.—He was a Representative in Congress, from Virginia, from 1789 to 1791, and again from 1793 to 1797.

Coles, Walter.—He was born in Virginia, and was a Representative in Congress, from that State, from 1835 to 1845.

Colfax, Schuyler.—Born in New York City, March 23, 1823; received a good common school education; was bred a printer, and settled in Indiana in 1836. He has been the editor and publisher of the South Bend Register ever since he became of age; was a member, in 1850, of the Indiana Constitutional Convention; in 1848 and 1852 he was a Delegate to the Whig National Convention of those years, and the Secretary of each Convention. He was elected a Representative, from Indiana, to the Thirty-fourth Congress, and was re-elected to each successive Congress, including the Thirty-eighth, serving during two of his terms as Chairman of the Committee on Post-offices and Post-roads. He is also a Regent of the Smithsonian Institution; was elected Speaker of the Thirty-eighth Congress.

Collamer, Jacob.—He was born in Troy, New York, in 1792, but when a child removed with his father to Burlington, Vermont. He graduated at the University of Vermont in 1810; served as a subaltern during the first campaign of the last war with England; studied law, and was admitted to the bar in 1813; practised the profession until 1833, during which time he was for several years a member of the State Legislature; and from 1833 to 1841 he was Judge of the Supreme Court of Vermont. In 1843 he took his seat as a Representative in Congress, from Vermont, serving by re-elections until 1849; in March of that year he was appointed Postmaster-General in the cabinet of President Taylor; resigned in 1850, with the rest of the cabinet, on the death of the President; and was soon afterwards reappointed on the Supreme Bench of his State, which office he held until 1854, when he was elected a Senator in Congress, from Vermont, for six years, from 1855; and in 1861 he was re-elected for the term ending in 1867, serving as Chairman of the Committee on Post-offices and Post-roads, also that on the Library, and as a member of several other important committees. He received the degree of LL.D. from the University of Vermont, and from Dartmouth College, New Hampshire.

Collier, John A.—He was a Representative in Congress, from New York, from 1831 to 1833.

Collin, John F.—Born in Hillsdale, Columbia County, New York, April 30, 1802. He received a common school education, and has devoted himself to agricultural pursuits. He served in the State Legislature in 1834, was a member, for some years, of the County Board of Supervisors, and was a Representative in Congress, from New York, from 1845 to 1847.

Collins, Ela.—Born in Meriden, Connecticut, February 14, 1786; studied law and commenced practice in Oneida County, New York; was for twenty years a District Attorney, displaying ability as an advocate; and during the latter part of his life devoted much attention to farming. He commanded a regiment of militia near Sackett's Harbor, New York, in 1814; represented Lewis County in the Legislature of the State, and in 1821 was a member of the State Constitutional Convention; he was in Congress, from 1823 to 1825; and died at Lowville, Lewis County, November, 23, 1848.

Collins, John.—Governor of Rhode Island, from 1786 to 1789, succeeding William Greene. He was a patriot of the Revolution, and a Representative in Congress in 1789. He died at Newport, in March, 1795, aged seventy-eight.

Collins, William.—He was the son of Ela, and born in Oneida County, New York, and was a Representative in Congress, from that State, from 1847 to 1849. He studied law, and was District Attorney for Lewis County, until he removed to Cleveland, Ohio.

Colquit, Alfred H.—He was a native of Georgia, and a Representative in Congress, from that State, from 1853 to 1855.

Colquitt, W. T.—He was born in Halifax County, Virginia, December 27, 1799; was educated at Princeton College, and admitted to the bar in 1820. He was a Brigadier-General of militia at the age of twenty-one; in 1826 was appointed a District Judge, and held the first court ever held in Columbus; was appointed to the same office in 1829; was a member of the State Senate in 1834 and 1837; a Representative in Congress, from Georgia, from 1839 to 1843, and a Senator in Congress from 1843 to 1849. He was also a member of the Nashville Convention in 1850; and he died at Macon, Georgia, May 7, 1855.

Colston, Edward.—Born in Berkeley County, Virginia, in 1788, and graduated at Princeton College in 1806. He served for a long time as magistrate of the county, and in the capacity of High Sheriff; was frequently a member of the State Legislature; and was a Representative in Congress from 1817 to 1819. He died April 23, 1851.

Comegys, Joseph P.—Son of Cornelius P. Comegys, formerly Governor of the State of Delaware; was born in St. Jones's Neck, at Cherbourg, near Dover, Delaware, December 29, 1813; was educated at Dover Academy. In May, 1831, entered the office of J. M. Clayton as a student of law, and was admitted to the bar in 1835. Elected a member of the House of Representatives of the State in 1842 and 1848. In January, 1851, was appointed by the General Assembly one of a committee of three to revise the statutes of the State. In November, 1856, was chosen by the Governor to fill the vacancy in the United States Senate occasioned by the death of John M. Clayton.

Comins, Linus B.—Born in Charlton, Massachusetts, in 1817; graduated at the "Worcester County Manual Labor High School;" and has devoted himself to mercantile business, and to manufacturing. He was of the Roxbury City Council in 1846, and in 1847 and 1848 President of the Council; in 1854 he was Mayor of Roxbury; and having been, soon after, elected to Congress, continued in that position to the close of the Thirty-fifth Congress, serving on the Committee on Commerce.

Comstock, Oliver C.—He was a member of the New York Assembly in 1810 and 1812, and a Representative in Congress, from that State, from 1813 to 1819.

Condict, John.—He was born in 1755; was a soldier and surgeon during the Revolutionary war; he was a member of the New Jersey Legislature for several years; a Representative in Congress, from that State, from 1799 to 1803; a Senator in Congress, from 1803 to 1817; and again a Representative during the years 1819 and 1820. He died May 4, 1834.

Condict, Lewis.—Born at Morristown, New Jersey, in March, 1773, and was a physician of eminence. From 1805 to 1810 he was a member of the New Jersey Legislature, the two latter years officiating as Speaker; in 1807 was a Commissioner for settling the boundary between New York and New Jersey; and he was a Representative in Congress from 1811 to 1817, and from 1821 to 1833. He was also at one time Sheriff of Morris County, and died at Morristown, New Jersey, May 26, 1862.

Condict, Silas.—Born in New Jersey in 1777; was a Representative in Congress, from New Jersey, from 1831 to 1833. He was a member of the Convention which formed the State Constitution of 1844; for many years President of the Newark Banking Company; and was frequently elected to the Legislature of New Jersey. Died at Newark, New Jersey, November 29, 1861.

Conger, Harmon S.—He was a Representative in Congress, from New York, from 1847 to 1851. His native State was Connecticut.

Conger, James L.—He was born in New Jersey, and, on removing to Michigan, was elected a Representative in Congress, from 1851 to 1853.

Conkling, Alfred.—He was a Representative in Congress, from New York, from 1821 to 1823, and was subsequently appointed a Judge of the United States District Court for New York. In 1852 he was appointed Minister to Mexico.

Conkling, Frederick A.—He was born in Montgomery County, New York, August 22, 1816; was bred a merchant, and has followed that occupation in the city of New York; was a member of the Assembly of New York in 1854, 1859, and 1860; and was elected a Representative, from New York, to the Thirty-seventh Congress, serving as a member of the Committee on Naval Affairs.

Conkling, Roscoe.—Was born in Albany in 1828; received a good education; adopted the profession of law; in 1849 he was appointed District Attorney for Oneida County; in 1858 he was elected Mayor of Utica, to which place he had removed in 1846; and at the close of 1858 he was elected a Representative, from New York, to the Thirty-sixth Congress, serving as a member of the Committee on the District of Columbia. Re-elected to the Thirty-seventh Congress, serving as Chairman of the Committee on a Bankrupt Law, and also as Chairman of that on the District of Columbia.

Conner, Henry W.—Born in Prince George County, Virginia, in August, 1793; educated at the University of South Carolina, where he graduated in 1812; in 1814 he was aide-de-camp to General Joseph Graham in the Creek war; was a Representative in Congress, from North Carolina, from 1821 to 1841, when he declined a re-election; and having, in 1848, served in the General Assembly, he also declined a re-election to that office, and retired to private life.

Conner, Samuel S.—He was born in New Hampshire; graduated at Yale College in 1806; was a Lieutenant-Colonel in the United States Army in 1812 (18th Infantry); was a Representative in Congress, from Massachusetts, from 1815 to 1817. He also held the office of Surveyor-General in Ohio in 1819. He died at Covington, Kentucky, December 17, 1820.

Conness, John.—He was born in Ireland in 1819, but came to this country when ten years of age; was among the first emigrants to California, where he became engaged in mining and mercantile pursuits. In 1854 he was elected to the State Legislature, and was re-elected two or three times. In 1859 he was elected to the State Senate; and in 1863 he was elected a Senator in Congress, from California, for the term ending in 1869, serving on the Committee on Finance.

Conrad, Charles M.—He was born in Winchester, Virginia, and when an infant went with his father, first to Mississippi, and then to Louisiana, where he has since resided. In 1828 he was admitted to the bar in New Orleans; served a number of years in the State Legislature; was a Senator in Congress in 1842 and 1843; was a member of the State Constitutional Convention in 1844; and a Representative in Congress, from Louisiana, from 1849 to August, 1850, when he became Secretary of War under President Fillmore. Served in the Southern Rebellion as a Brigadier-General.

Conrad, Frederick.—He was a Representative in Congress, from Pennsylvania, from 1803 to 1807.

Conrad, John.—He was a Representative in Congress, from Pennsylvania, from 1813 to 1815.

Constable, Albert.—He was born in Maryland, and was a Representative in Congress, from that State, from 1845 to 1847.

Contee, Benjamin.—He was a Representative in Congress, from Maryland, from 1789 to 1791.

Conway, Henry W.—He was born in Greene County, Tennessee, and was a Delegate to Congress, from the Territory of Arkansas, from 1823 to 1829.

Conway, Martin F.—Was born in Charleston, South Carolina, about the year 1830; removed to Baltimore in his fourteenth year; was bred a printer; followed that business for a time, and took part in originating the National Typographical Union. He subsequently studied law and practised for several years; went to Kansas in 1854, and was elected to the Council of the first Territorial Legislature. Under the Topeka Convention he was chosen Chief Justice of the Supreme Court. In 1856 he was President of the Leavenworth Constitutional Convention; and in 1859 he was elected a Representative, from Kansas, to the Thirty-seventh Congress, serving on the Committee on Indian Affairs.

Cook, Daniel P.—He was born in Scott County, Kentucky, and was a Representative in Congress, from Illinois, from 1820 to 1827, and filled with great ability the post of Chairman of the Committee of Ways and Means. By such men as Mr. Calhoun and Judge McLean he was considered a man of remarkable talents. He died at the age of thirty-two years in October, 1827.

Cook, E. Bates.—He was a Representative in Congress, from New York, from 1831 to 1833. At one time he held the office of Comptroller of New York. Died in 1841.

Cook, John B.—He was born in New York, and on taking up his residence in Iowa, was elected a Representative in Congress, from 1853 to 1855.

Cook, Orchard.—He was a Representative in Congress, from Massachusetts, from 1805 to 1811. He was a merchant by occupation, and for some years Sheriff of Lincoln County.

Cook, Thomas B.—He was a Representative in Congress, from New York, from 1811 to 1813, and a member of the Assembly of that State in 1838 and 1839.

Cook, Zadock.—Born in 1769; was frequently in the Legislature of Georgia; and a Representative in Congress, from 1817 to 1819. His memory is said to have been remarkable, as he could, after reading a chapter in the Bible, repeat the same from beginning to end. In 1854 he was still living.

Cooke, Eleutheros. — Born in Granville, Washington County, New York, December 25, 1787. He received a liberal education, and having studied law, practised it with success both in New York and Ohio, until 1830. He was a Representative in Congress, from Ohio, from 1831 to 1833; served for many years in the Legislature of that State, before and after entering Congress; and though ostensibly living in retirement, he has been for many years, and is still, very frequently called upon to address the citizens of Ohio on topics of a varied nature, on account of his popularity as an orator.

Cooke, Joseph P.—He was born in 1730; graduated at Yale College in 1750; was a Representative in Congress, from New York, from 1811 to 1813, and died at Danbury, Connecticut, in 1816.

Cooper, George B.—Born at Long Hill, Morris County, New Jersey, June 6, 1808; received a good common school education; removed to Michigan in 1830; served in the two houses of the State Legislature; served two terms as State Treasurer of Michigan; held the position of Postmaster at Jackson for eleven years, which he resigned when chosen Treasurer; and was elected a Representative, from Michigan, to the Thirty-sixth Congress. His seat, however, was contested by William A. Howard, and before the close of the first session the latter was admitted.

Cooper, James.—He was born in Frederick County, Maryland, May 8, 1810. He commenced his education at the common schools of the county, spent some little time at St. Mary's College, and graduated at Washington College, Pennsylvania. He studied law, and was admitted to the bar in Pennsylvania in 1834; was elected a Representative in Congress, from Pennsylvania, in 1838, and re-elected in 1840; in 1843 he was elected to the State Legislature, and re-elected in 1844, 1846, and 1848, serving in 1847 as Speaker; in 1848 he was appointed Attorney-General of Pennsylvania, and in 1849 was chosen a Senator in Congress for the term of six years. During his service in Congress his health was feeble, so that he could not participate in the debates of the Senate to the extent that he desired, and on his return to Pennsylvania, settled in Philadelphia. He subsequently became a Brigadier-General in the army, and died at Cincinnati, Ohio, March 1, 1863.

Cooper, Mark A.—He was born

in Georgia, and was a Representative in Congress, from that State, from 1839 to 1841, and again from 1842 to 1843.

Cooper, Richard M.—Born in Gloucester County, New Jersey; was a member of the Society of Friends; and was a Representative in Congress, from New Jersey, from 1829 to 1833. He also served in the Legislature, and was President of the State Bank at Camden. Died March 10, 1844, aged seventy-six years.

Cooper, Thomas.—He was a Representative in Congress, from Delaware, from 1813 to 1817.

Cooper, Thomas B.—He was born in Cooperstown, Lehigh County, Pennsylvania, December 29, 1823; was educated at Pennsylvania College at Gettysburg, and also at the University of Pennsylvania, where he graduated in 1843; and having adopted the profession of a physician, he was successful therein. He was elected a Representative in Congress, from Pennsylvania, for the term ending in 1863, but died at Cooperstown, April 4, 1862, during the second session of the Thirty-seventh Congress.

Cooper, William.—Born in New Jersey; and having removed to Otsego County, New York, became the founder of Cooperstown. He was a Representative in Congress, from New York, from 1795 to 1797, and again from 1799 to 1801. He was the father of the eminent author, James Fenimore Cooper.

Cooper, W. R.—He was a Representative in Congress, from New Jersey, from 1839 to 1841.

Corning, Erastus.—Born in Norwich, Connecticut, December 14, 1794. When thirteen years of age he went to Troy, New York, and entered the hardware store of his uncle Benjamin Smith, the bulk of whose property he subsequently inherited. In 1814 he removed to Albany, and continued in the same business, establishing the well-known house, still in existence, of Erastus Corning & Co. His first public position was that of Alderman of the City of Albany; from that he was promoted to Mayor, which office he held for three years. He was also for several years an influential railroad, bank, and canal company President; for several terms a member of the State Legislature; and was elected a Representative to the Thirty-fifth Congress, serving on the Committee on Naval Affairs. In 1860 he was re-elected to the Thirty-seventh Congress, serving on the Committee of Ways and Means; and was also a member of the Peace Congress of 1861. Re-elected in 1862 to the Thirty-eighth Congress.

Corwin, Moses B.—He was born in Bourbon County, Kentucky, January 5, 1790; spent his boyhood on a farm in Ohio; received a good education; studied law, and was admitted to the bar in 1812. In 1838 and 1839 he was elected to the Legislature; and was a Representative in Congress, from Ohio, from 1849 to 1855, serving as a member of the Committee on the Post-office Department.

Corwin, Thomas.—Born in Bourbon County, Kentucky, July 29, 1794. Rising from humble life, he became distinguished as a lawyer, having come to the bar in 1817; was elected to the Ohio Legislature in 1822, and afterwards a Representative to Congress, from the Warren District, in 1831. He continued a member of the House until 1840; was a Presidential Elector in 1840, when he was chosen Governor of Ohio, in October of that year. He was Governor but two years, Wilson Shannon succeeding him in 1842. The Whigs having a majority in the Legislature of Ohio in 1845, elected him United States Senator, which office he held till his appointment in the cabinet, in 1850, as Secretary of the Treasury, under President Fillmore. He was long known in Congress as an advocate of the Whig measures of policy. As a stump speaker and before a jury, his eloquence is singularly effective. In October, 1858, he was elected a Representative in Congress, from Ohio, for the term commencing in 1859; and during that year a volume of his Speeches was published. He was Chairman of the Committee on Foreign Affairs. Re-elected to the Thirty-seventh Congress, but in 1861 was appointed by President Lincoln Minister to Mexico.

Cotteral, J. L. T.—He was a Representative in Congress, from Alabama, from 1846 to 1847.

Cottman, Joseph S.—Born in Somerset County, Maryland, August 16, 1803; received a classical education; admitted to the bar in 1826; served in the Maryland Legislature; was a Presidential Elector in 1849; and a member of Congress, from 1851 to 1853. Died in Somerset County, Maryland, in 1863.

Coulter, Richard.—He attained eminence as a lawyer, and was a Representative in Congress, from Pennsylvania, from 1827 to 1835, and died in Westmoreland County, Pennsylvania, April 21, 1852. At the time of his death, he was Judge of the Supreme Court of Pennsylvania.

Covington, Leonard.—He was born at Aquasco, Prince George County, Maryland, October 30, 1768. In 1793 he obtained, from General Washington, the commission of Lieutenant of dragoons, and joined the army under General Wayne; he distinguished himself at Fort Recovery and the battle of Miami, and was honorably mentioned in the official report of General Wayne. After the war he was promoted to the rank of Captain, by Washington, in 1794, and retired to the pursuits of agriculture. He was for many years a member of the Legislature of Maryland, and was elected a Representative in Congress, from that State, from 1805 to 1807. He was appointed, by President Jefferson, in 1809, Lieutenant-Colonel of a regiment of cavalry, and in 1810 was in command at Fort Adams, on the Mississippi, and took possession of Baton Rouge, and a portion of West Florida. In 1813 he was ordered to the northern frontier, and appointed, by President Madison, Brigadier-General. At the battle of Williamsburg, he received a mortal wound while animating his men, and leading them to the charge, and died at French Mills, November 13, 1813, two days after his fall. His remains were removed to Sackett's Harbor, August 13, 1820, and the place of his burial is now known as Mount Covington. He had the reputation of being one of the best officers in the service.

Covode, John.—Born in Westmoreland County, Pennsylvania, March 17, 1808; a farmer and manufacturer by occupation; and extensively engaged in the coal business. He was elected a member of the Thirty-fourth and re-elected to the Thirty-fifth Congress, serving on the Committee on Public Expenditures. He was also re-elected to the Thirty-sixth Congress, and was made Chairman of a Special Committee appointed to investigate certain charges made against President Buchanan and his administration. Re-elected to the Thirty-seventh Congress, serving as Chairman of the Committee on Public Expenditures.

Cowan, Edgar.—He was born in Greensburg, Pennsylvania, and adopted the profession of law; and he was elected a Senator in Congress, from Pennsylvania, for the term ending in 1869, serving on the Committee on Foreign Relations, and as Chairman of the Committee on Patents and the Patent-office.

Cowen, Benjamin S.—He was a Representative in Congress, from Ohio, from 1841 to 1843.

Cowles, Henry B.—Born at Hartford, Connecticut, March 18, 1798; when eleven years old he removed to Dutchess County, New York, with his father; and graduated at Union College in 1816. He studied law, and was admitted to the bar in 1819; in 1826, 1827, and 1828, he served as a member of the New York Legislature, from Putnam County, and during his first term was Chairman of the Select Committee raised to investigate the "Astor Claim;" and he was a Representative in Congress, from New York, from 1829 to 1831. In 1834 he took up his residence in the city of New York, where he continues in the practice of his profession.

Cox, Anleder M.—He was born in Virginia, and removing to Kentucky, was elected a Representative, from that State, to the Thirty-third and Thirty-fourth Congresses.

Cox, James.—He was a native of Monmouth County, New Jersey, having been born in 1753; several years a member of the State Legislature, and Speaker of the Assembly; commanded a company of militia in the Revolution, having been engaged in the battles of Germantown and Monmouth; was subsequently a Brigadier-General of militia; and was a Representative in Congress, from New Jersey, during the years 1809 and 1810. Died September 12, 1810.

Cox, Samuel S.—He was born in Zanesville, Ohio; graduated at Brown University; adopted the profession of law, and was also an editor in Ohio. He was appointed Secretary of Legation to Peru in 1855; and elected a Representative, from Ohio, to the Thirty-fifth and Thirty-sixth Congresses, serving as Chairman of the Committee on Revolutionary Claims. As an author, he published a book of foreign travel, called "The Buckeye Abroad," and on literary topics is an occasional lecturer. He was elected to the Thirty-seventh Congress, serving on the Committee on Foreign Affairs, and was re-elected to the Thirty-eighth Congress, serving on the same Committee. He is also a Regent of the Smithsonian Institution; and was a Delegate to the Chicago Convention in 1864.

Coxe, William.—He was a Representative in Congress, from New Jersey, from 1813 to 1815; served in the State Legislature, and was chosen Speaker of the Assembly; and died at Burlington.

Crabb, George W.—He was born in Virginia, and was a Representative in Congress, from Alabama, from 1839 to 1841.

Crabb, Jeremiah.—He was a Representative in Congress, from Maryland, from 1795 to 1796.

Cradlebaugh, John.—He was born in Ohio, and elected a Delegate, from the Territory of Nevada, to the Thirty-seventh Congress.

Crafts, Samuel C.—He was born in Windham County, Connecticut; and graduated at Harvard University in 1790. His father effected the settlement of Craftsbury, Vermont, and upon the organization of the town, in 1792, Mr. Samuel C. Crafts was chosen Town Clerk, and held the office for thirty-seven successive years. He was the youngest delegate to the Convention for revising the State Constitution in 1793. In 1796, 1800, 1801, 1803, and 1805, he was elected a member of the House of Representatives of the State. From 1796 to 1815 he was Register of Probate for Orleans District. In 1798 and 1799 he was Clerk of the House of Representatives. From 1809 to 1812, and from 1825 to 1827, he was a member of the Executive Council. In 1800 he was appointed a Judge of Orleans County Court, and remained such till 1816, during the last six years as Chief Judge. From 1825 to 1828 he was again Chief Judge, and from 1836 to 1838 Clerk of the Court. In 1816 he was elected Representative to Congress, and served for that and the three succeeding terms; *i. e.*, from 1817 to 1825, inclusive. In 1828 he was elected Governor of Vermont, and was re-elected in 1829 and 1830. In 1829 he was President of the Constitutional Convention. In 1842 he was appointed by Governor Paine, and afterwards elected by the Legislature, a Senator in Congress, for the unexpired term of one year. He thus filled every office in the gift of Vermont. He died in Craftsbury, Vermont, November 19, 1853, aged eighty-four years.

Cragin, Aaron H.—Born in Weston, Vermont, February 3, 1821. He is a lawyer by profession; was a member of the New Hampshire Legislature, from 1852 to 1855, and was elected a Representative, from that State, to the Thirty-fifth Congress, serving on the Committee on Revolutionary Claims. In 1864 he was elected a Senator in Congress, from New Hampshire, for the term commencing in 1865.

Craig, Hector.—He was a Representative in Congress, from New York, from 1823 to 1825, and again from 1829 to 1830.

Craig, James.—Born in Pennsylvania; is a lawyer by profession; and was a member of the Missouri Legislature in 1846 and 1847; was Captain of a volunteer company in the Mexican war; Circuit Attorney for the Twelfth Judicial Circuit in Missouri, from 1852 to 1856; and was a Representative in the Thirty-fifth Congress, serving on the Committee on Post-offices and Post-roads. He was also re-elected to the Thirty-sixth Congress, serving on the Committee on Post-offices and Post-roads.

Craig, Robert.—He was born in Virginia, and was a Representative in

Congress, from that State, from 1829 to 1833, and again from 1835 to 1841.

Craige, Burton.—Born in Rowan County, North Carolina, March 13, 1811; graduated at Chapel Hill in 1829; is a lawyer by profession; was a member of the State Legislature in 1832 and 1834; and was elected to the Thirty-third, Thirty-fourth, and Thirty-fifth Congresses, serving as a member of the Judiciary Committee; re-elected to the Thirty-sixth Congress, serving on the Committee on Revolutionary Pensions. He took part in the Rebellion of 1861 as a member of the Confederate Congress.

Craik, William.—He was a Representative in Congress, from Maryland, from 1796 to 1801.

Cramer, John.—He was a Representative in Congress, from New York, from 1833 to 1837; having been elected to the State Constitutional Convention in 1821, and having served three years in the Assembly, and three years in the Senate of the State of New York.

Crane, Joseph H.—Born in Elizabethtown, New Jersey; was a Representative in Congress, from Ohio, from 1829 to 1837; and died at Dayton, Ohio, November 12, 1851, aged seventy years.

Cranston, Henry Y.—Born in Newport, Rhode Island, October 9, 1789; received a limited education; worked at a trade for five years from the age of twelve, then commenced the business of commission merchant; studied law, and was admitted to the bar in three years. In 1818 he was elected Clerk of the Court of Common Pleas, and held the office until 1833; he was for twenty-five years annually elected Moderator for the town of Newport; was a member of the several conventions for framing and remodelling the State Constitution; and was Vice-President of the Convention in 1842. From 1827 to 1843 he was a member of the lower branch of the Legislature; and was a Representative in Congress, from 1843 to 1847, when he was returned to the Legislature, and was several times Speaker of that body until 1854, after which time he lived in retirement. Died at Newport, February 12, 1864.

Cranston, Robert B.—He was born in Rhode Island, and was a Representative in Congress, from that State, from 1837 to 1843, and again from 1847 to 1849.

Crary, Isaac E.—Was a Delegate to Congress, from the Territory of Michigan, in 1835 and 1836, and a Representative from that State from the time of its admission into the Union in 1836, to 1841. He died in Michigan, May 8, 1854.

Cravens, James A.—Born in Rockingham County, Virginia, November 4, 1818; removed with his father to Indiana in 1820; spent his boyhood in Washington County, where he received a common school education, and has devoted much of his life to agricultural pursuits, and especially to the raising of the best breeds of cattle. He served as a Major in the Mexican war under General Taylor, and was present at the battle of Buena Vista. In 1848 and 1849 he was elected to the Legislature of Indiana; in 1850 elected to the State Senate, serving three years; in 1854 he was commissioned a Brigadier-General of militia; frequently presided over the Board of School Trustees for his township; was Vice-President and President of the Washington and Orange Counties Agricultural Societies; in 1859 he was appointed by the Legislature of Indiana to the important position of agent for the State, which he resigned, and in 1860 he was elected a Representative, from Indiana, to the Thirty-seventh Congress, serving on the Committee on Territories. He was re-elected to the Thirty-eighth Congress, and was a member of the Committee on Territories. His father, James H. Cravens, was also in Congress.

Cravens, James H.—He was born in Rockingham County, Virginia, in 1798, and was a Representative in Congress, from Indiana, from 1841 to 1843.

Crawford, George W.—Born in Columbia County, Georgia, December 22, 1798. He graduated at Princeton in 1820; studied law, and commenced the practice at Augusta, in 1822. In 1827 he was elected Attorney-General, and continued in that office until 1831; he was in the State Legislature from 1837 to 1842; and in 1843 was elected to Congress to fill a vacancy. He was elected Governor of the State in 1843, and re-elected in 1845. He was a member of President Taylor's cabinet, as Secretary of War, and subsequently visited Europe, since which time he has lived in retirement.

Crawford, Joel.—Born in Columbia County, Georgia, June 15, 1783. He was educated by private tutors; became a student of law, and was admitted to practice in 1808. In 1813 he joined the army of General Floyd, and served through the whole campaign as aide-de-camp to the General. After the war he resumed the practice of his profession; served three years in the State Legislature, and was a Representative in Congress, from Georgia, from 1817 to 1821.

Crawford, Martin J.—He was born in Jasper County, Georgia, March 17, 1820; was educated at the Mercer University; is a lawyer by profession, and was a member of the Georgia Legislature, from 1845 to 1847. In 1853 he was appointed Judge of the Superior Court for the Chattahoochee Circuit, and was elected a member of the Thirty-fourth and Thirty-fifth Congresses, serving in the last on the Committees of Ways and Means, and Roads and Canals. He was also elected to the Thirty-sixth Congress, still serving on the Committee of Ways and Means. Resigned in 1861 and joined the Great Rebellion of that year as a member of the Rebel Congress, and a Commissioner to Washington.

Crawford, Thomas H.—Born at Chambersburg, Pennsylvania, November 14, 1786. He graduated at Princeton College in 1804; studied law for three years and was admitted to the bar in 1807; and was a Representative in Congress, from Pennsylvania, from 1829 to 1833. During the last year named, he was elected to the State Legislature; in 1836 he was appointed a Commissioner to investigate certain alleged frauds in the purchase of the reservation of land of the Creek Indians; in 1838 he was appointed, by President Van Buren, Commissioner of Indian Affairs, and took up his residence in Washington, holding that office for seven years; and in 1845 he was appointed, by President Polk, Judge of the Criminal Court of the District of Columbia, which arduous position he occupied until his death, which took place in Washington, January 27, 1863.

Crawford, William.—He was a Representative in Congress, from Pennsylvania, from 1809 to 1817.

Crawford, William H.—Born in Amherst County, Virginia, February 24, 1772, and with his father settled in Georgia in 1783. He received an academical education, and subsequently had the management of Richmond Academy. He studied law and took a high position as a lawyer. He served four years in the State Legislature, and was a Senator in Congress from 1807 to 1813, and during a part of the Twelfth Congress, officiated as President *pro tem.* of the Senate. President Madison invited him into his cabinet as Secretary of War, but he declined the honor, accepting, instead, the post of Minister to France, in 1813; on his return, however, at the end of two years, he went into the War Department. In 1817 he was appointed, by President Monroe, Secretary of the Treasury, where he served with marked ability until 1825, during which year he received a flattering vote for President of the United States. In 1827 he was appointed Judge of the Northern Circuit of Georgia, which office he held until his death, which occurred in Albert County, Georgia, September 15, 1834.

Creighton, William.—Born in Berkeley County, Virginia, October 29, 1778; graduated at Dickinson College, when quite young; studied law and was admitted to the bar at the age of twenty; and in 1798 he settled in Chillicothe, Ohio, devoting himself to his profession, and holding many positions of public trust. He was the first Secretary of State for Ohio; and was a Representative in Congress, from that State, from 1813 to 1817, and again from 1827 to 1833. Died at Chillicothe, October 8, 1851, having for many years previously declined all public office.

Creswell, John A. J.—Was born in Port Deposit, Cecil County, Maryland, November 18, 1828; graduated at Dickinson College, Pennsylvania, in 1848; studied law and came to the bar of Maryland, in 1850. He was a member of the Maryland House of Delegates in 1861 and 1862. From August, 1862, to April, 1863, he was an Assistant Adjutant-General for Maryland, and was elected a Representative, from Maryland, to the Thirty-eighth Congress, serving on the Committees on Commerce, and Invalid Pensions. He was also a Delegate to the Baltimore Convention of 1864.

Crisfield, John W.—Was born in Kent County, Maryland, November 6, 1808; received his education at Washington College, Chestertown; studied law and was admitted to the bar in 1830; settled in the practice of his profession, in Somerset County; was elected to the Maryland Legislature, in 1836; he was a Representative in Congress, from Maryland, from 1847 to 1849; in 1850 he was a Delegate to the State Constitutional Convention; in 1861 he was a Delegate to the Peace Congress; and was elected a Representative from Maryland, to the Thirty-seventh Congress, serving on the Committees on Public Lands, and on Public Expenditures.

Crittenden, John J.—He was born in Woodford County, Kentucky, in September, 1786. When quite young he entered the army, and during the war of 1812 served as Major under General Hopkins, in his expedition, and was aide-de-camp to Governor Shelby, at the battle of the Thames. After adopting the profession of law, he served a number of years in the State Legislature, and was chosen Speaker of the House; he entered Congress as a member of the Senate, from Kentucky, in 1817, serving then but two years. From 1819 to 1835 he continued in the practice of his profession, residing principally at Frankfort, and again occasionally representing his county in the State Legislature. In 1835 he was again elected to the United States Senate, and continued to serve in that body until March, 1841, when he was appointed Attorney-General by President Harrison. In September, 1841, he resigned with the other members of the cabinent, except Mr. Webster, and retired to private life, from which, however, he was soon called by the Legislature, to resume his seat in the United States Senate, in 1842. He was also elected a Senator for another term of six years, from March, 1843, but, in 1848, having received the Whig nomination for Governor of Kentucky, he retired from the Senate, and was elected to that office, which he held until his appointment as Attorney-General by President Fillmore. He was again elected to the United States Senate in 1855, for the term ending in 1861, and was, when he retired, the oldest member of that body. He was elected in 1860 a Representative, from Kentucky, to the Thirty-seventh Congress. Died at Louisville, Kentucky, July 25, 1863.

Crocheron, Henry.—He was a Representative in Congress, from New York, from 1815 to 1817.

Crocheron, Jacob.—He was a Representative in Congress, from New York, from 1829 to 1831.

Crocker, Samuel L.—Was born in Taunton, Massachusetts, March 31, 1804; graduated at Brown University in 1822; held various municipal offices; and in 1849 was elected a member of the Executive Council of Massachusetts; has been devoted to the manufacturing business; and was a Representative from Massachusetts to the Thirty-third Congress.

Crockett, David.—Born in Greene County, Tennessee, August 17, 1786, of Irish descent, his father having fought in the Revolutionary war. He commenced the active duties of life, when twelve years old, by turning drover, and, instead of going to school, he chose the fortunes of an adventurer. He served under General Jackson in some of the Indian wars, and became his fast friend. He had a natural bias for politics, and his smartness and eccentricities made him very popular on the frontiers, and caused him to be elected to the Legislature of Tennessee. He was fond of the woods, and had no equal as a bear-hunter. He was elected to Congress in 1827, and served until 1831, and then again in 1833, serving until 1835. While in Washington he was always at his post of duty, never forgetting the welfare of his constituents, and he was one of the most popular men in Congress. The most striking features of his disposition and mind were, undoubtedly, of a whimsical character;

but behind these there was much to command respect and admiration. He told stories, or related his wild adventures, with wonderful effect. He was killed at the Alamo, Texas, March 1, 1836.

Crockett, John W.—He was the son of the celebrated David Crockett, a Representative in Congress, from Tennessee, from 1838 to 1843, and died at Memphis, November 24, 1852.

Cross, Edward.—He was born in Tennessee, and, on taking up his residence in Arkansas, was elected a Representative in Congress, from 1839 to 1845.

Crouch, Edward.—He was a Representative in Congress, from Pennsylvania, from 1813 to 1815.

Crowell, John.—Born in Halifax County, Alabama; was chosen Delegate to Congress, when the Territory of Alabama was established in 1817, and served till 1819, when the State Constitution was formed, and he was elected first Representative to Congress, serving till 1821, and was a member of the Committee on Private Land Claims. Soon afterwards he was appointed Agent for the Creek Indians, then inhabiting large portions of Alabama and Georgia, and exercised extensive influence over them, until their removal west of the Mississippi, in 1836. He died near Fort Mitchell, Alabama, June 25, 1846.

Crowell, John.—He was born in Connecticut, and was a Representative in Congress, from Ohio, from 1847 to 1851, and was a member of the Committee on Indian Affairs.

Crowninshield, Benjamin W.—Born in Essex County, Massachusetts, in 1774. He filled with general acceptance the office of Secretary of the Navy, to which he was appointed in December, 1814, by President Madison, and served until his resignation, in November, 1818. In 1823, he was elected a Representative in Congress, from the Salem District of Massachusetts, and continued in that position until 1831. He died in Boston, February 8, 1851.

Crowninshield, Jacob.—He was a member of the Massachusetts Legislature in 1801, and was elected a Representative in Congress, from Massachusetts, from 1803 to 1805, and appointed Secretary of the Navy by President Jefferson, March 3, 1805. Died April 14, 1808.

Crozier, John.—He was born in Tennessee, and was a Representative in Congress, from that State, from 1845 to 1847, and for a second term, ending in 1849.

Crudup, Josiah.—He was born in Wake County, North Carolina; a Representative in Congress, from North Carolina, from 1821 to 1823, and was a member of the Committee on Private Claims.

Cruger, Daniel.—He was a member of the New York Assembly a number of years, and a Representative in Congress, from that State, from 1817 to 1819.

Crump, John.—He was born in Powhatan County, Virginia, and was a Representative in Congress, from Virginia, from 1826 to 1827.

Culbreth, Thomas. — Born in Kent County, Delaware, and was a Representative in Congress, from Maryland, from 1817 to 1821.

Cullen, Elisha D.—He was born in Delaware, and elected a Representative from that State to the Thirty-fourth Congress.

Cullom, Alvan.—He was a native of Kentucky; adopted the law as his profession; served frequently in the Legislature of Tennessee, and was a Representative in Congress, from Tennessee, from 1845 to 1847. He was a Delegate to the Peace Congress of 1861.

Cullom, William.—He was a Representative in Congress, from Tennessee, from 1851 to 1855, and Clerk of the House of Representatives during the Thirty-fourth Congress.

Culpepper, John.—He was born in Anson County, North Carolina, and represented that State in Congress, from 1807 to 1808, when his seat was vacated by resolution of the House; but he was re-elected, and served from

1813 to 1817, from 1819 to 1821, and from 1823 to 1825. He was a Baptist preacher, and elected to the General Assembly, but his seat was vacated on constitutional grounds.

Culver, Erastus D.—He was born in New York; graduated at the University of Vermont in 1826; served in the Assembly of New York in 1838 and 1841, and was a Representative in Congress, from New York, from 1845 to 1847.

Cumback, William.—He was born in Franklin County, Indiana, March 24, 1829; was educated at the Miami University, Ohio; taught school for one or two years; attended the Law School at Cincinnati, and adopted the legal profession; and he was elected a Representative from Indiana, in the Thirty-fourth Congress.

Cummings, Thomas W.—He was born in Maryland, and was a Representative in Congress, from New York, from 1853 to 1855.

Cummins, John D.—He was born in Pennsylvania, and was a Representative, from Ohio, during the Thirtieth Congress. He died of cholera at Milwaukee, Wisconsin, September 11, 1848.

Cunningham, Francis A.—He was born in South Carolina, and was a Representative in Congress, from Ohio, from 1845 to 1847.

Curry, J. L. M.—Born in Lincoln County, Georgia, June 5, 1825, and removed with his father, in 1838, to Talladega County, Alabama, where he has since resided; he graduated at the University of Georgia in 1843, and at the Dane Law School, Harvard University, in 1845, and practised law with success in Alabama. In 1846 he joined the Texas Rangers for the Mexican war, but soon returned on account of ill health. He was a member of the lower branch of the Legislature of Alabama in 1847, 1853, and 1855; and in 1857 was elected a Representative in Congress, serving on the Committees on Revolutionary Claims, and Expenditures in the State Department. Re-elected to the Thirty-sixth Congress, serving on the Committee on Naval Affairs. Resigned in 1861, and took part in the Rebellion of that year as a member of the Rebel Congress.

Curtis, Carlton B.—He was born in New York, and was a Representative in Congress, from Pennsylvania, from 1851 to 1855.

Curtis, Edward.—Born in Vermont, graduated at Union College, New York, and practised law in New York City. He took a prominent part in the councils of that city, and was a Representative in Congress, from New York, from 1837 to 1841. He was appointed Collector of New York by President Harrison, and removed by President Polk. He was an intimate friend of Daniel Webster.

Curtis, Samuel R.—Born in Ohio (while his parents were emigrating to the West from Connecticut), February 3, 1807. He graduated at the West Point Academy in 1831, and was appointed a Lieutenant in the United States infantry, but resigned in 1832. He studied and pursued the profession of law in Ohio; was subsequently an engineer in Ohio and Iowa; from 1837 to 1840, chief engineer of the Muskingum Works; during the Mexican war he served as an Adjutant-General in mustering the State troops; he went to Mexico as a Colonel under General Taylor, and acted for a time as Governor of Matamoras, Camargo, Monterey, and Saltillo, performing much important service; on his return from Mexico, he practised law for a time, but was called to Iowa and Missouri to perform important labors as an engineer, in improvements of harbors and the building of railroads; and having finally settled at Keokuk, in Iowa, he was elected from that State a member of the House in the Thirty-fifth Congress. He was also re-elected to the Thirty-sixth Congress, serving on the Committee on Military Affairs. He was also a Delegate to the Peace Congress in 1861. Re-elected to the Thirty-seventh Congress, but resigned to serve as a Brigadier-General in the Union army in 1861.

Cushing, Caleb.—Was born in Salisbury, Essex County, Massachusetts, January 17, 1800. He graduated at Harvard College in 1817, and was subsequently a tutor there of mathematics and natural philosophy; studied law at Cambridge, and settled in Newburyport to practice, having come to the bar in 1822. In 1825 and 1826 he served in the State Legislature, and in 1829 visited Europe for pleasure, publishing, on his return, "Reminiscences of Spain," and "Review of the Revolution in France." He also wrote for the North American Review. In 1833 and 1834, he was again elected to the Legislature; and was a Representative in Congress, from 1835 to 1843. He was appointed by President Tyler Commissioner to China, and as such negotiated an important treaty. In 1846, he was again elected to the Legislature. In 1847 he was chosen Colonel of the Massachusetts Regiment of Volunteers for the Mexican war, and was afterwards appointed Brigadier-General by President Polk. In 1850, he was for the fifth time elected to the Legislature, and in 1851 was made a Justice of the Supreme Court of the State. When President Pierce came into power, he invited General Cushing into his Cabinet, as Attorney-General; and on his return home, he was again re-elected to the Legislature of his native State. In office, or out of it, he has the reputation of being a hard student, and his ability as a lawyer is unquestioned. In 1860, he was elected President of the Charleston Convention to nominate a President.

Cushman, John Paine.—He was born in Pomfret, Connecticut, in 1784, and graduated at Yale College in 1807. He studied law and removed to Troy, New York, where he practised his profession. He served in Congress, from 1817 to 1819; and in 1838, was appointed Judge of the Circuit Court, having previously been Recorder of the City of Troy, and one of the Regents of the State University. Died in Troy, New York, September 16, 1848. He was a man of eminence in his profession, and discharged with ability the various offices with which he was intrusted.

Cushman, Joshua.—He was born in Plymouth, Massachusetts; graduated at Cambridge in 1787; studied divinity; was a Representative in Congress, from Massachusetts, from 1819 to 1821; and represented Maine, in Congress, from 1821 to 1825, after its separation from Massachusetts. He was also a State Senator in 1809, 1810, 1828, and 1829, and a member of the Assembly in 1811 and 1834, when he died.

Cushman, Samuel.—Born in 1783; was Judge of the Police Court of Portsmouth, New Hampshire, and held several offices of trust in the State; such as Councillor, from 1833 to 1835; County Treasurer, from 1823 to 1828; and Navy Agent at Portsmouth, from 1845 to 1849. He was a Representative in Congress, from 1835 to 1839, and died in Portsmouth, May 20, 1851.

Cuthbert, Alfred.—Born in Savannah, Georgia; he graduated at Princeton College in 1803; and was a Representative in Congress, from Georgia, from 1814 to 1817; again, from 1821 to 1827, and a Senator of the United States, from 1837 to 1843. Died in 1856.

Cuthbert, John A.—He was born in Savannah, Georgia; graduated at Princeton College in 1805; and was a Representative in Congress, from his native State, from 1819 to 1821, and was appointed, by the President, in 1822, a Commissioner to treat with the Creek and Cherokee Indians.

Cutler, Manasseh.—He was born in Killingly, Connecticut, in 1742, and graduated at Yale College in 1765; studied law, and was admitted to the bar in 1767; removed to Dedham, Massachusetts, in 1769; studied for the ministry, and was ordained in 1771; and was settled as a pastor of a church in Hamilton, Massachusetts, September 11, 1771. He distinguished himself by his attention to several branches of natural history, particularly by making the first essay toward a scientific description of the plants of New England, an account of several hundred of which, communicated by him, was published by the American Academy, of which he was a member. He was one of the first scientific explorers of the White Mountains. In 1787 he organized an expedition for the Northwest Territory, and in 1788, with General Rufus Putnam, commenced a settlement at Marietta, on the Muskingum, Ohio. In 1790 he returned, with his family, to New England, served a number of years in the Legislature, and was pastor of the church at Hamilton, Massachusetts, until his death. In 1800 he was elected to a seat in Congress, and retained it till 1804, when he declined any further political employment, from its interference with his professional duties. He died July 28, 1823.

Cutler, William P.—Born near Marietta, Ohio, July 12, 1813; was elected to the Ohio Legislature in 1844, 1845, and 1846, officiating as Speaker of the House during the last term; he was a member of the Constitutional Convention of 1850; from that period until elected to Congress, he was President of the Marietta and Cincinnati Railroad Company; and he was elected a Representative, from Ohio, to the Thirty-seventh Congress, serving on the Committees on the Militia, and on Invalid Pensions.

Cutting, Francis B.—He was born in New York; was liberally educated, and adopted the profession of law; in 1836 and 1837 he was a member of the Legislature of New York, from the city of New York; and was a Representative in Congress, from his native State, from 1853 to 1855.

Cutts, Charles.—Born in Massachusetts, in 1769; entered Harvard College in 1786; graduated in 1790; studied law with Judge Pickering; was elected a member of the Legislature in 1804, and then Speaker of the House; was sent to the United States Senate in 1810, from New Hampshire, and served till 1813; and chosen Secretary of the Senate, from 1814 to 1825. By appointment, he entered the Senate, for a second term, in 1813, but resigned in June of that year. He died in Virginia, in 1846.

Cutts, Richard.—Born June 22, 1771, at Cutts Island, Saco, in the province or district of Maine, then constituting a part of the Commonwealth of Massachusetts, and received his early education at Harvard University, at which institution he graduated in 1790, and in the twentieth year of his age. He studied law, was extensively engaged in commerce, and took an active part in politics. He visited Europe, and on his return, after serving two successive years as a member of the General Court of Massachusetts, he was, at the age of twenty-nine, in 1800, elected by the people of his district a member of the House of Representatives of the United States. He took his seat in the House, December 7, 1801, and through six successive Congresses, constantly sustained by the continued confidence of his constituents, he gave a firm support to President Jefferson's administration, and to that of his successor, President Madison, until the close of his first term, March 3, 1813, having patriotically sustained, by his votes, non-importation, non-intercourse, the embargo, and finally war, as measures called for by the honor and interest of the nation, although ruinous to his private fortune. On the 3d of June, of that year, he was appointed Superintendent-General of Military Supplies, an office created by the act of March 3, 1813, the functions of which were required only during the continuance of the war. The office was accordingly abolished by the act of March 3, 1817, to provide for the prompt settlement of public accounts. By the same act, the office of Second Comptroller of the Treasury was created, to which Mr. Cutts was immediately appointed by President James Monroe, and which he held until 1829; after which he resided in the city of Washington, in the retirement of private life, until his death, April 7, 1845.

Daggett, David.—Born in Attleborough, Massachusetts, December 31, 1764; graduated at Yale College in 1783, and was professor of law in that institution. He was State's Attorney and Mayor of New Haven, and frequently a member of the Legislature, and member of the Council. From 1813 to 1819 he was a Senator in Congress, from Connecticut; from 1826 to 1832 he was a Judge of the Supreme Court of the State, and was Chief Judge from 1832 to 1834, when he attained the age of seventy years. He died April 12, 1851.

Daily, Samuel G.—He was elected a Delegate, from the Territory of Nebraska, to the Thirty-seventh Congress, and re-elected to the Thirty-eighth Congress.

Dallas, George Mifflin.—He was born, July 10, 1792, in the city of Philadelphia, where he received his early education. He graduated at Princeton College in 1810; commenced the study of law in his father's office in Philadelphia; and was admitted to the bar in 1813. In the same year he accompanied Mr. Gallatin to Russia as his private secretary, when that gentleman was appointed a member of the commission to negotiate a peace under the mediation of Alexander. During his absence, he visited Russia, France, England, Holland, and the Netherlands. He returned to the United States in 1814, and after assisting his father for a time in his duties as Secretary of the Treasury, he commenced the practice of his profession at Philadelphia. In 1817 he was appointed the deputy of the Attorney-General of Philadelphia, and soon won a high reputation as a criminal lawyer. He took an active part in politics, and in 1825 he was elected Mayor of Philadelphia, and on the accession of General Jackson, in 1829, he was appointed to the office of District Attorney, the same office which had been held by his father. This post he held until 1831, when a vacancy having occurred in the representation from Pennsylvania in the United States Senate, Mr. Dallas was chosen to fill it. He took an active part in the debates of the stormy session of 1832–33. On the expiration of his term of office in 1833, he declined a re-election, and resumed the practice of his profession. In 1837 he was appointed by President Van Buren, Ambassador to Russia, and remained in that country until October, 1839, when he returned home, and once more devoted himself to the practice of law. In 1844 he was elected Vice-President of the United States, and entered upon the duties of his office in March of the following year. His term of office expired in March, 1849, when he was succeeded by Mr. Fillmore. He was appointed by President Pierce, in 1856, to succeed Mr. Buchanan as Minister at the Court of St. James, in which position he was retained by Mr. Buchanan, when he became President.

Dalton, Tristam.—Was born in that portion of Newbury, Massachusetts, now Newburyport, in 1783, and at the early age of seventeen graduated at Harvard University. He studied law as an accomplishment, the fortune which he inherited from his father not requiring him to practise it as a profession, and he took a deep interest in the cultivation of a large landed estate, in what is now the town of West Newbury. Washington, John Adams, Louis Philippe, Talleyrand, and other distinguished guests partook of his hospitalities. As eminent for piety as he was for mental endowments, the Episcopal Church, of which he was a warden, shared in his generous liberality; and he was also noted for the affectionate interest which he took in the welfare of his servants, both black and white. He was a Representative, Speaker of the House of Representatives, and a Senator in the Legislature of Massachusetts, and a Senator of the United States in the First Congress after the adoption of the Federal Constitution. When Washington City was founded, Mr. Dalton invested his entire fortune in lands there, and lost it by the mismanagement of a business agent. At the same time a vessel, which was freighted with his furniture and valuable library, was lost on her voyage from Newburyport to Washington, and he thus found himself, after having lived sixty years in affluence, penniless. Several offices of profit and honor were immediately tendered him by the Government, and he accepted the Surveyorship of Boston. He died in Boston in June, 1817, and his remains were taken to Newburyport, where they were interred in the burial-ground of St. Paul's Church.

Damrell, William S.—Born in Portsmouth, New Hampshire, November 20, 1809; never had the privilege of even a common school education; was by trade a printer; and was elected a Representative, from Massachusetts, to the Thirty-fourth Congress, where he served on the Committee on Engraving, and to the Thirty-fifth Congress, serving on the Committee on Roads and Canals. Died at Boston, May 17, 1860.

Dana, Amasa.—He was a member of the New York Assembly in 1828 and 1829, and a Representative in Congress, from that State, from 1839 to 1841, and again from 1843 to 1845.

Dana, Judah.—Born in Massachusetts in 1772; graduated at Dartmouth College in 1795; commenced the practice of law in Fryeburg; was Attorney for Oxford County for six years; Judge of Probate for twenty years; Judge of the Common Pleas for nine years; one of the Committee which drafted the Constitution of Maine; a member of the Executive Council of the State in 1834; and by appointment of the Governor, was a Senator in Congress during the years 1836 and 1837. He died at Fryeburg, Maine, December 27, 1845.

Dana, Samuel.—He was a respectable lawyer and a judge, and during the years 1814 and 1815 a Representative in Congress, from Massachusetts. He died at Charlestown in November, 1835, in the sixtieth year of his age.

Dana, Samuel W.—He was born in Connecticut in 1747, and died July 21, 1830. He graduated at Yale College in 1775, and was a Senator in Congress, from Connecticut, from 1810 to 1821.

Dane, Joseph.—He was born in Beverly, Essex County, Massachusetts, October 25, 1778, and graduated at Harvard University in 1799. He adopted the profession of law, and removing to Kennebunk, Maine, was a member of the State Constitutional Convention of 1816 and 1819, and from 1820 to 1823 he represented the York District of Maine in Congress; was subsequently in the Legislature as a member of the House for six years, and was a member of the Senate in 1829. He was chosen a member of the Executive Council of Massachusetts in 1817, and to a similar station in Maine in 1841, but he declined both offices. He settled in Kennebunk early in the present century, where he died, May 1, 1858.

Daniel, Henry.—He was born in 1793, and was a Representative in Congress, from Kentucky, from 1827 to 1833, where he had a famous encounter with Tristam Burgess.

Daniel, John R. J.—Born in Halifax County, North Carolina; graduated at the University of that State in 1821; studied law, and practised it with success. He served for several years in the General Assembly, and was elected Attorney-General of the State; and was a Representative in Congress, from 1841 to 1853, serving through several sessions as Chairman of the Committee on Claims.

Danner, Joel B.—He was a Representative in Congress, from Pennsylvania, from 1850 to 1851.

Darby, Ezra.—He was a Representative in Congress, from New Jersey, from 1804 to 1808. Died January 28, 1808.

Darby, John Fletcher.—Born in Person County, North Carolina, December 10, 1803. In 1818 he removed with his father to Missouri, and settled in St. Louis County, where, until 1823, he worked on a farm, pursuing his studies under many difficulties, having previously received a good English education in his native town. After the death of his parents, in 1825, he applied for an appointment at West Point, but being unsuccessful, sold out his father's estate, and went to Frankfort, Kentucky, and studied law with Mr. Crittenden. In May, 1827, having a license to practise from the Supreme Court of Kentucky, he returned to Missouri and commenced his professional life. He was four times chosen Mayor of the City of St. Louis, and once a member of the State Senate, and was a Representative in Congress, from 1851 to 1853.

Dargan, Edward S.—He was born in North Carolina, removed in early youth to Alabama, where he subsequently taught school and studied law. In 1844 he was elected Mayor of Mobile; from 1845 to 1847 he was a Representative in Congress; and during the latter year was elected a Judge of the Supreme Court of Alabama.

Darling, Mason C.—Born in Bellingham, Massachusetts, May 18, 1801; received a common school education; commenced active life as a school teacher in New York; and having studied medicine, graduated at the Berkshire Medical Institution of Massachusetts in 1824. He practised his profession for thirteen years, when he removed to Wisconsin, and aided in establishing the towns of Sheboygan and Fond du Lac. The principal offices held by him, in Wisconsin, were those of Judge of Probate, Mayor of Fond du Lac, a member, for several years, of the Territorial Legislature, and a Representative in Congress, from the State of Wisconsin, from 1847 to 1849.

Darlington, Edward.—He was born in Pennsylvania, and was a Representative in Congress, from that State, from 1833 to 1839.

Darlington, Isaac. — Born in Westtown, Chester County, Pennsylvania, December 13, 1781, and died April 27, 1839. He was brought up to hard labor, partly on a farm, and in the shop of his father, a worthy blacksmith, and was a Quaker in religion. He educated himself, taught school, studied law, and was successful as a practitioner. In 1807 he was elected to the State Legislature; served as a volunteer Lieutenant in the last war with England; and was a member of Congress, from 1817 to 1819,—declining a re-election. In 1820 he was appointed Deputy Attorney-General for Chester County, and in 1821 was appointed President Judge of the County Court, which he held until his death.

Darlington, William.—Born in Birmingham, Chester County, Pennsylvania, April 28, 1782. He was brought up on a farm until eighteen years old, trained in the religion of George Fox, and when young had but a limited education. He studied medicine, and in 1804 graduated at the University of Pennsylvania. In 1806 he was *disowned* by the Society of Friends for accepting the appointment of surgeon to a military regiment; in 1807 he went to India as surgeon of a merchant ship; in 1811 and 1812 he assisted in establishing the West Chester Academy, Pennsylvania, of which he was long a Trustee and the Secretary; in 1813 he prepared a catalogue of plants of his native county; in 1814 he took part in establishing the Bank of West Chester, and was its President. When Washington City was attacked by the British, he went to camp as a volunteer; and he was a member of Congress, from Pennsylvania, from 1815 to 1817, and again from 1819 to 1823. He was also a member of the "American Philosophical Society;" was a Canal Commissioner in 1825. In 1826 he aided in forming a Natural History Society in West Chester, and was elected President of the same; and on account of his devotion to science and his scientific learning, a number of rare plants were named after him by leading naturalists of Switzerland and America. He also held the office of Clerk of the Court of Chester County; aided in founding and was President of the "West Chester Medical Society;" was President of a railway company; in 1847 he was robbed of $50,000 belonging to the bank of which he was president; his publications on botany and kindred subjects are quite numerous; in 1848 he received from Yale College the degree of Doctor of Laws, and in 1855 that of Doctor of Physical Science from Dickinson College; and he has been elected a member of some forty learned societies, in America and Europe. Died in 1863.

Darragh, Cornelius. — He was born in Pennsylvania, and was a Representative in Congress, from that State, from 1843 to 1847.

Davee, Thomas.—Born in Plymouth, Massachusetts, December 9, 1797; removed to Maine, and was bred a merchant; served six years in the two Houses of the Maine Legislature; served a second term in the State Assembly, and was chosen Speaker; he was also High Sheriff of Somerset County; and a Representative in Congress, from 1837 to 1841. He was also, for many years, a Postmaster in Maine, and at the time of his death was a Senator elect of the State Legislature. He died, supported by the hopes of the Christian, December 9, 1841.

Davenport, Franklin.—He was a Senator in Congress, from New Jersey, from 1798 to 1799, but was superseded, and a Representative in Congress, from 1799 to 1801.

Davenport, James.—He was a graduate of Yale College in 1777, and was a Representative in Congress, from Connecticut, from 1796 to 1797, in which year he died.

Davenport, John.—He was born in Connecticut; graduated at Yale College in 1770; was a tutor in that College; and a Representative in Congress, from Connecticut, from 1799 to 1817. He died in 1830.

Davenport, John.—He was a Representative in Congress, from Ohio, from 1827 to 1829.

Davenport, Thomas.—He was born in Cumberland County, Virginia, and was a Representative in Congress, from Virginia, from 1825 to 1835, and died in Halifax County, in November, 1838.

Davidson, Thomas G.—Born in Jefferson County, Mississippi, August 3, 1805; studied law, and was admitted to the bar in 1827; in 1833 was Register of the Land-office at Greensburg, Louisiana; was elected to the Legislature of that State in 1833, where he served, from different parishes, some thirteen years; and he was elected a Representative in Congress, in 1855; re-elected in 1857, and was Chairman of the Committee on Enrolled Bills, and member of the Committee on Claims. Re-elected to the Thirty-sixth Congress, but resigned in February, 1861.

Davidson, William.—He was a native of Mecklenburg County, North Carolina, having been born September 12, 1778; represented that County in the State Legislature, as a Senator, in 1813, 1815, 1816, and 1817; and was a Representative in Congress, from his native State, from 1818 to 1821. He served again in the State Senate, in 1827, 1828, and 1829. He died in Charlotte, Mecklenburg County, September 16, 1857, from injuries which he received by being thrown from his carriage, while taking a drive with a fractious horse. Though leading the quiet life of a planter, he was a man of great influence and usefulness.

Davies, Edward.—He was born in Pennsylvania, and was a Representative in Congress, from that State, from 1837 to 1841.

Davis, Amos.—He represented Kentucky in Congress, from 1833 to 1835, and died in Owingsville, Kentucky, June 5, 1835.

Davis, Garret.—He was born at Mount Stirling, Kentucky, September 10, 1801; received an English and classical education; while yet a boy, he was employed as a writer in the County and Circuit Courts of his district; studied law, and came to the bar in 1823. In 1833 he was elected to the State Legislature, and was twice re-elected; in 1839 he was a member of the State Constitutional Convention; from 1839 to 1847 he was a Representative in Congress, from Kentucky, and declined a re-election; and, though always actively engaged in the practice of his profession, he has ever devoted much attention to the pursuits of agriculture. In 1861 he was elected a Senator in Congress, from Kentucky, for the term ending in 1867, serving on the Committees on Foreign Relations and on Territories. From early manhood until the death of Henry Clay, he was one of the most intimate personal and political friends of that statesman.

Davis, George T.—He was born in Sandwich, Massachusetts, January 12, 1810; graduated at Harvard College in 1829; studied law, and was admitted to the bar in 1832; was elected to the Senate of Massachusetts in 1839 and 1840; and was a Representative in Congress from 1851 to 1853. He is now devoted to his profession.

Davis, H. Winter.—He was born in Annapolis, Maryland, in 1817; graduated at Hampden Sidney College; was elected a Representative, from Maryland, to the Thirty-fourth and Thirty-fifth Congresses, serving as a member of the Committee of Ways and Means. He was also elected to the Thirty-sixth Congress, serving on the same Committee; and in 1863 he was re-elected to the Thirty-eighth Congress, serving as Chairman of the Committee on Foreign Affairs. As an author he published, in 1852, a book entitled "The War of Ormuzd and Ahrinam in the Nineteenth Century."

Davis, Jefferson.—He was born in Christian County, Kentucky, June 3, 1808, but his father removed to Mississippi in his infancy. He commenced his education at the Transylvania University, Kentucky, but left it for the West Point Academy, where he graduated in 1828. He followed the fortunes of a soldier until 1835, when he became a planter. He was a cadet from 1824 to 1828; Second Lieutenant of infantry from 1828 to 1833; First Lieutenant of dragoons from 1833 to 1835, serving in various campaigns against the Indians; was Adjutant of dragoons, and at different times served in the Quartermaster's Department; in 1844 was a Presidential Elector; in 1845 was elected a Representative in Congress, from Mississippi, for one term, but resigned in 1846, to become Colonel of a volunteer regiment to serve in Mexico; in Mexico he received the appointment of Brigadier-General; in 1847 was appointed a Senator in Congress, to fill a vacancy, and was elected for the term ending in 1851, but resigned in 1850; was re-elected for a term of six years, but resigned; was appointed Secretary of War by President Pierce, serving throughout his administration; and in 1857 again took his seat in the United States Senate for the term of six years, serving as Chairman of the Committee on Military Affairs, and a member of those on Public Buildings and Grounds and on Printing. In February, 1861, he resigned his seat in the Senate, became identified with the Great Rebellion, and was elected President of the so-called "Southern Confederacy."

Davis, John.—Born in Northborough, Massachusetts, January 13, 1787; graduated at Yale College in 1812; adopted the profession of law; admitted to the bar in 1815; was a Reprensentative in Congress from 1825 to 1833; Governor of Massachusetts during the years 1833 and 1834, and 1841 and 1842; a Senator in Congress from 1835 to 1841, and again from 1845 to 1853, always serving on important committees and exerting much influence. On account of his many popular qualities, he was called "Honest John Davis." He died suddenly, at Worcester, April 19, 1854.

Davis, John.—He was born in Pennsylvania, and was a Representative in Congress, from that State, from 1839 to 1841.

Davis, John G.—Born in Fleming County, Kentucky, October 10, 1810. His education was obtained at a country school, where, during the winter months, he studied the rudiments of reading, writing, and arithmetic. He was bred to the occupation of a farmer; was elected Sheriff of Parke County, Indiana, where he now resides, and resigned in 1832. He was Clerk of the Superior and Inferior Courts of that county, from 1833 to 1851, and was a Representative, from Indiana, in the Thirty-second, Thirty-third, and Thirty-fifth Congresses, and was a member of the Committee on Public Lands, and also served on the Committee to Examine into the Accounts of the late Clerk of the House. He was also re-elected to the Thirty-sixth Congress, serving as a member of the Committee on Public Lands.

Davis, John W.—He was born in Lancaster, Pennsylvania, in 1799; after completing his medical studies in Baltimore, in 1821, at the Medical College, he emigrated to Indiana. He served first as a Surrogate and then in the Legislature of that State, and was Speaker of the lower branch, both before and after his services in Congress, viz., in 1832 and 1841; and was also a Commissioner to make a treaty with the Indians. He was a Representative in Congress, from Indiana, from 1835 to 1837, from 1839 to 1841, and again from 1843 to 1847, and was Speaker of the House of Representatives during the Twenty-ninth Congress. He was, in 1848, appointed Minister to China, and, subsequently, held the position of Governor of Oregon Territory. He was also President of the Baltimore Convention which nominated Franklin Pierce for President, in 1852. Died at Carlisle, Indiana, August 22, 1859.

Davis, Reuben.—Born in Tennessee, January 18, 1813. He was self-educated, owing to the limited means of his father. He studied and practised medicine for a few years, and, afterwards, pursued the law as a profession. In 1835 was chosen District Attorney for the Sixth Judicial District of Mississippi. In 1837 he was re-elected to the same office; served for four months, in 1842, on the bench of the High Court of Errors and Appeals; was in the Mexican war as Colonel commandant of the Mississippi Rifles, but resigned on account of sickness, and was in no battle; was elected to the lower branch of the State Legislature from 1855 to 1857; and was elected a member of the Thirty-fifth Congress, serving on the Committees on Post-offices and Post-roads and Expenditures in the Navy Department. Re-elected to the Thirty-sixth Congress. Joined the Rebellion in 1861.

Davis, Richard D.—He was born in New York, graduated at Yale College in 1818, and was a Representative in Congress, from his native State, from 1841 to 1845.

Davis, Roger.—He was a Representative in Congress, from Pennsylvania, from 1811 to 1815.

Davis, Samuel.—He was born in Massachusetts, and was a Representative in Congress, from that State, from 1813 to 1815. In 1803, from 1808 to 1812, and in 1815 and 1816, he was a member of the State Legislature.

Davis, Samuel B.—He was born in Virginia, and was a Representative in Congress, from Louisiana, from 1853 to 1855.

Davis, Thomas.—He was born in Ireland, and having emigrated to Rhode Island, was elected a Representative in Congress, from 1853 to 1855.

Davis, Thomas T.—He was a Representative in Congress, from Kentucky, from 1797 to 1803, and was appointed in that year Judge in the Territory of Indiana.

Davis, Thomas T.—Was born in Middlebury, Addison County, Vermont, August 22, 1810; graduated at Hamilton College, New York, in 1831; studied law in Syracuse, and was admitted to the bar in 1833. As a public man, his time has been chiefly devoted to business connected with railroads, with various kinds of manufacturing, and with the mining of coal; and in 1862 he was elected a Representative, from New York, to the Thirty-eighth Congress, serving on the Committee for the District of Columbia.

Davis, Timothy.—He was born in Newark, New Jersey, in March, 1794; received a common school education; removed to Kentucky in 1816, and was there admitted to the bar in 1817; spent twenty years of his life in Missouri; and, having removed to Iowa, was elected a Representative, from that State, to the Thirty-fifth Congress, and was a member of the Committee on the Post-office and Post-roads.

Davis, Timothy.—He was born in Gloucester, Massachusetts, April 12, 1821; was educated at a district school, which he did not attend after reaching the age of twelve years; spent two years in a printing-office; lived a number of years in Boston as a clerk and as a merchant; in 1854, by an unusually large majority, he was elected a Representative in Congress, from his native district; was re-elected to the Thirty-fifth Congress, and served as a member of the Committee on Naval Affairs. He was appointed by President Lincoln to a place in the Boston Custom-house in 1861.

Davis, Warren R.—He was born in South Carolina; graduated at the College of South Carolina in 1810; adopted the profession of law; came to the bar in 1814; was appointed Solicitor for South Carolina in 1818; and was a Representative in Congress, from South Carolina, from 1825 to 1835, and died in Washington, District of Columbia, January 29, 1835, aged forty-two years. It was while attending his funeral that President Jackson was fired at by a man named Lawrence.

Davis, William M.—Was born in Pennsylvania, and elected a Representative, from that State, to the Thirty-seventh Congress, serving on the Committee on the District of Columbia.

Dawes, Henry L.—Born in Cummington, Hampshire County, Massachusetts, October 30, 1816. He graduated at Yale College in 1839, and adopted the profession of law. He taught school for a time, and edited a paper called the Greenfield Gazette. He was a member for three years of the Legislature of Massachusetts, during the years 1848, 1849, and 1852; of the State Senate in 1850, and also of the State Constitutional Convention in 1853. He was also District Attorney for the Western District of his native State, from 1853 until elected to the Thirty-fifth Congress, wherein he served as a member of the Committee on Revolutionary Claims; was re-elected to the Thirty-sixth Congress; serving on the Committee on Elections; re-elected to the Thirty-seventh Congress, serving as Chairman of the Committee on Elections; and was re-elected to the Thirty-eighth Congress, serving again as Chairman of the Committee on Elections.

Dawson, John.—He graduated at Harvard University in 1782; was elected a Representative in Congress, from Virginia, from 1797 to 1814; served in one of the State Conventions of Virginia, and in the General Assembly; was a member of the Executive Council of Virginia; rendered service in the war of 1813, as aid to the commanding General, on the Lakes; and was appointed bearer of despatches to France in 1801, by President Adams. He died in Washington City, March 30, 1814, aged fifty-two years.

Dawson, John B.—He was born at Nashville, Tennessee, in 1800, and was a Representative in Congress, from Louisiana, from 1841 to the time of his death, which occurred at St. Francisville, Louisiana, June 26, 1845.

Dawson, John L.—He was born in Uniontown, Fayette County, Pennsylvania, February 7, 1813; was educated at Washington College; adopted the profession of law; was appointed by President Polk, in 1845, United States Attorney for the Western District of Pennsylvania; was elected a Representative, from Pennsylvania, to the Thirty-second and Thirty-third Congresses, serving during the last term as Chairman of the Committee on Agriculture; and in 1862 was re-elected to the Thirty-eighth Congress, and was a member of the Committee on Foreign Affairs. He was the author of the Homestead Bill which passed in 1854; and a Delegate to the Baltimore Conventions of 1844, 1848, and 1860, and of the Cincinnati Convention of 1856, when, on the part of Pennsylvania, he delivered the speech acknowledging the nomination of Mr. Buchanan. He was appointed Governor of Kansas, by President Pierce, in 1855, but declined the appointment.

Dawson, William C.—Born in Greene County, Georgia, January 4, 1798, and died May 5, 1856. He graduated at Franklin College in 1816; studied law at home and at Litchfield, Connecticut; and having been admitted to the bar, settled at Greensborough, in 1818, where he was eminently successful as a jury lawyer. He was for twelve years Clerk of the House of Representatives of Georgia, and several times Senator and Representative in the Legislature. He was a Representative in Congress from 1837 to 1842; and in 1845 he was appointed Judge of the Ockmulgee Circuit; and from 1849 to 1855 he was a Senator of the United States, where he served on important committees, and spoke on many important questions of national interest, and commanded a wide influence.

Dawson, William J.—A Representative in Congress, from North Carolina, from 1793 to 1795.

Day, Rowland.—He was a member of the New York Assembly in 1816 and 1817, and was a Representative in Congress, from that State, from 1823 to 1825, and again from 1833 to 1835.

Day, Timothy C.—He was born in Ohio, and was elected a Representative, from that State, to the Thirty-fourth Congress.

Dayan, Charles.—Born at Amsterdam, New York, July 16, 1792; until fourteen years of age he worked in a mill; at that time he began to study, and was successful; taught school for four winters at a monthly price of two dollars per month; studied law, and was a successful practitioner for many years. He was a Representative in Congress, from New York, from 1831 to 1833; a State Senator in 1827 and 1828; acting Lieutenant-Governor in 1829; and a member of the Assembly in 1835 and 1836. He was also District Attorney for Lewis County for five years.

Dayton, Jonathan.—A native of New Jersey; graduated at Princeton College in 1776; was a member of the State Convention in 1787; a Representative in Congress from 1791 to 1799; Speaker of the House of Representatives from 1795 to 1797; and was a Senator of the United States from 1799 to 1805. He was a distinguished statesman, and died at Elizabethtown, New Jersey, October 9, 1824, aged about sixty-eight years.

Dayton, William L.—Born in Somerset County, New Jersey, February 17, 1807; graduated at Princeton College in 1825; is a lawyer by profession, having come to the bar in 1830; was a member of the State Senate of New Jersey in 1837; was appointed one of the Justices of the Superior Court of the State February 28, 1838, and resigned said office in 1841, and resumed the practice of law; was a Senator in Congress from 1842 to 1851. In March, 1857, was appointed Attorney-General of New Jersey, which office he held until 1861, when he was appointed, by President Lincoln, Minister to France.

Dean, Ezra.—He was born in New

York, and was a Representative in Congress, from Ohio, from 1841 to 1845.

Dean, Gilbert.—Is a native of Pleasant Valley, Dutchess County, New York. In May, 1837, he entered the Amenia Seminary, and in September of the same year he went to Yale College, and graduated in 1841. He studied law in Pine Plains, and commenced practice in Poughkeepsie in 1844, attaining eminence in his profession; and was elected a Representative in Congress from 1851 to 1853. Was re-elected for a second term, but resigned in 1854.

Dean, Josiah.—He was born in Baynham, Massachusetts, March 16, 1748, and was a Representative in Congress, from Massachusetts, from 1807 to 1809. From 1804 to 1807 he was a State Senator; and in 1810 and 1811 was a member of the State Legislature. Died October 14, 1818.

Dean, Sidney.—He was born in Glastenbury, Hartford County, Connecticut, November 16, 1818. He received only a common school education; entered upon active life as a manufacturer; but subsequently became a clergyman. He served one year in the Legislature of Connecticut, and was elected a Representative in Congress, from that State, in 1855, and re-elected in 1857; officiating during his first term as Chairman of the Committee on Public Expenditures, and as a member of the Committee on the District of Columbia. In 1860 he settled in Rhode Island as a clergyman.

Dearborn, Henry.—Was a native of New Hampshire, and settled, in the practice of physic, at Portsmouth. He was a Captain in Stark's regiment at the battle of Bunker Hill; he accompanied Arnold in the expedition through the wilderness of Maine to Quebec; he was captured by the British, and put into close confinement; but in May, 1776, was permitted to return on parole; in March, 1777, he was exchanged; he served as a Major in the army under Gates at the capture of Burgoyne. He distinguished himself at the battle of Monmouth by a gallant charge on the enemy. Dearborn being sent to ask for further orders, Washington inquired, by way of commendation, "What troops are those?" "Full-blooded Yankees from New Hampshire, sir," was the reply. In 1779 he accompanied Sullivan in his expedition against the Indians; in 1780 he was with the army in New Jersey; in 1781 he was at Yorktown, at the surrender of Cornwallis; in 1789 Washington appointed him Marshal of the District of Maine. He was elected a member of Congress from 1793 to 1797. In 1801 he was appointed Secretary of War, and held the office till 1809, when he was appointed to the lucrative office of Collector of Boston. In 1812 he received a commission as senior Major-General in the army of the United States. In the spring of 1813 he captured York, in Upper Canada, and Fort George, at the mouth of the Niagara. He was recalled by Mr. Madison in July. He was ordered to assume the command of the military district of New York City. In 1822 he was appointed Minister Plenipotentiary to Portugal; two years after he returned to America at his own request. He died in 1829, aged seventy-eight years.

Dearborn, Henry A. S.—Born in 1783, in Exeter, New Hampshire; was educated at William and Mary College, Virginia, and commenced the study of law in Washington, while his father was Secretary of War under Jefferson. He finished his studies at Salem, Massachusetts, in the office of Judge Story, and commenced to practise in that city. He removed to Portland, and superintended the erection of the forts in the harbor. He was appointed Collector of Boston by President Madison (having been previously made Deputy Collector by his father, when Collector), as an inducement for his father to accept the command of the army, and he held the office until removed by General Jackson in 1829. In 1812 he was Brigadier of militia, and had the command of the troops in Boston harbor. In 1821 was a member of the Convention for revising the Constitution of Massachusetts. In 1829 was a Representative in the Legislature from Roxbury; and the same year chosen Executive Councillor, and the following year a State Senator. From 1831 to 1833 he was a Representative in Congress. He was soon appointed Adjutant-General of Massachusetts, and continued in that office till 1843, when he was removed for lending some of the State arms during the Dorr Rebellion in Rhode

Island. In 1847 was chosen Mayor of Roxbury, which office he held until his death. While in the Custom-house, in Boston, he wrote and published three volumes on the "Commerce of the Black Sea." He also wrote a biography of Commodore Bainbridge, and one of his father; a book on Architecture, and a Life of Christ. He died in Portland, Maine, July 29, 1851.

Deberry, Edmund. — Born in Montgomery County, North Carolina, August 14, 1787. He was educated at the ordinary schools of the county, and having entered public life, in 1806, as a member of the State Legislature, he continued to serve there, with occasional intermissions, until 1828; and was a Representative in Congress from 1829 to 1831, from 1833 to 1845, and again from 1849 to 1851. Died in his native county in 1859.

De Graff, John J.—He was a Representative in Congress, from New York, from 1827 to 1829, and again from 1837 to 1839.

Deitz, William.—He was born in Schoharie County, New York, and was a member of the New York Assembly in 1814 and 1815; a Representative in Congress, from that State, from 1825 to 1827; and a State Senator from 1830 to 1833.

De Jarnette, Daniel C.—Born in Caroline County, Virginia, in 1822; received a liberal education; adopted the occupation of a farmer; served many years in the Legislature of Virginia; and was elected a Representative, from that State, to the Thirty-sixth Congress, serving on the Committee on Revolutionary Claims. Re-elected to the Thirty-seventh Congress, serving on the Committee on the District of Columbia.

Delano, Charles.—Born in Braintree, Massachusetts, in 1820; graduated at Amherst College in 1840; studied law and came to the bar in 1842; in 1850 he was appointed Treasurer of Hampshire County; and he was elected a Representative, from Massachusetts, to the Thirty-sixth Congress, serving as a member of the Committee on Revolutionary Pensions. Re-elected to the Thirty-seventh Congress.

Delano, Columbus. — Born in Shoreham, Vermont, June 5, 1809; removed to Knox County, Ohio, in 1817; studied law and was admitted to the bar in 1831, and settled in the town of Mount Vernon. In 1836 he was elected for two years Prosecuting Attorney for Knox County; re-elected in 1838; and in 1844 was elected a Representative, from Ohio, to the Twenty-ninth Congress. In 1860 he was a Delegate to the Chicago Convention; in 1863 was elected to the Ohio Legislature; and was a Delegate to the Baltimore Convention of 1864.

Delaplaine, Isaac C.—He was born in New York, and was elected a Representative, from that State, to the Thirty-seventh Congress, serving on the Committee on Public Buildings and Grounds.

Dellet, James.—He was a native of Ireland; and one of the early graduates of the University of South Carolina, having left it in 1810; he adopted the profession of law, coming to the bar in 1813; was a Commissioner in Equity; removed to Alabama in 1818, where he was appointed a Judge of the Circuit Court, and frequently represented his county in the State Legislature; and was a Representative in Congress, from Alabama, from 1839 to 1841, and again from 1843 to 1845. He died at Claiborne, December 21, 1848, aged sixty years.

Deming, Henry C.—He was born in Connecticut; graduated at Yale College in 1836, and at the Law School of Harvard College in 1838; he was a member of the Connecticut Legislature in 1849 and 1850, and also from 1859 to 1861, serving as Speaker during the latter year. In 1851 he was a member of the State Senate. He subsequently presided over the city of Hartford as Mayor for six years. In 1861, as Colonel of the Twelfth Regiment of Connecticut Volunteers, he went to New Orleans, and participated in the capture of that city. In October, 1862, he was appointed Mayor of New Orleans, which position he held until February, 1863, when he resigned both that office and his commission in the army and returned home. Two months afterwards he was elected a Representative, from Connecticut, to the Thirty-eighth Congress, serving on the Committee on

Military Affairs, and as Chairman of the Committee on Expenditures in the War Department.

Demming, Benjamin F.—He was born at Danville, Vermont; received a common school education; served a number of years as a clerk in a store; was Clerk of the court in his native county for sixteen years; and was elected a Representative in Congress for the term from 1833 to 1835, but died at Saratoga Springs, whither he had gone for his health, July 11, 1834.

De Mott, John.—He was born in New Jersey; was a member of the New York Assembly, in 1833; and a Representative in Congress, from that State, from 1845 to 1847.

Denison, Charles.—Was born in Wyoming Valley, Pennsylvania, January 23, 1818; graduated at Dickinson College in 1839; adopted and practised the profession of law; and was elected a Representative, from Pennsylvania, to the Thirty-eighth Congress, serving on the Committee on Indian Affairs.

Dennis, John.—He was born in Somerset County, Maryland, in 1807; and was a Representative in Congress, from that State, from 1837 to 1841. He was also twice elected to the State Legislature, and was a member of the Maryland State Convention in 1850. He was educated for the bar, but relinquished professional life for the pursuits of agriculture. Died of consumption November 1, 1859.

Dennis, Littleton P.—He graduated at Yale College in 1803; served many years in the Legislature of Maryland; and was elected a Representative to Congress, from Maryland, in 1833; and died at Washington, April 14, 1834, before the expiration of his term in Congress.

Dennison, George.—He was born in Luzerne County, Pennsylvania, and was a Representative in Congress, from that State, from 1819 to 1823. He was for many years Register and Recorder of Luzerne County, and before as well as after his service in Congress, was frequently returned to the Legislature, and he died at Wilkesbarre, Pennsylvania, in 1831, while in office.

Denny, Harmar.—Born in Pittsburg, Pennsylvania, in 1794; graduated at Dickinson College; was a member of the Legislature of his native State, and a Representative in Congress, from 1829 to 1837; and a member of the Convention which formed the present Constitution of Pennsylvania. He died in Pittsburg, January 29, 1852.

Dent, George.—He was a Representative in Congress, from Maryland, from 1793 to 1801, and was appointed in the latter year United States Marshal for the Potomac District. During the third session of the Fifth Congress he was elected Speaker of the House of Representatives.

Dent, William B. W.—He was born in Maryland, and was a Representative in Congress, from Georgia, from 1853 to 1855.

Denver, James W.—Born in Winchester, Virginia, in 1818. When quite young he emigrated to Ohio with his parents; received a good education; in 1841 he went to Missouri, where he taught school and studied law; he served in the Mexican war as a Captain, under appointment from President Polk; in 1850 he went to California, where he was appointed a member of a relief committee to protect emigrants; and, afterwards, Secretary of State of California; he was a Representative, from California, in the Thirty-fourth Congress; by President Buchanan he was appointed a Commissioner of Indian Affairs, which office he resigned to accept the appointment of Governor of the Territory of Kansas, which position he resigned in November, 1858, and was reappointed Commissioner of Indian Affairs. Resigned, March, 1859.

Desaussure, William F.—He was born in South Carolina; graduated at Harvard University in 1810; and was a Senator in Congress, from his native State, from 1850 to 1853.

Desha, Joseph.—He was born in Pennsylvania, December 9, 1768, and emigrated to Kentucky in 1781; in 1794 he served as a volunteer in the expedition against the Indians, under General Wayne; served for a time in the State Legislature; fought at the battle of the Thames, as a Major-General; was a Representative in Congress, from 1807 to 1819; was Governor of Kentucky for four years, from 1824; and died at Georgetown, Kentucky, October 13, 1842.

Desha, Robert.—He was a prominent merchant of Mobile, and a Representative in Congress, from Tennessee, from 1827 to 1831. He was the brother of Joseph Desha. He died, February 8, 1849.

Destrihan, John Noel.—He was a Senator in Congress, from Louisiana, for a part of the year 1812.

Dewart, Lewis.—He was a native of Pennsylvania, and a Representative in Congress, from that State, from 1831 to 1833.

Dewart, William L.—He was born in Pennsylvania; was a lawyer by profession, and was a member of the Thirty-fifth Congress, from his native State. He was Chairman of the Committee on Unfinished Business.

Dewey, Daniel.—Was a lawyer, having studied under Theodore Sedgwick, and attained a high rank in his profession. He was a member of the Council of the State, and a Representative in Congress, from Berkshire District, Massachusetts, in 1813 and 1814; was appointed Judge of the Supreme Court of Massachusetts in 1814. He died June 3, 1815.

De Witt, Alexander.—Born in Worcester County, Massachusetts, April 2, 1797; was a Representative in the Massachusetts Legislature from 1830 to 1836; devoted himself to the manufacturing business; was a bank President; and was a Representative in Congress, from 1853 to 1857. He was also a State Senator in 1842, 1844, 1850, and 1851; and a member of the Constitutional Convention of 1853.

De Witt, Charles G.—He was a Representative in Congress, from New York, from 1829 to 1831, and appointed Chargé d'Affaires, for Central America, in 1833. He died at Newburg, April 13, 1839.

De Witt, Jacob H.—He was born in Ulster County, New York, and was a Representative in Congress, from that State, from 1819 to 1821; and a member of the New York Assembly in 1839 and in 1847. He died at Kingston, New York, January 30, 1857, aged seventy-three years.

De Wolfe, James.—He was a Senator of the United States, from Rhode Island, from 1821 to 1825, when he resigned, and died in the city of New York, December 21, 1837, aged seventy-four years.

Dexter, Samuel.—Was a native of Massachusetts, and born in 1761; he graduated at Harvard College in 1781; and, having studied law at Worcester, with Levi Lincoln, he soon rose to professional eminence. He was a member of the House of Representatives in Congress, from 1793 to 1795, and was elected to the Senate, serving from 1799 to 1800. During the administration of John Adams he was appointed Secretary of War, in 1800, and Secretary of the Treasury, in January, 1801; and, for a short time, also, had the charge of the Department of State. On the accession of Mr. Jefferson to the Presidency, he held the office of Secretary of the Treasury, and not complying with an intimation to resign, Mr. Gallatin was appointed in his place. In 1812 he abandoned the party to which he had always been attached, and became a leader on the other side, and, as such, was the candidate for Governor of Massachusetts, in 1815 and 1816, in opposition to Governor Brooks. A mission to Spain was offered him, by Mr. Madison, in 1815. He died May 3, 1816.

Dick, John.—Was born in Pennsylvania, was bred a merchant, and was a member of Congress, from said State, in 1854 and 1855, and was re-elected to the Thirty-fourth and Thirty-fifth Congresses, serving as a member of the Committee on Accounts.

Dickens, Samuel.—A Representative in Congress, from North Carolina, during the years 1816 and 1817.

Dickerson, Mahlon.—Born in Morris County, New Jersey, in 1769; graduated at Princeton College in 1789; studied law, and in early life he resided in Pennsylvania, where he was Recorder of the city of Philadelphia, and subsequently Quartermaster-General of the State; he returned to New Jersey, and was elected to the Legislature of that State. He was Judge of the Supreme Court of New Jersey, and was elected Governor of that State in 1815, and held the office until 1817, when he was chosen United States Senator, and continued in that office for sixteen years. In 1834 he became Secretary of the Navy, in the cabinet of President Jackson, and held that department until 1838, some two years after the accession of President Van Buren. For two years he was President of the American Institute. He died in Morris County, New Jersey, October 5, 1853.

Dickerson, Philemon.—He was the brother of Mahlon Dickerson, a native of New Jersey, and a Representative in Congress, from the Paterson District in that State, from 1833 to 1835, and again from 1839 to 1841. In 1836 he was Governor of New Jersey, and was subsequently appointed Judge of the United States District Court for New Jersey. Died at Paterson, New Jersey, December 10, 1862, aged about seventy years.

Dickey, Jesse C.—He was born in Pennsylvania, and was a Representative in Congress, from 1849 to 1851.

Dickey, John.—He was a member of Congress, from Pennsylvania, from 1843 to 1845, and from 1847 to 1849; and at the time of his death, was United States Marshal for Western Pennsylvania. He died in Beaver County, March 14, 1853.

Dickinson, Daniel S.—He was born in Goshen, Litchfield County, Connecticut, September 11, 1800; removed with his family to New York in 1806; he was self-educated, and adopted the profession of law, coming to the bar in 1830. He was at one time in the State Senate; was Judge of the Court of Errors from 1836 to 1841; he was Lieutenant-Governor, President of the Senate and of said court, from 1842 to 1844; was a Democratic Elector in 1844; and a Senator in Congress, from New York, from 1844 to 1851, since which time he has lived in retirement. He was a Delegate to the Baltimore Convention of 1864.

Dickinson, David W.—He was a Representative in Congress, from Tennessee, from 1833 to 1835, and again from 1843 to 1845, and died at Franklin, Tennessee, April 27, of the latter year.

Dickinson, Edward.—He was born in Massachusetts; adopted the profession of law; was a member of the Massachusetts Legislature, in 1838 and 1839; a State Senator in 1842 and 1843; a State Councillor in 1845 and 1846; and a Representative in Congress, from Massachusetts, from 1853 to 1855. He was a graduate of Amherst College, and a lawyer by profession.

Dickinson, John D.—He was born in Middlesex County, Connecticut, in 1767; graduated at Yale College in 1785; and was a member of Congress, from New York, from 1819 to 1823, and again from 1827 to 1831; and died at Troy, January 28, 1841.

Dickinson, Philemon.—A native of New Jersey; was an officer in the American Revolution, and enjoyed a great reputation for courage and zeal in the cause of liberty. He commanded the Jersey militia at the battle of Monmouth. He was a Delegate from Delaware, to the Continental Congress, from 1782 to 1783; and after the organization of the National Government in its present form, he was appointed a Senator in Congress, from 1790 to 1793. Having discharged in a satisfactory manner the duties of the several civil and military stations which he held, he enjoyed several years of retirement from public life, and died at Trenton in 1809.

Dickinson, Rudolphus.—He was born in Massachusetts, and having removed to Ohio, was elected a Representative in Congress, from 1847 to 1849. Died in August, 1849.

Dickson, David.—He was a member of Congress, from Mississippi, in 1835 and 1836, and died at Little Rock, Arkansas, July 31, 1836.

Dickson, John.—He was a Representative in Congress, from New York, from 1831 to 1835, and died at West

Bloomfield, New York, February 22, 1852.

Dickson, Samuel.—He was a Representative in Congress, from New York, during the Thirty-fourth Congress. He died at his residence, in New Scotland, New York, May 3, 1858, in consequence of spinal injuries received while in the faithful discharge of his public duties at Washington. He had been bred a physician, and was universally respected.

Dickson, William.—He was a Representative in Congress, from Tennessee, from 1801 to 1807.

Dillingham, Paul, Jr.—He was born in Shutesbury, Franklin County, Massachusetts, August, 1800; removed to Waterbury, Vermont, with his father, in 1805; received a good education; adopted the profession of law; and was admitted to practice, in Washington County, in 1824. He was Town Clerk of Waterbury, from 1829 to 1844, and Justice of the Peace eighteen years. He was State's Attorney, for Washington County, from 1835 to 1838; and was a member of the Constitutional Convention in 1836 and 1837. He was a Representative to the General Assembly six years, and State Senator in 1841 and 1842; and elected a Representative in Congress, from 1843 to 1847, and was a member of the Committee on the Judiciary. He has since that time devoted himself to the practice of his profession.

Dimmick, Milo M.—He was born in Pennsylvania, and was a Representative in Congress, from that State, from 1849 to 1853.

Dimmick, William H.—He was born in Milford, Pike County, Pennsylvania, December 20, 1815. He received an academical education, and adopted the profession of law. He was Prosecuting Attorney, for the Commonwealth of Pennsylvania, for Wayne County, in 1836 and 1837; was a member of the State Senate in 1845, 1846, and 1847; and was elected a Representative, from Pennsylvania, in the Thirty-fifth Congress, officiating as Chairman of the Joint Committee on the Library. He was also re-elected to the Thirty-sixth Congress, serving on the Committee on Printing. Died at Honesdale, Pennsylvania, August 2, 1861.

Dimock, Davis, Jr.—He was a Representative in Congress, from Pennsylvania, from 1841 to 1842. Died January 13, 1842.

Dinsmoor, Samuel.—He was born at Londonderry, New Hampshire, in 1766; graduated at Dartmouth College in 1789; was for many years a Major-General of militia; a Representative in Congress, from New Hampshire, from 1811 to 1813; a Judge of Probate; and served as Governor of his native State during the years 1831, 1832, and 1833. He died at Keene, March 15, 1835.

Disney, David T.—He was a native of Baltimore, Maryland, and removed to Cincinnati, Ohio, in 1820. He was frequently a member of both branches of the State Legislature of Ohio, and three times elected Speaker. He represented his adopted State in Congress, from 1849 to 1855. He died in Washington, March 14, 1857, aged fifty-four years.

Diven, Alexander S.—He was born at the head of Seneca Lake, town of Catharine, and County of Tioga, New York, February 15, 1809; received an academical education; studied law and adopted that profession; was a Senator in the New York Legislature, in 1858; and was elected a Representative, from New York, to the Thirty-seventh Congress, serving as a member of the Committee on the Judiciary.

Dix, John A.—Born in Boscawen, New Hampshire, July 24, 1798. He commenced his education by attending the academies at Salisbury and Exeter; spent one year in a French college at Montreal; and, in 1812, was appointed a cadet in the army, but, instead of going to West Point, preferred to join the army on the frontier as an Ensign; and in 1813, he was acting Adjutant of an independent battalion. In 1819 he was aide-de-camp to Major-General Brown, but devoted his leisure to the study of law; from that time until 1828, he visited Cuba and travelled in Europe for his health, when he settled at Cooperstown, as a lawyer. In 1831 he was Adjutant-General under Governor

Throop; in 1833 he was appointed Secretary of State of New York, and was a Regent of the State University; in 1841 he was elected to the Assembly, from Albany; and after making another visit abroad, was elected to the United States Senate, where he served from 1845 to 1849. Of late years, he has been chiefly engaged in the management of large estate. In 1820 he received from Brown University the degree of Master of Arts, and in 1845, from Geneva College, the degree of Doctor of Laws. In 1860 he was appointed by President Buchanan, Postmaster of New York; and in January, 1861, was appointed by Mr. Buchanan, Secretary of the Treasury. He served in 1861 and 1862 as a Major-General of volunteers, and was appointed to the same position in the regular army.

Dixon, Archibald.—Was born in Caswell County, North Carolina, April 2, 1802, and removed with his father to Henderson County, Kentucky, in 1805. He received only a plain English education at the county schools, but made good use of his advantages, and at the age of twenty, entered upon the study of law, and acquired considerable reputation as a lawyer. In 1830 he was a Representative in the Legislature, and in 1836 in the State Senate, and again in the Lower House in 1841. In 1843 was elected Lieutenant-Governor of Kentucky. In 1849 was a member of the Constitutional Convention for reforming State laws, and was a member of the United States Senate, from 1852 to 1855, being elected to fill the vacancy occasioned by the resignation of his friend, Henry Clay.

Dixon, James.—Born in Enfield, Connecticut, in 1814; graduated at Williams College, Williamstown, Massachusetts, in 1834; is a lawyer by profession; and was a member of the House in the Legislature of Connecticut, in 1837, 1838, and 1844, and of the State Senate in 1849 and 1854; and a Representative in Congress, from 1845 to 1849; also elected a Senator for six years, from March 4, 1857; and he was re-elected for a second term in 1862. He has served on several committees and was Chairman of the Committee on Contingent Expenses of the Senate.

Dixon, Joseph Henry.—A Representative in Congress, from North Carolina, from 1799 to 1801.

Dixon, Nathan F.—Born at Plainfield, Connecticut, in 1774; graduated at Brown University in 1799; studied law, and established himself in Rhode Island, in 1802, to practise his profession. In 1813 he was elected a member of the General Assembly of that State. From 1839 to 1842 he was a Senator of the United States. He died at Washington, District of Columbia, January 29, 1842.

Dixon, Nathan F.—Born in Westerly, Rhode Island, May 1, 1812; fitted for College at Plainfield Academy, in Connecticut, and graduated at Brown University in 1833. He attended the Law Schools at New Haven and Cambridge, and was admitted to the bar in New London in 1837, and engaged in the practice of his profession in Connecticut and Rhode Island. He was a member of the General Assembly of Rhode Island from 1840 to 1849, and was elected a Representative, from Rhode Island, to the Thirty-first Congress. He was again elected to the General Assembly of his State in 1851, and, with the exception of two years, held the office until 1859. In 1863 he was re-elected to the Thirty-eighth Congress, serving as a member of the Committee on Commerce.

Doane, William.—He was born in Maine, and having removed to Ohio, was elected a Representative in Congress, from that State, from 1839 to 1843.

Dobbin, James C.—He was born in 1814; graduated at the University of North Carolina in 1832. He was a lawyer by profession, and was elected a Representative in Congress, from his native State, in 1845, and declined a re-election. He served in the State Legislature in 1848 and 1850, and during the last session officiated as Speaker. His eloquence at the bar and in the legislative hall, is said to have been of the most winning character, and his urbane manners and amiable disposition made him a general favorite. He was Secretary of the Navy during the whole of President Pierce's administration, and he died in Fayetteville, North Carolina, August 4, 1857.

Dockery, A.—He was a native of North Carolina, and a Representative in Congress, from that State, from 1845 to 1847, and again from 1851 to 1853.

Dodd, Edward.—Born in Salem, Washington County, New York, in 1805; was bred a merchant; chosen County Clerk of the County of Washington for three terms of three years each, commencing January 1, 1835; was a member of the Constitutional Convention of New York in 1846; and a Representative in Congress, in 1855, serving on the Committee on the District of Columbia.

Doddridge, Philip.—He was a Representative in Congress, from Virginia, in 1829, and continued in that position until his death, which occurred in Washington, November 19, 1832. He was a distinguished lawyer, and commanded great influence in Congress. He was about sixty years of age.

Dodge, Augustus C.—He was born in Missouri, and was a Delegate to Congress, from the Territory of Iowa, from 1841 to 1847; a Senator in Congress, from the State of Iowa, from 1848 to 1855; after which he received, from President Pierce, the appointment of Minister to Spain, which he resigned. He was a Delegate also to the Chicago Convention of 1864.

Dodge, Henry.—He was born in Indiana, and removing to Wisconsin, served, with great credit, as an officer of volunteers, on the Northwestern frontiers. He distinguished himself especially in the Black Hawk war, and, as an Indian fighter, was thought to have no superior. When the first regiment of dragoons was raised in 1833, he was appointed Colonel, which office he resigned in 1836, when he was appointed Governor of Wisconsin Territory and Superintendent of Indian Affairs. He was a Delegate to Congress, from Wisconsin, from 1841 to 1845, and a Senator in Congress, from the State of Wisconsin, from 1849 to 1857.

Doe, Nicholas B.—Born in New York, and elected a Representative, from that State, to the Twenty-sixth Congress, in place of A. Brown, deceased.

Doig, Andrew W.—He was born in Washington County, New York, and was a Representative in Congress, from that State, from 1839 to 1843, having previously served one year, 1832, in the State Assembly. He was many years a teacher and surveyor, a County Clerk for one year, and held the office of Surrogate from 1835 to 1840. He went to California in 1849, but subsequently returned to his native county.

Doneyelles, Peter.—He was a Representative in Congress, from New York, from 1813 to 1815.

Donnell, Richard S.—He was born in North Carolina, and was a Representative in Congress, from that State, from 1847 to 1849. In 1863 he published a Letter on the Rebellion, which attracted great attention.

Donnelly, Ignatius.—He was born in Philadelphia, Pennsylvania, November 3, 1831; graduated at the Central High School in that city; studied law, and was admitted to the bar in 1853; emigrated to Minnesota in 1857; was elected Lieutenant-Governor of that State in 1859; re-elected in 1861, and in 1862 was elected a Representative, from Minnesota, to the Thirty-eighth Congress, and served on the Committees on the Post-office and Post-roads, and Expenditures in the Interior Department.

Doolittle, J. R.—Born in Hampton, Washington County, New York, January 3, 1815; graduated at Geneva College in 1834; is a lawyer by profession, and was admitted to the Supreme Court of New York in 1837. He was District Attorney, for several years, for Wyoming County, New York; and removed to Wisconsin in 1851; was chosen Judge of the First Judicial Circuit of that State in 1853, but resigned in 1856. He was elected a Senator of the United States in 1857, for six years, serving as Chairman of the Committee on Indian Affairs. He was also a member of the Peace Congress of 1861. In 1863 he was re-elected for the term ending in 1869.

Dorsey, Clement.—He was born

in Anne Arundel County, Maryland, and was a Representative in Congress, from Maryland, from 1825 to 1831. Died August 6, 1846.

Doty, James D.—He was born in New York, was a Delegate to Congress, from the Territory of Wisconsin, from 1839 to 1841, and a Representative in Congress, from the State of Wisconsin, from 1849 to 1853. He was also, for many years, United States Judge for Northern Michigan; also Superintendent of Indian Affairs; and from 1841 to 1844 Governor of Wisconsin.

Doubleday, Ulysses F.—He was born in New York, and was a Representative in Congress, from that State, from 1831 to 1833, and again from 1835 to 1837.

Douglas, Stephen A.—Was born at Brandon, Rutland County, Vermont, April 23, 1813. He lost his father while an infant, and his mother being left in destitute circumstances, he entered a cabinet shop at Middlebury, in his native State, for the purpose of learning the trade. After remaining there for several months, he returned to Brandon, where he continued for a year at the same calling, but his health obliged him to abandon it, and he became a student in the academy. His mother having married a second time, he followed her to Canandaigua, in the State of New York. Here he pursued the study of the law until his removal to Cleveland, Ohio, in 1831. From Cleveland he went still farther west, and finally settled in Jacksonville, Illinois. He was at first employed as clerk to an auctioneer, and afterwards kept school, devoting all the time he could spare to the study of the law. In 1834 he was admitted to the bar, soon obtained a lucrative practice, and was elected Attorney-General of the State. In 1837 he was appointed, by President Van Buren, Register of the Land-office, at Springfield, Illinois. He afterwards practised his profession, and, in 1840, was elected Secretary of State, and the following year Judge of the Supreme Court. This office he resigned, after sitting upon the bench for two years, in consequence of ill health. In 1843 he was elected to Congress, and continued a member of the Lower House for four years. In December, 1847, he was elected to the United States Senate. He was Chairman of the Committee on Territories. In 1860 he was the candidate of his own party for the office of President, but was defeated.

Dowdell, James F.—Born in Jasper County, Georgia, November 26, 1818; graduated at Randolph Macon College in 1840, and is a lawyer by profession; he removed to Alabama in 1846, and took charge of a female college for one year, and afterwards engaged in farming and planting. He was a Representative, from Alabama, in the Thirty-third, Thirty-fourth, and Thirty-fifth Congresses, and was a member of the Committee of Ways and Means, and also that of Inquiry into the Cost of Public Printing and Laws relating thereto.

Downing, Charles.—He was born in Virginia, and was a Delegate to Congress, from the Territory of Florida, from 1837 to 1841. Died October 24, 1841.

Downs, Solomon W.—He was Collector of the Port of New Orleans, and from 1847 to 1853 a Senator in Congress, from Louisiana. He died at Orchard Springs, Kentucky, August 14, 1854.

Dowse, Edward.—He was a Representative in Congress, from Massachusetts, from 1819 to 1821.

Drake, John R.—He was one of the earliest settlers in Tioga County, New York; was a Representative in Congress, from that State, from 1817 to 1819; was elected Judge of Tioga County in 1833; and was a member of the New York Assembly in 1834. He was in ill health for eight years before his death, which occurred at Oswego, March 21, 1857, in the seventy-fourth year of his age.

Draper, Joseph.—He was a Representative in Congress, from Virginia, from 1830 to 1831, and again from 1832 to 1833.

Drayton, William.—Born in St. Augustine, Florida, December 30, 1776; went to school in England, and on returning to South Carolina was for a time Assistant Clerk in a Court of Sessions; studied law, and came to the bar in 1797; was a Captain in the South Carolina militia; in 1812 was commissioned a Colonel in the United States Army, and Inspector-General in 1814; assisted Generals Scott and Macomb in preparing a System of Infantry Tactics for the army; was elected Recorder of Charleston in 1819; was a Representative in Congress, from South Carolina, from 1825 to 1833; and was chosen President of the United States Bank in 1840. Died in Philadelphia, May 24, 1846.

Driggs, John F.—Was born in Kinderhook, New York, March 3, 1813; was apprenticed to a mechanical business connected with building in New York City, and was a master mechanic until 1856; in 1844 he was appointed Superintendent of the New York Penitentiary, holding the office one year; settled in East Saginaw, Michigan, in 1856; was President of that village in 1858; during the two following years he was a member of the Michigan Legislature; and in 1862 he was elected a Representative, from Michigan, to the Thirty-eighth Congress, and was a member of the Committee on Public Lands.

Drum, Augustus.—He was born in Pennsylvania, and was a Representative in Congress, from that State, from 1853 to 1855.

Drumgoole, George C.—He was born in Virginia; educated a lawyer; and was a Representative in Congress, from Virginia, from 1835 to 1841, and also from 1843 to 1847; and died April 28, 1847.

Dudley, Charles E.—He was born in Rhode Island, but early settled in Albany, New York. He was a merchant by occupation, and attained great wealth. He was at one time Mayor of Albany, served in the New York Legislature from 1820 to 1825, and was a Senator in Congress, from that State, from 1828 to 1833. Died at Albany, January 23, 1841. His widow founded an astronomical observatory at Albany, to which she gave the name of her husband.

Dudley, Edward B.—He was a Representative in Congress, from 1829 to 1831; and in 1836 was elected the first Governor of North Carolina under the amended Constitution of that State. He was subsequently appointed President of the Wilmington and Raleigh Railroad Company, and died at Wilmington, North Carolina, in November, 1855.

Duell, R. Holland.—Born in Warren, Herkimer County, New York, December 20, 1823; received an academic education; studied law and was admitted to the bar in 1845; in 1850 he was elected District Attorney for Cortland County, and held the office six years; in 1856 he was elected County Judge for said county; and in 1858 he was elected a Representative, from New York, to the Thirty-sixth Congress, serving as a member of the Committee on Revolutionary Claims. Re-elected to the Thirty-seventh Congress, serving as Chairman of the Committee on Revolutionary Pensions.

Duer, William.—Born in the city of New York, May 25, 1805. He graduated at Columbia College in 1824; studied law, and in 1828, removed to Oswego, soon after returning to New York; he subsequently removed to New Orleans, and again returned to Oswego; he served in the Legislature of New York on two occasions; was District Attorney for Oswego County, and a Representative in Congress, from 1847 to 1851.

Dumont, Ebenezer.—Born in Vevay, Switzerland County, Territory of Indiana, November 23, 1814; attended the Indiana University at Bloomington, but did not graduate; adopted the profession of law; was a member of the State Legislature in 1838; from 1839 to 1845 was Treasurer of his county; served in the war with Mexico as a Lieutenant-Colonel, and was in several battles; was a Presidential Elector in 1852; in 1850 and 1853 he was again elected to the Legislature; was President for nine years of the State Bank of Indiana; when the Rebellion broke out, he was appointed Colonel of the Seventh Indiana Volunteers, and was at the battle of Philippi in West Virginia; was subsequently in charge of a brigade at Murfreesboro, and after the battle at that place, was assigned to the command of the troops at Nashville; from that place he led an expedition against John Morgan, taking nearly his whole command; and in 1862, while yet in the field, he was elected a Representative, from Indiana, to the Thirty-eighth Congress, serving on the Committees on the District of Columbia, and on Revolutionary Pensions.

Dunbar, William.—He was a Representative in Congress, from Louisiana, from 1853 to 1855.

Duncan, Alexander.—He was a member of the House of Representatives in Congress, from Ohio, from 1837 to 1841, and from 1843 to 1845. He died in Cincinnati, Ohio, March 2, 1852.

Duncan, Daniel.—Born in the town of Shippensburg, Cumberland County, Pennsylvania, July 22, 1806, and died in Washington, June 18, 1849. He was bred a merchant, and in 1843 was elected to the Legislature of Ohio, from Licking County. He was a Representative in Congress from 1847 to 1849; and more a man of action than of words.

Duncan, Garnett.—He was born in Kentucky, and was a Representative in Congress, from that State, from 1847 to 1849.

Duncan, James H.—He was born in Haverhill, Massachusetts, December 5, 1793; adopted the profession of law; served four years in the State Legislature; was a State Senator from 1828 to 1831; State Councillor in 1840 and 1841; and was a Representative in Congress, from his native State, from 1849 to 1853.

Duncan, Joseph.—He served in the army with credit during the late war with England; held various offices of distinction and trust; was at one time Governor of Illinois, and a Representative in Congress, from that State, from 1827 to 1835. He died at Jacksonville, Illinois, January 15, 1844.

Dunham, Cyrus L.—He is a native of New York State. As a farmer's boy he worked laboriously during the summer months, to obtain means for his education during the winter; after acquiring the rudiments, he filled the humblest position on board a fishing craft from one of the seaports of Massachusetts to Newfoundland, and after completing his studies, he removed to Salem, Indiana, taught school and studied law, and was admitted to the bar. He was elected to the Legislature of Indiana, in 1846 and 1847, and was a Representative in Congress, from that State, from 1849 to 1855.

Dunlap, George W.—He was born in Fayette County, Kentucky, February 22, 1813; graduated at Transylvania University, Lexington; studied law and adopted that profession; was a member of the Kentucky Legislature; also of the Border State Convention held in May, 1861; and was elected a Representative, from Kentucky, to the Thirty-seventh Congress, serving as Chairman of the Committee on the Navy Department, and also as a member of the Committee on Accounts.

Dunlap, Robert P.—He was born in Maine; graduated at Bowdoin College in 1815; studied law and was admitted to the bar in 1818; in 1821, 1822, and 1823, was a member of the State Legislature; in 1823 he was elected a State Senator, serving nine years, and presided over that body four years; in 1833 he was a member of the Executive Council of Maine; in 1834 he was elected Governor of Maine, and served four years; and he was a Representative in Congress, from 1843 to 1847. During the years 1848 and 1849, he was Collector of Customs for Portland; and from 1853 to 1857, Postmaster of Brunswick; after which he became President of the Board of Overseers of Bowdoin College. Died in Brunswick, Maine, October 20, 1859, aged seventy years.

Dunlap, William C.—He was born in Tennessee, and was a Representative in Congress, from that State, from 1833 to 1837.

Dunn, George G.—He was born in 1813, and died in Lawrence County, Indiana, in September, 1857. He had held many high official trusts, and was a Representative in Congress, from 1847 to 1849. He was a lawyer, and noted for his abilities as an orator.

Dunn, George H.—He was a Representative in Congress, from Indiana, from 1837 to 1839.

Dunn, William McKee.—Born in the Territory of Indiana, December 12, 1814; graduated at the State College of Indiana in 1832; taught school for two years, and having entered Yale College, received from College the degree of A. M. in 1835; adopted the profession of law; was elected to the Indiana Legislature in 1848; a member of the State Constitutional Convention in 1850; and in 1858 was elected a Representative, from Indiana, to the Thirty-sixth Congress, serving on the Committees on Manufactures and Roads and Canals. Re-elected to the Thirty-seventh Congress, serving as Chairman of the Committee on Patents, after which he became a Judge-Advocate in the army.

Durell, Daniel M.—He was born in Massachusetts; graduated at Dartmouth College in 1794; studied law and entered upon the practice at Dover in 1797; and was a Representative in Congress, from New Hampshire, from 1807 to 1809. He also held the post of United States District Attorney from 1830 to 1834. He died in 1841, aged seventy-one years.

Durfee, Job.—He was born at Tiverton, Rhode Island, in 1790; graduated at Brown University in 1813; adopted the profession of the law; and though for a long time Chief Justice of Rhode Island, he devoted much attention to poetry and belles-lettres generally. He was a Representative in Congress, from Rhode Island, from 1821 to 1825. He died in 1847.

Durfee, Nathaniel B.—He was born in Tiverton, Rhode Island, September 29, 1812; received a good classical education at Newport; from 1838 to 1850 devoted himself to the pursuits of agriculture; he represented the town of Warwick, some seven or eight years, in the State Legislature, and the town of Tiverton, four years; and, having been elected a member of the Thirty-fourth Congress, served his term, and was re-elected to the Thirty-fifth Congress, serving on the Committee on Manufactures.

Durkee, Charles.—Born in Royalton, Vermont, December 5, 1807; was a merchant; removed to Wisconsin, and was elected to the Legislature of that State in 1837 and 1838; a Representative in Congress in 1848 and 1850; and a United States Senator for six years, commencing March, 1855, serving as a member of the Committees on Revolutionary and Private Land Claims. He was a Delegate also to the Peace Congress of 1861.

Duval, William P.—Born in Virginia in 1784, but in early life went to Kentucky, where he studied and practised law; he was a Representative in Congress, from 1813 to 1815; and in 1822 was appointed Governor of Florida by President Monroe, and reappointed by Adams and Jackson. In 1848 he removed to Texas; and died in Washington, District of Columbia, March 19, 1854.

Duvall, Gabriel.—He was born in 1751, of a Huguenot family; served as a clerk to the first Legislature of Maryland, before the Declaration of Independence; he was a Representative in Congress, from Maryland, from 1794 to 1796; Comptroller of the United States Treasury in 1802; and in 1811 was appointed a Judge of the Supreme Court of the State, which office he held for twenty years. He died in Prince George County, Maryland, March 6, 1844.

Dwight, Henry W.—Born in Berkshire County, Massachusetts; was a member of the Massachusetts Legislature in 1818 and 1834; and a Representative in Congress, from Massachusetts, from 1821 to 1831, and died in New York, February 21, 1845.

Dwight, Theodore.—Born in Northampton, Massachusetts, in 1765. Soon after the Revolution he studied law, and attained a high position as a lawyer; for a great number of years he was a State Senator in Connecticut; and he was a Representative in Congress, during the years 1806 and 1807. He was a ready and brilliant writer; conducted for a time the Hartford Mirror; was Secretary of the Hartford Convention, of which he wrote the authentic history; in 1815, at the suggestion of leading men, he established the Albany Daily Advertiser; and in 1817 founded the New York Daily Advertiser, which he conducted with signal ability until 1836, when he removed to Hartford, Connecticut, and retired from active life. About three years before his death he went to New York to reside with his son, and died in that city, June 11, 1846.

Dwight, Thomas.—He graduated at Harvard University in 1778; was a member of the Massachusetts Legislature in 1794 and 1795; a State Senator from 1796 to 1803 and 1813; and a member of the Executive Council in 1808 and 1809; and was a Representative in Congress, from Massachusetts, from 1803 to 1805; and died in 1819.

Dwinell, Justin.—He graduated at Yale College in 1805; was a member of the New York Assembly in 1821 and 1822; and was a Representative in Congress, from that State, from 1823 to 1825.

Eager, S. W.—He graduated at Princeton College in 1809; and was a Representative in Congress, from New York, from 1829 to 1831.

Earle, Elias.—He was born in Frederick County, Virginia, and was a Representative in Congress, from South Carolina, from 1805 to 1807, from 1811 to 1815, and again from 1817 to 1821.

Earle, John B.—He was a Representative in Congress, from South Carolina, from 1803 to 1805.

Earle, Samuel.—He was a Representative in Congress, from South Carolina, from 1795 to 1797.

Earll, Jonas.—Born in 1786; was at one time a Senator in the New York Legislature; a member of Congress, from that State, from 1827 to 1831; and a Canal Commissioner at the time of his death, which occurred at Syracuse, New York, in October, 1846.

Earll, Nehemiah H.—He was born in New York, and was a Representative in Congress, from that State, from 1839 to 1841.

Early, Peter.—Born in Madison County, Virginia, June 20, 1773, and emigrated to Georgia with his father in 1795. He graduated at Nassau Hall, Princeton, and studied law in Philadelphia. He served in the United States House of Representatives, from Georgia, from 1802 to 1807; and was one of the most conspicuous among its members who supported the Administration. On his return to Georgia, he was made a Judge of the Supreme Court of the State, and in 1813 was elected Governor of his adopted State. He was subsequently a State Senator, but for several years before his death lived in retirement. He died August 15, 1817.

Easterbrook, Experience.—Born in Lebanon, Grafton County, New Hampshire, April 30, 1813; received a good academic education; studied law in Buffalo, and graduated at the Law School of Marshall College, Pennsylvania; removed to Wisconsin in 1840, where he practised his profession until 1854; besides holding a number of county offices he was a member of the Convention that formed the Constitution of that State; served also in the Legislature of Wisconsin, and was Attorney-General of the State. In 1854 he was appointed United States District Attorney for the Territory of Nebraska, which office he held until 1859, when he was elected a Delegate to the Thirty-sixth Congress from Nebraska.

Eastman, Benjamin C.—A Representative in Congress, from Wisconsin, from 1851 to 1855. He died February 5, 1856, at Platteville, in that State.

Eastman, Ira A.—He was born in New Hampshire; graduated in Dartmouth College in 1829; served in the State Legislature, and was Speaker of the House from 1837 to 1839; he was at one time Secretary of the State Senate; Register of Probate; and from 1844 to 1859 was a Judge of the Circuit and Supreme Court; and elected a Representative in Congress, from New Hampshire, from 1839 to 1843.

Eastman, Nehemiah.—Was born in Strafford County, New Hampshire; was a lawyer by profession; settled at Farmington, New Hampshire; was a Senator in the State Legislature from 1820 to 1825; a Representative in Congress, from New Hampshire, from 1825 to 1827. Died January 11, 1856, aged sixty-five years.

Easton, Rufus.—He was a Delegate to Congress, from Missouri Territory, from 1814 to 1816.

Eaton, John H.—He was a Senator in Congress, from Tennessee, from 1818 to 1829; was Secretary of War under President Jackson (as well as a warm personal friend), from 1829 to 1831; from 1834 to 1836 was Governor of the Territory of Florida; and from 1836 to 1840, Minister Plenipotentiary to Spain. He died in Washington, District of Columbia, November 17, 1856, aged sixty-six years.

Eaton, Lewis.—He was a Representative in Congress, from New York, from 1823 to 1825.

Eckert, George N.—He was born in Pennsylvania, and was a Representative in Congress, from that State, from 1847 to 1849.

Eckley, Ephraim R. — Born in Jefferson County, Ohio, December 9, 1812; received his education in the West; read law, and came to the bar in 1837; was a member of the Ohio Senate in 1843, 1845, and 1849, serving until 1851; and in 1853 he was elected to the State House of Representatives. After the Rebellion broke out he had charge, as Colonel, of the Twenty-sixth and Eightieth Regiments of Ohio volunteers, serving through several battles, and at the battle of Corinth he had command of a brigade. In 1862 he was elected a Representative, from Ohio, to the Thirty-eighth Congress, serving on the Committees on Private Land Claims, and on Roads and Canals; and in March, 1863, resigned his position in the army.

Eddy, Norman.—He was born in New York, and having removed to Indiana, was a Representative in Congress, from that State, from 1853 to 1855.

Eddy, Samuel.—Born in Providence, Rhode Island, March 31, 1769; graduated at Brown University in 1787; studied law, but did not long engage in practice. In 1798 he was chosen Secretary of State, and held the office for twenty-one years, when he resigned, and was elected a Representative in Congress, from his native State, from 1819 to 1825. He was subsequently Chief Justice of the Supreme Court of Rhode Island, for eight years. He devoted some attention to literary pursuits, and published a work on "Antiquities," and was honored, in 1801, with the degree of LL.D. He died in Providence, February 3, 1839.

Eden, John R.—Was born in Bath County, Kentucky, February 1, 1826; went with his parents at an early age to Indiana, and received a common school education; studied law, and commenced the practice of it in Illinois. In 1856 he was appointed State Attorney for the Seventeenth District, which office he held four years; and in 1862 he was elected a Representative, from Illinois, to the Thirty-eighth Congress, serving as a member of the Committees on Accounts and Revolutionary Pensions.

Edgerton, Alfred P. — He was born in New York, and removing to Ohio, was elected a Representative in Congress, from that State, from 1851 to 1855.

Edgerton, Joseph Ketchum.—Born in Vergennes, Vermont, February 16, 1818; spent his youth in Clinton County, New York, and received a common school education, chiefly at Plattsburg; read law; settled in New York City in 1835, and came to the bar in 1839, and removed to Fort Wayne, Indiana, in 1844. In 1855 he was President of the Fort Wayne and Chicago Railroad Company, and subsequently financial agent of the same when consolidated with the Pittsburg road, and in 1862 he was elected a Representative, from Indiana, to the Thirty-eighth Congress, serving on the Committee on Naval Affairs.

Edgerton, Sidney.—Born in Cazenovia, Madison County, New York, in 1818; became an orphan when a mere boy, and acquired an academic education by means of his own exertions, teaching school and studying at the same time; removed to Ohio in 1844 and studied law, spending one year at the Law School in Cincinnati; he was a Prosecuting Attorney for four years in Summit County; and was elected a Representative, from Ohio, to the Thirty-sixth Congress, serving as a member of the Committee on the District of Columbia. Re-elected to the Thirty-seventh Congress, serving on the Committees on Revolutionary Claims and

Private Land Claims. He was appointed by President Lincoln a Judge for the Territory of Idaho, and subsequently Governor of Montana.

Edie, John R.—He was born in Pennsylvania, and elected a Representative to the Thirty-fourth and Thirty-fifth Congresses, serving as a member of the Committee on Patents.

Edmond, William.—Born at South Britain, Connecticut, September 28, 1755, and graduated at Yale College in 1773. He was a volunteer soldier at the burning of Danbury, and received a wound in the leg, which made him lame for life. He was a lawyer by profession; was chosen a member of the Legislature, member of the Council, and Judge of the Supreme Court of the State; and a member of Congress, from 1798 to 1801. He died in Newton, Connecticut, August 1, 1838.

Edmonds, J. Wiley.—He was born in Massachusetts, and was a Representative in Congress, from that State, from 1853 to 1855.

Edmundson, Henry A.—He was born in Virginia, and having been elected a Representative in Congress, from that State, in 1849, has been re-elected to each successive Congress, serving in the Thirty-sixth Congress as a member of the Committee on Public Expenditures.

Edsall, Joseph E.—He was born in Sussex County, New Jersey, and was elected a Representative in Congress, from that State, from 1837 to 1839. He was also a member of the State Legislature, and of the Convention which framed the last State Constitution.

Edwards, Benjamin.—Born in Stafford County, Virginia, in 1752, and died in Todd County, Kentucky, November 13, 1826. He had not the advantage of a classical education, and his pursuits were those of agriculture and merchandise. He was a member of the Maryland Legislature; also of the State Convention which ratified the Federal Constitution; and a member of Congress, from Maryland, from 1793 to 1795. He spent the later years of his life in Kentucky, but held no public positions in that State.

Edwards, Francis S.—He was born in Norwich, Connecticut, May 28, 1818; adopted the profession of law; and removing to New York, was appointed a Master in Chancery in 1841 for the County of Chenango; in 1851 was elected Surrogate of Chautauque County; and in 1854 to the Thirty-fourth Congress.

Edwards, Henry W.—He was born at New Haven, Connecticut, in 1779; graduated at Princeton College in 1797; studied his profession at the Litchfield Law School, and settled in New Haven. He was a Representative in Congress, from 1819 to 1823; United States Senator from 1823 to 1827; member of the State Senate in 1828 and 1829; Speaker of the Connecticut House of Representatives in 1830; Governor in 1833, and from 1835 to 1838; and upon his recommendation a geological survey of the State was taken. He died in New Haven, July 22, 1847.

Edwards, John.—He was a Senator in Congress, from Kentucky, from 1792 to 1795.

Edwards, John.—He was born in New York, and was a Representative in Congress, from that State, from 1837 to 1843.

Edwards, John.—He was a Representative in Congress, from Pennsylvania, from 1839 to 1843, and died in Chester, Pennsylvania, June 25, 1843.

Edwards, John C.—He was a Representative in Congress, from Missouri, from 1841 to 1843, and Governor of that State, from 1844 to 1848.

Edwards, Ninian.—Born in Montgomery County, Maryland, March, 1775. He was in early life the intimate friend of William Wirt, and graduated at Dickinson College. He studied both medicine and law, but devoted himself to the practice of the law with eminent success. Removing to Kentucky, he was twice elected to the Legislature; was appointed a Circuit Clerk, and subsequently Judge of the General Court of Kentucky, of the Circuit Court, of the Court of Appeals, and, finally, Chief Justice of the State, and all before reaching the thirty-second year of his age. In 1809 President Madison appointed him Governor of the Territory of Illinois, to which office he was three times reappointed. Before Congress had adopted any measures on the subject of volunteer rangers, he organized companies, supplied them with arms, built stockade forts, and established a line of posts from the mouth of the Missouri to the Wabash River. He was thus prepared for defence, and during the Indian wars on the frontiers, was most devoted to his country's service. In 1816 he was appointed a Commissioner to treat with the Indian tribes. When Illinois became a State, he was elected a Senator in Congress, serving from 1818 to 1824, when he was appointed Minister to Mexico, but declined the office. In 1826 he was elected Governor of the State of Illinois, which office he filled until 1831. He died of cholera, July 20, 1833.

Edwards, Samuel.—He was born in Delaware County, Pennsylvania, and was a Representative in Congress, from that State, from 1819 to 1827.

Edwards, Thomas M.—Born in Cheshire, New Hampshire; graduated at Dartmouth College; adopted the profession of law; served eight years in the New Hampshire Legislature, between the years 1834 and 1856; was a Presidential Elector in 1856; and in 1859 was elected a Representative from New Hampshire to the Thirty-sixth Congress, serving as a member of the Committee on Indian Affairs. Re-elected to the Thirty-seventh Congress.

Edwards, Thomas O.—He was born in Maryland, and having taken up his residence in Ohio, was elected a Representative in Congress, from that State, from 1847 to 1849.

Edwards, Weldon N.—Born in Northampton County, North Carolina, in 1788; educated at Warrenton Academy; read law, and came to the bar in 1810; was in the Legislature for two years; and was a member of Congress, from 1816 to 1827. He again went into the Legislature, serving there from 1833 to 1844; and was re-elected in 1850, when he was made President of the State Senate.

Effner, Valentine.—He was born in New York; a member of the Assembly of that State in 1829; and a Representative in Congress, from 1835 to 1837.

Egbert, Joseph.—He was born in New York, and was a Representative in Congress, from that State, from 1841 to 1843.

Ege, George.—He was a Representative in Congress, from Pennsylvania, during the years 1796 and 1797.

Eggleston, Joseph.—Born in Amelia County, Virginia, November 24, 1754, and died February 15, 1811. He was educated at the College of William and Mary; served in the Revolutionary war as a Captain and Major of cavalry under Colonel Henry Lee; was in several of the battles fought by Gates and Greene; he served in the Virginia Assembly for several years; and was a Representative in Congress, from 1798 to 1801. From the time of his leaving Congress until his death, he was a Justice of the Peace.

Eldredge, Charles A.—He was born in Bridgeport, Addison County, Vermont, February 27, 1821. When a child he removed with his parents to St. Lawrence County, New York; studied law in that State, and came to the bar in 1846. In 1848 he removed to Fond du Lac, Wisconsin; in 1854 and 1855 he was a member of the State Senate; and in 1862 he was elected a Representative from Wisconsin to the Thirty-eighth Congress, serving on the Committee on Revolutionary Claims.

Eliot, Samuel A.—Born in Boston, Massachusetts, March 5, 1798; educated at Harvard College, and engaged in commercial and manufacturing business. He was Mayor of Boston, from 1837 to 1839; Representative and Senator in the Legislature for three or four years; and a Representative in Congress, from 1850 to 1851. He was also Treasurer of Harvard College eleven years. Died at Cambridge in 1861.

Eliot, Thomas D.—Born in Boston, Massachusetts, March 20, 1808; graduated at Columbia College, Washington, in 1825; adopted the profession of law, and settled at New Bedford; served in both houses of the Massachusetts Legislature; served as a Representative in Congress for the unexpired term of Zeno Scudder, in 1855; and was elected a Representative, from Massachusetts, to the Thirty-sixth Congress, serving on the Committee on Commerce; re-elected to the Thirty-seventh Congress, serving as Chairman of the Special Committee on Confiscation of the property of rebels; and was re-elected to the Thirty-eighth Congress, serving on the Committees on Commerce and on Expenditures in the Treasury Department.

Ellery, Christopher.—He graduated at Yale College in 1787; was a Senator in Congress, from Rhode Island, from 1801 to 1805; and was appointed, in the latter year, United States Commissioner of Loans. He was appointed Collector of Newport in 1828; and died in 1840.

Ellicott, Benjamin.—He was a Representative in Congress, from New York, from 1817 to 1819.

Elliot, John.—He graduated at Yale College in 1794; resided in Sunbury, Liberty County, Georgia, and was a Senator in Congress, from that State, from 1819 to 1825, serving on several important committees. He died August 9, 1827.

Elliot, Thomas D.—He was born in Massachusetts; adopted the profession of law; was a State Senator in 1846; and was a Representative in Congress, from Massachusetts, from 1854 to 1855. He was also elected to the Thirty-sixth Congress in 1859.

Elliott, James.—He was a Representative in Congress, from Vermont, from 1803 to 1809, and died at Newfane, Vermont, November 10, 1839.

Elliott, John M.—Born in Scott County, Virginia, May 16, 1820. He was educated in the county schools of Kentucky; studied law, and commenced the practice in 1843; was elected to the State Legislature in 1847; and in 1853 was elected a Representative in Congress, serving as Chairman of the Committee on Public Expenditures.

Ellis, Caleb.—Born at Walpole, Massachusetts, and graduated at Harvard College in 1793; when admitted to the bar he settled at Claremont, New Hampshire. He was a Representative in Congress, from 1805 to 1809; was a member of the Council, and in 1811 elected to the State Senate. In 1812 he was one of the Electors of President and Vice-President; and in 1813 was Judge of the Supreme Court of New Hampshire, and continued in that office until his death, which occurred May 9, 1816, aged forty-nine years.

Ellis, Cheselden.—He was born in New York, and was a Representative in Congress, from that State, from 1843 to 1845.

Ellis, Powhatan.—He was born in Virginia, but removing at an early day to Mississippi, there devoted himself to the practice of law. He became one of the Judges of the Supreme Court of that State; in 1825 he was appointed to a seat in the United States Senate, but was displaced by the Legislature; in 1827, however, the Legislature elected him a Senator in Congress, where he served until 1833. In 1836 he was appointed Chargé d'Affaires to Mexico, and in 1839 full Minister to that republic.

Ellis, William C.—He was a Representative in Congress, from Pennsylvania, from 1823 to 1825.

Ellison, Andrew.—He was born in Ireland, and having emigrated to Ohio, was elected a Representative in Congress, from 1853 to 1855.

Ellsworth, Oliver.—Born at Windsor, Connecticut, April 29, 1745, and graduated at Princeton College, New Jersey, in 1766. He studied law, and soon became eminent in the practice. In 1777 he was chosen a Delegate in Congress, from Connecticut. In 1780 he was elected to the Council of Connecticut, and was a member of that body till 1784, when he was appointed a Judge of the Superior Court of that State. In 1787 he was elected a member of the Convention which framed the Federal Constitution. In an assembly illustrious for talents, erudition, and patriotism, he held a distinguished place. His exertions essentially aided in the production of an instrument which has been the main pillar of American prosperity and glory. He was afterwards a member of the State Convention of Connecticut, and contributed his efforts toward procuring the ratification of the Constitution by that State. When the Federal Government was organized, in 1789, he was a member of the Senate, from Connecticut. In 1796 he was appointed, by Washington, Chief Justice of the Supreme Court of the United States, but resigned the office, on account of ill health, in 1800. In 1799 he was appointed, by President Adams, Envoy Extraordinary to France, for the purpose of settling a treaty with that nation. He received the degree of LL.D., in 1790, from Yale College, and in 1797 from Dartmouth. He died November 26, 1807.

Ellsworth, Samuel S.—He was born in Vermont; was a member of the New York Assembly in 1840, and a Representative in Congress, from that State, from 1845 to 1847.

Ellsworth, William W.—He was born in Windsor, Hartford County, Connecticut, November 10, 1791; graduated at Yale College in 1810; adopted the profession of law, and was Professor of Law in Trinity College, and was a Representative in Congress, from Connecticut, from 1829 to 1833. In 1838 he was elected Governor of Connecticut, and re-elected four years; and for many years past has been a Judge of the Supreme Court of Connecticut.

Elmaker, Amos.—He was a native of Pennsylvania, and a lawyer by profession; was an officer in the army which marched from Pennsylvania to the defence of Baltimore in 1812. He was a Representative in Congress, from the Dauphin District of Pennsylvania, from 1814 to 1815, having been elected to fill the vacancy caused by the resignation of James Whitehill. He was appointed President Judge of the Dauphin, Lebanon, and Schuylkill District; was Attorney-General of the State; and in 1832 was a candidate for the Vice-Presidency of the United States. He retired from the active duties of his profession, and resided in Lancaster City, where he died in 1851. Some authorities give this name as Slaymaker; but it is presumed that the above spelling is correct.

Elmendorf, Lucas.—He graduated at Princeton in 1782, and was a Representative in Congress, from New York, from 1797 to 1803; a member of the Assembly of that State in 1804 and 1805; and a State Senator from 1814 to 1817.

Elmer, Ebenezer.—He was born in Cedarville, New Jersey, in 1752; was educated a physician; was a field-officer in the Revolutionary war; also a surgeon in the army; was President of the Society of the Cincinnati for New Jersey; a Representative in Congress, from that State, from 1801 to 1807; served a number of years in the State Assembly, and was chosen Speaker; he was also for a long time Adjutant-General of the New Jersey militia; during the war of 1812, he commanded the troops on the Delaware; in 1807 and 1815 he was a member and Vice-President of the State Council; in 1808 he was appointed Collector of Bridgeton, and held the office for many years; and he died at Bridgeton, New Jersey, October 18, 1843. He was one who always seemed to think more of his duty as a public officer than of his private interests.

Elmer, Jonathan.—He was born in Cumberland County, New Jersey, in 1745; was a prominent physician, and practised in his native county, having graduated with honors at the University of Pennsylvania; was a member of the Continental Congress; and a Senator in Congress under the Federal Constitution, from 1789 to 1791. During the Revolution, he was a Sheriff, a Surrogate, and a Judge; was a man of learning, and member of the Philosophical Society of America. He died in 1817.

Elmer, Lucius Q. C.—Born in Bridgeton, New Jersey, in 1793; graduated at Princeton College; was educated a lawyer, which profession he practised in his native town. For many years he was Prosecutor for the State; was in the Assembly from 1820 to 1823, the last year being Speaker of that body; and in 1824 he was appointed Attorney of the United States for New Jersey, which office he filled until 1829. He was a Representative in Congress, from New Jersey, from 1843 to 1845; in 1850 was appointed Attorney-General of the State; and in 1852 one of the Justices of the Supreme Court of his State, which office he continued to hold until 1859.

Elmore, Franklin Harper.—Born in Laurens District, South Carolina, in 1799; entered South Carolina College in November, 1817, and graduated in 1819; he was a lawyer by profession, and admitted to the bar in 1821; was a Colonel of militia, and also a Trustee of the South Carolina College. In 1822 he was elected Solicitor of the Southern Circuit, and was continued in this office, by re-elections, until 1837, when he was elected to the House of Representatives in Congress, and served till 1839; he was that year elected President of the Bank of the State of South Carolina, which office he held till his nomination to the Senate in 1850, to fill the vacancy occasioned by the death of the Hon. John C. Calhoun. His voice was heard but once in the Senate, and then in answering to his name when called by the Secretary. He died in Washington, District of Columbia, May 29, 1850.

Ely, Alfred.—Was born in Lyme, New London County, Connecticut, February 18, 1815; removed to Rochester, New York, in 1835; studied law, and was admitted to the bar in 1841, where he has since practised his profession. In 1840, while a student at law, he was appointed Clerk of the Recorder's Court of Rochester; in 1858 was elected a Representative, from New York, to the Thirty-sixth Congress; was re-elected, and while in the Thirty-seventh Congress served as Chairman of the Committee on Invalid Pensions. In July, 1861, he was a witness of the battle of Bull Run, where he was captured and taken as a prisoner of war to Richmond; after a confinement of more than five months, he was exchanged in December, 1861, for the Hon. Charles J. Faulkner, the American Minister to France, who had been imprisoned for disloyalty. After his return home, Mr. Ely published a book with this title, "Journal of Alfred Ely, a Prisoner of War in Richmond," edited by the author of this Dictionary.

Ely, John.—He was born in Connecticut, and was a Representative in Congress, from New York, from 1839 to 1841, having previously served two years in the Assembly of that State.

Ely, William.—He graduated at Yale College in 1787; was a Representative in Congress, from Massachusetts, from 1805 to 1815, and died in 1817.

Embree, Elisha.—Born in Lincoln County, Kentucky, September 28, 1801, and removed with his father, in 1811, to the southwestern portion of Indiana Territory, where he has continued to reside. He received a common school education, after which he studied and practised law. In 1813 he was elected to the State Senate of Indiana; in 1835 was chosen, by the Legislature, Circuit Judge, which office he held for ten years. In 1847 he was elected Representative in the Thirtieth Congress, and after the expiration of that term became engaged in agricultural pursuits. Died at Princeton, New Jersey, March 7, 1863.

Emott, James.—Born in Albany, New York, in 1770; he did not receive a collegiate education, but in 1800 Union College conferred on him the degree of A. M. He was a distinguished member of the bar, and under the old Constitution of New York he, for several years, filled the office of first Judge of the Court of Common Pleas for his county, and in that capacity gave that court a rank among the best of the State. Under the Constitution of 1821 he was appointed Judge for the Second District, which station he filled until he reached the age of sixty years, which required him to retire. He was a Representative in Congress, from his native State, from 1809 to 1813, and died in Poughkeepsie, April 7, 1850.

Emrie, J. Reece.—He was born in Ohio, and elected a Representative, from that State, to the Thirty-fourth Congress.

English, James E.—Was born in New Haven, Connecticut, in March, 1812; entered early in life into mercantile pursuits, and continued to do business as a merchant until 1855; since which he has been extensively engaged in several branches of manufacture. In 1855 he was a member of the Legislature; in 1856 was elected to the State Senate, and declined a re-election; was a candidate for Lieutenant-Governor of Connecticut in 1860, but was not elected; and was elected a Representative, from his native State, to the Thirty-seventh Congress; and re-elected to the Thirty-eighth Congress, serving on the Committees on Public Lands, and Expenditures in the State Department.

English, William H.—Born in Scott County, Indiana, August 27, 1822. He received a good common school education, and spent three years at the University of South Hanover; studied law, and was admitted to practice in 1845, but when at home is chiefly devoted to agricultural pursuits; in 1843 he was elected Clerk of the House of Representatives of Indiana; during President Polk's administration he was a Clerk in the Treasury Department; he was the Clerk of the State Constitutional Convention in 1850; in 1851 he was elected to the State Legislature, and officiated as Speaker; in 1852 he was elected a Representative in Congress, re-elected in 1854, and made a Regent of the Smithsonian Institution; again elected in 1856, and during the first session of the Thirty-fifth Congress took part in the Kansas Compromise measure, and officiated at the same time as Chairman of the Committee on Post-offices and Post-roads. He was re-elected to the Thirty-sixth Congress, serving on the Committee on Post-offices and Post-roads.

Eppes, John W.—He was a Representative in Congress, from Virginia, from 1803 to 1811, and again from 1813 to 1815; was a Senator in Congress from 1817 to 1819, when he resigned from ill health; he died near Richmond, Virginia, September, 1823, aged fifty years.

Erdman, Jacob.—He was born in Pennsylvania, and was a Representative in Congress, from that State, from 1845 to 1847.

Ervin, James.—Born in South Carolina in October, 1778; graduated at Brown University in 1797; studied law, and admitted to the bar in 1800; served in the State Legislature in 1801 and 1802, and from 1804 to 1816; was a Solicitor of the Northern Circuit; eight years a Trustee of the South Carolina College; a Representative in Congress, from South Carolina, from 1817 to 1821, and died in 1841.

Estill, Benjamin.—He was born in Washington County, Virginia, and was a Representative in Congress, from Virginia, from 1825 to 1827.

Etheridge, Emerson.—He was born in Currituck, North Carolina, September 28, 1819; when thirteen years of age he removed to Tennessee, where he received a common school education; and having studied law, was admitted to the bar in 1840. In 1845 he was elected to the State Legislature, and was at once nominated for Speaker, which he lost by two votes; re-elected in 1846; and in 1853 he was elected a Representative, from Tennessee, to the Thirty-third Congress, re-elected to the Thirty-fourth, and also to the Thirty-sixth Congress, serving, during his last term, as Chairman of the Committee on Indian Affairs. On the meeting of the Thirty-seventh Congress, he was elected Clerk of the House of Representatives.

Eustis, George, Jr.—He was born in Louisiana, and was educated at Harvard University; practised law in New Orleans, and was elected a Representative to the Thirty-fourth and Thirty-fifth Congresses, serving on the Committee of Commerce.

Eustis, William.—Was born in Cambridge, Massachusetts, June 10, 1753. After graduating at Harvard College in 1772, he studied medicine with Dr. Joseph Warren. At the beginning of the war he was appointed surgeon of a regiment, and afterwards hospital surgeon. In 1777, and during most of the war, he occupied, as a hospital, the spacious house of Colonel Robinson, a royalist, opposite to West Point; Arnold had his headquarters in the same house. At the termination of the war, he commenced the practice of his profession in Boston. In 1800 he was elected a Representative in Congress, from Massachusetts, serving until 1805. In 1809 he was appointed Secretary of War by President Madison, and continued in office until, in the late war, the army of Hull was surrendered, when he resigned. In 1815 he was sent as Ambassador to Holland. After his return, he was a Representative in Congress, from 1820 to 1823. He was chosen Governor of Massachusetts in 1823, and died in Boston, after a short illness, February 6, 1825.

Evans, Alexander.—He was born at Elkton, Cecil County, Maryland, his ancestors having settled in that county more than a hundred years ago. His education was received at a village school, until fifteen years of age, and his first avocation was that of a civil engineer. In 1842 he commenced the study of law in his native town, and was admitted to the bar in 1845. He was a Representative in Congress, from Maryland, from 1847 to 1853, since which time he has practised his profession at Elkton. In 1842 he was elected Corresponding Member of the National Institute at Washington, and in 1849 received the degree of A. M. from Delaware College. In 1851 he was elected a member of the American Association for the Advancement of Science, and also a member of the Historical Society of Baltimore.

Evans, David R.—Born in Westmoreland, England, February 20, 1769; and, having removed to South Carolina, was educated at Mount Zion College; studied law and came to the bar in 1796; served in the State Legislature from 1800 to 1803; from 1804 to 1811 was Solicitor for the Middle District of South Carolina; was a Representative in Congress, from that State, from 1813 to 1815; in 1818 and 1822 was a member of the State Senate; and was for many years the President of a Bible Society, and also of Mount Zion Society. Died March 8, 1843.

Evans, George.—Born in Hallowell, Maine, January 12, 1797; graduated at Bowdoin College, September 3, 1815; is a lawyer by profession; was Speaker of the House of Representatives of Maine in 1829; a Representative in Congress, from 1829 to 1841, and United States Senator, from 1841 to 1847. From 1849 to 1850 he was a Commissioner of the Board of Claims against Mexico; and Attorney-General of Maine in 1853, 1854, and 1856.

Evans, Joshua.—He was a Representative in Congress, from Pennsylvania, from 1829 to 1833.

Evans, Josiah J.—He was born in the District of Marlborough, South Carolina, November 27, 1786; he was for a time a merchant's clerk, but graduated at South Carolina College in 1808; taught school for one year; studied law and rose to a high legal position; at an early age, in 1812, 1813, and 1816, he was sent to the Legislature; by that body made Solicitor for the State from his district, which position he held for thirteen years; in 1830 he was chosen a Judge of the Supreme Court, which office he held until 1852, when he was elected to the United States Senate. He died May 6, 1858, of disease of the heart, having, only an hour before his death, been partaking of the hospitalities at dinner of his friend and colleague, Senator Hammond. He was Chairman of the Committees on Revolutionary Claims and on Contingent Expenses of the Senate, and also a member of the Committees on Patents and on Naval Affairs.

Evans, Lemuel D.—He was born in Tennessee, and was elected a Representative, from Texas, to the Thirty-fourth Congress.

Evans, Nathan.—Born in Belmont County, Ohio, June 24, 1804; received a common school education, and studied law, being admitted to practice in 1831. He was Prosecuting Attorney for Guernsey County for four years, and was a Representative in Congress, from 1847 to 1849, and now follows his profession in Cambridge, Ohio.

Evans, Thomas.—He was a Representative in Congress, from Virginia, from 1797 to 1801.

Everett, Edward.—Born in Dorchester, Massachusetts, April, 1794. He received his early education at Boston, and entered Harvard College when little more than thirteen years old, leaving it with first honors four years later, undecided as to a pursuit for life. He turned his attention for two years to the profession of divinity; but, in 1814, he was invited to accept the new professorship of Greek literature at Cambridge, Massachusetts, with permission to visit Europe. He accepted the office, and, before entering on its duties, embarked at Boston for Liverpool. He passed more than two years at the famous University of Göttingen, engaged in the study of the German language and the branches of learning connected with his department. He passed the winter of 1817–18 at Paris. The next spring he again visited London, and passed a few weeks at Cambridge and Oxford. In the autumn of 1818 he returned to the continent, and divided the winter between Florence, Rome, and Naples. In the spring of 1819 he made a short tour in Greece. He came home in 1819, and entered at once upon the duties of his professorship. Soon after his return, he became the editor of the North American Review, a journal which, though supported by writers of great ability, had acquired only a limited circulation. Under its new editor the demand increased so rapidly that a second and sometimes a third edition of its numbers was required. In 1824 he delivered the annual oration before the Phi-Beta-Kappa Society, at Cambridge, Massachusetts. This was the first of a series of orations and addresses delivered by him on public occasions of almost every kind during a quarter of a century, and afterwards collected in several volumes. Up to 1824 he had taken no active interest in politics, but the constituency of Middlesex, Massachusetts, without any solicitation on his part, returned him to Congress. For ten years he sat in Congress, and was a working member. In 1835 he retired from Congress, and was for four successive years chosen Governor of Massachusetts. In 1841 he was appointed to represent the United States at the Court of St. James. Although the Secretaryship of State at Washington was held by four different statesmen, of various politics, during his mission, he enjoyed the confidence and approbation of all. His scholarship was recognized by the bestowal of the degree of D. C. L. by the Universities of Oxford and Cambridge. He returned to America in 1845, and was chosen President of Harvard College, which office he resigned in 1849. On the death of Mr. Webster, he was appointed Secretary of State by President Fillmore, which office he resigned for a seat in the Senate. This position he also resigned, since which time, although leading the quiet life of a scholar, he has greatly added to his reputation by delivering orations on the Life of Washington, and on other topics, all being for charitable purposes. He was the intimate friend of Daniel Webster, and wrote the best Life extant of that distinguished man, whose many collected writings he edited. In 1860 he was nominated by the Union party as their candidate for the office of Vice-President of the United States, but was defeated.

Everett, Horace.—A native of Vermont, was born in 1780; he was a lawyer by profession; settled in Windsor, and distinguished himself as one of the most successful jury advocates in Vermont. He served in the State Legislature in 1819, 1820, 1822, 1823, 1824, and 1834; was State's Attorney for Windsor County, from 1813 to 1817; and was a prominent member of the State Constitutional Convention of 1828. He was a Representative in Congress, from 1829 to 1843, and had the title conferred upon him of Doctor of Laws. Died at Windsor, Vermont, January 30, 1851.

Everhart, William.—He was born in Pennsylvania, and was a Representative in Congress, from that State, from 1853 to 1855. The circumstance is related of this gentleman, that it was his misfortune, many years ago, to be wrecked on the coast of Ireland, where he and five survivors of the ill-fated vessel were treated with great kindness; and that, during the famine in Ireland a few years ago, he loaded a ship with provisions, at his own expense, and sent her to Ireland, by way of expressing his gratitude.

Ewing, Andrew.—He was born in Tennessee, and was a Representative in Congress, from 1849 to 1851.

Ewing, Edwin H.—He was born in Tennessee, and was a Representative in Congress, from Tennessee, from 1845 to 1847.

Ewing, John.—He was born at sea, while his parents were on their way from Ireland to Baltimore. He was bred to mercantile pursuits, but acquired a taste for literature. He served in both branches of the Legislature of Indiana, and was a Representative of that State, in Congress, from 1833 to 1835, and again from 1837 to 1839. He died suddenly and alone, at Vincennes, in the winter of 1857, leaving on his table these lines:

> "Here lies a man who loved his friends,
> His God, his country, and Vincennes."

Ewing, John H.—He was born in Pennsylvania, and was a Representative in Congress, from that State, from 1845 to 1847.

Ewing, Presley.—Born in Kentucky, and was a Representative to the Thirty-third Congress; he died at the Mammoth Cave, September 27, 1854. He was considered one of the most promising young men of the State.

Ewing, Thomas.—He was born near West Liberty, Ohio County, Virginia, December 28, 1789; he received his early education chiefly from an elder sister, and, with his father's family, settled in the wilds of Ohio, about 1792, where he enjoyed the advantages of a winter school and an academy; his life, during his youth and early manhood, was one of continuous toil; in 1814 he was a school teacher; in 1815 he received the degree of A.B. from the Athens Academy, the first ever granted in Ohio; and he studied law and was admitted to the bar in 1816, practising with success in the courts of Ohio and the Supreme Court of the United States. In 1830 he was elected to a seat in the United States Senate, from Ohio, where he remained until 1837; he was a member of President Harrison's cabinet, as Secretary of the Treasury, in 1841; on the accession of President Taylor to the Presidency, in 1849, he was invited into the cabinet, and took charge of the new Department of the Interior; and, in 1850, he was appointed to a seat in the United States Senate, where he remained until 1851, when he retired from political life and resumed the practice of his profession in Ohio. He was a Delegate to the Peace Congress of 1861.

Ewing, William L. D.—He was a Representative in Congress, from Illinois, from 1836 to 1837. Died March 25, 1846.

Fairfield, John.—Born in Saco, Maine, January 30, 1797. He received a common school education, studied law, and was admitted to the bar in 1826. In 1832 he was appointed reporter of the decisions of the Supreme Court; from 1835 to 1839 he was a Representative in Congress; he was Governor of the State during the years 1839, 1840, 1842, and 1843; and he was elected a Senator in Congress, in 1843, to fill a vacancy, and in 1845 was re-elected for a term of six years; but he died at Washington, December 24, 1847, after a surgical operation for the relief of a local complaint.

Faran, James J.—He was born in Ohio, residing at Cincinnati, and was a Representative, from Ohio, to the Thirtieth Congress.

Farelly, John W.—He was born in Pennsylvania, and was a Representative in Congress, from that State, from 1847 to 1849.

Farelly, Patrick.—Born in Ireland in 1760; was a lawyer by profession, and was a Representative in Congress, from Pennsylvania, from 1821 to 1826. Died January 12, 1826, at Meadville, Pennsylvania, while in Congress.

Farlee, Isaac G.—He was born in New Jersey, and was a Representative in Congress, from that State, from 1843 to 1845.

Farley, E. Wilder.—He was born in Maine, in 1818; graduated at Bowdoin College in 1836; studied law, and was in the State Legislature in 1845 and from 1851 to 1853; and was a Representative in Congress, from Maine, from 1853 to 1855. He also served in the State Senate in 1856.

Farlin, Dudley.—He was a Representative in Congress, from New York, from 1835 to 1837, and died at Warrensburg, New York, September 26, 1837.

Farnsworth, John F.—Born in the township of Eaton, Lower Canada, March 27, 1820; is a lawyer by profession, and was a Representative to the Thirty-fifth Congress, from Illinois, serving as a member of the Committee on Revolutionary Pensions. He was also re-elected to the Thirty-sixth Congress, and in 1862 to the Thirty-eighth Congress, serving on the Committee on Military Affairs. In 1861 he took part in the war as a Colonel of volunteers.

Farrington, James.—He was

born in New Hampshire in 1791, and was a Representative in Congress, from that State, from 1837 to 1839. He was also a member of the State Legislature in 1830, 1832, and 1833. Died at Rochester, New York, October 29, 1859.

Farrow, Samuel.—Born in Virginia in 1760; served in the Revolutionary war and was wounded; studied law, and was admitted to the bar in 1793; was elected to Congress, from South Carolina, as a Representative for the terms from 1813 to 1817, but resigned in 1816; served in the State Legislature from 1817 to 1821; and died at Columbia, November 18, 1824.

Faulkner, Charles J.—Born in Berkeley County, Virginia, about the year 1805. He received a collegiate education; came to the bar in 1829; was, in 1832 and 1833, elected to the House of Delegates; soon afterwards appointed a Commissioner to report upon the boundary between Virginia and Maryland; in 1841 was elected to the Senate of Virginia, and in 1848 was again elected to the House of Delegates; in 1850 was a member of the Convention formed to revise the Constitution of the State; and having, in 1851, been elected a Representative in Congress, has been re-elected to each successive Congress, and was, during the first session of the Thirty-fifth Congress, a member of the Committee to Inquire into the Sale of the Fort Snelling Reservation, also serving on the Committee on Military Affairs, and in a subsequent Congress was Chairman of the Committee on Military Affairs. In January, 1860, he was appointed by President Buchanan Minister to France. He returned to America in 1861; was suspected of disloyalty, imprisoned at Fort Warren, and exchanged for Hon. Alfred Ely in December of that year.

Fay, Francis B.—He was born in Massachusetts; was a member of the Massachusetts Senate in 1842 and 1845; Mayor of Chelsea in 1857; and a Representative in Congress, from Massachusetts, from 1852 to 1853.

Fay, John.—He was born in Worcester County, Massachusetts, and was a Representative in Congress, from New York, from 1819 to 1821.

Fearing, Paul.—Born in Wareham, Massachusetts, February 28, 1762, graduated at Harvard University in 1785; studied law, and emigrated to Ohio, where he became distinguished in his profession. He settled in Marietta in 1788, after performing the journey, from Baltimore over the mountains, on foot. Soon after his arrival he was appointed United States Attorney for Washington County, in that Territory. In 1797 he was appointed Judge of Probate, for his county, and in 1801 was chosen a Delegate to Congress, serving until 1803. In 1814 he was appointed Master Commissioner in Chancery, and from 1810 to 1817 was Judge in one of the State Courts. In 1808 he engaged extensively in the raising of merino sheep, producing the best description of wool, and stimulating others to unite in the business. He died August 21, 1822.

Featherstone, W. S.—He was born in Tennessee, and on taking up his residence in Mississippi, was elected a Representative in Congress, from 1847 to 1851. Took part in the Rebellion of 1861 as a Brigadier-General.

Felch, Alpheus.—Born in Limerick, York County, Maine, September 28, 1806. He graduated at Bowdoin College, and adopted the law as a profession. He emigrated to Michigan when quite young; was a member of the State Legislature in 1836 and 1837; was appointed Bank Commissioner of Michigan in 1838, and resigned in 1839; for a short time in 1842 was Auditor-General of the State, but relinquished that position for a seat on the bench of the Supreme Court of Michigan; in 1845 he was elected Governor of Michigan, and having resigned in 1847, was elected a Senator in Congress for six years. He was appointed, by President Pierce, one of the Commissioners to settle land claims in California, under the Act of Congress and the Treaty of Guadalupe Hidalgo, in March, 1853, the business of which commission was closed by disposing of all the cases before it in March, 1856, since which time he has lived in retirement. He was also a Delegate to the Chicago Convention of 1864.

Felder, John M.—Born in Orangeburg District, South Carolina, July 7,

1782; graduated at Yale College in 1804; studied law, and was admitted to the bar in 1808; was a member of the State Assembly in 1812, and subsequently of the Senate; was a Trustee of South Carolina College; and served as a Major of the militia; and was a Representative in Congress, from South Carolina, from 1831 to 1835. Died at Union Point, September 1, 1851.

Fenner, James.—Born in Providence, Rhode Island, in 1771; graduated at Brown University, from which Institution he received the degree of LL.D. He was for more than half a century actively connected with the public affairs of his native State; was United States Senator from 1805 to 1807, when he was elected Governor of Rhode Island, which office he held four years; was re-elected in 1824, and served seven years, and was again elected in 1844. He died in Providence, April 17, 1846.

Fenton, Reuben E.—Born in Carroll, Chautauque County, New York, July 1, 1819; was educated at Pleasant Hill and Fredonia Academies, and adopted the profession of law, but pursued the mercantile business. In 1843 he was elected Supervisor of the town of Carroll. He was elected a Representative, in the Thirty-third and Thirty-fifth Congresses, from New York, serving on the Committee on Private Land Claims; was re-elected to the Thirty-sixth Congress, serving as Chairman of the Committee on Invalid Pensions; was also elected to the Thirty-seventh Congress, serving as Chairman of the Committee on Claims. Re-elected to the Thirty-eighth Congress, serving on the Committee of Ways and Means.

Ferguson, Fenner.—Born in Rensselaer County, New York, April 25, 1814. His education was academic, and he is a lawyer by profession; he was Master in Chancery in Albany, New York, in 1844; also Master in Chancery in Michigan; a member of the Michigan Legislature, and Prosecuting Attorney. June 29, 1854, he was appointed, by President Pierce, Chief Justice of the Territory of Nebraska, which office he resigned, after being elected a Delegate to the Thirty-fifth Congress, from that Territory.

Ferris, Charles G.—He was born in New York, and was a Representative in Congress, from that State, from 1841 to 1843.

Ferry, Orris S.—Born in Bethel, Connecticut, August 15th, 1823; graduated at Yale College in 1844; studied law, and was admitted to the bar in 1846. In 1847 he received the appointment of Lieutenant-Colonel of the First Division Connecticut Militia; in 1849 was appointed Judge of Probate for the District of Norwalk; elected to the State Senate in 1855 and 1856; in 1856 he was appointed State Attorney for the County of Fairfield, which position he continued to occupy until 1859, when he was elected a Representative to the Thirty-sixth Congress, from Connecticut, serving as a member of the Committee on Revolutionary Claims.

Fessenden, Samuel C.—Was born in New Gloucester, Maine, March 7, 1815; graduated at Bowdoin College in 1834, and completed his education at the Bangor Theological Seminary in 1837; in 1838 he was ordained and installed as Pastor of the Second Congregational Church, in Thomaston, now Rockland, and dismissed at his own request in 1856; during that year he established the Maine Evangelist; in 1858 he entered upon the practice of the law; soon after taking that step he was elected Judge of the Municipal Court of Rockland; and he was elected a Representative, from Maine, to the Thirty-seventh Congress, serving as a member of the Committee on Unfinished Business.

Fessenden, T. A. D.—Was born in Portland, Maine, January 23, 1826; graduated at Bowdoin College in 1845; adopted the profession of law; was a member of the Convention that nominated General Fremont for President; in 1858 was appointed aide-de-camp to the Governor of Maine; in 1860 was elected to the Maine Legislature; and in 1861 was chosen Attorney for the County of Androscoggin; which position he held until 1862, when he was elected a Representative, from Maine, to the Thirty-seventh Congress, for the unexpired term of C. W. Walton, resigned, serving on the Committee on Private Land Claims.

Fessenden, William P.—Born at

Boscawen, New Hampshire, October 16, 1806; graduated at Bowdoin College in 1823; studied law, and was admitted to practice in Portland, in 1827, where he has continued the practice to the present time; was a member of the Maine Legislature in 1832, and re-elected in 1840; was a Representative in Congress from 1841 to 1843, declining further service; was again in the State Legislature in 1845 and 1846, and re-elected in 1853 and 1854; and was elected a Senator in Congress for six years, from March, 1853, serving as a member of the Committee on Finance; and in 1859 was re-elected for the term of six years, serving as Chairman of the Committee on Finance. He was a member, in 1832, of the Convention which nominated Henry Clay for President, and also of the Conventions that nominated Generals Taylor and Scott. During the summer of 1858, the degree of LL.D. was conferred upon him by Bowdoin College, of which iustitution he is an overseer. He was also a member of the Peace Congress of 1861. In July, 1864, he was appointed, by President Lincoln, Secretary of the Treasury, in the place of S. P. Chase, resigned; and soon afterward received from Harvard University the degree of LL.D.

Few, William.—Born in Maryland, June 8, 1748. When he was ten years of age he removed with his father to North Carolina, where he received a good education. He was a Colonel in the Revolutionary army, and distinguished himself in several actions with the British and Indians. He settled in Georgia in 1776, and in 1778 was Surveyor-General of the State, and Presiding Judge of the Richmond County Court; in 1780 he was sent as Delegate to Congress, and remained in that body until the peace; and was again appointed in 1786; and in the next year he assisted in forming the National Constitution, after the adoption of which he was elected a Senator in Congress, serving from 1789 to 1793; in 1796 he was a member of the Convention which framed the Constitution of the State of Georgia, and subsequently served three years upon the Bench, as well as in the Legislature of that State. He resided during his later years in the city of New York, of which he was Mayor, and whence he went to the Legislature of that State, and where he also held the office of Commissioner of Loans. He died at Fishkill, New York, July 16, 1828.

Ficklin, Orlando B.—A native of Kentucky, and born in 1808; he received a plain English education; studied law, and graduated at the Transylvania Law School, commencing to practice in 1830, in Mount Carmel, Illinois. In 1834 he was a member of the Legislature, and was Attorney for the Wabash Circuit in 1835. In 1838 and in 1842, was again elected to the Legislature; and in 1843 was elected a Representative in Congress, serving six consecutive years, and was re-elected in 1850. In 1853 he was Colonel of militia; since which time he has been engaged in the practice of his profession, and in agricultural pursuits.

Field, Richard S.—He was born in New Jersey, and held a seat in the United States Senate, for a few months, in 1862–3, by appointment; when he was appointed, by President Lincoln, Judge of the District Court of the United States for New Jersey.

Fillmore, Millard.—Born January 7, 1800, at Summer Hill, Cayuga County, in the State of New York. At an early age he was sent to Livingston County, at that time a wild region, to learn the clothier's trade, and about four months later he was apprenticed to a wool-carder, in the town in which his father lived. During the four years that he worked at his trade, he did what he could to supply the defects of his early education. At the age of nineteen he commenced the study of law, and devoted a portion of his time to teaching school. In 1821 he removed to Erie County, and pursued his legal studies in the city of Buffalo. Two years later he was admitted to the Common Pleas, and commenced the practice of the law at Aurora, in the same county. In 1827, he was admitted as an Attorney, and in 1829 as a Counsellor in the Supreme Court, and in the following year he removed to Buffalo. His political life commenced with his election to the State Assembly, in which he took his seat in 1829. In 1832 he was elected to Congress, and took his seat the following year. In 1835, at the close of his term in office, he resumed the practice of the law, but was re-elected to Congress in 1837. During this term, he took a more prominent part in the business of the

House than during his former term, and was assigned a place on the Committee on Elections. He was successively re-elected to the Twenty-sixth and Twenty-seventh Congresses. At the close of the first session of the Twenty-seventh Congress he declined a re-election, returned to Buffalo, and again devoted himself to his profession. In 1847 he was elected to the office of Comptroller of the State. In 1848 he was nominated by the Whigs as their candidate for Vice-President, and elected to that office in the autumn of the same year. In March, 1849, he resigned his office of Comptroller, to assume the duties of his new position, where he remained until the death of President Taylor, in July, 1850, by which he was elevated to the Presidential chair. His term of office expired March 4, 1853. Since his retirement from public life he has visited Europe.

Finch, Isaac.—He was a native of New York; a member of the Assembly of that State, in 1822 and 1824; and a Representative in Congress, from New York, from 1829 to 1831.

Finck, William E.—He was born in Ohio, in 1822; studied law, and was admitted to the bar of that State when twenty-one years of age; in 1851 he was elected to the Senate of Ohio; in 1852 was a member of the National Convention which nominated General Scott for the Presidency; in 1861 he was again elected a State Senator, and in 1862 he was chosen a Representative, from Ohio, to the Thirty-eighth Congress, and was a member of the Committee on the Post-office and Post-roads.

Findlay, James.—He was a native of Franklin County, Pennsylvania, and a member of Congress, from Ohio, from 1825 to 1833. He died at Cincinnati, Ohio, December 21, 1835.

Findlay, John.—He was a Representative in Congress, from Pennsylvania, from 1823 to 1827. He was born in Franklin County, Pennsylvania, and brother of James and John.

Findlay, William.—He was born in Franklin County, Pennsylvania; Governor of Pennsylvania, from 1817 to 1820; and a Senator in Congress, from that State, from 1821 to 1827.

Findley, William.—He came in early life from Ireland. In the Revolution he engaged with zeal in the cause of his adopted country, and at the close of the war he removed to Pennsylvania. He was a member of the Convention which framed the new Constitution of Pennsylvania, and a member of Congress, from 1791 to 1799, and from 1803 to 1817. In his politics he opposed the administration of Mr. Adams, and supported Mr. Jefferson. He published a Review of the Funding System in 1794, and a History of the Insurrection of the Four Western Counties of Pennsylvania, in 1796. He died at Unity Township, Greensburg, April 5, 1821, aged upwards of seventy.

Fine, John.—Born in New York, August 26, 1784; graduated at Columbia College, New York, in 1809; studied law, and settled in St. Lawrence County, New York; was a Judge in that county for eighteen years; was County Treasurer from 1821 to 1833; and a Representative in Congress, from 1839 to 1841. He published a volume of law lectures.

Fish, Hamilton.—He was born in New York City in 1809; graduated at Columbia College; studied law, and was admitted to the bar in 1830; in 1837 was elected to the State Legislature; was a Representative in Congress, from 1843 to 1845; Governor of New York in 1849; and a Senator in Congress, from 1851 to 1856. Of late years he has been travelling in Europe.

Fisher, Charles.—Born in Rowan County, North Carolina, October 20, 1789. He received an academical education, and studied law, but did not practise to any extent. He commenced public life by going into the State Senate in 1818, and in 1819 was elected to Congress, where he served during his term. In 1821 he was elected again to the State Legislature, when he served almost continuously until 1836. He was a Delegate to the Convention to amend the State Constitution in 1835; and, from 1839 to 1841, was again a Representative in Congress. He died at Hillsborough, Scott County, Mississippi, May 7, 1849, while returning home from an extended tour in the Southwest.

Fisher, David.—He was born in Somerset County, Pennsylvania, December 3, 1794; received an English education, chiefly in a log school-house; brought up to clearing land and farming in Ohio; he has done something also as a lay preacher; in 1842 he was elected to the Legislature of Ohio; and he was a Representative in Congress, from 1847 to 1849. His chair in the House of Representatives was next to that of the late John Quincy Adams, and when the great statesman fainted, before his death, he fell into the arms of Mr. Fisher. He is the author of a theological work on the "Divinity of Christ."

Fisher, George.—He was a Representative in Congress, from New York, from 1829 to 1830, and a member of the New York Assembly, from Tioga County, in 1835.

Fisher, George P.—Born in Milford, Kent County, Delaware, October 13, 1817; graduated at Dickinson College, Pennsylvania, in 1838; studied law, and was admitted to the bar in 1841; in 1840 he was clerk of the Delaware Senate; in 1843 and 1844 he was elected to the Delaware House of Representatives; in 1846 he became Secretary of State for Delaware; in 1849 he went into the State Department at Washington as the confidential clerk of Secretary Clayton; in 1850 he was appointed by President Taylor a Commissioner to settle claims against Brazil, which office expired in 1852; from 1855 to 1860 he held the position of Attorney-General for the State of Delaware; and was elected a Representative from that State to the Thirty-seventh Congress, serving as a member of the Committee on Foreign Affairs. He was subsequently appointed by President Lincoln a Judge for the District of Columbia.

Fisk, James.—Born about the year 1762; received a limited education, but studied law, and from his superior natural talents, rose to eminence in his profession; he was a Representative in Congress, from Vermont, from 1805 to 1809, and from 1811 to 1815, when he was appointed one of the Judges of the Supreme Court of Vermont. He was a Senator in Congress during the years 1817 and 1818, and resigned. In 1812 he was appointed by President Madison Judge of the Territory of Indiana, and in 1817, Collector of the Port of Alburg, which office he held eight years. He died December 1, 1844.

Fisk, Jonathan.—He was a Representative in Congress, from New York, from 1809 to 1811, and again from 1813 to 1815, when he was appointed United States Attorney for the Southern District of New York.

Fitch, Asa.—He was a Representative in Congress, from New York, from 1811 to 1813.

Fitch, G. N.—Born in Le Roy, Genesee County, New York, in December, 1810. He received his education at Middlebury and Geneva, but did not graduate; he studied medicine, and was a Medical Professor in the Rush Medical College at Chicago, Illinois, from 1844 to 1849. In 1844, 1848, and 1856, he was chosen a Presidential Elector, and in 1836 and 1839 was elected to the Legislature of Indiana. He was a Representative in Congress, from 1849 to 1853, and in 1857 was chosen a Senator of the United States, serving as a member of the Committees on Post-offices and Post-roads, and on Indian Affairs.

Fitzgerald, Thomas H.—He was a lawyer by profession; served in the war of 1812, under General W. H. Harrison; and in 1848 and 1849, was a Senator in Congress, from Michigan, under the appointment of the Governor. Died at Niles, Michigan, March 25, 1855.

Fitzgerald, William.—He was born in Tennessee, and was a Representative in Congress, from that State, from 1831 to 1833, and was a member of the Committee on Expenditures in the Treasury Department. He was also Judge of the Circuit Court of Tennessee.

Fitzpatrick, Benjamin.—He was born in Greene County, Georgia, June 30, 1802; having been left an orphan when quite young, he emigrated with an elder brother, in 1815, to the valley of the Alabama River, near Montgomery, where he has ever since resided. He received as good an education as new countries generally afford; studied law and was admitted to practice in 1821; was shortly afterwards elected Solicitor of the Judicial District in which he lived; was again elected to the same office in 1825, and held it until 1829; after which his health compelled him to relinquish his profession, and settle upon a farm. He was a Presidential Elector in 1840; in 1841 was elected Governor of Alabama; in 1843 was re-elected to the same position; in 1852 he was appointed a Senator in Congress, to succeed Honorable W. R. King, which appointment was confirmed by the Legislature of his State, and at the conclusion of that term, he was elected, in 1855, to the same position, for the term ending in 1861; retired from the Senate in February, 1861, and took an active part in the Rebellion of that year. For several sessions he served as President *pro tem.* of the Senate.

Fitzsimmons, Thomas.—He was a Delegate to the Continental Congress, from Pennsylvania, from 1782 to 1783; a Representative in Congress, from that State, from 1789 to 1795; and died in August, 1811, aged seventy years.

Flagler, Thomas T.—He was born in New York, served in the Assembly of that State in 1842 and 1843, and was a Representative in Congress from 1853 to 1857.

Flanders, Benjamin F.—Born in Bristol, New Hampshire, January 26, 1816; graduated at Dartmouth College in 1842; studied law and settled in New Orleans; taught school in that city for a time, and became the editor of the Tropic newspaper; served as a member of the city government; was superintendent of a public school, and also of a railroad company; and towards the close of the year 1862, he was elected, under a new order of things, a Representative, from Louisiana, to the Thirty-seventh Congress, taking his seat within a fortnight of its final adjournment.

Fletcher, Isaac.—He was formerly a member of the Vermont Legislature, and a member of Congress, from that State, from 1837 to 1841. He died at Lyndon, Vermont, October 19, 1842.

Fletcher, Richard.—He was born in Cavendish, Vermont, January 8, 1788; graduated at Dartmouth College in 1806; served in the Legislature of Massachusetts; was a Judge of the Superior Court from 1848 to 1853; and a Representative in Congress, from Massachusetts, from 1837 to 1839.

Fletcher, Thomas.—He was a Representative in Congress, from Kentucky, from 1816 to 1817.

Florence, Elias.—He was born in Virginia, and having taken up his residence in Ohio, was elected a Representative in Congress, from 1843 to 1845.

Florence, Thomas B.—Born in Philadelphia, Pennsylvania, January 26, 1812. He had not the benefit of a college education; for a time he devoted himself to the occupation of a hatter; he published and edited, for several years, a Democratic newspaper; was for nine years Secretary of the Board of Controllers of Public Schools in Pennsylvania; and was elected to Congress in 1850, where he served continuously until 1859, acting as a member of the Committees on Naval Affairs and Invalid Pensions. He was also re-elected to the Thirty-sixth Congress; and while occupying his seat as a Representative, established in Washington the National Democratic Review.

Flournoy, Thomas S.—He was born in Virginia, and was a Representative in Congress, from that State, from 1847 to 1849. He participated in the great Rebellion, and was killed in battle in Virginia in June, 1864.

Floyd, Charles A.—He was born in New York, served in the Assembly of that State in 1836 and 1838, and was a Representative in Congress, from 1841 to 1843.

Floyd, John.—Born in Virginia, October 3, 1769. In consequence of the pecuniary losses of his father, he learned the trade of a carpenter, and in 1791 removed to Georgia, and acquired wealth from the manufacture of boats. He served in the State Legislature, and was a Representative of Georgia, in Congress, from 1827 to 1829. He was Brigadier-General of militia, and subsequently Major-General, and served during the war of 1812. He died in Camden County, Georgia, June 24, 1839.

Floyd, John.—He was born in Jefferson County, Virginia, and was a Representative in Congress, from Virginia, from 1817 to 1829; served many years in the Legislature of that State, and was Governor of Virginia from 1829 to 1834. He died at the Sweet Springs, in that State, August 16, 1837.

Floyd, John G.—He was a native of New York, served in the Assembly of that State, and was a Representative in Congress, from the same, from 1839 to 1843, and from 1851 to 1853.

Floyd, William.—He was born in Suffolk County, New York, December 17, 1734; was a Delegate to the Continental Congress, from 1774 to 1783, and signed the Declaration of Independence; was a Representative in Congress, from New York, from 1789 to 1791; a Presidential Elector in 1800 and 1804; and, for three years, a member of the New York State Senate; in 1801 he was a member of the State Constitutional Convention. He died in Oneida County, New York, August 4, 1821, aged eighty-seven years.

Foley, James B.—He was born in Kentucky, and having taken up his residence in Indiana, was elected a Representative in Congress, from that State, in 1857, and was a member of the Committees on Agriculture and Expenditures in the Post-office Department.

Folger, Walter.—He was born at Nantucket, Massachusetts; was a member of the Massachusetts Senate from 1809 to 1815, and also in 1822; and was a Representative in Congress, from that State, from 1817 to 1821.

Foot, Solomon.—Born in Cornwall, Addison County, Vermont, November 19, 1802; graduated at Middlebury College; a lawyer by profession; a member of the House of Representatives of Vermont, during the years 1833, 1836, 1837, 1838, and 1847; Speaker of the House in 1837, 1838, and 1847; member of the Convention for altering the State Constitution in 1836; State's Attorney for Rutland, from 1836 to 1842; a Representative in Congress, from 1843 to 1847; and was appointed United States Senator, in 1850, serving as a member of the Committees on Foreign Relations and the Pacific Railroad, and Chairman of the Committee on Public Buildings and Grounds. He was re-elected to the Senate for the term commencing in 1863, and ending in 1869. During a part of the Thirty-sixth, and the whole of the Thirty-seventh Congress, he was President *pro tem.* of the Senate. He was also a Delegate to the Baltimore Convention of 1864.

Foote, Charles A.—He was born in New York, and was a Representative in Congress, from that State, from 1823 to 1825. Died August 1, 1828.

Foote, Henry S.—He was born in Fauquier County, Virginia, September 20, 1800, and was educated at Washington College, in that State; studied law, was admitted to the bar, and settled in Alabama in 1824; in 1826 he removed to Mississippi, and there continued the practice of his profession; was elected, in 1847, a Senator in Congress, where he remained until 1852, officiating as Chairman of the Committee on Foreign Relations; and he was elected Governor of Mississippi in 1852. He subsequently spent a few years in California. In 1859 he was a member of the Southern Convention held at Knoxville, Tennessee, and during his life has fought three duels. He identified himself with the Great Rebellion, and was a member of the Confederate Congress.

Foote, Samuel A.—Born in Cheshire, Connecticut, November 8, 1780; graduated at Yale College in 1797, and commenced the practice of law in his native town. He was chosen a Representative in Congress, in 1819, 1823, and 1833; was Speaker of the Connecticut House of Representatives in 1825 and 1826; and Senator in Congress, from 1827 to 1833. In 1834 he was elected Governor of the State. He died September 16, 1846. He it was who offered, on the floor of Congress, the famous resolutions, upon which was founded the great debate between Hayne and Webster.

Ford, James.—He served two years in the Pennsylvania Legislature, and was a Representative in Congress, from Pennsylvania, from 1829 to 1833. His life was honorably interwoven with the history of his State, and he died at Lawrenceville, Pennsylvania, August, 1859, aged seventy-six years.

Ford, William D.—He was born in Providence, Rhode Island; served in the New York Assembly in 1816 and 1817; and was a Representative in Congress, from that State, from 1819 to 1821.

Fornance, Joseph.—He was born in Pennsylvania, and was a Representative in Congress, from that State, from 1839 to 1841.

Forney, Daniel M.—Born in Lincoln County, North Carolina, May, 1784. During the late war with England, he served as a Major in the State line, and was a Representative in Congress, from 1815 to 1818, and in 1820 was appointed Commissioner to treat with the Creek Indians. From 1823 to 1826 he was a member of the State Legislature. In 1834 he removed to Lowndes County, Alabama, where he died in October, 1847.

Forney, Peter.—Born in Lincoln County, North Carolina, April, 1756. He was a patriot and soldier of the Revolution. He served as a member of the State Legislature for several years, and was a Representative in Congress, from 1813 to 1815. He served as an Elector during the Presidential campaigns of Jefferson, Madison, Monroe, and Jackson. Died February 1, 1834.

Forrest, Thomas.—He was born in Philadelphia, Pennsylvania, and was a Representative in Congress, from that State, from 1819 to 1821, and again from 1822 to 1823. Died March 20, 1825. He was elected to Congress by *one* vote.

Forrest, Uriah.—He was a General in the Revolutionary war; was wounded at the battle of Germantown, from the effects of which he never recovered; was a Representative in Congress, from Maryland, during the years 1793 and 1794; and died at his seat near Georgetown, District of Columbia, in 1805.

Forrester, J. B.—He was born in Tennessee, and was a Representative in Congress, from that State, from 1833 to 1837, and was a member of the Committee on Claims. Died August 31, 1845.

Forsyth, John.—He was born in Fredericksburg, Virginia, October, 2, 1780; graduated at Princeton College in 1799; removed with his father to Charleston, South Carolina, and afterwards to Augusta, Georgia. He studied law, and from 1802 to 1808 distinguished himself at the Georgia bar; and in 1808 was Attorney-General of the State; he was a Representative in Congress, from Georgia, from 1813 to 1818, and from 1823 to 1827; a Senator in Congress, during the years 1818 and 1819, and from 1829 to 1837; Governor of Georgia in 1827, 1828, and 1829; Minister to Spain from 1819 to 1822; and was Secretary of State under President Jackson; in which position he was continued by President Van Buren, until the end of his administration. His superior abilities were universally acknowledged, and the dignity and elegance of his manners added much to his popularity. He died in Washington City, of bilious fever, October 21, 1841.

Fort, Tomlinson.—He was a Representative in Congress, from Georgia, from 1827 to 1829.

Forward, Chauncey.—He was a native of Pennsylvania, and a Representative in Congress, from that State from 1825 to 1831.

Forward, Walter.—He was born in Connecticut in 1786, where he received a liberal education. He removed to Pittsburg in 1803, and studied law. In 1805 he became editor of the Democratic paper called the Tree of Liberty; from 1806 to 1822 he was engaged in the practice of law, and, as a pleader, had few equals. In 1822 he was elected to Congress, as a Representative, where he continued till March, 1825. In 1837 he bore a prominent part in the Pennsylvania Convention to reform the State Constitution. In March, 1841, President Harrison named him First Comptroller of the Treasury, which post he held until he was appointed by President Tyler Secretary of the Treasury. On retiring from Mr. Tyler's cabinet, he resumed and continued his practice at the bar, until appointed by President Taylor Chargé d'Affaires to Denmark, where he spent several years, resigning his situation to return home in order to accept the office of President Judge of the District Court of Alleghany County, to which he had been called by popular election. While in court, employed in his judicial duties, he was suddenly taken ill, and died in forty-eight hours, at Pittsburg, Pennsylvania, November 24, 1852.

Fosdick, Nicoll.—Born in New London, Connecticut, November 9, 1785, of direct Puritan stock; in 1809 removed to Herkimer County, New York; was a Presidential Elector in 1816; a member of the Legislature of New York in 1818, again in 1819, and declined a re-election; was a Representative from New York in the Nineteenth Congress; returned to his native place in 1843, and from 1849 to 1853 was Collector of Customs for the District of New London.

Foster, Abiel.—Born in Andover, Massachusetts, August 8, 1735; graduated at Harvard University in 1756; studied theology and was a pastor for eighteen years over the Congregational Church in Canterbury, New Hampshire; and in 1780 was a Representative to the General Court; was a Delegate from New Hampshire to the Continental Congress, from 1783 to 1785; and was present at Washington's resignation of the command of the army at Annapolis; he was a Representative in Congress, from New Hampshire, from 1789 to 1791, and was again a Representative in the Legislature, and a Delegate to revise the State Constitution; was a member of the State Senate, from 1793 to 1794, and in both years was President of that body; and was re-elected to Congress, from 1795 to 1803. He died at Canterbury, February 6, 1806.

Foster, A. Lawrence.—He was born in New York, and was a Representative in Congress, from that State, from 1841 to 1843.

Foster, Dwight.—He was born in Massachusetts in 1757, and died at Brookfield, in that State, in April, 1823. He graduated at Brown University in 1774; studied and practised law; was County Sheriff, and Judge of the Common Pleas; and was a Representative in Congress, from Massachusetts, from 1793 to 1799; and a Senator in Congress, from 1800 to 1803, when he resigned.

Foster, Ephraim H.—He entered public life when quite young, and in 1829 was Speaker of the House of Representatives of Tennessee. In 1837 he was elected to the United States Senate, but in 1839 resigned his seat because he could not obey the instructions of the State Legislature; and in 1843 he was re-elected for two years. On his return from Washington he was a candidate for Governor, but failed of an election. He died at Nashville, September 4, 1854.

Foster, Henry A.—He was born in New York; served in the Senate of that State from 1831 to 1834, and from 1841 to 1844; was a Representative in Congress, from New York, from 1837 to 1839; and was a Senator in Congress during the years 1844 and 1845.

Foster, Henry D.—He was born in Pennsylvania, and was a Representative in Congress, from that State, from 1843 to 1847.

Foster, Lafayette S.—Born in Franklin, New London County, Connecticut, November 22, 1806, and is a direct descendant of Miles Standish. He graduated at Brown University; is a lawyer by profession; was a member of the General Assembly of Connecticut in 1839, 1840, 1846, 1847, 1848, 1854; Speaker of the House in 1847, 1848, 1854; Mayor of the City of Norwich, Connecticut, for two years, and chosen a Senator in Congress, from March 4, 1855, for six years, and serving as a member of the Committees on Public Lands, Pensions, and the Judiciary. In 1860 he was re-elected to the Senate for a second term of six years. During the Thirty-seventh Congress he was Chairman of the Committee on Pensions.

Foster, Nathaniel G.—Born at "The Fork," in Greene County, Georgia, August 25, 1809; graduated at Franklin College in 1839; read law, and was admitted to the bar in 1831, and settled in Madison, Georgia, where he obtained a high reputation as an advocate and jury lawyer. He served three years as Solicitor-General of Ocmulgee Circuit, five years in the State Senate, and one year in the House, and was a Representative in the Thirty-fourth Congress.

Foster, Stephen C.—Born in Machias, Maine, December 24, 1799; commenced life as a blacksmith, but for the last twenty-five years has been a lumber merchant and ship-builder; was in the Maine Legislature from 1834 to 1837, again in 1840, when he was President of the Senate, and again in 1847; was elected to Congress, from Maine, in 1856, serving through the Thirty-fifth Congress, as a member of the Committee on Manufactures. He is now President of the Washington Agricultural Society of his native State. He was also elected to the Thirty-sixth Congress, and was also a member of the Peace Congress of 1861.

Foster, Theodore.—He was born in Massachusetts, and was a Senator in Congress, from Rhode Island, from 1790 to 1803, and died in 1828.

Foster, Thomas F.—Born in Greensborough, Georgia, November 23, 1790. He graduated at Franklin College in 1812; read law at home, and at Litchfield, Connecticut, and was admitted to the bar in 1816. He was for many years a member of the Georgia Legislature; and a Representative in Congress, from 1829 to 1835, and again from 1841 to 1843. He died in 1847.

Fouke, Philip B.—Born in Kaskaskia, Illinois, January 23, 1818; was chiefly self-educated; was first a clerk, and then a civil engineer; in 1841 he established a paper called the Belleville Advocate, which he printed and edited for four years; he then studied law, and after being admitted to practice, he was elected in 1846 Prosecuting Attorney for his District and re-elected; in 1851 he was elected a member of the Illinois Legislature; in 1856 he was again elected Prosecuting Attorney; and in 1858 was elected a Representative, from Illinois, to the Thirty-sixth Congress, serving on the Committee on Public Expenditures. Re-elected to the Thirty-seventh Congress, but served as a Colonel of volunteers in 1861, resigning his commission in 1862.

Fowler, John.—He was a soldier in the war of the Revolution; attained the rank of Captain; and was a member of Congress, from Kentucky, from 1797 to 1807. He died at Lexington, Kentucky, August 22, 1840, aged eighty-five years.

Fowler, Orin.—He was born in Connecticut in 1795; graduated at Yale College in 1815; studied divinity, but turned his attention to politics; was elected to the Senate of Massachusetts in 1848; and was a Representative in Congress from 1849 to the time of his death, which occurred in Washington City, September 3, 1852. He was at one time settled over a church in Plainfield, Connecticut.

Fowler, Samuel.—Born in New Jersey in 1779; was a distinguished member of the medical profession; and a Representative in Congress, from New Jersey, from 1833 to 1837. Died in Sussex County, New Jersey, February 21, 1844.

Franchot, Richard.—Was born in Morris, Otsego County, New York, in 1816; received an English education; served as a civil engineer for seven years; subsequently turned his attention to farming; was President of the Albany and Susquehanna Railroad Company; and was elected a Representative, from New York, to the Thirty-seventh Congress, serving on the Committees on the District of Columbia, and the Pacific Railroad.

Francis, John B.—He was born in Rhode Island, and was a Senator in Congress, from that State, from 1844 to 1845, having been Governor of Rhode Island, from 1833 to 1838. Died in Providence, Rhode Island, August 9, 1864.

Frank, Augustus.—He was born in Warsaw, Wyoming County, New York, July 17, 1826; early became engaged in mercantile pursuits, to which he was devoted for many years. In 1858 he was elected a Representative, from New York, to the Thirty-sixth Congress, serving as a member of the Committee on Patents; re-elected to the Thirty-seventh Congress, serving on the Committees on the Library and on Mileage; and for a third term, was re-elected to the Thirty-eighth Congress, when he was made Chairman of the Committee on the Library, serving also on the Committee on Mileage, and the Select Committee on the Bankrupt Law.

Franklin, Jesse.—He was born in Surry County, North Carolina; served with credit in the Revolutionary war, as a Major; was a member of the House of Delegates of that State in 1794; represented that State in Congress, from 1795 to 1797, and then returned to the Legislature. From 1799 to 1805, and from 1807 to 1813, he was United States Senator, officiating in the Eighth Congress as President *pro tem.* of the Senate. In 1816 he was appointed, by President Madison, a Commissioner to treat with the Chickasaws, and was elected Governor of North Carolina in 1820. He died in Surry County, in 1823, aged sixty-five years.

Franklin, John A.—He was born in Worcester County, Maryland, May 6, 1820; graduated at Jefferson College, Pennsylvania, in 1836; studied law, and was admitted to the bar in 1841; served in the State Legislature of Maryland in 1843, and also in 1849, when he was elected Speaker; in 1851 he was chosen President of the Board of Public Works of the State, and was a Representative in Congress, from Maryland, from 1853 to 1855.

Franklin, Meshack.—A Representative in Congress, from North Carolina, from 1807 to 1815. He served in the House of Commons of that State in 1800, and in the State Senate in 1828 and 1829. He was also a member of the Executive Council of North Carolina, and a Delegate to the Convention for revising the State Constitution. He died in Surry County, December 18, 1839.

Freedley, John.—He was born (according to an interesting work published by E. T. Freedley, Esq.), in Norristown, Montgomery County, Pennsylvania, May 22, 1793. He commenced life as a brickmaker; studied law, and was admitted to the bar in 1820; he entered extensively into various kinds of business, especially that of quarrying marble, and was successful; and was a Representative in Congress, from Pennsylvania, from 1847 to 1851. He died December 8, 1851.

Freeman, John D.—He was born in New Jersey, and, having removed to Mississippi, was elected a Representative in Congress, from that State, from 1851 to 1853.

Freeman, Jonathan.—He was a Representative in Congress, from New Hampshire, from 1797 to 1801. From 1789 to 1797 he was a State Councillor; from 1793 to 1808 one of the Overseers of Dartmouth College; and died in 1808, aged sixty-three years.

Freeman, Nathaniel.—He was born at Dennis, Massachusetts, in April, 1741, and died September 27, 1820. He graduated at Harvard University; studied medicine; and was a patriot in the Revolutionary war; performed various services in the Legislature and as a Brigadier-General of militia; he was also a Judge of Probate for forty-seven years, and a Judge of the Common Pleas for thirty years; he was twice married, and had twenty children; and was a member of Congress, from Massachusetts, from 1795 to 1799.

Frelinghuysen, Frederick.—Born in New Jersey, April 13, 1753; graduated at Princeton College in 1770. When twenty-two years of age he was sent to the Continental Congress; and as Captain of a volunteer corps of artillery, he was at the battles of Trenton and Monmouth, and it is said that it was he who killed Rhalle, the Hessian commander at Trenton. He was a Senator in Congress, from 1793 to 1796, when he resigned on account of domestic bereavements. He stood among the first at the bar of New Jersey, and held various State and County offices. He died April 13, 1804.

Frelinghuysen, Theodore.—He was born in Millstown, Somerset County, New Jersey, March 28, 1787; graduated at Princeton College, Nassau Hall, in 1804; studied law, and was admitted to the bar in 1808; was Attorney-General of New Jersey, from 1818 to 1829; and a Senator in Congress, from New Jersey, from 1829 to 1835. Mr. Frelinghuysen was Chancellor of the University of New York, from 1839 to 1850, and while in that position was the candidate of the Whig party for Vice-President upon the ticket with Henry Clay.

In 1850 he was elected President of Rutgers College, where he officiated until his death, devoting much of his time and means to the benevolent and educational interests of his native State and of the Union. He resided for some years at Newark, New Jersey, and was Mayor of that city in 1837 and 1838. He also served as President of the American Temperance Union, of the American Tract Society, the Board of Foreign Missions, and of the American Bible Society. In the church, he was for many years recognized as the great leader in all the moral movements of the country, and was universally beloved. Died at New Brunswick, New Jersey, April 12, 1862.

Fremont, John Charles.—Born in Savannah, Georgia, January 21, 1813. His father was an emigrant from France. He received a good education, though left an orphan at four years of age; and at the age of seventeen he graduated at Charleston College. From teaching mathematics he turned his attention to civil engineering, and was recommended to the Government for employment in the Mississippi survey. He was afterwards employed at Washington in constructing maps of that region. Having received the commission of a Lieutenant of engineers, he proposed to the Secretary of War to penetrate the Rocky Mountains. His plan was approved, and in 1842, with a few men, he explored the South Pass. Impatient of quiet, he planned a new expedition to the Territory of Oregon. He approached the Rocky Mountains by a new line, scaled the summits south of the South Pass, deflected to the Great Salt Lake, and connected his survey with that of Wilkes's Exploring Expedition. He also performed another expedition, in which he revealed the grand features of Alta California, its great basin, the Sierra Nevada, the valleys of the San Joaquin and Sacramento, and established the geography of the western portion of the continent. In August, 1844, he was planning a third expedition, while writing the history of the second, and before its publication, in 1845, was again on his way to the Pacific, collecting his mountain comrades, to examine in detail the Asiatic slope of the continent, which resulted in giving a new volume of science to the world, and California to the United States. After the conquest of California, in which he bore a part, he was the victim of a quarrel between two American commanders, and stripped of his commission by court-martial. The President reinstated him, but he declined returning. He determined to retrieve his honor. One line more would complete his survey, the route for a great road from the Mississippi to San Francisco. Again he appeared in the far West. He refitted his expedition, and started again; pierced the country of the Apaches; met, awed, or defeated savage tribes; and, in a hundred days from Santa Fé, stood on the banks of the Sacramento. The people of California reversed the judgment of the court-martial, and he was made the first Senator of the Golden State, in 1850 and 1851. He was subsequently a candidate for President in opposition to Mr. Buchanan, and, though he received a large vote, was defeated. In 1861 he served in the Union army as a Major-General; and by the Cleveland Convention of 1864 was again nominated for the office of President of the United States.

French, Ezra B.—He was a Representative, from Maine, in the Thirty-sixth Congress, serving as a member of the Committee on Manufactures. He was also a member of the Peace Congress of 1861. By President Lincoln he was appointed Second Auditor of the Treasury.

French, Richard.—He was a native of Kentucky, and was a Representative in Congress, from that State, from 1835 to 1837, from 1843 to 1845, and again from 1847 to 1849.

Frey, Joseph.—He was born in Pennsylvania, and was a Representative in Congress, from that State, from 1827 to 1831.

Frick, Henry.—Born in Northumberland County, Pennsylvania, in 1796; was educated as a printer; became an editor of a newspaper; served for three sessions in the State Legislature; and was a Representative in Congress at the time of his death, which occurred at Washington City, March 1, 1844.

Fries, George.—He was born in Pennsylvania, and, having removed to

Ohio, was elected a Representative in Congress, from that State, from 1845 to 1847, and for a second term ending in 1849.

Fromentin, Eligius.—A Senator of the United States, from Louisiana, from 1813 to 1819. In 1821 he was Judge of the Criminal Court of New Orleans, and was appointed Judge of the Western District of Florida. He shortly resigned his office and returned to the practice of law, at New Orleans, where he died, of the yellow fever, October 6, 1822.

Frost, Joel.—He was born in New York; served in the State Assembly, in 1806 and 1808, and was a Representative in Congress, from that State, from 1823 to 1825.

Fry, Jacob, Jr.—He was a native of Pennsylvania, and was elected a Representative in Congress, from that State, from 1835 to 1839.

Fuller, George.—He was born in Pennsylvania, and was a Representative in Congress, from that State, from 1843 to 1845.

Fuller, Henry M.—He was born in Bethany, Wayne County, Pennsylvania, January 3, 1820; graduated at Nassau Hall, Princeton, in 1839; studied law, and was admitted to the bar in 1842; in 1848 was elected to the Legislature of Pennsylvania; and was a Representative in Congress, from that State, from 1851 to 1853, and from 1855 to 1857. Died in Philadelphia, December 26, 1860.

Fuller, Philo C.—He was a member of the New York Assembly in 1830; a Representative in Congress, from New York, from 1833 to 1837; the Second Postmaster-General, from 1841 to 1843; and died at Geneva, August 16, 1855.

Fuller, Thomas J. D.—He was born in Hardwick, Caledonia County, Vermont, March 17, 1808; was left an orphan when seven years of age; spent his boyhood and youth upon a farm; on attaining manhood, studied and adopted the profession of law, having been admitted to the bar in 1833; and, removing to Maine, was elected State's Attorney for his county for three years; was elected a Representative, from Maine, to the Thirty-first, Thirty-second, Thirty-third, and Thirty-fourth Congresses, serving as an active member of the Committee on Commerce. In 1857 he was appointed, by President Buchanan, Second Auditor of the Treasury, which office he held until 1861.

Fuller, Timothy.—He was born at Chilmark, Martha's Vineyard, Massachusetts, July 11, 1778, and graduated at Harvard University in 1801; was a member of the Massachusetts Senate from 1813 to 1817; Speaker of the Lower House in 1825; again a State Representative in 1831; a State Councillor in 1831; and he was a Representative in Congress, from Massachusetts, from 1817 to 1825; and died at Groton, Massachusetts, October 1, 1835, aged fifty-seven years.

Fuller, William K.—He was a member of the Assembly of New York in 1829 and 1830; at one time Adjutant-General of the State Militia; and from 1833 to 1837 a Representative in Congress.

Fullerton, David.—Born in 1771; was for several years a member of the State Legislature of Pennsylvania; and represented that State in Congress, from 1819 to 1820. He died at Greencastle, Pennsylvania, February 1, 1843.

Fullton, Andrew S.—He was born in Virginia, and was a Representative in Congress, from that State, from 1847 to 1849.

Fulton, John H.—He was a Representative in Congress, from Virginia, from 1833 to 1835, and died at Abingdon, January 28, 1836.

Fulton, William S.—He was born in Cecil County, Maryland, June 2, 1795; graduated at Baltimore College in 1813, and commenced the study of law with William Pinckney; but before coming of age, he served with great credit in a volunteer company, which was assigned to the defence of Fort McHenry. He was aid to Colonel Armisted, taking charge of the company during the illness of that commander, and returned with them to the city of Baltimore. After peace was restored in 1815, he removed to Tennessee with his father's family, and resumed the study of law with Felix Grundy. In 1818 he volunteered with the Nashville Guards, and was private secretary to General Jackson during the Florida campaign. He settled in Alabama for the practice of law, and was appointed by President Jackson, in 1829, Secretary of the Territory of Arkansas, and, in 1835, Governor of the same, which office he held until the Territory was admitted into the Union as a State, when he was elected a Senator, from Arkansas, from 1836 to 1844. He died at Rosewood, near Little Rock, Arkansas, August 15, 1844.

Gage, Joshua.—He was a Representative in Congress, from Massachusetts, from 1817 to 1819, having been a member of the Legislature from 1805 to 1808, in 1813, 1814, 1820, and 1821; and was a State Councillor in 1822 and 1823.

Gaillard, John.—A Senator of the United States, from South Carolina, from 1804 to 1826. He voted for the war of 1812, and was repeatedly called to preside over the Senate, in the absence of the Vice-President. He died at Washington, February 26, 1826.

Gaines, John P.—He was born in Kentucky; was a Representative in Congress, from that State, from 1847 to 1849; and was subsequently appointed Governor of Oregon Territory.

Gaither, Nathan.—He was born in Kentucky, and was a Representative in Congress, from that State, from 1829 to 1833. Died at Columbia, Adair County, Kentucky, in 1862, aged seventy-seven years.

Galbraith, John.—He was born in Pennsylvania, and was a Representative in Congress, from that State, from 1833 to 1837, and again from 1839 to 1841. Died at Erie, June 15, 1860, while holding the office of United States Judge for the District of Pennsylvania.

Gale, George.—He was a Representative in Congress, from Maryland, from 1789 to 1791.

Gale, Levin.—He was born in Maryland, and was a Representative in Congress, from that State, from 1827 to 1829.

Gallatin, Albert.—Born at Geneva, January 29, 1761; graduated at the University of his native city, in 1779, and during the next year emigrated to America. He commenced his career in Maine, then a part of Massachusetts, having been placed in command of a small fort at Machias, and while there he furnished funds of his own to American troops, and acted as a volunteer also. He was appointed a tutor at Harvard University in 1782, and removed to Pennsylvania in 1783, where he acted a prominent part in the State Convention of 1789, and served in the lower branch of the Legislature in 1790 and 1791. He also spent several years in Virginia, and in that State took the oath of allegiance. In 1793 he was elected a Senator in Congress, from Pennsylvania, but his seat was vacated, in 1794, by a resolution of the Senate, on the ground of want of citizenship for a sufficient length of time; and soon after, without his knowledge, he was elected a Representative in Congress, from Pennsylvania, serving from 1795 to 1801. He was, in the latter year, appointed Secretary of the Treasury, under President Jefferson, and, as an executive councillor, and subsequently diplomatist and statesman, he obtained a very high reputation. In 1813 he went to St. Petersburg as one of the Envoys Extraordinary, to negotiate with Great Britain, under the mediation of Russia, and, during the following year, with Adams, Bayard, Clay, and Russell, signed the Treaty of Ghent. He assisted also in concluding the Commercial Convention with England, at London, in 1815, and resided at Paris, as Minister of the United States, from 1816 to 1823. In 1827 he obtained full indemnification from England, for injuries sustained by our citizens for violating the Treaty of Ghent. President Madison offered him a seat in his cabinet, as Secretary of State; President Monroe offered him the post of Secretary of the Navy, and he was also nominated for Vice-President, all which honors he declined. In 1828 he became a citizen of New York, and took an active part in promoting the literary and commercial interests of the Empire City, and of the Union at large. In 1831 he was a member of the Free Trade Convention, and drew up the memorial to Congress, which embodies the views of the Democratic party; he was President of the National Bank of New York, and also of the New York Historical Society, and the Ethnological Society, and advocated the establishment of the New York University; and, just before his death, became identified with the Smithsonian Institution. He was a fine scholar, and published many papers on the currency and finance, on Indian languages, and other important subjects. He died at Astoria, Long Island, August 12, 1849.

Gallegos, Jose Manuel.—He was born in New Mexico, and was a Delegate, from that Territory, to the Thirty-third and Thirty-fourth Congresses.

Galloway, Samuel.—He was born in Pennsylvania, and, having removed to Ohio, was elected a Representative, from that State, to the Thirty-fourth Congress.

Gallup, Albert.—He was at one time Sheriff of Albany County, New York; a Representative in Congress, from New York, from 1837 to 1841, and was appointed by President Polk Collector of Providence, Rhode Island. He died at Providence, in November, 1851.

Gamble, James.—He was born in Pennsylvania, and was a Representative in Congress, from that State, from 1851 to 1855.

Gamble, Roger L.—Was a member of the House of Representatives in Congress, from Georgia, from 1833 to 1835, and from 1841 to 1843; and afterwards Judge of the Superior Court of that State. He died December 20, 1847.

Gannett, Barzillai.—He graduated at Harvard University in 1785; served four years in the State Legislature; and was a Representative in Congress, from Massachusetts, from 1809 to 1811.

Ganson, John.—He was born in Le Roy, Genesee County, New York, January 1, 1818; graduated at Harvard College in 1839; adopted the profession of law; was a member of the State Legislature in 1862; and was elected a Representative, from New York, to the Thirty-eighth Congress, serving on the Committee of Elections. He was also a Delegate to the Chicago Convention of 1864.

Gardenier, Barent.—He was a Representative in Congress, from New York, from 1807 to 1811.

Gardner, Francis.—He was born in Leominster, Massachusetts, December 27, 1771; graduated at Harvard College; was a preacher of the Gospel in New Hampshire for half a century; a Representative in Congress, from that State, from 1807 to 1809; and died at Roxbury, Massachusetts, June 25, 1835.

Gardner, Gideon.—He was a Representative in Congress, from Massachusetts, from 1809 to 1811.

Garfield, James A.—He was born in Orange, Cuyahoga County, Ohio, November 19, 1831; graduated at Williams College, Massachusetts, in 1856, and adopted the profession of law; in 1859 and 1860 he was a member of the Ohio Senate; in 1861 he entered the army as Colonel of the Forty-second Regiment of Volunteers; was appointed a Brigadier-General in 1862, the day that he fought in the battle of Middle Creek, Kentucky. He subsequently served at Shiloh, Corinth, and in Alabama, and early in 1863 he was appointed chief of staff to General Rosecrans, with whom he served up to the battle of Chickamauga. In 1862 he was elected a Representative, from Ohio, to the Thirty-eighth Congress, serving as a member of the Committee on Military Affairs. Before taking his seat in Congress he was appointed a Major-General of volunteers "for gallant and meritorious services in the battle of Chickamauga, Georgia, from September 19, 1863."

Garland, David S.—He was a Representative in Congress, from Virginia, from 1809 to 1811. Died in October, 1841.

Garland, James.—He was a native of Virginia, and a Representative in Congress, from that State, from 1845 to 1847.

Garland, Rice.—He was born in Virginia, and, having taken up his residence in Louisiana, was a Representative in Congress, from that State, from 1834 to 1840, having resigned to become

Judge of the Superior Court of Louisiana.

Garnett, James M.—Born at Elmwood, in Essex County, Virginia, June 8, 1770. He served for several years as a member of the Legislature of his native State, and was a Representative in Congress, from Virginia, from 1805 to 1809. He was a member of the Convention assembled at Richmond in 1829 to revise the Constitution of Virginia. He was interested in the cause of education, and devoted to the pursuits of agriculture, having presided over the Agricultural Society of Fredericksburg for more than twenty years, and toiled laboriously for the formation of a National Agricultural Society. He died at Elmwood, May, 1843, aged sixty-two years.

Garnett, Muscoe R. H.—He was born in Essex County, Virginia; was educated at the University of Virginia, and studied law as a profession; he was a member of the Constitutional Convention of the State in 1850; a member of the House of Delegates in 1853 and 1854, 1855 and 1856, and during the latter session was Chairman of the Committee on Finance. He was elected to the Thirty-fifth Congress as a Representative, from Virginia, serving as a member of the Committee on Claims, and also elected to the Thirty-sixth Congress. He was a Delegate to the Democratic Conventions at Baltimore and Cincinnati, in 1852 and 1856.

Garnett, Robert S.—He was a native of Essex County, Virginia, and a Representative in Congress, from that State, from 1817 to 1827.

Garnsey, Daniel G.—He was born in Saratoga County, New York, and was a Representative in Congress, from New York, from 1825 to 1830.

Garrison, Daniel.—He was born in Salem County, New Jersey, and was a Representative in Congress, from New Jersey, from 1823 to 1827.

Garrow, Nathaniel.—He was a Representative in Congress, from New York, from 1827 to 1829.

Gartlin Alfred.—He was born in North Carolina; graduated at the University of that State; and was a Representative in Congress, from North Carolina, from 1823 to 1825.

Gartrell, Lucius J.—Born in Wilkes County, Georgia, January 7, 1821; educated at Randolph Macon College, Virginia, and Franklin College, Athens, Georgia; is a lawyer by profession; and in 1843 was elected, by the General Assembly of Georgia, Solicitor-General of the Northern Judicial Circuit. He resigned in 1847, on being elected a Representative to the Legislature, and was re-elected in 1849; was a Presidential Elector for the State of Georgia in 1856; and in 1857 was elected a Representative in the Thirty-fifth Congress. He was one of the Regents of the Smithsonian Institution, and a member of the Committee on Expenditures in the Treasury Department; re-elected to the Thirty-sixth Congress, serving on the Committee on Elections. Resigned in 1861, and retired to Georgia.

Garvin, William S.—He was a Representative in Congress, from Pennsylvania, from 1845 to 1847.

Gaston, William.—Born in Newbern, North Carolina, September 19, 1778. His early education was conducted by his mother; advanced at the Catholic College of Georgetown, District of Columbia; and he graduated at Princeton College. He studied law, and was admitted to practice in 1798. He served a number of years in the State Legislature, and was a Representative in Congress, from 1813 to 1817. In 1834 he was appointed Judge of the Supreme Court, and in 1835 was a member of the State Convention to amend the Constitution. He continued on the Bench until the time of his death, which occurred January 23, 1844. He was an able and successful lawyer, and an upright judge, had a taste for polite literature, and is remembered in North Carolina as one of its most distinguished citizens. He was a Presidential Elector in 1808, and later in life received from Princeton the degree of Doctor of Laws.

Gates, Seth Merrill.—He was born in Winfield, Herkimer County, New York, October 16, 1800; was self-educated; studied law, and commenced practice in 1827; was elected to the State Legislature in 1832, declining a re-election; in 1838 he purchased and became editor of the Le Roy Gazette; was elected a Representative, from New York, to the Twenty-sixth Congress, and was elected to the Twenty-seventh Congress. In his paper and in Congress he advocated the right of petition, and on account of his hostility to slavery a reward of five hundred dollars was offered by a Southern planter for his person. At the close of the Twenty-seventh Congress he drew up a protest against the annexation of Texas, which was signed by twenty-two Representatives, John Quincy Adams heading the list of names. In 1848 he was the Free-soil candidate for Lieutenant-Governor of New York; and he has been a resident of the "Old Genesee" District for fifty-eight years.

Gayarre, Charles E. A.—Born in Louisiana, January 3, 1805; educated at the College of New Orleans; in 1826 he went to Philadelphia and studied law; was admitted to the bar in 1829, and returned home; in 1830 he was elected to the Legislature; in 1831 was appointed Deputy Attorney-General; in 1833 Presiding Judge of the City Court of New Orleans; and in 1835 he was elected a Senator in Congress, but ill health prevented him from taking his seat. He went to Europe, where he spent a number of years, and on his return, in 1843, was again returned to the State Legislature; and in 1846 he was appointed Secretary of State, in which capacity he served seven years. As an author, he has acquired a high position, his leading works being as follows: "History of Louisiana," "Romance of the History of Louisiana," "Spanish Domination in Louisiana," a dramatic novel called "The School of Politics," and a work on "The Influence of the Mechanic Arts."

Gayle, John.—Born in Sumter District, South Carolina, September 11, 1792; educated at South Carolina College; and emigrated to Alabama in 1813. In 1817 he was appointed a member of the Territorial Legislature; was Solicitor of the First Judicial District on the organization of the State Government; and in 1823 was elected Judge of the Supreme Court of the State. In 1829 was elected to the State Legislature, and was Speaker of the House. In 1831 was elected Governor, and reelected in 1833. He was Presidential Elector in 1836 and in 1840, and in 1847 was elected, from Mobile County, a Representative in Congress. In 1849 he was appointed Judge of the United States District Court of Alabama, and died near Mobile, July 21, 1859.

Gaylord, James M.—He was born in Ohio, and was a Representative in Congress, from that State, from 1851 to 1853.

Gazley, James W.—He was a Representative in Congress, from Ohio, from 1823 to 1825.

Gebhard, John.—He was born in Claverack, New York, and was a Representative in Congress, from New York, from 1821 to 1823.

Geddes, James.—Born near Carlisle, Pennsylvania, July 22, 1763; obtained a limited education while working upon a farm; removing to New York, he organized, in 1794, a company for the manufacture of salt at Onondaga; in 1800 was elected a magistrate; in 1804 and in 1821 he was in the State Legislature; in 1809 an Associate County Justice; in 1812 Judge of the Common Pleas; and he was a Representative in Congress from 1813 to 1815. In 1822 he was appointed Chief Engineer of the Ohio Canal; and in 1827 assisted in locating the Chesapeake and Ohio Canal, as well as the Pennsylvania Canal. He died August 19, 1838.

Gentry, Meredith P.—He was born in North Carolina; studied law, and settled in the practice of his profession in Tennessee; and was a Representative in Congress, from that State, from 1839 to 1843, from 1845 to 1847, and from 1847 to 1853.

German, Obadiah.—He was a Senator in Congress, from New York, from 1809 to 1815, and died September 24, 1842.

Gerry, Elbridge.—Born at Marblehead, Massachusetts, July, 1744, and graduated at Harvard College in 1762. He devoted himself for several years to commercial pursuits; was a member of the Legislature in 1773, and was appointed on the Committee of Correspondence. From 1776 to 1785 he was a Delegate to the Continental Congress, and signed the Declaration of Independence; while in that body he was a member of the Committee of Public Safety and Supplies, and when the Committee were in session at Menotomy, he, with Colonel Orne, escaped from the British troops at night by fleeing to a corn-field, while the house was searched for them. He was a member of the Convention which framed the Constitution of the United States, but declined subscribing to it. He was a Representative in the Federal Congress from 1789 to 1793; and in 1797 he was appointed Minister to France. In 1804 he was one of the Presidential Electors, and was Governor of Massachusetts in 1810 and 1811. In 1813 he was inaugurated Vice-President of the United States, and filled the office until his death, which took place at Washington, November 23, 1814.

Gerry, Elbridge.—Born in Waterford, Oxford County, Maine, December 6, 1815; received a good academical education; studied law, and was admitted to the bar in 1839; in 1840 was Clerk of the House of Representatives of Maine; in 1842 was appointed State's Attorney for Oxford County, and reelected by the people during the following year; in 1846 he was elected to the State Legislature; and he was a Representative in Congress, from Maine, from 1849 to 1851. Of late years he has resided in Portland, engaged in the practice of his profession.

Gerry, James.—He was born in Maryland, and was a Representative in Congress, from Pennsylvania, from 1839 to 1843.

Geyer, Henry S.—He was born in Frederick County, Maryland, in 1798, and early in life removed to Missouri. He saw some service in the war of 1812, and was Captain of the first militia company formed in the State of his adoption. He adopted the profession of law, and became eminent as a practitioner. He took an active part in politics, and was a member of the Convention which formed a State Constitution; and he was an active member of the first two sessions of the State Legislature, and was chosen Speaker during his second term. He succeeded Mr. Benton in the United States Senate, where he served irom 1851 to 1857; and while in Washington, officiated as Attorney in the Dred Scott case. He was a man of ability, of pleasing manners, and of high character. He died at St. Louis, March 5, 1859.

Gholson, James H.—He was born in Virginia; graduated at Princeton College in 1820; and was a Representative in Congress, from Virginia, from 1833 to 1835; and died at Brunswick, Virginia, July 2, 1848, aged fifty years.

Gholson, S. H.—He was a Representative in Congress, from Mississippi, from 1837 to 1838.

Gholson, Thomas.—He was a Representative in Congress, from Virginia, from 1808 to 1816.

Giddings, Joshua R.—Born at Athens, Bradford County, Pennsylvania, October 6, 1795; was a lawyer by profession; practised in Ohio; was elected to the Ohio Legislature in 1826; and was a Representative in Congress, from Ohio, from 1838 to 1859. He was for many years recognized as one of the leaders of the Anti-slavery party, and was the author of a book on Florida. In 1861 he was appointed by President Lincoln, Consul-General of British North America; and died at Montreal, while playing billiards, May 27, 1864.

Gilbert, Edward.—He was a Representative in Congress, from California, from 1850 to 1851.

Gilbert, Ezekiel.—He was born in 1755, in Middletown, Connecticut; graduated at Yale College in 1778; and was a member of Congress, from New York, from 1793 to 1797. He suffered for thirty years from a stroke of paralysis, and died at Hudson, New York, in July, 1842.

Gilbert, Sylvester.—Born in 1756, at Hebron, Connecticut; graduated at Dartmouth College in 1775; studied law, and was admitted to practice in 1777, at Hebron. In 1780 he was a member of the General Assembly, being the youngest member in the House. In 1788 he was appointed State's Attorney for Toland County, and filled that office twenty-one years. In 1807 he was appointed Chief Judge of the County Court, and Judge of Probate, which offices he held until 1825, with the exception of his term as Representative in Congress, in 1818 and 1819; and in 1810 he was a teacher of a law school, which he continued about seven years, during which time fifty-six students were prepared for the bar under his tuition. In 1826 he was again elected to the Legislature, and was then the oldest member in the House; to which body he had, from the year 1780, been re-elected thirty times. He died in January, 1846.

Gilbert, William A.—He was born in Connecticut, and, removing to New York, was elected a Representative, from that State, to the Thirty-fourth Congress.

Giles, John.—Born in Rowan County, North Carolina, about the year 1788; graduated at Chapel Hill University in 1808; was a lawyer by profession, and engaged in the practice for more than thirty years. In 1829 he was elected a member of the House of Representatives in Congress, but resigned before taking his seat, on account of ill health. In 1835 he was a member of the Convention which met to revise the State Constitution. He died March 2, 1846, in Stanley County, North Carolina, where his professional duties required his attendance before the Circuit Court.

Giles, William Branch.—Born in Amelia County, Virginia, August 12, 1762; graduated at Princeton in 1781; studied law, but abandoned the profession after practising about six years. From 1826 to 1829 he was Governor of his native State; was a Representative in Congress, from 1790 to 1798, and again from 1801 to 1802; and United States Senator, from 1804 to 1815; and was subsequently a member of the Legislature. He published a Speech on the Embargo Laws in 1808, and, in 1813, Political Letters to the People of Virginia, and subsequently an invective letter against President Monroe, and others, of a political character, to John Marshall and John Quincy Adams. He died in Albemarle County, Virginia, December 4, 1830.

Giles, William D.—He was born in Maryland, and was a Representative in Congress, from that State, from 1845 to 1847.

Gillespie, James.—He was a member of the Provincial Congress of North Carolina, and a Representative in the United States Congress, from 1793 to 1799, and from 1803 to 1805. Died January 10, 1805.

Gillet, Ransom H.—Was born in New Lebanon, Columbia County, New York, January 27, 1800. His early employment was farming on his father's farm, in Saratoga County, in the summer, and lumbering in the pine forest during the winter. In 1819 he removed to St. Lawrence County, where he was employed to teach school, during the winter, while he attended the St. Lawrence Academy during the summer. In 1821 he engaged in the study of the law with the late Silas Wright, at Canton, still continuing to teach for his support. He was soon admitted to the bar, and settled in Ogdensburg, where he continued, mainly devoted to his profession, for about twenty years. In 1827 he was appointed Brigade-Major and Inspector of the 49th Brigade of Militia, and for ten years drilled and inspected six large regiments in St. Lawrence and Jefferson Counties; February 27, 1830, he was appointed Postmaster of Ogdensburg, which office he filled about three years; in 1832 he was a member of the first Baltimore Convention, which nominated General Jackson for President; he was elected, in November of that year, to Congress; re-elected in 1834, and served, while in Congress, as a member of the Committee on Commerce; in 1837 he was appointed, by President Van Buren, a Commissioner to treat with the Indian tribes in New York, and continued in that service until March, 1839; in 1840 he was a member of the Baltimore Convention which renominated Mr. Van Buren; he then engaged in practising law, and continued to do so until 1845, when President Polk appointed him Register of the Treasury, in which office he served until 1847, when he was promoted to the office of Solicitor of the Treasury, in which place he continued to serve until the autumn of 1849; he then resumed the practice of law in New York; in 1855 he became Assistant to the Attorney-General of the United States, and continued in that office until he resigned, in 1858; and President Buchanan tendered him the place of Solicitor of the Court of Claims, which he accepted and held until 1861.

Gillette, Francis.—He was a Senator in Congress, from Connecticut, during the session of 1854–5.

Gillis, James L.—Born at Hebron, Washington County, New York, October 2, 1792. He received a common school education; served an apprenticeship to the currying and tanner's trade; during the campaigns of 1812 and 1813, served as a volunteer from New York; in 1814 he was commissioned a Lieutenant by the Governor of New York, and, having been taken prisoner by the British, was transported to Halifax, where he remained until the close of the war; he subsequently returned to Ontario County, and established himself as a farmer; in 1823 he removed to Pennsylvania; in 1840 was elected to the Legislature of that State; in 1842 was appointed one of the Judges of Jefferson County; elected to the State Senate in 1845; re-elected to the Lower House in 1851; and elected a Representative in the Thirty-fifth Congress, serving on the Committee on Agriculture.

Gillon, Alexander.—He was a Representative in Congress, from South Carolina, from 1793 to 1794, having died during the latter year.

Gilman, Charles J.—He was born in New Hampshire; served in the Legislature of that State in 1854; and having removed to Maine, was elected a Representative to the Thirty-fifth Congress, from that State, and was a member of the Committee on Private Land Claims.

Gilman, Nicholas.—He was a Delegate, from New Hampshire, to the Continental Congress, from 1786 to 1788; after the adoption of the Constitution, was elected a Representative in Congress, from 1789 to 1797; and was a Senator in Congress, from New Hampshire, from 1805 to 1814. He died at Philadelphia, Pennsylvania, May 2, 1814, aged fifty-two years.

Gilmer, George R.—He was born in Wilkes County (now Oglethorpe), Georgia, April 11, 1790. He received an academical education, but did not enter college, on account of ill health. He studied law, and settled in Lexington, Oglethorpe County, Georgia. In 1813, as First Lieutenant of the Forty-third Regiment, United States Army, he participated in the Creek war, and in 1818 entered upon the practice of his profession. He was elected to the State Legislature in 1818, 1819, and 1824; was Governor of the State for the terms commencing in 1829 and 1837, and during the latter term removed the Cherokee Indians from Georgia. He was President of the Board of Presidential Electors in 1836; and was a Representative in Congress, from 1821 to 1823, from 1827 to 1829, and from 1833 to 1835. He was also a Presidential Elector in 1836 and 1840, and for thirty years performed the duties of trustee of the Georgia College. He was the author of a book, published in 1855, entitled "Georgians," which contains much useful and interesting information touching the early settlement of his native State. Died at Lexington, Georgia, November 15, 1859.

Gilmer, John A.—Born in Guilford County, North Carolina, November 4, 1805; acquired a good English education at winter schools, working on a farm and in the shop during the summers; then taught a school, and thus obtained the means to enter the academy at Greensborough for three years, and became a good linguist and mathematician, and taught for three years in a grammar school; afterwards studied law, and was admitted to the bar in 1832. Was a member of the State Senate, from 1846 to 1856, and was elected a Representative to the Thirty-fifth Congress, serving as a member of the Committee on Elections. In 1856 he was the Whig candidate for Governor of North Carolina, but defeated. He was re-elected to the Thirty-sixth Congress, and made Chairman of the Committee on Elections.

Gilmer, Thomas W.—He was a native of Virginia, in which State he held many positions of high character, having been Governor of the State in 1840, and was a Representative in Congress, from 1841 to 1843, from Virginia; and was Secretary of the Navy under

President Tyler. He was killed by the accident on board the United States steamer Princeton, February 28, 1844.

Gilmore, Alfred.—He was born in Pennsylvania, and was a Representative in Congress, from that State, from 1849 to 1853.

Gilmore, John.—He was a Representative in Congress, from Pennsylvania, from 1829 to 1833. Died May 18, 1845.

Gist, Joseph.—Born in Union District, South Carolina, in 1775; educated at the Charleston College; studied law and admitted to the bar in 1799; served in the Legislature of his native State for eighteen years; was a Representative in Congress, from South Carolina, from 1821 to 1827; served as a Trustee of the State College; and died May 8, 1836.

Glascock, Thomas. — He was a soldier and statesman of Georgia; served at the siege of Savannah, under Count Pulaski, as Lieutenant, and exhibited great skill and bravery; he was appointed Colonel of the troops ordered out by the Legislature, in defence of the State against the Indians, on the western frontier; and was afterwards elected General of militia. He was a Representative in Congress, from Georgia, from 1836 to 1839, and highly respected for his talents and character. He died at Decatur, Georgia, May 9, 1841.

Glasgow, Hugh.—He was a Representative in Congress, from Pennsylvania, from 1813 to 1817.

Glenn, Henry.—He took an active part in the Revolutionary war, and was a Representative, from New York, in Congress, from 1793 to 1801. He died at Schenectady, in 1814, aged seventy-three years.

Gloninger, John.—He was born in Pennsylvania, and was a Representative, from that State, in the Twelfth Congress, but resigned before the expiration of his term, and E. Crouch was elected in his place.

Goddard, Calvin. — Born in Shrewsbury, Massachusetts, July 17, 1768; and graduated at Dartmouth, in 1786. He was admitted to the bar in Norwich, Connecticut, in 1790, and settled in Plainfield, from which place he was elected a Representative in the Legislature, for nine sessions, during three of which he was Speaker of the House. He removed to Norwich in 1807. From 1801 to 1805 he was a Representative in Congress, and from 1808 to 1815 he was a member of the State Council, and from 1815 to 1818 Judge of the Superior Court. He was State's Attorney for the County of New London for five years, and Mayor of Norwich for seventeen years. He died at Norwich, May 2, 1842.

Goggin, William L. — Born in Bedford County, Virginia, May 31, 1807; received an academic education; studied law in Winchester, and was admitted to the bar in 1828, and practised in several of the Circuit and District Courts of the State. In 1836 he was a member of the Legislature, and in 1837 declined a re-election. In 1839 he was elected a Representative in Congress, from Virginia, and was re-elected in 1841, 1843, and 1847, being Chairman of the Committee on Post-offices and Post-roads during his last term. He was afterwards appointed one of the Visitors of West Point, under the administration of President Fillmore, and since that time he has pursued his profession, in connection with agricultural pursuits. In 1859 he was nominated as the Whig candidate for Governor of Virginia.

Gold, Thomas R.—He was a native of New York; graduated at Yale College in 1786; was a member of the State Senate from 1797 to 1802; a member of the Assembly in 1808; and a Representative in Congress, from 1809 to 1813, and again from 1815 to 1817. He died in 1826.

Goldsborough, Charles W.—He was Governor of the State of Maryland, and a Representative in Congress, from 1805 to 1817. He died at Shoal Creek, Maryland, December 13, 1834.

Goldsborough, Robert H.—He was a Senator of the United States, from Maryland, from 1813 to 1819, and again from 1835 to 1836. He died at New Easton, Maryland, October 5, 1836.

Gooch, Daniel W.—Born in Wells, State of Maine, in January, 1820. He graduated at Dartmouth in 1843; studied law, and came to the bar in 1846; commenced the practice of his profession in Boston; was elected in 1852 to the Legislature of Massachusetts; in 1853 to the Constitutional Convention of the State; and subsequently a Representative in the Thirty-fifth Congress, from Massachusetts, for an unexpired term. He was also elected to the Thirty-sixth Congress, serving as a member of the Committee on Territories; re-elected to the Thirty-seventh Congress, serving on the Special Committee on the Conduct of the War; and was re-elected to the Thirty-eighth Congress, serving on the Committees on Private Land Claims, and Foreign Affairs.

Goode, Patrick G.—He was born in Virginia, and was elected a Representative in Congress, from Ohio, from 1837 to 1843.

Goode, Samuel.—He was a Representative in Congress, from Virginia, from 1799 to 1801.

Goode, William O.—He was born at Inglewood, Mecklenburg County, Virginia, September 16, 1798; was educated at the College of William and Mary; studied law, and commenced the practice in 1821; he was, early in life, elected for several terms a member of the State Legislature. He was a member, in 1829, of the State Reform Convention of Virginia; in 1832 he was again elected to the State Legislature, and took an active part in the debates on slavery of that year; he was reelected to the Legislature in 1838; and he was first elected a Representative in Congress, from Virginia, in 1841, serving until 1843. He was subsequently again elected to the Legislature, and was Speaker of the House of Delegates for several sessions; he was also a member of the State Reform Convention of 1850, and was chosen Chairman of the Legislative Committee; and he was a member of the House of Delegates, called to put the New Constitution into operation, and Chairman of the Committee on Finance. In 1853 he was again elected a Representative in Congress, from Virginia, and was regularly reelected until the Thirty-fifth Congress, in which he served as Chairman of the Committee on the District of Columbia. Died near Boydtown, Virginia, July 3, 1859.

Goodenow, John M.—He was a Representative in Congress, from Ohio, from 1829 to 1831.

Goodenow, Robert.—He was born in Farmington, New Hampshire, in 1800; admitted to the bar in 1821; was County Attorney from 1828 to 1834, and in 1841; and, having taken up his residence in Maine, was a Representative in Congress, from that State, from 1851 to 1853. In 1857 he was appointed Bank Commissioner for the State.

Goodenow, Rufus K.—Born in Henniker, New Hampshire, April 24, 1790, but removed with his father to Brownfield, Maine, where he was educated in a country school. He was a farmer, and for many years a common sailor. He entered the army in 1812 as Captain in the Thirty-third Regiment of United States Infantry, and served in that capacity until 1815. Upon the organization of a State Government he was appointed Clerk of the Courts for Oxford County, and removed to Paris, and held this office sixteen years. He was a member of the Legislature, and a Presidential Elector in 1840, and represented his district in the Thirty-first Congress.

Goodhue, Benjamin.—Born at Salem, Massachusetts, October 1, 1748; graduated at Harvard University in 1766; and received literary honors from Yale College in 1804. Early in life he engaged in commercial pursuits. He was a Whig during the Revolution; represented his native county in the State Senate, from 1784 to 1789, when he was elected a Representative to Congress under the new Constitution, and, assisted by Mr. Fitzsimmons, of Philadelphia, formed our code of revenue laws, the majority of which have never been abrogated. In 1796 he was elected a Senator of the United States, and became distinguished as Chairman of the Committee on Commerce; but in 1800 he resigned his seat, and retired from public life. He died at Salem, July 28, 1814.

Goodrich, Chauncey.—Born at Durham, Connecticut, October 20, 1759;

graduated at Yale College in 1776, with a high reputation for genius and acquirements. After spending several years as tutor in that institution he established himself as a lawyer at Hartford, and soon attained to eminence in the profession. He was a Representative in the Legislature in 1793, and a Representative in Congress, from 1795 to 1801. From 1802 to 1807 was a Councillor of the State; and he was elected United States Senator from 1807 to 1813. He received the office of Mayor of Hartford in 1812, and resigned his seat in Congress. He was elected Lieutenant-Governor of the State in 1813. He died August 18, 1815.

Goodrich, Elizur.—He was one of the very few survivors among the men who figured in public life under the administrations of Washington and the elder Adams. He belonged to the Washington school of Federalists, and his removal from the office of Collector of Customs, at New Haven, immediately on the accession of Jefferson to the Presidency, gave occasion to the famous letter, in which Jefferson avowed his principle of removal for political opinions. Besides being honored with various offices of trust and responsibility, he was for some time Professor of Law in Yale College, and for many years the efficient Mayor of New Haven. He was a Representative in Congress, from Connecticut, from 1799 to 1801. Died in New Haven, November 1, 1849.

Goodrich, John Z.—He was born in Sheffield, Massachusetts, September 27, 1801; adopted the profession of law, but turned his attention to manufacturing; served in the State Legislature in 1848 and 1849; and was a Representative in Congress, from 1851 to 1855, from his native State. In 1861 he was appointed, by President Lincoln, Collector of Boston, and was a Delegate to the Peace Congress of 1861.

Goodwin, Henry C.—Born in De Ruyter, Madison County, New York, June 25, 1824, received an academic education, and studied law, having been admitted to the bar in 1846. In 1847 he was elected District Attorney of Madison County, and held the office three years. He was a Representative, from New York, to the second session of the Thirty-third Congress, and was re-elected to the Thirty-fifth, serving as a member of the Committee on Claims. Died at Hamilton, Canada West, November 12, 1860.

Goodwin, John N.—Was born in South Berwick, Maine; graduated at Dartmouth College in 1844; studied law, and commenced practice in South Berwick; was elected in 1854 to the Senate of Maine; and in 1860 a Representative, from Maine, to the Thirty-seventh Congress, serving on the Committees on the Militia, and Invalid Pensions. He was subsequently appointed, by President Lincoln, Chief Justice of the Territory of Arizona.

Goodwin, Peterson.—He was a Representative in Congress, from Virginia, from 1803 to 1818. Died February 21, 1818.

Goodyear, Charles.—He was born in New York, and was a member of the New York Assembly, from Schoharie County, in 1840, and a Representative in Congress from 1845 to 1847.

Gordon, James.—He was a member, for seven years, of the State Senate of New York, twelve years in the State Assembly, and was a Representative in Congress, from New York, from 1791 to 1795.

Gordon, Samuel.—He was born in New York, served in the State Assembly in 1834, and was a Representative in Congress, from that State, from 1841 to 1843, and again from 1845 to 1847.

Gordon, William.—He was a graduate of Harvard College in 1779; was Attorney-General for the State of New Hampshire; a Representative in Congress, from New Hampshire, from 1797 to 1800; and died at Boston, in May, 1802, aged thirty-nine years.

Gordon, William F.—He was a native of Virginia, and a Representative in Congress, from that State, from 1829 to 1835. He is said to have been the originator of the Sub-treasury System. Died in Albemarle County, July 2, 1858.

Gore, Christopher.—Born in Boston, Massachusetts, in 1758; graduated at Harvard College in 1776; Governor of Massachusetts under the Constitution of 1780. He settled in Boston as a lawyer, and, in 1789, was appointed District Attorney for the District of Massachusetts, under the new Constitution of the United States. In 1796 he was appointed a Commissioner under the fourth article of Jay's Treaty. This appointment obliged him to go to London, where he remained eight years, during the last of which he was left Chargé d'Affaires. He was again chosen Governor in 1809, but only served one term. In 1813 he was chosen a Senator of the United States, in which capacity he served until 1816, when he retired to private life. He died March, 1, 1827, aged sixty-eight. Having no children, Mr. Gore left valuable bequests to the American Academy and the Historical Society, of which he was a member; and he made Harvard College, of which institution he had been a Fellow and Trustee, his residuary legatee. He was for a time the legal tutor and adviser of Daniel Webster.

Gorham, Benjamin.—He was born in Charlestown, Massachusetts, February 13, 1775, and died in Boston, September 27, 1855. He graduated at Cambridge in 1795, studied law with Theophilus Parsons, of Newburyport, and rose to eminence at the bar of Boston. He was a Representative in Congress, from the Suffolk District, from 1820 to 1823, from 1827 to 1831, and from 1833 to 1835. He was afterwards, for a short time, member of the State Legislature, but spent the closing years of his life in retirement.

Gorman, William A.—He was born in Kentucky, and having removed to Indiana, was elected a Representative in Congress, from that State, from 1849 to 1853.

Gott, Daniel.—He was born in Connecticut, and on removing to New York, was elected a Representative in Congress, from 1847 to 1851.

Gould, Herman D.—He was born in Connecticut, and having taken up his residence in New York, was elected a Representative in Congress, from that State, from 1849 to 1851.

Gourdin, Theodore.—He was a Representative in Congress, from South Carolina, from 1813 to 1815. Died January 17, 1826.

Govan, A. R.—He was born in Orangeburg, South Carolina, and was a Representative in Congress, from South Carolina, from 1822 to 1827.

Graham, James.—Born in Lincoln County, North Carolina, in January, 1793. He graduated at the University of that State in 1814; studied law, and practised with success for many years; served four years in the State Legislature; and was a Representative in Congress, from 1833 to 1843, and from 1845 to 1847. He spent the close of his life engaged in agricultural pursuits, and died September 25, 1851.

Graham, James H.—He was elected a Representative, from New York, to the Thirty-sixth Congress, serving as a member of the Committee on Accounts.

Graham, William.—He was born in 1783; received a limited education; was a member of the Convention which framed the State Constitution of Indiana; served many years in both branches of the State Legislature, and was Speaker in 1820; and was a Representative in Congress, from Indiana, from 1837 to 1839. Died near Valonia, Indiana, in 1857.

Graham, William A.—Was born in 1800, in North Carolina, and represented that State in the United States Senate two years, viz., from 1841 to 1843. In August, 1844, he was elected Governor of the State, to which office he was re-elected in 1846, retiring at the expiration of his second term, in January, 1849. He was Secretary of the Navy under President Fillmore, and subsequently, candidate for Vice-President on the ticket with General Scott.

Granger, Amos P.—He was born in Suffield, Hartford County, Connecticut, in June, 1789; received a common school education; devoted the most of his life to farming and merchandizing; and having removed to New York, was elected a Representative, from that State, to the Thirty-fourth and Thirty-fifth Congresses, and was a member of the Committee on Territories.

Granger, Bradley F.—He was born in New York, and elected a Representative, from Michigan, to the Thirty-seventh Congress, serving on the Committee on Revolutionary Pensions.

Granger, Francis.—He was born in Suffield, Hartford County, Connecticut, in 1787; graduated at Yale College in 1811; and, on removing to New York, was for five years, from 1826, a member of the General Assembly of that State. He was a Representative in Congress, from New York, from 1835 to 1837, and again from 1839 to 1841, when he resigned, to receive from President Harrison the appointment of Postmaster-General. Since that time he has lived in retirement.

Grant, Abraham P.—He was born in New York, and was a Representative in Congress, from that State, from 1837 to 1839.

Grantland, Seaton.—He was born in Virginia, and having taken up his residence near Milledgeville, in Georgia, was elected a Representative in Congress, from that State, from 1835 to 1839. He was also a Presidential Elector.

Graves, William J.—He represented the State of Kentucky in Congress, from 1835 to 1841, and died at Louisville, September 27, 1848, aged forty-three years.

Gray, Edward.—He was a Representative in Congress, from Virginia, from 1799 to 1813.

Gray, Hiram.—He was a Representative in Congress, from New York, from 1837 to 1839.

Gray, John C.—He was born in Southampton County, Virginia, and was a Representative in Congress, from that State, from 1820 to 1821.

Grayson, William.—Was a native of Virginia, and a member of the Continental Congress. In 1788 was a member of the Convention of Virginia which assembled to consider the Constitution of the United States, and made himself conspicuous both by his talents and his union with Henry in opposing the adoption of the Constitution. From 1789 to 1790 he was a Senator of the United States, and died at Dumfries, while on his way to the seat of Government, March 12, 1790.

Grayson, William J.—He is a native of Beaufort, South Carolina; graduated at the South Carolina College in 1809; was bred to the legal profession; was a Commissioner in Equity of South Carolina; a member of the State Legislature; and a Representative in Congress, from 1833 to 1837; and by President Taylor he was appointed Collector of the Customs at Charleston. Of late years he has devoted himself to planting. In 1856 he published "The Hireling and the Slave," "Chicora, and other Poems."

Greeley, Horace.—Was born at Amherst, in New Hampshire, February 3, 1811. Until the age of fourteen, he attended a common school in his native State. About that time, his parents having removed to the State of Vermont, Horace, who had early shown a fondness for reading, especially newspapers, and had resolved to be a printer, endeavored to find employment as an apprentice in a printing-office in Whitehall, but without success. He afterwards applied at the office of the Northern Spectator, in Pultney, Vermont, where his services were accepted, and where he remained until 1830, when the paper was discontinued, and he returned to work on his father's farm. During the following year he arrived in the city of New York, where he obtained work as a journeyman printer, and was employed in various offices, with occasional intervals, for the next eighteen months. In 1834, in connection with Jonas Winchester, he started The New Yorker, a weekly journal of literature and general intelligence, and became its editor. After struggling on for several years, the journal was abandoned. During its existence, Mr. Greeley published several political campaign papers, The Constitution, The Jeffersonian, and The Log Cabin. In 1841 he commenced the publication of the New York Tribune. In 1848 he was chosen to fill a vacancy in the Thirtieth Congress, and served through the short term preceding President Taylor's inauguration. In 1851 he visited Europe, and was chosen chairman of one of the juries at the World's Fair. He gave an account of his travels in a series of letters to the Tribune, which were afterwards collected into a volume. He has also published a collection of his addresses, essays, &c., under the title of "Hints towards Reforms."

Green, Byram.—He was born in New York; served five years in the Assembly of that State; and was a Representative in Congress, from 1843 to 1845.

Green, Frederick W.—He was born in Maryland, and having removed to Ohio, was elected a Representative in Congress, from that State, from 1851 to 1855.

Green, I. L.—He was born in Massachusetts; graduated at Harvard University in 1781; was a Representative in Congress, from Massachusetts, from 1805 to 1809, and again from 1811 to 1813. He died in 1841.

Green, Innis.—He was born in Pennsylvania, and was a Representative in Congress, from that State, from 1827 to 1831.

Green, James S.—He was born in Fauquier County, Virginia, February 28, 1817; and in 1836, with no fortune but a common English education, he removed to Alabama, where he remained one year, and then took up his residence in Missouri, with which State he has since been identified. After many struggles with the world, he was admitted to the bar in 1840, and soon thereafter entered upon a lucrative practice. He was a member of the Convention, held in 1845, for the revision of the Constitution of Missouri; and was elected a member of Congress in 1846, serving through two terms. He argued a boundary dispute case in the Supreme Court, by appointment of the Governor of Missouri; and in 1849 took the stump against the late Hon. Thomas H. Benton. In 1853 President Pierce appointed him to be Chargé d'Affaires, and subsequently Minister Resident at Bogota, New Granada. He was again elected a member of Congress in 1856, but before taking his seat he was chosen by the Legislature to represent the State of Missouri in the Senate of the United States. During the first session of the Thirty-fifth Congress he was a member of the Committees on the Judiciary, and on Territories, and at the commencement of the second session of that Congress, he was chosen Chairman of the Committee on Territories.

Green, Willis.—He was born in Kentucky, and was a Representative in Congress, from that State, from 1839 to 1845.

Greene, Albert C.—He was born in East Greenwich, Rhode Island, in 1792; read law in New York, where he was admitted to the bar; returned to his native State, and there commenced the practice of his profession; in 1815 he was elected to the General Assembly of the State; in 1816 was elected a Brigadier-General of militia, and subsequently became a Major-General; from 1822 to 1825 he served again in the Legislature of the State, and was chosen Speaker; from 1825 to 1843 he was Attorney-General of the State; from 1845 to 1851 he was a Senator in Congress, from Rhode Island; and having again served a term in each of the two Houses of the State Legislature, he retired from public life in 1857. Died at Providence, January 8, 1863.

Greene, Ray.—He graduated at Yale College in 1784; and was a Senator in Congress, from Rhode Island, from 1797 to 1801, when he resigned.

Greene, Thomas M.—He was a Delegate to Congress, from the Territory of Mississippi, from 1802 to 1803.

Greenup, Christopher.—He was Governor of Kentucky from 1804 to 1808; was a patriot of the American Revolution, and participated in the perils of the war. He was at various times a member of the Legislature of Kentucky, and a Representative of that State in Congress, from 1792 to 1797. He was a man of great usefulness in his native State, and died at Frankfort, Kentucky, April 24, 1818.

Greenwood, A. B.—Born in Franklin County, Georgia, July 11, 1811; graduated at the Athens University, Georgia; is a lawyer by profession; and was a member of the Legislature of the State of Arkansas from 1842 to 1845.

He was Prosecuting Attorney for said State from 1845 to 1851; Circuit Judge from 1851 to 1853; and elected a Representative in Congress from 1853 to 1858, serving a portion of the time as Chairman of the Committee on Indian Affairs. In 1859 he was appointed, by President Buchanan, Commissioner of Indian Affairs.

Gregg, Andrew.—Born in Carlisle, Pennsylvania, June 10, 1755; he received a good classical education, and for several years was tutor in the University of Pennsylvania. In 1783 he opened a country store in Middletown, Dauphin County, whence he removed, in 1789, to a wilderness valley, where he commenced agricultural pursuits. In 1790 he was elected a Representative in Congress, from Pennsylvania, serving from 1791 to 1807, and a Senator of the United States from 1807 to 1813, serving for a time as President *pro tem.* of the Senate. In 1814 he removed to Bellefonte, and in 1816 he was appointed Secretary of State of Pennsylvania. He was remarkable for a sound and discriminating mind, agreeable and dignified manners, and performed his duties with talent and integrity. He died at Bellefonte, May 20, 1835.

Gregg, James M.—Born in Patrick County, Virginia, June 26, 1806. He received only a common school education, and was bred a practical farmer, but studied the profession of law; and in 1830 he settled in Hendrick County, Indiana. From 1834 to 1837 he was County Surveyor, and then chosen Clerk of the Circuit Court, serving till 1845. He was elected a Representative of the Thirty-fifth Congress, and was a member of the Committee on Public Expenditures.

Gregory, Dudley S.—He was born in Connecticut; was at one time engaged in the iron business among the Adirondack Mountains of New York, and having settled in New Jersey, was elected a Representative in Congress, from that State, from 1847 to 1849.

Greig, John.—Born in Dumfriesshire, Scotland, August 6, 1779; educated at the Edinburgh High School; emigrated to America in 1797; settled in Canandaigua, New York; studied law, and came to the bar in 1804: practised his profession until 1820, when he became President of the Ontario Bank, which he held until 1856; he was for many years a Regent of the New York University, and also a Vice-Chancellor; was long the active head of an Agricultural Society, and was one of the founders and corporators of the Ontario Female Seminary. His service in Congress was for the term commencing in 1841, but he resigned at the close of the first session. Died at Canandaigua, April 9, 1858.

Grennell, George.—Born in Greenfield, Franklin County, Massachusetts, December 25, 1786; graduated at Dartmouth College in 1808; studied law, and came to the bar in 1811; was Prosecuting Attorney for Franklin County from 1820 to 1828; was a member of the State Senate from 1824 to 1827; and was a Representative in Congress, from Massachusetts, from 1829 to 1839. He was for many years a member of the Board of Trustees of Amherst College, and in 1854 the degree of LL. D. was conferred upon him by that institution. From 1849 to 1853, he was Probate Judge for his county, and subsequently settled down as Clerk of the Franklin County Court. He was the first man who proposed and advocated on the floor of Congress the recognition of Hayti.

Grey, Benjamin E.—He was born in Kentucky, and was a Representative in Congress, from that State, from 1851 to 1855.

Grider, Henry.—Was born in Garrard County, Kentucky, July 16, 1796; received a good desultory education at Bowling Green, and elsewhere; studied law, and while engaged in practice, also devoted some attention to farming. He rendered his first public service as a private in the army, during the last war with England, having served with Shelby in his campaign to Canada; in 1827 and 1831 he was elected to the Legislature of Kentucky, and in 1833 to the State Senate, where he served four years. He was a Representative in Congress, from Kentucky, from 1843 to 1847, and was also reelected to the Thirty-seventh Congress, serving on the Committees on Revolutionary Claims, and on Mileage. Reelected to the Thirty-eighth Congress;

was a member of the Committee on the Territories.

Griffin, Isaac.—He was born in Pennsylvania, and was a Representative in Congress, from that State, from 1813 to 1817.

Griffin, John K.—He was a Representative in Congress, from South Carolina, from 1831 to 1841, and died at Milton, South Carolina, August 1, 1841.

Griffin, Samuel.—He was a Representative in Congress, from Virginia, from 1789 to 1795.

Griffin, Thomas.—He was a Representative in Congress, from Virginia, from 1803 to 1805.

Grimes, James W.—He was born in Deering, Hillsborough County, New Hampshire, October 16, 1816, and commenced his education at Hampton Academy, and graduated at Dartmouth College in 1836. Soon after that time he emigrated to the West, and in 1838 was elected to the first General Assembly of the Territory of Iowa, to which he was frequently re-elected. He was Governor of the State of Iowa from 1854 to 1858, and in 1859 he was elected a Senator in Congress, from that State, for six years, serving as Chairman of the Committee on the District of Columbia. He was also a Delegate to the Peace Congress of 1861.

Grinnell, Joseph.—He was born in New Bedford, Massachusetts, November 17, 1788. His early education was received at private schools, and was moulded in view of a mercantile life; he commenced business in New York as a commission merchant in 1809, and continued there until 1829, for five years being connected with John H. Howland, eleven years with Preserved Fish, and four years with his brothers, Moses H. and Henry Grinnell; in 1829 he retired from the New York concern, and visited Europe; on his return, he settled in his native place, devoting himself to commerce generally, and especially to the whale fishery. Among the laborious positions which he has long held in New Bedford, are those of President of the Marine Bank, of the New Bedford and Taunton Railroad, and of the Wamsutta Cotton-mill. In 1839, 1840, and 1841, he was a member of the Governor's Council of Massachusetts; he was elected a Representative to Congress in 1843, and was three times re-elected, serving on the Post-office and Commerce Committees, and originating the idea of a reduction of postage and the establishment of life-boats. Indeed, so great was Mr. Grinnell's influence on the floor of Congress, as every measure he proposed seemed to succeed, he was playfully designated by his friends as one of the most dangerous men in the House.

Grinnell, Josiah B.—He was born in New Haven, Vermont, December 22, 1821; received a collegiate and theological education; went to Iowa in 1855, and turned his attention to farming, having been the most extensive wool-grower in the State, to which he has devoted special attention; was a member of the State Senate for four years; a special agent for the General Post-office for two years; and was elected a Representative, from Iowa, to the Thirty-eighth Congress, serving on the Committee on Post-offices and Post-roads.

Grinnell, Moses H.—Born in New Bedford, Massachusetts, March 3, 1803; was educated at private schools and at Friends' Academy; was bred a merchant, and frequently went abroad as supercargo; and he was a Representative in Congress, from New York, from 1839 to 1841. Moses H., Henry Grinnell, and Robert B. Minturn, were the gentlemen composing the distinguished firm of Grinnell, Minturn & Co., the house taking that title in 1829, though in reality founded many years before by Joseph Grinnell and Preserved Fish.

Griswold, Gaylord.—He graduated at Yale College in 1787; was a member of the New York Assembly, from 1796 to 1798; and a Representative in Congress, from New York, from 1803 to 1805; and died in 1809.

Griswold, John A.—He was born in Rensselaer County, New York, about the year 1822; was educated for the mercantile profession; settled himself in the iron trade, to which, in connection with banking, he has ever been devoted. He served one term as Mayor of the City of Troy, and in 1862 he was elected a Representative, from New York, to the Thirty-eighth Congress, serving on the Committee on Naval Affairs.

Griswold, Roger.—Born in Lyme, Connecticut, May 21, 1762; graduated at Yale College in 1780, and studied law. From 1795 to 1805 he was a Representative in Congress, from Connecticut. In 1801 he declined the appointment of Secretary of War, offered him by President Adams, a few days previous to the accession of President Jefferson. In 1807 he was chosen a Judge of the Supreme Court of the State; was Lieutenant-Governor from 1809 to 1811, and then elected Governor; while holding that office, he refused to place four companies under General Dearborn, at the requisition of the President, for garrison purposes, deeming the requisition unconstitutional, as they were not wanted to "repel invasion," &c. He died in 1812.

Griswold, Stanley.—Born in Torringford, Connecticut, November, 1768; graduated at Yale College in 1786; and was a clergyman. In 1804 he became the editor of a Democratic paper in Walpole, New Hampshire, but soon after was appointed, by President Jefferson, Secretary of the Territory of Michigan. He was a Senator in Congress, from Ohio, in 1809; and United States Judge for the Northwestern Territory. He died at Shawneetown, Illinois, August 21, 1814.

Groesbeck, William S.—He was born in New York about the year 1826; studied law and removed to Cincinnati, where he engaged in the practice of his profession; in 1852 he was a member of the Commission appointed to codify the laws of Ohio; was a member in 1851 of the State Constitutional Convention; was elected a Representative, from Ohio, to the Thirty-fifth Congress, serving on the Committee on Foreign Affairs; was a member of the Peace Congress of 1861, and in 1862 was elected to the Senate of Ohio.

Gross, Ezra C.—He was born in Windsor County, Vermont; graduated at the University of Vermont in 1806; was a Representative in Congress, from New York, from 1819 to 1821; and was elected to the Assembly of that State in 1828 and 1829, but died before the close of his second term.

Gross, Samuel.—He was a native of Montgomery County, Pennsylvania, and was a Representative in Congress, from 1819 to 1823.

Grosvenor, Thomas P.—Born in Pomfret, Connecticut, in 1780, and died April 25, 1817. He graduated at Yale College in 1800; and, after studying law, removed to New York; served a number of years in the Legislature of that State, and was elected to Congress as a Representative, serving from 1813 to 1817.

Grout, Jonathan.—He was a Representative in Congress, from Massachusetts, from 1789 to 1791. He was also a State Representative in 1781 and 1784, and a State Senator in 1787 and 1788.

Grove, William B.—He was a Representative in Congress, from North Carolina, from 1791 to 1803.

Grover, Lafayette.—Was born in Bethel, Oxford County, Maine; graduated at Bowdoin College; studied law in Philadelphia, where he was admitted to the bar in 1850; and soon afterwards took up his residence in Salem, Oregon Territory. In 1851 he was elected Prosecuting Attorney for the Territory; in 1852 Auditor of Public Accounts; served three years in the Territorial Legislature; saw some service in the Indian wars of Oregon; was a Commissioner in 1854 to adjust the claims of citizens of Oregon against the United States; he was appointed in 1856 one of the Commissioners to investigate the Indian war claims against the General Government; and, having been an active member of the Convention of 1857 to form a State Constitution, he was subsequently elected the first Representative in Congress from the prospective State, and took his seat as such in February, 1859.

Grover, Martin.—He was a native of New York, and a Representative in Congress, from that State, from 1845 to 1847.

Grow, Galusha A.—Born in Ashford, Windham County, Connecticut, August 31, 1823; was educated at Amherst College, graduating in 1844; adopted the law as a profession, and was admitted to the bar in 1847; and having settled among the mountains of Pennsylvania, and his health, in 1850, being delicate, he amused himself by surveying wild lands and rafting; and in 1850 he was elected a Representative in Congress, where he served as a member of the Committees onTerritories and Public Printing. When Mr. Banks was Speaker of the House of Representatives, Mr. Grow was Chairman of the Committee on Territories; and, during one of the recesses of Congress, he visited Europe. He was re-elected to the Thirty-sixth Congress, serving as Chairman of the Committee on Territories. Re-elected to the Thirty-seventh Congress, and was chosen Speaker of the House of Representatives. He was also a Delegate to the Baltimore Convention of 1864.

Grundy, Felix. — Born in Virginia, September 11, 1770; he removed with his father to Kentucky, and was educated at Bardstown Academy; studied law, and soon became distinguished at the bar. He commenced his public career at the age of twenty-two, as a member of the Convention for revising the Constitution of Kentucky; was afterwards, for six or seven years, a member of the Legislature of that State. In 1806 he was elected one of the Judges of the Supreme Court of Kentucky, and was soon after Chief Justice. In 1807 he removed to Nashville, Tennessee, and became eminent as a lawyer. From 1811 to 1814 he was a Representative in Congress, from Tennessee, and during several years after was a member of the Legislature of that State. From 1829 to 1838 he was United States Senator, and in the latter year was appointed, by President Van Buren, Attorney-General of the United States; in 1840 he resigned this position, and was again elected Senator. He died at Nashville, Tennessee, December 19, 1840.

Gunn, James.—He was a Senator of the United States, from Georgia, from 1789 to 1801, and died in Louisville, in that State, July 30, 1801.

Gurley, Henry H.—He was born in Lebanon, Connecticut, in 1787; was educated at Williamstown College; studied law, and settled at an early day in Louisiana; and he was a Representative in Congress, from that State, from 1823 to 1831. He previously held the office of United States Judge of the District Court of Louisiana, and died in 1832.

Gurley, John A.—Born in East Hartford, Connecticut, December 9, 1813; received an academic education; studied for the ministry, and was settled as a preacher at Methuen, Massachusetts, from 1834 to 1837, when he removed to Cincinnati, Ohio, where he published a paper, called the Star of the West, for fifteen years. In 1858 he was elected a Representative, from Ohio, to the Thirty-sixth Congress, officiating as Chairman of the Committee on Printing. Re-elected to the Thirty-seventh Congress, serving on the Committees on Commerce and on Roads and Canals. Died at Cincinnati, August 19, 1863, while holding the office of Governor of Arizona, conferred upon him by President Lincoln.

Gustine, Amos.—He was a Representative in Congress, from Pennsylvania, from 1841 to 1843, and died in Lost Creek Valley, Pennsylvania, March 3, 1844.

Guyon, James.—He was born in Richmond County, New York, in 1777; represented Staten Island, in the Legislature of New York, a number of years, and was a member of Congress, from 1819 to 1821. He died on Staten Island, March 8, 1846.

Gwin, William M. — Born in Sumner County, Tennessee, October 9, 1805; graduated at Transylvania University, Lexington, Kentucky, and studied medicine as a profession; he was appointed United States Marshal for Mississippi; and elected a Representative in Congress, from that State, serving from 1841 to 1843. He was Commissioner of Public Buildings to superintend the erection of the New Orleans Custom-house; a member of the Convention for framing the Constitution of California, and was one of the first United States Senators from that State, having been elected, in 1850, for six years, and re-elected in 1856, for the term which expired in 1861. He was

Chairman of the Committee on the Pacific Railroad, and a member of the Committees on Finance and on Post-offices and Post-roads.

Habersham, Richard W.—He was born in Savannah, Georgia, in 1786, and was educated at Nassau Hall, New Jersey, where he graduated in 1805. He distinguished himself as a lawyer, and occupied many stations of trust in his native State, and was a Representative in Congress, from 1839 to 1843, where he commanded great respect for his political integrity and gentlemanly character. He died in Habersham County, Georgia, December 2, 1844.

Hacket, Thomas C.—He was born in Georgia, and was a Representative in Congress, from that State, from 1849 to 1851, and was a member of the Committee on Indian Affairs. Died at Marietta, Georgia, October 8, 1851.

Hackley, Aaron.—Born in New Haven, Connecticut, and was a member of the New York Legislature in 1814, 1815, and 1818, and a Representative in Congress, from that State, from 1819 to 1821.

Hahn, John.—He was a Representative in Congress, from Pennsylvania, from 1815 to 1817.

Hahn, Michael.—Born in Bavaria, in November, 1830; was brought to the United States when a child, and settled in Louisiana; received a public school education in New Orleans, and received the degree of LL.B. in the University of Louisiana; adopted the profession of law; and in 1862 was chosen a Representative to the Thirty-seventh Congress, he and B. F. Flanders having been elected during the military rule in Louisiana. He took his seat at the close of the session.

Haight, Edward.—Born in New York City, March 26, 1817; was educated at a private school; entered a counting-house, and turned his whole attention to mercantile pursuits; became a Director in the National Bank of New York, and subsequently Vice-President of the Bank of the Commonwealth, and finally President, which position he still occupies. Besides acting as a Director in six or seven banks and insurance companies, he has frequently served as an officer in various benevolent institutions. In 1860 he was elected a Representative, from New York, to the Thirty-seventh Congress, serving on the Committee on Manufactures.

Haile, William.—He was born in 1797, and died at Woodville, Mississippi, March 7, 1837. He was a member of Congress, from Mississippi, from 1826 to 1828.

Hale, Artemas.—Born in Winchendon, Worcester County, Massachusetts, October 20, 1783, and pursued the occupation of a farmer until twenty-one years of age, having received only a common school education. He was a teacher in Hingham for ten years, and then removed to Bridgewater, where he engaged in manufacturing. He was a Representative in the Legislature for several years, and a State Senator in 1833 and 1834. In 1853 he was a member of the State Constitutional Convention, and a Representative in Congress, from 1845 to 1849.

Hale, James T.—He was born in Bradford County, Pennsylvania, in October, 1810; received a common school education; studied law, and was admitted to the bar in 1832; in 1851 he was appointed President Judge in the Twentieth Judicial District of Pennsylvania, and in 1858 was elected a Representative, from Pennsylvania, to the Thirty-sixth Congress, serving as a member of the Committee on Claims. Re-elected to the Thirty-seventh Congress, serving on the Committees on Claims and on Roads and Canals. Re-elected to the Thirty-eighth Congress, and was Chairman of the Committee on Claims.

Hale, John P.—Born in Rochester, Stafford County, New Hampshire, March 31, 1806. After preparing himself at Exeter Academy, he entered Bowdoin College, and graduated in 1827. He studied law, and was admitted to the bar in 1830; in 1832 he was elected to the State Legislature; in 1834 he was appointed, by President Jackson, District Attorney for New Hampshire, and reappointed by President Van Buren; in 1843 he was elected a Representative in Congress; in

1846 he was again elected to the State Legislature and chosen Speaker; in 1847 he was elected a Senator in Congress, and after serving until 1853, devoted himself for two years to his profession, and was re-elected in 1855 to the United States Senate, and in 1859 was re-elected for the term ending in 1865, serving as Chairman of the Committee on Naval Affairs, and member of that on Post-offices and Post-roads. In 1852 he was the Free-soil candidate for Vice-President of the United States.

Hale, Salma.—He was a Representative in Congress, from New Hampshire, from 1817 to 1819, and a member of the State Legislature in 1823, 1824, and 1845, serving in both Houses.

Hale, William.—He was one of the most influential men of New Hampshire, and a member of Congress, from 1809 to 1811, and again from 1813 to 1817. Died at Dover, November 8, 1848, aged eighty-four years.

Haley, Elisha.—He was born in Connecticut, and was a Representative in Congress, from that State, from 1835 to 1839.

Hall, Augustus.—He was born in New York, and elected a Representative in Congress, from Iowa, to the Thirty-fourth Congress.

Hall, Bolling.—He was a member of Congress, from Georgia, from 1811 to 1817; died near Montgomery, Alabama, March 25, 1836, aged sixty-seven years.

Hall, Chapin.—Born in Ellicott, Chautauque County, New York, July 12, 1816; received a good English education; has devoted his life to mercantile pursuits in connection with lumbering; and was elected a Representative, from Pennsylvania, to the Thirty-sixth Congress, serving as a member of the Committee on Invalid Pensions.

Hall, George.—He was born in New Haven, Connecticut; was a member of the Assembly of New York in 1816, and a Representative in Congress, from that State, from 1819 to 1821.

Hall, Hiland.—He was born in Bennington, Vermont, July 20, 1795. He spent his boyhood on his father's farm, receiving, as he could, a good English education; studied law, and was admitted to the bar in 1819; in 1827 he was elected to the State Legislature, and afterwards, for several years, was State's Attorney; and he was a Representative in Congress, from Vermont, from 1833 to 1843, officiating for several sessions as Chairman of the Committee on Revolutionary Claims. He was also Bank Commissioner for Vermont, from 1843 to 1846; four years Judge of the Supreme Court; in 1850 Second Comptroller of the Treasury; and in 1851 was appointed, by President Fillmore, Land Commissioner for California, where he remained until 1854. He is now residing on the farm where he was born, and was elected Governor of Vermont in 1858; and served as a Delegate to the Peace Congress of 1861.

Hall, Joseph.—He was born in Essex County, Massachusetts, June 26, 1793; received a limited education; after leaving Andover Academy, went to Maine, and was a clerk in a store until twenty-one years of age; served as a Lieutenant of militia in 1813–14; from 1817 until 1819 was engaged in mercantile pursuits; was Sheriff of two counties for twelve years; and was a Representative in Congress, from Maine, from 1833 to 1837, having been the first Northern man who voted against receiving slavery petitions. Before entering Congress he was for four years Postmaster of Camden, Maine; and, by President Polk, was appointed Navy Agent of Boston in 1849. He has since been connected with the Boston Custom-house.

Hall, Lawrence W.—He was born in Lake County, Ohio, in 1819; was educated in that State; graduated at Hudson in 1839; was admitted to the bar in 1843; practised his profession until 1851, when he was elected Judge of the Court of Common Pleas, which position he held until 1856, when he was elected a Representative, from Ohio, to the Thirty-fifth Congress, serving as a member of the Committees on Agriculture, and on Public Buildings and Grounds. During the troubles of 1862 he was imprisoned for alleged disloyalty, and died soon after his release, in Ohio, January 26, 1863.

Hall, Nathan K.—Born March 28, 1810, at Marcellus, Onondaga County, New York. He read law in the office of Mr. (afterwards President) Fillmore, and became his partner in the practice of their profession, at Buffalo, Erie County, New York, in 1832. He has held different administrative and judicial offices in his native State, served as a member of the State Legislature, and was a Representative in Congress, from 1847 to 1849. On Mr. Fillmore's accession to the Presidency, in July, 1850, he was appointed to the office of Postmaster-General.

Hall, Obed.—He was a Representative in Congress, from New Hampshire, from 1811 to 1813.

Hall, Robert B.—Born in Boston, Massachusetts, January 28, 1812; was educated for the ministry; was a member of the Massachusetts Senate in 1855; was elected a Representative to the Thirty-fourth Congress in that year, and was re-elected to the Thirty-fifth Congress in 1857, serving as a member of the Committee on Revolutionary Pensions.

Hall, Thomas H.—Born in Edgecombe County, North Carolina, in 1773; was educated for the medical profession; and was a Representative in Congress, from 1817 to 1825, and again from 1827 to 1835. In 1836 he served as a member of the State Senate, and voted against the reception of any of the surplus revenue of the United States Treasury by the State of North Carolina. He died in Tarborough, June 30, 1853.

Hall, Willard.—He was born in Westford, Massachusetts, December 24, 1780; graduated at Harvard College in 1799; he studied law, and was admitted to the bar in 1803; he removed to Delaware and practised his profession there; in 1811 he was elected Secretary of State in Delaware, and held that office three years; he was elected a Representative in Congress in 1816, and re-elected in 1818; he was again Secretary of State in 1821; in 1822 was elected to the Legislature; and in 1823 was appointed by President Monroe District Judge of the United States for Delaware; in 1829 he revised the State Laws of Delaware, and in 1831 he was a member of the State Constitutional Convention.

Hall, Willard P.—He was born in Virginia, and on taking up his residence in Missouri, was elected a Representative in Congress, from 1847 to 1853.

Hall, William.—He was born in 1774, and died in Sumner County, Tennessee, in October, 1856. He was a General of Militia, and a Representative in Congress, from Tennessee, from 1831 to 1833.

Hall, William A.—He was born in Maine; taken to Virginia in early childhood; and emigrated to Missouri in 1841. In 1844 he was a Presidential Elector; in 1847 was appointed a Judge of the Circuit Court; was a member of the Missouri Convention of 1861; was elected a Representative, from Missouri, to the Thirty-seventh Congress, in the place of J. B. Clark, expelled; and in 1863 was re-elected to the Thirty-eighth Congress, serving on the Committees on Roads and Canals, and Expenditures in the Post-office Department. He was also a Delegate to the Chicago Convention of 1864.

Hallock, John, Jr.—He was born in Orange County, New York, and was a member of the Assembly of New York State, from Orange County, in 1816 and 1817, and from 1820 to 1821; and a Representative in Congress, from 1825 to 1829.

Halloway, David P.—Born in Waynesville, Warren County, Ohio, December 6, 1809, but removed with his parents to Cincinnati in 1813. In 1823 he went to Richmond, Indiana, and learned the printing business, and subsequently served four years in the office of the Cincinnati Gazette. He commenced the publication of the Richmond Palladium in 1832, and is still the editor. In 1843 he was elected to the lower branch of the State Legislature of Indiana, and in 1844 to the State Senate, serving nine years. In 1855 he was elected a Representative in Congress, and was Chairman of the Committee on Agriculture during that term. He was eight years President of the Agricultural Society of Wayne County. In 1861 he was appointed by President Lincoln Commissioner of Patents.

Halloway, Ransom.—A Representative in Congress, from the Eighth

Congressional District of New York, from 1849 to 1851. He died in Mount Pleasant, Prince George County, Maryland, April 6, 1851.

Halsey, Jehiel H.—He was a member of the New York Senate from 1832 to 1835, having previously been a Representative in Congress, from that State, from 1829 to 1831.

Halsey, Nicoll.—He was a member of the New York Assembly, from Tompkins County, in 1824, and a Representative in Congress, from that State, from 1833 to 1835.

Halsey, Silas.—He was a Representative in Congress, from New York, from 1805 to 1807, and having previously been in the Assembly of that State for several years, was subsequently, for one year, a member of the State Senate.

Halsted, William.—He was born in New Jersey, and was a Representative in Congress, from that State, from 1837 to 1839, and again from 1841 to 1843. He was a candidate for election to the Twenty-sixth Congress, and although he came with the broad seal of his State, he was not admitted.

Hamer, Thomas L.—He was a Representative in Congress, from Ohio, from 1833 to 1839, and died at Monterey, Mexico, while serving in the war, December 3, 1846.

Hamilton, Andrew J.—Born in Madison County, Alabama, January 28, 1815; received a good common school education, spending his earlier years on his father's farm. He held for some years the position of Clerk of the Circuit Court, and did business as a merchant; he subsequently studied law, and was admitted to the bar; in 1846 he removed to Texas, and devoted himself to his profession. In that State he has held the office of Attorney-General; served frequently in the Legislature; in 1856 was a Presidential Elector; and was elected a Representative from Texas to the Thirty-sixth Congress. In 1862 he was appointed by President Lincoln Military Governor of Texas.

Hamilton, James. — Born in Charleston, South Carolina, in 1789; was liberally educated; and adopted the law as a profession. In 1812 he served with distinction on the Canadian frontier; was for several years Mayor of Charleston; in 1823 was elected to the State Legislature; and from that position was transferred to the National House of Representatives, where he remained until 1829. He was subsequently chosen Governor of South Carolina, and, becoming interested in the Republic of Texas, helped to promote her independence, and went to Europe as Minister Plenipotentiary from that Republic. He did much to promote the interests of his native city and State, and was one of the founders of the Southern Quarterly Review, and also of the Bank of Charleston. At the time of his death he was a Senator elect in Congress, but was drowned on his passage to Texas, November 15, 1857, by a collision between the steamers Galveston and Opelousas, having been a passenger on board the latter steamer.

Hamilton, John.—He was at one time High Sheriff of Washington County, Pennsylvania, and a Representative in Congress, from that State, from 1805 to 1807. He died at home, August 31, 1837.

Hamilton, William T.—He was born in Maryland, and was a Representative in Congress, from that State, from 1849 to 1855.

Hamlin, Edward S.—He was a Representative in Congress, from Ohio, from 1844 to 1845.

Hamlin, Hannibal. — Born in Paris, Oxford County, Maine, August 27, 1809; prepared himself for a collegiate education, but, owing to his father's death, was obliged to take charge of his farm, where he remained until he was of age; he then spent a year in a printing-office as a compositor; studied law, and was admitted to the bar in 1833, and continued in active practice until 1848; was a member of the Maine Legislature from 1836 to 1840; and Speaker of the House in 1837, 1839, and 1840; was elected a Representative to the Twenty-eighth Congress, and re-elected to the Twenty-ninth Congress; was again a member of the House of Representatives in the State Legislature in 1847; and elected to the United States Senate, May 26, 1848, for four years, to fill a vacancy occasioned by the decease of John Fairfield. He was re-elected for six years in 1851, and elected Governor of Maine, January 7, 1857, resigning his seat in the Senate and being inaugurated Governor the same day. On the sixteenth of the same month, was re-elected United States Senator for six years, and resigned the office of Governor, February 20, 1857. He has served as a member of the Committees on Commerce, and on the District of Columbia. In 1860 he was nominated by the Republican Party as their candidate for the office of Vice-President, and was elected.

Hammet, William J.—He was born in Virginia; studied divinity; was Chaplain of the University of Virginia when he finished his education; was at one time Chaplain of Congress; and a Representative in Congress, from Mississippi, from 1843 to 1845.

Hammond, Edward.—He was born in Maryland, and was a Representative in Congress, from that State, from 1849 to 1853.

Hammond, Jabez D.—He was a lawyer and popular political writer of New York; did not receive a collegiate education, but Union College conferred on him the degree of A. M. He was a Representative in Congress, from New York, from 1815 to 1817, and on the expiration of his term, he was elected to the State Senate, of which he was a member until 1821. He visited Europe, in 1830, to restore his health. He was elected County Judge in 1838, and about that time commenced his "Political History of the State of New York." In 1845 he was elected to succeed Mr. Van Buren as a Regent of the University of New York, and held the office until his death. After his return from Europe, having withdrawn in a great measure from public and professional life, he devoted himself to literary pursuits, and published works entitled "Julius Melbourn," "The Political History of New York," and the "Life and Times of Silas Wright." He died August 18, 1855, in Cherry Valley, New York, his place of residence.

Hammond, James H.—Born in Newbury District, South Carolina, November 15, 1807; graduated at the State College, Columbia, in 1827; practised law from 1828 to 1830; was editor of the Southern Times; served his native State in Congress, from 1835 to 1837; after which he visited Europe for his health. In 1841 he was appointed a General of militia; and in 1842 elected Governor of South Carolina. After spending about fifteen years in the quiet enjoyment of his plantation, on the Savannah River, devoting himself to agricultural and literary pursuits, he was, in November, 1857, elected to the United States Senate, but resigned in December, 1860.

Hammond, Robert H.—He was born in Pennsylvania, and was a Representative in Congress, from that State, from 1837 to 1841. Died June 2, 1847.

Hammond, Samuel.—Born in Richmond County, Virginia, September 21, 1757; received as good an education as the country afforded at the time; when quite young he volunteered in an expedition against the Indians under Governor Dunmore, and acquired distinction at the battle of the Kanawha; when the Revolution broke out he displayed great bravery and ability at the battle of Long Bridge, at the siege of Savannah, where he was made Assistant Quartermaster; at the battle of Black Stocks, where he had three horses shot from under him, and was wounded; he was a member of the Council of Capitulation at Charleston; was at the battle of King's Mountain; he was also at the siege of Augusta; at the battle of Cowpens; the battle of Eutaw, where he was again badly wounded; and also at many others. After the war he settled at Savannah, and held many positions of trust and honor; in 1793 he headed a volunteer corps, and did good service in the Creek country; served a number of years in the Georgia Legislature; was one of the early Governors of the State; and he was a Representative in Congress, from that State, from 1803 to 1805. He was also appointed, by President Jefferson, Military and Civil Commandant of Upper Louisiana; and Receiver of Public Money in Missouri. He was also President of the Bank of St. Louis. In 1824 he returned to South Carolina, and was elected to the

Legislature of that State; was appointed Surveyor-General; and in 1831 Secretary of State. He retired from public life in 1835, and died September 11, 1842, leaving behind a brilliant reputation, both as a patriot and a man.

Hammons, David.—He was born in Oxford County, Maine, in 1807; received a limited education; studied law and commenced the practice in Lovell, Oxford County, in 1836; was a member of the Senate of Maine in 1840 and 1841; and was a Representative in Congress, from Maine, from 1847 to 1849. Now living in Bethel, Maine, devoted to his profession.

Hammons, Joseph.—He was a Representative in Congress, from New Hampshire, from 1829 to 1833; and died at Farmington, in that State, April, 1836.

Hampton, James G.—He was born in New Jersey; graduated at Princeton College in 1835; and was a Representative in Congress, from his native State, from 1845 to 1849.

Hampton, Moses.—Born in Beaver County, Pennsylvania, October 28, 1803, but removed, with his father, to Trumbull County, Ohio, so that his opportunities for even a common school education were limited; he, however, by his own exertions, obtained a classical education, and graduated at Washington College, Pennsylvania. He studied law at Uniontown, and was admitted to the bar in 1829, and commenced to practise in Somerset, Pennsylvania, where he remained until 1838, and then went to Pittsburg, and pursued the practice of his profession. From 1847 to 1851, he was a Representative in Congress, and declined a re-election. In 1853, he was elected President Judge of the District Court for Alleghany County, and still holds that office.

Hampton, Wade.—He was born in South Carolina in 1755; he took an active part in the war of the Revolution; commanded a brigade in 1812 on the Northern frontier; he spent the larger part of his life engaged in agricultural pursuits, by which he amassed a very large fortune, having been called the richest planter in the United States; and he died at Columbia, South Carolina, February 4, 1834.

Hanchett, Luther.—Was born in Portage County, Ohio, October 25, 1825; received a good education at Fremont; studied law and commenced the practice when twenty-one years of age; emigrated to Wisconsin in 1849; spent some time engaged in the lead and lumbering business; was four years District Attorney for Portage County, in his adopted State; from 1856 to 1860 was a member of the Wisconsin Senate; and in 1860 he was elected a Representative, from Wisconsin, to the Thirty-seventh Congress, serving on the Committees on Public Expenditures, and Private Land Claims. Died at Madison, Wisconsin, November 26, 1862.

Hancock, George.—He was a Representative in Congress, from Virginia, from 1793 to 1797. He served as a Colonel in the Revolution; was greatly beloved by his associates, and died at Fotheringay, Virginia, August 1, 1820, in the sixty-sixth year of his age.

Hand, Augustus C.—He was a member of the State Senate of New York, from Essex County, from 1845 to 1848, and a Representative in Congress, from 1839 to 1841. His native State was Vermont.

Hanna, John A.—He was a Representative in Congress, from Pennsylvania, from 1797 to 1805.

Hanna, Robert.—He was a member of the Indiana Constitutional Convention of 1816; a General of militia; was for many years in the State Legislature; was a Senator in Congress, from Indiana, by appointment, from 1831 to 1832; took an active part for many years in the public affairs of his State; and was killed by the cars, while walking on the track of a railroad at Indianapolis, November 19, 1858.

Hannegan, Edward A.—He was born in Ohio, but spent his boyhood in Kentucky; received a good education, studied law and was admitted to the bar in his twenty-third year, settling in Indiana. He was frequently a member of the State Legislature, and a Representative in Congress, from Indiana, from 1833 to 1837, and a Senator in Congress, from 1843 to 1849, officiating a part of the time as Chairman of the Committee on Roads and Canals, and on Enrolled Bills. On his retirement from the Senate, he was appointed Minister to Prussia, and on his return from Europe, took up his residence in Missouri. He died at St. Louis, February 25, 1859.

Hanson, Alexander Contee.—He was a lawyer by profession, and at one time edited a political newspaper called the Federal Republican, first in Baltimore and then at Georgetown, District of Columbia. He was a bitter opponent of the administration, and in 1812 published an article, which so irritated the populace, that his printing-office in Baltimore was destroyed. He resolved to reissue the paper, and took possession of a house for that purpose, supported by several political friends, well armed; the paper appeared next morning with an article against the people and police of Baltimore, and in the evening the house was attacked by a mob, which was, however, repelled; but Mr. Hanson and his friends were obliged to surrender to the civil authorities, for security, and were conducted to jail. That building was also attacked, and he was thrown in front of the jail, with others, and left by the mob, supposed to be dead. Then it was that he issued his paper in Georgetown. He afterwards settled in Baltimore, and was elected a Representative in Congress, serving from 1813 to 1816, when he was elected a Senator of the United States. He died at Belmont, April 23, 1819, aged thirty-three years.

Haralson, Hugh A.—Born in Greene County, Georgia, November, 13, 1805. He graduated at the University of Georgia, in 1825, and adopted the law as a profession, having, by an act of the Legislature, been permitted to practise before he was twenty-one. He was for many years a member of the Georgia Legislature, and a Representative in Congress, from 1843 to 1851. He died at home in October, 1854. He also participated in the military affairs of the State, and was a Major-General of militia; and when in Congress, was Chairman of the Committee on Military Affairs.

Hard, Gideon.—He was a Representative in Congress, from New York, from 1833 to 1837, and a Senator from that State, from 1842 to 1847.

Hardeman, Thomas, Jr.—He was born in Bibb County, Georgia, January 12, 1825, and elected a Representative, from that State, to the Thirty-sixth Congress, serving on the Committee on Mileage. He had before served in the State Legislature. Joined the Great Rebellion in 1861.

Hardin, Benjamin. — He was born in Westmoreland County, Pennsylvania, and was a Representative in Congress, from Kentucky, from 1815 to 1817, from 1819 to 1823, and again from 1833 to 1837, and died at Bardstown, Kentucky, September 24, 1852.

Hardin, John J.—He was born in Kentucky, and having removed to Illinois, was elected a Representative in Congress, from 1843 to 1845. Died in February, 1847.

Hardin, Martin D.—He was born on the Monongahela River, Western Pennsylvania, June 21, 1780. He was educated chiefly at Transylvania Seminary, in Kentucky; studied law; served for several years in the Legislature of Kentucky; was at one time Secretary of State for Kentucky; served in the Northwestern army as a Major; and was a Senator in Congress, during the years 1816 and 1817. He had a superior mind, and as a lawyer was eminently successful. He died in Franklin County, Kentucky, October 8, 1823.

Harding, Aaron.—Was born in Greene County, Kentucky; spent his boyhood on a farm; studied law, and came to the bar in 1833, locating in Greene County; in 1840 he was elected to the State Legislature, and in 1861 he was elected a Representative, from Kentucky, to the Thirty-seventh Congress, serving on the Committee on Territories. Re-elected to the Thirty-eighth Congress, serving on the Committee on the Post-office and Post-roads.

Harding, Benjamin F.—Born in Wyoming County, Pennsylvania, January 4, 1823; studied law in his native county, and came to the bar in 1847; emigrated to Illinois in 1848, and during the following year settled in

Oregon; in 1850 was chosen a member of the Legislative Assembly; in 1851 was Chief Clerk of the Legislative Assembly; in 1852 was chosen a member of the Legislature, and made Speaker. In 1853 he was appointed by President Pierce United States District Atorney for the Territory of Oregon; in 1854 was appointed Secretary of the Territory, which office he held until Oregon was admitted as a State. From 1859 to 1862 he was a member of the State Legislature, serving the two last years as Speaker; and in 1862 he was elected a Senator in Congress, from Oregon, taking his seat during the third session of the Thirty-seventh Congress, serving on the Committee on Naval Affairs, and that on Public Lands.

Harlan, Aaron.—He was born in Warren County, Ohio, September 8, 1802; received a good English education; adopted the profession of law, and was admitted to the bar in 1825; in 1831 he was elected a member of the State Legislature, and in 1838 and 1839 was elected to the State Senate; was a Presidential Elector in 1844, from Ohio; in 1849 was again elected to the State Senate; in 1850 was a member of the State Constitutional Convention; and in 1852 he was elected a Representative in Congress, from Ohio, where he continued to serve the people of his native district until the close of the Thirty-fifth Congress, serving as a member of the Committee on Private Land Claims.

Harlan, Andrew J.—He was born in Chester, Clinton County, Ohio, March 29, 1815; received a limited education; studied law, but abandoned the practice for politics; in 1842 he was elected Clerk of the Indiana House of Representatives; was elected to the Legislature in 1846, 1847, and 1848; and was elected a Representative in Congress, from Indiana, from 1849 to 1851, and again from 1853 to 1855.

Harlan, James.—Born in Mercer County, Kentucky, June 22, 1800; received a good English education, and engaged in mercantile pursuits from 1817 to 1821. He then commenced the study of the law, and was admitted to the bar in 1823. In 1829 he was appointed Prosecuting Attorney for the Circuit in which he resided, and held the office four years. In 1835 he was elected a Representative to Congress from Kentucky, and in 1837 he was re-elected; during the last session he was Chairman of the Committee for Investigating Defalcations. From 1840 to 1844 he was Secretary of State of Kentucky. In 1845 he was elected to the lower branch of the Legislature; and in 1850 he was appointed Attorney-General of that State, which office he held until his death, which occurred at Frankfort, Kentucky, February 18, 1863.

Harlan, James.—Born in Clarke County, Illinois, August 26, 1820; graduated at Indiana University in 1845; a lawyer by profession; was Superintendent of Public Instruction in the State of Iowa in 1847; President of Iowa Wesleyan University in 1853; and was elected a United States Senator in 1854, serving as Chairman of the Committee on Public Lands. He was also a Delegate to the Peace Congress of 1861. Re-elected to the Senate for the term ending in 1867, serving as Chairman of the Committee on Public Lands.

Harmanson, John H.—Born in Norfolk, Virginia, in January, 1803. He was educated at Jefferson College, Mississippi, and having removed to Louisiana, devoted himself first to one of the mechanic arts, then to law, and afterwards to agriculture. He served in the State Senate in 1844; and was elected to the National House of Representatives in 1845, and re-elected in 1847 and 1849, ever keeping a watchful eye upon the interests of his adopted State, and proposed in Congress a project to secure a grant from the United States to Louisiana of all the submerged lands in that State, with a view to their redemption from that condition, and thus promoting the public health. He died in New Orleans, October 25, 1850.

Harper, Alexander.—He was born in Ireland, and having emigrated to Ohio, was elected a Representative in Congress, from 1837 to 1839, from 1843 to 1847, and again from 1851 to 1853.

Harper, Francis J.—He was elected a member of Congress from Pennsylvania, but died before taking his seat, March 18, 1837, aged thirty-eight years.

Harper, James.—He was born in Ireland, and having emigrated to Pennsylvania, was elected a Representative in Congress, from 1833 to 1837.

Harper, John A.—He was a Representative in Congress, from New Hampshire, from 1811 to 1813.

Harper, Joseph M. — Born in Limerick, Maine, June 21, 1787; commenced active life by working on his father's farm in summer, and going to the district school in winter; he was also at the Fryeburg Academy, and taught school; he studied medicine and law, and practised both professions; he was a judge, at one time, of the United States District Court of New Hampshire, and a Representative in Congress, from New Hampshire, from 1831 to 1835. In 1858 was President of the Mechanics' Bank, Concord.

Harper, Robert G.—He was born near Fredericksburg, Virginia, in 1765; was a graduate of Princeton College in 1785, and for a time a teacher in that institution; removing to Charleston, South Carolina, he studied law, and was admitted to the bar of that State; he was a leading Representative in Congress, from South Carolina, from 1794 to 1801; he subsequently removed to Baltimore, Maryland, and was a Senator in Congress, from that State, during the years 1815 and 1816; in 1819 he visited Europe, and, on his return, devoted himself to the cause of the Colonization Society, and to literary pursuits, publishing a number of interesting addresses and papers, which were subsequently collected in a volume. He served with credit in the war of 1812, having attained the rank of Major-General. He died suddenly, January 15, 1825, having been engaged the preceding day in the Circuit Court.

Harper, William.—He was a native of South Carolina; born January 17, 1790; graduated at the South Carolina College in 1808, and became one of the Board of Trustees of that institution in 1813; adopted the profession of law; served in the State Legislature, and was elected Speaker of the Lower House. He was a Senator in Congress, from South Carolina, during the year 1826, and was appointed Chancellor of that State in 1835. He was, in 1830, elected a Judge of the Court of Appeals, and for a time State Reporter. For domestic reasons, he spent a few years in Missouri, from 1818 to 1823, and while in that State was made Chancellor of the State. He was an eminent jurist, and died October 10, 1847.

Harrington, Henry W. — Was born in Otsego County, New York, September 12, 1825; studied law, and came to the bar in 1849; in 1856 he took up his residence in Indiana, and continued the prosecution of his profession there; after serving in a local Convention, he was chosen a Delegate to the Charleston Convention in 1860; and in 1862 he was elected a Representative, from Indiana, to the Thirty-eighth Congress, serving on the Committee on Private Land Claims.

Harris, Benjamin Gwinn.—Born near Leonardtown, St. Mary's County, Maryland, December 13, 1806; after receiving an academical education at Charlotte Hall, he spent a few months in St. Mary's College, and went to Yale College, from which he was dismissed with one hundred and forty others, in 1829, on account of their seceding from Commons Hall; and although a compact was entered into that they would not return unless their wishes were respected, all of them did return, excepting Mr. Harris and one other, a Georgian. He subsequently spent fourteen months at the Cambridge Law School, and then settled in his native county as a lawyer. In 1832 he was elected to the House of Delegates of Maryland, and re-elected in 1833, 1836, 1849, 1852, and 1856. With his profession and public duties he ever combined agricultural pursuits; and in 1863 he was elected a Representative, from Maryland, to the Thirty-eighth Congress, serving on the Committee on Manufactures. He was a Delegate to the Chicago Convention of 1864.

Harris, Charles M.—He was born in Munfordsville, Hart County, Kentucky, April 10, 1821; received a common school education; adopted the profession of law; and having become a citizen of Illinois, he was elected, in 1862, a Representative, from that State, to the Thirty-eighth Congress, serving on the Committees on Public Expenditures, and on Expenditures in the War Department.

Harris, Ira.—He was born in Charleston, Montgomery County, New York, May 31, 1802, tracing his lineage to the colony of Roger Williams; when a boy, he labored upon a farm in summer and attended school in winter; in his seventeenth year he entered Cortland Academy, to prepare for college; graduated at Union College in 1824; studied law, and was admitted to the bar in Albany, where he settled. For seventeen years he devoted his whole attention to his profession, in which he was eminently successful, avoiding all political entanglements. In 1844 he was elected to the State Legislature; re-elected in 1845; was a Delegate in 1846 to the Convention for revising the Constitution of the State; before the Convention adjourned was elected to the State Senate; in 1847 he was elected Judge of the Supreme Court, and held the position twelve years and a half; and in 1861 he was elected, for six years, a Senator in Congress, from New York, serving as Chairman of the Committee on Private Land Claims, and member of the Committees on the Judiciary, and Foreign Relations.

Harris, Isham G.—He was born in Tennessee, and was a Representative in Congress, from that State, from 1849 to 1853.

Harris, J. Morrison.—Born in the city of Baltimore, in 1821; was educated at Lafayette College, Pennsylvania, and studied law, being admitted to the bar in 1843. He was a Presidential Elector in 1848, and in 1855 was elected a Representative, from Maryland, in the Thirty-fourth Congress, and returned to the Thirty-fifth Congress in 1857, serving as a member of the Committee on Mileage. Also elected to the Thirty-sixth Congress, serving on the Committee on Naval Affairs.

Harris, John.—He was born in New York, and was a Representative in Congress, from that State, from 1807 to 1809.

Harris, John T.—Born in Albemarle County, Virginia, in 1823; received a good English education, going to school and working on his father's farm alternately; taught school for a while; studied law, and was licensed to practise in 1845; was a State Elector in 1848, 1851, and 1855; a Presidential Elector in 1852 and 1856; was twice elected Attorney for the Commonwealth; and was elected a Representative, from Virginia, to the Thirty-sixth Congress, serving on the Committee on Expenditures on the Public Buildings.

Harris, Mark.—He was born in Ipswich, Massachusetts, in 1779; removed to Portland in 1800; went into trade as a grocer; took an active part in politics; held the offices of County and State Treasurer for twenty years; was a State Senator in 1816 and 1819; a State Councillor in 1820; served also in the State Legislature; and was a Representative in Congress, from Maine, from 1822 to 1823. Died in New York, March 2, 1843.

Harris, Robert.—He was born in Dauphin County, Pennsylvania, and was a Representative in Congress, from that State, from 1823 to 1827.

Harris, Sampson W.—Born in Elbert County, Georgia, February 23, 1809, and died in Washington City, April 1, 1857. He graduated at Franklin College in 1828; adopted the profession of law; served one term in the Georgia Legislature, and then removed to Alabama. He was there appointed Prosecuting Attorney for the State; and in 1847 he was elected a Representative in Congress, from Alabama, where he continued until his death.

Harris, Thomas K.—He was a Representative in Congress, from Tennessee, from 1813 to 1815.

Harris, Thomas L.—He was born in Norwich, Connecticut, October 29, 1816; graduated at Trinity College, Hartford, in 1841; studied law, in Connecticut, with Governor Isaac Toucey; was admitted to the bar, in Virginia, in 1842, and during that year commenced the practice of his profession in Petersburg, Menard County, Illinois. In 1845 he was chosen School Commissioner for his county; and in 1846 he raised and commanded a company, and joined the Fourth Regiment of Illinois Volunteers to serve in the war with Mexico;

he was afterwards elected Major of the regiment, and, owing to the sickness of his superior officers, was chief in command during most of the campaign. He was at the taking of Vera Cruz, and served in the navy battery with a detachment during the day of its terrible fire; was also at Cerro Gordo, and after the wounding of General Shields took command of the regiment, and was honorably mentioned in Government despatches, for placing a twenty-four pounder battering cannon on the heights of Cerro Gordo, during the night preceding the battle. While absent in the army, in 1846, he was elected a Senator in the Illinois Legislature, and in 1848 was chosen a Representative in Congress, serving through the Thirty-first, and was re-elected to the Thirty-fifth Congress; during his second term he officiated as Chairman of the Committee on Elections. He took a special interest in the election in Illinois when he was re-elected to the Thirty-sixth Congress; and it is supposed that, owing to his declining health, the efforts he made to attend the polls were the more immediate cause of his death, which occurred at Springfield, Illinois, November 24, 1858. His disease was pulmonary consumption.

Harris, W. L.—He was appointed, by the acting Governor of Mississippi, in 1851, to fill a vacancy in the United States Senate, caused by the resignation of Mr. J. Davis; but the writer is not certain that he occupied his seat in the Senate.

Harris, Wiley P.—He was born in Mississippi, and was a Representative in Congress, from that State, from 1853 to 1855.

Harris, William A.—He was born in Fauquier County, Virginia, August 8, 1805; received a classical education; he adopted the profession of law, and practised it for ten years; he was twice elected to the Legislature of Virginia; and he was a Representative in Congress, from 1841 to 1843. He was editor, for several years, of a journal called the Spectator, and subsequently of the Constitution; and in 1845 he was appointed, by President Polk, Chargé d'Affaires to Buenos Ayres, where he remained until 1851. After the election of Mr. Buchanan to the Presidency, he became the editor and proprietor of the Washington Union, which continued in his possession until he was elected Printer to the United States Senate, which office he held for two years. In 1854 he removed to Missouri, and died in Pike County, March 28, 1864.

Harrison, Albert G.—He was a native of Kentucky; a lawyer by profession; and a member of Congress, from Missouri, from 1835 to 1839. He died at Fulton, Missouri, September 7, 1839, highly esteemed.

Harrison, Carter B.—He was a Representative in Congress, from Virginia, from 1793 to 1799.

Harrison, John S.—He was born in Ohio, and was a Representative in Congress, from that State, from 1853 to 1857.

Harrison, Richard A.—He was born in England in 1827, and emigrated to Ohio in 1836; received a good English education; served for a time in a printing-office in Clarke County; graduated at the Cincinnati Law School in 1846; in 1857 he was elected to the Ohio House of Representatives; subsequently to the State Senate; and he was elected a Representative, from Ohio, to the Thirty-seventh Congress, serving on the Committees on Invalid Pensions, and the Militia.

Harrison, S. S.—He was born in Maryland; and was a Representative in Congress, from Pennsylvania, from 1833 to 1837.

Harrison, William Henry.—Was born in Charles County, Virginia, February 9, 1773; was educated at Hampden Sydney College, and afterwards studied medicine. He received, from Washington, a military commission in 1791, and fought under Wayne in 1792. After the battle of Miami Rapids, he was made Captain, and placed in command of Fort Washington. In 1797 he was appointed Secretary of the Northwest Territory; and in 1799 and 1800 he was a Delegate to Congress. Being appointed Governor of Indiana, he was also Superintendent of Indian Affairs, and negotiated thirteen treaties. He gained a great victory in the battle of Tippecanoe, November 7, 1811. In the war with Great Britain he was commander of the Northwest army, and was distinguished in the defence of Fort Meigs, and the victory of the Thames. From 1816 to 1819, he was a Representative in Congress, from Ohio; and from 1825 to 1828, United States Senator. In 1828 he was Minister to the Republic of Colombia; and on his return he resided upon his farm, at North Bend, Ohio. In 1840 he was elected President of the United States, by 234 votes out of 294, and inaugurated March 4, 1841. He died in the Presidential mansion, April 4, 1841.

Hart, Emanuel B.—Born in New York City, October 29, 1811; entered early upon a mercantile occupation; went to the Spanish Main as a supercargo, and settled in New York as a commission merchant; served for a time in the Board of Aldermen; was a Representative in Congress, from 1851 to 1853; he was at one time a Lieutenant-Colonel of the State militia; and was appointed, by President Buchanan, Surveyor of the Port of New York. Mr. Hart has also frequently been a member of the State and National Conventions of the Democratic party.

Hartley, Thomas.—He was born in Reading, Pennsylvania; served in the Revolutionary war as a Colonel from 1776 to 1779; was a lawyer of eminence; and a Representative in Congress, from Pennsylvania, from 1789 until his death, which occurred at York, Pennsylvania, in 1800.

Harvey, Jonathan.—He was born in Merrimack County, New Hampshire; served seven years in the two Houses of the State Legislature; was President of the Senate from 1817 to 1823; was a State Councillor from 1823 to 1825; and a Representative in Congress, from New Hampshire, from 1825 to 1831, during his last term serving as a member of the Committee on Commerce. Died in Sutton, New Hampshire, August 23, 1859, aged seventy-nine years.

Harvey, Matthew.—He was born in Hillsborough County, New Hampshire, and was for many years a member of the New Hampshire Legislature; Speaker of the House from 1818 to 1821, and President of the Senate from 1825 to 1828; a State Councillor in 1828; Governor of the State in 1830; and in 1831 was appointed Judge of the United States District Court. His services as a Representative in Congress, from New Hampshire, were rendered from 1821 to 1825.

Hasbrouck, Abraham.—He was a member of the New York Assembly, from Ulster County, in 1781 and 1782, and again in 1811; and a Representative in Congress, from 1813 to 1815; and State Senator in 1822.

Hasbrouck, Abraham B.—He graduated at Yale College in 1810; and was a Representative in Congress, from New York, from 1825 to 1827. He was a native of Ulster County, New York; but he spent a few years of his life in New Jersey, and was President of Rutgers College, which office he resigned.

Hasbrouck, Josiah.—He was for four years a member of the New York Assembly, and a Representative in Congress, from that State, from 1803 to 1805, and again from 1817 to 1819.

Hascall, Augustus P.—He was born in Massachusetts; and was a Representative in Congress, from New York, from 1851 to 1853.

Haskell, William T.—He was born in Tennessee, received a liberal education, and adopted the profession of law; he commanded, as Colonel, a regiment of Tennessee volunteers, in the late war with Mexico, having distinguished himself at Medelin and at Cerro Gordo; and was a Representative in Congress, from Tennessee, from 1847 to 1849. He died at Hopkinsville, Tennessee, March 20, 1859.

Haskin, John B.—Born at Fordham, Westchester County, New York, August 7, 1821; educated at a public school in New York City; he was a lawyer by profession; held several important city offices from 1846 to 1856, and was then elected a Representative in the Thirty-fifth Congress, from New York, officiating as Chairman of the Committee on Expenditures in the Navy Department; and was also elected to the Thirty-sixth Congress, serving as Chairman of the Committee on Public Expenditures.

Hastings, George.—He was born in Clinton, Oneida County, New York, March 18, 1807; graduated at Hamilton College in 1826; studied law, and was admitted to the bar in 1830; he was District Attorney for Oneida County nine years; and he was a Representative in Congress, from New York, from 1853 to 1855. Late in the latter year he was elected Judge for Livingston County, which office he now holds.

Hastings, John.—He was a Representative in Congress, from Ohio, from 1839 to 1843, and died at Columbus, December 29, 1854.

Hastings, L. Clinton.—He was a Representative in Congress, from Iowa, from 1846 to 1847.

Hastings, Seth.—He graduated at Harvard University in 1782; was a Representative in Congress, from Massachusetts, from 1801 to 1807. After his service in Congress, he was elected a State Senator in 1810 and 1814; was appointed Chief Justice of the Court of Sessions; and died in 1831, aged seventy years, at Mendon, Massachusetts.

Hastings, William Soden.—He was frequently a member of the Legislature of Massachusetts, in the Senate from 1829 to 1834, and was a Representative in Congress, from that State, from 1837 to 1842. He died at the Sulphur Springs, Virginia, June 17, 1842.

Hatch, Israel T.—He was born in New York; was a member of the Assembly of that State in 1852; and elected a Representative to the Thirty-fifth Congress, serving as Chairman of the Committee on the Militia, and as member of the Committee on Engraving. In 1859 he was appointed, by President Buchanan, to examine and report upon the working of the Reciprocity Treaty, and a few weeks later was appointed Postmaster at Buffalo.

Hathaway, S. G.—He was, for three years, a member of the Assembly of New York, one year a State Senator, and a Representative in Congress, from that State, from 1833 to 1835.

Hathorn, John.—He was a member of the State Senate of New York in 1787; a Representative in Congress, from New York, from 1789 to 1791, and again from 1795 to 1797; and was again elected to the State Senate in 1804.

Hatton, Robert.—Born in Sumner County, Tennessee, in 1827; graduated at Cambridge University; studied law, and was admitted to the bar in 1849; served in the Tennessee Legislature in 1856; and in 1859 was elected a Representative, from Tennessee, to the Thirty-sixth Congress, serving on the Committee on Expenses in the Navy Department. He served in the Rebellion of 1861, and was killed at the battle before Richmond in 1862.

Haun, H. P.—Born in Scott County, Kentucky; read law at the Transylvania University of that State, and was admitted to the bar in 1839; he was for a time Attorney for his native county; removed to Iowa in 1845, and was a member of the Convention which formed the Constitution of that State in 1846; removed to California in 1850, and was there elected a County Judge; and in 1859 was elected a Senator in Congress, from California, for the unexpired term of the late Mr. Broderick. He served as a member of the Committees on Indian Affairs, and on Territories. Died at Marysville, California, May 6, 1860.

Haven, Jonathan N.—He graduated at Yale College in 1777, and was for nine years a member of the New York Assembly, from Suffolk County, and a Representative in Congress, from 1795 to 1799, the year of his death.

Haven, Nathaniel A.—He was a native of New Hampshire; graduated at Harvard University in 1779; was a member of Congress, from that State, from 1809 to 1811, and died March, 1831, aged sixty-nine years.

Haven, Solomon G.—He was born in New York, and was a Representative in Congress, from that State, from 1851 to 1857. Died at Buffalo, New York, December 24, 1862.

Hawes, Albert G.—He was a Representative in Congress, from Kentucky, from 1831 to 1837, and died in Davis County, Kentucky, April 14, 1849.

Hawes, Aylett.—Was a Representative in Congress, from Virginia, from 1811 to 1817. He was a physician by profession, and died in Culpeper County, Virginia, August 31, 1833.

Hawes, Richard.—He was born in Caroline County, Virginia, February 6, 1797; removed with his family to Kentucky in 1810; received a good collegiate education; adopted the profession of law; was a member of the Kentucky Legislature in 1828, 1829, and 1836; and was a Representative in Congress, from Kentucky, from 1837 to 1841.

Hawkins, Benjamin.—Born in Yates County, North Carolina, August 15, 1754; was educated at Princeton College; and was an excellent French scholar, which occasioned his becoming a personal friend of Washington, that he might act as interpreter in his intercourse with the French officers of his army. He was with him at the battle of Monmouth. In 1780 he was chosen Commercial Agent by the Legislature of North Carolina; and from 1781 to 1784, and 1786 to 1787, he was a Delegate in the First Congress; and as a Senator of the United States, under the Constitution, from North Carolina, he served from 1789 to 1795; and having been appointed, by Washington, Agent for Superintending all the Indians south of the Ohio, he retained that office until his death,—having tendered his resignation, without its being accepted, to each successive President, from 1796 to 1816. He was a man of superior abilities and lofty character, and left behind him some valuable writings on "Topography," and "Indian Character." He died June 6, 1816.

Hawkins, George S.—He was born in New York, and, having become a citizen of Florida, was elected a Representative to the Thirty-fifth and Thirty-sixth Congresses, from that State, serving on the Committees on Private Land Claims, and on Naval Affairs.

Hawkins, Joseph.—He was a Representative in Congress, from New York, from 1829 to 1831.

Hawkins, Joseph W.—He was a Representative in Congress, from Kentucky, from 1814 to 1815.

Hawkins, M. T.—He entered public life, in 1819, as a member of the House of Commons of North Carolina; was a member of the State Senate from 1823 to 1827; and a Representative in Congress, from North Carolina, from 1831 to 1841. He served again in the State Senate in 1846. He was also at one time a General of militia.

Hawks, John.—He was born in Worcester, Massachusetts, and was a Representative in Congress, from New York, from 1821 to 1823.

Haws, J. H. Hobart.—He was born in New York, and was a Representative in Congress, from that State, from 1851 to 1853.

Hay, Andrew K.—He was born in Massachusetts, and, having become a resident of New Jersey, was elected a Representative in Congress, from 1849 to 1851.

Hayden, Moses.—He was born in Hampshire County, Massachusetts, and was a member of the New York State Senate in 1829 and 1830, and a Representative in Congress, from 1823 to 1827.

Haymond, Thomas S.—He was born in Virginia, and was a Representative in Congress, from that State, from 1849 to 1851.

Hayne, Arthur P.—He was born in Charleston, South Carolina, March 12, 1790, received a good education, and commenced active life in a counting-house. He early formed an attachment for military life, and, on entering the army, rendered good service during the last war with England, at Sackett's Harbor, as First Lieutenant; on the St. Lawrence, as Major of cavalry; in the Creek Nation, as Inspector-General, and also at the storming of Pensacola, and at New Orleans. After the war he studied law, and was admitted to the bar in Pennsylvania. During the Florida war he was again called into the field, and had command of the Tennessee volunteers, and he retired from the army in 1820. He subsequently served in the Legislature of South Carolina, and was chosen a Presidential Elector in 1832, voting for Jackson; and he was appointed to a seat in the United States Senate, from South Carolina, in May, 1858, in the place of Senator Evans.

Hayne, Robert Y.—He was born near Charleston, South Carolina, November 10, 1791; his early advantages for education were limited; he studied law with Langdon Cheves, and was admitted to the bar before he was twenty-one years of age, attaining a high rank as a lawyer. In the war of 1812 he held the commission of Lieutenant. In 1814 he was elected to the State Legislature, and in 1818 Speaker, and was also Attorney-General of the State. He was elected to the United States Senate in 1823, and continued there until 1832. In 1832, as a member of the "Union and State Rights Convention" of South Carolina, he reported the ordinance of Nullification, and was soon afterwards elected Governor of the State. He was subsequently Mayor of Charleston, and President of the Charleston, Louisville, and Cincinnati Railroad Company. He died at Ashville, North Carolina, September 24, 1839. His abilities were of a high order, and he acquired distinction by his participation in a debate in the Senate with Daniel Webster.

Haynes, Charles E.—He was born in Brunswick, Virginia, and was a Representative in Congress, from Georgia, from 1825 to 1829, and again from 1835 to 1839.

Hays, Samuel.—He was born in Virginia, and was a Representative in Congress, from that State, from 1841 to 1843.

Hays, Samuel.—He was born in Pennsylvania, and was a Representative in Congress, from that State, from 1843 to 1845.

Haywood William H., Jr.—Born in Wake County, North Carolina, in 1801; graduated at the University of North Carolina in 1819; studied law; entered public life as a member of the House of Commons in 1834, continuing there three years; in 1836 was Speaker of the House; and a Senator in Congress, from 1843 to 1845.

Hazard, Nathaniel.—He was born in Newport, Rhode Island, and was elected a Representative in Congress, from 1819 to 1821. Died December 17, 1820, in Washington City.

Hazeltine, Abner.—He was a member of the New York Assembly in 1829 and 1830, and a Representative in Congress, from that State, from 1833 to 1837.

Healey, Joseph.—He was born in Cheshire, New Hampshire; was a Representative in Congress, from New Hampshire, from 1825 to 1829, and was a member of the Committee on Revolutionary Claims. He was also a State Councillor from 1829 to 1832, and State Senator in 1824.

Heath, James P.—He was born in Delaware, December 21, 1777. In 1799 he was appointed a Lieutenant in the regiment of artillerists and engineers, which he resigned in 1802; he was Register in Chancery, at Annapolis, at the commencement of the war of 1812; he served through the whole war as aide-de-camp to General Winder; in 1838 he was wrecked on the steamer Pulaski, and spent five days and nights afloat upon a piece of the wreck; when nineteen years of age he fought a duel with John Knight, and received a ball which never left him; and he was a Representative in Congress, from Maryland, from 1833 to 1835, serving as a member of the Committee on Commerce. He died in Georgetown, June 12, 1854.

Heath, John.—He was a Representative in Congress, from Virginia, from 1793 to 1797.

Hebard, William.—He was born in Connecticut, and having settled in Vermont, was elected a Representative in Congress, from that State, from 1849 to 1853. He was also Judge of the Supreme Court from 1842 to 1845; Judge of Probate for seven years; served seven years in the two houses of the Legislature; and was two years Attorney for Randolph County.

Heister, Daniel.—He was a native of Berks County, Pennsylvania, and a Representative in Congress, from that State, from 1789 to 1796, having resigned.

Heister, Daniel.—He was a Representative in Congress, from Maryland, from 1801 to 1804. He died March 8, 1804.

Heister, Daniel.—He was a Representative in Congress, from Chester County, Pennsylvania, from 1809 to 1811.

Heister, John.—He was a Representative in Congress, from Pennsylvania, from 1807 to 1809, and father of Daniel Heister, of Chester County.

Heister, Joseph.—He was born in Reading, Pennsylvania, November 18, 1752; was a General in the Revolutionary war, having organized a company at his own expense, which fought on Long Island, where he was wounded and taken prisoner. He was a Representative in the Pennsylvania Legislature soon after the close of the war, and served for several years; was a member of the Convention which formed the State Constitution, and a Representative in Congress, from that State, from 1797 to 1805, and again from 1815 to 1820. He was Governor from 1820 to 1823, and died in Reading, June 10, 1832.

Heister, William.—He was, for many years, an active politician, and a leader of the Anti-masonic party. He was a member of the Convention to revise the Constitution of Pennsylvania, and a Representative in Congress, from that State, from 1831 to 1837. He died October 14, 1853, in Pennsylvania, aged sixty-two years.

Helmick, William.—Born in Jefferson County, Ohio, September 6, 1817; received a common school education, and taught school for seven years; studied law and was admitted to the bar in 1845; in 1851 he was elected a Prosecuting Attorney; and in 1858 he was elected a Representative, from Ohio, to the Thirty-sixth Congress, serving as a member of the Committee on Post-offices and Post-roads. He subsequently accepted a clerkship in the Interior Department.

Helms, William.—He was an officer in the Revolutionary army; a Representative in Congress, from New Jersey, from 1801 to 1811; and removing to Tennessee, died there at an advanced age.

Hemphill, John.—He was a Senator in Congress, from Texas, from 1859 until that State seceded, when he became identified with the Great Rebellion. Expelled from the Senate in July, 1861.

Hemphill, Joseph.—He was born in Delaware County, Pennsylvania, and was a leading member of the old Federal party; he was a Representative of Pennsylvania in Congress, from 1801 to 1803, again from 1819 to 1827, and from 1829 to 1831. He distinguished himself particularly by a speech on the Judiciary Bill in 1801; and was for some time Judge of the District Court of Philadelphia. He died in Philadelphia, May 29, 1842, aged seventy-two years.

Hempstead, Edward.—He was born in New London, Connecticut, June 3, 1780; received a classical education from private tutors, and having studied law, was admitted to the bar in 1801. After spending three years in Rhode Island practising his profession, he removed in 1804 to the Territory of Louisiana, travelling on horseback, and tarrying for a time at Vincennes, Indiana Territory. He first settled at St. Charles, on the Missouri River, but in 1805, he removed to St. Louis, where he resided the balance of his life. In 1806 he was appointed Deputy Attorney-General for the District of St. Louis and St. Charles, and in 1809 Attorney-General for the Territory of Upper Louisiana, which office he held until 1811; and he was the first Delegate to Congress from the western side of the Mississippi River, representing Missouri Territory from 1811 to 1814. After his service in Congress, he went upon several expeditions against the Indians; was elected to the Territorial Assembly, and chosen Speaker; and he died on the 10th August, 1817. He was a man of ability, pure, and without reproach, and his loss was deeply lamented by all who knew him.

Henderson, Archibald.—Born in Granville County, North Carolina, August 7, 1768, and died October 21, 1822. He was educated in his native county, studied law, and rose to a high position at the bar of his State. He was a Representative in Congress, from North Carolina, from 1799 to 1803;

and subsequently elected to the General Assembly for several terms. His learning was extensive, and his character as a man above reproach.

Henderson, Bennett H.—He was a Representative in Congress, from Tennessee, from 1815 to 1817.

Henderson, John.—He was a lawyer by profession; a General of militia in Mississippi; a Senator in Congress, from Mississippi, from 1839 to 1845; and during the latter part of his life, practised his profession in Louisiana. After his service in Congress, he was engaged in an unlawful expedition against Cuba, for which he was tried, but acquitted by a New Orleans jury. He died at Pass Christian, in 1857, aged sixty-two years.

Henderson, John B.—Was born in Virginia, November 16, 1826; in 1836 removed with his parents to Missouri; spent a part of his boyhood on a farm. While obtaining an academical education, he taught school for his support; studied law, and came to the bar in 1848, and was soon afterwards elected to the State Legislature; re-elected in 1856; he was a Delegate to the Charleston Convention in 1860; had command for a time of a brigade of militia. On the expulsion of Trusten Polk from the United States Senate, he was appointed to fill the vacancy, and in 1863 was elected for the full term ending in 1869, serving on the Committees on the Post-office and Post-roads, and that on the District of Columbia.

Henderson, Joseph.—He was born in Pennsylvania, and was a Representative in Congress, from that State, from 1833 to 1837.

Henderson, J. Pinckney.—Born in Lincoln County, North Carolina, March 31, 1808. He received a liberal education, but did not graduate, and adopted the law as a profession, first visiting Cuba for his health, and settling in Mississippi. He emigrated to Texas in 1836, and his first civil office was that of Attorney-General of the Republic of Texas, having been appointed by President Houston in 1836; in 1837 he was appointed Secretary of State of the Republic; soon afterwards Minister Plenipotentiary to England and France, clothed with the additional powers of Commissioner to solicit the recognition of the independence of Texas; in 1838 he made a commercial arrangement with England, and in 1839 a commercial treaty with France; in 1844 he was appointed a Special Minister to the United States, which mission resulted in the annexation of Texas; in 1845 he was a member of the Convention which framed the Constitution of the State of Texas; in November, of the same year, was elected Governor of the State; and when the Mexican war broke out, in 1846, as Governor of the State, and by permission of the Legislature, he took command in person of the volunteer troops, called for by General Taylor, served six months as Major-General, and distinguished himself at the battle of Monterey, subsequently receiving from Congress, for his services, a vote of thanks, and a sword valued at fifteen hundred dollars. He was elected a Senator in Congress, in 1857, but owing to ill health, did not take an active part in its proceedings, and he died in Washington City, June 4, 1858, deeply lamented by all who knew him.

Henderson, Samuel.—He was a Representative in Congress, from Pennsylvania, from 1814 to 1815.

Henderson, Thomas.—He was a graduate of Princeton College in 1761; was Judge of the Court of Common Pleas; a Delegate to the Continental Congress, from 1779 to 1780; a Representative of New Jersey in Congress, under the Constitution, from 1795 to 1797; and was once Lieutenant-Governor of that State.

Hendricks, Thomas A.—He was born in Muskingum County, Ohio, September 7, 1819; was educated at South Hanover College; studied law, and completed his legal studies at Chambersburg, Pennsylvania, in 1843; settled in Indiana, and practised his profession with success; in 1848 he was chosen to the State Legislature, and declined a re-election; was an active member of the Constitutional Convention of 1850; and was a Representative in Congress, from Indiana, from 1851 to 1855; he was appointed by President Pierce, in 1855, Commissioner of the General Land Office, in which he was continued by President Buchanan until 1859, when he resigned. He was subsequently elected a Senator in Congress for the long term, ending 1869, serving on the Committees on Claims, and on Public Buildings and Grounds.

Hendricks, William.—Born in Westmoreland County, Pennsylvania, in 1783. He was one of the early settlers of Madison, Indiana, having removed there in 1814. During his residence in that State, he filled many high and important offices; he was Secretary of the Convention which formed the present Constitution of the State; the first and sole Representative of Indiana in Congress, from 1816 to 1822; Governor of the State from 1822 to 1825, when he was elected a member of the United States Senate, and served until 1837. He died in Madison, May 16, 1850.

Henley, Thomas, Jr.—He was born in Indiana, and was a Representative in Congress, from that State, from 1843 to 1847.

Henley, Thomas J.—He was born in Ohio, and was a Representative in Congress, from Indiana, from 1847 to 1849. He subsequently removed to California, and held the offices of Indian Agent and Postmaster of San Francisco.

Henn, Bernhardt.—He was born in New York, and on emigrating to Iowa, he was elected a Representative in Congress, from that State, from 1849 to 1853.

Henry, John.—He was a graduate of Princeton College in 1769; was for several years, from 1778, a Delegate to the old Congress; a Senator in Congress under the Constitution, from Maryland, from 1789 to 1797, when he resigned; and elected Governor of Maryland in the latter year. He died at Easton, December, 1798.

Henry, John F.—He was the brother of Robert P. Henry, and was elected to Congress for the unexpired term of the same, from 1826 to 1827. He was born in Scott County, Kentucky, January 17, 1793; received his education at the Georgetown Academy of Kentucky; studied medicine, and in 1813 was appointed Surgeon's mate in Boswell's Regiment of Kentucky troops, serving at Fort Meigs. Subsequently graduated at the New York University; settled in Hopkinsville, Kentucky, in 1822; and subsequently to his service in Congress, removed to Burlington, Iowa.

Henry, Robert P.—Born in Scott County, Kentucky, November 24, 1788; graduated at the University of Transylvania; studied law with Henry Clay, and was admitted to the bar in 1809; served that year as Prosecuting Attorney for his district; served in the war of 1812 as an aide-de-camp to his father, Major-General William Henry; subsequently settled in Christian County, and became Prosecuting Attorney for that circuit; was a Director of the Princeton Branch of the Commonwealth Bank; and was elected a Representative in Congress, from Kentucky, for the term from 1823 to 1827. As a member of the Committee on Roads and Canals, he obtained the first appropriation ever granted for improving the Mississippi River. While in Congress he received the appointment of Judge of the Court of Appeals, which he declined; and he died of fever August 25, 1826, before the expiration of his term in Congress.

Henry, Thomas.—Born in Ireland in 1785. He served his adopted State in Congress from 1837 to 1843. Died in Beaver County, Pennsylvania, February 27, 1849.

Henry, William.—He was born in New Hampshire, and having settled in Vermont, devoted himself to mercantile pursuits. Was for many years Cashier of the Bank of Bellows Falls, where he resides; was elected a Representative in Congress, from Vermont, from 1847 to 1853, accomplishing much work as a member of several committees.

Herbert, John C.—He was a Representative in Congress, from Maryland, from 1815 to 1819.

Herbert, Philip T.—Born in Alabama, and was a Representative in Congress, from California, from 1855 to 1857.

Hereford, Jedediah.—He was born in Vermont, and having removed to New York, was elected a Representative in Congress, from that State, from 1851 to 1853.

Herkimer, John.—Born in Herkimer County, New York, in 1773; was for many years a Judge of the Circuit Court; and a Representative in Congress, from New York, from 1817 to 1819, and again from 1823 to 1825. Died at Danube, New York, June 8, 1845.

Hernandez, Joseph M.—He was one of the prominent Spanish citizens who remained in the Territory of Florida at the time of its transfer to the United States. He was the first Delegate to Congress, from Florida, and subsequently a leading member and presiding officer of the Territorial Legislature. At the breaking out of the Indian hostilities, he was made a Brigadier-General in the United States service. He was a man of refined and elegant manners; resided at St. Augustine; and died near Matanzas, Cuba, June 8, 1857, at an advanced age.

Herod, William.—He was a Representative in Congress, from Indiana, from 1837 to 1839.

Herrick, Anson.—He was born in Lewiston, Maine, January 21, 1812; received a common school education; at the age of fifteen years he was apprenticed to the business of a printer; settled in New York City in 1836, and continued in the same employment until 1838, when he commenced the publication of a weekly journal, now called the New York Atlas, of which he has since been the editor and proprietor. In 1853 he was chosen one of the Aldermen of the city, and served three years, and by President Buchanan he was appointed Naval Storekeeper for New York, which he held until 1861. In 1862 he was elected Representative, from New York, to the Thirty-eighth Congress, serving on the Committees on Revolutionary Pensions, and Expenditures in the Navy Department. Ebenezer Herrick, who served in Congress from 1821 to 1827, was his father.

Herrick, Ebenezer.—He was born in Lincoln County, Maine, and was a Representative in Congress, from Maine, from 1821 to 1827, and died at Lewiston, in that State, May 7, 1839. In 1820 he held the office of Secretary of the State Senate, and was a State Senator in 1828 and 1829.

Herrick, Joshua.—He was born in Beverly, Essex County, Massachusetts, in 1794; received a common school education; removed to Maine, and became a Sheriff in that State; was Collector of the Port of Kennebunk from 1829 to 1841; was Chairman of a Board of County Commissioners from 1842 to 1843; and was a Representative in Congress, from Maine, from 1843 to 1845, serving on the Committees on Naval Affairs, and Accounts. He was again Collector of Kennebunk from 1847 to 1849; and from 1850 to 1857 he was Register of Probate for York County, State of Maine.

Herrick, Richard P.—Born in 1791; a man of remarkable business enterprise; and a member of Congress, from New York, from 1845 to the time of his death, which occurred at Washington, June 22, 1846.

Herrick, Samuel.—He was born in Dutchess County, New York, April 14, 1779. He read law at Carlisle, Pennsylvania, and was admitted to the bar in 1805; in 1810 he settled at Zanesville, Ohio, and was appointed Collector of Taxes for that county; soon afterwards, Prosecuting Attorney for the same county; and soon after that, by President Madison, was appointed United States District Attorney for Ohio; in 1812 he was appointed one of a Board of Commissioners, for settling the Northwestern boundary line; in the autumn of that year, he succeeded Lewis Cass as Prosecuting Attorney for Muskingum County; in 1814 he was appointed to the same office in Licking County; and he was a Representative in Congress, from 1817 to 1821. After his second election, his seat was contested by Charles Hammond, but the House sustained his claim. He was a Presidential Elector in 1828, and in 1829 was appointed, by President Jackson, United States District Attorney for Ohio. The remainder of his life was spent in retirement, and he died in December, 1851.

Heyward, William H.—He graduated at Princeton College in 1808, and was a Representative in Congress, from Maryland, from 1823 to 1825.

Hibbard, Henry.—He was born in Vermont, graduated at Dartmouth

College in 1835; was Assistant Clerk of the New Hampshire House of Representatives in 1839; Clerk of the same from 1840 to 1843; Speaker of the House in 1844 and 1845; in the State Senate from 1846 to 1849, officiating two years as President; and was a Representative in Congress, from New Hampshire, from 1849 to 1855.

Hibshman, Jacob.—He was born in Lancaster, Pennsylvania, and was a Representative in Congress, from that State, from 1819 to 1821.

Hickman, John.—Born in Chester County, Pennsylvania, near the Brandywine battle-ground, September 11, 1810; received a thorough mathematical and classical education; commenced the study of medicine, but finding his health too feeble for the dissecting-room, he studied law and was admitted to the bar in 1833. In 1845 he was appointed District Attorney for Chester County, holding the office fifteen months; in 1854 he was elected a Representative, from Pennsylvania, to the Thirty-fourth Congress, serving on the Committee on Elections; re-elected to the Thirty-fifth Congress, serving as Chairman of the Committee on Revolutionary Pensions; to the Thirty-sixth Congress, and was Chairman of the Judiciary Committee; and to the Thirty-seventh Congress, again serving as Chairman of the Judiciary Committee. He declined a re-election to the Thirty-eighth Congress.

Hicks, Thomas H.—He was born in Maryland; frequently served in the Legislature of that State; was Governor thereof, from 1858 to 1862; and was elected a Senator in Congress, in the place of James A. Pearce, deceased, taking his seat during the third session of the Thirty-seventh Congress, and was re-elected for the term ending in 1867, serving on the Committee on Naval Affairs, and that on Claims.

Hiester, Isaac E.—He was born in Pennsylvania, and was a Representative in Congress, from that State, from 1853 to 1855. He was the son of William Heister, M. C., but changed the spelling of his name.

Higby, William.—Was born in Essex County, Vermont, August 18, 1813; spent his boyhood on a farm, and subsequently engaged in the lumber and iron business; graduated at the University of Vermont in 1840; adopted the profession of law, which he practised in his native county until 1850; during that year he emigrated to California, and was District Attorney of Calaveras County, from 1853 to 1859; in 1862 he was a member of the State Senate; and in 1863 was elected a Representative, from California, to the Thirty-eighth Congress, serving on the Committees on Public Lands, and Expenditures in the Navy Department.

Hill, Clement S.—Born in Kentucky, and was a Representative in Congress, from that State, from 1853 to 1855.

Hill, Hugh L. W.—Born in Tennessee, and was a Representative in Congress, from that State, from 1847 to 1849.

Hill, Isaac.—Born in Somerville, Massachusetts, April 6, 1788. In 1798 his parents removed to a farm in Ashburnham, Massachusetts; his education was exceedingly limited, and at the age of fourteen he was apprenticed in a printing-office, and in 1809, at the expiration of his apprenticeship, he went to Concord, New Hampshire, and purchased the American Patriot, which was afterwards issued as The New Hampshire Patriot, and became a paper of immense circulation and influence during the twenty years of his editorship. During that time he was twice chosen Clerk of the State Senate; was once a Representative in the Legislature, and was elected a member of the State Senate in 1820, 1821, 1822, and 1827. In 1828 he was a candidate for the United States Senate, but not elected. In 1829 he was appointed, by President Jackson, Second Comptroller of the Treasury, and held the office until April, 1830. He returned to New Hampshire, and was elected by the Legislature United States Senator for six years, from 1831. In 1836 he resigned his senatorship, being elected Governor of New Hampshire, and re-elected in 1837 and 1838. In 1840 he was appointed by President Van Buren, Sub-Treasurer at Boston, and in that year established, in connection with his two oldest sons, Hill's New Hampshire Patriot, which they published and edited until 1847, when that paper was united with the

Patriot. He also published the Farmers' Monthly Visitor, an agricultural paper, for ten years; and during the last fifteen years of his life, devoted much attention to agriculture. He died in Washington, District of Columbia, March 22, 1851.

Hill, John.—He was born in Virginia, and was a Representative in Congress, from that State, from 1839 to 1841.

Hill, John.—Born in Stokes County, North Carolina, served many years in the Legislature of the State; was a Representative in Congress, from 1839 to 1841, and in 1850 held the position of Reading Clerk in the State Senate.

Hill, Joshua.—Born in Abbeville District, South Carolina, January 10, 1812; he had not a collegiate education, but studied law as a profession. He was elected a Representative to the Thirty-fifth Congress, from Georgia, and was a member of the Committee on Public Lands. Re-elected to the Thirty-sixth Congress, serving on the Committee on Foreign Affairs. Resigned in February, 1861, and returned to Georgia.

Hill, Mark L.—He was born in Biddeford, Maine, June 30, 1772. From the year 1792 to the close of his life, he had been almost constantly in the exercise of some public employment, either by popular election or executive appointment. Though denied the advantages of a liberal education, he succeeded, by assiduous self-culture, in making himself useful to his country, and gaining honor to himself in the various posts of high responsibility to which he was successively elevated. He was, at various periods, a member of the Senate and House of Representatives of Massachusetts, a Judge of the Court of Common Pleas, member of Congress, from Massachusetts, from 1819 to 1821, and from Maine, from 1821 to 1823; Postmaster at Phippsburg, Maine, Collector of the Port at Bath, and held several other town and county offices. He was one of the Overseers of Bowdoin College from the first, until 1821, when he became a Trustee, in which office he continued till his decease, and during the whole period of forty-nine years, regularly attended every meeting except one. He died at Phippsburg, Maine, November 26, 1842, in the seventy-first year of his age.

Hill, Thomas.—He was born in Pennsylvania, and was a Representative in Congress, from that State, from 1824 to 1826.

Hill, William H.—He was a Representative in Congress, from North Carolina, from 1799 to 1803, and he was also appointed Judge of the United States District Court for the District of North Carolina. He died in 1809.

Hillen, Solomon, Jr.—He was born in Maryland, and was a Representative in Congress, from that State, from 1839 to 1841.

Hillhouse, James.—He was born at Montville, Connecticut, October 21, 1754; graduated at Yale College in 1773; after due preparation, entered upon the practice of law; took an active part in the Revolutionary struggle, and when New Haven was invaded by the British, was commander of the Governor's Guards. He became a Representative in Congress in 1791, and three years afterwards he was chosen a Senator of the United States, from Connecticut, and continued a distinguished member for sixteen years; and in the Sixth Congress was President *pro tem.* of the Senate. In 1810 he resigned his seat in the Senate, and took the office of Commissioner of the School Fund of Connecticut, which he managed with great ability and fidelity for fifteen years; and in 1825 he undertook to conduct the construction of the Farmington and Hampshire Canal. He was chosen Treasurer of Yale College in 1782, and continued to hold the office until his death, having done much to promote the interests of that institution. He died at New Haven, December 29, 1832.

Hilliard, Henry W.—He was born in North Carolina, but spent his boyhood in South Carolina, at the College of which State he graduated. He studied law, and settled in Georgia, but in 1836 became a citizen of Alabama, occupying for several years a professorship in the University of that State. In 1838 he was elected to the State Legislature, and in 1840 a Presidential Elector. In 1842 he was appointed, by

President Tyler, Minister to Belgium; and was a Representative in Congress, from Alabama, from 1843 to 1851. He was also a Regent of the Smithsonian Institution, and devoted some attention to the pursuits of literature. A volume of his speeches was published in 1855.

Hillyer, Junius.—He was born in Wilkes County, Georgia, April 23, 1807; graduated at the State University at Athens in 1828; having studied his profession while in college, he was admitted to the bar within one week after graduating; in 1834 he was elected by the Legislature Solicitor-General for the Western District of the State; and he was a Representative in Congress, from Georgia, from 1851 to 1855, during his second term serving as Chairman of the Committee on Private Land Claims. In 1857 he was appointed, by President Buchanan, Solicitor of the United States Treasury.

Hindman, Thomas C.—He was born in Tennessee, in 1818; served in the Mexican war as a Second Lieutenant of Mississippi volunteers; and was a Representative, from Arkansas, to the Thirty-sixth Congress; was re-elected to the Thirty-seventh, but when the Rebellion broke out he entered the Confederate service, and was at once made a Brigadier-General, and subsequently a Major-General; and he died in 1863.

Hindman, William.—He was a Delegate, from Maryland, to the Continental Congress; a Representative in Congress, from 1792 to 1799; and a Senator in Congress during the years 1800 and 1801. He died January 26, 1822.

Hinds, Thomas.—Born about the year 1775; was a distinguished officer in the battle of New Orleans; and a Representative in Congress, from Mississippi, from 1828 to 1831. He died in Jefferson County, Mississippi, August 23, 1840.

Hines, Richard.—He was born in North Carolina, and was a Representative in Congress, from North Carolina, from 1825 to 1827.

Hitchcock, Peter.—Born in Cheshire, Connecticut, October 19, 1780; and graduated at Yale College in 1801. He was admitted to the bar in 1804, and commenced the practice of law in his native town. In 1806 he removed to Geauga County, Ohio, and in 1810 he was elected to the General Assembly of that State; from 1812 to 1816 he was a member of the State Senate, and President of that body one session. He was a Representative in Congress, from 1817 to 1819, and then chosen Judge of the Supreme Court of Ohio, for seven years; was re-elected to the same office in 1826, and retired from the bench in 1852, after a judicial service of twenty-eight years; having been for a portion of that time Chief Justice. From 1833 to 1835 he was again a member of the State Senate, and once again President. In 1850 he was a Delegate to the Constitutional Convention of the State. He died in Painesville, Ohio, May 11, 1853.

Hoagland, Moses.—He was born in Ohio, and was a Representative in Congress, from that State, from 1849 to 1851.

Hoar, Samuel.—Born in Lincoln, Massachusetts, May 18, 1788. He graduated at Cambridge in 1802, and was for two years thereafter a private tutor in Virginia. He studied law with Artemas Ward, and was admitted to the bar in 1805, and opened an office in Concord. He soon attained high rank, and was for forty years one of the most eminent and successful practitioners in Middlesex County, as well as in the whole State. He was a member of the Convention for revising the State Constitution in 1820; State Senator in 1825 and 1833; member of the Executive Council in 1845 and 1846; State Representative in 1850; and a Representative in Congress, from 1835 to 1837. In 1844 he was appointed by the Legislature of Massachusetts to proceed to South Carolina and aid the colored citizens of Massachusetts, imprisoned by the authorities of South Carolina, by testing, in the courts of the United States, the constitutionality of the acts of South Carolina, authorizing the imprisonment of colored persons who should enter that State. His appearance in Charleston caused great excitement, and he was expelled from that city by its citizens, December 5, 1844; the Legislature having passed resolutions on that day authorizing the Governor to expel him. He was a member of various religious and charitable societies, of the American

Academy of Arts and Sciences, of the Massachusetts Historical Society, and, at the time of his death, one of the Overseers of Harvard College; the degree of Doctor of Laws having, in 1838, been conferred upon him by that institution. He died in Concord, Massachusetts, November 2, 1856.

Hoard, Charles B. — Born in Springfield, Vermont, June 28, 1805; he was a mechanic, and for several years in early life a clerk in a private land office at Antwerp, New York. He was Postmaster under Presidents Jackson and Van Buren; Justice of the Peace for several years; a member of the Legislature of New York in 1838, and County Clerk of Jefferson County, New York, in 1844, 1845, and 1846. He has been an active politician, and was elected a Representative to the Thirty-fifth Congress, serving on the Committee on Expenditures in the State Department. He was also re-elected to the Thirty-sixth Congress, serving as a member of the Committee on Claims.

Hobart, Aaron.—He was born in Abington, Plymouth County, Massachusetts, June 26, 1787; graduated at Brown University in 1805; adopted the profession of law; served in the State Senate; as a State Councillor; was Judge of Probate; and was a Representative in Congress, from Massachusetts, from 1821 to 1827. Died at East Bridgewater, September 19, 1858.

Hobart, John Sloss. — He graduated at Yale College in 1757; was Judge of the District Court of New York, and held several important stations in that State during the Revolutionary war; after which he was appointed one of the three Judges of the Supreme Court. He was elected a member of the United States Senate for the term commencing January, 1798, but resigned May 5, not having taken his seat, and was then appointed Judge of the United States District Court of New York. He died February 4, 1805, aged sixty-six.

Hobbie, Selah R.—Born in Newburg, New York, March 10, 1797, and at an early day established himself at Delhi, Delaware County, in the practice of law, where he was soon appointed District Attorney and Brigade Major and Inspector. He was a Representative in Congress, from 1827 to 1829, when, on the accession of General Jackson to the Presidency, he was appointed Assistant Postmaster-General, which he held until 1850, when he retired on account of ill health, but assumed the duties of the office under President Pierce. He died in Washington, District of Columbia, March 23, 1854.

Hodges, Charles D. — He was elected a Representative in Congress, from Illinois, and took his seat during the second session of the Thirty-fifth Congress.

Hodges, George T.—He was born in Clarendon, Vermont, July 4, 1789; he was bred to active business, and was a merchant in Rutland for many years; served frequently in both Houses of the State Legislature; and was a Representative in Congress, from Vermont, during the second session of the Thirty-fourth Congress. For more than a quarter of a century he was President of the Bank of Rutland; was a large contributor to the success of the Burlington Railroad, and a warm supporter of the Vermont Agricultural Society. Died at Rutland, September 9, 1860.

Hodges, James L. — He was a State Senator in 1823 and 1824, and a Representative in Congress, from Massachusetts, from 1827 to 1831. He died March 8, 1846, aged fifty-six years.

Hoffman, Henry W. — He was born in Maryland, and was a Representative in Congress, from that State, from 1855 to 1857.

Hoffman, Martin. — He was a Representative in Congress, from New York, from 1825 to 1829.

Hoffman, Michael.—Born in the town of Clifton Park, Saratoga County, New York, in 1788. He was educated as a physician, but afterwards studied law, and settled in Herkimer County, where he occupied a high position. He was elected to Congress in 1824, and continued a member for eight years, serving a portion of the time as Chairman of the Committee on Naval Affairs. He was appointed a Canal Commissioner for the State of New York, wrote several able reports, and resigned the office in 1835. In 1841 he went into the House of Assembly, from Herkimer County, and accomplished much good for the service and credit of his State. He was also a Delegate to the Constitutional Convention of 1846, and was Naval Officer in the city of New York; he was a powerful and effective debater, and, as a man, unselfish and of high character. He died at Brooklyn, September 27, 1848.

Hoffman, Ogden.—He was born in New York City in 1794, and graduated at Columbia College in 1812; he soon after entered the navy as a midshipman, but in three years he resigned, and studied law. He commenced to practise in Orange County, and was appointed District Attorney, but removed to New York City in 1826, and was a partner of Hugh Maxwell, and became eminently successful in his profession. In 1828 he was a Representative in the Legislature; from 1829 to 1835 was District Attorney; and was appointed United States District Attorney by President Harrison. From 1837 to 1841 he was a Representative in Congress, and was a member of the Committee on Foreign Affairs; he was re-elected in 1848, and in 1854 was appointed Attorney-General of the State. He was remarkable for his eloquence and learning; and for more than a quarter of a century occupied a high position at the bar of New York. He died in that city, May 1, 1856.

Hogan, William.—He was a Representative in Congress, from New York, from 1831 to 1833.

Hoge, John.—He was a Representative in Congress, from Pennsylvania, from 1804 to 1805.

Hoge, Joseph R.—He was born in Ohio, and, having removed to Illinois, was elected a Representative in Congress, from that State, from 1843 to 1847.

Hoge, William.—He was a Representative in Congress, from Pennsylvania, from 1801 to 1804, and again from 1807 to 1809.

Hogeboom, J. L.—He was a member of the New York Constitutional Convention of 1821, and was a Representative in Congress, from that State, from 1823 to 1825.

Hogg, Samuel.—He was a Representative in Congress, from Tennessee, from 1817 to 1819.

Holcomb, George.—Born in Hunterdon County, New Jersey; graduated at Princeton College in 1805; was a Representative in Congress, from New Jersey, from 1821 to 1828, and died January 14, 1828.

Holladay, Alexander R.—He was born in Virginia, and was a Representative in Congress, from that State, from 1849 to 1853, and was Chairman, during his first term, of the Committee on Expenditures in the Navy Department.

Holland, Cornelius.—Born July 9, 1782; established himself as a physician at Canton, Maine; was a member of the Maine Constitutional Convention of 1819; a member of the State Legislature in 1820 and 1821; and a State Senator in 1822, 1825, and 1826. He was a Representative in Congress, from Maine, from 1831 to 1833, serving on the Committee on Elections, as well as on the Committee of Representation under the Fifth Census.

Holland, James.—He was a Representative in Congress, from North Carolina, from 1795 to 1797, and again from 1801 to 1811.

Holleman, Joel.—Born in the County of Isle of Wight, Virginia, October 1, 1799; was educated at Chapel Hill, North Carolina; taught school for some years, and then studied law, in the practice of which he was successful; and was a Representative in Congress, from Virginia, from 1839 to 1840, when he resigned, "because he could not represent the feelings and wishes of a majority of his constituents." He was subsequently in the State Legislature for several years, and Speaker of the House when he died, August, 1844.

Holley, John M.—He graduated at Yale College in 1822; was a member of the New York Assembly, from 1838 to 1841; and elected a Representative in Congress, from New York, from 1847 to 1848. He died at Jacksonville,

Florida, March 8, 1848, before the expiration of his term.

Holman, William S.—Born in Verdstown, Indiana, September 6, 1822; received a good English education at common schools; adopted the profession of law; was a member of the Convention to revise the Constitution of Indiana in 1850; was a member of the State Legislature in 1851; was a Judge of the Court of Common Pleas from 1852 to 1856; and was elected a Representative, from Indiana, to the Thirty-sixth Congress, serving as a member of the Committee on Revolutionary Claims. Re-elected to the Thirty-seventh Congress, serving on the Committee on Claims; and he was also re-elected to the Thirty-eighth Congress, serving on the Committee on Claims.

Holmes, Elias B.—Born in Fletcher, Vermont, May 27, 1807. He commenced life as a teacher, and at the age of twenty emigrated to Monroe County, New York, where he studied law, and was admitted to practice in 1830. He was a Representative in Congress, from New York, from 1845 to 1849.

Holmes, Gabriel.—Born in Sampson County, North Carolina; was a Representative in Congress, from North Carolina, from 1825 to 1829. Educated at Harvard University, and was a lawyer by profession. He was in the State Senate in 1807, and Governor of the State in 1821. He died September 26, 1829, in Sampson County. North Carolina, aged sixty-five years.

Holmes, Isaac E. — Born in Charleston, South Carolina, April 5, 1796; educated at the best schools of his native city, and graduated with honors, at Yale College, in 1815; he studied law, and was admitted to the bar in 1818, in Charleston. He was one of the originators of the "South Carolina Association;" and was elected to the State Legislature in 1826. For a time he devoted himself to planting, but his most distinguished public service was as a Representative in Congress, from South Caroiina, from 1839 to 1851, during which period he served with ability at the head of the Committees of Commerce, and the Navy, and also on that for Foreign Affairs. He subsequently took up his residence in California.

Holmes, John.—He was born on Cape Cod in March, 1773; graduated at Brown University in 1796; studied law, and commenced the practice in Alfred, Maine, in 1799; was a member of the Massachusetts Legislature in 1802 and 1803, and State Senator from 1813 to 1817; was a Boundary Commissioner under the Treaty of 1815; was a member of the Convention to form the Constitution of Maine, and Chairman of the Committee that drafted the document in 1820; having been a Representative in Congress, from Massachusetts, from 1817 to 1820; and he was a Senator in Congress, from Maine, from 1820 to 1833. For a part of 1829, and from 1835 to 1838, he was a member of the Maine Legislature; and he was United States District Attorney, for Maine, from 1841 till his death, which occurred at Portland, July 7, 1843. He was a prominent member of the bar for forty years, and distinguished for his eloquence and wit.

Holmes, Uriel.—He graduated at Yale College in 1784, and was a Representative in Congress, from Connecticut, from 1817 to 1818, when he resigned. He died in 1827.

Holsey, Hopkins.—He was born in Virginia in 1799, and was a Representative in Congress, from Georgia, from 1837 to 1839. He subsequently edited the Athens Banner, and filled a large space in the politics of Georgia. Died in Columbus, Georgia, March 31, 1859.

Holt, Orrin.—He was born in Connecticut, and was a Representative in Congress, from that State, in 1836, to fill an unexpired term, and from 1837 to 1839.

Holten, Samuel.—Born in Danvers, Massachusetts, June 9, 1738, and was bred a physician. During the Revolution he zealously espoused the cause of his country, and was a member of the old Congress from 1778 to 1787, officiating, at one time, as its President. He was a Representative, under the Constitution, from 1793 to 1795; and spent the closing years of his life as Judge of Probate for Essex County, and died January 2, 1816.

Hook, Enos.—He was born in Pennsylvania, and was a Representative in Congress, from that State, from 1839 to 1841.

Hooks, Charles.—Born in Bertie County, North Carolina, served for many years in the State Legislature, and was a Representative in Congress during the years 1816 and 1817, and from 1819 to 1825. He subsequently removed to Alabama, where he died in 1851.

Hooper, Samuel.—Was born in Marblehead, Massachusetts, February 3, 1808; received his education in that town; spent four years in a counting-room in Boston; subsequently made repeated visits to Europe and the West Indies, attending to commercial business; and in 1832 settled finally in Boston as a merchant, chiefly engaged in the China trade, the last house of which he formed a part having long been known as William Appleton & Co. In 1851 he was elected to the State House of Representatives, served three years, and declined a re-election; in 1857 was elected to the State Senate, and declined to serve a second term; in 1861 he was elected a Representative, from Massachusetts, to fill the vacancy caused by the resignation of William Appleton in the Thirty-seventh Congress, serving on the Committee of Ways and Means; and in 1862 he was re-elected to the Thirty-eighth Congress, serving on the same Committee.

Hooper, W. H.—Born in Cambridge, Dorchester County, Maryland, December 25, 1813; received a common school education; was for several years a clerk in a store at Baltimore; when seventeen years of age built a schooner; was for some years a merchant on the Eastern Shore of Maryland; emigrated to Illinois in 1835, from which time, until 1849, he was engaged in mercantile pursuits and steamboating on the Mississippi; in 1850 he removed to Utah; was a member of the Legislature, and Acting Secretary of the Territory; and in 1859 entered Congress as a Delegate from the Territory of Utah.

Hopkins, George W.—Born in Goochland County, Virginia, February 22, 1804. He was educated at the "old field schools" of that day, and, for some years, alternately taught school and studied law. During the years 1833 and 1834 he served in the House of Delegates, and was elected a Representative in Congress in 1835, and was re-elected until 1847, serving during one session as Speaker of the House of Representatives, after which he was appointed by President Polk Chargé d'Affaires of the United States to Portugal. On his return from Europe, in 1849, he went a second time into the House of Delegates of Virginia, and was elected Speaker of the House. He was subsequently elected a Judge of the Circuit Court, and, in 1857, was re-elected to the Thirty-fifth Congress, serving as Chairman of the Committee on Foreign Relations. Died March 2, 1861, at which time he was a member of the Virginia Legislature.

Hopkins, Samuel.—He was born in Albemarle County, Virginia. He served with distinction in the Revolutionary war, having fought at Princeton, Trenton, Monmouth, Brandywine, and Germantown, and also as Lieutenant-Colonel of a Virginia regiment at the siege of Charleston. He removed to Kentucky in 1797, and served a number of years in the State Legislature; in 1812 led two thousand troops against the Kickapoo Indians; and was a Representative in Congress, from Kentucky, from 1813 to 1815. He died at an advanced age in October, 1819.

Hopkins, Samuel M.—He graduated at Yale College in 1791, and was a Representative in Congress, from New York, from 1813 to 1815. He was an eminent lawyer, and much respected as a philanthropist and a Christian. He died at Geneva, New York, October 8, 1837, aged sixty-five years.

Hopkinson, Joseph.—Born in Philadelphia, Pennsylvania, November 12, 1770; was educated at the University of his native State, from which institution, as well as from Nassau Hall and Harvard University, he subsequenty received the degree of LL.D. He studied law, and commenced to practise at the age of twenty, at Easton, and afterwards at Philadelphia, and became eminent in his profession. He was the leading counsel of Dr. Rush in his famous suit against William Cobbett, in 1799, and was also engaged by Judge Chase in his impeachment case before the United States Senate. In 1815 he was a Representative in Congress, and served until 1819, after which he resided in Bordentown, New Jersey, until appointed by President John Quincy Adams Judge of the District Court of the United States for the Eastern District of Pennsylvania, when he returned to Philadelphia, and held this office until his death. In 1837 he was a member of the Constitutional Convention of the State; was one of the Trustees of the University of Pennsylvania; was President of the Philadelphia Academy of Fine Arts, and Vice-President of the American Philosophical Society. He published many interesting addresses, and wrote the song "Hail, Columbia." He died at Philadelphia, January 15, 1842.

Horn, Henry.—He was a Representative in Congress, from Pennsylvania, from 1831 to 1833.

Hornbeck, John W.—He was a member of the House of Representatives in Congress, from Pennsylvania, from 1847 to 1848, and died at Allentown, Pennsylvania, January 16, 1848.

Horsey, Outerbridge.—He was a native of Delaware, and born in 1777; after completing his classical education, he studied law, under Honorable James A. Bayard, and rose to eminence in his profession. He was for many years Attorney-General of the State, and was a Senator in Congress, from Delaware, from 1810 to 1821. He died at Needwood, Maryland, June 9, 1842.

Horton, Thomas R.—He was born in New York, and was a Representative in Congress, from that State, from 1855 to 1857.

Horton, Valentine B.—He was born at Windsor, Vermont, January 29, 1802; was educated at Partridge's Military Academy, in that State; and after that institution was removed to Middletown, Connecticut, he became a teacher therein. He studied law at Middletown, and was admitted to the bar in 1830, after which he removed to and practised his profession in Pittsburg. He removed to Cincinnati, Ohio, in 1833, where he followed his profession for two years, and in 1835 removed to Pomeroy, Ohio, his present residence, where he engaged in mining and manufacturing. He was a member of the Ohio Constitutional Convention of 1850, and in 1854 he was elected a Representative to the Thirty-fourth Congress, and was re-elected to the Thirty-fifth, his business affairs causing him to decline a nomination for the next Congress. He was, however, re-elected to the Thirty-seventh Congress, serving on the Committee of Ways and Means. In 1861 he was a member of the Peace Congress, held in Washington.

Hosmer, Hezekiah L.—He was a Representative in Congress, from New York, from 1797 to 1799.

Hostetter, Jacob.—He was born in York, Pennsylvania, and was a Representative in Congress, from that State, from 1819 to 1821.

Hotchkiss, Giles W.—A lawyer by profession; and in 1862 he was elected a Representative, from New York, to the Thirty-eighth Congress, serving as a member of the Committees on Claims, and on Private Land Claims.

Houck, Jacob, Jr.—He was born in New York, and was a Representative in Congress, from 1841 to 1843.

Hough, David.—He was a Representative in Congress, from New Hampshire, from 1803 to 1807.

Hough, William J.—He was born in New York; served in the Assembly of that State, in 1835 and 1836; and was a Representative in Congress, from New York, from 1845 to 1847.

Houston, George S.—He was born in Williamson County, Tennessee, January 17, 1811, but removed, when quite young, to the Fifth Congressional District of Alabama, where he was educated, and has since resided. Soon after attaining the age of twenty-one, he was admitted to the bar, and elected to the Alabama Legislature, and served two sessions; he was also, for a time, Attorney for the State, or Solicitor; and was a second time elected to the Legislature. He was elected a Representative to Congress, in 1841, and continued to serve, by successive elections, until 1849, when he voluntarily retired, for the purpose of resuming the practice of law. He was again elected to Congress, in 1851, and subsequently re-elected, serving on several of the leading committees, and officiating during the Thirty-fifth Congress as Chairman of the Committee on the Judiciary; having, during a former session, acted as Chairman of the Committee of Ways and Means. Resigned in February, 1861.

Houston, John W.—Born in Sussex County, Delaware; studied at Newark Academy, and graduated at Yale College in 1834. He studied law with Hon. John M. Clayton, and was admitted to the bar in 1837. He was Secretary of State in 1841; and a Representative in Congress, from Delaware, from 1845 to 1851. He was a Delegate to the Peace Congress of 1861.

Houston, Sam.—Born in Rockbridge County, Virginia, March 2, 1793. He lost his father when quite young, and his mother removed with her family to the banks of the Tennessee, at that time the limit of civilization. Here he received but a scanty education; he passed several years among the Cherokee Indians, and in fact, through all his life, he seems to have held opinions with Rousseau, and retained a predilection for life in the wilderness. After having served for a time as clerk to a country trader, and kept a school, in 1813 he enlisted in the army, and served under General Jackson, in the war with the Creek Indians. He distinguished himself on several occasions, and at the conclusion of the war he had risen to the rank of Lieutenant, but soon resigned his commission, and commenced the study of law at Nashville. It was about this time that he began his political life. After holding several minor offices in Tennessee, he was, in 1823, elected to Congress, and continued a member of that body until, in 1827, he became Governor of Tennessee. In 1829, before the expiration of his gubernatorial term, he resigned his office, and went to take up his abode among the Cherokees in Arkansas. During his residence among the Indians, he became acquainted with the frauds practised upon them by the government agents, and undertook a mission to Washington for the purpose of exposing them. In the execution of this project, he met with but little success; he became involved in lawsuits, and returned to his Indian friends. During a visit to Texas, he was requested to allow his name to be used in the canvass, for a Convention which was to meet to form a Constitution for Texas, prior to its admission into the Mexican Union. He consented, and was unanimously elected. The Constitution drawn up by the Convention was rejected by Santa Anna, at that time in power, and the disaffection of the Texans caused thereby was still further heightened by a demand upon them to give up their arms. They determined upon a resistance; a militia was organized, and Austin, the founder of the colony, was elected commander-in-chief, in which office he was shortly after succeeded by General Houston. He conducted the war with vigor, and finally brought it to a successful termination by the battle of San Jacinto, which was fought in April, 1836. In May, 1836, he signed a treaty, acknowledging the independence of Texas, and in October of the same year he was inaugurated the first President of the Republic. At the end of his term of office, as the same person could not constitutionally be elected President twice in succession, he became a member of the Texas Congress. In 1841, however, he was again elevated to the Presidential chair. During the whole time that he held that office it was his favorite policy to effect the annexation of Texas to the United States, but he retired from office before he saw the consummation of his wishes. In 1846 Texas became one of the States of the Union, and General Houston was elected to the Senate, of which body he remained a member until the close of the Thirty-fifth Congress, serving on the Committee on Indian Affairs. In 1859 he was elected Governor of Texas. Died in Huntersville, Texas, July 25, 1863.

Howard, Benjamin.—He was a Representative in Congress, from Kentucky, from 1807 to 1810, when he was appointed Governor of Indiana Territory. He was appointed Brigadier-General in the United States Army in 1813; and was once Governor of Missouri Territory. He died at St. Louis, Missouri, September 18, 1814.

Howard, Benjamin C.—He was born in Maryland; graduated at Princeton College in 1809; and was a Representative in Congress, from Maryland, from 1829 to 1833, and again from 1835 to 1839. He was also a Delegate to the Peace Congress of 1861.

Howard, Jacob M.—He was born in Shaftsbury, Vermont, July 10, 1805; was educated at the Academies of Bennington and Brattleborough, and at Williams College, where he graduated in 1830; studied law, and taught in an academy in Massachusetts for a time; removed to Michigan in 1832, and came to the bar of that Territory in 1833; in 1838 he was a member of the Legislature of the State; from 1841 to 1843 he was a Representative in Congress, from Michigan; in 1854 he was elected Attorney-General of the State, twice re-elected, and serving in all six years; and in 1862 he was elected a Senator in Congress, in the place of K. S. Bingham, deceased, for the term ending in 1865, serving as Chairman of the Committee on the Pacific Railroad, and as a member of the Committees on Military Affairs, the Judiciary, and Private Land Claims.

Howard, John Eager.—He was born June 4, 1752, in Baltimore County, Maryland; and graduated at Princeton College. He entered the army in 1776, as a Captain in the regiment of Colonel J. C. Hall; in the following year he was promoted, till finally he succeeded to the command of the Second Maryland Regiment. He was an efficient coadjutor of Greene during the campaign in the South, distinguishing himself at the battle of Cowpens, when, says Lee, "he seized the critical moment, and turned the fortune of the day;" also at Guilford, and the Eutaws. He was in the engagement of White Plains, Germantown, Monmouth, Camden, and Hobkirk's Hill. Having been trained to the infantry service, he was remarkably apt at charging into close battle with fixed bayonet; at Cowpens this mode of fighting was resorted to for the first time in the war, and in this battle he had in his hands at one time the swords of seven officers who had surrendered to him personally. On this occasion he saved the life of the British General O'Hara, whom he found clinging to his stirrup and asking quarter. When the army was disbanded he retired to his patrimonial estate near Baltimore. In 1788 he was chosen Governor of Maryland, and held the office three years. He was a Senator of the United States, from Maryland, from 1796 to 1803, and was President *pro tem.* of the Senate in the Sixth Congress. He died October 12, 1827.

Howard, Tilghman A.—Born near Pickensville, South Carolina, November 14, 1797. He received a limited education, and commenced active life as a clerk in a store, and as a schoolmaster; removed to Tennessee and devoted himself to the law; when twenty-seven years of age was elected a member of the Tennessee Legislature; was a Jackson Elector in 1830; during that year removed to Indiana, and was appointed, by President Jackson, District Attorney for that State; and was appointed Chargé d'Affaires to Texas in 1844, in which Republic he died August 16, 1844. His term of service as a Representative in Congress from Indiana was from 1839 to 1841.

Howard, Volney E.—He was born in Norridgewock, Maine; studied law; emigrated to Mississippi, where he distinguished himself as an editor, and fought two duels, first with S. S. Prentiss, and next with Governor McNutt; and having emigrated to Texas, was elected a Representative in Congress, from that State, from 1849 to 1853.

Howard, William.—Born in Virginia, and was elected a Representative, from Ohio, to the Thirty-sixth Congress, serving on the Committee on Revisal and Unfinished Business.

Howard, William A.—He was born in Vermont, and having taken up his residence in Michigan, was elected a Representative, from that State, to the Thirty-fourth and Thirty-fifth Congresses, and was a member of the Committee of Ways and Means. Having contested the seat of G. B. Cooper in 1860, he became a member of the Thirty-sixth Congress. In 1861 he was appointed, by President Lincoln, Postmaster at Detroit.

Howe, John W.—He was born in New Hampshire, and having settled in Pennsylvania, was elected a Representative in Congress, from 1849 to 1853.

Howe, Thomas M.—He was born in Vermont, and having settled in Pennsylvania, was elected a Representative in Congress, from 1851 to 1855. He was for many years Cashier, and then President, of the Exchange Bank of Pittsburg.

Howe, Thomas Y., Jr.—He was a native of New York, and was a Representative in Congress, from that State, from 1851 to 1853.

Howe, Timothy O.—Was born in Livermore, Oxford County, Maine, February 7, 1816; received an academical education at the Readfield Seminary; studied law and was admitted to the bar in 1839; settled at Readfield, and was elected to the Legislature of Maine in 1845; in the latter part of that year, he removed to Green Bay, Wisconsin; was elected a Circuit Judge in that State in 1850, holding the office until 1855, when he resigned; and in 1861, he was elected a Senator in Congress, from Wisconsin, serving on the Committees on Finance, Pensions, and Claims.

Howell, Edward.—He was a member of the New York Assembly in 1832, and a Representative in Congress, from that State, from 1833 to 1835.

Howell, Elias.—He was born in New Jersey, and having taken up his residence in Ohio, was elected a Representative in Congress, from 1835 to 1837.

Howell, Jeremiah B.—He was a Senator in Congress, from Rhode Island, from 1811 to 1817.

Howell, Nathaniel W.—He was a Representative in Congress, from New York, from 1813 to 1815, and died at Canandaigua, New York, October 16, 1851, aged eighty-one years.

Howland, Benjamin.—He was a Senator in Congress, from Rhode Island, from 1804 to 1809, and died 6th of May, 1821.

Hubard, Edmund W.—He was born in Virginia, and was a Representative in Congress, from that State, from 1841 to 1847.

Hubbard, A. B.—He was born in Haddam, Connecticut, January 18, 1819; received a district school education; removed to Indiana in 1838, and taught school for a time; studied law and came to the bar in 1841; in 1847 he was elected to the Indiana Legislature, and served three years; in 1857 he removed to Iowa, and was chosen Judge of the Fourth Judicial District of that State; and in 1862 he was elected a Representative, from Iowa, to the Thirty-eighth Congress, serving as a member of the Committee on Foreign Affairs.

Hubbard, David.—He was born in Virginia, and was a Representative in Congress, from Alabama, from 1839 to 1841, and for a second term, from 1849 to 1851.

Hubbard, Henry.—He was born in Charlestown, New Hampshire, May 3, 1784; graduated at Dartmouth College in 1803; studied law, and commenced practice in Charlestown. He came early into public life. He was frequently a member of the State Legislature, and for some years Speaker of the House. He was Judge of Probate for Sullivan County, from 1827 to 1829; a Representative in Congress, from 1829 to 1835; and a Senator in Congress, from 1835 to 1841. He was also Governor of New Hampshire, in 1842 and 1843; and from 1846 to 1849 United States Assistant Treasurer in Boston. For a part of the time, during the Twenty-eighth Congress, he was chosen Speaker of the House of Representatives. He died at Charlestown, New Hampshire, June 5, 1857.

Hubbard, John H.—He was born in Salisbury, Litchfield County, Connecticut, in 1805; received a good common school education; studied law and was admitted to the bar in 1826, and was a regular practitioner of his profession until 1855. For five years he was Attorney for the county of Litchfield; was twice elected to the State Senate; and early in 1863 he was elected a Representative, from Connecticut, to the Thirty-eighth Congress, serving on the Committees on Patents, and Expenditures in the Post-office Department.

Hubbard, Jonathan H.—Born in 1768. He was one of the oldest and most esteemed citizens of Vermont, and was distinguished as a jurist; he was a Representative in Congress, from 1809 to 1811, and for many years was one of the Judges of the Supreme Court of Vermont. His death occurred where most of his life was spent, at Windsor, Vermont, September 20, 1849.

Hubbard, Levi.—He was a Representative in Congress, from Massachusetts, from 1813 to 1815; a State Senator in 1806, 1807, 1811, and 1816; also for some years a County Treasurer; a State Councillor in 1819; a Presidential Elector in 1820 and 1828; having also been in 1804 and 1805 a member of the State Assembly.

Hubbard, Samuel Dickinson.—Born at Middletown, Connecticut, August 10, 1799, and died at the same place, October 8, 1855. Graduated at Yale College in 1819, studied law, but did not practice, devoting himself chiefly to the manufacturing business. He served as a Representative through the Twenty-ninth and Thirtieth Congresses. In 1852 he was appointed Postmaster-General, and held the office until the close of President Fillmore's administration, after which he retired to private life. He was zealous in the cause of education, and assisted in the establishment of the City High School at Middletown.

Hubbard, Thomas H.—He was a native of New Haven, Connecticut, and a graduate of Yale College in 1798. He studied law, and settled at Hamilton, Madison County, New York, and was there Surrogate for ten years. In 1823 he removed to Utica, and was a Representative in Congress, from New York, from 1817 to 1819, and from 1821 to 1823. He was chosen Presidential Elector in 1812, 1844, and 1852. He died in Utica, May 22, 1857, aged seventy-six years.

Hubbell, William S.—He was born in New York; was a member of the Assembly of that State in 1841, and a Representative in Congress, from the same, from 1843 to 1845.

Hubley, Edward B.—From 1835 to 1839, a Representative in Congress, from Pennsylvania, and died February 23, 1856, in Philadelphia.

Hudson, Charles.—Born in Marlborough, Massachusetts, November 14, 1795. He spent his youth as a student in a village school, and also as a teacher, and at the age of twenty-one was a day laborer on a farm. In 1819 he was licensed as a preacher of the Universalist persuasion; was a member of the Massachusetts Legislature from 1828 to 1833; a State Senator from 1833 to 1839; a State Councillor from 1839 to 1841; and was elected to Congress in 1841, where he remained until 1849. He was subsequently appointed Naval Officer for Boston, Massachusetts, by the Federal Government, serving from 1849 to 1853.

Hufty, Jacob.—He was a Representative in Congress, from New Jersey, from 1809 to 1814.

Huger, Benjamin.—He was a Representative in Congress, from South Carolina, from 1799 to 1805, and for a second term, from 1815 to 1817.

Huger, Daniel.—He was a member of the Continental Congress, and a Representative in the Congress of the United States, from South Carolina, from 1789 to 1793.

Huger, Daniel Elliot.—Was a citizen of Charleston, South Carolina; graduated at Princeton College in 1789; and for nearly half a century was identified with the public service of his State, as a member of the Legislature, State Senate, and Judge of her Courts; and was a Senator in Congress, from 1843 to 1846. He died in Charleston, in August, 1854.

Hughes, Charles.—He was born in Georgia, and having settled in New York, was elected a Representative in Congress, from that State, from 1853 to 1855. In 1862 he was appointed Provost Marshal for the Sixteenth District of New York.

Hughes, George W.—He was elected a Representative, from Maryland, to the Thirty-sixth Congress, serving as a member of the Committee on Expenditures in the Navy Department.

Hughes, James.—He was born at Hampstead, Maryland, November 24, 1823, and was educated at the State University of Indiana. He began the practice of law at Bloomington, Indiana, in 1842; was appointed First Lieutenant of the 16th Regiment of United States infantry, one of the ten regiments in the Mexican war, and served till the close of the war, and then returned to the practice of law in Bloomington. He was elected Circuit Judge, in 1852, for six years; in 1853 was elected Professor of Law in the University of Indiana, and served three years. He was elected a Representative, from Indiana, in the Thirty-fifth Congress, serving as a member of the Committee on Territories. In 1863 he was appointed, by President Lincoln, a Judge of the Court of Claims.

Hughes, James M.—He was a native of Kentucky, and a Representative in Congress, from Missouri, from 1843 to 1845.

Hughes, Thomas H.—He was a Representative in Congress, from New Jersey, from 1829 to 1833.

Hughston, Jonas A.—He was born in New York, and was a Representative, from that State, to the Thirty-fourth Congress.

Huguenin, Daniel.—He was born in Montgomery County, New York, and was distinguished as an officer in the war of 1812, and participated in the stirring events on the Niagara frontier, and the battle of Queenstown, with General Scott, where he was taken prisoner. He was a member of Congress, from New York, from 1825 to 1827, and a member of the New York Legislature, and at a later period United States Marshal for the Territory of Wisconsin, under an appointment from President Harrison. He died at Kenosha, Wisconsin, June, 1850, aged fifty-nine.

Hulbert, John W.—He was a Representative in Congress, from Massachusetts, from 1814 to 1817.

Hulburd, Calvin T.—He was born in Stockholm, St. Lawrence County, New York, June 5, 1809; graduated at Middlebury College, Vermont; read law at Yale College, and adopted the occupation of farming; was a member of the State Legislature from 1842 to 1844, and again in 1862; and in the latter year was elected a Representative, from New York, to the Thirty-eighth Congress, serving on the Committee on Agriculture, and as Chairman of the Committee on Public Expenditures.

Humphrey, Charles.—He was born in Orange County, New York, and was a Representative in Congress, from New York, from 1825 to 1827, and subsequently served four years in the Assembly of that State,—one year as Speaker. He died at Albany, July 18, 1850, aged fifty-nine years.

Humphrey, James.—Born in Fairfield, Connecticut, October 9, 1811; graduated at Amherst College in 1831, of which his father, Rev. Heman Humphrey, was for many years President; had charge, in 1832, of Plainfield Academy, in Connecticut; studied law, and settled for practice in Louisville, Kentucky, where he remained only one year. In 1838 he removed to the city of New York, where he has since practised his profession; and in 1858 he was elected a Representative, from New York, to the Thirty-sixth Congress, serving as a member of the Committee on Foreign Affairs.

Humphrey, Reuben.—He was for four years a Senator in the Legislature of New York, from Onondaga County, and a Representative in Congress, from that State, from 1807 to 1809.

Humphreys, Jacob.—He was a Representative in Congress, from Pennsylvania, from 1819 to 1821.

Humphreys, Perry W.—He was a Representative in Congress, from Tennessee, from 1813 to 1815.

Hungerford, John P.—He was an officer in the Revolutionary war, and a member of Congress, from Virginia, from 1813 to 1817. He died at Twiford, in Westmoreland County, December 21, 1833, aged seventy-four years.

Hungerford, Orville.—He was born in Connecticut in 1790, and was a Representative in Congress, from New York, from 1843 to 1847. He died at Watertown, April 6, 1851.

Hunt, Hiram P.—He was born in New York, and was a Representative in Congress, from that State, from 1835 to 1837, and again from 1839 to 1843.

Hunt, James B.—He was a native of New York, and for many years law-partner with Michael Hoffman. He removed to Michigan about the time of its admission into the Union, and was soon called to responsible public trusts. He was a member of Congress, from Michigan, from 1843 to 1847. He died in Washington, August 15, 1857, aged fifty-eight years.

Hunt, Jonathan.—He represented the State of Vermont in Congress, from 1827 to 1832, serving on the Committee on Public Lands, and died at Washington, May 14, of the latter year. He was a graduate of Dartmouth College in 1807.

Hunt, Samuel.—He was a Representative in Congress, from New Hampshire, from 1802 to 1805.

Hunt, Theodore G.—He was born in South Carolina, and was a Representative in the Thirty-third Congress, from Louisiana.

Hunt, Washington.—Born in Windham, Greene County, New York, August 5, 1811. At the age of eighteen he entered upon the study of law, and was admitted to the bar at Lockport in 1834. In 1836 he was appointed first Judge of Niagara County, and was a Representative in Congress, from 1843 to 1849, serving during his last term as Chairman of the Committee on Commerce. In 1849 he was elected Comptroller of New York, and, in 1850, Governor of the State. Since that time he has lived in retirement upon a handsome farm near Lockport, dividing his attention between his friends, his books, and the pursuits of horticulture. He was a Delegate to the Chicago Convention in 1864.

Hunter, John.—He was a Representative in Congress, from South Carolina, from 1793 to 1795, and a Senator in Congress, from that State, from 1795 to 1796.

Hunter, Naisworthy.—He was a Delegate in Congress, from the Territory of Mississippi, from 1801 to 1802. Died March 11, 1802.

Hunter, Robert M. T.—He was born in Essex County, Virginia, April 21, 1809; was educated at the University of Virginia; adopted the profession of law and came to the bar in 1830; served three years in the State Legislature; and was first elected a Representative in Congress, from his native State, in 1837, when he served two terms, and was re-elected in 1845, officiating during the Twenty-sixth Congress as Speaker. In 1847 he was elected a Senator in Congress for a long term, and re-elected for the term ending in 1859, serving as Chairman of the Committee on Finance, and as a member of the Committees on the Library, and on the Pacific Railroad. He was re-elected to the Senate in 1859 for another long term, but was expelled July, 1861. He took part in the Rebellion as Secretary of State and a member of Congress in the Rebel government.

Hunter, William.—He was a Representative in Congress, from Vermont, from 1817 to 1819. He was also a member of the State Legislature in 1807 and 1809, and a State Councillor in 1809, 1814, and 1815.

Hunter, William.—Born in Newport, Rhode Island, November 23, 1775; graduated at Brown University in 1791; went to London, and studied medicine, but soon changed to the law, and entered at the Inner Temple in London; and on his return to Newport, at the age of twenty-one, was admitted to the bar. In 1799 he was a Representative in the General Assembly of Rhode Island, and re-elected at different periods from that time to the year 1811, when he was chosen a Senator in Congress, and held his seat till 1821. His speeches, especially those on the acquisition of Florida, and the Missouri Compromise, won him a high reputation as a sagacious statesman and finished orator. In 1834 he was Chargé to Brazil, an office which was, in 1842, raised to a full mission, and he was continued as Minister till 1845, when he retired from public life, and resided at Newport until his death, which occurred December 3, 1849.

Hunter, William F.—He was born in Alexandria, Virginia, December 10, 1808; had few educational advantages; practised the trade of a cabinet-maker until 1840; and having studied law, removed to Ohio, and was a Representative in Congress, from that State, from 1849 to 1853; since which time he has devoted himself to his profession.

Hunter, William G.—He was born in New York, and was a Representative in Congress, from that State, from 1843 to 1844.

Hunter, William H.—He was a Representative in Congress, from Ohio, from 1837 to 1839.

Huntington, Abel.—He was born in Norwich, Connecticut, but at an early age removed to East Hampton, Long Island, and for sixty years was a practising physician. He was a Representative in Congress, from New York, from 1833 to 1837. He was Collector of Sag Harbor, under President Polk; and member of the New York Constitutional Convention of 1846. He died at East Hampton, May 18, 1858, aged eighty-two years.

Huntington, Benjamin.—Was a native of Norwich, Connecticut; graduated at Yale College in 1761, and practised law in his native town. He was a Judge of the Superior Court of the State, from 1793 to 1798, and was a member of the Continental Congress, from 1780 to 1784, and also from 1787 to 1788; and a Representative in Congress, under the Constitution, from 1789 to 1791. He was Mayor of Norwich for twelve years, and he died in 1800.

Huntington, Ebenezer.—He was born in Norwich, Connecticut, and died there in May, 1834, aged ninety-seven years. He graduated at Yale College in 1775; joined the army the same year as a volunteer; was soon commissioned as a Lieutenant; in 1776 he was appointed a Captain, and also, deputy Adjutant-General; in 1777 a Major; in 1779 a Lieutenant-Colonel; and he was present at the surrender of Cornwallis, at Yorktown. He was twice elected to Congress, from Connecticut, serving from 1810 to 1811, and again from 1817 to 1819. In 1799 he was, at the recommendation of Washington, appointed a Brigadier-General in the army raised by Congress, when expectations were entertained of a war with France.

Huntington, Jabez W.—Born in Norwich, Connecticut, November 8, 1788, and graduated at Yale College in 1806. He studied law at Litchfield, and commenced to practise there, where he remained thirty years. In 1828 he was elected to the State Legislature, and in 1829 was a Representative in Congress; which office he filled until 1834, when he removed to Norwich, and became a Judge of the Supreme Court of Errors, and was chosen a Judge of the Superior Court of his State. He was a Senator in Congress from 1840 until his death, which occurred at Norwich, November 1, 1847.

Huntsman, Adam.—He was a native of Virginia, and a Representative in Congress, from Tennessee, from 1835 to 1837.

Hutchins, John.—Born in Vienna Township, Trumbull County, Ohio, July 25, 1812; was chiefly educated by private tutors, although he spent one year at the Western Reserve College; studied law, and was admitted to the bar in 1837; in 1838 was appointed Clerk of the Court of Common Pleas for Trumbull County, holding the position five years; in 1849 he was elected to the Ohio Legislature; served a number of years as a Bank Director; and in 1858 he was elected a Representative, from Ohio, to the Thirty-sixth Congress, serving as a member of the Committee on Claims. Re-elected to the Thirty-seventh Congress, serving as Chairman of the Committee on Manufactures.

Hutchins, Wells A.—Was born in Hartford, Trumbull County, Ohio, October 8, 1818; received a common school education; taught school for several years in Ohio and Indiana; studied law, and came to the bar in his twenty-third year; was elected to the Ohio Legislature in 1851; in 1862 he was appointed one of the six Provost Marshals for Ohio; and in 1862 he was elected a Representative, from Ohio, to the Thirty-eighth Congress, serving on the Committee on Commerce.

Huyler, John.—He was born in New York, and having become a citizen of New Jersey, was elected a Representative to the Thirty-fifth Congress, from that State, and was a member of the Committee on Agriculture.

Hyneman, John M.—He was a Representative in Congress, from Pennsylvania, from 1811 to 1813, when he resigned, and D. Udree was elected in his place.

Ihrie, Peter.—He was a native of Pennsylvania, and was a Representative in Congress, from that State, from 1829 to 1833.

Ilsley, Daniel. — Born in Falmouth, Massachusetts, in 1740; was a distiller by occupation; served three years in the State Legislature; was a Representative in Congress, from Massachusetts, from 1807 to 1809. Died in 1813.

Imlay, James H.—He graduated at Princeton College in 1786; was for a time tutor in that institution; and was a Representative in Congress, from New Jersey, from 1797 to 1801.

Inge, Samuel W.—He was born in North Carolina, and on removing to Alabama was elected a Representative in Congress, from that State, from 1847 to 1851.

Inge, William M.—He was born in Tennessee, and was a Representative in Congress, from that State, from 1833 to 1835.

Ingersoll, Charles J.—Born in Philadelphia, October 3, 1782; received a liberal education; was a Representative in Congress, from Pennsylvania, from 1813 to 1815, when he was appointed United States District Attorney for Pennsylvania, which he held until 1829. In 1837, he was appointed Secretary of Legation to Prussia. He was afterwards re-elected a Representative in Congress, from 1841 to 1847, serving as Chairman of the Committee on Foreign Affairs. He has published a "History of the Second American War with Great Britain," and several other works of minor importance, including some poetry. He has also served as a member of various Internal Improvement Conventions; and in 1847 was appointed by President Polk Minister to France, but was rejected by the Senate. Died in Philadelphia, May 14, 1862.

Ingersoll, Colin M.—He was born in Connecticut in 1820; received a liberal education, and adopted the profession of law; was Secretary of Legation at St. Petersburg, by appointment of President Polk; and was a Representative in Congress, from Connecticut, from 1851 to 1855.

Ingersoll, Ebon C.—Born in Oneida County, New York, December 12, 1831; removed with his father to Illinois in 1843; finished his education at Paducah, Kentucky; studied law, and came to the bar in 1854; in 1856 he was elected to the Illinois Legislature; and in 1864 he was elected a Representative, from Illinois, to the Thirty-eighth Congress, for the unexpired term of Owen Lovejoy.

Ingersoll, Joseph R.—Born in Philadelphia, June 14, 1786; graduated at Yale College in 1804; is a lawyer by profession, and was a Representative in Congress, from Pennsylvania, from 1835 to 1837, and from 1842 to 1849, and for a time Chairman of the Judiciary Committee. He was appointed by President Fillmore Minister to England. The titles of LL.D. and D.C.L. Oxon. have been conferred upon him.

Ingersoll, Ralph J.—He was born in New Haven, Connecticut; graduated at Yale College in 1808; served in the Legislature of Connecticut; was a Representative in Congress, from that State, from 1825 to 1833, and was appointed, by President Polk, Minister Plenipotentiary to Russia.

Ingham, Samuel.—He was born in Hebron, Connecticut, September 5, 1793; received a good English education in Vermont, and studied law in Connecticut, having been admitted to the bar in 1815; and in 1817 he settled at Saybrook, which has since been his home. From 1827 to 1835 he was State's Attorney for the County of Middlesex, and again in 1843 and 1844; he was a Judge of Probate from 1829 to 1833; Judge of the Middlesex County Court from 1849 to 1853; and was a Representative in Congress, from Connecticut, from 1835 to 1839, having officiated as Chairman of the Committee on Naval Affairs, and as a member of the Committee on Commerce. He also served a number of years in the Senate and House of Representatives of Connecticut, three years as Speaker, and was one year Clerk of the House; he was appointed in 1837, by the State, an agent to prosecute certain claims against the United States, and was successful; and in 1857 he was appointed, by President Buchanan, Commissioner of Customs. In 1854 he was a candidate for the office of United States Senator, and received the entire vote of his party in the Legislature, but Senator Foster was elected.

Ingham, Samuel D.—He was born in Pennsylvania, September 16, 1773; received a good education; had the management for some years of a paper-mill in Eastern New Jersey; served three years in the Pennsylvania Legislature; held for a time the office of Prothonotary to one of the Courts of that State; and was a Representative in Congress, from 1813 to 1818, and from 1822 to 1829, serving as Chairman of several Committees, when he was appointed, by President Jackson, Secretary of the Treasury. Died at Trenton, New Jersey, June 5, 1860.

Iredell, James.—Born in Chowan County, North Carolina, in 1788. He was for several years in the Legislature of that State, part of the time Speaker of the House; in 1812 commanded a company of volunteers, who went to Norfolk to repel the British; in 1819 he was appointed Judge of the Superior Court; in 1827 was elected Governor of North Carolina; and was a Senator in Congress, from 1828 to 1831. Toward the close of his life he was a Reporter of the Decisions of the Supreme Court, and died at Edenton, April 13, 1853.

Irvin, Alexander.—He was born in Pennsylvania, and was a Representative in Congress, from that State, from 1847 to 1849.

Irvin, James.—He was born in Pennsylvania, and was a Representative in Congress, from that State, from 1841 to 1845.

Irvine, William.—Born in Ireland; educated for the medical profession; served as surgeon on board of a British ship, in the war which began in 1754, and after the peace of 1763 settled at Carlisle, Pennsylvania. In 1774 he was a member of the State Convention; in 1776 he served in Canada, and accompanied Colonel Thompson from Sorelle to dislodge the enemy from Trois Rivières; but was taken prisoner, June 16, and remained as such at Quebec until exchanged in 1778. On his release he was promoted to the command of the Second Pennsylvania Regiment, and in 1781 the defence of the northwestern frontier was intrusted to him, and he attained the rank of Major-General. He was a Representative in Congress, after the war, from 1793 to 1795. He was a Commissioner during the Whiskey Insurrection of 1794, and removed shortly after to Philadelphia, and was appointed Superintendent of Military Stores. He died July 30, 1804, aged sixty-three years.

Irvine, William.—He was elected a Representative, from New York, to the Thirty-sixth Congress, serving as a member of the Committee on the Militia.

Irvine, William W.—He was a member of the State Legislature of Ohio, and Judge of the Supreme Court of the State, and a Representative in Congress, from Ohio, from 1829 to 1833. In 1843 he was appointed Chargé d'Affaires to Denmark. He died at Lancaster, Ohio, April, 1842.

Irving, William.—He was born in the city of New York, August 16, 1766; from 1787 to 1791 was an Indian trader on the Mohawk; was subsequently a merchant in New York City, and a Representative in Congress, from 1813 to 1819, and a member of the Committee of Commerce and Manufactures. He was a brother of Washington Irving, for whose "Salmagundi" he wrote several poems and essays. He was distinguished for his colloquial powers, and was a popular as well as an influential member of Congress, but he resigned before the expiration of his term, on account of his health. He died November 9, 1821.

Irwin, Jared.—He was a member of the Convention which adopted the Constitution of 1789; was Governor of Georgia, from 1796 to 1798, and also from 1806 to 1809. He removed to Pennsylvania, and was a Representative in Congress, from that State, from 1813 to 1817; and died March 1, 1818, aged sixty-eight years.

Irwin, Thomas.—He was born in Pennsylvania, and was a Representative in Congress, from 1829 to 1831, and was in the latter year appointed, by President Jackson, United States Judge of the Western District of Pennsylvania.

Irwin, William W.—He was a member of Congress, from Pennsylvania, from 1841 to 1843; and from 1843 to 1847 he was Chargé d'Affaires of the United States to Denmark. He died in Pittsburg, September 15, 1856.

Isaacs, Jacob C.—He was born in Montgomery County, Pennsylvania, and was a Representative in Congress, from that State, from 1823 to 1833.

Iverson, Alfred.—Born in Burke County, Georgia, December 3, 1798; graduated at Princeton College in 1820; a lawyer by profession; served three years as a member of the House of Representatives, and one year as Senator in the Legislature of Georgia. Twice elected Judge of the Superior Court of that State for terms of three and four years; was one of the Electors at large in the Presidential election of 1844; elected a Representative to the Thirtieth Congress, and served two years. In 1854 he was elected to the United States Senate for six years, from March 4, 1855; and for a long time acted as Chairman of the Committee on Claims, and as a member of the Committees on Military Affairs, and the Pacific Railroad. Resigned in February, 1861, and joined the Great Rebellion.

Ives, Willard.—He was born in Watertown, New York, July 7, 1806; received a good English education; is a farmer by occupation; and was a Representative in Congress, from New York, from 1851 to 1853. In 1846 he was elected by the Methodist Episcopal Church, a Delegate to the Christian World's Convention, which was held in London.

Izard, Ralph.—A Senator of the United States, from South Carolina, from 1789 to 1795, President of the Senate *pro tem.* during the first session of the Third Congress, and a distinguished and eloquent statesman. In the judgment of Washington no man was more honest in public life. He died at South Bay, May 30, 1804, aged sixty-six years.

Jack, William.—He was born in Pennsylvania, and was a Representative in Congress, from that State, from 1841 to 1843.

Jackson, Andrew.—Born at the Waxsaw Settlement, North Carolina, March 15, 1767. When fourteen years of age he left the academy where he had been placed, and entered the Revolutionary army, and at the age of twenty-one established himself as a lawyer in Western North Carolina. When that part of the country became a Territory in 1790, President Washington appointed him Attorney of the United States for the new district. When said Territory was formed into the State of Tennessee, he was a member of the Convention which drew up the new Constitution, and he was immediately chosen a Representative in Congress, serving one term, when he was transferred to the United States Senate, where he continued until 1798. His next public position was that of Judge of the Supreme Court; and having been chosen Major-General of one of the divisions of the Tennessee militia, he retained the office until 1814, when he went into the regular army with the same rank. He was assigned to the command of the army at New Orleans, and January 8, 1815, obtained his famous victory over the British. In 1817–18 he conducted the Seminole war in Florida, and soon after retired from the army. In 1823 he was again elected a Senator in Congress, and remained there two years. He was elected President in 1828, and re-elected in 1832. The events which marked his administration were, the difficulties with France, the suppression of the Nullification movement in South Carolina, the Indian war in Florida, and the removal of the deposits from the United States Bank. He retired to private life in 1836, and in the peaceful shades of the Hermitage, in Tennessee, he died, June 8, 1845. That he was a remarkable man is the undisputed verdict of his countrymen throughout the Union.

Jackson, David S.—He was born in New York, and was a Representative in Congress, from that State, from 1847 to 1848.

Jackson, Ebenezer, Jr.—He was born in Connecticut, and was a Representative in Congress, from that State, to fill an unexpired term, from 1834 to 1835.

Jackson, Edward B.—He was born in Harrison County, Virginia, and was a Representative in Congress, from that State, from 1819 to 1823. Died September 8, 1826.

Jackson, Jabez.—He was born in Georgia, and was a Representative in Congress, from that State, from 1836 to 1839.

Jackson, James.—Born in Devon, England, in 1757, and came to this country in 1772. Early in the American Revolution he joined the army; in 1778 was made Brigade-Major; and in 1781 commanded the Legionary Corps of the State of Georgia. When the British evacuated Savannah, July 12, 1782, he received the keys. For his various services the Assembly of the State presented him with a house and lot in Savannah. On the return of peace he engaged with success in the practice of law; in 1780 he fought a duel with Lieutenant-Governor Wells, whom he slew, but was wounded himself in both knees; and he was a member of the Convention which formed the first Constitution of Georgia. He was chosen a Representative in Congress in 1789, from Georgia, and soon after a Senator, which office he resigned in 1795. He was Major-General of the Georgia militia; and Governor of the State from 1798 till his election as Senator in 1801. He died March 18, 1806, aged forty-eight.

Jackson, James.—He was born in Jefferson County, Georgia, in 1819; graduated at the University of Georgia in 1837; and, having studied law, commenced the practice in 1840. In 1842 he was elected Secretary of the Senate of Georgia, holding the office one year; in 1845 he was elected to the State Legislature, and re-elected to the same position in 1847; in 1849 he was chosen by the Legislature Judge of the Western Circuit of his State, and was elected to the same office by the people in 1853, and again in 1857. In June of that year he was nominated for Congress, resigned his judgeship, and in October following was elected a Representative to the Thirty-fifth Congress, and was a member of the Committees on Claims, and Revolutionary Claims. Re-elected to the Thirty-sixth Congress. Resigned in February, 1861, and returned to Georgia.

Jackson, James S.—He was born in Madison County, Kentucky, and adopted the profession of law. He served in the Mexican war as a Captain of volunteers. In 1861 he was elected a Representative, from Kentucky, to the Thirty-seventh Congress; but, while the Rebellion was progressing, he recruited a regiment of Kentucky cavalry; was subsequently appointed a Brigadier-General, and was killed at the battle of Perryville, in 1862, bravely fighting in the service of his country.

Jackson, John G.—He was a Representative in Congress, from Virginia, from 1795 to 1797, from 1799 to 1810, and again from 1813 to 1817.

Jackson, Joseph W.—He was frequently a member of the City Council of Savannah; at one time Mayor of the city; served a number of years in the State Legislature; and was a Representative in Congress, from Georgia, from 1850 to 1853. Died at Savannah, December 28, 1854.

Jackson, Richard S.—Born in 1764, and died at Providence, April 18, 1838. He was a member of Congress, from Rhode Island, from 1808 to 1815. In early life he was engaged in mercantile business, and was among the first, in this country, who embarked in the manufacture of cotton. He filled several important public offices, and was distinguished for his benevolence.

Jackson, Thomas B.—He was born in New York, and was a Representative in Congress, from that State, from 1837 to 1841; and was also, for three years, a member of the Assembly of New York.

Jackson, William.—He was born in Massachusetts, September 6, 1783; was one of the pioneers of railroad enterprise in Massachusetts; and from 1834 to 1837, and 1841 to 1843, was a Representative in Congress, from that State. He was also a member of the State Legislature from 1829 to 1832; and, at the time of his death, President of the Newton Bank. He died at Newton, Massachusetts, February 27, 1855.

Jackson, W. T.—Born in Chester, Orange County, New York, December 29, 1794; received a common school education; and has been chiefly employed in mercantile business. He was Justice of the Peace several years in Havana, New York, and held the office of County Judge four years. In 1848 he was elected a Representative in Congress, and served one term.

Jacobs, Israel.—He was born in Germany, and was a Representative in Congress, from Pennsylvania, from 1791 to 1793.

James, Charles T.—Was born in West Greenwich, Rhode Island, in 1806; received a limited education; early turned his attention to mechanics as connected with the cotton interest; wrote a series of papers on the culture and manufacture of cotton in the South; and he was a Senator in Congress, from 1851 to 1857, from Rhode Island. He subsequently invented a rifled cannon, and he met his death from the explosion of a shell of his own invention, while trying experiments at Sag Harbor, New York, October 17, 1862.

James, Francis.—He was a native of Pennsylvania, and a Representative in Congress, from that State, from 1839 to 1843.

Jameson, John.—He was born in Kentucky, and was a Representative in Congress, from Missouri, from 1830 to 1831, and again from 1843 to 1845, and for another term from 1847 to 1849.

Janes, Henry F.—He was born at Brimfield, Hampden County, Massachusetts, in October, 1792; studied law in Montpelier, Vermont, and was admitted to the bar in Washington County in 1817, and commenced to practise at Waterbury in that year. From 1820 to 1830 he was Postmaster at Waterbury; he was a member of the Legislative Council from 1830 to 1834, and was a Representative in Congress, from Vermont, from 1835 to 1837. He was State Treasurer from 1838 to 1841; a member of the Council of Censors in 1848; and a member of the Legislature, from Waterbury, in 1855; since which time he has practised his profession.

Jarnagin, Spencer.— Born in Granger County, Tennessee; graduated at Greenville College in 1813; studied law, and was admitted to the bar in 1817; and was United States Senator, from Tennessee, from 1841 to 1847. He died in Memphis, Tennessee, June 24, 1851.

Jarvis, Leonard.—He was born in 1782; graduated at Harvard University in 1800; and died in Surry, Maine, September 18, 1854. He was Sheriff of Hancock County from 1821 to 1829; Collector of Customs for the Penobscot District from 1829 to 1831; and a Representative in Congress, from Maine, from 1831 to 1837, serving as Chairman of the Committee on Naval Affairs. From 1838 to 1841 he held the office of Navy Agent for the Port of Boston.

Jayne, William.—Born in Springfield, Illinois, October 8, 1826; adopted the profession of medicine, and practised eleven years in Springfield; in 1859 was elected Mayor of that city; was elected to the State Senate in 1860 and 1861; during the latter year was appointed Governor of Dakota Territory; and in 1862 he was elected a Delegate from Dakota to the Thirty-eighth Congress. After occupying his seat for some time, he was superseded by J. B. S. Todd.

Jefferson, Thomas.—He was born at Shadwell, Virginia, in 1743. His education was principally conducted by private tutors, although he passed two years at the College of William and Mary. He adopted the law as his profession; was a member of the Legislature of Virginia from 1769 to the commencement of the American Revolution. In 1775 he was a Delegate in Congress; and on May 15, 1776, the Convention of Virginia instructed their delegates to propose a Declaration of Independence. In June, Mr. Lee accordingly made the motion, and it was voted that a committee be appointed to prepare one. The committee was elected by ballot, and consisted of Thomas Jefferson, John Adams, Benjamin Franklin, Roger Sherman, and Robert R. Livingston. The Declaration was exclusively the work of Jefferson, to whom the right of drafting it belonged, as Chairman of the Committee, though alterations and amendments were made in it by Adams, Franklin, and other members of the Committee, and afterwards by Congress. Jefferson retired from Congress September, 1776, and took a seat in the Legislature of his State in October. In 1779 he was chosen Governor, and held the office two years. He declined a foreign appointment in 1776, and again in 1781. He accepted the appointment of one of the Commissioners for negotiating peace, but before he sailed, news was received of the signing of the provisional treaty, and he was excused from proceeding on the mission. He returned to Congress. In 1784 he wrote notes on the establishment of a money-unit, and of a coinage for the United States; in May of that year he was appointed, with Adams and Franklin, a Minister Plenipotentiary to negotiate treaties of commerce with foreign nations. In 1785 he was Minister to the French Court. In 1789 he returned to America, and received from Washington the appointment of Secretary of State, which he held till December, 1793, and then resigned. In September, 1794, when an appointment was offered him by Washington, he replied, "No circumstance will ever more tempt me to engage in anything public." Notwithstanding this determination, he suffered himself to be a candidate for President, and was chosen Vice-President in 1796. At the election in 1801 he and Aaron Burr having an equal number of electoral votes, the House of Representatives, after a severe struggle, finally determined in his favor. He was reelected in 1805. At the end of his second term he retired from office. He died July 4, 1826, at one o'clock in the afternoon, just fifty years from the date of the Declaration of Independence. Preparations had been made throughout the United States to celebrate this day as a jubilee; and it is a most remarkable fact, that on the same day John Adams, a signer with Jefferson of the Declaration, and the second on the Committee for drafting it, and his immediate predecessor in the office of President, also died. Jefferson's publications were: Summary View of the Rights of British America, 1774; Declaration of Independence, 1776; Notes on Virginia, 1781; Manual of Parliamentary Practice, for the Use of the Senate; Life of Captain Lewis, 1814; and some papers of a philosophical character. His works, chiefly letters, were first published by his grandson, Thomas Jefferson Randolph, four volumes, 8vo., 1829.

Jenckes, Thomas A.—He was born in Providence, Rhode Island, in 1818; received a liberal education; studied law, and practised the profession until elected, in 1863, a Representative, from Rhode Island, to the Thirty-eighth Congress, serving as Chairman of the Committee on Patents.

Jenifer, Daniel.—Was frequently a member of the State Legislature of Maryland, and represented that State in Congress, from 1831 to 1833, and from 1835 to 1841. During the administrations of Presidents Harrison and Tyler, he was the United States Minister to Austria. He died December 18, 1855, near Port Tobacco, Maryland.

Jenkins, Albert G.—Was born in Cabell County, Virginia, November 10, 1830; graduated at Jefferson College, Pennsylvania, and in law at Cambridge, in 1850; never practised law, but has been devoted to agricultural pursuits; was a member of the Cincinnati National Convention in 1856; and was elected a Representative, from Virginia, to the Thirty-fifth Congress, serving as a member of the Committee on the Militia; and also to the Thirty-sixth Congress, serving on the same Committee.

Jenkins, Lemuel.—He was a Representative in Congress, from New York, from 1823 to 1825.

Jenkins, Robert.—He was a Representative in Congress, from Pennsylvania, from 1807 to 1811.

Jenkins, Timothy. — Born in Barre, Worcester County, Massachusetts, January 29, 1799; received an academic education; studied law, and was admitted to the bar in 1824, practising his profession in Oneida County, New York; he was District Attorney for that county six years, and resigned the office on being elected a Representative in the Twenty-ninth Congress, and was re-elected to the Thirtieth and Thirty-second. Died at Martinsburg, New York, December 24, 1859.

Jenks, Michael H.—He was born in Pennsylvania, and was a Representative in Congress, from that State, from 1843 to 1845.

Jenness, Benning W.—He was Judge of Probate in Strafford County, New Hampshire, from 1841 to 1845, and a Senator in Congress, from New Hampshire, during the years 1845 and 1846.

Jennings, David.—He was born in Hunterdon County, New Jersey, and was a Representative in Congress, from Ohio, from 1825 to 1826.

Jennings, Jonathan.—He was born in Hunterdon County, New Jersey, and was the first Governor of Indiana, and twice elected a Representative in Congress, from that State, from 1809 to 1816, and from 1822 to 1831. In 1818 he was appointed, by President Monroe, Indian Commissioner. He died near Charlestown, Clarke County, Indiana, July 26, 1834.

Jewett, Freeborn G.—He was born in New York; was a member of the Assembly of that State in 1826 and 1827; and a Representative in Congress, from the same, from 1831 to 1833. From 1846 to 1856 he was a Judge of the Supreme Court of New York; and died February 23, 1858, aged sixty-eight years.

Jewett, Joshua H.—He was born at Deer Creek, Harford County, Maryland, September 13, 1812, and, having adopted the profession of law, removed to Kentucky, and was elected a Representative, from that State, to the Thirty-fourth and Thirty-fifth Congresses. He was Chairman of the Committee on Invalid Pensions.

Jewett, Luther.—He was born in Vermont; graduated at Dartmouth College in 1795; was both a clergyman and a physician; for fifteen years a member of the Vermont Legislature; and was a Representative in Congress, from Vermont, from 1815 to 1817.

Johns, Kensey.—Was born in Delaware, December 10, 1791; graduated at Princeton College in 1810; studied law, and was admitted to practice in 1813; was a Representative in Congress, from Delaware, from 1827 to 1831; in 1832 he was appointed Chancellor of the State of Delaware, in which capacity he was still serving at the time of his death, which occurred at New Castle, March 28, 1857.

Johnson, Andrew.—He was born in Raleigh, North Carolina, December 29, 1808; when ten years of age he was apprenticed to a tailor, and worked at that business, in South Carolina, until his seventeenth year; he never attended school, but acquired a good common education by studying alone. Having removed to Greenville, Tennessee, he was elected Mayor of that place in 1830; was elected to the State Legislature in 1835; to the State Senate in 1841; and he was a Representative in Congress, from Tennessee, from 1843 to 1853. During the latter year he was elected Governor of Tennessee, and re-elected in 1855. He was elected a Senator in Congress in 1857, for the term ending in 1863. He has served on the Committees on Public Lands, and on the District of Columbia. In 1862 he was appointed, by President Lincoln, Military Governor of Tennessee; and by the Baltimore Convention of 1864 was nominated for the office of Vice-President of the United States.

Johnson, Cave.—He was born in Robertson County, Tennessee, January 11, 1793; received a liberal education, and adopted the profession of law; was a Circuit Judge for a few years; and he was a Representative in Congress, from Tennessee, from 1829 to 1837, and again from 1839 to 1845, after which he went into the Cabinet of President Polk as Postmaster-General. He also held for many years the position of President of the Bank of Tennessee, which he resigned in 1859.

Johnson, Charles.—He was born in Connecticut, and was a Representative in Congress, from New York, from 1839 to 1841.

Johnson, Francis.—He was born in Caroline County, Virginia, and was a Representative in Congress, from Kentucky, from 1821 to 1827.

Johnson, Harvey A.—He was born in Vermont, and having removed to Ohio, was elected a Representative in Congress, from that State, from 1853 to 1855.

Johnson, Henry.—He was born

in Virginia in 1781; removed to Louisiana when quite young, and adopted the profession of law; he was a member, in 1812, of the Convention called to form a Constitution for Louisiana; from 1818 to 1824 he served the State as a Senator in Congress; from 1824 to 1828 he was Governor of Louisiana; from 1835 to 1839 he was a Representative in Congress; and was a second time elected to the United States Senate, serving from 1843 to 1849. He died at his residence in Louisiana, on the 21st of August, 1864, commanding in his old age, as he did in the Senate, the highest respect of all who knew him.

Johnson, Herschel V.—Born in Burke County, Georgia, September 18, 1812. He graduated at the University of Georgia in 1834, and adopted the profession of law. He was a Presidential Elector in 1844; in 1848 was appointed to fill a vacancy in the United States Senate; and in 1849 he was elected a Judge of the Superior Court. In 1860 he was a candidate for the office of Vice-President on the ticket with Mr. Douglas, but was defeated; and subsequently served in the Confederate Senate.

Johnson, James.—He was born in Virginia, and was a Representative in Congress, from Virginia, from 1813 to 1820, and in the latter year was appointed Collector of Norfolk and Portsmouth, Virginia. He also served in the State Legislature. Died at Norfolk, December 7, 1825.

Johnson, James.—He was born in Orange County, Virginia; served as Lieutenant-Colonel under Colonel R. M. Johnson, at the battle of the Thames; and was a Representative in Congress, from Kentucky, during the years 1825 and 1826, his death having been announced in the House in December, 1826.

Johnson, James.—He was a native of Georgia, and a Representative in Congress, from that State, from 1851 to 1853.

Johnson, James H.—He was born in New Hampshire, and was a Representative in Congress, from that State, from 1845 to 1847, serving on the Committee on Manufactures. He was also a State Councillor in 1842 and 1843, and a State Senator in 1839.

Johnson, James L.—He was born in Kentucky, and was a Representative in Congress, from that State, from 1849 to 1851.

Johnson, Jeromus.—He was born in King's County, New York, and was a Representative in Congress, from New York City, from 1825 to 1829, and died in Goshen, Orange County, New York, September 7, 1846.

Johnson, John.—He was born in the County of Tyrone, Ireland, in 1808; received a common school education, and emigrated to Ohio, in 1824, where he is devoted to agricultural pursuits. He has served as a member of the Ohio Senate, and in the last Constitutional Convention of that State, and was a Representative in Congress, from Ohio, from 1851 to 1853.

Johnson, John T.—He was born in Scott County, Kentucky; was brother of Richard M. Johnson; once Judge of the Court of Appeals of Kentucky, and represented that State in Congress, from 1821 to 1825. For thirty years he was a preacher of the Gospel, without a salary. He died in Lexington, Missouri, December 18, 1857.

Johnson, Joseph.—He was born in Orange County, New York, and on removing to Virginia, was elected a Representative in Congress, from 1823 to 1827, from 1835 to 1841, and from 1845 to 1847. He was also Governor of Virginia from 1852 to 1856.

Johnson, Noadiah.—He served in the Legislature of New York; was a member of Congress, from 1833 to 1835; and died at Albany, April 4, 1839.

Johnson, Perley B.—He was born in Ohio, and was a Representative in Congress, from that State, from 1843 to 1845.

Johnson, Philip.—Was born in Warren County, New Jersey, January 17, 1818; in 1839 he removed with his father to Pennsylvania, settling in Northampton County; and he was educated at Lafayette College, where he spent two years, after which he spent two years teaching school in the South. On his return home he studied law, was admitted to the bar in 1848, and soon afterwards elected Clerk of the Court of Sessions and of the Oyer and Terminer. In 1853 and 1854 he was elected to the State Assembly. In 1857 he was Chairman of the Democratic State Convention. In 1860 he was the Revenue Commissioner for the Third Judicial District of the State, and was elected a Representative, from Pennsylvania, to the Thirty-seventh Congress, serving on the Committees on Roads and Canals, and on Patents; he was re-elected to the Thirty-eighth Congress, and was a member of the Committee on the Territories. He was also a Delegate to the Chicago Convention of 1864.

Johnson, Reverdy.—Born in Annapolis, Maryland, May 21, 1796; was educated at St. John's College, Annapolis; studied law with his father; and having been admitted to the bar, has practised his profession without intermission to the present time; his first appointment was that of State Attorney; in 1817 he removed to Baltimore (where he has since resided), and in 1820 was appointed Chief Commissioner of Insolvent Debtors, which office he held until 1821, when he was elected to the State Senate, serving two years; was re-elected, and resigned in the second year of that term; in 1845 he was chosen a Senator in Congress, where he remained until 1849, when he resigned to accept the post of Attorney-General of the United States, bestowed upon him by President Taylor. On his leaving the latter position, he turned his whole attention to his profession, practising chiefly in the Supreme Court of the United States. Mr. Johnson has also taken an active part in the preparation of seven volumes of Reports of Decisions in the Court of Appeals of Maryland. He was a Delegate to the Peace Congress of 1861, and in 1862 he was again elected a Senator in Congress, from his native State, for the term commencing March, 1863, and ending 1869, and serving on the Library Committee, and that on the Judiciary.

Johnson, Richard M.—He was born in Kentucky, in 1780, and died at Frankfort, November 19, 1850. In 1807 he was chosen a Representative in Congress, from Kentucky, which post he held until 1813. In 1813 he raised a volunteer regiment of cavalry, of one thousand men, to fight the British and Indians on the Lakes, and during the campaign that followed, served with great credit, under General Harrison, as a Colonel of that regiment. He greatly distinguished himself at the battle of the Thames, and the chief Tecumseh is said to have been killed by his hand. In 1814 he was appinted Indian Commissioner, by President Madison. He was again a Representative in Congress, from 1815 to 1819. In 1819 he went from the House into the United States Senate, to fill an unexpired term; was re-elected, and served as Senator until 1829. He was re-elected to the House, and remained there until 1837, when he became Vice-President, and as such presided over the Senate. At the time of his death he was a member of the Kentucky Legislature, and he died from a second attack of paralysis. He was a kind-hearted, courageous and talented man.

Johnson, R. W.—He was born in Kentucky, in 1814; and was elected a Representative in Congress, from Arkansas, in 1847, and served until 1853, when he was elected a Senator in Congress, serving as Chairman of the Committee on Printing, and as a member of the Committees on Military Affairs, and on Public Lands.

Johnson, William C.—Born in Frederick County, Maryland, in 1806; received an academic education; studied law, and was admitted to practice in the Supreme Court in 1831; and was a Representative in Congress, from 1833 to 1835, and from 1837 to 1843. He served in the State Legislature before entering and after he left Congress; was a member of the last Convention for revising the Constitution of Maryland; and was President of the National Convention of Young Men, which met in Washington to nominate Henry Clay for President. When in Congress, Mr. Johnson officiated, for a number of years, as Chairman of the Committee on Public Lands, and also as a member of the Judiciary Committee. Died in Washington, April 16, 1860.

Johnson, William S.—Born at Stratford, Connecticut, October 7, 1727;

graduated at Yale College in 1744; studied law, and acquired distinction as a pleader and orator. In 1765 he was a Delegate to the Congress at New York, and in 1766 an agent for the Colony to England. In 1772 he was appointed Judge of the Supreme Court of Connecticut; was again a Delegate to the New York Congress in 1785, and was a member in 1787 of the Convention which framed the Constitution of the United States. He was a Senator in Congress, from 1789 to 1791, and from 1792 to 1800, President of Columbia College, in New York; after which he returned to his native village, where he died, November 14, 1819.

Johnston, Charles. — Born in Chowan County, North Carolina; was a member of the State Legislature for many years, and a Representative in Congress during the years 1801 and 1802, having died before the expiration of his term.

Johnston, Charles C.—A member of Congress, from Virginia, from 1831 to 1832, having died at Washington, June 18, of the latter year. He was Chairman of the Committee on Imprisonment for Debt. He was found drowned in the Potomac, near Alexandria.

Johnston, Josiah S.—He was born in Salisbury, Connecticut, November 25, 1784, but was taken by his father, in infancy, to Kentucky. He graduated at Transylvania University, and studied law. He removed to Louisiana in 1805, and commenced his professional career at Alexandria, on the Red River; and, in 1812, was a leading man in the State Legislature; he was next appointed District Judge, and represented Louisiana, in Congress, from 1821 to 1823; and in 1824 he was elected to the United States Senate, retaining that position until his death, which occurred May 19, 1833, by the explosion of gunpowder on board the steamboat Lioness, on Red River.

Johnston, Samuel.—Governor of North Carolina, from 1787 to 1789; was President of the Convention of that State which ratified the Federal Constitution, and had been a member of Congress previous to 1789, when he was appointed Senator, from North Carolina, and served till 1793; was afterwards a Judge of the Supreme Court of Law and Equity. He was a native of Edenton, and died at Sherwarkey, August 18, 1816, aged eighty-three.

Johnston, William. — He was born in Ireland in 1819; removed to Ohio in early life; received a good education; held a variety of local offices in Richmond County, where he has long resided; adopted the profession of law, and in 1862 was elected a Representative, from Ohio, to the Thirty-eighth Congress, serving on the Committees on Revolutionary Claims, and on Expenditures on the Public Buildings.

Jones, Benjamin.—He was born in Virginia, and, having removed to Ohio, was elected a Representative in Congress, from that State, from 1833 to 1837.

Jones, Daniel T.—He was born in Connecticut, and, having settled in New York, was elected a Representative in Congress, from that State, from 1851 to 1855.

Jones, Francis.—He was a Representative in Congress, from Tennessee, from 1817 to 1823.

Jones, George.—He was a Senator in Congress, from Georgia, during the session of 1807.

Jones, George W.—Born at Vincennes, Indiana, and graduated at Transylvania University, Kentucky, in 1825. He was bred to the law, but ill health prevented him from practising. He was Clerk of the United States District Court, in Missouri, in 1826; served as an aide-de-camp to General Henry Dodge in the Black Hawk war; was chosen Colonel of militia in 1832; subsequently Major-General; also a Judge of the County Court; in 1835 was elected a Delegate to Congress, from the Territory of Michigan, and served four years; in 1839 was appointed, by President Van Buren, Surveyor-General of the Northwest; was removed in 1841 for his politics, but reappointed, by President Polk, and remained in the office until 1849; in 1848 he was elected a United States Senator, from Iowa, for six years, and re-elected in 1852, officiating as Chairman of the Committees on

Pensions, and on Enrolled Bills, and as a member of the Committee on Territories. At the conclusion of his last term he was appointed, by President Buchanan, Minister to New Granada. In 1861 he was charged with disloyalty, and imprisoned in Fort Warren.

Jones, George W.—Born in King and Queen County, Virginia, March 15, 1806. He began life by adopting the occupation of a saddler; was a Justice of the Peace for three years; in 1834 a Justice to hold the Quorum Court in Lincoln County; in 1835 and 1837 was elected to the Tennessee Legislature; in 1839 to the State Senate; in 1840 and 1842 was elected Clerk of the Lincoln County Court; and was elected a Representative to Congress, in 1843, to which position he has been regularly re-elected to 1859, serving, during the Thirty-fifth Congress, as Chairman of the Committee on Roads and Canals. In 1853, upon the inauguration of President Pierce, Mr. Jones was appointed special bearer of despatches to the American Consul at Havana, having been authorized to administer the official oath to the Vice-President, W. R. King, who had visited Cuba for his health. In 1861 he was a Delegate to the Peace Congress held in Washington.

Jones, Isaac D.—He was born in Maryland, and was a Representative in Congress, from that State, from 1841 to 1843. He was a Delegate also to the Chicago Convention of 1864.

Jones, James.—Born in Maryland, and removed to Georgia when young. He studied law, and settled in Savannah. He was often a member of the Legislature of Georgia, and was a Representative in Congress, from 1799 to the time of his death, which occurred at Washington, January 12, 1801.

Jones, James.—He was born in Amelia County, Virginia, and was a Representative in Congress, from that State, from 1819 to 1823.

Jones, James C.—Born in Wilson County, Tennessee, June 8, 1809; received a good education; devoted himself in early life to farming; first entered public life in 1839 as a member of the Tennessee Legislature; was Governor of Tennessee, from 1841 to 1845, serving two terms; was a Presidential Elector in 1841 and 1849; and in 1851 he was elected a Senator in Congress, from Tennessee, serving the whole of his term of six years. Died at Memphis, Tennessee, October 29, 1859. He was for many years devoted to the public interests of Memphis, and his native State, and was distinguished for his abilities.

Jones, J. Glancy.—He was born on the Conestoga River, Pennsylvania, October 7, 1811. By his early education he was prepared for the church, but preferred the law, to which he devoted himself with success; and while Deputy Attorney-General of the State, was elected a Representative in Congress, from Pennsylvania, serving (excepting a part of the Thirty-third Congress, when Henry W. Muhlenburg succeeded him), from 1850 to 1858. He was the author, in the House, of the bill creating the Court of Claims, when a member of the Committee on Claims; and by Mr. Speaker Orr, was placed at the head of the Committee of Ways and Means. He was a Presidential Elector in 1856, and was tendered, by President Buchanan, the Mission to Berlin, which he declined; but in October, 1858, he was offered the mission to Austria, and accepted the appointment.

Jones, John J.—Born in Burke County, Georgia, November 13, 1824; graduated at Emory College; studied law, and was admitted to practice in 1848; and was a Representative, from that State, to the Thirty-sixth Congress, serving on the Committee on Revisal and Unfinished Business. Resigned in February, 1861, and returned to Georgia.

Jones, John W.—He was born in Virginia, and was a Representative in Congress, from that State, from 1835 to 1845. He was also Speaker of the House of Representatives, during the Twenty-eighth Congress. He was an eminent politician, and died January 29, 1848.

Jones, John W.—Born on Rock Creek, Montgomery County, Maryland, April 14, 1806; when quite young he removed, with his father, to Kentucky, where he received a good English and classical education, at the Carlisle Seminary; as his health would permit, he devoted himself to the study of medicine, attended lectures at the Pennsylvania Academy, and from Jefferson College received the degree of Doctor of Medicine. In 1840 he was elected to the Georgia Legislature, and he was a Representative in Congress, from Georgia, from 1847 to 1849. In 1849 he removed to Alabama, and devoted himself to agriculture; but, returning to Georgia, was appointed a medical professor in the Atlanta Medical College. He enjoys the reputation of having done much for the cause of education in the States of Georgia and Alabama.

Jones, Nathaniel.—He was a member of the New York Assembly in 1827 and 1828; a Representative in Congress, from New York, from 1837 to 1841; a State Senator in 1852 and 1853; and also held the offices of Surveyor-General of the State, and Canal Commissioner.

Jones, Owen.—Born in Pennsylvania; a lawyer by profession, and Representative, in the Thirty-fifth Congress, from his native State.

Jones, Roland.—He was born in North Carolina, and was a Representative, in the Thirty-third Congress, from that State.

Jones, Seaborn.—He was born in Columbus, Georgia, and was a Representative in Congress, from that State, from 1833 to 1835, and again from 1845 to 1847.

Jones, Walter.—Born in Virginia, and educated as a physician at Edinburgh, about the year 1770; on his return he settled in Northumberland County, where he had extensive practice in his profession. He was a Representative in Congress, from 1797 to 1799, and again from 1803 to 1811. He died in Westmoreland County, Virginia, December 31, 1815, aged seventy-six years.

Jones, William.—Born in Philadelphia; took an active part in the Revolutionary struggle, having fought at Trenton and Princeton as a volunteer, and served in several vessels; he was a Lieutenant under Commodore Truxton, and was twice wounded and twice made prisoner; in 1790 settled in Charleston, South Carolina, whence he returned to Philadelphia in 1793; was a Representative in Congress, from Pennsylvania, from 1801 to 1803; and was for a short time Secretary of the Navy, under President Madison. He was also President of the Bank of the United States; Collector of Customs at Philadelphia; and for twenty-six years was a member of the American Philosophical Society, before which he read many valuable communications, which were published. Died at Bethlehem, Pennsylvania, in 1831.

Judson, Andrew T.—Born at Eastford, Connecticut, November 29, 1784; his education was obtained at the common schools, and under the instructions of his father and brother. He studied law, and was admitted to the bar in 1806, when he removed to Montpelier, Vermont, and practised in that State; he afterwards returned to his native town, and in 1809 went to Canterbury, which he made his permanent residence. In 1819 he received the appointment of State's Attorney for Windham County, which office he held for fourteen years. He was at different times a member of both branches of the Legislature, and was a Representative in Congress, from 1835 to 1839, when he was elected Judge of the District Court, and continued in that position until his death. In October, 1850, he was designated, by the Circuit Judge of the Second Circuit, to hold the Courts of the United States in the Southern District of New York, during the illness of the distinguished Judge of that District, and he officiated at the trial of Mr. O'Sullivan, and others, for the attempted Cuban invasion. Among the causes which were brought before him for adjudication, was the libel of the Amistad, and the fifty-four Africans on board. He died at home, March 17, 1853.

Julian, George W.—Was born in Centreville, Wayne County, Indiana, May 5, 1817; received a good common school education; spent three years as school teacher; studied law, and was admitted to the bar in 1840. In 1845 he was elected to the Legislature of Indiana; was a Delegate to the Buffalo Convention of 1848; was a Representative in Congress, from Indiana, from 1849 to 1851. In 1852 he was nominated by the Pittsburg Convention for the office of Vice-President of the United States, on the ticket with J. P. Hale for President; and in 1856 he was Vice-President of the Republican Convention held at Pittsburg. In 1860 he was elected a Representative, from Indiana, to the Thirty-seventh Congress, serving on the Committees on Public Lands, and on Public Expenditures; and in 1862 was re-elected to the Thirty-eighth Congress, and was Chairman of the Committee on Public Lands, and a member of the Committee on Public Expenditures.

Junkin, Benjamin T.—Born in Cumberland County, Pennsylvania, November 12, 1822; educated at Fayette College; studied law at Carlisle, and was admitted to the bar in 1844; was elected District Attorney for Perry County in 1850, and held the office three years; and was elected, from Pennsylvania, to the Thirty-sixth Congress, serving on the Committee on Revolutionary Pensions.

Kalbfleisch, Martin.—He was born in Flushing, Netherlands, February 6, 1804; received a common school education, and adopted the profession of a chemist. He came to the United States early in life, and his first public position was that of Health Warden in New York City in 1832. In 1836 he was Trustee of one of the common schools in New York; in 1852, and the two following years, Supervisor of the town of Bushwick, King's County. In 1854 he was appointed President of a Board of Commissioners for consolidating the cities of Brooklyn, Williamsburg, and Bushwick. In 1855 he was elected an Alderman of Brooklyn, and having been re-elected, was President of the Board of Aldermen from 1857 to 1861; during the latter year he was elected Mayor of Brooklyn; and in 1862, was elected a Representative, from New York, to the Thirty-eighth Congress, serving on the Committees on Revolutionary Claims, and Expenditures in the Treasury Department.

Kane, Elias K.—He was born in New York State about the year 1795, and was bred to the legal profession. At an early period of his life he went to Tennessee, and finally settled in Kaskaskia, in Illinois Territory, in 1815. In 1818 he was a member of the Convention for framing a State Constitution, and when that Government was organized, he was appointed Secretary of State. He was subsequently elected a member of the Legislature; and from 1825 to 1836 he was a Senator in Congress, from Illinois, officiating as Chairman of the Committee on Private Land Claims. He died at Washington, District of Columbia, December 12, 1835.

Kasson, John A.—He was born near Burlington, Vermont, January 11, 1822; graduated at the University of Vermont; studied law in Massachusetts, and practised the profession in St. Louis, Missouri, until 1857, when he removed to Iowa. In 1858 he was appointed a Commissioner to report upon the condition of the Executive Departments of Iowa; assisted in 1859 in organizing the State Bank of Iowa, and became Director for the State. In 1861 he was appointed Assistant Postmaster-General, which office he resigned in 1862, when he was elected a Representative, from Iowa, to the Thirty-eighth Congress, serving on the Committee of Ways and Means. During the summer of 1863 he was appointed, by President Lincoln, a Commissioner to the International Postal Congress at Paris, returning in August.

Kaufman, David S.—Born in Cumberland, Pennsylvania, in 1813; graduated at Princeton College in 1833; not long after he removed to Natchez, Mississippi, and read law in the office of General Quitman. In 1835 he settled in Natchitoches, Louisiana. In 1837 he emigrated to Nacogdoches, in Texas, and in 1838 was elected a Representative in the Texan Congress; he was twice re-elected, and twice chosen Speaker of the House. In 1843 he was elected to the Senate, and from the Committee on Foreign Relations, in 1844, presented a report in favor of annexation, and took an active part in its consummation. In 1845 he was appointed Chargé to this Government, but that office was superseded by the final act of annexation, and he was elected one of the first members of the House of Representatives, from Texas, serving from 1846 to 1851. He died in Washington, District of Columbia, January 13, 1851.

Kavanagh, Edward.—He was

born April 27, 1795; adopted the profession of law; was a member of the Maine Legislature in 1826, 1828, 1842, and 1843; Secretary of the State Senate in 1830; and he was a Representative in Congress, from 1831 to 1835; when he was appointed Chargé d'Affaires to Portugal, where he remained until 1841. In 1842 he was a Commissioner for settling the Northeast Boundary; and was acting Governor of Maine from 1843 to 1844; and for a short time President of the State Senate. He died at Newcastle, Maine, January 20, 1844.

Keese, Richard.—Born in New York, and was a Representative in Congress, from that State, from 1827 to 1829.

Keim, George M.—He was born in Pennsylvania, and was a Representative in Congress, from that State, from 1838 to 1843.

Keim, William H.—He was born in Reading, Berks County, Pennsylvania, June 25, 1813; was educated at the Mount Airy Military Academy; but he turned his attention to mercantile pursuits, and continued in active business until 1855. He held almost continually, for thirty years, a number of military offices, among others that of Major-General of the Fifth Division of Pennsylvania Volunteers; in 1848 he was elected Mayor of Reading; and in November, 1858, he was elected to fill the unexpired term of the Hon. J. Glancy Jones (appointed Minister to Austria), and took his seat at the commencement of the second session of the Thirty-fifth Congress.

Keitt, Lawrence M.—He was born in Orangeburg District, South Carolina, October 4, 1824; graduated at the College of South Carolina in 1843; studied law, and was admitted to practice in 1845; was elected to the State Legislature in 1848; and in 1853 to a seat in the National House of Representatives, having been regularly re-elected until December, 1860, when he resigned, serving in the Thirty-fifth Congress as Chairman of the Committee on Public Buildings and Grounds. Just before leaving Congress, he was elected to the Seceding Convention of South Carolina, and subsequently took an active part in the Great Rebellion as a member of the Confederate Congress. Killed in battle, in Virginia, in June, 1864.

Kelley, William D.—Was born in Philadelphia in the spring of 1814; received a good English education; commenced life as a reader in a printing-office; spent seven years as an apprentice in a jewelry establishment; removed to Boston, and followed his trade there for four years, devoting some attention to literary matters; returned to Philadelphia, studied law, and was admitted to the bar in 1841, and held the office for some years of Judge of the Court of Common Pleas in Philadelphia. In addition to his many political speeches, a number of literary addresses have been published from his pen. He was elected a Representative, from Pennsylvania, to the Thirty-seventh Congress, serving as a member of the Committees on Indian Affairs, and Expenditures on Public Buildings. Re-elected to the Thirty-eighth Congress, serving on the Committees on Agriculture, and on Naval Affairs.

Kellogg, Charles.—He was a native of Berkshire County, Massachusetts; served six years in the New York Assembly, from Cayuga County, and was a Representative in Congress, from that State, from 1825 to 1827.

Kellogg, Francis W.—Born in Worthington, Hampshire County, Massachusetts, May 30, 1810; received a limited education, and having removed to Michigan, entered into the business of lumbering. He served in the Legislature of Michigan, and was elected a Representative, from that State, to the Thirty-sixth Congress, serving as a member of the Committee on Invalid Pensions; was re-elected to the Thirty-seventh Congress, serving on the Committees on Public Lands, and on Expenditures in the Post-office Department; and was also re-elected to the Thirty-eighth Congress, and was a member of the Committee on Military Affairs.

Kellogg, Orlando.—Was born in Elizabethtown, New York, in 1809; was elected a Representative, from New York, to the Thirtieth Congress; and re-elected to the Thirty-eighth Congress, serving on the Committee on Manufactures, and that on the Militia.

Kellogg, William.—Born in Ashtabula County, Ohio, July 8, 1814, and removed to Illinois in 1837. His education was obtained in the common schools of the country, and having studied law, acquired an extensive practice in the district of disputed land titles in Illinois. He served in the State Legislature in 1849 and 1850, and was three years Judge of the Circuit Court of Illinois, and elected a Representative, from that State, to the Thirty-fifth Congress, serving as a member of the Committee on Public Expenditures. Re-elected to the Thirty-sixth Congress, serving on the Judiciary Committee. Re-elected to the Thirty-seventh Congress, serving on the Judiciary Committee, and that on Government Expenditures. In 1864 he was appointed by President Lincoln Minister to Guatemala.

Kelly, James.—He was a Representative in Congress, from Pennsylvania, from 1805 to 1809.

Kelly, John.—Born in the city of New York, April 21, 1821; educated at the public schools in that city; by trade a mason; was Alderman of the city for two years; and elected a Representative in the Thirty-fourth and Thirty-fifth Congresses, serving on the Committee of Ways and Means. In October, 1858, he was elected High Sheriff for the City and County of New York. He was also a Delegate to the Chicago Convention of 1864.

Kelly, William.—He was a Representative in Congress, from Louisiana, during the years 1821 and 1822; and a Senator in Congress, from 1822 to 1825.

Kelsey, William H.—He was born in New York, and was elected a Representative, from that State, to the Thirty-fourth and Thirty-fifth Congresses, and was a member of the Committee on Agriculture.

Kemble, Gouverneur.—He was born in New York, and was a Representative in Congress, from that State, from 1837 to 1841.

Kempshall, Thomas.—He was born in England, and having emigrated to New York, was a Representative in Congress, from that State, from 1839 to 1841.

Kenan, Thomas.—Born in Duplin County, North Carolina, in 1771. In 1799 he was a member of the House of Delegates; served in the State Senate in 1804; and was a Representative in Congress, from 1805 to 1811. He subsequently removed to Alabama, where he served for many years in the Legislature of that State, but declined a re-election to Congress. Died near Selma, October 22, 1843.

Kendall, Jonas.—He was born at Worcester, Massachusetts, in 1757; obtained a finished education by his own unaided exertions; served thirteen years in the Legislature of Massachusetts; and was a Representative in Congress, from that State, from 1819 to 1821. Died in Leominster, Massachusetts, October 22, 1844.

Kendall, Joseph G.—Born in 1788; graduated at Harvard College in 1810, and was a tutor in that University from 1812 to 1819. He was a Representative in Congress, from the Northern District of Worcester County, Massachusetts, from 1829 to 1833; and then appointed Clerk of the State Courts. He died at Worcester, Massachusetts, October 2, 1847.

Kennedy, Andrew.—Born in Ohio in 1810; was bred a blacksmith, and at the age of nineteen could neither read nor write. He subsequently studied law, and was a member of the State Senate of Indiana; and represented that State in Congress, from 1841 to 1847. He died at Muncietown, Indiana, December 31, 1847.

Kennedy, Anthony.—Born in Baltimore, Maryland, in 1811; removed, when ten years of age, to Virginia; educated at Jefferson Academy, Charlestown, Virginia; studied law, but abandoned it, and subsequently engaged in the manufacture of cotton and in planting. He was a member of the Legislature of Virginia, from 1839 to 1843, and an unsuccessful candidate for Congress, from Virginia; removed to Baltimore in 1850, and was elected to the Maryland Legislature in 1856, serving as Chairman of the Committee of Ways and Means; and by that body elected to the United States Senate, for six years, from March 4, 1857, serving as a member of the Committees on Private Land Claims, and on the District of Columbia.

Kennedy, John P.—He was born in Baltimore, October, 1795. He studied law, and practised in that city until 1838, when he was elected to the House of Representatives, in the Federal Legislature, and served in that body through the Twenty-fifth, Twenty-seventh, and Twenty-eighth Congresses; elected in 1846 to the House of Delegates of Maryland (of which he had been a member in the sessions of 1820 and 1822); he was made Speaker, and took an active part in the measure which was then adopted to resume the payment of the State debt, and the restoration of the public credit. Since 1847, he has held no local political post, but has devoted his time to literary pursuits. His last national position was that of Secretary of the Navy, under President Fillmore. In 1849, he was chosen by the Regents of the University of Maryland to preside over that institution, as provost, which position he now occupies. Among his various political tracts, speeches, reports, and addresses, which have been published, are "A Review of Mr. Cambreling's Free-Trade Report, by Mephistopheles," in 1830; "The Memorial of the Permanent Committee of the New York Convention of Friends of Domestic Industry," in 1833; an elaborate report on "The Commerce and Navigation of the United States, by the Committee of Commerce" (of which Mr. Kennedy was chairman), in 1842; and a report from the same Committee, on "The Warehouse System," in 1843. Besides these, he has published several pamphlets and tracts, in defence of the protective system. In the field of general literature, he is known to the public as the author of "Swallow Barn, a Sojourn in the Old Dominion," "Horse-shoe Robinson," "Rob of the Bowl," "Quod Libet," "Memoirs of the Life of William Wirt, late Attorney-General of the United States," sundry historical, biographical, and literary discourses, essays, and reviews, which have not yet been collected into volumes. He is an active member of the Historical Society of Maryland, of which he is the Vice-President.

Kennedy, William.—He was a Representative in Congress, from North Carolina, from 1803 to 1805, from 1809 to 1811, and from 1813 to 1815.

Kennett, Luther M.—He was born in Falmouth, Pendleton County, Kentucky, March 15, 1807; received a good English and classical education; was for a number of years Deputy Clerk of Pendleton and Campbell counties; he studied law, and in 1825 removed to Missouri, where he engaged in mercantile pursuits; having settled in St. Louis in 1842, he was elected to the Councils of that city; in 1849 he was Chairman of the Pacific Railroad Convention, held in St. Louis, and subsequently Vice-President of the company formed for commencing the work; in 1850 he was elected Mayor of St. Louis, and re-elected in 1851 and 1852. In 1853 he was elected President of the St. Louis and Iron Mountain Railroad; and he was a Representative in Congress, from Missouri (St. Louis District), from 1855 to 1857.

Kennon, William.—He was born in Pennsylvania, and having emigrated to Ohio, was elected a Representative in Congress, from that State, from 1829 to 1833, from 1833 to 1837, and from 1847 to 1849.

Kent, Joseph.—Born in 1779, in Calvert County, Maryland; was educated for a physician, and combined the practice of his profession with the pursuits of agriculture. He was a Representative in Congress, from his native State, from 1811 to 1815, and from 1821 to 1826; Governor of Maryland from 1826 to 1829; and United States Senator from 1833 to 1837. He died near his residence, in the vicinity of Bladensburg, Maryland, November 24, 1839.

Kent, Moss.—He was a member of the New York Assembly in 1807 and 1810, and was a Representative in Congress, from that State, from 1813 to 1817.

Kenyon, William S.—He was elected a Representative, from New York, to the Thirty-sixth Congress, serving as a member of the Committee on Private Land Claims.

Kernan, Francis.—He was born

in Steuben County, New York, January 14, 1816; received his education at the Georgetown College, District of Columbia; adopted and practised the profession of law; held for a time the office of Reporter of the Court of Appeals; served in the State Legislature; and was elected a Representative, from New York, to the Thirty-eighth Congress, serving on the Committee on the Judiciary.

Kerr, John.—He was a Representative in Congress, from Pennsylvania, from 1813 to 1817.

Kerr, John. — He was born in North Carolina, received a liberal education, and adopted the profession of law; was a Representative in Congress, from his native State, from 1853 to 1855; and was subsequently elected to the House of Commons of that State.

Kerr, John Bozman.—Born at Easton, Talbot County, Maryland, March 5, 1809; graduated at Harvard University in 1830. He studied law at Easton, and was admitted to the bar in 1833; was a member of the General Assembly of Maryland from 1836 to 1838; and from 1847 to 1849 he acted as deputy for the Attorney-General of Maryland, for Talbot County. From 1849 to 1851 he was a Representative in Congress, and at the end of the session was appointed by President Fillmore Chargé d'Affaires to the Republic of Nicaragua. During the revolution of 1851 he had the good fortune, as the National Representative in Central America, to bring about an armistice, and was instrumental in saving the lives of leading officers of the revolutionary party, for which he received a formal expression of thanks from the Executive on leaving the country; and in 1853 the Congress of the United States voted him an extra sum for services in Central America. In 1854 he resumed the practice of his profession in the city of Baltimore, and subsequently held an office under the Attorney-General in Washington, after which he was appointed Deputy Solicitor of the Court of Claims.

Kerr, John L.—He was born at Greenbury Point, near Annapolis, Maryland, January 15, 1780; graduated at St. John's College in 1799; studied law with John Leeds Bozman, and practised the profession with success; and was a Representative in Congress, from Maryland, from 1825 to 1829, and again from 1831 to 1833; he was also a Senator in Congress from 1841 to 1843. He was a member of the National Convention, held at Harrisburg in 1839, and at the head of the Electoral ticket for President during the same year. Before entering Congress, he was the agent of Maryland in the prosecution of militia claims against the United States. He died at his homestead, in Maryland, February 21, 1844.

Kerr, Joseph.—He was a Senator in Congress, from Ohio, from 1814 to 1815, having succeeded Thomas Worthington.

Kerrigan, James E.—He was elected a Representative, from New York, to the Thirty-seventh Congress, leaving his seat for a time to serve as a Colonel of volunteers in the troubles of 1861.

Kershaw, John.—He was a native of South Carolina, and a Representative in Congress, from that State, from 1813 to 1815, when he was appointed by President Madison one of the three Commissioners to run the Creek boundary lines.

Key, Philip.—Was born in Saint Mary's County, Maryland, in 1750; received a classical and commercial education; was devoted to agricultural pursuits; served a number of years in the Legislature of Maryland, and was for one or two terms Speaker. He also rendered some service in the municipal courts of his native county. His service as a Representative in Congress, from Maryland, was from 1791 to 1793. Died in his native place in January, 1820.

Key, Philip Barton.—Born in Cecil County, Maryland, in 1765; was liberally educated; entered the English army as a Captain, and when the Revolutionary war broke out, he refused to bear arms against the Colonies; he had a small command and some service at Pensacola, Florida, where he was a hard student; and after the peace he returned to Maryland, where he took a high position as a lawyer. He also represented Annapolis in the State Legislature. He was a Representative in Congress, from Maryland, from 1807 to 1813, and died at Georgetown, District of Columbia, July 28, 1815.

Keyes, Elias.—He was born in Ashford, Connecticut; a Representative in Congress, from Vermont, from 1821 to 1823. From 1803 to 1818 he was a State Councillor; and a member of the Legislature of Vermont for a period of eighteen years, from Stockbridge County.

Kidder, David.—He was born in Dresden, Lincoln County, Maine, December 8, 1787; received a classical education from private tutors; studied law, and settled in Somerset County, where he was County Attorney from 1811 to 1823; was a Representative in Congress, from Maine, from 1823 to 1827; and a member of the State Legislature in 1829.

Kidwell, Zedekiah.—He was born in Fairfax County, Virginia, January 4, 1814; was educated by his father; studied medicine, and graduated at the Jefferson Medical College of Philadelphia in 1839; after practising medicine some years, he commenced in 1848 the study of law, and began to practise as a lawyer in 1849; he served a number of years in the Legislature of Virginia; was a member of the State Constitutional Convention in 1829; was a Presidential Elector in 1852; and a Representative in Congress, from Virginia, from 1853 to 1857. In 1857 he was elected one of three Commissioners to superintend the public works for the State of Virginia, representing in that board the Third District.

Kilbourn, James.—Born in New Britain, Connecticut, October 19, 1770; while apprenticed as a farmer's boy he received instruction in Latin and Greek and mathematics, from the son of his employer; was next a mechanic, then a merchant and manufacturer, and finally studied divinity, and became a clergyman of the Episcopal Church. In 1803 he was instrumental in forming an emigrating colony to Central Ohio, called the "Scioto Company;" a town was soon organized, and named Worthington. In 1805 he was appointed by Congress to the office of United States Surveyor of Public Lands; and in 1806 he was chosen by the Legislature a member of the Board of Trustees of Ohio College, at Athens. In 1812 he was appointed, by the President, a Commissioner to settle the boundary between the Public Lands and the Virginia Reservation, and also commissioned as Colonel of the frontier regiment. He was one of the Commissioners for locating Miami University, and President of the Board of Trustees of Worthington College. From 1813 to 1817 he was a Representative in Congress. In 1823 he was elected to the Ohio Legislature, serving on fourteen committees, and was re-elected in 1838; and subsequently devoted much attention to matters of State policy. He died in Worthington, Ohio, April 24, 1850.

Kilgore, David.—He was born in Harrison County, Kentucky, April 3, 1804, and removed with his father to Indiana in 1819, and settled in Franklin County. He received a common school education, and commenced the study of law in 1825, and was admitted to practice in 1830, and removed to Delaware County. In 1833 he was elected to the State Legislature, and served several years. In 1839 he was elected by the Legislature President Judge of the Judicial Circuit in which he resided, and held the office seven years. In 1850 he was a Delegate to the Constitutional Convention of the State. In 1854 was again elected to the Legislature, and was Speaker of the House. In 1856 he was elected a Representative, from Indiana, to the Thirty-fifth Congress, and has been re-elected to the Thirty-sixth, serving as a member of the Committee on Expenditures in the Treasury Department, and that on the District of Columbia.

Kilgore, Daniel.—He was born in Virginia, and was a Representative in Congress, from Ohio, from 1835 to 1839. Died in New York, December 12, 1851.

Kille, Joseph.—He was born in New Jersey, and was a Representative in Congress, from that State, from 1839 to 1841.

Killinger, John W.—Born in Pennsylvania, and was elected a Representative, from that State, to the Thirty-sixth Congress, serving on the Committee on Public Expenditures. Re-elected to the Thirty-seventh Congress, serving on the Committee on Mileage, and as Chairman of the Committee on Expenditures in the Post-office Department. In 1863 he was appointed Assessor of Internal Revenue for the Tenth District of Pennsylvania.

Kincaid, John.—He was a Representative in Congress, from Kentucky, from 1829 to 1833.

King, Adam.—He was a Representative in Congress, from Pennsylvania, from 1827 to 1833, and died May 6, 1835.

King, Austin A.—He was born in Sullivan County, Tennessee, September 20, 1801; received as good an education as the country then afforded; studied law, and was licensed to practise on becoming of age; removed to Missouri in 1830; in 1834 was elected to the Missouri Legislature; re-elected to the same position in 1836; in 1837 he was appointed a Circuit Judge for Ray County, which position he held until 1848, when he was elected Governor of Missouri, the term of that office expiring in 1853; in 1862 he was again placed upon the Bench in his old circuit, and during that year was elected a Representative, from Missouri, to the Thirty-eighth Congress, serving on the Committee on the Judiciary; was subsequently reported against by the Committee on Elections.

King, Cyrus.—Born in Scarborough, Massachusetts, September 6, 1772; graduated at Columbia College in 1794; was private secretary to Rufus King, his half brother, in 1796; studied law, and practised twenty years in Saco; was a Major-General of militia; and was a Representative in Congress, from Massachusetts, from 1813 to 1817. Died April 25, 1817.

King, Daniel Putnam.—Born in Danvers, Massachusetts, in 1800; graduated at Harvard in 1823. At first he contemplated the study of the law, but soon abandoned it for the practice of agriculture. In 1836 and 1837 he was a member of the Massachusetts Legislature; in 1838 and 1839 a member of the State Senate; and in 1840 and 1841 President of that body. Speaker of the House in 1843, and during that year he was elected a Representative in Congress, and held that position until his death, which occurred in Danvers, July 25, 1850.

King, George G.—He was born in Rhode Island, and was a Representative in Congress, from that State, from 1849 to 1853.

King, Henry.—He was a Representative in Congress, from Pennsylvania, from 1831 to 1835, and also served in the Legislature of that State. Died at Allentown, Pennsylvania, July 13, 1861, aged seventy-one years.

King, James G.—He was born at Highwood, New Jersey, in 1791; was taken to England by his father when American Minister, and was educated there, and graduated at Harvard College in 1810; was an eminent merchant and banker in New York City, and a Representative in Congress, from New Jersey, from 1849 to 1851. He died in Highwood, New Jersey, October 3, 1853, aged sixty-two years.

King, John.—He was born in 1775; served in Congress, from New York, from 1831 to 1833; and died at New Lebanon, New York, September, 1, 1836.

King, John A.—He was born in New York in 1788, and educated at Harrow, England. He was a member of the New York Assembly from 1819 to 1821; and re-elected in 1832 and in 1840, from Queen's County; and in 1823 he was elected to the State Senate. He was a Representative in Congress, from New York, from 1849 to 1851; and was also Governor of New York, from 1856 to 1858. Rufus King, the diplomatist, was his father, and James G. King, of New Jersey, was his brother. He was also appointed Secretary of Legation at London, in 1826, and on the return of his father acted as Chargé d'Affaires. He was also a Delegate to the Peace Congress of 1861.

King, John P.—He was a Senator in Congress, from Georgia, from 1833 to 1837.

King, Perkins.—He was a member of the New York Assembly in 1827, and a Representative in Congress, from that State, from 1829 to 1831.

King, Preston.—Born at Ogdensburg, St. Lawrence County, New York, October 14, 1806. He graduated at Union College; is a lawyer by profession; was for several years a member of the New York Legislature; also a Representative, from that State, from 1843 to 1847, and from 1849 to 1853; after which he was elected to the United States Senate, which position he still retains, serving as Chairman of the Committee on Revolutionary Pensions. He was also a Delegate to the Baltimore Convention of 1864.

King, Rufus.—He was born in Scarborough, Maine, in 1755; was educated at Dummer Academy, in Newbury, Massachusetts; graduated at Harvard College in 1777; in 1778 he was aide-de-camp to Sullivan in his expedition against the British in Rhode Island; he studied law, and was admitted to the bar, in Newburyport, Massachusetts, in 1780; he was elected, from that town, to the State Legislature; in 1784 was elected a Delegate to Congress, at Trenton; was a member of the State Convention of Massachusetts, held in 1787; he was a member of the Convention which formed the Federal Constitution; removing to New York City in 1788, he was, in 1789, elected a Senator in Congress, and served his entire term, and was re-elected to the same position in 1813, remaining in that capacity until 1825. At the close of his first term in the Senate he was appointed, by President Washington, Minister to England, where he remained through the whole of President Adams's term, and during two years of President Jefferson's term. In 1825 President John Quincy Adams again appointed him Minister to England, but bad health prevented him from entering upon his duties; and, returning home, he died at Jamaica, Long Island, April 29, 1827. As a statesman, diplomatist, and political writer, he displayed great abilities, and he was the author of many of the papers written on the British Treaty in 1794, over the signature of Camilius; as a man, he was universally respected and beloved.

King, Rufus H.—He was born in New York, and was a Representative in Congress, from that State, from 1855 to 1857.

King, T. Butler.—He was born in Hampden, Hampshire County, Massachusetts, August 27, 1804; was educated at Westfield Academy; studied law, and removed to Georgia in 1823, where he devoted himself to planting. In the years 1832, 1834, 1835, and 1837, he was a member of the State Senate; and he was a Representative in Congress, from Georgia, from 1839 to 1843, and again from 1845 to 1847, and for another term ending with 1849, serving much of the time on the Committee on Naval Affairs, in which he took especial interest. He was also a member, in 1833, of the Milledgeville Convention; in 1836, of the Macon Railroad Convention; and, in 1840, of the Young Men's Convention at Baltimore; besides serving as the President of various canal and railroad companies. He subsequently became a resident of California, but returned to Georgia, and was elected, in 1859, a Senator in the State Legislature. He was for two years Collector of the Port of San Francisco; was identified with the Great Rebellion as a Commissioner to Europe; and died in Georgia, May 10, 1864.

King, William R.—Born in North Carolina, April 7, 1786; received a good education; studied law and was admitted to the bar in 1806; was a Representative in Congress, from his native State, from 1811 to 1816; he resigned that position and accompanied William Pinckney to Europe, as Secretary of Legation; and, on his return from Europe, he settled in the Territory of Alabama, and devoted himself to planting. He was a member of the Convention which formed the State Constitution of Alabama; in 1819 he was elected a Senator in Congress, from Alabama, where he continued until 1844; in that year he was appointed Minister to France, and continued there two years; in 1846 he was again elected to the United States Senate, where he remained until elected Vice-President of the United States, in 1852. During the Twenty-fourth, Twenty-fifth, Twenty-sixth, Thirty-first, and Thirty-second Congresses, he officiated as President, *pro tem.*, of the Senate, and as a presiding officer, as well as a man, commanded universal respect. At the time of his election, as Vice-President, his health was feeble, and, when the time arrived for taking the constitutional oath of that office, he was in Cuba, and the oath was administered by the American Consul there. He returned to his plantation at Cahawba, Alabama, April 17, 1852, and died on the following day.

Kingsbury, William W.—Born in Towanda, Bradford County, Pennsylvania, June 4, 1828. He was self-educated; he was bred a farmer, emigrated to Minnesota, and in the year 1855 was first elected a member of the Minnesota Legislature, and again in 1856. In 1857 was Delegate to the Convention for framing a Constitution for Minnesota, and elected a Delegate to the Thirty-fifth Congress.

Kinnard, George L.—He was a Representative in Congress, from Indiana, from 1833 to 1837, and died at Cincinnati, November 26, 1838, from injuries received on the sixteenth of that month on board the steamboat Flora, which exploded near that city.

Kinney, John Fitch.—Born in New Haven, Oswego County, New York, April 2, 1816; received an academical education, studied law, settled in Marysville, Ohio, and was admitted to practice at "Court and Bank" in 1837. In 1839 he removed to Lee County, Iowa; held the office of Secretary of the Legislative Council for the Territory, and also that of District Attorney. Upon the admission of Iowa as a State he was appointed one of the Judges of the Supreme Court, holding the office two years, when he was elected to the same by the Legislature for six years. In 1853 he was appointed, by President Pierce, Chief Justice of the Supreme Court of Utah, and went to that Territory in 1854; in 1857 removed to Nebraska Territory, and settled in the practice of law; in 1860, by President Buchanan, he was again appointed Chief Justice of Utah, holding that office until 1863, when he was elected, by a unanimous vote, a Delegate from Utah to the Thirty-eighth Congress.

Kinsey, Charles.—He was a Representative in Congress, from New Jersey, from 1817 to 1819, and from 1820 to 1821.

Kinsley, Martin.—He was born in Bridgewater, Massachusetts, June 2, 1754; graduated at Harvard University in 1778, and studied medicine; performed some service in the Revolutionary war, and was chosen a Delegate to the Convention for forming the Constitution of his native State; served in the Legislature of Massachusetts about thirty years; he was also at different periods a member of the State Council; a Judge of the Court of Common Pleas; Judge of Probate; and a Representative in Congress, from Massachusetts, from 1819 to 1821. He died June 20, 1835.

Kirkland, Joseph.—He was born in Old Norwich, Connecticut, in 1771; graduated at Yale College in 1790; removed to Utica, New York, and was the first Mayor of that city; served frequently in the State Legislature; and was a Representative in Congress, from New York, from 1821 to 1823. He died at Utica, January 26, 1844.

Kirkpatrick, Littleton.—Born in New Brunswick, New Jersey; graduated at Princeton College in 1815; and was a Representative in Congress, from New Jersey, from 1843 to 1845. He was also for five years Surrogate of the County of Middlesex.

Kirkpatrick, W.—He was born in Amwell, Hunterdon County, New Jersey, in November, 1768; was educated at Princeton College, graduating in 1788; studied medicine, and was admitted to practice in 1795; in 1806 he removed to Salina, New York, and became Superintendent of the Salt Springs; was a Representative in Congress, from 1807 to 1809, from New York; and died of cholera, at Salina, September 2, 1832.

Kirtland, Dorrance.—He was born in New York; graduated at Yale College, in 1789; and was a Representative in Congress, from that State, from 1817 to 1819.

Kitchell, Aaron.—Born in Morris County, New Jersey; was a warm supporter of the Revolution; a Representative in Congress, from New Jersey, from 1791 to 1793, from 1794 to 1797, and from 1799 to 1801; and a Senator in Congress from 1805 to 1809, when he resigned. He was also a member of the State Legislature.

Kittera, John W.—He was a graduate of Princeton College in 1776; and a Representative in Congress, from Pennsylvania, from 1791 to 1801, when he was appointed United States District Attorney for the Eastern District of Pennsylvania.

Kittera, Thomas.—He was a Representative in Congress, from Pennsylvania, from 1826 to 1827.

Kittredge, George W.—He was born in New Hampshire; a physician by profession; a member of the Legislature for three years, in 1847, 1851, and 1852, officiating as Speaker in 1852; and was a Representative in Congress, from that State, from 1853 to 1855.

Klingensmith, John, Jr.—He was born in Pennsylvania, and was a Representative in Congress, from that State, from 1835 to 1839.

Knapp, Anthony L.—Born in Middletown, Delaware County, New York, June 14, 1828; removed with his father to Illinois, in 1839; studied law, and was admitted to the bar in 1849, settling in the town of Jerseyville; in 1858 he was elected to the Senate of Illinois, attending the sessions of 1859 and 1861; and in the latter year he was elected a Representative, from Illinois, to the Thirty-seventh Congress, serving on the Committee on Revolutionary Pensions. In 1862 he was re-elected to the Thirty-eighth Congress, serving on the Committee on Private Land Claims.

Knapp, Chauncey L.—He was born in Berlin, Vermont, February 26, 1809. He commenced the active business of life by serving an apprenticeship of seven years in a printing-office in Montpelier; was elected Reporter for the Legislature in 1833; was co-proprietor and editor for some years of the State Journal; was elected Secretary of the State in 1836, in which capacity he served four years; and removing to Massachusetts he was elected Secretary of the Massachusetts Senate in 1851; and was elected a Representative to the Thirty-fourth, and re-elected to the Thirty-fifth Congress, and was a member of the Committee on Territories. To him was awarded the credit, while editing the Journal, of first nominating General Harrison for the Presidency, which resulted in his obtaining the electoral votes of Vermont four years before he was really elected. Mr. Knapp's tastes have led him to the study of mechanics, and in all his public positions he has paid particular attention to the mechanical interests of his constituents.

Knickerbocker, Herman.—He was born in New York in 1780, and was a descendant, in the third generation, of one of the original emigrants to New York. He early engaged in politics, and was a member of Congress, from 1809 to 1811, as a Federalist; but during President Jackson's administration he became a Democrat. He died in Williamsburg, New York, January 30, 1855. This was the person to whom Irving playfully alluded in the preface to his Knickerbocker as "my cousin the Congressman."

Knight, Jonathan.—Born in Bucks County, Pennsylvania, November 22, 1787, and removed with his parents, in 1801, to East Bethlehem, Washington County. He was mostly self-educated, and became a school teacher, and surveyor of lands. In 1816 he was appointed by the State Government to make and report a map of his county. He served three years as County Commissioner, and was appointed, in 1827, a Commissioner to extend the National Road between Cumberland and Wheeling, through Ohio and Indiana to the eastern line of Illinois. In 1822 he was elected to the Legislature, and served six years. In 1828 he visited England to acquire a thorough knowledge of civil engineering, and on his return was appointed Chief Engineer on the Baltimore and Ohio Road. He was elected, in 1854, a Representative in the Thirty-fourth Congress; after that time he was engaged in agriculture. He died in Washington County, November 22, 1858.

Knight, Nehemiah.—He was a native of Rhode Island; a farmer by occupation; a prominent politician of the Federal school, and a Representative in Congress, from 1803 to 1808.

Knight, Nehemiah R.—Born in Cranston, Rhode Island, December 31, 1780; was chiefly self-educated; at the age of twenty-two was elected to the State Legislature; in 1805 he was elected Clerk of the Court of Common Pleas in

Providence; in 1812 he was chosen Clerk of the Circuit Court, and served until 1817; he was also for many years President of the Roger Williams Bank; he was elected Governor of Rhode Island in 1817, and re-elected in 1819 and 1820; he was appointed, by President Madison, during the war with England, Collector of Providence; and he was a Senator in Congress, from 1821 to 1841. He was a member, in 1843, of the State Constitutional Convention, after which he retired to private life. He died at Providence, Rhode Island, April 19, 1854. He was a man of sterling character, and a true patriot.

Knowlton, Ebenezer.—He was born in New Hampshire; was educated for the ministry; was elected to the Maine Legislature in 1844, 1846, and 1848, serving during his second year as Speaker; and was a Representative in Congress, from Maine, from 1855 to 1857.

Knox, James.—Born in Canajoharie, Montgomery County, New York, July 4, 1807; graduated at Yale College in 1830; studied law at Utica, New York, and was admitted to the bar in 1833. In 1836 he located at Knoxville, Illinois, where he has since resided, giving his attention chiefly to mercantile and agricultural pursuits. In 1847 he was a member of the Constitutional Convention of Illinois, and in 1852 was elected a Representative in the Thirty-third Congress, and re-elected to the Thirty-fourth. He subsequently became blind, and visited Europe with a view of recovering his sight.

Knox, Samuel.—He was elected a Representative, from Missouri, to the Thirty-eighth Congress, having successfully contested the seat occupied by F. P. Blair, Jr., and taking his own seat near the close of the first session.

Krebs, Jacob.—He was a Representative in Congress, from Pennsylvania, from 1826 to 1827.

Kremer, George.—Born in Dauphin County, Pennsylvania, in 1775, and died in Union County, Pennsylvania, September 11, 1854. He was a Representative in Congress, from Pennsylvania, from 1823 to 1829.

Kuhns, Joseph H.—He was born in Pennsylvania, and was a Representative in Congress, from that State, from 1851 to 1853.

Kunkel, Jacob M.—Was born in Frederick, Maryland, July 23, 1822; graduated at the University of Virginia in 1843; studied law, and commenced practice in 1846; and in 1850 was elected to the Maryland Senate for six years, but the change in the State Constitution cut short his term. He was elected a Representative, from Maryland, to the Thirty-fifth Congress, serving as a member of the Committees on Revolutionary Claims, and Expenditures in the Treasury Department. Also elected to the Thirty-sixth Congress, serving on the Committee on Accounts.

Kunkel, John C.—Born in Pennsylvania, a lawyer by profession, and a member of the Thirty-fifth Congress, from his native State, and a member of the Committee on Claims.

Kurtz, William H.—He was born in Pennsylvania, and was a Representative in Congress, from that State, from 1851 to 1855.

Labranch, Alcea.—He was born in Louisiana, and was a Representative in Congress, from that State, from 1843 to 1845.

Lacock, Abner.—Born in Virginia in 1770. Without the advantage of much early education, he raised himself by his talents to eminence as a legislator, statesman, and civilian. He filled various public stations for a period of nearly forty years; was a Representative in Congress, from Pennsylvania, from 1811 to 1813, and United States Senator from 1813 to 1819. He died in Beaver County, Pennsylvania, April 12, 1837.

Lahm, Samuel.—Born in Leitersburg, Maryland, April 22, 1812. His education was limited, yet his first earnings were the result of teaching school. In March, 1835, he removed to Indiana, and studied law, and then settled in Ohio. In 1837 he was elected Master in Chancery; in 1842 a State Senator; at various times to high positions in the militia; and to Congress, as a Representative, in 1847, where he remained until 1849.

Lake, William A.—He was born in Maryland; graduated at Washington College, in Pennsylvania; studied law; served in the Legislature of Maryland; removed to Mississippi; practised his profession there with success; was elected to the Senate of that State; and was a Representative in Congress, from Mississippi, during the Thirty-fourth Congress.

Lamar, Henry G.—He was born in Georgia, and was a Representative in Congress, from that State, from 1829 to 1833.

Lamar, L. Q. C.—He is a native of Georgia, having been born in 1820; but removed to Mississippi, studied law, and was elected a Representative to the Thirty-fifth Congress, from that State, serving on the Committee on Elections. Re-elected to the Thirty-sixth Congress, serving on the Committee on Commerce. Joined the Great Rebellion in 1861.

Lamb, Alfred W.—He was born in New York, and was a Representative in Congress, from Missouri, from 1847 to 1849.

Lambert, John.—He was a Representative in Congress, from New Jersey, from 1805 to 1809; and from 1809 to 1815 he was a member of the United States Senate. During the years 1802 and 1803 he performed the duties of Governor of New Jersey, served many years in the Legislature of that State, and died in February, 1823, aged seventy-five years.

Lancaster, Columbia.—He was a Delegate to Congress, from the Territory of Washington, during the years 1854 and 1855.

Landrum, John M.—He was born in Edgefield District, South Carolina, July 3, 1815; obtained the greater part of his education after he became of age, by his own exertions; graduated at the South Carolina College in 1842; taught school and studied law at the same time; in 1845 removed to Louisiana, and settled at Shreveport, and was elected a Representative, from Louisiana, to the Thirty-sixth Congress, serving as a member of the Committee on Expenses in the Post-office Department. Resigned in February, 1861.

Landry, J. Aristide.—He was born in Louisiana, and was a Representative in Congress, from that State, from 1851 to 1853.

Landy, James.—He was born in Philadelphia, Pennsylvania, October 13, 1813; received his education in his native city; devoted himself, for a time, to the occupation of a builder; studied law, but abandoned the profession, and turned his attention to mercantile pursuits. He has devoted much of his attention to the Public School System of Philadelphia, and has held the positions of Commissioner and President of the Board of School Commissioners. In 1856 he was elected a Representative to the Thirty-fifth Congress, from Pennsylvania, and was a member of the Committee on Commerce.

Lane, Amos.—He was a Representative in Congress, from Indiana, from 1833 to 1837, having previously been a member of the State Legislature, and served one session as Speaker. He was a lawyer of the first ability, and filled a conspicuous place in the history of Indiana. He died in Lawrenceburg, in that State, in 1850.

Lane, Henry S.—He was born in Montgomery County, Kentucky, February 24, 1811; received a good common school education, and under a tutor, some knowledge of the classics; studied law in Kentucky, but removed to Indiana, and was admitted to the bar in that State; in 1837 he was elected to the Indiana Legislature; was a Representative in Congress, from Indiana, from 1841 to 1843; served as a Lieutenant-Colonel of volunteers under General Taylor, in the war with Mexico, in 1846; in 1859 he was elected to the United States Senate, to contest the seat of J. D. Bright, but was denied the seat; in 1861 he was elected Governor of Indiana; but, two days after his inauguration, he was again elected a Senator in Congress, from Indiana, serving on the Committees on Military Affairs, and of Pensions, and as Chairman of the Committee on Enrolled Bills.

Lane, James H.—He was born in

Indiana, and was a Representative in Congress, from Indiana, from 1853 to 1855; settled in Kansas, and took an active part in politics; and on the admission of that State into the Union, he was chosen a Senator in Congress, for the term ending in 1865, serving on the Committees on Indian Affairs, and Agriculture. During the early part of the Rebellion he was commissioned a Brigadier-General of volunteers. He was also a Delegate to the Baltimore Convention of 1864.

Lane, Joseph.—Born in Buncombe County, North Carolina, December 14, 1801. In his fifteenth year he became a clerk in a mercantile house in Indiana, and in 1822 was chosen a member of the Legislature of that State, serving in that capacity, with occasional intervals, until 1846. He participated in the war with Mexico, acquitting himself with credit at Buena Vista and on other fields, and was appointed, by President Polk, a Brigadier-General. In 1849 he was appointed Governor of the Territory of Oregon, without his solicitation, and organized the government; and was elected a Delegate to Congress, in 1851, where he was retained by his constituents until the admission of Oregon as a State, when he took his seat as a Senator in Congress in 1859. In 1860 he was nominated for Vice-President on the ticket with Mr. Breckenridge, but was defeated.

Langdon, Chauncey.—He graduated at Yale College in 1787; was a Representative in Congress, from Vermont, from 1815 to 1817, and died in 1830. He also served seven years in the Legislature of the State, and was a State Councillor for nine years.

Langdon, John.—He was educated for mercantile pursuits, and afterwards prosecuted business upon the sea, until the commencement of the controversy with Great Britain. He was one of the party which removed the powder and the military stores from Fort William and Mary, at New Castle, in 1774. In 1775 and 1776 he was chosen a Delegate to Congress. Commanding a company of volunteers, he served, for awhile, in Vermont and Rhode Island. In his own State, he was, in 1776 and 1777, Speaker of the House, and Judge of the Court of Common Pleas. In 1779 he was Continental agent in New Hampshire, and contracted for the building of several ships of war. In 1783 he was again appointed Delegate to Congress, and was afterwards repeatedly a member of the Legislature, and Speaker. In March, 1788, he was chosen Governor of the State, and from 1789 to 1801 he was Senator of the United States and President of the Senate *pro tem.* during the First Congress, and part of the Second. From 1805 to 1808, and again in 1810 and 1811, he was Governor of the State. He died in 1819, aged seventy-eight.

Lanman, James.—Born in Norwich, Connecticut, June 14, 1769; graduated at Yale College, in 1788; studied law and was admitted to the bar in 1791, and settled as a lawyer in his native town; he was a member of the Convention which formed the first Constitution of Connecticut in 1818; served two years in the Lower House of the Legislature in 1817 and 1832, and one year as a State Senator in 1819; and was for five years Attorney for the State, for New London County, from 1814 to 1819, acquiring great local distinction by his abilities. He was elected a Senator in Congress, serving from 1819 to 1825, during one Congress as Chairman of the Committees on Post-offices and Post-roads, and Contingent Expenses of the Senate, and voted with the South on the Missouri Compromise; during the Seventeenth Congress, he was at one time member of four committees, viz., that of Commerce and Manufactures, the Militia, District of Columbia, and the Contingent Expenses of the Senate. He was appointed, by the Governor, to a second term in the Senate, in recess of the Legislature and before the vacancy occurred, and by a small majority the Senate decided that the appointment was without authority of law. He was subsequently Judge of the Supreme and Superior Courts of Connecticut, for three years, from 1826 to 1829, and three years, from 1831 to 1834, Mayor of Norwich, where he died, August 7, 1841.

Lansing, Gerrit Y.—He was born in New York, served four years in the Legislature of that State, and was a Representative in Congress, from New York, from 1831 to 1837. He has also been a Regent of the University of New York.

Lansing, William E.—Was born in the town of Sullivan, Madison County, New York, in 1822; studied law at Utica, and commenced the practice in 1845; in 1850 he was elected District Attorney of Madison County; in 1857 Clerk of the same County; and in 1860 he was elected a Representative, from New York, to the Thirty-seventh Congress, serving as a member of the Committee on Indian Affairs.

Laporte, John.—He was born in Pennsylvania, and was a Representative in Congress, from that State, from 1833 to 1837.

Larrabee, Charles H.—Born in Rome, Oneida County, New York, November 9, 1820; when quite young, accompanied his father to Ohio, and was educated at Granville College; after devoting some attention to practical engineering, he studied law, and was admitted to the bar in 1841, at Pontotoc, Mississippi; in 1844 he settled in Chicago, Illinois, and edited for a time, the Democratic Advocate; served one term as City Advocate for Chicago; in 1847 he settled in Wisconsin, and became a member of the Convention to form a State Constitution; in 1848 he was elected a Circuit Judge, and after serving ten years, resigned, and was elected a Representative, from Wisconsin, to the Thirty-sixth Congress, serving as a member of the Committee on Expenses in the War Department. He subsequently entered the army in the volunteer service, and had command as Colonel, of a regiment from his State.

La Sere, Emile.—He was born in Louisiana, and was a Representative in Congress, from that State, from 1846 to 1847, and also for the two following terms, ending in 1851.

Latham, Milton S.—Was born in Columbus, Ohio, May 23, 1827; graduated at Jefferson College, Pennsylvania, in 1845; soon afterwards removed to Alabama, where he studied law; was appointed in 1848, Clerk of the Circuit Court for Russell County; removed to California in 1850, and was there appointed Clerk of the Recorder's Court in San Francisco; he was soon afterwards chosen District Attorney for the counties of Sacramento and El Dorado, which he held until 1851. In 1852 he was elected a Representative, from California, to the Thirty-seventh Congress, declining a re-election; he was appointed in 1855, by President Pierce, Collector of San Francisco, which office he held until 1857; having been elected Governor of California, three days after his inauguration, in January, 1860, he was elected a Senator in Congress, from California, for six years, serving on the Committees on Military Affairs, and on the Post-office and Post-roads.

Lathrop, Samuel. — Born in Hampden County, Massachusetts, in 1771; graduated at Yale College in 1792; studied law, and attained a high position at the bar; was a Representative in Congress, from Massachusetts, from 1818 to 1826. He was also a member of the Massachusetts Senate for ten years, and President of that body in 1829 and 1830. He died in West Springfield, July 11, 1846.

Lattimer, Henry.—He was a Representative in Congress, from Delaware, from 1794 to 1795, and a Senator in Congress, from 1795 to 1801, when he resigned.

Lattimore, William.—Born in Norfolk, Virginia, February 9, 1774, where he received a limited education; he studied medicine; removed to the Territory of Mississippi; and was a Delegate to Congress, from that Territory, from 1803 to 1807, and from 1813 to 1817. He was also a Delegate to the Convention which formed the first Constitution of Mississippi; after which he retired to private life, and died April 3, 1843.

Law, John.—Was born in New London, Connecticut, in 1798; graduated at Yale College in 1814; studied law, and was admitted to practice in the Supreme Court of Connecticut in 1817, and soon afterwards emigrated to the Territory of Indiana, locating himself at Vincennes. Soon after arriving in the West he was elected a Prosecuting Attorney, and in 1823 a member of the Legislature; he was again elected Attorney for his district, and held that position until promoted to a Judgeship, which office he held by re-elections for eight years. He subsequently removed to Evansville, where he resumed the practice of his profession. In 1860 he was elected a Representative, from Indiana, to the Thirty-seventh Congress, serving on the Committees on the Library, and on Revolutionary Pensions. Like Mr. Charles F. Adams, Mr. John Law can mention the fact, with excusable pride, that his father, as well as his grandfather, both served their country as members of Congress, and witnessed the same events in our country's history. Amasa Learned, who was also his grandfather on his mother's side, was in the first Congress that sat under the Constitution. He was re-elected to the Thirty-eighth Congress, serving on the Committees on Agriculture, and Revolutionary Pensions, and the Select Committee on Emigration.

Law, Lyman.—Born at New London, Connecticut, August 19, 1770; graduated at Yale College in 1791; studied law with his father, Richard Law (who was a member of the Continental Congress), and practised at New London; after serving in the Legislature of the State, and being Speaker of the House of Representatives, he was elected to Congress, and represented his State, in that body, from 1811 to 1817. He died in New London, February 3, 1842.

Lawler, Joab.—Born in North Carolina, June 12, 1796; was educated for the ministry, and became a clergyman of the Baptist Church. In 1826 he was elected to the lower house of the Alabama Legislature, and was re-elected until 1831, in which year he was elected to the State Senate. In 1832 he was appointed Receiver of Public Moneys for the Coosa Land District, and held the office until 1835. In 1833 he was elected Treasurer of the University of Alabama. He was a Representative in Congress, from Alabama, from 1835 to 1838. He died in Washington, May 8, 1838, during the first session of his second term.

Lawrance, John.—He was born in the county of Cornwall, England, in 1750, and emigrated to the city of New York in 1767. He studied law, and was admitted to the bar in 1772, and in 1775 was commissioned in the First New York Regiment, and served to the end of the Revolutionary war, his several grades having been Aide-de-camp to his relative, Colonel McDougal, Judge-Advocate, and General, in which latter capacity he conducted the court-martial called to try Major André. In 1783 he resumed the practice of his profession in New York. In 1785 and 1786 he was a member of the First Congress. In 1789 he was elected a State Senator, and during that year was elected, by a five-sixths vote, a Representative in the Federal Congress, serving from 1789 to 1793; was appointed by Washington in 1794 Judge of the United States District Court for New York; and was a Senator in Congress, from 1796 to 1800, serving for a short time as President *pro-tem.* of that body, when he resigned, and retired to private life. He died in 1810.

Lawrence, Abbott.—Born in Groton, Massachusetts, December 16, 1792. His education was obtained at a district school and at Groton Academy, and in 1808 he went to Boston, and became a clerk in the store of his brother Amos. In 1814 he was admitted as a partner in the concern, and for many years the twain prosecuted a very extensive importing business, and laid the foundations of their several fortunes. He was the travelling partner, and visited Europe a number of times. He subsequently became one of the foremost men in building up American manufactures, and the flourishing city of Lawrence was the offspring of his enterprise. In 1827 he was a Delegate to the Harrisburg Convention. He served in the Common Council of Boston in 1831, and was a Representative in Congress, from 1835 to 1837, and again in 1839 and 1840. In 1842 he was appointed a Commissioner to arrange the Northeastern boundary question; in 1849 he was invited by President Taylor into his cabinet, but declined; he subsequently accepted, however, the appointment of Minister to England, where he acquitted himself with credit. He founded a scientific school in Cambridge, and his gifts and bequests to various charitable and religious societies proved him to be a man of many noble qualities. Died in Boston, August 18, 1855.

Lawrence, Cornelius Van Wyck.—He was born in Flushing, Long Island, February 28, 1791; spent his boyhood working on his father's farm, and acquiring a good English education; and, on arriving at the age of manhood, removed to New York City, with which, as a business man, he has been identified ever since. He was a Representative in Congress, from New York City, from 1832 to 1834; for two years following he was Mayor of the City of New York; in 1836 President of the Electoral College for President; and for twenty years he held the honorable position of President of the Bank of the State of New York. Among other positions of trust and responsibility which, with the above, have tended to give him a high reputation, may be mentioned the following: Director of the Branch Bank of the United States and the Bank of America, Trustee of the New York Life and Trust Company, and of numerous Fire and Marine Insurance Companies. In 1856 ill health compelled Mr. Lawrence to retire from the pursuits of active life, and he spent the closing years of his life in peace, on the spot where his ancestors have resided for two hundred years. Died at Flushing, February 20, 1861.

Lawrence, John W.—He was born in New York; served two years in the Assembly of that State, from Queen's County; and was a Representative in Congress, from 1845 to 1847.

Lawrence, Joseph.—He was born in Adams County, Pennsylvania, in 1788; he served for nine years in the State Legislature, one year as State Treasurer, and was a Representative in Congress, from Pennsylvania, from 1825 to 1829, and again from 1841 to the time of his death, which occurred in Washington, District of Columbia, April 17, 1842.

Lawrence, Samuel.—He was born in New York; served seven years in the Assembly of that State, and was a Representative in Congress, from the same, from 1823 to 1825.

Lawrence, Sidney.—He was born in Vermont, but removed to New York, and was elected a Representative in Congress, from that State, from 1847 to 1849.

Lawrence, William.—Born in Washington, Guernsey County, Ohio, September 2, 1814; graduated at Jefferson College, Pennsylvania, in September, 1835; engaged in mercantile and agricultural pursuits; and served in the Ohio Legislature in 1843. He was a Presidential Elector in 1848, a member of the Constitutional Convention of Ohio in 1850–51, State Senator in 1856–57, and elected a Representative to the Thirty-fifth Congress, officiating as Chairman of the Committee on Expenditures in the State Department.

Lawrence, William T.—Born in New York City, May 7, 1788; he was bred a merchant, and continued such until called into the service of the United States, in the war of 1812, as a militia Captain of artillery. In 1823 he removed to Cayuga County, New York, and settled on a farm. In 1838 he was chosen County Judge, and from 1847 to 1849 he was a Representative in Congress; he also served as delegate to several nominating conventions.

Lawyer, Thomas.—He was a member of the New York Assembly, from Schoharie County, in 1816, and was a Representative in Congress, from New York, from 1817 to 1819.

Lay, George W.—He was born in New York; liberally educated; a lawyer by profession; and was a member of the New York Assembly, from Genesee County, in 1840, having been a Representative in Congress, from 1833 to 1837. He was also appointed Chargé d'Affaires to Sweden, by President Tyler, in 1842. Died at Batavia, New York, October 21, 1860.

Lazear, Jesse.—Was born in Greene County, Pennsylvania, December 12, 1804; received his early education from his parents, and worked on a farm until he became of age; served as a Clerk in the Recorder's office; in 1829 and 1832 he was appointed Register and Recorder for his county; and since that time (until 1864), he has held the position of Cashier of the Farmers' and Drovers' Bank of Waynesburg. In 1860 he was elected a Representative, from Pennsylvania, to the Thirty-seventh Congress, serving on the Committee on Private Land Claims, and Chairman of that on Expenditures on the Public Buildings; and in 1862 he was re-elected to the Thirty-eighth Congress, serving on the Committee on

Public Expenditures, and again on that relating to Public Buildings.

Lea, Luke.—He was born in Surry County, North Carolina, January 26, 1782; removed at an early day with his father to Tennessee, where he was for several years Clerk of the House of Representatives; he served gallantly in Florida and in the Creek country, under General Jackson, in the Indian wars. He was a Representative in Congress, from 1833 to 1837, and for thirty years discharged the duties of Cashier of the State Bank, and Register of the State Land-office of Tennessee. In 1849, he was appointed, by President Taylor, Indian Agent of the Fort Leavenworth Agency, and was highly esteemed by the Indians under his charge. He was returning to his residence, after making the Indian payments of his agency, when he was killed by a fall from his horse, June 17, 1851.

Lea, Pryor.—Born in Knox County, Tennessee, in 1794; was educated at Greenville College; studied law as a profession, and was admitted to the bar in 1817. He served with General Jackson in the Creek war, in 1813; was Clerk to the Legislature in 1816; United States District Attorney in 1824; and a Representative in Congress, from 1827 to 1831. In 1837 he removed to Jackson, Mississippi, and in 1847 to Goliad, Texas. He projected the work called the "Central Transit," for building a railroad from Arkansas Bay to Mazatlan, and was President of the Company.

Leach, De Witt C.—Born in Clarence, Erie County, New York, November 23, 1822. He was self-educated; bred a farmer; chosen a member of the Michigan Legislature in 1849 and 1850; and a member of the Convention to revise the State Constitution, in 1850; he was also State Librarian in 1855 and 1856; and was elected a Representative to the Thirty-fifth Congress, from Michigan, serving as a member of the Committee on Revisal and Unfinished Business; also elected to the Thirty-sixth Congress, serving on the Committee on Indian Affairs.

Leach, James M.—Born in Landsdowne, Randolph County, North Carolina; received a good classical education; studied law and was admitted to the bar in 1842; served ten years in the Legislature of North Carolina; and in 1859 was elected a Representative, from that State, to the Thirty-sixth Congress, serving as a member of the Committee on Revolutionary Claims.

Leadbetter, D. P.—He was born in Pennsylvania, and having removed to Ohio, was elected a Representative in Congress, from 1837 to 1841.

Leake, Shelton F.—Born in Albemarle County, Virginia, November 30, 1812; received a good English education; taught for three years an "old field school;" studied law, and in his twenty-fifth year was admitted to the bar; in 1842 he was elected to the Virginia House of Delegates; was a Representative in Congress, from Virginia, from 1845 to 1847; in 1851 he was elected Lieutenant-Governor of Virginia; was a candidate for Governor in 1854, but was defeated; and in 1859 he was re-elected to the Federal House of Representatives for the Thirty-sixth Congress, serving as a member of the Committee on Manufactures.

Leake, Walter.—He was a soldier in the Revolutionary war; in 1821 was elected Governor of Mississippi, having previously served as Senator of the United States, from 1817 to 1820. He died at Mount Salus, Hines County, Mississippi, November 17, 1825.

Learned, Amasa.—Born in Killingly, Connecticut, November 15, 1750, and died at New London, May 4, 1825. He graduated at Yale College in 1772; studied divinity, but preached for only a short time; and was a Representative in Congress, from Connecticut, from 1801 to 1805. He had been a member of the Convention which ratified the Constitution of the United States; in 1818 was a member of the Connecticut Constitutional Convention; and afterwards frequently sat in the Assembly of his native State.

Leary, Cornelius L. L.—Born in Baltimore, October 22, 1813; was educated at St. Mary's College, in that city; in 1835 he engaged in business in Louisville, Kentucky, but returned to Baltimore in 1837; in 1838 he was chosen a Delegate to the Maryland Assembly;

in 1847 he came to the bar; was a Presidential Elector in 1856; and in 1861, at a special election, he was elected a Representative, from Maryland, to the Thirty-seventh Congress, serving on the Committee on Commerce.

Leavitt, Humphrey H.—He was born in Suffield, Connecticut, in June, 1796; removed at an early day with his father to the Western Reserve of Ohio; received an academical education; and adopted the profession of the law, having been admitted to the bar in 1816; and he was a Representative in Congress, from 1831 to 1834. He also served in the State Legislature, in the House in 1825 and 1826, and in the Senate in 1827; and he has for many years been Judge of the District Court of Ohio, having been appointed, in 1834, by President Jackson.

Le Blonde, Francis C. — Was born in Ohio, and adopted the profession of law; in 1851 he was elected for two years to the State Legislature; was re-elected in 1853, and served as Speaker of that body; and in 1862 he was elected a Representative, from Ohio, to the Thirty-eighth Congress, serving on the Committee on Public Expenditures.

Lecompte, Joseph.—He was born in Woodford County, Kentucky; and was a Representative in Congress, from Kentucky, from 1825 to 1833.

Lee, Gideon.—He was born in Amherst, Massachusetts, in 1777; in early life removed to the city of New York, where he became a leather merchant, and amassed a large fortune. He was at one time Mayor of New York, a Presidential Elector, and a member of Congress during the years 1836 and 1837. He died at Geneva, New York, August 21, 1841.

Lee, Henry. — Born in Virginia, January 29, 1756, and graduated at Princeton College in 1773. In 1776 he was appointed a Captain of cavalry, under Colonel Bland, and in September, 1777, he joined the main army. His skill in discipline and gallant bearing attracted the notice of Washington, and he was soon promoted to the rank of Major, with the command of a separate corps of cavalry, and then advanced to the rank of Lieutenant-Colonel. From 1780 to the end of the war he served under Greene. The services of Lee's Legion in various actions were very important. He particularly distinguished himself in the battle of Guilford; afterwards, he succeeded in capturing Fort Cornwallis, and other forts; he was also conspicuous at Ninety-six, and at the Eutaw Springs. In 1786 he was appointed a Delegate in Congress, from Virginia, in which body he remained till the Constitution was adopted, having in the Convention of Virginia advocated its adoption. In 1791 he was chosen Governor of Virginia, and remained in office three years. By appointment of Washington, he commanded the forces sent to suppress the Whiskey Insurrection in Pennsylvania. He was a member of Congress at the period of Washington's death, in 1799, and was appointed, by Congress, to deliver a eulogy on the occasion. He it was who first uttered the memorable saying in regard to Washington, "First in peace, first in war, and first in the hearts of his countrymen." In 1801 he retired to private life, and in his last years he was distressed with pecuniary embarrassments; while confined in 1809 within the bounds of Spottsylvania County, for debt, he wrote his valuable "Memoirs of the Southern Campaigns." In 1814, during the mob at Baltimore, he was one of the defenders, and was severely wounded, and carried to the jail for safety. Returning from the West Indies, where he had gone for health, he died at Cumberland Island, near St. Mary's, Georgia, March 25, 1818.

Lee, John.—He was a Representative in Congress, from Maryland, from 1823 to 1825.

Lee, Joshua.—He was born in New York, and served three years in the Legislature of that State, from Ontario and Yates counties, and was a Representative in Congress, from New York, from 1835 to 1837.

Lee, M. Lindley.—Born in Minisink, Orange County, New York, May 29, 1805; spent his boyhood alternately working upon a farm in summer and attending the district school in winter; when sixteen years of age commenced an academical course of study, and graduated at Union College in 1827; and having studied medicine and surgery, obtained a degree in 1830 from the College of Physicians and Surgeons of Western New York. While devoting himself to his profession he was appointed Postmaster of Fulton, Orange County, New York, serving from 1840 to 1844; he was elected in 1846 and 1847 to the Assembly of New York; subsequently held the position, for three terms, of Commissioner of Loans for the State; was a member of the State Senate in 1855; and in 1858 was elected a Representative to the Thirty-sixth Congress, from New York, serving as a member of the Committee on Post-offices and Post-roads.

Lee, Richard Henry.—Was born at Stratford, Westmoreland County, Virginia, January 20, 1732, and was educated at Wakefield, Yorkshire, England. He had a seat in the House of Burgesses, of Virginia, in 1757, and proposed there, in 1773, the formation of a Committee of Correspondence. He had the honor of originating the first resistance to British oppression, in the time of the Stamp Act, in 1765. He was a member of the First Congress, in 1774, and in October prepared the draft of the memorial to the people of British America. In accordance with instructions from the Virginia Convention, he first proposed in Congress a declaration of independence, June 7, 1776, and a committee was appointed to prepare it. The second eloquent address to the people of Great Britain was drawn up by him; and after the adoption of the Articles of Confederation, he withdrew from Congress, but was re-elected in 1784, and chosen President of that body, serving till 1787. He contended for the necessity of amendments to the Constitution previously to its adoption in 1789; and was a Senator, from Virginia, from 1789 to 1792, serving one session as President *pro tem.* of that body. He was the author of a number of political pamphlets, and his correspondence was published in 1825. He died at Chantilly, Westmoreland County, Virginia, June 9, 1794.

Lee, Silas.—He graduated at Harvard University in 1784; served in the Massachusetts Legislature in 1793, 1797, and 1798; was a Representative in Congress, from Massachusetts, from 1799 to 1802; Judge of Probate from 1805 to 1814; for some years Chief Judge of the Court of Common Pleas; and he was appointed, by President Adams, United States District Attorney for Maine. Died in 1814.

Lee, Thomas.—He was a Representative in Congress, from New Jersey, from 1833 to 1837; and died at Port Elizabeth, November 2, 1855.

Lee, Thomas Bland.—He was a native of Virginia, and a Representative in Congress, from 1789 to 1795, having previously served in the Continental Congress, and died in 1827.

Leet, Isaac.—Born in Pennsylvania in 1802; was for several years in the Senate of that State; a Representative in Congress, from 1829 to 1831; and died at Washington, Pennsylvania, June 10, 1844.

Lefevre, Joseph.—He was a Representative in Congress, from Pennsylvania, from 1811 to 1813.

Lefferets, John.—He was a Representative in Congress, from New York, from 1813 to 1815; a member of the State Constitutional Convention of 1821; and a State Senator, from 1822 to 1825.

Leffler, Isaac.—Born in Washington County, Pennsylvania, in November, 1788; was educated at Jefferson College; studied law and settled in Wheeling, Virginia; in 1817 was elected to the Virginia Legislature, where he served eight years; in 1827 was elected a member of the Board of Public Works; and he was a Representative in Congress, from Virginia, from 1827 to 1829. In 1832 again elected to the Virginia Legislature; in 1835 removed to Burlington, Iowa; served two years in the Legislature of Wisconsin Territory; one year as Speaker; one year in the Legislature of Iowa; in 1843 was appointed Marshal of Iowa; in 1849 Register of the Land Office at Stillwater, but declined; in 1852 appointed Receiver of the same office, whence he was removed for opinion's sake.

Leffler, Shepherd.—He was born in Pennsylvania; and was a Representative in Congress, from Iowa, from 1846 to 1851.

Leftwich, Jabez.—He was born in Bedford County, Virginia, and was a Representative in Congress, from that State, from 1821 to 1825.

Legare, Hugh Swinton. — He was born at Charleston, South Carolina, January 2, 1797; graduated at the College of that State in 1814, and, after having studied law, went to Europe, where he remained until 1820, occupied with the pursuits of literature. On his return to Charleston, he devoted himself to the practice of his profession and to agricultural pursuits. In 1830 he was appointed Attorney-General of the State, and was the principal editor of the Southern Review. In 1832 he was appointed Chargé d'Affaires of the United States to Belgium; from 1837 to 1839 was a Representative of his native State in Congress; and in 1841 was appointed Attorney-General of the United States by President Tyler, and also Acting Secretary of State. He died, suddenly, at Boston, June 20, 1841, while accompanying the President in his journey to attend the Bunker Hill Celebration. His fine taste as a writer, his eminent acquirements as a scholar, and his learning and eloquence as a lawyer, were known and appreciated throughout the Union. His writings were collected and published in 1846.

Lehman, William E.—Born in Philadelphia, August 21, 1822; graduated at the University of Pennsylvania in 1843; studied law, and, after practising with success, retired from the bar and travelled in Europe. By President Polk he was appointed an Examiner of Post-offices in New York and Pennsylvania, his only office by appointment; and he was elected a Representative, from Pennsylvania, to the Thirty-seventh Congress, serving as a member of the Committee on Accounts. His family was one of note in Dresden, his father and grandfather having acquired distinction in the civil and military service.

Leib, Michael.—He was a Representative in Congress, from Pennsylvania, from 1799 to 1806, and a Senator of the United States from 1808 to 1814, and in the latter year he was appointed Postmaster at Philadelphia. He also served in the Legislature of Pennsylvania both before and after his election to Congress. Died in Philadelphia, December 28, 1822, aged sixty-three years.

Leib, Owen D.—He was born in Pennsylvania, and was a Representative in Congress, from that State, from 1845 to 1847. Died June 17, 1848.

Leidy, Paul.—Born in Hemlock, Columbia County, Pennsylvania, November 21, 1813. He was educated at a common school; the early part of his life was devoted to agricultural pursuits; from the age of sixteen to twenty-four he followed the business of a tailor; taught school, and having studied law at the same time, has since practised that profession. He was for five years District Attorney for Montour County; for a short time Superintendent of Common Schools for the same county; and was elected a Representative to the Thirty-fifth Congress, serving as a member of the Committee on Roads and Canals.

Leigh, Benjamin Watkins. — Born in Virginia in 1782, and died at Richmond, February 2, 1849. He was one of the most eminent men of his State, well known as a lawyer and public man. From 1829 to 1841 he was Reporter of the State; frequently a member of the House of Delegates; a member of the Convention of 1830 for revising the State Constitution; and a Senator in Congress from 1834 to 1837.

Leiper, George G.—He was a Representative in Congress, from Pennsylvania, from 1829 to 1831.

Leiter, Benjamin F. — He was born in Leitersburg, Washington County, Maryland, October 13, 1813. He was chiefly educated by his father; taught school in Maryland, from 1830 to 1834; removed to Ohio and taught there until 1842, after which he was admitted to the bar and devoted himself to the practice of law, in which he was successful; he was elected to the Ohio Legislature in 1848, and was chosen temporary Chairman, by the Democrats, acting as such throughout the long contest of that year between his party and the Whigs, which is now spoken of in Ohio as the "days of the Revolution;" in 1849 he was re-elected and chosen Speaker; and in 1854 he was elected to Congress, and re-elected to each successive Congress, serving as a member of the Committee on Indian Affairs.

Lent, James.—He was a member of Congress, from New York, from 1829 to 1833, and died in Washington, February 24, 1833. He was Chairman of the Committee on Expenditures in the Department of State.

Leonard, George.—Born in Boston, July 4, 1729; graduated at Harvard College in 1748; a Representative in Congress, from 1789 to 1793, and from 1795 to 1797; a man of unusual wealth; for his learning was made a Doctor of Laws; and died at Newton, Massachusetts, July 26, 1819. His descendants are numerous, and many of them distinguished.

Leonard, Moses G.—He was born in Connecticut; was a Representative in Congress, from New York, from 1843 to 1845, and was for several years Commissioner of Emigration in the city of New York.

Leonard, Stephen B.—He was born in New York, and was a Representative in Congress, from that State, from 1835 to 1837, and again from 1839 to 1841.

Letcher, John.—Born in Lexington, Rockbridge County, Virginia, March 29, 1813; he commenced his classical studies at Washington College, and completed his education at Randolph Macon College; adopted the profession of law, and was admitted to practice in 1839; during that year he established, and for a time edited, the Valley Star, in Lexington; a member of the Convention for reforming the Constitution of Virginia in 1850; and was elected a Representative in the Thirty-second, Thirty-third, Thirty-fourth, and Thirty-fifth Congresses, serving generally as a member of the Committee of Ways and Means. He was, in 1859, elected by the democracy of Virginia Governor of that Commonwealth.

Letcher, Robert P.—He was born in Goochland County, Virginia; received a good education, and adopted the profession of law. He served a number of years in the State Legislature, and was at one time elected Speaker of the House; was a Representative in Congress, from 1823 to 1835; Governor of Kentucky from 1840 to 1844; and in 1849 was appointed Minister to Mexico. Died in Frankfort, Kentucky, January 24, 1861.

Levin, Lewis C.—He was born in Charleston, South Carolina, November 10, 1808; received a liberal education, having graduated at Columbia College, South Carolina; adopted the profession of law, and practised the same in Maryland, Louisiana, Kentucky, and Pennsylvania; and was a Representative in Congress, from Pennsylvania, from 1845 to 1847, and again from 1847 to 1851, generally serving on the Committee on Naval Affairs. To him is generally awarded the credit of having founded, in 1843, the Native American Party. Died in Philadelphia, March 14, 1860.

Lewis, Abner.—He was born in New York; was a member of the Assembly of that State, from Chautauque County, in 1838 and 1839, and was a Representative in Congress, from New York, from 1845 to 1847.

Lewis, Dixon H.—Born in Dinwiddie, County, Virginia, in 1802, and was educated at the South Carolina College. He studied law, removed to Alabama, and became eminent in his profession. He was an able and amiable man, and physically very large and fleshy; and the story is related of him, that when returning home on one of the Southern steamers, which was wrecked, he refused to take a seat in a small boat, because the lives of several persons would thereby be jeopardized, and though for a time he was in great danger, he was rescued. He represented Alabama in Congress, from 1829 to 1843, and from 1844 until his death was a Senator in Congress. Died in New York, October 25, 1848.

Lewis, Joseph, Jr.—He was born in Virginia, and was a Representative, from that State, to the Thirteenth Congress.

Lewis, William J.—He was a Representative in Congress, from Virginia, from 1817 to 1819.

Ligon, Thomas W.—He was born in Prince Edward County, Virginia, placed at an early age at Hampden Sydney College, but finished his education at the University of Virginia. He studied law, and after spending a year and a half at the Yale Law School, settled in Baltimore. He was a Representative in Congress, from Maryland, from 1845 to 1849, having been re-elected for a second term; and was elected in 1854 Governor of that State.

Lilly, Samuel.—Was born in New York, adopted the medical profession, and was a Representative in Congress, from New Jersey, from 1853 to 1855.

Lincoln, Abraham. — He was born in Hardin County, Kentucky, February 12, 1809; removed with his father to Indiana in 1816; received a limited education; spent two years at school in Stafford County, Virginia; taught school and studied law for a time in Culpeper County, of that State; removed to Illinois in 1830, and turned his attention to agricultural pursuits; he served as a Captain of volunteers in the Black Hawk war; was at one time Postmaster in a small village; and he served four years in the Illinois Legislature, during which time he turned his attention again to the study of law, and settled at Springfield in the practice of his profession. He was a member of the National Convention which nominated General Taylor for President in 1848, and was a Representative in Congress, from Illinois, from 1847 to 1849, serving on the Committees on the Post-office and Post-roads, and on Expenses in the War Department. In 1858 he acquired distinction by stumping the State of Illinois, for the United States Senate, against S. A. Douglas; and in 1860 he was nominated by the Republican Party as their candidate for President of the United States, and was duly elected to that position for the term commencing the 4th of March, 1861. By the Baltimore Convention, held in 1864, he was nominated for re-election to the Presidency.

Lincoln, Enoch.—Born in Worcester, Massachusetts, December 28, 1788; and, after studying law, settled in Fryeburg, Maine, and afterwards removed to Paris. He was a member of the United States House of Representatives, from Massachusetts, from 1818 to 1820, and from 1821 to 1826 from the new State of Maine, when he was elected Governor of Maine, and re-elected in 1828. He published, while at Fryeburg, a poem, entitled "The Village;" he was also the author of some historical recollections of Maine. He died at Augusta, October 8, 1829.

Lincoln, Levi. — Born May 15, 1749, at Hingham, Massachusetts; graduated at Harvard College in 1772; and settled as a lawyer in Worcester, where he rose to distinction; was Judge of Probate; a State Senator in 1797; County Prosecutor in 1775; a State Councillor in 1806, 1810, and 1811; and he was a Representative in Congress, from 1799 to 1801; and during the administration of President Adams he wrote a series of political papers, called "Farmer's Letters." In 1801 he was appointed Attorney-General of the United States, and acted as Secretary of State until Mr. Madison reached Washington; and in 1807 was Lieutenant-Governor of Massachusetts; acting as Governor in 1809, after the death of Governor Sullivan. In 1811 he was appointed Associate Judge of the Supreme Court, but declined the office. He died at Worcester, Massachusetts, April 14, 1820, aged seventy-one years.

Lincoln, Levi.—He was born in Massachusetts; was a State Senator in 1812; a State Representative from 1814 to 1823, and two years Speaker; Lieutenant-Governor of Massachusetts in 1823; Judge of the Supreme Court of the State in 1824; Collector at Boston, from 1841 to 1843; a State Senator in 1844 and 1845, and President thereof; Mayor of Worcester in 1848; and Governor of Massachusetts, from 1825 to 1834; and from 1834 to 1841 was a Representative in Congress.

Lindley, James J. — Born at Mansfield, Ohio, January 1, 1822; went with his parents to Kentucky when a boy, and lived at Cynthiana several years; was a student in Woodville College, Ohio, for two years; studied law, and located at Monticello, Missouri, in 1846. In 1848 he was elected Circuit Attorney for eight counties, and re-elected in 1852. He was a Representative in the Thirty-third Congress, and was re-elected to the Thirty-fourth. He afterwards removed to Davenport, Iowa, and engaged in the practice of his profession.

Lindsley, William D.—He was born in Connecticut, and having removed to Ohio, was elected a Representative in Congress, from that State, from 1853 to 1855.

Linn, Archibald L.—He was born in New York; was a Representative in Congress, from that State, from 1841 to 1843; and was a member of the State Assembly, from Schenectady, in 1844.

Linn, James.—He graduated at Princeton College in 1769, and was a Representative in Congress, from New Jersey, from 1799 to 1801, when he was appointed, by President Jefferson, Supervisor of the Revenue. He also held the office, for many years, of Secretary of State of New Jersey. Died at Trenton, December 28, 1820.

Linn, John.—He was for many years a member of the New Jersey Assembly and a Representative in Congress, from New Jersey, of which State he was a native, from 1817 to 1821. Died, January 6, 1821.

Linn, Lewis F.—Born near Louisville, Kentucky, November 5, 1795. He was educated chiefly by an elder brother, and studied medicine. In 1809 he removed to Missouri; and in 1814 helped to fight the battles of his country; after successfully practising his profession, he was elected to the State Legislature in 1827; and in 1833 was elected a Senator in Congress; in which capacity he served until his death, which occurred at St. Genevieve, Missouri, October 3, 1843. He proved himself to be a man of remarkable abilities, identified himself throughout his whole career in Congress with the interests of the valley of the Mississippi, and when he died, many of the best men in the country eulogized him for his manifold virtues.

Litchfield, Elisha.—He was born in Canterbury, Connecticut, in 1795; served five years in the State Legislature, from Onondaga County; was Speaker in 1848; was many years a Justice of the Peace at Delphi, New York, and was a Representative in Congress, from New York, from 1821 to 1823, and again from 1823 to 1825. Died at Cazenovia, New York, August 4, 1859.

Little, Edward P.—He was born in Massachusetts in 1788, and was a Representative, in Congress, from that State, from 1852 to 1853. He was a State Representative from 1829 to 1834, and from 1835 to 1838; and Collector at Plymouth from 1853 to 1857.

Little, Peter.—He was born in Petersburg, Pennsylvania; removed to Maryland; and was elected a Representative in Congress, from that State, from 1811 to 1813, and was in the latter year appointed, by President Madison, Colonel of infantry; and again a Representative in Congress, from 1816 to 1829. Died, February 5, 1830, in Baltimore County, Maryland.

Littlefield, Nathaniel S.—Born in Wells, York County, Maine, September 20, 1804; received a common school education; studied and adopted the profession of law; was a member of the Maine Senate in 1837, 1838, and 1839; President of the same a part of the time; a Representative, from Maine, to the Twenty-seventh and Thirty-first Congresses; and a member of the Maine House of Representatives in 1854. Now devoted to his profession.

Littlejohn, De Witt C.—Was born in Bridgewater, Oneida County, New York, February 7, 1818; received a thorough academic education, and since 1839 has been largely engaged in the commerce of the lakes and canals, as well as in the manufacture of flour. He served as President of the village of Oswego, and when it became a city he became an Alderman, and was twice elected Mayor. He was seven times elected to the Assembly of New York, presiding as Speaker during five terms; and in 1862 he was elected a Representative, from New York, to the Thirty-eighth Congress, serving on the Committee on Roads and Canals, and as Chairman of the Committee on Revolutionary Pensions.

Livermore, Arthur.—Born in Londonderry, New Hampshire, July 26, 1776. He was a Judge of the Supreme Court of New Hampshire from 1799 to 1816; from 1825 to 1833 Judge of the Common Pleas; and a Representative in Congress from 1817 to 1821, and from 1823 to 1825. He died at Campton, New Hampshire, July 1, 1853.

Livermore, Edward S.—He was Judge of the Supreme Court of New Hampshire from 1797 to 1799; and a Representative in Congress, from Massachusetts, from 1807 to 1811. Died in 1832, aged eighty years.

Livermore, Samuel.—Born in Waltham, New Hampshire, in 1732; graduated at Princeton College in 1752; was Judge-Advocate of the Admiralty before the Revolution; subsequently Judge of the Superior Court of New Hampshire; and a Senator in Congress, from 1793 to 1801, when he resigned; and was President *pro tem.* of that body during two sessions. He died at Holderness, May, 1803.

Livingston, Edward.—Born at Claremont, Livingston Manor, New York, in 1764; graduated at Princeton College in 1781; studied law, and was admitted to the bar in 1785, and pursued his profession till 1795, when he was elected a Representative to Congress, from New York City, serving until 1802. He was then appointed United States Attorney for the District of New York, and was also Mayor of the city. Removing to New Orleans in 1804, he became eminent there as a lawyer; at the invasion of Louisiana he acted as the aid to General Jackson; was employed in negotiations for the exchange of prisoners after the war; and was elected a Representative, from Louisiana, in Congress, from 1823 to 1829, and as a Senator of the United States, from 1829 to 1831, when he was appointed by President Jackson Secretary of State, and in 1833 Minister to France. His "Penal Code" is considered a monument of his profound learning. He died at Rhinebeck, May 23, 1836.

Livingston, Henry Walter.—Was born in 1764; graduated at Yale College in 1786, and was educated to the law; he was secretary in 1792 to Mr. Morris, Ambassador to France; a Representative in Congress, from New York, from 1803 to 1807. He died at Livingston Manor, New York, December 22, 1810, aged forty-two.

Livingston, Robert Le Roy.—He was elected a Representative in Congress, from the Sixth Congressional District of New York, from 1809 to 1813 but resigned in 1812, when he was succeeded by T. P. Grosvenor; he was then appointed by President Madison Lieutenant-Colonel of infantry.

Lloyd, Edward.—He was at one time Governor of Maryland; a member of Congress from 1806 to 1809; and served as United States Senator, from Maryland, from 1819 to 1826, when he resigned. He was highly respected both in public and private life. He died June 2, 1834.

Lloyd, James.—He was a Senator in Congress, from Maryland, from 1797 to 1800, when he resigned.

Lloyd, James.—He was born in Boston, Massachusetts, in 1769; graduated at Harvard University in 1787; and devoted himself to mercantile pursuits, and resided in Russia a number of years. He devoted some attention to literature; was elected a member of the American Academy of Arts and Sciences; and received from his Alma Mater, in 1826, the degree of Doctor of Laws. He was a Senator in Congress, from Massachusetts, from 1808 to 1813, when he resigned, and again from 1822 to 1826, serving as Chairman of the Committees on Commerce, and Naval Affairs. His reputation was that of an able statesman and a wealthy and benevolent man. He died in New York City, April 5, 1831.

Loan, Benjamin F.—Born in Hardinsburg, Breckinridge County, Kentucky, in 1819; settled in Missouri in 1838, and adopted the legal profession. When the Rebellion broke out in 1861, he took an active part in military affairs, and was appointed a Brigadier-General; and in 1862 he was elected a Representative, from Missouri, to the Thirty-eighth Congress, serving on the Committee on Military Affairs. Was subsequently reported against by the Committee on Elections.

Locke, Francis.—Born in Rowan County, North Carolina, October 31, 1766. He was elected Judge of the Superior Court in 1803, and, having resigned, was chosen a Senator in Congress, for the years 1814 and 1815, from his native State, but appears not to have taken his seat. Died January, 1823.

Locke, John.—He was born in Hopkinton, Massachusetts, in 1764; graduated at Cambridge in 1792; was admitted to the bar in 1796, and opened an office in Ashby. He represented that town in the Legislature in 1804, 1805, 1813, and 1823. In 1820 he was a member of the Constitutional Convention of the State; and from 1823 to 1829 was a Representative in Congress, from the Worcester North District. In 1830 he was State Senator from Middlesex County; and in 1831 was a member of the Executive Council. He removed to Lowell in 1837, and thence, in 1849, to Boston, where he died, March 29, 1855.

Locke, Matthew.—Born in Rowan County, North Carolina, in 1730, and died in 1801. He was a member of the Congress at Halifax, in 1776, which formed the Constitution of North Carolina, and was a Representative in the Congress of the United States, from 1793 to 1799. He also served in the Legislature, and had four sons, at one time, in the Revolutionary war.

Lockhart, James.—He was born in New York, but removed to Indiana, and was elected a Representative in Congress, from 1851 to 1853. Died at Evansville, Indiana, September 7, 1857.

Logan, George.—Born at Stanton, near Philadelphia, September 9, 1753. He was educated at Edinburgh for the medical profession, but devoted a great portion of his time to agriculture; and was a member of the Legislature of Pennsylvania. In 1798 he embarked for Europe for the sole purpose of preventing a war between America and France, and prepared the way for a negotiation which terminated in peace. He was a Senator of the United States, from 1801 to 1807. He went to England in February, 1810, on the same peaceful mission which led him to France, but not with the same success. He was an active member of the Philosophical Society and the State Board of Agriculture; and in 1797 published "Experiments on Gypsum" and "Rotation of Crops." He died at Stanton, April 9, 1821.

Logan, Henry.—He was born in Pennsylvania, and was a Representative in Congress, from that State, from 1835 to 1839.

Logan, John A.—Born in Jackson County, Illinois; received a common school education; went with the army as a private in the war with Mexico, and was made Quartermaster of his regiment; in 1849 was elected County Clerk of Jackson County, but resigned; in 1850 studied law, and came to the bar in 1852, having graduated at the Louisville University; in 1852 was elected to the Illinois Legislature; in 1853 was appointed a Prosecuting Attorney; in 1856 was a Presidential Elector; was a second time elected to the Legislature; and in 1858 he was elected a Representative, from Illinois, to the Thirty-sixth Congress, serving as Chairman of the Committee on Unfinished Business; reelected to the Thirty-seventh Congress, and resigning, served as a Colonel in the Union army in 1861, and subsequently as a General.

Logan, William.—He was born in Harrodsburg, Kentucky, December 8, 1776; was a member of the State Constitutional Convention in 1799; studied law, and practised with success; was frequently in the Legislature, and officiated as Speaker; was twice chosen Judge of the Court of Appeals; was a Senator in Congress during the years 1819 and 1820; and died August 8, 1822.

Long, Alexander.—He was born in Greenville, Mercer County, Pennsylvania, December 24, 1816; was educated at Cary's Academy (now Farmer's College), Ohio; adopted the profession of law, practising in Cincinnati; was elected to the Ohio Legislature in 1848 and 1849, and in 1862 was elected a Representative, from Ohio, to the Thirty-eighth Congress, serving on the Committee of Claims. He was also a Delegate to the Chicago Convention of 1864.

Long, Edward H.—He was born in Maryland, and was a Representative in Congress, from that State, from 1845 to 1847.

Long, John.—Born in Loudon County, Virginia; was a farmer by profession; entered public life as a Senator in the Assembly, in 1815, and in 1821 was elected to Congress, as a Representative, from North Carolina, where he remained until 1829.

Longfellow, Stephen. — He was born in Gorham, Massachusetts, June 28, 1775; graduated at Harvard University in 1798; studied law, and was admitted to the bar in 1801; was for many years a leading politician and lawyer in Maine; and a member of the Hartford Convention in 1814, of which body, at the time of his death, he was the only surviving Delegate from Massachusetts. From 1817 to 1836 he was a member of the Corporation of Bowdoin College, from which institution he received the degree of LL.D.; he was also a member of the State Constitutional Convention of 1819; a Representative in the Maine Legislature in 1826; and a Representative in Congress, from Maine, from 1823 to 1825; and died at Portland, August 2, 1849.

Longnecker, Henry C. — Born in Allentown, Lehigh County, Pennsylvania, in 1825; graduated at Lafayette College; adopted the profession of law; served as a Lieutenant and also as Adjutant in the war with Mexico; was appointed District Attorney for Lehigh County on his return; and was elected a Representative, from Pennsylvania, to the Thirty-sixth Congress, serving as a member of the Committee on Military Affairs.

Longyear, John W. — He was born in Shandaken, Ulster County, New York, October 22, 1820; received a good academic education; removed to Michigan in 1844; studied law, and came to the bar in 1846; and was elected a Representative, from Michigan, to the Thirty-eighth Congress, serving on the Committee on Commerce, and as Chairman of the Committee on Expenditures on the Public Buildings.

Loomis, A.—He was a Representative in Congress, from Ohio, from 1837 to 1838.

Loomis, Arphaxad.—He was for three years a member of the Legislature of New York, from Herkimer County, and a Representative in Congress, from that State, from 1837 to 1839.

Loomis, Dwight. — Born in Columbia, Tolland County, Connecticut, July 27, 1821; received a common school education; spent the most of his youth on a farm, and taught school for about one year; commenced the study of law in 1844, and having finished his legal studies at New Haven, was admitted to the bar in 1847; since which time he has practised his profession at Rockville, Connecticut. In 1851 he was elected to the Connecticut Legislature; was a Delegate in 1856 to the "People's Convention" in Philadelphia; was a State Senator in 1857; and was elected a Representative, from Connecticut, to the Thirty-sixth Congress, serving as a member of the Committee on Mileage. Re-elected to the Thirty-seventh Congress, serving on the Committees on Elections, and on Agriculture.

Lord, Frederick W. — Born in Lyme, Connecticut, December 11, 1800; graduated at Yale College in 1821; was for two years Professor of Mathematics in Washington College; had charge for three years of an academy in the city of Baltimore; devoted himself, in Baltimore, for several years, to the study of medicine, and received a diploma from Yale College, in 1829; spent fifteen years in the practice of his profession at Sag Harbor, New York, when he retired; and was a Representative in Congress, from New York, from 1847 to 1849. He was also a Delegate to the Baltimore National Convention for nominating a President in 1840. Died at New York, May 24, 1860.

Love, James.—He was a Representative in Congress, from Kentucky, from 1833 to 1835.

Love, John.—He was a Representative in Congress, from Virginia, from 1807 to 1811.

Love, P. E.—Born near Dublin, Laurens County, Georgia, July 7, 1818; was educated at Franklin College; studied medicine and attended medical lectures in Philadelphia; relinquished that profession, and turned his attention to law, having been admitted to the bar in 1839; in 1843 he was chosen Solicitor-General for the Southern District of Georgia; in 1849 he was elected to the State Senate; in 1853 he was appointed a Judge for the Southern Circuit of Georgia; and was elected a Representative, from Georgia, to the Thirty-sixth

Congress, serving on the Committee on Expenses in the State Department.

Love, Thomas C.—He was a Representative in Congress, from New York, from 1835 to 1837.

Love, William C.—Born in Virginia, educated at the University of North Carolina, of which his father was steward; was a lawyer by profession, and a Representative in Congress, from North Carolina, from 1815 to 1817.

Lovejoy, Owen.—He was born in Albion, Kennebec County, Maine, January 6, 1811; labored on a farm until eighteen years of age; taught school, and thereby received the means for a college education, which he received at Bowdoin. He was a clergyman of the Congregational church at Princeton, Illinois, from 1838 to 1854, having resigned his pastoral duties to take a seat in the Illinois Legislature, in that year; and in 1856 he was elected a Representative, from that State, to the Thirty-fifth Congress; re-elected to the Thirty-sixth, Thirty-seventh, and the Thirty-eighth Congresses, serving on the Committees on Revolutionary Claims, and Public Lands, and as Chairman of the Committees on Agriculture, and for the District of Columbia, and also a member of the Committee on the Territories. Died in Brooklyn, New York, March 25, 1864.

Lovett, John.—He was born in Norwich, Connecticut; graduated at Yale College, and was a member of the New York Assembly in 1800 and 1801, and a Representative in Congress, from that State, from 1813 to 1814, and from 1815 to 1817. He died in 1818, in Ohio.

Lowell, Joshua A.—He was born in Thomaston, Maine, March 20, 1801; his educational advantages were limited, but he commenced active life by teaching school; he adopted the profession of law, having come to the bar in 1826; was a member of the Maine Legislature in 1826, 1831, 1832, 1833, 1835, and 1836; and a Representative in Congress, from Maine, from 1839 to 1843. He was also a Presidential Elector in 1844.

Lower, Christian.—He was a Representative in Congress, from Pennsylvania, from 1805 to 1807.

Lowndes, Thomas.—He was born in Charleston, South Carolina, in 1765; received a thorough education, and was one of the chivalrous citizens of his native city. He was a Representative in Congress, from South Carolina, from 1801 to 1805, and was distinguished for his talents. He died in Charleston, July 8, 1843.

Lowndes, William.—He was a native of Charleston, South Carolina, having been born February 7, 1782; educated by a private tutor; served in the State Legislature in 1806 and 1808; and was a Representative in Congress, from that State, from 1811 to 1822, when, from ill health, he resigned. In 1818 he was Chairman of the Committee of Ways and Means. He died while on a voyage, with his family, from Philadelphia to London, in the ship Moss, October 27, 1822, aged forty-two. He had a memory of uncommon power, was an eloquent debater, and stood in the first rank of American statesmen.

Lowrie, Walter.—He was a Senator in Congress, from Pennsylvania, from 1819 to 1825. He was afterwards Secretary of the United States Senate from 1825 to 1836.

Loyall, George.—Born in Norfolk, Virginia, May 29, 1789; graduated at William and Mary College in 1808. In 1815 he visited England, and on his return in 1817, was elected a member of the House of Delegates of Virginia, and served ten years. In 1829 was a member of the Convention to amend the State Constitution, and from 1831 to 1837 he was a Representative in Congress. In 1837 he was appointed Navy Agent at Norfolk, and with the exception of two years, he occupied that position until the breaking out of the Rebellion.

Lucas, Edward.—He was born in Virginia, and was a Representative in Congress, from that State, from 1833 to 1837. He was subsequently appointed Government Superintendent at Harper's Ferry, where he died March 4, 1858.

Lucas, John B. C.—He was born in Normandy, France, in 1762; was educated at the University of Caen, where he graduated as Doctor of Civil and Common Law in 1782. He practised his profession in his native country two years, and then emigrated to the United States, and settled on a farm near Pittsburg, Pennsylvania, where, in connection with agricultural pursuits, he devoted himself to acquiring the English language, and making himself acquainted with the history, constitution, and laws of his adopted country. He soon gained the confidence of the people, and in 1792 was elected to the Legislature of Pennsylvania, and served as a Judge of the Court of Common Pleas, for his district. In 1802 he was elected a Representative in Congress, and re-elected in 1804. In 1805 he was appointed, by President Jefferson, Judge of the United States Court in Upper Louisiana, when he resigned his seat in Congress, and removed to St. Louis. He was also Commissioner of Land Titles in that Territory. He held the office of Judge until 1820, when he retired to private life, on a farm adjoining the city of St. Louis, where he died in September, 1842.

Lucas, William.—He was born in Virginia, and was a Representative in Congress, from that State, from 1839 to 1841, and for a second term, from 1843 to 1845.

Lumpkin, John H.—He was born in Oglethorpe County, Georgia, June 13, 1812; he was educated at Franklin and Yale Colleges; served for a time as Secretary in the Executive Department of Georgia; studied law, and was admitted to the bar in 1834; was elected to the State Legislature in 1853; in 1838 he was Solicitor-General of the Cherokee Circuit; and he was a Representative in Congress, from Georgia, from 1843 to 1849, and re-elected to the Thirty-fourth Congress. He also held the office, for three years, of Judge of the Cherokee Circuit Court, and that of Judge of the Supreme Court of the State. Died in Rome, Georgia, in 1860.

Lumpkin, Wilson.—Born in Pittsylvania County, Virginia, January 14, 1783. He received a common school education, and while engaged as a copying clerk, in his father's office, studied law. Soon after attaining the age of twenty-one, he was sent to the State Legislature, and continued in that capacity a number of years. He was twice elected Governor of Georgia. In 1823 he was appointed, by President Monroe, to mark out the boundary line between Georgia and Florida; and by President Jackson, was appointed a Commissioner, under the Cherokee treaty of 1835. He was also a member of the Board of Public Works. He served in the Federal House of Representatives, from 1815 to 1817, and from 1827 to 1831; and was a Senator in Congress from 1837 to 1841.

Lyle, Aaron.—He was a soldier in the Revolution, and a Representative in Congress, from Pennsylvania, from 1809 to 1817. Died September 24, 1825.

Lyman, J. S.—He was born in Hampden, Massachusetts, and was a Representative in Congress, from New York, from 1819 to 1821.

Lyman, Samuel.—He was a graduate of Yale College in 1770; a Representative in Congress, from Massachusetts, from 1795 to 1800. From 1786 to 1788 he served in the Legislature, and from 1790 to 1793 as State Senator.

Lyman, William.—A native of Northampton, Massachusetts; graduated at Yale College in 1776, and was Brigadier-General of militia. He was a Representative in Congress, from 1793 to 1797; and appointed Consul to London in 1805, where he died, October, 1811, aged about fifty-eight years. He was also a member of the Legislature in 1787, and a State Senator in 1789.

Lynde, William P.—He was a Representative in Congress, from Wisconsin, from 1848 to 1849.

Lyon, Asa.—Was a native of Connecticut; a graduate of Dartmouth College in 1790, and shortly after his graduation, removed to South Hero, Vermont. He was appointed Chief Judge of Grand Isle County, in 1805, 1806, 1808, and 1813. He was elected a Representative, from South Hero, in 1802, 1804, 1805, 1806, and 1808, and from Grand Isle in 1810, 1811, 1812, 1813, and 1814. He was a member of the Executive Council in 1808; and was elected a member of Congress, from 1815 to 1817. He was a member of the Corporation of the University of Vermont, from 1814 to 1821 inclusive. He is said to have been a second cousin of Robert Burns, the Scotch poet. He was for many years, and until his death, an able preacher of the Gospel. Although never regularly installed, he preferred the Calvinistic form of worship. He was distinguished for his ripe scholarship and eloquence. By rigid economy and prudence, he amassed wealth, and died at South Hero, April 4, 1841. His published sermons and patriotic addresses indicate a high order of talent, and an intimate acquaintance with modern and classic literature.

Lyon, Caleb, of Lyonsdale.—The grandfather of this gentleman, who bore the same name, was a Lieutenant of the Massachusetts militia, and was wounded at Bunker Hill ; and his father, also named Caleb, was a member of the New York Legislature, and an ardent friend of De Witt Clinton. He was born in Lyonsdale, New York, December 7, 1822; graduated at the University of Vermont, in 1841; travelled extensively in Europe; was appointed by President Polk, Consul at Shanghai, China; on his return he visited Mexico, Brazil, Chili, Peru, the Sandwich Islands, and California, and was Secretary of the Convention called in 1849 to form a Constitution, and designed the coat of arms for the Golden State. He made a second visit to Europe, and extended his travels to Egypt and the Holy Land. From his native State, he was elected to the Assembly, but on the question of enlarging the Erie Canal, which he favored, he resigned, and was, during the same year, elected to the State Senate as its youngest member, and for his services he was presented by his brother Senators, in the State Capitol, with a service of plate; and was the author of the bill for purchasing Washington's headquarters at Newburg, by the State; and was subsequently elected a Representative in the Thirty-third Congress, from New York. While abroad he was identified with the Kosta affair as the friend of Captain Duncan N. Ingraham. He writes poetry, lectures on the East, translates Oriental literature, and is a member of several Historical Societies, with a passion for archæologic and antiquarian lore. The title of LL.D. has been conferred upon him by the University of Vermont. In February, 1864, he was appointed, by President Lincoln, Governor of Idaho.

Lyon, Chittenden.—He was a Representative in Congress, from Kentucky, from 1827 to 1835, and died in Caldwell County, Kentucky, in November, 1842.

Lyon, Francis S.—He was born in North Carolina, and having settled in Alabama, was elected a Representative in Congress, from 1835 to 1839.

Lyon, Lucius.—He was born in Vermont, but emigrated to Michigan when quite a young man; devoted himself for a number of years to the business of surveying the wild lands of the Territory; was a Delegate in Congress, from that Territory, during the years 1833, 1834, and 1835; and a Senator in Congress, from the State of Michigan, from 1836 to 1840; and a Representative in Congress, from 1843 to 1845. His last public position was that of Surveyor-General in the Northwest. Died at Detroit, September 25, 1851.

Lyon, Matthew.—He was born in Wicklow County, Ireland, in 1746, and having emigrated to this country when thirteen years of age, participated to some extent in the Revolutionary struggle, having, in 1777, been appointed temporary Paymaster of the Northern army, and in 1778 Deputy Secretary of the Governor of Vermont, and at the same time Clerk of the Court of Confiscation. He settled in Vermont after the war, and was elected a member of the State Legislature, in 1799 and the three following years. In 1783 he founded the town of Fairhaven, where he built saw-mills, grist-mills, established a forge or iron foundry, manufactured paper from basswood, and established a newspaper, called The Farmers' Library. He served that town in the Legislature ten years. In 1786 he was Assistant Judge of Rutland County. He was a Representative in Congress, from Vermont, from 1799 to 1801, and it was during his first term that he had a personal difficulty, on the floor of Congress, with Roger Griswold, of Connecticut, when an unsuccessful effort was made to have him expelled. The fact of his giving the vote that made Jefferson President, is well known. At the end of his second term as a Representative, from Vermont, he removed to Kentucky, served two years in the Legislature of that State, and was a Representative in Congress, from that State, from 1803 to 1811. After his final retirement from Congress, and on November 13, 1811, the Speaker of the House of Representatives presented a petition from him, setting forth that he had, many years before, been prosecuted and convicted under the sedition law (see "State Trials of the United States"); that he had suffered imprisonment, and been made to pay the sum of $1060.90, and that he wished to have the money refunded to him. On July 4, 1840, a law was passed, paying to his heirs the specified sum, with interest from February, 1799. It was while in prison at Vergennes, that he was elected to Congress, from Vermont, and at the close of his services in Congress, from Kentucky, he was employed to build gunboats for the war, but became bankrupt from the speculation. In 1820 he was appointed a Factor among the Cherokee Indians in Arkansas; when that Territory was organized, he was elected the first Delegate to Congress, but did not live to take his seat, having died at Spadra Bluff, Arkansas, August 1, 1822.

Lytle, Robert T.—He was distinguished as a public speaker, and was a member of Congress, from Ohio, from 1833 to 1835. He died in New Orleans, December 21, 1839.

Mace, Daniel.—Was a native of Ross County, Ohio; he commenced life as a merchant, in Warren County, Indiana, but subsequently became a successful lawyer. He was a Representative in Congress, from Indiana, from 1851 to 1855.

Machir, James.—He was a Representative in Congress, from Virginia, from 1797 to 1799. Died June 25, 1827.

Maclay, Samuel.—He was a Representative in Congress, from Pennsylvania, from 1795 to 1798, and a Senator in Congress, from 1803 to 1808, when he resigned.

Maclay, William.—He was a Senator in Congress, from Pennsylvania, from 1789 to 1791, and died in April, 1804.

Maclay, William.—He was a native of Pennsylvania; held the offices of County Commissioner and Associate Judge; was a member of the Assembly; and a Representative in Congress, from Pennsylvania, from 1815 to 1817, and again from 1817 to 1819. Died January 4, 1825, aged fifty-nine years.

Maclay, William B.—Born in New York City in 1815; graduated at the University of New York, where he subsequently officiated for a time as Professor of Latin; he was also a Trustee, as well as Secretary of the University; he adopted the profession of the law; and in 1836 he was associate editor of the New York Quarterly Magazine. He was also an active member of the Legislature of New York for several years, and was elected a Representative in Congress, from that State, in 1843; was re-elected in 1845, 1847, and also in 1857, serving generally on important committees. He was re-elected a Representative to the Thirty-sixth Congress.

Maclay, William P.—He was born in Northumberland County, Pennsylvania, and was a Representative in Congress, from that State, from 1816 to 1821.

Macon, Nathaniel.—He was born in Warren County, North Carolina, in 1757. His early youth was marked by diligence in the acquisition of knowledge, and he was sent to Princeton College to complete his education; but the troubles of the Revolution closed the halls of that institution, and he returned home and volunteered as a private in a company commanded by his brother, having refused a higher position. While in the army, he was elected a member of the General Assembly, in which he served for several years. In 1791 he was elected a Representative in Congress, and continued a member of that body until transferred to the United States Senate, in 1815, where he served until 1828. From 1801 to 1805 he was Speaker of the House, and from 1825 to 1828 he was President *pro tem.* of the Senate. He was for thirty-seven years a member of the House or Senate, and was called the Father of the House, having served a longer time in that body than any other man. In 1828 his native State, in honor of his services, named a county for him. He afterwards returned to the General Assembly, and in 1835 was President of the

Constitutional Convention of the State. He died suddenly, at his residence, June 29, 1837.

Macy, John B.—He was a Representative in Congress, from Wisconsin, from 1853 to 1855. He resided at Fond du Lac, and was lost, September 24, by the burning of the steamboat Niagara, on Lake Michigan.

Madison, James.—He was born on the Rappahannock River, in Virginia, March 16, 1751; and, after due preparation, he entered Princeton College in 1769, and graduated in 1771, going through the junior and senior studies in one year. He remained at the College until 1772, for the purpose of studying Hebrew. In 1776 he was sent to the General Assembly, and in 1778 was a member of the Executive Council; from 1779 to 1785 he was a member of the Continental Congress, and was chosen a second time in 1786; in 1789 he was a member of the Convention at Philadelphia which formed the Federal Constitution, and he was a Representative in Congress, under the Constitution, from 1789 to 1797. In 1798 he went again into the Assembly, and in 1800 was an Elector for President. In 1801 he was Secretary of State of the United States, which office he held until 1809, when he was elected President of the United States, and served two entire terms. After leaving the Executive chair, he retired to private life on his estate, known as Montpelier. He was subsequently a Visitor and Rector of the University of Virginia; and in 1829 a member of the State Convention, which was the last public position he held. He was one of the contributors to the Federalist, and his collected state papers and miscellaneous writings have been published in six volumes. He died at Montpelier, Orange County, Virginia, June 28, 1836.

Magee, John.—He was born in New York, and was a Representative in Congress, from that State, from 1827 to 1831.

Magruder, Allan B.—A native of Kentucky, and a lawyer by profession. He removed to Louisiana, and in 1805 published "Reflections on the Cession of Louisiana to the United States;" and was a Senator in Congress, from that State, from 1812 to 1813. He had collected materials for a general history of the Indians. He died at Opelousas, Louisiana, in April, 1822.

Magruder, Patrick.—He was born in Montgomery County, Maryland, in 1768; educated at Princeton College; adopted the profession of law; and was a Representative in Congress, from Maryland, from 1805 to 1807; and was Clerk of the United States House of Representatives, from 1807 to 1815. He died in Petersburg, Virginia, in 1819 or 1820.

Malbone, Francis.—He was a Senator in Congress, from Rhode Island, in 1809, having previously been a Representative in Congress, from that State, from 1793 to 1797. He died June 4, 1809.

Mallary, Rollin C.—He was born in New Haven, Connecticut, in 1784, and died in Baltimore, April 16, 1831. He represented the State of Vermont in Congress, from 1819 to 1831, and took an active part in all matters appertaining to commerce as chairman of an important committee. He was held in the highest estimation both for his public acts and private virtues.

Mallory, Francis.—He was born in Virginia, and was a Representative in Congress, from that State, from 1837 to 1839, and again from 1841 to 1843. Died at Norfolk, March 26, 1860.

Mallory, Meredith.—Born in Connecticut, and was a Representative in Congress, from New York, from 1839 to 1841.

Mallory, Robert.—He was born in Madison County, Virginia, November 15, 1815; graduated at the University of Virginia in 1827; removed to Kentucky in 1839, where he has devoted the most of his life to agricultural pursuits; and he was elected a Representative, from Kentucky, to the Thirty-sixth Congress, serving as a member of the Committee on Roads and Canals; re-elected to the Thirty-seventh Congress, serving as Chairman of the Committee on Roads and Canals; and also elected to the Thirty-eighth Congress, serving on the Committee of Ways and Means.

Mallory, Stephen R.—He was a Senator in Congress, from Florida, having been elected in 1851, serving continuously, by re-election, until 1861. He was Chairman of the Committee on Naval Affairs, and a member of the Committee on Claims. He resigned in February, 1861, and took part in the Rebellion as Secretary of the Rebel Navy.

Mangum, Willie P.—Born in Orange County, North Carolina, in 1792, and graduated at the University of that State in 1815. He studied law, rose to eminence in his profession, entered into politics, and was elected to the House of Commons in 1818. In 1819 he was elected a Judge of the Superior Court; and from 1823 to 1826, served as a Representative in Congress. He was elected a United States Senator in 1831, re-elected in 1841, and for a third term in 1848, serving, on one occasion, as President, *pro tem.*, of that body. In 1837 he received eleven electoral votes for President of the United States; and, during the administration of President Tyler, was President of the United States Senate. He subsequently lived in retirement at his home in North Carolina. Died September 14, 1861.

Mann, Abijah, Jr.—Born at Fairfield, Herkimer County, New York, September 24, 1793; he received a good common school education, and became a teacher in the district school in Oneida County; he was afterwards a merchant, Postmaster, and Justice of the Peace; and elected to the Legislature in 1827, serving by re-elections until 1830. He was a Representative in Congress, from 1833 to 1837, during which time he served on several committees, being once Chairman of the Committee on Rules and Orders of the House. In 1837, on returning to his native county, he was again re-elected to the Legislature. He afterwards removed to New York City, and declined all official employments.

Mann, Horace.—Born in Franklin, Norfolk County, Massachusetts, May 4, 1796. He was, to some degree, self-educated, but graduated at Brown University in 1819, where he subsequently held the position of Tutor of Latin and Greek; he studied law at Litchfield, Connecticut, and while counsellor-at-law, in Dedham, Massachusetts, where he settled in 1826, was elected to the State Legislature. He removed to Boston in 1834, where he was elected to the State Senate, chosen President of that body, and also President of the Massachusetts Board of Education, which he was foremost in founding; he also rendered important services in behalf of the Normal Schools of Massachusetts, and was elected a member of Congress, from 1848 to 1853. After that time he continued to be devoted to matters connected with education, having been appointed President of Antioch College and the Northwestern Christian University at Indianapolis. He wrote much and well, and is remembered as a benefactor to his race. Died at Yellow Springs, Ohio, August 2, 1859.

Mann, Job.—Born in Bethel Township, Bedford County, Pennsylvania, March 31, 1795; received a common school education; in 1816 was appointed Clerk to a board of county commissioners; two years afterwards he was appointed Register, Recorder, and Clerk, for the courts of Bedford County, all of which positions he continued to hold until 1835, when he was elected a Representative in Congress, where he served one term. In 1839 he was admitted to the bar; in 1842 was appointed State Treasurer, which office he held for three terms; and in 1847 was again elected to Congress, where he served until 1851, declining a re-election.

Mann, Joel K.—He was born in Pennsylvania in 1780, and was a Representative in Congress, from that State, from 1831 to 1835. He died in Montgomery County, Pennsylvania, September 4, 1857.

Manning, Richard I.—He was born in Sumter District, South Carolina, May 1, 1789; graduated at the State College at Columbia in 1811; commanded a volunteer company in the war of 1812; was frequently in the upper and lower House of the State Legislature; was Governor of South Carolina for two years from 1824; a Representative in Congress, from 1834 to 1836; and died May 1, 1836, at Philadelphia, before the expiration of his term, very suddenly, while seated at the table with his family. He was greatly respected for his talents and virtues, Mr. Preston and Mr. Pinckney both eulogizing him in Congress.

Marable, John H.—He was born in Brunswick County, Virginia, and was a Representative in Congress, from Tennessee, from 1825 to 1829.

Marchand, Albert G.—He was a Representative in Congress, from Pennsylvania, from 1839 to 1843, and died at his residence, in Greensburg, Pennsylvania, February 5, 1848.

Marchand, David.—He was born in Westmoreland County, Pennsylvania, and was a Representative in Congress, from that State, from 1817 to 1821.

Marcy, Daniel.—Born in New Hampshire, November 7, 1809; became a sailor when twelve years of age, and at twenty was master of a ship; in 1853 and 1854 he was a member of the New Hampshire Legislature; in 1856 and 1857 of the State Senate; was subsequently engaged in the mercantile and ship-building business; and was elected a Representative, from New Hampshire, to the Thirty-eighth Congress, serving on the Committees on Revolutionary Pensions, and on Expenditures in the Navy Department.

Marcy, William Larned.—He was born in Sturbridge, Worcester County, Massachusetts, in 1786, and died in Ballston Spa, New York, July 4, 1857. He graduated at Brown University in 1808; taught school for awhile in Newport, Rhode Island; studied law, and commenced practice in Troy, New York. He was appointed Recorder of that city in 1816; made Comptroller in 1823, and removed to Albany. In 1829 he was appointed Judge of the Supreme Court of the State. He was elected to the United States Senate in 1831. Elected Governor of New York in 1832, and re-elected in 1834. He was Secretary of War, under President Polk, from 1845 to 1849; and Secretary of State, under President Pierce, from 1853 to 1857. He was a hard-working, careful, plain man, and a good scholar. As a statesman and diplomatist, he had the reputation of displaying both judgment and skill; but his crowning virtue was his incorruptible integrity.

Mardis, Samuel W.—Born in Alabama in 1801, and died at Talladega, in that State, November 14, 1837. He was a Representative in Congress, from Alabama, from 1831 to 1835, and was much respected for his manly virtues.

Marion, Robert.—He was a native of South Carolina, and a Representative in Congress, from that State, from 1805 to 1810.

Markell, Henry.—He was born in Montgomery County, New York, and was a Representative in Congress, from New York, from 1825 to 1829.

Markell, Jacob.—He was a Representative in Congress, from New York, from 1813 to 1815.

Markley, Philip S.—He was born in Montgomery County, Pennsylvania, and was a Representative in Congress, from Pennsylvania, from 1823 to 1827, and was in the latter year appointed Naval Officer for the Port of Philadelphia.

Marks, William.—Was a Senator in Congress, from Pennsylvania, from 1825 to 1831.

Marr, Alem.—He graduated at Princeton College in 1807; was a Representative in Congress, from Pennsylvania, from 1829 to 1831.

Marr, George W. L.—He was a Representative in Congress, from Tennessee, from 1817 to 1819.

Marrow, John.—He was a Representative in Congress, from Virginia, from 1805 to 1809.

Marsh, Charles.—Born at Lebanon, Connecticut, July 10, 1765, but with his father's family removed to Vermont, before the Revolution. He graduated at Dartmouth College in 1786, studied law, and commenced practice in Woodstock, Vermont. He was for fifty years devoted to his profession, and for a long time at the head of the bar in the State. He served as a member of Congress, from 1815 to 1817, and while in Washington became identified with the American Colonization Society as one of its founders. He acquired great popularity as a patron of benevolent societies generally, and was a highly influential and useful citizen. Died at Woodstock, Vermont, January 11, 1849. The degree of LL. D. was conferred upon him by Dartmouth College.

Marsh, George P. — Born in Woodstock, Vermont, March 15, 1801; was educated at Dartmouth College, where he graduated in 1820. He afterwards removed to Burlington, Vermont, where he commenced the study of the law; and afterwards made that place his home. After his admission to the bar, he came into an extensive practice, and devoted much of his time to politics. He was a member of the State Legislature in 1835, and in 1842 he took his seat in the United States House of Representatives, which he continued to occupy until he was sent as Resident Minister to Turkey, in 1849, by President Taylor. At this post he rendered essential service to the cause of civil and religious toleration in the Turkish Empire. He was also charged with a special mission to Greece in 1852. He is well known as an author and a scholar. He has devoted much attention to the languages and literature of the North of Europe, and his sympathies appear to be with the Goths, whose presence he traces in whatever is great and peculiar in the character of the founders of New England. In a work entitled "The Goths in New England," he has contrasted the Gothic and Roman characters, which he appears to regard as the great antagonistic principles of society at the present day. He is also the author of a grammar of the old Northern or Icelandic language, and of various essays, literary and historical, relating to the Goths and their connections with America. He is the author of an interesting work on the Camel, also of a work on the English Language, which occupies a very high rank, and his miscellaneous published addresses and speeches are quite numerous. After his return from Turkey, he performed the duties of Commissioner of Railroads for the State of Vermont. His library is said to be one of the finest in this country, rich beyond compare in Scandinavian literature. In 1861 he was appointed, by President Lincoln, Minister to Sardinia.

Marshall, Alexander K. — He was born in Kentucky, and was a Representative in Congress, from that State, from 1855 to 1857.

Marshall, Alfred. — He served four years in the Maine Legislature, viz., 1827, 1828, 1834, and 1835; was a Representative in Congress, from Maine, from 1841 to 1843, acting as a member of the Committee on the Militia; and from 1846 to 1849 he was Collector at Belfast. He was also for some years a General of the State militia.

Marshall, Edward C.—He was born in Kentucky, and was a Representative in Congress, from California, from 1851 to 1853.

Marshall, Humphrey.—He was among the earliest pioneers to Kentucky, having gone there in 1780; he was a member of the State Convention in 1787; served for many years in the State Legislature; and was a Senator in Congress, from 1795 to 1801. He was the author of the first published History of Kentucky, and died at an advanced age.

Marshall, Humphrey.—Born at Frankfort, Kentucky, January 13, 1812. He graduated at the West Point Academy, but resigned his military commission of Lieutenant, and studied law, which he practised with success. During the ten years preceding the Mexican war, and while devoting himself to his profession in Louisville, he took an active part in the military affairs of the State as Captain, Major, and Lieutenant-Colonel; he served in the Mexican war as Colonel of cavalry, fighting at Buena Vista, and leading the charge of the Kentucky volunteers; in 1847, after declining several important nominations, he retired to a farm; he was elected to Congress in 1849, as a Representative, and re-elected in 1851; he was appointed by President Fillmore Commissioner to China, which was immediately raised to a first-class mission; on his return he was elected a Representative in the Thirty-fourth Congress; in 1856 he was a member of the American National Council held in New York, where he caused to be thrown off all secrecy in the politics of his party; and in 1857 he was re-elected to Congress, serving as a member of the Committee on Military Affairs. He took part in the Rebellion of 1861 as a General of volunteers.

Marshall, John.—He was born in Fauquier County, Virginia, September 24, 1755, and was the eldest of fifteen children. He had some classical education in his youth, but his opportunities for learning were limited, and he never entered college; his father, Thomas Marshall, having been a poor man, but possessed of superior talents. At the commencement of the American war, he espoused it with ardor; in 1776 he was appointed Lieutenant, and in 1777 promoted to the rank of Captain. In 1780 he was admitted to the bar, and in 1781 resigned his commission, and entered upon the practice of his profession, soon rising to distinction. He was a member of the Virginia Convention to ratify the Constitution of the United States, and as such produced a deep impression by his logic and eloquence. He also entered the Legislature of Virginia, where he was a leader. President Washington invited him to become Attorney-General, and offered him the mission to France, after Mr. Monroe's return, both of which honors he declined. President Adams appointed him an Envoy to France, with Pickering and Gerry, but they were not accredited, and he returned to the United States in 1798. He was a Representative in Congress in 1799; in 1800 he was appointed Secretary of War; soon afterwards Secretary of State; and, January 31, 1801, upon the nomination of President Adams, was confirmed as Chief Justice of the Supreme Court of the United States. He wrote a "Life of George Washington," and a "History of the American Colonies." He died in Philadelphia, July 6, 1835. As a Judge, he was the most illustrious in America, and for his public services was ranked by many with Washington. He was the object of universal affection, respect, and confidence, and in every particular one of the greatest and best of men.

Marshall, S. S.—He was born in Illinois; educated at Cumberland College, Kentucky; studied law, and devoted himself to its practice in his native State. He was elected to the State Legislature in 1846; by the Legislature he was elected State Attorney, serving two years; in 1851 he was elected a Judge of the Circuit Court, in which position he remained until 1854; and having been elected to the Thirty-fourth Congress, was re-elected to the Thirty-fifth, and was Chairman of the Committee on Claims. He was also a Delegate to the Chicago Convention of 1864.

Marshall, Thomas A.—He was born near Versailles, Kentucky, January 15, 1794; graduated at Yale College in 1815; studied law, and entered upon the practice in 1816; and he was a Representative in Congress, from Kentucky, from 1831 to 1835. He has been a Judge and Chief Justice of the Court of Appeals of Kentucky for about twenty years; and a Professor of Law in the Transylvania College.

Marshall, Thomas F.—He was a native of Kentucky; Judge of the Louisville Circuit Court; and a Representative in Congress, from Kentucky, from 1841 to 1843. He died near Versailles, Woodford County, Kentucky, September 22, 1864, in the sixty-fourth year of his age.

Marston, Gilman.—Born in New Hampshire, and was elected a Representative, from New Hampshire, to the Thirty-sixth Congress, serving as a member of the Committee on Elections. During the Rebellion of 1861 he served as the Colonel of a New Hampshire regiment, retaining his seat in Congress.

Martin, Alexander.—Born in Guilford County, North Carolina, and died in November, 1807. He was educated at Princeton College, and devoted much attention to the pursuits of literature. He was a member of the Colonial Assembly, and Colonel of a regiment in the Continental line, having been at the battles of Brandywine and Germantown. He was subsequently in the State Senate, and was elected Speaker; he was elected Governor of North Carolina in 1782, and again in 1789, and was a member of the Convention which framed the Constitution of the United States. From 1793 to 1799 he was United States Senator; also President of the Senate. In 1793 the degree of Doctor of Laws was conferred on him by Princeton College, and at the time of his death he was a Trustee of the University of North Carolina.

Martin, Barclay.—He was born

in South Carolina, and was a Representative in Congress, from Tennessee, from 1845 to 1847.

Martin, Charles D.—Born in Ohio, and was elected a Representative, from that State, to the Thirty-sixth Congress, serving on the Committee on Invalid Pensions.

Martin, Elbert S.—Born in Virginia, and elected a Representative, from that State, to the Thirty-sixth Congress, serving as a member of the Committee on Expenditures in the Post-office Department.

Martin, Frederick S.—He was born in Rutland County, Vermont, April 25, 1794; after spending his early life as a sailor on Lake Champlain and at sea, he settled at Olean, New York, as a hotel-keeper and merchant; in 1830 he was appointed Postmaster at that place; he served three years in the State Legislature; and was a Representative in Congress, from New York, from 1851 to 1853.

Martin, John P.—Born in Lee County, Virginia, October 11, 1811; removed to Kentucky in 1828; in 1841 was elected to the Legislature of that State, and re-elected the following year; and he was a Representative in Congress, from Kentucky, from 1845 to 1847. In 1857 he was elected to the Senate of Kentucky, which was his last public position.

Martin, Joshua L.—He was a member of Congress, from Alabama, from 1835 to 1839, and from 1845 to 1847 Governor of that State. He died at Tuscaloosa, November 2, 1856.

Martin, Morgan L.—He was born in New York, and was a Delegate to Congress, from the Territory of Wisconsin, from 1845 to 1847.

Martin, Robert N.—He was born in Dorchester County, Maryland, and was a Representative in Congress, from Maryland, from 1825 to 1827.

Martin, William D.—He was a Judge of the Court of Common Pleas, and a Representative in Congress, from South Carolina, from 1827 to 1833. He was distinguished for his talents and public usefulness. He retired to bed slightly indisposed, and was found dead in the morning. He died at Charleston, November 17, 1833, aged forty-five years.

Martindale, Henry C.—He was born in Berkshire County, Massachusetts, and was a Representative in Congress, from New York, from 1823 to 1831, and again from 1833 to 1835.

Marvin, Dudley.—Was a native of Lyme, Connecticut, from which place he removed to Canandaigua, New York, in 1807. He was admitted to the bar, and commenced the practice of law in 1811, and soon attained eminence in his profession. He was a Representative in Congress, from 1823 to 1829. In 1844 he removed to Ripley, Chautauque County, and was again elected to Congress, serving from 1847 to 1849. He died at Ripley, New York, June 25, 1852, aged sixty-five years.

Marvin, James M.—Born in Ballston, Saratoga County, New York, February 27, 1809; spent a portion of his boyhood on a farm, but received a good education. In 1846 he was elected to the House of Assembly; was a County Supervisor for three terms; is proprietor of one of the large Saratoga hotels, and has chiefly been engaged for years past in taking care of a large estate. In 1862 he was elected a Representative, from New York, to the Thirty-eighth Congress, serving on the Committee on Territories.

Marvin, Richard P.—He was born in New York, served in the Assembly of that State, from Chautauque County, in 1836, and was a Representative in Congress, from New York, from 1837 to 1841.

Mason, Armistead L.—Born in Loudon County, Virginia, in 1785, and educated at William and Mary College; was a farmer by occupation, and a Colonel in the war of 1812; and a United States Senator, from 1816 to 1817. He fell in the memorable duel with Colonel McCarty, February 6, 1819.

Mason, James B.—He was a Representative in Congress, from Rhode Island, from 1815 to 1819.

Mason, James M.—Born on Analoston Island, Fairfax County, Virginia, November 3, 1798. He received a good education, and graduated at the University of Pennsylvania in 1818; he studied law at the College of William and Mary, and obtained a license to practise in 1820; in 1826 he was elected to the House of Delegates, and twice re-elected; he was a Representative in Congress, from 1837 to 1839; in 1847 he was elected a Senator in Congress, in the place of Senator Pennypacker, and re-elected in 1849, in which position he continued until 1861, having for several sessions been Chairman of the Committee on Foreign Relations. He took part in the Rebellion of 1861; went to England as a Minister of the Rebel government, was captured by the San Jacinto, imprisoned in Fort Warren, and after his release took up his residence in Europe. He was expelled from the Senate in July, 1861.

Mason, Jeremiah.—Born at Lebanon, Connecticut, April 27, 1768, and died at Boston, November 14, 1848. Destined for professional life, he entered Yale College, and after graduating in 1788, entered upon the study of law, and acquired the reputation of being profoundly learned in common law. He went to Vermont, and was admitted to the bar of that State, but subsequently removed to Portsmouth, New Hampshire, where he became the friend of Daniel Webster, who always spoke of him in extravagant terms of praise. In 1802 he was appointed Attorney-General of the State, and from 1813 to 1817, was a Senator in Congress, having resigned for the purpose of devoting himself to his profession. He removed to Boston in 1832, and on reaching the age of seventy he left the bar, though he was consulted as chamber-counsel to the close of his life.

Mason, John C.—He was born in Kentucky, and elected a Representative, from that State, to the Thirty-fifth Congress, and is Chairman of the Committee on Accounts.

Mason, John Thomson.—Born at Montpelier, Washington County, Maryland, in May, 1815; graduated at Princeton College in 1836; read law in Hagerstown, and was admitted to the bar in 1838; the same year was elected a member of the Legislature of Maryland, and re-elected in 1839. He was a Representative in Congress, from 1841 to 1843, being at that time the youngest man in Congress. In 1851 he was elected by the people, under the new Constitution of the State, a Judge of the Court of Appeals, which position he filled till 1857, when he resigned, and was appointed Collector of the port of Baltimore.

Mason, John Y.—He was born at Greensville, Sussex County, Virginia, April 18, 1799; graduated at the University of North Carolina in 1816, from which institution he received the degree of LL.D.; adopted the profession of law, and was a Federal Judge of the Eastern District Court of Virginia; Judge also of the General Court of Virginia; served about ten years in the State Legislature; he was a Representative in Congress, from Virginia, from 1831 to 1837; was a Delegate to the Conventions of 1828 and 1849 for revising the State Constitution; a member of President Tyler's cabinet, as Secretary of the Navy; a member of President Polk's cabinet, first as Attorney-General, and secondly as Secretary of the Navy; was subsequently President of the James River and Kanawha Company; and was appointed, by President Pierce, Minister to France, in which position he was continued by President Buchanan. Died in Paris, of apoplexy, October 3, 1859.

Mason, Jonathan.—He was born in 1757; graduated at Princeton College in 1774; and died at Boston, November 1, 1831. He was a Senator of the United States, from Massachusetts, from 1800 to 1803; and a Representative in Congress, from that State, from 1817 to 1820.

Mason, Moses.—He was a County Commissioner from 1831 to 1834; a Representative in Congress, from Maine, from 1834 to 1837; and a member of the State Executive Council in 1834 and 1845.

Mason, Samson.—He was born in Ohio, and was a Representative in Congress, from that State, from 1835 to 1843. He was afterwards a member of the Convention which formed the State Constitution.

Mason, Stevens Thomson.—He

was born in Chapawansick, Stafford County, Virginia, in 1760; educated at William and Mary College; he was a lawyer by profession, and an officer in the Revolutionary war, attaining to the rank of General; was a member of the Virginia House of Burgessess; and a Senator of the United States, from 1794 to 1803; also a member of the Convention to form the Constitution of Virginia, and a member of the Legislature. He died in 1803.

Mason, William.—He was born in Connecticut; served in the Legislature of New York, from Chenango County, from 1820 to 1822; and was a Representative in Congress, from that State, from 1835 to 1837.

Masters, Josiah.—Born in Woodbury, Connecticut, October 22, 1763; graduated at Yale College in 1784, soon after which he removed to Schaghticoke, Rensselaer County, New York, which was thereafter his place of residence. He was a prominent member of the State Legislature in 1792, 1800, and 1801, when he was appointed Associate Judge of Rensselaer County; and from 1805 to 1809 was a Representative in Congress. In 1808 he was chosen first Judge of the County Court of Common Pleas, which office he held until his death. He was a zealous supporter of the general measures against Great Britain, during the war of 1812, yet he opposed with great earnestness, in several able speeches, the embargo, non-intercourse, and other commercial restrictions. He numbered among his personal friends such patriots as Jefferson, Randolph, Madison, Clay, &c., and was a co-operator and adviser of De Witt Clinton in the system of internal improvements, which gave to New York the rank of the Empire State. He died June 30, 1822.

Mathews, George.—He was a Representative in Congress, from Georgia, from 1789 to 1791.

Mathews, James.—He was born in Ohio, and was a Representative in Congress, from that State, from 1841 to 1845.

Mathews, Vincent.—Born in Orange County, New York, June 29, 1766. He studied law and was admitted to the bar in 1790; and fixing his residence near Elmira, Tioga County, was elected a State Representative in 1793, and in 1796 chosen a State Senator. In 1798 he was elected a Commissioner to settle certain claims for bounty land; and from 1809 to 1811 he was a Representative in Congress. In 1812 he was appointed District Attorney for a number of counties in Western New York; and in 1816 he removed from Elmira to Bath, and thence to Rochester, pursuing the practice of his profession, in different places, for no less a period than fifty-six years. Toward the close of his life, he served a second time in the Assembly of the State, and was District Attorney for Monroe County. The College of Geneva conferred upon him the degree of Doctor of Laws when he was nearly seventy-five years old; and he died at Rochester, August 23, 1846.

Mathewson, Elisha.—He was at different periods a member of the General Assembly of Rhode Island; once a Speaker in the House; and a Senator in Congress, from that State, from 1807 to 1811. He died at Scituate, Rhode Island, October 14, 1853.

Mathiot, Joshua.—He was born in Ohio, and was a Representative in Congress, from that State, from 1841 to 1843. Died July 30, 1849, at Newark, Ohio.

Matlack, James.—He was born in Gloucester County, New Jersey, and was a Representative in Congress, from that State, from 1821 to 1825, and died at Woodbury, in same State, January 15, 1840.

Matson, Aaron.—He was born in Plymouth County, Massachusetts; for many years Judge of Probate in Cheshire County; a Representative in Congress, from New Hampshire, from 1821 to 1825; a State Councillor from 1819 to 1821; and died at Newport, Rhode Island, July 18, 1855, aged eighty-five years.

Matteson, Orasmus B.—He was born in New York, and was elected a Representative in Congress, from that State, in 1849, and subsequently re-elected to the same position.

Matthews, William.—He was a Representative in Congress, from Maryland, from 1797 to 1799.

Mattocks, John.—Born in Hartford, Connecticut, in 1776, and was a resident of Peacham, Vermont; he was for many years distinguished as a successful lawyer; had held various public trusts, being for two years Judge of the Supreme Court of Vermont; and a Representative in Congress, from 1821 to 1825, and from 1841 to 1843; also Governor of the State one year, declining a re-election to that office. He died at Peacham, Vermont, August 14, 1847.

Mattoon, Ebenezer.—Born in Amherst, Massachusetts; graduated at Dartmouth College in 1776; he was a Major in the war of 1812, and Sheriff of Hampshire; and a Representative in Congress, from Massachusetts, from 1800 to 1803; and, in 1816, Adjutant-General of militia. He died in Amherst, September 11, 1843, aged eighty-eight years.

Maurice, James.—He was born in New York, and was a Representative in Congress, from that State, from 1853 to 1855.

Maury, Abraham P.—A Representative in Congress, from Tennessee, from 1835 to 1839; died at his residence, in Williamson County, Tennessee, July 22, 1848.

Maxwell, Augustus E.—Born in Elberton, Georgia, September 21, 1820; received the benefit of country schools in Alabama, and graduated at the University of Virginia; studied law; removing to Florida, was elected in 1847 to the Assembly of that State; was Secretary of State in 1848; a State Senator in 1849; was a member of Congress, from 1853 to 1857, refusing a re-nomination; and in 1857 was appointed, by President Buchanan, Navy Agent at Pensacola, Florida.

Maxwell, George C.—He was a native of New Jersey, and was a Representative in Congress, from that State, from 1811 to 1813.

Maxwell, J. P. B.—Born in New Jersey in 1805; graduated at Princeton College in 1823; studied law, and was admitted to the bar in 1827; and was a Representative in Congress, from 1837 to 1839, and again from 1841 to 1843. He died at Belvidere, New Jersey, November 14, 1845. He was a candidate for election to the Twenty-sixth Congress, and although he came with the broad seal of his State, he was not admitted.

Maxwell, Lewis.—He was a native of Virginia, and a Representative in Congress, from that State, from 1827 to 1833.

Maxwell, Thomas.—He was a Representative in Congress, from New York, from 1829 to 1831.

May, Henry.—He was born in the District of Columbia; received a liberal education; adopted the profession of law; and was a Representative in Congress, from Maryland, from 1853 to 1855. Re-elected to the Thirty-seventh Congress.

May, William L.—He was born in Kentucky, and was a Representative in Congress, from that State, from 1835 to 1839.

Mayall, Samuel.—He was born in Maine; served in the State Legislature in 1845, 1847, and 1848; and was a Representative in Congress, from Maine, from 1853 to 1855.

Maynard, Horace.—He was born in Westborough, Massachusetts, August 30, 1814; graduated at Amherst College in 1838, and soon afterwards emigrated to Tennessee. He entered the University of East Tennessee as a tutor, and subsequently received the appointment of Professor of Mathematics in that institution; during that period he studied law, and was admitted to the bar in 1844. He acquired an extensive practice in his profession; held a number of local offices in his adopted State; and was elected a Representative, from Tennessee, to the Thirty-fifth Congress. During the first session of that Congress he was Chairman of the Special Committee to investigate the accounts of William Cullum, late Clerk of the House of Representatives, and was a member of the Committee on Claims. He was re-elected to the Thirty-sixth Congress, serving on the same Committee; and also re-elected to the Thirty-seventh Congress. For his loyalty during the troubles of 1861, his property was confiscated, and he as well as his family, were driven from Eastern Tennessee by the Rebel government. He was a Delegate to the Baltimore Convention of 1864.

Maynard, John.—He was a resident of Western New York, and graduated at Union College in 1810; he studied law and commenced practice at Seneca Falls, and then removed to Auburn. He was a Representative in Congress, from New York, from 1827 to 1829, and gave a zealous support to the administration of Mr. Adams; he was subsequently a member of the New York Senate for four years, and again from 1841 to 1843 a member of Congress; he was Judge of the Supreme Court of New York, and from January, 1850, a Judge of the Court of Appeals. He died in Auburn, New York, March 24, 1850.

Mayrant, William.—He was a native of South Carolina, and a Representative in Congress, from that State, during the years 1815 and 1816.

McAllister, Archibald.—He was born in Dauphin County, Pennsylvania, in 1814; and having settled in Blair County, was for thirty-three years engaged in the manufacture of iron. In 1862 he was elected a Representative, from Pennsylvania, to the Thirty-eighth Congress, serving on the Committee on Military Affairs.

McArthur, Duncan.—He was born in Dutchess County, New York, in 1772. When he was eight years of age he removed with his father to Pennsylvania, and at the age of eighteen he volunteered in defence of the frontier settlements of Ohio, against the Indians. He studied surveying, and acquired great wealth in the business of buying and selling lands, in addition to surveying them. In 1805 he was a member of the Legislature, and in 1806 was appointed Colonel, and in 1808 Major-General of the State militia. He performed valuable services during the war of 1812, in which he held a General's commission, and although elected to Congress in 1813, declined leaving his command; in 1815 was again a member of the Legislature, and in 1816 was appointed Commissioner to conclude treaties with the Indians; from 1817 to 1819 was in the Legislature, and Speaker of the House in 1817. He was a Representative in Congress, from Ohio, from 1823 to 1825, and in 1830 was chosen Governor of the State, which position he held until 1833, and while in that service met with an accident, from the effects of which he never recovered.

McBride, John R.—Was born in Franklin County, Missouri, August 22, 1832; emigrated to Oregon in 1846; in 1854 he was chosen Superintendent of Common Schools; studied law and came to the bar in 1855; in 1857 he was a Delegate to the Convention which formed the Oregon State Constitution; was chosen to the State Senate for four years after its adoption; and in 1862 he was elected a Representative, from Oregon, to the Thirty-eighth Congress, serving on the Committee on Indian Affairs.

McBryde, Archibald.—Born in Moore County, North Carolina, and was a Representative in Congress, from that State, from 1809 to 1813, and subsequently a member of the State Senate for two years.

McCarty, Andrew Z.—He was born in New York, and was a Representative in Congress, from that State, from 1855 to 1857. He was also a member of the New York Assembly in 1848.

McCarty, Jonathan.—Was a native of Tennessee, but removed, with his father, at an early age to Indiana. He engaged in mercantile pursuits, and was for a time Clerk of the Circuit or County Court, at Connersville. He was a Representative in Congress, from Indiana, from 1831 to 1837. He left Indiana for Iowa, where he died in 1855.

McCarty, Richard.—Was born in Albany, New York, and was a Representative in Congress, from that State, from 1821 to 1823.

McCarty, William M.—He was a Representative in Congress, from Virginia, from 1840 to 1841.

McCauslen, William C.—He was born in Ohio, and was a Representative in Congress, from that State, from 1843 to 1845.

McLean, Moses.—He was born in

Pennsylvania, and was a Representative in Congress, from that State, from 1845 to 1847.

McClellan, Abraham.—He was born in Tennessee, and was a Representative in Congress, from that State, from 1837 to 1843.

McClellan, Robert.—He was a native of Schoharie County, New York, and a Representative in Congress, from that State, from 1837 to 1839, and again from 1841 to 1843.

McClelland, Robert.—Born in Franklin County, Pennsylvania. He graduated at Dickinson College; practised law for a year or so in Pittsburg, and in 1833 removed to Michigan, and established himself at Monroe. He served for several years in the Legislature of that State; and was a Representative in Congress, from 1843 to 1849. He was twice elected Governor of Michigan, in 1851 and 1852; and was appointed Secretary of the Interior Department, by President Pierce, the arduous duties of which position he performed with fidelity and ability.

McClenachan, Blair.—He was a Representative in Congress, from Pennsylvania, from 1797 to 1799.

McClernand, John A.—Born in Breckenridge County, Kentucky, May 30, 1812; brought up at Shawneetown, Illinois, and had only the advantages of a common school education. He studied law, and was admitted to the bar in 1832, and served as a private, but with credit, in the Black Hawk war. He established the first Democratic press in Shawneetown, and edited his paper and practised law until 1843, when he was elected to Congress, and served as a Representative until 1851. He had also, before going to Congress, been elected to the State Legislature. In 1859 he was again elected to Congress, serving on the Committee on Claims. Re-elected to the Thirty-seventh Congress, but resigned to accept the commission of Brigadier-General in the Union army in 1861.

McClurg, Joseph W.—Born in St. Louis County, Missouri, February 22, 1818; received a good education, chiefly at Oxford College, Ohio; in his seventeenth year he went to Louisiana and Mississippi, and spent nearly two years as a teacher; went to Texas in 1841, where he was admitted to the bar, and was Clerk of the Circuit Court; in 1844 he settled in Missouri as a merchant; when the Rebellion broke out his interests suffered greatly from the plunder of the Rebels; took part in the war as Colonel of the Osage regiment of infantry, and also of a cavalry regiment; was a member of the Missouri State Convention in 1862, and was elected a Representative, from Missouri, to the Thirty-eighth Congress, serving on the Committee on Territories. He was also a Delegate to the Baltimore Convention of 1864.

McComas, William.—Was born in Virginia, and was a Representative in Congress, from that State, from 1833 to 1837, and was a member of the Committee on Manufactures.

McConnell, Felix G.—Was a native of Lincoln County, Tennessee, but removed in 1824 to Talladega County, Alabama. He was a Representative in Congress, from that State, from 1843 to 1846. He died, by his own hand, in Washington, District of Columbia, September, 1846, aged thirty-six.

McCord, Andrew.—He was a member of the New York Assembly, during the years 1800, 1801, 1802, and 1807, part of the time Speaker; and was a Representative in Congress, from that State, from 1803 to 1805.

McCorkle, Joseph W.—He was born in Ohio, and was a Representative in Congress, from California, from 1851 to 1853.

McCoy, Robert.—He resided at one time in Carlisle, Pennsylvania, and held several public positions in that State, such as Brigadier-General of militia, and Canal Commissioner. He was a member of Congress, from Pennsylvania, from 1831 to 1833, and died at Wheeling, Virginia, June 7, 1849.

McCoy, William.—He was born in Augusta County, Virginia, and was a Representative in Congress, from that State, from 1811 to 1833.

McCrate, John D.—He was born

in Wiscasset about 1800; graduated at Bowdoin College in 1819; adopted the profession of law; was a member of the State Legislature, from 1831 to 1836; Collector of Customs at Wiscasset, from 1836 to 1841; and was a Representative in Congress, from Maine, from 1845 to 1847.

McCreary, John.—He was born in Chester District, South Carolina, and was a Representative in Congress, from that State, from 1819 to 1821.

McCreary, William.—He was a Representative in Congress, from Maryland, from 1803 to 1809.

McCreedy, William.—He was a Representative in Congress, from Pennsylvania, from 1829 to 1831.

McCulloch, George.—He was born in Pennsylvania, and was a Representative in Congress, from that State, irom 1840 to 1841.

McCulloch, John.—He was born in Pennsylvania, and was a Representative in Congress, from that State, from 1853 to 1855.

McCulloch, Thomas G.—He was born in Franklin County, Pennsylvania, and was a Representative in Congress, from that State, from 1820 to 1822.

McDonald, Joseph E.—Born in Ohio, and was a Representative in Congress, from that State, from 1849 to 1851.

McDonald, Moses.—Born in Limerick, York County, Maine, April 8, 1815. Practised law from 1837 to 1845; and was a member of the Maine Legislature in 1841 and 1842. In 1845 was Speaker of the House. In 1847, 1848, and 1849, served as Treasurer of the State; represented the First Congressional District in the Thirty-second and Thirty-third Congresses; and in April, 1857, was appointed, by President Buchanan, Collector for the District of Portland and Falmouth.

McDougall, James A.—Was born in Bethlehem, Albany County, New York, November 19, 1817; received his education at the Albany grammar school; assisted in the survey of the first railway ever built in this country, that of Albany and Schenectady; studied law, and adopted that profession; removed to Pike County, Illinois, in 1837; in 1842 he was chosen Attorney-General of Illinois; re-elected in 1844; in 1849 he originated and accompanied an exploring expedition to Rio del Norte, the Gila, and Colorado; he afterwards emigrated to California, and followed his profession at San Francisco; in 1850 was elected Attorney-General of California; was a Representative in Congress, from California, from 1853 to 1855, declining a re-nomination; and in 1861 he was elected a Senator in Congress, for six years, serving on the Committees on Finance, and Naval Affairs, and as Chairman of the Committee on the Pacific Railroad. He was also a Delegate to the Chicago Convention of 1864.

McDowell, James.—He was born in Rockbridge County, Virginia, in 1796, and graduated at Princeton College in 1816. He was Governor of Virginia from 1842 to 1845, and from 1845 to 1851 he was a Representative in Congress, from the Eleventh Congressional District of Virginia. In 1846 his Alma Mater conferred on him the degree of LL.D. He was an eloquent speaker, an upright man, and a true patriot. He died near Lexington, Virginia, August 24, 1851.

McDowell, James Foster.—Born in Mifflin County, Pennsylvania, December 3, 1825; went with his parents to Ohio in 1835; served for a time in a printing-office; during which apprenticeship he studied law, and came to the bar in his twenty-first year, and his first office was that of County Attorney. In 1851 he settled in Indiana, and established the Marion Journal; was a Presidential Elector in 1852; and in 1862 he was elected a Representative, from Indiana, to the Thirty-sixth Congress, serving on the Committee on Invalid Pensions.

McDowell, Joseph.—Born in Winchester, Virginia, and emigrated with his father to North Carolina, where he took an active part in the military operations of the time, and was at the battle of King's Mountain. He was a member of the House of Commons from 1782 to 1788, and a Representative in Congress from 1793 to 1795, and again from 1797 to 1799.

McDowell, Joseph J.—He was born in North Carolina, and on removing to Kentucky was elected a Representative in Congress, from that State, from 1843 to 1847.

McDuffie, George.—He was born in Columbia County, Georgia, in 1788; was for a time a clerk in Augusta; graduated at the South Carolina College in 1813; adopted the profession of law; served a number of years in the State Legislature; was a Trustee of his Alma Mater; a Major of militia; was elected a Representative in Congress, from South Carolina, in 1821, and served until 1835, when he was chosen Governor of the State. In 1843 he was elected a Senator of the United States, but was compelled by ill health to resign that station before the expiration of his term of office. His ill health was partly the result of a duel which he fought in Augusta, Georgia, with Colonel Cumming, in which he was wounded. He was a co-worker and friend of Calhoun and Hayne, and an eloquent defender of the peculiar institutions of the South. He died in Sumter District, South Carolina, March 11, 1851.

McFarlan, Duncan.—A Representative in Congress, from North Carolina, from 1805 to 1807, and subsequently a member of the State Senate for three years.

McGaughey, Edward W.—He was born in Indiana, and was a Representative in Congress, from that State, from 1845 to 1847, and for another term ending in 1851.

McHatton, Robert.—He was a Representative in Congress, from Kentucky, from 1826 to 1829.

McHenry, John H.—He was born in Kentucky, and was a Representative in Congress, from that State, from 1843 to 1847.

McIlvane, Abraham R.—Born at Crum Creek, Delaware, August 14, 1804. He was bred a farmer, in which pursuit he was eminently successful, and was a Representative in Congress, from Pennsylvania, from 1843 to 1849. Died in Chester County, Pennsylvania, in August, 1863.

McIlvane, Joseph.—Was born in Bristol, Bucks County, Pennsylvania, in 1768; received a good education, and was admitted to the bar in New Jersey in 1791; he took an interest in military matters, and in 1798 attained the rank of Captain in McPherson's Regiment of Blues; in 1800 he was elected Clerk of Burlington County, and held the office twenty-four years; in 1801 he was appointed, by President Jefferson, Attorney of the United States for New Jersey, which office he also held for twenty years; in 1804 he was appointed aide-de-camp of the Governor of New Jersey, with the title of Colonel; in 1818 he was appointed Judge of the Superior Court of New Jersey, but declined the appointment; and he was a Senator in Congress, from New Jersey, from 1823 to 1826, having died in Burlington on the 19th of August of the latter year. He was a man of high character and great influence.

McIndoe, Walter D.—Was born in Scotland, March 30, 1819; emigrated to New York City in his fifteenth year; and was a clerk in a large mercantile house; followed the same pursuit in Charleston, South Carolina, and in St. Louis, Missouri, and subsequently settled in Wisconsin, and engaged in the lumber business; served in the Wisconsin Legislature in 1850, 1854, and 1855; was a Presidential Elector in 1856 and 1860; and was elected a Representative, from Wisconsin, to the Thirty-seventh Congress (in place of Luther Hanchett, deceased), and was re-elected to the Thirty-eighth Congress, serving on the Committees on Indian Affairs, and Revolutionary Pensions.

McIntyre, Rufus.—Born in York, County of York, Maine, December 19, 1784; received a common school education, and by teaching for two or three years, acquired the means to fit himself for college at South Berwick Academy, and graduated at Dartmouth in 1809. He studied law, and was admitted to practice in 1812. In the mean time war was declared, and he was appointed Captain of militia, and remained in service on the frontier until peace was declared, after which he returned to the practice of his profession at York. He represented that town in the Brunswick Convention; and after the separation from Massachusetts, he was a Representative in the Legislature at its first session; he was then appointed County Attorney, which office he held till elected to Congress as Representative of Maine, serving from 1826 to 1835. In 1826 he was a Commissioner for settling the boundary line of his State, and in 1836 was a member of the Legislature, and was appointed Land Agent for two years, in 1839. He was subsequently United States Marshal for Maine, and Surveyor of the port of Portland four years. He has been connected with two or three academies as overseer, and is a member of the Board of Overseers of Bowdoin College. He is now devoted to agriculture.

McKay, James J.—Born in Bladen County, North Carolina, in 1793. He was bred to the law; and served from 1815 to 1831 in the State Senate, and was at one time United States District Attorney. He was a Representative in Congress, from 1831 to 1849, and was for a time Chairman of the Committee of Ways and Means. At the Baltimore Convention, which nominated Lewis Cass for President, he received the vote of the North Carolina delegation as candidate for Vice-President. He died in Goldsborough, North Carolina, September 14, 1853.

McKean, James Badell.—Born in Hoosic, Rensselaer County, New York, August 5, 1821; during his youth he worked upon his father's farm in Saratoga County, receiving his education chiefly from the district school and academies; taught school for a time, and became a school Superintendent for the town where he lived; served one term as a Professor in Jonesville Academy; was a Colonel of infantry; he studied law, and was admitted to the bar in 1849; in 1855 he was elected County Judge for Saratoga County for four years; and in 1858 was elected a Representative, from New York, to the Thirty-sixth Congress, serving as Chairman of the Committee on Expenditures in the State Department. Re-elected to the Thirty-seventh Congress, serving as Chairman of the Committee on Expenditures in the State Department.

McKean, Samuel.—He was born in Huntingdon County, Pennsylvania, and was a Representative in Congress, from Pennsylvania, from 1823 to 1829, and a Senator of the United States, from 1833 to 1839. He died June 23, 1840, in McKean County. He was a man of talent and influence.

McKee, John.—He was born in Rockbridge County, Virginia, and was at one time a Government Agent among the Choctaw Indians, also a Commissioner for settling the boundary line of Tennessee, and a Representative in Congress, from that State, from 1823 to 1829.

McKee, Samuel.—He was a Representative in Congress, from Kentucky, from 1809 to 1817.

McKennan, Thomas M. T.—He was a Representative in Congress, from Pennsylvania, from 1831 to 1839, and from 1841 to 1843, and died at Reading, July 9, 1852.

McKenney, John F.—He was born near Piqua, Ohio, April 12, 1827; spent his boyhood chiefly on a farm; received an academic education, and spent one year at the Ohio Wesleyan University; adopted the profession of law; and in 1862 he was elected a Representative, from Ohio, to the Thirty-eighth Congress, serving on the Committees on Unfinished Business, and on the Militia.

McKeon, John.—He was born in New York, and was educated a lawyer. In 1832, 1833, and 1834, he served in the Legislature of New York, and was a Representative in Congress, from that State, from 1835 to 1837, and again from 1841 to 1843. He has twice been appointed United States District Attorney for the Southern District of New York. He was also a Delegate to the Chicago Convention of 1864.

McKibbin, Joseph C.—He was born in Pennsylvania, and having taken up his residence in California, was elected a Representative, from that State, to the Thirty-fifth Congress, and was a member of the Committee on Public Lands and on Private Land Claims.

McKim, Alexander.—Born in 1748, and died at Baltimore, January 18, 1832. He was a member of Congress, from Maryland, from 1809 to 1815.

McKim, Isaac.—He was a much-respected and wealthy merchant of Baltimore; a member of Congress, from Maryland, from 1823 to 1825, and again from 1835 to 1838; and died in Washington, April 1, 1838.

McKinley, John.—Born in Virginia; removed to Kentucky, thence to Alabama; and he was a Senator in Congress, from Alabama, from 1826 to 1837. In 1837 he was appointed a Justice of the Supreme Court of the United States, and died in Louisville, Kentucky, July 19, 1852.

McKinley, William.—He was a Representative in Congress, from Virginia, from 1810 to 1811.

McKissock, Thomas.—He was born in Ulster County, New York, in 1798. He received a classical education; was bred first to the medical, and afterwards to the legal profession; was, under the old organization, a Judge of the Supreme Court of New York; and a Representative in Congress, from 1849 to 1851.

McKnight, Robert. — Born in Pittsburg, Pennsylvania, in 1820; graduated at Princeton College in 1839; studied law, and was admitted to the bar in 1842; from 1847 to 1849, both inclusive, he was a member of the City Councils of Pittsburg, the last two years President of that body; and was elected a Representative, from Pennsylvania, to the Thirty-sixth Congress, serving as a member of the Committee on Elections. Re-elected to the Thirty-seventh Congress, serving on the Committees on Foreign Affairs, and on Public Buildings.

McLanahan, James X. — He was born in Antrim, Franklin County, Pennsylvania, in 1809; graduated at Dickinson College in 1826; he studied law, and settled in Chambersburg; in 1841 he was elected to the State Senate; and in 1849 he was elected to Congress, and re-elected in 1851, and was Chairman of the Committee on the Judiciary. He is now living in retirement.

McLane, Louis.—He was born in Smyrna, Kent County, Delaware, May 28, 1784. When twelve years of age, he was appointed a midshipman in the navy, on leaving which, in 1801, he studied law, and was admitted to the bar in 1807; in 1812 he was a volunteer in a company commanded by Cæsar H. Rodney, and marched to the relief of Baltimore when threatened by the British. He was a Representative in Congress, from Delaware, from 1817 to 1827; and was chosen, by the Legislature, a Senator in Congress, from 1827 to 1829; was appointed in 1829, by President Jackson, Minister to England, where he remained two years; and in 1831 he received the appointment of Secretary of the Treasury; and in 1833, that of Secretary of State under President Jackson. In June, 1834, he retired from political life, and in 1837 was chosen President of the Baltimore and Ohio Railroad Company, and, removing to Maryland, discharged the duties of that office until 1847. During the administration of President Polk, he accepted the mission to England while the Oregon negotiations were pending; after which he returned to Maryland, and in 1850 represented Cecil County in the State Constitutional Convention, and then retired to private life. He held a high rank as a statesman, and died in Baltimore, Maryland, in 1857.

McLane, Robert M.—Born in Delaware, June 23, 1815; was educated at Washington College, District of Columbia, and at St. Mary's College, Baltimore; went to Europe with his father, Louis McLane, in 1829, and on his return entered the West Point Academy, which he left in 1837; he served as an army officer in Florida, the Cherokee Country, and in the Northwest; in 1843 was admitted to the bar of Baltimore; in 1845 and 1846 was elected to the Maryland Legislature; and from 1847 to 1851 was a Representative in Congress, from Maryland. In 1853 he was appointed by President Pierce Minister to China, and on his return resumed the practice of his profession in Baltimore. In March, 1859, he was appointed by President Buchanan Minister to Mexico, but resigned in November, 1860.

McLean, Alney.—He was born in Burke County, North Carolina, and was a Representative in Congress, from Kentucky, from 1815 to 1817, and again from 1819 to 1821.

McLean, Finis E.—He was born in Kentucky, and was a Representative in Congress, from that State, from 1849 to 1851.

McLean, John.—Born in Morris County, New Jersey, in 1785. Four years after his birth his father emigrated with his family to Virginia, whence he removed to Kentucky, and finally settled in the State of Ohio. Here the son received a scanty education; and, having determined to pursue the legal profession, he engaged at the age of eighteen to write in the clerk's office at Cincinnati, in order to maintain himself, by devoting a portion of his time to that labor, while engaged in his studies. In 1807 he was admitted to the bar, and entered upon the practice of the law at Lebanon, Ohio. In 1812 he became a candidate to represent his district in Congress, and was elected by a large majority. He professed the political principles of the Democratic party, being an ardent supporter of the war, and of President Madison's administration. In 1814 he was again elected to Congress by a unanimous vote, a circumstance of rare occurrence, and remained a member of the House of Representatives until 1816, when the Legislature of Ohio having elected him a Judge of the Supreme Court of the State, he resigned his seat in Congress at the close of the session. He remained six years upon the Supreme Bench of Ohio. In 1822 he was appointed Commissioner of the General Land Office by President Monroe; and in 1823 he became Postmaster-General. In the year 1829 he was appointed by President Jackson a Justice of the United States Supreme Court, after he had refused the offer of the War and Navy Departments. He entered upon the discharge of his duties at the January Term of 1830, and died at Cincinnati, April 4, 1861.

McLean, John.—He was a Representative in Congress, from Illinois, during the years 1818 and 1819; was a Senator in Congress, from that State, from 1824 to 1825, and again from 1829 to 1830, having died on the 4th of October of the latter year.

McLean, William.—He was a native of Morris County, New Jersey; a Representative in Congress, from Ohio, from 1823 to 1829, and died at Cincinnati, October 12, 1839. He was a brother of Judge McLean, and when in Congress was mainly instrumental in procuring an appropriation of half a million of acres of land for the extension of the Ohio Canal from Cincinnati to Cleveland. After his service in Congress he was engaged in business in Cincinnati.

McLene, Jeremiah.—He was born in 1767, and died in Washington City, March 19, 1837. He was for twenty-one years Secretary of State for Ohio, and a Representative in Congress, from that State, from 1833 to 1837.

McManus, William.—He was born in Rensselaer County, New York, and was a Representative in Congress, from New York, from 1825 to 1827.

McMullen, Fayette.—He was born in Virginia, and was a Representative in Congress, from that State, from 1849 to 1855, and in May, 1857, he was appointed by President Buchanan Governor of the Territory of Washington.

McNair, John.—He was born in Pennsylvania in 1800, and was a Representative in Congress, from that State, from 1851 to 1855. Died at Evansport, Prince William County, Virginia, in August, 1861.

McNiel, Archibald.—Born in Cumberland County, North Carolina; entered the House of Commons in 1808; re-elected in 1809; served in the State Senate in 1811 and 1815, and was a Representative in Congress, from 1821 to 1823, and again from 1825 to 1827.

McPherson, Edward.—Born in Gettysburg, Adams County, Pennsylvania, July 31, 1830; graduated at Pennsylvania College in 1848; devoted some attention to the printing business, and edited a paper at Harrisburg in 1851, and for several years afterwards. On account of his health he subsequently turned his attention to agricultural pursuits; and in 1858 was elected a Representative, from Pennsylvania, to the Thirty-sixth Congress, serving on the Committee on Public Buildings and Grounds. He has delivered many public addresses on literary and other topics, and is the author of several letters touching the internal affairs of his native State, which have exerted a wide influence for good. Re-elected to the Thirty-seventh Congress, serving as Chairman of the Committee on the Library, and as a member of the Committee on Military Affairs; and in 1863 he was appointed Deputy Commissioner of the Revenue in the Treasury Department; and on the meeting of the Thirty-eighth Congress, he was elected Clerk of the House of Representatives. During his last term in Congress he was a Regent of the Smithsonian Institution.

McQueen, John.—He was born in Robinson County, North Carolina, in 1808. He claims descent in a direct line from the heroic Robert Bruce of Scotland, and his father, James McQueen, was a nephew of the celebrated Flora MacDonald. He received a good education under the guidance of an elder brother, Rev. A. McQueen, who was a graduate of the Chapel Hill University, North Carolina. He commenced the study of law in his native State, and completed his course of study in South Carolina, to which he removed at an early day. He was admitted to the bar in 1828, and having settled in Marlborough District, he there commenced, and has ever since, as his public calls have permitted, continued the practice of his profession with success. During the Nullification times of 1833, he was elected a Colonel of the State militia, in 1834 a Brigadier-General, and in 1835 a Major-General, which last position he held for ten years, and then resigned. He was elected a Representative in Congress in 1849, and has continued a member down to the Thirty-sixth Congress, serving on leading committees. Re-elected to the Thirty-seventh Congress. Resigned in December, 1860.

McRae, John J.—He was born in Wayne County, Mississippi; received a good education; adopted the profession of law; was elected frequently to the State Legislature, and during two sessions officiated as Speaker; was also elected to the State Senate; was Governor of Mississippi, from 1844 to 1848; was, by appointment, for a short time in the United States Senate; and was elected to the second session of the Thirty-fifth Congress, from Mississippi, as the successor to General Quitman; and was re-elected to the Thirty-sixth Congress, serving on the Committee on Military Affairs. Joined the Great Rebellion in 1861.

McReady, James.—He was a Representative in Congress, from South Carolina, from 1819 to 1821.

McRoberts, Samuel.—He was a Senator in Congress, from Illinois, from 1841 to the time of his death, which occurred March 27, 1843, in Cincinnati, Ohio, aged about forty years.

McSherry, James.—He was a native of Adams County, Pennsylvania; served twenty years in the Legislature of that State; was a Delegate to reform the Constitution of the same; and a Representative in Congress, from Pennsylvania, from 1821 to 1823. Died at Littlestown, Pennsylvania, February 3, 1849.

McVean, Charles.—He was born at Johnstown, New York, in 1802, and died in the city of New York, December 20, 1848. He was bred to the law, which he practised with success in Montgomery County, until he removed to New York. He held the office of Surrogate; served as a Representative in Congress, from 1833 to 1835; and at the time of his death was District Attorney for Southern New York.

McWillie, William.—He was born in Kershaw District, South Carolina, November 17, 1795; graduated at the South Carolina College in 1817; adopted the profession of law; came to the bar in 1818; was an Adjutant of militia; was a Representative and Senator in the Legislature of South Carolina; and, on removing to Mississippi, in 1845, was elected a Representative in Congress, from that State, from 1849 to 1851. He was also President of a bank for several years; and elected Governor of the State in 1858.

Meacham, James.—Born in Rutland, Vermont, in 1810; graduated at Middlebury College in 1822; was tutor there; studied theology; was settled in New Haven, Vermont; was called from his parish to the Professorship of Elocution and English Literature in Middlebury College, when, in 1849, he was elected a Representative in Congress, and twice re-elected. At the time of his death, August 22, 1856, he was a member of Congress, and a Regent of the Smithsonian Institution.

Mead, Cowles.—He was elected a Representative in Congress, from Georgia, in 1805, but his election was successfully contested by Thomas Spalding; and in 1806 he was appointed, by President Jefferson, Secretary of Mississippi Territory.

Meade, Richard K.—He was born in Virginia; received a liberal education; and adopted the profession of law; he was a Representative in Congress, from Virginia, from 1847 to 1853; was appointed, by President Pierce, in 1853, Chargé d'Affaires to Sardinia; and in 1857 was appointed, by President Buchanan, Minister to Brazil, which mission he held until 1861.

Mebane, Alexander.—Born in Hawfields, Orange County, North Carolina, November 26, 1767, and died July 5, 1795. He was a member of the Convention, in 1776, that met to form the State Constitution; served a number of years in the Legislature; and was in Congress during the years 1793 and 1794. He was distinguished for his sense, integrity, and firmness.

Medill, William.—He was born in New Castle County, Delaware; received an academical education; he studied law, and having removed to Ohio, was admitted to the bar of that State in 1832; he was soon after elected to the State Legislature, serving a number of years, and was twice elected Speaker; he was elected a Representative in Congress, from that State, from 1839 to 1843; by President Polk, he was appointed First Assistant Postmaster-General, and subsequently held the office of Commissioner of Indian Affairs; in 1850 he was a member of the Convention called to revise the State Constitution, and chosen Chairman; in 1851 and 1852 he was elected Lieutenant-Governor of Ohio; in 1853 he was elected Governor of Ohio; and, by President Buchanan, was appointed First Comptroller of the United States Treasury.

Meech, Ezra.—He was born in New London, Connecticut, July 26, 1773; was associated in early life with John Jacob Astor in the fur trade; in 1806 became agent of the Northwest Fur Company; and in 1809 was agent for supplying the British Government with spars and timber. Having settled in Vermont, he was, in 1822 and 1823, elected Chief Justice of Chittenden County; and was a member of the Constitutional Conventions of 1822 and 1826. He was elected, in 1805 and 1807, to the State Legislature; and was a Representative in Congress, from Vermont, from 1819 to 1821, and again from 1825 to 1827. During the latter years of his life he was devoted to agricultural pursuits, and owned one farm, kept in a high state of cultivation, which contained three thousand acres, and upon which have been seen a flock of three thousand sheep and a herd of eight hundred oxen. He was remarkable for his intelligence and hospitality, and not less so for his personal appearance, as he measured six feet five inches in height, and weighed three hundred and seventy pounds; and, strange as it may seem, he was one of the most expert trout fishers in the county. He died at Shelburne, Vermont, September 23, 1856.

Meigs, Henry.—Born in New Haven, Connecticut, October 28, 1782; graduated at Yale College in 1798; educated a lawyer, and was elected a Representative in Congress, from New York City, from 1819 to 1821, and for many years past has been an active officer, Recording Secretary, and Trustee of the American Institute in New York. It was said of him, as something remarkable, that he never wore an overcoat, never had a sore throat or headache, and, when seventy years of age, did not use glasses. Died in New York, May 20, 1861.

Meigs, Return J.—Was a native of Middletown, Connecticut; graduated at Yale College in 1785, and was a lawyer by profession. He removed to Ohio, and became a Judge of the Supreme Court of the State; was a Senator in Congress, from 1808 to 1810; and was Governor of the State, from 1810 to 1814. He was appointed Postmaster-General of the United States in 1814, and held the office nine years. He died at Marietta, March 29, 1825.

Mellen, Prentiss.—Born in Sterling, Massachusetts, October 11, 1764; graduated at Cambridge in 1784; studied law, and settled at Bridgewater; in 1792 he became a citizen of Biddeford, Maine, and in 1806 settled at Portland. In 1817 he was chosen a Senator in Congress, from Massachusetts; and on the separation of Maine, in 1820, he resigned his seat in the Senate, and was elected the first Chief Justice of the Supreme Court of Maine. He occupied a high position as a lawyer and jurist; and in 1834, after becoming disqualified by age to serve as judge, he resumed the practice of law. His decisions may be found in the first eleven volumes of the Maine Reports. He was also a Trustee of Bowdoin College, from 1817 to 1836; and in 1828 received the degree of LL.D. from that institution. He died at Portland, December 31, 1840.

Menifee, Richard H.—He was a member of Congress, from Kentucky, from 1837 to 1839, and died at Frankfort, February 21, 1841.

Menzies, John W.—Was born in Fayette County, Kentucky, April 12, 1819; graduated at the University of Virginia in 1840; studied law and came to the bar in 1841, establishing himself in Covington, Kentucky, where he has ever since practised his profession. In 1848 and 1855 he was elected to the General Assembly of Kentucky; and in 1861 he was elected a Representative, from Kentucky, to the Thirty-seventh Congress, serving on the Committees on Elections, and Unfinished Business. He was also a Delegate to the Chicago Convention of 1864.

Mercer, Charles Fenton.—Born in Fredericksburg, Virginia, June 6, 1778; graduated at Princeton in 1797. In 1798, while a student of law, he tendered his services to General Washington for the defence of the country against a threatened invasion by the French, and received from him a commission as first Lieutenant of cavalry, and soon after that of Captain, which he declined, not intending to devote his life to the military profession. In 1803, after spending a year in Europe, he returned and practised law. From 1810 to 1817 he was a member of the General Assembly of Virginia. In 1811 he was again called to military duty by the General Government; and in 1813 was appointed aid to the Governor, and rose to the rank of Brigadier-General of militia, having command of the forces at Norfolk. In 1816, as Chairman of the Committee on Finance, in the Legislature, he devoted his time to the promotion of internal improvements, and was chief supporter of the measure for the Chesapeake and Ohio Canal, and was appointed President of the Canal Company. He was a member of Congress, from 1817 to 1840. In 1853 he visited Europe from philanthropic motives, at his own expense, and used his efforts for the entire abolition of the African slave trade, conferring with the chief executive officers of most of the kingdoms of Europe on the subject. He died at Howard, near Alexandria, Virginia, May 4, 1858.

Mercer, John F.—He was a soldier of the Revolution; was a member of the old Congress, in 1782; was a member, from Maryland, of the Convention which formed the Federal Constitution; a Representative in the new Congress, from 1792 to 1794; Governor of Maryland, from 1801 to 1803; also a member of the Legislature of that State; and died at Philadelphia, August 30, 1821, in the sixty-fourth year of his age.

Meriwether, David.—He was a Representative in Congress, from Georgia, from 1802 to 1807; and was appointed, by President Jefferson, in 1804, a Commissioner to treat with the Creek Indians.

Meriwether, David.—He was a Senator in Congress, from Kentucky, by appointment, for one session, in 1852, and was appointed, by President Pierce, May 6, 1853, Governor of the Territory of New Mexico.

Meriwether, I. A.—He was born in Georgia, and was a Representative in Congress, from that State, from 1841 to 1843.

Meriwether, James.—He was born in Wilkes County, Georgia, and was a Representative in Congress, from Georgia, from 1825 to 1827.

Merrick, William D.—He filled several prominent positions in the State of Maryland, and served in the United

States Senate, from 1838 to 1845. He died in Washington, District of Columbia, February 5, 1857, at an advanced age.

Merrill, Orsamus C.—He was a Representative in Congress, from Vermont, from 1817 to 1819; and also held the positions in that State of County Attorney for two years; State Councillor for four years; State Senator for one year; Register of Probate for two years; and Judge of Probate for six years.

Mervin, Orange.—He was born in Litchfield, Connecticut, and was a Representative in Congress, from Connecticut, from 1825 to 1829.

Metcalf, Arunah.—He was a native of New York; a Representative in Congress, from that State, from 1811 to 1813, and subsequently served four years in the Assembly of New York, from Otsego County.

Metcalf, Thomas.—He was born in Fauquier County, Virginia, March 20, 1780. When he was quite young, his parents emigrated to Kentucky, and settled in Fayette, where his education was restricted to the advantages of a few months' attendance at a country school. He worked at the trade of a mason, but employed his leisure hours in study, and soon developed remarkable intellectual abilities. In 1809 he first appeared as a public speaker, in defence of his country against British oppression; served in the war of 1812, and in 1813 commanded a company of infantry at the battle of Fort Meigs, and greatly distinguished himself for his bravery. He was subsequently a member of the Kentucky Legislature for several years, and was a Representative in Congress, from 1819 to 1829, when he was elected Governor of Kentucky, which office he held until 1833. In 1834 he was elected to the State Senate, and in 1840 was chosen President of the Board of Internal Improvement. In 1848 he was appointed to fill the unexpired term of Mr. Crittenden, in the Senate of the United States, after which he retired to his farm, between Maysville and Lexington. He boasted of his service as a stone-mason, and delighted in being called the "Old Stone Hammer." He died in Nicholas County, Kentucky, August 18, 1855.

Middleswarth, Ner.—He was born in New Jersey, and on removing to Pennsylvania, was elected a Representative in Congress, from that State, from 1853 to 1855.

Middleton, George.—Was born in Philadelphia, October 14, 1811; came of the old stock of the Society of Friends; received a common school education; while yet a boy removed with his father to New Jersey, and settled in Burlington; was engaged for many years in the business of tanning; was twice elected to the Legislature of New Jersey; has been noted in his district as a local peace-maker among his neighbors; and was elected a Representative, from New Jersey, to the Thirty-eighth Congress, serving on the Committees on Agriculture, and on the Expenditures in the Interior Department.

Middleton, Henry.—A native of South Carolina; was chosen a Representative in the State Legislature in 1801; then State Senator until elected Governor in 1810. From 1815 to 1819 he was a Representative in Congress, and in 1820 was appointed, by President Monroe, Minister to Russia, which position he filled for many years. He died in Charleston, South Carolina, June 14, 1846.

Miles, W. Porcher.—Born in Charleston, South Carolina, in July, 1822; prepared for college at the "Wellington School," and graduated at the Charleston College; studied law; was for several years Assistant Professor of Mathematics in Charleston College; he was Mayor of Charleston in 1856 and 1857, and inaugurated the present police system of that city, and also the present system of tidal drains for the same; and he was elected a Representative, from South Carolina, to the Thirty-fifth Congress, and re-elected to the Thirty-sixth. Mr. Miles has been a frequent contributor to the "Southern Quarterly Review," and has delivered a number of literary and patriotic addresses. It ought to be mentioned, that when the yellow fever was raging in Norfolk in 1855, Mr. Miles visited that city as a humanitarian, and for that conduct was rewarded with the office of Mayor of

Charleston. His Committees have been those of Commerce, and Foreign Affairs. Re-elected to the Thirty-seventh Congress. Was elected a member of the South Carolina Seceding Convention in 1860, and resigned his seat in Congress. Served as a Colonel in the Rebellion, and as a member of the Confederate Congress.

Milledge, John.—He was born in Savannah, Georgia, and descended from one of the early settlers of the colony. He frequently served in the Legislature, and in 1780 he was appointed Attorney-General of the State, and Governor in 1802. He was a Representative in Congress, from 1792 to 1802, excepting one term, and a Senator of the United States, from 1806 to 1809, serving for a session as President *pro tem.* of the Senate. He was the principal founder of the University of Georgia, and presented the land which forms its site. He died at his country-seat, at the Sand Hills, February 9, 1818. His memory was honored by an Act of the Legislature, calling the capital of the State Milledgeville.

Millen, John.—He was born in 1804; educated a lawyer; served in the Legislature of Georgia; and died near Savannah, October 15, 1843, about ten days after his election to a seat in the National House of Representatives.

Miller, Daniel F.—Born in Alleghany County, Maryland, October 4, 1814; studied law in Pittsburg, and admitted to the bar in 1838; emigrated to Iowa in 1839; and during the following year was elected to the Legislature of that Territory. In 1848 he was the Whig candidate for Congress, but his seat having been contested, a new election took place in 1850, when he was elected for the term ending in 1851. In 1856, he was a Presidential Elector, since which time he has resided in Fort Madison.

Miller, Daniel H.—He was a native of Philadelphia, Pennsylvania, and was a Representative in Congress, from that State, from 1823 to 1831. Died many years ago.

Miller, Jacob W.—Born in Morris County, New Jersey; bred a lawyer; and was a Senator in Congress, from New Jersey, from 1841 to 1847; and having been re-elected, served until 1853. Died at Morristown, New Jersey, September 30, 1862.

Miller, Jesse.—He was a Representative in Congress, from Pennsylvania, from 1836 to 1837, and died at Harrisburg, August 20, 1850. By President Jackson, he was appointed First Auditor of the Treasury.

Miller, John.—He was born in Dutchess County, New York, and was a Representative in Congress, from New York, from 1825 to 1827, having previously, as well as subsequently, served both in the Assembly and Senate of New York for a number of years.

Miller, John. — He was distinguished for his courage as an officer, in the last war with England; soon after the struggle, he was appointed Register of the Land-office in Missouri; subsequently elected Governor of the State; and he was a Representative in Congress, from 1837 to 1843. Died near Florissant, Missouri, March 18, 1846.

Miller, John G.—Born in Kentucky, and in 1835 emigrated to Missouri. In 1840 was elected to the State Legislature, and from 1853 to the time of his death he was a Representative in Congress, from Missouri. Died in Saline County, Missouri, May 11, 1856, aged forty-four.

Miller, John K.—He was born in Ohio, and was a Representative in Congress, from that State, from 1847 to 1851.

Miller, Joseph.—He was born in Ohio, was elected a Representative, from that State, to the Thirty-fifth Congress, and was a member of the Committees on Unfinished Business, and Expenditures in the Navy Department.

Miller, Killian.—Born in Claverack, Columbia County, New York, July 30, 1785; received a good common school education, with instruction in the Latin and Greek languages. He studied law, and was admitted to practice in 1806; from that time continued to pursue his profession, removing from Livingston to Hudson City in 1833. In 1824 and in 1827 he was a member of the General Assembly, and in 1837 was elected County Clerk, which office he held for three years. In 1854 he was chosen a Representative in the Thirty-fourth Congress.

Miller, Morris S.—He was a Representative in Congress, from New York, from 1813 to 1815; and in 1819 was appointed a Commissioner to superintend a treaty with the Seneca Indians. He was also Judge of a County Court, and died at Utica, November 15, 1824, aged forty-five years.

Miller, Pleasant M.—He was a Representative in Congress, from Tennessee, from 1809 to 1811.

Miller, Rutger B.—Born in New York, and was a Representative, from that State, in the Twenty-fourth Congress, in the place of S. Beardsley, resigned.

Miller, Samuel F.—He was born in Franklin, Delaware County, New York, May 27, 1827; graduated at Hamilton College in 1852; studied law, and came to the bar in 1853, but instead of practising the profession turned his attention to farming and lumbering. In 1854 he was elected to the New York Legislature; in 1850 and 1857 he was Supervisor of Franklin; was for fifteen years identified as a Colonel with the State militia; and in 1862 he was elected a Representative, from New York, to the Thirty-eighth Congress, serving on the Committee on Public Lands.

Miller, Smith.—He is a native of North Carolina, but when a youth removed with his father to Indiana. His school education was limited, and he engaged in farming as an occupation. He was a member of both branches of the Legislature of Indiana, and a Representative in Congress, from 1853 to 1855.

Miller, Stephen D.—He was born in the Waxsaw Settlement, South Carolina, in May, 1787; graduated at the South Carolina College in 1808; adopted the profession of law; came to the bar in 1812; served in the South Carolina Senate in 1822; represented his native State in the Lower House of Congress from 1819 to 1820; was Governor of South Carolina from 1828 to 1830; and elected a Senator in Congress for the term from 1831 to 1837, but resigned on account of his health at the end of two years. He died at Raymond, Mississippi, March 8, 1838, having removed to that State in 1835, where he was an extensive planter.

Miller, William H.—Born in Perry County, Pennsylvania, January 29, 1828; graduated at Marshall College, Franklin, Pennsylvania; in 1854 was appointed Clerk of the Supreme Court of his native State, which office he held until 1863; and he was elected a Representative, from Pennsylvania, to the Thirty-eighth Congress, serving on the Committee on Invalid Pensions. His father, Jesse Miller, was also a Representative in Congress.

Miller, William S.—He was a Representative in Congress, from New York, from 1845 to 1847, and a man of high cultivation. He died in New York City, November 9, 1854.

Milligan, John J.—Born in Cecil County, Maryland, December 10, 1795; after receiving an academical education, he entered Princeton College, and remained three years; he then studied law, and was admitted to practice in New Castle County, Delaware, in 1818, and pursued his profession for several years, but subsequently retired to a country-seat near Wilmington. In 1830 he was elected a member of the House of Representatives in Congress, and served from 1831 to 1839. In 1839 he was appointed, by the Governor, Judge of the Superior Court of the State of Delaware, and has continued in this position ever since.

Mills, Elijah H.—Born in 1778; graduated at Williams College in 1797; studied law; was a Representative in Congress, from Massachusetts, from 1815 to 1819, and a Senator in Congress, from 1820 to 1827. He died at Northampton, May 5, 1829.

Millson, John S.—Born in Norfolk, Virginia, October 1, 1808, and commenced the study of law before the age of sixteen; he held no public office until elected a Representative, from Virginia, in the Thirty-first Congress, which position he has filled, by re-elections, to the present time, 1860, serving as a member of the Committees on Commerce, and Ways and Means.

Millward, John.—Born in Pennsylvania, and elected a Representative, from that State, to the Thirty-sixth Congress, serving as Chairman of the Committee on Patents.

Millward, William. — He was born in Pennsylvania, and was a Representative in Congress, from that State, from 1855 to 1857.

Milnor, James.—He was born in Philadelphia, June 20, 1773; he received his education at a grammar school and at the University of Pennsylvania, and subsequently studied law. In 1794 he commenced the practice of his profession, before he was twenty-one years of age. From 1811 to 1813 he was a Representative, from Pennsylvania, in Congress. In 1811 he was elected a Delegate to the General Convention of the Episcopal Church, and in 1814 was ordained a clergyman by Bishop White, and in 1816 was called to the rectorship of St. George's Church, in New York. He was one of the founders of the New York Deaf and Dumb Institution, and after spending the evening in company with its directors, in apparent good health, died suddenly, April 8, 1845.

Milnor, William.—He was born in Philadelphia, and was a Representative in Congress, from Pennsylvania, from 1807 to 1811, from 1815 to 1817, and again from 1821 to 1822.

Miner, Ahiman L.—He was born in Vermont; was Clerk of the Vermont House of Representatives, in 1836 and 1837; a State Representative, in 1838, 1839, and 1846; a State Senator in 1840; County Attorney for two years; Register of Probate for seven years; Judge of Probate, from 1846 to 1849; and was a Representative in Congress, from Vermont, from 1851 to 1853.

Miner, Charles.—He was born in Norwich, Connecticut, about the year 1800; when a boy, removed with his father to Wilkesbarre, Pennsylvania, and subsequently settled in West Chester, and for many years published the "Village Record," in that place, which attained a high position. He was a Representative in Congress, from Pennsylvania, from 1825 to 1829, and declined a re-election on account of deafness. He is the author of an interesting work, entitled "History of Wyoming."

Miner, Phineas.—He was an eminent lawyer, and a Representative in Congress, from Connecticut, during the years 1834 and 1835, for an unexpired term. He died at Litchfield, in that State, September 16, 1839, aged sixty years.

Mitchell, Anderson. — Born in Caswell County, North Carolina, in 1800. He graduated at the University of that State in 1821; studied law, and settled in Wilkes County in 1840, when he was immediately elected to the Legislature. He was a member of Congress in 1842 and 1843, and since that time has devoted all his attention to his profession.

Mitchell, Charles F. — He was born in New York, and was a Representative in Congress, from that State, from 1837 to 1841.

Mitchell, George E.—He was born in Cecil County, Maryland, and was a Representative in Congress, from Maryland, from 1823 to 1827, and again from 1829 to 1832. He died in Washington, June 28, 1832.

Mitchell, Henry.—He was a Representative in Congress, from New York, from 1833 to 1835.

Mitchell, James C.—He was born in Mecklenburg County, North Carolina, and was a Representative in Congress, from Tennessee, from 1825 to 1829.

Mitchell, James S.—He was born in York County, Pennsylvania, and was a Representative in Congress, from Pennsylvania, from 1821 to 1827.

Mitchell, John.—He was born in Perry County, Pennsylvania, and was a Representative in Congress, from Pennsylvania, from 1825 to 1829. He died at Beaver, Pennsylvania, in August, 1849.

Mitchell, Nahum.—Born in East Bridgewater, Massachusetts, February 12, 1769; graduated at Harvard University in 1789; taught school, studied law, and was admitted to the bar in

1792. From 1811 to 1821 he was Judge of the Circuit Court of Common Pleas, and afterwards Chief Justice. From 1798 to 1812 he was a Representative in the General Court; and a Representative in Congress, from 1803 to 1805. In 1813 and 1814 he was State Senator; and from 1814 to 1820 he was one of the Governor's Council; and from 1822 to 1827 he was Treasurer of the State. In 1840 he published a History of Bridgewater, Massachusetts; was a member of the Massachusetts Historical Society; and published a volume of sacred music, entitled the "Bridgewater Collection." He fell and died suddenly in one of the streets of Plymouth, August 1, 1853, while attending the first celebration of the embarkation of the Pilgrims at Delft Haven.

Mitchell, Stephen M.—He was born at Wethersfield, Connecticut, December 27, 1743; graduated at Yale College in 1763; was chosen a tutor in the College in 1766, in which station he continued three years; he entered upon the practice of law in 1772; was appointed in 1779 a Judge of the Hartford County Court, and in 1790 placed at the head of that Court; in 1795 he was appointed Judge of the Superior Court of Connecticut, and in 1807 Chief Justice of that Court, which office he held until 1814, when he became disqualified by age. He was a Delegate to the old Congress, in 1783 and 1785; and in 1793 he was appointed to the United States Senate, which position he held until 1795, when he was made Judge of the Superior Court. It was to his services, while in Congress, that Connecticut was greatly indebted for the establishment of her title to the tract of land in Ohio called the "Western Reserve." He died in the place of his birth, September 30, 1835. In him were combined the dignity of the Christian, the purity of the patriot, and the virtues of the faithful public servant and useful citizen.

Mitchell, Thomas R.—Born in Georgetown, South Carolina; he graduated at Harvard University in 1802; was a Representative in Congress, from South Carolina, from 1821 to 1823, from 1825 to 1829, and again from 1831 to 1833; he died in 1837.

Mitchell, William.—He was born in New York, and elected a Representative from Indiana, to the Thirty-seventh Congress, serving on the Committee on Indian Affairs.

Mitchill, Robert.—He was born in Pennsylvania, and was a Representative in Congress, from 1833 to 1835, from Ohio.

Mitchill, Samuel Latham.—Born on Long Island in 1763, and was well educated; after the close of the war he went to Edinburgh, and there studied medicine and natural history. On his return he was appointed Professor of Chemistry and Natural History in Columbia College; and his practice as a physician was extensive; he edited, with Dr. Smith, fourteen volumes of the "Medical Repository;" he also published a Life of Tammany, the Indian chief, and other useful works, historical and scientific. He was a Representative in Congress, from New York, from 1801 to 1804, and again from 1810 to 1813; and a Senator, from 1804 to 1809. He died in New York, September 8, 1831.

Moffit, Hosea.—He was born in New York; served six years in the Legislature of that State; and was a Representative in Congress, from 1813 to 1817.

Molony, Richard S.—He was born in New Hampshire, and was a Representative in Congress, from Illinois, from 1851 to 1853.

Monell, Robert.—He was a native of Columbia County, New York, and a Representative in Congress, from that State, from 1819 to 1821, and again from 1829 to 1831.

Monroe, James.—Born April 28, 1758, in Westmoreland County, Virginia. He was educated at William and Mary College. In 1776 he joined the army in the Revolutionary war, and continued with it till 1778, having displayed great bravery, when he retired and engaged in the study of law. In 1780 he held the office of Military Commissioner for Virginia, and in that capacity visited the Southern army. In 1782 he was a member of the Virginia Assembly; and in 1783 a Delegate to Congress. In 1788 he was a member of the Convention, in Virginia, to deliberate on the proposed Constitution for the United States. In 1790 he was elected a Senator of the United States, from Virginia. In 1794 he received the appointment of Minister Plenipotentiary to France, and was recalled in 1797. In 1799 he was elected Governor of Virginia. In 1802 he was sent on a special mission to France, which resulted in the purchase of Louisiana. In 1803 he was appointed Minister to England; and in 1805 he was associated with Charles Pinckney to negotiate with Spain. During his residence in England, he and Mr. William Pinckney negotiated a commercial treaty with Great Britain, but it was never submitted to the Senate by President Jefferson. He returned to America in 1808. In 1811 he was Governor of Virginia, and the same year received, from President Madison, the appointment of Secretary of State, which office he held till his election as President, March 4, 1817. During a part of the time, in 1814 and 1815, he also performed the duties of Secretary of War. He was again elected President in 1821. He died July 4, 1831.

Monroe, James.—He was born in Virginia, and having removed to New York, was elected a Representative in Congress, from that State, serving from 1839 to 1841; he was a member of the Assembly of New York in 1850 and 1852, and a State Senator during the three subsequent years.

Montanya, J. L. D.—He was born in New York, served two years in the Assembly of that State, and was a Representative in Congress, from New York, from 1839 to 1841.

Montgomery, Daniel.—He was a Representative in Congress, from Pennsylvania, from 1807 to 1809.

Montgomery, John.—He was a Representative in Congress, from Maryland, from 1807 to 1811.

Montgomery, John G.—He was elected a member of the Thirty-fifth Congress, from Pennsylvania, but died before taking his seat, of the mysterious National Hotel disease, at Danville, Pennsylvania, April 24, 1857, aged fifty-two years. He was an excellent lawyer, of great experience and learning, and a brilliant career was anticipated for him in the arena of national politics.

Montgomery, Thomas.—He was born in Nelson County, Virginia, and was a Representative in Congress, from Kentucky, from 1813 to 1815, and again from 1821 to 1823. Died April 2, 1828.

Montgomery, William.—He was a Representative in Congress, from Pennsylvania, from 1793 to 1795.

Montgomery, William.—Born in Guilford County, North Carolina, and was educated for the medical profession. He was elected to the General Assembly in 1824, where he served, with but one intermission, until 1834, when he was elected a Representative in Congress, and continued in that position until 1841. He died November 27, 1844, aged fifty-three years.

Montgomery, William.—Born in Canton Township, Pennsylvania, April 11, 1819; graduated at Washington College, Pennsylvania, in 1839; he studied law, and was admitted to the bar in 1842, and he was elected a Representative in Congress, in 1856, serving in the Thirty-fifth Congress on the Committee on Public Lands. He was re-elected to the Thirty-sixth Congress, serving as a member of the Committee on Roads and Canals.

Moor, Wyman B. S.—Born in Waterville, Maine, November 3, 1814; graduated at Waterville College; studied law at Cambridge, and admitted to the bar in 1834; was a member of the Maine Legislature, in 1839; was Attorney-General of that State, from 1844 to 1848; and by appointment, succeeded John Fairfield, as a Senator in Congress, serving during the session of 1848 and 1849. He subsequently devoted much attention to the railroad interests of his State, and in 1857 was appointed by President Buchanan, Consul-General for the British American Provinces.

Moore, Andrew.—He was a Representative in Congress, from Virginia, from 1789 to 1797, and again from 1803 to 1804; when he was chosen to the United States Senate, and served until 1809. Died in May, 1821.

Moore, Eli.—He was born in New Jersey, and educated as a printer; was a Representative in Congress, from New York, from 1835 to 1839; was appointed Marshal of New York by President Polk; subsequently edited a newspaper in New Jersey; was appointed Indian Agent in Kansas Territory; and at the time of his death, in 1859, was Register of a Land, office in Kansas.

Moore, Gabriel.—He was born in Stokes County, North Carolina, and was a Representative in Congress, from Alabama, from 1822 to 1829; a Senator in Congress, from 1831 to 1837; and died at Caddo, Texas, in 1844.

Moore, Henry D.—He was born in Goshen, Orange County, New York, April 17, 1817; received his education at one of the public schools of New York City; when sixteen years of age, he acquired a knowledge of the tailoring business, which he followed until 1843; in that year he removed to Philadelphia, and became interested in the marble business; and he was a Representative in Congress, from Pennsylvania, from 1849 to 1853.

Moore, Heman A.—He was born in Vermont, in 1810, studied law in Rochester, New York, and removing to Columbus, Ohio, obtained distinction as a lawyer, and was a Representative in Congress, from that State, from 1843 to the time of his death, which occurred in Columbus, April 3, 1844.

Moore, John.—He was a Representative in Congress, from Louisiana, from 1841 to 1843.

Moore, John.—He was born in Virginia, and was a Representative in Congress, from that State, from 1851 to 1853.

Moore, Laban T.—Born in Cabell County, Virginia, January 13, 1829; received a limited education; removed to Kentucky and adopted the profession of law; and was elected a Representative, from Kentucky, to the Thirty-sixth Congress, serving on the Committee on Manufactures.

Moore, Nicholas R.—He was a Representative in Congress, from Maryland, from 1803 to 1811, and again from 1813 to 1816. Died at Baltimore, in 1816.

Moore, Oscar F.—He was born in Ohio, and was a Representative in Congress, from that State, from 1855 to 1857.

Moore, Robert.—He was born in Washington County, Pennsylvania, and was a Representative in Congress, from that State, from 1817 to 1821.

Moore, Samuel.—He was born in Cumberland County, New Jersey, and was a Representative in Congress, from Pennsylvania, from 1819 to 1822.

Moore, S. McD.—He was born in Virginia, and was a Representative in Congress, from that State, from 1833 to 1835.

Moore, Sydenham.—Born in Rutherford County, Tennessee, but removed to Alabama with his parents, soon after its admission as a State; he was educated at the University of Alabama; was bred to the profession of the law; was Judge of the County Court of Greene County, Alabama, for six years, and for a short time also of the Circuit Court of that State; resigned his judgeship, and went to Mexico as Captain of a volunteer company, and served one year, a portion of the time in General Taylor's line, on the Rio Grande, and also in General Scott's line at Tampico, Vera Cruz, Alvarado, and Jalapa; and, on his return home, was elected Brigadier-General of militia; and was chosen, in 1857, a member of the Thirty-fifth Congress; and re-elected to the Thirty-sixth Congress, serving as a member of the Committee on Claims. Took part in the Rebellion as a Colonel.

Moore, Thomas.—He was a Representative in Congress, from South Carolina, from 1801 to 1813, and again from 1815 to 1817.

Moore, Thomas P.—He was born in Charlotte County, Virginia, in 1795; was an officer in the war of 1812; member of Congress, from 1823 to 1829, from Kentucky; Minister to the Republic of Colombia in 1829; and Lieutenant-Colonel in the regular army during the war with Mexico. His last public position was that of member of the Convention for revising the Constitution of

Kentucky. He died in Harrodsburg, Kentucky, July 21, 1853.

Moore, Thomas S.—He was born in Jefferson County Virginia, and was a Representative in Congress, from that State, from 1820 to 1823.

Moorhead, J. Kennedy.—Born on the Susquehanna River, Pennsylvania, in 1806; received a limited education; spent the most of his youth on a farm, and as an apprentice to a tanner; was one of the contractors for building the Susquehanna branch of the Pennsylvania Canal; was the originator of a passenger packet line on said canal; in 1836 he removed to Pittsburg, and there took an active part in improving the navigation of the Monongahela, and was made President of a company bearing that name, and established in that city the Union Cotton Factory; in 1838 he received the militia title of Adjutant-General, and subsequently, taking a great interest in the business of telegraphing, became the President of several telegraphic companies. In 1859 he was elected a Representative, from Pennsylvania, to the Thirty-sixth Congress, serving as a member of the Committee on Commerce; was re-elected to the Thirty-seventh Congress, serving as Chairman of the special Committee on National Armories; re-elected to the Thirty-eighth Congress, serving as Chairman of the Committee on Manufactures, and as a member of the Committee on Naval Affairs.

Moorhead, Charles S.—He was born in Nelson County, Kentucky, in 1802; he adopted the profession of law, and after practising it for a few years he was elected to the State Legislature, serving during 1828 and 1829; he was appointed, in 1832, Attorney-General of Kentucky, which office he held five years; in 1838, 1839, and 1840, he was again returned to the Legislature, officiating during the latter year as Speaker; was re-elected and made Speaker in 1841; was again re-elected in 1842 and 1844, and for the third time chosen Speaker; and he was a Representative in Congress, from Kentucky, from 1847 to 1851; in 1853 he was once more returned to the Legislature; and in 1855 was elected Governor of Kentucky. He was for many years one of the most devoted friends and supporters of Henry Clay. In 1861 he was a Delegate to the Peace Convention held in Washington.

Morehead, I. T.—A Representative in Congress, from North Carolina, from 1851 to 1853.

Morehead, James T.—Born in Covington, Kentucky, May 24, 1797; studied law and entered upon the practice in 1818. He served three years in the State Legislature; in 1832 he was elected Lieutenant-Governor of Kentucky, and after the death of Governor Breathitt, in 1834, became Governor. In 1837 he was again elected to the Legislature; and in 1838 he was appointed President of the Board of Internal Improvements, which office he held until 1841, when he was elected to the United States Senate for the term of six years. He subsequently resumed the practice of his profession, and died at Covington, Kentucky, December 28, 1854.

Morgan, Christopher.—He was born in Groton, Connecticut; graduated at Yale College in 1828; and was a Representative in Congress, from New York, from 1839 to 1843.

Morgan, Daniel.—Was a native of New Jersey, but removed in early life to Virginia. Having neither the advantages of wealth nor of a good education, he was dependent for his support on hard labor. In 1755 he served as a private soldier under General Braddock. At the close of the campaign he retired to a farm in Frederick County. At the commencement of the Revolution he commanded a troop of cavalry, under General Washington, at Boston. He was detached on the expedition against Quebec, and when Arnold was wounded he took command of his division; but the retreat of the other division, after the fall of Montgomery, left Morgan to contend with the whole force of the enemy, and he was taken prisoner; on being exchanged, he was appointed to the command of a regiment. He was with General Gates at the capture of Burgoyne. In 1778 he commanded a corps on the Schuylkill to cut off supplies from the British in Philadelphia. He served in the Southern campaign, under General Greene, and advanced to the rank of Brigadier-General, receiving from Congress a gold medal, for the skill and bravery he displayed at the battle of Cowpens in the defeat of Tarleton. In 1794 he commanded the militia of Virginia, ordered out by President Washington, for the purpose of suppressing the Whiskey Insurrection in Pennsylvania. He was a Representative in Congress from 1795 to 1799. In 1799 he published an address to his constituents, vindicating the administration of Mr. Adams. He died at Winchester, Virginia, in 1802, aged sixty-nine.

Morgan, Edwin B.—Born at Aurora, Cayuga County, New York, May 2, 1806. He was a merchant by occupation, until his election to the Thirty-third Congress as Representative; and he was re-elected to the Thirty-fourth and Thirty-fifth Congresses, and was a member of the Committee on Public Buildings and Grounds.

Morgan, Edwin D. — Born in Washington, Berkshire County, Massachusetts, February 8, 1811; at the age of seventeen years he entered a wholesale grocery house, in Hartford, Connecticut, as a clerk, and in three years became a partner; soon after reaching his majority he was chosen a member of the City Council of Hartford; in 1836 he settled in New York City, and was extensively devoted to mercantile pursuits; in 1849 he was chosen an Alderman of the city; during the same year he was elected to the State Senate, serving two terms; in 1855 he was appointed Commissioner of Emigration, and held the office until 1858; was a Vice-President of the National Republican Convention, held at Pittsburg in 1856; and has since then been Chairman of the National Republican Committee; in 1858 he was elected Governor of New York; re-elected in 1860; in 1861 he was appointed, by President Lincoln, Major-General of volunteers, and though he rendered much service, declined all compensation, the number of troops sent to the war during his administration having amounted to 223,000; and in 1863 he was elected a Senator in Congress, for New York, for the term ending in 1869, serving on the Committees on Finance, Military Affairs, and on Printing. He was also a Delegate to the Baltimore Convention of 1864.

Morgan, James.—He was born in New Jersey, and was a Representative in Congress, from that State, from 1811 to 1813.

Morgan, John J.—He was born in Queen's County, New York, and was a member of the New York Assembly; a Representative in Congress, from that State, from 1821 to 1825; and again in the Assembly in 1836 and 1840. Died in July, 1849.

Morgan, William S. — Born in Monongalia County, Virginia, September 7, 1801. He was self-educated; served as a Representative in Congress, from Virginia, from 1835 to 1839, and was Chairman of the Committee on Revolutionary Pensions, and declined a re-election; in 1840 he was appointed a Clerk in the House of Representatives, from which position he was transferred to the Legislature of Virginia, and declined a re-election; he was a Democratic Elector in 1844; and in 1845, having injured his health by public speaking, he was appointed to a clerkship in the Treasury Department.

Morril, David L.—Born in Epping, New Hampshire, June 10, 1772, and died February 4, 1849. He attended Exeter Academy, studied medicine, and commenced the practice at Epsom in 1793. He also studied theology, and was ordained a pastor, but resigned his charge in 1811, and resumed the practice of medicine. He was a Representative to the General Court, in 1811, 1812, and 1816; and in 1816 was chosen to the United States Senate for six years. He subsequently became a member of the State Senate, and its President, and afterwards, for four successive terms, was elected Governor of New Hampshire. He wrote and published many occasional discourses and essays, on various religious and secular topics.

Morrill, Anson P.—Was born in Belgrade, Maine, June 10, 1803; received the advantages of a common school education; has been chiefly devoted to mercantile and manufacturing pursuits; was for several years a member of the Maine Legislature; was Governor of Maine from 1855 to 1857; and in 1860 was elected a Representative, from Maine, to the Thirty-seventh Congress, serving on the Committees on Post-offices and Post-roads, and Revolutionary Claims.

Morrill, Justin S.—He was born in Strafford, Vermont, April 14, 1810; received an academic education, and engaged in mercantile pursuits until the year 1848, when he turned his attention to agriculture. He was elected a Representative, from Vermont, to the Thirty-fourth Congress; and re-elected to the Thirty-fifth, the Thirty-sixth, the Thirty-seventh, and the Thirty-eighth Congresses, serving on the special Committee on the Sale of Fort Snelling, and on the regular Committees on Agriculture, and on Ways and Means.

Morrill, Lot M. — Was born in Belgrade, Kennebeck County, Maine, in 1815; entered Waterville College in 1834, but soon after commenced the study of law, and in 1839 was admitted to the bar. He was a member of the Maine Legislature in 1854; of the Senate in 1856, and made its President; he was elected Governor of Maine in 1858, and re-elected in 1859 and 1860; and in 1861 was elected a Senator in Congress, for the unexpired term of Hannibal Hamlin, elected Vice-President of the United States. In the Senate, Mr. Morrill has served on the Committees on Commerce, District of Columbia, and Claims. He was also a member of the Peace Congress of 1861. He was re-elected to the United States Senate in 1863, for the term ending in 1869.

Morris, Calvary.—He was born in Virginia, and was a Representative in Congress, from Ohio, from 1837 to 1844.

Morris, Daniel.—Born in Seneca County, New York, January 4, 1812; settled when quite young in Yates County, and was bred a farmer; having educated himself, he taught school for a while, and then adopted the profession of law; was at one time District Attorney for Yates County; served one term in the State Legislature; and was elected a Representative, from New York, to the Thirty-eighth Congress, serving on the Committee on the Judiciary.

Morris, Edward Joy.—Born in Philadelphia, Pennsylvania, July 15, 1817; graduated at Harvard University; was a member of the House of Representatives of Pennsylvania in 1841, 1842, and 1843; and elected to the Twenty-eighth Congress, as Representative from the First Congressional District; was appointed United States Chargé d'Affaires to Naples in 1850, where he remained four years. On his return to Philadelphia, was chosen a member of the Board of Directors of Girard College. In 1856 was again elected to the State Legislature, and in the fall of that year was elected to the Thirty-fifth Congress, and was a member of the Committee for the District of Columbia. As an author, his publications are, "A Tour through Turkey, Greece, and Egypt, Arabia Petræa," &c.; "The Turkish Empire, Social and Political;" "Afraja, or Life and Love in Norway" (a translation); and also a translation from the German of Gregozovius, "Corsica, Social and Political," &c. He was re-elected to the Thirty-sixth Congress, serving as a member of the Committee on Foreign Affairs. Re-elected to the Thirty-seventh Congress.

Morris, Gouverneur.—Minister from the United States to France, and an eminent American statesman and orator. Born in Morrisania, New York, in 1752, and graduated at King's College, in the city of New York, in 1768. He was bred to the law, came to the bar in 1771, and attained great celebrity in the profession. In 1775 he was a Delegate to the Provincial Congress, from New York, and was employed in the public service in various capacities during the Revolutionary contest, and in all of them displayed great zeal and ability. After the war of the Revolution he retired from public life, although an active member of the Convention which formed the present Constitution of the United States. In 1792 he was appointed Minister to France, and remained in that capacity till October, 1794. He returned to America in 1798, and in 1800 was chosen a Senator of the United States, from New York, serving three years. After retiring from Congress, he spent seven years in Philadelphia. He died November 6, 1816, aged sixty-four. His publications were numerous. Selections from his papers, with a sketch of his life, have been published by Jared Sparks.

Morris, Isaac N.—He is the fourth son of Thomas Morris, and brother of Jonathan D. Morris; was born in Ohio,

January 22, 1812. He studied law, and was admitted to the bar in 1835; in 1836 he emigrated to Illinois, and settled in Quincy, where he still resides. In 1840 he was appointed Secretary of State for Illinois, but declined the position; in 1841 he was chosen President of the Illinois and Michigan Canal Company; in 1846 he was elected to the State Legislature from Adams County; in 1856 he was elected a Representative, from Illinois, to the Thirty-fifth Congress, and re-elected to the Thirty-sixth Congress, serving as a member of the Committee on Roads and Canals.

Morris, James R.—He was born in Greene County, Pennsylvania, January 10, 1820 (his father, Joseph Morris, having been a member of Congress in 1843 and 1845), and having become a resident of Ohio, he was elected in 1848 to the Legislature of that State; and in 1860 he was elected a Representative, from Ohio, to the Thirty-seventh Congress, serving on the Committee on Public Buildings and Grounds. In 1862 he was re-elected to the Thirty-eighth Congress, serving on the Committee for the District of Columbia.

Morris, Jonathan D.—He was born in Ohio, and was a Representative, from that State, to the Thirty-first Congress.

Morris, Jonathan D.—He is the eldest son of Thomas Morris, was born in Ohio, and is a lawyer by profession. He served for twenty years as Clerk of the Court of Common Pleas, and of the Supreme Court of Clermont County, Ohio; and he was a Representative in Congress, from Ohio, from 1847 to 1851. Now devoted to the practice of his profession.

Morris, Joseph.—Born in Greene County, Pennsylvania, October 16, 1795. He was left an orphan at the age of ten years, and having been apprenticed to the trade of a wheelwright, he continued to follow the business until he was twenty-five years old. In 1824 he was elected Sheriff of his native county. In 1829 he removed to Ohio, and devoted himself to merchandizing; he was elected to the Ohio Legislature in 1833 and 1834; he was Treasurer for Monroe County for one year, and, while in that office, was elected to Congress in 1843, and re-elected in 1845, serving two entire terms. He died at Woodfield, Ohio, October 23, 1854.

Morris, Lewis R.—He was a Representative in Congress, from Vermont, from 1797 to 1803.

Morris, Mathias.—A Representative in Congress, from Pennsylvania, from 1835 to 1839, and was much respected for his talents. He died at Doylestown, Pennsylvania, November 9, 1839, aged fifty-four years.

Morris, Robert.—He was a native of England, but came to the United States when a boy of thirteen, and settled in Philadelphia as a clerk, where he spent the most of his life as an influential merchant and financier. He was a member of the Congress of 1776, and signed the Declaration of Independence. In 1781 he obtained the control of the American finances, and rendered important services to his adopted country. He was a member of the Convention which formed the present Constitution, and was chosen a United States Senator, serving from 1789 to 1795. Notwithstanding his valuable services to his country, he passed the latter years of his life in imprisonment for debt. Until the period of his impoverishment, his house had been the scene of most liberal hospitality. He died May 8, 1806, aged seventy-one years.

Morris, Samuel W. — Born in 1788; was for many years Judge of the District Court of Tioga County, Pennsylvania, and was a member of the House of Representatives, in Congress, from 1837 to 1841. He died in Wellsborough, Pennsylvania, May 25, 1847.

Morris, Thomas.—He was for three years a member of the New York Assembly, from Ontario County, and a Representative in Congress, from 1801 to 1803.

Morris, Thomas.—He was born in Virginia, January 3, 1776, and was the son of a Baptist clergyman. When nineteen years of age he emigrated to the valley of the Ohio, and settled near the present site of Cincinnati, but two years afterwards removed to the county of Clermont. In 1802, while engaged in the avocation of a day laborer, and without an instructor, he commenced the study of law, adopted the profession, and became eminent. In 1806 he was elected to the Legislature of Ohio, and represented Clermont County, either in the Senate or House, for a period of twenty-four years, doing much to develop the resources of his adopted State. He was also Chief Judge of Ohio, and he was elected a Senator in Congress for the long term, from 1833 to 1839. He died December 7, 1844, and his Life and collected speeches and writings have been published in one volume, under the supervision of his son, Rev. B. F. Morris. While in Congress he ably defended the freedom of the press, the freedom of speech, and the right of petition. Isaac N. and Jonathan D. Morris were his sons.

Morrison, George W.—He was born in Vermont, and was a Representative in Congress, from New Hampshire, from 1850 to 1851, and again from 1853 to 1855.

Morrison, John A.—He was born in Pennsylvania, and was a Representative in Congress, from that State, from 1851 to 1853.

Morrison, William Balls.—Was born in Monroe County, Illinois, September 14, 1825; received a liberal education, and adopted the profession of law; in 1852 was chosen Clerk of Monroe County, which office he resigned to go into the State Legislature, where he served three years, and was Speaker of the House in 1859; served as a private in the Mexican war, fighting under Colonel Bissell at Buena Vista; after the Rebellion broke out, he organized the Forty-ninth Regiment Illinois Volunteers, and was severely wounded at Fort Donelson; and while in command of his regiment in the field was elected a Representative, from Illinois, to the Thirty-eighth Congress, serving on the Committee on the Militia.

Morrow, Jeremiah. — Born in Pennsylvania in 1770, but removed to the Northwest Territory, now the State of Ohio, in 1795, and was chosen a member of the Territorial Legislature in 1800. He was the first Representative in Congress, from Ohio, serving from 1803 to 1813; and was a Senator in Congress, from 1813 to 1819, being appointed, in 1814, a Commissioner to treat with the Indians. He was Governor of Ohio, from 1822 to 1826; subsequently a Canal Commissioner; served a second time as a Representative in Congress, from 1841 to 1843, officiating as Chairman of the Committee on Public Lands; and for several years before his death was President of the Little Miami Railroad Company. He died in Ohio, March 22, 1852.

Morse, Freeman H. — He was born in Bath, Maine, February 18, 1807; was in the State Legislature from 1840 to 1844, and also in 1853 and 1856; was Mayor of Bath three years; was elected to Congress in 1843, serving one term; and was re-elected a Representative to the Thirty-fifth Congress, from Maine, serving as a member of the Committee on the Cost of Public Printing, and that on Naval Affairs. He was also re-elected to the Thirty-sixth Congress. He was also a member of the Peace Congress of 1861.

Morse, Isaac E.—He was born in Louisiana, and was a Representative in Congress, from that State, from 1843 to 1851.

Morse, O. A. — Born in Cherry Valley, Otsego County, New York, March 26, 1815; graduated at Hamilton College, New York; studied law, but has not practised of late years; and was elected a Representative to the Thirty-fifth Congress, serving as a member of the Committee on Invalid Pensions.

Morton, Jackson.—He was born in Virginia, and, removing to Florida, was a Senator in Congress, from that State, from 1849 to 1855. He subsequently entered extensively into the business of manufacturing lumber in Florida. Served in the Rebellion as a member of the Confederate Congress.

Morton, Jeremiah.—He was born in Virginia, and was a Representative in Congress, from that State, from 1849 to 1851.

Morton, Marcus.—He was born in Freetown, Massachusetts, December 19, 1784; graduated at Brown University in 1804; studied law, and devoted himself to politics; in 1811 he was chosen Clerk of the Massachusetts Senate; he was a Representative in Congress, from Massachusetts, from 1817 to 1821; in 1823 was a member of the Executive Council of that State; in 1824 was elected Lieutenant-Governor; subsequently a Judge of the Supreme Court of Massachusetts, from 1825 to 1840; and was Governor of the State from 1840 to 1841, and again from 1843 to 1844; and was Collector of Boston from 1845 to 1849. He was also a member of the Constitutional Convention of 1853; and a member of the State Legislature in 1858.

Mosely, Jonathan Ogden.—Born at East Haddon, Middlesex County, Connecticut; was a graduate of Yale College in 1780; and a Representative in Congress, from his native State, from 1805 to 1821. He subsequently removed to Michigan, and died at Saginaw, in that State, September 9, 1839, aged seventy-seven years.

Mosely, William A.—He graduated at Yale College in 1816; was a member of the New York Assembly in 1835; of the State Senate, from 1838 to 1841; and a Representative in Congress, from 1843 to 1847.

Mott, Gordon N.—Was born in Zanesville, Ohio, October 21, 1812; studied law, and came to the bar in 1836; during the troubles in that year between Mexico and Texas, he served nine months as a volunteer in the Texan service; and soon after that returned to Ohio, and settled in the practice of his profession in Miami County. He also served as a Captain in the war with Mexico, having raised the company he commanded, after which he again returned to his native State. In 1849 he emigrated to California; in 1850 was elected Judge of Sutter County; in 1851 appointed a District Judge; in 1861 he was appointed, by President Lincoln, a Justice of the Supreme Court of Nevada Territory; and in 1862 was elected a Delegate, from that Territory, to the Thirty-eighth Congress.

Mott, James.—He was a Representative in Congress, from New Jersey, from 1801 to 1805. He had previously been Treasurer of the State, and was a Presidential Elector in 1809.

Mott, Richard.—Born in Mamaroneck, Westchester County, New York, July 21, 1804. He was educated at the Quaker Seminary of "Nine Partners," in Dutchess County, New York; bred a merchant, and has resided in Toledo, Ohio, for twenty years; was elected to the Thirty-fourth Congress, and re-elected to the Thirty-fifth.

Moulton, Mace.—He was born in New Hampshire; was Sheriff of Hillsboro County in 1845; a State Councillor in 1848 and 1849; and was a Representative in Congress, from that State, from 1845 to 1847.

Mouton, Alexander.—He was a Senator in Congress, from Louisiana, from 1837 to 1842.

Muhlenberg, Francis S.—Born in Reading, Pennsylvania; received a liberal education; was private Secretary to Governor Heister; removed to Ohio; served in the Legislature of that State; was a Representative in Congress, from Ohio, during the session of 1828–9; and died in Pickaway County, Ohio, in 1832, aged thirty-two years.

Muhlenberg, Frederick A.—Born in Philadelphia, Pennsylvania; was Treasurer of the State; President of the Convention which ratified the Constitution of the United States; was a Representative in Congress, from 1789 to 1797; and Speaker of the House during the First and Third Congresses. He died at Lancaster, Pennsylvania, June 4, 1801, aged fifty-one years.

Muhlenberg, Henry A.—He was born in Reading, Pennsylvania, and was Representative in Congress, from that State, from 1853 to 1854. He died January 9, 1854, in the prime of life.

Muhlenberg, Henry Augustus.—He was born in Lancaster, Pennsylvania, May 13, 1782. Under the instruction of his father, a learned clergyman of the Lutheran Church, he completed the usual course of collegiate studies at an early age; and in 1802 he was ordained as a Lutheran clergyman, and had the pastoral charge of Trinity Church at Reading, in which position he remained until 1828, when, on account of ill health, he resigned, and retired to a farm. In 1829 he was elected a Representative in Congress, serving until 1838, when he resigned his seat, having, during his term of office, been Chairman of several important Committees. In 1835 he was the Democratic candidate for Governor, but the Whig party was successful. In 1837 President Van Buren tendered him a place in his cabinet as Secretary of the Navy, and also the mission to Russia, both of which he declined, but in 1838 he accepted the mission to Austria, and was recalled at his own request in 1841. In 1844 he was again a candidate for Governor, but he died suddenly at Reading, August 12, 1844, a few weeks before the election, leaving the reputation of an upright and able statesman.

Muhlenberg, Peter.—He was born at the Trappe, Montgomery County, Pennsylvania, October 1, 1746. He was educated in Germany, and on his return home, studied theology with his father. In 1772 he went to London with Bishop White, who was also a candidate for holy orders, and was ordained, by the Bishop of London, as an Episcopal clergyman. He was for a few years settled over a parish in Virginia, but at the commencement of the Revolution, he was urged to take a military command; and he accordingly preached his last sermon to his parishioners, throwing off his clerical robes, and appearing in the pulpit in full uniform, saying; "There is a time for all things, and now is the time to fight;" read his commission as Colonel, and ordered the drummers to beat for recruits; his parishioners crowded to the standard, and he had no difficulty in forming a regiment. His first campaigns were fought in Georgia and South Carolina. In 1777 he was promoted to the rank of Brigadier-General, and participated in the battles of Brandywine, Germantown, Monmouth, and Stony Point; and in 1780, held the chief command, when Leslie invaded Virginia, and was next in command to Lafayette when Cornwallis entered Virginia. He commanded the First Brigade of Light Infantry at Yorktown; and when the army was disbanded, he received the commission of Major-General. After returning to his abode in Pennsylvania, he was elected a member of the Supreme Executive Council of the State. In 1785 he was chosen Vice-President of the Commonwealth, and upon the adoption of the Federal Constitution, he was elected a Representative in Congress, serving from 1789 to 1791, from 1793 to 1795, and from 1799 to 1801. In 1797 he was a Presidential Elector; and in 1801 he was elected United States Senator, but resigned in 1802, and was appointed Supervisor of the Revenue for the District of Pennsylvania. In 1803 he was made Collector of the Port of Philadelphia, and held this office until his death, which occurred October 1, 1807.

Mullen, Joseph.—He was a native of Ireland, and a Representative in Congress, from New York, from 1847 to 1849.

Mumford, George.—Born in Rowan County, North Carolina. He represented it in the General Assembly in 1810 and 1811; and was a Representative in Congress, from 1817 to 1819, having died in Washington before the expiration of his term, December 31, 1818.

Mumford, Gurdon S.—He was born in New York, and was a Representative in Congress, from that State, from 1805 to 1811.

Murfree, William H.—Born in Hertford County, North Carolina; graduated at Chapel Hill in 1801, and having studied law, was a successful advocate. He served in the State Legislature in 1805, and was a Representative in Congress, from 1813 to 1817. In 1825 he emigrated to Tennessee, and soon after died at Nashville.

Murphy, Charles.—He was born in South Carolina, and was a Representative in Congress, from Georgia, from 1851 to 1853.

Murphy, Henry C.—He was born in Brooklyn, New York, in 1810; graduated at Columbia College in 1830; studied law, and was admitted to the bar in 1833; was at one time Attorney for the city of Brooklyn; was elected Mayor of that city in 1842; was a Representative in Congress, from New York, from 1843 to 1849; and by President Buchanan was appointed Minister to the Hague. In his tastes he was decidedly literary, and has devoted much attention to the investigation of the early history of his native State. On his return from Europe, he was elected to the Legislature of New York.

Murphy, John.—He was a native of South Carolina; graduated at the South Carolina College in 1808; was Clerk of the Senate of South Carolina; Trustee of his Alma Mater; removed to Alabama in 1817; was Governor of Alabama, from 1825 to 1829, and a Representative in Congress, from that State, from 1833 to 1835. He died in Clark County Alabama, September 21, 1841, in the fifty-sixth year of his age.

Murray, Ambrose S.—He was born in New York, and was elected a Representative, from that State, to the Thirty-fourth and Thirty-fifth Congresses, and was a member of the Committee on Mileage.

Murray, John.—He was born in Lancaster, Pennsylvania, and was a Representative in Congress, from that State, from 1817 to 1821.

Murray, John L.—He was a Representative in Congress, from Kentucky, from 1838 to 1839.

Murray, Thomas.—He was born in Northumberland County, Pennsylvania, and was a Representative in Congress, from that State, from 1821 to 1823.

Murray, William.—He was born in New York, and was a Representative in Congress, from that State, from 1851 to 1855.

Murray, William Vans.—He was born in Maryland, about the year 1761. In 1783 he went to London, and entered as a student of law at the Temple, and remained three years. On returning to his native State, he engaged in the practice of law, but was soon elected to a seat in the Legislature. In 1791 he was elected a Representative to Congress, and continued in that position until 1797, when he declined being a candidate. He was appointed, by Washington, Minister to the Netherlands; and, in connection with Mr. Ellsworth and Mr. Davie, he negotiated a treaty with France in 1800. He returned to the United States in 1801, and died December 11, 1803. He possessed great keenness of wit and delicacy of taste, and was distinguished for his eloquence, having a mind well stored with science and literature.

Myers, Amos.—Born in Lancaster County, Pennsylvania, April 23, 1824; received a good academic education; studied law and came to the bar in 1846. In 1847 he was appointed a District Attorney, and in 1862 he was elected a Representative, from Pennsylvania, to the Thirty-eighth Congress, serving as Chairman of the Committee on Expenditures in the Navy Department, and a member of the Committee on Mileage.

Myers, Leonard.—He was born in Attleborough, Bucks County, Pennsylvania, November 13, 1827; received a liberal education, and adopted the profession of law; was Solicitor for two municipal districts in Philadelphia; digested the ordinances for the consolidation of the city, and has translated several works from the French. He was elected, in 1862, a Representative, from Pennsylvania, to the Thirty-eighth Congress, serving on the Committees on Patents, and Expenditures in the Post-office Department.

Nabers, Benjamin D.—He was born in Tennessee, and, on removing to Mississippi, was elected a Representative in Congress, from that State, from 1851 to 1853.

Naudain, Arnold.—He was born in Delaware; graduated at Princeton College in 1806, and was a Senator in Congress, from that State, from 1829 to 1836.

Naylor, Charles.—Born in the County of Philadelphia, Pennsylvania, October 6, 1806; educated a lawyer, admitted in 1828 to the bar of Philadelphia, and was there for some years extensively engaged in practice. He represented his native district in Congress, from 1837 to 1841. In 1846 he raised in Philadelphia a company of volunteers, and, as their Captain, took part in the war with Mexico; rendezvoused at the Island of Lobos, in the Gulf of Mexico; landed with the invading army at Vera Cruz; was active in the operations before that city, and in most of the engagements on General Scott's line. Upon the fall of the city of Mexico, September 14, 1847, he was appointed

Governor of the National Palace (the "Halls of the Montezumas"), and keeper of the archives and property of that Republic; and continued to hold that place, and to aid in the administration of the government of the city, till the final evacuation of it by the American army, June 12, 1848. He has filled many posts of trust and honor in his native State, and is at present engaged in the practice of his profession in the city of Washington.

Neal, Raphael.—He was born in St. Mary's County, Maryland; and was a Representative in Congress, from that State, from 1819 to 1825.

Nelson, Homer A.—He was born in Poughkeepsie, New York, August 31, 1829; adopted the profession of law. In 1855 he was elected Judge of Dutchess County for four years, and in 1859 was re-elected for a second term; and in 1862 he was elected a Representative, from New York, to the Thirty-eighth Congress, serving on the Committees on Indian Affairs, and Unfinished Business. In 1857 Rutgers College, of New Jersey, conferred upon him the degree of Master of Arts, and at the time of his election to Congress he was Colonel of the One Hundred and Fifty-ninth regiment of New York volunteers, which he resigned.

Nelson, Hugh.—He was born in Virginia; and was at one time Speaker of the House of Delegates of Virginia; a Judge of the General Court; a member of Congress, from 1811 to 1823, and immediately afterwards appointed American Minister to Spain. He died in Albemarle County, March 18, 1836.

Nelson, Jeremiah.—He was born in Rowley, Essex County, Massachusetts, in 1768; graduated at Dartmouth College in 1790; settled in Newburyport, Massachusetts, as a merchant; served as a Representative in Congress, from Massachusetts, from 1805 to 1807, and again from 1815 to 1823; and died at Newburyport, October 2, 1838.

Nelson, John.—He was born in Frederick, Maryland; was a Representative in Congress, from that State, from 1821 to 1823; in 1831 was appointed Chargé d'Affaires to the Two Sicilies; and in 1844 was Attorney-General of the United States under President Tyler.

Nelson, Roger.—He was a General in the Revolutionary war; and a Representative in Congress, from Maryland, from 1804 to 1810, and died at Fredericktown, June 7, 1815, at an advanced age.

Nelson, Thomas A. R.—He was born in Tennessee; was bred a lawyer, and served as a Representative, from that State, in the Thirty-sixth Congress. He was re-elected to the Thirty-seventh Congress, but was prevented from taking his seat by the forcible action of the Rebel Government.

Nelson, Thomas M.—He was born in Virginia in 1782; served with distinction in the war of 1812, as a Captain of infantry; after the war he was promoted to the rank of Major, but resigned his commission; was a Representative in Congress, from his native State, from 1816 to 1819, when he declined a re-election and retired to private life. He died November 10, 1853.

Nelson, William.—Born in Clinton, Dutchess County, New York, June 29, 1784; he received an academical education; studied law and was admitted to the bar in 1807; was District Attorney for the counties of Westchester, Putnam, and Rockland, for a period of thirty years; was a member of the Assembly of New York in 1819 and 1820; and a State Senator in 1823; and he was a Representative in Congress, from New York, from 1847 to 1851. He is at the present time a resident of Peekskill.

Nes, Henry.—Born in York, Pennsylvania, in 1799, and was educated a physician. He was frequently called to fill places of trust and responsibility in his native town, and was a Representative in Congress, from 1843 to 1845, and again, from 1846 to 1850. He was retiring in his habits, but had many devoted friends. He died September 10, 1850.

Nesbitt, Wilson.—He was a Representative in Congress, from South Carolina, from 1817 to 1819.

Nesmith, James W.—Was born

in Washington County, Maine, July 23, 1820; when quite young removed to New Hampshire, and in 1838 emigrated to Ohio; subsequently spent some time in Missouri; and in 1843 emigrated to Oregon. In 1848 and 1853 he commanded, as a Captain, two expeditions against the Indians; in 1853 he was appointed United States Marshal for Oregon, which he resigned in 1855, and had the command of a regiment; in 1857 he was appointed Superintendent of Indian Affairs for Oregon and Washington Territories; and was elected a Senator in Congress, from Oregon, for the full term, beginning in 1861, serving on the Committees on Military Affairs, and Indian Affairs.

Nevell, Joseph.—He was a Representative in Congress, from Virginia, from 1793 to 1795. Died March 4, 1819.

New, Anthony.—He was born in Gloucester County, Virginia, and was a Representative in Congress, from Virginia, from 1793 to 1805; and on taking up his residence in Kentucky, was elected a Representative in Congress, from that State, from 1811 to 1813, from 1817 to 1818, and from 1821 to 1823.

Newbold, Thomas.—He was a Representative in Congress, from New Jersey, from 1807 to 1813; after which he served in the Legislature of that State. Died in Burlington County, of apoplexy, in December, 1823.

Newell, William A.—He was born in Ohio; graduated at Rutgers College; was educated for the medical profession, and on taking up his residence in New Jersey, was elected a Representative in Congress, from 1847 to 1851. In 1856 was elected Governor of New Jersey for the term ending in 1860; and was a Delegate to the Baltimore Convention of 1864.

Newhard, Peter.—He was born in Pennsylvania, and was a Representative in Congress, from that State, from 1839 to 1843.

Newman, Daniel.—He served as a soldier in the early Indian wars in Georgia, held many high positions in the State, and was a member of Congress, from 1831 to 1833. He died in Walker County, Georgia.

Newton, Eben.—Born in Goshen, Litchfield County, Connecticut, October 16, 1795; his early education was limited, having been obtained while working on a farm; his first earnings, off the farm, were obtained from teaching school in the winter; in 1814 he emigrated to Portage County, Ohio, and turned his attention to farming exclusively; he studied law, and in 1823 was admitted to the bar, and became the partner of Elisha Whittlesey, at Canfield, Ohio. In 1842 he was elected a member of the Ohio Senate; was soon afterwards elected President Judge of the Third Circuit; and was elected a Representative in Congress, for the term from 1851 to 1853, but before taking his seat visited Europe. In 1856 he was elected President of the Ashtabula and New Lisbon Railroad Company, in which position he remained until 1859, when he declined a re-election. He has of late years devoted himself to the pursuits of agriculture, in which he is eminently successful.

Newton, Thomas.—Born in Norfolk, Virginia, in 1769; was a Representative in Congress, from Virginia, from 1801 to 1829, and again from 1831 to 1833. He served for many years as Chairman of the Committee on Commerce and Manufactures. He died in Norfolk, Virginia, August 5, 1847.

Newton, Thomas W.—He was a Representative in Congress, from Arkansas, from 1845 to 1846.

Newton, Willoughby.—He was born in Virginia, and was a Representative in Congress, from that State, from 1843 to 1845.

Niblack, William E.—Born in Dubois County, Indiana, May 19, 1822. He studied law and was admitted to practice in 1843; during that year he was appointed County Surveyor; in 1849 he was elected to the State Legislature, where he served until 1852; in 1854 he was appointed a Circuit Judge, and subsequently elected for six years. He was elected a Representative in the Thirty-fifth Congress, from Indiana, serving on the Committee on Mileage, and re-elected to the Thirty-sixth Congress, serving on the Committee on Patents. He was also a Delegate to the Chicago Convention of 1864.

Nicholas, John.—He was a Representative in Congress, from Virginia, from 1793 to 1801. He subsequently removed to Geneva, Ontario County, New York, whence he was elected to the State Senate, from 1806 to 1809. Died May 27, 1821.

Nicholas, R. C.—He was born in Virginia, and appointed Captain of infantry in 1812, serving in different grades until the reduction of the army in 1815. Settling in Louisiana, he was elected to the United States Senate, serving from 1835 to 1841, and in 1851 was appointed State Superintendent of Public Schools.

Nicholas, Wilson C.—A Governor of Virginia; an officer in the war of the Revolution, and a member of the Convention which ratified the Constitution of the United States. He was a distinguished member of the National House of Representatives, from 1807 to 1809, and of the Senate of the United States, from 1799 to 1804, and ably supported the measures of President Jefferson's administration. In 1804 he resigned his seat in the Senate, and accepted the office of Collector of the ports of Norfolk and Portsmouth. He was afterwards a member of the House; but he resigned his seat in 1809. In 1814 he was Governor, and remained in office until 1817. He died at Milton, October 10, 1820.

Nichols, Matthias H.—Born in Salem County, New Jersey, October 3, 1824. His education was acquired in a printing-office and by the aid of friends, who instructed him after the ordinary hours of labor. He studied law, and in 1849 was licensed to practice in Auglaize County, Ohio. He was Prosecuting Attorney for Allen County; resigned the office in 1852 to become a candidate for Congress, and was elected a Representative to the Thirty-third, Thirty-fourth, and Thirty-fifth Congresses, and was a member of the Joint Committee on Printing.

Nicholson, A. O. P.—He was born in Williamson County, Tennessee, August 31, 1808; graduated at Chapel Hill University, North Carolina, in 1827; settled in Tennessee as a lawyer; was a member of the Tennessee Legislature from 1833 to 1839; was a Senator in Congress, from that State, from 1840 to 1842; was a member of the Tennessee Senate from 1843 to 1845; was Chancellor of the middle division of the State in 1845; was President of the Bank of Tennessee in 1846 and 1847; was elected Printer of the House of Representatives, by the Thirty-third Congress, and Printer of the Senate, by the Thirty-fourth Congress; and from 1853 to 1856 he was editor of the Washington Daily Union. He was elected a Senator in Congress, from Tennessee, for the term commencing in 1859 and ending in 1865, but was expelled in July, 1861.

Nicholson, John.—He was a member for several years of the New York Assembly, and a Representative in Congress, from that State, from 1809 to 1811. Died January, 1820, aged fifty-five years.

Nicholson, Joseph Hopper.—A native of Maryland; received a good education, and was a lawyer by profession. In 1805 he was appointed Chief Judge of the Sixth Judicial District, and was also a Judge of the Court of Appeals of Maryland. From 1799 to 1806 he was a Representative in Congress, and died March 4, 1817, aged forty-seven years.

Nicoll, Henry.—Born in the city of New York, October 23, 1812; graduated at Columbia College in 1830; studied law, and has practised with success; was a member of the New York Constitutional Convention in 1846; and a Representative in Congress, from New York, from 1847 to 1849.

Niles, John M.—He was born in Windsor, Connecticut, in 1787, and was bred to the bar, and went to Hartford in 1816 to practise law. In 1817 he was there concerned in publishing the Times, which he edited for a time. In 1820 he was a commissioned Judge of the County Court. He was appointed Postmaster at Hartford, by President Jackson, and held the office until made a Senator in Congress, in 1835, in which position he remained until 1839. In 1840 he was appointed Postmaster-General by President Van Buren. In 1842 he was again elected to the United States Senate, served six years, retired to private life, and died May 31, 1856. He was fond of literary pursuits, and his contributions to the periodical press were abundant. He edited a Gazetteer of Connecticut and Rhode Island, and wrote a History of South America. In his will he gave $20,000 for the benefit of the poor of Hartford, and bequeathed his library to the Historical Society of Connecticut.

Niles, Nathaniel.—He was born in South Kingston, Rhode Island, in 1741; graduated at Princeton College in 1766; was a student of law, medicine, and theology; was the inventor of making wire from bar iron, by water power, and erected at Norwich, Connecticut, a woollen card manufactory; he was a member of the Vermont Legislature, and Speaker of the House; a Judge of the Supreme Court of that State; was six times a Presidential Elector; and a Representative in Congress, from Vermont, from 1791 to 1795. He wrote poetry and many sermons, and preached in his own house twelve years. He died at West Fairlee, Vermont, in November, 1828.

Nisbet, E. A.—He was born in Georgia; and was a Representative in Congress, from that State, from 1839 to 1842.

Niven, Archibald C.—He was born in New York; and was a Representative in Congress, from that State, from 1845 to 1847.

Nixon, John I.—Born in Cumberland County, New Jersey, in 1820; graduated at Princeton College in 1841; studied law, and came to the bar in 1845; served in the New Jersey Legislature, from 1848 to 1850, during the last year as Speaker; and was elected a Representative, from New Jersey, to the Thirty-sixth Congress, serving as a member of the Committee on Commerce. Re-elected to the Thirty-seventh Congress, serving on the Committee on Commerce.

Noble, David A.—He was born in Massachusetts; liberally educated; adopted the profession of law; and on removing to Michigan, was elected a Representative in Congress, from that State, from 1853 to 1855.

Noble, James.—He was a Senator in Congress, from Indiana, from 1816 to 1831, having died in Washington, February 26, of the latter year. He was a native of Battletown, Clark County, Virginia, but removed when a youth to Kentucky, and subsequently to Indiana. He was a self-educated man, and very influential in his adopted State.

Noble, Warren P.—He was born in Pennsylvania, June 14, 1821; received a good English education in the State of Ohio; studied law, and has practised ever since his admission to the bar; was elected to the Ohio Legislature in 1856, serving two terms, and in 1860 was elected a Representative, from Ohio, to the Thirty-seventh Congress, serving on the Committee on Patents; re-elected to the Thirty-eighth Congress, serving on the same Committee.

Noble, William H.—He was born in New York; served three years in the Assembly of that State, from Cayuga County; and was a Representative in Congress, from New York, from 1837 to 1839.

Noell, John W.—Born in Bradford County, Virginia, February 15, 1816; emigrated to Missouri with his parents in 1832; received a liberal education; adopted the profession of law; from 1841 to 1850 he was Clerk of the Circuit Court of Perry County, Missouri; served four years in the State Senate of Missouri; and in 1858 he was elected a Representative, from Missouri, to the Thirty-sixth Congress, serving as a member of the Committee on Expenses of the Public Buildings. Re-elected to the Thirty-seventh Congress, serving as a member of the Committee on Claims. He was also re-elected to the Thirty-eighth Congress, but died in Washington, March 14, 1863.

Norris, Moses.—Born in Pittsfield, New Hampshire, in 1799; graduated at Dartmouth College in 1828; studied law, and devoted himself successfully to the practice; in 1839 he was elected to the State Legislature, and in 1840 was elected Speaker of the House; in 1841 he was elected a member of the State Council; and in 1844 he was elected a

Representative in Congress, where he continued four years. In 1847 he was again a member of the Legislature, and Speaker; and while serving in that capacity he was elected a Senator in Congress, serving from 1849 to 1855; and he died at Washington, January 11, 1855.

North, William.—He was aid to Baron Steuben, in the Revolutionary war, and afterwards appointed Adjutant-General. He was a Senator in Congress, by appointment, from New York, in 1798; died at New York, January 4, 1836, aged eighty-three years; and was buried at Duanesburg.

Norton, Ebenezer F.—He was born in New York; served in the State Assembly, from Erie County, in 1823; and was a Representative in Congress, from New York, from 1829 to 1831.

Norton, Elijah H.—Was born in Logan County, Kentucky, November 24, 1821; received a liberal classical education, graduating at the Transylvania Law School in 1841; removed to Missouri in 1845; practised law until 1852, when he was chosen a Judge of the Circuit Court of Missouri; re-elected to the same position in 1857; and after resigning the judgeship, in 1860 he was elected a Representative, from Missouri, to the Thirty-seventh Congress, serving on the Committee on Post-offices and Post-roads.

Norton, Jesse O.—Was born in Vermont; graduated at Williams College, Massachusetts; emigrated to Illinois in 1839; studied law, and came to the bar of Illinois in 1840; was a member, in 1847, of the State Constitutional Convention; was a member of the State Legislature in 1851 and 1852; was elected a Representative, from Illinois, to the Thirty-third and Thirty-fourth Congresses, serving on the Committees on Post-offices and Post-roads; in 1857 was elected Judge of the Eleventh Judicial District of Illinois, holding the office until 1862; and in 1863 was re-elected a Representative to Congress, serving on the Committees on Post-offices and Post-roads, and Revolutionary Pensions.

Norvell, John.—He was bred a printer; was for a time the editor of a newspaper in Philadelphia; was appointed, by President Jackson, Postmaster of Detroit, in Michigan; and having become identified with the Territory of Michigan, became one of the Senators in Congress, from the new State, having served in that capacity from 1835 to 1841. He died of apoplexy, in April, 1850.

Nott, Abraham.—He graduated at Yale College in 1787; was Judge of the Supreme Court of South Carolina, and was a Representative in Congress, from that State, from 1799 to 1801. Died June 19, 1830.

Nourse, Amos.—He graduated at Harvard, in 1812; studied medicine; was a Medical Lecturer at Bowdoin College from 1846 to 1854, and Medical Professor since 1854. He was also Postmaster at Hallowell, and Collector of Customs at Bath, and a Senator in Congress, from January to March in 1857.

Noyes, John.—He was a graduate of Dartmouth College in 1795; was subsequently a tutor in that institution; and was elected a Representative in Congress, from Vermont, from 1815 to 1817. He died in 1841, aged seventy-eight years.

Noyes, Joseph C.—He was born in Portland, in 1800; and was a Representative in Congress, from Maine, from 1837 to 1839, serving as a member of the Committee on Agriculture. He was a merchant by occupation; a member of the State Legislature in 1833; and Collector of the Passamaquoddy District from 1841 to 1843.

Nuckolls, William C.—He was born in South Carolina; graduated at the University of that State in 1820; adopted the profession of law; and was a Representative in Congress, from South Carolina, from 1827 to 1833.

Nugen, Robert H.—He was born in Washington County, Pennsylvania, in 1809; with his parents removed to Columbiana County, Ohio, in 1811; settled in Tuscarawas County in 1828; and in 1860 was elected a Representative, from Ohio, to the Thirty-seventh Congress, serving on the Committee on Roads and Canals. Declined a re-election.

Oakley, Thomas Jackson.--Born in Dutchess County, New York, in 1783; graduated at Yale College in 1801; studied law, and entered on the practice at Poughkeepsie, New York. In 1810 he was appointed Surrogate of Dutchess County, and in 1813 was elected a Representative in Congress, where he continued until 1815, when he resumed his profession, and was elected a member of the Assembly. He was appointed Attorney-General of the State of New York in 1819; in 1820 again served in the Assembly, and in 1827 he was again elected to Congress. In 1828, when the Superior Court of New York City was organized, he was appointed one of its Judges; and on the reorganization of the Court, under the Constitution of 1846, he was elected the Chief Justice, and continued in that position until his death, which occurred in New York City, May 11, 1857. The duties of the various stations to which he was called he discharged with fidelity and marked ability.

O'Brien, Jeremiah. — Born at Machias, Maine, in 1768, and died at Boston, May 30, 1858. He was a Representative in Congress, from Maine, from 1823 to 1831. Early in life, and after the separation of Maine from Massachusetts, he was for six years in the Legislature of the State. His educational advantages were limited, but he was a man of sound sense and solid judgment. He was both a farmer and a merchant.

Odell, Moses F.—Born in Tarrytown, Westchester County, New York, February 24, 1818; received a common school education; from a clerk he rose to the position of Assistant Collector of New York City, under President Polk; under President Buchanan he held the post of Public Appraiser, and he was elected a Representative, from New York, to the Thirty-seventh Congress, serving as Chairman of the Committee on the Treasury Department, and member of that on Indian Affairs; re-elected to the Thirty-eighth Congress, serving on the Committee on Military Affairs.

Ogden, Aaron.—He was born in Elizabethtown, New Jersey, December 3, 1756; graduated at Nassau Hall in 1773; taught school for a time; served as an officer in the army, during the whole Revolutionary war; had a horse shot from under him at the battle of Springfield, New Jersey; participated in the Sullivan campaign against the Indians; and for his services at Yorktown was complimented by Washington; after the war he pursued the legal profession with distinction; was a Presidential Elector in 1800; was a Senator in Congress, from 1801 to 1803; was Governor of New Jersey in 1812; and at the time of his death was President-General of the Society of Cincinnati. He died at Jersey City, April 19, 1839. During the war of 1812, President Madison offered him a commission as Major-General in the Army of the United States, which honor he declined, preferring to continue, as he had been, commander-in-chief of the militia of his own State.

Ogden, David A.—He was born in Morristown, New Jersey; studied law, and took up his residence in St. Lawrence County, New York, in 1812; was a member of the Assembly in 1814 and 1815; and a Representative in Congress, from 1817 to 1819. He died at Montreal, Canada, June 9, 1829.

Ogle, Alexander.—He was a Representative in Congress, from 1817 to 1819, and died in Somerset, Pennsylvania, October 14, 1852.

Ogle, Andrew J.—He was born in Pennsylvania, and was a Representative in Congress, from that State, from 1849 to 1851.

Ogle, Charles.—He was a Representative in Congress, from Pennsylvania, from 1837 to 1841, also a General of militia; and died at Somerset, May 10, 1841.

Olcott, Simeon.—He was born in 1737; graduated at Yale College in 1761; studied law, and settled in the practice at Charlestown, New Hampshire; he was appointed, in 1784, Chief Justice of the Court of Common Pleas; in 1790 a Judge of the Superior Court; Chief Judge of the same Court in 1795; and was a Senator in Congress, from New Hampshire, from 1801 to 1805. He died in New Hampshire in 1815.

Olds, Edson B.—He was born in Vermont, and was a Representative in

Congress, from Ohio, from 1849 to 1855. In 1862 he was for a short time imprisoned in Fort Lafayette for supposed disloyalty, and while there confined, he was elected a member of the Assembly of Ohio, having previously served six years in the State Legislature, and been Speaker of the Senate.

Olin, Abraham B.—He was born in Shaftsbury, Bennington County, Vermont in 1812; graduated at Williams College, Massachusetts, in 1835; commenced the practice of law at Troy, New York, in 1838; was for three years Recorder of the City of Troy; and was elected a Representative to the Thirty-fifth Congress, from New York, serving as a member of the Committee on Expenditures on the Public Buildings. He was also re-elected to the Thirty-sixth Congress, serving as a member of the Committee on Military Affairs. Re-elected to the Thirty-seventh Congress also. His father, Gideon Olin, was in Congress, from Vermont, during the administration of President Jefferson.

Olin, Gideon.—He was born in Rhode Island, and removing to Vermont, became one of its founders. He was a member of the State Legislature, and Speaker of the House, a Judge of the County Court, and a Representative in Congress, from 1803 to 1807. He died at Shaftsbury, Vermont, in 1822.

Olin, Henry.—His boyhood was spent in Addison County, Vermont; he was elected to the General Assembly of that State in 1799, and, excepting four years, continued to serve in that capacity until 1825; he was also a member of the State Constitutional Convention of 1814, 1822, and 1828; was an Associate Judge of Addison County, from 1801 to 1806; Chief Judge of said court in 1807, and from 1810 to 1824; and he was chosen a Representative in Congress, to fill a vacancy, in 1824, and served through the term, ending in 1825. He died at Salisbury, Vermont, in 1837, aged seventy years.

Oliver, Andrew.—Born at Springfield, Otsego County, New York. Soon after his birth, in 1819, his parents removed to Pen Yan, in Yates County. He received a classical education, and graduated at Union College in 1835; he studied law, and was admitted to the bar in 1838, and entered upon a successful practice. He was appointed to succeed his father as First Judge of the Court of Common Pleas in 1843, which position he held till the adoption of the new State Constitution. In 1846 he was elected Judge of the Surrogate and County Courts. In 1852 he was elected a Representative in the Thirty-third Congress, and was re-elected to the Thirty-fourth. Since that time he has been devoted to the practice of his profession.

Oliver, Mordecai.—Born in Anderson County, Kentucky, October 22, 1819, and emigrated to Missouri in 1832. He received as good an education as that country afforded, and entered upon the study of law at the age of nineteen, and was admitted to the bar in 1842. He was elected Circuit Attorney for the Fifth Judicial Circuit of Missouri in 1848; and in 1852 was elected a member of the Thirty-third Congress, and re-elected to the Thirty-fourth. Upon retiring from Congress, he resumed the duties of his profession in Richmond, Missouri.

Oliver, William M.—He was a native of Springfield, Otsego County, New York; was a lawyer by profession, and for a long time the First Judge of the Court of Common Pleas. He was State Senator and Lieutenant-Governor, and a Representative, of New York, in the Twenty-seventh Congress.

O'Neill, Charles.—Born in Philadelphia, March 21, 1821; graduated at Dickinson College in 1840; studied law, and came to the bar in 1843; in 1850, 1851, and 1852 he was elected to the State Legislature, and in 1853 to the State Senate; re-elected to the Legislature in 1859; and in 1862 elected a Representative, from Pennsylvania, to the Thirty-eighth Congress, serving on the Committee on Commerce.

O'Neill, John.—Was born in Philadelphia, December 17, 1821. In 1827 his father settled in Frederick City, Maryland, and at St. John's College, in that place, he received his education; studied law, and came to the bar of Maryland in 1842; in 1844 he removed to Ohio, and there practised his profession in the Supreme Court; in 1855 he was elected Prosecuting Attorney for Muskingum County; and in 1862 he was elected a Representative, from Ohio, to the Thirty-eighth Congress, serving on the Committee on Private Land Claims.

Ormsby, Stephen.—He was a Judge of the Circuit Court of Kentucky, a Representative in Congress, from 1811 to 1817, lived to an advanced age, and died in Kentucky. He was defeated in 1813, but his successful competitor, John Simpson, having been killed at the battle of River Raisin, he was re-elected before the opening of Congress.

Orr, Alexander D.—He was a Representative in Congress, from Kentucky, from 1792 to 1797, and died at Paris, in that State, June 21, 1835, aged seventy years.

Orr, Benjamin.—A native of Bedford, New Hampshire; graduated at Dartmouth College in 1798, and settled as a lawyer in Brunswick, Maine, attaining a high rank in his profession. He was a Representative in Congress, from Massachusetts, from 1817 to 1819, and died at Brunswick in 1828, aged fifty years. .

Orr, James L.—He was born at Craytonville, South Carolina, May 12, 1822; received his education chiefly in the University of Virginia; studied law, and was admitted to the bar in 1843. In 1844 he was elected to the State Legislature; re-elected in 1845; and in 1848 he was elected a Representative in Congress, from South Carolina, to which position he was subsequently re-elected. During the Thirty-second Congress he was frequently Chairman of the Committee of the Whole on the State of the Union, and during the next Congress was Chairman of the Committee on Indian Affairs; and on the assembling of the Thirty-fifth Congress, he was elected Speaker. In December, 1860, he was appointed one of the Commissioners to visit Washington in behalf of South Carolina.

Orr, Robert.—He was born in Westmoreland County, Pennsylvania, and was a Representative in Congress, from Pennsylvania, from 1825 to 1829.

Orth, Goodlove S.—Born near Lebanon, Pennsylvania, April 22, 1817; was educated chiefly at the Pennsylvania College, Gettysburg; studied law, and came to the bar in 1839, locating in Indiana. In 1843 and 1846 he was elected to the State Senate, serving six years in all, and one year as President of that body; was a Presidential Elector in 1848; was a member of the Peace Congress of 1861; rendered some service in 1861 as Captain of the United States Ram Horner; and in 1862 he was elected a Representative, from Indiana, to the Thirty-eighth Congress, serving on the Committee on Foreign Affairs.

Osborne, Thomas B.—He was born in Connecticut, and was a Representative in Congress, from that State, from 1839 to 1843.

Osgood, Gayton P.—He graduated at Harvard University in 1815; served in the Massachusetts Legislature in 1829 and 1831; and was a Representative in Congress, from Massachusetts, from 1833 to 1835.

Otero, Miguel A.—He was born at Valencia, New Mexico, June 21, 1829; was educated at the St. Louis University, in Missouri; studied law, and was admitted to practice in Missouri in 1852; returning to New Mexico, he was elected to the Territorial Legislature; was appointed, by President Pierce, United States District Attorney for the Territory, but declined to serve; held the office for a time of Attorney-General for the Territory; and in 1855 he was elected a Delegate to Congress, from New Mexico.

Otis, Harrison Gray.—He was born in Boston, Massachusetts, October 8, 1765, and died at Boston, October 28, 1848. His father, Samuel A. Otis, was the first Secretary of the Senate of the United States, which office he held for twenty-five years. Harrison Gray graduated at Harvard University in 1783, and soon became a successful practitioner at the bar. He was for many years an active and leading member of the State Legislature, serving as Speaker and President of the Senate. He was chosen a Representative in Congress, for the Suffolk District, in 1797, and served through President Adams's administration; and in 1817 he was chosen a Senator in Congress, where he remained for five years. He was also Judge of the Court of Common Pleas, and Mayor of Boston, for whose prosperity he accomplished much good; displaying, in all his public stations, great ability, and the utmost fidelity to the public interests. He was also appointed, by President Adams, United States District Attorney for Massachusetts. He was distinguished for his scholarly acquirements, and for his eloquence as an orator.

Otis, John.—He was born in Maine in 1801; graduated at Bowdoin College in 1823; adopted the profession of law; served five years in the Maine Legislature; was a Commissioner for settling the Northeastern Boundary; and was a Representative in Congress, from Maine, from 1849 to 1851, and died October 17, 1856.

Outlaw, David.—Born in Bertie County, North Carolina, and graduated at the University of that State in 1824. He read law at Newbern, and was admitted to the bar in 1827. He served three years in the House of Commons; was elected Solicitor of Edenton District in 1836; and was a Representative in Congress, from 1847 to 1853.

Outlaw, George B.—He was born in Bertie County, North Carolina; was a member of the House of Commons in 1796, in the State Senate a number of years thereafter, and a Representative in Congress, during the years 1824 and 1825. Died August 15, 1835.

Overstreet, James.—He was a native of Barnwell District, South Carolina, and a Representative in Congress, from that State, from 1819 to 1822. Died in 1822.

Overton, Walter H.—He was a Representative in Congress, from Louisiana, from 1829 to 1831.

Owen, Allen F.—He was born in North Carolina, and having removed to Georgia, was elected a Representative in Congress, from 1849 to 1851.

Owen, George W.—Born in Brunswick County, Virginia, in 1798; was Speaker of the House of Representatives in Alabama; Mayor of Mobile; and a Representative in Congress, from that State, from 1823 to 1829, when he was appointed Collector of the port of Mobile. He died August 18, 1839, at Mobile, Alabama.

Owen, James.—Born in Bladen County, North Carolina, in December, 1784. He was well educated, and adopted the occupation of a planter. He was a General of militia, four years a member of the Legislature, and a Representative in Congress, from 1817 to 1819.

Owen, Robert Dale.—He was born in Scotland; was a Representative in Congress, from Indiana, from 1843 to 1847. He was one of the first Regents of the Smithsonian Institution, and took a prominent part in its organization; and was appointed Minister-Resident at Naples. He wrote a work entitled "Footfalls on the Boundary of another World."

Owens, George W.—A prominent member of the Georgia bar, and a Representative in Congress, from that State, from 1835 to 1839. Died at Savannah in 1856.

Owsley, Bryan Y.—He was born in Kentucky, and was a Representative in Congress, from that State, from 1841 to 1843.

Packer, Asa.—He was born in Connecticut, and was a Representative in Congress, from Pennsylvania, from 1853 to 1857.

Page, John.—He was one of the first Representatives in Congress, from Virginia, under the present Constitution, serving from 1789 to 1797. In 1800 he was chosen one of the Electors for President, and from 1802 to 1805 was Governor of Virginia. He published addresses to the people in 1796 and 1799. He died at Richmond, Virginia, October 11, 1804, aged sixty-four years.

Page, John.—He was a Senator in Congress, from New Hampshire, during the years 1836 and 1837; Governor of the State from 1839 to 1842; a State Councillor in 1838; and for some years Register of Deeds for Grafton County, New Hampshire.

Page, Robert.—He was a Representative in Congress, from Virginia, from 1799 to 1801.

Page, Sherman.—He was born in Connecticut, served in the Assembly of New York, from Otsego County, in 1827, and was a Representative in Congress, from that State, from 1833 to 1837.

Paine, Elijah.—Born in Brooklyn, Connecticut, January 21, 1757, and graduated at Harvard College in 1781. He was the first President of the Phi Beta Kappa Society of Harvard, and pronounced the first oration before the same. He was a lawyer by profession; and having settled in Vermont, was one of the most useful pioneers of the new State, following the practice of his profession, and the employments of farmer, road-maker, and cloth manufacturer. In 1786 he was a member of the Convention called to revise the State Constitution, and of which he was Secretary. In 1787 he was elected to the State Legislature, and so continued until 1791, when he was appointed Judge of the Supreme Court. He was one of the Commissioners to settle the controversy between Vermont and New York in 1789; was a Trustee of Dartmouth College; President of the Vermont Colonization Society; a pecuniary benefactor to the University of Vermont; received from Harvard College the degree of LL.D., and was elected a Fellow of the American Academy of Arts and Sciences, and an honorary member of several other literary institutions. He was a Senator in Congress, from Vermont, from 1795 to 1801. In 1801 he was appointed, by President, Adams, Judge of the District Court of Vermont, which office he held till within a month of his death, when he resigned. He died at Williamstown, Vermont, April 21, 1842.

Paine, Robert T.—He was born in North Carolina, and was a Representative in Congress, from that State, from 1855 to 1857.

Palen, Rufus.—He was born in New York, and was a Representative in Congress, from that State, from 1839 to 1841.

Palfrey, John G.—Born in Boston, May 2, 1795. He was prepared for college at Exeter Academy, and graduated at Harvard in 1815; he studied theology, and was ordained a Unitarian preacher in 1818; he was subsequently, for a number of years, editor of the North American Review; delivered a course of lectures before the Lowell Institute; during the years 1842 and 1843, he was a member of the General Court; was elected Secretary of the Commonwealth of Massachusetts; and he was a member of Congress, from 1847 to 1849. His published writings are numerous, chiefly of a theological and political character. His last work is a History of New England.

Palmer, Beriah.—Born in New York; served four years in the Assembly of New York, from Saratoga County; and was a Representative in Congress, from 1803 to 1805.

Palmer, George W.—Born in Hoosick, Rensselaer County, New York, January 13, 1818; received a common school education; adopted the profession of law; was Surrogate of Clinton County from 1843 to 1847; and a Representative in the Thirty-fifth Congress, from New York, serving as a member of the Committee on Expenditures in the Post-office Department. He was re-elected to the Thirty-sixth Congress, serving as a member of the Committee on Public Expenditures. He was also a Delegate to the Baltimore Convention of 1864.

Palmer, John.—He was born in Hoosick, Rensselaer County, New York, in 1785; received a good education, and studied law, and having settled in Plattsburg, Clinton County, in 1810, formed a law partnership with Chancellor Walworth, which continued until 1820. He was elected a Representative to Congress, in 1817, but before the expiration of his term, he was chosen District Attorney for Clinton County, in which capacity he served until 1831, and during that year he was made the first Judge of said county, and held the office until 1836. He was again elected to Congress in 1837, and served one term. He died of consumption, at St. Bartholomew, West Indies, December 8, 1840.

Palmer, William A.—He was a Senator in Congress, from Vermont, from 1818 to 1825. He was also a member of the Vermont Legislature for six years; Judge of the Supreme Court in 1816; Governor of Vermont from 1831 to 1835; member of the Constitutional Conventions of 1828 and 1836; Judge of Probate and of the County Court; two years a State Senator; and for eight years Clerk of the Courts. Died at Danville, Vermont, at an advanced age, in December, 1860.

Parish, Isaac.—He was born in Ohio, and was a Representative in Congress, from that State, from 1839 to 1841, and again from 1845 to 1847.

Parke, Benjamin.—He was a native of New Jersey, and was born in 1777; he was one of the early pioneers to the Western territory, and settled in that portion which now forms the State of Indiana, in 1800. From 1805 to 1808 he was a Delegate in Congress, from that Territory, and was soon after appointed, by President Jefferson, Judge of the District Court, which office he held until his death, which occurred in Salem, Indiana, July 12, 1835. He was at one time President of the State Historical Society.

Parker, Amasa J.—Born in 1807, at Sharon, Connecticut, and graduated at Union College, New York. He was admitted to the bar in Delhi, New York, in October, 1828. In 1833 he was elected a Representative in the State Legislature, and in 1835 was chosen a Regent of the University. From 1837 to 1839 he was a Representative in Congress, and in 1844 he was appointed a Circuit Judge and Vice-Chancellor of the Court of Equity. Soon after the adoption of a new State Constitution, he became a Judge of the Supreme Court of New York. In 1859 he was appointed United States Attorney for the District of New York. He was also a Delegate to the Chicago Convention of 1864.

Parker, Andrew.—He was born in Pennsylvania, and was a Representative in Congress, from that State, from 1851 to 1853.

Parker, Isaac.—Born in Boston, Massachusetts, June 17, 1768, and graduated at Harvard College in 1786. He commenced the practice of law at Castine, in the District of Maine, and was elected to Congress, serving as Representative, from 1797 to 1799. He was appointed, by President Adams, Marshal for the District of Maine, which office he held till 1801. He afterwards removed to Portland, and in 1806 was chosen a Judge of the Supreme Court, and in 1814 Chief Justice, which position he occupied for sixteen years. In 1820 he was President of the Massachusetts Convention for the revision of the Constitution, and for several years he was Professor of Law in Harvard University. He was a distinguished scholar and friend of literature, and for eleven years was a Trustee of Bowdoin College, and for twenty years an Overseer of Harvard. He died in Boston, May 26, 1830.

Parker, James.—He was born in the Township of Bethlehem, Hunterdon County, New Jersey, March 1, 1776. He was a student in Columbia College, New York, and graduated in 1793; he entered the counting-house of a merchant in New York, and remained there until 1797, when he settled in Perth Amboy, where he has since resided; he was for a few years engaged in trade; was a member of the New Jersey Legislature in 1806, 1807, 1808, 1809, 1810, 1812, 1813, 1815, 1816, 1818, and 1827,—in all eleven years; was a Jackson Elector in 1824; Collector of the Customs at Perth Amboy, from 1829 to 1833; and was a Representative in Congress, from 1833 to 1837. He also served as one of the Commissioners, on the part of New Jersey, to settle the boundary and jurisdiction between New York and New Jersey, at the different periods of 1807, 1827, and 1833, obtaining an agreement during the year last named; and he was member of the Constitutional Convention of the State in 1844. Mr. Parker is still living, in the enjoyment of a pleasant home and troops of friends.

Parker, James.—A native of Boston, Massachusetts; was a physician by profession; and was a Representative in Congress, from Massachusetts, from 1813 to 1815, and from 1819 to 1821. He was for fifty years a resident of Gardiner, Maine, where he died, November 9, 1837, aged sixty-nine years.

Parker, John M.—Born in Granville, Washington County, New York, June 14, 1805; graduated at Middlebury College, Vermont, in 1828; was a lawyer by profession, and a Representative in the Thirty-fifth Congress, from New York, serving on the Committees of Public Expenditures and Revolutionary Pensions.

Parker, Josiah.—He was a Representative in Congress, from Virginia, from 1789 to 1801.

Parker, Nahum.—He was a Senator in Congress, from New Hampshire, from 1807 to 1810, having also held the positions of State Councillor from 1805 to 1807, President of the State Senate in 1828, and Judge of the Court of Common Pleas for Hillsborough County, from 1822 to 1825. Resigned his seat in the Senate, June, 1860.

Parker, Richard.—He was born in Virginia, and was a Representative in Congress, from that State, from 1849 to 1851.

Parker, Richard E.—Born in 1777; in early life was a member of the Virginia House of Delegates; for many years a Judge of the General and Circuit Courts of Virginia; also, a Judge of the Supreme Court of Appeals; and for a brief period, from 1836 to 1837, a Senator in Congress. He died in Virginia, in November, 1840.

Parker, Samuel W.—He was born in Jefferson County, New York, September 9, 1805; graduated at the Miami University, in Ohio, in 1828; settled in Indiana, and, while studying law, taught school and edited a newspaper; he was admitted to the bar in 1831; was elected to the Legislature in 1836, where he served five years; and was two years Attorney for the State. He was a Representative in Congress, from Indiana, from 1851 to 1855; he was, in 1846, President of the White Water Canal Company, the charter for which he had passed by the Legislature; in 1844 he was a Clay Elector, and in 1856 an Elector for Fremont; and, at the present time, is President of the Junction Railway Company of Indiana, where he resides, chiefly engaged in agricultural pursuits.

Parker, Severn E.—He was born in Northampton County, Virginia, and was a prominent member of the Virginia Legislature, an eminent lawyer, and a Representative in Congress, from 1819 to 1821. He died, October 21, 1836, in Northampton County, Virginia.

Parks, Gorham.—He was born in the western part of Massachusetts in 1793; graduated at Harvard College in 1813; adopted the profession of law, and commenced practice at Bangor; and was a Representative in Congress, from Maine, from 1833 to 1837. From 1838 to 1841 he was United States Marshal for the District of Maine; from 1843 to 1845, United States Attorney; and from 1845 to 1849, United States Consul at Rio Janeiro.

Parmenter, William.—He was born in Massachusetts, and was a Representative in Congress, from that State, from 1837 to 1845. He was also a State Senator in 1836; and Naval Officer at Boston, from 1845 to 1849.

Parris, Albion K.—He was born in Hebron, Oxford County, Maine, January 19, 1788; graduated at Dartmouth College in 1806; studied law, and was admitted to the bar in 1809; in 1811 he was appointed Attorney for Oxford County; in 1813 was elected to the General Court; in 1814 was chosen a State Senator; was elected a Representative in Congress in 1815, and again in 1817; in 1816 he was a member of the State Constitutional Convention; was appointed Judge of the Federal District Court in 1818. In 1819 he was a member of the State Convention for framing a Constitution; and in 1820 was appointed Judge of Probate for Cumberland County. He was five times elected Governor of Maine, from 1822 to 1827; was a Senator in Congress in 1827 and 1828; was appointed Judge of the Supreme Court of the State in 1828, holding the office until 1836, when he became Second Comptroller in the Federal Treasury Department. He left this office in 1850, and returned to Portland, of which city, in 1852, he was elected Mayor. He died in Portland, February 11, 1857.

Parris, Virgil D.—Born in Maine; adopted the profession of law; was Assistant Secretary of State Senate in 1831; was a member of the Maine Legislature, from 1833 to 1839; a Representative in Congress, from Maine, from 1838 to 1841; a State Senator in 1842 and 1843; United States Marshal for Maine, from

1844 to 1848; United States Special Mail Agent from 1853 to 1856; and subsequently held the office of Naval Storekeeper at Kittery, Maine. When in the State Senate he was President *pro tem.*, and for a short time acting Governor of the State.

Parrott, John F.—He was a member, in 1811, of the New Hampshire Legislature; a Representative in Congress, from New Hampshire, from 1817 to 1819; and a Senator of the United States, from 1819 to 1825; and in 1826 was appointed Postmaster at Portsmouth, New Hampshire. He died in Greenland, New Hampshire, July 9, 1836, aged sixty-eight years.

Parrott, Marcus J.—Born at Hamburg, South Carolina, October 27, 1828; graduated at Dickinson College, Pennsylvania, in 1849; is a lawyer by profession, having studied at Cambridge; was a member of the Ohio Legislature in 1853 and 1854; and was elected a Delegate to the Thirty-fifth Congress, from Kansas Territory. Elected also to the Thirty-sixth Congress.

Partridge, George.—He graduated at Harvard College in 1762; was a Delegate to the Continental Congress, from Massachusetts; and a Representative in Congress, after the adoption of the Constitution, from 1789 to 1791. He died at Duxbury, Massachusetts, July 7, 1828, aged eighty-eight years.

Partridge, Samuel.—He was born in New York; and was a Representative in Congress, from that State, from 1841 to 1843.

Paterson, William.—Born at sea, of Irish parents, in 1745. He graduated at Princeton in 1763; studied law and admitted to the bar in 1769; was a member of the Convention which formed the first Constitution of New Jersey in 1776; from that time until the year 1786 he was Attorney-General of the State; and was one of the first Senators in Congress, from 1789 to 1790, when he resigned, having previously been a member of the Convention which formed the Federal Constitution. He was Governor of New Jersey, from 1791 to 1794, when he was appointed, by the President, a Judge of the Supreme Court of the United States, which he held until his death in 1806. In 1798 and 1799 he revised, by authority of the Legislature, the laws of New Jersey, a work highly esteemed and the foundation of the jurisprudence of the State. He received the degree of LL.D. from Harvard and Dartmouth.

Paton, John.—He was a Representative in Congress, from Delaware, from 1793 to 1794, and for a second term from 1795 to 1797. His seat was successfully contested by H. Lattimer, in 1794.

Patterson, John.—He was a member, for four years, of the Assembly of New York; and a Representative in Congress, from that State, from 1803 to 1805.

Patterson, John.—He was a Representative in Congress, from Ohio, from 1823 to 1825.

Patterson, J. W.—He was born in Henniker, Merrimack County, New Hampshire, July 2, 1823; was educated at Dartmouth College, graduating in 1848. From 1854 to 1859 he was a Professor of Mathematics in Dartmouth College, after which he was transferred to the chair of Professor of Astronomy and Meteorology, in the same college, which he still holds. From 1858 to 1861 he was School Commissioner for Grafton County, and at the same time was Secretary of the Board of Education for the State. In 1862 he served in the State Legislature, and was elected a Representative, from New Hampshire, to the Thirty-eighth Congress, serving on the Committees on Expenditures in the Treasury Department, and for the District of Columbia.

Patterson, Thomas.—He was born in Lancaster County, Pennsylvania; and was a Representative in Congress, from that State, from 1817 to 1825.

Patterson, Thomas J.—He was born in New York; and was a Representative in Congress, from that State, from 1843 to 1845.

Patterson, Walter.—He was born in Columbia County, New York, and was a member of the Assembly of New York, in 1818, from Columbia County;

and a Representative in Congress, from 1821 to 1823.

Patterson, William.—He was born in Maryland, and having settled in Ohio, was elected a Representative in Congress, from that State, from 1833 to 1838.

Patterson, William.—He was born in Londonderry, New Hampshire, June 4, 1789; removed to the State of New York in 1815, and subsequently settled in Warsaw, Genesee, now Wyoming County. He was elected a Representative in Congress, from New York, from 1837 to 1839, but died before the expiration of his term, at Warsaw, New York, August 14, 1838.

Patton, John.—He was born in Pennsylvania, and elected a Representative, from that State, to the Thirty-seventh Congress, serving on the Committee on Indian Affairs.

Patton, John M.—He was born in Virginia; received a liberal education, and adopted the profession of law, in which he was successful; and was a Representative in Congress, from that State, from 1830 to 1838. He died in October, 1858, in the sixty-second year of his age. He was for some years, and at the time of his death, Judge of the Court of Appeals.

Paulding, William.—Born in Tarrytown, Westchester County, New York, in 1769; was educated for the law and engaged in a lucrative practice in New York City. He was a delegate to the New York Convention for revising the State Constitution in 1821; and elected a Representative in Congress, from that State, from 1811 to 1813, but he was absent from his seat during the session in which war was declared, and served as General of militia during its prosecution. In 1823 he was chosen Mayor of New York, after which he held no public office. He died at Tarrytown, February 11, 1854.

Pawling, Levi.—He was a Representative in Congress, from Pennsylvania, from 1817 to 1819.

Payne, Winter W.—He was born in Warrenton, Virginia, which he left when young, and was a Representative in Congress, from Alabama, from 1841 to 1847.

Paynter, Lemuel.—He was born in Delaware, and on removing to Pennsylvania, was elected a Representative in Congress, from that State, from 1837 to 1841.

Pearce, Dutee J.—Born in Portsmouth, Rhode Island, in 1789, and died at Newport, Rhode Island, May 9, 1849. He was a prominent lawyer; at one time Attorney-General of the State, and United States District Attorney for that district, and a Representative in Congress, from Rhode Island, from 1825 to 1833, and again from 1835 to 1837. He was a graduate of Brown University, and served in the Legislature of Rhode Island.

Pearce, James A.—He was born in Alexandria, Virginia, December 14, 1805, although of a Maryland family by his father's side. He graduated at Princeton College, with the first honors, in 1822; was bred to the law, but was much engaged in the pursuits of agriculture; he was a member of the Maryland Legislature in 1831; a Representative in Congress, from that State, from 1835 to 1839, and from 1841 to 1843; and a Senator in Congress, from 1843 to 1862, having served for a number of years as Chairman of the Joint Committee on the Library. He also held the post of Professor of Law in Washington College, Chestertown, and was a Regent of the Smithsonian Institution. Was re-elected to the Senate for the term commencing March, 1863, but died at Chestertown, Maryland, December 20, 1862.

Pearce, John J.—He was born in Pennsylvania, and was a Representative in Congress, from that State, from 1855 to 1857.

Pearson, Joseph.—Born in Rowan County, North Carolina, and died at Salisbury, October 27, 1834. He was a lawyer by profession, served two years in the State Legislature, and was a Representative in Congress, from 1809 to 1815. While in Congress he fought a duel with the Hon. John G. Jackson, the result of a political quarrel.

Peaslee, Charles H.—He was

born in Gilmanton, New Hampshire, in February, 1804; graduated at Dartmouth College in 1824; and was a Representative in Congress, from that State, from 1847 to 1853. He was also a State Representative from 1833 to 1837; Adjutant-General of the State from 1839 to 1847; and Collector of Customs, at Boston, from 1853 to 1857.

Peck, George W.—He was born in New York about the year 1818; removed to Michigan, and was a member of the Legislature of that State in 1846 and 1847, serving as Speaker during the latter year; was afterwards chosen Secretary of State; and was a Representative in Congress, from Michigan, from 1855 to 1857.

Peck, Jared V.—He was born in New York, and was a Representative in Congress, from that State, from 1853 to 1855.

Peck, Lucius B.—He was born in Vermont, and was a Representative in Congress, from that State, from 1847 to 1851. From 1853 to 1857 he was United States Attorney for Vermont.

Peck, Luther C.—He was born in Connecticut, and was a Representative in Congress, from New York, from 1837 to 1841.

Peckham, Rufus W.—He was born in New York, and was a Representative in Congress, from that State, from 1853 to 1855.

Peek, Hermanus.—He was born in Albany, New York, and was for two years a member of the New York Assembly, from Schenectady County, and a Representative in Congress, from New York, from 1819 to 1821.

Pegram, John.—He was a native of Virginia, and a Representative in Congress, from that State, from 1818 to 1819.

Pelton, Guy R.—Born at Great Barrington, Berkshire County, Massachusetts, August 3, 1825. His tastes, from early boyhood, had inclined him to the study of law, but it was not until he had attained his twentieth year that he was enabled to prosecute his plans for a professional life, having previously to that time remained upon the homestead farm with his father. He spent two years in the academy of his native town, and three years in the Connecticut Literary Institute, after which he devoted one year to teaching at Lee, Massachusetts, and at Dover Plains, New York, employing his leisure in reading elementary works on law. He then entered a law office at Kinderhook, and completed his studies, being admitted to the bar in 1850. In 1851 he opened a law office in New York City, and in 1854 was elected a Representative to the Thirty-fourth Congress, after which he returned to New York, and resumed his professional labors.

Pendleton, Edmund H.—He was a Representative in Congress, from New York, from 1831 to 1833.

Pendleton, George H.—Born in Cincinnati, Ohio, July 25, 1825; is a lawyer by profession; was a member of the State Senate of Ohio in 1854 and 1855; was elected a Representative, from Ohio, to the Thirty-fifth, Thirty-sixth, and Thirty-seventh Congresses, serving as a member of the Committee on Military Affairs during each term. Re-elected to the Thirty-eighth Congress, serving on the Committee of Ways and Means. His father, Nathaniel Greene Pendleton, was also a Representative in Congress. In 1864 he was nominated for the office of Vice-President of the United States, on the ticket with George B. McClellan.

Pendleton, John S.—He was born in Virginia; in 1841 was appointed Chargé d'Affaires to the Republic of Chili; and was a Representative in Congress, from that State, from 1845 to 1847, and for a second term, ending in 1849.

Pendleton, Nathaniel Greene.—Born in Savannah, Georgia, in August, 1793; removed with his father to New York in his childhood; was educated at Columbia College; adopted the profession of law; was an aid to General E. P. Gaines, from 1813 to 1815; removed to Ohio in 1818; in 1825 was elected to the Senate of Ohio, and re-elected; and was a Representative in Congress, from Ohio, from 1841 to 1843, after which he voluntarily retired from public life. He was a man of high character and uncommon ability, and died in Cincinnati, June 16, 1861. His father, Nathaniel, was an officer in the Revolutionary war, a Judge, and second of General Alexander Hamilton in his duel with Aaron Burr.

Penn, Alexander G.—He was born in Virginia, and, having settled in Louisiana, was elected a Representative in Congress, from that State, from 1851 to 1853.

Penniman, Ebenezer J.—He was born in New York, and was a Representative in Congress, from Michigan, from 1851 to 1853.

Pennington, Alexander C. M.—He was born in Newark, New Jersey; a lawyer by profession; and was a Representative in Congress, from that State, from 1853 to 1857. He also served two years in the State Legislature.

Pennington, William.—He was born in Newark, New Jersey, in 1797; received a liberal education, and adopted the profession of law; in 1837 he was elected Governor of New Jersey, and annually re-elected until 1843, acting at the same time as Chancellor of the State, *ex officio*, and taking a prominent part in what was known as the "Broad Seal Controversy." By President Taylor, he was appointed Governor of Minnesota Territory, and by President Fillmore a Judge to settle land claims in California, both of which positions he declined to accept. In 1858, contrary to his wishes, he was elected a Representative, from New Jersey, to the Thirty-sixth Congress; and after the lapse of two months after taking his seat, he was elected Speaker of the House of Representatives. Died at Newark, New Jersey, February 16, 1862. He had been indisposed, and having taken an overdose of morphine for some other medicine, died from its effects.

Pennybacker, Isaac S.—Born in 1806, in Shenandoah County, Virginia; was a lawyer by profession; and a Representative in Congress, from 1837 to 1839; and then Judge of the District Court of Western Virginia; and a Senator in Congress, from 1845 to 1851. He died in Washington, District of Columbia, January 12, 1847.

Perea, Francisco.—Was born in Zadillas, County of Bernalillo, New Mexico, January 9, 1831, and in 1863 he was elected a Delegate, from New Mexico, to the Thirty-eighth Congress.

Perham, Sidney.—Was born in Woodstock, Oxford County, Maine, March 27, 1819; until his thirty-fourth year he followed the double occupation of farmer and teacher; in 1852 he was chosen a member of the Maine Board of Agriculture, which position he held for two years; in 1855 he was a member of the State Legislature, and officiated as Speaker; in 1856 he was a Presidential Elector; in 1858 was elected County Clerk for Oxford County, and re-elected in 1861; and in 1862 was elected a Representative, from Maine, to the Thirty-eighth Congress, serving on the Committees on Agriculture, and Invalid Pensions.

Perkins, Bishop.—He was born in New Hampshire, and having settled in New York, was elected a Representative in Congress, from that State, from 1853 to 1855.

Perkins, Elias.—He was a Representative in Congress, from Connecticut, from 1801 to 1803, having graduated at Yale College in 1786. He died in 1845.

Perkins, Jared.—He was born in New Hampshire, and was a Representative in Congress, from that State, from 1851 to 1853. He also held the position of State Councillor from 1846 to 1849; State Representative in 1850; and died at Nashua, October 14, 1854.

Perkins, John, Jr.—He was born in Louisiana, July 1, 1819. He graduated at Yale College in 1840, and subsequently at the Law School of Harvard College; he settled for the practice of his profession in New Orleans, but his health compelled him to travel in Europe; on his return, in 1851, he was chosen a Judge of the Circuit Court of Louisiana, which position he held until elected to Congress, in 1853, where he advocated Democratic measures, and remained until 1855, serving on the Committee on Foreign Affairs. He is now devoted to planting in Louisiana.

Perrill, Augustus L.—He was born in Virginia, and was a Representative in Congress, from that State, from 1845 to 1847.

Perry, John J.—He was born in Portsmouth, New Hampshire, August 2, 1811, but when a child removed with his father, Rev. Daniel Perry, to Oxford, Maine; he received a common school education, and of his own accord spent three years at the "Maine Wesleyan Seminary," paying for his tuition by laboring on the farm belonging to the institution, and also by teaching school in the winter. Having spent three years engaged in mercantile pursuits, he turned his attention to the law; was admitted to the bar at Oxford in 1844, where he has practised his profession ever since. He was elected to the Maine Legislature in 1839, 1842, and 1843; was afterwards for seven years Major-General of the Maine militia; in 1846 and 1847 he was elected to the State Senate; in 1854 he was elected Clerk of the Maine House of Representatives; and he was a Representative in Congress, from 1855 to 1857. Of late years he has been connected with the press, as editor of the "Oxford Democrat," a paper published at Paris, Maine; and he was also elected a Representative in the Thirty-sixth Congress, serving as a member of the Committee on Territories. He was also a member of the Peace Congress of 1861.

Perry, Nehemiah.—He was born at Ridgefield, Connecticut, March 30, 1816; received a good education at the West Lane Seminary; has been chiefly engaged in the cloth and clothing business; was for many years the presiding member of the Common Council of Newark, New Jersey; served a number of years in the Legislature of that State; and was elected a Representative, from New Jersey, to the Thirty-seventh Congress, serving on the Committees on Revolutionary Claims, and Expenditures on Public Buildings. Re-elected to the Thirty-eighth Congress, serving on the Committee on Commerce.

Perry, Thomas.—He was born in Maryland, and was a Representative in Congress, from that State, from 1845 to 1847.

Peter, George.—Born in Georgetown, Montgomery County, Maryland (now District of Columbia), September 28, 1779. He was educated at private institutions and Georgetown College; entered the United States Army in 1799, and resigned in 1809; served as a Major of volunteers during the war of 1812; was a Representative in Congress, from 1816 to 1819, and again from 1825 to 1827; was elected twice to the State Legislature; and also served the public as Commissioner of Public Works for the State of Maryland.

Petrie, George.—He was born in New York, and was a Representative in Congress, from that State, from 1847 to 1849.

Petriken, David.—He was born in Pennsylvania, and was a Representative in Congress, from that State, from 1837 to 1841. Died January 3, 1849.

Pettigrew, Ebenezer.—He was a Representative in Congress, from North Carolina, from 1835 to 1837, and was a member of the Committee on Expenses in the Navy Department.

Pettis, Spencer.—He was born in Virginia, and educated a lawyer, and, on taking up his residence in Missouri, was elected a Representative in Congress, where he served from 1829 to 1831. Died August 26, 1831, aged twenty-nine years, having fallen in a duel with Major Thomas Biddle at St. Louis.

Pettit, John.—Born at Sackett's Harbor, Jefferson County, New York, July 24, 1807; he received a good education, and studied law, and removed to Lafayette, Indiana, in 1831, where he has since resided. He was a member of the State Legislature, United States District Attorney, and served in the House of Representatives in Congress, from 1843 to 1847, and in the United States Senate, from 1853 to 1855. In 1850 he was a member of the State Constitutional Convention, and has twice held the office of Circuit Judge; and in 1859 he was appointed, by President Buchanan, Chief Justice of the Federal Courts of Kansas. He was also a Delegate to the Chicago Convention of 1864.

Pettit, John U.—He was born in New York; graduated at Union College in 1839; studied law, and commenced the practice of his profession in

Wabash, Indiana, in 1841. He went as United States Consul to Maranham, Brazil, in 1850; and on his return, in 1853, was appointed Judge of the Upper Wabash Circuit Court of Indiana; and was elected to Congress, as a Representative of that State, in 1854; and was re-elected to the Thirty-fifth Congress. He was a member of the Joint Committee on the Library. He was re-elected to the Thirty-sixth Congress, serving as Chairman of the Library Committee.

Peyton, Bailie.—He was born in Sumner County, Tennessee, received a liberal education, and adopted the profession of law; he was a Representative in Congress, from that State, from 1833 to 1837; he was appointed, by President Fillmore, Minister to Chili; was subsequently elected United States District Attorney for Louisiana; was for a time settled at San Francisco, California, in the practice of his profession, but is now residing in his native State.

Peyton, Joseph H.—Born in Sumner County, Tennessee, in 1818; was frequently elected to the Senate of Tennessee; held many other local positions of high character; and was a Representative in Congress, from 1843 to 1845. He received a medical education, but abandoned that profession for politics. Died in October, 1845, having been re-elected to Congress.

Peyton, Samuel O.—Born in Bullitt County, Kentucky, in 1804; received a good common school education; settled in Hartford and devoted two years to the duties of a clerk; studied medicine, and graduated at Transylvania University in 1827; in 1835 he was elected to the State Legislature; was a Representative in Congress, from Kentucky, from 1847 to 1849; and was re-elected to the Thirty-fifth and Thirty-sixth Congresses, serving during his last term as a member of the Committee on Public Buildings and Grounds.

Phelps, Elisha.—He was a native of Simsbury, Connecticut; born in November, 1779; graduated at Yale College in 1800, and studied law at Litchfield. He was several times a member of the House of Representatives and of the Senate of his native State. He was Speaker of the House of Representatives in the Legislature in 1821 and 1829; was a Representative in Congress, from Connecticut, from 1819 to 1821, and also from 1825 to 1829; was Comptroller of the State from 1830 to 1834, and in 1835 was appointed one of the Commissioners to revise the statutes of Connecticut. He died at Simsbury, in April, 1847.

Phelps, John Smith. — He was born in Simsbury, Hartford County, Connecticut, December 22, 1814; was educated at Washington (now Trinity) College, Hartford, Connecticut, and studied law in the office of his father, Elisha Phelps. He practised law a short time in his native State, and in 1837 emigrated to Missouri, and settled at Springfield, Greene County, near which town he now resides. In 1840 he was chosen by the people of Greene County to represent them in the Legislature; and having been appointed Brigade Inspector of militia in 1841 he has since borne the title of Major. In 1844 he was elected Representative to the Twenty-ninth Congress, serving in that position until the close of the Thirty-sixth Congress. He was also re-elected to the Thirty-seventh Congress. He served as a Colonel of volunteers in 1861, and in 1862 was appointed by President Lincoln Military Governor of Arkansas. He was during the Thirty-fifth Congress Chairman of the Committee of Ways and Means, and has generally served on important committees.

Phelps, Launcelot.—He was born in Connecticut, and was a Representative in Congress, from that State, from 1835 to 1839.

Phelps, Oliver.—He was a Representative in Congress, from New York, from 1803 to 1805, and a member of the Assembly of that State, from Ontario County, in 1834.

Phelps, Samuel S.—He was born in Litchfield, Connecticut, May 13, 1793, and died March 25, 1855, in Middlebury, Vermont. He graduated at Yale College in 1811, and while studying law, in 1812, he entered the American army, and before the close of his military career was appointed Paymaster. He settled in Middlebury, and practised law. In 1827 he was member of the Council of Censors, and wrote the address issued by that body. In 1831 he was chosen a member of the Legislative Council of Vermont, and was soon afterwards appointed Judge of the Supreme Court of the State, in which position he remained until 1838. He was a Senator in Congress, from 1839 to 1854, in which body he displayed abilities of a high order.

Phelps, Timothy J.—He was born in New York, and removing to California was elected a Representative, from that State, to the Thirty-seventh Congress.

Phelps, William W.—He was born in Oakland County, Michigan, June 1, 1826; he graduated at the University of Michigan in 1846; studied law, and was admitted to the bar in 1848; and edited a Democratic newspaper, in Oakland County, from 1851 to 1855. In 1852 and 1853 he held the office of Commissioner for his native county, performing the duties of Judge at chambers; in 1854 was appointed, by President Pierce, Register of the United States Land Office at Red Wing, in Minnesota; and in 1857 he was elected a Representative to the Thirty-fifth Congress, from that State, and was a member of the Committee on Mileage. In 1860 he assumed the editorship of the Red Wing Sentinel.

Phillips, Henry M.—He was born in Pennsylvania; elected a Representative, from that State, to the Thirty-fifth Congress, and was a member of the Committee on Finance.

Phillips, John.—He was born in Chester County, Pennsylvania, and was a Representative in Congress, from Pennsylvania, from 1821 to 1823.

Phillips, Philip.—He was born in Charleston, South Carolina, December 13, 1807, and was educated at the Norwich Military Academy, in Vermont, and at Middletown, Connecticut. In 1825 he commenced the study of law in Charleston, and on the day after attaining his majority was admitted to the bar. He entered public life by becoming a member of the Nullification Convention in 1832, and voted with the minority; in 1834 he was elected, for two years, to the State Legislature; in 1835 he resigned; removed to Mobile, Alabama, and practised his profession with success; in 1837 was elected President of the Alabama Democratic State Convention; in 1844 was elected to the Legislature, and was Chairman of the Committee on Federal Relations; in 1849 was President of an Internal Improvement Convention; in 1851 was again elected to the Legislature; in 1852 went to the Baltimore Convention; and was a Representative in Congress, from Alabama, from 1853 to 1855, and declined a re-election. Since that time he has practised his profession in Washington City.

Phillips, Stephen Clarendon.—He was born in Salem, Massachusetts, November 1, 1801; graduated at Harvard College in 1819, with high honors; began to study law, but soon became a merchant. From 1824 to 1829, by annual re-elections, he was chosen a Representative to the State Legislature from Salem; from 1830 to 1831 he was State Senator, and in 1832 and 1833 was again a member of the House. From 1834 to 1838 he worthily represented Massachusetts in Congress. From December, 1838, to March, 1842, he was Mayor of Salem, and upon his voluntary retirement devoted the whole of his salary as Mayor to the public schools of the city. In 1840 he was one of the Presidential Electors for Massachusetts, and in 1848 and 1849 was the Free-soil candidate for Governor. He held various State and private trusts, in the discharge of which, by his ability, sagacity, experience, and integrity, he rendered signal service. He was for many years a member of the State Board of Education, and a Trustee of the State Lunatic Hospital at Worcester. He retired from public life in 1849, and was extensively engaged in the lumbering business. He was lost by the burning of the steamer Montreal, on the St. Lawrence River, June 26, 1857, while returning from Quebec, whither he had been on business to Three Rivers, the head-quarters of his operations in Canada.

Philson, Robert.—He was born in Donegal, Ireland, and was a Representative in Congress, from Pennsylvania, from 1819 to 1821.

Phœnix, J. Phillips.—He was born in Morristown, New Jersey; was for many years a leading merchant in New York City; served several years in the Councils of the city; was a Representative in Congress, from New York, from 1843 to 1845; a member of the State Assembly in 1848, from New York City; and again in Congress, from 1849 to 1851, serving as Chairman of the Committee on Commerce. Died suddenly in New York, May 4, 1859, at an advanced age.

Pickens, Andrew.—He was born at Paxton, Pennsylvania, September 19, 1739, and removed with his father, in 1752, to the Waxsaw Settlement, in South Carolina; he served as a volunteer in Grant's expedition against the Cherokees, and was an active military partisan during the Revolution. He was a member of the State Legislature, from the close of the war until 1793, when he was elected a Representative in Congress, from 1793 to 1795. In 1795 he was commissioned Major-General of the South Carolina militia, and was frequently a Commissioner to treat with the Indians. It was his son and not himself who was Governor of the State, from 1816 to 1817. He died in Pendleton District, South Carolina, August 17, 1817.

Pickens, Francis W.—He was born in South Carolina, and was a Representative in Congress, from that State, from 1835 to 1845. In 1858 he was appointed by President Buchanan Minister to Russia; and in December, 1860, was elected Governor of South Carolina.

Pickens, Israel.—Born in Cabarrus County, North Carolina; served one year in the State Legislature; was a Representative, from that State, in Congress, from 1811 to 1817, in which year he was appointed Register of the Land-office of Mississippi Territory; on removing to Alabama, he was elected Governor of that State, in 1821, and in 1826 was a Senator in Congress, from Alabama.

Pickering, Timothy.—Was born in Salem, Massachusetts, July 17, 1745; graduated at Harvard College in 1763, and after the usual course of professional studies, was admitted to the practice of law. When the dissensions between the mother country and our own commenced, he soon became the champion and leader of the Whigs of the quarter where he lived. He was a member of the Committees of Inspection and Correspondence, and bore the entire burden of writing. The addresses which, in 1774, the inhabitants of Salem, in full town meeting, voted to Governor Gage, on the occasion of the Boston Port-bill, proceeded from his pen. A part of it, disclaiming any wish on the part of the inhabitants of Salem to profit by the closing of the port of Boston, is quoted by Dr. Ramsay, in his History of the American Revolution. In April, 1775, on receiving intelligence of the battle of Lexington, he marched with the regiment of which he was at the time commander, to Charlestown, but had not an opportunity of coming to action. Before the close of the same year, when the provisional government was organizing, he was appointed one of the Judges of the Court of Common Pleas for Essex, his native county; and sole Judge of the Maritime Court (which had cognizance of all prize causes) for the Middle District, comprehending Boston, with Salem and the other ports in Essex. These offices he held until he accepted an appointment in the army. In 1777 he was named Adjutant-General, by Washington, and joined the army, then at Middlebrook, New Jersey. He continued with the Commander-in-chief until the American forces went into winter quarters at Valley Forge, having been present at the battles of Brandywine and Germantown. He then proceeded to discharge the duties of a member of the Continental Board of War, to which he had been elected by Congress, then sitting at York, Pennsylvania. In this station he remained until he was appointed to succeed General Greene in the office of Quartermaster-General, which he retained during the residue of the war, and in which he contributed much to the surrender of Cornwallis at Yorktown. From 1790 to 1794 he was charged, by President Washington, with several negotiations with the Indian nations on our frontiers. In 1791 he was also made Postmaster-General; and in 1794 removed from that station to the Secretaryship of War, on the resignation of General Knox. In 1795 he was appointed Secretary of State in the place of Mr. Randolph. From that office he was removed, by President Adams, in 1800. At the end of the year 1801 he returned to Massachusetts. In 1803 the Legislature of that State chose him a Senator to Congress, for the residue of the term of Dwight Foster, who had resigned; and in 1805 re-elected him to the same station for the term of six years. After its expiration, in 1811, he was chosen, by the Legislature, a member of the Executive Council, and during the war of 1812 he was appointed a member of the Board of War for the defence of the State. In 1814 he was returned to Congress, and held his seat until March, 1817. He then finally retired to private life. His death took place January 29, 1829. In his manners, Colonel Pickering was plain and unassuming. In public life he was distinguished for energy, ability, and disinterestedness; as a soldier he was brave and patriotic; and his writings bear ample testimony to his talents and information. He was one of the leaders of the Federal party of the United States.

Pickman, Benjamin.—He was born in 1763; graduated at Cambridge in 1784; visited Europe, and on his return studied law, and, though admitted to the bar, abandoned that profession, devoting himself to mercantile pursuits. In 1800 he was elected to the State Legislature, and re-elected a number of years to the State Senate; in 1807 he became a member of the Executive Council; was a Representative in Congress, from 1809 to 1811; and in 1820 was a member of the Convention for revising the State Constitution. He also held many other offices of trust and honor, and died at Salem, Massachusetts, in August, 1843.

Pierce, Franklin.—Was born in the town of Hillsborough, New Hampshire, in 1804, and, after completing his academical studies, entered Bowdoin College, Maine. On leaving college he commenced his legal studies at Northampton, Massachusetts, but subsequently returned to his native State, and finished his studies at Amherst. He was admitted to the bar, and commenced the practice of his profession in his native town; but before the end of two years he was elected a Representative in the State Legislature, and during his second year's service was chosen Speaker of the House. In 1833 he was elected to Congress, and remained a member of the House of Representatives four years. In 1837 he was elected a member of the United States Senate, but, after five years' service in that body, resigned his seat. He settled in Concord, and resumed his practice at the bar. He adhered to his resolution of accepting no political office, declined to be a candidate for Governor of the State, or United States Senator, and refused the offices of Attorney-General and Secretary of War, which were tendered him by President Polk. On the breaking out of the Mexican war, however, he enrolled himself as a private soldier in the New England Regiment, but President Polk sent him a Colonel's commission, and subsequently raised him to the rank of Brigadier-General in March, 1847. He was in most of the battles which were fought between Vera Cruz and the city of Mexico. On the restoration of peace between the two countries, he resigned his commission, and returned home, where he remained, comparatively unobserved, until the action of the Baltimore Democratic Convention gave him a new importance throughout the Union. He was nominated by that body as the Democratic candidate for the Presidency. He was elected President of the United States in November, 1852, was inaugurated March 4, 1853, and served to the end of his term, after which he retired to private life. The best biography of him was written by his personal friend, Nathaniel Hawthorne.

Pierce, Joseph.—He was a Representative in Congress, from New Hampshire, during the years 1801 and 1802.

Pierson, Isaac.—He was born August 15, 1770, and died September 22, 1833, in New Jersey. He was educated at Princeton College, graduating in 1789, and was subsequently a Fellow of the College of Surgeons and Physicians of New York. He practised medicine for forty years; and was a Representative in Congress, from New Jersey, from 1827 to 1831.

Pierson, Jeremiah H.—He was born in Essex County, New Jersey, and was a Representative in Congress, from New York, from 1821 to 1823.

Pierson, Job.—He was a Representative in Congress, from New York, from 1831 to 1835.

Pierson, Joseph.—He was a Representative in Congress, from North Carolina, from 1809 to 1815, and died October 27, 1834.

Pike, Frederick A.—Born in Calais, Maine, where he has always resided; was for several years a member of the Maine Legislature, serving one term as Speaker of the House of Representatives. He adopted the profession of law, and was for several years attorney for the county in which he lived. He was elected a Representative, from Maine, to the Thirty-seventh Congress, serving on the Committee on Naval Affairs. Re-elected to the Thirty-eighth Congress, serving as Chairman of the Committee on Expenditures in the State Department, and a member of the Committee on Naval Affairs.

Pike, James.—He was born in Salisbury, Massachusetts, in November, 1818; was educated at the Wesleyan University, in Connecticut; was a minister in the Methodist Episcopal Church from 1841 to 1854; and was elected a Representative, from New Hampshire, in the Thirty-fourth and Thirty-fifth Congresses, and was a member of the Committee on Enrolled Bills.

Pilsbury, Timothy.—He was born in Newbury, Massachusetts, April 12, 1789; received a common school education; spent two years as a clerk in a store, and several subsequent years as a sailor and coasting trader, making one trip to Europe as captain of a brig; settled in Maine, and was appointed a member of the Executive Council; also served in the State Legislature; went from Maine to Ohio, thence to Louisiana, and finally to Texas; he served a number of years in the Senate and House of Representatives of Texas; and when that Republic came into the Union he was elected a Representative in Congress, from 1846 to 1849. He died near Danville, Texas, November 23, 1858.

Pinckney, Charles.—Born in Charleston, South Carolina, in 1758; was a patriot in the Revolutionary struggle; was taken prisoner, and sent to St. Augustine, Florida; served in the Provincial Legislature; was a member of the Provincial Congress in 1785; received the degree of LL.D. from Princeton College in 1787; and in 1787 was a Delegate to the Convention which framed the Constitution of the United States. He was President of the State Convention which ratified the Federal Constitution; and Governor of South Carolina, from 1789 to 1792, and from 1796 to 1798. He was a Senator in Congress, from 1798 to 1801, and was appointed in 1802 Minister to Spain, by President Jefferson, holding that position till 1805. He was subsequently a Representative in Congress, from 1819 to 1821; served in the State Legislature in 1810 and 1812; and died October 29, 1824.

Pinckney, H. L.—He was born in South Carolina, and was a Representative in Congress, from that State, from 1833 to 1837. He was the founder of the Charleston Mercury, and died in Charleston, February 3, 1863.

Pinckney, Thomas.—He was a soldier of the American Revolution; was elected Governor of South Carolina in 1787; was appointed Minister to Great Britain by Washington; and was a Representative in Congress, from 1799 to 1801. He died in 1828.

Pindell, James.—He was born in Virginia, and was a Representative in Congress, from that State, from 1817 to 1820.

Pinkney, William.—Born in Annapolis, Maryland, March 17, 1765. Having prepared himself for the bar, under the instruction of Judge Chase, he was admitted to practice in 1786, and immediately gave promise of high distinction. He was a member of the Convention which ratified the Federal Constitution, and from 1789 to 1792, was a Representative in Congress; and then a member of the Executive Council, and made its President. In 1795 he was a member of the State Legislature. In 1796 he was a Commissioner under Jay's treaty, in conjunction with Mr. Gore, and remained in London eight years. He recovered for Maryland a claim on the Bank of England for $800,000. In 1806 he was Envoy Extraordinary to England, and in 1808, on the return of Mr. Monroe, was made Minister Plenipotentiary. He returned to the United States, and settled in Baltimore, in 1811, and was soon after a member of the State Senate. In December, 1811, he was appointed Attorney-General, and remained in that position until 1814. He commanded a battalion of riflemen, and was wounded at Bladensburg, in August, 1814. He was a Representative in Congress, from 1815 to 1816, and then made Minister to Russia and Envoy to Naples. On his return in 1819, he was elected a member of the United States Senate, and continued in that station until his death, February 25, 1822. He possessed splendid talents, and was one of the most accomplished orators and statesmen of his time.

Piper, William.—He was a Representative in Congress, from Pennsylvania, from 1811 to 1819.

Pitcher, Nathaniel.—He was born at Litchfield, Connecticut; and was a member of the New York Legislature in 1806, 1815, 1816, and 1817; a Delegate to the State Constitutional Convention of 1821; at one time Lieutenant-Governor and acting Governor of the State; at another, Commissioner to survey the State roads; and a Representative in Congress, from New York, from 1819 to 1823, and again from 1831 to 1833.

Pitkin, Timothy.—Born in Farmington, Connecticut, in 1765, and graduated at Yale College in 1785. He was for several years a member of the State Legislature, and Speaker of the House during five sessions, and a Representative in Congress, from 1805 to 1819. In 1816 he published "A Statistical View of the Commerce of the United States," and in 1828 his "Political and Civil History of the United States, from 1763 to the close of Washington's Administration." He died in New Haven, December 18, 1847.

Pitman, Charles W.—He was born in New Jersey, and was a Representative in Congress, from Pennsylvania, from 1849 to 1851.

Plant, David.—Was a native of Stratford, Connecticut, and graduated at Yale College in 1804. In 1819 and 1820 he was Speaker of the House of Representatives; in 1821 a member of the State Senate, and was twice re-elected. From 1823 to 1827 he was Lieutenant-Governor of the State, and from 1827 to 1829 a Representative in Congress. He died October 18, 1851.

Plater, Thomas.—He was a Representative in Congress, from Maryland, from 1801 to 1805.

Platt, Jonas.—Judge of the Supreme Court of New York; was a Representative in Congress, from New York, from 1799 to 1801, and died in Peru, Clinton County, New York, in 1834.

Pleasants, James.—Born in Virginia, in 1769, and died in Goochland County, November 9, 1836. He was a Representative in Congress, from 1811 to 1819, United States Senator, from 1819 to 1822, Governor of Virginia, from 1822 to 1825, and a member of the Convention of 1829–30 for amending the State Constitution. He was twice appointed to the bench, but declined, from a distrust of his own qualifications. He was a man of rare modesty, greatly respected and esteemed for public and private virtues.

Plumer, Arnold.—He was born in Pennsylvania, and was a Representative in Congress, from 1837 to 1839, and again from 1841 to 1843.

Plumer, George.—He was born in Alleghany County, Pennsylvania, and was a Representative in Congress, from Pennsylvania, from 1821 to 1827.

Plumer, William.—He was born at Newburyport, Massachusetts, June 25, 1759; received a good education; studied law, and was admitted to the bar in 1787; was for many years Solicitor for the County of Rockingham; he was for eight years a member of the State Legislature, and two years Speaker of the House; served as a member, and President of the State Senate. He was also Governor of New Hampshire in 1813, and from 1816 to 1819; and was a Senator in Congress, from that State, from 1802 to 1807. He died at Epping, New Hampshire, December 22, 1850.

Plumer, William.—Born in Epping, New Hampshire, in 1790, and died, September 18, 1854. He graduated at Cambridge in 1809; studied law, but never practised his profession. He frequently served in the State Legislature, and was a Representative in Congress, from 1819 to 1825,—his father, whose name he bore, having been a United States Senator in 1802, from the same State. He was also a member of the Convention to form a new State Constitution, in 1850.

Plummer, Franklin E.—He was at one time a Judge of the Circuit Court of Mississippi, and a Representative in Congress, from that State, from 1831 to 1833, and again from 1833 to 1835. He died at Jackson, Mississippi, September 24, 1852.

Poindexter, George.—He was the second Governor of Mississippi, under the State Constitution, from 1819 to 1821; was a Delegate to Congress, from the Territory, from 1807 to 1813, when he was appointed Federal Judge of the Territory; he was a Representative in Congress, from 1817 to 1819, and United States Senator, from Mississippi, from 1830 to 1835, serving for a time as President *pro tem.* of the Senate. He died in Jackson, Mississippi, September 5, 1853.

Poinsett, Joel R.—He was born in Statesburg, South Carolina, in 1779; spent the most of his youth in travelling in foreign countries; was a Representative in Congress, from South Carolina, from 1821 to 1825; was appointed, by President John Quincy Adams, United States Minister to Mexico; he was Secretary of War under President Van Buren; and from 1840 until his death he lived in retirement. He was a man of letters, and among other things, wrote an interesting book on Mexico. He died in Statesburg, South Carolina, December 14, 1851.

Polk, James Knox.—Born in Mecklenburg County, North Carolina, November 2, 1795; removed with his father, in 1806, to Tennessee, and lived in the valley of Duck River, a branch of the Cumberland. He graduated at the University of North Carolina in 1815; studied law in Tennessee with Felix Grundy, and was admitted to the bar in 1820; he was a member of the House of Representatives in Congress, from 1825 to 1839, and Speaker in that body from 1835 to 1837; and was elected Governor of Tennessee, in 1839, for two years. In December, 1844, the Electors chose him President of the United States; and during his eventful administration the Oregon question was settled, Texas annexed, war with Mexico declared, and New Mexico and California were acquired. He died at Nashville, Tennessee, June 15, 1849.

Polk, Trusten.—He was born in Sussex County, Delaware, May 29, 1811; graduated at Yale College in 1831; studied law at the Yale Law School; and in 1835 he emigrated to Missouri, where he commenced the practice of his profession. In 1845, while absent from Missouri for the benefit of his health, he was elected a member of the Convention called to remodel the State Constitution; in 1856 he was elected Governor of Missouri, and inaugurated January, 1857, but soon resigned for a seat in the United States Senate, to which he was elected for the term of six years, from March 4, 1857. He was a member of the Committees on Foreign Affairs, and on Claims.

Polk, William H.—He was born in Maury County, Tennessee, May 24, 1815; educated at Chapel Hill, North Carolina, and the University of Tennessee; studied law, and was admitted to the bar in 1839; in 1841 and 1843, he was elected to the State Legislature; was appointed, by President Tyler, Chargé d'Affaires to Naples, where he negotiated a treaty with the Two Sicilies; served as a Major of dragoons in the Mexican war; was a Delegate to the Nashville Convention, in 1850; and a Representative in Congress, from Tennessee, from 1851 to 1853. He was a brother of President Polk, and opposed to the Great Rebellion. Died at Nashville, December 16, 1862.

Pollock, James.—He was born in Pennsylvania; graduated at Princeton College in 1831; was a Judge of the Court of Common Pleas; was a Representative in Congress, from that State, from 1843 to 1849; and Governor of Pennsylvania from 1855 to 1858. Was a Delegate to the Peace Congress of 1861.

Pomeroy, Samuel C.—Was born in Southampton, January 3, 1816; spent his boyhood on his father's farm; after receiving an academic education, he entered Amherst, and graduated in 1836; spent four years in Onondaga, New York; returned to his native town, and held various local offices; in 1851 he was elected to the Massachusetts Legislature; in 1854 he engaged in organizing the New England Emigrant Aid Society, and became its financial agent; removed to Kansas the same year, and participated in its affairs; was a member of the Territorial Defence Committee; a Delegate to the Pittsburg and Philadelphia Conventions in 1856; also to that of Chicago in 1860. During the famine in Kansas he was Chairman of the Relief Committee; and in 1861 he took his seat as a Senator in Congress, from Kansas, for six years, serving on the Committees on Pensions, Claims, and Territories.

Pomeroy, Theodore M.—Born in Cayuga, New York, December 31, 1824; graduated at Hamilton College; adopted the profession of law; was District Attorney for Cayuga County from 1850 to 1856; was a member of the State Legislature in 1857; and was elected a Representative, from New York, to the Thirty-seventh Congress, serving on the Committee on Foreign Affairs. Re-elected to the Thirty-eighth Congress, serving as Chairman of the Committee on Expenditures in the Post-office Department, and a member of the Committee on Foreign Affairs.

Pond, Benjamin.—He served four years in the Assembly of New York, from Essex County, and was a Representative in Congress, from that State, from 1811 to 1813.

Pope, John.—He was born in Prince William County, Virginia, in 1770. Having lost one arm by accident, he determined to study law, and attained eminence at the bar; he removed to Kentucky, and served a number of years in the Legislature; was a Senator in Congress, from that State, from 1807 to 1813, officiating for a time as President *pro tem.* of that body; and a Representative in Congress, from 1837 to 1843. In 1829 he was appointed Governor of the Territory of Arkansas, and died in Kentucky, July 12, 1845.

Pope, Nathaniel.—He was a Delegate to Congress, from the Territory of Illinois, from 1816 to 1818, in which year he was appointed Register of the Land-office in Edwardsville, Illinois; and was appointed, in 1819, Federal Judge of the Illinois District.

Pope, Patrick H.—He was a Representative in Congress, from 1833 to 1835, and died at Louisville, Kentucky, in May, 1841.

Porter, Albert G.—Born in Lawrenceburg, Indiana, April 20, 1824; graduated at the Asbury University in 1843; studied law, and was admitted to the bar in 1845, settling at Indianapolis; in 1853 he was appointed Reporter of the Decisions of the Supreme Court of Indiana, publishing five volumes; served two terms as City Attorney of Indianapolis; was twice elected a member of the City Council; and in 1858 he was elected a Representative, from Indiana, to the Thirty-sixth Congress, serving on the Judiciary Committee. Re-elected to the Thirty-seventh Congress, serving on the Committees on the Judiciary, and on Manufactures.

Porter, Alexander.—Born in Ireland in 1786; and his father having fallen a victim there during the disturbances of 1798, he emigrated to America, and settled at Nashville, Tennessee, as a clergyman. He soon engaged in commerce, but afterwards studied law, and removed to Louisiana about the year 1809, where he soon acquired distinction. He assisted in forming the Constitution of the State, and became a Judge of the Supreme Court of Louisiana, serving as such for fifteen years; and was a Senator in Congress, from 1833 to 1837. He died at Attakapas, Louisiana, January 13, 1844.

Porter, Augustus S.—Born in Canandaigua, New York, January 18, 1798; graduated at Union College in 1818; studied law as a profession, and practised for twenty years in Detroit, Michigan; of which city he was chosen Mayor in 1838. He was a Senator in Congress, from Michigan, from 1840 to 1845; and in 1848 he removed to Niagara Falls, the residence of his father, where he has since lived in retirement.

Porter, Gilchrist.—He was born in Virginia, and was a Representative in Congress, from Missouri, from 1851 to 1857.

Porter, James.—He was a member of the New York Assembly in 1814 and 1815, and was a Representative in Congress, from that State, from 1817 to 1819.

Porter, John.—He was a Representative in Congress, from Pennsylvania, from 1806 to 1811.

Porter, Peter B.—He was born in 1773; a native of Salisbury, Connecticut; and graduated at Yale College in 1791. He completed his law studies at Litchfield, and emigrated to Western New York. He was a Representative in Congress, from that State, from 1809 to 1813, and from 1815 to 1816. As Chairman of the Committee on Foreign Relations, he reported the resolutions authorizing immediate and active preparations for war; and in 1816 was appointed Commissioner under the treaty of Ghent. In 1813 he was made Major-General, and chief in command of the State troops; and in 1815 he received from President Madison the appointment of Commander-in-chief of the United States Army, which he declined. Soon after the war he was chosen Secretary of the State of New York. In 1828 he was appointed Secretary of War by President Adams. He died at Niagara Falls, March 20, 1844, aged seventy-one years.

Porter, Timothy H.—He was born in New Haven, Connecticut; served five years in the Assembly of New York, and also five years in the State Senate; and was a Representative in Congress, from New York, from 1825 to 1827.

Posey, Thomas.—He was a Senator in Congress, from Louisiana, from 1812 to 1813. He died March 19, 1818.

Post, Jotham.—Born in New York, a graduate of Columbia College, and a member of the New York Assembly for four years, from the city of New York, and a Representative in Congress, from 1813 to 1815, from his native State.

Potter, Elisha R.—He filled for forty years a large space in the political transactions of Rhode Island, having been for twenty-five years a member of the General Assembly, and a Representative in Congress, from that State, from 1796 to 1797, and from 1809 to 1815. He was a man of superior talents, and died at South Kingston, Rhode Island, September 26, 1835.

Potter, Elisha R., Jr.—He was born in Rhode Island; graduated at Brown University; served many years in both branches of the Legislature; and was a Representative in Congress, from that State, from 1843 to 1845.

Potter, Emery D.—He was born in Ohio, and was a Representative in Congress, from that State, from 1843 to 1845, and again from 1849 to 1851.

Potter, John F.—Born in Augusta, Maine, May 11, 1817; educated at Phillips's Academy, New Hampshire; is a lawyer by profession; was a member of the Legislature of Wisconsin in 1856, and Judge of Walworth County, from 1842 to 1846, and elected a Representative in the Thirty-fifth Congress, serving as a member of the Committee on Revolutionary Pensions. He was re-elected to the Thirty-sixth Congress, serving on the Committee on Revolutionary Pensions. Elected also to the Thirty-seventh Congress, and made Chairman of a special Committee on Government Employees, and also of that on Public Lands. He was a Delegate also to the Peace Congress of 1861. He was appointed Governor of Nevada Territory by President Lincoln, but declined, and was subsequently appointed Consul-General of British North America.

Potter, Robert.—Born in Granville County, North Carolina. He entered the navy as a midshipman, but resigned this position, and studied law. He entered the State Legislature in 1826, and was in Congress, from 1829 to 1831. He was a second time in the Legislature, but owing to an outrage that he committed upon the persons of two men, of whom he was jealous, he lost all political influence, and, removing to Texas, was killed in a private brawl.

Potter, Samuel I.—He was a Senator in Congress, from Rhode Island, during the years 1803 and 1804, having died October 29th of the latter year, aged fifty-four years.

Potter, William W.—He was a Representative in Congress, from Pennsylvania, from 1837 to 1839, and died at Bellefonte, in that State, October 28, 1839.

Pottle, Emory B.—He was born in Naples, New York; is a lawyer by profession; was once in the Legislature of New York; and was elected a Representative in the Thirty-fifth Congress, from that State, serving on the Committee on Expenditures in the Navy Department. He was also re-elected to the Thirty-sixth Congress, serving as a member of the Committee on Naval Affairs.

Potts, David, Jr.—He was born in Chester County, Pennsylvania, in 1793, and was a Representative in Congress, from that State, from 1831 to 1839. Died in 1863.

Potts, Richard.—He was Governor of Maryland during the years 1781 and 1782; and a Senator in Congress, from that State, from 1792 to 1796, when he resigned. He received from Princeton College, in 1805, the degree of LL.D.

Powell, Alfred H.—He was born in Loudon County, Virginia; graduated at Princeton College; studied law in Alexandria, Virginia; settled in Winchester, Virginia, in 1800; served in the State Legislature, and one or two State Conventions; and was a Representative in Congress, from Virginia, from 1825 to 1827. He died at Winchester while arguing a cause in court in 1831, aged fifty years.

Powell, Cuthbert.—He was at one time Mayor of Alexandria, in Virginia, and, on his removal to Loudon County, was elected to the Legislature; was subsequently a Representative in Congress, from 1841 to 1843. He died at Langollen, Virginia, May 8, 1849.

Powell, Lazarus W.—Born in Henderson County, Kentucky, October 6, 1812; graduated at St. Joseph's College, Bardstown, in 1833; studied law at the Transylvania University, and came to the bar in 1835, following his profession and carrying on a farm at the same time; in 1836 he was elected to the Kentucky Legislature; was a Presidential Elector in 1844; was Governor of Kentucky from 1851 to 1855; and he was chosen a Senator in Congress for the long term commencing in 1859, serving on the Committees on the Judiciary, Pensions, and Printing.

Powell, Levin.—He was born in Loudon County, Virginia, and was a Representative in Congress, from Virginia, from 1799 to 1801.

Powell, Paulus.—He was born in Virginia, and, having been elected a Representative in Congress, from that State, in 1849, continued in that capacity to the close of the Thirty-fifth Congress, serving as a member of the Committee on Expenditures in the Navy Department, and that on Post-offices and Post-roads.

Powell, Samuel.—He was a Representative in Congress, from Tennessee, from 1815 to 1817.

Powers, Gershom.—He was a Representative in Congress, from New York, from 1829 to 1831.

Poydras, Julian.—He was a Delegate in Congress, from the Territory of Louisiana, from 1809 to 1812.

Pratt, James T.—He was born in Middletown in 1805; was bred a farmer, which occupation he still follows; has served in the Connecticut Legislature; and was a Representative in Congress, from 1853 to 1855. He was also a Delegate to the Peace Congress of 1861.

Pratt, Thomas G.—He was born in Washington City in 1800; was educated at Princeton College; was bred a lawyer; was Governor of Maryland, from 1844 to 1848; and was a Senator in Congress, from that State, from 1851 to 1857. He was also a Delegate to the Chicago Convention of 1864.

Pratt, Zadock.—Was born at Stephentown, Rensselaer County, New York, October 30, 1790. He commenced in early life without means, but by his industry gained a large fortune. Devoting his attention to tanning, he attained eminent success in that branch of the mechanic arts, and his name will ever be associated with Prattsville, and that vast tannery, where, previous to the close of it, in 1846, he had tanned more than a million sides of leather. He was elected to Congress in 1836, and labored successfully for the public good. His career in Congress will be remembered for his efforts in behalf of the reduction of postage, his plans for the new Post-office buildings, and the Bureau of Statistics, which owes its origin to him.

Prentiss, John H.—He was born in Massachusetts, and was a Representative in Congress, from New York, from 1837 to 1841.

Prentiss, Samuel.—He was born in Stonington, Connecticut, March 31, 1782; removed with his father to Worcester, Massachusetts, and subsequently to Northfield, where he commenced the study of law. He completed his professional studies in Brattleborough, Vermont, and commenced practice at Montpelier in 1803, where he soon attained success, and became one of the foremost men of the bar. In 1824 and 1825 he represented Montpelier in the State Legislature. In 1829 he was elected Chief Justice of the Supreme Court of the State, having several years before declined the office of Associate Justice of that Court. He was a Senator in Congress, from Vermont, from 1831 to 1842. While Senator, he did much to effect the passage of the law against duelling in the District of Columbia. In 1842 he was appointed Judge of the Federal District Court in Vermont, which office he held at the time of his death. He died in Montpelier, Vermont, January 15, 1857.

Prentiss, Sergeant S.—Born in Portland, Maine, September 30, 1808, and died at Longwood, near Natchez, Mississippi, July 1, 1850. He graduated at Bowdoin College in 1826, when, after studying law at Gorham, he removed to Mississippi, and passed two years as tutor in a private family. He studied law at Natchez, and on removing to Vicksburg, became from the start the leader of the bar in his adopted State, acquiring by his profession a large property. He entered into politics, was elected to the State Legislature in 1835, and in 1837 was chosen a Representative in Congress, for the years 1838 and 1839. From that period until the close of his life he was devoted wholly to his profession, appearing frequently in court at New Orleans; and, as a jury orator, he was acknowledged as having no equal in the Southwestern States.

Preston, Francis.—He was a member of Congress, from Virginia, from 1793 to 1797, and died at Columbia, South Carolina, May 26, 1835, whither he had gone upon a visit to his son, the distinguished William C. Preston. He was in the seventieth year of his age.

Preston, Jacob A.—He was born in Maryland, and was a Representative in Congress, from that State, from 1843 to 1845.

Preston, William.—He was born near Louisville, Kentucky, October 16, 1816; was liberally educated at St. Joseph College, Kentucky, in New Haven, and at Harvard University; he settled, in the practice of law, at Louisville, and there remained until the Mexican war, when he went to Mexico as Lieutenant-Colonel of the Kentucky volunteers; he served in the Convention called to frame anew the Constitution of Kentucky; in 1850 and 1851 he was elected to the State Legislature; he was a Presidential Elector in 1852, voting for Scott; was a member of the Cincinnati Convention which nominated Mr. Buchanan in 1856; and was appointed, by President Buchanan, Minister to Spain. On his return, in 1861, he took part in the Rebellion, and was a Brigadier-General.

Preston, William B.—He was born in Virginia, and was a Representative in Congress, from that State, from 1847 to 1849; and Secretary of the Navy, under President Taylor, in 1849 and 1850. He took part in the Rebellion of 1861, as a member of the "Confederate" Congress. He died in Montgomery County, Virginia, November 16, 1862.

Preston, William C.—Was born December 27, 1794, in Philadelphia, while his father was attending Congress at that place, as a member from Virginia. His maternal grandmother was the sister of Patrick Henry. He was educated at the University of South Carolina. In 1812 he graduated, and returned to Virginia, where he studied law in the office of William Wirt, at Richmond. In 1816 he went to Europe, and after visiting France, England, and Switzerland, resided for some time in Edinburgh, where he attended the lectures of Hope, Playfair, and Brown. In 1819 he returned to the United States, and being admitted to the bar in 1821, commenced the practice of law in Virginia. In 1822 he removed to Columbia, in South Carolina, where he continued the practice of his profession with great distinction and success. In 1832 he was elected to the Senate of the United States, where he assumed a high position as a debater. In 1842 he resigned his place in the Senate, and returned to the practice of his profession in South Carolina. In 1855 he became President of the University of South Carolina, which office he filled with great credit until he was forced to resign, in consequence of ill health, after which time he lived in retirement. Died at Columbia, South Carolina, May 22, 1860.

Price, Hiram.—He was born in Washington County, Pennsylvania, January 10, 1814; is President of the State Bank of Iowa; and in 1862 he was elected Representative, from Iowa, to the Thirty-eighth Congress, serving as Chairman of the Committee on Revolutionary Claims.

Price, Rodman M.—Born in Sussex County, New Jersey, November 5, 1816. He attended Princeton College until his health compelled him to retire, and he devoted some attention to the study of law; was appointed Purser in the Navy in 1840; is said to have been the first person to exercise judicial functions under the American flag on the Pacific Coast, as Alcalde; in 1848 was made Navy Agent for the Pacific Coast; was a Representative in Congress, from his native State, from 1851 to 1853; and subsequently elected Governor of New Jersey. He caused the establishment, in that State, of a Normal School, and has done much to improve the militia of the State. He was a Delegate to the Peace Congress of 1861.

Price, Sterling.—He was born in Virginia; was a Representative in Congress, from Missouri, from 1845 to 1847; and Governor of that State, from 1853 to 1857. Was identified with the Great Rebellion of 1861 as a Major-General.

Price, Thomas L.—He was elected a Representative, from Missouri, to the Thirty-seventh Congress. He was also a Delegate to the Chicago Convention of 1864.

Prince, Oliver H.—He was a Senator in Congress, from Georgia, during the years 1828 and 1829, and died at sea, October 9, 1837.

Prince, William.—He was a Representative in Congress, from Indiana, from 1823 to 1824, having died in Princeton, Indiana, before the expiration of his term, September 8, 1824.

Pringle, Benjamin. — Born in Richfield, Otsego County, New York, November 9, 1807; received a good English and classical education; studied law, and practised for several years, but relinquished the profession on being made President and financial officer of the Bank of Genesee, at Batavia. He held the office of Judge of the County Courts of Genesee for five years, and served one year in the State Assembly; and he was elected a Representative, from New York, to the Thirty-third and Thirty-fourth Congresses.

Proffit, George H.—He was a Representative in Congress, from Indiana, from 1839 to 1843; and in 1843 was United States Minister to Brazil. He died at Louisville, Kentucky, September 5, 1847.

Pruyn, John V. L.—He was born in Albany, New York; was chiefly educated at private schools, and received a degree at Rutgers College, New Jersey; studied law, and came to the bar in Albany in 1832; in 1835 he was Counsel and Director of the Mohawk and Hudson Railroad, and subsequently became Treasurer of the New York Central Railroad Company; he was also a Master in Chancery during the Governorship of W. L. Marcy; in 1844 was made a member of the Board of Regents; and in 1862 a Chancellor of the University of New York, and was a State Senator in 1862. At a special election in 1863 he was elected a Representative, from New York, to the Thirty-eighth Congress, to fill the vacancy caused by the resignation of Erastus Corning, serving on the Committee of Claims.

Pryor, Roger A.—Born in Dinwiddie County, Virginia, July 19, 1828; graduated at Hampden Sidney College in 1845; adopted the profession of law, but relinquished the practice on account of his health; in 1851 became an editor in Petersburg; in 1852 connected himself with the Washington Union as a writer; in 1853 he joined the Richmond Enquirer; in 1855 he was appointed by President Pierce a special Commissioner to Greece, to adjust certain difficulties with that country; on his return he established a political journal called "The South," which stopped in eighteen months; was connected for four months with the "Washington States;" and was elected a Representative, from Virginia, to the Thirty-sixth Congress, serving as a member of the Committee on the District of Columbia. He took part in the Rebellion as a member of the "Confederate" Congress, and also as a Brigadier-General.

Pugh, George Ellis. — Born in Cincinnati, Ohio, November 28, 1822; graduated at Miami University in 1840, and is a lawyer by profession. He was Captain of the Fourth Regiment of Ohio volunteers, in the Mexican war, in 1847; Representative in the Legislature in 1848 and 1849; was appointed Solicitor to the City of Cincinnati, in 1850; was Attorney-General of the State in 1851; and elected a Senator in Congress, from March 4, 1855, for six years, and was a member of the Committees on Public Lands and on the Judiciary.

Pugh, James L.—Born in Burke County, Georgia, in 1820; received an academical education; adopted the profession of law, and removing to Alabama, was elected a Representative, from that State, to the Thirty-sixth Congress, serving on the Committee on the Library. Resigned in February, 1861, to take part in the Rebellion of that year.

Pugh, John.—He was a Representative in Congress, from Pennsylvania, from 1805 to 1809.

Purdy, Smith M.—He was born in New York, and was a Representative in Congress, from that State, from 1843 to 1845.

Purviance, Samuel A.—Born in Butler, Pennsylvania, November 8, 1809. He was a student of Washington College, but did not graduate; is a lawyer by profession, and has practised for twenty-five years; was a member of the Convention to amend the State Constitution, in 1836, and served in the Legislature in 1838 and 1839; was a member of the Electoral College in 1848; and a Representative from Pennsylvania, in the Thirty-fifth Congress. He was a member of the Committee on Public Buildings and Grounds.

Purviance, Samuel D.—A member of Congress, from North Carolina, from 1803 to 1805.

Puryear, Richard C. — He was born in Mecklenburg, Virginia, February 9, 1801; received a good English education; has spent the most of his life engaged in merchandizing and farming. In 1838, having removed to North Carolina, he was elected to the Legislature of that State; in 1840 to the State Senate; in 1844, 1846, and 1852, he was again chosen to the Legislature; and was a Representative in Congress, from North Carolina, from 1853 to 1857. He took part in the Rebellion of 1861 as a member of the "Confederate" Congress.

Putman, Harvey. — For many years a leading member of the Genesee County bar; was elected several times to both branches of the New York Legislature; and was a Representative in Congress, from New York, from 1847 to 1851. He died in Attica, New York, September 21, 1855, aged sixty-two years.

Quarles, James M. — Born in Louisa County, Virginia, February 8, 1823; removed with his father to Kentucky in 1833; received a common school education; adopted the profession of law; on removing to Tennessee, in 1846, he became Attorney-General of the Tenth District; was a Presidential Elector in 1852; and was elected a Representative, from Tennessee, to the Thirty-sixth Congress, serving on the Committee on the Militia.

Quarles, Tunstall.—He was born in Virginia; was a Representative in Congress, from Kentucky, from 1817 to 1820, and was subsequently Receiver of Public Moneys at Cape Girardeau, Missouri.

Quincy, Josiah.—Born in Boston, Massachusetts, February 4, 1772. He graduated at Harvard in 1790, and entered on the practice of law in Boston. In 1804 he was chosen a Representative, from Boston, in the Congress of the United States, and held that station eight successive years, until he declined a re-election in 1813. He was chosen State Senator, for Suffolk, from 1814 to 1819; Representative, from Boston; and was Speaker of the House, in 1820; Judge of the Municipal Court, in Boston, in 1821; and Mayor of that city in 1823. He held the office of Mayor six successive years, until he declined a re-election, in December, 1828. In 1829 he was chosen President of Harvard University, and held that office until his resignation in 1845. His published works are "Speeches in Congress, and Orations on Various Occasions," "Memoir of Josiah Quincy, Jr., of Massachusetts," "Centennial Address on the Two Hundredth Anniversary of the Settlement of Boston," "A History of Harvard University, from 1636 to 1836," "Memoir of James Grahame, Historian of the United States Army," "Memoir of Major Samuel Shaw," "History of the Boston Athenæum," "A Municipal History of the Town and City of Boston, from 1630 to 1830." Died in Boston, July 1, 1864.

Quitman, John A.—He was born in Rhinebeck, Dutchess County, New York, September 1, 1799; had a liberal education; studied theology, but preferred the law, and in his twentieth year was a Professor of Law in Mount Airy College, Pennsylvania. In 1820 he emigrated to Ohio, and was admitted to the bar of that State, but soon afterwards removed to Natchez, Mississippi. In 1827 he was elected to the State Legislature; in 1828 was appointed Chancellor of the State, serving three years; in 1835 he was elected to the State Senate, and as President of that body was called upon to perform the duties of Governor; in 1836 he distinguished himself as a soldier and leader in behalf of Texas against Mexico; in 1839 he visited Europe on business for the Mississippi Railroad; on his return was appointed Judge of the High Court of Errors and Appeals; he served with distinction in the Mexican war; had a horse shot from under him at Monterey; commanded at Victoria; was at Vera Cruz and Ojo Del Agua; commissioned, by the President, Major-General in the army; he also acquitted himself with great credit at Chapultepec; he was Governor of Mississippi in 1850; and in 1855 he was elected a Representative in Congress, from Mississippi, and re-elected in 1857, serving both terms at the head of the Committee on Military Affairs. By virtue of his experience and strict integrity he ever commanded the respect of all, and the kindness of his heart and amiable manners won for him troops of friends among all parties. He was spoken of on two occasions as the Democratic candidate for Vice-President, and was the recognized leader of those favorable to the annexation of Cuba. He died at his residence, in Mississippi, July 17, 1858.

Radford, William.—Was born in Poughkeepsie, Dutchess County, New York, June 24, 1814; received a good common school education; settled in New York City in 1829, and was for a long time engaged in mercantile pursuits; and in 1862 he was elected a Representative, from New York, to the Thirty-eighth Congress, serving on the Committee on Public Buildings and Grounds.

Ramsay, Alexander.—He was born near Harrisburg, Pennsylvania, and was a Representative in Congress, from that State, from 1843 to 1847. He was educated at Lafayette College; served as a Presidential Elector in 1840; was Clerk of the Pennsylvania House of Representatives in 1841; and was the first Territorial Governor of Minnesota, serving from 1849 to 1853. In 1863 he was elected a Senator in Congress, from Minnesota, for the term ending in 1869, serving on the Committee on Post-offices and Post-roads.

Ramsay, Robert.—He was born in Pennsylvania, and was a Representative in Congress, from that State, from 1833 to 1835, and again from 1841 to 1843.

Ramsey, William.—Born at Sterrett's Gap, Cumberland County, Pennsylvania, September 7, 1779. In 1803 he was appointed Surveyor of his native county, an office held by his father during the Revolution; and he also held the offices of Prothonotary, Register, Recorder, and Clerk of the Orphans' Court; studied law, and practised with success. In 1826 he was elected a member of Congress, from Pennsylvania; re-elected in 1828 and 1830, and died in September, 1831, at Carlisle, Pennsylvania.

Ramsey, William S.—Born in Carlisle, Pennsylvania, June 12, 1810; was educated at Dickinson College, but on account of bad health, did not graduate; he travelled in Europe; was an attaché to the American Legation in London, and formed the acquaintance of Walter Scott and General Lafayette; returning to Carlisle, he was admitted to the bar in 1832; elected a Representative to Congress, in 1838; re-elected in 1840, but died in Baltimore, October 17, 1840, a few weeks after his election.

Randall, Alexander.—He was born in Maryland, and was a Representative in Congress, from that State, from 1841 to 1843.

Randall, Benjamin.—He was born in Massachusetts in 1789; graduated at Bowdoin College in 1809; studied law, and was admitted to the bar in 1814, and commenced practice in Bath, Maine, where he resided forty-five years. He was a member of the State Senate in 1833, and a Representative in Congress, from Maine, from 1839 to 1843, and a member of the Committee on Invalid Pensions. He was appointed by President Taylor, Collector of the Port of Bath, and died at that place, October 14, 1857.

Randall, Samuel J.—Was born in Philadelphia in 1828; educated in that city; was brought up a merchant, and has ever been engaged in that pursuit; served four years in the Councils of his native city; one term in the State Senate; and in 1862 he was elected a Representative, from Pennsylvania, to the Thirty-eighth Congress, serving on the Committee on Public Buildings and Grounds.

Randall, William H.—Was born in Kentucky; studied law, and came to the bar in 1835; in 1836 was appointed Clerk of the Circuit and County Court of Laurel County, which position he held until 1851; after the adoption of the State Constitution, held the office one year by election; and was elected a Representative, from Kentucky, to the Thirty-eighth Congress, serving on the Committee on Foreign Affairs.

Randolph, James F.—Born in Middlesex County, New Jersey, June 26, 1791; received a common school education; served an apprenticeship to the printing business, and became editor of the "Fredonia," a weekly newspaper, in 1812, and continued in that capacity for thirty years. He was appointed Collector of the Internal Revenue of the United States in 1815, and held that office till the close of the war in Texas. He was subsequently Clerk of the Court of Common Pleas for the County, and for two years a member of the State Legislature. He was a Representative in Congress, from 1828 to 1833, and was afterwards President of a bank in New Brunswick, New Jersey, for ten years.

Randolph, John, of Roanoke.—He was born in Chesterfield, Virginia, June 2, 1773, and claimed descent through his grandmother, from Pocahontas, the daughter of Powhatan, the great Indian chief. His father died in 1775, leaving three sons and a large estate; and his mother was married in 1783 to St. George Tucker, who was his guardian during his minority. His early life was spent at different places, under different instructors, of most of whom he said "he never learned anything." He passed a short time at Princeton College, Columbia College, and at William and Mary College; and for a time he studied law with Edmund Randolph. He was elected a Representative in Congress, in 1799, and he continued a member of the House of Representatives, with the exception of two intervals of two years each, until 1829; in that year he was a member of the Convention to revise the Constitution of Virginia, and he was afterwards appointed Minister Plenipotentiary to Russia, by President Jackson, in 1830. During one of the intervals alluded to, from 1825 to 1827, he was a Senator of the United States. He was never married, and was possessed of a large estate on the Roanoke. He died at Philadelphia, May 24, 1833, while about to depart for Europe for the restoration of his feeble health. He was distinguished alike for his genius, his effective eloquence, and for many eccentricities of thought and manner.

Randolph, Joseph Fitz.—Born in 1803, in New Jersey, and obtained an ordinary school education, after which he studied law, and was licensed to practise in 1825; he settled at Monmouth Court-house, and was appointed State's Attorney for the County. He was a Representative in Congress, from 1837 to 1843, and during one term he was Chairman of the Committee on Revolutionary Claims. In 1844 he was a member of the Convention which framed the State Constitution; and in 1845 was appointed a Judge of the Supreme Court of New Jersey, for seven years, after which he resumed the practice of his profession at Trenton, where he now resides. He was also a member of the Peace Congress of 1861.

Randolph, Thomas M.—He was a native of Virginia; Governor of that State; and a Representative in Congress, from 1803 to 1807, and died at Monticello, June 20, 1828.

Rankin, Christopher.—He was born in Washington County, Pennsylvania, and was a Representative in Congress, from Mississippi, from 1819 to 1826. Died March 14, 1826, in Washington City.

Rantoul, Robert.—Born in Beverly, Massachusetts, May 13, 1805. He graduated at Harvard University in 1826; studied law; was admitted to the bar in 1827, and settled in practice in South Reading, and removed to Gloucester in 1832; was elected to the State Legislature in 1834, and in 1837 a member of the Masssachusetts Board of Education. In 1838 he removed to Boston, and in 1843 was appointed Collector of that port; in 1845 was appointed, by President Polk, United States District Attorney for Massachusetts; in 1851 succeeded Mr. Webster in the United States Senate, but remained there only a short time; and was a Representative in Congress, from 1851 to the time of his death, which occurred at Washington, August 7, 1852. His writings have since been published in a large volume.

Rariden, James.—He was a native of Kentucky, and was an early settler of the White Water Valley, Indiana; he was self-educated, and became eminent as a lawyer. He was a Representative in Congress, from Indiana, from 1837 to 1841, and died at Cambridge City, in that State.

Rathbun, George.—He was born in New York, and was a Representative in Congress, from that State, from 1843 to 1847.

Rayner, Kenneth.—Born in Bertie County, North Carolina, in 1808; received an academical education; and though he studied law, he did not practise. He entered public life, in 1835, as a member of the House of Commons, and the same year was a member of the Convention to revise the State Constitution. He served again in the local Legislature in 1836 and 1838, and was a Representative in Congress, from 1839 to 1845. In 1846 he went for the third time into the Legislature.

Rea, John.—He was a Representative in Congress, from Pennsylvania, from 1803 to 1811, and again from 1813 to 1815.

Read, Almon H.—He was born in Vermont in 1790; graduated at Williamstown College; studied law, and removing to Pennsylvania, was frequently elected to the State Legislature; in 1840 was appointed Treasurer of the State; and in 1841 was elected to fill a vacancy in the National House of Representatives. Died at Montrose, Pennsylvania, June 3, 1844.

Read, George.—Born in Cecil County, Maryland, in 1734, but, with his father, removed to New Castle County, Delaware. He was educated for the law, and was admitted to the bar in Philadelphia, at the age of nineteen, and practised his profession in New Castle; was made Attorney-General of the three lower counties on the Delaware, in 1763, and held the office until he was chosen a Delegate to Congress, in 1775. In 1776 he was a signer of the Declaration of Independence. He was President of the Convention which formed the first Constitution of Delaware, and also a member of the Convention which framed the Federal Constitution, and was elected a member of the United States Senate, serving from 1789 to 1793. He was then appointed Chief Justice of the Supreme Court of Delaware, in which office he remained until his death, in 1798.

Read, Jacob.—He was elected a Senator in Congress, from South Carolina, for the term from 1795 to 1802, serving a short time as President *pro tem.* of that body, and was appointed, by President Adams, Judge of the United States District Court of South Carolina, in 1801.

Read, Nathan.—Born in Essex County, Massachusetts, in 1760; graduated at Harvard University in 1781, and two years afterwards officiated as tutor in that institution. He was a Representative in Congress, from Massachusetts, from 1800 to 1803; and having removed to Hallowell, Maine, was for many years Judge of the Court of Common Pleas. He was devoted to science, and a petitioner for a patent for an invention, before the patent laws were enacted; and before the time of Fulton's experiments, he had tried the effect of steam upon a boat in Wenham Pond. He died at Hallowell, January 20, 1849.

Read, Thomas B.—He was a Senator in Congress, from Mississippi, from 1826 to 1827, and also during the session of 1829, and died suddenly on his way to Washington, at Lexington, Kentucky, November 26, 1829. He was in the meridian of life and a man of talents.

Reade, Edwin G.—Born in Orange County, North Carolina, November 13, 1812; he had a liberal education; studied law, and was admitted to the bar in 1836, in Person County, and engaged in a lucrative practice. He was elected a Representative in Congress, in 1855, serving until 1857.

Ready, Charles.—Born at Readyville, Rutherford County, Tennessee, December 22, 1802. He graduated at Greenville College, and received from the Nashville University the degree of Master of Arts. He was bred a lawyer, and has practised his profession with success. He was a member of the Tennessee Legislature in 1835, and closely identified with the organization of the Judiciary. By special commission he has twice presided in the Supreme Court of Tennessee, and was elected a Representative in Congress, from that State, in 1853, to which position he has been twice re-elected, and was a member of the Committee on the Judiciary.

Reagan, John H.—Born in Sevier County, Tennessee, October 8, 1818; a lawyer by profession; was appointed Deputy Surveyor in the Republic of Texas, in 1840; and in 1843 was a Justice of the Peace and militia Captain; in 1846, Probate Judge and Colonel of militia; and elected a member of the Legislature in 1847; was a Judge of the District Court from 1852 to 1857, when he was elected a member of the Thirty-fifth Congress, serving on the Committees on Indian Affairs, and Expenditures in the Post-office Department. Re-elected to the Thirty-sixth Congress. Resigned in February, 1861, and became Postmaster-General of the Rebel government.

Reding, John R.—He was born in New Hampshire, and was a Representative in Congress, from that State, from 1841 to 1845. From 1853 to 1858 he held the office of Naval Storekeeper, at Portsmouth.

Reed, Charles M.—He was born in Pennsylvania, and was a Representative in Congress, from that State, from 1843 to 1845.

Reed, Edward C.—He was a native of New York; graduated at Dartmouth College in 1812; and was a Representative in Congress, from New York, from 1831 to 1833.

Reed, Isaac.—Born in Waldoborough, Maine, in 1810; was a merchant by occupation; and a Representative in Congress, from Maine, from 1852 to 1853. He served six years in the State Legislature; was State Treasurer in 1856; and President of the Waldoborough Bank.

Reed, John.—Born in Plymouth County, Massachusetts; graduated at Yale College in 1772; was ordained as a minister of the Gospel in 1780, and settled at West Bridgewater, Massachusetts. He was a Representative in Congress, from that State, from 1795 to 1801. He died February 17, 1831, aged eighty years.

Reed, John.—He was a native of Bridgewater, Massachusetts, having been born in 1781; was a graduate of Brown University, in 1803; a lawyer by profession; and a Representative in Congress, from Massachusetts, from 1813 to 1817, and again from 1821 to 1841. He was the son of the foregoing, and was Lieutenant-Governor of Massachusetts, from 1845 to 1851. Died at Bridgewater, November 25, 1860.

Reed, Philip.—He was born in Kent County, Maryland, and was a Senator in Congress, from Maryland, from 1806 to 1813, and a Representative in Congress, from 1817 to 1819, and again from 1821 to 1823. He died November 2, 1829.

Reed, Robert R.—He was born in Pennsylvania, and was a Representative in Congress, from that State, from 1849 to 1851.

Reed, William.—He was a native of Massachusetts, an eminent merchant, and highly esteemed for his benevolent and religious character. He was a member of Congress, from Massachusetts, from 1811 to 1815; was President of the Sabbath-school Union of Massachusetts, and of the American Tract Society; Vice-President of the American Education Society; a member of the Board of Visitors of the Theological Seminary at Andover, and of the Board of Trustees of Dartmouth College. Besides liberal bequests to heirs and relatives, he left $68,000 to benevolent objects, of which $17,000 were to Dartmouth College, $10,000 to Amherst College, $10,000 to the Board of Commissioners for Foreign Missions, $9000 to the First Church and Society in Marblehead, $7000 to the Second Congregational Church of Marblehead, and $5000 to the Library of the Theological Seminary at Andover. He died at Marblehead, February 18, 1837, very suddenly, while attending a Sabbath-school meeting.

Reese, David A.—He was born in South Carolina, and was a Representative in Congress, from Georgia, from 1853 to 1855.

Reid, David S.—Born in Rockingham County, North Carolina, April 19, 1813. He studied law, and was admitted to practice in 1843; he was elected to the State Legislature in 1835, and served continuously until 1842. In 1843 he was elected a Representative in Congress, from North Carolina, serving that term; and was re-elected in 1845 for a second term; he was, in 1850, elected Governor of North Carolina, and re-elected in 1852, serving until 1855, when he was elected a Senator in Congress. He was Chairman of the Committee on Patents and the Patent-office, and a member of the Committee on Commerce. He was also elected a Delegate to the Peace Congress of 1861.

Reid, John W.—Was born in Lynchburg, Virginia, June 14, 1821; received a good English education; removed to Missouri in 1840; studied law and came to the bar in 1844; served with credit in the Mexican war in 1846, as Captain of a company of mounted volunteers, with Colonel Doniphan; settled in Jackson County, practising his profession; served two sessions in the Missouri Legislature; and was elected a Representative, from Missouri, to the Thirty-seventh Congress. Expelled from the House in December, 1861.

Reid, Robert R.—He was born in Beaufort District, South Carolina, in 1789; removed early in life to Georgia; was a Representative in Congress, from that State, from 1818 to 1823; was elected Mayor of Augusta, on his retirement from Congress; was also a Judge of the Superior Court of Georgia; was appointed, in 1832, by President Jackson, District Judge for Eastern Florida; and was appointed, by President Van Buren, Governor of the Territory of Florida; and was a member of the Convention which formed a State Constitution for Florida, over which body he presided in a creditable manner. He died near Tallahassee, July 1, 1841.

Reilly, Wilson.—Born in Pennsylvania; followed for a time the business of a hatter; and was elected a Representative in Congress, in 1857, from Pennsylvania, serving as a member of the Committee on Patents. Of late years, he has been devoted to the practice of law.

Reily, Luther.—He was born in Pennsylvania, and was a Representative in Congress, from that State, from 1837 to 1839.

Relfe, James H.—He was born in Virginia, and, having settled in Missouri, was elected a Representative in Congress, from that State, from 1843 to 1847.

Rencher, Abraham.—Born in Wake County, North Carolina, and in 1822 graduated at the University of that State. He practised law for a time, but taking an interest in politics, was elected to Congress, where he served from 1829 to 1839, and again from 1841 to 1842; Chargé d'Affaires to Portugal in 1843; and he was appointed, by President Buchanan, Governor of the Territory of New Mexico.

Reynolds, Gideon.—He was born in New York, and was a Representative in Congress, from that State, from 1847 to 1851.

Reynolds, James B.—He was a Representative in Congress, from Tennessee, from 1815 to 1817, and again from 1823 to 1825.

Reynolds, John.—He was born in Montgomery County, Pennsylvania, February 28, 1788; and was a Representative in Congress, from Illinois, from 1835 to 1837, and again from 1839 to 1843. Before entering Congress he was Governor of Illinois, from 1830 to 1834.

Reynolds, John H.—Born in Moreau, Saratoga County, New York, June 21, 1819; received his education at the academies of Evansville, Sandy Hill, and Kinderhook, New York, and was also at Bennington, Vermont; studied law, and was admitted to the bar in 1843; in 1853 was appointed Postmaster at Albany by President Pierce, but removed in 1854 for insubordination as a party man; and in 1858 was elected a Representative, from New York, to the Thirty-sixth Congress, serving as a member of the Committee on the Judiciary.

Reynolds, Joseph.—He was born in New York, and was a Representative in Congress, from that State, from 1835 to 1837. He also served in the Assembly of that State, in 1819.

Rhea, John.—He was a Representative in Congress, from Tennessee, from 1803 to 1815, and from 1817 to 1823. In 1816 he was appointed United States Commissioner to treat with the Choctaws.

Rhett, Robert B.—He was born in Beaufort, South Carolina, December 24, 1800; received a liberal education, and adopted the profession of law; in 1826 he was elected to the State Legislature, and in 1832 he was elected Attorney-General of South Carolina; and was a Representative in Congress, from 1838 to 1847, and for a second term, ending in 1849; and was a Senator in Congress during the years 1850 and 1851, having resigned, contrary to the wishes of his State. He is said to have been the first man who proposed, and advocated on the floor of Congress, a dissolution of the Union. Of late years he has lived wholly retired from public life, on an extensive plantation. He took part in the Rebellion of 1861, as a member of the "Confederate" Congress.

Ricaud, James B.—Born in Baltimore, Maryland, February 11, 1808; graduated at Washington College, Maryland, and is a lawyer by profession; was a member of the House of Delegates of Maryland, in 1834, and of the State Senate of Maryland, from 1836 to 1844, inclusive; was an Elector of President and Vice-President in 1836 and 1844; and a Representative in the Thirty-fourth and Thirty-fifth Congresses, serving on the Committee on Manufactures, and also that for Investigating the Accounts of the late Clerk of the House. In 1864 he resigned his seat in the Maryland Senate, and was appointed Judge of the Circuit Court.

Rice, Alexander H.—Born in Newton, Massachusetts, in August, 1818; received a common school education; served in his father's paper mill as a clerk while yet a mere boy; subsequently graduated at Union College in 1844, after which he entered on his own account into the paper business; in 1853 was elected to the Common Council of

Boston, and became the President of that body; was Mayor of Boston in 1856 and 1857; and was elected a Representative, from Massachusetts, to the Thirty-sixth Congress, serving on the Committee on the District of Columbia; re-elected to the Thirty-seventh Congress, serving on the Committees on Naval Affairs, and on Expenditures in the Treasury Department; re-elected to the Thirty-eighth Congress, serving as Chairman of the Committee on Naval Affairs.

Rice, Henry M.—He was born in Vermont, November 29, 1816; emigrated to Michigan when it was a Territory, and since that time has lived in three other Territories, viz., Iowa, Wisconsin, and Minnesota, much of his life having been spent among the wild Indian tribes of the Northwest; in 1840 he was appointed a sutler in the army; has been employed as Commissioner in making many Indian treaties of great importance; in 1853 he was elected a Delegate to Congress, from Minnesota; re-elected in 1855, having secured the passage of the act authorizing the people of Minnesota to form a State Constitution; and in 1857 he was elected a Senator in Congress, from Minnesota, for the term of six years. At the commencement of the second session of the Thirty-fifth Congress, he was appointed a member of the Committees on Indian Affairs, and on Post-offices and Post-roads.

Rice, John H.—Born in Mount Vernon, Kennebec County, Maine, February 5, 1816; received a good common school education; between the years 1832 and 1838 he held a variety of local offices at Augusta; devoted some attention to the study of law; served as a staff officer during the troubles connected with the Northeastern boundary; in 1840 was appointed Deputy Sheriff of Kennebec County; in 1842 settled in Piscataquis County, and devoted himself to the lumbering business until 1848; subsequently practised law; in 1852 was elected a State Attorney for three years; and, having been re-elected, held the office until he was chosen a Representative, from Maine, to the Thirty-seventh Congress, serving on the Committees on Revolutionary Claims, and on Patents. Re-elected to the Thirty-eighth Congress, serving as Chairman of the Committee on Public Buildings and Grounds, and a member of the Committee on the Territories.

Rice, Thomas.—He graduated at Harvard University in 1791; adopted the profession of law; was in the State Legislature in 1813; was a Representative in Congress, from Massachusetts, from 1815 to 1819; and died in 1854.

Rich, Charles.—He was born in Hampshire County, Massachusetts, in 1771, and was a Representative in Congress, from Vermont, from 1813 to 1815, and again from 1817 to 1824. He died at Sherburne, Vermont, October 15, 1824.

Richard, Gabriel.—He was a Roman Catholic priest, and a man of learning. He was born at Saintes, in France, October 15, 1764; was educated at Angiers; received orders at a Catholic seminary in Paris, in 1790; came to America after the commencement of the French Revolution; labored in Illinois as a missionary; was for a time Professor of Mathematics in St. Mary's College, Maryland; went to Detroit, Michigan, in 1798, whence he was sent as a Delegate to Congress, in 1823. He died in Detroit, September 13, 1832, aged sixty-eight years. During his ministry, it became his duty, according to the Roman Catholic religion, to excommunicate one of his parishioners, who had been divorced from his wife. The parishioner prosecuted the priest for defamation of character, which resulted in his obtaining a verdict of $1000. This money the priest could not pay, and was consequently imprisoned in the common jail; as he had already been elected a Delegate to Congress, he went from his prison, in the wilds of Michigan, to his seat on the floor of Congress. In 1809 he visited Boston, and took a printing-press to Michigan, and started a journal called the "Michigan Essay," which failed for the want of readers; he then published some Catholic books, and the laws of the Territory, all in French; in 1812, after Hull's surrender, was taken prisoner, and after his release, finding his people destitute, purchased wheat and gave it to the destitute. He wrote several languages, and was a man of superior ability and rare benevolence.

Richards, Jacob.—He was a Representative in Congress, from Pennsylvania, from 1803 to 1809.

Richards, John.—He was a Representative in Congress, from Pennsylvania, from 1795 to 1797.

Richards, John.—He was a member of the New York Assembly in 1814 and 1815, and a Representative in Congress, from that State, from 1823 to 1825.

Richards, Mark.—He was born in New Haven, Connecticut, and was a Representative in Congress, from Vermont, from 1817 to 1821. He was also a member of the State Legislature for eight years; County Sheriff for five years; a State Councillor in 1813 and 1815; and Lieutenant-Governor of Vermont in 1830.

Richards, Matthias.—He was a Representative in Congress, from Pennsylvania, from 1807 to 1811.

Richardson, John P.—He graduated at the South Carolina College in 1819; was a Judge; a member of the House of Representatives, in Congress, from South Carolina, from 1837 to 1840; Governor of that State from 1840 to 1842; and died in South Carolina in 1850.

Richardson, John S.—Born in South Carolina in 1777, and died at Charleston, May 11, 1850. He was an Associate Judge of the General Sessions and the Common Pleas, and Presiding Judge of the Court of Appeals; and was elected a member of Congress in 1820, but owing to some exigency in his private affairs, he was not qualified. He was also a member of the State Legislature, and Attorney-General for the State.

Richardson, Joseph.—Born at Billerica, Massachusetts, February 1, 1778; graduated at Dartmouth College in 1802; and was a Representative in Congress, from Massachusetts, from 1827 to 1831. He was senior Pastor over the First Church at Hingham, Massachusetts, for fifty years.

Richardson, William A.—Born in Fayette County, Kentucky; graduated at the Transylvania University; studied law, and came to the bar before attaining his twentieth year, and soon after settled in Illinois. In 1835 he was elected State Attorney; in 1836 a member of the State Legislature; in 1838 he was elected to the State Senate; and in 1844 was again elected to the Legislature, and made Speaker of the House. In 1846 he served as Captain in the Mexican war, and on the battle-field of Buena Vista was promoted by the unanimous vote of his regiment; in 1847 he was elected a Representative in Congress, from Illinois, where he continued to serve by re-election until 1856, when he resigned; in 1857 he was appointed, by President Buchanan, Governor of Nebraska, which he resigned in 1858; in 1860 he was, against his consent, re-elected to the House of Representatives, but before the expiration of his term in 1863, was elected a Senator in Congress, from Illinois, for the unexpired term of his friend, S. A. Douglas, serving on the Committees on Territories, and the District of Columbia.

Richardson, William M.—He was born at Pelham, New Hampshire, January 4, 1774, and graduated at the University of Cambridge in 1797. He practised law for a few years at Groton, Massachusetts, and was a member of Congress from 1811 to 1814. He removed to Portsmouth, New Hampshire, in 1814, and was appointed Chief Justice in 1816; and he discharged the duties of the office with high reputation nearly twenty-two years. He was a man of distinguished talents, great industry, and extensive acquirements, and highly respected for his integrity and estimable character. He was the author of "The New Hampshire Justice," and "The Town Officer." A considerable portion of the first and second volumes of the New Hampshire Reports were drawn up by the Chief Justice; nearly all the cases of the third, fourth, and fifth were furnished by him; and of the matter for, perhaps, four volumes more, he prepared a large share. He died at Chester, New Hampshire, March 23, 1838.

Richmond, Jonathan.—He was born in Bristol, Massachusetts, in 1774; was one of the pioneers to Western New York in 1813; was once Collector of the Customs for the United States; and a Representative in Congress, from New York, from 1819 to 1821. He died in Cayuga, New York, July 29, 1853.

Riddle, Albert G.—He was born in Massachusetts, and elected a Representative, from Ohio, to the Thirty-seventh Congress, serving on the Committee on Revolutionary Claims.

Riddle, George R.—He was born in New Castle, Delaware, in 1817; educated at Delaware College; studied surveying, and was engaged for years in locating canals and roads in Pennsylvania, Maryland, and Virginia; he studied law, and was admitted to the bar in 1848; he was soon afterwards appointed Deputy Attorney-General for his native county, which he held until 1850; and he was elected a Representative in Congress, from Delaware, from 1851 to 1855. He was also a Delegate to the several National Conventions of 1844, 1848, and 1856. In 1864 he was elected a Senator in Congress, in the place of J. A. Bayard, resigned, for the term ending in 1869.

Ridgeley, Henry M.—Born in 1778; a lawyer by profession, and for many years was a distinguished member of the Delaware bar. He was a Representative in Congress, from Delaware, from 1811 to 1815; and supplied a vacancy as Senator in Congress, from 1826 to 1829. He died at his residence in Dover, Delaware, August 7, 1847.

Ridgway, Joseph.—He was born on Staten Island, New York, May 6, 1783; received a limited education, and acquired the trade of a house carpenter. In 1811 he emigrated to Cayuga County, New York, and devoted himself to making fanning mills; and in 1822 settled in Columbus, Ohio, and established an extensive iron foundry, which subsequently became an establishment for manufacturing railroad carriages. In 1828 he was elected to the Legislature of Ohio, and re-elected in 1830; and was a Representative in Congress, from Ohio, from 1837 to 1843. He failed in business in 1811, and though exonerated by the bankrupt law, he thought proper, in 1857, to pay up his old debts, at the rate of two dollars for one; and of seventy creditors, he only found four living, so that he had to hunt up and pay the heirs, which occupied four months of his time.

Riggs, Jetur R.—Born in Morris County, New Jersey, June 20, 1809; studied medicine, and graduated at the Barclay Street Medical University of New York. In 1828 he made an extensive sea-voyage over the world; practised his profession from 1832 to 1849; served two years in the New Jersey Legislature; spent one or two years in charge of the hospital at Sutter's Fort, California; in 1855 was elected for three years to the Senate of New Jersey; and in 1858 was elected a Representative in Congress, from that State, serving as a member of the Committee on Manufactures.

Riggs, Lewis.—Was born in New York, and was a Representative in Congress, from that State, from 1841 to 1843.

Riker, Samuel.—He was a member of the New York Assembly in 1784, and a Representative in Congress, from that State, from 1804 to 1805, and again from 1807 to 1809.

Ringgold, Samuel.—He was a Representative in Congress, from Maryland, from 1810 to 1815, and again from 1817 to 1821.

Ripley, Eleazar W.—He graduated at Dartmouth College in 1800; studied law, and settled in the District of Maine; was Speaker of the Massachusetts House of Representatives in 1811; acquitted himself with credit as an officer in the last war with England; removed to Louisiana, whence he was elected to Congress, serving from 1835 to the time of his death, which occurred at New Orleans, March 2, 1839, aged fifty-seven years.

Ripley, James W.—He was a lawyer; served four years in the Legislature of Maine; was an officer in the late war with England, and a member of Congress, from Maine, from 1826 to 1830, when he was appointed Collector of Customs for the Passamaquoddy District of Maine. He died in June, 1835.

Risley, Elijah.—He was born in Connecticut, and was a Representative in Congress, from New York, from 1849 to 1851.

Ritchey, Thomas.—He was born in Pennsylvania, and having settled in Ohio, was elected a Representative in Congress, from that State, from 1847 to 1849, and again from 1853 to 1855.

Ritchie, David.—He was born at Canonsburg, Washington County, Pennsylvania, August 19, 1812; graduated at Jefferson College in 1829; admitted to the bar, at Pittsburg, in 1835; received the degree of S.W.D. from the University of Heidelberg, Germany, in 1837; and has been a Representative, from Pittsburg, in the Thirty-third, Thirty-fourth, and Thirty-fifth Congresses, and was a member of the Committee on Foreign Affairs.

Ritter, John.—He was a Representative in Congress, from Pennsylvania, from 1843 to 1847, and died in Reading, Pennsylvania, November 24, 1851.

Rivers, Thomas.—He was born in Tennessee, and was a Representative in Congress, from 1855 to 1857.

Rives, Francis E.—He was born in Virginia, and was a Representative in Congress, from that State, from 1837 to 1841.

Rives, William C.—He was born in Nelson County, Virginia, May 4, 1793; was educated at Hampden Sidney and William and Mary Colleges; studied law and politics under the direction of Thomas Jefferson; was aide-de-camp in 1814 and 1815 with a body of militia and volunteers, called out for the defence of Virginia; and was a member, in 1816, of the Staunton Convention, called to reform the State Constitution. He was elected to the Legislature of Virginia in 1817, 1818, and 1819, from Nelson County; in 1822 to the same position from Albemarle County; in 1823 he was elected a Representative in Congress, and he served for three successive terms; in 1829 he was appointed by President Jackson Minister to France; on his return in 1832 he was elected a Senator in Congress, and resigned in 1834; was re-elected in 1835, and served to the end of the term, in 1839; in 1840 was elected to the Senate for a third term, where he remained until 1845. In 1849 he was a second time appointed Minister to France, and returned in 1853, when he finally retired from political life. He has also added to his reputation by publishing a History of the Life and Times of James Madison. He took part in the Rebellion of 1861 as a member of the so-called Confederate Congress, having previously been a Delegate to the Peace Congress of that year.

Roane, John.—He was born in Virginia, and was a Representative in Congress, from that State, from 1815 to 1817, from 1827 to 1831, and for a third term, from 1835 to 1837.

Roane, John J.—He was a Representative in Congress, from Virginia, his native State, from 1831 to 1833.

Roane, John T.—He was a Representative in Congress, from Virginia, from 1809 to 1815.

Roane, William H. — Born in Virginia in 1788; was twice elected a member of the Executive Council of that State; once a Delegate to the General Assembly; a Representative in Congress, from 1815 to 1817; and a Senator of the United States, from 1837 to 1841. He died at Tree Hill, near Richmond, Virginia, May 11, 1845.

Robbins, Asher.—Born in Wethersfield, Connecticut, in 1757, and graduated at Yale College. He was a lawyer by profession, was United States District Attorney in 1812; held many other important public positions, and was a leading Senator in Congress, from Rhode Island, from 1825 to 1839. He was also a member of the Rhode Island Legislature for many years. Died at Newport, Rhode Island, February 25, 1845.

Robbins, George R.—Born near Allentown, Monmouth County, New Jersey, September 24, 1812; graduated at the Jefferson Medical College, Philadelphia, in 1837, and pursued the practice of medicine until his election to the House of Representatives, during the Thirty-fourth Congress, and was re-elected to the Thirty-fifth, and was a member of the Committee on Invalid Pensions.

Robbins, John, Jr.—He was born in Pennsylvania, and was a Representative in Congress, from that State, from 1849 to 1855.

Roberts, Anthony E.—Born in Chester County, Pennsylvania, October, 1803, but removed with his parents to Lancaster County in his infancy. He received a common school education, and commenced life as a merchant. In 1839 he was elected Sheriff of Lancaster County, and held the office till 1842. In 1849 he was appointed by President Taylor Marshal of the Eastern District of Pennsylvania, and remained in that position until 1853, and collected the statistics for the Seventh Census of that District. He was a Representative in the Thirty-fourth Congress, and re-elected to the Thirty-fifth, and was a member of the Committee on the Militia.

Roberts, Jonathan.—Born in 1771, and early in the present century was elected to both branches of the Legislature of Pennsylvania; was a Representative in Congress, from 1811 to 1814, and an advocate of the war of 1812. From 1814 to 1821 he was a Senator of the United States; and in 1841 he was appointed Collector of the Port of Philadelphia by President Harrison. He died in Philadelphia, July, 1854.

Roberts, Robert W.—He was born in Delaware, and having settled in Mississippi, was elected a Representative in Congress, from that State, from 1843 to 1847.

Robertson, George.—Born in Mercer County, Kentucky, November 18, 1790, and completed his education in Transylvania University. He studied law, and commenced practice in 1809. In 1816 he was elected a Representative in Congress, and served from 1817 to 1821. He was a member of the Legislature, and Speaker of the House four sessions, ending in 1827. In 1828 he was Secretary of State, and the same year chosen Judge of the Court of Appeals, and in 1829 commissioned Chief Justice of Kentucky, which position he resigned in 1843, and resumed the practice of law in Lexington in 1835. He was Professor of Law in Transylvania University for twenty-three years, and is still engaged in teaching law. He has repeatedly declined important offices, including missions to Colombia and Peru.

Robertson, John.—He was born in Virginia, and was a Representative in Congress, from that State, from 1834 to 1839.

Robertson, Thomas B.—He was a Representative in Congress, from Louisiana, from 1812 to 1818, having been the first member elected under the State Constitution.

Robie, Reuben.—He was born in Vermont, and, having settled in New York, was elected a Representative in Congress, from that State, from 1851 to 1853.

Robinson, Christopher.—He was elected a Representative, from Rhode Island, to the Thirty-sixth Congress, serving as a member of the Committee on the Judiciary.

Robinson, Edward.—He was a shipmaster and merchant; served two years in the Maine Senate; and was a Representative in Congress, from Maine, during the years 1838 and 1839. In 1840 he was a Presidential Elector; and died February 20, 1857, aged sixty-one years.

Robinson, James C.—Was born in Edgar County, Illinois, in 1822; served as a private in the Mexican war; studied law and came to the bar in 1854; was elected a Representative, from Illinois, to the Thirty-sixth Congress, and re-elected to the Thirty-seventh and Thirty-eighth Congresses, serving as Chairman of the Committee on Mileage, and as a member of the Committee on Expenditures in the State Department.

Robinson, John L.—He was born in Kentucky, and was a Representative in Congress, from Indiana, from 1847 to 1853.

Robinson, John M.—He was born in 1793, and was one of the early settlers of Illinois; and one of the Judges of the Supreme Court of that State. He was a Senator in Congress, from 1830 to 1842, and died at Ottawa, Illinois, April 26, 1843.

Robinson, Jonathan.—He was appointed Chief Justice of Vermont in

1801, in the place of Judge Smith, who resigned, and in 1806 was elected to succeed Mr. Smith as Senator in Congress, serving from 1807 to 1815. He died at Bennington, November 3, 1819, aged sixty-four.

Robinson, Moses.—He was Governor of Vermont, having succeeded Mr. Chittenden, in 1789. He was a member of the Senate of the United States under the administration of Washington, from 1791 to 1796, when he resigned. He was one of the minority who were opposed to the ratification of Jay's Treaty. He died at Bennington, May 26, 1813, aged seventy-two.

Robinson, Orville.—He was born in New York, and was a Representative in Congress, from that State, from 1843 to 1845. He also served four years in the Assembly of New York, from Oswego County.

Robinson, Thomas.—He was a Representative in Congress, from Delaware, from 1839 to 1841, and died in Sussex County, of that State, October 28, 1843.

Robison, David F.—He was born in Pennsylvania, and was a Representative in Congress, from that State, from 1855 to 1857.

Rochester, William B.—He was born in Washington County, Maryland, and was a man of legal acquirements, much respected for his abilities, and a Representative in Congress, from New York, from 1821 to 1823. He subsequently held the office of Circuit Judge in New York. He was lost, with many others, off the coast of North Carolina, by the explosion of the steamer Pulaski, June 15, 1838.

Rockhill, William.—He was born in New Jersey, and, having settled in Indiana, was elected a Representative in Congress, from that State, from 1847 to 1849.

Rockwell, John A.—Born in Norwich, Connecticut, in 1804; graduated at Yale College in 1822; studied law, which he practised with ability and success; was twice elected to the State Senate; was at one time Judge of the County Court for New London County; and was a Representative in Congress, from Connecticut, from 1845 to 1849, serving as Chairman of the Committee on Claims. He subsequently practised in the Court of Claims, and was the author of a work on Spanish law. Died in Washington of apoplexy, February 10, 1861.

Rockwell, Julius.—Born at Colebrook, Litchfield County, Connecticut, April 26, 1805. Entered Yale College in 1822, and graduated in 1826; studied law at the New Haven Law School, and was admitted to the bar in Litchfield County, in 1829, commencing practice in 1830, at Pittsfield, Massachusetts. He was a member of the House of Representatives of Massachusetts, from 1834 to 1838, and was Speaker, from 1835 to 1838, and in that year was appointed Bank Commissioner, and held the office three years. He was a Representative in Congress, from 1847 to 1851, and United States Senator for two sessions, to succeed Mr. Everett. In 1853 he was a member of the Convention to revise the Constitution of Massachusetts; and in 1858 was again elected to the House of Representatives of that State.

Rodgers, James.—He was born in South Carolina; graduated at the University of that State in 1813; adopted the profession of law; and was a Representative in Congress, from that State, from 1835 to 1837, and again from 1839 to 1843.

Rodman, William.—Born in Bensalem, Bucks County, Pennsylvania, October 7, 1757, his parents being of the Society of Friends. He received a liberal education; served in the Revolutionary war as a soldier; under the call from Washington, he raised and commanded a company, during the "Whiskey Insurrection" in Western Pennsylvania; he was, for many years, in the Legislature of his native State; and he was a Representative in Congress, from 1811 to 1813. He died at the place of his birth, July 27, 1824.

Rodney, Cæsar A.—He was a Representative in Congress, from Delaware, from 1803 to 1805. He was appointed Attorney-General of the United States, by President Jefferson; and in 1812 commanded a company of volunteers in defence of Baltimore; again a Representative in Congress, from Delaware, from 1819 to 1821; and a Senator of the United States, from 1821 to 1823, in which year he was appointed United States Minister to Buenos Ayres, where he died June 10, 1824.

Rodney, Daniel.—He was a Representative in Congress, from the State of Delaware, from 1822 to 1823, and a Senator in Congress, from 1826 to 1827.

Rodney, George B.—He was born in Delaware; graduated at Princeton College in 1820, and was a Representative in Congress, from his native State, from 1841 to 1845. He was a Delegate in 1861 to the Peace Congress of Washington.

Rogers, Andrew J.—He was born in Hamburg, Sussex County, New Jersey, July 1, 1828; received a limited education; spent the most of his youth as an assistant in a hotel and in a country store; taught school for two years and a half, during which time he studied law, and was admitted to the bar in 1852; and in 1862 he was elected a Representative, from New Jersey, to the Thirty-eighth Congress, serving on the Committee on Public Expenditures.

Rogers, Charles.—He was born in New York, and was a Representative in Congress, from that State, from 1843 to 1845. He also served in the Assembly of New York, from Washington County, in 1833 and 1837.

Rogers, Edward.—He was born in Connecticut; received a classical education, studied law, and settled in Madison County, New York. He was, for many years, County Judge; and was a Representative in Congress, from New York, from 1843 to 1845. He died in Galway, Saratoga County, New York, May 23, 1857, aged seventy years.

Rogers, Sion H.—He was born in North Carolina, and was a Representative in Congress, from that State, from 1853 to 1855.

Rogers, Thomas J.—He was born in Waterford, Ireland, and came to this country when three years of age; was a Representative in Congress, from Pennsylvania, from 1818 to 1824, and died in New York City, December 7, 1832, aged fifty-one years.

Rollins, Edward H.—He was born in Somersworth, now Rollingford, Strafford County, New Hampshire, October 3, 1824; received an academical education, and for a short time taught school; was devoted for several years to mercantile pursuits, first as a clerk and then as an apothecary; was a member of the State Legislature in 1855, 1856, and 1857, serving as Speaker during the last two years; was chosen Chairman of the State Republican Committee in 1856, which position he held until he entered Congress; elected a Representative, from New Hampshire, to the Thirty-seventh Congress, serving on the Committee on the District of Columbia; and re-elected to the Thirty-eighth Congress, serving as Chairman of the Committee on Accounts.

Rollins, James Sidney.—Was born in Madison County, Kentucky, April 19, 1812; graduated at the State University of Indiana, at Bloomington, in 1830; studied law, and graduated at the Transylvania Law School, in Kentucky, in 1833; and soon afterwards settled in Boone County, Missouri. In 1838 he was elected to the State Legislature, and re-elected in 1840 and 1842; in 1846 he was elected to the State Senate, and served four years; in 1854 he was again elected to the Legislature; in 1857 he was defeated as the Whig candidate for Governor by two hundred and thirty votes, 100,000 having been polled, though many thought him legally elected; in 1860 he was elected a Representative, from Missouri, to the Thirty-seventh Congress, serving on the Committees of Commerce and on Expenditures in the War Department. He was re-elected in 1862 to the Thirty-eighth Congress, serving on the Committee on Naval Affairs.

Roman, James D.—He was born in Maryland; was educated a lawyer; was a Presidential Elector on two occasions; and was a Representative in Congress, from that State, from 1847 to 1849. He is at the present time President of the Hagerstown Bank. He was also a Delegate to the Peace Congress of 1861.

Roosevelt, James I.—Born in the

city of New York, December, 1796; was educated at Columbia College; studied law with Peter Augustus Jay, and was for several years his partner. In 1835 and 1840 he was a member of the State Legislature, and in 1842 and 1843 was a Representative in Congress, from New York City. He declined a re-election, and went abroad in 1843. On his return he retired from the practice of law to private life; but was induced to accept the appointment of Judge of the Supreme Court of the State in 1851. He was also for several years in early life a member of the city government.

Root, Erastus.—Born in Hebron, Connecticut, March 16, 1772; graduated at Dartmouth College in 1793; after which he taught school for some time, and then studied law and settled in Delaware County, New York, in 1796. He was a Representative in the Assembly eleven years; Speaker of the House three years; State Senator eight years; and a Representative in Congress, from 1803 to 1805, from 1809 to 1811, 1812 to 1813, 1815 to 1817, in which year he was appointed Postmaster at Delhi, New York, and was re-elected to Congress, from 1831 to 1833. In 1822 he was chosen Lieutenant-Governor of the State, and he was also Major-General of militia. He died in New York City, December 24, 1846. His intellect and tastes were highly cultivated.

Root, Joseph M.—Born in Cayuga, New York, October 7, 1817; read law at Auburn, and removed to Ohio in 1829; was appointed Prosecuting Attorney in that State; in 1840 chosen to the State Senate; and served as a Representative in Congress, from 1845 to 1851. He was for a time Chairman of the Committees on the Post-office, and Expenditures in the Treasury Department.

Rose, Robert L.—Born in Geneva, New York, October 12, 1804; is a farmer by occupation; has held the office of Supervisor for the town of Allen's Hill; and was a Representative in Congress, from New York, from 1847 to 1851.

Rose, Robert R.—He was born in Henrico County, Virginia; and was a Representative in Congress, from the State of New York, from 1823 to 1827, and again from 1829 to 1831. He died at Waterloo, New York, November 24, 1835, aged sixty-three years.

Ross, Henry H.—He was born in Essex County, New York, and was a Representative in Congress, from New York, from 1825 to 1827.

Ross, James.—Born about the year 1761, in Pensylvania. He was a Senator in Congress, from 1794 to 1803, serving during one session as President *pro tem.* of that body, and died at his residence, near Pittsburg, November 27, 1847.

Ross, John.—He was a Representative in Congress, from Pennsylvania, from 1809 to 1811, and again from 1815 to 1818.

Ross, Lewis W.—He was born in Seneca County, New York, December 8, 1812; removed with his father to Illinois when a boy; was educated at the Illinois College; adopted the profession of law. In 1840 and 1844 he was elected to the State Legislature; was a Presidential Elector in 1848; and a Delegate in 1860 to the Charleston and Baltimore Conventions. In 1861 was elected to the State Constitutional Convention; and in 1862 was elected a Representative, from Illinois, to the Thirty-eighth Congress, serving on the Committee on Invalid Pensions.

Ross, Thomas.—He was a native of Pennsylvania; graduated at Princeton College in 1825; and was a Representative in Congress, from that State, from 1849 to 1853.

Ross, Thomas R.—He was born in Chester County, Pennsylvania, and was a Representative in Congress, from Ohio, from 1819 to 1825.

Rowan, John.—He was born in Pennsylvania, in 1773; emigrated to Kentucky when quite young; he was a member of the Convention which formed the Constitution of 1799; he was Secretary of State in 1804; elected a member of Congress, from 1807 to 1809; for many years a member of the General Assembly; Judge of the Court of Appeals in 1819; and was a Senator in Congress, from 1825 to 1831. His last public position was that of Commissioner for carrying out a late treaty with Mexico. He died in Louisville, Kentucky, July 13, 1843.

Rowe, Peter.—He was a Representative in Congress, from New York, from 1853 to 1855.

Royce, Homer E.—He was born in Berkshire, Vermont, in 1819; received a common school education; studied law, and was admitted to the bar in 1842; was a member of the State Legislature in 1846 and 1847; was Prosecuting Attorney for the State in 1848; a State Senator in 1849, 1850, and 1851; and was elected a Representative, from Vermont, to the Thirty-fifth Congress, serving as a member of the Committee on Foreign Affairs. He was also re-elected to the Thirty-sixth Congress, serving as a member of the same Committee.

Ruffin, Thomas.—Born in Edgecombe County, North Carolina; graduated at Chapel Hill University; is a lawyer by profession, and served as Circuit Attorney of the Seventh Judicial Circuit of the State of Missouri, from December, 1844, to December, 1848; and was elected a Representative, from North Carolina, to the Thirty-third, Thirty-fourth, Thirty-fifth, and Thirty-sixth Congresses, serving as a member of the Committees on Public Lands, on Accounts, and on the Militia. He took part in the Rebellion of 1861, as a member of the Rebel Congress, having previously been a Delegate to the Peace Congress of 1861. He also served as a Colonel in the Southern army, and from the effects of a wound, died at Alexandria, Virginia, in October, 1863.

Ruggles, Benjamin.—Born in Windham County, Connecticut. He obtained the means for receiving a classical education by teaching a school in winter. He studied law, and after his admission to the bar removed to Marietta, Ohio; he subsequently settled at St. Clairsville; and in 1810 was elected President Judge of the Court of Common Pleas for the Third Circuit. He was elected, by the Legislature, a Senator of the United States, from Ohio, serving from 1815 to 1833; and from his well-known habits of industry and constant devotion to the interests of his clients, he was called "The Wheel-horse of the Senate." From his youth he was a member of the Masonic fraternity. He died at St. Clairsville, September 2, 1857, aged seventy-four years.

Ruggles, Charles H.—He was born in Litchfield County, Connecticut, and was a member of the New York Assembly in 1820; a Representative in Congress, from that State, from 1821 to 1823, and also Judge of the Supreme Court of New York.

Ruggles, John.—Born in Westboro, Massachusetts; was well educated, but possessed a taste for the mechanic arts; and was a Senator in Congress, from Maine, from 1835 to 1841, and a member of the Committee on Commerce. He took a special interest in, and was the originator, when in Congress, of the idea of a reorganization of the Patent-office, and the very first patent granted after the reorganization, July 28, 1836, was granted to him for a locomotive steam-engine. He was nine times elected to the Maine Legislature, and officiated as Speaker three years; and from 1835 to 1841 was Judge of the Court of Common Pleas.

Ruggles, Nathaniel.—He was a native of Massachusetts; graduated at Harvard University in 1781; was a Representative in Congress, from Massachusetts, from 1813 to 1819, and died at Roxbury, Massachusetts, December 19, of the latter year, aged fifty-eight years.

Rumsey, David.—He was born in New York, and was a Representative in Congress, from that State, from 1847 to 1851.

Rumsey, Edward.—He was born in Kentucky, and was a Representative in Congress, from that State, from 1837 to 1839.

Runk, John.—He was born in New Jersey, and was a Representative in Congress, from that State, from 1845 to 1847.

Rusk, Thomas J.—He was born in South Carolina; studied law, and practised with success in Georgia. In the early part of 1835 he removed to Texas, and was a prominent actor in all the important events in the history of the Republic and the State of Texas. He was a member of the Convention that declared Texas an independent Republic, in March, 1836; was the first Secretary of War; participated in the battle of San Jacinto, and took command of the army after General Houston was wounded. He continued in command of the army until the organization of the Constitutional Government, in October, 1836, when he was again appointed Secretary of War, and resigned after a few months. He afterwards commanded several expeditions against the Indians; served as a member of the House of Representatives, and as Chief Justice of the Supreme Court, which last office he resigned early in 1842. In 1845 he was President of the Convention that consummated the annexation of Texas to the United States. Upon the admission of Texas into the Union in 1845, he was elected one of the Senators in the Congress of the United States, in which office he served two terms, and was elected for the third term. He was Chairman of the Committee on the Post-office. He took a deep interest in the wagon-road to the Pacific, and the overland mail. At the time of his death, which occurred in Nacogdoches, Texas, July 29, 1856, he was President, *pro tem.*, of the Senate. In a moment of insanity, caused by overwhelming grief at the death of his wife, he took his own life, aged fifty-four.

Russ, John.—He was a native of Ipswich, Massachusetts, and was a Representative in Congress, from Connecticut, from 1819 to 1823. He died at Hartford, Connecticut, June 22, 1832, aged sixty-eight years.

Russell, David.—He was born in Massachusetts, and was a Representative in Congress, from New York, from 1835 to 1841, serving as Chairman of the Committee on Claims. He was also in the Assembly of that State, in 1816 and 1830, from Washington County, and District Attorney for Northern New York. Died at Salem, Washington County, New York, November 24, 1861, aged sixty-one years.

Russell, James M.—He was born in Pennsylvania, and was a Representative in Congress, from that State, from 1842 to 1843.

Russell, Jeremiah.—He was born in New York, and was a Representative in Congress, from that State, from 1843 to 1845.

Russell, John.—He was a Representative in Congress, from New York, from 1805 to 1809.

Russell, Jonathan.—He was appointed Minister Plenipotentiary to Sweden in 1814, and was a Representative in Congress, from Massachusetts, from 1821 to 1823. Died February 16, 1832. His birthplace was Middlesex County, Massachusetts.

Russell, Joseph.—He was a Representative in Congress, from New York, from 1845 to 1847, and from 1851 to 1853.

Russell, Samuel.—He was born in Pennsylvania, and was a Representative in Congress, from that State, from 1853 to 1855.

Russell, William.—He was born in Ireland, and having emigrated to Ohio, was a Representative in Congress, from that State, from 1827 to 1833, and again from 1841 to 1843.

Russell, William F.—Born in Saugerties, Ulster County, New York; was a merchant for twenty years, and a member of the Legislature of New York, in 1850, serving one term; was elected a Representative, from New York, in the Thirty-fifth Congress, serving on the Committee on Indian Affairs.

Rust, Albert.—He was born in Virginia, and removing to Arkansas, was a Representative in Congress, from that State, from 1855 to 1857, and again from 1859 to 1861, serving on the Committee on Roads and Canals. He took part in the Rebellion of 1861, and was a Brigadier-General.

Rutherford, John.—He was a native of New York City; a nephew of William Alexander, Earl of Stirling; graduated at New Jersey College in 1776; was educated a lawyer; was one of the first Presidential Electors, and a Senator of the United States, from New Jersey, from 1791 to 1798; and was the last survivor of the Senators in Congress during the administration of Washington. He early retired from public life, and, being one of the largest landholders in New Jersey, was actively engaged in agricultural and internal improvements. He died at Ederston, New Jersey, February 23, 1840, in the eightieth year of his age.

Rutherford, Robert.—He was a Representative in Congress, from Virginia, from 1793 to 1797.

Rutledge, John.—He was born in Ireland in 1739; emigrated to South Carolina; studied law in England, and, returning to South Carolina in 1761, took an active part in the Revolutionary cause, and was a Delegate to the Continental Congress. In 1776 he was appointed President of South Carolina, and Commander-in-chief of that Colony, having also been a member of the Convention of 1774. He was Governor of the State in 1779; Chancellor of the State in 1784; a Representative in Congress, from 1797 to 1803; and, after having been Judge of the Court of Chancery, Chief Justice of South Carolina, and Judge of the Supreme Court of the United States, was finally promoted to the position of Chief Justice, in which capacity he died January 23, 1800.

Ryall, D. B.—He was born in Trenton, New Jersey; adopted the profession of law; and was a Representative in Congress, from that State, from 1839 to 1841.

Sabin, Alvah.—He was born in Georgia, Vermont, October 23, 1793; was educated for the ministry; and was a Representative in Congress, from that State, from 1853 to 1857. He served ten years in the State Legislature; and was Secretary of State for Vermont, in 1841.

Sabine, Lorenzo.—He was born in Lisbon, New Hampshire, February 28, 1803; was entirely self-educated; was bred a merchant; was for many years a bank officer; and was for some time Secretary of the Boston Board of Trade. He was three times elected to the Legislature of Maine, from Eastport, and was at one time Deputy Collector of the port of Passamaquoddy. He has held, in Massachusetts, the position of Confidential Agent of the Treasury Department; and was a Representative, from that State, to the Thirty-second Congress. He has devoted much of his time to literary pursuits, and is the author of a "Life of Commodore Preble," "The American Loyalists," "Report on the American Fisheries," and "Notes on Duels and Duelling," and has been a contributor to the North American Review. The degree of A.M. was conferred upon him by Bowdoin and Harvard Colleges.

Sackett, William A.—Born in New York, and was a Representative in Congress, from that State, from 1849 to 1853, and was a member of the Committee on Revolutionary Pensions.

Sage, Ebenezer.—He graduated at Yale College in 1778, and was a Representative in Congress, from New York, from 1809 to 1815, and again from 1819 to 1820. He died in 1834.

Sage, Russell.—Born in Oneida County, New York, August 4, 1816; received a common school education; commenced active life as a clerk in a store at Troy, and until 1853 was wholly devoted to mercantile pursuits. In 1841 he was elected an Alderman in the city of Troy, and, by annual elections, served seven years in that capacity; he was also Treasurer of Rensselaer County for seven years, in which office he was especially popular; and he was a Representative in Congress, from New York, from 1853 to 1857, serving on the Committees on Invalid Pensions, and on Ways and Means. He was the first man who advocated, on the floor of Congress, the purchase by the General Government, of Mount Vernon; and he was among the most active supporters of Mr. Banks for the office of Speaker of the House of Representatives. He is at the present time wholly devoted to his private affairs.

Sailly, Peter.—He was born in Loraine, France; first came to the United States in 1783, and settled in Clinton County, New York. Having been well educated, and possessing a decided talent for business, he acquired considerable influence, and held several offices of public trust in his adopted State. He was a Representative in Congress, from New York, from 1805 to 1807, and on his retirement from that position, he was appointed, by President Jefferson, Collector of Customs for the District of Champlain, holding the office until his death, which occurred at Plattsburg, in 1826.

Saltonstall, Leverett.—Born in Massachusetts, in 1781; graduated at Harvard College in 1802; commenced the practice of law in Salem in 1805, and was distinguished as a lawyer; he frequently served in the State Legislature, and was a Representative in Congress, from 1839 to 1843. He was also an active member of the American Academy of Arts and Sciences, and of the Massachusetts Historical Society, and the degree of Doctor of Laws was conferred upon him by Harvard College, to which he left a legacy, and he also made a bequest of valuable books to Phillips's Academy, at Exeter, where he commenced his education. He died at Salem, Massachusetts, May 8, 1845.

Sammons, Thomas.—He was a Representative in Congress, from New York, from 1803 to 1807, and again from 1809 to 1813.

Sample, Samuel C.—He was born in Maryland, and was a Representative in Congress, from Indiana, from 1843 to 1845.

Sampson, Zabdiel.—He was born in Plympton, Massachusetts; graduated at Brown University in 1803, and adopted the profession of law. He was a Representative in Congress, from his native State, from 1817 to 1819; and in 1820 he was appointed Collector of Customs at Plymouth, where he died, while in office, July 19, 1828.

Samuel, Green B.—Born in Virginia, and was elected a Representative in Congress, from 1839 to 1841.

Sandford, John.—He was a native of New York, and was a Representative in Congress, from that State, from 1841 to 1843, and a member of the New York Senate, in the extra session of 1851. He died in Amsterdam, Montgomery County, New York, October, 1857.

Sandford, Jonah.—He was a member of the New York Assembly in 1827 and 1830, from the County of St. Lawrence, and was a Representative in Congress, from 1830 to 1831.

Sandidge, John M.—Born in Franklin County, Georgia, January 7, 1817; was a planter by occupation, and served as a member of the Legislature of Louisiana from 1846 to 1855. In 1852 he was a member of the Convention that framed the present Constitution of that State; Speaker of the House in 1854 and 1855; and elected a Representative to the Thirty-fourth and Thirty-fifth Congresses, and was Chairman of the Committee on Private Land Claims. Died in Louisiana in the autumn of 1861.

Sands, Joshua.—He was born in Queen's County, New York, and was a member of the New York Senate, from King's County, from 1792 to 1799, and a Representative in Congress, from 1803 to 1804, and again from 1825 to 1827.

Sanford, James T.—He was born in Virginia, but removed to Tennessee at an early day. He was a Representative in Congress, from Tennessee, from 1823 to 1825. He was liberally educated, and having acquired a large property in the pursuits of agriculture, he appropriated a part of his wealth to the establishment of "Jackson College," where many prominent men have been educated. He died many years ago.

Sanford, Nathan.—He was a native of New York, and held successively the public positions of Speaker of the New York Assembly, District Attorney of the United States for his State, United States Senator from 1815 to 1821, Chancellor of the State, and was again a Senator in Congress, from 1825 to 1831. He died on Long Island, in October, 1838.

Sanford, Thomas.—He was a Representative in Congress, from Kentucky, from 1803 to 1807.

Sapp, William R.—He was born in Ohio, and was a Representative in Congress, from that State, from 1853 to 1857.

Sargent, Aaron A.—Was born in Newburyport, Massachusetts, September 28, 1827; early acquired a knowledge of the printing business; emigrated to California in 1849; studied law, and came to the bar in 1854; and in 1861 was elected a Representative, from California, to the Thirty-seventh Congress, serving as a member of the Select Committee on the Pacific Railroad, to which enterprise he was particularly devoted.

Saulsbury, Willard.—Was born in Kent County, Delaware, June 2, 1820; was educated at Delaware College and also at Dickinson College; studied law, and was admitted to the bar in 1845; in 1850 he was appointed Attorney-General of Delaware, and held the office five years; and in 1859 he was elected a Senator in Congress, for the term ending in 1865, serving on the Committees on Commerce, Pensions, and Patents, and the Patent-office. He was also a Delegate to the Chicago Convention of 1864.

Saunders, Romulus M.—Born in Caswell County, North Carolina, March, 1791. He received an academical education, and spent two years in the University of that State. He studied law in Tennessee, and was admitted to practice there in 1812. He returned to North Carolina; was in the House of Commons from 1815 to 1820, and for two years Speaker of the House. He was a Representative in Congress, from 1821 to 1827, and from 1841 to 1845. In 1828 he was Attorney-General of the State; in 1833 was President of the Board of Commissioners to settle the claims of American citizens under the treaty of July 4, 1831, with France; in 1835 he was elected a Judge of the Supreme Court; in 1846 he was appointed by President Polk Minister to Spain, where he remained four years; on his return he was again elected to the Legislature of North Carolina, and since then has been devoting much attention to the railroad improvements of the State.

Savage, John.—He was a member of the New York Assembly in 1814; and from 1815 to 1819 a Representative in Congress, from that State. He subsequently held the positions of District Attorney, Comptroller of the State, Chief Justice of the Supreme Court, and Treasurer of the United States for New York.

Savage, John H.—He is a native of Warren County, Tennessee. During his minority he volunteered as a private soldier under General Gaines to defend the Texan frontier; also served during a campaign in Florida. He afterwards studied law, and commenced practice, in 1837, at Smithville, Tennessee. He was elected Colonel of the Tennessee militia; was elected by the Legislature Attorney-General of the Fourth District of his State in 1841, and held the office until 1847. During that year he received from President Polk the appointment of Major in the Fourteenth Regiment United States Infantry, and joining the American army in Mexico, was present at the battles of Contreras, Churubusco, and Molina del Rey, and was wounded at Chapultepec. He was promoted to the position of Lieutenant-Colonel, and as such, had command of his regiment, after the death of Colonel Graham, until the close of the war. On returning to Tennessee, he resumed the practice of his profession, and was first elected a Representative in Congress in 1849; he was re-elected in 1851; declined being a candidate in 1853; and was re-elected in 1855 and 1857. He was a member of the Committee on Military Affairs.

Sawtelle, Cullen.—He was born in Norridgewock, Maine; graduated at Bowdoin College in 1825; studied law, and admitted to the bar in 1829; served eight years as Judge of Probate; was a State Senator during the years 1843 and 1844; and was a Representative in Congress, from Maine, from 1845 to 1847, and again from 1849 to 1851.

Sawyer, Lemuel.—Was born in Camden County, North Carolina, in 1777; educated at Flatbush, New York; studied law; was in the State Legislature in 1801, and voted in the Electoral College for Thomas Jefferson in 1804. He was elected a Representative to Congress in 1807, serving until 1813; and subsequently served in the same capacity from 1817 to 1823, and from 1825 to 1829. About the year 1850 he removed to Washington, and held a clerkship in one of the departments.

Sawyer, S. T.—He was born in North Carolina, and was a Representative in Congress, from that State, from 1837 to 1839.

Sawyer, William.—Born in Ohio, and was a Representative in Congress, from that State, from 1845 to 1849.

Say, Benjamin.—He was a Representative in Congress, from Pennsylvania, from 1808 to 1809.

Scales, Alfred M., Jr.—He was born in Rockingham County, North Carolina, November 26, 1827; was educated chiefly at the Chapel Hill University; adopted the profession of law, and was admitted to the bar in 1851; was elected to the Legislature of North Carolina in 1852 and 1856; and in 1857 he was elected a Representative, from his native State, to the Thirty-fifth Congress, and was a member of the Committee on the District of Columbia.

Scammon, John F.—Born in Saco, Maine; was bred a merchant; served in the Massachusetts Legislature as Representative during 1817, and in the Maine Legislature in 1820 and 1821; was Collector of Customs at Saco from 1829 to 1841; was a Representative in Congress, from Maine, from 1845 to 1847; a State Senator in 1855; and Secretary and Treasurer of an insurance company at the time of his death, May 23, 1858.

Schenck, Abraham H.—He was born in 1777; was a member of the New York Assembly in 1804, 1805, and 1806; and a Representative in Congress, from that State, from 1815 to 1817. He was among the first who engaged in the manufacture of cotton under the non-intercourse laws. Died in 1831.

Schenck, Ferdinand S.—Born in Middlesex County, New Jersey, February 11, 1790; he received a common school education; and having studied medicine, was for many years devoted to the practice. In 1829 he was elected to the State Legislature, and re-elected in 1830 and 1831; and was a Representative in Congress, from New Jersey, from 1833 to 1837. He was a member, in 1844, of the Convention to revise the State Constitution, and was soon after elected a Judge of the Court of Errors and Appeal, which position he held for eight years. Died at Camden, May 17, 1860.

Schenck, Robert C.—Born in Franklin, Warren County, Ohio, October 4, 1809; graduated at Miami University in 1827, where he remained one or two years as a tutor; he studied law, and was admitted to the bar in 1831, and settled in Dayton. In 1840 he was elected to the Ohio Legislature; re-elected in 1842, and was a Representative in Congress, from his native State, from 1843 to 1851, serving on many committees; during the Thirtieth Congress as Chairman of the Committee on Roads and Canals. On his retirement from Congress, he was appointed, by President Fillmore, Minister to Brazil, and during his residence in South America, he took part in negotiating a number of treaties. On his return in 1853, he became extensively engaged in the railway business. During the troubles of 1861, he served as a Brigadier and Major-General in the Union army, and in 1862 was elected to the Thirty-eighth Congress, serving as Chairman of the Committee on Military Affairs.

Schermerhorn, Abraham M.—He was a Representative in Congress, from New York, from 1849 to 1853, and died in Rochester, New York, August 22, 1855.

Schley, William.—Born in Frederick City, Maryland, December 15, 1786. He received an academical education in Georgia; studied law, and was admitted to the bar at Augusta in 1812; continued the practice of his profession until 1825, when he was elected a Judge of the Superior Court of the Middle District of Georgia. He was elected to the State Legislature in 1830, and was a Representative in Congress, from 1833 to 1835, and during the two following years was Governor of Georgia. He published a "Digest of the English Statutes." He was, when Governor, one of the most active supporters of the Western and Atlantic Railroad, and at the time of his death, was President of the Medical College of Georgia. He died at Augusta, Georgia, November 20, 1858.

Schoolcraft, John L.—He was born in Albany, New York, and was all his life identified with that city as a merchant. He was for many years President of the Commercial Bank of Albany; and was a Representative in Congress, from New York, from 1849 to 1853. Died at St. Catharine's, Canada West, in May, 1860.

Schoonmaker, Cornelius C.—He was a Representative in Congress, from New York, from 1791 to 1793, and was for fourteen years, before and after the above term, a member of the New York Assembly, from the County of Ulster.

Schoonmaker, Marius.—Born in New York, and was a Representative in Congress, from that State, from 1851 to 1853.

Schureman, James.—He was a prominent man in New Jersey during the Revolution, and was a graduate of Queen's College. He was a Representative in Congress, from New Jersey, from 1789 to 1791, and from 1797 to 1799; a Senator in Congress from 1799 to 1801, when he resigned; and again a Representative, from 1813 to 1815. He was also, at one time, Mayor of New Brunswick.

Schureman, Martin G.—He was a Representative in Congress, from New York, from 1805 to 1807.

Schuyler, J.—He was a Representative in Congress, from New York, from 1817 to 1819, and died in New York City, February 21, 1835, aged sixty-seven years.

Schuyler, Philip.—Was a native of Albany, New York. He was appointed Major-General in the army of the Revolution in 1775, and despatched to the fortifications in the north of New York, to prepare for the invasion of Canada. By the loss of his health, the command soon devolved upon Montgomery. On his recovery, he directed the operations against Burgoyne, and in consequence of the evacuation of Ticonderoga, he unreasonably fell under some suspicion, and was superseded in command by General Gates. He afterwards rendered important services, though not in command. He was a Delegate to Congress previous to the present Constitution, and a Senator of the United States, from 1789 to 1791. He died at Albany in 1804, aged seventy-three.

Schwarts, John.—Born in Berks County, Pennsylvania, October 27, 1793; received a common school education; served as a Lieutenant in the last war with Great Britain; was engaged in mercantile pursuits from 1806 to 1829, and from that year to 1857 was wholly devoted to farming. He was elected a Representative, from Pennsylvania, to the Thirty-sixth Congress, but died before the expiration of his first session, in July, 1860.

Scofield, Glenni W.—He was born in Chautauque County, New York, March 11, 1817; graduated at Hamilton College in 1840, and removed to Warren, Pennsylvania, where he was admitted to the bar in 1843. In 1850 and 1851 he was a member of the State Assembly; and from 1857 to 1859 he was in the State Senate. In 1861 he was appointed President Judge of the Eighteenth Judicial District of the State, and in 1862 he was elected a Representative, from Pennsylvania, to the Thirty-eighth Congress, serving on the Committees of Elections, and Expenditures in the War Department.

Scott, Charles L.—He was born in Richmond, Virginia, January 23, 1827; graduated at William and Mary College; studied law, and formed a partnership with his father in the practice of his profession, at Richmond. In 1849 he embarked, as a member of the Madison Mining and Trading Company, for California. In 1851 he abandoned the mines, and resumed the practice of law in Tuolumne County, California. He was elected a Representative in the Thirty-fifth and Thirty-sixth Congresses, from California, serving as a member of the Committees on Indian Affairs, and on Post-offices and Post-roads.

Scott, Harvey D.—He was born in Ohio, and having removed to Indiana, was elected a Representative to the Thirty-fourth Congress, from that State.

Scott, John.—He was born in Hanover County, Virginia, in 1782; moved with his parents to Indiana in 1802; settled at St. Genevieve, Missouri, in 1805; was a Delegate to Congress, from the Territory of Missouri, from 1816 to 1821, and a Representative in Congress, from the same State, from 1821 to 1827. Died at St. Genevieve in 1861.

Scott, John.—He was a Representative in Congress, from Huntingdon County, Pennsylvania, from 1829 to 1831.

Scott, John G.—Was born in Philadelphia, December 26, 1819; left that city when seventeen years of age to seek his fortune in the West; settled in Missouri, and for many years resided at the Iron Mountain; engaged in the business of iron-master, and developing the mineral resources of the State; and in 1862 he was, at a special election, elected a Representative, from Missouri, to the Thirty-eighth Congress, in the place of J. W. Noell, deceased. He ran for Congress, at the regular election, against Mr. Noell, and was beaten by a small majority. His committee duties have been rendered as a member of the Committee on Revolutionary Pensions.

Scott, Thomas.—He was a Representative in Congress, from Pennsylvania, from 1789 to 1791, and again from 1793 to 1795.

Scranton, George W.—Born in Madison, New Haven County, Connecticut, May 23, 1811; received a common school education, and when eighteen years of age removed to New Jersey; he subsequently removed to Pennsylvania, and engaged in the iron and railroad business, having extensive interests at Oxford, New Jersey, and at Scranton, Pennsylvania; he held the positions severally of President of the Lackawanna and Western Railroad Company, and of the Cayuga and Susquehanna Railway Company; and in 1858 he was elected a Representative, from Pennsylvania, to the Thirty-sixth Congress, serving on the Committee on Manufactures. Re-elected to the Thirty-seventh Congress, but died at Scranton, Pennsylvania, March 24, 1861.

Scudder, John A.—He was a native of New Jersey; a physician by profession; served a number of years in the Assembly of his native State; and was a Representative in Congress, from New Jersey, for the unexpired term of James Cox, who died in 1810.

Scudder, Treadwell.—He was for six years a member of the New York Assembly, and a Representative in Congress, from New York, from 1817 to 1819.

Scudder, Zeno.—He filled with credit various public positions. He was President of the Massachusetts Senate, and a Representative in Congress, from 1851 to 1854, when he was compelled, by failing health, to resign his seat. He was a good lawyer, enjoyed the confidence and respect of the community in which he lived, and died at Barnstable, Massachusetts, June 26, 1857.

Scurry, Richardson.—Born in Tennessee, and was elected a Representative in Congress, from Texas, from 1851 to 1853.

Seaman, Henry J.—He was born in New York, and was a Representative in Congress, from that State, from 1845 to 1847.

Searing, John A.—Born in Queen's County, New York, May 14, 1814. His father died when he was young, and he was educated at the common schools of New York, by his grandparents. He was bred a farmer, held several public positions previously to his election as a member of the State Legislature in 1853, and was chosen a Representative to the Thirty-fifth Congress, serving on the Committees on Revolutionary Pensions, and Accounts.

Seaver, Ebenezer.—Born in 1763; graduated at Harvard University in 1784; was a member of the State Legislature, from 1794 to 1802; member of the State Constitutional Convention of 1820; and a Representative in Congress, from Massachusetts, from 1803 to 1813. He died in Roxbury, Massachusetts, March 1, 1844.

Sebastian, W. K.—Born in Vernon, Tennessee, and educated at Columbia College, in that State. He settled as a lawyer in Arkansas, in 1835, and was soon after appointed Prosecuting Attorney, and held the office until 1837; he was Circuit Judge from 1840 to 1842, and was appointed in the latter year Supreme Judge. He was a State Senator, and President of the body in 1846; and Presidential Elector in 1848. He was a United States Senator from 1848 to 1852, and re-elected for a term of six years, serving as Chairman of the Committee on Indian Affairs, and a member of the Committee on Territories. Expelled July, 1861.

Seddon, James A.—He was born in Virginia, and was elected a Representative in Congress, from that State, from 1845 to 1847, and again from 1849 to 1851; was a member of the Rebel Government as member of Congress in 1861, having previously been a Delegate to the Peace Congress of that year. In 1862 he became the Confederate Secretary of War.

Sedgwick, C. B.—Born in Pompey, New York, March, 1815; adopted the profession of law; and was elected a Representative, from New York, to the Thirty-sixth Congress, serving as a member of the Committee on Naval Affairs. Re-elected to the Thirty-seventh Congress, serving as Chairman of that Committee. In 1863 he was appointed, by President Lincoln, a Commissioner to look after certain naval affairs.

Sedgwick, Theodore.—Was born at West Hartford, Connecticut, in May, 1746. He was educated at Yale College, but did not graduate. On leaving this institution, he commenced the study of theology, but soon relinquished it, and studied law, and was admitted to the bar before reaching the age of twenty-one. He commenced practice at Great Barrington, Massachusetts, then settled at Sheffield, and afterwards at Stockbridge, in the same county. He was a zealous patriot in the Revolutionary war. He was a member of the Provincial Congress, in 1785 and 1786; and a Representative in Congress, after the adoption of the Constitution, from 1789 to 1796. He was a Senator of the United States, from 1796 to 1798, and served as President *pro tem.* during one session. In 1799 he was again a member of the House, and was chosen Speaker. From 1802 until his death, he was a Judge of the Supreme Court of Massachusetts. He died at Boston, January 24, 1813. He received the degree of LL.D. from Princeton and Cambridge. As a statesman and jurist he was highly valued by his country. His life was in an uncommon degree varied and active; his industry was unwearied, and an ardent enthusiasm was the basis of his character.

Segar, Joseph E.—Born in King William County, Virginia, June 1, 1804. In 1836 he was elected to the House of Delegates of Virginia, and served a number of years; was again elected to the same position in 1848, and continued to serve almost uninterruptedly until the State rebelled against the Union. After Eastern Virginia was restored to the Federal authority he was elected a Representative, from Virginia, to the Thirty-seventh Congress.

Selden, Dudley.—Formerly a prominent member of the New York bar, and a Representative in Congress, from New York, from 1833 to 1835. He died in Paris, France, November 7, 1855.

Semmes, Benedict J.—Was born in Charles County, Maryland, November 1, 1789. He was bred to the profession of medicine, and graduated at the Medical School in Baltimore, about the year 1811. He settled in Piscataway, Maryland, where he acquired an extensive practice, but subsequently relinquished his profession. In the year 1821 he was elected to the State Legislature; was again elected in 1825, 1827, and 1828, and during one session was chosen Speaker of the House of Delegates. In 1821 he introduced and carried through a bill for removing religious tests, as applicable to office in Maryland. In 1829 he was elected to Congress, from the district composed of Prince George and Anne Arundel Counties, and the City of Annapolis. He was re-elected in 1831, but his health soon after failing, he found it necessary to retire, at a time when there was no opposition to him in his district. He again served in the State Legislature in 1842 and 1843, since which time he has lived in retirement on his estate, in the County of Prince George.

Semple, James.—He was a Senator in Congress, from Illinois, from 1843 to 1847.

Seney, Joshua.—He was a Representative in Congress, from Maryland, from 1789 to 1792.

Senter, William T.—Born in Granger County, Tennessee, in 1802, and died there August 28, 1849. He was a Representative in Congress, from that State, from 1843 to 1845.

Sergeant, John.—He was born in Philadelphia in 1779; graduated at

Princeton College in 1795; he was for a short time a clerk in a store, but studied law, and was admitted to the bar in 1799. His first appointment was that of Prosecutor for the Commonwealth, which he held several years. He was for more than half a century known and honored for his extraordinary ability in his profession of the law, for his habitual courtesy, his liberal fairness, and his integrity. Elected to Congress, he served there from 1815 to 1823, from 1827 to 1829, and from 1837 to 1842. He was especially famous for his part in the great Missouri Compromise of 1820. For the Panama Congress, Mr. Sergeant was selected by President Adams to represent the United States. The measures of international law which were proposed to be settled in that Congress were deemed so important, that Mr. Clay, the Secretary of State, had filled eighty pages of instructions to Mr. Sergeant on the subject. In 1832 Mr. Sergeant was the Whig candidate for Vice-President, being upon the same ticket with Henry Clay. Forty-nine electoral votes were cast for these candidates. At the outset of Harrison's administration, Mr. Sergeant was tendered the mission to England, which he declined. In the cause of charity he was never appealed to in vain; and, for many years before his death, took an active interest in all the public affairs of his native city. He died in Philadelphia, November 23, 1852.

Settle, Thomas.—He was born in Rockingham County, North Carolina. He was a Representative in the State Legislature of that State in 1815, and in 1826, 1827, and 1828, at which last session he was Speaker of the House of Commons. He was a Representative in Congress from 1817 to 1821. In 1832 he was chosen Judge of the Superior Court of Law and Equity, and held the office for twenty years, when he resigned. He was highly esteemed for his many virtues. He died in Rockingham County, August 5, 1857, aged sixty-five.

Severance, Luther.—He was born in Montague, Massachusetts, October 28, 1797; and having been bred a printer, was the founder and editor of the Kennebec Journal from 1825 to 1849, and a Representative in Congress, from Maine, from 1843 to 1847. He was frequently a member of the Maine Legislature—five years in the Assembly, and two years in the Senate—and, by President Taylor, was appointed Commissioner to the Sandwich Islands. He died of a cancer, January 25, 1855, at Augusta, Maine.

Sevier, Ambrose H.—Born in Tennessee in 1802. He had few early advantages of education, but he relied on his own energies, and removed to the Territory of Arkansas, where, before the age of twenty-one, he was admitted to the bar as an attorney. He was first elected Clerk of the Legislature, and, so soon as he was eligible, was elected a member of that body, first in 1823, and again in 1825. From 1827 to 1836 he was a Delegate to Congress, from Arkansas; and when the Territory became a State, in 1836, he was elected a Senator in Congress. He was Chairman, for many years, of the Committee on Indian Affairs, and afterwards of the Committee on Foreign Relations. He resigned his seat in the Senate in 1848, to accept the appointment, from President Polk, of a special mission to Mexico, to negotiate a peace. He possessed the unbounded confidence of his constituents and party. He died at Little Rock, December 21, 1848.

Sevier, John.—A native of Tennessee, having been born in 1744; was an officer in the Revolutionary war, and distinguished himself in the battle at King's Mountain, in 1780. For his services, on that occasion, the Legislature of North Carolina, in 1813, voted him a sword. He commanded the forces which defeated the Creek and Cherokee Indians, in 1789. He was afterwards a General in the Provisional army; and from 1796 to 1801, and 1803 to 1809, Governor of Tennessee; he was a Representative in Congress, from 1811 to 1815, and was then appointed, by President Monroe, one of the Commissioners to ascertain the boundary line of the Creek territory, and died while engaged in that service, at Fort Decatur, September 24, 1815.

Sewall, Samuel.—Born in Boston, December 11, 1757. He graduated at Harvard College in 1776; was a lawyer by profession, and settled at Marblehead; in 1796 was elected a Representative in Congress, serving till 1800, and was distinguished in that body by his knowledge of commercial law. In 1800 he was placed upon the bench of the Supreme Court of Massachusetts, and in 1813 was appointed Chief Justice. He died at Wiscasset, June 8, 1814, where the gentlemen of the bar erected a monument to his memory.

Seward, James L.—He was born in Georgia, and bred a lawyer. He first entered Congress in 1853, as a Representative, from Georgia, and continued there to the close of the Thirty-fifth Congress, serving as a member of the Committee on Naval Affairs.

Seward, William H.—Born in Florida, Orange County, New York, May 16, 1801. He graduated at Union College in 1820; was admitted to the bar in 1822, and entered upon the practice of his profession at Auburn, in his native State, the following year. In 1830 he was elected to the New York Senate for four years. In 1834 he was nominated by the Whig party their candidate for Governor of the State, but failed of an election. In 1838, however, on a second nomination for the same office, he was elected, and entered upon the discharge of his duties in January, 1839. During the four years that he held that office, he upheld the system of internal improvements, and devoted himself to reforming and improving the system of public education. His plan for taking the management of the public schools in New York out of the hands of the Public School Society, and subjecting them to the control of the State, caused considerable feeling on the subject at the time, and gave rise to an animated contest between the Protestants, who maintained the existing system, and the Roman Catholics, who favored the change. On the expiration of his second term of office, Mr. Seward declined to be a candidate for re-election, and resumed the practice of his profession at Auburn, in 1843. He had an extensive practice, chiefly in the Federal courts. In March, 1849, he was chosen United States Senator for six years, and took his seat at the extra session called to consider the nominations of President Taylor. He was re-elected in 1855, and held the position until he became Secretary of State under President Lincoln. In 1860 he was spoken of by a large party as a candidate for the Presidency, and during that year made a pilgrimage to Egypt and the Holy Land.

Seybert, Adam.—He was a citizen of Philadelphia, and a Representative in Congress, from Pennsylvania, from 1809 to 1815, and again from 1817 to 1819. He died at Paris, May 2, 1825, bequeathing $1000 for educating the deaf and dumb, and $500 to the Orphan Asylum in Philadelphia. He was a man of science, and was particularly skilful as a chemist and mineralogist. He published Statistical Annals of the United States, from 1789 to 1818.

Seymour, David L.—He was a member of the New York Assembly in 1836, from Rensselaer County, and a Representative in Congress, from 1843 to 1845.

Seymour, David L.—He was born in Connecticut; served repeatedly in the State Legislature, having been made Speaker in 1852; was a Representative in Congress, from Connecticut, from 1851 to 1853; and in 1856 he was chosen a Judge of the Superior Court of Connecticut for a term of eight years.

Seymour, Horatio.—Born in Litchfield, Connecticut, May 31, 1778; graduated at Yale College in 1797; studied law at the Litchfield school, and settled in Middlebury, Vermont. He was a Judge of Probate, member of the Council, and a Senator in Congress, from 1821 to 1833. He died at Middlebury, November 21, 1857.

Seymour, Origen S.—He was born in Litchfield, Connecticut, in 1804; was bred a lawyer; served in the State Legislature, and as Speaker in 1850; and was a Representative in Congress, from Connecticut, from 1851 to 1855. He was subsequently chosen a Judge of the Superior Court of Connecticut.

Seymour, Thomas H.—He was born in Hartford, Connecticut, in 1808; was educated at the Middletown Military Academy; studied law, and practised the profession; was a Judge of Probate; a Representative in Congress, from Connecticut, from 1843 to 1845; in 1846 went to Mexico as a Major of the New England Regiment, and was with General Scott at the City of Mexico; he was elected Governor of the State in 1850, and re-elected three times; and was appointed, by President Pierce, Minister to Russia.

Seymour, William. — He was born in Connecticut, served as a member of the New York Assembly, in 1832 and 1834, and was a Representative in Congress, from 1835 to 1837.

Shadwick, William.—He was a member of Congress, from North Carolina, during the years 1796 and 1797.

Shanks, John P. C. — Born in Martinsburg, Virginia, June 17, 1826; was for the most part self-educated; removed to Indiana, where he studied law, and commenced practice in 1850; was elected to the Indiana Legislature in 1853 and 1854; and in 1860 he was elected a Representative, from Indiana, to the Thirty-seventh Congress, serving on the Committees on Private Land Claims, and on Agriculture. He visited the field of Bull Run, in July, 1861, as a spectator, but became a participant; during the subsequent recess of Congress he served in Missouri as a member of General Fremont's staff, performing some other military service until he resumed his seat in Congress in December, 1861.

Shannon, Thomas. — He was a Representative in Congress, from Ohio, from 1826 to 1827.

Shannon Thomas B.—Born in Westmoreland County, Pennsylvania, in 1827; emigrated to Illinois in 1844; in 1849, to California; from 1854 to 1861, was engaged in merchandizing; served four sessions in the California Legislature; and in 1863 he was elected a Representative, from California, to the Thirty-eighth Congress, serving on the Committee on Indian Affairs.

Shannon, Wilson.—He was born in Belmont County, Ohio, February 24, 1802; educated at Athens College, in Ohio, and Transylvania University, in Kentucky; adopted the profession of law, and in 1835 was Prosecuting Attorney for the State of Ohio; was elected Governor of Ohio in 1837, and again in 1842; by President Tyler was appointed Minister to Mexico; and was a Representative in Congress, from Ohio, from 1853 to 1855. In 1855 he was appointed, by President Pierce, Governor of the Territory of Kansas.

Sharpe, Peter.—He was a member of the Assembly of New York, from 1814 to 1820, officiating a number of sessions as Speaker; he was also a member of the State Constitutional Convention of 1821; a Representative in Congress, from 1823 to 1825; and a member of the Tariff Convention held in 1827.

Sharpe, Solomon P. — He was born in Virginia, but removed to Kentucky when a child; he received a limited education, but studied law, and was admitted to the bar when nineteen years of age, and was successful; he served a number of years in the State Legislature; was Attorney-General of the State; and a Representative in Congress, from Kentucky, from 1813 to 1817. He fell by the hand of an assassin, while a member of the Legislature, in November, 1835, aged fifty-five years; and a legislative reward of $3000, for the arrest of the murderer, was offered, but in vain.

Shaw, Aaron.—Born in Orange County, New York, in 1811; a lawyer by profession; was State's Attorney for eight years, in the Fourth Judicial Circuit of Illinois; and was a member of the State House of Representatives, in 1849–50. He was elected a Representative to the Thirty-fifth Congress, from Illinois, serving as a member of the Committee on the Militia.

Shaw, Henry.—He was born in Windham County, Vermont; studied law with Judge Foot, in Albany, New York, and settled in practice in Lanesborough, Berkshire County, Massachusetts, at the age of twenty-two; he was nominated for Congress before he was eligible, and was subsequently elected, in 1816, to the Sixteenth Congress, and voted for the Missouri Compromise, which prevented his re-election. He was an intimate friend of Henry Clay, and was a personal friend and acquaintance of ten of the Presidents of the United States. He was a member of the Massachusetts Legislature for eighteen years, also a member of the Governor's Council, and was the pioneer in the manufacturing prosperity of Western

Massachusetts. In 1848 he removed to New York, and resided at Fort Washington, on the Hudson; was a member of the Board of Education in New York City, and two years in the Common Council, and in 1853 was a member of the Assembly. He removed to Newburg in 1854, where he resided until within a few months of his death, which occurred at Peekskill, October 17, 1857, aged sixty-nine years.

Shaw, Henry M.—He was born at Newport, Rhode Island, November 20, 1819; studied medicine, and graduated at the University of Pennsylvania; removed to North Carolina, and was a State Senator in 1852, and a Representative, from that State, in the Thirty-third and Thirty-fifth Congresses, and was a member of the Committees on Manufactures, and Revolutionary Pensions.

Shaw, Samuel.—He was born in Dighton, Massachusetts, in December, 1768, and removed to Putney, Vermont, at the age of ten years; he received a limited education; commenced the study of medicine at the age of seventeen, and in two years entered upon the practice of his profession at Castleton, Vermont, and became eminent as a surgeon. He entered early into politics, and was one of the victims of the Sedition Law; for his denunciation of the administration of John Adams, he was imprisoned, and liberated by the people without the forms of law; and in 1799 was returned as a member of the State Legislature. He was for some time a member of the State Council, and was a Representative in Congress, from Vermont, from 1808 to 1813. He was a personal friend of Jefferson and Madison, and gave his earnest support to the measures for the prosecution of the war. On his retirement from Congress, he was appointed surgeon in the army, and removed to the city of New York; he was subsequently stationed at Greenbush, St. Louis, and at Norfolk, and held this office until 1816. As an instance of his physical endurance, it may be mentioned that he, on one occasion, rode on horseback from St. Louis, Missouri, to Albany, New York, in twenty-nine consecutive days. He died at Clarendon, Vermont, October 22, 1827.

Shaw, Tristam.—Born in New Hampshire in 1787; was a Representative in Congress, from that State, from 1839 to 1843; and died at Exeter, New Hampshire, March 14, 1843.

Sheafe, James.—He was born in 1755; was a Representative in Congress, from New Hampshire, from 1799 to 1801; a Senator in Congress in 1801 and 1802, resigning June, 1802; and died at Portsmouth, New Hampshire, in 1829.

Sheffer, Daniel.—He was born in Pennsylvania, and was a Representative in Congress, from that State, from 1837 to 1839.

Sheffey, Daniel.—He was born at Frederick, Maryland, in 1770; had a limited education; was bred to the trade of a shoemaker, and settled in Augusta, Virginia; he afterwards studied law, engaged in a lucrative practice; and frequently represented his county in the House of Delegates. He was a Representative in Congress, from Virginia, from 1809 to 1817, and took a high rank. His speech in favor of the renewal of the first Bank of the United States was a masterly production. He was opposed to the war of 1812. He died at his home, December 3, 1830.

Sheffield, William P.—Was born at New Shoreham (Block Island), Newport County, Rhode Island, August 30, 1820. His education was obtained first at Kingston Academy, and then from a private tutor; studied law at Harvard University, and was admitted to the bar in 1844. In 1841 and 1842 he was elected to Conventions called to frame a State Constitution; in 1845 he was elected, from his native town, to the State Assembly; removing his residence to Tiverton, he was again elected to the Assembly in 1849, where he continued to serve until 1853, when he resigned his seat, and settled in Newport. That city he represented in the Assembly from 1857 to 1861, when he was elected a Representative, from Rhode Island, to the Thirty-seventh Congress, serving as a member of the Committees on Commerce, and on Foreign Affairs.

Shellabarger, Samuel.—Born in Clark County, Ohio, December 10, 1817; graduated at the Miami University, Ohio, in 1841; adopted the profession of law; was a member of the Ohio Legislature in 1852 and 1853; and was elected a Representative, from Ohio, to the Thirty-seventh Congress, serving on the Committee on Expenses in the Interior Department.

Shepard, Charles B.—Born in Newbern, North Carolina, December 5, 1807; graduated at Chapel Hill in 1827; was elected to Congress in 1837, where he continued to serve until 1841; and died in October, 1843.

Shepard, William B.—Born in Newbern, North Carolina, in 1799; educated at Chapel Hill; studied law, and became eminent in his profession; was a Representative in Congress, from 1827 to 1837, when he declined a re-election; in 1838 he was elected to the State Senate, and served five terms. He died at Elizabeth City, June 20, 1852.

Shepherd, William.—Born in Massachusetts, December 1, 1737; he served six years as a Captain in the Revolutionary army, and distinguished himself at William Henry and Crown Point; in 1783 he was chosen a Brigadier-General, having fought in twenty-two battles; he was subsequently a Major-General of militia; and a Representative in Congress, from 1797 to 1803. Died at Westfield, Massachusetts, November 11, 1817.

Shepley, Ether.—A Senator in Congress, from Maine, from 1833 to 1836. He was born in Groton, Massachusetts, November 2, 1789; graduated at Dartmouth College in 1811; studied law, and commenced the practice in Saco, but subsequently settled in Portland; he was in the Massachusetts Legislature in 1819; a member of the Convention that formed the first Constitution of Maine in 1820; he was for thirteen years Attorney of the United States for Maine; after leaving the Senate of the United States, he was chosen a Justice of the Supreme Court of Maine, and subsequently Chief Justice of the same, which latter position he held until 1855. While on the bench he furnished the materials for twenty-six volumes of Reports, and as sole Commissioner, was appointed to revise the statutes of Maine. He was Trustee of Bowdoin College, from which institution he received the degree of LL.D.

Sheplor, Matthias.—Born in Pennsylvania, and was a Representative in Congress, from Ohio, from 1837 to 1839.

Shepperd, Augustus H.—He was born in Surry County, North Carolina; educated a lawyer; served in the House of Commons from 1822 to 1826; and was a Representative in Congress from 1829 to 1839; again from 1841 to 1843, and again from 1847 to 1851.

Sherburne, John S.—He was born in New Hampshire; graduated at Dartmouth College in 1776; attended the law school at Harvard; was a Representative in Congress, from New Hampshire, from 1793 to 1797; was United States District Attorney in 1803, and Judge of the United States District Court from 1803 to 1830. He died in 1830, aged seventy-three years.

Sheredine, Upton.—He was a Representative in Congress, from Maryland, from 1791 to 1792.

Sherman, John.—He was born in Lancaster, Ohio, May 10, 1823; received a good education; adopted the profession of law, and came to the bar in 1844. In 1848 and 1852 he was a Delegate to the Whig Conventions of those years; in 1854 he was elected a Representative, from Ohio, to the Thirty-fourth Congress; re-elected to the Thirty-fifth; and on being returned for the Thirty-sixth Congress, he was the Republican candidate for Speaker, and after an unprecedented contest, wanted only one or two votes to secure his election; and during that Congress, he was Chairman of the Committee of Ways and Means. In 1860 he was elected to the Thirty-seventh Congress, but in 1861, on the resignation of Senator Chase, he was chosen a Senator in Congress, for the term expiring in 1867, serving as Chairman of the Committee on Agriculture, and as a member of the Committee on Finance.

Sherman, J. W.—He was born in New York, and elected a Representative, from that State, to the Thirty-fifth Congress, and was a member of the Committee on Unfinished Business.

Sherman, Roger.—Born at Newton, Massachusetts, April 19, 1721. He had no advantages for education, yet he was eager in the pursuit of knowledge, and while apprenticed to a shoemaker, he often had a book open before him while at his work. In 1743 he removed to New Milford, Connecticut, carrying his tools upon his back. He afterwards studied law, and settled at New Haven, and was admitted to the bar in 1754. He was Judge of the County and Superior Courts; and a member of the first Congress, in 1774, and continued a member for many years. He signed the Declaration of Independence in 1776. After the adoption of the Constitution of the United States, in regard to which he took a prominent part, he was elected a Representative to Congress; and chosen a Senator in 1791, continuing in that station till his death, July 23, 1793. He was a profound and sagacious statesman, an able and upright judge, and an exemplary Christian. He was made Master of Arts by Yale College, and was for many years Treasurer of that institution.

Sherman, Socrates N.—He was born in Vermont, and elected a Representative, from New York, to the Thirty-seventh Congress, serving on the Committee on Expenditures in the Interior Department.

Sherrill, Eliakim.—He was born in New York, and was a Representative in Congress, from that State, from 1847 to 1849, and was a member of the Committee on Manufactures.

Sherwood, Samuel.—He was a Representative in Congress, from New York, from 1813 to 1815. Died in New York in November, 1862.

Sherwood, Samuel B.—He was born in Connecticut; graduated at Yale College in 1786; was a Representative in Congress, from that State, from 1817 to 1819, and died in 1833.

Shiel, George K.—He was born in Ireland, and was elected a Representative, from Oregon, to the Thirty-seventh Congress, serving on the Committee on the Pacific Railroad.

Shields, Benjamin G.—He was a Representative in Congress, from Alabama, from 1841 to 1843.

Shields, Ebenezer J.—Born in Georgia, and was elected a Representative in Congress, from Tennessee, from 1835 to 1839. Died May 20, 1846.

Shields, James.—He was a Representative in Congress, from Ohio, from 1829 to 1831. Died in Butler County, Ohio, in 1831.

Shields, James.—Was born in County Tyrone, Ireland, in 1810, and emigrated to America about 1826. He pursued his mathematical and classical studies until the year 1832, when he went to Illinois, and commenced the practice of the law at Kaskaskia. In 1836 he was elected a member of the Illinois Legislature, and Auditor of the State in 1839. In 1843 he was appointed Judge of the Supreme Court; and in 1845 Commissioner of the General Land Office. At the commencement of the Mexican war he was appointed by President Polk a Brigadier-General in the United States army, and, for his distinguished services during the course of the war, was promoted to the rank of Brevet Major-General. In 1848 he was appointed Governor of Oregon Territory, which he resigned. In 1849 he was elected to a seat in the United States Senate, for the term of six years, from the State of Illinois. He subsequently took up his residence in the Territory of Minnesota, and in 1857 was elected to represent the same in the Senate of the United States, when she became a State, in which position he served two years. During the troubles of 1861 he served as a General in the Union army.

Shinn, William N.—He was born in New Jersey; a farmer by occupation; and was a Representative in Congress, from that State, from 1833 to 1837.

Shipperd, Zebulon R.—He was a Representative in Congress, from New York, from 1813 to 1815.

Shorter, Eli S.—Born in Monticello, Georgia, March 15, 1823; graduated at Yale College in 1843; was a lawyer by profession, but engaged in the planting business. He was elected a Representative, from Alabama, to the Thirty-fourth and Thirty-fifth Congresses, and was a member of the Committee on Indian Affairs.

Showers, Jacob.—He was a Representative in Congress, from Maryland, from 1853 to 1855.

Sibley, Henry H.—He was born in February, 1811, in Detroit, Michigan; spent much of his early life on the Northwestern frontiers; was for many years an Indian trader in the employ of the American Fur Company, at Mackinaw and Fort Snelling; was a Delegate to Congress, from Minnesota Territory, from 1849 to 1853; and, having witnessed the progress of Minnesota from a wilderness to an organized State, he was elected, in 1857, its first Governor.

Sibley, Jonas.—He was born in Sutton, Massachnsetts, March 17, 1762; for thirty-five years held a variety of town offices; from 1806 to 1823 was a member of the Massachusetts Legislature; was an Elector for President in 1820; served again in both houses of the Legislature; was a member of the State Constitutional Convention of 1820; a member of Congress, from Worcester County, Massachusetts, from 1823 to 1825; and died at Sutton, in that State, February 10, 1834, aged seventy-two years.

Sibley, Mark H.—Born in Great Barrington, Massachusetts, in 1796, and removed to Canandaigua, New York, in 1814. He studied law, and was distinguished as an advocate. He was a member of the New York Assembly in 1834 and 1835; a Representative in Congress, from 1837 to 1839; subsequently a State Senator; and in 1846 a County Judge. He died in Canandaigua, New York, September 8, 1852.

Sibley, Solomon.—He was born in Sutton, Massachusetts, October 7, 1769. He studied law, and removed to Ohio in 1795, establishing himself first at Marietta, and then at Cincinnati, in the practice of his profession. He removed to Detroit in 1797, and in 1799 was elected to the first Territorial Legislature of the Northwestern Territory. He was a Delegate to Congress, from the Territory of Michigan, from 1820 to 1823; in 1824 he was appointed Judge of the Supreme Court, and held the office until 1836, when he resigned in consequence of increasing deafness. He died at Detroit, April 4, 1846. He was universally respected for his talents and manifold virtues.

Sickles, Daniel E.—He was born in New York, in October, 1821; acquired the printer's trade, which he followed for some years; he studied law, and was admitted to the bar in 1843; in 1847 he was elected to the Assembly of New York, and in 1856 to the State Senate. For a short time, when Mr. Buchanan was the American Minister in England, he was the Secretary of that legation; and was elected a Representative, from New York, to the Thirty-fifth Congress, and was a member of the Committee on Foreign Affairs. He was re-elected to the Thirty-sixth Congress; before the expiration of his first term, in February, 1859, he killed Philip Barton Key for "dishonoring his bed." His trial lasted twenty days, and he was acquitted. He served in the army during the Rebellion, and attained the rank of Major-General.

Sickles, Nicholas.—He was born in Kinderhook, New York; was a Representative in Congress, from 1835 to 1837; and died at Kingston, New York, May 13, 1845.

Sill, Thomas H.—He was a native of Connecticut; a lawyer by profession; and settled in the practice at Erie, Pennsylvania, in 1812. He was a member of the Convention to revise the State Constitution; and a Representative in Congress, from Pennsylvania, from 1829 to 1831, having served in the same capacity for an unexpired term in 1826.

Silsbee, Nathaniel.—Born in Essex County, Massachusetts, in 1773, and died at Salem, Massachusetts, July 1, 1850. He was a distinguished and successful merchant, and frequently elected to the State Legislature, and was for three years President of the State Senate; he served as a Representative in Congress, from 1816 to 1820; and was a Senator of the United States, from 1826 to 1835. He was the firm supporter of the administration of John Quincy Adams, and when his term expired, Mr. Silsbee offered to vacate his seat in the Senate in his favor, but the ex-President declined the proposal.

Silvester Peter.—He was born in New York; was a member of the Albany Committee of Safety in 1774, and of the New York Provincial Congress; was a Judge of the Common Pleas in 1776; and elected a member of the First Congress under the Federal Constitution. He was subsequently a State Senator, and died at Kinderhook, January 30, 1845.

Silvester, Peter H.—He was born at Kinderhook, Columbia County, New York, February 17, 1807; graduated at Union College in 1827; studied law, and was admitted to the bar in 1830; and he was a Representative, in Congress, from New York, from 1847 to 1851.

Simkins, Eldred.—He was born in Edgefield District, South Carolina, August 29, 1779; was educated for the bar at Litchfield, Connecticut; was partner of Mr. McDuffie; served frequently in the Legislature; was Lieutenant-Governor of South Carolina in 1812; a General of militia; and was a Representative in Congress, from South Carolina, from 1817 to 1821. Died at Edgefield in 1832.

Simmons, George A.—He was born in New York; graduated at Dartmouth College in 1816; served a number of years in the Assembly of that State; and was elected a Representative in Congress to the Thirty-third and Thirty-fourth Congresses, from that State. In 1852 he received from his Alma Mater the degree of LL.D., and died, October 27, 1857, aged sixty-six years, at Keesville, New York.

Simmons, James F.—Born in Little Compton, Rhode Island, September 10, 1795. His employments were farming and manufacturing; he was a member of the General Assembly, from 1828 to 1841; elected to the United States Senate in 1841, for six years, to March 4, 1847; again chosen for another term, beginning March 4, 1857, and served as a member of the Committees on Claims, on Patents and the Patent-office, and on Finance. During the Thirty-seventh Congress he was Chairman of the Committee on Patents. Died in Johnson, R. I., July 10, 1864.

Simms, William E.—Born in Kentucky, and elected a Representative, from that State, to the Thirty-sixth Congress, serving on the Committee on the Militia.

Simons, Samuel.—He was a Representative in Congress, from Connecticut, from 1843 to 1845; and died in Bridgeport, Connecticut, January 13, 1847, aged fifty-five years.

Simonton, William.—He was a member of Congress, from Pennsylvania, from 1839 to 1843, and died at South Hanover, Pennsylvania, May 18, 1846.

Simpson, Richard F.—He was born in South Carolina, and was a Representative in Congress from 1843 to 1847. He graduated at the University of South Carolina in 1816; adopted the profession of law; and before entering Congress had been a member of the Senate of his native State.

Sims, Alexander D.—He was born in Brunswick County, Virginia, June 12, 1803, and died at Kingstree, South Carolina, November 22, 1849. He went through a course of studies at Chapel Hill, North Carolina, and finished his education at Union College, New York. He read and practised law in Virginia, and removing to South Carolina, taught an academy at Darlington Court-house. In 1829 he commenced the practice of law in South Carolina, and became a prominent member of the bar in that State. He had a taste for politics, and during the Nullification times was active and decided; and he was a member of Congress from 1845 to 1849. He also served in the State Legislature in 1840 and 1842.

Sims, Leonard H.—Born in North Carolina, and was elected a Representative in Congress, from Missouri, from 1845 to 1847.

Singleton, Otho R.—Born in Jessamine County, Kentucky; graduated at St. Joseph College, Bardstown, Kentucky, and adopted the law as a profession; he was two years in the lower house of the Mississippi Legislature; six years in the State Senate; a Presidential Elector in 1852; and was elected a Representative to the Thirty-third Congress, and re-elected to the Thirty-fifth Congress, from the same State, serving as a member of the Joint Committee on Printing. Re-elected to the

Thirty-sixth Congress, serving on the Committee on Roads and Canals. Joined the Great Rebellion in 1861.

Singleton, Thomas D.—He was elected to Congress, from South Carolina, in 1833, and while on his way to Washington to take his seat, in December, he died at Raleigh, North Carolina.

Sinnickson, Thomas.—Born in Salem County, New Jersey; received a classical education, and was bred a merchant. He served in the Revolutionary war at the battles of Trenton and Princeton, in the capacity of Captain; was for many years a member of the Council and Assembly of New Jersey, and the Presiding Judge of the Court of Common Pleas; he was a Correspondent of the Committee of Safety, during the Revolution; and a Representative in the First Congress, after the adoption of the Constitution, from 1789 to 1791, and again from 1797 to 1799.

Sinnickson, Thomas.—Born in Salem, New Jersey, December 13, 1786; received a common school education; commenced active life as a merchant; was a Judge of the Court of Common Pleas for twenty years; a member of the New Jersey Legislature; Judge of the Court of Errors and Appeals; and a Representative in Congress, during the years 1828 and 1829.

Sitgreaves, Samuel.—He was a Representative in Congress, from Pennsylvania, from 1795 to 1798; and was then appointed, by President Adams, Commissioner to treat with Great Britain. Died, April 4, 1827.

Skelton, Charles.—Born in Pennsylvania, and was a Representative in Congress, from New Jersey, from 1851 to 1855.

Skinner, Richard.—He was born at Litchfield, Connecticut, May 30, 1788, and received his education at the celebrated law school of his native town; he was admitted to the bar in 1800, and removed to Manchester, Vermont. In 1801 he was appointed State's Attorney for Bennington County, and in 1809 Judge of Probate; and was elected a Representative in Congress, from 1813 to 1815; Judge of the Supreme Court in 1816; and Chief Justice in 1817. In 1818 he was elected to the lower branch of the Legislature, and was Speaker. He was Governor in 1820, 1821, and 1822; was reappointed Chief Justice in 1824, and resigned in 1829. He died at Manchester, May 23, 1833, much respected for his public services and private worth. He was President of the Northeastern Branch of the American Education Society; was a member of the Board of Trustees of Middlebury College, from which institution he received the degree of LL.D. He was also interested in various local benevolent associations.

Skinner, Thompson J., Jr.—He was a Representative in Congress, from Massachusetts, from 1796 to 1799, and again from 1803 to 1805; in 1804 he was appointed, by President Jefferson, Commissioner of Loans.

Slade, Charles.—He was a Representative in Congress, from Illinois, from 1833 to 1834, and died in July of the same year, on his return from Washington, in Knox County, Indiana, after an illness of only twenty-four hours.

Slade William.—Born in Cornwall, Vermont, May 9, 1786; graduated at Middlebury College in 1807; and having studied law was admitted to the bar in 1810. From 1814 to 1816 he published and edited the Columbian Patriot, and at the same time kept a bookstore; in 1815 he was elected Secretary of State, which office he held eight years, during six of which, he officiated as Judge of the Addison County Court; and was subsequently State's Attorney for the same County. From 1823 to 1829 he was a clerk in the State Department at Washington. His service in Congress, as a Representative from Vermont, was from 1831 to 1843. On his retirement from Congress, he was elected Reporter of the Decisions of the Supreme Court of Vermont, which office he held one year; and in 1844 he was chosen Governor of Vermont. He was subsequently made Secretary of the National Board of Popular Education, having for its object, the furnishing of the West with teachers from the East. In 1823 he published the "Vermont State Papers;" in 1825 the "Statutes of Vermont," and in 1844 a volume of "Vermont Reports." He died at Middlebury, Vermont, January 18, 1859.

Slaymaker, Amos.—He was born in the London Lands, Lancaster County, Pennsylvania, March 11, 1755; received a good common school education; served as a soldier in the Revolutionary army; paid much attention to farming, and officiated as a magistrate; and was a Representative in Congress, from Pennsylvania, during a part of two terms, in 1810 and 1814. He died in Salisbury, Lancaster County, Pennsylvania, June 12, 1837.

Slidell, John.—Born in New York about the year 1793, and on reaching the age of manhood removed to New Orleans, where he established himself as a lawyer, and practised his profession with success. He was appointed, by President Jackson, United States District Attorney; was frequently elected to the Legislature of Louisiana; was a Representative in Congress, from 1843 to 1845; while in Congress he was appointed, by President Polk, Minister to Mexico; and in 1853 was elected to the United States Senate for the unexpired term of Senator Soulé, and was re-elected for six years, and was Chairman of the Committee on the Condition of the Banks, and a member of the Committees on Naval Affairs, and Foreign Relations. He resigned, and became identified with the Rebellion of 1861. He went to France as a Minister from the Rebel government, was captured by the San Jacinto, on his passage out, imprisoned in Fort Warren, and after being released took up his residence in Paris.

Slingerland, John I.—He was born in Albany County, New York, March 1, 1804; received a good common school education; and as a business, has devoted nearly his whole life to agricultural pursuits. He was a member of the New York Legislature in 1843, and was a Representative in Congress, from New York, from 1847 to 1849.

Sloan, A. Scott.—Born in Morrisville, Madison County, New York, in 1820; adopted the profession of law; in 1847 was elected Clerk of Madison County; removed to Wisconsin in 1854; elcctcd to the Wisconsin Legislature in 1856; appointed a Circuit Judge in 1858; and in 1860 was elected a Representative, from Wisconsin, to the Thirty-seventh Congress, serving on the Committee on Territories.

Sloan, Ithamar C.—Born in Madison County, New York; received a common school education; adopted the profession of law; removed to Wisconsin in 1854; in 1858 and 1860 he was chosen District Attorney of Rock County; and in 1862 was elected a Representative, from Wisconsin, to the Thirty-eighth Congress, serving on the Committee on Public Lands, and also that on Expenses in the War Department.

Sloan, James.—He was a Representative in Congress, from New Jersey, from 1803 to 1809; a resident of Gloucester County, and a member of the Society of Friends. Died in New Jersey, in November, 1811.

Sloane, John.—Born in York, Pennsylvania, but removed to Ohio, while yet a Territory. He was elected a member of the General Assembly in 1804, and in 1805 and 1806 was Speaker. He was a Receiver of Public Moneys at Canton, from 1808 to 1816, and afterwards at Wooster, until 1819, when he was elected to Congress as a Representative, continuing a member until 1829. He was Clerk of the Common Pleas for seven years, Secretary of State for three years, and Treasurer of the United States under President Fillmore. He was a Colonel of militia during the war of 1812, and died in Wooster, May 15, 1856, aged seventy-seven years.

Sloane, Jonathan.—He was born in Massachusetts, and having settled in Ohio, was a Representative in Congress, from that State, from 1833 to 1837.

Slocum, Jesse.—Was a Representative in Congress, from North Carolina, from 1817 to 1820, and died in Washington before the expiration of his term, December 20, of the latter year.

Smart, Ephraim K.—Born at Prospect (now Searsport), Maine, in 1813. He was thrown upon his own resources to obtain means of education, which he received at the Maine Wesleyan Seminary. After the study of law for three years, he was admitted to the bar in Camden. He was appointed Postmaster in 1838, and in 1841 was elected State Senator. In 1842 he was aid to the Governor, with the rank of Lieutenant-Colonel, and was re-elected to the Senate the same year. In 1843 he went to Missouri, and practised law, as an attorney, and counsellor and solicitor in Chancery; but returned to Camden, and was again Postmaster in 1845. He was a Representative, from Maine, in Congress, from 1847 to 1849, and from 1851 to 1853. From 1853 to 1858 he was Collector at Belfast. In 1854 he established the Maine Free Press, and was its editor three years; and in 1858 returned to the practice of law in Camden, and in September of that year was again elected to the Legislature.

Smelt, Dennis.—He was a Representative in Congress, from Georgia, from 1806 to 1811.

Smilie, John.—He was born in Ireland, but emigrated to this country when young; held many civil and military positions during the Revolution; served in the Legislature of Pennsylvania, his adopted State, and was a Representative in Congress, from Pennsylvania, from 1793 to 1795, and again from 1799 to 1813. Died in Washington, December 30, 1813, aged seventy-six years.

Smith, Albert.—Born in Hanover, Plymouth County, Massachusetts, January 3, 1793; graduated at Brown University in 1813; admitted to the bar in 1816; removed to Maine in 1817; and was sent to the General Court of Massachusetts in 1820; was for many years a Postmaster in Maine; from 1830 to 1838 he was Marshal of the United States for Maine; was a Representative in Congress, from 1839 to 1841; and in 1842 he was appointed the United States Commissioner to settle the Northeastern Boundary, under the Ashburton Treaty, which business was completed in 1847.

Smith, Albert.—He was born in New York, and was a member of the New York Assembly, from Genesee County, in 1842, and a Representative in Congress, from that State, from 1843 to 1847.

Smith, Arthur.—Born in the County of Isle of Wight, Virginia, November 15, 1785; was educated at the College of William and Mary; served with credit at the head of a militia force at Norfolk, in 1812; was a member of the Privy Council of Virginia, and subsequently a member of the State Legislature; and was a Representative in Congress, from 1821 to 1825. He was a lawyer by profession, but never practised. Died in Virginia, March 30, 1853.

Smith, Ballard.—He was a Representative in Congress, from Virginia, from 1815 to 1821.

Smith, Bernard.—He was born in Morristown, New Jersey, and was a Representative in Congress, from his native State, from 1819 to 1821, when he was appointed, by President Monroe, Register of the Land-office in Arkansas.

Smith, Caleb B.—He was born in Boston, Massachusetts, April 16, 1808; emigrated with his parents to Ohio in 1814; and was educated at the Cincinnati College and Miami University; adopted the profession of law, and settled in Indiana; in 1832 he established and edited a Whig journal called the Indiana Sentinel; in 1833 he was elected a member of the Legislature; re-elected in 1834, 1835, and 1836, during the latter year officiating as Speaker; in 1847 and 1848 he was a member of the Board of Fund Commissioners; and he was a Representative in Congress, from Indiana, from 1843 to 1849. He was also a Presidential Elector in 1840 and 1856; and after leaving Congress, in 1849, he was appointed, by President Taylor, one of the members of the Board for Investigating the Claims of American citizens against Mexico. He subsequently practised his profession in Cincinnati, Ohio; and in 1861 was appointed Secretary of the Interior Department, by President Lincoln. He was also a member of the Peace Congress held in Washington in February, 1861. In December, 1862, he resigned the office of Secretary, and was appointed Judge of the United States District Court for the District of Indiana. Died January 8, 1864.

Smith, Daniel.—He was one of the earliest emigrants to Tennessee; a General of militia; and a Senator in Congress, from Tennessee, during the years 1798 and 1799, and again from 1805 to 1809. He died in July, 1818.

Smith, Delazon.—Was born in New Berlin, Chenango County, New York; graduated at the Oberlin Collegiate Institute, of Ohio, in 1837; he studied law, but becoming a writer for the press, was associated with the Rochester True Jeffersonian, in New York, and the Western Empire, in Dayton, Ohio; he was appointed, by President Tyler, Special Commissioner to Quito; in 1846 he removed to Iowa Territory, where he remained until 1852, when he emigrated to Oregon Territory; in 1854 he was elected to the Assembly of Oregon, and re-elected in 1855 and 1856; he was a member of the Convention in 1857 which formed a State Constitution; and in July, 1858, he was chosen one of the Senators in Congress for the prospective State, and took his seat as such in February, 1859. Died in Portland, Oregon, November 17, 1860.

Smith, Edward Henry.—He was born at Smithtown, Long Island, in 1809; received a good common school education; was bred a farmer, to which occupation he has devoted his whole life; and in 1860 was elected a Representative, from New York, to the Thirty-seventh Congress, serving on the Committees on Agriculture, and Expenditures in the Post-office Department.

Smith, F. O. J.—He was born in Massachusetts; bred to the law; was elected to the Assembly of Maine in 1831; was President of the State Senate in 1833; and was a Representative in Congress, from Maine, from 1833 to 1839. Of late years he has been much interested in telegraph and railroad enterprises.

Smith, George.—He was a Representative in Congress, from Pennsylvania, from 1809 to 1813.

Smith, Gerritt. — Born in New York, and was a Representative in Congress, from that State, from 1853 to 1855.

Smith, Green Clay. — Born in Richmond, Kentucky, July 2, 1830; graduated at Transylvania University in 1849, and in the Law Department of the same institution in 1852; was a School Commissioner from 1853 to 1857, establishing a great number of schools; served as Second Lieutenant in the Mexican war; after the breaking out of the Rebellion, in 1861, he had command of the Fourth Kentucky Cavalry; and was elected to the State Legislature; was appointed a Brigadier-General in 1862; was present at the battle of Ball's Bluff and about fifty other engagements; and in 1863 he was elected a Representative, from Kentucky, to the Thirty-eighth Congress, serving on the Committees on Elections, and on the Militia. His commission as General he resigned on the 1st December, 1863. He was a Delegate to the Baltimore Convention of 1864. His father, John Speed Smith, was also in Congress.

Smith, Isaac.—He was a graduate of Princeton College in 1755, and a tutor in that institution; a Representative in Congress, from New Jersey, from 1795 to 1797; was appointed, by President Washington, in the latter year, a Commissioner to treat with the Seneca Indians; and was a Judge of the Superior Court of New Jersey. He died in 1807.

Smith, Isaac.—He was a native of Pennsylvania, and a Representative in Congress, from that State, from 1813 to 1815.

Smith, Israel.—Born in Connecticut, April 4, 1759. He graduated at Yale College in 1781, studied law, and settled at Rupert, Vermont. He subsequently settled at Rutland, and was sent to the State Legislature from that town. He was a Representative in Congress, from 1791 to 1797, again in 1800, and a Senator in Congress, during the years 1801 and 1802, and from 1803 to 1807, when he resigned. He was also appointed Chief Justice of the Supreme Court in 1797, and was Governor of Vermont in 1807. He died December 2, 1810.

Smith, James S.—He was born in Orange County, North Carolina, and was educated for the medical profession; served in the Legislature of North Carolina in 1821; and was a Representative in Congress, from that State, from 1817 to 1821.

Smith, Jedediah K.—He was a Representative in Congress, from New Hampshire, from 1807 to 1809; and from 1822 to 1825 he held the office of Judge and Chief Judge of the Court of Common Pleas for Hillsborough County; from 1810 to 1814 he was also a State Councillor; and died in 1828, aged fifty-eight years.

Smith, Jeremiah.—Born in Peterborough, New Hampshire, and graduated at Rutgers College, New Jersey, in 1780, and also received, from Harvard College, the degree of Doctor of Laws. He was a Representative in Congress, from New Hampshire, in 1791, and continued there till 1797, being one of the last survivors of the distinguished men who participated with Washington in the administration of the government. He was appointed, by John Adams, in 1801, a Judge of the United States Circuit Court, but did not serve, as the office was soon afterwards abolished by Congress. He was chosen Governor of New Hampshire in 1809, and was for several years Chief Justice of the Superior Court of the State. His extraordinary mental endowments not only remained unimpaired, but even shone forth brightest when he was near the close of his long life. Few persons have been more widely known as statesmen and jurists, or have left behind them a more enduring reputation. His acquaintance with books was extensive, and his literary taste remarkably correct and pure. He was highly esteemed, not only as a lawyer and judge, but for his eminent social qualifications, and for all the attributes of a great and good man. He was a patron and friend of Daniel Webster, and died at Dover, New Hampshire, September 21, 1843.

Smith, John.—He was a Representative in Congress, from New York, from 1799 to 1804; from 1804 to 1813 he was a Senator in Congress; and was appointed, in the latter year, by President Madison, United States Marshal for New York. He died in 1816.

Smith, John,—He was a Representative in Congress, from Virginia, from 1801 to 1815.

Smith, John.—He was born in 1735, was a Senator in Congress, from Ohio, from 1803 to 1808, and died in July, 1816.

Smith, John.—He was born at Barre, Massachusetts, in August, 1789; received a limited education, and removed in early life to St. Alban's, Vermont, where he was admitted to practice as a lawyer in 1810. He represented St. Alban's in the Legislature for nine successive years, and was elected State's Attorney of Franklin County in 1826, and served six years. In 1831, 1832, and 1833, he was Speaker in the General Assembly. He was a Representative in Congress, from Vermont, from 1839 to 1841, after which he resumed the practice of his profession. In 1846 he became enlisted in important railroad projects, and was so engaged at the time of his sudden death, which occurred at St. Alban's, November 20, 1858. He received the degree of A.M. from Middlebury College and the University of Vermont.

Smith, John B.—He was a Representative in Congress, from Louisiana, from 1853 to 1855.

Smith, John Cotton.—He was born in Sharon, Connecticut, February 12, 1765, and graduated at Yale College in 1783. He studied law, and was admitted to practice, in Litchfield County, in 1786. He was a member of the General Assembly in 1793, and from 1796 to 1800 was a member of the Lower House, and in 1799 was elected Speaker. He was a Representative in Congress, from Connecticut, from 1800 to 1806, and was again a member of the Legislature until 1809, when he was chosen a member of the Council. He also held the several offices of Governor of Connecticut, from 1812 to 1817, Lieutenant-Governor, and Judge of the Superior Court. He received the degree of LL.D. from Yale College; was a member of the Northern Society of Antiquaries in Copenhagen; also of the Connecticut Historical Society, and of various religious associations. He died at Sharon, Connecticut, November 7, 1845, and had devoted the latter years of his life to agricultural and literary pursuits.

Smith, John Speed.—Was born in Jessamine County, Kentucky, July 31, 1792; served as a soldier under General Harrison, and was at the battle of Tippecanoe; was aide-de-camp to the same General at the battle of the Thames, in 1813. In 1819 he was elected to the Legislature of Kentucky; and was a Representative in Congress, from Kentucky, from 1821 to 1823. In 1827 he was again elected to the State Legislature, and made Speaker of the House; and subsequently served several terms both in the House and Senate. By President Jackson, he was appointed

United States Attorney for the District of Kentucky; was at one time a Commissioner to the Legislature of Ohio, on a mission of local interest; and also Superintendent of Public Works in Kentucky for several years. Died in Madison County, Kentucky, June 6, 1854.

Smith, John T.—He was born in Pennsylvania, and elected a Representative in Congress, from that State, from 1843 to 1845, and was a member of the Committee on Expenditures in the State Department.

Smith, Josiah.—He was born at Pembroke, Massachusetts, in 1745; graduated at Harvard University in 1774; was a Representative in Congress, from Massachusetts, from 1801 to 1803. On his return from Washington, in March, 1803, he took the small-pox in New York, and died at home before the close of the month.

Smith, Nathan.—He was born at Roxbury, Connecticut, in 1770; received his professional education at the Law School in Litchfield; was a member of the Convention that formed the State Constitution; for many years State's Attorney for the County of New Haven; frequently in the State Legislature, and for several years United States Attorney for the District of Connecticut. He represented his native State in the Senate of the United States, from 1833 to 1835. He was long known as an eminent lawyer, respected for his integrity and ability. He died at Washington, District of Columbia, December 6, 1836.

Smith, Nathaniel.—He was born in Woodbury, Connecticut, January 6, 1762. His education was limited, but he obtained distinction by the energy of his talents. He studied law, and settled in practice in his native town, in 1789. He was for many years a member of the State Legislature, having served in both Houses. He was a Representative in Congress, from that State, from 1795 to 1799. In 1806 he was elected Judge of the Supreme Court of the State, and held the office until 1819. His legal knowledge was extensive, and he was greatly esteemed for his integrity and piety. He died March 9, 1822.

Smith, Oliver Hampton.—He was born near Trenton, New Jersey, October 23, 1794, and died at Indianapolis, Indiana, March 19, 1859, having, from 1817 and the balance of his life, been honorably identified with the public history of that State. He studied law, and in 1824 he was Prosecuting Attorney for the Third District of Indiana. He was elected to the State Legislature in 1822; was a Representative in Congress, from Indiana, from 1827 to 1829; and a Senator in Congress, from 1837 to 1843. He was the author of a work giving his "Recollections of Congressional Life," originally published in the Indianapolis Journal. When in the Senate he was Chairman of the Committee on Public Lands, and he subsequently devoted much attention to the internal affairs of his adopted State.

Smith, Perry.—Born in Washington, Connecticut; attended the Litchfield Law School, and settled in New Milford in 1807. He was a State Representative for four years, Judge of Probate for two years, and a Senator in Congress, from 1837 to 1843. He died in New Milford in 1852.

Smith, Robert.—Born in Peterborough, New Hampshire, June 12, 1802, and received a limited education. He was a farmer by occupation until he attained his twentieth year, but subsequently engaged in manufacturing and merchandizing. Removing to Illinois in 1832, he served in the Illinois Legislature from 1836 to 1840; was Enrolling and Engrossing Clerk of the House of Representatives of Illinois, from 1840 to 1843, and was then elected to Congress, and served till March 4, 1849, and was re-elected to the Thirty-fifth Congress, being Chairman of the Committee on Mileage. Of late years he has taken an active part in organizing the railroads in his adopted State.

Smith, Samuel.—He was born in Pennsylvania, July 27, 1752. He was a distinguished merchant of Baltimore, and contributed largely to the advancement of that city, of which he was once Mayor. He rose from the rank of Captain to that of Brigadier-General in the Revolutionary war. In 1776 he was a member of the Convention for framing the Constitution of Maryland; and was a Representative in Congress, from that State, from 1793 to 1803, and again from 1816 to 1822; and a Senator in Congress from 1803 to 1815, and again from 1822 to 1833. During a part of the Ninth and Tenth Congresses, he officiated as President *pro tem.* of the Senate. He died suddenly, at Baltimore, April 25, 1839.

Smith, Samuel.—He was a Representative in Congress, from Pennsylvania, from 1805 to 1809.

Smith, Samuel.—Born in 1767, in Peterborough, New Hampshire; held many public positions; was for many years a manufacturer of paper; and a Representative in Congress, from that State, from 1813 to 1815. He died in 1842.

Smith, Samuel A.—He was born in Pennsylvania, and was a Representative in Congress, from Bucks County, Pennsylvania, from 1829 to 1833, serving, during his second term, on the Committee on Agriculture.

Smith, Samuel A.—He was born in Monroe County, Tennessee, June 26, 1822. He lost his father when quite young, and, with limited opportunities for attending school, spent the most of his time on a farm, until he became of age. At that time he began to attend school in earnest, and at the end of three months became a teacher, and for two years alternately attended and taught school in his native county. He also taught school, for awhile, during ten months that he studied law, and was admitted to the bar in 1845. During that year he was elected Attorney-General for the Third Judicial District of Tennessee, which office he held until 1848. He was a Delegate to the National Convention of that year held at Baltimore, and was soon afterwards elected a Presidential Elector, and was again chosen an Elector in 1852. In 1850 he took a deep interest in the affairs of the East Tennessee and Georgia Railroad; and he was elected a Representative, from Tennessee, to the Thirty-third Congress, and re-elected to the Thirty-fourth and Thirty-fifth Congresses, and was Chairman of the Joint Committee on Printing. In 1859 he was appointed, by President Buchanan, Commissioner of the General Land-office, and resigned in February, 1860.

Smith, Thomas.—He was a Representative in Congress, from Pennsylvania, from 1815 to 1817.

Smith, Thomas.—Born in Pennsylvania, and was a Representative in Congress, from Indiana, from 1839 to 1841, and again from 1843 to 1847.

Smith, Truman.—He was born in Roxbury, Litchfield County, Connecticut, November 27, 1791; graduated at Yale College in 1815; he studied law, and was admitted to the bar in 1818; he was elected to the State Legislature in 1831, and re-elected in 1832 and 1834; in 1839 he was elected a Representative in Congress, and re-elected in 1841, 1845, and 1847; in 1849 he took his seat in the United States Senate, for a full term of six years, resigning in 1854. Of late years he has been engaged in the practice of his profession in New York City.

Smith, William.—He was a Delegate to the Continental Congress, from Maryland, from 1777 to 1778, and a Representative under the Constitution, from 1789 to 1791, when he was appointed, by President Washington, Auditor of the Treasury.

Smith, William.—He was a Representative in Congress, from South Carolina, from 1789 to 1799, and resigned on being appointed United States Minister to Portugal, by President John Adams.

Smith, William.—He was born in North Carolina, in 1762; emigrated to South Carolina, and was educated at Mount Zion College. He studied law, and came to the bar in 1792. He was a Senator in Congress, from that State, from 1816 to 1823, and again from 1826 to 1831, officiating on two occasions as President *pro tem.* of the Senate. In 1837 he received the electoral vote of Virginia for Vice-President of the United States. He served in the Legislature of South Carolina, and was Judge of the Superior Court of that State. He was a distinguished supporter of the doctrine of State Rights. He was offered a seat on the bench of the Supreme Court of the United States, but declined it. He spent the latter years of his life in Alabama, and died at Huntsville, in July, 1840.

Smith, William.—Was born in Chesterfield, Virginia, and was a Representative, from that State, to the Nineteenth Congress.

Smith, William.—Born in King George County, Virginia, September 6, 1797. After prosecuting his studies at Plainfield Academy, in Connecticut, and at private schools in Virginia, he studied law, and commenced the practice in 1818. Soon after he was the means of establishing a line of post-coaches through Virginia, the Carolinas, and Georgia, by which he made a fortune; and in 1836 he was elected to the State Legislature; and re-elected in 1840. He was a Representative in Congress, during the term of 1842 and 1843; in 1845 he was elected Governor of Virginia for three years; and in 1853 was re-elected a Representative in Congress, in which position he continued until the breaking out of the Rebellion in 1861. He was Chairman of the Committee on the Laws of Public Printing, and a member of the Committee on Territories, in the Thirty-sixth Congress. He subsequently served as a Brigadier-General in the Virginia army, and was wounded at Antietam.

Smith, William N. H.—Born in Murfreesboro, Hertford County, North Carolina, September 24, 1812; graduated at Yale College in 1834; studied law in New Haven for two years, and was admitted to the bar in 1839; in 1840 he was elected a member of the State House of Commons; in 1848, to the State Senate; before the expiration of his senatorial term he was chosen Solicitor of the First Judicial District, holding the office for eight years; in 1858 he was re-elected to the House of Commons, but resigned his seat; and was elected a Representative, from North Carolina, to the Thirty-sixth Congress, serving as a member of the Committee on Commerce. He took part in the Rebellion of 1861 as a member of the so-called Confederate Congress.

Smith, William R.—He was a Representative in Congress, from Alabama, his native State, from 1851 to 1855, where he acquired reputation by making a demonstration against Kossuth. He has chiefly devoted himself to literature and law, and has had a seat on the bench of Alabama.

Smith, William S.—He was for three years a member of the New York Assembly, and a Representative in Congress, from that State, from 1813 to 1816.

Smithers, Nathaniel B.—He was born in Dover, Delaware, October 8, 1818; graduated at Lafayette College, Pennsylvania, in 1836; studied law, and came to the bar in 1840; was Clerk of the Delaware House of Representatives in 1845 and 1847; in January, 1863, he was appointed Secretary of State for Delaware, which position he resigned, and was elected a Representative, from Delaware, to the Thirty-eighth Congress, serving on the Committee on Elections. He was also a Delegate to the Baltimore Convention of 1864.

Smyth, Alexander.—He was a Representative in Congress, from Virginia, from 1817 to 1825, and again from 1827 to 1830. Died April 17, 1830, in Washington, aged sixty-five years.

Smyth, George W. — Born in North Carolina, and was elected a Representative in Congress, from Texas, from 1853 to 1855.

Sneed, William H.—He was born in Tennessee, and was a Representative in Congress, from that State, from 1855 to 1857.

Snodgrass, John Fryall.—Born in Berkeley County, Virginia, March 2, 1804; was a lawyer by profession, and practised in Parkersburg, Virginia. He was a member of the Virginia Constitutional Convention assembled at Richmond, in 1850; and was a Representative in Congress, from 1853 until his death, which occurred while trying a case in court, in Parkersburg, June 5, 1854.

Snow, William W.—He was born in Massachusetts, and having removed to New York, was elected a Representative, from that State, to the Thirty-second Congress.

Snyder, Adam W.—Born in 1801; frequently served in the State Legislature of Illinois, and was a Representative in Congress, from that State, from 1837 to 1839. He was a candidate for Governor of the State at the time of his death, which occurred at Belleville, Illinois, May 14, 1842.

Snyder, John.—He was born in Pennsylvania, and was elected a Representative in Congress, from that State, from 1841 to 1843, and was a member of the Committee on the Militia.

Sollers, Augustus R.—Born in Maryland, and was elected a Representative in Congress, from his native State, from 1841 to 1843, and again from 1853 to 1855.

Somes, Daniel E.—He was a Representative, from Maine, in the Thirty-sixth Congress, serving as a member of the Committee on Public Expenditures. He was also a member of the Peace Congress of 1861.

Soule, Nathan.—He was a Representative in Congress, from New York, from 1831 to 1833. He was also a member of the State Assembly, from Onondaga, in 1837.

Soulé, Pierre.—Born at Castillon, in the Pyrenees, during the First Consulate of Napoleon. He was destined for the church, and in 1816 was sent to the Jesuits' College at Toulouse. He was afterwards sent to complete his studies at Bordeaux. At the age of fifteen he took part in a conspiracy against the Bourbons, and the plot having been discovered, he was obliged to take refuge in a little village of Navarre, where he remained for more than a year, following the occupation of a shepherd. He was permitted to return to Bordeaux; but he longed for a more exciting scene of action, and accordingly repaired to Paris. Here, in conjunction with Barthelemy and Mery, he established a paper advocating liberal republican sentiments. This soon brought him under the eye of the authorities, and he was put upon his trial. His advocate appealed to the clemency of the court in behalf of the prisoner on the score of his youth. This line of defence did not suit the prisoner, who rose from his seat and addressed the court, denying the criminality of his opinions and conduct. His eloquence did not save him from St. Pelagie, whence he succeeded in making his escape to England. Disappointed in his expectations of obtaining a situation in Chili, which had been promised him, and finding himself alone in a strange country, wholly ignorant of the language, he returned to France. At Havre he met a friend, a captain in the French navy, who advised him to seek an asylum in the United States, and offered him a passage in his ship as far as St. Domingo. He accepted the proposition, and arrived at Port-au-Prince, in September, 1825. From this place he took passage to Baltimore, and finally removed to New Orleans, in the fall of 1825. Having determined to make the law his profession, he first applied himself assiduously to the study of English, and passed his examination for the bar in that language, and was admitted. In 1847 he was elected a Senator in Congress, from Louisiana, to fill a vacancy, and was re-elected, in 1849, for the term of six years. In 1853 he was appointed, by President Pierce, Minister to Spain. In 1862 he was arrested in New Orleans for disloyalty to the Government, and after an imprisonment of some months in Fort Lafayette, he was released, on condition that he would not return to Louisiana until the end of the Rebellion.

Southard, Henry.—Born on Long Island, October, 1749. When he was eight years of age his father removed to Baskingridge, in the Colony of New Jersey. He received but an ordinary education, and, as a day laborer, earned the money to buy a farm. He took an active part in the Revolutionary war, and after the adoption of the Constitution, served nine years in the State Legislature, and was a Representative in Congress, from 1801 to 1811, and from 1815 to 1821. A short time before retiring from Congress, he met his son in joint committee, and they voted together on the Missouri Compromise. He died June 2, 1842. He was a man of superior talents and remarkable memory.

Southard, Isaac.—He was a Representative in Congress, from New Jersey, from 1831 to 1833. Died September 18, 1850.

Southard, Samuel L.—Was the son of Henry Southard; born in Baskingridge, New Jersey, June 9, 1787. He graduated at Princeton in 1804, and soon afterwards removed to Virginia, where he was admitted to the bar. In 1811 he returned to his native State, and rose to a high position as a lawyer. He was, for several years, Deputy Attorney, and in 1814 was admitted as counsellor-at-law, and appointed Law Reporter by the Legislature. In 1815 he was elected to the Legislature, and, in a week after taking his seat, was placed on the bench of the Supreme Court of New Jersey. In 1820 he was a Presidential Elector; in 1821 he was elected a Senator in Congress, serving as President *pro tem.* of that body; remained there until 1823, when he was appointed by President Monroe Secretary of the Navy; he was also acting Secretary of the Treasury, and for a short period acting Secretary of War. In 1822 he was elected a Trustee of Nassau Hall, and also of the Theological Seminary of Princeton. In 1830 he was elected Attorney-General of the State; and in 1832 was Governor of the State. In 1833 he was re-elected to the United States Senate, and served until 1842, and on the death of President Harrison he became the President of the Senate. He is remembered in New Jersey as the "favorite son" of that State. He died at Fredericksburg, Virginia, June 26, 1842.

Southgate, William W.—Born in Kentucky, and was a Representative in Congress, from that State, from 1837 to 1839.

Spaight, Richard D.—He commenced his academic studies in Ireland, and finished his education at the University of Glasgow. He joined the American army in 1778, as aide-de-camp to General Caswell, and was at the battle of Camden in 1780. In 1781 he entered the House of Commons of North Carolina; from 1782 to 1784 was a member of the Continental Congress, and also during the years 1785 and 1786; and he was one of the Delegates to form the Constitution of the United States, to which his name is appended. In 1792 he was again elected to the local Legislature, and was the same year elected Governor of North Carolina. He was a Representative in Congress, from 1798 to 1801, after which he was elected to the State Senate. On Sunday, September 5, 1802, he fought a duel with the Honorable John Stanley, was wounded in the side, and died in about twenty hours.

Spaight, Richard D.—He was the son of the above, and born in Newbern, North Carolina, in 1796. He graduated at the University of that State in 1815; studied law; served four years in the State Legislature; was a Representative in Congress, from 1823 to 1825; he subsequently served ten years in the State Senate, and was Governor of North Carolina in 1835 and 1836. After retiring from that office, he declined all public positions, and devoted himself to agricultural pursuits. He died in 1850.

Spalding, Rufus Paine.—He was born in West Tisbury, Martha's Vineyard, Massachusetts, May 3, 1798. Went with his parents to Connecticut when young; was educated at the Plainfield and Colchester Academies; and graduated at Yale College in 1817; studied law, and, removing to Ohio, commenced the practice of his profession in Trumbull County in 1821; in 1839 he was elected to the Ohio Legislature; re-elected in 1841, and was Speaker of the House; in 1849 he was elected a Judge of the Superior Court, and held the position three years, until the new State Constitution was adopted; and in 1862 he was elected a Representative, from Ohio, to the Thirty-eighth Congress, serving on the Committees on Naval Affairs, and Revolutionary Pensions.

Spalding, Thomas.—He was a Representative in Congress, from Georgia, from 1805 to 1806.

Spangler, David.—He was a Representative in Congress, from Ohio, from 1833 to 1837, and in 1844 was nominated by the Whig party for Governor of the State, but declined the nomination. He died in Coshocton, Ohio, October 18, 1856.

Spangler, Jacob.—Born in 1768; was a Representative in Congress, from Pennsylvania, from 1816 to 1818, and subsequently Surveyor-General of the State. Died at York, Pennsylvania, June 17, 1843.

Spaulding, Elbridge G.—He was born at Summer Hill, Cayuga County, New York, February 24, 1809; was educated at Auburn Academy; taught school, studied law, and was admitted to practice in Genesee County. In 1834 he removed to Buffalo, and in 1836 was Attorney of the Supreme Court of New York, and also Solicitor in Chancery, and in 1839 was Counsellor of the same. In 1836 he was appointed City Clerk of Buffalo; in 1841 he was Alderman, and in 1847 was elected Mayor. In 1848 he was a member of the Assembly of the State; and from 1849 to 1851 he was a Representative in Congress, serving on the Committee on Foreign Relations. In 1853 he was elected Treasurer of the State of New York, and was a member of the Canal Board for two years, and is now President of the Farmers' and Mechanics' Bank of Genesee, at Buffalo. He was also elected to the Thirty-sixth Congress, serving as a member of the Committee of Ways and Means. Re-elected to the Thirty-seventh Congress.

Speed, Thomas.—He was a Representative in Congress, from Kentucky, from 1817 to 1819.

Speight, Jesse.—Born in Greene County, North Carolina, September 22, 1795. His education was limited, but his natural abilities were of a high order. In 1822 he was a member of the House of Commons; in 1823 of the Senate, where he continued until 1827, officiating several years as Speaker; and he was a Representative in Congress, from North Carolina, from 1829 to 1837. He declined a re-election; removing to Mississippi, was elected to the Legislature there, and made Speaker; and from 1845 to 1847, was a Senator in Congress, from his adopted State. He died at Columbus, Mississippi, May 5, 1847.

Spence, John S.—He was a Senator in Congress, from Maryland, from 1837 to 1841, and a Representative from 1823 to 1825, and again from 1836 to 1840. Died October 29, 1840.

Spence, Thomas A.—He graduated at Yale College in 1829; and was elected a Representative in Congress, from Maryland, from 1843 to 1845.

Spencer, Ambrose.—Born in Salisbury, Connecticut, December 13, 1765; in 1799 entered Yale College, and remained three years, but graduated at Harvard University in 1783; studied law, and settled at Hudson, New York. He was a member of the Assembly in 1793; from 1795 to 1798, State Senator; in 1796 Assistant Attorney-General of the Counties of Columbia and Rensselaer, and a member of the Council of Appointment; in 1802 was Attorney-General for the State; in 1804 was chosen Judge, and in 1810 Chief Justice of the Supreme Court of the State. In 1823 he retired from the bench, and was engaged at the bar; and was elected a Representative in Congress, from New York, from 1829 to 1831. He was also Mayor of Albany one term. He retired to the village of Lyons in 1839, and engaged in agricultural pursuits, and in 1844 was President of the National Whig Convention at Baltimore. He died at Lyons, March 13, 1848.

Spencer, Elijah.—He was born in Columbia County, New York, and was a member of the New York Assembly in 1819; and a Representative in Congress, from that State, from 1821 to 1823.

Spencer, J. B.—He served as a Captain in the war of 1812, and was in several engagements; he was in the Legislature of New York in 1831 and 1832; and was a Representative in Congress, from that State, from 1837 to 1839. He subsequently held the various positions of Elector, Magistrate, County Judge, Collector, and Indian Agent. He died at Fort Covington, Kentucky, in March, 1848.

Spencer, John C.—He was born in Hudson, New York, January 8, 1783. He entered Williams College, but soon went to Union College, where he graduated in 1806. President Nott was then at the head of the College, and one of the last professional acts of Mr. Spencer, was to defend in court the President's administration for many years of the affairs of the College. Mr. Spencer was admitted to the bar in 1809, and opened an office in Canandaigua. He lived in Canandaigua until 1845, when he removed to Albany, where he resided until his death. He was Private Secretary to Governor Daniel D. Tompkins, and at the age of nineteen, became connected with public affairs, and from that time until his last illness, no prominent public event occurred in which he did not take an interest. In 1811 he was made Master in Chancery; in 1813 he was Brigade Judge-Advocate in active service on the frontier; in 1814 he was appointed Postmaster of Canandaigua; in 1815 was Assistant Attorney-General for the western part of the State; and in 1816 was elected to Congress, where he remained two years. While there he was one of the Committee who examined into the affairs of the United States Bank, and their report was drawn by his hand. In 1820 he was first elected to the Assembly, and was chosen Speaker. The next year he was returned, but was in the minority. In 1824 he was elected to the State Senate, and served four years. He joined the Anti-masonic party, and was appointed, by Governor Van Buren, Special Attorney-General, under the law passed for that purpose, to prosecute those connected with the alleged abduction of Morgan. In 1832 he was again elected to the Assembly. In 1839 he was appointed Secretary of State and Superintendent of Common Schools, and did much to reduce them to a system. He served for two years. He was appointed Regent of the University in 1840. In October, 1841, he was made Secretary of War, by President Tyler, and in March, 1843, was transferred to the Treasury Department, but resigned in 1844, from his opposition to the annexation of Texas. Mr. Spencer was a successful lawyer, but he achieved his highest fame from his connection with the revision of the statutes of New York. Not content with merely preparing the statutes, he followed them up with a series of essays explaining their purposes. So great confidence was placed in him by the people, that he was selected to revise the whole body of the law of the State; but his advancing age compelled him to decline the task. He was industrious, and a man of intellect and intense energy. He died at Albany, May 18, 1855.

Spencer, Richard.—He was a Representative in Congress, from Maryland, from 1829 to 1831.

Spinner, Francis E.—Born in the town of German Flats, Herkimer County, New York (where the village of Mohawk now stands), January 21, 1802; and received most of his instruction from his father, who was a highly educated German clergyman. For twenty years he was the executive officer of the Mohawk Valley Bank; he held all the commissions, from the Governors of New York, from a Lieutenant to a Major-General of the State Artillery; was County Sheriff, and Commissioner for building the State Lunatic Asylum. From 1845 to 1849 he was Auditor in the Naval Office at New York; and in 1854 was elected a Representative to the Thirty-fourth Congress, and was re-elected to the Thirty-fifth, serving as a member of the Committee on Accounts. He was re-elected to the Thirty-sixth Congress, serving as Chairman of the Committee on Accounts. In 1861 he was appointed, by President Lincoln, United States Treasurer.

Sprague, Peleg.—He was a Representative in Congress, from New Hampshire, from 1797 to 1799, and is supposed to have been the father of the Representative from Maine of the same name.

Sprague, Peleg.—He was born in Duxbury, Massachusetts, son of Seth Sprague, in 1792; graduated at Harvard University with honor in 1812; and having adopted the profession of law, settled in the practice first at Augusta, Maine, and then at Hallowell; he was a member of the Maine Legislature in 1821 and 1822; a Representative in Congress, from Maine, from 1825 to 1829; and a Senator in Congress, from 1829 to 1835. On completing his Senatorial term he settled in Boston, and in 1841 he was appointed Judge of the District Court of the United States for Massachusetts, which office he now holds. In 1847 he received from Harvard the degree of Doctor of Laws.

Sprague, William.—He was born in Cranston, Rhode Island, in 1800. When quite young he was elected to the General Assembly, and in 1832 was chosen Speaker of the House. In 1835 he was chosen Representative to Congress, and declined a re-election. He was Governor of Rhode Island, in 1838 and 1839, and in 1842 was elected to the United States Senate, serving two years.

He was a member of the Assembly of his State at the time of his death, which occurred in Providence, October 19, 1851.

Sprague, William.—He was born in Rhode Island, and, removing to Michigan, was a Representative in Congress, from that State, from 1849 to 1851.

Sprague, William.—Was born in Cranston, Rhode Island, September 11, 1830, his ancestors having been for several generations honorably associated with the manufacturing business of New England; was educated chiefly at the Irving Institute, Tarrytown, New York, and subsequently spent several years in the counting-room of an uncle, on the death of whom one of the largest manufacturing interests in the country came into his possession. Having a taste for military affairs, he joined an artillery company in Providence in his eighteenth year, and became a Colonel; in 1859 he visited Europe, and was friendly to the cause and person of Garibaldi. In 1861 he was elected Governor of Rhode Island, and, on the breaking out of the Rebellion, he took a great interest in the national cause; was with the troops of Rhode Island at the first battle of Bull Run; and in 1862 he was elected a Senator in Congress, from Rhode Island, for the term ending in 1869, serving as Chairman of a newly-formed Committee on Manufactures, and as a member of the Committees on Commerce, and Military Affairs. He is the President of several banks, and, when at home, takes an active part as a Director in various Insurance Companies. His father, bearing the same name, was also a Senator in Congress.

Sprigg, James C.—Born in Maryland, and was elected a Representative in Congress, from Kentucky, from 1841 to 1843.

Sprigg, Michael C.—He was frequently a member of the Maryland Legislature; at one time President of the Chesapeake and Ohio Canal; and a Representative in Congress, from 1827 to 1831. He died at Cumberland, Maryland, in December, 1845.

Sprigg, Richard.—He was a Representative in Congress from Maryland, from 1796 to 1799, and from 1801 to 1802.

Sprigg, Thomas.—He was a Representative in Congress, from Maryland, from 1793 to 1796.

Spruance, Presley.—He was a Senator in Congress, from Delaware, from 1847 to 1853. Died in Smyrna, Delaware, February 13, 1863, aged seventy-eight years.

Stallworth, James A.—Born in Conecuh County, Alabama, April 7, 1822. He received an academic education; studied law; served in the Legislature during the years 1845–6, and 1847–8; was twice elected Solicitor for his District; and was elected a Representative to the Thirty-fifth Congress, serving as a member of the Committee on Commerce. Re-elected to the Thirty-sixth Congress, but resigned in February, 1861, to take part in the Rebellion of that year.

Stanberry, William.—Born in Essex County, New Jersey, and was a Representative in Congress, from Ohio, from 1827 to 1833. He resided in Licking County.

Standifer, James.—He was a Representative in Congress, from Tennessee, from 1823 to 1825, and again from 1829 to 1837. He died near Kingston, Tennessee, August 24, 1836.

Stanford, Richard.—He was a Representative in Congress, from North Carolina, from 1797 to 1816. Died April 9, 1816, in Georgetown, District of Columbia, aged forty-seven years.

Stanley, Edward.—Born in North Carolina, and served three years in the House of Commons, most of the time as Speaker; and was a Representative in Congress, from 1837 to 1843, and again from 1847 to 1853. He subsequently left his native State, and emigrated to California.

Stanley, John.—He was born in North Carolina; was a distinguished member of the Legislature of North Carolina; and a Representative in Congress, from that State, from 1801 to 1803, and again from 1809 to 1811. He was an able and eloquent debater, greatly respected for his talents and private character. While delivering a speech in the Legislature, in 1826, he was arrested by an attack of hemiplegia, from the effects of which he suffered until his death, August 3, 1834, at Newbern, North Carolina.

Stanton, Benjamin.—Born at Mount Pleasant, Jefferson County, Ohio, June 4, 1809. He lived on a farm until the age of seventeen, and then worked at the trade of a tailor until he was twenty-one. He studied law, and settled in Bellefontaine, Ohio, in April, 1834, where he practised his profession. He was elected to the State Senate in 1841; resigned in 1842, but was re-elected the same year. In 1850 he was a Delegate to the Ohio Constitutional Convention, and in October of that year was elected to the House of Representatives of the Thirty-second Congress. He was re-elected to the Thirty-fourth and Thirty-fifth Congresses; and was one of the Regents of the Smithsonian Institution, and a member of the Committee on Military Affairs. He was also re-elected to the Thirty-sixth Congress, serving as Chairman of the Committee on Military Affairs. In 1862 he was Lieutenant-Governor of Ohio.

Stanton, Frederick P.—Born in the District of Columbia, and was elected a Representative in Congress, from Tennessee, from 1845 to 1847, and again from 1847 to 1855.

Stanton, Joseph.—He was a Senator in Congress, from Rhode Island, from 1790 to 1793, and was a Representative in Congress, from 1801 to 1807.

Stanton, Richard H.—Born in the District of Columbia, and was a Representative in Congress, from Kentucky, from 1849 to 1855.

Stark, Benjamin.—Born in the city of New Orleans, June 26, 1820; received an academic education in New London, Connecticut, and a commercial education in the city of New York. In 1845 he settled in Oregon and established commercial relations with the Sandwich Islands, and with California when a Mexican province; in 1850 he abandoned commercial pursuits, studied law and came to the bar in 1851; in 1852 he was a member of the Territorial Legislature of Oregon; in 1860 of the State Legislature of that State; and he was a Senator in Congress, from Oregon, during a part of the years 1861–2, the Thirty-seventh Congress. In 1845 he erected in Portland, Oregon, his present residence, the first building, which was a log trading-house. He was also a Delegate to the Chicago Convention of 1864.

Starkweather, David A.—Born in Connecticut, and was elected a Representative in Congress, from Ohio, from 1839 to 1841, and again from 1845 to 1847.

Starkweather, George A.—Born in Connecticut, and was a Representative in Congress, from New York, from 1847 to 1849, and was a member of the Committee on Accounts.

Starr, John F.—Born in Philadelphia in 1818; removed to New Jersey in 1844; has been engaged in business pursuits; and in 1863 he was elected a Representative, from New Jersey, to the Thirty-eighth Congress, serving on the Committee on Manufactures, and that on Public Buildings and Grounds.

Stearns, Asahel.—He was born at Lunenburg, Massachusetts, in 1774; graduated at Cambridge University in 1797; was educated as a lawyer; practised with reputation many years at Chelmsford; was several years County Attorney for Middlesex County; was a Representative in Congress, from Massachusetts, from 1815 to 1817; was appointed Professor of Law at Cambridge in 1817, and continued in the office till 1829, when he resigned. In 1824 he published a volume on Real Actions,—a learned work. He was afterwards appointed one of the Commissioners for revising the statutes of the Commonwealth. After this work was completed, his health declined, and he continued very feeble till his decease. He died at Cambridge, Massachusetts, February 5, 1839.

Stebbins, Henry G.—Was born in the city of New York in 1812; received a good education; was brought up to the business of banking, and has been identified with many of the important financial events and trusts of his native city. He was at one time identified with the militia of New York, and was Colonel of the Twelfth Regiment. He was one of the Commissioners of the Park, and long President of the Board of Commissioners. He was one of the originators and President of the Dramatic Fund Association, and an active manager of the New York Academy of Music. In 1862 he was elected a Representative, from New York, to the Thirty-eighth Congress, serving on the Committee of Ways and Means. In October, 1864, he resigned his seat in Congress, because he had declared himself in favor of the war, and therefore supposed that he did not represent the peace principles of his constituents.

Stedman, William.—He graduated at Harvard University in 1784; was a lawyer of extensive practice; served in the State Legislature; was for several years Clerk of the Supreme Judicial Court in Worcester; and was a Representative in Congress, from Massachusetts, from 1803 to 1810; and died in 1831, at Newburyport, Massachusetts, aged sixty-six years. He came to the bar in 1787, and was in the Legislature in 1802.

Steele, John.—A Representative in Congress, from North Carolina, from 1790 to 1793. He was born in Salisbury, November 1, 1764, and died August 14, 1815. He was brought up a merchant, but turned his attention to agricultural pursuits. He served a number of years in the State Legislature, part of the time as Speaker; was a member of the State Convention to consider the Constitution of the United States; he was, in 1806, Commissioner to adjust the boundaries between the States of North and South Carolina; was a General of the militia; and held the office of First Comptroller of the Treasury, under Presidents Washington and Adams. On August 14, 1815, he was again elected to the Legislature, but on that day he died.

Steele, John B.—Was born in Delhi, Delaware County, New York, March 28, 1814; was educated at Delaware Academy and at Williams College, Massachusetts; studied law, and came to the bar in 1839; in 1841 was appointed District Attorney for Otsego County, and served his term; in 1847 removed to Kingston, Ulster County, and there pursued his profession; in 1850 was elected Special Judge of that county; and in 1860 was elected a Representative, from New York, to the Thirty-seventh Congress, serving on the Committees on the District of Columbia, and on Revolutionary Pensions. Re-elected to the Thirty-eighth Congress, again serving on the Committees for the District of Columbia, and on Expenditures in the War Department.

Steele, John N.—Born in Maryland, and elected a Representative in Congress, from that State, from 1835 to 1837.

Steele, William G.—Was born in Somerset County, New Jersey, December 17, 1820; educated at the Somerville Academy; entered early into the mercantile business, to which he subsequently added that of banking; was appointed, for several years, by the Governor of the State, a State Director for the Delaware and Raritan Canal, and the Camden and Amboy Railroad Company; was elected a Representative, from New Jersey, to the Thirty-seventh Congress, serving on the Select Committee on Army Contracts; and he was re-elected to the Thirty-eighth Congress, serving on the Committees on Accounts, and Enrolled Bills. He was also a Delegate to the Chicago Convention of 1864.

Steenrod, Lewis.—Born in Virginia, and elected a Representative in Congress, from that State, from 1839 to 1845.

Stephens, Abraham P.—Born in New York, and elected a Representative in Congress, from that State, from 1851 to 1853.

Stephens, Alexander H.—Born in Taliaferro County, Georgia, February 11, 1812. He was left an orphan at the age of fourteen, when kind friends, unsolicited, furnished him with the means to obtain an education, all of which he subsequently returned with interest. He prepared himself for college in nine months, and graduated at Franklin College in 1832. He studied law, and was admitted to practice in 1834. After paying his debts, his first earnings were devoted to redeeming from the hands of strangers the home of his childhood, which had been sold after his father's death, and upon which he still resides. In 1836 he was elected to the lower house of the State Legislature, where he served five years, devoting himself especially to the internal interests of his native State. In 1839 he was chosen a Delegate to the Commercial Convention at Charleston, where he is said to have made a deep impression by his peculiar eloquence. In 1842 he was elected to the Senate of his State; and in 1843 he was elected a Representative in Congress, from Georgia, to which position he was regularly re-elected to the close of the Thirty-fifth Congress. He has served on many committees, delivered many speeches; and it was while he officiated as Chairman of the Committee on Territories that the Territories of Minnesota and Oregon were admitted into the Union. He subsequently became identified with the Rebellion of 1861, and was chosen Vice-President and member of Congress of the so-called "Southern Confederacy."

Stephens, Philander. — Was a member of the House of Representatives in Congress, from Pennsylvania, from 1829 to 1833. He died at Springfield, Pennsylvania, July 8, 1842, aged fifty-four years.

Stephenson, Benjamin.—He was a Delegate in Congress, from Illinois Territory, from 1815 to 1816, when he was appointed Receiver of Public Moneys in Edwardsville, Illinois.

Stephenson, James. — He was born in Gettysburg, Pennsylvania, March 20, 1764; and having removed to Virginia at an early day, commanded a company in the campaign of General St. Clair; was present at the quelling of the Whiskey Insurrection in Pennsylvania, and was promoted to the office of Brigade Inspector; he served for many years as a Delegate to the Virginia Assembly; and was a Representative in Congress, from Virginia, from 1803 to 1805, from 1809 to 1811, and again from 1822 to 1825. He died in August, 1833.

Stephenson, James S. — He was born in York County, Pennsylvania; and was a Representative in Congress, from Pennsylvania, from 1825 to 1829; and died at Pittsburg, October 17, 1831.

Sterigere, John B.—He was born in Pennsylvania, and was a Representative in Congress, from Montgomery County, Pennsylvania, from 1827 to 1831; and a member, in 1829, of the Committee on Private Land Claims.

Sterling, Ansel.—He was a native of New London County, Connecticut, and a Representative in Congress, from that State, from 1821 to 1825.

Sterling, Micah.—Born at Lyme, Connecticut, in 1781, and graduated at Yale College in 1804. He removed to the State of New York, and was for some years a member of the Legislature; and a Representative in Congress, from 1821 to 1823. He died at Watertown, New York, April 10, 1844.

Sterrett, Samuel.—He was a member of the House of Representatives of the United States, from Maryland, from 1791 to 1793; and died at Baltimore, July 12, 1833, aged seventy-seven years.

Stetson, Charles.—Born in New Hampshire, and was a Representative in Congress, from Maine, from 1849 to 1851.

Stetson, Lemuel B.—He was born in New York; bred to the law; served for three years in the Assembly of that State; and was a Representative in Congress, from 1843 to 1845, from the same State.

Stevens, Hestor L.—He was born in Lima, Livingston County, New York, in October, 1803; received a good English and classical education; adopted the profession of law; was for several years connected with the press in Rochester; and having taken up his residence in Michigan, was elected a Representative in Congress, from that State, from 1853 to 1855. Died in Georgetown, D. C., May 7, 1864.

Stevens, Isaac I.—He was born in North Andover, Massachusetts, in 1818; graduated at the West Point Military Academy in 1839, and entered the Corps of Engineers, in which service he continued until 1853, when he was appointed Governor and Superintendent of Indian Affairs for the Territory of Washington. This office he resigned in 1857, having previously been elected a Delegate to Congress, from Washington Territory, where he continued until the breaking out of the Rebellion in 1861. As an officer of the army, he was at the siege of Vera Cruz, under General Scott; fought in several subsequent battles; was severely wounded in the final assault upon the city of Mexico, and was twice breveted for gallant services. He also served for a time as an assistant in the Coast Survey Office in Washington City. When Governor of Washington Territory, he travelled throughout its whole extent, and as Commissioner made many treaties with the Indian tribes. In September, 1861, he was appointed a Brigadier-General in the volunteer service, and was killed in battle, in Virginia, in 1862.

Stevens, James.—He was born in Fairfield, Connecticut; served in Congress as a Representative, from that State, from 1819 to 1821, voting with the South on the Missouri Compromise; and in 1822 was appointed Postmaster at Stamford; he died at that place, in April, 1835, aged sixty-seven years.

Stevens, Thaddeus.—Born in Caledonia County, Vermont, April 4, 1793; graduated at Dartmouth College in 1814; during that year removed to Pennsylvania; studied law and taught in an academy at the same time; in 1816 was admitted to the bar in Adams County; in 1833 was elected to the State Legislature, and also in 1834, 1835, 1837, and 1841; in 1836 was elected a member to the Convention to revise the State Constitution; in 1838 was appointed a Canal Commissioner; in 1842 he removed to Lancaster; and in 1848 was elected a Representative, from Pennsylvania, to the Thirty-first Congress, also to the Thirty-second; and in 1858 was re-elected to the Thirty-sixth Congress, and also to the Thirty-seventh, during which he was Chairman of the Committee of Ways and Means, having previously served on various important committees. In 1862 he was re-elected to the Thirty-eighth Congress, again serving as Chairman of the Committee of Ways and Means. He was also a Delegate to the Baltimore Convention of 1864.

Stevenson, Andrew.—He was a native of Culpeper County, Virginia, and entered public life in 1804, as a member of the State Legislature, where, after several sessions, he was elected Speaker of the House. He was a Representative in Congress, from Virginia, from 1821 to 1834; and for the Twentieth, Twenty-first, and Twenty-second Congresses, from 1828 to 1834, was Speaker. He was appointed Minister to Great Britain in 1836, and remained there till he was succeeded by Mr. Everett in 1841. After his return to America, he devoted himself chiefly to agricultural pursuits, and to the interests of the University of Virginia, of which institution he was Rector at the time of his death. As a friend and neighbor he was much beloved. He died at Blenheim, Albemarle County, Virginia, January 25, 1857, aged seventy-three.

Stevenson, John W.—Born in Richmond, Virginia; graduated at the University of Virginia; read law; and settled in Covington, Kentucky in 1841, practising his profession with success; was elected to the Kentucky Legislature in 1845, 1846, and 1847; in 1849 he was elected to the State Constitutional Convention, in which he took a leading part; he was a member of the Democratic National Conventions of 1848, 1852, and 1856; he was twice a Senatorial Elector; and was one of three Commissioners appointed to revise the Civil and Criminal Code of Kentucky; and was elected a Representative to the Thirty-fifth Congress, from that State, and was a member of the Committee on Elections. He was also re-elected to the Thirty-sixth Congress, serving on the same Committee.

Stewart, Andrew.—Born in Fayette County, Pennsylvania, in June, 1792. He studied law, and was admitted to the bar in 1815; was soon afterwards elected to the State Legislature, and served three years; he was appointed, by President Monroe, District Attorney for Western Pennsylvania; and was a Representative in Congress, from 1821 to 1829, from 1831 to 1835, and from 1843 to 1847. In Congress and out of it, he was ever a warm advocate of what is known as the "American Protective System," and of late years he has been devoted chiefly to the congenial pursuits of agriculture, though paying some attention to the business of manufacturing.

Stewart, David.—He was a lawyer by profession, and a Senator in Congress, from Maryland, from 1849 to 1850, by Executive appointment. Died in Baltimore, Maryland, January 6, 1858.

Stewart, James.—He was a Representative in Congress, from North Carolina, during the years 1818 and 1819. Died in North Carolina in February, 1822, aged fifty-two years.

Stewart, James A.—He was born in Dorchester County, Maryland, November 24, 1808; received a good education, and studied law; served in the State Legislature; was a Judge of the Circuit Court of Maryland; and was elected a Representative, from Maryland, to the Thirty-fourth and Thirty-fifth Congresses, serving as Chairman of the Committee on Patents. He was also elected to the Thirty-sixth Congress, serving on the same Committee.

Stewart, John.—He was a Representative in Congress, from Pennsylvania, from 1800 to 1805.

Stewart, John.—Born in Chatham, Connecticut, in 1795; was by occupation a farmer; served many years in the Connecticut Legislature; was Judge of Middlesex County Court; and was a Representative in Congress, from Connecticut, from 1843 to 1845. Died at Chatham, September 16, 1860.

Stewart, William.—He was born in the town of Mercer, Mercer County, Pennsylvania, September 16, 1811; was educated at Jefferson College, in that State; studied law, and was admitted to practice in 1835. He was a member of the State Senate of Pennsylvania for three years, and was elected a Representative, from that State, to the Thirty-fifth Congress, and re-elected to the Thirty-sixth, serving as a member of the Committees on Expenses in the War Department, and on Agriculture.

Stiles, John D.—Was born in Luzerne County, Pennsylvania, January 15, 1823; received an academic education; studied law, and was admitted to the bar in 1844; in 1853 he was elected District Attorney for Lehigh County, and held the office three years; he was a Delegate in 1856 to the National Convention which nominated Mr. Buchanan for President, and was elected to the Thirty-seventh Congress, for the unexpired term of T. B. Cooper, deceased (against whom he had run in the previous election), serving on the Committee on Revolutionary Claims. In 1862 he was re-elected to the Thirty-eighth Congress, serving on the Committees on Expenditures in the State Department, and Revolutionary Claims. He was also a Delegate to the Chicago Convention of 1864.

Stiles, William H.—He was born in Georgia, and was elected a Representative in Congress, from that State, from 1843 to 1845, and before leaving Washington, was appointed Chargé d'Affaires to Austria.

St. John, Daniel B.—Born in Sharon, Litchfield County, Connecticut, October 8, 1808; removed to New York; became a merchant's clerk, and then followed the mercantile business until 1847; in 1839 was elected to the State Legislature; served four years as a member of the Board of Supervisors for Sullivan County; and was a Representative, from New York, to the Thirtieth Congress. From 1849 until 1855, he had charge of the Bank Department of New York, since which time he has been devoted to agricultural pursuits in Newburg, New York.

St. John, Henry.—He was born in New York, and was a Representative in Congress, from Ohio, from 1843 to 1847.

St. Martin, Louis.—He was born in Louisiana, and was a Representative in Congress, from that State, from 1851 to 1853.

Stockton, Richard. — Born at Princeton, New Jersey, April 17, 1764, and graduated at Nassau Hall in 1779; on leaving college he studied law, and was admitted to practice at the age of twenty. In 1792 he was a Presidential Elector. He was a Senator of the United States from 1796 to 1799, and a Representative in Congress, from 1813 to 1815. In 1827 he was a Commissioner for settling the boundary line between

New York and New Jersey. He was eminently distinguished for his talents, was an eloquent and profound lawyer, and during more than a quarter of a century, was at the head of the bar in New Jersey. He died at Princeton, March 7, 1828.

Stockton, Robert Field.—He was born at Princeton, New Jersey. Early in life he entered the United States Navy, and was actively engaged in some of the most important naval battles during the war of 1812. He commanded the American squadron on the coast of Africa, and he was one of the founders of the colony of Liberia. He was one of the first of our commanders to introduce and apply steam to naval purposes, the famous sloop-of-war Princeton having been built under his supervision. When war was declared with Mexico, he was placed in command of our fleet in the Pacific, and performed the duties of Commodore, General, and Governor, and the foundation of religion, education, and social progress were laid by his instrumentality in many of those outposts of our Western world. Soon after his return from the Pacific, he resigned his commission in the navy, and devoted himself to the internal improvement of his native State. He was elected United States Senator from 1851 to 1857, serving as a member of several important committees. The bill to abolish flogging in the navy was introduced by him. He was also elected a Delegate to the Peace Congress of 1861.

Stoddart, Ebenezer. — Born in West Woodstock, Connecticut, May 6, 1786, and graduated at Brown University in 1806; he was a lawyer by profession, and practised extensively; had several years been a member of the State Legislature; and was Lieutenant-Governor of the State for one year. He was a Representative in Congress, from 1821 to 1825, and died at Woodstock, August, 1848.

Stoddart, John T.—He was a Representative in Congress, from Maryland, from 1833 to 1835, and was a member of the Committees on Claims, and on the District of Columbia.

Stokely, Samuel.—He was born in Ohio; received a liberal education; adopted the profession of law; served in the State Legislature; and was a Representative in Congress, from Ohio, from 1841 to 1843, serving on two prominent committees.

Stokes, Montford.—Born in North Carolina in 1760; was for several years Clerk of the Superior Court, and subsequently of the Senate; in which capacity he became so popular as to be elected to the United States Senate, which honor he declined. He was again elected in 1816 to the same position, and served until 1823. In 1826 he went into the General Assembly as Senator; in 1829 into the Commons; also in 1830, when he was elected Governor of the State. In 1831 he was appointed by President Jackson Indian Agent in Arkansas, where he died, in 1842.

Stokes, William B.—He was born in Chatham County, North Carolina, September 9, 1814; received, when young, only a limited education; has devoted the most of his life to agricultural pursuits; served three sessions in the Legislature of Tennessee, twice as a Representative and once as a Senator; and was elected a Representative, from Tennessee, to the Thirty-sixth Congress, serving as a member of the Committee on Invalid Pensions. During the Rebellion of 1861 he served as a Colonel in the Union army.

Stone, Alfred P.—He was a Representative in Congress, from Ohio, from 1844 to 1845.

Stone, David. — Born in Bertie County, North Carolina, February 17, 1770; graduated at Princeton College in 1788; studied law, and rose to a high position at the bar. He was four years in the State Legislature; Judge of the Supreme Court from 1795 to 1798; a Representative in Congress, from 1799 to 1801; a Senator in Congress, from 1801 to 1807; Governor of North Carolina in 1808; and served a second term as United States Senator, from 1813 to 1814, which position he resigned on account of disagreements with his constituents. Died October 7, 1818.

Stone, James.—Born in Kentucky, and was a Representative in Congress, from that State, from 1843 to 1845.

Stone, James W.—Born in Kentucky in 1813, and died October 13, 1854. He was a Representative in Congress, from 1843 to 1845, and again from 1851 to 1853.

Stone, Michael.—He was born in Charles County, Maryland, about the year 1750, and died in 1812. He was a Representative in Congress, from his native State, from 1789 to 1791; and was subsequently, for many years, Judge of the Charles County Court.

Stone, William.—He was a Representative in Congress, from Tennessee, from 1838 to 1839.

Storer, Bellamy.—He was a Representative in Congress, from Ohio, from 1835 to 1837, and was a member of the Committee on Revolutionary Pensions. He adopted the profession of law, and was a Judge in Cincinnati.

Storer, Clement.—He was born in 1760, and died at Portsmouth, New Hampshire, November 22, 1830. He was a United States Senator, from New Hampshire, from 1817 to 1819.

Storrs, Henry R.—Born in Middletown, Connecticut, in 1787. He graduated at Yale College in 1804; practised law some years at Utica, New York; and during his residence there, was a Representative in Congress, from 1819 to 1821, and from 1823 to 1831. He afterwards established himself in the city of New York, where he soon became a very eminent practitioner in his profession. He was possessed of extensive and various acquirements, uncommon powers of discrimination, great logical exactness, and a ready and powerful elocution; and as a debater in Congress, he stood conspicuous in the first rank. He died July 29, 1837, at New Haven.

Storrs, William L.—He was born in Connecticut; graduated at Yale College in 1814; adopted the law as a profession; was a Representative in Congress, from Connecticut, from 1829 to 1833, and again from 1839 to 1840; and was for many years the Chief Justice of the Supreme Court of Connecticut.

Story, Joseph.—Born in Marblehead, Massachusetts, September 18, 1779. He graduated at Harvard College in 1798; studied law; was a member of the State Legislature in 1805, and elected Speaker; and during the years 1808 and 1809 he was a Representative in Congress. In 1811 he was appointed by President Madison a Judge of the Supreme Court of the United States, which office he held until his death. He acquired a large fortune from his practice as a lawyer, and it is said that his income from the sale of his legal writings, which are numerous and of the highest order, numbering twenty-seven volumes, with thirty-four volumes of Decisions, has amounted to ten thousand dollars per annum. In 1830 he was appointed Dane Professor in the Law School of Harvard University, and subsequently published his Commentaries on the Constitution of the United States. In early life he was a writer of poetry, and in his later years, was considered, even in England, "the first of living writers on law." He received the degree of LL.D. from the Colleges of Harvard, Brown, and Dartmouth. He died in Cambridge, September 10, 1845. His Life was published by his son, W. W. Story, in 1851.

Stout, Lansing. — Born in Pamelia, New York, March 27, 1828; received a limited education, and commenced active life by working on a farm and teaching school; became a Superintendent of public schools, and studied law; went to California in 1851, and in 1856 was elected to the California Legislature; in 1857 he went to Oregon, and turned his attention to the practice of law; in 1858 was elected Judge of Multnomah County; and before the close of that year was elected a Representative, from Oregon, to the Thirty-sixth Congress, serving as a member of the Committee on Expenses in the State Department.

Stow, Silas.—He was a Representative in Congress, from New York, from 1811 to 1813.

Stower, John G.—He was a Representative in Congress, from New York, from 1827 to 1829, and was a State Senator, from Madison County, in 1833 and 1834.

Stranahan, J. S. T.—He was born in New York, and was a Representative in Congress, from that State, from 1855 to 1857.

Strange, Robert.—Born in Virginia, September 20, 1796; educated at Hampden Sidney College; studied law, and removed to North Carolina, where he took a high position in his profession; he served a number of years in the State Legislature; was elected in 1826 a Judge of the Superior Court; and held the office until he was elected a Senator of the United States, from 1836 to 1841, but resigned his seat in 1840, having received from his State instructions incompatible with his ideas of duty. He was subsequently appointed Solicitor for the Fifth Judicial District of the State, and toward the close of his life, was wholly devoted to his profession. He died in 1854.

Stratton, Charles C.—Born in New Jersey in 1796; was an active politician; served a number of years in the State Legislature; and was a Representative in Congress, from New Jersey, from 1837 to 1839, and again from 1841 to 1843. He was also a member of the Constitutional Convention of 1844, and Governor of New Jersey, from 1844 to 1848, after which he retired to his farm in Gloucester County, where he died, March 30, 1859. He was a candidate for election to the Twenty-sixth Congress, and although he appeared with the broad seal of his State, he was not admitted.

Stratton, John.—He was a Representative in Congress, from Virginia, from 1801 to 1803.

Stratton, John L. N.—Born in Mount Holly, New Jersey, in 1817; graduated at Princeton College in 1836; studied law, and was admitted to the bar in 1839; and in 1858 he was elected a Representative, from New Jersey, to the Thirty-sixth Congress, serving as a member of the Committee on Elections. Re-elected to the Thirty-seventh Congress, serving on the Committees of Ways and Means, and on National Armories.

Stratton, Nathan T.—Born in New Jersey, and was a Representative in Congress, from that State, from 1851 to 1855.

Straub, Christian M.—Born in Pennsylvania, and was a Representative in Congress, from that State, from 1853 to 1855.

Street, Randall S.—He was born in New Haven, Connecticut, and was a Representative in Congress, from New York, from 1819 to 1821.

Strohm, John.—He was born, October 16, 1793, in Lancaster County, Pennsylvania, in what is now Fulton Township; received a common school education, and taught a school for six years. In 1831 he was elected a Representative in the Legislature of his native State, serving three sessions in the House and eight in the Senate, and during one term as Speaker. He was a Representative in Congress, from 1845 to 1847, and for a second term ending in 1849.

Strong, Caleb.—Born in Northampton, Massachusetts, January, 1745, and graduated at Harvard College in 1764. In consequence of poor health he did not commence the practice of law for eight years afterwards. He spent his life at Northampton, where his paternal ancestors had lived from the year 1659. In 1775 he was a member of the Committee of Safety; and in 1780 he was chosen one of the Council of Massachusetts. In 1779 he assisted in forming the Constitution of that State; and in 1787 he also assisted in forming the Constitution of the United States. From 1789 to 1797 he was a Senator in Congress, and from 1800 to 1807 he was Governor of the State; also, from 1812 to 1816. Governor Strong was a man of unimpeachable moral character, and he possessed a vigorous and well-cultivated mind. He died November 7, 1819.

Strong, James.—He was born in Windham, Connecticut, in 1783, and graduated at the University of Vermont in 1806; was a Representative in Congress, from New York, from 1819 to 1821; and again from 1823 to 1831. He died in Chester, New Jersey, August 8, 1847.

Strong, Selah B.—He was born in Brookhaven, Long Island, May 1, 1792; graduated at Yale College in 1811; studied law, and was admitted to the bar in 1814; was at one time Attorney for

Suffolk County; a Representative, in Congress, from 1843 to 1845; and was appointed, in 1847, a Judge of the Supreme Court of New York.

Strong, Solomon.—He was a Representative in Congress, from Massachusetts, from 1815 to 1819. He was also a member of the State Legislature in 1812, 1813, 1843, and 1844; Judge of the Court of Common Pleas from 1818 to 1842; and died September 16, 1850, aged seventy-one years.

Strong, Stephen.—He was born in Connecticut, and was a Representative in Congress, from New York, from 1845 to 1847.

Strong, Theron R.—He was born in Connecticut; served in the Assembly of New York, from Wayne County, in 1842; and was a Representative in Congress, from New York, from 1839 to 1841.

Strong, William.—He was born in Windham County, Connecticut, and was a Representative in Congress, from Vermont, from 1811 to 1815, and again from 1819 to 1821. He was also a Sheriff for eight years in Hartford County; Judge of the same County; and member of the State Legislature for eight years.

Strong, William.—Born in Somers, Tolland County, Connecticut, May 6, 1808; attended Plainfield Academy, and graduated at Yale College in 1828; taught school in Connecticut and New Jersey; studied law in New Haven, and was admitted to the bar, in Philadelphia, in 1832; and was a Representative in Congress, from Pennsylvania, from 1847 to 1851.

Strother, George F.—He was a native of Culpeper County, Virginia, a lawyer by profession, and a Representative in Congress, from Virginia, from 1817 to 1820, when he was appointed Receiver of Public Moneys at St. Louis, Missouri.

Strother, James F.—He was born in Culpeper County, Virginia, September 4, 1811; received a collegiate education, and adopted the profession of law. He served ten years in the Legislature of Virginia, having occupied the chair of Speaker during the sessions of 1847 and 1848. He was a member, in 1850, of the Convention which formed the present Constitution of the State; and a Representative in Congress, from 1851 to 1853. Died in Culpeper County, September 20, 1860.

Strouse, Myer.—Was born in Germany, December 16, 1825; came with his father to the United States in 1832, and settled in Pottsville, Pennsylvania; received an academic education and studied law; from 1848 to 1852 he edited a newspaper in Philadelphia, called the North American Farmer, after which he devoted himself to the practice of his profession; and in 1862 he was elected a Representative, from Pennsylvania, to the Thirty-eighth Congress, serving on the Committee on Roads and Canals.

Strudwick, William E.—He was a Representative in Congress, from Maryland, from 1796 to 1797.

Stuart, Alexander H. H.—He was born in Staunton, Virginia, April 2, 1807; his early education was received at the Staunton Academy, and in 1824 he spent one session at William and Mary College; he then commenced the study of law, which he finished at the University of Virginia, in 1828, and was admitted to practice in Staunton in that year. His political career began as a member of the Young Men's Convention in Washington, in 1832. In 1836 he was elected a member of the House of Delegates, of Virginia, from the County of Augusta, and was reelected in 1837 and 1838. In 1839 he declined a re-election and pursued the practice of law. He took an active part in the canvass of 1840, for President Harrison. In 1841 he was elected a Representative in Congress, from Virginia, and served till 1843. In 1844 he delivered the annual address before the American Institute in New York City. He was Presidential Elector on the Clay ticket, in 1844, having been from the outset of life, a devoted personal friend of that statesman. He was also a Presidential Elector in 1848. In 1850 he was invited, by President Fillmore, to fill the office of Secretary of the Interior, which he held until 1853, and then returned to his profession in Staunton. In 1856 he was a member of the Convention which nominated Mr. Fillmore. In 1857 was elected to the State Senate of Virginia, for four years, and devoted himself especially to the subject of internal improvements.

Stuart, Andrew.—Born in Pennsylvania; and was elected a Representative in Congress, from Ohio, from 1853 to 1855.

Stuart, Archibald.—He was born in Virginia, and elected a Representative in Congress, from that State, from 1837 to 1839.

Stuart, Charles E.—He was born in Columbia County, New York, November 25, 1810, and adopted the profession of law. He was a member of the Michigan Legislature in 1842; a Representative in the Thirtieth and Thirty-second Congresses; and was elected, in 1853, a Senator in Congress, serving as Chairman of the important Committee on Public Lands.

Stuart, David.—He was born in New York, and was a Representative in Congress, from Michigan, from 1853 to 1855.

Stuart, John T.—Was born in Fayette County, Kentucky, November 10, 1807; graduated at the Centre College, Danville, in 1826; and, having studied law, settled in Illinois, where he has since practised his profession. In 1832 and 1834 he was a member of the Illinois Legislature; he was elected a Representative, from Illinois, to the Twenty-sixth and Twenty-seventh Congresses, serving on the Committee on Territories. In 1848 he was elected to the State Senate, serving four years; and in 1862 he was re-elected a Representative to the Thirty-eighth Congress, serving on the Committee on Foreign Affairs.

Stuart, Philip.—He was a Representative in Congress, from Maryland, from 1811 to 1819.

Sturgeon, Daniel.—He was a Senator in Congress, from Pennsylvania, from 1840 to 1851.

Sturges, Jonathan.—Born at Fairfield, Connecticut, August 23, 1740; graduated at Yale College in 1759, and became a lawyer. In 1775 he was chosen a Delegate to Congress; he espoused and supported the cause of Independence, and was a Representative in Congress, from 1789 to 1793, when he was appointed a Judge of the Supreme Court of Connecticut, and continued in the office until 1805. He died at Fairfield, October 4, 1819.

Sturges, Lewis Burr.—Born in Fairfield, Connecticut, in 1762, and graduated at Yale College in 1782. He was a Representative in Congress, from Connecticut, from 1805 to 1817; and subsequently emigrated to the State of Ohio. He died in Norwalk, Ohio, March 30, 1844.

Sullivan, George.—He was born in Durham, New Hampshire, in 1772; graduated at Harvard University in 1790, and commenced in early life the practice of law in Exeter, which he continued for more than forty years, and acquired a high reputation. He was a Representative in the General Court, in 1805 and 1813; a Representative in Congress, in 1811 and 1812; and a member of the State Senate, in 1814 and 1815. He was twenty-one years Attorney-General of the State, which office he resigned in 1836. He died at Exeter, June 14, 1838, highly esteemed for his talents and public usefulness.

Summers, George W.—He was born in Fairfax County, Virginia, near Alexandria, but has lived from infancy in Kanawha County, in the western part of the State. He was educated for the legal profession, and came to the bar in 1827. In 1830 he was elected a member of the House of Delegates, and continued to represent Kanawha County in the Legislature for several years. He was elected to the House of Representatives in the spring of 1841, and re-elected in 1843, serving throughout the Twenty-seventh and Twenty-eighth Congresses. In 1850 he was elected a member of the State Convention which framed the present Constitution of Virginia. In 1851 he was unanimously nominated as the Whig candidate for Governor, at the first election of the Governor by the people, that officer having been previously chosen by the Legislature, but was defeated. In May, 1852, he was elected Judge of the Eighteenth Judicial Circuit in Virginia, and having served in that capacity for six years, he resigned his office, July 1, 1858, there being two years of the term for which he had been elected unexpired. He has of late devoted himself to agriculture, and the practice of law, and was a Delegate to the Peace Congress of 1861.

Sumner, Charles.—Was born in Boston, Massachusetts, January 6, 1811; graduated at Harvard College in 1830; spent the three following years at the Cambridge Law School; had the editorial charge for three years of the American Jurist; was admitted to the bar in 1834, and settled in Boston; was subsequently the Reporter of the United States Circuit Court, and published three volumes, which now bear his name; was for three winters a teacher at the Cambridge Law School; soon afterwards edited Dunlap's Treatise on Admiralty Practice; and about this time declined a Professorship tendered to him by his Alma Mater. In 1837 he visited Europe, was received with marked attention in England, and remained abroad until 1840. During the years 1844–46 he produced an edition of Vesey's Reports, in twenty volumes; from that time onward, he frequently appeared in public as a speaker on various philanthropic and literary subjects, and two volumes of his orations were published in 1850. In 1851 he was elected a Senator in Congress, from Massachusetts; in 1856, for words uttered in debate on the subject of Slavery, he was assaulted at his desk in the Senate Chamber, by Preston Brooks, a Representative from South Carolina, from the effects of which his health suffered, and he again visited Europe, having been, just before his departure, re-elected for a second term to the Senate. In 1853 he published a work on "White Slavery in the Barbary States," and in 1856, a volume of "Speeches and Addresses." In 1863 he was re-elected to the Senate for the third term, ending in 1869, serving as Chairman of the Committee on Foreign Affairs.

Sumter, Thomas.—A distinguished soldier of the American Revolution; was a citizen of South Carolina; and was promoted, by Governor Rutledge, in 1780, from the office of Colonel to that of Brigadier-General. For his services he received the thanks of Congress, and the applause of his country. In 1801 he was elected a Senator in Congress, serving until 1809, when he was appointed Minister to Brazil. He died suddenly, June 1, 1832, aged ninety-seven.

Sumter, Thomas D.—Born in Pennsylvania, and elected a Representative in Congress, from South Carolina, from 1840 to 1843.

Sutherland, Joel B.—He was a Representative in Congress, from Philadelphia County, Pennsylvania, from 1827 to 1837, and was Chairman of the Committee on Commerce during the Twenty-fourth Congress. Died in Philadelphia, November 15, 1861.

Sutherland, Josiah.—He was born in New York, and was elected a Representative to the Thirty-second Congress, from that State.

Swan, Samuel.—Born in Somerset County, New Jersey, in 1771; was a Representative in Congress, from New Jersey, from 1821 to 1831, and died at Brunswick, New Jersey, August 24, 1844.

Swanwick, John.—He was a Representative in Congress, from Pennsylvania, from 1795 to 1798.

Swart, Peter.—He was a member of the New York Senate, from Schoharie County, from 1817 to 1820, and had been a Representative in Congress, from that State, from 1807 to 1809.

Swearingen, Henry.—Born in Pennsylvania, and was a Representative in Congress, from Ohio, from 1839 to 1841.

Swearingen, Thomas V.—He was born in Jefferson County, Virginia, and was elected a Representative in Congress, from that State, from 1819 to 1821. Died, August 19, 1822, in Virginia.

Sweat, Lorenzo D. M.—Born in Parsonsfield, York County, Maine, May 26, 1818; graduated at Bowdoin College in 1837, and at the Harvard Law School in 1840; during the next two years he practised law in New Orleans; in 1856 and 1860 he was City Solicitor in Portland; in 1861 and 1862 a member of the

State Senate; and was elected a Representative, from Maine, to the Thirty-eighth Congress, serving on the Committee on Private Land Claims.

Sweeny, George.—Born in Pennsylvania, and was a Representative in Congress, from Ohio, from 1839 to 1843.

Sweetser, Charles.—Born in Vermont, and was a Representative in Congress, from Ohio, from 1849 to 1853.

Swift, Benjamin.—He was born in Amenia, New York, April 5, 1781; he received an academic education; studied law, and was admitted to practice at Bennington in 1806; he was settled for a time in Manchester, and subsequently in St. Alban's, where he rose to eminence in his profession. In 1813 and 1814, 1825 and 1826, he was a Representative to the General Assembly; and was a Representative in Congress, from Vermont, from 1827 to 1831. He received the degree of A.M. from Middlebury College in 1820, and was a member of the Corporation of that institution from 1830 to 1839. In 1833 he was elected to the Senate of the United States for six years, after which he retired to private life. While in apparent good health he died suddenly, in an open field on his farm, November 11, 1847.

Swift, Zephaniah.—He was born in Wareham, Massachusetts, in 1759; graduated at Yale College in 1778, and established himself as a lawyer at Windham, Connecticut, where his superior talents gained him a lucrative practice in his profession. He was a Representative in Congress, from Connecticut, from 1793 to 1797, and in 1800 was Secretary to Ellsworth, Davie, and Murray, in their mission to France. Soon after his return he was placed on the bench of the Superior Court of the State, where he continued eighteen years, during the last five of which he was Chief Justice. He was afterwards a member of the State Legislature, and was one of a Committee to revise the Statute Laws of the State. He published several works; among them was a "Digest of the Laws of Connecticut, on the model of Blackstone." He died at Warren, Ohio, September 27, 1823.

Swoope, Jacob.—He was a Representative in Congress, from Virginia, from 1809 to 1811.

Swope, Samuel F.—He was born in Kentucky, and was a Representative in Congress, from that State, from 1855 to 1857.

Sykes, George.—He was born in New Jersey, and was a Representative in Congress, from that State, from 1843 to 1847.

Taggart, Samuel.—Born in Londonderry, Massachusetts, and graduated at Dartmouth in 1774; he studied for the ministry, and settled in Coleraine in 1777. He was elected a Representative in Congress, from Massachusetts, serving from 1803 to 1817, and died in 1825, aged seventy-one years.

Tait, Charles.—He was born in Louisa County, Virginia, but removed at an early age to Georgia. He was for several years a Judge of the Superior Court of Georgia, and a Senator in Congress, from that State, from 1809 to 1819. He distinguished himself as a supporter of the administrations of Madison and Monroe. In 1819 he removed to Alabama, and was appointed a Judge of the District Court, when first established in that State, which office he resigned in 1826. He died in Wilcox County, Alabama, October 7, 1835, in the sixty-eighth year of his age.

Talbot, Albert G.—He was born in Kentucky, and was elected a Representative, from that State, to the Thirty-fourth and Thirty-fifth Congresses, and was Chairman of the Committee on Expenditures in the War Department, and a member of that on Roads and Canals.

Talbot, Isham.—He was born in Bedford County, Virginia, in 1773; received a good education; studied law, and practised with success; he was a member of the Kentucky Senate, from 1812 to 1815; from 1815 to 1819 a member of the United States Senate, and for a second term, from 1820 to 1825. He died near Frankfort, September 27, 1837.

Talbot, Silas.—He was a Representative in Congress, from New York, from 1793 to 1794, when he was appointed, by President Washington, Captain in the navy, having previously served a number of years in the State Assembly, from Montgomery County.

Taliaferro, Benjamin.—He was a Representative in Congress, from Georgia, from 1799 to 1802. Died September 3, 1821.

Taliaferro, John.—He was born in Spottsylvania County, Virginia, in 1768; was a Representative in Congress, from that State, from 1801 to 1803, from 1811 to 1813, from 1824 to 1831, and from 1835 to 1843. For three years before his death he was Librarian of the Treasury Department in Washington. He died at his residence in Virginia, August 18, 1853.

Tallmadge, Benjamin.—He was born in Suffolk County, New York, February 25, 1754. His military services were very valuable; he acted a prominent part in the capture of André; planned and conducted the expedition in 1780, which resulted in the capture of Fort George and the destruction of the British stores on Long Island; and was a member of Washington's military family. After the war, having attained the rank of General, he engaged in mercantile pursuits, and acquired a large property. He was a Representative in Congress, from Connecticut, from 1801 to 1817. He was highly respected for his public services and private character, and died at Litchfield, Connecticut, March 6, 1835.

Tallmadge, James.—He was born in Stanford, Dutchess County, New York, January 28, 1788; graduated at Brown University in 1798, and was by by profession a lawyer. He was, early in life, private Secretary to Governor Clinton, and during the war of 1812 commanded a portion of the force detailed for the defence of New York City. From 1817 to 1819 he was a Representative in Congress, from New York, and declined a re-election; he was a member of the Convention which framed the Constitution of the State, and in 1823 was elected to the Assembly from Dutchess County. From 1825 to 1828 he was Lieutenant-Governor, under Clinton, and in 1846 a member of the Constitutional Convention of New York. For the last twenty years of his life he was President of the American Institute in New York. He visited Europe, and benefited the United States by his introduction of a knowledge of American machinery into Russia, and induced that government to adopt it in their manufacture of cotton goods. He was one of the founders of the University of New York, and was President of the Council. He was honored with the degree of LL.D. from that institution. He died, suddenly, in New York City, September 29, 1853.

Tallmadge, Nathaniel P.—He was born in Chatham, Columbia County, New York, February 8, 1795; graduated at Union College; studied law, and was admitted to the bar in 1818; was a member of the Assembly of New York in 1828; of the State Senate, from 1830 to 1833; a Senator in Congress, from New York, from 1833 to 1844; and was subsequently appointed, by President Tyler, Territorial Governor of Wisconsin, where he now resides, devoted to his profession.

Tallman, Peleg.—He was born at Tiverton, Rhode Island, in 1764; in 1778, at the age of fourteen, he entered into the privateering service for employment; in 1780 he had his left arm shot off; and in 1781 he was taken prisoner, and was confined in Ireland and England till the peace in 1783. He soon afterwards became commander of a merchant vessel, and, after following a seafaring life for many years, he devoted himself to the business of a merchant, and acquired a large fortune. He was a Representative in Congress, from Massachusetts, from 1811 to 1813, and died at Bath, Maine, March 8, 1841.

Talmadge, Frederick A.—He was born in Litchfield, Connecticut, August 29, 1792; graduated at Yale College in 1811, and having studied law, settled in practice, in New York, in 1814; in 1836 he was elected an Alderman of the city, and also a State Senator; was, subsequently, five years Recorder of the city; a Representative, from New York, in the Thirtieth Congress; was again Recorder for three years; and in 1857 was appointed General Superintendent of the Metropolitan Police, and was subsequently appointed Clerk of the Court of Appeals.

Tannehill, Adamson.—He was a Representative in Congress, from Pennsylvania, from 1813 to 1815. Died December 23, 1820.

Tappan, Benjamin.—Born at Northampton, Massachusetts, May 25, 1773; was taught the business of copperplate engraving and printing; devoted some attention to portrait painting; and subsequently studied and adopted the profession of law. In 1799 he emigrated to Ohio, and was one of the earliest settlers there; in 1803 was elected to the Legislature of the new State; he served in the war of 1812 as aide-de-camp to General Wadsworth; was for seven years President Judge of the Fifth Ohio Circuit; in 1833 he was appointed, by President Jackson, United States Judge for the District of Ohio; and he was a Senator in Congress, from Ohio, from 1839 to 1845, serving as Chairman of the Committee on the Library. He died at Steubenville, Ohio, April 12, 1857.

Tappan, Mason W.—Born in Newport, Sullivan County, New Hampshire; fitted for college, and studied law as a profession; he was a member of the State Legislature in 1853, 1854, and 1855; and a Representative, from New Hampshire, in the Thirty-fourth Congress, and re-elected to the Thirty-fifth and Thirty-sixth, serving as a member of the Committee on the Judiciary, and in the last Congress as Chairman of the Committee on Claims.

Tarr, Christian.—He was born in Baltimore, Maryland, and was a Representative in Congress, from Pennsylvania, from 1817 to 1819, and again from 1820 to 1821.

Tate, Magnus.—He was a Representative in Congress, from North Carolina, from 1815 to 1817.

Tatnall, Edward F.—He was born in Savannah, Georgia, and was a Representative in Congress, from Georgia, from 1821 to 1827.

Tatnall, Josiah.—He was born at Bonaventure, near Savannah, and died in the West Indies, in 1804. His boyhood was full of adventure, and at the age of eighteen he joined the army of General Wayne, at Ebenezer. In 1793 he was appointed Colonel of a Georgia regiment, and in 1800 a Brigadier-General, participating extensively in the military affairs of the State, and serving occasionally in the Legislature. He also served in 1796 at Louisville, in the General Assembly that rescinded the Yazoo Act of 1795; and was a Senator in Congress, from Georgia, from 1796 to 1799.

Tatum, Absalom.—A Representative in Congress, from North Carolina, during the years 1795 and 1796.

Taul, Micah.—He was a Representative in Congress, from Kentucky, from 1815 to 1817.

Taylor, George.—He was born in Wheeling, Virginia, October 19, 1820, and after receiving a liberal education, turned his attention to the study of medicine, but subsequently adopted the profession of law; he was admitted to the bar in 1840, and removed to Indiana, where he was successful as a special pleader. In 1844 he removed to Alabama, and there practised his profession for four years, after which he removed to New York, where he now resides. In 1856 he was elected a Representative to the Thirty-fifth Congress, and was a member of the Committees on Revolutionary Claims, and on the Cost of Public Buildings. As an author, writing upon topics connected with the natural sciences, he has been successful. A work published in 1851, and entitled "Indications of the Creator," has passed through four editions, and been highly applauded by the critics of England and France. He has also written much in behalf of popular education, and his collected addresses and lectures make quite a large and interesting volume.

Taylor, John.—He was born in Orange County, Virginia; was distinguished for his attention to agriculture, and published a work entitled "Constructor Construed: an Inquiry into the Principles and Policy of the Government of the United States, 1814;" and was a Senator of the United States, from Virginia, from 1792 to 1794, when he resigned, and in 1803, and from 1822 to 1824. He died in Caroline County, Virginia, August 20, 1824, at an advanced age.

Taylor, John.—Born in South Carolina in 1770; graduated at Princeton College in 1790; studied law, and was admitted to the bar in 1793, but turned his attention chiefly to planting; served in the State Legislature a number of years; was a Representative in Congress, from South Carolina, from 1807 to 1809, and also from 1817 to 1821; was a Senator in Congress, from 1810 to 1816; was a trustee of the South Carolina College in 1806; a State Senator in 1810 and 1822; Governor of the State, from 1826 to 1828; and died in 1832. He was also at one time Receiver of Public Moneys in Mississippi Territory.

Taylor, John J.—He was born in Massachusetts, and having settled in New York, was elected a Representative in Congress, from that State, from 1853 to 1855.

Taylor, John L.—Born in Stafford County, Virginia, March 7, 1805; was educated in the common schools and seminaries of the neighborhood; studied law in Washington City, and was admitted to the bar in 1828; settled in Chillicothe, Ohio, in 1829; he was for six years Major-General of the Ohio militia; and he was a Representative in Congress, from Ohio, from 1847 to 1855, serving from time to time on important committees.

Taylor, John W.—Born in Saratoga County, New York, in 1784, and graduated at Union College in 1803. He studied law in Albany; was elected to the State Legislature in 1811, and while in that body was elected to Congress, where he served from 1813 to 1833. He was Speaker of the House during the second session of the Sixteenth Congress, during the passage of the Missouri Compromise. He removed to Cleveland, Ohio, in 1843, where he died in September, 1854. He was for many years a leading and prominent statesman of New York, and was esteemed for his personal virtues and liberal hospitality.

Taylor, Jonathan.—He was a native of Connecticut, and having removed to Ohio, was elected a Representative in Congress, from that State, from 1839 to 1841.

Taylor, Miles.—He was born in New York, and having taken up his residence in Louisiana, was elected a Representative, from that State, to the Thirty-fourth and Thirty-fifth Congresses, and he was a member of the Committees on Claims, and on the Judiciary.

Taylor, Miles.—He was elected a Representative, from Louisiana, to the Thirty-sixth Congress, serving as a member of the Committee on the Judiciary. Resigned in February, 1861.

Taylor, Nathaniel G.—Born in Carter County, Tennessee, December 29, 1819; studied at Washington College in that State, but graduated at Princeton College in 1840; studied law, and was admitted to the bar in 1843; and was a Representative in Congress, from Tennessee, from 1854 to 1855, as the successor of Brookins Campbell. He was also a Presidential Elector in 1853, and of late years has been a minister in the Methodist Episcopal Church South.

Taylor, Robert.—He was a Representative in Congress, from Virginia, his native State, from 1825 to 1827.

Taylor, Waller.—He was a Senator in Congress, from Indiana, from 1816 to 1825, and died in Lunenburg County, Virginia, August 26, 1826. He held offices of trust in the Territory of Indiana, served as aide-de-camp to General Harrison at the battle of Tippecanoe, and was a man of high literary attainments.

Taylor, William.—He was born in Connecticut; was a Representative in Congress, from New York, from 1833 to 1839, and served two years in the Assembly of that State, from New York City, and two years from Onondaga County.

Taylor, William.—He was born in Virginia, and was a Representative in Congress, from that State, from 1833 to 1835.

Taylor, William.—Born in Alexandria, District of Columbia; was elected a Representative in Congress, from Virginia, from 1843 to 1847, but died in Washington City, January 17, 1846.

Tazewell, Henry.—He was a Senator in Congress, from Virginia, from 1794 to 1799, and President *pro tem.* of the Senate during a part of the Third Congress. He died January 24, 1799, in Washington.

Tazewell, Littleton W.—Born in Williamsburg, Virginia, in 1774; educated at William and Mary College; studied law, and attained great success in his profession; was a member of the Virginia Legislature in 1798; a Representative in Congress, from Virginia, from 1799 to 1801; a Senator in Congress, from 1824 to 1832; and Governor of Virginia, from 1834 to 1836. In the Senate he was Chairman of the Committee on Foreign Relations, and President *pro tem.* of that body during a part of the Twenty-second Congress. In 1820 he was one of the Commissioners under the Florida Treaty, and his last great effort as a lawyer was made in the Supreme Court of the United States, in what was known as the "Cochineal case." He died at Norfolk, Virginia, May 6, 1860.

Telfair, Thomas.—He was a Representative in Congress, from Georgia, from 1813 to 1817. Died at Savannah, Georgia, in April, 1818.

Temple, William.—Born in Queen Anne County, Maryland, February 28, 1815; received a good academic education, and adopted the occupation of a merchant in Smyrna, Delaware. In 1844 he was elected to the State Legislature, and was Speaker of the House; and the Governor of the State and the President of the Senate having died, he became acting Governor for the balance of the term. During the next ten years he was a member of the State Senate, and declined a re-election in 1854; and he was elected a Representative, from Delaware, to the Thirty-eighth Congress, but died, before taking his seat, at Smyrna, Delaware, in the summer of 1863.

Ten Eyck, E.—He was born in Rensselaer County, New York, April 18, 1779; graduated at Williams College; studied law in Albany; was a member of the Assembly in 1812 and 1813, and Speaker; member also of the Constitutional Convention of 1822; and a Representative in Congress, from New York, from 1823 to 1825. He also held the offices of Judge of the Jefferson County Court, and President of a county agricultural society. He died at Watertown, New York, April 11, 1844.

Ten Eyck, John C.—Born in Freehold, New Jersey, March 12, 1814; obtained a classical education under private tutors; studied law, and was admitted to the bar in 1835. In 1839 he was appointed Prosecutor of the Pleas for Burlington County, holding the position for ten years; he was a member of the New Jersey Constitutional Convention of 1844; and was elected a Senator in Congress for the term commencing in 1859, and ending in 1865, serving on the Committees on Commerce, and the Judiciary.

Tenney, Samuel.—Was born in Byfield Parish, Newbury, Massachusetts; and having received a collegiate education at Harvard University, graduating in 1772, commenced the study of medicine. When the Revolutionary war began, he was found among the assertors of his country's rights; and was present at the battle of Bunker's Hill, where he was employed in attending upon the wounded. He served during the whole war, and was attached to the Rhode Island line of the Provincial army. At the close of the war he retired from his profession, and settled at Exeter, New Hampshire. For many years he was Judge of Probate; and in 1800 was elected a Representative in the Congress of the United States, serving until 1807. His death, which occurred in 1816, was universally regretted. An ardent lover of his country, a faithful expounder of her laws and institutions, and an elegant scholar, his memory is still fondly cherished by many who knew him.

Terrill, William.—He was frequently a member of the Georgia Legislature, and was a Representative in Congress, from that State, from 1817 to 1821. Becoming tired of politics, he took great interest in the promotion of agricultural science, and in 1853 he made a donation of $20,000 for the establishment of an agricultural professorship in the University of Georgia, which professorship bears his name. He was one of the most accomplished and useful citizens of his State, and died at Sparta, Georgia, July 4, 1855.

Terry, Nathaniel.—Born in Enfield, Connecticut, in 1768, and graduated at Yale College in 1786. He resided in Hartford, Connecticut, and held various offices in his native State; from 1817 to 1819 was a Representative in Congress, and died in New Haven, June 14, 1844.

Test, John.—He was a native of Salem, New Jersey, and emigrated to Indiana; was a Representative in Congress, from that State, from 1823 to 1827, and from 1829 to 1831. He was Presiding Judge of one of the Circuit Courts of Indiana; and afterwards removed to Mobile, Alabama, where he gained a high reputation for his learning and talents as a lawyer. He died near CambridgeCity, Indiana, October 9, 1849.

Thacher, George.—Born in Yarmouth, Massachusetts, April 12, 1754; graduated at Harvard College in 1776; studied law, and established himself in practice in Biddeford, Maine; he was a Delegate to the old Congress, and on the adoption of the Constitution, served as a Representative in Congress, from Massachusetts, from 1789 to 1801; in 1792 he was elected a District Judge in Maine, serving until 1800, when he was chosen a Judge of the Supreme Court in Massachusetts; and he held the latter office until January, 1824, when he resigned, and died on the 6th of April following. He was also a member of the Convention which formed the Constitution of Maine in 1819. He was a man of superior abilities, and performed all his duties to the entire satisfaction of the public. He was famous for his wit, and when a bill was reported in Congress respecting the use of the eagle on American coin, he playfully recommended a goose, for which he was challenged by the reporter of the bill, and the challenge he ridiculed.

Thacher, Samuel.—He was born in Cambridge, Massachusetts, July 1, 1776; graduated at Harvard University in 1793; adopted the profession of law; and was a Representative in Congress, from Massachusetts, from 1802 to 1805. He also served eleven years in the Massachusetts Legislature, and was Sheriff of Lincoln County from 1814 to 1821.

Thayer, Eli.—Born in Mendon, Worcester County, Massachusetts, June 11, 1819; graduated at Brown University in 1845; was a teacher in the Worcester Academy for three years; was a farmer by occupation; served as Alderman of the city of Worcester in 1853; he was a Representative in the Massachusetts Legislature during the years 1853 and 1854; elected a Representative to the Thirty-fifth Congress, from that State, serving as a member of the Committee on Militia; and was re-elected to the Thirty-sixth Congress, serving as Chairman of the Committee on Public Lands. He was the founder of the New England Emigrant Aid Society; and has been identified with other societies of a benevolent character.

Thayer, M. Russell.—He was born in Petersburg, Virginia, January 27, 1819; graduated at the University of Pennsylvania in 1840; studied law, and was admitted to the bar in 1842; and was elected a Representative, from Pennsylvania, to the Thirty-eighth Congress, serving as Chairman of the Committee on Private Land Claims. He received from his Alma Mater the two degrees of Bachelor and Master of Arts.

Theaker, Thomas C.—Born in York County, Pennsylvania, February 1, 1812; received a good English education; removed to Ohio in 1830; has devoted the most of his life to the occupation of a millwright and machinist; and he was elected a Representative, from Ohio, to the Thirty-sixth Congress, serving on the Committees on the Militia, and Enrolled Bills.

Thibodeaux, B. G.—Born in Louisiana, and was a Representative in Congress, from that State, from 1845 to 1847, and for a second term ending in 1849.

Thomas, Benjamin F.—Was born in Boston, February 12, 1813; removed to Worcester in 1819; graduated at Brown University in 1830; studied law, and was admitted to practice in 1833; was a member of the Massachusetts Legislature in 1842; was appointed Judge of Probate for the County of Worcester in 1844, resigning the office in 1848; was a Presidential Elector on the Taylor ticket in that year; and in 1853 he was appointed to the bench of the Supreme Court of Massachusetts, holding the office six years, when he resigned. He subsequently returned to Boston to practise his profession, residing in West Roxbury, and in 1861 he was elected a Representative, from Massachusetts, to the Thirty-seventh Congress, serving as a member of the Committee on the Judiciary, and the Special Committee on the Bankrupt Law.

Thomas, David.—He was a Representative in Congress, from New York, from 1801 to 1808; served four years in the Assembly of that State; and also held the position of State Treasurer.

Thomas, Francis.—He was born in Frederick County, Maryland, February 3, 1799; was educated at St. John's College, in that State; studied law, and was admitted to the bar in 1820; was a member of the House of Delegates in 1822, 1827, and 1829; and was a Representative in Congress, from Maryland, from 1831 to 1841. During one term, he was Chairman of the Judiciary Committee, and a report made by him led to the settlement of the boundary difficulties between Ohio and Michigan. From 1841 to 1844 he was Governor of Maryland; was elected, for the sixth time, a Representative to the Thirty-seventh Congress, and re-elected to the Thirty-eighth Congress, serving on the Judiciary Committee.

Thomas, Isaac.—He was a Representative in Congress, from Tennessee, from 1815 to 1817.

Thomas, James Houston.—Was born in Iredell County, North Carolina, September 22, 1808; received the degree of A. B. from Columbia College, Tennessee, in 1830; studied and adopted the profession of law; in 1836 was elected Attorney-General for the State, holding the office six years; was for many years the law partner of James K. Polk; was a Representative in Congress, from Tennessee, from 1847 to 1851; was a Presidential Elector in 1856; and in 1859 he was elected a Representative, from Tennessee, to the Thirty-sixth Congress, serving on the Committee on Revolutionary Pensions.

Thomas, Jesse B.—He was a Delegate to Congress, from the Territory of Indiana, from 1808 to 1809, and was then appointed United States Judge of Illinois Territory. He was also one of the first Senators in Congress, from Illinois, having held the position from 1818 to 1829, serving on important committees. He died in February, 1850.

Thomas, John C.—He was a Representative in Congress, from Maryland, from 1799 to 1801.

Thomas, Philemon.—A native of North Carolina, where, during the Revolutionary war, he was engaged in many skirmishes with the British. He resided some years in Kentucky, and was a member of the Legislature of that State; he afterwards removed to Louisiana, and, in 1810 and 1811, headed the insurrection at Baton Rouge, which threw off the yoke of Spain from West Florida. He was a Representative in Congress, from Louisiana, from 1831 to 1835, and died at Baton Rouge, Louisiana, November 18, 1847, aged eighty-three years.

Thomas, Philip Francis.—He was born in Talbot County, Maryland, September 12, 1810; was educated at Dickinson College; studied law, and was admitted to the bar in 1831; in 1836 was a member of the State Constitutional Convention; in 1838 was elected to the State Legislature; was a Representative in Congress, from 1839 to 1841; was, subsequently, Judge of the Land-office Court of the Eastern Shore of Maryland; in 1843 and 1845 was elected to the House of Delegates; and in 1847 was elected Governor of Maryland. In the early part of 1860 he was appointed, by President Buchanan, Commissioner of the Patent Office, and on the resignation of Howell Cobb as Secretary of the Treasury, in December, 1860, he was appointed Secretary of the Treasury in Mr. Buchanan's Cabinet.

Thomas, Richard.—He was a soldier in the Revolutionary war, and a Representative in Congress, from Pennsylvania, from 1795 to 1801. Died in Philadelphia in 1832, aged eighty-seven years.

Thomasson, William P.—Born in Henry County, Kentucky; commenced the study of law at an early age; and when eighteen, was licensed to practise at Corydon, Indiana, from which place he was elected to the Legislature. He removed to Louisville about the year 1841, and was chosen a Representative in Congress, from Kentucky, from 1843 to 1847. He afterwards went to Chicago, where he is now engaged in the practice of his profession.

Thompson, Alexander. — He was born in Franklin County, Pennsylvania, and a Representative in Congress, from Pennsylvania, from 1824 to 1826; died at his residence, in Chambersburg, Pennsylvania, August 2, 1848, aged sixty-three years.

Thompson, Benjamin. — Born in Massachusetts in 1798. He held many responsible offices in the town of Charlestown, and was several times a Representative in the State Legislature. He was twice elected to Congress as a member from the Fourth District of Massachusetts, serving from 1845 to 1847; and again from March, 1851, till his death. He united mental cultivation and sound judgment with great business talent. His services upon the Committee on Military Affairs, during the Mexican war, were especially valuable. He died in Charlestown, September 24, 1852.

Thompson, George W.—He was born in Ohio, and, removing to Virginia, was elected a Representative in Congress, from that State, from 1851 to 1852.

Thompson, Hedge.—He was a Representative in Congress, from New Jersey, during the years 1827 and 1828. Died at Salem, July 20, 1828.

Thompson, Jacob.—He was born in Caswell County, North Carolina, May 15, 1810, and received his education at the University of Chapel Hill. He studied law, and was admitted to the bar in 1834, and during the following year removed to the State of Mississippi. Locating himself in what was known as the Chickasaw Country, he applied himself to the task of making the wilderness blossom like the rose, and through his influence the Indian lands were divided into counties, and became politically identified with the State. The consequence was that a grateful constituency called upon him to represent them in Congress, and, having been elected in 1839, he continued to serve in that capacity, with ability and fidelity, until 1851. On first taking his seat in Congress he was placed on the Committee on Public Lands, and was for some years Chairman of the Committee on Indian Affairs. He was one of the most devoted defenders of Mississippi and of the Democratic party, at the time when the cry of *repudiation* was ringing throughout the land; and as he had, in 1845, declined going into the United States Senate, by appointment of the Governor of Mississippi, so did he, in 1851, decline a re-election to the House of Representatives, preferring to lead the more peaceful life of a man of fortune, in the midst of troops of friends. But this retirement did not happen to coincide with the views of President Buchanan when he came into power, and as he was familiar with Mr. Thompson's career in Congress and the National Nominating Conventions, the natural result was his appointment as Secretary of the Interior Department. That position he resigned in January, 1861, and served in the Rebellion as aide-de-camp to General Beauregard.

Thompson, J. B.—He was born in Kentucky, and was a Representative in Congress, from that State, from 1841 to 1843, and again from 1847 to 1851; and in 1853 he was elected a Senator in Congress for a long term. He was a member of the Committee on Private Land Claims and of that on Pensions.

Thompson, James. — Born in Middlesex, Butler County, Pennsylvania, October 1, 1806. He received a good education, and commenced life as a printer; he studied law, and was admitted to the bar in 1828; he was elected to the Assembly of his native State, in 1832, 1833, and 1834, presiding during the last session as Speaker; in 1836 he was a Presidential Elector; he was Presiding Judge of the District Court for six years, and a Representative in Congress, from 1845 to 1851. Of late years he has been chiefly devoted to the practice of his profession, and in 1847 was elected a Judge of the Supreme Court of Pennsylvania, for fifteen years.

Thompson, Joel.—He was a Representative in Congress, from New York, from 1813 to 1815, having previously served one year in the State Assembly, from Albany, and two years from Chenango County.

Thompson, John.—He was a member of the New York Assembly, from Albany, in 1788 and 1789, in 1827, from Delaware County, in 1802 and 1841 from Dutchess County; and was a Representative in Congress, from New York, from 1799 to 1801, and again from 1807 to 1811.

Thompson, John.—He was born in Franklin County, Pennsylvania, in 1777, and was a Representative in Congress, from Ohio, from 1825 to 1827, and again from 1829 to 1837. He died at New Lisbon, Ohio, December 2, 1852.

Thompson, John.—He was born in Rhinebeck, Dutchess County, New York, July 4, 1809. He was educated at Yale and Union Colleges; lived on a farm until sixteen years of age, since which time he has devoted himself to the law; and against his own wishes and consent was elected a Representative in Congress, from New York, to the Thirty-fifth Congress, serving on the Committee on Roads and Canals.

Thompson, John R.—Born in Philadelphia, September 5, 1800; entered Princeton College, but left in the junior year, and devoted himself to mercantile pursuits, making a voyage to China in 1817, and in 1820 established himself as a merchant in Canton; was appointed Consul of the United States at that port in 1823, and remained there until 1825. Since the year 1830 he has been engaged in the management of several railways, and of the New Jersey Canal. In 1844 he was a member of the Constitutional Convention of New Jersey, and was United States Senator from 1853 to 1857, and was re-elected for the term ending in 1863. He was a member of the Committees on Naval Affairs, and on Post-offices and Post-roads. He was offered a seat in the Cabinet by President Buchanan, which he declined. Died at Trenton, September 13, 1862.

Thompson, Mark.—He was a Representative in Congress, from New Jersey, from 1795 to 1799.

Thompson, Philip.—He was a native of Kentucky, and a Representative in Congress, from that State, from 1823 to 1825.

Thompson, Philip R.—Born in 1766, and died in Kanawha County, Virginia, July 22, 1837. He was a Representative in Congress, from Virginia, from 1801 to 1807.

Thompson, Richard W.—He was born in Culpeper County, Virginia, June 9, 1809; received a good English and classical education; and his love of adventure led him into the wilds of Kentucky before he became of age. In 1831 he settled in Louisville, and became a clerk in an extensive mercantile house; tiring of this, he removed to Lawrence County, Indiana, taught school for a few months, but again turned his attention to merchandizing, selling goods and studying law at the same time. He was admitted to the bar in 1834, and was almost immediately elected to the Indiana Legislature; was re-elected in 1835; in 1836 he was elected to the State Senate, served two years, and was for a time President *pro tem.* of the Senate, and Acting Lieutenant-Governor; he was a Presidential Elector in 1840, and voted for General Harrison, whose election he zealously advocated with his pen and on the stump; and in 1841 he was elected a Representative in Congress, for the term ending in 1843. In 1844 he was again chosen a Presidential Elector; was again a Representative in Congress, from Indiana, from 1847 to 1849, when he declined a re-election. Since that time he has held no public office, but has been devoted to the practice of his profession at Terre Haute. President Taylor offered him the appointment of Chargé d'Affaires to Austria, and President Fillmore, the office of Recorder of the General Land-Office, both of which honors he declined.

Thompson, Robert A.—He was born in Virginia, and was a Representative in Congress, from that State, from 1847 to 1849. Now Land Commissioner in California.

Thompson, Thomas W.—He graduated at Harvard University in 1786; was a Representative in Congress, from New Hampshire, from 1805 to 1807; State Treasurer in 1809; and a United States Senator from 1814 to 1817. He was a neighbor and one of the earliest friends of Daniel Webster. Died at Concord, in October, 1820, aged fifty-five years.

Thompson, Waddy. — He was born at Pickensville, South Carolina, September 8, 1798; graduated at the South Carolina College in 1814, and having studied law, was admitted to the bar in 1819. He has served in the Legislature of his native State; was at one time Solicitor for the Western Circuit of South Carolina; was chosen a Presidential Elector; attained the military title of Brigadier-General; and was appointed, in 1842, Minister Plenipotentiary to Mexico, about which he published an interesting work. He was a Representative in Congress, from 1835 to 1841, serving, in 1840, as Chairman of the Committee on Military Affairs.

Thompson, Wiley. — He was a native of Amelia County, Virginia, and a Representative in Congress, from Georgia, from 1821 to 1833.

Thompson, William. — He was born in Pennsylvania, and having settled in Iowa, was elected a Representative in Congress, from that State, from 1847 to 1851.

Thorington, James. — He was born in North Carolina, and removing to Iowa, was elected a Representative from that State to the Thirty-fourth Congress.

Throop, Enos T. — He was born in Johnstown, Montgomery County, New York, August 21, 1784; while performing the duties of an attorney's clerk, he acquired a classical education; studied law, and settled in Auburn; was a Representative in Congress during the years 1815 and 1816; in 1823 was elected Circuit Judge; in 1829, Lieutenant-Governor of New York; and in 1831 was Governor of that State. In 1838 he was appointed Chargé d'Affaires to the two Sicilies.

Thruston, Buckner. — Born in Virginia, about the year 1763. He emigrated in early life to Kentucky, and being possessed of superior talents, he was soon called into the public service. He was appointed Federal Judge in the Territory of Orleans, in 1805, and was the same year elected a member of the United States Senate, from Kentucky, for six years, but he resigned in 1809, on being appointed, by President Madison, Judge of the United States Circuit Court of the District of Columbia, which office he held until his death, which occurred at Washington, August 30, 1845.

Thurman, Allen G. — He was born in Virginia, and having taken up his residence in Ohio, was elected a Representative in Congress, from that State, from 1845 to 1847.

Thurman, John R.—He was a Representative in Congress, from New York, from 1849 to 1851, and died in New York, July 25, 1854.

Thurston, Benjamin B. — He was born in Hopkinton, Rhode Island, June 29, 1804; he received a common school education; was bred a merchant; was elected fourteen years in succession to the Assembly of his native State; and in 1838 was Lieutenant-Governor; and he was a Representative in Congress, from Rhode Island, from 1847 to 1849, and again from 1851 to 1857. He was subsequently elected a member of the Senate of Rhode Island.

Thurston, John B.—He was born in Virginia in 1757; studied law, and emigrated to Kentucky, whence he was sent to the United States Senate, in 1805, for a long term. He was subsequently elected a Judge of the Circuit Court of Kentucky, in which position he continued until his death, which occurred at Washington, August 30, 1845.

Thurston, Samuel R. — He was born in Maine; graduated at Bowdoin College in 1843, and was a Delegate in Congress, from the Territory of Oregon, from 1849 to 1851. He died on board the steamer California, on her passage from Panama to San Francisco, April 9, 1851.

Tibbatts, John W.—He was born in Kentucky, and was a Representative in Congress, from that State, from 1843 to 1847.

Tibbetts, George.—He was a Representative in Congress, from New York, from 1803 to 1805, and a member of the State Assembly, from Rensselaer County, in 1802 and 1820, and of the State Senate, from 1815 to 1818.

Tichenor, Isaac.—He was born in 1754; graduated at Princeton College in 1775; and died at Bennington, Vermont, in December, 1838. He was an officer of the Revolution; a Judge of the Supreme Court of Vermont; a Representative in the State Legislature; and a Senator in Congress, during the sessions of 1796 and 1797, when he resigned; Governor of Vermont from 1797 to 1808; and again in the United States Senate, from 1815 to 1821.

Tiffin, Edward.—He was born in 1765; was Governor of Ohio, from 1803 to 1807; and a Senator in Congress, from that State, from 1807 to 1809. He died 9th July, 1829.

Tilden, Daniel R.—He was born in Connecticut, and, having settled in Ohio, was elected a Representative in Congress, from that State, from 1843 to 1847.

Tillinghast, Joseph L.—Born in Taunton, Massachusetts, in 1791, and removed to Rhode Island in his boyhood. He graduated at Brown University in 1819, and in 1833 was elected a member of the Board of Trustees of that institution. He studied law, and devoted himself to its practice in Providence, with marked success, for thirty years; and was a Representative in Congress, from Rhode Island, from 1837 to 1843. He was also for many years a member of the State Legislature, and was elected Speaker on several occasions; and to him was awarded the authorship of the free schools and improved judiciary systems of his native State. Died December 30, 1844, at Providence, Rhode Island.

Tillinghast, Thomas.—He was a Representative in Congress, from Rhode Island, from 1797 to 1799, and again from 1801 to 1803.

Tipton, John.—He was a Senator in Congress, from Indiana, from 1831 to 1839; and died at Logansport, of apoplexy, in 1839.

Titus, Obadiah.—He was a Representative in Congress, from New York, from 1837 to 1839.

Todd, John. — He was born in Hartford, Connecticut, and was a Representative in Congress, from Pennsylvania, from 1821 to 1824. Died March 28, 1830.

Todd, John B. S.—He was born in Kentucky, and, having settled in Dakota, was elected a Delegate to the Thirty-seventh Congress. During the first session of the Thirty-eighth Congress he contested the seat, as Delegate, which had been assigned to William Jayne, and was admitted as the duly elected Delegate from Dakota.

Todd, Lemuel.—Born in Carlisle, Pennsylvania, July 29, 1817; educated at Dickinson College; studied law, and was admitted to the bar in 1841, and practised in his native town. In 1854 he was elected a Representative to the Thirty-fourth Congress.

Toland, George W.—He was born in Pennsylvania, and was a Representative in Congress, from that State, from 1837 to 1843.

Tomlinson, Gideon. — He was born at Stratford, Connecticut, December 31, 1780, and graduated at Yale College in 1802. He studied law, and practised the profession in Fairfield. He was then called to public life, and in 1818 was chosen a Representative in Congress, in which office he was continued till 1827. In that year he was chosen Governor of Connecticut, and remained in that station until March, 1831, when, on being appointed a Senator of the United States, he resigned his office as Governor. After six years' service he returned to private life. Died October 8, 1854, at Fairfield, Connecticut.

Tomlinson, Thomas A.—He was born in New York; served in the State Assembly, from Essex County, in 1835 and 1836, and was a Representative in Congress, from 1841 to 1843.

Tompkins, Caleb.—He was born in Westchester County, New York, and was a member of the New York Assembly, from that county, from 1804 to 1806; and was elected a Representative in Congress, from New York, from 1817 to 1821.

Tompkins, Christopher. — He was a Representative in Congress, from Kentucky, from 1831 to 1835, and died at Glasgow, Kentucky, in 1845.

Tompkins, Cydnor B.—Born in Belmont County, Ohio, November 8, 1810, and was educated at the Ohio University, at Athens; was bred a farmer, and afterwards studied law, having practised for twenty-two years; and was elected a Representative, from Ohio, to the Thirty-fifth Congress, serving as a member of the Committee on the Militia. Re-elected to the Thirty-sixth Congress, serving on the Committee on Military Affairs.

Tompkins, Daniel D.—He was born in Westchester County, New York, June 21, 1774. His father was a farmer, and he was his seventh son. He graduated at Columbia College in 1795, then studied law, and was admitted to practice in the city of New York in 1797. In 1821 he was a member of the Constitutional Convention of the State, and also served in the State Legislature. He was elected a Representative in Congress, from 1805 to 1807, but resigned to accept an appointment as Associate Judge of the Supreme Court of the State. In 1807 he was elected Governor of the State, and held that office ten years. His aid in support of the National Government, during the war of 1812, gave him prominence as a statesman. He prorogued the State Legislature in 1812 for the space of ten months, to prevent the establishment of the Bank of America in the city of New York; his opposition postponed, but did not defeat the measure, and a charter was granted in 1813. In 1817 he resigned the office of Governor, and was elected Vice-President of the United States, and served two terms; by virtue of which office he was also President of the Senate. He died in New York, June 11, 1825.

Tompkins, Patrick W.—He was born in Kentucky, and settling in Mississippi, was elected a Representative in Congress, from that State, from 1847 to 1849.

Toombs, Robert.—He was born in Wilkes County, Georgia, July 2, 1810. The first three years of his collegiate life were spent at the University of Georgia, but he left it during the senior year, and went to Schenectady, New York, and graduated at Union College. He read law at the University of Virginia under Judge Lomas; was admitted to the bar of Georgia in 1829, and practised regularly until his election to Congress in 1845. His first public service was as Captain of volunteers in the Creek war, in 1836, under General Winfield Scott. In 1837 he was elected to the Legislature, from his native county, where he now resides, and with the exception of 1841, continued a member of the lower branch, until his election to the Federal House of Representatives, where he served during the Twenty-ninth, Thirtieth, Thirty-first, and Thirty-second Congresses. He entered the Senate during the Thirty-third Congress for six years, and was re-elected for a second term, ending March 4, 1865. In the House and also in the Senate he always served on important committees. He resigned in 1861, and became Secretary of State in the Rebel government, and was also a Brigadier-General in the Great Rebellion.

Toucey, Isaac.—He was born in Connecticut in 1798. He received a common school education; adopted the profession of law, and early in life was State's Attorney for his native county. He was a Representative in Congress, from 1835 to 1839; in 1846 was elected Governor of Connecticut; in 1848 went into President Polk's cabinet as Attorney-General; in 1850 he was elected to the State Senate of Connecticut; he was a Senator in Congress, from 1852 to 1857; and in March of the latter year went into President Buchanan's cabinet as Secretary of the Navy.

Towns, George W. B.—Born in Wilkes County, Georgia, May 4, 1802. He was prevented by ill health from receiving a collegiate education, and commenced life as a merchant; afterwards studied law; was admitted to the bar of Alabama in 1824, and for a time performed the duties of editor of a political paper. In 1826 he returned to Georgia, and settled in Talbot County. He served for several years in both branches of the Legislature of that State, and was a Representative in Congress, from 1835 to 1839, and was re-elected in 1846; his last public position was that of Governor of Georgia, to which office he was elected in 1847, and was re-elected in 1849. He died at Macon, July 15, 1854.

Townsend, George. — He was a Representative in Congress, from New York, from 1815 to 1819.

Townsend, N. S.—He was born in England, and having settled in Ohio, was elected a Representative in Congress, from that State, from 1851 to 1853.

Tracy, Albert H.—He was born in Norwich, Connecticut, June 17, 1793; received a good classical education; studied medicine with his father, but when eighteen years of age he removed to New York State, studied law, and was admitted to the bar in 1815; and he served three terms in Congress as a Representative from a district comprehending almost the whole of that part of New York west of Seneca Lake, from 1819 to 1825; and in 1829 he was elected to the Senate of New York for four years, and was re-elected for a second term of four years. He was a supporter of Mr. Adams for President, and declined a seat in his cabinet; he also declined a Judgeship tendered by Governor Clinton. Died at Buffalo, September 19, 1859.

Tracy, Andrew.—He was born in Vermont; educated a lawyer; and was a Representative in Congress, from that State, from 1853 to 1855. He also served ten years in both branches of the State Legislature, and was Speaker from 1842 to 1845.

Tracy, H. W.—He was born in Luzerne County, Pennsylvania, September 24, 1807; was bred a farmer, and devoted some attention to mercantile pursuits; in 1861 and 1862 he was elected to the State Legislature; was a member of the Chicago Convention which nominated Mr. Lincoln for President; and was elected a Representative, from Pennsylvania, to the Thirty-eighth Congress, serving on the Committees for the District of Columbia, and on Expenditures in the Navy Department.

Tracy, Phineas L.—He was born in Norwich, Connecticut; graduated at Yale College in 1806; and was a Representative in Congress, from Genesee County, New York, from 1827 to 1833, and was a member of the Committee on Expenditures on Public Buildings.

Tracy, Uri.—He was born in Franklin, Connecticut, and graduated at Yale College in 1789; was a Representative in Congress, from New York, from 1805 to 1807, and again from 1809 to 1813, and died in 1813.

Tracy, Uriah.—Born in Franklin, Connecticut, February 2, 1755; graduated at Yale College in 1778; read law in Litchfield, and settled in that town. He was often chosen a State Representative, and in 1793 was Speaker of the House. He was a Representative in Congress from 1793 to 1796, and from 1796 to 1807 a Senator of the United States, officiating for a short time as President *pro tem.* of the Senate. He was also a Major-General of militia; commanded the respect and enjoyed the friendship of the leading men of his time; and died at Washington City, July 19, 1807, and was the first person buried in the Congressional burying-ground.

Trafton, Mark.—He was born in Maine, and elected a Representative, from Massachusetts, to the Thirty-fourth Congress.

Train, Charles R.—Born in Framingham, Massachusetts, in 1817; worked on a farm until fifteen; graduated at Brown University in 1837; studied law, and finished his legal education at Cambridge, coming to the bar in 1841; he was elected to the Massachusetts Legislature in 1847; from 1848 to 1851 was District Attorney for Northern Massachusetts; in 1852 he was appointed by President Fillmore an Associate Judge of the United States Court in Oregon, but declined the office; he was a member of the State Constitutional Convention of 1853; was a second time appointed District Attorney; in 1857 and 1858 he served as a member of the State Council; and he was elected a Representative, from Massachusetts, to the Thirty-sixth Congress, serving as Chairman of the Committee on Public Buildings and Grounds. Re-elected to the Thirty-seventh Congress, serving as Chairman of the Committee on Public Buildings. During the autumn of 1862 he served in the army as a volunteer aid on the staff of his friend, General Gordon, and was present at the battle of Antietam. He was also a Delegate to the Baltimore Convention of 1864.

Treadway, William M. — He was born in Virginia, and was a Representative in Congress, from that State, from 1845 to 1847.

Tredwell, Thomas.—He was for seven years a member of the New York Assembly, from 1776 to 1783, from Suffolk County, and was a Representative in Congress, from New York, from 1791 to 1795.

Trezvant, James.—He was born in Sussex County, Virginia; was a lawyer by profession; was Attorney for the State; member of the State Legislature, and of the Constitutional Convention of 1830; a Representative in Congress, from Virginia, from 1825 to 1831, serving during his last term as Chairman of the Committee on Military Pensions. He died in 1838.

Trigg, Abram.—He was a Representative in Congress, from Virginia, from 1797 to 1809.

Trigg, John.—He was a Representative in Congress, from Virginia, from 1797 to 1804.

Trimble, Cary A.—Born in Hillsborough, Ohio, September 13, 1813; graduated at the Ohio University in 1833; studied medicine, and received a medical diploma from the Cincinnati Medical College in 1836; in 1837 was appointed Demonstrator of Anatomy in his Alma Mater, which position he held until 1841, when he settled in Chillicothe; in 1839, on account of his health, he retired from his profession, and devoted himself to farming; and was elected a Representative, from Ohio, to the Thirty-sixth Congress, serving on the Committee on Public Lands. Re-elected to the Thirty-seventh Congress.

Trimble, David.—He was born in Frederick County, Virginia, about the year 1782; educated at William and Mary College; studied law, and when he came of age removed to Kentucky. He was engaged in the war of 1812, serving two campaigns under General Harrison. In 1817 he was chosen a member of Congress, from Kentucky, and served without interruption till 1827, being highly esteemed for the integrity of his principles and his devotion to his public duties. After his retirement from Congress, he became engaged in agriculture and the iron manufacture, and in the latter interest he did much to develop the resources of the State. He died at Trimble's Furnace, Kentucky, October 26, 1842.

Trimble, William A. — He was born in 1786; he served with credit in the army of the United States during the war of 1812; occupied, as commander, several frontier posts; was a Senator in Congress, from Ohio, from 1819 to 1821, having died December 13 of the latter year.

Triplett, Philip.—He was born in Virginia, and was a Representative in Congress, from Kentucky, from 1839 to 1843.

Trippe, Robert P.—He was born in Georgia, and was elected a Representative in Congress, from that State, to the Thirty-fourth and Thirty-fifth Congresses.

Trotter, F. James.—He was a Senator in Congress, from Mississippi, during the year 1838.

Troup, George M.—Born on the Tombigbee River, September 8, 1780; graduated at Princeton College; studied law; and in 1800 was elected to the Legislature of Georgia, and re-elected for four terms; was a Representative in Congress, from Georgia, from 1807 to 1815; and a Senator from 1816 to 1818, and from 1829 to 1834. From 1823 to 1827 he was Governor of that State. He died in Laurens County, Georgia, May 3, 1856. He was an advocate of State rights, and the champion of State sovereignty.

Trout, Michael C.—He was born in Pennsylvania, and was a Representative in Congress, from that State, from 1853 to 1855.

Trowbridge, R. E.—Was born in Elmira, New York, June 18, 1821; removed with his parents to Michigan when a mere child; graduated at Kenyon College, Ohio, in 1841; has been devoted all his life to the business of farming; was elected to the Senate of Michigan in 1856 and 1858; and in 1860 was elected a Representative, from Michigan, to the Thirty-seventh Congress, serving on the Committee on the Post-office and Post-roads.

Trumbo, Andrew.—A native of Kentucky; was born in Montgomery County, now Bath, September 13, 1799; he had a limited English education, and at the age of fifteen went into the County Clerk's office, and afterwards became clerk; studied law, and commenced practice in 1824. He was a Representative in the Twenty-ninth Congress, and one of the Presidential Electors of Kentucky, in 1848.

Trumbull, Jonathan.—Born in Lebanon, Connecticut, March 26, 1740, and graduated at Harvard College in 1759. In 1775 he was appointed, by Congress, Paymaster in the Northern department of the army, and not long after was attached to the family of Washington as secretary and first aid, with whom he continued until the close of the war. He was for several years a Representative in the State Legislature of Connecticut, and Speaker of the House; was a Representative in Congress, from that State, from 1789 to 1795; elected Speaker of the House of Representatives in 1791, and continued in that station till he was transferred to the United States Senate, in 1795, where he served only one year, having been elected Lieutenant-Governor of Connecticut, and in 1798 Governor, in which position he remained until his death, which occurred August 7, 1809.

Trumbull, Joseph.—Born in Lebanon, Connecticut, December 7, 1783; graduated at Yale College in 1801; studied law, and practised with success, in Ohio; was President of the Hartford Bank for eleven years; served in the General Assembly in 1832, 1848, and 1851; in 1849 he was elected Governor of Connecticut; was President of a railroad company; received from Yale College the degree of LL.D.; and was a Representative in Congress, from Connecticut, in 1834, for an unexpired term, and from 1839 to 1843.

Trumbull, Lyman.—Born in Colchester, Connecticut, in 1813; is a lawyer by profession; was a member of the Illinois Legislature in 1840; Secretary of State in 1841–42; Justice of the Supreme Court of Illinois, from 1848 to 1853; elected to the House of Representatives of the United States, in 1854; and chosen United States Senator, by the Illinois Legislature, in 1855, serving as Chairman of the Committee on the Judiciary. He was also re-elected for the term ending in 1867.

Tuck, Amos. — He was born in Maine; graduated at Dartmouth College in 1835; was for some time a tutor in that institution; and removing to New Hampshire, was elected a Representative in Congress, from that State, from 1847 to 1853. He was also a member of the Peace Congress of 1861.

Tucker, Ebenezer.—He was born in Burlington, New Jersey, in 1758; he was a soldier in the Revolutionary war, and served at the battle of Long Island; he filled many offices of distinction and trust, among them those of Collector and Postmaster of New Jersey; and he was a member of Congress, from New Jersey, from 1825 to 1829. He also held the offices of Judge of the Common Pleas, Justice of the Court of Quarter Sessions, and Judge of the Orphans' Court. He died at Tuckerton, New Jersey, September 5, 1845.

Tucker, George.—He was a native of Virginia, and a Representative in Congress, from that State, from 1819 to 1825.

Tucker, Henry St. George.—Born in Virginia in 1779; received a liberal education, and became a prominent lawyer. He was at one time President of the Court of Appeals; also Professor of Law in the University of Virginia; the author of several valuable works on law; and a Representative in Congress, from Virginia, from 1815 to 1819. He died at Winchester, Virginia, August 28, 1848.

Tucker, Starling.—He was born in Halifax County, North Carolina, and was a Representative in Congress, from the Laurens District of South Carolina, from 1817 to 1831. He died February 4, 1834.

Tucker, Thomas T.—He was a Delegate to the Continental Congress, from 1787 to 1788; and was a Representative in Congress, from South Carolina, from 1789 to 1793. Died May 2, 1828.

Tucker, Tilghman W.—He was born in North Carolina, and was a Representative in Congress, from Mississippi, from 1843 to 1845.

Turner, Charles.—Graduated at Harvard University in 1752, studied for the ministry, and settled in Duxbury, Massachusetts; was elected a Representative in Congress, from Massachusetts, serving from 1809 to 1813, and died in 1816, aged about sixty-six years.

Turner, Daniel.—Born in Warren County, North Carolina, September 26, 1796. He commenced his education at Warrenton Academy; completed it at West Point; in 1814 was appointed Lieutenant of artillery, as such, served at Brooklyn Heights, and at Plattsburg, and resigned in 1815; after leaving the army, he spent two years at William and Mary College; from 1819 to 1823 he served in the Legislature of North Carolina; and was a member of Congress, from 1827 to 1829. He subsequently had charge of the Warrenton Female Seminary.

Turner, James.—Born in Virginia, in the year 1766. His education was such as could be afforded by the common schools of the country; he served in the Revolution as a private soldier; entered public life in 1800, as a member of the Legislature of North Carolina; in 1802 was elected Governor of the State; and was a Senator in Congress, from 1805 to 1816. He died at Bloomsbury, January 15, 1824, much respected for his talents and personal worth.

Turner, James.—He was born in Maryland, and was a Representative in Congress, from that State, from 1833 to 1837.

Turner, Thomas J.—Born in Trumbull County, Ohio, April 5, 1815, where he resided until ten years of age, receiving all his school education within that time. In 1825 he removed with his father's family to Butler County, Pennsylvania, where he worked on a farm until fourteen years old, when the destitute circumstances of his father compelled him to make unusual exertions to assist in the support of the family, which he did by working as a laborer on the Pennsylvania Canal, and contributed his earnings to his father until the age of eighteen. Leaving his father comfortable, he went to the "far West," and spent three years in St. Paul's County, Indiana, and finally settled in Freeport, Stevenson County, Illinois. He was made Justice of the Peace, which office he held for several years; in 1838 he studied law as a profession, and obtained a lucrative practice. In 1842 he was elected Probate Justice of the Peace, and in 1844 was appointed Postmaster. In 1845 he was chosen State's Attorney for the Sixth Judicial District, and in 1846 he was elected a Representative in the Thirtieth Congress. In 1854 he was a member of the lower house of the Legislature, and chosen Speaker. Since that time he has devoted himself to the practice of law.

Turney, Hopkins L.—Born in Smith County, Tennessee, October 3, 1797. He was in his boyhood bound to a tailor, and served at that business several years; in 1818 he entered upon the campaign against the Seminole Indians; he did not learn to write until twenty-two years of age, and yet soon after studied law, and was very successful at the bar; he served about ten years in the Legislature, from 1828 to 1838, and he was a Representative in Congress, from Tennessee, from 1837 to 1843, and in the Senate of the United States, from 1845 to 1851. He died in Winchester, Tennessee, August 1, 1857, leaving behind him a high reputation for his abilities and virtues.

Turpie, D.—Was born in Hamilton County, Ohio, July 8, 1829; graduated at Kenyon College in 1848; studied law, and was admitted to practice at Logansport, Indiana, in 1849; was appointed, by Governor Wright, whom he succeeded in the Senate, Judge of the Court of Common Pleas in 1854, and was Judge of the Circuit Court in 1856, both of which offices he resigned; in 1852, and also 1858, he was a member of the Legislature of Indiana; and in 1863 he was elected a Senator in Congress, for the unexpired term of J. D. Bright, and immediately succeeding J.

A. Wright, who served by appointment of the Governor.

Turrell, Joel.—He was born in Vermont, and was a Representative in Congress, from New York, from 1833 to 1837, having been a member of the State Assembly, from Oswego County, in 1831.

Tuthill, Selah. — Born in New York, and was elected a Representative, from that State, to the Seventeenth Congress, but died in December, 1821.

Tweed, William M.—Born in the city of New York, April 3, 1823; received a common school education; is by occupation a chair manufacturer; was an Alderman in New York City in 1852; a member of the Thirty-third Congress; a member of the State Board of Education in 1857; and a Supervisor of New York County in 1858.

Tweedy, Samuel.—He was born in Connecticut, and was a Representative in Congress, from that State, from 1833 to 1835.

Tyler, Asher.—He was born in New York, and was a Representative in Congress, from that State, from 1843 to 1845.

Tyler, John.—Born in Charles City County, Virginia, in 1790. He commenced his political life at an early age, having been elected to the Virginia Legislature at the age of twenty-one years, and five years later to Congress. In 1826 he was elevated to the station of Governor of his native State. He discharged the duties of his office but one year and a half, when, in 1847, the Legislature selected him to fill a vacancy in the Senate of the United States, where he officiated as President *pro tem.* of that body. He served in this capacity until a difference of opinion having arisen between General Jackson and himself, he resigned his seat in 1836, and went into voluntary retirement. Mr. Tyler did not again make his appearance in public life until 1840, when he was selected by the Whig party as their candidate for Vice-President. He was elected to that office by a large majority, and entered upon the discharge of his duties in March, 1841, when the death of the President, General Harrison, shortly after, raised him to the chief magistracy of the Republic. His term of office expired in 1845, after which he lived in retirement in Virginia until 1861. He was elected in that year a Delegate to the Peace Congress held in Washington, and officiated as its President; and on his return to Virginia, he became a member of the Virginia Convention of 1861, and the Rebel Congress, and died in Richmond, January 17, 1862.

Tyson, Jacob.—He was a member of the New York Senate, from Richmond County, in 1828, and a Representative in Congress, from New York, from 1823 to 1825.

Tyson, Job R.—He was born in Montgomery County, Pennsylvania, in 1804, and died near Philadelphia, in 1858. He was educated a lawyer, frequently served in the City Councils of Philadelphia, and was a member of the Twenty-fourth Congress. He commanded uncommon influence in Congress, and was a man of refined tastes in literature and the fine arts. He also served in the Legislature of Pennsylvania, and through his exertions the archives of that State were first published.

Udree, Daniel.—He was born in Philadelphia, and was a Representative in Congress, from Pennsylvania, from 1813 to 1815, from 1819 to 1821, and from 1823 to 1825. Died July 22, 1828.

Underhill, Walter.—He was born in New York, and was a Representative, in Congress, from that State, from 1849 to 1851.

Underwood, John W. H.—Born in Elbert County, Georgia, November 20, 1816; received a good English and classical education; studied law and was admitted to the bar in 1834; in 1843 was elected Solicitor-General for the Western Circuit, resigning in 1847; was a member of the Georgia Constitutional Convention of 1850; declined two Judicial appointments tendered to him by Presidents Pierce and Buchanan; was a member of the Georgia Legislature in 1857, and chosen Speaker; and in 1859 was elected a Representative from Georgia, to the Thirty-sixth Congress, serving on the Committee on Expenses in the Navy Department. Resigned in February, 1861, on the breaking out of the Rebellion, and returned to Georgia.

Underwood, Joseph R.—Born in Goochland County, Virginia, October 24, 1791. He was adopted by his maternal uncle in 1803, who resided in Barren County, Kentucky. He received his education at various schools in that State, and ended his scholastic course at the University of Lexington, in 1811; and then read law with Robert Wickliffe. In 1813 he entered the service of the United States, as Lieutenant of a volunteer company, and was badly wounded and taken by the enemy at Dudley's defeat, commanding his company after the Captain was mortally wounded. He was released from captivity, and landed from the prison-ships on Lake Erie, near Cleveland, where he was lodged in a hospitable cabin until sufficiently recovered to return home. In the fall of 1813 he located at Glasgow, Kentucky, and practised law for ten years, during which time he was Trustee of the town, and County Attorney; and was a member of the Legislature from 1816 to 1819. In 1823 he removed, with his family, to Bowling Green, and was elected a member of the General Assembly in 1825 and 1826. From 1828 to 1835 he was Judge of the Court of Appeals, and resigned on being elected a Representative in Congress, in which position he served for ten sessions. In 1846 he was again elected to the Legislature of Kentucky, and was Speaker of the House. In 1847 he was elected a member of the United States Senate, for six years, and at the expiration of the term returned to the practice of law. In 1824 and in 1844 he was a Presidential Elector. He was also a Delegate to the Chicago Convention of 1864.

Underwood, Warner L.—Born in Goochland County, Virginia, August 7, 1808; graduated at the University of Virginia, where he received the first honors in the studies of law, mathematics, and the modern languages, in 1830. He removed to Bowling Green County, Kentucky, at the age of seventeen; a lawyer by profession, with an extensive practice. In 1833 he visited Texas, and spent most of the time, until 1840, in that Republic. He was appointed, by President Lamar, Attorney-General for the Eastern District of that Republic, but held the office only a short time, and also declined the offer of a place in General Houston's cabinet, being unwilling to relinquish his citizenship of the United States. In 1848 he was a Representative in the Kentucky Legislature, and in 1849 a member of the State Senate; and was elected a Representative to the Thirty-fourth and Thirty-fifth Congresses, serving as a member of the Committee on Engraving.

Upham, Charles W.—Born in St. John, New Brunswick, May 4, 1802. He commenced life by becoming a merchant's clerk; graduated at Harvard College in 1821; in 1824 he was settled over the First Church in Salem, Massachusetts; and in 1844 he relinquished the ministry on account of loss of voice. He has also, at different times, edited the Christian Review (Unitarian); was Mayor of Salem in 1852; in 1840, 1849 and 1850 was in the State Legislature; in 1851, 1857, and 1858, President of the Senate; and he was a member of the Thirty-third Congress, serving upon the Committee on Post-roads and the Post-office, and was Chairman of a Special Committee on the Smithsonian Institution. As an author he has been industrious, and among his publications are the following: "Letters on the Logos," "Lectures on Witchcraft," "Life of Sir Henry Vane," and "Life of John C. Fremont."

Upham, George B.—He graduated at Harvard University in 1789; served a number of years in the New Hampshire Legislature, having been Speaker in 1809 and 1815; and a Representative in Congress, from New Hampshire, from 1801 to 1803. He died February 10, 1848, at Claremont, New Hampshire, aged seventy-nine years.

Upham, Jabez.—He was born in Massachusetts; graduated at Harvard University in 1785; and was a Representative in Congress, from that State, from 1807 to 1810. He died in 1811.

Upham, Nathaniel.—Born in Deerfield, Rockingham County, New Hampshire, June 9, 1774. He was educated at the schools of his native town, and at Phillips's Exeter Academy. At an early age he engaged in mercantile pursuits. He was a member of the Legislature of New Hampshire, and of the Governor's Council, from 1811 to 1812; and a Representative in Congress, from that State, from 1817 to 1823. Died in 1829.

Upham, William.—He was born at Leicester, Massachusetts, in 1792; in 1802 removed with his father to Vermont; spent some time in the University of Vermont; and was a lawyer by profession. He was a member of the Vermont Assembly in 1827, 1828, and 1830; and was State's Attorney, for Washington County, in 1829. He was a Senator in Congress, from 1843 to the time of his death, which occurred in Washington City, January 14, 1853.

Upson, Charles.—Born in Southington, Hartford County, Connecticut, March 19, 1821; received a good English education; removed to Michigan in 1845; studied law, and came to the bar in 1847; in 1849 and 1850 was County Clerk for St. Joseph County; in 1853 and 1854 was Prosecuting Attorney for the same; in 1855 and 1856 held the office of State Senator; in 1861 and 1862 he was Attorney-General for Michigan, and was elected a Representative from Michigan to the Thirty-eighth Congress, serving on the Committees of Elections, and Unfinished Business.

Vail, George.—He was born in New Jersey, and was elected a Representative in Congress, for the terms between 1853 and 1857.

Vail, Henry.—He was born in New York, and was a Representative in Congress, from that State, from 1837 to 1839. Died June 25, 1853.

Valk, William W.—He was born in South Carolina, and, on removing to New York, was a Representative in Congress, from that State, from 1855 to 1857.

Vallandigham, Clement L.—He came of a Huguenot family, and was born in New Lisbon, Columbia County, Ohio, in 1822. He received a good education; spent one year in Jefferson College, in Ohio; spent two years as principal of an academy at Snow Hill, Maryland; returned to Ohio in 1840; studied law, and was admitted to the bar in 1842; was elected to the State Legislature in 1845 and 1846; was editor of the Dayton Enquirer from 1847 to 1849; for some years subsequent to that date he devoted himself wholly to his profession and politics; was a member of the National Democratic Convention held at Cincinnati in 1856; ran for the Thirty-fifth Congress against L. C. Campbell, whose seat he successfully contested; and he was re-elected to the Thirty-sixth Congress. At the commencement of the second session of the Thirty-fifth Congress, and during the Thirty-sixth, he was placed on the Committee on Territories. Re-elected to the Thirty-seventh Congress. In 1863 he was arrested by military authority for expressing his opinions against the war, was banished to the Southern States, and by way of Bermuda went to Canada. During his exile he was nominated for Governor of Ohio and defeated. He subsequently returned and was a Delegate to the Chicago Convention of 1864.

Van Allen, James I.—He was a Representative in Congress, from New York, from 1807 to 1809, having been a member of the State Assembly, in 1804, from Columbia County.

Van Allen, John E.—He was a Representative in Congress, from New York, from 1793 to 1799, and was a member of the State Assembly in 1800 and 1801, from Rensselaer County.

Van Buren, John.—He was one of the ablest lawyers of the Ulster County bar, in New York, and a Representative in Congress, from 1841 to 1843. He died at Kingston, January 16, 1855.

Van Buren, Martin.—Was born at Kinderhook, New York, December 5, 1782. His father's circumstances were humble, and the son was only able to obtain an ordinary education at the common school and academy of his native village. In 1796 he left the academy, and commenced the study of law. In 1800 he represented the Republicans of his native town in the Congressional Convention for that District. A part of the years 1802 and 1803 he spent in New York, still engaged in the study of his profession, and in November of the latter year he was admitted to the bar. He still continued to take an active part in politics. The first official distinction which he received was conferred upon him by Governor Tompkins, who appointed him Surrogate of Columbia County, in 1808. He took his next step in public life in 1812. In the spring of that year he was elected to the State Senate. He continued a member of that body until 1820, having been, during that period, a supporter of the war and the canal project. A portion of this time he also held the office of Attorney-General. He was a member of the Constitutional Convention of the State of New York, in 1821, and in February of the same year he was elected to the United States Senate, and re-elected in 1827, serving until 1829. The following year the Gubernatorial chair of the State of New York became vacant, by the death of Governor Clinton, and Mr. Van Buren was selected as the candidate for that office, by the Democratic party of the State. He was elected, but his career as Governor was brief. Scarcely was his administration commenced, when President Jackson offered him the appointment of Secretary of State, and Mr. Van Buren at once accepted it. The President appointed him Ambassador to England, but the Senate refused to confirm the nomination. He received a large majority of the electoral votes for Vice-President in 1832, which office he continued to fill during President Jackson's term. In 1836 he was nominated for the office of President, and elected. The principal measure of his administration was the establishment of the Independent Treasury. In 1840 he was again nominated for the same office, but defeated by the Whig candidate, General Harrison. After the close of his Presidential term, in 1841, he lived in retirement at Kinderhook, his place of birth, on an estate to which he gave the name of Lindenwald. In 1848 he was the Presidential candidate of the section of the Democratic party styling themselves "Barnburners," or, on that occasion, "Free-soilers," but was unsuccessful. Died near Kinderhook, July 24, 1862.

Vance, Joseph.—He was born in Washington County, Pennsylvania, and was one of the earliest residents of the State of Ohio; served frequently in the Legislature of that State; was a Representative in Congress, from 1821 to 1835; Governor of the State in 1836; and again in Congress, from 1843 to 1847, serving as Chairman of the Committee on Claims. In every public position he acquitted himself with ability, and died near the town of Urbanna, Ohio, August 24, 1851.

Vance, Robert B.—He was born in North Carolina, and was a Representative in Congress, from that State, from 1823 to 1825.

Vance, Zebulon B.—He was born in Buncombe County, North Carolina, May 13, 1830; received a limited education, and spent one year at the State University, through the friendship of its distinguished President; he studied law, and was admitted to the bar in 1853; in 1854 he was elected to the Legislature, from Buncombe County; and, on the resignation of Hon. T. L. Clingman, in 1858, he was elected to succeed him in the Federal House of Representatives. Re-elected to the Thirty-sixth Congress, serving on the Committee on Revolutionary Claims; and was Governor of North Carolina from 1861 to 1863.

Van Cortlandt, Philip. — He served through the Revolutionary war as a Colonel in the New York line, fighting at Saratoga and Bemis Heights; was a member of the State Convention which ratified the United States Constitution, and was a member of the New York Assembly, from Westchester County, in 1788, 1789, and 1790; of the State Senate, from 1791 to 1794; and a Representative in Congress, from New York, from 1793 to 1809. Died November 5, 1831, in Westchester County, aged eighty-two years. The latter part of his life was devoted to agriculture.

Van Cortlandt, Pierre.—He was a Representative in Congress, from New York, from 1811 to 1813, having been a member of the State Assembly in 1777.

Vanderpool, Aaron. — He was born at Kinderhook, New York, February 5, 1799; received a classical education; he studied law, and was admitted to the bar in 1820; he served in 1825, 1829, and 1830, in the State Legislature; and he was a Representative in Congress, from 1833 to 1837, and again from 1839 to 1841. On his retirement from Congress he settled in New York City, and was appointed one of the Judges of the Superior Court, which office he held until 1850.

Vanderveer, Abraham.—He was born in New York, and was a Representative in Congress, from that State, from 1837 to 1839. Died July 20, 1839.

Vandever, William. — Born in Maryland, and removing to Iowa, was elected a Representative, from that State, to the Thirty-sixth Congress, serving as a member of the Committee on Public Lands. Re-elected to the Thirty-seventh Congress. Served also as a Colonel in the Union army in 1861.

Van Dyke, John.—He was born in New Jersey; adopted the legal profession; and was a Representative in Congress, from that State, from 1847 to 1851. He is now a Judge of the Supreme Court of the State.

Van Dyke, Nicholas.—He graduated at Princeton College in 1788; was a Representative in Congress, from Delaware, from 1807 to 1811; a Senator in Congress, from 1817 to 1826; and died in May, 1826.

Van Gaasbeck, Peter.—He was a Representative in Congress, from New York, from 1793 to 1795.

Van Horn, Burt.—Was a Representative, from New York, to the Thirty-seventh Congress, and also served as a Colonel of volunteers in 1861.

Van Horne, Archibald.—He was a Representative in Congress, from Maryland, from 1807 to 1811.

Van Horne, Espy.—He was born in Lycoming County, Pennsylvania, and was a Representative in Congress, from Pennsylvania, from 1825 to 1829. Died at Williamsport, Pennsylvania, July 25, 1829.

Van Horne, Isaac.—He was a Captain in the Revolutionary war, and a Representative in Congress, from Pennsylvania, from 1801 to 1805, and was then appointed Receiver of Public Moneys in Zanesville, Ohio.

Van Houton, Isaac B.—He was a Representative in Congress, from New York, from 1833 to 1835.

Van Metre, John J.—He was a Representative in Congress, from Ohio, from 1843 to 1845, and was a member of the Committee on Expenses in the Navy Department.

Van Ness, John P.—He was born in Ghent, Columbia County, New York, in 1770. He was educated at Columbia College, and studied law, but gave up the practice on account of ill health. He was a Representative in Congress, from 1801 to 1803; and having taken up his residence in Washington City, became the first President of the Bank of the Metropolis in 1814; he was also elected Mayor of Washington, and both as a public and private citizen did much to promote the prosperity of the seat of Government. While a member of Congress he received, from President Jefferson, a commission as Major of militia for the District of Columbia, which, with the fact that he married a Washington lady, was the cause of his change of residence. He died in Washington, March 7, 1846.

Van Rensselaer, Henry. — He was born in New York; entered West Point as a cadet in 1827; was commissioned a Lieutenant in 1831, but resigned the following year; and was a Representative in Congress, from New York, from 1841 to 1843.

Van Rensselaer, Jeremiah.—He was born in 1741; was a patriot of the Revolution; Lieutenant-Governor of New York; a member of Congress, from that State, from 1789 to 1791. He died in Albany, February 22, 1810.

Van Rensselaer, Solomon.—He was born in Rensselaer County, New York, in 1774; he served as an officer under General Wayne in 1794, and was wounded through the lungs, and received four wounds at the battle of Queenstown Heights. In 1799 he was promoted to the rank of Major. He was Adjutant-General of New York, from 1801 to 1810, and in 1813. He was a Representative in Congress, from that State, from 1819 to 1822, when he was appointed Postmaster at Albany. He died near Albany, April 23, 1852.

Van Rensselaer, Stephen.—He was born in the city of New York, in November, 1764, and graduated at the

University in Cambridge, Massachusetts, in 1782; was elected a member of the New York Senate in 1795; was six years Lieutenant-Governor of New York; a member of Congress, from 1822 to 1829; was appointed, in 1810, one of the Canal Commissioners, and, for the last fourteen years of his life, was President of the Board; and during the last war with England he commanded, with reputation, as Major-General on the Niagara frontier. He was distinguished for his wealth and munificent charities, and enjoyed the inherited title of Patroon. He died at Albany, January 26, 1839.

Van Rensselaer, William.—He was born in 1763; was a member of Congress, from New York, from 1801 to 1811, after which he retired to private life, and died in New York City, June 18, 1845.

Vansant, Joshua.—He was born in Maryland, and was a Representative in Congress, from that State, from 1853 to 1855; was also for many years President of the Maryland Institute.

Van Valkenburgh, Robert B.—Born in Steuben County, New York, September 4, 1821; adopted the profession of law; served three terms in the Legislature of New York; when the Rebellion broke out he was placed by the Governor of New York in charge of affairs at Elmira, and there organized seventeen regiments for the war, and was elected a Representative, from New York, to the Thirty-seventh Congress, serving as Chairman of the Committee on the Militia. In 1862, and while in Congress, he took command, as Colonel, of the One Hundred and Seventh Regiment New York Volunteers, and was present at the battle of Antietam. He was re-elected to the Thirty-eighth Congress, serving as Chairman of the Committees on the Militia, and Expenditures in the State Department.

Van Winkle, Peter G.—Was born in the city of New York, September 7, 1808; removed to Parkersburg, now West Virginia, in 1835; was a member of the Virginia Constitutional Convention of 1850; also of the Wheeling Convention of 1861; and also of the Convention which formed the Constitution of West Virginia in 1862; was a member of the Legislature of that State from its organization to June, 1863; and in November of that year was elected a Senator in Congress for the term ending in 1869, serving on the Committees on Finance and Pensions.

Van Wyck, Charles H.—He was elected a Representative, from New York, to the Thirty-sixth Congress, serving as a member of the Committee on Mileage; also elected to the Thirty-seventh Congress, and appointed Chairman of the Committee on Government Contracts. While in Congress he served in the volunteer service as the Colonel of a regiment.

Van Wyck, William H.—He was born in Dutchess County, New York, and was a Representative in Congress, from that State, from 1821 to 1825.

Varnum, John.—He was a Representative in Congress, from Massachusetts, from 1825 to 1831. He was a native of Essex County, Massachusetts; educated at Harvard University; practised law for some years at Haverhill, Massachusetts; was frequently a member of the State Legislature. He removed to Niles, in the State of Michigan, where he died, July 23, 1836, aged sixty-three years.

Varnum, Joseph Bradley.—Born in 1759, in Dracut, Massachusetts; he was a General in the Revolutionary war, and a Representative in Congress, from 1795 to 1811, being four years Speaker, during the Tenth and Eleventh Congresses. He was chosen Senator in 1811, served till 1817, and was President *pro tem.* of the Senate. Of three conventions of Massachusetts he was a useful member. He died suddenly, September 11, 1821, being then Major-General of a division of the militia.

Venable, Abraham B.—He was a graduate of Princeton College in 1780; a Representative in Congress, from Virginia, from 1791 to 1799, and a Senator of the United States, from 1803 to 1804. He perished in the conflagration of the theatre at Richmond, Virginia, December 26, 1811.

Venable, Abraham W.—Born in Prince Edward County, Virginia, October 17, 1799; graduated at Hampden Sidney College in 1816; studied medicine for two years, and then went to Princeton College, where he graduated in 1819; he then studied law, and was admitted to the bar in North Carolina in 1821. He was a Presidential Elector in 1832, and also in 1836; and a Representative in Congress, from North Carolina, from 1847 to 1853. His father and six uncles were in the Revolutionary war, serving their country faithfully. He took part in the Rebellion of 1861 as a member of the so-called Confederate Congress.

Verplanck, Daniel C.—He was born in New York in 1761, and was a Representative in Congress, from that State, from 1803 to 1809. He subsequently served for many years as Judge of the County Court of Dutchess County, New York, and died near Fishkill, March 29, 1834.

Verplanck, Gulian C.—An American author, and born in the city of New York. He graduated at Columbia College, pursued the study of the law, and, after his admission to the bar, he passed several years abroad, in Great Britain and on the continent. On his return home, he became interested in politics, and, in 1814, was a candidate of the "malcontents" in New York for the Assembly. In 1819 he wrote the "State Triumvirate, a Political Tale," being a satire on the political parties of the day, and other works of a similar description. In 1820 he was a prominent member of the New York Legislature, in which he was Chairman of the Committee on Education. He soon after became Professor of the Evidences of Christianity in the Theological Seminary of the Protestant Episcopal Church in New York, and, in 1824, he published his "Essays on the Nature and Uses of the various Evidences of Revealed Religion," a work written with simplicity and elegance. The following year appeared his "Essay on the Doctrine of Contracts, being an Inquiry how Contracts are affected, in Law and Morals, by Concealment, Error, or Inadequate Price." Besides these works, he contributed much to various magazines, and in conjunction with Mr. Bryant and Mr. Sands, he published the Talisman, a sort of annual, three volumes of which appeared. From 1825 he was for eight years a member of Congress, from the city of New York, and he was afterwards, for several years, a member of the New York Senate. He also published, in 1833, a collection of his discourses and addresses on various subjects, and in 1844–46, a handsome edition of Shakspeare.

Verree, John P.—Born in Philadelphia, Pennsylvania, in 1819; is an iron manufacturer by occupation—the business of his whole life heretofore; was for six years a member of the Philadelphia Select Council, and four years the presiding officer of that body; and was elected a Representative, from Pennsylvania, to the Thirty-sixth Congress, serving as a member of the Committee on Revolutionary Pensions. Re-elected to the Thirty-seventh Congress.

Vibbard, Chauncey.—Was born at Galway, Saratoga County, New York, November 11, 1811; received a common school education; was employed for several years as a clerk in a store, and afterwards in a railroad office, in Albany; in 1848 he became the Superintendent of the Utica and Schenectady Railway Company; and was afterwards called to the same position in the New York Central Railway Company, in which capacity he continued until elected a Representative, from New York, to the Thirty-seventh Congress, serving as a member of the Committee on the Post-office and Post Roads.

Vining, John.—He was a Representative in Congress, from Delaware, from 1789 to 1792, and a Senator in Congress, from 1795 to 1798, when he resigned. He had previously been elected a Delegate to the Continental Congress, from 1784 to 1786.

Vinton, Samuel F.—Born at South Hadley, Massachusetts, September 25, 1792. He graduated at Williams College, Massachusetts, in 1814; studied law in Middletown, Connecticut, and was admitted to the bar in 1816, when he removed to Ohio, and practised his profession with eminent success. He was first elected a Representative in Congress, in 1823, and served fourteen years, when he declined a re-election; he was re-elected in 1843, and served eight years in succession, when he again declined a re-election, and retired to private life, where his tastes and wishes inclined him to remain. While in Congress, Mr. Vinton served as chairman of several of the most important committees. In 1862 he was appointed a Commissioner under the act emancipating the slaves in the District of Columbia, and died in Washington in May, 1862.

Voorhees, Daniel W.—Was born in Fountain County, Indiana, September 26, 1828; graduated at the Indiana Asbury University in 1849; read law, and commenced the practice in 1851; in 1858 he was appointed United States District Attorney for Indiana by President Buchanan, which office he held three years; in 1859 he was engaged in the defence of John E. Cook, at Harper's Ferry, for participation in the John Brown raid. In 1860 he was elected a Representative, from Indiana, to the Thirty-seventh Congress, serving on the Committee on Elections, and was re-elected to the Thirty-eighth Congress, serving on the same Committee. Occasionally, by way of relieving the monotony of professional life, he is in the habit of addressing literary societies on subjects of general interest.

Vose, Roger.—He graduated at Harvard University in 1790; was for many years Chief Justice of the Court of Common Pleas in New Hampshire; and was a Representative in Congress, from that State, from 1813 to 1817; and died April 17, 1842.

Vroom, Peter D.—He was born in New Jersey; graduated at Columbia College, New York; and was a Representative in Congress, from New Jersey, from 1839 to 1841. He was also Governor of New Jersey, from 1829 to 1832, and for a second term, from 1833 to 1836; and a member of the State Constitutional Convention of 1844. In 1853 he was appointed Minister to Prussia. He was also a Delegate to the Peace Congress of 1861.

Wade, Benjamin F.—He was born in Feeding Hills Parish, Massachusetts, October 27, 1800; received a limited education, and commenced active life by teaching school and attending to agricultural pursuits, in Ohio, to which he removed when twenty-one years of age; he studied law, and was admitted to the bar in 1828; and he was elected a Senator in Congress, from Ohio, in 1851, for the term ending in 1857, and re-elected for a second and third term, ending in 1869, serving as Chairman of the Committee on Territories, and of the Special Committee on the Conduct of the War. The other public positions held by him are Justice of the Peace, Prosecuting Attorney for Ashtabula County, State Senator, and President of a Judicial Circuit.

Wade, Edward.—He was born in West Springfield, Massachusetts, November 22, 1803, and received a common school education; he removed with his father to Andover, Ashtabula County, Ohio, in 1821, where he remained until 1824, and engaged in clearing the land. He studied law in Albany and Troy, New York, and was admitted to the bar in Jefferson, Ohio, in 1827, and was elected Justice of the Peace in that county; in 1832 he removed to Unionville, and remained until 1837, and finally settled in Cleveland. He was elected a Representative, from Ohio, in the Thirty-third Congress, to which position he has been re-elected, serving in the Thirty-sixth Congress on the Committee on Commerce.

Wadsworth, Jeremiah.—He was a Delegate, from Connecticut, to the Continental Congress, from 1786 to 1788, and a Representative in Congress, from that State, from 1789 to 1795.

Wadsworth, Peleg.—Was born in Duxbury, Massachusetts, May 6, 1748; graduated at Harvard College in 1769, and afterwards engaged in commercial pursuits. He joined the army as Captain of a company of minute men, at Roxbury, in the beginning of the war, and by his skill and courage rose rapidly in the service. He was second in command of the forces sent to Penobscot by Massachusetts, in 1779, on which occasion he displayed great courage, and was taken prisoner. He rose to the rank of Brigadier-General. After the war, in 1784, he established himself in Portland, Maine, in mercantile business; and was employed much in surveying, in which he was quite skilful.

In 1792 he was elected a Senator in the Legislature of Massachusetts, and the same year was chosen the first Representative in Congress from his district. He was successively re-elected until 1806, when he declined a further nomination. In 1798, the citizens of Portland gave him a public dinner, in approbation of his conduct as their Representative. In 1807 he removed to the county of Oxford, Maine, to improve a large tract of land granted to him by Government, for his services. Here he passed the remainder of his days in retirement, enjoying the respect of a large circle of his friends and fellow-citizens. He died in 1829.

Wadsworth, W. H.—Was born in Maysville, Mason County, Kentucky, July 4, 1821, but came of the old family of Wadsworths who founded the city of Hartford, Connecticut. He received his education from the Maysville Seminary and the Augusta College of Kentucky; adopted the profession of law; sat in the Senate of Kentucky in 1853 and 1855; was a Presidential Elector in 1860, presiding over the Electoral College; and was elected a Representative, from Kentucky, to the Thirty-seventh Congress, serving on the Committee on Naval Affairs. Re-elected to the Thirty-eighth Congress, serving on the Committees on Public Lands, and the Joint Committee on the Library.

Wagener, D. D.—He was born in Pennsylvania, and was a Representative in Congress, from that State, from 1833 to 1841. He was a merchant, and for many years President of the Easton Bank. Died at Easton, Pennsylvania, October 1, 1860.

Waggamann, George A.—He was Secretary of State of Louisiana, under three administrations; held various other public positions; and was a Senator in Congress, from 1831 to 1835. He died at New Orleans, March 23, 1843, from the effects of a wound received in a duel, aged fifty-three years.

Wagner, Peter J.—He was born in New York, and was a Representative in Congress, from that State, from 1839 to 1841.

Wakeman, Abram. — Born in Fairfield, Connecticut, May 31, 1824. He received a district school education; when sixteen years of age he removed to New Rochelle, New York, and taught school; he subsequently attended an academy in Herkimer County, as pupil, working a part of the time on a farm to pay his expenses; he then went into the wilderness and took charge of a saw-mill; after that he went into the business of selling books by subscription, travelling through much of the Union; in 1844 he commenced the study of the law in Herkimer County, New York; went to New York City in 1846, and was admitted to the bar in 1847; in 1850 he was elected to the Legislature; re-elected in 1851; in 1854 was elected an Alderman in New York, serving two years; and in 1856 was elected a Representative to the Thirty-fifth Congress. He has also frequently served as a member of State conventions.

Walbridge, David S.—Born in Bennington, Vermont, July 30, 1802; received his education from the common schools of the vicinity; has devoted himself to the various employments of the farmer, the merchant, and the miller; he removed to Michigan in 1842; and was elected a Representative in Congress, from that State, in 1854, and served until 1859.

Walbridge, Henry S.—He was a Representative in Congress, from New York, from 1851 to 1853.

Walbridge, Hiram. — Born at Ithaca, Tompkins County, New York, February 2, 1821; commenced life by learning the trade of a mechanic; subsequently received a good education at the Ohio University; when twenty-three years of age was elected Brigadier-General of the Ohio militia; and removing to New York City, was elected a Representative in Congress, from New York, serving from 1853 to 1855.

Walden, Hiram.—He was born in Rutland County, Vermont, August 29, 1800; received a limited education, and having removed with his father to New York, devoted himself to the business of cloth dressing and wool carding; he took an interest in military affairs, and attained the office of Major-General of militia; in 1836 he was elected to the State Legislature; in 1842 he was elected a Supervisor in the county of Schoharie;

and was a Representative in Congress, from New York, from 1849 to 1851.

Waldo, Lorin P.—Was born in Canterbury, Windham County, Connecticut, February 2, 1802; received a thorough English education in the common schools, and pursued the study of the classics to some extent under private instructors; read law, and was admitted to practice in the courts of the State of Connecticut, in September, 1825; located in Tolland County, Connecticut, where he was State's Attorney from 1837 to 1849; was two years Judge of the Court of Probate in his district, and six years a member of the Legislature of his State. In April, 1849, he was elected to the Thirty-first Congress, and served the term. In 1852 he was elected Commissioner of the School Fund of Connecticut; was, in March, 1853, appointed, by President Pierce, Commissioner of Pensions; and in June, 1855, was elected, by the Legislature of Connecticut, to the office of Judge of the Supreme Court, which office he now holds.

Waldron, Henry.—He was born in Albany, New York, October 11, 1819; graduated at Rutgers College, New Brunswick, New Jersey, in July, 1836; became a civil engineer by profession; was elected to the Legislature of Michigan in 1843; and served as a Representative in Congress, during the years 1855, 1856, 1857, and 1858, and was a member of the Committee on Mileage. He was re-elected to the Thirty-sixth Congress, serving on the Committee on Territories.

Wales, George E.—He was born in Windham County, Vermont, and was a Representative in Congress, from Vermont, from 1825 to 1829. He also served six years in the State Legislature, and was Speaker in 1823 and 1824; and was Judge of Probate, for Hartford County, from 1843 to 1848.

Wales, John.—He was a Senator in Congress, from Delaware, from 1849 to 1851. Died December 3, 1863.

Walker, Amasa.—He was elected a Representative, from Massachusetts, to the Thirty-seventh Congress, for the unexpired term of G. F. Bailey, deceased.

Walker, Benjamin.—He was a Representative in Congress, from New York, from 1801 to 1803.

Walker, David.—He was a Representative in Congress, from Kentucky, from 1817 to 1820. Died March 1, 1820, having sent a request to Congress that his death should not be officially noticed, which request was complied with.

Walker, Felix.—He was born in Hampshire County, Virginia, July 19, 1753, and was a Representative in Congress, from North Carolina, from 1817 to 1823; was the friend and companion of Daniel Boone, when he explored Kentucky and founded Boonsborough; he served as a soldier in the Indian wars in the Carolinas; settled in Tryon County, North Carolina; and was for many years in the State Legislature; and subsequently removing to the State of Mississippi, he died there in 1830.

Walker, Francis.—He was a Representative in Congress, from North Carolina, from 1793 to 1795.

Walker, Freeman.—He was a Senator in Congress, from Georgia, from 1819 to 1821.

Walker, George.—He was a Senator in Congress, from Kentucky, from 1814 to 1815.

Walker, Isaac P.—He was a Senator in Congress, from Wisconsin, from 1848 to 1855, and Chairman of the Committee on Revolutionary Claims.

Walker, John.—He was a Senator in Congress, from Virginia, during the year 1790.

Walker, John.—He was a Senator in Congress, from Georgia, from 1790 to 1791.

Walker, John W.—He was a Senator in Congress, from Alabama, from 1819 to 1822, and died in April, 1823. He resigned his seat in Congress on account of ill health. It was said that he sometimes addressed the Senate when it was thought he would die before finishing.

Walker, Percy.—Born near Huntsville, Alabama; received an academic education, and in 1835 graduated in the medical department of the University of Pennsylvania, and removed to Mobile. He served as an officer in a volunteer company during the Creek war. He afterwards studied law as a profession, and was admitted to the bar in 1842; he was elected by the Legislature to the office of State's Attorney for the Sixth Judicial Circuit, which he held four years. In 1839, 1847, and 1853, he represented Mobile County in the General Assembly, and in 1855 was elected a Representative, from Alabama, to the Thirty-fourth Congress. At the next election he declined being a candidate, and resumed the practice of law.

Walker, Robert J.—Was born at Northumberland, in the State of Pennsylvania, in 1801. He entered the University of Pennsylvania, in Philadelphia, where he graduated in 1819. On leaving college, he settled in Pittsburg, studied law, and was admitted to practice in 1821. He interested himself in politics at a very early period, and became Chairman of a Democratic Committee, during a State election, when only twenty-two years of age. A year or two later he took part in the movement in favor of nominating General Jackson to the Presidency, and was instrumental in bringing about the action of the Harrisburg Convention, which nominated Jackson for that office in 1824. In the spring of 1826 he moved to the State of Mississippi. He uniformly refused political office until 1836, when he was chosen a Senator in Congress, serving until 1845. In that body he was one of the leaders of his party. In March, 1845, on President Polk's accession to office, he was called upon to take charge of the Treasury Department, which he administered for four years. He subsequently visited England, where he met with flattering attentions. After having been for some years out of the pale of politics, he was appointed, by President Buchanan, in 1857, Governor of the Territory of Kansas, which office he resigned.

Walker, William A.—He was born in New Hampshire, and was a Representative, in Congress, from New York, from 1853 to 1855. Died at New York, December 18, 1861.

Wall, Garret D.—Born in Monmouth County, New Jersey, March 10, 1783; received an academical education, and in 1798 commenced the study of law at Trenton; in 1804 was licensed as an attorney, and in 1807 as counsellor-at-law. Was appointed Clerk of the Supreme Court in 1812, which office he held for five years. He commanded a volunteer company at the defence of Sandy Hook, in the last war; and was Quartermaster-General of the State from 1815 to 1837. In 1827 he was elected to the General Assembly. In 1829 was appointed United States District Attorney for New Jersey, and the same year elected Governor of the State, by the Legislature, but declined the appointment. He was a member of the United States Senate from 1835 to 1841. In 1843 his health was greatly impaired by a stroke of paralysis; but in 1848 he was appointed Judge of the Court of Errors and Appeals, which office he occupied until his death, which occurred in Burlington, New Jersey, November 22, 1850. His disease was dropsy on the chest.

Wall, James W.—Was born in Trenton, New Jersey in 1820; his father, Garret D. Wall, having been a Senator before him; graduated at Princeton College in 1839; studied law, and commenced the practice in Trenton; his first public position was that of Commissioner of Bankruptcy; in 1847, he settled in Burlington, and devoted some attention to literary pursuits; in 1850 he was elected Mayor of Burlington; and in 1854 he visited Europe, and published a volume, entitled, "Foreign Etchings, or Visits to the Old World's Pleasant Places." During the early part of the Rebellion, he wrote against the administration in power for interfering with the freedom of the press, and was imprisoned for a few weeks in Fort Lafayette, and on his release was welcomed home with great enthusiasm by his fellow-citizens; and in January, 1863, he was elected a Senator in Congress, from New Jersey, for the unexpired term of John W. Thompson, deceased, but which seat was for a short time occupied by R. S. Field.

Wall, William.—Was born in Philadelphia, March 20, 1801; served seven years as an apprentice to a ropemaker; removed to King's County, Long Island, in 1822, where he followed his business of rope-making so successfully that when he gave it up in 1856 he had acquired a large fortune. While thus engaged in active business, he was called upon to fill a great number of local offices, such as Commissioner of Highways, School Trustee, Supervisor, Commissioner of Water-works, &c.; and in 1860 he was elected a Representative, from New York, to the Thirty-seventh Congress, serving on the Committees on Revolutionary Claims, and Expenditures on Public Buildings.

Wallace, Daniel.—He was born in South Carolina, and was a Representative in Congress, from that State, from 1847 to 1853.

Wallace, David.—He was born in Philadelphia, April 4, 1799; graduated at West Point in 1821, and served for a time as Professor of Mathematics. In 1828 he was a member of the Indiana Legislature; elected Lieutenant-Governor of the State in 1830 and 1833; Governor of the State from 1837 to 1840; and was a Representative in Congress, from Indiana, from 1841 to 1843; and subsequently to his service in Congress was Prosecuting Attorney for the State; a member of the State Constitutional Convention; and in 1856 was elected Judge of the Court of Common Pleas at Indianapolis, where he died, September 5, 1859.

Wallace, James M.—He was born in Dauphin County, Pennsylvania, and was a Representative in Congress, from that State, from 1815 to 1821. It is said he always protested against the initial M. in his name, but never got rid of it in the Journals of Congress.

Wallace, John W.—He was born in Pennsylvania, and elected a Representative, from that State, to the Thirty-seventh Congress, serving on the Committee on Claims.

Wallace, William H.—Born in Miami County, Ohio, July 17, 1811; spent his early life in Indiana; removed to Iowa in 1837; was elected to the State Legislature of Iowa, and served as Speaker, and also as President of the State Council; was appointed, by President Taylor, Receiver of Public Moneys at Fairfield, Iowa; removed to Washington Territory in 1853; served several sessions in the Territorial Legislature; was appointed, in 1861, by President Lincoln, Governor of Washington Territory; was elected a Delegate therefrom to the Thirty-seventh Congress; was appointed the first Governor of Idaho Territory; and re-elected to the Thirty-eighth Congress, as a Delegate from Idaho.

Walley, Samuel H.—Born in Boston, Massachusetts, August 31, 1805; fitted for college at Andover Academy; graduated at Harvard College in 1826; studied law; officiated for twenty years as Treasurer of a savings bank in Boston for the benefit of seamen; was also Treasurer for a long time of a railroad in Vermont, and one in New York; he was also a member of the State Legislature for eight sessions, and Speaker of the House for two years; and a Representative in Congress from 1853 to 1855. On his return from Washington he was the Whig candidate for Governor of Massachusetts, but was defeated; was a Bank Commissioner in 1858; and in 1859 became President of the Revere Bank of Boston.

Waln, Robert.—He was a prominent merchant in Philadelphia, and a member of Congress, from Pennsylvania, from 1798 to 1801, and died, January 24, 1836, aged seventy-one years.

Walsh, Mike.—Born in Yanghull, Ireland, but brought to this country when a child; spent his boyhood as a wanderer; conducted a paper in New York called the "Subterranean," in which he published certain libels, for which he was imprisoned two years; and he was a Representative in Congress, from New York, from 1853 to 1855. He subsequently visited Europe, and also Mexico, and on March 17, 1859, was found dead in the yard of a public house in New York. The cause of his death unknown.

Walsh, Thomas Y.—He was a native of Maryland, and a Representative in Congress, from that State, from 1851 to 1853.

Walton, Charles W.—Was born in Mexico, Oxford County, Maine, December 9, 1819; was bred a printer; studied law, and was admitted to the bar in 1843; in 1847 was elected Attorney for Oxford County, which he held for four years; removing to Androscoggin County in 1855, was elected Attorney for that county in 1857, which office he held until 1860, when he was elected a Representative, from Maine, to the Thirty-seventh Congress, serving on the Committee on Private Land Claims. In May, 1862, he resigned his seat in Congress, and was appointed, by the Governor, a Judge of the Supreme Court of Maine.

Walton, E. P.—Born at Montpelier, Vermont, February 17, 1812; studied law, but was a practical printer and editor, having for several years edited the "Vermont Watchman;" he served in the State Legislature, as Representative, one term; and was then elected a Representative to the Thirty-fifth Congress, and was a member of the Committee on Public Expenditures. He was also re-elected to the Thirty-sixth and Thirty-seventh Congresses, and serving as a member of the Committee on Claims, and Chairman of that on Printing. He was also a Delegate to the Baltimore Convention of 1864.

Walton, George.—He was a native of Virginia; born in 1740; he served an apprenticeship to the carpenter's trade, after the expiration of which he removed to Georgia, studied law, and was admitted to the bar in 1774. He was one of the signers of the Declaration of Independence, and one of the four individuals who called a public meeting at Savannah to concert measures for the defence of the country, in 1774; was one of the Committee who prepared a petition to the King, and drew up the patriotic resolutions adopted on that occasion. He was active in promoting the Revolution at home, and in 1776 was a Delegate to Congress, from Georgia. When the enemy attacked Savannah he was dangerously wounded and taken prisoner, but was released in 1779, and the same year was chosen Governor of the State; in 1780 was again sent to Congress; and in 1783 was appointed Chief Justice of the State; in 1787 was a Delegate to the Convention for framing the Constitution of the United States, but declined taking his seat; in 1793 was again Judge of the Supreme Court; and in 1795 was elected to succeed General Jackson as a Senator in Congress, serving one year. He died February 2, 1804.

Walton, Matthew.—He was a Representative in Congress, from Kentucky, from 1803 to 1807. Died January 18, 1819.

Walworth, Reuben Hyde.—He was born at Bozrah, Connecticut, in October, 1789. He spent his earlier years on a farm, and had few advantages of education. He commenced the study of law at the age of seventeen, and when twenty was admitted to practice, and when twenty-two was licensed as an attorney of the Supreme Court of New York. He settled at Plattsburg in 1811, and held successively the offices of Master in Chancery, officer of militia during the siege of Plattsburg in 1814, and Adjutant-General of the combined forces, having as such participated in the battles of Beekmanstown and Pike's Cantonment. He was a member of the House during the Seventeenth Congress, declined a re-election, and was appointed a Circuit Judge in 1823; and in 1828 he was made Chancellor of the State of New York, which he held for twenty years, when the office was abolished. His opinions as Chancellor were published in fourteen volumes, while his other opinions occupy as many more.

Ward, Aaron.—He was born at Sing Sing, New York; was educated at Mount Pleasant Academy, and adopted the profession of law. He served, in 1813, in the regular army as a Captain; was, for a time after the war, District Attorney for the County of Westchester, and subsequently attained the position of Major-General of the New York militia. His terms of service as a Representative in Congress were from 1825 to 1829, from 1831 to 1837, and from 1841 to 1843.

Ward, Artemas.—Graduated at Harvard College in 1748. He was a Representative in the Massachusetts Legislature; a member of the Common Council of Boston; and a Judge of the Court of Common Pleas for the County of Worcester. June 17, 1775, he was appointed Major-General of the American army, and was intrusted with the command of the right wing of the troops stationed at Roxbury for the siege of Boston. He was a Delegate to the Provincial Congress, and a Representative in the United States Congress, from Massachusetts, from 1791 to 1795. He was much esteemed by Washington, and although he resigned his commission in April, 1776, yet at the request of the Commander-in-chief he continued some time longer in the service. He was a man of exemplary piety and incorruptible integrity. After a long and patient endurance of many sufferings, he died, October 28, 1800, aged seventy-three years.

Ward, Artemas.—He was a native of Massachusetts, and born in 1763; graduated at Harvard University in 1783; he studied law, and was admitted to practice, and soon became eminent in his profession. He was elected a Representative in Congress, from Massachusetts, from 1813 to 1817; in 1821 he was appointed Chief Justice of the Court of Common Pleas, which office he held for nineteen years. He died in Boston, October 7, 1847. He was honored with the degree of LL.D. from Harvard University.

Ward, Elijah.—He was born in Sing Sing, New York, September 16, 1816; received an academic education, and was bred a merchant, chiefly in the city of New York, where he was President of the Mercantile Library Association in 1839; he studied law at the University of New York, and was admitted to the bar in 1843. He was elected a Representative, from New York, to the Thirty-fifth Congress, serving on the Committee on the District of Columbia. In 1860 he was re-elected to the Thirty-seventh Congress, and in 1862 to the Thirty-eighth Congress, serving on the Committees on Roads and Canals, and on Commerce.

Ward, Jonathan.—He was a native of New York, and a Representative in Congress, from 1815 to 1817, having been a State Senator, from Westchester County, from 1807 to 1810.

Ward, Matthias.—He was born in Elbert County, Georgia, but grew up to manhood in Madison County, Alabama. He received an academic education; was a school teacher for two years; studied law, and became a citizen of the Republic of Texas, in 1836. He served a number of years in the Congress of that Republic, and when it became a State, was elected to the Legislature as a Senator. He was a member of the two Conventions which nominated Mr. Pierce and Mr. Buchanan for the office of President; in 1856 he was chosen President of the State Democratic Convention held at Austin; and in 1858 was appointed a Senator in Congress, from Texas, for the term ending in 1863. Died at Raleigh, North Carolina, October 13, 1861.

Ward, Thomas.—Was a Representative in Congress, from New Jersey, from 1813 to 1817. He died at Newark, New Jersey, February 4, 1842, aged eighty-three.

Ward, William T.—He was born in Kentucky; and was a Representative in Congress, from that State, from 1851 to 1853.

Wardwell, Daniel.—He was born in Rhode Island, and having taken up his residence in New York, was elected a Representative in Congress, from that State, from 1831 to 1837, and was Chairman of the Committee on Revolutionary Pensions. He was also a member of the New York Assembly for four years, from Jefferson County.

Ware, Nicholas.—He was a Senator in Congress, from Georgia, from 1821 to the time of his death, which occurred in New York City, September 7, 1824.

Warfield, Henry R.—Was born in Anne Arundel County, Maryland; and was a Representative in Congress, from that State, from 1819 to 1825. On the morning of March 18, 1839, he was found dead in his bed, at Frederick, Maryland.

Warner, Hiram.—Born in Hampshire County, Massachusetts, October 29, 1802; he received a good common school education, with some knowledge of the classics, and emigrated to Georgia at the age of seventeen, and there taught school for three years; with his earnings he was enabled to study the profession of law, and was admitted to practice in 1825, and opened an office at Knoxville, in Crawford County. From 1828 to 1831, he was a Representative in the General Assembly, and declined a re-election. In 1833 he was elected by the

Legislature one of the Judges of the Superior Courts of the State, and was reappointed in 1836, holding the office until 1840. From that time till 1845 he was engaged in a lucrative practice, and was that year appointed one of the Judges of the Supreme Court, serving for eight years, and then resigned. In 1855 he was elected a Representative in the Thirty-fourth Congress, and declined a re-election in 1857.

Warren, Cornelius.—Born in Putnam County, New York, in 1790, and died at Cold Spring, July 28, 1849. He was a member of Congress, from New York, from 1847 until his death.

Warren, Edward A.—Born in Greene County, Alabama, May 2, 1818; received a liberal education, and studied the profession of law. He served in the Mississippi Legislature in 1845 and 1846, and in the Legislature of Arkansas in 1848 and 1849, as Speaker of the House. In 1850 he was elected State's Attorney for the Sixth Judicial District of Arkansas; and was a Representative, from that State, in the Thirty-third Congress, and was re-elected to the Thirty-fifth. He was a member of the Committees on the Militia, and Railroads and Canals.

Warren, Lott.—Born in Burke County, Georgia, October 30, 1797; commenced life as a clerk in a store; served in the Seminole war as a Second Lieutenant of militia in 1818; studied law, and was admitted to the bar in 1821; in 1823 he was elected a Major of battalion; in 1824 went to the State Legislature; in 1825 was appointed Solicitor-General to fill a vacancy; in 1830 he was sent to the State Senate; in 1831 again elected to the Lower House; and he was a Representative in Congress, from 1839 to 1843. He is still devoted to the profession of law.

Washburn, Cadwallader C.—Born in the town of Livermore, Maine, April 22, 1818. He was a lawyer by profession; removed to Wisconsin, and was elected a Representative, from that State, to the Thirty-fourth and Thirty-fifth Congresses. He was a member of the Committees on Private Land Claims, and Expenditures on the Public Buildings. He was re-elected to the Thirty-sixth Congress, serving as Chairman of the Committee on Private Land Claims. He was also a Delegate to the Peace Congress of 1861.

Washburn, Israel, Jr.—Born June 6, 1813, at Livermore, County of Oxford (now Androscoggin), Maine. He received a classical education; studied law, and in October, 1834, was admitted to the bar; he commenced the practice of law in Orono, Penobscot County, December, 1834, where he has since resided. He was a member of the Legislature in 1842, and elected to the Federal House of Representatives, from Maine, for the Thirty-second, Thirty-third, Thirty-fourth, Thirty-fifth, and Thirty-sixth Congresses, serving in the latter Congress as a member of the Committee of Ways and Means. In 1860 he was elected Governor of Maine, and in 1863 was appointed, by President Lincoln, Collector of Portland.

Washburn, William B.—He was born in Winchendon Massachusetts, January 31, 1820; graduated at Yale College in 1844; has always been engaged in the manufacturing business; was a member of the State Senate in 1850, and of the Lower House in 1854; was subsequently President of the Greenfield Bank; and was elected a Representative, from Massachusetts, to the Thirty-eighth Congress, serving on the Committees on Invalid Pensions, and Roads and Canals.

Washburne, Elihu B.—Born in Livermore, Oxford County, Maine, September 23, 1816; served an apprenticeship in the printing-office of the Kennebec Journal; studied law at Harvard University, and removing to the West, practised at Galena, Illinois. He was elected a Representative to the Thirty-third Congress, from that State, and re-elected to the Thirty-fourth, Thirty-fifth, and Thirty-sixth Congresses, serving on two occasions as Chairman of the Committee on Commerce. He was also elected to the Thirty-seventh Congress, again serving as Chairman of the Committee on Commerce, and re-elected to the Thirty-eighth Congress, serving again as Chairman of the Committee on Commerce, and as a member of the Joint Committee on the Library. On account of his having served continuously for a longer period than any other member of this Congress, usage awarded to him the title of "Father of the House."

Washington, George C.—Born in Westmoreland County, Virginia, August 20, 1789, and died in Georgetown, District of Columbia, July 17, 1854. He was educated at Cambridge, and became a lawyer by profession, though partial to the pursuit of agriculture. At the time of his death, he was the oldest and nearest surviving male relative of his granduncle, General Washington. He represented Maryland in Congress, from 1827 to 1833, and from 1835 to 1837. He was also President of the Chesapeake and Ohio Canal, and a Commissioner for the settlement of Indian Claims. When General Scott was nominated for the Presidency, Mr. Washington was spoken of as the candidate for Vice-President.

Washington, William H.—Born in North Carolina; graduated at Yale College in 1834, and is a lawyer by profession. He was in Congress from 1841 to 1843, and subsequently five or six years in the State Legislature.

Watkins, Albert G.—He was born in Jefferson County, Tennessee, May 5, 1818; was educated at Holston College, Tennessee; adopted the profession of law; was elected to the Legislature, from his native county, in 1845; was a Presidential Elector in 1848; and was first elected a Representative in Congress in 1849, and has been re-elected to each succeeding Congress, excepting the Thirty-third, when he declined the nomination. He was a member of the Committees on Manufactures, and on the Militia.

Watmough, John G.—He was born on the banks of the Brandywine, Delaware, December 6, 1793, and educated at the University of Pennsylvania and Princeton. He served in the war of 1812, as a Lieutenant in the Second Artillery, and while doing service on the frontiers, in 1813 and 1814, was wounded by receiving in his body three musket-balls, the last of which was extracted in 1835; he resigned his commission in 1816, and was elected a Representative in Congress, from Pennsylvania, in 1831, where he remained four years, during the whole of which period his wounds were open and constantly giving him pain. His other public positions were those of aide-de-camp to General Gaines at New Orleans, and in the Creek Nation in 1814 and 1815; High Sheriff of Philadelphia City and County, in 1835; and Surveyor of that port in 1841. During the latter part of his life he lived in retirement, and died at Philadelphia, November 29, 1861.

Watson, Cooper K.—He was born in Ohio, and was a Representative in Congress, from that State, from 1855 to 1857.

Watson, James.—He was a Senator in Congress, from New York, from 1798 to 1800, when he resigned; had previously been a member of the Assembly of New York, during the years 1791, 1794, 1795, and 1796; was a State Senator in 1797.

Watterson, Harvey M.—He was born in Tennessee, and was a Representative in Congress, from that State, from 1839 to 1843.

Watts, John.—He was born in New York in 1749, and died in New York City, September 3, 1836. He was a member of Congress, from 1793 to 1795.

Watts, John S.—He was born in Kentucky, and elected a Delegate, from the Territory of New Mexico, to the Thirty-seventh Congress.

Wayne, Anthony.—Born in Easttown, Chester County, Pennsylvania, in 1746. In 1773 he was elected a Representative in the General Assembly, where he took an active part against the claims of Great Britain. In 1775 he entered the army as Colonel, and in the battle at the Three Rivers, in June, 1776, received a wound in the leg, and at the close of the campaign he was made a Brigadier-General. In the battles of Brandywine, Germantown, and Monmouth, and especially at Stony Point, he greatly distinguished himself, in the latter assault receiving a severe wound in the head. In 1781 he led the Pennsylvania line, to form a junction with Lafayette in Virginia, and engaged in the capture of Cornwallis; after which he conducted the war in Georgia with equal success, receiving from the

Legislature of that State a valuable farm as a reward for his services, upon which he retired after the war. In 1787 he was a member of the Convention for framing the Constitution, and served as a Representative in Congress, from Georgia, in 1791, but his seat was vacated by a resolution of the House. In 1792 he was again called into military service, and succeeded St. Clair in the command of the army against the Indians, gaining a complete victory over them in 1794, at the battle of the Miami; he concluded a treaty, August 3, 1795, with the hostile tribes northwest of the Ohio. While in the service of his country, having attained the rank of Major-General, he died in a hut at Presque Isle, and was buried on the shore of Lake Erie, in December, 1796.

Wayne, Isaac.—He was a Representative in Congress, from Pennsylvania, from 1823 to 1825.

Wayne, James M.—He was born in Savannah, Georgia. Having obtained an excellent preliminary education, under the instruction of a private tutor, he entered Nassau Hall (now Princeton College), where he counted among his fellow-students some of the leading men of the present day. On his return home, at the close of his collegiate course, he commenced the study of law with one of the most distinguished lawyers of Savannah; but his father having died a few months afterwards, he left, by the advice of his friends, to prosecute his studies at the North. On his return home, he commenced the practice of his profession, and also took much interest in politics. After three or four years, he was elected a member of the General Assembly, as an opponent of the "relief law," which had created much feeling throughout the State. He was re-elected the following year, but declined being a candidate the third time. He was next Mayor of the city. On his resignation of that office, he was chosen Judge of the Superior Court, and served for five years and a half. He was then elected a member of Congress, in the session of 1829–30. He took a prominent position in the House as a debater, and also proved himself a good business member on various committees. He was a supporter of President Jackson, by whom he was appointed to a seat on the bench of the United States Supreme Court in 1835. He has proved himself a sound and accomplished jurist. He has especially devoted his attention to the subject of admiralty jurisprudence, and his opinion on points connected with that subject are everywhere cited as high authority.

Weakley, Robert.—He was a Representative in Congress, from Tennessee, from 1809 to 1811, and in 1819 was appointed United States Commissioner to treat with the Chickasaws.

Webster, Daniel.—Born in the town of Salisbury, New Hampshire, January 18, 1782. His opportunities for education were very deficient, and he was indebted for his earliest instruction to his mother. For a few months only, in 1796, he enjoyed the advantages of Phillips's Exeter Academy; here his education for college commenced, and it was completed at Boscawen. He entered Dartmouth College in 1797, and graduated in 1801. Soon after he engaged in professional studies, first in his native village, and afterwards at Fryeburg, in Maine, where, at the same time, he had the charge of an academy, and was also a copyist in the office of the Register of Deeds. Having completed his studies in the office of Governor Gore, of Boston, he was admitted to the bar of Suffolk, Massachusetts, in the year 1805. He commenced the practice of law in his native State, and county; in 1807 he removed to Portsmouth, New Hampshire, and soon became engaged in a respectable but not lucrative practice. In 1812 he was chosen a Representative in Congress, from Massachusetts, and was re-elected. He removed to Boston in 1816, and was placed at once beside the leaders of the Massachusetts bar, having already appeared before the Supreme Court of the United States, at Washington. By his argument in the Dartmouth College case, carried by appeal to Washington, in 1817, he took rank among the most distinguished jurists in the country. In 1820 he was chosen a member of the Convention for revising the Constitution of Massachusetts. He was offered, about this time, a nomination as a Senator of the United States, but declined. In 1822 he was elected a Representative in Congress, from the city of Boston; he took his seat in December, 1823, and early in the session made his celebrated speech on the Greek Revolution, which at once established his reputation as one of the first statesmen of the age. In the autumn of the same year he was re-elected. In 1826 he was again elected, and under the Presidency of Mr. Adams, he was the leader of the friends of the administration, first in the House of Representatives, and afterwards in the Senate, to which he was elected in 1827. His speech on the Panama Mission was made in the first session of the Nineteenth Congress. When the tariff law of 1824 was brought forward he spoke against it, on the ground of expediency. He remained in the Senate a period of twelve years. In 1830 he made what is generally regarded the ablest of his parliamentary efforts, his second speech in reply to Colonel Hayne, of South Carolina. Mr. Webster, although opposed to the administration of General Jackson, gave it a cordial support in its measures for the defence of the Union, in 1832 and 1833, but opposed its financial system. In 1839 he made a short visit to Europe. His fame had preceded him, and he was received, in the Old World, with the attention due to his character and talents, at the French and English courts. On the accession of President Harrison, he was appointed Secretary of State, and was continued in this office by President Tyler. President Tyler's cabinet was broken up in 1842, but Mr. Webster remained in office till the spring of 1843, being desirous of putting some other matters, connected with our foreign relations, in a prosperous train. Mr. Webster returned to the Senate of the United States in 1845, and he remained in that body until 1850, when he was appointed Secretary of State, by President Fillmore. In December, 1850, the famous Hülsemann letter was written. In 1851, by his judicious management of the Cuba question, he obtained of the Spanish Government the pardon of the followers of Lopez, who had been deported to Spain. About the same time he received from the English Government an apology for the interference of a British cruiser with an American steamer, in the waters of Nicaragua. This was the second time that the British Government had made a similar concession at the instance of Mr. Webster. The first was in reference to the destruction of the "Caroline," at Schlosser. He paid much attention to agriculture, and his residence, when not engaged in public business at Washington, was either at Marshfield, in Massachusetts, or the place of his birth, in New Hampshire. The works of Mr. Webster were published in six volumes, with a biographical memoir by Edward Everett. He died October 23, 1852, at Marshfield; and in 1857, two volumes of Mr. Webster's private correspondence were published by his son, Fletcher Webster, Esq.

Webster, Edwin H.—He was born in Harford County, Maryland, March 31, 1829; was educated at Dickinson College, and was a member of the Maryland Senate from 1855 to 1859, serving two years as the President of that body. In 1856 he was chosen a Presidential Elector. His term in Congress commenced with the Thirty-sixth Congress, as a Representative from Maryland, and he was re-elected to the Thirty-seventh Congress, serving on the Committees on Claims, and on Public Expenditures. For a time he rendered the State some service in a military capacity, and was Colonel of a Maryland regiment. In 1863 he was re-elected to the Thirty-eighth Congress, serving on the Committees of Claims, and on the Militia.

Webster, Taylor.—He was born in Pennsylvania, and having settled in Ohio, was elected a Representative in Congress, from that State, from 1833 to 1839.

Weeks, John W.—He was a County Sheriff in New Hampshire from 1820 to 1825; a State Senator in 1827 and 1828; a Representative in Congress, from New Hampshire, from 1829 to 1833; and Judge of Probate in Coos County in 1854.

Weeks, Joseph.—He was born in Massachusetts, and was a Representative in Congress, from New Hampshire, from 1835 to 1839, having previously been for two years Judge of the County Court for Cheshire County.

Weems, John C.—He was born in Calvert County, Maryland, and was a Representative in Congress, from that State, from 1826 to 1829.

Weightman, Richard Hanson.—Born in Maryland, and educated at West Point; was a Captain in the Missouri battalion of light artillery volunteers in the Mexican war, and distinguished himself under Colonel Donophan in the battle of Sacramento; subsequently held the position of additional Paymaster; and was a Delegate to Congress, from New Mexico, from 1851 to 1853.

Welch, John.—He was born in Jefferson County, Ohio, October, 28, 1805; was educated at Franklin College, Ohio; studied law, and was admitted to the bar in 1833; he was a member of the State Senate of Ohio in 1846 and 1847; and a Representative in Congress, from 1851 to 1853. He was subsequently one of the Trustees of the Ohio University.

Welch, William W.—He was born in Norfolk, Connecticut, December 10, 1818; received the rudiments of his education at the common schools and from private instructors, and having turned his attention to the science of medicine, received the degree of M.D. from the medical institution of Yale College, in 1838; and, excepting when interrupted by his public duties, has ever been a practising physician. He has twice been elected to the House of Representatives, and twice to the Senate of Connecticut; and he was a Representative, from that State, during the Thirty-fourth Congress.

Wellborn, M. J.—Born in Georgia, and was a Representative in Congress, from that State, from 1849 to 1851.

Weller, John B.—He was born in Ohio; was a Representative in Congress, from that State, from 1839 to 1845; was the first United States Commissioner to Mexico, under the treaty of Guadalupe Hidalgo; and having taken up his residence in California, was elected to the United States Senate, in 1851, for a long term; and was subsequently elected Governor of California. In December, 1860, he was appointed Minister to Mexico; and was a Delegate to the Chicago Convention in 1864.

Welles, William H.—He was a Senator in Congress, from Delaware, from 1799 to 1804, when he resigned, and again from 1813 to 1817; he died March 11, 1829.

Wells, Alfred.—Born in Dagsboro, Sussex County, Delaware, May 27, 1814; adopted the profession of law, and settled at Ithaca, New York; and in 1858 was elected a Representative, from New York, to the Thirty-sixth Congress, serving as a member of the Committee on the Militia. He has also held the positions of Deputy Clerk, District Attorney, and Judge of Tompkins County, New York.

Wells, Daniel, Jr.—He was born in Maine, and adopted the profession of law. In 1836 he removed to Wisconsin, and was a Representative in Congress, from that State, from 1853 to 1855. He subsequently held the offices of Judge of Probate and County Judge, and died in 1858.

Wells, John.—He was born in New York, and was a Representative in Congress, from that State, from 1851 to 1853.

Wells, John S.—He was a Senator in Congress, from New Hampshire, from January to March, in 1855, by executive appointment. He filled many local offices, and died at Exeter, New Hampshire, in 1860, aged fifty-six years.

Wendover, Peter H.—He was born in New York City; was a member of the State Assembly, from the city of New York, in 1804; and a Representative in Congress, from that State, from 1815 to 1821.

Wentworth, John.—He was born in Sandwich, New Hampshire, March 5, 1815. He received an academic education; taught school for a while, and having entered Dartmouth College, graduated in 1836. Removing soon afterwards to Illinois, he studied law and settled in Chicago, where he has ever since been connected with the press, and practised his profession, excepting when in Congress, his service, as a Representative, having extended from 1843 to 1855. He was subsequently twice elected Mayor of Chicago.

Wentworth, Tappan.—He was born in Dover, New Hampshire, February 24, 1802; and was a Representative in Congress, from Massachusetts, from 1853 to 1855. He followed the law as a profession, and was President of the Common Council of Lowell in 1842; and served four years in the State Senate.

Westbrook, John.—He was born in Pennsylvania, and was a Representative in Congress, from that State, from 1841 to 1843.

Westbrook, Theodoric R.—He was a native of New York, and was a Representative in Congress, from that State, from 1853 to 1855.

Westcott, James D.—He was born at Alexandria, Virginia, in May, 1802. He removed with his father to New Jersey, and was at an early age admitted to the bar of the Supreme Court of that State, where he practised his profession until 1829; and he afterwards held, for a short time, a position in the Consular Bureau of the State Department at Washington. He was appointed, by President Jackson, Secretary of the Territory of Florida, and held the office four years, performing the duties of the Governor during his temporary absence. He was a member of the Territorial Legislature in 1832. He was appointed United States District Attorney for the Middle District of the Territory, which office he held until 1836. He was again a member of the Legislature, and a member of the Convention for framing a State Constitution in 1838 and 1839. On the admission of Florida into the Union as a State, in 1845, he was elected a Senator in Congress, and served until 1849.

Westerlo, Rensselaer.—He was born in New York, and was a Representative in Congress, from that State, from 1817 to 1819.

Wethered, John.—He was born in Maryland, and was a Representative in Congress, from that State, from 1843 to 1845.

Whaley, Killian V.—Was born in Onondaga County, New York, May 6, 1821. While yet young, he removed with his father to Ohio, and received a limited education, and when twenty-one years old he settled in Western Virginia, devoting himself to the lumber and mercantile business. When the Rebellion broke out he took the Union side of the question, and was elected to the Thirty-seventh Congress, serving on the Committee on Invalid Pensions. He afterwards acted as an aid to Governor Pierpoint, in organizing and equipping regiments, and was in command at the battle of Guyandotte, when he was taken prisoner, in November, 1861. After travelling with his captors sixty miles towards Richmond, he made his escape at night when surrounded with guards, and after six days and nights spent in the mountains, suffering much from hunger, fatigue, and cold, he arrived safely at Catlettsburg, Kentucky, and was soon able to resume his seat in the House of Representatives. He was re-elected to the Thirty-eighth Congress, serving as Chairman of the Committee on Invalid Pensions, and as a member of the Committee on Agriculture. He was also a Delegate to the Baltimore Convention of 1864.

Whallon, Reuben.—Born in New Jersey, and was a Representative in Congress, from New York, from 1833 to 1835, and died in Essex County, New York, April 15, 1843, aged sixty-six years.

Wharton, Jesse.—He represented the State of Tennessee, in Congress, from 1807 to 1809, and was a United States Senator in 1814 and 1815. He died at Nashvile, July 22, 1833.

Wheaton, Horace.—He was born in New York, and was a Representative in Congress, from that State, from 1843 to 1847.

Wheaton, Laban.—He was born at Marshfield, Massachusetts, and graduated at Harvard University in 1774. He studied both theology and law. He was a County Judge, and a Representative in Congress, from 1809 to 1817. He died at Norton, Massachusetts, March 23, 1846, aged ninety-two years.

Wheeler, Ezra.—He was born in Chenango County, New York, in 1820; emigrated to Berlin, Wisconsin, in 1849; adopted the profession of law; in 1852 he was elected to the Legislature of Wisconsin; in 1854 he was elected to the office of County Judge, holding the same for eight years; and he was elected a Representative, from Wisconsin, to the Thirty-eighth Congress, serving on the Committee on the District of Columbia.

Wheeler, Grattan H.—He was a native of New York, and a Representative in Congress, from that State, from 1831 to 1833. He was also a member of the State Assembly, from Steuben County, for four years, and one year a member of the State Senate.

Wheeler, John.—Born in 1823, at Darby, Connecticut; received a good commercial education, and at the age of twenty entered the mercantile business in New York City; he subsequently engaged in hotel keeping, which he followed at the time of his election, and during his service as a member of Congress, having been a Representative from 1853 to 1857.

Wheeler, William A.—Born in Malone, Franklin County, New York, in 1820; adopted the profession of law; in 1850 and 1851 he was elected to the State Legislature; in 1857 and 1858 to the State Senate; and in 1860 he was elected a Representative, from New York, to the Thirty-seventh Congress. He was for many years engaged in the banking business, and was President of the Ogdensburg and Rouse Point Railroad Company.

Whipple, Thomas.—He was born in Berkshire County, Massachusetts; was bred a physician, and served the State of New Hampshire, as a Representative in Congress, from 1821 to 1829. He died at Wentworth, New Hampshire, January 23, 1835, aged fifty years.

White, Addison.—He was born in Kentucky, and was a Representative in Congress, from that State, from 1851 to 1853.

White, Albert S.—Was born in Blooming Grove, Orange County, New York, October 24, 1803; graduated at Union College in 1822; studied law and was admitted to the bar at Newburg in 1825; removed to Indiana in 1829; and was a Representative in Congress, from that State, from 1837 to 1839; was a Senator in Congress, from 1839 to 1845; during his service in Congress, he was instrumental in securing grants of land for the Wabash and Erie Canal; and after leaving Congress, he abandoned politics and turned his attention to the railroad business, becoming President of the Wabash and Indianapolis, and of the Lake Erie, Wabash and St. Louis Companies. Earlier in life he was for five years Clerk of the Indiana House of Representatives; and was elected a Representative, from Indiana, to the Thirty-seventh Congress, serving as a member of the Committee on Foreign Affairs, and Chairman of a Select Committee on Emancipation. After leaving Congress, he was appointed by President Lincoln, a Commissioner to settle certain claims against the Sioux Indians. In January, 1864 he was appointed, by President Lincoln, Judge of the District Court of Indiana. He died in Stockwell, Indiana, September 4, 1864.

White, Alexander.—He was a Delegate to the Continental Congress, from North Carolina, from 1786 to 1788, and a Representative in Congress, from 1789 to 1793, and distinguished for his eloquence and patriotism. He died at Woodville, Virginia, in 1804, aged sixty-six years.

White, Alexander.—He was born in Tennessee, and having settled in Alabama, was elected a Representative in Congress, from that State, from 1851 to 1853.

White, Allison.—He was born in Pennsylvania, December 21, 1816; received a common school education; studied law, and practised his profession for twelve years. He was elected a Representative from Pennsylvania to the Thirty-fifth Congress, from the Fifteenth Congressional District of that State, and was Chairman of the Committee on Expenditures on the Public Buildings.

White, Bartow.—He was born in Westchester County, New York; and was a Representative in Congress, from that State, from 1825 to 1827.

White, Benjamin.—He was born in Maine; a farmer by occupation; and was a Representative in Congress, from that State, from 1844 to 1845. During the years 1841 and 1842 he was also a member of the Maine Legislature.

White, Campbell P.—Was born in New York; for many years a prominent merchant in that city; and was a Representative in Congress, from that State, from 1829 to 1835. He also took a leading part in the New York Convention of 1846. He died February 12, 1859, leaving an exalted reputation for abilities, and sterling qualities of heart and manners.

White, Chilton A.—Was born in Georgetown, Brown County, Ohio, February, 1826; studied law with General Thomas L. Hamer, under whom he served one year as a private soldier in Mexico; was admitted to the bar in 1848, and settled in his native town. In 1852 and 1853 he was the Prosecuting Attorney for Brown County; in 1859 and 1860 was chosen a Senator in the State Legislature; but before the expiration of his second term, he was elected a Representative, from Ohio, to the Thirty-seventh Congress, serving on the Committee on Public Expenditures. He was re-elected to the Thirty-eighth Congress, serving on the Committees on Manufactures, and Expenditures in the Post-office Department.

White, David.—He was one of the Judges of the Circuit Court of Kentucky, and represented that State in Congress, from 1823 to 1825. He died in Franklin County, Kentucky, February 17, 1835, aged fifty years.

White, Edward D.—Governor of Louisiana, and a Representative in Congress, from that State, from 1829 to 1834, and again from 1839 to 1843. His popularity was great and well deserved. He died in New Orleans, April 18, 1847.

White, Francis.—He was a Representative in Congress, from Virginia, his native State, from 1813 to 1815.

White, Hugh.—He was born in New York, followed the plough until he was nineteen years of age, and was a Representative in Congress, from his native State, from 1845 to 1851.

White, Hugh Lawson.—He was born in Iredell County, North Carolina, October 30, 1773; removed with his father to Knox County, Tennessee, in 1786; volunteered as a private soldier during the Indian hostilities in 1792. In 1794 he went to Philadelphia, and pursued a course of mathematical studies, and then went to Lancaster, Pennsylvania, and studied law. He commenced the practice of his profession at Knoxville, in 1796. In 1801 he was appointed Judge of the Supreme Court of the State, and served until 1807. In 1808 he was appointed District Attorney, and in 1809 was elected to the State Senate; he again served six years in the Supreme Court as Judge, and in 1815 was chosen President of the State Bank of Tennessee. In 1820 he was again a member of the State Senate, and about that time was appointed, by President Monroe, a Commissioner to adjust the claims of our citizens against Spain. He was elected a Senator in Congress, from 1825 to 1835, and from 1836 to 1840, serving on one occasion as President *pro tem.* of the Senate. At the election for President of the United States, in 1836, he received all the votes (twenty-six) of Georgia and Tennessee. He resigned his seat in the Senate in 1839, having received instructions to vote against his own judgment. Soon after reaching his home, in Knoxville, he died, April 10, 1840.

White, James.—He was a Representative in Congress, from Tennessee, from 1792 to 1794.

White, John.—He was born in 1805; served from 1835 to 1845, as a Representative in Congress, and was Speaker of the House during the Twenty-seventh Congress. He was Judge of the Nineteenth Judicial District at the time of his death, which occurred at Richmond, Kentucky, by suicide, September 22, 1845. His talents and attainments were of a high order.

White, Joseph L.—Was born in Cherry Valley, New York; studied law in Utica, and settled in Indiana; was a Representative in Congress, from that State, from 1841 to 1843. After leaving Congress, he settled in New York City, and practised his profession with success. He subsequently entered into an India-rubber speculation, and while on a business visit to Nicaragua, he was shot by a drunken man, from the effects of which he died in January, 1861.

White, Joseph M.—He was born in Franklin County, Kentucky, and was a Delegate to Congress, from the Territory of Florida, from 1823 to 1837, and died at St. Louis, Missouri, October 18, 1839, while on a visit to his brother. He was an eminent lawyer, and noted for his eloquence and acquirements.

White, Joseph W.—Was born in Cambridge, Guernsey County, Ohio, October 2, 1822; studied law, and came to the bar in 1844; in 1845 and 1847 he was appointed Prosecuting Attorney for his native county; and was elected a Representative, from Ohio, to the Thirty-eighth Congress, serving on the Committees on Mileage, and Expenditures in the Treasury Department.

White, Leonard.—Born in Haverhill, Massachusetts, in 1767. He was a fellow-student of John Quincy Adams, under the tuition of the Rev. Mr. Shaw, of Haverhill, and at Harvard they were of the class of 1787. He was for many years Town Clerk and Treasurer, and represented his town in the Legislature, and his district in Congress, from 1811 to 1813, and then he was appointed Cashier of the Merrimack Bank, which office he held until the infirmities of age obliged him to retire. He died in Haverhill, October 10, 1849.

White, Phineas.—He graduated at Dartmouth College in 1797, and was a Representative in Congress, from Vermont, from 1821 to 1823. He was Register of Probate for Pomfret County, from 1800 to 1809; County Attorney in 1813; served eight years in the two branches of the State Legislature; and died in 1847, aged seventy-seven years. He was born in Hampshire County, Massachusetts.

White, Samuel.—Was a United States Senator, from Delaware, from 1801 until his death, which occurred at Wilmington, Delaware, November 4, 1809, aged thirty-nine years.

Whitecomb, James.—Was born in 1795. He removed with his father to Ohio, in 1806; had a country school education, and prepared himself for college by teaching school, and graduated at Transylvania University with the highest honors. He studied law, and settled in practice in Bloomington, Indiana, in 1824. In 1826 he was appointed Prosecuting Attorney, and in 1830 was chosen a member of the State Senate, and served five years. He was appointed Commissioner of the General Land Office in 1836; and in 1841 returned to the practice of his profession at Terre Haute, Indiana. In 1843 he was chosen Governor of the State, and was re-elected in 1846. He was elected a Senator of the United States in 1849, which position he held until his death, which occurred in New York, October 4, 1852. He was much interested in the American Bible Society, of which association he was Vice-President.

Whitehill, James.—He was a Representative in Congress, from Pennsylvania, from 1813 to 1814. He was also Judge of a County Court, and a General of militia. Died at Strasburg, Pennsylvania, March 5, 1822, at a very advanced age.

Whitehill, John.—He was a Representative in Congress, from Pennsylvania, from 1803 to 1807.

Whitehill, Robert.—He was a Representative in Congress, from Pennsylvania, from 1805 to 1813, the year in which he died.

Whiteley, William G.—Born in Newark, New Castle County, Delaware; graduated at Nassau Hall, Princeton, in 1838. He is a lawyer by profession, and was elected a member of the Thirty-fifth Congress, serving as Chairman of the Committee on Agriculture. He was re-elected to the Thirty-sixth Congress, serving on the same Committee.

Whiteside, Jenkins.—He was a Senator in Congress, from Tennessee, from 1809 to 1811, and died September 24, 1822.

Whiteside, John.—He was a Representative in Congress, from Pennsylvania, from 1815 to 1819.

Whitfield, J. W.—He was born in Tennessee, and was a Delegate, from the Territory of Kansas, to the Thirty-fourth Congress.

Whitman, Ezekiel.—Born in East Bridgewater, Massachusetts, March 11, 1776; graduated at Brown University in 1795; settled as a lawyer in the District of Maine in 1798; he was Chief Justice of the Common Pleas, and also of the Supreme Court of Maine, presiding as such for twenty-five years;

and was a Representative in Congress, from Massachusetts, from 1809 to 1811, and from 1817 to 1821; and was a Representative in Congress, from Maine, from 1821 to 1823. He was also a member of the Executive Council of Maine in 1815 and 1816, and a member of the Convention to form a Constitution in 1819. He is still living in the enjoyment of a happy old age.

Whitman, Lemuel.—He was a graduate of Yale College in 1800; was a Representative in Congress, from Connecticut, from 1823 to 1824; and died at Farmington, November 18, 1841.

Whitney, Thomas R.—He was born in New York City in 1804; served two years in the Assembly of that State, and was a Representative in Congress, from New York, from 1855 to 1857. He devoted much of his life to literary pursuits, having been at one time editor of the New York Sunday News, and was the author of a poem called the "Ambuscade," and a political work entitled "The American Policy Vindicated." He died April 12, 1858.

Whittemore, Elias.—He was born in Rockingham County, New Hampshire, and was a Representative in Congress, from New York, from 1825 to 1827.

Whittlesey, Elisha.—He was born in Washington, Connecticut, October 19, 1783; he spent a part of his boyhood on a farm; received an academical education; studied law; and in 1806 removed to the Western Reserve of Ohio, from which district he was a Representative in Congress, from 1823 to 1839. He served in the war of 1812 as aide-de-camp to General E. Wadsworth; was for sixteen years a Prosecuting Attorney; and was elected to the State Legislature in 1820 and 1821. He was appointed by President Harrison Auditor for the Post-office Department, and, by President Taylor, was appointed First Comptroller of the Treasury, which office he continued to hold until the accession of President Buchanan. He was reappointed to the same position by President Lincoln in 1861.

Whittlesey, Frederick.—He was born in Washington, Connecticut, in June, 1799; graduated at Yale College in 1818; studied law, and was admitted to the bar at Utica, New York, in 1821; settled in Rochester in 1822; was a Representative in Congress, from 1831 to 1835; in 1839 he was chosen Vice-Chancellor of the Eighth Judicial District of New York, and retained the office eight years; he was also a Judge of the Supreme Court of the State; and in 1850 he was elected Professor of Law in Genesee College. He died in Rochester, New York, September 19, 1851.

Whittlesey, Thomas T.—He was born in Connecticut; graduated at Yale College in 1817; and was a Representative in Congress, from his native State, from 1836 to 1839.

Whittlesey, W. A.—He was born in Connecticut; graduated at Yale College; studied law, and settled in practice in Ohio; and was a Representative in Congress, from that State, from 1849 to 1851.

Wick, William W.—Born in Canonsburg, Washington County, Pennsylvania, February 23, 1796. He received a classical education, and was pursuing a collegiate course when the death of his father threw him upon his own resources; he then followed the occupation of a teacher, and devoted his leisure hours to the study of medicine until 1818, when he was induced to adopt the law as his profession, and prosecuted his studies with the Hon. Thomas Corwin, and located, for practice, in Fayette County, Indiana, in 1820. He was that year Assistant Clerk of the House of Representatives, and in 1821 Assistant Secretary of the State Senate. In 1822 he was chosen President Judge of the Fifth Judicial Circuit, and in 1825 became Secretary of State; in 1829 he was Attorney for the State in the same circuit, from which office he retired in 1831, and was again President Judge for three years; in 1839 he was elected a Representative in Congress, and again in 1845 and 1847; in 1850 he was again chosen President Judge, and from 1853 to 1857 Postmaster at Indianapolis. He has served in the militia of the State as Brigadier-General, Quartermaster, and Adjutant-General. In 1857 he resumed the practice of the legal profession.

Wickes, Eliphalet.—He was a Representative in Congress, from New York, from 1805 to 1807.

Wickliffe, Charles A.—He was born in Bardstown, Kentucky, June 8, 1788; was educated at the Bardstown grammar school; studied law, and attained a high position at the bar. In 1812 he was appointed aide-de-camp to General Winlock, and during the same year was elected to the State Legislature, and re-elected in 1813. He was at the battle of the Thames as aid to General Caldwell, after which he was again elected to the Legislature, where he continued until elected to Congress, from Kentucky, in 1823, and to which he was four times re-elected. He was for several sessions Chairman of the Committee on Public Lands. On his retirement from Congress, in 1833, he was again elected to the Legislature, and was Speaker in 1834; in 1836 he was elected Lieutenant-Governor of Kentucky; on the death of Governor Clark, in 1839, he became Acting Governor, and in 1841 was appointed Postmaster-General by President Tyler. In 1845 he was sent by President Polk on a secret mission to Texas, to look after annexation; in 1849 he was a member of the Convention called to revise the State Constitution; and in 1861 he once again became a Representative in Congress, from Kentucky, having previously occupied a seat in the Peace Convention of February in that year, and served to the close of the Thirty-seventh Congress. He was also a Delegate to the Chicago Convention of 1864.

Widgery, William.—He was a Lieutenant of a privateer in the Revolutionary war; served in the Massachusetts Legislature in 1789, 1791, 1793, 1794, and 1797; a State Councillor in 1806 and 1807; Judge of the Court of Common Pleas from 1813 to 1822; and a Representative in Congress, from Massachusetts, from 1811 to 1813. He was born in Philadelphia in 1753, and died in Boston, August 7, 1822.

Wigfall, Lewis T.—He was a Senator in Congress, from Texas, from 1859 until that State seceded, when he became identified with the Great Rebellion as a Brigadier-General. Refused all appeals for information. Was expelled from the Senate in July, 1861.

Wilbur, Isaac.—He was a Representative in Congress, from Rhode Island, from 1807 to 1809.

Wilcox, Jeduthun.—Born in New Hampshire, in 1769, and died at Orford, in the same State, in July, 1838. He was a Representative in Congress, from 1813 to 1817.

Wilcox, John A.—He was born in North Carolina, and on removing to Mississippi, was elected a Representative in Congress, from that State, from 1851 to 1853.

Wilcox, Leonard.—He was a native of New Hampshire; graduated at Dartmouth College in 1817; was a member of the State Legislature; was a Judge of the Superior Court; and was a Senator in Congress, from New Hampshire, during the years 1842 and 1843. He died in 1850, aged fifty years.

Wilde, Richard Henry. — He was born in the city of Dublin, September 24, 1789. His childhood was passed in Baltimore. His father having died, he obtained the rudiments of learning from his mother and a private tutor, and in his eleventh year was placed as a clerk in a store; in 1802 he went with his mother to Augusta, Georgia, and the twain obtained a living by merchandizing, in a small way, the boy devoting all his leisure to books. Under many difficulties he studied law, and practised with success; also devoted himself to polite literature; as an advocate he rose to eminence; was made Attorney-General of Georgia; and, in 1815, was elected a Representative in Congress, from that State; was re-elected in 1823, and again in 1827, serving with marked ability until 1835. After leaving Congress he visited Europe, and on his return devoted himself to literature, politics, and law. In 1843 he removed to New Orleans, where he added to his reputation as a lawyer, and was elected Professor of Constitutional Law in the University of Louisiana. He died in New Orleans, September 10, 1847, leaving a reputation composed of the elements of the statesman, the orator, and the poet. One of his lyrics, entitled "My Life is Like a Summer Rose," attracted the praise of Lord Byron. His literary productions were quite numerous, and they all bear the impress of a gifted and highly educated mind. His principal work was a "Life of Tasso," which evinced his familiarity with Italian literature, and gave him a rank among the best scholars.

Wilder, A. Carter.—He was born in Mendon, Worcester County, Massachusetts, March 18, 1828; in 1850 removed to Rochester, New York, and in 1857 to Kansas, where he was engaged in mercantile pursuits; was a Delegate to the Chicago Convention in 1860, and in 1862 he was elected a Representative, from Kansas, to the Thirty-eighth Congress, serving on the Committee on Indian Affairs. He was also a Delegate to the Baltimore Convention of 1864.

Wildman, Zalmon. — He was from Danbury, Connecticut, and was elected a Representative in Congress, from that State, from 1835 to 1836. He died at Washington, District of Columbia, December 10, 1835, before the expiration of his term.

Wildrick, Isaac.—He was born in New Jersey, and was a Representative in Congress, from that State, from 1849 to 1853.

Wiley, James S.—He was born in Maine; graduated at Waterville College in 1836; studied law, and was a Representative in Congress, from Maine, from 1847 to 1849.

Wilkin, James W.—Born in 1762; was a member of the Legislature of New York in 1800, and held many other places in the gift of his fellow-citizens, and was a Representative in Congress, from 1815 to 1819. He died at Goshen, New York, February 23, 1845.

Wilkin, Samuel J.—He was born in New York; graduated at Princeton College in 1812, and was a Representative in Congress, from New York, from 1831 to 1833; having been in the State Assembly, from Orange County, in 1824 and 1825.

Wilkins, William.—He was a Senator in Congress, from Pennsylvania, from 1831 to 1834; a Representative in Congress, from 1843 to 1844; Secretary of War, from 1844 to 1845, under President Tyler; and was appointed American Minister Plenipotentiary to Russia in 1834.

Wilkinson, Morton S. — Was born in Skaneateles, Onondaga County, New York, January 22, 1819; received an academical education, working occasionally upon his father's farm; in 1837 he removed to Illinois, and was employed for two years upon the railroad works then commenced in that State; returned to his native town, studied law, and was admitted to the bar, after which he removed to the West again, and settled at Eaton Rapids, in Michigan; in 1847 he settled in Minnesota, and in 1849, when that Territory was organized, he was elected to the Legislature, and the laws adopted by the Territory as its code were of his drafting; and in 1859 he was chosen a Senator in Congress, from Minnesota, for the term ending in 1865, serving as Chairman of the Committee on Revolutionary Claims, and as a member of the Committee on Indian Affairs. He was also a Delegate to the Baltimore Convention of 1864.

Willey, Calvin. — Born at East Haddam, Connecticut, September 15, 1776; he read law and was admitted to the bar in 1798; he served in the State Legislature and Senate a number of years, and was Postmaster at Stafford Springs eight years; Judge of Probate for seven years; in 1824 he was a Presidential Elector; and a Senator in Congress, from 1825 to 1831. He died at Stafford, Connecticut, August 23, 1858.

Willey, Waitman T.—Was born on Buffalo Creek, Monongalia County, Virginia, October 18, 1811; received a common school education, and graduated at Madison College in 1831; studied law and came to the bar in 1833; in 1841 he was elected Clerk of the Monongalia County Court; subsequently Clerk of the Circuit Court, holding the two fourteen years; in 1850 he was elected to the Convention to reform the Constitution of Virginia; in 1853 he delivered a series of lectures on Methodism, took part in various local societies, lectured on various topics, and wrote for the reviews; in 1858 he was a Delegate to the National Convention of that year; in the winter of 1860–61 he was a Delegate to the Richmond Convention; and in 1861 he was elected by the reorganized Legislature of Virginia a Senator in Congress, and at the close of that year was a Delegate to the Wheeling Constitutional Convention; and in 1863 he was elected a Senator in Congress from West Virginia, serving on the Committees on Naval Affairs, and on the District of Columbia. In 1863 the degree of LL.D. was conferred upon him by Alleghany College of Pennsylvania.

William, Benjamin.—He was a native of North Carolina, a patriot of the Revolution, and a member of Congress, from 1793 to 1795. He also served many years in the State Legislature, and was twice elected Governor of North Carolina, in 1799 and 1807. He died in Moore County, of that State.

Williams, Christopher H.—He was born in Tennessee, and a Representative in Congress, from that State, from 1837 to 1843, and again from 1849 to 1853.

Williams, David R.—He was a Representative in Congress, from South Carolina, from 1805 to 1809, and again from 1811 to 1813, in which year he was appointed, by President Madison, Brigadier-General. He was also Governor of South Carolina from 1814 to 1816.

Williams, Henry.—He was born in Taunton, Massachusetts, in November, 1804; adopted the profession of law; and was a Representative in Congress, from that State, from 1839 to 1841, and from 1843 to 1845. He was also a Senator for two years, and a Representative in the State Legislature for three years.

Williams, Hezekiah.—He was born in Vermont; graduated at Dartmouth College in 1820; studied law; was Register of Probate from 1824 to 1838; a State Senator from 1839 to 1841; and was a Representative in Congress, from Maine, from 1845 to 1849. He died October 24, 1856, aged fifty-eight years.

Williams, Isaac.—He was a native of New York; and was a Representative in Congress, from that State, from 1814 to 1815, and from 1817 to 1819, and again from 1823 to 1825.

Williams, James W.—While on his way to Washington, December 2, 1843, he was stricken with paralysis, while in his carriage, and survived the attack but a short time. His age was about fifty-five years. He was a native of Maryland, and was for many years a prominent member of the Legislature of that State, being for a time Speaker of the House of Delegates. In May, 1841, he was elected to Congress, and continued a member of that body until the time of his death. As a faithful public servant, a sagacious statesman, and an upright man, he commanded the confidence of his neighbors, and the esteem and respect of all who knew him.

Williams, Jared.—He was born in Montgomery County, Maryland, March 4, 1766, and died in Frederick County, Virginia, January 2, 1831. In 1811 he was elected to the House of Delegates of Virginia, and served a number of years; and he was a Representative in Congress, from Virginia, from 1819 to 1825. In 1829 he was a Presidential Elector, voting for General Jackson, and was appointed, by the Electoral College, to transmit the vote to Washington. When not in public life, he was devoted to the pursuits of agriculture.

Williams, Jared W.—He was born in New Hampshire; graduated at Brown University in 1818; settled as a lawyer in Lancaster; and was a Representative in Congress, from that State, from 1837 to 1841; and a Senator in Congress, from 1853 to 1854. He was Governor of New Hampshire from 1847 to 1849; served several terms in the State Legislature; and died in Lancaster, New Hampshire, September 29, 1864.

Williams, John.—He was a member of the New York Senate, from 1777 to 1779, and from 1783 to 1795, from Washington County; of the Assembly, from 1781 to 1782; and a Representative in Congress, from New York, from 1795 to 1799.

Williams, John.—He was a Senator in Congress, from Tennessee, from 1815 to 1823, and was highly respected for his talents and character. He died at Knoxville, August 7, 1837.

Williams, John.—He was born in New York, and was a Representative in Congress, from that State, from 1855 to 1857.

Williams, Joseph L.—He was born in Tennessee, and was a Representative in Congress, from that State, from 1837 to 1843.

Williams, Lemuel.—He graduated at Harvard University in 1765, and was a Representative in Congress, from Massachusetts, from 1799 to 1805. He died in 1827.

Williams, Lewis.—Born in Surry County, North Carolina; graduated at the University of North Carolina, in 1808; entered the House of Commons, of his native State, in 1813; was re-elected in 1814; and was a Representative in Congress, from 1815 to 1842, where, for his many good qualities and his long service, he was known as the "Father of the House." He died in Washington, while representing his State in Congress, February 23, 1842, aged nearly sixty years. He was for fifteen years Chairman of the Committee on Claims.

Williams, Marmaduke.—Born April 6, 1772, in Caswell County, North Carolina; he was a lawyer by profession, and served as a Representative in Congress, from his native State, from 1803 to 1809. In 1810 he removed, with his family, to Madison County, Alabama, and thence to Tuscaloosa, in 1818. He was repeatedly elected to the Legislature, and was a Delegate, from Tuscaloosa County, to the Convention which formed the State Constitution. Was a candidate for Governor, but defeated by William W. Bibb. In 1826 was appointed a Commissioner to adjust the unsettled accounts between Alabama and Mississippi, growing out of their territorial relationship. In 1832 was elected Judge of the County Court, which office he held until April, 1842, when he resigned, having attained the age of seventy, which the Constitution declares a disqualification for the bench. He died in Tuscaloosa, October 29, 1850.

Williams, Nathan.—He was born in New York; served in the State Assembly, from Onondaga, in 1816, 1817, and 1818; and was a Representative in Congress, from New York, from 1805 to 1807.

Williams, Reuel.—Born in Hallowell (now Augusta), Maine, June 2, 1783; had an academic education, and was a lawyer by profession. He was a Representative and Senator in the Legislature of Maine for twelve years, and a Senator in Congress, from 1837 to 1843. He received from Bowdoin College the degree of LL.D., and was a Trustee of that institution. He was also a Presidential Elector in 1836. Died at Augusta in 1862.

Williams, Robert.—He was born in Caswell County, North Carolina, and bred to the law. He was the brother of Marmaduke Williams, and distinguished for his attainments; was an Adjutant-General of North Carolina; and a Representative in Congress, from that State, from 1797 to 1803, and was appointed Commissioner of Land Titles in Mississippi Territory in 1803. He was also Governor of the Territory of Mississippi, from 1805 to 1809. He emigrated to Tennessee toward the close of his life, and died in Louisiana.

Williams, Sherrod.—He was born in Kentucky, and was a Representative in Congress, from that State, from 1835 to 1841.

Williams, Thomas.—Was born in Greensburg, Westmoreland County, Pennsylvania, August 28, 1806; graduated at Dickinson College in 1825; studied law, and came to the bar in 1828; settled in Pittsburg, from which place he was sent, as Senator, to the State Legislature in 1838 and the three following years; in 1860 he was re-elected to the lower House of the Legislature; and in 1862 he was elected a Representative, from Pennsylvania, to the Thirty-eighth Congress, serving on the Committee on the Judiciary.

Williams, Thomas Hill.—Was a native of North Carolina, and read law, but relinquished the profession for a clerkship in the War Department at Washington. In 1805 he was appointed, by President Jefferson, Register of the Land Office, and Commissioner for deciding Land Claims in the Territory of Mississippi; he subsequently held the office for a few years of Collector at

New Orleans; and was a Senator in Congress, from Mississippi, from 1817 to 1831. Late in life he removed to Tennessee, and there died.

Williams, Thomas H.—He emigrated to the northern part of Mississippi soon after the cession of Indian territory in that quarter, and held the office of a Senator in Congress, from Mississippi, during the years 1838 and 1839, by executive appointment.

Williams, Thomas Scott.—Born at Wethersfield, Connecticut, June 26, 1777; graduated at Yale College in 1794; studied law at Litchfield; was admitted to the bar in Windham County, in 1799, and commenced practice at Mansfield, whence he removed to Hartford in 1803. In 1809 he was appointed Attorney of the Board of Managers of the School Fund. He represented the town of Hartford in the General Assembly for seven terms, from 1813 to 1829; and was elected a Representative in Congress, from Connecticut, from 1817 to 1819. In 1829 he was appointed an Associate Judge of the Supreme Court of Errors, and in 1834 was appointed Chief Justice; and in the same year he received the degree of LL.D. from Yale College. He was Mayor of the city of Hartford, from 1831 to 1835. In 1847 he resigned his position as Chief Justice, his term having expired by constitutional limitation. He was for twenty years President of the American Asylum for the Deaf and Dumb, and Vice-President for a long time of the Insane Retreat at Hartford, and of the Board of Foreign Missions, and subsequently President of the American Tract Society. He lived in retirement at Hartford, until December 15, 1861, when he died, leaving a much-loved name for his benevolence.

Williams, Thomas W.—Born in Stonington, Connecticut, September 28, 1790; was educated at Plainfield and Stonington Academies; received a commercial education in New York City, and has been engaged in mercantile business at New London, Connecticut, since 1809. He was a Representative in Congress, from 1839 to 1843; a member of the Legislature in 1846; and chosen Presidential Elector in 1848.

Williamson, Hugh. — Born in Pennsylvania, December 5, 1735, and died suddenly, May 22, 1819. He graduated at the University of Pennsylvania in 1757; studied divinity, and preached two years; in 1760 was appointed Professor of Mathematics in the University of Pennsylvania; resigned in 1764, and went to Edinburgh to study medicine; on his return, in 1772, settled in practice in his profession in Philadelphia; he again visited Europe, and had much to do with matters connected with the Revolution; he subsequently engaged in commercial pursuits, and an accident took him to Edenton, North Carolina. With that State he was long and honorably identified. He served a number of years in the House of Commons; also for three years in the Continental Congress; was a Delegate to the Convention which formed the Constitution of the United States; and was a Representative in Congress, from 1790 to 1793. In 1811 he published a work on the Climate of America; in 1812 a History of North Carolina; and he was associated with De Witt Clinton, in 1814, in forming the Literary and Philosophical Society of New York. He enjoyed the respect of all who knew him, and died universally lamented.

Williamson, William D.—Born in Canterbury, Connecticut, July 31, 1779; graduated at Brown University in 1804; studied and adopted the law as a profession, commencing practice, in 1807, at Bangor; he was for seven years in the Senate of Massachusetts, before the separation of Maine; also a Senator in the Maine Legislature in 1821; part of that year Acting Governor of Maine; a member of Congress from 1821 to 1823; Judge of Probate from 1827 to 1840; and a Bank Commissioner from 1838 to 1841. He was the author, also, of a History of Maine. Died at Bangor, May 27, 1846.

Willis, Francis.—He was born in Frederick County, Virginia, January 5, 1825; received a good education; and, removing to Georgia in 1784, he was a Representative in Congress, from that State, from 1791 to 1793. In 1811 he took up his residence in Tennessee, and led the life of a retired gentleman. He died in Maury County, Tennessee, January 25, 1829.

Willoughby, Westel.—He was a

Representative in Congress, from New York, from 1816 to 1817.

Wilmot, David.—Born at Bethany, Wayne County, Pennsylvania, January 20, 1814. He was educated at Bethany Academy, and at Aurora, Cayuga County, New York; read law, and was admitted to the bar in 1834; he was a member of Congress, from 1845 to 1851; and subsequently President Judge of the Thirteenth Judicial District of Pennsylvania, which position he resigned, but to which he was re-elected. He was the author of a slavery proviso which caused some excitement in Congress when he was a member. In 1860 he was elected a Senator in Congress, serving on the Committees on Foreign Affairs, on Claims, and on Pensions. He was also a Delegate to the Peace Congress of 1861. In 1863 he was appointed, by President Lincoln, a Judge of the Court of Claims.

Wilson, Alexander.—He was a Representative in Congress, from Virginia, from 1804 to 1809.

Wilson, Edgar C.—He was a native of Virginia, and was a Representative in Congress, from that State, from 1833 to 1835. Died at Morgantown, Virginia, in May, 1860.

Wilson, E. K.—He graduated at Princeton College in 1789, and was a Representative in Congress, from Maryland, from 1827 to 1831.

Wilson, Henry.—He was born in Dauphin County, Pennsylvania, and was a Representative in Congress, from that State, from 1823 to 1826. Died in Allentown, Pennsylvania, August 14, 1826.

Wilson, Henry.—Born February 16, 1812, in Farmington, New Hampshire; was brought up on a farm, and when twenty-one, went to Natick, Massachusetts, where he learned to make shoes. In 1840 he was elected to the Massachusetts House of Representatives, in which he served four years, and then served four years in the State Senate, of which he was President two sessions. He was the candidate of the Free-soil party, for Congress, in 1852, and was beaten by only 92 votes, although his party was in a minority of more than 7000. In 1853 he was a member of the State Constitutional Convention, and he has taken an active part in many of the political conventions held since he entered public life. After having been defeated as the Free-soil candidate for Governor in 1853 and 1854, he was elected in 1855 to the United States Senate, to succeed Edward Everett, and was re-elected in 1859. From 1842 to 1851 he was actively connected with the militia of Massachusetts, as Major, Colonel, and Brigadier-General. In 1861 he raised the Twenty-second regiment of Massachusetts volunteers, of which he was made Colonel, and after joining the Army of the Potomac, he was made a member of General McClellan's staff, on which he served until after the meeting of Congress. Since the commencement of the war he has been Chairman of the Senate Committee on Military Affairs, which has had to pass upon thousands of military appointments, and to devise important measures of legislation. In 1856 he was challenged by Mr. Brooks, of South Carolina, for pronouncing his assault upon Mr. Sumner, "murderous, brutal, and cowardly," but he replied, that while he religiously believed in the right of self-defence, he must decline to accept the challenge, believing duelling to be not only a violation of the laws of the land, but the relic of a barbarous age.

Wilson, Isaac.—During the war of 1812 he commanded a company of cavalry, and was in some of the severest actions on the Northern frontier. He was subsequently elected a member of the Assembly of New York, and also of the Senate. He was elected a Representative in Congress, in 1823, and at the end of his term, his seat having been successfully contested by P. Adams, was appointed first Judge of Genesee County, and held it until his removal to Batavia, Illinois, where he died October 25, 1848.

Wilson, James.—Born in 1757; graduated at Harvard University in 1789; was a lawyer by profession; and a Representative in Congress, from New Hampshire, from 1809 to 1811. He died at Keene, New Hampshire, January 4, 1839.

Wilson, James.—He was born

in York County, now Adams County, Pennsylvania, April 28, 1779; received a good English education; in his fourteenth year he was bound to learn the trade of cabinet-maker, in Maryland; from 1811 to 1822 he was a Justice of the Peace; and was a Representative, from Pennsylvania, to the Eighteenth, Nineteenth, and Twentieth Congresses, serving chiefly on the Committee on Claims. Soon after returning to private life, he was again elected a Justice of the Peace, the duties of which office he continued to fill until 1859. It is said of him, that he never solicited a vote for office, nor attended a political meeting to promote his own advancement.

Wilson, James.—He was born in New Hampshire; was Speaker of the State House of Representatives in 1828; and in the Legislature a number of years; practised law at Keene; was a General of militia; and a Representative in Congress, from New Hampshire, from 1847 to 1849. He subsequently settled in California.

Wilson, James.—He was born in Crawfordsville, Montgomery County, Indiana, April 9, 1822; graduated at Wabash College in 1842; was admitted to the bar in 1845; went to Mexico in 1846 as a private in the Indiana Regiment, and before his return home was promoted to the office of Quartermaster; and was elected a Representative, from Indiana, to the Thirty-fifth Congress, and was a member of the Committee on Elections. He was also re-elected to the Thirty-sixth Congress, serving on the Committee on Naval Affairs.

Wilson, James F.—Was born in Newark, Ohio, October 19, 1828; resided there until 1853, when he removed to Iowa; in 1856 was elected a member of the Convention to revise the State Constitution; in 1857 he was appointed, by the Governor of the State, Assistant Commissioner of the Des Moines River Improvement; in 1857 he was elected to the State Legislature; in 1859 he was elected to the State Senate, and in 1861 was President of the Senate; during that year he was elected a Representative, from Iowa, to the Thirty-seventh Congress, for the unexpired term of S. R. Curtis; and re-elected to the Thirty-eighth Congress, serving as Chairman of the Committee on the Judiciary.

Wilson, James J.—Born in Essex County, New Jersey; for many years editor of the True American, at Trenton; and he was a Senator in Congress, from New Jersey, from 1815 to 1821, when he resigned and was appointed Postmaster at Trenton, New Jersey. He was also, for many years, Clerk of the State Assembly, and died July 28, 1824. He was also at one time Adjutant-General of the State, and always a man of influence.

Wilson, John.—He was born in 1777; graduated at Harvard University in 1799; studied law, and attained a high position in his profession; and was a Representative in Congress, from Massachusetts, from 1813 to 1815, and from 1817 to 1819. He died at Belfast, Maine, July 9, 1848.

Wilson, John.—He was born in York District, South Carolina, and a Representative in Congress, from that State, from 1821 to 1827.

Wilson, Nathan.—He was a Representative in Congress, from New York, from 1808 to 1809.

Wilson, R.—He was elected a Senator in Congress, from Missouri, taking his seat in 1861, and serving on the Committee on the Pacific Railroad.

Wilson, Thomas.—He was a Representative in Congress, from Virginia, from 1811 to 1813. Died January 24, 1826.

Wilson, Thomas.—He was a Representative in Congress, from Pennsylvania, from 1813 to 1817. Died at Erie, October 4, 1824, aged fifty-three years.

Wilson, William.—He was a Representative in Congress, from Pennsylvania, from 1814 to 1819.

Wilson, William.—He was born in Hillsborough County, New Hampshire, and was a Representative in Congress, from Ohio, from 1823 to 1827.

Windom, William.—Born in Belmont County, Ohio, May 10, 1827; received an academic education; studied law, and was admitted to the bar in 1850; was elected Prosecuting Attorney for Knox County in 1852; removed to Minnesota in 1853, and was elected a Representative, from that State, to the Thirty-sixth Congress, serving as a member of the Committee on Public Lands; re-elected to the Thirty-seventh Congress, serving on the Committee on Public Expenditures; and also to the Thirty-eighth Congress, serving as Chairman of the Committee on Indian Affairs.

Winfield, Charles H.—He was born in Crawford, Orange County, New York, April 22, 1822; studied law and came to the bar in 1846; he was for six years District Attorney for Orange County, from 1850 to 1856; and in 1862 he was elected a Representative, from New York, to the Thirty-eighth Congress, serving on the Committee on Private Land Claims.

Wing, Austin E.—He was born in Hampshire County, Massachusetts; was a Delegate to Congress, from the Territory of Michigan, in 1832; resided at Monroe, and was for many years a leading man in all its local affairs. He died at Cleveland, Ohio, August 25, 1849.

Wingate, Joseph F.—He was born in Massachusetts; was a member of the Legislature of that State, in 1818 and 1819; Collector of Customs at Bath, Maine, from 1820 to 1824; member of the Maine Legislature in 1825 and 1826; and was a Representative in Congress, from Maine, from 1827 to 1831.

Wingate, Paine.—He was born at Amesbury, Massachusetts, May 14, 1739; graduated at Harvard University in 1759; ordained as a Congregational minister at Hampton Falls, New Hampshire, in 1763; and afterwards removed to Stratham, and engaged in agricultural pursuits. He was appointed a member of Congress under the Confederation in 1787; after the adoption of the Constitution, he was elected a member of the United States Senate, in 1789, and served till 1793, when he was elected a Representative in Congress, in 1793, serving until 1795. In 1798 he was appointed a Judge of the Superior Court of New Hampshire, and continued in office till May, 1809, when he attained the age of seventy. He survived all others who were members of the United States Senate at the time of his taking his seat in that body upon its first organization; and he was for some years the oldest graduate of his college. He was a man of talents and extensive information; highly esteemed and respected for his character, and his honorable and useful life. Hé died at Stratham, New Hampshire, March 7, 1838.

Winslow, Warren.—He was born in Fayetteville, North Carolina, January 1, 1810; entered Chapel Hill University, and graduated in 1827; having studied law, was soon afterwards admitted to the bar. In 1854 he was appointed, by President Pierce, a confidential agent to Madrid, on business connected with the Black Warrior affair; during his absence abroad he was nominated for the Senate of North Carolina, was elected a member thereof, and placed in the chair of Speaker; while in that position, Governor Reid was elected to the United States Senate, and the duties of Governor devolved upon and were performed by Mr. Winslow. He was elected, in 1855, to the Thirty-fourth Congress, serving on the Committee on Naval Affairs; and was re-elected to the Thirty-fifth and Thirty-sixth Congresses, serving as a member of the Committees on Naval Affairs, and on the Library. He was offered, by President Buchanan, the mission to Sardinia, but declined. He took part in the Rebellion of 1861, in some military capacity.

Winston, Joseph.—Born in Virginia, in 1746. In 1760 joined a company of rangers, and marched to the frontier of the State; in a battle on the Greenbrier, was twice wounded, and had a horse killed under him; had a pension granted to him by the Legislature, for his gallantry in battle; in 1766 removed to North Carolina; took an active part in the Revolution; raised a regiment, and marched against the Cherokee Indians; was appointed a Major in 1776, and had various actions with the forces of the Tories; commanded the right wing of the American troops in the battle of King's Mountain, and for his bravery had a sword voted to him by the Legislature; was elected to

Congress in 1792, and again in 1803, and served till 1807.

Winter, Elisha J.—He was a Representative in Congress, from New York, from 1813 to 1815.

Winthrop, Robert C.—Born in Boston, Massachusetts, May 12, 1809; graduated at Harvard College in 1828, and studied law with Daniel Webster. He entered the Legislature of Massachusetts in 1835, and was Speaker of the House from 1838 to 1840; was a member of the United States House of Representatives, from 1840 to 1842, when he resigned on account of domestic circumstances, but was re-elected the same year, and continued in that body until 1850, having been Speaker during the Congress commencing in 1847. He was appointed to the Senate of the United States to fill the vacancy occasioned by the resignation of Mr. Webster, and served from 1850 to 1851. He was President of the Electoral College of Massachusetts which voted for General Scott; and was President of the Historical Society of Massachusetts, and other literary and charitable associations; also President of the Commissioners chosen by the City of Boston for building a Public Library. He delivered the Inaugural of the Franklin Statue in 1856, and also that of the Washington Monument in 1848.

Wise, Henry A.—Born December 3, 1806, in Drummondtown, Accomac County, Virginia; graduated at Washington College, Pennsylvania, at the age of nineteen; studied law, and was admitted to the bar at Winchester, Virginia, in 1828; the same year removed to Nashville, Tennessee, and practised his profession for two years, when, from local attachment, he returned to Accomac, and became a Representative in Congress, serving from 1833 to 1843, when he resigned his seat for the mission to Brazil, which post he occupied until the fall of 1847. In 1848 he was one of the Presidential Electors of Virginia. In 1850 he was a member of the Reform Convention of Virginia, which adopted the present Constitution of the State. In 1852 he was again Presidential Elector; and in 1855 was elected Governor of Virginia, which office he held until 1860. Served in the Great Rebellion as a Brigadier-General.

Witherell, James.—He was a Representative in Congress, from Vermont, during the years 1807 and 1808, and was in the latter year appointed Federal Judge in Michigan Territory. From 1798 to 1803 he was a member of the State Legislature; two years a County Judge; and a State Councillor from 1802 to 1807.

Witherspoon, Robert.—He was a Representative in Congress, from South Carolina, from 1809 to 1811.

Witte, William H.—He was born in New Jersey, and having settled in Pennsylvania, was elected a Representative in Congress, from 1853 to 1855.

Wolf, George.—He was born in Allen Township, Northampton County, Pennsylvania, August 12, 1777. After pursuing a course of classical education in his own county, he studied law, became eminent, and engaged in a lucrative practice. In 1814 he was elected a member of the Legislature of his native State; and he was a Representative in Congress, from Pennsylvania, from 1824 to 1829; Governor of that State from 1829 to 1835; in 1836 was appointed First Comptroller of the United States Treasury; and subsequently Collector of Customs for Philadelphia, in which city he died of an affection of the heart, March 14, 1840.

Wood, Abiel.—He was a distinguished merchant of Wiscasset, Massachusetts, and a member of Congress, from that State, from 1813 to 1815. From 1807 to 1811, and in 1816, he was a member of the State Legislature; a State Councillor in 1820 and 1821; and a member of the Constitutional Convention of 1819. He died at Belfast, Maine, November, 1834, aged sixty-two years.

Wood, Amos E.—Born in Jefferson County, New York, in 1800; he removed with his father in 1812 to Portage County, Ohio. In 1833 he settled permanently in Woodville, Sandusky County; he twice represented his district in the lower branch of the Legislature, and once for a term of two years in the State Senate; and was elected a Representative in Congress, from Ohio, from 1850 to 1852. He died in Fort Wayne, Indiana, November 19, 1850.

Wood, Benjamin.—He was born in Shelbyville, Kentucky, October 13, 1820; received a good English education; has acquired some reputation as a novelist; and was elected a Representative, from New York, to the Thirty-seventh Congress, and re-elected to the Thirty-eighth Congress. He has served on the Committees on Mileage, and on Invalid Pensions.

Wood, Bradford R.—He was born in Connecticut, and was a Representative in Congress, from New York, from 1845 to 1847.

Wood, Fernando.—Born in Philadelphia in 1812; and from the humble employment of a segar maker, he rose to the position of clerk in a counting-house, and was for many years a ship-owner and successful merchant in New York. He was a Representative in Congress, from New York, from 1841 to 1843; and in 1854 was elected Mayor of the city of New York, and re-elected to that office. In 1862 he was elected for a second time a Representative, from New York, to the Thirty-eighth Congress, serving on the Committee on Public Lands.

Wood, John.—Born in Philadelphia in 1816; was educated for the counting-room, in which he had an experience of twenty-five years, devoting himself chiefly to the manufacture of iron; and never held any public position but that of Representative to the Thirty-sixth Congress, from Pennsylvania, to which he was elected contrary to his wishes, serving on the Committee on Public Expenditures.

Wood, John J.—He was a Representative in Congress, from New York, from 1827 to 1829.

Wood, John M.—He was born in Minnisink, Orange County, New York, November 17, 1813; received a good common school education; was a member of the Legislature of Maine; and has for years been occupied as a constructor of railroads and other public works. He was elected in 1854 a Representative, from Maine, in the Thirty-fourth Congress; was re-elected to the Thirty-fifth Congress; and was a member of the Committee on Post-offices and Post-roads.

Wood, Silas.—He was born in Suffolk County, New York; graduated at Princeton College in 1789; was the author of a History of Long Island; and was a Representative in Congress, from New York, from 1819 to 1829. He died at Huntington, Suffolk County, Long Island, March 2, 1847, aged seventy-eight years.

Woodbridge, F. E.—He was born in Vergennes, Vermont, August 29, 1818; graduated at the University of Vermont in 1840; studied law, and came to the bar in 1842; served three years in the State Legislature, two years in the State Senate, three years as State Auditor; and in 1863 he was elected a Representative, from Vermont, to the Thirty-eighth Congress, serving on the Committee on the Judiciary.

Woodbridge, William.—Born in Norwich, Connecticut, August 20, 1780; and his father becoming one of the earliest emigrants to the Northwest Territory, he removed to Marietta in 1791. He received his earliest education in Connecticut; studied law at Litchfield, Connecticut, and was admitted to the bar, in Ohio, in 1806. In 1807 he was elected to the Assembly of Ohio; in 1808 was Prosecuting Attorney for his county, which office he held until 1814, and during the same period he was also a member of the State Senate. In 1814 he received, from President Madison, unexpectedly, the appointment of Secretary of the Territory of Michigan, and removed to Detroit; and in 1819 he was elected the first Delegate, from Michigan, to Congress, where he was very active in promoting the interests of his constituents. In 1828 he was appointed Judge of the Supreme Court of Michigan Territory, and held the office four years; in 1835 he was a member of the Convention called to form a State Constitution; in 1837 he was elected to the State Senate of Michigan; in 1839 he was chosen Governor of the State; and he was a Senator in Congress, from 1841 to 1847. He was a working member on many important committees, and his reports and speeches were numerous; and Daniel Webster, in a note to his speech in defence of the Ashburton Treaty, attributed to Mr. Woodbridge the first suggestion that was ever made to him for inserting in that treaty a provision for the surrender of fugitives, under certain circumstances, upon the demand of foreign governments. For many years before his death he lived in retirement at Detroit. Died October 20, 1861.

Woodbury, Levi.—Born in Francestown, New Hampshire, December 22, 1789; he graduated at Dartmouth College in 1809; attended the Law School at Litchfield; continued to study law in Boston, Exeter, and Francestown, and entered upon the practice in 1812, in which he was successful. In 1816 he was appointed Judge of the Superior Court of New Hampshire, and in 1819 settled in Portsmouth. In 1823 he was elected Governor of New Hampshire; was Speaker of the State House of Representatives in 1825; was a Senator in Congress, from 1825 to 1831; was appointed Secretary of the Navy by President Jackson in 1831; was transferred to the Treasury Department, as Secretary, in 1834, by President Van Buren, and served until 1841; he was again a Senator in Congress, from 1841 to 1845, when he was appointed by President Polk a Justice of the Supreme Court of the United States. He was also tendered the appointment of Minister to England, but declined it. He received the degree of LL.D. from Dartmouth College and the Wesleyan University of Connecticut, and was a member of various literary societies. He died at Portsmouth, New Hampshire, September 7, 1851.

Woodcock, David.—He was born in Berkshire County, Massachusetts, and was a member of the New York Assembly, from Seneca County, in 1814 and 1815, and from Tompkins County, in 1826; and a Representative in Congress, from New York, from 1821 to 1823, and again from 1827 to 1829.

Woodruff, George C.—Was born in Litchfield, Connecticut, December 1, 1805; graduated at Yale College in 1825; studied law at the Litchfield School, and came to the bar in 1827; he was for fourteen years Postmaster of Litchfield; was a Clerk and Representative in the State Legislature; President for years of a bank; Judge of Probate for several years; and in 1861 he was elected a Representative, from Connecticut, to the Thirty-seventh Congress, serving on the Committee on Public Lands.

Woodruff, John.—He was born in Hartford, Connecticut, February 12, 1826; was a member of the Connecticut Legislature in 1854; in 1855 was elected a Representative, from Connecticut, to the Thirty-fourth Congress; re-elected to the Thirty-sixth Congress, serving on the Committee on the Post-office.

Woodruff, Thomas M.—He was a resident of New York City, a furniture dealer by occupation, a member of Congress from 1845 to 1847, and died some time ago.

Woods, Henry.—He was a Representative in Congress, from Pennsylvania, from 1790 to 1803.

Woods, John.—He was a Representative in Congress, from Pennsylvania, from 1815 to 1817.

Woods, John.—He was born in Dauphin County, Pennsylvania, in 1794, and removed with his father to Ohio in his infancy. He was admitted to the bar in 1819, settled in Hamilton County, and at once took a high stand in his profession. In 1824 he was elected to Congress, and served two terms. In 1829 he became the editor and publisher of the "Hamilton Intelligencer," and so continued until 1832, when he returned to his profession, which he successfully practised until 1845, when he was elected Auditor of the State, which office he held for two terms. While Auditor, he did much to preserve the credit of the State. He died in Hamilton, Ohio, July 30, 1855.

Woods, William.—He was a Representative in Congress, from New York, from 1823 to 1825, and a member of the State Assembly, from Steuben County, in 1828.

Woodson, Samuel B.—Born in Jessamine County, Kentucky, October 24, 1815; graduated at Centre College, and became a lawyer by profession. He was a member of the Constitutional Convention of Missouri, in 1855; and a member of the Missouri General Assembly, in 1853 and 1854; and was elected a Representative to the Thirty-fifth Congress, from that State, serving as a member of the Committee on Indian Affairs. He was re-elected to the Thirty-sixth Congress, serving on the Committee on Indian Affairs.

Woodson, Samuel H.—He was a Representative in Congress, from Kentucky, from 1820 to 1823, having been elected the first time for the unexpired term of Henry Clay, and re-elected to the next Congress.

Woodward, Joseph A.—He was born in South Carolina, and was a Representative in Congress, from that State, from 1843 to 1847.

Woodward, William.—He was a Representative in Congress, from South Carolina, from 1815 to 1817.

Woodworth, James H.—He was born December 4, 1804, in Greenwich, Washington County, New York. He lived on a farm until twenty-one years of age; received a limited education at the schools in the vicinity, and removed to Fabius, Onondaga County, New York; taught a village school for a few months, and then engaged in mercantile business. In 1827 he went to Erie County, Pennsylvania, residing there four years, and removed to Chicago, Illinois, in 1833. In 1839 he was elected to the State Senate, and in 1842 was a member of the Lower House. From 1845 to 1850 he was connected with the city government of Chicago, being two years Mayor. He was a Representative, from Illinois, to the Thirty-fourth Congress.

Woodworth, William W.—He was born in Connecticut, and was a Representative in Congress, from New York, from 1845 to 1847.

Worcester, Samuel T.—Born in Hollis, Hillsborough County, New Hampshire, August 30, 1804; graduated at Cambridge University in 1830; for two years he was a Preceptor at the Weymouth Academy, Massachusetts; he studied law at Cambridge, and came to the bar in 1834; went to Ohio that year, and settled at Norwalk, in the practice of his profession; in 1848 and 1849 he was elected to the State Senate; in 1859 was elected Judge of the Court of Common Pleas, which he held until elected a Representative, from Ohio, to the Thirty-seventh Congress, serving on the Committees on Elections, Accounts, and Agriculture.

Word, Thomas J.—He was a Representative in Congress, from Mississippi, from 1838 to 1839.

Worman, Ludwig.—He was born in Bucks County, Pennsylvania; and was a Representative in Congress, from Pennsylvania, from 1820 to 1822. Died in 1822.

Wortendyke, J. R.—Born at Chestnut Ridge, in the Township of Harrington, Bergen County, New Jersey, November 27, 1818; graduated at Rutgers College in 1839; and was for several years teacher of the classics and mathematics. He commenced the study of law in 1849, and was admitted to the bar in 1852; was Alderman of Jersey City, where he practised law; and was elected a Representative in the Thirty-fifth Congress, from New Jersey, serving on the Committee on Public Expenditures.

Worthington, J. T. H.—He was born in Maryland, and was a Representative in Congress, from that State, from 1831 to 1833, and again from 1837 to 1841.

Worthington, Thomas.—He was born in Jefferson County, Virginia, about 1769; emigrated to Ohio, and settled in Ross County in 1798. In 1803 he was a member of the State Constitutional Convention. He was a Senator in Congress, from Ohio, from 1803 to 1807, and again from 1810 to 1814, when he resigned; and from 1814 to 1818, he was Governor of Ohio. After his retirement from that office, he was appointed a member of the first Board of Canal Commissioners, in which capacity he served until his death, which occurred in 1827.

Worthington, Thomas C.—He was born in Prince George County, Maryland, and was a Representative in Congress, from that State, from 1825 to 1827. Died June 19, 1827.

Wright, Augustus R.—Born at Wrightsborough, Columbia County, Georgia, June 16, 1813; commenced his education at a grammar school; afterwards entered Franklin College, but left in the latter part of the junior year without graduating. He is a lawyer by profession; and at the age of twenty-nine, was elected Circuit Judge. He resigned before the expiration of the second term, and was elected a Representative, from Georgia, to the Thirty-fourth Congress, and re-elected to the Thirty-fifth, serving as a member of the Committee on the District of Columbia.

Wright, Daniel B.—He was born in Tennessee, and was a Representative in Congress, from Mississippi, from 1853 to 1857.

Wright, George H.—He was born in Concord, Massachusetts, June 4, 1817; spent seven years on a farm; settled in Boston, as a merchant, in 1822; was connected with the Boston Courier for two years, from 1837, after which he settled in Nantucket, in the whaling business; went to California in 1849; and was a Representative in Congress, from that State, during the years 1850 and 1851.

Wright, Hendrick B.—Born in Luzerne County, Pennsylvania, April 24, 1808; graduated at Dickinson College in 1829; studied law, and came to the bar in 1831; in 1834 he was appointed Deputy Attorney-General for Luzerne County; was elected to the State Legislature in 1841 and 1842; re-elected in 1843, and made Speaker of the House; he was a member of all the National Democratic Conventions between 1840 and 1860; and of that Convention which nominated Mr. Polk for President he was the President. In 1852 he was elected a Representative, from Pennsylvania, to the Thirty-third Congress; and he was re-elected to the Thirty-seventh Congress, to fill the vacancy caused by the death of George W. Scranton, and was a member of the Committee on Military Affairs.

Wright, John C.—He was born in 1783; attained eminence as a lawyer, and early rose to the Supreme Bench of Ohio. His Law Reports are a part of all good libraries in the Western States. He was a Representative in Congress, from Ohio, from 1823 to 1829, and was for many years the owner and editor of the Cincinnati Gazette. He took an active part, as Delegate from Ohio, in the Peace Congress of February, 1861, but died in Washington before the adjournment of that body, on the 13th of that month.

Wright, John V.—Born in McNairy County, Tennessee, June 28, 1828; was a lawyer by profession; was elected a Representative to the Thirty-fourth and Thirty-fifth Congresses, from his native State; and was a member of the Committees on Revolutionary Pensions, and Expenditures in the War Department. Re-elected to the Thirty-sixth Congress, serving on the Committee on the District of Columbia.

Wright, Joseph A.—He was born in Pennsylvania, and having settled in Indiana, was elected a Representative in Congress, from that State, from 1843 to 1845; was Governor of Indiana from 1849 to 1857; and in 1857 he was appointed, by President Buchanan, Minister to Prussia. In 1861 he was elected a Senator in Congress, from Indiana, serving one session; and in 1863 he was appointed, by President Lincoln, Commissioner to attend the Hamburg Exhibition.

Wright, Robert.—He was born in Kent County, Maryland; a Senator in Congress, from Maryland, from 1801 to 1806, when he resigned; at one time member of the State Executive Council; was Governor of Maryland from 1806 to 1809; a Representative in Congress, from Maryland, from 1810 to 1817; re-elected for the term from 1821 to 1823; and died September 7, 1826.

Wright, Samuel G. — Born in 1787, and at the time of his death, was a member elect of Congress, from New Jersey. Died near Allentown, New Jersey, July 30, 1845.

Wright, Silas.—Was born at Amherst, Massachusetts, May 24, 1795. He worked upon his father's farm, in Vermont, in the summer, and attended school in the winter. He prepared for and entered college in August, 1811, and graduated at Middlebury College in 1815. He read law in Washington County, New York, teaching school one or two winters to aid in defraying his own expenses. In 1819, he settled, in the practice of the law, at Canton, St. Lawrence County, New York, where he continued his residence until his death. He was soon made a Magistrate and Postmaster of his town, and Surrogate of his county. He early raised a uniformed militia rifle company, of which he was unanimously chosen Captain, from which position he rose to be Colonel of a rifle regiment, and became a Brigadier-General of infantry in 1827. He was elected to the State Senate in November, 1823, and served until March 4, 1827, when he resigned that office, having been elected to Congress in November, 1826. He took his seat in Congress in December, 1827. He was re-elected in November, 1828. Having been elected State Comptroller, January 27, 1829, he resigned his seat in Congress before serving out his term. While in Congress, he served as a member of the Committee on Manufactures, and took an active part in the tariff investigations and discussions of 1828. He served as Comptroller from the time of his election until he was chosen United States Senator, in the early part of January, 1833, when he immediately took his seat in that body. He was re-elected in February, 1837, and again in February, 1843, and continued to serve until December, 1844, when he resigned. In November, 1844, he was elected Governor of New York, and entered upon his duties, January 1, 1845. In 1846 he retired to private life, devoting himself to the cultivation of his farm, and enjoying the society of his early friends and neighbors. On August 27, 1847, he died suddenly, at his residence in Canton. While in the United States Senate, he served most of his time on the Committee on Finance, and introduced the first Sub-Treasury bill, which became a law. President Tyler offered him a seat upon the bench of the Supreme Court, which he declined. By other Presidents he was offered seats in their cabinets and missions abroad, all of which he refused. His last labor for the public was the preparation of an address for the State Agricultural Society, which, having been finished, was read to that body a short time after his death, by his friend, Gèneral Dix. He appeared twice in the Supreme Court of the United States to argue cases of high importance, and established in that tribunal a high reputation as a lawyer.

Wright, William.—He was born in Clarksville, Rockland County, New York, and having removed to New Jersey, in 1794, was a Representative in Congress, from that State, from 1843 to 1847; and in 1853 was elected a Senator in Congress for the term ending in 1859. He was Chairman of the Committee on Engrossed Bills, and of that on the Contingent Expenses of the Senate. In 1863 he was re-elected to the Senate for the term ending in 1869, serving on the Committees on Public Lands, and Revolutionary Claims.

Wurtz, John.—He was born in Morris County, New Jersey; graduated at Princeton College in 1813; and was a Representative in Congress, from Pennsylvania, from 1825 to 1827. Died in Rome, Italy, April 23, 1861.

Wynkoop, Henry.—He was a Delegate to the Continental Congress, from 1779 to 1783, and a Representative in Congress, from Pennsylvania, from 1789 to 1791.

Wynn, Richard.—He was a Representative in Congress, from South Carolina, from 1793 to 1797, and again from 1802 to 1813.

Wynn, Thomas.—He was born, lived, and died, in Hertford County, North Carolina. He was a General of militia; a planter by occupation; served a number of years in the House of Commons and Senate; and was a Representative in Congress, from 1802 to 1807. Died June 3, 1825.

Yancey, William L. — Born at Ogeechee Shoals, Georgia, August 10, 1814; received a good education in the Northern States; studied law, and practised in South Carolina; in 1837 he settled in Alabama, and edited the Cahawba Democrat and Wetumpka Argus; and was a Representative in Congress, from Alabama, from 1844 to 1847. Before entering Congress, he had served in the Alabama Legislature, and since that time has served as a member of various political conventions, first at Baltimore in 1848, then at Cincinnati in 1856, and at Charleston in 1860, in which he bore a conspicuous part. He subsequently visited Europe as an agent of the Southern States during the Great Rebellion of 1861; also held several other appointments and positions under the Confederate Government, and died in July, 1863.

Yancy, Bartlett.—He was born in Virginia, and educated at the University of North Carolina, where he was, for a time, a tutor. His first appearance in public life was as a member of Congress, from North Carolina, in 1813, where he served four years; he served for many years in the State Legislature, and frequently as Speaker of the House; and his position as a lawyer was unsurpassed. He died in Caswell County, August 30, 1828.

Yancy, Joel.—He was a Representative in Congress, from Kentucky, from 1827 to 1831.

Yates, John B.—He was born in New York, and was a Representative in Congress, from New York, from 1815 to 1817, and was a member of the Assembly of that State in 1836, from Madison County.

Yates, Richard.—He was born in Kentucky, and was a Representative in Congress, from Illinois, from 1851 to 1855; and in 1861 he was chosen Governor of Illinois for four years.

Yeaman, George H.—He was born in Hardin County, Kentucky, November 1, 1829; received his early education under many difficulties; studied law, and came to the bar in his twenty-third year, entering upon the practice of his profession at Owensboro, Davies County, Kentucky. In 1854 he was elected Judge of Davies County, and from that time until 1858 devoted his whole attention to the law, acquiring an extensive practice in the Circuit Court and Court of Appeals. In 1861 he was elected to the Legislature of Kentucky, and in 1862 he was engaged in raising a regiment for the Union service; but when J. S. Jackson resigned he was elected as his successor a Representative, from Kentucky, to the Thirty-seventh Congress, serving on the Committee on Military Affairs, and was re-elected to the Thirty-eighth Congress, serving on the same Committee.

Yell, Archibald.—He was born in Tennessee, and, removing to Arkansas, was elected a Representative in Congress, from 1836 to 1839, and was re-elected in 1845, serving only until 1846. He was also Governor of Arkansas in 1842 and 1844. Died February 23, 1847.

Yorke, Thomas J.—He was born in New Jersey, and was a Representative in Congress, from that State, from 1837 to 1839, and again from 1841 to 1843. He was a candidate for election to the Twenty-sixth Congress, and, although he came with the Broad Seal of his State, he was not admitted.

Yost, Jacob S.—He was born in Pennsylvania, and was a Representative in Congress, from that State, from 1843 to 1847.

Young, Augustus.—He was born in Arlington, Vermont, March 20, 1785, and was admitted to the bar in St. Alban's in 1810; he commenced practice at Stowe, and in about eighteen months removed to Craftsbury, which town he represented in the General Assembly during eight sessions. He was four years State's Attorney for Orleans County, and Judge of Probate in 1830. In 1836 he was chosen State Senator, and was twice re-elected. He was a Representative in Congress, from Vermont, from 1841 to 1843, and declined a re-election. In 1847 he removed to St. Alban's, and was for several years Judge of Franklin County Court. He subsequently devoted himself to literary and scientific pursuits, and being a learned geologist and mineralogist, was appointed, in 1856, State Naturalist. He died at St. Alban's, June 17, 1857. He was highly popular, possessed great talents, and his scientific books and tracts indicate that he was a great mathematician and a profound reasoner.

Young, Bryan R.—He was born in Kentucky, and was a Representative in Congress, from that State, from 1845 to 1847.

Young, Ebenezer.—Born in Killingly, Connecticut, in 1784, and graduated at Yale College in 1806. In 1823 he was elected to the State Senate, and twice re-elected; he was also two years Speaker of the House; and was a Representative in Congress, from 1829 to 1835. He died at West Killingly, August 18, 1851.

Young, John.—He was born in Vermont in 1802; when quite a boy he moved with his father to Livingston County, New York, and received a common school education at Conesus; studied law, and was admitted to the bar in 1829; was in the State Legislature in 1831, 1844, and 1845; was a Representative in Congress, from New York, from 1841 to 1843; Governor of the State, from 1847 to 1849; and Assistant Treasurer of the United States, in New York City, at the time of his death, which occurred April 23, 1852.

Young, Richard M.—He was a Senator in Congress, from Illinois, from 1837 to 1843; and Clerk of the United States House of Representatives in 1850 and 1851.

Young, Timothy R.—He was born in New Hampshire; graduated at Bowdoin College in 1835; and was a Representative in Congress, from Illinois, from 1849 to 1851.

Young, William S.—He was born in Nelson County, Kentucky, and was a Representative in Congress, from that State, from 1825 to 1827.

Yulee, David L.—He was born in the West Indies, of Hebrew extraction, in 1811, but when quite young was removed to Virginia, where he received the rudiments of a classical education. He emigrated to Florida in 1824, and though he studied law, he divided his time between the practice of his profession and the pursuits of agriculture. He was a Delegate to Congress, from the Territory of Florida, from 1841 to 1845, bearing the name of Levy, and as Yulee was a Delegate to the Convention which formed the State Constitution, and was elected a Senator in Congress in 1845, where he continued until 1861, officiating as Chairman of the Committee on Post-offices and Post-roads. He was also President of the Atlantic and Gulf Railroad in Florida. Resigned his seat in the Senate to take part in the Rebellion of 1861.

Zollicoffer, Felix K.—Born in Maury County, Tennessee, May 19, 1812, and received an academical education. He served for a few months in a printing-office, and in 1829 took upon himself the management of a newspaper at Paris, Tennessee. In 1834 he was editor and publisher of the Columbian Observer, in the same State; in 1835 he was elected State printer, and re-elected in 1837; in 1842 he removed to Nashville, and edited the Banner; in 1843 he was elected Comptroller of the State Treasury, and was re-elected in 1845 and 1847; in 1849 was elected to the State Senate; in 1850 was a contractor for building the Suspension Bridge at Nashville; in 1851 and 1852, again edited the Nashville Banner, and was elected a Representative in Congress, from Tennessee, in 1853, where he continued until the close of the Thirty-fifth Congress, serving in the same as a member of the Committee on Territories. He subsequently joined the Great Rebellion, and served as a General of volunteers, having been killed at the battle of Somerset, Kentucky. He was a Delegate to the Peace Congress of 1861.

APPENDIX.

APPENDIX.

SUCCESSIVE SESSIONS OF CONGRESS.

STATEMENT

Showing the Commencement and Termination of each Session of Congress, held under the Present Constitution, with the Number of Days in each.

Congress.	Session.	From	To	Year of Independence.	Number of Days in each Session.	Where held.
1	1	March 4, 1789	Sept. 29, 1789	13	210	New York.
	2	January 4, 1790	August 12, 1790	14	221	do.
	3	Dec. 6, 1790	March 3, 1791	15	88	Philadelphia.
2	1	Oct. 24, 1791	May 8, 1792	16	197	do.
	2	Nov. 5, 1792	March 2, 1793	17	119	do.
3	1	Dec. 2, 1793	June 9, 1794	18	190	do.
	2	Nov. 3, 1794	March 3, 1795	19	121	do.
4	1	Dec. 7, 1795	June 1, 1796	20	177	do.
	2	Dec. 5, 1796	March 3, 1797	21	89	do.
5	1	May 15, 1797	July 10, 1797	21	57	do.
	2	Nov. 13, 1797	July 16, 1798	22	246	do.
	3	Dec. 3, 1798	March 3, 1799	23	91	do.
6	1	Dec. 2, 1799	May 14, 1800	24	164	do.
	2	Nov. 17, 1800	March 3, 1801	25	107	Washington.
7	1	Dec. 7, 1801	May 3, 1802	26	148	do.
	2	Dec. 6, 1802	March 3, 1803	27	88	do.
8	1	Oct. 17, 1803	March 27, 1804	28	163	do.
	2	Nov. 5, 1804	March 3, 1805	29	119	do.
9	1	Dec. 2, 1805	April 21, 1806	30	141	do.
	2	Dec. 1, 1806	March 3, 1807	31	93	do.
10	1	Oct. 26, 1807	April 25, 1808	32	182	do.
	2	Nov. 7, 1808	March 3, 1809	33	117	do.
11	1	May 22, 1809	June 28, 1809	33	38	do.
	2	Nov. 27, 1809	May 1, 1810	34	156	do.
	3	Dec. 3, 1810	March 3, 1811	35	91	do.
12	1	Nov. 4, 1811	July 6, 1812	36	245	do.
	2	Nov. 2, 1812	March 3, 1813	37	122	do.
13	1	May 24, 1813	August 2, 1813	37	71	do.
	2	Dec. 6, 1813	April 18, 1814	38	134	do.
	3	Sept. 19, 1814	March 3, 1815	39	166	do.

Statement of the Successive Sessions of Congress—(Continued).

Congress.	Session.	From	To	Year of Independence.	Number of Days in each Session.	Where held.
14	1	Dec. 4, 1815	April 30, 1816	40	148	Washington.
	2	Dec. 2, 1816	March 3, 1817	41	92	do.
15	1	Dec. 1, 1817	April 30, 1818	42	141	do.
	2	Nov. 16, 1818	March 3, 1819	43	108	do.
16	1	Dec. 6, 1819	May 15, 1820	44	162	do.
	2	Nov. 13, 1820	March 3, 1821	45	111	do.
17	1	Dec. 3, 1821	May 8, 1822	46	157	do.
	2	Dec. 2, 1822	March 3, 1823	47	92	do.
18	1	Dec. 1, 1823	May 27, 1824	48	178	do.
	2	Dec. 6, 1824	March 3, 1825	49	88	do.
19	1	Dec. 5, 1825	May 22, 1826	50	169	do.
	2	Dec. 4, 1826	March 3, 1827	51	90	do.
20	1	Dec. 3, 1827	May 26, 1828	52	175	do.
	2	Dec. 1, 1828	March 3, 1829	53	93	do.
21	1	Dec. 7, 1829	May 31, 1830	54	176	do.
	2	Dec. 6, 1830	March 3, 1831	55	88	do.
22	1	Dec. 5, 1831	July 16, 1832	56	225	do.
	2	Dec. 3, 1832	March 3, 1833	57	91	do.
23	1	Dec. 2, 1833	June 30, 1834	58	211	do.
	2	Dec. 1, 1834	March 3, 1835	59	93	do.
24	1	Dec. 7, 1835	July 4, 1836	60	211	do.
	2	Dec. 5, 1836	March 3, 1837	61	89	do.
25	1	Sept. 4, 1837	October 16, 1837	62	43	do.
	2	Dec. 4, 1837	July 9, 1838	62	218	do.
	3	Dec. 3, 1838	March 3, 1839	63	91	do.
26	1	Dec. 2, 1839	July 21, 1840	64	233	do.
	2	Dec. 7, 1840	March 3, 1841	65	87	do.
27	1	May 31, 1841	Sept. 13, 1841	65	106	do.
	2	Dec. 6, 1841	August 31, 1842	66	269	do.
	3	Dec. 5, 1842	March 3, 1843	67	89	do.
28	1	Dec. 4, 1843	June 17, 1844	68	196	do.
	2	Dec. 2, 1844	March 3, 1845	69	92	do.
29	1	Dec. 1, 1845	August 10, 1846	70	253	do.
	2	Dec. 7, 1846	March 3, 1847	71	87	do.
30	1	Dec. 6, 1847	August 14, 1848	72	254	do.
	2	Dec. 4, 1848	March 3, 1849	73	90	do.
31	1	Dec. 3, 1849	Sept. 30, 1850	74	302	do.
	2	Dec. 2, 1850	March 3, 1851	75	92	do.
32	1	Dec. 1, 1851	August 31, 1852	76	275	do.
	2	Dec. 6, 1852	March 3, 1853	77	88	do.
33	1	Dec. 5, 1853	August 7, 1854	78	246	do.
	2	Dec. 4, 1854	March 3, 1855	79	90	do.
34	1	Dec. 3, 1855	August 18, 1856	80	260	do.
	2	August 21, 1856	August 30, 1856	81	10	do.
	3	Dec. 1, 1856	March 3, 1857	82	93	do.
35	1	Dec. 7, 1857	June 1, 1858	82	177	do.
	2	Dec. 6, 1858	March 3, 1859	83	88	do.
36	1	Dec. 5, 1859	June 18, 1860	84	196	do.
	2	Dec. 3, 1860	March 4, 1861	85	93	do.
37	1	July 4, 1861	August 6, 1861	85	34	do.
	2	Dec. 2, 1861	July 17, 1862	86	228	do.
	3	Dec. 1, 1862	March 4, 1863	87	94	do.

SPEAKERS OF THE HOUSE OF REPRESENTATIVES.

Congress	Speaker	State
1st Congress.	F. A. Muhlenberg,	Pennsylvania.
2d "	Jonathan Trumbull,	Connecticut.
3d "	F. A. Muhlenberg,	Pennsylvania.
4th "	Jonathan Dayton,	New Jersey.
5th "	Jonathan Dayton, George Dent, *pro tem.*,	" " Maryland.
6th "	Theodore Sedgwick,	Massachusetts.
7th "	Nathaniel Macon,	North Carolina.
8th "	Nathaniel Macon,	" "
9th "	Nathaniel Macon,	" "
10th "	Joseph B. Varnum,	Massachusetts.
11th "	Joseph B. Varnum,	"
12th "	Henry Clay,	Kentucky.
13th "	Henry Clay, 1st session, Langdon Cheves, 2d "	" South Carolina.
14th "	Henry Clay,	Kentucky.
15th "	Henry Clay,	"
16th "	Henry Clay, 1st session, John W. Taylor, 2d "	" New York.
17th "	P. P. Barbour,	Virginia.
18th "	Henry Clay,	Kentucky.
19th "	John W. Taylor,	New York.
20th "	Andrew Stevenson,	Virginia.
21st "	Andrew Stevenson,	"
22d "	Andrew Stevenson,	"
23d "	Andrew Stevenson, 1st session, John Bell, 2d session, Henry Hubbard, *pro tem.*,	" Tennessee. New Hampshire.
24th "	James K. Polk,	Tennessee.
25th "	James K. Polk,	"
26th "	R. M. T. Hunter,	Virginia.
27th "	John White,	Kentucky.
28th "	John W. Jones, George W. Hopkins, *pro tem.*,	Virginia. "
29th "	John W. Davis,	Indiana.
30th "	Robert C. Winthrop, Armisted Burt, *pro tem.*,	Massachusetts. South Carolina.
31st "	Howell Cobb, R. C. Winthrop, *pro tem.*,	Georgia. Massachusetts.
32d "	Linn Boyd,	Kentucky.
33d "	Linn Boyd,	"
34th "	Nathaniel P. Banks,	Massachusetts.
35th "	James L. Orr,	South Carolina.
36th "	William Pennington,	New Jersey.
37th "	Galusha A. Grow,	Pennsylvania.
38th "	Schuyler Colfax,	Indiana.

PRESIDENTS OF THE SENATE.

VICE-PRESIDENTS OF THE UNITED STATES.

Congresses.		
1 to 4.	John Adams,	Massachusetts.
5 and 6.	Thomas Jefferson,	Virginia.
7 and 8.	Aaron Burr,	New York.
9 to 12.	George Clinton,*	" "
13 and 14.	Elbridge Gerry,*	Massachusetts.

* Died in office.

Congresses.		
15 to 18.	Daniel D. Tompkins,	New York.
19 to 22.	John C. Calhoun,*	South Carolina.
23 and 24.	Martin Van Buren,	New York.
25 and 26.	Richard M. Johnson,	Kentucky.
27.	John Tyler,†	Virginia.
29 and 30.	George M. Dallas,	Pennsylvania.
31.	Millard Fillmore,‡	New York.
32.	William R. King,§	Alabama.
33.	(Vacant.)	
34.	(Vacant.)	
35.	John C. Breckinridge,	Kentucky.
36.	John C. Breckinridge,	"
37.	Hannibal Hamlin,	Maine.
38.	Hannibal Hamlin,	"

PRESIDENTS OF THE SENATE, PRO TEM.

1st Congress.	John Langdon,	New Hampshire.
2d "	Richard Henry Lee, John Langdon,	Virginia. New Hampshire.
3d "	Ralph Izard, Henry Tazewell,	South Carolina. Virginia.
4th "	Samuel Livermore, William Bingham,	New Hampshire. Pennsylvania.
5th "	William Bradford, Jacob Read, Theodore Sedgwick, John Lawrence, James Ross,	Rhode Island. South Carolina. Massachusetts. New York. Pennsylvania.
6th "	Samuel Livermore, Uriah Tracy, John E. Howard, James Hillhouse,	New Hampshire. Connecticut. Maryland. Connecticut.
7th "	Abraham Baldwin, Stephen R. Bradley,	Georgia. Vermont.
8th "	John Browne, Jesse Franklin, Joseph Anderson,	Kentucky. North Carolina. Tennessee.
9th "	Samuel Smith, Samuel Smith,	Maryland. "
10th "	Samuel Smith, Stephen R. Bradley, John Milledge,	" Vermont. Georgia.
11th "	Andrew Gregg, John Gaillard, John Pope,	Pennsylvania. South Carolina. Kentucky.
12th "	William H. Crawford, Joseph B. Varnum,	Georgia. Massachusetts.
13th "	John Gaillard,	South Carolina.
14th "	John Gaillard,	" "
15th "	John Gaillard, James Barbour,	" " Virginia.
16th "	James Barbour, John Gaillard,	" South Carolina.
17th "	John Gaillard,	" "
18th "	John Gaillard,	" "
19th "	Nathaniel Macon,	North Carolina.
20th "	Nathaniel Macon, Samuel Smith,	" " Maryland.

* Resigned December 28, 1832. † Became President by death of Harrison.
‡ Became President by death of Taylor. § Died in office.

21st Congress.	Samuel Smith,	Maryland.
22d "	Littleton W. Tazewell,	Virginia.
	Hugh L. White,	Tennessee.
23d "	George Poindexter,	Mississippi.
	John Tyler,	Virginia.
24th "	William R. King,	Alabama.
25th "	William R. King,	"
26th "	William R. King,	"
27th "	Samuel L. Southard,	New Jersey.
28th "	Willie P. Mangum,	North Carolina.
29th "	David R. Atchison,	Missouri.
30th "	David R. Atchison,	"
31st "	William R. King,	Alabama.
32d "	William R. King,	"
33d "	David R. Atchison,	Missouri.
34th "	Jesse D. Bright,	Indiana.
35th "	Benjamin Fitzpatrick,	Alabama.
36th "	Jesse D. Bright,	Indiana.
	Solomon Foot,	Vermont.
37th "	Solomon Foot,	"
38th "	Solomon Foot,	"
	Daniel Clark,	New Hampshire.

SECRETARIES OF THE SENATE.

Names.	States.	Time of appointment.	Expiration of service.
Samuel Allyne Otis . . .	Massachusetts .	8 April, 1789	18 April, 1814
Charles Cutts	New Hampshire	11 Oct. 1814	12 Dec. 1825
Walter Lowrie	Pennsylvania .	12 Dec. 1825	5 Dec. 1836
Asbury Dickens	North Carolina	12 Dec. 1836	July, 1861
John W. Forney	Pennsylvania .	July, 1861	

CLERKS OF THE HOUSE OF REPRESENTATIVES.

Names.	States.	Time of appointment.	Expiration of service.
John Beckley	Virginia . . .	1 April, 1789	15 May, 1797
Jonathan Williams Condy .	Pennsylvania .	15 May, 1797	9 Dec. 1800
John Holt Oswald . . .	Pennsylvania .	9 Dec. 1800	7 Dec. 1801
John Beckley	Virginia . . .	7 Dec. 1801	26 Oct. 1807
Patrick Magruder . . .	Maryland . .	26 Oct. 1807	28 Jan. 1815
Thomas Dougherty . . .	Kentucky . .	30 Jan. 1815	3 Dec. 1822
Matthew St. Clair Clarke .	Pennsylvania .	3 Dec. 1822	2 Dec. 1833
Walter S. Franklin . . .	Pennsylvania .	2 Dec. 1833	20 Sept. 1838
Hugh A. Garland	Virginia . . .	3 Dec. 1838	31 May, 1841
Matthew St. Clair Clarke .	Pennsylvania .	31 May, 1841	6 Dec. 1843
Caleb J. McNulty . . .	Ohio	6 Dec. 1843	18 Jan. 1845
Benjamin B. French . . .	New Hampshire	18 Jan. 1845	7 Dec. 1847
Thomas Jefferson Campbell	Tennessee . .	7 Dec. 1847	13 April, 1850
Richard M. Young . . .	Illinois . . .	17 April. 1850	1 Dec. 1851
John W. Forney	Pennsylvania .	1 Dec. 1851	4 Feb. 1856
William Cullom	Tennessee . .	4 Feb. 1856	6 Dec. 1857
James C. Allen	Illinois . . .	6 Dec. 1857	3 Feb. 1860
John W. Forney	Pennsylvania .	3 Feb. 1860	4 July, 1861
Emerson Etheridge . . .	Tennessee . .	4 July 1861	8 Dec. 1863
Edward McPherson . . .	Pennsylvania .	8 Dec. 1863	

CHAPLAINS TO CONGRESS.

Showing the Names of Clergymen who have served as Chaplains to the Senate since 1789; *also, the Churches to which they belonged; in the order of their appointment.*

The initials opposite the name signify: B. for Baptist, C. for Congregationalist, D. for Dutch Reformed, E. for Episcopalian, L. for Lutheran, M. for Methodist, P. for Presbyterian, R. C. for Roman Catholic, U. for Universalist, Un. for Unitarian.

Names.	Church.	Names.	Church.
Rt. Rev. Bishop Provost,	E.	Rev. William Ryland,	M.
Rt. Rev. Bishop White,	E.	Rev. C. P. McIlvaine,	E.
Rt. Rev. Bishop Clagett,	E.	Rev. W. Staughton,	B.
Rev. Dr. E. Gantt,	E.	Rev. C. P. McIlvaine,	E.
Rev. A. T. McCormick,	E.	Rev. W. Staughton,	B.
Rev. Dr. Gantt,	E.	Rev. W. Ryland,	M.
Rev. John J. Sayrs,	E.	Rev. H. V. D. Johns,	E.
Rev. Dr. Gantt,	E.	Rev. J. P. Durbin,	M.
Rev. A. T. McCormick,	E.	Rev. C. C. Pise,	R. C.
Rev. R. Elliott,	P.	Rev. T. W. Hatch,	E.
Rev. M. Wilmer,	E.	Rev. E. Y. Higby,	E.
Rev. O. B. Brown,	B.	Rev. Henry Slicer,	M.
Rev. Walter Addison,	E.	Rev. G. G. Cookman,	M.
Rev. J. Breckenridge,	P.	Rev. S. Tustin,	P.
Rev. Jesse Lee,	M.	Rev. Henry Slicer,	M.
Rev. J. Glendy,	P.	Rev. C. M. Butler,	E.
Rev. J. Glendy,	P.	Rev. Henry Slicer,	M.
Rev. S. E. Dwight,	C.	Rev. Henry C. Dean,	M.
Rev. William Hawley,	E.	Rev. Stephen P. Hill,	B.
Rev. John Clark,	P.	Rev. R. R. Gurley,	P.
Rev. B. Allison,	B.	Rev. Mr. Sunderland,	P.

Showing the Names of Clergymen who have served as Chaplains to the House of Representatives since 1789.

Names.	Church.	Names.	Church.
Rev. William Linn,	P.	Rev. Reuben Post,	P.
Rev. Samuel Blair,	P.	Rev. R. R. Gurley,	P.
Rev. Ashbel Green,	P.	Rev. Reuben Post,	P.
Rev. Thomas Lyell,	M.	Rev. W. Hammett,	M.
Rev. W. Parkinson,	B.	Rev. T. H. Stockton,	M.
Rev. W. Bentley,	C.	Rev. E. D. Smith,	P.
Rev. W. Parkinson,	B.	Rev. T. H. Stockton,	M.
Rev. James Laurie,	P.	Rev. O. C. Comstock,	B.
Rev. J. Glendy,	P.	Rev. S. Tustin,	P.
Rev. R. Elliott,	P.	Rev. L. R. Reese,	M.
Rev. O. B. Brown,	B.	Rev. Joshua Bates,	C.
Rev. Jesse Lee,	M.	Rev. T. W. Braxton,	B.
Rev. N. Sneathen,	M.	Rev. J. W. French,	E.
Rev. Jesse Lee,	M.	Rev. J. N. Maffit,	M.
Rev. O. B. Brown,	B.	Rev. J. S. Tiffany,	E.
Rev. S. H. Cone,	B.	Rev. J. S. Tinsley,	B.
Rev. B. Allison,	B.	Rev. W. M. Daily,	M.
Rev. J. N. Campbell,	P.	Rev. W. H. Milburn,	M.
Rev. Jared Sparks,	Un.	Rev. W. S. S. Sprole,	P.
Rev. J. Breckenridge,	P.	Rev. R. R. Gurley,	P.
Rev. H. B. Bascom,	M.	Rev. L. F. Morgan,	M.

Names.	Church.	Names.	Church.
Rev. James Gallagher, . . .	P.	Rev. Daniel Waldo, ...	C.
Rev. W. H. Milburn, . . .	M.	Rev. T. H. Stockton, . . .	M.
Rev. Daniel Waldo, ...	C.	Rev. Mr. Chauncey, . . .	U.

NOTE. The Thirty-fifth Congress discontinued the usage of electing Chaplains, and extended an invitation to the Clergy of the District of Columbia to alternate in opening the daily sessions by prayer, and in preaching on the Sabbath; which they continued to do until the Thirty-sixth Congress.

SUCCESSIVE ADMINISTRATIONS.

FIRST ADMINISTRATION—1789 to 1797.—EIGHT YEARS.

President—GEORGE WASHINGTON, Virginia.

Vice-President—JOHN ADAMS, Massachusetts.

*Secretaries of State**—Thomas Jefferson, of Virginia, appointed September 26, 1789; Edmund Randolph, of Virginia, January 2, 1794; Timothy Pickering, of Massachusetts, December 10, 1795.

Secretaries of the Treasury—Alexander Hamilton, of New York, September 11, 1789; Oliver Wolcott, of Connecticut, February 3, 1795.

Secretaries of War and of the Navy†—Henry Knox, of Massachusetts, September 12, 1789; Timothy Pickering, of Massachusetts, January 2, 1794; James McHenry, of Maryland, January 27, 1796.

Postmasters-General‡—Samuel Osgood, of Massachusetts, September 26, 1789; Timothy Pickering, of Massachusetts, November 7, 1791; Joseph Habersham, of Georgia, February 25, 1795.

Attorneys-General—Edmund Randolph, of Virginia, September 26, 1789, made Secretary of State, January 2, 1794; William Bradford, of Pennsylvania, January 28, 1794; died. Charles Lee, of Virginia, December 10, 1795.

SECOND ADMINISTRATION—1797 TO 1801.—FOUR YEARS.

President—JOHN ADAMS, Massachusetts.

Vice-President.—THOMAS JEFFERSON, Virginia.

Secretaries of State.—Timothy Pickering, continued in office; John Marshall, of Virginia, May 13, 1800.

Secretaries of the Treasury—Oliver Wolcott, continued in office; S. Dexter, of Massachusetts, December 31, 1800.

Secretaries of War—James McHenry, continued in office; S. Dexter, of Massachusetts, May 13, 1800; Roger Griswold, of Connecticut, February 3, 1801.

Secretaries of the Navy—George Cabot, of Massachusetts, May 3, 1798, declined; Benjamin Stoddert, of Maryland, May 21, 1798.

Postmaster-General—Joseph Habersham, continued.

Attorney-General—Charles Lee, continued.

THIRD ADMINISTRATION—1801 TO 1809.—EIGHT YEARS.

President—THOMAS JEFFERSON, Virginia.

Vice-Presidents—AARON BURR, New York; GEORGE CLINTON, New York.

Secretary of State—James Madison, of Virginia, March 5, 1801.

---

* The Department of State was created by the Act of September 15, 1789, previously to which, by Act of July 27, 1789, it was denominated the Department of Foreign Affairs.

† The War Department, as created by Act of Congress of August 7, 1789, had also the superintendence of Naval Affairs. A separation took place in April, 1798, when a Navy Department was established.

‡ From the organization of the Government down to the year 1829 the Postmasters-General were not recognized as members of the Cabinet, but are herein printed as such for the sake of uniformity.

Secretaries of the Treasury—S. Dexter, continued in office; Albert Gallatin, of Pennsylvania, January 26, 1802.

Secretary of War—Henry Dearborn, of Massachusetts, March 4, 1801.

Secretaries of the Navy—Benjamin Stoddert, continued in office; Robert Smith, of Maryland, January 26, 1802; Jacob Crowninshield, of Massachusetts, March 2, 1805.

Postmasters-General—Joseph Habersham, continued in office; Gideon Granger, of Connecticut, January 26, 1802.

Attorneys-General—Theophilus Parsons, of Massachusetts, February 20, 1801, declined; Levi Lincoln, of Massachusetts, March 5, 1801; resigned in 1805. Robert Smith, of Maryland, March 2, 1805; John Breckenridge, of Kentucky, December 25, 1805; Cæsar A. Rodney, of Pennsylvania, January 20, 1807.

FOURTH ADMINISTRATION—1809 TO 1817.—EIGHT YEARS.

President—JAMES MADISON, Virginia.

Vice-Presidents—GEORGE CLINTON, New York, ELBRIDGE GERRY, Massachusetts.

Secretaries of State—Robert Smith, of Maryland, March 6, 1809; James Monroe, of Virginia, November 25, 1811.

Secretaries of the Treasury—Albert Gallatin, continued in office; George W. Campbell, of Tennessee, February 9, 1814; Alexander J. Dallas, of Pennsylvania, October 6, 1814.

Secretaries of War—William Eustis, of Massachusetts, March 7, 1809; John Armstrong, of New York, January 19, 1813; James Monroe, of Virginia, September 26, 1814; William H. Crawford, of Georgia, March 2, 1815.

Secretaries of the Navy—Paul Hamilton, of South Carolina, March 7, 1809; William Jones, of Pennsylvania, January 12, 1813; Benjamin W. Crowninshield, of Massachusetts, December 17, 1814.

Postmasters-General—Gideon Granger, continued in office; R. J. Meigs, of Ohio, March 17, 1814.

Attorneys-General—Cæsar A. Rodney, continued in office; William Pinkney, of Maryland, December 11, 1811; Richard Rush, February 10, 1814.

FIFTH ADMINISTRATION—1817 TO 1825.—EIGHT YEARS.

President—JAMES MONROE, Virginia.

Vice-President—DANIEL D. TOMPKINS, New York.

Secretary of State—John Q. Adams, of Massachusetts, March 3, 1817.

Secretary of the Treasury—William H. Crawford, of Georgia, March 5, 1817.

Secretaries of War—Isaac Shelby, of Kentucky, March 5, 1817, declined the appointment; John C. Calhoun, of South Carolina, December 16, 1817.

Secretaries of the Navy—Benjamin W. Crowninshield, continued in office; Smith Thompson, of New York, November 30, 1818; Samuel L. Southard, of New Jersey, December 9, 1823.

Postmasters-General—Return J. Meigs, continued in office; John McLean, of Ohio, December 9, 1823.

Attorney-General—William Wirt, of Virginia, December 15, 1817.

SIXTH ADMINISTRATION—1824 TO 1829.—FOUR YEARS.

President—JOHN QUINCY ADAMS, Massachusetts.

Vice-President—JOHN C. CALHOUN, South Carolina.

Secretary of State—Henry Clay, of Kentucky, March 8, 1825.

Secretary of the Treasury—Richard Rush, of Pennsylvania, March 7, 1825.

Secretaries of War—James Barbour, of Virginia, March 7, 1825; Peter B. Porter, of New York, May 26, 1828.

Secretary of the Navy—Samuel L. Southard, continued in office.

Postmaster-General—John McLean, continued in office.

Attorney-General—William Wirt, continued in office.

SEVENTH ADMINISTRATION—1829 TO 1837.—EIGHT YEARS.

President—ANDREW JACKSON, Tennessee.

Vice-Presidents—JOHN C. CALHOUN, South Carolina; MARTIN VAN BUREN, New York.

Secretaries of State—Martin Van Buren, of New York, March 6, 1829; Edward Livingston, of Louisiana, 1831; Louis McLane, of Delaware, 1833; John Forsyth, of Georgia, 1834.

Secretaries of the Treasury—Samuel D. Ingham, of Pennsylvania, March 6, 1829; Louis McLane, of Delaware, 1831; William J. Duane, of Pennsylvania, 1833; Roger B. Taney, of Maryland, 1833 (not confirmed by the Senate); Levi Woodbury, of New Hampshire, 1834.

Secretaries of War—John H. Eaton, of Tennessee, March 9, 1829; Lewis Cass, of Ohio, 1831.

Secretaries of the Navy—John Branch, of North Carolina, March 9, 1829; Levi Woodbury, of New Hampshire, 1831; Mahlon Dickerson, of New Jersey, 1834.

Postmasters-General—William T. Barry,* of Kentucky, March 9, 1829; Amos Kendall, of Kentucky, 1835.

Attorneys-General—John M. Berrien, of Georgia, March 9, 1829; Roger B. Taney, of Maryland, December 27, 1831; Benjamin F. Butler, of New York, June 24, 1834.

EIGHTH ADMINISTRATION—1837 TO 1841.—FOUR YEARS.

President—MARTIN VAN BUREN, New York.

Vice-President—RICHARD M. JOHNSON, Kentucky.

Secretary of State—John Forsyth, June 27, 1834.

Secretary of the Treasury—Levi Woodbury, June 27, 1834.

Secretary of War—Joel R. Poinsett, March 7, 1837.

Secretaries of the Navy—Mahlon Dickerson, June 30, 1834; James K. Paulding, June 30, 1838.

Postmasters-General—Amos Kendall, May 1, 1835; John M. Niles, May 25, 1840.

Attorneys-General—Felix Grundy, of Tennessee, September 1, 1838; Henry D. Gilpin, of Pennsylvania, January 10, 1840.

NINTH ADMINISTRATION.—1841 TO 1845—FOUR YEARS.

President—GENERAL WILLIAM HENRY HARRISON, Ohio. Died April 4, 1841.

Vice-President—JOHN TYLER, Virginia.

President—JOHN TYLER, Virginia (from April 4, 1841).

Secretaries of State—Daniel Webster, March 5, 1841; Hugh S. Legaré, May 9, 1843, died June 20, 1843; Abel P. Upshur, June 24, 1843, died February 28, 1844; John Nelson, acting, February 29, 1844; John C. Calhoun, March 6, 1844.

Secretaries of the Treasury—Thomas Ewing, March 5, 1841; Walter Forward, September 13, 1841; George M. Bibb, June 15, 1844.

Secretaries of War—John Bell, March 5, 1841; John C. Spencer, October 12, 1841, transferred to Treasury Department; James M. Porter, March 8, 1843, rejected by the Senate; William Wilkins, February 15, 1844.

Secretaries of the Navy—George E. Badger, March 5, 1841; Abel P. Upshur, September 13, 1841, transferred to Department of State; David Henshaw, July 24, 1843, rejected by the Senate; Thomas W. Gilmer, February 15, 1844, died February 28, 1844; John Y. Mason, March 14, 1844.

Postmasters-General—Francis Granger, March 6, 1841; Charles A. Wickliffe, September 13, 1841.

---

* Before the accession of Andrew Jackson to the Presidency, the Postmaster-General was looked upon as the head of a bureau, but President Jackson invited Mr. Barry to a seat in his cabinet meetings, since which time the head of the Post-office Department has been considered a regular member of the cabinet.

Attorneys-General—John J. Crittenden, of Kentucky, March 5, 1841; Hugh S. Legaré, of South Carolina, September 13, 1841, died; John Nelson, of Maryland, January 2, 1844.

TENTH ADMINISTRATION—1845 TO 1849.—FOUR YEARS.

President—JAMES KNOX POLK, Tennessee.
Vice-President—GEORGE M. DALLAS, Pennsylvania.
Secretary of State—James Buchanan, of Pennsylvania, March 5, 1845.
Secretary of the Treasury—Robert J. Walker, of Mississippi, March 5, 1845.
Secretary of War—William L. Marcy, of New York, March 5, 1845.
Secretary of the Navy—George Bancroft, of Massachusetts, March, 1845; John Y. Mason, of Virginia, in 1846.
Postmaster-General—Cave Johnson, of Tennessee, March 5, 1845.
Attorneys-General—John Y. Mason, of Virginia, March 5, 1845; Nathan Clifford, of Maine, December 23, 1846; Isaac Toucey, of Connecticut, June 21, 1848.

ELEVENTH ADMINISTRATION—1849 TO 1853.—FOUR YEARS.

President—ZACHARY TAYLOR, Louisiana. Died July 9, 1850.
Vice-President—MILLARD FILLMORE, New York.
President—MILLARD FILLMORE, New York. Succeeded Zachary Taylor, on his death, July 9, 1850.
Secretaries of State—John M. Clayton, of Delaware, March 7, 1849; Daniel Webster, of Massachusetts, July 20, 1850, died October 24, 1852; Edward Everett, of Massachusetts, November, 1852.
Secretaries of the Treasury—William M. Meredith, of Pennsylvania, March 7, 1849; Thomas Corwin, of Ohio, July 20, 1850.
Secretaries of War—George W. Crawford, of Georgia, March 7, 1849; Charles M. Conrad, of Louisiana, August 15, 1850.
Secretaries of the Navy—William B. Preston, of Virginia, March 7, 1849; William A. Graham, of North Carolina, July 20, 1850; John P. Kennedy, of Maryland, in 1852.
Secretaries of the Interior—Thomas Ewing, of Ohio, March 7, 1849; Alexander H. H. Stuart, of Virginia, September 12, 1850.
Postmasters-General—Jacob Collamer, of Vermont, March 7, 1849; Nathan K. Hall, of New York, July 20, 1850; Samuel D. Hubbard, of Connecticut, 1852.
Attorneys-General—Reverdy Johnson, of Maryland, March 7, 1849; John J. Crittenden, of Kentucky, July 20, 1850.

TWELFTH ADMINISTRATION—1853 TO 1857.—FOUR YEARS.

President—FRANKLIN PIERCE, New Hampshire.
Vice-President—WILLIAM R. KING, Alabama. Died April 18, 1853.
Secretary of State—William L. Marcy, of New York, March 7, 1853.
Secretary of the Treasury—James Guthrie, of Kentucky, March 7, 1853.
Secretary of War—Jefferson Davis, of Mississippi, March 7, 1853.
Secretary of the Navy—James C. Dobbin, of North Carolina, March 7, 1853.
Secretary of the Interior—Robert McClelland, of Michigan, March 7, 1853.
Postmaster-General—James Campbell, of Pennsylvania, March 7, 1853.
Attorney-General—Caleb Cushing, of Massachusettts, March 7, 1853.

THIRTEENTH ADMINISTRATION—1857 TO 1861.—FOUR YEARS.

President—JAMES BUCHANAN, Pennsylvania.
Vice-President—JOHN C. BRECKINRIDGE, Kentucky.
Secretaries of State—Lewis Cass, of Michigan, March, 1857; Jeremiah S. Black, of Pennsylvania, December, 1860.
Secretaries of the Treasury—Howell Cobb, of Georgia, March, 1857; Philip F. Thomas, of Maryland, December, 1860; John A. Dix, of New York, January, 1861.

Secretaries of War—John B. Floyd, of Virginia, March, 1857; Joseph Holt, of Kentucky, December, 1860.

Secretary of the Navy—Isaac Toucey, of Connecticut, March, 1857.

Secretary of the Interior—Jacob Thompson, of Mississippi, March, 1857.

Postmasters-General—Aaron V. Brown, of Tennessee, March, 1857, died; Joseph Holt, of Kentucky, March, 1859.

Attorneys-General—Jeremiah S. Black, of Pennsylvania, March, 1857; Edwin M. Stanton, of Ohio, December, 1860.

FOURTEENTH ADMINISTRATION—1861 TO 1865.—FOUR YEARS.

President—ABRAHAM LINCOLN, Illinois.

Vice-President—HANNIBAL HAMLIN, Maine.

Secretary of State—William H. Seward, of New York.

Secretaries of the Treasury—Salmon P. Chase, of Ohio; William P. Fessenden, of Maine.

Secretaries of War—Simon Cameron, of Pennsylvania; Edwin M. Stanton, of Ohio, 1861.

Secretary of the Navy—Gideon Welles, of Connecticut.

Secretaries of the Interior—Caleb B. Smith, of Indiana; John P. Usher, of Indiana, 1863.

Postmasters-General—Montgomery Blair, of Maryland; William Dennison, of Ohio.

Attorney-General—Edward Bates, of Missouri.

PRESIDENTIAL ELECTORS.

THE election of the President and of the Vice-President, by Colleges of Electors, chosen in each State, was first proposed in the Convention for the formation of the Constitution, by James Wilson, a delegate from Pennsylvania. It was adopted after a prolonged discussion, and was regulated by an Act of Congress, of March 1, 1792. The Electors must be chosen within thirty-four days preceding the first Wednesday of December of the year in which an election of President and Vice-President takes place. They must be equal in number to all the Senators and Representatives in Congress, but no Senator or person holding an office of trust or profit under the United States can be appointed an Elector. The Electors were at first chosen in four different modes, viz.: by joint ballot of the State Legislature, by a concurrent vote of the two branches of the State Legislature, by the people of the State, voting by general ticket, and by the people, voting in districts. This latter mode was evidently that which gave the fairest expression to public opinion, by approaching nearest to a direct vote. But those States which adopted it were placed at the disadvantage of being exposed to a division of their strength, and neutralization of their vote; while the Electors chosen by either of the other methods voted in a body on one side or the other, thus making the voice of the State decisively felt. This consideration induced the leading States of Massachusetts and of Virginia, which originally adopted the district system, to abandon it in 1800.

An Act of Congress was approved January 23, 1845, to establish a uniform time for holding elections for Electors in all the States of the Union, whereby they are appointed in each State on the Tuesday next after the first Monday in the month of November of the year in which they are to be appointed. Each State may also by law provide for the filling of any vacancy or vacancies which may occur in its College of Electors, when such College meets to give its electoral vote; and when any State shall have held an election for the purpose of choosing Electors, and shall fail to make a choice on the day aforesaid, then the Electors may be appointed on a subsequent day in such manner as the State shall by law provide.

The Electors meet at the capitals of their respective States, on the first Wednesday of December, and vote by distinct ballots for President and Vice-President, one of whom shall not be an inhabitant of the same State with themselves. They make lists of the number of votes given, and of the persons voted for, which they transmit sealed, by a special messenger, to the President of the Senate at Washington.

The Senate and House of Representatives, having met in convention on a day fixed, the President of the Senate opens all the certificates, and the votes are counted. The person having the greatest number of votes for President is duly elected, if such a number be a majority of the whole number of Electors appointed. If no person have such a majority, then from the persons having the highest number, not exceeding three, in the list of those voted for as President, the House of Representatives shall choose immediately, and by ballot, the President. If the House of Representatives shall not choose a President, whenever the right of choice devolves upon them, before the 4th of March next following, then the Vice-President shall act as President, as in the case of the death, or other constitutional disability of the President.

Should the offices of President and Vice-President both become vacant, it then becomes the duty of the Secretary of State to communicate information thereof to the Executive of each State, and to cause the same to be published in at least one newspaper in every State, giving two months' previous notice that Electors of President shall be chosen or appointed in the several States, within thirty-four days next preceding the first Wednesday in December ensuing, when the choice of President must proceed as usual.

FIRST PRESIDENTIAL ELECTION.

GEORGE WASHINGTON was unanimously elected President, receiving 69 votes. JOHN ADAMS was elected Vice-President, receiving 34 votes; while John Jay had 9 votes, Robert H. Harrison 6, John Rutledge 6, John Hancock 4, George Clinton 3, Samuel Huntington 2, James Armstrong 1, Edward Telfair 1, and Benjamin Lincoln 1. The Electors were:

NEW HAMPSHIRE.

Benjamin Bellows, Ebenezer Thompson.
1. John Pickering, 2. John Parker, 3. John Sullivan.

MASSACHUSETTS.

Caleb Davis, David Sewall.
1. Samuel Phillips, Jr., 2. Walter Spooner, 3. Francis Dana, 4. Moses Gill, 5. Samuel Henshaw, 6. William Cushing, 7. William Sever, 8. William Shepard.

CONNECTICUT.

Samuel Huntington, Erastus Wolcott.
1. Oliver Wolcott, 2. Thaddeus Burr, 3. Richard Law, 4. Jedediah Huntington, 5. Matthew Griswold.

NEW JERSEY.

David Brearley, David Moore.
1. James Kinsey, 2. John Rutherford, 3. John Neilson, 4. Matthias Ogden.

PENNSYLVANIA.

Edward Hand, James Wilson.
1. George Gibson, 2. James O'Harra, 3. John Arndt, 4. David Grier, 5. Collinson Read, 6. Samuel Potts, 7. Lawrence Keene, 8. Alexander Graydon.

DELAWARE.

Gunning Bedford, George Mitchell.
1. John Baning.

MARYLAND.

John Rogers, Philip Thomas.

1. George Plater, 2. Robert Smith, 3. William Tilghman, 4. William Richardson, 5. Alexander C. Hanson, 6. William Matthews.

VIRGINIA.

Patrick Henry, W. Tikhugh.

1. John Pride, 2. Edward Stevens, 3. Zachariah Johnston, 4. Anthony Walke, 5. James Wood, 6. David Stuart, 7. John Harvie, 8. John Roane.

SOUTH CAROLINA.

Christopher Gadsden, Edward Rutledge.

1. Henry Laurens, 2. Arthur Simkins, 3. Charles C. Pinckney, 4. Thomas Heyward, Jr., 5. John F. Grimke.

GEORGIA.

George Handley, John Wilson.

1. George Walton, 2. H. Osborne, 3. John King.

SECOND PRESIDENTIAL ELECTION—1793.

GEORGE WASHINGTON was again unanimously elected President, receiving 132 votes. JOHN ADAMS was elected Vice-President, receiving 77 votes; while George Clinton had 50 votes, Thomas Jefferson 4, and Aaron Burr 1. The Electors were:

NEW HAMPSHIRE.

Josiah Bartlett, Benjamin Bellows.

1. John T. Gilman, 2. John Pickering, 3. Jonathan Freeman, 4. Ebenezer Thompson.

MASSACHUSETTS.

Azor Orne, Francis Dana.

1. Samuel Holten, 2. Ebenezer Mattson, Jr., 3. Thomas Dawes, 4. William Sever, 5. Increase Sumner, 6. Walter Spooner, 7. Moses Gill, 8. Solomon Freeman, 9. William Shepard, 10. Nathaniel Wells, 11. Thompson J. Skinner, 12. Daniel Cony, 13. Dwight Foster, 14. Peleg Wadsworth.

RHODE ISLAND.

Arthur Fenner, Samuel J. Potter.

1. George Champlin, 2. William Greene.

CONNECTICUT.

Samuel Huntington, John Davenport, Jr.

1. Oliver Wolcott, 2. Thomas Grosvenor, 3. David Austin, 4. Elijah Hubbard, 5. Thomas Seymour, 6. Sylvester Gilbert, 7. Marvin Wait.

VERMONT.

Samuel Hitchcock, Lemuel Chipman.

1. Lot Hall, 2. Paul Brigham.

NEW YORK.

Jesse Woodhull, David Van Ness.

1. Edward Savage, 2. Samuel Clark, 3. Johannes Bruyn, 4. Abraham Yates, Jr., 5. William Floyd, 6. Volkert Veeder, 7. Abraham Ten Eyck, 8. Stephen Ward, 9. John Bay, 10. Samuel Osgood.

NEW JERSEY.

Thomas H. Sanderson, Aaron D. Woodruff.

1. Richard Stockton,
2. John W. Vancleve,
3. Joseph Bloomfield,
4. Samuel Dick,
5. Franklin Davenport.

PENNSYLVANIA.

William Henry, Robert Coleman.

1. Joseph Heister,
2. Thomas Bull,
3. Thomas McKean,
4. Cornelius Coxe,
5. Henry Miller,
6. Robert Johnston,
7. John Wilkins, Jr.,
8. John Boyd,
9. David Stewart,
10. James Morris,
11. George Latimer,
12. Robert Hare,
13. Hugh Lloyd.

DELAWARE.

James Sykes, Gunning Bedford.

1. William Hill Wells.

MARYLAND.

Alexander C. Hanson, John Seney.

1. John E. Howard,
2. Levin Winder,
3. Thomas Lee,
4. William Smith,*
5. Richard Potts,
6. Samuel Hughes,*
7. William Richardson,
8. Donaldson Yates.

VIRGINIA.

John Wise, George Carrington.

1. Nathaniel Wilkinson,
2. John Early,
3. William O. Callis,
4. Catesby Jones,
5. Elias Langham,
6. Daniel C. Brent,
7. John Dawson,
8. Stephen T. Mason,
9. John Roane, Jr.,
10. Moses Hunter,
11. James Murdough,
12. Archibald Stuart,
13. Michael Bailey,
14. John Bowyer,
15. Thomas Claiborne,
16. Maxwell Armstrong.
17. John Pride,
18. Claiborne Watkins,
19. Tarlton Woodson.

NORTH CAROLINA.

Stephen Cahames, John L. Taylor.

1. Alfred Moore,
2. John Mocon,
3. Joel Sane,
4. R. D. Spaight,
5. Benjamin Smith,
6. John M. Binford,
7. Matthew Lock,
8. Peter Dange,
9. James Taylor,
10. William Porter.

SOUTH CAROLINA.

Charles C. Pinckney, John Chestnut.

1. Andrew Pickens,
2. John Hunter,
3. John Barnwell,
4. Edward Rutledge,
5. Robert Anderson,
6. John Julius Pringle.

GEORGIA.

Benjamin Taliaferro, William Gibbons.

1. John King.
2. Seaborn Jones.

KENTUCKY.

R. C. Anderson, Charles Scott.

1. Benjamin Logan,
2. Notley Conn.

THIRD PRESIDENTIAL ELECTION—1797.

JOHN ADAMS was elected President, receiving the entire vote of New Hampshire, Massachusetts, Rhode Island, Connecticut, Vermont, New York, New Jer-

* Not present.

sey, and Delaware, with 10 scattering votes from other States, making 71 of the 140 votes cast. THOMAS JEFFERSON was elected Vice-President, having the next highest number of votes, 68; while Thomas Pinkney had 58, Aaron Burr 30, Samuel Adams 15, Oliver Ellsworth 11, George Clinton 7, John Jay 5, James Iredell 3, Samuel Johnston 2, George Washington 2, John Henry 2, Charles C. Pinckney 1. The Electors were:

NEW HAMPSHIRE.

John T. Gilman, Timothy Farrar.
1. Oliver Peabody,
2. Ebenezer Thompson,
3. Benjamin Bellows,
4. Timothy Walker.

VERMONT.

Elijah Dewey, John Bridgman.
1. Elisha Sheldon,
2. Oliver Gallup.

MASSACHUSETTS.

William Sever, Stephen Longfellow.
1. Samuel Holton,
2. Edward H. Robbins,
3. Elbridge Gerry,
4. Ebenezer Mattoon,
5. Samuel Phillips,
6. Increase Sumner,
7. Thomas Dawes,
8. David Rosseter,
9. Nathaniel Wells,
10. Ebenezer Hunt,
11. Elisha May,
12. Joseph Allen,
13. Thomas Rice,
14. Ebenezer Bacon.

RHODE ISLAND.

Arthur Fenner, Samuel J. Potter.
1. George Champlin,
2. William Greene.

CONNECTICUT.

Oliver Wolcott, Jonathan Trumbull.
1. Jeremiah Wadsworth,
2. Heman Swift,
3. Elizur Goodrich,
4. William Hart,
5. Elias Perkins,
6. Jesse Root,
7. Jonathan Sturges.

NEW YORK.

Lewis Morris, R. Van Rensselaer.
1. Richard Thorne,
2. Peter Cantine, Jr.,
3. A. Ten Broeck,
4. Obijah Hammond,
5. A. Van Vechten,
6. William Root,
7. Peter Smith,
8. St. John Honeywood,
9. Charles Newkirk,
10. Johannes Miller.

NEW JERSEY.

John Neilson, Caleb Newbold.
1. Aaron Ogden,
2. John Blackwood,
3. Jonathan Rhea,
4. William Colefax,
5. Elisha Lawrence.

PENNSYLVANIA.

Thomas McKean, John Smilie.
1. James Boyd,
2. Joseph Heister,
3. William Brown,
4. John Piper,
5. John Whitehill,
6. William Irvine,
7. Peter Muhlenberg,
8. Robert Coleman,
9. Abraham Smith,
10. Samuel Miles,
11. Jacob Morgan,
12. William Maclay,
13. James Hanna.

DELAWARE.

Thomas Robinson, Isaac Cooper.
1. Richard Bassett.

MARYLAND.

John R. Plater, John Archer.
1. Francis Deakins,
2. John Gilpin,
3. George Murdock,
4. John Roberts,
5. John Lynn,
6. John Eccleston,
7. Gabriel Duvall,
8. John Done.

VIRGINIA.

William Nimmo, William Terry.

1. Nathaniel Wilkinson,
2. David Saunders,
3. John Taylor,
4. Catesby Jones,
5. Wilson C. Nicolas,
6. D. Carroll Brent,
7. William Madison,
8. Levin Powell,
9. Benjamin Temple,
10. Moses Hunter,
11. Josiah Riddick,
12. Archibald Stuart,
13. John Mason,
14. John Bowyer,
15. Robert Walker,
16. John Brown,
17. George Markham,
18. Robert Crockett,
19. Peter Johnson.

NORTH CAROLINA.

James Martin, Richard D. Spaight.

1. Gabriel Raysdale,
2. John Gray Blout,
3. John Hamilton,
4. William Edmunds,
5. James Bradley,
6. John Hamilton,
7. William Martin,
8. Evan Alexander,
9. Anthony Brown,
10. Sterling Harwell.

SOUTH CAROLINA.

Edward Rutledge, Arthur Simkins.

1. Andrew Pickens,
2. William Thomas,
3. John Chesnut,
4. John Mathews,
5. Thomas Taylor,
6. John Rutledge, Jr.

GEORGIA.

James Jackson, Charles Abercombie.

1. Edward Telfair,
2. William Barnett.

KENTUCKY.

Stephen Ormsby, Caleb Wallace.

1. Isaac Shelby,
2. John Coburn.

TENNESSEE.

Daniel Smith, Hugh Neilson.

1. Joseph Greer.

FOURTH PRESIDENTIAL ELECTION—1801.

THOMAS JEFFERSON and AARON BURR having each received 73 of the 128 electoral votes cast, the choice devolved upon the House of Representatives. The 73 votes comprised all from the States of New York, Virginia, Kentucky, Tennessee, South Carolina, and Georgia, with 8 from Pennsylvania, 5 from Maryland, and 8 from North Carolina. John Adams had 65 votes, Charles C. Pinckney 64, and John Jay 1. The Electors were:

NEW HAMPSHIRE.

Oliver Peabody, Benjamin Bellows.

1. John Prentice,
2. Timothy Farrar,
3. Ebenezer Thompson,
4. Arthur Livermore.

VERMONT.

Elijah Dewey, Roswell Hopkins.

1. Jonathan Hunt,
2. William Chamberlain.

MASSACHUSETTS.

Samuel Philips, Francis Dana.

1. E. H. Robbins,
2. Samuel Sewall,
3. David Rosseter,
4. Theophilus Bradbury,
5. Ebenezer Hunt,
6. John Hooker,
7. Walter Spooner,
8. Joseph Allen,
9. William Sever,
10. S. S. Wilde,
11. William Baylies,
12. Lemuel Weeks,
13. Thomas Dawes,
14. Andrew P. Fernald.

RHODE ISLAND.

George Champlin, Oliver Davis.

1. Edward Manton,
2. William Greene.

CONNECTICUT.

Jonathan Trumbull, Jonathan Ingersoll.

1. John Treadwell,
2. Tapping Reeve,
3. Jesse Root,
4. Matthew Griswold,
5. Jonathan Sturges,
6. J. O. Moseley,
7. Stephen M. Mitchell.

NEW YORK.

Isaac Ledyard, Peter Van Ness.

1. Anthony Lispenard,
2. Robert Ellis,
3. P. Van Cortlandt, Jr.,
4. John Woodworth,
5. James Burt,
6. J. Van Rensselaer,
7. Gilbert Livingston,
8. Jacob Eaker,
9. Thomas Jenkins,
10. William Floyd.

NEW JERSEY.

Isaac Smith, Samuel S. Smith.

1. Thomas Sinnickson,
2. M. Williamson, Jr.,
3. Richard Stockton,
4. William Griffith,
5. Joshua L. Howell.

PENNSYLVANIA.

Frederick Kuhn, Samuel Wetherill.

1: James Armstrong,
2. John Kean,
3. George Ege,
4. Jonas Hartzell,
5. John Hubley,
6. Gabriel Heister,
7. William Hall,
8. Presly Carr Lane,
9. Samuel W. Fisher,
10. N. B. Boileau,
11. James Crawford, Sr.,
12. Isaac Van Horn,
13. Robert Whitehill.

DELAWARE.

Kensey Johns, Nathaniel Mitchell.

1. Samuel White.

MARYLAND.

Edmund Plowden, Francis Deakins.

1. George Murdock,
2. John Gilpin,
3. Martin Kershner,
4. Perry Spencer,
5. Gabriel Duvall,
6. William M. Robertson,
7. Nicholas B. Moore,
8. Littleton Dennis.

VIRGINIA.

George Wythe, Walter Jones.

1. William Newsum,
2. Richard Brent,
3. William H. Cabell,
4. William Ellzey,
5. James Madison, Jr.,
6. John Brown,
7. John Page,
8. John Preston,
9. Thomas Newton,
10. Hugh Holmes,
11. Joseph Jones,
12. Archibald Stuart,
13. William B. Giles,
14. John Shore,
15. Creed Taylor,
16. John Bowyer,
17. Thomas Reade, Sr.,
18. Daniel Coleman,
19. George Penn.

NORTH CAROLINA.

William Tate, Thomas Brown.

1. Joseph Winston,
2. William Martin,
3. Absalom Tatom,
4. Bryan Whitfield,
5. Spruce Macay,
6. Nathan Mayo,
7. Joseph Taylor,
8. Thomas Wynns,
9. Gideon Alston,
10. John Hamilton.

SOUTH CAROLINA.

John Hunter, Arthur Simkins.

1. Paul Hamilton,
2. Andrew Love,
3. Robert Anderson,
4. Joseph Blyth,
5. Theodore Gaillard,
6. Wade Hampton.

GEORGIA.

John Morrison, Henry Graybill.

1. Dennis Smelt,
2. David Blackshear.

KENTUCKY.

John Coburn, Charles Scott.

1. John Pope,
2. Isaac Shelby.

TENNESSEE.

Daniel Smith, Robert Love.
1. John Locke.

The House of Representatives, on which devolved the choice between Jefferson and Burr, voted to commence balloting on Wednesday, the eleventh day of February, to attend to no other business while the election was pending, and not to adjourn until a choice was effected. Seats were provided upon the floor for the President and the Senators, but during the act of balloting the galleries were cleared of spectators, and the doors were closed. Upon the first ballot, New York, New Jersey, Pennsylvania, Virginia, North Carolina, Georgia, Kentucky, and Tennessee (8), voted for Thomas Jefferson; New Hampshire, Massachusetts, Rhode Island, Connecticut, Delaware, and South Carolina (6), voted for Aaron Burr; and the votes of Vermont and Maryland (the representatives of which were divided) were given blank. The balloting was continued, and the House remained in session, nominally without adjournment, for seven days, during which one hundred and four members were present. Some of them were so infirm or indisposed that it was necessary to provide beds for them, and one member, who was quite ill, was attended by his wife. On the thirty-sixth ballot, which was taken on the afternoon of the seventeenth, the votes of Delaware and South Carolina were given blank, while those of Vermont and Maryland were given to Mr. Jefferson, and elected him. The Vice-Presidency, of course, devolved upon Mr. Burr.

FIFTH PRESIDENTIAL ELECTION—1805.

THOMAS JEFFERSON was re-elected President, receiving 162 of the 176 votes cast. This comprised the entire electoral vote of all the States, except Connecticut, Delaware, and Maryland; the two first of which threw their full vote for Charles Cotesworth Pinckney, and the last gave nine votes for Mr. Jefferson and two for Mr. Pinckney. GEORGE CLINTON was elected Vice-President by the same majority and vote, Rufus King receiving fourteen votes. The Electors were:

NEW HAMPSHIRE.

John Goddard, Robert Alcock.
1. Levi Bartlet,
2. George Aldrich,
3. Timothy Walker,
4. Jonathan Steele,
5. William Tarlton.

VERMONT.

Josiah Wright, Nathaniel Niles.
1. Samuel Shaw,
2. William Hunter,
3. Ezra Butler,
4. John Noyes.

MASSACHUSETTS.

James Sullivan, Timothy Newell.
1. Elbridge Gerry,
2. John Whiting,
3. James Bowdoin,
4. John Bacon,
5. John Hathorne,
6. William Heath,
7. Thomas Kitteridge,
8. John Woodman,
9. James Winthrop,
10. Charles Turner,
11. Edward Upham,
12. Thomas Fillebrown,
13. James Warren,
14. John Farley,
15. John Davis,
16. Jonathan Smith,
17. Josiah Deane.

RHODE ISLAND.

Constant Taber, James Helme.
1. James Aldrich,
2. Benjamin Remington.

CONNECTICUT.

Jonathan Trumbull, Lewis B. Sturges.
1. John Treadwell,
2. David Smith,
3. Oliver Ellsworth,
4. Asher Miller,
5. David Daggett,
6. Sylvester Gilbert,
7. Joshua Huntington.

New York.

Sylvester Dening, John Cramer.

1. James Fairlie,
2. Thomas Brooks,
3. Cornelius Bergen,
4. Matthias B. Hildreth,
5. John Herring,
6. William Floyd,
7. Ezra Thompson,
8. Jonas Earl,
9. John Wood,
10. Joseph Ellicott,
11. Conrad I. Elmendorff,
12. Henry Quackinboss,
13. Stephen Miller,
14. Adam Comstock,
15. Albert Pawling,
16. Abraham Bancker,
17. Isaac Sargent.

New Jersey.

Solomon Freligh, Thomas Newbold.

1. Alexander Carmichael,
2. Moore Furman,
3. Phineas Manning,
4. Jacob Hufty,
5. William Rossell,
6. Abijah Smith.

Pennsylvania.

Charles Thomson, Casper Shaffner, Jr.

1. William Montgomery,
2. John Bowman,
3. Matthew Lawler,
4. William Brown,
5. Robert McMullen,
6. George Smith,
7. William Brooke,
8. Jacob Hostetter,
9. Thomas Long,
10. Jacob Bonnett,
11. Francis Swaine,
12. James Montgomery,
13. Henry Spering,
14. John Minor,
15. James Boyd,
16. John Hamilton,
17. Peter Frailey,
18. Nathaniel Irish.

Delaware.

Maxwell Bines, Thomas Fisher.

1. George Kennard.

Maryland.

John Parnham, Tobias E. Stansbury.

1. Joseph Wilkinson,
2. John Gilpin,
3. John Johnson,
4. William Gleaves,
5. Edward Johnson,
6. Perry Spencer,
7. John Tyler,
8. Ephraim K. Wilson,
9. Frisby Tilghman.

Virginia.

Richard Evers Lee, Richard Field.

1. John Goodrich,
2. Thomas Read,
3. Edward Pegram,
4. Creed Taylor,
5. William H. Cabell,
6. John Taliaferro, Jr.,
7. George Penn,
8. Richard Brent,
9. George Wythe,
10. Hugh Holmes,
11. John Taylor,
12. James Dailey,
13. Larkin Smith,
14. James Allen,
15. John Minor,
16. Archibald Stuart,
17. William Ellzey,
18. James McFarlane,
19. William Dudley,
20. John Preston,
21. Mann Page,
22. William McKinley.

North Carolina.

Felix Walker, Robert Cochran.

1. Peter Forney,
2. Lemuel Sawyer,
3. Joseph Williams,
4. James Jones,
5. Montford Stokes,
6. Reading Blount,
7. Solomon Graves,
8. Bryan Whitfield,
9. Joseph Taylor,
10. Samuel Ashe, Sr.,
11. Joseph John Alston,
12. Gideon Alston.

South Carolina.

John Blake, Samuel Warren.

1. John Gaillard,
2. Arthur Simkins,
3. Thomas Taylor,
4. William Hill,
5. Joseph Blythe,
6. James Miles,
7. Joseph Calhoun,
8. John Taylor.

Georgia.

Edward Telfair, James B. Maxwell.

1. David Emanuel,
2. John Rutherford,
3. Henry Graybill,
4. David Cresswell.

KENTUCKY.

Charles Scott, Isaac Shelby.
1. John Coburn, 3. Hubbard Taylor, 5. William Irvine,
2. Ninian Edwards, 4. Joseph Lewis, 6. William Roberts.

TENNESSEE.

David Deaderich, William Martin.
1. Richard Mitchell, 2. George Ridley, 3. Robert Houston.

OHIO.

William Goforth, James Pritchard.
1. Nathaniel Massie.

SIXTH PRESIDENTIAL ELECTION—1809.

JAMES MADISON was elected President, having received the entire electoral vote of Vermont, Pennsylvania, South Carolina, Georgia, Tennessee, Kentucky, and Ohio, and 13 of the 19 votes of New York, 9 of the 11 of Maryland, and 11 of the 14 of North Carolina; in all 122 of the 175 votes cast; George Clinton received 6 votes of New York, and the balance (47) were given to Charles Cotesworth Pinckney. GEORGE CLINTON was elected Vice-President, receiving 113 votes, while Rufus King had 47, James Madison 3, and James Monroe 3. The Electors were:

NEW HAMPSHIRE.

Jeremiah Smith, Timothy Farrar.
1. Oliver Peabody, 3. Samuel Hale, 5. Robert Wallace.
2. Benjamin West, 4. Jonathan Franklin,

VERMONT.

Israel Smith, Samuel Shepardson.
1. Jonas Galusha, 3. John White, 4. William Cahoon.
2. James Tarbox,

MASSACHUSETTS.

Caleb Strong, Daniel Dewey.
1. Francis Dana, 7. William Bartlett, 13. Josiah Stearns,
2. Ebenezer Warren, 8. Lemuel Williams, 14. Samuel S. Wilde,
3. John Brooks, 9. Ebenezer Bridge, 15. John Hooker,
4. Samuel Tobey, 10. Andrew Fernald, 16. Jeremiah Bailey,
5. Moses Brown, 11. Benjamin Heywood, 17. John Barrett.
6. Joshua Thomas, 12. Samuel Freeman,

RHODE ISLAND.

Thomas P. Ives, James Rhodes.
1. C. Fowler, 2. Thomas Noyes.

CONNECTICUT.

Jonathan Trumbull, John Cotton Smith.
1. John Treadwell, 4. Jesse Root, 7. Samuel W. Johnson.
2. Stephen T. Hosmer, 5. Roger Griswold,
3. David Daggett, 6. Frederick Wolcott,

NEW YORK.

Ambrose Spencer, Henry Yates, Jr.
1. Henry Huntington, 7. John Garretson, 13. James Tallmage,
2. Benjamin Mooers, 8. William Hallock, 14. Hugh Jamison,
3. John W. Seaman, 9. Ebenezer White, 15. Jonathan Rouse,
4. Adam B. Vroman, 10. Russel Atwater, 16. Matthew Carpenter,
5. Henry Rutgers, 11. Thomas Lawrence, 17. Micajah Petit.
6. Thomas Shankland, 12. Joseph Simonds,

New Jersey.

James Mott, Benjamin Egbert.

1. James Morgan,
2. Thomas Hendry,
3. Amos Harrison,
4. George Burgin,
5. David Welsh,
6. Abijah Smith.

Pennsylvania.

Charles Thomson, Adamson Tannehill.

1. Thomas Leiper,
2. James Cowden,
3. Michael Leib,
4. William Wilson,
5. Joseph Engle,
6. Robert Griffen,
7. William Rodman,
8. Jacob Hostetter,
9. Archibald Darrah,
10. David Fullerton,
11. Jacob Weygandt,
12. Peter Kenimell,
13. Joseph Lefevre,
14. Joseph Huston,
15. Gabriel Heister, Jr.,
16. William Montgomery,
17. George Hartman,
18. John McDowell.

Delaware.

James Booth, Daniel Rodney.

1. Nicholas Ridgely.

Maryland.

John R. Plater, Tobias E. Stanbury.

1. Robert Bowie,
2. Thomas W. Veazey,
3. Edward Johnson,
4. Richard Tilghman,
5. John Johnson,
6. Earle Perry Spencer,
7. John Tyler,
8. Henry James Carroll,
9. Nathaniel Rochester.

Virginia.

Joseph Goodwin, Sr., Benjamin Harrison.

1. Edward Pegram, Sr.,
2. Robert Nelson,
3. Richard Field,
4. Mann Page,
5. Thomas Read,
6. Richard Barnes,
7. Joseph Eggleston,
8. John T. Brooks,
9. Hugh Nelson,
10. Hugh Holmes,
11. George Penn,
12. Osborn Sprigg,
13. Philip N. Nicholas,
14. James Allen,
15. Spencer Roane,
16. Archibald Stuart,
17. John Roane,
18. Andrew Russell,
19. Robert Taylor,
20. John Preston,
21. Gustavus B. Horner,
22. William McKinley.

North Carolina.

Francis Locke, Robert Cleveland.

1. Thomas Wynns,
2. Kemp Plummer,
3. Samuel Ashe, Sr.,
4. Joseph Taylor,
5. Murdock McKenzie,
6. Peter Forney,
7. Robert Love,
8. James Rainey,
9. John Winslow,
10. Joseph Riddick,
11. William Gaston,
12. Henry I. Toole.

South Carolina.

Joseph Gist, Joseph Bellinger.

1. John Wilson,
2. Langdon Cheves,
3. John McMonies,
4. Paul Hamilton,
5. William Strother,
6. Samuel Mays,
7. William Zimmerman,
8. William Rouse.

Georgia.

John Rutherford, David Meriwether.

1. John Twiggs,
2. Christopher Clark,
3. Henry Graybill,
4. James E. Houston.

Kentucky.

Samuel Hopkins, Charles Scott.

1. William Logan,
2. Robert Trimble,
3. Matthew Walton,
4. Hubbard Taylor,
5. Robert Ewing,
6. Christopher Greenup.

Tennessee.

James Robertson, Joseph Greer.

1. William Martin,
2. James Sevier,
3. Baldwin Hale.

Ohio.

Nathaniel Massie, Thomas McCune.

1. Stephen Wood.

SEVENTH PRESIDENTIAL ELECTION—1813.

JAMES MADISON was re-elected President, having received the entire electoral vote of Vermont, Pennsylvania, Virginia, North and South Carolina, Georgia, Kentucky, Tennessee, Ohio, and Louisiana, and 6 of the 11 votes of Maryland—in all 128 of the 217 votes cast; the balance (89) were given for De Witt Clinton, of New York. ELBRIDGE GERRY was elected Vice-President, receiving 131 votes; while Jared Ingersoll had 86. The Electors were:

NEW HAMPSHIRE.

John Goddard, Timothy Farrar.
1. Oliver Peabody,
2. Benjamin West,
3. Samuel Hale,
4. Caleb Ellis,
5. Nathan Taylor,
6. Jonathan Franklin.

VERMONT.

Nathaniel Niles, Josiah Wright.
1. Noah Chittenden,
2. William A. Griswold,
3. William Slade,
4. Elihu Luce,
5. John H. Andrus,
6. Mark Richards.

MASSACHUSETTS.

William Heath, John W. Hurlburt.
1. Harrison G. Otis,
2. Joshua Thomas,
3. Nathan Dane,
4. David Scudder,
5. Jeremiah Nelson,
6. Lathrop Lewis,
7. Abraham Bigelow,
8. Nathaniel Goodwin,
9. John Walker,
10. Samuel Parris,
11. George Bliss,
12. Abiel Wood,
13. Benjamin Heywood,
14. Lemuel Paine,
15. Eleazer James,
16. James McLellan,
17. E. Williams,
18. William Crosby,
19. Isaac Maltby,
20. Israel Thorndike.

RHODE ISLAND.

Christopher Fowler, William Rhodes.
1. Samuel G. Arnold,
2. Ephraim Bowen.

CONNECTICUT.

Nathaniel Terry, Daniel Putnam.
1. Theodore Dwight,
2. James Gould,
3. David Daggett,
4. Stephen T. Hosmer,
5. Calvin Goddard,
6. Jonathan Barnes,
7. S. B. Sherwood.

NEW YORK.

Joseph C. Yates, David Van Ness.
1. Simeon De Witt,
2. Robert Jenkins,
3. Archibald McIntyre,
4. M. S. Van Dercook,
5. John C. Hodgeboom,
6. George Palmer, Jr.,
7. G. S. Mumford,
8. James Hill,
9. J. Delamontagnie,
10. William Kirby,
11. P. Van Cortlandt,
12. Henry Frey,
13. John Chandler,
14. Thomas H. Hubbard,
15. Henry Huntington,
16. John Russell,
17. John Woodworth,
18. James S. Kipp,
19. David Boyd,
20. Jotham Jayne,
21. Cornelius Bergen,
22. Jonathan Stanley, Jr.,
23. Joseph Perine,
24. William Burnet,
25. Chauncey Belknap,
26. George Rosecrantz,
27. John Dill.

NEW JERSEY.

Matthew Whillden, William Griffith.
1. William B. Ewing,
2. Elias Conover,
3. Franklin Davenport,
4. Andrew Howell,
5. Jacob Losey,
6. William McGill.

PENNSYLVANIA.

Walter Franklin, Hugh Glasgow.
1. David Mitchell,
2. David Fullerton,
3. Paul Cox,
4. Samuel Smyth,
5. Isaac Worrell,
6. Robert Smith,
7. Michael Baker,
8. Nathaniel Mickler,
9. Joseph Engle,
10. Chas. Shoemaker, Jr.,
11. James Fulton,
12. James Mitchell,
13. Isaiah Davis,
14. John Murray,
15. John Whitehill,
16. Clement Paine,
17. Edward Crouch,
18. Joseph Reed,
19. Henry Allshouse,
20. Alexander Dysart,
21. James Stephenson,
22. David Mead,
23. Abia Minor.

Delaware.

James L. Clayton, James Sykes.

1. Benjamin Blakiston,
2. Thomas Fisher.

Maryland.

Henry H. Chapman, Tobias E. Stansbury.

1. •Edward H. Calvert,
2. Thomas W. Veazey,
3. Edward Johnson,
4. Thomas Worrell,
5. John Stephen,
6. Edward Lloyd,
7. Henry Williams,
8. Littleton Dennis,
9. Daniel Kentch.

Virginia.

Richard Henry Lee, Gustavus B. Horner.

1. Benjamin Harrison,
2. Robert Nelson,
3. Edward Pegram,
4. Mann Page,
5. Richard Field,
6. Walter Jones,
7. Thomas Read,
8. John T. Brooke,
9. Matthew Cheatham,
10. Hugh Holmes,
11. William Armistead,
12. Daniel Morgan,
13. Charles Yancey,
14. Archibald Rutherford,
15. George Penn,
16. Archibald Stuart,
17. W. G. Poindexter,
18. Andrew Russell,
19. Spencer Roane,
20. Charles Taylor,
21. Sthreshly Rennolds,
22. W. McKinley,
23. Robert Taylor.

North Carolina.

William H. Murfree, James Mebane.

1. Redar Ballard,
2. James Rainey,
3. James Bright,
4. Francis Locke,
5. Thomas D. King,
6. Montford Stokes,
7. James W. Clarke,
8. Joseph Uniston,
9. H. G. Burton,
10. Jonathan Hampton,
11. Thomas Davis,
12. Henry Massey,
13. Kemp Plummer.

South Carolina.

James Campbell, Reuben Starke.

1. John Johnson,
2. John McCreary,
3. Andrew Pickens,
4. William Smith,
5. William Caldwell,
6. William Alston,
7. Samuel Johnson,
8. Richard Singleton,
9. Sampson Butler.

Georgia.

Daniel Stewart, John Twiggs.

1. Henry Graybill,
2. Oliver Porter,
3. Charles Harris,
4. Henry Mitchell,
5. John Rutherford,
6. John Howard.

Kentucky.

Robert Ewing, William Irvine.

1. William Casey,
2. Robert Mosby,
3. Samuel Murrell,
4. Hubbard Taylor,
5. Samuel Caldwell,
6. Duval Payne,
7. Richard Taylor,
8. Walker Baylor,
9. William Logan,
10. T. D. Owings.

Tennessee.

E. K. Dulany, William Trigg.

1. Henry Bradford,
2. Thomas Washington,
3. James Trimble,
4. David McEwen,
5. James McCampbell,
6. Thomas Johnson.

Ohio.

John Jones, James Pritchard.

1. Matthias Corwin,
2. D. Abbott (not present),
3. David Purviance,
4. Thomas Ijams,
5. James Dunlap,
6. John Hamm.

Louisiana.

Julien Poydras, Stephen A. Hopkins.

1. Philemon Thomas.

EIGHTH PRESIDENTIAL ELECTION—1817.

JAMES MONROE was elected President, having received the entire electoral vote of every State except Massachusetts, Connecticut, and Delaware—in all 183 of the 217 votes cast; the remaining 34 being given for Rufus King. DANIEL D. TOMPKINS was elected Vice-President, receiving 183 votes; while John E. Howard had 22 votes, James Ross 5, John Marshall 4, and Robert G. Harper 3. The Electors were:

NEW HAMPSHIRE.

Thomas Manning, Richard H. Ayer.
1. Benjamin Butler,
2. Jacob Tuttle,
3. William Badger,
4. Thomas C. Drew,
5. Amos Cogswell,
6. Dan Young.

VERMONT.

J. Robinson, James Roberts.
1. Apollos Austin,
2. Asaph Fletcher,
3. Robert Holly,
4. John H. Cotton,
5. William Brayton,
6. Isaiah Fisk.

MASSACHUSETTS.

Christopher Gore, Bezabeel Taft.
1. Prentiss Mellen,
2. Jonas Kendall,
3. Israel Thorndike,
4. E. H. Robbins,
5. Benj. Pickman, Jr.,
6. John Low,
7. David A. White,
8. S. Longfellow, Jr.,
9. Joseph Locke,
10. William Abbot,
11. Thomas Dwight,
12. Timothy Boutelle,
13. Peter Bryant,
14. Luther Carey,
15. Daniel Howard,
16. William Phillips,
17. Wendell Davis,
18. Josiah Stebbins,
19. Seth Washburn,
20. Thomas H. Perkins.

RHODE ISLAND.

James Fenner, Edward Wilcox.
1. Thomas Pitman,
2. Dutee Arnold.

CONNECTICUT.

Jonathan Ingersoll, William Perkins.
1. Nathaniel Terry,
2. Elisha Sterling,
3. Seth P. Staples,
4. Elijah Hubbard,
5. Jirah Isham,
6. Asa Willey,
7. S. W. Johnson.

NEW YORK.

Henry Rutgers, Alexander McNish.
1. Lemuel Chipman,
2. Artemus Aldrich,
3. John W. Seaman,
4. Henry Becker,
5. Jacob Drake,
6. Aaron Searing,
7. James Farlie,
8. Israel W. Clark,
9. Augustus Wright,
10. Daniel Root,
11. P. S. Van Orden,
12. Montgomery Hunt,
13. J. W. Van Wyck,
14. Nicholl Fosdick,
15. J. D. Monell,
16. E. Edmonds,
17. John Blake, Jr.,
18. George Petit,
19. Jacob Wertz,
20. Richard Townley,
21. Gabriel North,
22. Samuel Lawrence,
23. Charles E. Dudley,
24. Nathaniel Rochester,
25. Benjamin Smith,
26. Worthy L. Churchel,
27. Samuel Lewis.

NEW JERSEY.

Lewis Moore, Charles Ogden.
1. Aaron Kitchell,
2. Daniel Garrison,
3. David Welsh,
4. William Rossell,
5. John Crowell,
6. Robert McNeeley.

PENNSYLVANIA.

Paul Cox,
M. Fackenthal.

1. David Mitchell,
2. James Wilson,
3. John Geyer,
4. Gabriel Heister,
5. Daniel Bussier,
6. James Meloy,
7. John Conrad,
8. James Banks,
9. William Brooke,
10. Robert Clark,
11. Isaac Anderson,
12. Abiel Fellows,
13. Matthew Roberts,
14. David Marchand,
15. John Mohler,
16. Thomas Patterson,
17. John Harrison,
18. Joseph Huston,
19. Jacob Hostetter,
20. Samuel Scott,
21. John Rea,
22. James Alexander,
23. William Gilliland.

DELAWARE.

Thomas Robinson,
Andrew Barratt.

1. Isaac Tunnell,
2. Nicholas Ridgely.

MARYLAND.

William D. Beall,
George Warner.

1. Joseph Kent,
2. William C. Miller,
3. Edward Johnson,
4. Benjamin Massy,
5. John Stephen,
6. Thomas Ennalls,
7. John Buchanan,
8. Littleton Dennis,
9. Lawrence Brengle.

VIRGINIA.

George Newton,
John T. Brooke.

1. Charles H. Graves,
2. Hugh Holmes,
3. John Pegram,
4. Archibald Rutherford,
5. John Purnall,
6. Archibald Stuart,
7. Joseph C. Cabell,
8. Andrew Russell,
9. Charles Yancey,
10. Charles Taylor,
11. Spencer Roane,
12. Robert B. Starke,
13. Sthreshly Reynolds,
14. William Archer,
15. Robert Taylor,
16. Benjamin Cook,
17. Isaac Foster,
18. Wm. Brockenbrough,
19. Brazure W. Pryor,
20. Daniel Morgan,
21. William Jones,
22. John Edie,
23. William Lee Ball.

NORTH CAROLINA.

Robert Love,
Nathaniel Jones.

1. Jesse Franklin,
2. John Hall,
3. Peter Forney,
4. Thomas Wynns,
5. Francis Locke,
6. Joseph Riddick,
7. Abraham Phillips,
8. James Hoskins,
9. Alexander Gray,
10. Vine Allen,
11. Joseph Pukett,
12. Thomas D. King,
13. Thomas Ruffin.

SOUTH CAROLINA.

William Garrett,
James Duff.

1. Philemon Bradford,
2. Thomas Evans,
3. William McKeralls,
4. Thomas Lee,
5. Frederick Nance,
6. John L. Wilson,
7. John Thomas,
8. Joseph Reid,
9. Richard B. Screven.

GEORGIA.

David Adams,
Charles Harris.

1. John McIntosh,
2. John Clark,
3. Jared Irwin,
4. John Rutherford,
5. Henry Mitchell,
6. David Meriwether.

KENTUCKY.

Duvall Payne,
Richard Taylor.

1. Hubbard Taylor,
2. William Logan,
3. Robert Trimble,
4. Alexander Adair,
5. Thomas Bodley,
6. Samuel Caldwell,
7. Willis A. Lee,
8. Samuel Murrell,
9. William Irvine,
10. Robert Ewing.

TENNESSEE.

Alfred M. Carter,
Robert Allen.

1. Joseph Hamilton,
2. M. McClanohan,
3. David Campbell,
4. Samuel Buchanan,
5. Adam Huntsman,
6. James Baxter.

OHIO.

John G. Young, Abraham Shepherd.

1. Aaron Wheeler,
2. Othniel Looker,
3. John Patterson,
4. Benjamin Haugh,
5. William Skinner,
6. James Curry.

INDIANA.

Jesse L. Holman, Thomas H. Blake.

1. Joseph Bartholomew.

LOUISIANA.

Garrigues Flanjac, Squire Lea.

1. John R. Grimes.

NINTH PRESIDENTIAL ELECTION—1821.

JAMES MONROE was re-elected President, receiving the entire electoral vote of every State (228) except New Hampshire, of which one vote was thrown for John Quincy Adams. DANIEL D. TOMPKINS was elected Vice-President, receiving 215 votes; while Richard Stockton had 8 votes, Daniel Rodney 4, Robert G. Harper 1, and Richard Rush 1. The Electors were:

NEW HAMPSHIRE.

William Plumer, John Pendexter.

1. David Barker,
2. Nathaniel Shannon,
3. William Fisk,
4. Ezra Bartlett,
5. Samuel Dinsmoor,
6. James Smith.

VERMONT.

James Galusha, William Slade, Jr.

1. Gilbert Denison,
2. Daniel A. A. Buck,
3. Pliny Smith,
4. Ezra Butler,
5. Aaron Leland,
6. Timothy Stanley.

MASSACHUSETTS.

John Adams, Seth Sprague.

1. William Phillips,
2. Thomas H. Blood,
3. William Gray,
4. Jonas Sibley,
5. Daniel Webster,
6. Ezra Starkweather,
7. B. W. Crowninshield,
8. Wendell Davis,
9. John Heard,
10. John Davis,
11. Samuel Dana,
12. Joseph Woodbridge,
13. Ebenezer Mattoon.

RHODE ISLAND.

James Fenner, Robert F. Noyes.

1. Dutee J. Pearce,
2. Dutee Arnold.

CONNECTICUT.

Henry Seymour, Isaiah Loomis.

1. Samuel Welles,
2. William Cogswell,
3. William Moseley,
4. John Alsop,
5. Ebenezer Brockway,
6. S. W. Crawford,
7. Samuel H. Phillips.

NEW YORK.

William Floyd, John Baker.

1. Henry Rutgers,
2. John Walworth,
3. Abel Huntington,
4. Daniel McDougall,
5. Edward Severich,
6. Seth Wetmore,
7. Isaac Lawrence,
8. Latham A. Burrows,
9. John Targee,
10. Ferrand Stranahan,
11. Jacob Odell,
12. Henry Wager,
13. Peter Waring,
14. Elisha Harnham,
15. Edward P. Livingston,
16. Jonathan Collins,
17. Peter Millikin,
18. Samuel Nelson,
19. David Hammond,
20. Wm. B. Rochester,
21. Mark Spencer,
22. Charles Thompson,
23. Benjamin Knower,
24. Philetas Swift,
25. Gilbert Eddy,
26. James Brisban,
27. Howell Gardner.

New Jersey.

David Mills, Samuel L. Southard.

1. John Wilson,
2. Joseph Budd,
3. John Crowell,
4. Isaiah Shinn,
5. Aaron Vansyckel,
6. John L. Smith.

Pennsylvania.

Thomas Leiper, James P. Sanderson.

1. Paul Cox,
2. William Clingan,
3. Daniel Groves,
4. George Barnitz,
5. Chandler Price,
6. James Griffen,
7. Pierce Crosby,
8. John Miley,
9. Andrew Gilkerson,
10. George Plumer,
11. John Hamilton,
12. George Hebb,
13. James Kerr,
14. Andrew Sutton,
15. William Mitchell,
16. Joseph Huston,
17. D. W. Dingman,
18. Hugh Davis,
19. Gabriel Heister,
20. Patrick Farrelly,
21. John Todd,
22. Melchior Rahm (deceased),
23. Philip Benner.

Delaware.

Peter Robinson, Nicholas Ridgely.

1. John Clark,
2. Andrew Barratt.

Maryland.

James Forrest, Elias Brown.

1. Robert W. Bowie,
2. John Forward,
3. John Stephen,
4. William R. Stuart,
5. A. McKim,
6. John Boon,
7. William Gabby,
8. Joshua Prideaux,
9. Michael C. Sprigg.

Virginia.

William C. Holt, Thomas Brown.

1. Charles H. Graves,
2. Robert Shields,
3. John Pegram,
4. William Jones,
5. R. B. Stark,
6. John Taliaferro,
7. John Purnall,
8. John T. Brook,
9. B. T. Arthur,
10. Hugh Holmes,
11. William C. Rives,
12. W. Armstrong, Jr.,
13. Charles Yancey,
14. Archibald Rutherford,
15. Joseph Martin,
16. Archibald Stuart,
17. W. Breckenbrough,
18. Andrew Russell,
19. Armistead Hoomes,
20. Samuel Blackburn,
21. James Hunter,
22. John Edie,
23. Robert Taylor.

North Carolina.

Robert Love, Kinborough Jones.

1. Jesse Franklin,
2. John Hall,
3. Michael McLeary,
4. George Outlaw,
5. Francis Locke,
6. C. E. Johnson,
7. Abraham Phillips,
8. Lewis D. Wilson,
9. Alexander Gray,
10. H. J. G. Ruffin,
11. B. H. Covington,
12. Thomas Kenan,
13. James Mebane.

South Carolina.

Benjamin James, Benjamin Rynalds.

1. L. M. Ayer,
2. Isaac Smith,
3. John S. Glascock,
4. John Dunovant,
5. Matthew J. Kirth,
6. Rasha Cannon,
7. Benjamin Dickson,
8. William A. Ball,
9. Charles Miller.

Georgia.

Oliver Porter, John Graves.

1. Henry Mitchell,
2. John Rutherford,
3. John McIntosh,
4. John Foster,
5. David Meriwether,
6. Benjamin Whitaker.

Kentucky.

Samuel Murrel, Martin D. Hardin.

1. E. M. Ewing,
2. Willis A. Lee,
3. S. Caldwell,
4. James Johnson,
5. John E. King,
6. Jesse Bledsoe,
7. John Pope,
8. Thomas Bodley,
9. Richard Taylor,
10. Hubbard Taylor.

TENNESSEE.

A. M. Carter, Joseph Dickson.
1. J. Hamilton, Sr.,
2. German Lester,
3. David Campbell,
4. Henry Small,
5. John J. White.

MISSOURI.

William Shannon, John S. Brickey.
1. William Christy.

MAINE.

William Moody, Lemuel Trescott.
1. Joshua Wingate, Jr.,
2. Joshua Gage,
3. Elisha Allen,
4. Josiah Prescott,
5. William Chadwick,
6. Levi Hubbard,
7. Samuel Tucker.

OHIO.

Jeremiah Morrow, James Caldwell.
1. William H. Harrison,
2. James Kilbourne,
3. Alexander Campbell,
4. John McLaughlin,
5. Robert Lucas,
6. Lewis Dille.

INDIANA.

Nathaniel Ewing, John H. Thompson.
1. Daniel J. Caswell.

ILLINOIS.

James B. Moore, A. F. Hubbard.
1. Michael Jones.

ALABAMA.

John Scott, George Phillips.
1. Henry Minor.

MISSISSIPPI.

Duncan Stewart, Daniel Burnet.
1. Theodore Stark.

LOUISIANA.

Philemon Thomas, John R. Grymes.
1. Daniel L. Todd.

TENTH PRESIDENTIAL ELECTION—1825.

John Quincy Adams, Andrew Jackson, William H. Crawford, and Henry Clay were candidates, and the Electoral College not giving either of them the requisite majority (132 votes), the choice again devolved upon the House of Representatives, when MR. ADAMS was elected. Andrew Jackson received the entire electoral vote of New Jersey, Pennsylvania, North Carolina, South Carolina, Tennessee, Indiana, Mississippi, and Alabama, 1 of the 36 votes of New York, 7 of the 11 votes of Maryland, 3 of the 5 votes of Louisiana, and one of the 3 votes of Illinois. John Quincy Adams received the entire vote of Maine, New Hampshire, Vermont, Massachusetts, Rhode Island, and Connecticut, and 26 of the 36 votes of New York, 1 of the 3 votes of Delaware, 3 of the 11 votes of Maryland, 2 of the 5 votes of Louisiana, and 1 of the 3 votes of Illinois. William H. Crawford received the entire vote of Virginia and of Georgia, and 5 of the 36 votes of New York, 2 of the 3 votes of Delaware, and 1 of the 11 votes of Maryland. Henry Clay received the entire vote of Kentucky, Ohio, and Missouri, and 4 of the 36 votes of New York. JOHN C. CALHOUN was elected Vice-President, receiving 182 votes; while Nathan Sanford had 30 votes, Nathaniel Macon 24, Andrew Jackson 13, Martin Van Buren 9, and Henry Clay 2. The Electors were:

NEW HAMPSHIRE.

Josiah Bartlett, Abel Parker.
1. William Badger,
2. Caleb Reith,
3. Samuel Quarles,
4. Moses White,
5. William Fisk,
6. Hall Burgin.

MASSACHUSETTS.

William Gray, Oliver Smith.

1. Levi Lincoln,
2. Enos Foot,
3. T. L. Winthrop,
4. William Walker,
5. N. Silsbee,
6. John Endicot,
7. Joseph Kettredge,
8. Thomas Weston,
9. Augustus Tower,
10. Cornelius Grinnell,
11. Jonathan Davis,
12. Hezekiah Barnard,
13. Edmund Cushing.

RHODE ISLAND.

Caleb Earle, Elisha Watson.

1. Stephen B. Cornell,
2. Charles Eldridge.

CONNECTICUT.

Calvin Willey, David Keys.

1. Oliver Wolcott,
2. John Swathel,
3. Rufus Hitchcock,
4. Lemuel White,
5. David Hill,
6. Moses Warren.

VERMONT.

Jonas Galusha, John Mason.

1. Titus Hutchinson,
2. Dan Carpenter,
3. Joseph Burr,
4. Asa Aldis,
5. Jabez Proctor.

NEW YORK.

Nathan Thompson, William Townsend.

1. Darius Bentley,
2. Thomas Lawyer,
3. Micah Brooks,
4. E. B. Crandale,
5. Pierre A. Barker,
6. Samuel Hicks,
7. Joseph Sibley,
8. Edward Savage,
9. Timothy H. Porter,
10. Benjamin Mooers,
11. Samuel Russell,
12. Chester Patterson,
13. Marinus Willett,
14. Phineas Coon,
15. Ebenezer Sage,
16. Azariah Smith,
17. Richard Blanvelt,
18. Eleazar Burnham,
19. Abraham Stagg,
20. Solomon St. John,
21. John Drake,
22. Elisha B. Strong,
23. James Drake,
24. Clark Crandall,
25. Isaac Sutherland,
26. I. Sutherland,
27. William Walsh,
28. J. Lansing, Jr.,
29. Alexander J. Coffin,
30. Benjamin Bailey,
31. Benjamin Smith,
32. Samuel Smith,
33. Elisha Dorr,
34. Heman Cady.

NEW JERSEY.

Peter Wilson, John Buck.

1. Daniel Vliet,
2. James Cook,
3. Jacob Kline,
4. James Parker,
5. Joseph Kille,
6. J. W. Scott.

PENNSYLVANIA.

Thomas Leiper, William Beatty.

1. Cromwell Pearce,
2. Valentine Giesey,
3. Philip Peltz,
4. John Reed,
5. A. McCaraher,
6. James Duncan,
7. Daniel Sheffer,
8. John Boyd,
9. Daniel Raul,
10. Abraham Addams,
11. Joseph Engle,
12. Isaac Smith,
13. John Pugh,
14. William Thomson,
15. Adam Ritscher,
16. Asa Mann,
17. Charles Kenny,
18. John Fogel,
19. Adam King,
20. Philip Benner,
21. John Rush,
22. Henry Scheetz,
23. Peter Adams,
24. Adam Light,
25. James Ankrim,
26. James Murray.

DELAWARE.

John Caldwell, Isaac Tunnell.

1. Joseph G. Rowland.

MARYLAND.

Henry Brawner, William Brown.

1. John C. Herbert,
2. Thomas Hope,
3. George Winchester,
4. Samuel G. Osborn,
5. Dennis Claude,
6. James Sangston,
7. William Tyler,
8. Littleton Dennis,
9. Thomas Post.

Virginia.

William C. Holt, Robert Shield.

1. Charles H. Graves,
2. Ellison Currie,
3. John Cargill,
4. Robert Taylor,
5. W. H. Brodnax,
6. Isaac Foster,
7. Joseph Wyatt,
8. Daniel Morgan,
9. James Jones,
10. William Armstrong,
11. Charles Yancey,
12. Archibald Rutherford,
13. Joseph Martin,
14. John Bowyer,
15. Thomas M. Randolph,
16. James Hoge,
17. W. Brockenbrough,
18. Andrew Russell,
19. John T. Somax,
20. Joseph H. Samuels,
21. William Jones,
22. William Marteney.

North Carolina.

Montfort Stokes, William Martin.

1. Robert Love,
2. William A. Blount,
3. Peter Forney,
4. William B. Lockhart,
5. Vine Allen,
6. Edward B. Dudley,
7. James Mebane,
8. A. H. Shepperd,
9. John Giles,
10. Walter J. Leake,
11. William Drew,
12. John M. Morehead,
13. Josiah Crudup.

South Carolina.

Robert Clendinen, Evan Benbow.

1. John K. Griffen,
2. William Garrett,
3. Angus Patterson,
4. Eldred Simkins,
5. Joseph W. Alston,
6. William C. Pinckney,
7. M. J. Keith,
8. Thomas Benson,
9. William Laval.

Georgia.

Elias Beall, William Matthews.

1. Thomas Cumming,
2. John McIntosh,
3. John Floyd,
4. John Rutherford,
5. John Harden,
6. William Terrell,
7. Warren Jordan.

Kentucky.

J. R. Underwood, Richard Taylor.

1. John E. King,
2. Joseph Allen,
3. Alney McLean,
4. W. Moore,
5. Young Ewing,
6. Thomas Bodley,
7. Benjamin Lecher,
8. D. Payne,
9. James Smiley,
10. J. J. Crittenden,
11. Joshua Fry,
12. H. Taylor.

Tennessee.

John Rhea, William A. Sublett.

1. T. A. Howard,
2. Joseph Brown,
3. W. E. Anderson,
4. Joel Pinson,
5. B. C. Stout,
6. William Blout,
7. William Mitchell,
8. Robert H. Dyer,
9. Samuel Hogg.

Ohio.

W. H. Harrison, James Caldwell.

1. W. McFarland,
2. David Sloane,
3. Thomas Kirker,
4. Samuel Coulter,
5. James Heaton,
6. S. Kingsbury,
7. Henry Brown,
8. Ebenezer Merry,
9. E. Buckingham,
10. James Cooley,
11. William Kendall,
12. James Steele,
13. William Skinner,
14. John Bigger.

Louisiana.

William Nott, John B. Planche.

1. James H. Shepherd,
2. S. Heiriart,
3. Pierre Lacoste.

Missouri.

David Todd, James Logan.

1. David Musick.

Indiana.

Elias McNamee, John Carr.

1. David Robb,
2. Jonathan McCarty,
3. Samuel Milroy.

MISSISSIPPI.

Thomas Hinds, Bartlett C. Barry.
1. James Patton.

ILLINOIS.

William Harrison, Alexander P. Field.
1. Henry Eddy.

ALABAMA.

Reuben Safford, James Hill.
1. Henry Chambers, 2. John Murphy, 3. William Fleming.

MAINE.

James Campbell, Lemuel Trescott.
1. Thomas Fillebrown, 4. Benjamin Chandler, 6. Benjamin Nourse,
2. James Parker, 5. Rev. Joshua Taylor, 7. Stephen Parsons.
3. Nathaniel Hobbs,

The choice between Andrew Jackson, John Quincy Adams, and William H. Crawford, the three highest on the list of those voted for by the Electoral College for President, devolved on the House of Representatives. Twenty-four members, one from each State, were appointed Tellers, and they announced as the result of the first ballot: For John Quincy Adams: Maine, New Hampshire, Massachusetts, Rhode Island, Connecticut, Vermont, New York, Maryland, Ohio, Kentucky, Illinois, Missouri, and Louisiana,—13 States. For Andrew Jackson: New Jersey, Pennsylvania, South Carolina, Tennessee, Alabama, Mississippi, and Indiana,—7 States. For William H. Crawford: Delaware, Virginia, North Carolina, and Georgia,—4 States. The Speaker then declared that JOHN QUINCY ADAMS, having received a majority of the votes of all the States, was duly elected President.

ELEVENTH PRESIDENTIAL ELECTION—1829.

ANDREW JACKSON was elected President, receiving the entire electoral vote of Pennsylvania, Virginia, North Carolina, South Carolina, Georgia, Kentucky, Tennessee, Ohio, Louisiana, Mississippi, Indiana, Illinois, Alabama, and Missouri, 1 of the 9 votes of Maine, 20 of the 36 votes of New York, and five of the 11 votes of Maryland—178 in all; John Quincy Adams receiving the other 83 electoral votes. JOHN C. CALHOUN was re-elected Vice-President, receiving 171 votes; while Richard Rush had 83 votes, and William Smith 7. The Electors were:

MAINE.

Thomas Fillebrown, John S. Kimball.
1. Simon Nowell, 4. Levi Hubbard, 6. John Moore,
2. Joseph Southwick, 5. James C. Churchill, 7. Ebenezer Farley.
3. Joseph Prime,

VERMONT.

Jonas Galusha, Asa Aldis.
1. Ezra Butler, 3. John Phelps, 5. Apollos Austin.
2. Josiah Dana, 4. William Jarvis,

NEW HAMPSHIRE.

George Sullivan, William Bixby.
1. Samuel Quarles, 3. Nahum Parker, 5. Samuel Sparhawk,
2. Thomas Woolson, 4. Ezra Bartlett, 6. William Lovejoy.

MASSACHUSETTS.

Thomas L. Winthrop, Edmund Cushing.

1. Samuel Lathrop,
2. Eliel Frost,
3. Jesse Putnam,
4. John Gilbert,
5. Stephen White,
6. Samuel Jones,
7. Baily Bartlett,
8. E. H. Robbins,
9. Nathan Chandler,
10. Oliver Starkweather,
11. Jonathan Davis,
12. Bradford Dimmick,
13. Seth Sprague.

RHODE ISLAND.

Caleb Earle, Elisha Watson.

1. Stephen B. Cornell,
2. Charles Elbridge.

CONNECTICUT.

Sylvester Norton, Roger Taintor.

1. Rufus Hitchcock,
2. Homer Boardman,
3. Moses Warren,
4. George Pratt,
5. Charles Hawley,
6. W. R. Kibbee.

NEW YORK.

Moses Rolph, Asaph Stow.

1. John Garrison,
2. A. D. W. Bruyn,
3. Benjamin Bailey,
4. John Lloyd,
5. John Targee,
6. Alexander Coffin,
7. Gilbert Coutant,
8. Gilbert Eddy,
9. Jacob Odell,
10. A. Van Vechten,
11. Morgan Lewis,
12. E. B. Shearman,
13. Egbert Jansen,
14. A. McIntyre,
15. John E. Russell,
16. Salmon Childs,
17. Peter Pine,
18. Peter H. Myers,
19. J. C. Yates,
20. James Campbell,
21. Elkanah Brush,
22. Jesse Smith,
23. Rufus Crane,
24. Augustus Chapman,
25. Thomas Blakeslee,
26. Benjamin Cotton,
27. Freeborn G. Jewett,
28. John Beall,
29. William Hildreth,
30. John Taylor,
31. James H. Guernsey,
32. Charles Dayan,
33. Shubal Dunham,
34. Ebenezer Walden.

NEW JERSEY.

Theodore Frelinghuysen, J. J. Ely.

1. A. Leaming,
2. Abraham Brown,
3. A. White,
4. T. Elmer,
5. Gabriel Hoff,
6. C. Zabriskie.

PENNSYLVANIA.

John B. Gibson, William Thompson.

1. William Findlay,
2. Leonard Rupert,
3. Edward King,
4. Jacob Gearhart,
5. John Lisle,
6. George Barnitz,
7. Jacob Holgate,
8. Jacob Heyser,
9. Samuel Humes, Sr.,
10. John Harper,
11. John W. Cunningham,
12. John Scott,
13. George G. Leiper,
14. William Piper,
15. Henry Scheetz,
16. Valentine Giesey,
17. Adam Ritscher,
18. James Gordon,
19. David Hottenstein,
20. John M. Snowden,
21. Peter Frailey,
22. Robert Scott,
23. Francis Baird,
24. Henry Allshouse,
25. Henry Winters,
26. James Duncan.

DELAWARE.

James Canby, David Hazard.

1. John Adams.

MARYLAND.

William Fitzhugh, Jr., Benjamin F. Forrest.

1. William Tyler,
2. James Sewell,
3. John S. Sellman,
4. Thomas Emory,
5. Benjamin C. Howard,
6. T. R. Lockerman,
7. Elias Brown,
8. Littleton Dennis,
9. Henry Brawner.

VIRGINIA.

William C. Holt, Robert McCandlish.

1. Wm. H. McFarland,
2. Ellyson Currie,
3. John Cargill,
4. John W. Green,
5. Thomas M. Nelson,
6. John Gibson,
7. Richard Logan,
8. George Rust,
9. James Jones,
10. Jared Williams,
11. William Daniel,
12. Jacob D. Williamson,
13. Joseph Martin,
14. John Bowyer,
15. William F. Gordon,
16. John E. George,
17. Wm. Brockenbrough,
18. Andrew Russell,
19. Garret Minor,
20. Joel Shrewsbury,
21. William Jones,
22. John McMillan.

NORTH CAROLINA.

Robert Love, Josiah Crudup.

1. Montfort Stokes,
2. John Hall,
3. Peter Forney,
4. Joseph J. Williams,
5. John Giles,
6. Kedar Ballard,
7. Abraham Phillips,
8. Louis D. Wilson,
9. John M. Morehead,
10. R. D. Spaight,
11. Walter F. Leake,
12. E. B. Dudley,
13. Willie P. Mangum.

SOUTH CAROLINA.

Sanders Glover, William Pope.

1. David R. Evans,
2. John McComb,
3. John Stewart,
4. Arthur P. Hayne,
5. David Sloan,
6. Green B. Colmi,
7. William Johnston,
8. Henry L. Pinckney,
9. Wade Hampton, Jr.

GEORGIA.

John Rutherford, William Terrell.

1. Robert R. Reed,
2. John Moore,*
3. David Blackshear,
4. Augustus S. Clayton,
5. Solomon Graves,
6. John G. Maxwell,
7. Oliver Porter.

ALABAMA.

Thomas Miller, John A. Elmore.

1. Enoch Parsons,
2. Thomas D. Crabb,
3. William Y. Higgins.

MISSISSIPPI.

Joseph Dunbar, William Downing.

1. Wiley P. Harris.

LOUISIANA.

John B. Planche, Alexander Mouton.

1. Thomas W. Scott,
2. Placide Bossier,
3. Trasimon Landry.

TENNESSEE.

John Rhea, William A. Sublett.

1. Samuel Bunch,
2. Alfred Flournoy,
3. Thomas McCorry,
4. Joseph Brown,
5. Benjamin C. Stout,
6. Willie Blount,
7. Andrew J. Marchbanks,
8. Adam R. Alexander,
9. George Elliott.

KENTUCKY.

Thomas S. Slaughter, Reuben Munday.

1. Matthew Lyon,
2. Benjamin Chapeze,
3. Edmund Watkins,
4. John Younger,
5. Nathan Gaither,
6. John Sterrett,
7. Tunstall Quarles,
8. Benjamin Taylor,
9. Robert J. Ward,
10. Richard French,
11. Tandy Allen,
12. Thompson Ward.

OHIO.

Ethan Allen Brown, Robert Lucas.

1. George McCook,
2. John McElvain,
3. William Piatt,
4. Samuel Herrick,
5. James Shields,
6. George Sharp,
7. Henry Barrington,
8. Walter M. Blake,
9. Thomas Gillespie,
10. Benjamin Jones,
11. Thomas L. Hamer,
12. William Hayne,
13. Valentine Keffer,
14. Hugh McFall.

* John Moore declining to serve, Seaton Grantland was elected by the Legislature.

INDIANA.

Benjamin V. Beckes, Ratliff Boon.
1. Jesse B. Durham, 2. William Lowe, 3. Ross Smiley.

ILLINOIS.

John Taylor, Richard M. Young.
1. Alexander M. Houston.

MISSOURI.

John Bull, Augustus Jones.
1. Benjamin O'Fallon.

TWELFTH PRESIDENTIAL ELECTION—1833.

ANDREW JACKSON was re-elected President, receiving the entire electoral vote of Maine, New Hampshire, New York, New Jersey, Pennsylvania, Virginia, North Carolina, Georgia, Tennessee, Ohio, Louisiana, Mississippi, Indiana, Illinois, Alabama, and Missouri, with three of the eight votes of Maryland—219. Henry Clay, of Kentucky, received the entire vote of Massachusetts, Rhode Island, Connecticut, Delaware, and Kentucky, with five of the eight votes of Maryland—49; John Floyd received the entire vote of South Carolina—11; and William Wirt the entire vote of Vermont—7. MARTIN VAN BUREN was elected Vice-President, receiving 189 votes; while John Sergeant had 49 votes, William Wilkins had 30, Henry Lee had 11, and Amos Elmaker had 7. The Electors were:

MAINE.

Nathan Cutler, Samuel Moore.
1. Isaac Lane, 4. Elias Burgess, 7. Rowland H. Bridgham,
2. Silas Barnard, 5. Joseph Sewall, 8. E. Fletcher.
3. J. C. Churchill, 6. Joseph Kelsey,

NEW HAMPSHIRE.

Benjamin Peirce, John Holbrook.
1. Phineas Parkhurst, 3. Samuel Collins, 5. John Taylor.
2. Joseph Weeks, 4. Moses White,

VERMONT.

James Tarbox, Amos Thompson.
1. Nathan Leavenworth, 3. Ezra Butler, 5. William Strong.
2. John S. Pettibone, 4. Augustus Clarke,

MASSACHUSETTS.

Charles Jackson, E. Mattoon.
1. Thomas H. Perkins, 5. Ebenezer Moseley, 9. Aaron Tufts,
2. James Byers, 6. James Richardson, 10. Cornelius Grinnell,
3. Gideon Barstow, 7. Nathan Brooks, 11. Samuel Lee,
4. Henry Shaw, 8. Jotham Lincoln, 12. Nymphas Marston.

RHODE ISLAND.

Samuel Ward King, Nathaniel S. Ruggles.
1. William Peckham, 2. Peleg Wilbur.

CONNECTICUT.

Morris Woodruff, John D. Reynolds.
1. John Baldwin, 3. Eli Todd, 5. Erastus Sturges,
2. Chester Smith, 4. Oliver H. King, 6. E. Jackson, Jr.

NEW YORK.

Edward P. Livingston, Amos Buck.

1. Nathaniel Garron,
2. Theophilus S. Morgan,
3. Moses Ralph,
4. David Moulton,
5. Kenry Waring,
6. Ebenezer Wood,
7. Gideon Lee,
8. Peter Collier,
9. John Targee,
10. John Hyde,
11. Preserved Fish,
12. Thomas Humphrey,
13. J. W. Hardenbrook,
14. Joseph Reynolds,
15. Abraham Miller,
16. Darius Bentley,
17. William Taber,
18. Samuel Payne,
19. Samuel Hunter,
20. G. Curtis,
21. Peter Crispell, Jr.,
22. Seth Thomas,
23. William Deitz,
24. Jonas Seely,
25. Samuel Anable,
26. Oliver Phelps,
27. James Woods,
28. Truman.Spencer,
29. John N. Quackenbush,
30. Abel Baldwin,
31. Daniel D. Campbell,
32. James Sutherland,
33. John Gale,
34. Calvin T. Chamberlain,
35. Dudley Farlin,
36. Orris Crosby,
37. James B. Spencer,
38. M. A. Andrews,
39. John S. Veeder,
40. Asa Clark, Jr.

NEW JERSEY.

Daniel Vliet, Aaron Vansyckel.

1. Peter J. Terhune,
2. John M. Perrine,
3. Joseph Rogers,
4. James Newell,
5. William Munroe,
6. William L. Stiles.

PENNSYLVANIA.

Samuel McKean, David D. Wagener.

1. C. Garber,
2. William Swilland,
3. John T. Knight,
4. W. Brindle,
5. William Thomson,
6. Adam Light,
7. Edward King,
8. George Barnitz,
9. B. W. Richards,
10. D. Sheffer,
11. George W. Smick,
12. Frederick Orwan,
13. John Slaymaker,
14. George McCullock,
15. Oliver Alison,
16. John Murray,
17. George G. Leiper,
18. David Gilman,
19. Henry Scheetz,
20. David Frazier,
21. Adam Ritscher,
22. P. Mulvany,
23. William Addams,
24. J. Patten,
25. John Schall,
26. J. Y. Bauley,
27. J. Rooker,
28. Wilson Smith.

DELAWARE.

George Truitt, C. P. Comegys.

1. H. F. Hall.

MARYLAND.

R. H. Goldsborough, William Price.

1. J. S. Smith,
2. William B. Tyler,
3. William Frick,
4. Albert Constable,
5. U. S. Heath,
6. John L. Steele.

VIRGINIA.

George Loyall, Samuel Blackwell.

1. John Cargill,
2. John Gibson,
3. James Jones,
4. J. Horner,
5. Thomas M. Nelson,
6. H. L. Opie,
7. Archibald Austin,
8. James M. Mason,
9. Richard Logan,
10. John McMillan,
11. Joseph Martin,
12. J. D. Williamson,
13. William Jones,
14. Charles Beale,
15. W. H. Roane,
16. Thomas Bland,
17. Samuel Carr,
18. A. Russell,
19. L. T. Dade,
20. Philip N. Nicholas,
21. A. R. Harwood.

NORTH CAROLINA.

A. W. Venable, J. O. Watson.

1. Robert Love,
2. I. I. Daniel,
3. George L. Davidson,
4. W. B. Lockhart,
5. Peregrine Roberts,
6. F. Ward,
7. Thomas G. Polk,
8. R. D. Spaight,
9. Thomas Settle,
10. Owen Holmes,
11. J. M. Morehead,
12. Henry Skinner,
13. William H. Leak,

SOUTH CAROLINA.

Robert J. Turnbull, Elijah Watson.

1. W. Thompson, Jr., 4. Thomas Lyles, 7. Benjamin Hart,
2. Samuel Cherry, 5. W. B. Seabrook, 8. Joseph S. Shelton,
3. William Dubose, 6. Thomas Dugan, 9. Thomas Evans.

GEORGIA.

Beverly Allen, Henry Holt.

1. Elias Beall, 4. William Terrell, 7. John Floyd,
2. Henry Jackson, 5. W. B. Bullock, 8. Wilson Williams,
3. David Blackshear, 6. John Whitehead, 9. Seaton Grantland.

TENNESSEE.

M. Aiken, Daniel Bowman.

1. William Snodgrass, 6. William Pillow, 10. David Feutress,
2. J. G. Bostick, 7. Joseph McMillon, 11. John Heam,
3. Jesse Wallace, 8. Willie Blount, 12. B. Coleman,
4. Elliott Hickman, 9. William Stroud, Sr., 13. George Elliott.
5. W. B. A. Ramsey,

KENTUCKY.

Joseph Eve, Alney McLeon.

1. Benjamin Hardin, 6. William Ousley, 10. D. S. Patton,
2. W. K. Wall, 7. Burr Harrison, 11. E. M. Ewing,
3. M. P. Marshall, 8. Thomas Chilton, 12. M. Beatty,
4. J. L. Hickman, 9. John I. Marshall, 13. Thompson M. Ewing.
5. M. V. Thompson,

OHIO.

Benjamin Tappan, Joseph J. McDowell.

1. John M. Goodenow, 8. John Chaney, 14. William S. Tracy,
2. Valentine Keffer, 9. Alexander McConnell, 15. George Marshall,
3. I. D. Morris, 10. George Sharpe, 16. Jeremiah McLane,
4. Isaac Humphreys, 11. Michael Moore, 17. Eli Baldwin,
5. Mark T. Wills, 12. Fisher A. Blocksom, 18. H. J. Harman,
6. Alexander Elliott, 13. John Lavwell, 19. Jonathan Cilley.
7. R. D. Forman,

LOUISIANA.

J. B. Planche, Alexander Mouton.

1. Thomas W. Scott, 2. W. H. Overton, 3. T. Landry.

INDIANA.

George Boon, M. Crune.

1. W. Armstrong, 4. John Ketchum, 6. Thomas Givens,
2. Alexander J. Burnett, 5. Arthur Patterson, 7. N. B. Palmer.
3. James Blake,

MISSISSIPPI.

William Dowsing, Samuel Hunter.

1. Wiley P. Harris, 2. W. W. Cherry.

ILLINOIS.

James Evans, Adams Dunlap.

1. John C. Alexander, 2. Thomas Ray, 3. Abner Flack.

ALABAMA.

Henry King, William Edmondson.

1. John J. Winston, 3. William R. Pickett, 5. Theophilus Toulmin.
2. William P. Gould, 4. George Phillips,

MISSOURI.

Joel H. Haden, John Hume.

1. William Blackey, 2. Henry Shurlds.

THIRTEENTH PRESIDENTIAL ELECTION—1837.

Martin Van Buren was elected President, receiving the entire electoral vote of Maine, New Hampshire, Rhode Island, Connecticut, New York, Pennsylvania, Virginia, North Carolina, Louisiana, Mississippi, Illinois, Alabama, Missouri, Arkansas, Michigan—170. William H. Harrison received the entire vote of Vermont, New Jersey, Delaware, Maryland, Kentucky, Ohio, and Indiana—73; Hugh L. White, the vote of Georgia and of Tennessee—26; Daniel Webster, the vote of Massachusetts—14; and W. P. Mangum, the vote of South Carolina—11. Richard M. Johnson was chosen Vice-President by the Senate, no one having received a majority of the electoral votes, which stood: Richard M. Johnson, 147; Francis Granger, 77; John Tyler, 47; William Smith, 23. The Electors were:

Maine.

Reuel Williams, Shepherd Carey.

1. Sheldon Hobbs,
2. Joseph Tobin,
3. Jonathan Smith,
4. John Hamblen,
5. Benjamin Burgess,
6. William Thompson,
7. John H. Jarvis,
8. S. S. Heagan.

New Hampshire.

Jonathan Harvey, Josiah Russell.

1. Isaac Waldron,
2. G. Gilmore,
3. Tristam Shaw,
4. Ebenezer Carlton,
5. Stephen Gale.

Vermont.

Jabez Proctor, T. Howe.

1. S. Swift,
2. Titus Hutchinson,
3. David Crawford,
4. W. A. Griswold,
5. Edward Lamb.

Massachusetts.

Nathaniel Silsbee, Samuel Appleton.

1. E. A. Newton,
2. Leverett Saltonstall,
3. Benjamin Walker,
4. Isaac C. Bates,
5. Loammi Baldwin,
6. Thomas Longlay,
7. Samuel Lee,
8. Bezabeel Taft, Jr.,
9. J. G. Kendall,
10. Howard Lothrop,
11. Charles W. Morgan,
12. Charles J. Holmes.

Rhode Island.

James Fenner, Henry Bull.

1. John D'Wolf,
2. B. H. Thurston.

Connecticut.

Lorain T. Pease, Luther Warren.

1. Alfred Bassett,
2. Seth P. Beers,
3. Julius Clark,
4. R. P. Williams,
5. Moses Gregory,
6. Carlos Chapman.

New York.

Cornelius W. Lawrence, John Cox.

1. Jacob Sutherland,
2. Gideon Ostrander,
3. Moses Rolph,
4. John Targee,
5. Jacob Crocheron,
6. Jeremiah Anderson,
7. Stephen Allen,
8. James Hooker,
9. Nathaniel P. Hill,
10. Ichabod Bartlett,
11. Jeremiah Russell,
12. Augustus C. Welch,
13. Zadock Pratt,
14. Lyman Strabridge,
15. Lucas Hoes,
16. Whitcombe Phelps,
17. Henry Koon,
18. David Munro,
19. Peter Wendell,
20. Daniel Dickey,
21. Herman Gansevroot,
22. Peleg Slade,
23. John Gale,
24. Alanson M. Knapp,
25. Walcott Tyrrell,
26. Jared Willson,
27. David C. Judson,
28. Elisha Doubleday,
29. Frederick Lammons,
30. Joseph Sibley,
31. Henry Ellison,
32. Samuel Benedict, Jr.,
33. Parker Halleck,
34. Daniel H. Bissell,
35. George F. Falley,
36. Thomas J. Wheeler,
37. Orville Hungerford,
38. Guy H. Goodrich,
39. Joshua Babcock,
40. Hiram Gardner.

NEW JERSEY.

William Stevens, Allison Ely.

1. John H. Hall,
2. Joshua Burr,
3. William Brittan,
4. David Beevis,
5. Josiah S. Worth,
6. J. Leaming.

PENNSYLVANIA.

James Thompson, Henry Welsh.

1. Robert Patterson,
2. Thomas C. Miller,
3. Thomas D. Grover,
4. William Clark,
5. Joseph Burden,
6. John Mitchell,
7. John Naglee,
8. Leonard Rupert,
9. Samuel Badger,
10. George Kriner,
11. Gardner Furness,
12. Asa Mann,
13. Oliver Allison,
14. William R. Smith,
15. Henry Myers,
16. S. L. Carpenter,
17. John B. Sterigere,
18. Robert Patterson,
19. Henry Chapman,
20. Wallace M. Williams,
21. Jacob Kern,
22. James Power,
23. Jacob Dillinger,
24. Robert Orr,
25. Paul Geiger,
26. John Carothers,
27. Calvin Blythe,
28. John P. Davis.

DELAWARE.

William W. Morris, William Dunning.

1. H. F. Hall.

MARYLAND.

Elias Brown, David Hoffman.

1. J. B. Ricaud,
2. George Howard,
3. William Price,
4. J. M. Coale,
5. Anthony Kimmel,
6. Robert W. Bowie,
7. T. Burchenal,
8. Thomas G. Pratt.

VIRGINIA.

A. Smith, Samuel Carr.

1. John Cargill,
2. W. Holladay,
3. James Jones,
4. I. Horner,
5. Wm. R. Baskerville,
6. H. L. Opie,
7. Archibald Austin,
8. A. S. Baldwin,
9. Richard Logan,
10. J. D. Williamson,
11. A. Stuart,
12. D. B. Layne,
13. H. Hudgins,
14. A. Bierne,
15. A. R. Harwood,
16. James Hoge,
17. John Moncure,
18. John Gibson,
19. W. H. Roane,
20. Samuel L. Hays,
21. John Hindman.

NORTH CAROLINA.

Robert Love, Josiah O. Watson.

1. George Bower,
2. Nathaniel Macon,
3. John Wilson,
4. W. B. Lockhart,
5. A. Henderson,
6. G. C. Marchant,
7. John Hill,
8. L. D. Wilson,
9. John Parker,
10. W. P. Ferrand,
11. W. A. Morris,
12. Owen Holmes,
13. A. W. Venable.

SOUTH CAROLINA.

John Littlejohn, Thomas L. Gourdin.

1. Patrick Noble,
2. Thomas Dugan,
3. D. J. McCord,
4. B. T. Elmore,
5. Thomas F. Jones,
6. R. H. Goodwin,
7. John Frampton,
8. B. K. Hanegan,
9. John Maxwell.

GEORGIA.

George R. Gilmer, Thomas Stocks.

1. John W. Campbell,
2. Howell Cobb,
3. Gibson Clark,
4. William H. Holt,
5. E. Wimberly,
6. Ambrose Baber,
7. Thomas Hamilton,
8. David Meriwether,
9. C. Hines.

ALABAMA.

William Smith, Robert H. Watkins.

1. John McKinley,
2. John S. Hunter,
3. Thomas D. King,
4. William R. Hallett,
5. William R. Pickett.

TENNESSEE.

Robert J. McKinney, John Gordon.

1. John Netherland,
2. W. E. Anderson,
3. Alexander E. Smith,
4. Andrew J. Hoover,
5. James Park,
6. T. F. Bradford,
7. James A. Whiteside,
8. Neil S. Brown,
9. Asa Falkner,
10. S. D. Frierson,
11. Richard Cheatham,
12. L. P. Williamson,
13. William W. Lea.

KENTUCKY.

Burr Harrison, Thomas P. Wilson.

1. Henry Daniel,
2. William K. Wall,
3. Philip Triplett,
4. Robert Wickliff,
5. D. S. Patton,
6. Thomas Metcalf,
7. E. Rumsey,
8. M. P. Marshall,
9. Richard A. Buckner,
10. J. F. Ballinger,
11. C. Tompkins,
12. Robert P. Letcher,
13. M. Beaty.

OHIO.

Benjamin Ruggles, W. C. Kirker.

1. Joshua Collett,
2. Ira Belknap,
3. George P. Torrence,
4. Samuel Elliott,
5. Andrew McClany,
6. Mordecai Bartley,
7. Elijah Huntington,
8. John Codding,
9. Isaiah Morris,
10. Jared P. Kirtland,
11. Alexander Campbell,
12. D. Hasbough,
13. William Kendall,
14. John P. Coulter,
15. Abels Rennick,
16. John L. Lacy,
17. Christian King,
18. Andrew Donnelly,
19. Samuel Newell.

MISSISSIPPI.

Thomas Hinds, R. H. Grant.

1. B. W. Edwards,
2. H. G. Runnels.

LOUISIANA.

J. B. Planché, Alexander Mouton.

1. T. U. Scott,
2. P. E. Bossier,
3. T. Landry.

INDIANA.

John C. Clendenin, Achilles Williams.

1. Hiram Decker,
2. A. W. Morris,
3. Milton Stapp,
4. A. L. White,
5. Enoch McCarty,
6. M. G. Clark,
7. A. P. Andrews.

MISSOURI.

George F. Bollinger, William Monroe.

1. John Sappington,
2. A. Bird.

ARKANSAS.

John Miller, A. B. Anthony.

1. Joshua Morrison.

MICHIGAN.

Daniel Le Roy, William H. Hoeg.

1. David C. McKinstry.

ILLINOIS.

John Wyatt, Samuel Hachleton.

1. Samuel Leach,
2. John Pearson,
3. John D. Whitesides.

FOURTEENTH PRESIDENTIAL ELECTION—1841.

WILLIAM HENRY HARRISON was elected President, receiving the entire electoral vote of Maine, Massachusetts, Rhode Island, Connecticut, Vermont, New York, New Jersey, Pennsylvania, Delaware, Maryland, North Carolina, Georgia, Kentucky, Tennessee, Ohio, Louisiana, Mississippi, Indiana, and Michigan—234. Martin Van Buren received the entire vote of New Hampshire, Virginia, South Carolina, Illinois, Alabama, Missouri, and Arkansas—60. JOHN TYLER was elected Vice-President, receiving 234 votes; while R. M. Johnson had 48, L. W. Tazewell 11, and James K. Polk 1. The Electors were:

MAINE.

Isaac Ilsley, Thomas Fillebrown.

1. Isaac Hodson,
2. E. Robinson,
3. Samuel Small,
4. Benjamin P. Gilman,
5. Rufus K. Goodenow,
6. J. Huse,
7. Charles Trafton,
8. Thomas Robinson.

NEW HAMPSHIRE.

Samuel Burns, S. Perley.

1. John Scott,
2. J. W. Weeks,
3. Samuel Hatch,
4. F. Holbrook,
5. Andrew Paine, Jr.

VERMONT.

Samuel C. Crafts, John Conaut.

1. Ezra Meech,
2. A. B. W. Tenney,
3. William Henry,
4. William P. Briggs,
5. Joseph Reed.

MASSACHUSETTS.

Isaac C. Bates, Rufus Longley.

1. Peleg Sprague,
2. Sidney Willard,
3. Richard Houghton,
4. Ira M. Barton,
5. S. C. Phillips,
6. George Grinnel, Jr.,
7. Samuel Mixter,
8. Joseph Tripp,
9. Thomas French,
10. John B. Thomas,
11. W. Wood,
12. J. Z. Goodrich.

RHODE ISLAND.

Nicholas Brown, W. Weeden.

1. George Engs,
2. William Rhodes.

CONNECTICUT.

H. Spencer, Reuben Booth.

1. James Brewster,
2. P. Pearl,
3. A. Larrabee,
4. P. Bierce,
5. J. Green,
6. J. S. Peters.

NEW YORK.

James Burt, Elisha Jenkins.

1. Abraham Rose,
2. H. Watson,
3. John T. Harrison,
4. G. P. Griffith,
5. John L. Lawrence,
6. A. McIntyre,
7. Joseph Tucker,
8. E. Stimson,
9. J. P. Phœnix,
10. Josiah Hand,
11. Richard S. Williams,
12. K. P. Cool,
13. P. Van Cortlandt,
14. Jonathan Wallace,
15. B. White,
16. H. P. Voorhies,
17. N. Dubois,
18. Thomas Burch,
19. Peter G. Sharp,
20. P. B. Porter,
21. John I. Knox,
22. Albert Crane,
23. Peter Pratt,
24. Charles Bradish,
25. E. Merrick,
26. Gideon Lee,
27. J. Livingston,
28. Grattan H. Wheeler,
29. Isaac Ogden,
30. William Garbutt,
31. Samuel Balcom,
32. P. L. Tracey,
33. I. I. Speed, Jr.,
34. John Wheeler,
35. D. Hibbard,
36. Philo Orton,
37. John Williams,
38. H. R. Seymour,
39. B. D. Noxen,
40. Davis Hurd.

New Jersey.

Lewis Condict, John Runk.

1. C. Stepton,
2. Samuel G. Wright,
3. James Sliff,
4. Thomas Newbold,
5. J. M. Ryerson,
6. Joshua Townsend.

Pennsylvania.

J. A. Shulze, A. R. McIlvain.

1. J. Ritner,
2. J. K. Zeilin,
3. L. Passmore,
4. Robert Stimson,
5. J. P. Wetherell,
6. W. S. Hendrie,
7. Thomas P. Cope,
8. I. J. Ross,
9. F. Gillingham,
10. Peter Filbert,
11. A. Ellmaker,
12. William Addams,
13. John Harper,
14. B. Connelly, Jr.,
15. William McIlvain,
16. Joseph Markle,
17. J. Dickson,
18. J. G. Fordyce,
19. J. McKeehan,
20. T. M. T. McKennan,
21. John Reed,
22. H. Denny,
23. A. B. Wilson,
24. Joseph Buffington,
25. N. Middleswarth,
26. Henry Black,
27. George Walker,
28. John Dick.

Delaware.

Benjamin Caulk, H. F. Hall.

1. Peter J. Causey.

Maryland.

David Hoffman, J. P. Kennedy.

1. J. L. Kerr,
2. George Howard,
3. Theodore R. Lockerman,
4. Richard J. Bowie,
5. Jacob A. Preston,
6. James M. Coale,
7. W. T. Woolton,
8. Thomas A. Spence.

Virginia.

A. Smith, Richard Logan.

1. J. Cargill,
2. Archibald Stuart,
3. James Jones,
4. William Tod,
5. William R. Baskeville,
6. A. Brockenbrough,
7. Charles Yancey,
8. John Gibson,
9. J. B. Halybirton,
10. J. D. Williamson,
11. J. T. Randolph,
12. William Taylor,
13. W. Holliday,
14. A. C. Chapman,
15. J. Horner,
16. James Hoge,
17. Richard E. Byrd,
18. William Byers,
19. William A. Harris,
20. Benjamin Brown,
21. John Hurdman.

North Carolina.

James Welborn, D. F. Caldwell.

1. Charles McDowell,
2. J. B. Kelly,
3. D. Ramsour,
4. James Mebane,
5. A. Rencher,
6. William W. Cherry,
7. James S. Smith,
8. Thomas F. Jones,
9. Charles Manly,
10. Josiah Collins,
11. William L. Long,
12. James W. Bryan,
13. Daniel B. Baker.

South Carolina.

John Crawford, J. L. Jeter.

1. J. J. Caldwell,
2. W. H. Cannon,
3. A. Mazyck,
4. J. Buchanan,
5. H. J. Johnson,
6. F. J. Goodwyn,
7. W. McWillie,
8. J. Jenkins,
9. John L. Ashe.

Georgia.

George R. Gilmer, A. Miller.

1. D. L. Clinch,
2. W. W. Ezzard,
3. J. W. Campbell,
4. C. B. Strong,
5. Joel Crawford,
6. E. Wimberly,
7. Charles Dougherty,
8. J. Whitehead,
9. S. Grantland.

Alabama.

William K. Hallett, Joseph P. Frazier.

1. B. M. Lowe,
2. Benjamin Fitzpatrick,
3. M. F. Rainey,
4. Benjamin Reynolds,
5. J. Murphy.

MISSISSIPPI.

S. S. Prentiss, Thomas J. Word.
1. J. J. Stewart, 2. Henry Dickenson.

TENNESSEE.

E. H. Foster, Thomas I. Campbell.
1. S. Jarnagin, 5. William P. Senter, 9. J. H. Cahal,
2. J. F. Morford, 6. James O. Janes, 10. G. A. Henry,
3. Thomas D. Arnold, 7. A. A. Anderson, 11. E. J. Shields,
4. Thomas L. Bransford, 8. D. W. Dickenson, 12. George W. Gibbs.

KENTUCKY.

Richard A. Buckner, Charles G. Wintersmith.
1. James F. Morehead, 6. Daniel Breck, 10. M. P. Marshall,
2. Thomas W. Riley, 7. James W. Irwin, 11. James Harlan,
3. Robert Patterson, 8. R. H. Menefee, 12. A. Beatty,
4. William H. Field, 9. B. Y. Ousley, 13. W. W. Southgate.
5. Iredell Hart,

OHIO.

William R. Putnam, Reasin Beall.
1. Alexander Mayhew, 8. Aquila Toland, 14. John Carey,
2. Henry Harter, 9. Perley B. Johnson, 15. David King,
3. A. Spafford, 10. John Dukes, 16. Storm Rosa,
4. Joshua Collett, 11. Otho Brashear, 17. John Beatty,
5. Abram Miley, 12. James Raquet, 18. John Augustine,
6. Samuel F. Vinton, 13. C. S. Miller, 19. John Jameson.
7. John I. Vanmeter,

INDIANA.

J. McCarty, Joseph G. Marshall.
1. J. W. Payne, 4. James H. Cravens, 6. William Herod,
2. Joseph L. White, 5. Caleb B. Smith, 7. Samuel C. Sample.
3. Richard W. Thompson,

ILLINOIS.

A. W. Snyder, J. A. McClernand.
1. Isaac P. Walker, 2. James H. Ralston, 3. I. W. Eldridge.

MICHIGAN.

Thomas J. Drake, H. G. Wells.
1. J. Van Fassen.

LOUISIANA.

William De Buys, Jacques Dupré.
1. J. Birnard, 2. S. Lewis, 3. L. Barras.

MISSOURI.

A. Byrd, James Holman.
1. E. Dobyns, 2. W. G. Meriwether.

ARKANSAS.

John McClellen, Samuel M. Rutherford.
1. John Miller.

FIFTEENTH PRESIDENTIAL ELECTION—1845.

JAMES K. POLK was elected President, receiving the entire electoral vote of Maine, New Hampshire, New York, Pennsylvania, Virginia, South Carolina, Georgia, Louisiana, Mississippi, Indiana, Illinois, Alabama, Missouri, Arkansas, and Michigan—170. Henry Clay received the vote of Rhode Island, Massachusetts, Connecticut, Vermont, New Jersey, Delaware, Maryland, North Carolina,

Kentucky, Tennessee, and Ohio—105. GEORGE M. DALLAS was elected Vice-President, receiving 170 votes; while T. Frelinghuysen had 105. The Electors were:

MAINE.

James W. Bradbury, John Foster.
1. John Stickney,
2. Ichabod Jordan,
3. Alfred Pierce,
4. Levi Morrill,
5. J. A. Lowell,
6. Thomas Bartlett,
7. Nathaniel Robinson.

NEW HAMPSHIRE.

William Badger, Isaac Hale.
1. John McNeil,
2. E. Sawyer,
3. E. R. Currier,
4. J. L. Putnam.

MASSACHUSETTS.

Abbott Lawrence, A. R. Thompson.
1. Lewis Strong,
2. Charles Allen,
3. N. Appleton,
4. W. B. Calhoun,
5. J. P. Allen,
6. C. B. Rising,
7. Homer Bartlett,
8. Elijah Vose,
9. W. Baylies,
10. Seth Crowell.

RHODE ISLAND.

Benjamin Weaver, John Greene.
1. Stephen Steere,
2. N. F. Dixon.

CONNECTICUT.

Clark Bissell, N. O. Kellogg.
1. Charles W. Rockwell,
2. Joseph L. Gladding,
3. S. A. Foote,
4. Truman Smith.

VERMONT.

J. H. Harris, C. Coolidge.
1. John Pick,
2. Benjamin Swift,
3. C. Townsley,
4. E. Fairbanks.

NEW YORK.

Benjamin F. Butler, John Nellis.
1. Daniel S. Dickenson,
2. Clemence Whitaker,
3. Hugh Halsey,
4. A. Doane,
5. H. Thompson,
6. Thomas H. Hubbard,
7. George Douglass,
8. L. Pettengill,
9. Neil Cray,
10. William Mason,
11. W. S. Havemayer,
12. H. Potts,
13. J. J. Coddington,
14. Daniel Dana,
15. Daniel Johnson,
16. John Gillett,
17. J. Crawford,
18. J. E. Bogardus,
19. William Murrey,
20. J. Boynton,
21. JacobusHoerolnburgh,
22. E. Johnson,
23. J. L. Hogeboom,
24. John Lapham,
25. N. M. Martin,
26. J. D. Higgins,
27. J. K. Page,
28. R. H. Shankland,
29. John Savage,
30. J. Hascall, Jr.,
31. William Hedding,
32. Rufus H. Smith,
33. John Fay,
34. A. Hogeboom.

NEW JERSEY.

J. B. Aycrigg, John Emly.
1. Charles Reeves,
2. E. Y. Rogers,
3. E. Q. Keasbeg,
4. James Stewart,
5. A. Godwin.

PENNSYLVANIA.

Wilson McCandless, Jesse Sharp.
1. Asa Dimock,
2. N. W. Sample,
3. G. F. Lehman,
4. William Heidenrich,
5. Christian Kneass,
6. Conrad Shimer,
7. William H. Smith,
8. Stephen Baldy,
9. John Hill,
10. I. Brewster,
11. Samuel E. Leech,
12. George Schnable,
13. Samuel Camp,
14. N. B. Eldred,
15. William N. Irvine,
16. John Matthews,
17. James Woodburn,
18. William Patterson,
19. Hugh Montgomery,
20. A. Burke,
21. Isaac Ankeny,
22. John M. Gill,
23. C. Meyers,
24. Robert Orr.

DELAWARE.

Alfred Dupont, Thomas Davis.
1. Enoch Spruance.

MARYLAND.

William M. Gaither, William Price.
1. James B. Ricaud, 3. Thomas S. Alexander, 5. H. E. Wright,
2. C. K. Stewart, 4. A. W. Bradford, 6. Samuel Hambleton.

VIRGINIA.

John S. Millson, W. H. Roane.
1. Thomas Wallace, 6. G. B. Samuels, 11. William Smith,
2. Richard Coke, Jr., 7. A. Stuart, 12. R. A. Thompson,
3. R. H. Baptiste, 8. James Hoge, 13. William P. Taylor,
4. H. Bedinger, 9. Thomas J. Randolph, 14. Joseph Johnson,
5. William Daniel, 10. H. S. Kane, 15. William S. Morgan.

NORTH CAROLINA.

William W. Cheny, Josiah Collins.
1. R. B. Gilliam, 4. M. Q. Waddell, 7. James W. Osborne,
2. W. H. Washington, 5. John Kern, 8. J. Horton,
3. D. B. Baker, 6. A. H. Shepard, 9. John Baxter.

SOUTH CAROLINA.

F. H. Elmore, F. W. Pickens.
1. J. D. Wetherspoon, 4. T. B. Skipper, 6. William Cairn,
2. H. C. Young, 5. L. Boozer, 7. R. De Treville.
3. F. W. Huey,

GEORGIA.

Charles J. McDonald, Alfred Iverson.
1. B. Graves, 4. Charles Murphy, 7. William B. Wofford,
2. H. V. Johnson, 5. William F. Sandford, 8. Eli H. Baxter.
3. R. M. Charlton, 6. George W. Towers,

KENTUCKY.

P. Triplett, Greene Adams.
1. B. M. Crenshaw, 5. I. K. Underwood, 8. Leslie Coombs,
2. W. W. Southgate, 6. W. J. Gram, 9. John Kincard,
3. Benjamin Hardin, 7. R. A. Patterson, 10. L. W. Andrews.
4. W. R. Grigsby,

OHIO.

Thomas Corwin, Peter Hitchcock.
1. Bellamy Storer, 8. David Adams, 15. T. W. Bostwick,
2. Samson Mason, 9. Jos. Olds, 16. W. R. Sapp,
3. W. Bebb, 10. D. S. Norton, 17. J. W. Gill,
4. D. J. Cory, 11. W. W. Conklin, 18. Cyrus Spink,
5. A. Harlan, 12. James K. Holcombe, 19. J. H. Baldwin,
6. J. Scott, 13. H. Chapin, 20. W. S. Perkins,
7. R. W. Clark, 14. J. Crooks, 21. John Fuller.

TENNESSEE.

John Bell, Robert L. Caruthers.
1. G. A. Henry, 5. R. H. Hynds, 9. H. L. Bransford,
2. J. H. Crozier, 6. N. S. Brown, 10. William T. Haskell,
3. J. A. R. Nelson, 7. Thomas R. Jennings, 11. Robertson Topp.
4. D. L. Barringer, 8. J. D. Tyler,

LOUISIANA.

G. Leonard, J. B. Planché.
1. T. Landry, 3. A. E. Mouton, 4. S. W. Downes.
2. T. W. Scott,

MISSISSIPPI.

A. Fox, R. H. Boone.
1. J. W. Matthews,
2. Jos. Bell,
3. H. S. Foote,
4. Jefferson Davis.

INDIANA.

James G. Reed, G. N. Fitch.
1. William A. Bowles,
2. Elijah Newland,
3. J. M. Johnston,
4. Samuel E. Perkins,
5. William W. Wick,
6. P. C. Dunning,
7. Austin M. Puett,
8. H. W. Ellsworth,
9. Charles W. Cathcart,
10. John Gilbert.

ILLINOIS.

A. W. Cavarly, William A. Richardson.
1. J. D. Wood,
2. John Dement,
3. Willis Allen,
4. Isaac N. Arhold,
5. A. C. French,
6. John Calhoun,
7. Norman H. Purple.

MICHIGAN.

Lewis Beaufait, George Redfield.
1. P. S. Paulding,
2. Charles P. Burch,
3. Samuel Arford.

ALABAMA.

R. B. Wathall, Daniel Hubbard.
1. W. R. Hallett,
2. Dixon Hall,
3. Thomas S. Mays,
4. J. J. Winston,
5. J. A. Nooe,
6. Jeremiah Clemens,
7. William B. Martin.

ARKANSAS.

W. W. Izard, Solon Borland.
1. W. S. Oldham.

MISSOURI.

James S. Green, William A. Hall.
1. W. P. Hall,
2. William Shields,
3. W. C. Jones,
4. Franklin Cannon,
5. William L. Sublette.

SIXTEENTH PRESIDENTIAL ELECTION—1849.

ZACHARY TAYLOR was elected President, receiving the entire electoral vote of Massachusetts, Rhode Island, Connecticut, Vermont, New York, New Jersey, Pennsylvania, Delaware, Maryland, North Carolina, Georgia, Kentucky, Tennessee, Louisiana, and Florida—163 votes. Lewis Cass received the entire vote of Maine, New Hampshire, Virginia, South Carolina, Ohio, Mississippi, Indiana, Illinois, Alabama, Missouri, Arkansas, Michigan, Texas, Iowa, and Wisconsin—127 votes. MILLARD FILLMORE was elected Vice-President, receiving 163 votes; while William O. Butler received 127. The Electors were:

MAINE.

Rufus McIntire, Thomas D. Robinson.
1. H. J. Anderson,
2. A. Wiswell,
3. O. L. Sanborn,
4. A. Masters,
5. E. L. Osgood,
6. Asa Clark,
7. D. R. Straw.

NEW HAMPSHIRE.

Samuel Tilton, Jesse Bowers.
1. Joseph H. Smith,
2. J. Eastman,
3. R. H. Ayer,
4. Simeon Warner.

MASSACHUSETTS.

Levi Lincoln,
David Pingree.

1. E. Dwight,
2. D. Adams,
3. Albert Fearing,
4. Isaac Livermore.
5. B. F. Thomas,
6. M. Lawrence,
7. A. Howland,
8. H. A. S. Dearborn,
9. William Baylies,
10. William K. Easton.

RHODE ISLAND.

William Sprague,
George C. King.

1. I. T. Rhodes,
2. R. Babcock.

CONNECTICUT.

T. W. Williams,
Solomon Olmsted.

1. E. Jackson,
2. J. McClellan,
3. J. B. Ferris.

VERMONT.

Erastus Fairbanks,
Timothy Follett.

1. George T. Hodges,
2. A. Tracy,
3. A. L. Catlin,
4. E. Cleveland.

NEW YORK.

H. H. Ross,
George Griswold.

1. A. T. Rose,
2. George Benson,
3. J. M. Cross,
4. J. C. Cruger,
5. D. Lord,
6. T. D. Bull,
7. Jo. Hoxie,
8. J. S. Smith,
9. J. Whittemore,
10. Robert Dorlan,
11. J. Seymour,
12. C. F. Crosby,
13. J. McKie,
14. B. J. Clark,
15. S. Freeman,
16. J. A. Collier,
17. I. C. Duff,
18. J. Bradley,
19. William B. Welles,
20. Daniel Larkin,
21. Charles R. Barstow,
22. O. Poole,
23. D. Kellogg,
24. B. F. Harwood,
25. S. Francher,
26. J. Davenport,
27. E. Sheldon,
28. D. E. Sill,
29. M. Butterfield,
30. William Kelchum,
31. E. D. Smith,
32. O. P. Haskall,
33. Asa Chatfield,
34. Solomon Parmalee.

NEW JERSEY.

John Runk,
Isaac V. Brown.

1. J. Brick,
2. Robert V. Armstrong,
3. Charles Burroughs,
4. C. Howell,
5. Peter I. Ackerman.

PENNSYLVANIA.

Thomas M. T. McKennan,
Charles Snyder.

1. John P. Sanderson,
2. W. G. Hurly,
3. J. G. Clarkson,
4. Francis Tyler,
5. J. P. Wetherill,
6. H. Johnson,
7. J. M. Davis,
8. William Calder,
9. Thomas W. Duffield,
10. William McIlvaine,
11. J. Dungan,
12. Charles W. Fisher,
13. Daniel E. Hitner,
14. A. G. Curtin,
15. J. D. Steele,
16. Thomas R. Davidson,
17. I. Landes,
18. Joseph Markle,
19. Joseph Schomacher,
20. Daniel Agnew,
21. A. M. Loomis,
22. Thomas H. Sill,
23. Richard Irwin,
24. Samuel A. Purviance.

DELAWARE.

P. Reybold,
Samuel Cotts.

1. G. H. Wright.

MARYLAND.

W. L. Gaither,
A. G. Ege.

1. Joseph S. Cottman,
2. J. P. Roman,
3. J. M. S. Causin,
4. J. M. Starris,
5. B. C. Wicker,
6. J. C. Derickson.

Virginia.

J. S. Millson, R. G. Scott.

1. F. E. Rives,
2. Henry A. Wise,
3. H. L. Hopkins,
4. Thomas Sloane,
5. W. P. Bocock,
6. G. B. Samuels,
7. W. M. Tredway,
8. John Letcher,
9. S. F. Leake,
10. John B. Floyd,
11. J. S. Barbour, Sr.,
12. A. G. Pendleton,
13. H. A. Washington,
14. Samuel L. Haynes,
15. O. W. Largefit.

North Carolina.

Kenneth Rayner, H. W. Miller.

1. Edward Stanley,
2. W. H. Washington,
3. George Davis,
4. J. Winslow,
5. John Kerr,
6. Rawley Galloway,
7. Jas. W. Osborne,
8. Tod R. Caldwell,
9. John Baxton.

South Carolina.

Benjamin F. Perry, Alexander Ervins.

1. Thomas Lehre,
2. J. L. Manning,
3. P. C. Caldwell,
4. W. J. Hanna,
5. N. R. Eaves,
6. J. B. Campbell,
7. Benjamin G. Allston.

Georgia.

William Terrell, Seaton Grantland.

1. H. W. Sharpe,
2. W. Aiken,
3. William H. Crawford,
4. Asbury Hull,
5. A. W. Redding,
6. Y. P. King,
7. William Moseley,
8. George Stapleton.

Kentucky.

A. Dixon, M. V. Thomson.

1. L. Lindsay,
2. J. L. Johnson,
3. F. E. McLean,
4. William Chenault,
5. T. W. Lisle,
6. M. D. McHenry,
7. B. R. Young,
8. Leslie Coombs,
9. A. Trumbo,
10. W. C. Marshall.

Tennessee.

James C. Jones, John Netherland.

1. T. A. R. Nelson,
2. A. G. Watkins,
3. R. B. Brabson,
4. John L. Goodall,
5. William Kercheval,
6. S. E. Rose,
7. J. S. Brien,
8. William Cullom,
9. A. Goodrich,
10. G. D. Searcy,
11. C. H. Williams.

Ohio.

L. Byington, Samuel Starkweather.

1. J. Sniden,
2. George Kesling,
3. J. Kinney,
4. G. Volney Dorsey,
5. C. M. Godfrey,
6. S. Diffenderfer,
7. S. M. Littell,
8. D. T. Swinney,
9. Lewis Anderson,
10. John Lidey,
11. William Lawrence,
12. William J. Fry,
13. Joseph Burns,
14. W. McDonald,
15. D. A. Starkweather,
16. J. B. Butler,
17. H. B. Payne,
18. A. Ives,
19. John Caldwell,
20. John Glover,
21. Van S. Murphy.

Louisiana.

Jacques Joutant, J. P. Benjamin.

1. M. J. Carcia,
2. C. Adams, Jr.,
3. John Moore,
4. J. G. Campbell.

Mississippi.

J. A. Quitman, J. W. Chalmers.

1. D. B. Wright,
2. J. A. Ventress,
3. William McWillie,
4. G. W. L. Smith.

INDIANA.

Robert Dale Owen, E. M. Chamberlain.
1. N. Albertson, 5. James Ritchey, 8. Daniel Mace,
2. C. L. Dunham, 6. George W. Carr, 9. G. N. Fitch,
3. William M. McCarty, 7. I. M. Hanna, 10. A. J. Harlan.
4. Charles H. Test,

ILLINOIS.

I. Manning, Ferris Foreman.
1. M. Sweney, 4. H. W. Vandervier, 6. M. E. Hollister,
2. C. Lansing, 5. S. S. Hayes, 7. W. L. Furgerson.
3. William Martin,

ALABAMA.

John A. Winston, Columbus W. Lee.
1. J. E. Saunders, 4. James Armstrong, 6. C. C. Clay, Jr.,
2. Lewis M. Stone, 5. J. J. Seibels, 7. James F. Dowdell.
3. Francis S. Lyon,

MISSOURI.

J. C. Welborn, G. D. Hall.
1. Abraham McKinney, 3. E. B. Ewing, 5. Tristam Polk.
2. B. T. Massey, 4. James H. Rolfe,

ARKANSAS.

John Martin, John S. Krane.
1. James Yell.

MICHIGAN.

John S. Barry, L. M. Mason.
1. Rix Robinson, 2. H. C. Thurbur, 3. William T. Howell.

FLORIDA.

Jackson Morton, Samuel Spencer.
1. J. H. McIntosh.

TEXAS.

James B. Miller, T. G. Brooks.
1. William C. Young, 2. M. A. Dooley.

IOWA.

A. C. Dodge, J. J. Selman.
1. Joseph Williams, 2. Lincoln Clark.

WISCONSIN.

F. Huebschmann, Samuel F. Nicholas.
1. William Dinwiddie, 2. D. P. Mapes.

SEVENTEENTH PRESIDENTIAL ELECTION—1853.

FRANKLIN PIERCE was elected President, receiving the entire electoral vote of Maine, New Hampshire, Rhode Island, Connecticut, New York, New Jersey, Pennsylvania, Delaware, Maryland, Virginia, North Carolina, South Carolina, Georgia, Florida, Alabama, Mississippi, Louisiana, Texas, Arkansas, Ohio, Michigan, Indiana, Illinois, Missouri, Iowa, Wisconsin, and California—296. Winfield Scott received the vote of Vermont, Massachusetts, Tennessee, and Kentucky—42. WILLIAM R. KING was elected Vice-President, receiving 254 votes; while William A. Graham had 42. The Electors were:

MAINE.

R. McIntire, J. C. Talbot.
1. G. F. Shepley, 3. J. H. Fuller, 5. D. Richardson,
2. R. Lowell, 4. O. Moses, 6. J. W. Tabor.

NEW HAMPSHIRE.

H. Hubbard, L. Jones.

1. J. A. Douglass,
2. S. Webster,
3. N. B. Baker.

VERMONT.

Portus Baxter, A. P. Lyman.

1. E. P. Walton,
2. E. Kirkland,
3. L. Adams.

MASSACHUSETTS.

R. C. Winthrop, J. H. W. Page.

1. George Bliss,
2. J. Gardner,
3. R. G. Shaw,
4. George Coggswell,
5. E. Torrey,
6. George A. Crocker,
7. Amos Lawrence,
8. Daniel C. Baker,
9. J. Coggin,
10. R. Bullock,
11. E. R. Colt.

RHODE ISLAND.

George Turner, A. Ballou.

1. A. Eddy,
2. J. Spink.

CONNECTICUT.

Thomas H. Seymour, N. Belcher.

1. A. P. Hyde,
2. Charles Parker,
3. S. Bingham,
4. William F. Taylor.

NEW YORK.

S. B. Piper, Charles O'Connor.

1. P. S. Crooke,
2. E. B. Litchfield,
3. R. T. Compton,
4. J. M. Marsh,
5. I. Murphy,
6. William H. Cornell,
7. G. F. Conover,
8. A. F. Vache,
9. E. Suffern,
10. Alexander Thompson,
11. Zadock Pratt,
12. L. Van Buren,
13. J. Pierson,
14. J. W. Bishop,
15. C. Vosburgh,
16. Thomas Crook,
17. W. C. Crain,
18. William Taylor,
19. C. S. Grinnell,
20. W. C. Beardsley,
21. L. J. Walworth,
22. D. A. Ogden,
23. T. H. Hubbard,
24. T. G. McDowell,
25. S. G. Hathaway,
26. F. C. Divinny,
27. D. De Wolf,
28. D. Warners,
29. J. C. Collins,
30. T. B. Skinner,
31. William Vandervoort,
32. W. L. G. Smith,
33. Benjamin Chamberlain.

NEW JERSEY.

Peter D. Vroom, William Wright.

1. William S. Bowen,
2. G. Black,
3. P. B. Kennedy,
4. J. N. Taylor,
5. E. A. Stevens.

PENNSYLVANIA.

H. McCandless, Robert Patterson.

1. N. B. Eldred,
2. Peter Logan,
3. George H. Martin,
4. I. Miller,
5. F. W. Bockius,
6. R. McCoy, Jr.,
7. A. Apple,
8. N. Strickland,
9. A. Peters,
10. D. Fister,
11. R. E. James,
12. J. McReynolds,
13. Pardon Damon,
14. H. C. Eyer,
15. J. Clayton,
16. Isaac Robinson,
17. H. Fetten,
18. J. Burnside,
19. M. McCaslin,
20. J. McDonald,
21. W. S. Callahan,
22. A. Burke,
23. William Dunn,
24. J. S. McCalmont,
25. George K. Barrett.

DELAWARE.

J. Merritt, William I. Clark.

1. Henry Bacon.

MARYLAND.

R. M. McLane, C. Humphries.

1. J. Parren,
2. R. H. Alvey,
3. Carroll Spence,
4. C. J. M. Gwinne,
5. J. A. Wickes,
6. E. K. Wilson.

Virginia.

M. Cooke, A. H. Dillard.

1. T. Rives,
2. W. E. Flournoy,
3. J. Goode, Jr.,
4. R. G. Scott,
5. H. A. Wise,
6. R. L. Montague,
7. James Barbour,
8. R. Tucker,
9. George E. Deneale,
10. James McDowell,
11. J. B. Floyd,
12. M. H. Johnson,
13. Z. Kidwell.

North Carolina.

James C. Dobbin, William H. Thomas.

1. Burton Craige,
2. W. F. Leak,
3. Robert P. Dick,
4. A. Rencher,
5. L. O. B. Branch,
6. Samuel J. Person,
7. D. G. W. Ward,
8. Thomas Bragg.

South Carolina.

G. Cannon, Thomas P. Brockman.

1. J. H. Adams,
2. R. F. W. Allston,
3. I. F. Marshall,
4. M. E. Carn,
5. W. D. Porter,
6. C. G. Memminger.

Georgia.

Wilson Lumpkin, H. V. Johnson.

1. T. M. Forrman,
2. R. H. Clarke,
3. H. G. Lamar,
4. H. A. Haralson,
5. I. E. Brown,
6. William L. Mitchell,
7. R. W. Flournoy,
8. William Schley.

Florida.

Jesse Coe, McQueen McIntosh.

1. J. C. Smith.

Alabama.

J. A. Winston, E. Saunders.

1. F. S. Lyon,
2. J. S. Seibels,
3. C. W. Lee,
4. L. M. Stone,
5. Jas. Armstrong,
6. C. C. Clay, Jr.,
7. J. S. Dowdell.

Mississippi.

E. C. Wilkinson, A. M. Jackson.

1. W. H. Johnson,
2. O. K. Singleton,
3. J. H. R. Taylor,
4. U. S. Featherston,
5. Hiram Casseday.

Louisiana.

E. Warren Moise, T. G. Davidson.

1. J. B. Planché,
2. Thomas O. Moore,
3. T. Landry,
4. R. W. Richardson.

Texas.

George W. Smyth, R. S. Neighbors.

1. L. D. Evans.

Arkansas.

H. M. Rector, J. A. Carter.

1. T. B. Flournoy,
2. B. T. Duval.

Tennessee.

G. A. Henry, William T. Haskell.

1. N. G. Taylor,
2. H. Maynard,
3. George Brown,
4. S. M. Fite,
5. J. Stokes,
6. J. M. Davidson,
7. E. R. Osborne,
8. J. A. McEwen,
9. A. G. Shrewsbury,
10. J. R. Moseby.

Kentucky.

J. F. Bell, Charles S. Morehead.

1. L. Anderson,
2. J. S. McFarland,
3. J. G. Rogers,
4. Thomas E. Bramlette,
5. J. L. Helm,
6. C. F. Burnan,
7. Thomas F. Marshall,
8. J. Rodman,
9. L. M. Cox,
10. Thomas B. Stevenson.

OHIO.

W. McLean,		William Palmer.
1. B. Burns,	8. H. J. Jewett,	15. Joseph Kyle,
2. J. B. Damble,	9. E. G. Dial,	16. J. Finley,
3. Charles Rule,	10. W. O. Key,	17. F. Cleveland,
4. William Golden,	11. L. H. Steedman,	18. S. D. Harris,
5. G. W. Stokes,	12. C. H. Mitchener,	19. E. T. Wilder,
6. O. Keyser,	13. C. J. Orton,	20. E. H. Haines,
7. R. C. Cunningham,	14. E. T. McArtor,	21. B. T. Johnson.

MICHIGAN.

J. S. Barry,		D. J. Campau.
1. A. Edwards,	3. Salmer Sharpe,	4. John Stockton.
2. William McCauley,		

INDIANA.

John Pettit,		Nathaniel Balton.
1. J. H. Lane,	5. Jas. S. Athon,	9. E. Dumont,
2. A. F. Morrison,	6. George B. Buell,	10. A. H. Brown,
3. J. F. Read,	7. Jas. S. Hester,	11. J. M. Talbott.
4. W. C. Larabee,	8. Samuel A. Hall,	

ILLINOIS.

J. A. McClelland,		Richard J. Hamilton.
1. John Calhoun,	4. Vierby Benedict,	7. Jas. Mahon,
2. E. G. Sanger,	5. D. L. Gregg,	8. Joseph Knox,
3. E. P. Ferry,	6. E. O'Melveny,	9. C. A. Warren.

MISSOURI.

E. D. Bevritt,		Alexander Kayser.
1. H. F. Gary,	4. J. D. Stevenson,	6. J. M. Gatewood,
2. Wm. D. McCracken,	5. C. F. Holly,	7. Robert E. Acock.
3. C. F. Jackson,		

IOWA.

J. E. Fletcher,		George H. Williams.
1. A. Hall,	2. W. E. Leffingwell.	

WISCONSIN.

M. M. Cothren,		Charles Billinghurst.
1. B. Brown,	2. Philo White,	3. S. Clark.

CALIFORNIA.

W. S. Sherwood,		Thomas J. Henley.
1. J. W. Gregory,	2. Andrew Pico.	

EIGHTEENTH PRESIDENTIAL ELECTION—1857.

JAMES BUCHANAN was elected President, receiving the entire electoral vote of New Jersey, Pennsylvania, Delaware, Virginia, North Carolina, South Carolina, Georgia, Kentucky, Tennessee, Louisiana, Mississippi, Indiana, Illinois, Alabama, Missouri, Arkansas, Florida, Texas, and California—173. John C. Fremont received the entire vote of Maine, New Hampshire, Massachusetts, Rhode Island, Connecticut, Vermont, New York, Ohio, Michigan, Iowa, and Wisconsin—114. Millard Fillmore received the vote of Maryland—8. JOHN C. BRECKINRIDGE was elected Vice-President, receiving 173 votes; while W. L. Dayton had 114, and A. J. Donelson 8. The Electors were:

MAINE.

Noah Smith, Jr.,		S. Perham.
1. James Morton,	3. K. Crockett,	5. A. P. Emerson,
2. Isaac Gross,	4. E. Swan,	6. M. H. Pike.

NEW HAMPSHIRE.

W. H. H. Bailey, Thomas L. Whitton.

1. Daniel Clarke, 2. Thomas M. Edwards, 3. J. H. White.

VERMONT.

W. C. Bradley, George W. Strong.

1. L. Brainard, 2. John Porter, 3. Portus Baxter.

MASSACHUSETTS.

Thomas Colt, Julius Rockwell.

1. J. Vinson,
2. A. B. Wheeler,
3. G. R. Russell,
4. George Odiorne,
5. L. B. Marsh,
6. George H. Devereux,
7. James M. Usher,
8. J. Nesmith,
9. J. S. C. Knowlton,
10. Charles E. Forbes,
11. Franklin Ripley.

RHODE ISLAND.

E. W. Lawton, Isaac Saunders.

1. William P. Bullock, 2. William D. Brayton.

CONNECTICUT.

H. Dutton, J. Catlin.

1. Thomas Clark,
2. E. Spencer,
3. Wm. A. Buckingham,
4. S. W. Gold.

NEW YORK.

M. H. Grinnell, Thomas Carnley.

1. J. S. Wadsworth,
2. E. Field,
3. M. Tompkins,
4. J. P. Jones,
5. J. P. Stanton,
6. E. Cooke,
7. James Kennedy,
8. R. A. Barnard,
9. H. Raster,
10. J. G. McMurray,
11. J. Kelly,
12. H. H. Van Dyck,
13. J. S. Belcher,
14. J. C. Hulbert,
15. D. D. Conover,
16. J. D. Kingsland,
17. S. Stilwell,
18. D. Cady,
19. R. S. Hughston,
20. W. S. Sayre,
21. J. S. Lynch,
22. D. H. Marsh,
23. A. Davenport,
24. Le Roy Morgan,
25. E. Burnham,
26. M. H. Lawrence,
27. J. B. Williams,
28. Isaac L. Endress,
29. F. Clarke,
30. W. S. Mallory,
31. W. Keep,
32. R. Wheeler,
33. Delos E. Sill.

NEW JERSEY.

E. A. Stevens, G. F. Fort.

1. Benjamin F. Lee,
2. H. L. Little,
3. D. Von Fleet,
4. H. A. Ford,
5. George W. Savage.

PENNSYLVANIA.

Charles K. Buckalew, W. McCandless.

1. G. W. Nebinger,
2. P. Butler,
3. E. Wartman,
4. William H. Witte,
5. J. McNair,
6. J. H. Brinton,
7. D. Laury,
8. Charles Kessler,
9. James Patterson,
10. Isaac Stenker,
11. F. W. Hughes,
12. T. Osterhout,
13. A. Edinger,
14. R. Wilbur,
15. George A. Crawford,
16. James Black,
17. H. J. Stahle,
18. J. D. Roddy,
19. J. Turney,
20. James A. T. Buchanan,
21. William Wilkins,
22. J. C. Campbell,
23. Thomas Cunningham,
24. J. Keattey,
25. V. Phelps.

DELAWARE.

George C. Gordon, H. Ridgeley.

1. Charles Wright.

MARYLAND.

J. D. Roman, James Wallace.

1. R. Goldsborough,
2. E. H. Webster,
3. C. L. L. Leary,
4. Thomas Swann,
5. F. A. Schley,
6. A. R. Sollers.

VIRGINIA.

E. W. Massenburg, A. H. Dillard.

1. T. H. Campbell,
2. James Garland,
3. J. Goode, Jr.,
4. Alexander Jones,
5. William B. Taliaferro,
6. R. L. Montague,
7. James Barbour,
8. J. R. Tucker,
9. J. J. Harris,
10. A. G. Pendleton,
11. J. B. Floyd,
12. S. L. Hayes,
13. Sherrard Clemens.

NORTH CAROLINA.

H. M. Shaw, S. P. Hill.

1. W. F. Martin,
2. William P. Blow,
3. M. B. Smith,
4. G. H. Wilder,
5. S. E. Williams,
6. Thomas Settle, Jr.,
7. R. P. Waring,
8. W. W. Avery.

SOUTH CAROLINA.

J. A. Inglis, J. L. Noell.

1. W. A. Owens,
2. B. T. Watts,
3. J. J. Pickens,
4. J. Chesnut, Jr.,
5. F. W. Pickens,
6. J. L. Manning.

GEORGIA.

W. H. Stiles, J. N. Ramsay.

1. J. L. Harris,
2. L. J. Gartrell,
3. Thomas M. Fournan,
4. J. W. Lewis,
5. S. Hall,
6. J. P. Simmons,
7. J. P. Saffold,
8. T. W. Thomas.

FLORIDA.

M. A. Long, W. D. Barnes.

1. George W. Call.

ALABAMA.

W. L. Yancey, J. W. A. Sandford.

1. L. P. Walker,
2. J. G. Barr,
3. A. B. Meek,
4. J. D. Rathers,
5. J. L. Pugh,
6. W. O. Winston,
7. J. L. M. Curry.

MISSISSIPPI.

C. S. Tarpley, J. W. Matthews.

1. J. F. Cushman,
2. J. A. Orr,
3. B. Matthews,
4. William M. Estelle,
5. H. T. Ellett.

LOUISIANA.

C. J. Villerre, W. A. Elmore.

1. T. Landry,
2. J. McVea,
3. T. O. Moore,
4. H. Gray.

TEXAS.

William R. Scurry, M. D. Ector.

1. A. J. Hood,
2. A. J. Hamilton.

ARKANSAS.

L. H. Hempstead, N. B. Burrow.

1. J. J. Green,
2. J. McCoy.

TENNESSEE.

W. H. Polk, D. M. Key.

1. J. G. Harris,
2. E. L. Gardenhire,
3. S. Pawel,
4. E. A. Keeble,
5. J. M. McHenry,
6. J. H. Thomas,
7. J. J. Brown,
8. G. G. Poindexter,
9. J. D. C. Atkins,
10. D. M. Currin.

KENTUCKY.

E. Hise, J. A. Finn.

1. J. W. Stevenson,
2. S. Cravens,
3. I. T. Hawkins,
4. B. Magoffin,
5. George W. Williams,
6. Benjamin F. Rice,
7. William D. Reed,
8. R. W. Woolley,
9. R. H. Stanton,
10. Hiram Kelsey.

Ohio.

C. B. Smith, J. B. Stallo.

1. J. Perkins,
2. R. M. Corwine,
3. P. Odlin,
4. J. S. Conklin,
5. William Taylor,
6. E. P. Evans,
7. W. H. P. Denny,
8. J. R. Hubbell,
9. R. G. Pennington,
10. F. Cleaveland,
11. J. Welch,
12. D. Humphrey,
13. H. D. Cooke,
14. E. Pardee,
15. J. M. Hodge,
16. Davis Green,
17. M. Pennington,
18. J. S. Herrick,
19. A. Wilcox,
20. J. Dumas,
21. A. E. Burs.

Michigan.

F. C. Beaman, O. Johnson.

1. H. Chamberlain,
2. W. H. Withey,
3. C. H. Millen,
4. Thomas J. Drake.

Indiana.

G. N. Fitch, M. M. Ray.

1. S. H. Buskirk,
2. J. M. Hanna,
3. W. T. Parrett,
4. I. S. McClelland,
5. S. K. Wolfe,
6. O. Evarts,
7. S. W. Short,
8. F. P. Randall,
9. D. D. Jones,
10. S. Mickle,
11. E. Johnson.

Illinois.

A. M. Herrington, C. H. Constable.

1. M. L. Joslyn,
2. Hugh Maher,
3. R. Holloway,
4. I. P. Richmond,
5. S. W. Moulton,
6. O. B. Ficklin,
7. W. A. J. Sparks,
8. J. A. Logan.

Iowa.

D. F. Miller, H. T. Downey.

1. W. M. Stone,
2. H. O. Connor.

California.

A. Olvera, George Freaner.

1. P. Della Torre,
2. A. C. Bradford.

Missouri.

J. B. Henderson, J. B. Benjamin.

1. W. Y. Slack,
2. J. N. Burns,
3. J. W. Torbert,
4. J. T. Coffee,
5. F. Kenneth,
6. W. D. McCracken,
7. L. Cooke.

Wisconsin.

E. D. Holton, W. D. McIndoe.

1. I. H. Knowlton,
2. Billie Williams,
3. G. Menzel.

NINETEENTH PRESIDENTIAL ELECTION—1861.

Abraham Lincoln was elected President, receiving the vote of California, Connecticut, Illinois, Indiana, Iowa, Maine, Massachusetts, Michigan, Minnesota, New Hampshire, New Jersey (4), New York, Ohio, Oregon, Pennsylvania, Rhode Island, Vermont, and Wisconsin—180. John C. Breckinridge received the vote of Alabama, Arkansas, Delaware, Florida, Georgia, Louisiana, Maryland, Mississippi, North Carolina, South Carolina, and Texas—72. John Bell received the entire vote of Kentucky, Tennessee, and Virginia—39. Stephen A. Douglas received the vote of Missouri and New Jersey (3)—12. Hannibal Hamlin was elected Vice-President, receiving 180, while Joseph Lane received 72, Edward Everett 39, and Herschel V. Johnson 12. The Electors were:

Maine.

William Willis, Abner Coburn.

1. Louis O. Cowan,
2. Daniel Howes,
3. George W. Pickering,
4. William McGilvery,
5. Andrew Peters,
6. William M. Reed.

NEW HAMPSHIRE.

John Sullivan, Ebenezer Stevens.

1. David Gillis,
2. Nathaniel Tolles,
3. Daniel Blaisdell.

MASSACHUSETTS.

George Morey, Alfred Macy.

1. James H. Mitchell,
2. John M. Forbes,
3. Charles Mattoon,
4. John G. Whittier,
5. John Nesmith,
6. Charles B. Hall,
7. Reuben A. Chapman,
8. Gerry W. Cochrane,
9. Amasa Walker,
10. Peleg W. Chandler,
11. Charles Field.

RHODE ISLAND.

Thomas G. Turner, Latimer W. Ballou.

1. Elisha Harris,
2. David Buffum.

VERMONT.

William Henry, Henry G. Root.

1. Joseph Warner,
2. Edward A. Cahoon,
3. D. W. C. Clarke.

CONNECTICUT.

Chauncey F. Cleveland, Roger S. Baldwin.

1. Samuel Austin,
2. Augustus Brandegee,
3. Benjamin Douglas,
4. Frederick Wood.

NEW YORK.

William C. Bryant, James O. Putnam.

1. John A. King,
2. Andrew Carrigan,
3. Frederick Kapp,
4. Wm. A. Darling,
5. Rufus H. King,
6. John F. Winslow,
7. N. Edson Sheldon,
8. Henry Churchill,
9. Benjamin N. Huntington,
10. John J. Foote,
11. William Van Marter,
12. Frank L. Jones,
13. Ezra M. Parsons,
14. John Greiner, Jr.,
15. Edwards W. Fiske,
16. James Kelly,
17. Washington Smith,
18. William H. Robertson,
19. Jacob B. Carpenter,
20. Jacob H. Ten Eyck,
21. Robert S. Hale,
22. James R. Allaben,
23. Sherman D. Phelps,
24. Hiram Dewey,
25. John E. Seeley,
26. Jas. S. Wadsworth,
27. Charles C. Parker,
28. James Parker,
29. Sigismund Kaufmann,
30. George M. Grier,
31. Abijah Beckwith,
32. James L. Voorhees,
33. Elisha S. Whalen.

NEW JERSEY.

William Cook, Joel Parker.

1. Theodore Runyon,
2. Joseph C. Hornblower,
3. George H. Brown,
4. Edward W. Ivins,
5. Charles E. Elmer.

PENNSYLVANIA.

James Pollock, Thomas M. Howe.

1. Edward C. Knight,
2. Robert P. King,
3. Henry Bumm,
4. Robert M. Foust,
5. Nathan Hilles,
6. John M. Broomall,
7. James W. Fuller,
8. David E. Stout,
9. Francis W. Christ,
10. David Mumma, Jr.,
11. David Taggart,
12. Thomas R. Hull,
13. Francis B. Penneman,
14. Ulysses Mercur,
15. George Bressler,
16. A. Brady Sharpe,
17. Daniel O. Gehr,
18. Samuel Calvin,
19. Edgar Cowan,
20. William McKennan,
21. John M. Kirkpatrick,
22. James Kerr,
23. Richard P. Roberts,
24. Henry Souther,
25. John Greer.

DELAWARE.

Samuel Jefferson, John Mustard.

1. Robert B. Houston.

MARYLAND.

E. Lewis Lowe, James L. Martin.

1. Elias Griswold,
2. John Brooke Boyle,
3. Joshua Vansant,
4. T. Parkin Scott,
5. John Ritchie,
6. James S. Franklin.

VIRGINIA.

Thomas Bruce,
Marmaduke Johnson.

1. Lemuel J. Bowdon,
2. John J. Jackson,
3. F. T. Anderson,
4. B. H. Shackelford,
5. A. B. Caldwell,
6. L. H. Chandler,
7. Joseph Christian,
8. William Lamb,
9. John R. Edmunds,
10. James Lyons,
11. Richard B. Claybrook,
12. William H. Anthony,
13. J. W. Massie.

NORTH CAROLINA.

Alfred M. Scales,
Edward Naham Haywood.

1. John W. Moore,
2. William B. Rodman,
3. William A. Allen,
4. A. W. Venable,
5. J. R. McLean,
6. John M. Clement,
7. J. A. Fox,
8. John A. Dickson.

SOUTH CAROLINA.

Andrew P. Calhoun,
William E. Martin.

1. Thomas Y. Simmes,
2. John Williams,
3. George P. Elliott,
4. Tilman Watson,
5. Joseph F. Gist,
6. Robert G. McCaw.

GEORGIA.

A. H. Colquitt,
H. R. Jackson.

1. Peter Cone,
2. William M. Slaughter,
3. O. C. Gibson,
4. Hugh Buchanan,
5. Lewis Tumlin,
6. Hardy Strickland,
7. W. A. Lofton,
8. William M. McIntosh.

KENTUCKY.

W. H. Wadsworth,
E. L. Van Winkle.

1. Q. Q. Quigley,
2. S. A. Seavell,
3. William Sampson,
4. W. A. Hoskins,
5. Phil Lee,
6. William M. Fulkerson,
7. William C. Bullock,
8. John M. Harlan,
9. John B. Huston,
10. W. S. Rankin.

TENNESSEE.

Baylie Peyton,
N. G. Taylor.

1. J. W. Deaderich,
2. O. P. Temple,
3. Alfred Caldwell,
4. S. S. Stanton,
5. Ed. J. Golloday,
6. William F. Kercheval,
7. John C. Brown,
8. John F. House,
9. Alvin Hawkins,
10. Benjamin D. Nabors.

OHIO.

Frederick Hassaurek,
Joseph M. Root.

1. Benjamin Eggleston,
2. William M. Dickson,
3. Frank McWhiney,
4. John Riley Knox,
5. Dresden W. H. Howard,
6. John M. Kellum,
7. Nelson Rush,
8. Abraham Thomson,
9. John F. Henkle,
10. Hezekiah S. Bundy,
11. Daniel B. Stewart,
12. Richard P. L. Baber,
13. John Beatty,
14. Willard Slocum,
15. Joseph Ankeny,
16. Edward Ball,
17. John A. Davenport,
18. William K. Upham,
19. Samuel B. Philbrick,
20. George W. Brooke,
21. Norman K. Mackenzie.

LOUISIANA.

O. Rosseau,
B. Avegno.

1. Trasimond Landry,
2. B. B. Simmes,
3. J. G. Olivier,
4. W. M. Levy.

MISSISSIPPI.

A. K. Blythe,
J. A. Green.

1. Thomas W. Harris,
2. Richard Harrison,
3. P. F. Liddell,
4. J. B. Chrisman,
5. Livingston Mims.

INDIANA.

John L. Mansfield, Cyrus M. Allen.

1. M. C. Hunter,
2. Nelson Trusler,
3. John Hanna,
4. James N. Tyner,
5. David O. Dailey,
6. Will Cumback,
7. John W. Ray,
8. John H. Farquhar,
9. Reuben H. Riley,
10. Samuel A. Huff,
11. Isaac Jenkinson.

ILLINOIS.

Leonard Sweet, Allen C. Fuller.

1. Lawrence Weldon,
2. James Stark,
3. Henry P. H. Bromwell,
4. John M. Palmer,
5. William B. Plato,
6. William P. Kellogg,
7. James C. Conkling,
8. Thomas G. Allen,
9. John Olney.

ALABAMA.

David Hubbard, John T. Morgan.

1. J. S. Dickinson,
2. Ely S. Shorter,
3. C. A. Battle,
4. J. W. Garrott,
5. John S. Kennedy,
6. R. C. Brickell,
7. R. W. Cobb.

MISSOURI.

John B. Henderson, Robert S. Bevier.

1. John B. Hale,
2. James F. V. Thomson,
3. George G. Vest,
4. Mordecai Oliver,
5. E. T. Wingo,
6. Francis Hagan,
7. Richard H. Stevens.

ARKANSAS.

William W. Floyd, Theodric F. Sorrels.

1. William W. Leake,
2. George W. Taylor.

MICHIGAN.

Hezekiah G. Wells, Rufus Hasmer.

1. George W. Lee,
2. Edward Dorsch,
3. Philotas Hayden,
4. Augustus Coburn.

FLORIDA.

George W. Call, J. Patton Anderson.

1. J. Myrick Gorrie.

TEXAS.

M. D. Graham, Thomas M. Waul.

1. A. T. Rainey,
2. John A. Wharton.

IOWA.

Fitz Henry Warren, Joseph A. Chapline.

1. M. L. McPherson,
2. Charles Pomeroy.

WISCONSIN.

Walter McIndoe, Bradford Rixford.

1. J. Allen Barber,
2. William W. Vaughan,
3. Herman Linderman.

CALIFORNIA.

Charles A. Washburn, W. H. Weeks.

1. Charles A. Tuttle,
2. Antonio M. Pico.

MINNESOTA.

Stephen Miller, William Pfaender.

1. Clark W. Thompson,
2. Charles McClure.

OREGON.

T. J. Dryer, B. J. Pengra.

1. William H. Watkins.

THE SUPREME COURT OF THE UNITED STATES.

CHIEF JUSTICES.

JOHN JAY, of New York, appointed by the President, with the advice and consent of the Senate, September 26, 1789. Nominated April 16, and confirmed April 19, 1794, Envoy Extraordinary to England. Resigned as Chief Justice. Successor appointed July 1, 1795.

JOHN RUTLEDGE, of South Carolina, appointed July 1, 1795, in recess of Senate, in place of John Jay, resigned, and presided on the bench at August Term, 1795. Nominated December 10, and rejected by the Senate December 15, 1795.

WILLIAM CUSHING, of Massachusetts. Nomination confirmed and appointed, &c., January 27, 1796, in place of John Jay, resigned. Declined the appointment. He was then an Associate Justice.

OLIVER ELLSWORTH, of Connecticut. Nomination confirmed and appointed, &c., March 4, 1796, in place of W. Cushing, declined. Appointed Envoy Extraordinary and Minister Plenipotentiary to France, February 27, 1799. He presided on the bench at the August Term, 1799. Proceeded on his mission to France, November 3, 1799. Resigned as Chief Justice. Successor appointed December 19, 1800.

JOHN JAY, Governor of New York. Nomination confirmed and appointed, &c., December 19, 1800, in place of Oliver Ellsworth, resigned. Declined the appointment.

JOHN MARSHALL, Secretary of State.* Nomination confirmed January 27, and appointed, &c., January 31, 1801, in place of John Jay, declined. Died in 1835.

ROGER B. TANEY, of Maryland. Nomination confirmed and appointed, &c., March 15, 1836, in the place of John Marshall, deceased. Died in Washington City, October 12, 1864.

ASSOCIATE JUSTICES

OF THE SUPREME COURT OF THE UNITED STATES.

JOHN RUTLEDGE, of South Carolina. Nomination confirmed and appointed September 26, 1789. Resigned, and Thomas Johnson appointed.

WILLIAM CUSHING, of Massachusetts. Nomination confirmed September 26, and appointed September 27, 1789. Died, and Levi Lincoln appointed.

JAMES WILSON, of Pennsylvania. Nomination confirmed September 26, and appointed September 29, 1789. Died, and Bushrod Washington appointed.

JOHN BLAIR, of Virginia. Nomination confirmed September 26, and appointed September 30, 1789. Resigned, and Samuel Chase appointed.

ROBERT H. HARRISON, of Maryland. Nomination confirmed September 26, 1789. Resigned, and James Iredell appointed.

* John Marshall, Secretary of State, was nominated to the Senate as Chief Justice, January 20, 1801, was confirmed on the 27th, commissioned on the 31st, and presided on the bench of the Supreme Court from the 4th to the 9th of February, or during February Term, 1801. From a message of the President to Congress, accompanied by a report from John Marshall, Secretary of State, dated February 27, 1801, it appears that he also continued to act in the latter capacity until that day, and from other circumstances, that he continued to act as such until March 3, 1801, on which day the then administration terminated.

JAMES IREDELL, of North Carolina. Appointed in recess of Senate, in place of Robert H. Harrison, resigned. Nomination confirmed and appointed February 10, 1790. Died, and Alfred Moore appointed.

THOMAS JOHNSON, of Maryland. Appointed August 5, 1791, in recess of Senate, in place of John Rutledge, resigned. Nomination confirmed and appointed November 7, 1791. Resigned, and William Paterson appointed.

WILLIAM PATERSON, Governor of New Jersey. Nomination confirmed and appointed March 4, 1793, in place of Thomas Johnson, resigned. Died, and Brockholst Livingston appointed.

SAMUEL CHASE, of Maryland. Nomination confirmed and appointed January 27, 1796, in place of John Blair, resigned. Died, and Gabriel Duval appointed.

BUSHROD WASHINGTON, of Virginia. Appointed September 29, 1798, in recess of Senate, in place of James Wilson, deceased. Nomination confirmed and appointed December 30, 1798. Died, and Henry Baldwin appointed.

ALFRED MOORE, of North Carolina. Nomination confirmed and appointed December 10, 1799, in place of James Iredell, deceased. Resigned, and William Johnson appointed.

WILLIAM JOHNSON, of South Carolina. Nomination confirmed and appointed March 26, 1804, in place of Alfred Moore, resigned. (Confirmed and appointed Collector of the Customs, February 22, 1819, and declined the appointment.) Died in 1834, and James M. Wayne appointed.

THOMAS TODD, of Kentucky. Nomination confirmed March 2, and appointed March 3, 1807.

BROCKHOLST LIVINGSTON, of New York. Appointed November 10, 1806, in recess of Senate, in place of William Paterson, deceased. Nomination confirmed and appointed December 17, 1806. Died, and Smith Thompson appointed.

LEVI LINCOLN, of Massachusetts. Nomination confirmed and appointed January 3, 1811, in place of William Cushing, deceased. Declined the appointment, and John Quincy Adams appointed.

JOHN QUINCY ADAMS, of Massachusetts. Nomination confirmed and appointed February 22, 1811, in place of Levi Lincoln, declined. Declined the appointment, and Joseph Story appointed.

JOSEPH STORY, of Massachusetts. Nomination confirmed and appointed November 18, 1811, in place of John Quincy Adams, declined. Died, and Levi Woodbury appointed.

GABRIEL DUVAL, of Maryland. Nomination confirmed and appointed November 18, 1811, in the place of Samuel Chase, deceased. Resigned, and Philip P. Barbour appointed.

SMITH THOMPSON, of New York. Appointed September 1, 1823, in recess of the Senate, in place of Brockholst Livingston, deceased. Nomination confirmed and appointed December 9, 1823. Died, and Samuel Nelson appointed.

ROBERT TRIMBLE, of Kentucky. Nomination confirmed and appointed May 9, 1826, in the place of Thomas Todd, deceased. Died, and John McLean appointed.

JOHN MCLEAN, of Ohio. Nomination confirmed and appointed March 7, 1829, in the place of Robert Trimble, deceased.

HENRY BALDWIN, of Pennsylvania. Nomination confirmed and appointed January 6, 1830, in place of Bushrod Washington, deceased. Died, and R. C. Grier appointed.

JAMES M. WAYNE, of Georgia. Nomination confirmed and appointed January 9, 1835, in place of William Johnson, deceased.

PHILIP P. BARBOUR, of Virginia. Nomination confirmed and appointed March 15, 1836, in place of Gabriel Duval, resigned. Died, and P. V. Daniel appointed.

JOHN CATRON, of Tennessee. Nomination confirmed and appointed March 8, 1837.

WILLIAM SMITH, of Alabama. Nomination confirmed and appointed March 8, 1837. Declined the appointment, and John McKinley appointed.

JOHN MCKINLEY, of Alabama. Appointed April 22, 1837, in recess of the Senate, in place of William Smith, declined. Nomination confirmed and appointed September 25, 1837.

PETER V. DANIEL, of Virginia. Nomination confirmed and appointed March 3, 1841, in place of Philip P. Barbour, deceased.

SAMUEL NELSON, of New York. Nomination confirmed and appointed February 14, 1845, in place of Smith Thompson, deceased.

LEVI WOODBURY, of New Hampshire. Appointed September 20, 1845, in recess of the Senate, in place of Joseph Story, deceased. Nomination confirmed and appointed January 3, 1846.

ROBERT C. GRIER, of Pennsylvania. Nomination confirmed and appointed August 4, 1846, in place of Henry Baldwin, deceased.

BENJAMIN ROBBINS CURTIS, of Massachusetts. Appointed during the recess of the Senate, in place of Levi Woodbury, deceased. Nomination confirmed and appointed December 20, 1851. Resigned.

JAMES A. CAMPBELL, of Alabama. Appointed in 1853. Resigned May 1, 1861.

NATHAN CLIFFORD, of Maine. Appointed in 1858.

NOAH SWAYNE, of Ohio. Appointed in 1862.

SAMUEL H. MILLER, of Iowa. Appointed in 1862.

DAVID DAVIS, of Illinois. Appointed in 1862.

STEPHEN J. FIELD, of California. Appointed in 1863.

CLERKS OF THE SUPREME COURT OF THE UNITED STATES.

JOHN TUCKER, of Massachusetts, appointed February 3, 1790. Resigned.

SAMUEL BAYARD, of Delaware, appointed August 1, 1791. Resigned.

ELIAS B. CALDWELL, of New Jersey, appointed August 15, 1800. Died.

WILLIAM GRIFFITH, of New Jersey, appointed February 9, 1826. Died.

WILLIAM T. CARROLL, District of Columbia, appointed January 20, 1827.

T. WESLEY MIDDLETON, District of Columbia, appointed in 1862. Present incumbent.

REPORTERS OF DECISIONS OF THE SUPREME COURT.

ALEXANDER J. DALLAS,	reported	from	1789 to 1800,	inclusive.
WILLIAM CRANCH,	"	"	1801 to 1815,	"
HENRY WHEATON,	"	"	1816 to 1827,	"
RICHARD PETERS, JR.,	"	"	1828 to 1842,	"
BENJAMIN C. HOWARD,	"	"	1843 to 1862,	"
JEREMIAH S. BLACK,	"	"	1862 to 1864,	"
JOHN WILLIAM WALLACE,	"	"	1864. Present incumbent.	

MARSHALS OF THE UNITED STATES ATTENDANT ON THE SUPREME COURT.

Under the construction of the Judiciary Act of 1789, the Marshals of all the *Districts* were required to attend the sessions of the Supreme Court, until, by the

Act of June 9, 1794, the Marshal of the District alone in which the Court shall sit was required to attend its sessions.

DAVID LENOX, Marshal of the District of Pennsylvania, attended from January 28, 1794, to February, 1801.

DANIEL CARROLL BRENT, Marshal of the District of Columbia, attended from August 3, 1801, to August, 1808.

WASHINGTON BOYD, Marshal of the District of Columbia, attended from February 1, 1808, to August, 1818.

TENCH RINGGOLD, Marshal of the District of Columbia, attended from November 30, 1818, to August, 1831.

HENRY ASHTON, Marshal of the District of Columbia, attended from February 4, 1831, to February, 1834.

ALEXANDER HUNTER, Marshal of the District of Columbia, attended from March 6, 1834, to December, 1848.

ROBERT WALLACE, Marshal of the District of Columbia, attended from December 5, 1848, to December, 1849.

RICHARD WALLACH, Marshal of the District of Columbia, attended from December 4, 1849, to May, 1853.

JONAH D. HOOVER, Marshal of the District of Columbia, attended from May 31, 1853, to April, 1858.

WILLIAM SELDEN, Marshal of the District of Columbia, attended from April 1, 1858 to 1861.

WARD H. LAMON, attended from 1861.

Court meets first Monday in December, at Washington.

MINISTERS TO FOREIGN COUNTRIES.

A LIST OF DIPLOMATIC APPOINTMENTS MADE BETWEEN 1789 AND 1861, BOTH INCLUSIVE.

An asterisk prefixed to a name indicates that the individual has been a member of Congress, and that further information concerning him may be found, under the proper head, in the body of the work. En. Ex. and Min. Plen. signifies Envoy Extraordinary and Minister Plenipotentiary.

Name.	Office.	Place.	When appointed.	Remarks.
Adams, Charles F. . . .	En. Ex. and Min. Plen.	Great Britain.	1861	
*Adams, John Q.	Minister Resident.	Netherlands.	1794	Authorized in 1795 to exchange the ratifications of Jay's Treaty of 1794 with Great Britain; in 1797, to negotiate concerning the renewal of the treaty between the United States and Sweden; in 1813, jointly with Albert Gallatin and James A. Bayard, to meet, under the mediation of Russia, a Minister from Great Britain, and negotiate a treaty of peace; in 1814, jointly with James A. Bayard, Albert Gallatin, Henry Clay, and Jonathan Russel, to negotiate a treaty with Great Britain at Ghent.
" "	Minister Plenipotentiary.	Portugal.	1796	
" "	" "	Prussia.	1797	
" "	" "	Russia.	1809	
" "	En. Ex. and Min. Plen.	Great Britain.	1815	
Anderson, Charles E. . .	Secretary of Legation.	France.	1836	
*Anderson, Richard C. . .	Minister Plenipotentiary.	Colombia.	1823	Appointed in 1826, jointly with John Sergeant, En. Ex. and Min. Plen. to the Assembly of American Nations proposed to be held at Panama.

*Allen, Heman.	Minister Plenipotentiary.	Chili.	1823	
Angel, Benjamin F.	Minister Resident.	Sweden.	1857	
*Appleton, John.	Chargé d'Affaires.	Bolivia.	1848	
" "	Secretary of Legation.	Great Britain.	1853	
" "	Chargé d'Affaires.	Great Britain.	1855	
Appleton, J. A.	Minister Plenipotentiary.	Russia.	1860	
Appleton John J.	Secretary of Legation.	Portugal.	1819	
" "	" "	Spain.	1822	
" "	Chargé d'Affaires.	Two Sicilies.	1825	
" "	" "	Sweden.	1826	
*Armstrong, John.	Minister Plenipotentiary.	France.	1804	Appointed, jointly with James Bowdoin, Com. Plen. and Ex. to negotiate a treaty with Spain.
Aulick, John H.	Captain U. S. Navy.	Japan.	1851	Authorized to negotiate a treaty with Japan.
Baber, Ambrose.	Chargé d'Affaires.	Sardinia.	1841	
Bacon, John E.	Secretary of Legation.	Russia.	1858	
*Bagby, Arthur P.	Envoy and Minister Plenipotentiary.	Russia.	1848	
Bainbridge, William.	Captain U. S. Navy.	Algiers.	1815	Appointed, jointly with W. Shaler and S. Decatur, to negotiate a treaty with Algiers.
Balestier, Joseph.	Special Agent.		1849	Authorized to negotiate treaties with Siam, Anam, and Bruni.
Bancroft, George.	En. Ex. and Min. Plen.	Great Britain.	1846	In 1849 authorized, jointly with Richard Rush, to negotiate a postal treaty with Great Britain and France.
Banks, W. W.	Secretary of Legation.	Brazil.	1857	
*Barbour, James.	En. Ex. and Min. Plen.	Great Britain.	1828	
Barlow, Joel.	Minister Plenipotentiary.	France.	1811	
*Barnard, Daniel D.	En. Ex. and Min. Plen.	Russia.	1850	
*Barringer, Daniel M.	" "	Spain.	1849	
*Barrow, Washington.	Chargé d'Affaires.	Portugal.	1841	
*Barry, William T.	En. Ex. and Min. Plen.	Spain.	1835	
Barton, Seth.	Chargé d'Affaires.	Chili.	1847	
Barton, Thomas P.	Secretary of Legation.	France.	1833	

Ministers to Foreign Countries—Continued.

Name.	Office.	Place.	When appointed.	Remarks.
*Bayard, James A.	Minister Plenipotentiary.	France.	1801	Appointed in 1813, jointly with J. Q. Adams and Albert Gallatin, to negotiate with Great Britain, under the mediation of Russia; and in 1814, with Jonathan Russell, John Q. Adams, Henry Clay, and Albert Gallatin, to negotiate treaties with Great Britain, at Ghent.
*Bayard, James A.	En. Ex. and Min. Plen.	Russia.	1815	Appointed Envoy to Russia; declined.
*Bayard, Richard H.	Chargé d'Affaires.	Belgium.	1850	
*Baylies, Francis.	" "	Buenos Ayres.	1832	
*Bedinger, Henry.	" "	Denmark.	1853	
" "	Minister Resident.	Denmark.	1854	
Beelen, Frederic A.	Secretary of Legation.	Central America.	1853	
" "	" "	Chili.	1854	
Belmont, Augustus.	Chargé d'Affaires.	Netherlands.	1853	
Benton, Allen A.	Minister Resident.	New Granada.	1861	
Bergh, Henry.	Secretary of Legation.	Russia.	1863	
*Bidlack, Benjamin A.	Chargé d'Affaires.	New Granada.	1845	
Bigler, John.	En. Ex. and Min. Plen.	Chili.	1857	
*Bissell, William H.	Chargé d'Affaires.	Buenos Ayres.	1853	
Blackford, William M.	" "	New Granada.	1842	
Blatchford, R. M.	Minister Resident.	Rome.	1862	
*Bleecker, Hermanus.	Chargé d'Affaires.	Netherlands.	1839	
*Blow, Henry T.	Minister Resident.	Venezuela.	1861	
Blunt, Joseph.	Commissioner.	China.	1851	Appointment declined.
Borden, James W.	"	Hawaii.	1858	
*Borland, Solon.	En. Ex. and Min. Plen.	Central America.	1853	Authorized to negotiate treaties with Nicaragua and Honduras.
Boulware, William.	Chargé d'Affaires.	Two Sicilies.	1841	
Bowdoin, James.	Com. Plen. and Ex.	Spain.	1804	Appointed, jointly with John Armstrong, to negotiate a treaty with Spain.

*Bowlin, James B.	Minister Resident.	New Granada.	1854	
" "	Commissioner.	Paraguay.	1858	
Boyd, James McHenry.	Secretary of Legation.	Great Britain.	1846	
*Breckinridge, John C.	En. Ex. and Minister.	Spain.	1855	Appointment declined.
Brent, Thomas L. L.	Secretary of Legation.	Spain.	1814	Appointed in 1819 to exchange ratifications of a treaty with Spain.
" "	" "	Portugal.	1822	
" "	Chargé d'Affaires.	Portugal.	1825	
Brent, William, Jr.	" "	Buenos Ayres.	1844	
Brodhead, John R.	Secretary of Legation.	Great Britain.	1846	
Brown, Ethan A.	Chargé d'Affaires.	Brazil.	1830	
Brown, George.	Commissioner.	Sandwich Islands.	1843	
*Brown, James.	En. Ex. and Min. Plen.	France.	1823	
Brown, John P.	Dragoman.	Turkey.	1836	
" "	"	"	1842	
" "	Secretary and Dragoman.	"	1858	
Brown, Neil S.	En. Ex. and Min. Plen.	Russia.	1850	
Bryan, John A.	Chargé d'Affaires.	Peru.	1844	
*Buchanan, James.	En. Ex. and Min. Plen.	Russia.	1832	Authorized in 1853 to negotiate a treaty with Bavaria; in 1854, to negotiate a treaty with Hanover.
" "	" "	Great Britain.	1853	
Buchanan, James M.	Minister Resident.	Denmark.	1858	
*Buckalew, Charles R.	" "	Ecuador.	1858	
*Burlingame, Anson.	Minister Plenipotentiary.	China.	1861	
Burton, Allen A.	Minister Resident.	New Granada.	1861	
Butler, Anthony.	Secretary of Legation.	Russia.	1856	
Butler, Edward G. W.	" "	Prussia.	1856	
Calhoun, William R.	" "	France.	1857	
*Cambreling, Churchill C.	En. Ex. and Min. Plen.	Russia.	1840	
*Cameron, Simon.	Min. Plen. and Ex.	Russia.	1862	
*Campbell, G. W.	En. Ex. and Min. Plen.	Russia.	1818	
*Campbell, James H.	Minister Resident.	Sweden & Norway.	1864	
Carmichael, William.	Chargé d'Affaires.	Spain.	1790	Authorized, jointly with William Short, to negotiate with Spain concerning the navigation of the River Mississippi, etc.
Carr, Dabney S.	Minister Resident.	Turkey.	1843	

Ministers to Foreign Countries—Continued.

Name.	Office.	Place.	When appointed.	Remarks.
Cartter, D. K.	Minister Resident.	Bolivia.	1861	
*Cass, Lewis.	En. Ex. and Min. Plen.	France.	1836	
Cass, Lewis, Jr.	Chargé d'Affaires.	Papal States.	1849	
" "	Minister Resident.	Pontifical States.	1854	
Cathcart, James L.	Consul.	Tripoli.	1797	In 1797, authorized, jointly with S. O'Brien and W. Eaton, to negotiate a treaty with Tripoli.
" "	Consul General.	Algiers.	1802	
" "	Consul.	Tunis.	1803	
Caverly, Z. B.	Secretary of Legation.	Peru.	1855	
Cazneau, W. L.	Commissioner.	Dominican Rep.	1854	
*Chandler, Joseph R.	Minister Resident.	Two Sicilies.	1858	
Chauncey, Isaac.	Captain U. S. Navy.	Algiers.	1816	Authorized, jointly with William Shaler, to conclude a treaty with Algiers.
Chew, William W.	Secretary of Legation.	Russia.	1837	
Chinn, Thomas W.	Chargé d'Affaires.	Two Sicilies.	1849	
Clark, Franklin H.	Secretary of Legation.	Brazil.	1851	
Clarke, Beverly L.	Minister Resident.	Guatemala.	1858	
" "	" "	Honduras.	1858	
Clay, Cassius M.	Min. Plen. and En. Ex.	Russia.	1861	
Clay, Green.	Secretary of Legation.	Italy.	1861	
*Clay, Henry.	Min. Plen. and Ex.	Ghent.	1814	Authorized, jointly with John Q. Adams, Jonathan Russell, James A. Bayard, and Albert Gallatin, to negotiate a treaty with Great Britain.
*Clay, James B.	Chargé d'Affaires.	Portugal.	1849	
Clay, John R.	Secretary of Legation.	Russia.	1830	
" "	Chargé d'Affaires.	Russia.	1836	
" "	Secretary of Legation.	Austria.	1838	
" "	" "	Russia.	1845	
" "	Chargé d'Affaires.	Peru.	1847	
" "	En. Ex. and Min. Plen.	Peru.	1853	
Clay, Thomas H.	Minister Resident.	Honduras.	1863	
Clemson, Thomas G.	Chargé d'Affaires.	Belgium.	1844	

*Clifford, Nathan.	Commissioner.	Mexico.	1848	Appointed, with A. H. Sevier, Commissioners, with the rank of Envoy Extraordinary and Minister Plenipotentiary, to treat jointly or severally with Mexico.
" "	En. Ex. and Min. Plen.	Mexico.	1848	
Cogswell, Joseph G.	Secretary of Legation.	Spain.	1842	Appointment declined.
Collins, Samuel P.	Consul.	Morocco.	1854	
*Conklin, Alfred.	En. Ex. and Min. Plen.	Mexico.	1852	
Cooley, James.	Chargé d'Affaires.	Peru.	1826	
*Corwin, Thomas.	En. Ex. and Min. Plen.	Mexico.	1861	
Corwin, William H.	Secretary of Legation.	Mexico.	1861	
Cox, Ferdinand.	" "	Brazil.	1851	
*Cox, Samuel S.	" "	Peru.	1855	
*Crawford, William H.	Minister Plenipotentiary.	France.	1813	
Cripps, John.	Secretary of Legation.	Mexico.	1853	
Crosby, E. O.	Minister Resident.	Guatemala.	1861	
Crump, William.	Chargé d'Affaires.	Chili.	1844	
Culver, Erastus D.	Minister Resident.	Venezuela.	1862	
*Cushing, Caleb.	Commissioner.	China.	1843	In 1844, authorized to negotiate with Japan.
" "	En. Ex. and Min. Plen.	China.	1843	
Cushing, Courtland.	Chargé d'Affaires.	Ecuador.	1850	
Cushman, John F.	Minister Resident.	Argentine Confederation.	1859	
*Dallas, George M.	En. Ex. and Min. Plen.	Russia.	1837	
" "	" "	Great Britain.	1856	
*Dana, Francis,	" "	France.	1797	Declined the appointment.
Dana, John W.	Minister Resident.	Bolivia.	1854	
Daniel, John M.	" "	Sardinia.	1854	
Davezac, Auguste.	Secretary of Legation.	Netherlands.	1829	
" "	Chargé d'Affaires.	Netherlands.	1831	
" "	" "	Two Sicilies.	1833	
" "	" "	Netherlands.	1845	
Davie, William R.	En. Ex. and Min. Res.	France.	1799	
Davis, John C. B.	Secretary of Legation.	Great Britain.	1849	
*Davis, John W.	Commissioner.	China.	1848	
*Dayton, William L.	Min. Plen. and En. Ex.	France.	1861	

Ministers to Foreign Countries—Continued.

Name.	Office.	Place.	When appointed.	Remarks.
*Dearborn, Henry, Sr.	En. Ex. and Min. Plen.	Portugal.	1822	
Deas, William Allen.	Chargé d'Affaires.	Great Britain.	1795	
Decatur, Stephen,	Captain U. S. Navy.	Algiers.	1815	Authorized, jointly with William Shaler and William Bainbridge, to negotiate a treaty.
*De Witt, Charles G.	Chargé d'Affaires.	Central America.	1833	
*Dickerson, Mahlon.	En. Ex. and Min. Plen.	Russia.	1834	
Dickinson, Andrew B.	Minister Resident.	Nicaragua.	1861	
" "	Minister and En. Ex.	Nicaragua.	1863	
Dillon, Romain.	Secretary of Legation.	Brazil.	1858	
Dimitry, Alexander.	Minister Resident.	Costa Rica and Nicaragua.	1859	
*Dodge, Augustus C.	En. Ex. and Min. Plen.	Spain.	1855	
Donelson, Andrew J.	Chargé d'Affaires.	Texas.	1844	
" "	En. Ex. and Min. Plen.	Prussia.	1846	
" "	" "	Federal Gov't of Germany.	1848	Authorized to negotiate a treaty with Saxony, and exchange ratifications with Nassau.
Dryer, Thomas J.	Commissioner.	Sandwich Islands.	1861	
Eames, Charles.	"	Sandwich Islands.	1849	
" "	Chargé d'Affaires.	Venezuela.	1854	
" "	Minister Resident.	Venezuela.	1854	
Eaton, John H.	En. Ex. and Min. Plen.	Spain.	1836	
Edney, Balis M.	Chargé d'Affaires.	Guatemala.	1852	
Elliott, Jonathan.	Commercial Agent.	Dominican Rep.	1855	Authorized to negotiate a treaty.
*Ellis, Powhatan.	Chargé d'Affaires.	Mexico.	1836	
" "	En. Ex. and Min. Plen.	Mexico.	1839	
Ellis, Thomas H.	Secretary of Legation.	Mexico.	1839	
Ellis, Vespasian.	Chargé d'Affaires.	Venezuela.	1849	
*Ellsworth, Henry W.	" "	Sweden.	1845	
*Ellsworth, Oliver.	En. Ex. and Min. Plen.	France.	1799	

Erving, R. A.	Secretary of Legation.	Russia.	1853	
*Eustis, William.	En. Ex. and Min. Plen.	Netherlands.	1814	
Eve, Joseph.	Chargé d'Affaires.	Texas.	1841	
Everett, Alexander H.	Secretary of Legation.	Netherlands.	1814	
" "	Chargé d'Affaires.	Netherlands.	1818	
" "	En. Ex. and Min. Plen.	Spain.	1825	
" "	Commissioner.	China.	1845	In 1845, authorized to negotiate a treaty with Japan.
*Everett, Edward.	En. Ex. and Min. Plen.	Great Britain.	1841	
" "	Commissioner.	China.	1843	Appointment declined.
Ewing, George W.	Secretary of Legation.	Spain.	1804	
" "	Special Minister.	Denmark.	1811	
" "	Minister Plenipotentiary.	Spain.	1814	
Fair, Elisha Y.	Minister Plenipotentiary.	Belgium.	1858	
*Faulkner, Charles J.	En. Ex. and Min. Plen.	France.	1860	
Fay, Theodore S.	Secretary of Legation.	Great Britain.	1836	
" "	" "	Russia.	1837	
" "	Minister Resident.	Switzerland.	1853	
Fearn, Walter.	Secretary of Legation.	Mexico.	1856	
Fitzpatrick, Richard.	" "	Argentine Confederation.	1856	
Flenniken, Robert P.	Chargé d'Affaires.	Denmark.	1847	
Flood, G. W.	" "	Texas.	1840	
Fogg, G. G.	Minister Resident.	Switzerland.	1861	
Folsom, George.	Chargé d'Affaires.	Netherlands.	1850	
Foote, Thomas M.	" "	New Granada.	1849	
" "	" "	Austria.	1852	
Forbes, John M.	Secretary of Legation.	Buenos Ayres.	1823	
" "	Chargé d'Affaires.	Buenos Ayres.	1825	
*Forsyth, John.	Minister Plenipotentiary.	Spain.	1819	
Forsyth, John, Jr.	En. Ex. and Min. Plen.	Mexico.	1856	
*Forward, Walter.	Chargé d'Affaires.	Denmark.	1849	
Gadsden, James.	En. Ex. and Min. Plen.	Mexico.	1853	
*Gallatin, Albert.	" "	France.	1814	In 1813, appointed, jointly with John Q. Adams, Henry Clay, Jonathan Russell, and James A. Bayard, to negotiate with Great Britain.

Ministers to Foreign Countries—Continued.

Name.	Office.	Place.	When appointed.	Remarks.
*Gerry, Elbridge.	Secretary of Legation.	Belgium.	1797	Appointed, jointly with C. C. Pinckney and J. Marshall.
*Giddings, J. R.	Consul General.	British North America.	1861	
Goddard, C. W.	" "	Turkey.	1861	
Goodrich, Aaron.	Secretary of Legation.	Belgium.	1861	
Hadduck, Charles B.	Chargé d'Affaires.	Portugal.	1850	
Haldeman, J. S.	Minister Resident.	Sweden & Norway.	1861	
Hale, Charles.	Consul General.	Egypt.	1864	
Hall, Allen A.	Chargé d'Affaires.	Venezuela.	1843	
" "	Minister Resident.	Bolivia.	1863	
Hamilton, Alexander, Jr.	Secretary of Legation.	Spain.	1842	
*Hannegan, Edward A.	En. Ex. and Min. Plen.	Prussia.	1849	
Hardin, Benjamin R.	Secretary of Legation.	Chili.	1849	
Harper, Charles C.	" "	France.	1829	
Harris, Leavitt.	" "	Russia.	1813	Secretary of the Mission Extraordinary for entering into negotiations at St. Petersburg with Great Britain.
" "	Chargé d'Affaires.	France.	1833	
Harris, Townsend.	Consul General.	Japan.	1855	Authorized in 1857 to enter into negotiations with Siam.
" "	Minister Resident.	Japan.	1858	In 1858 negotiated a treaty with Japan.
" "	" "	Japan.	1861	
*Harris, William A.	Chargé d'Affaires.	Argentine Confederation.	1846	
Harrison, J. O.	Secretary of Legation.	Spain.	1835	
*Harrison, William H.	En. Ex. and Min. Plen.	Colombia.	1828	
Harum, John.	Chargé d'Affaires.	Chili.	1830	
Harvey, James E.	Minister Resident.	Portugal.	1861	
Hassaurek, Frederick.	" "	Ecuador.	1861	
Haywood, William H.	Chargé d'Affaires.	Belgium.	1837	
Heap, Samuel D.	Dragoman.	Turkey.	1852	
Henry, Patrick.	En. Ex. and Min. Plen.	France.	1799	Appointment declined.

*Hilliard, Henry W.	Chargé d'Affaires.	Belgium.	1842	
Hise, Elijah.	" "	Guatemala.	1848	Authorized to negotiate with San Salvador, Honduras, Nicaragua, and Costa Rica.
Hodgson, William.	Dragoman.	Turkey.	1832	
Holman, Jesse B.	Secretary of Legation.	Chili.	1852	
Homes, Henry A.	Assistant Dragoman.	Turkey.	1851	
Hopkins, George W.	Chargé d'Affaires.	Portugal.	1847	
Howard, Tilghman A.	" "	Texas.	1844	
Hughes, Christopher.	Secretary of Legation.	Sweden.	1814	Of the Mission Extraordinary to negotiate with Great Britain.
" "	" "	Sweden.	1816	
" "	Chargé d'Affaires.	Sweden.	1819	
" "	" "	Netherlands.	1825	
" "	Special Minister.	Denmark.	1835	
" "	Chargé d'Affaires.	Netherlands.	1842	
Humphreys, David.	Minister Resident.	Portugal.	1791	
" "	Commissioner Plen.	Algiers.	1793	Authorized to negotiate with Tripoli, Tunis, Algiers, and Morocco.
" "	" "	Spain.	1796	
*Hunter, William.	Chargé d'Affaires.	Brazil.	1834	
" "	En. Ex. and Min. Plen.	Brazil.	1841	
*Ingersoll, Charles J.	Secretary of Legation.	Prussia.	1837	
*Ingersoll, Colin M.	" "	Russia.	1848	
*Ingersoll, Joseph R.	En. Ex. and Min. Plen.	Great Britain.	1852	
*Ingersoll, Ralph J.	" "	Russia.	1846	
Irving, Washington.	Secretary of Legation.	Great Britain.	1829	
" "	En. Ex. and Min. Plen.	Spain.	1842	
Irwin, William W.	Chargé d'Affaires.	Denmark.	1843	
*Jackson, Andrew.	En. Ex. and Min. Plen.	Mexico.	1823	
Jackson, Henry.	Secretary of Legation.	France.	1813	
Jackson, Henry R.	Chargé d'Affaires.	Austria.	1853	
" "	Minister Resident.	Austria.	1854	
Jackson, Isaac R.	Chargé d'Affaires.	Denmark.	1841	
Jacobs, N. P.	Consul General.	East Indies.	1862	
Jay, John.	En. Ex. and Min. Plen.	Great Britain.	1799	
Jeffers, William N.	Chargé d'Affaires.	Rep. of Central America.	1831	

Ministers to Foreign Countries—Continued.

Name.	Office.	Place.	When appointed.	Remarks.
*Jenifer, Daniel.	Minister Plenipotentiary.	Austria.	1841	
Jewett, Albert G.	Chargé d'Affaires.	Peru.	1845	
*Jones, George W.	Minister Resident.	New Granada.	1859	
*Jones, J. Glancy.	En. Ex. and Min. Plen.	Austria.	1858	
Judd, Norman B.	" "	Prussia.	1861	
*Kavanagh, Edward.	Chargé d'Affaires.	Portugal.	1835	
*Kellogg, William.	Minister Resident.	Guatemala.	1864	
*Kennedy, John P.	Secretary of Legation.	Chili.	1823	
*Kerr, John B.	Chargé d'Affaires.	Nicaragua.	1851	
King, John A.	Secretary of Legation.	Great Britain.	1825	
*King, Rufus.	Minister Plenipotentiary.	Great Britain.	1796	In 1799 authorized to negotiate a treaty with Russia.
" "	En. Ex. and Min. Plen.	Great Britain.	1825	
" "	Minister Resident.	Rome.	1863	Second appointment.
*King, William R.	Secretary of Legation.	Russia.	1816	
" "	En. Ex. and Min. Plen.	France.	1844	
King, Yelverton P.	Chargé d'Affaires.	New Granada.	1851	
Kinney, William B.	" "	Sardinia.	1850	
Kirk, Robert C.	Minister Resident.	Argentine Confederation.	1863	
Koerner, Gustave.	En. Ex. and Min. Plen.	Spain.	1862	
Kriesmann, H.	Secretary of Legation.	Prussia.	1861	
*La Branch, Alcée.	Chargé d'Affaires.	Texas.	1837	
Lake, Shelton F.	Commissioner.	Hawaii.	1853	
Lamar, Mirabeau B.	Minister Resident.	Argentine Confederation.	1857	
" "	" "	Nicaragua.	1858	
" "	" "	Costa Rica.	1858	
Larned, Samuel.	Secretary of Legation.	Chili.	1823	
" "	Chargé d'Affaires.	Chili.	1828	
" "	" "	Peru.	1828	
*Lawrence, Abbott.	En. Ex. and Min. Plen.	Great Britain.	1849	
Lawrence, John L.	Secretary of Legation.	Sweden.	1814	

Lawrence, T. B.	Consul General.	Italy.	1862	
Lawrence, William B.	Secretary of Legation.	Great Britain.	1826	
*Lay, George W.	Chargé d'Affaires.	Sweden.	1842	
Ledyard, Henry.	Secretary of Legation.	France.	1839	
*Legaré, Hugh S.	Chargé d'Affaires.	Belgium.	1832	
*Letcher, Robert P.	En. Ex. and Min. Plen.	Mexico.	1849	
Lippitt, George W.	Secretary of Legation.	Austria.	1856	
*Livingston, Edward.	En. Ex. and Min. Plen.	France.	1833	
Livingston, Jasper H.	Secretary of Legation.	Spain.	1844	
*Livingston, Robert R.	Minister Resident.	France.	1801	Appointed in 1803, jointly with James Monroe, to negotiate with France.
Livingston, Van Brugh.	Chargé d'Affaires.	Ecuador.	1848	
Mackie, James S.	Commissioner.	Peru.	1862	
Mann, Dudley A.	Special Agent.	Austria.	1846	Full power to treat with Hanover, Oldenburgh, Mechlenburg-Schwerin, and Mechlenburg-Strelitz, and in 1847 authorized to exchange ratifications with the same States; also accredited to Saxony, Wurtemberg, Baden, Hesse-Darmstadt, Nassau, Brunswick, Hesse-Cassel, Frankfort-on-the-Maine, Hanover, Oldenburg, Mechlenburg-Schwerin, Mechlenburg-Strelitz, Hamburg, Bremen, and Lubec.
" "	Special and Confidential Agent.	Hungary.	1849	
" "	Special Agent.	Switzerland.	1850	
Mann, William G.	Secretary of Legation.	Brazil.	1854	
Marling, John L.	Minister Resident.	Guatemala.	1854	
Marriott, James G.	Secretary of Legation.	Peru.	1853	
*Marsh, George P.	Minister Resident.	Turkey.	1849	
" "	Min. Plen. and En. Ex.	Sardinia.	1861	
*Marshall, Humphrey.	Commissioner.	China.	1852	
*Marshall, John.	En. Ex. and Min. Plen.	France.	1797	Appointed jointly with Charles C. Pinckney and Francis Dana.
Martin, Jacob L.	Chargé d'Affaires.	Papal States.	1848	
Martin, John J.	Secretary of Legation.	Peru.	1853	
Mason, John.	" "	Mexico.	1823	
*Mason, John Y.	En. Ex. and Min. Plen.	France.	1853	

Ministers to Foreign Countries—Continued.

Name.	Office.	Place.	When appointed.	Remarks.
Massey, Thomas E.	Secretary of Legation.	Chili.	1853	
Maxcy, Virgil.	Chargé d'Affaires.	Belgium.	1837	
Maxwell, John S.	Secretary of Legation.	Russia.	1842	
McAfee, R. B.	Chargé d'Affaires.	New Granada.	1833	In 1836 appointed with full power to treat with Ecuador.
McBride, James.	Minister Resident.	Hawaiian Islands.	1863	
McCluny, Alexander K.	Chargé d'Affaires.	Bolivia.	1849	
McCurdy, Charles J.	" "	Austria.	1850	
*McLane, Louis.	En. Ex. and Min. Plen.	Great Britain.	1829	
" "	" "	Great Britain.	1845	
*McLane, Robert M.	Commissioner.	China.	1853	
" "	En. Ex. and Min. Plen.	Mexico.	1859	Resigned in 1860.
*Meade, Richard K.	Chargé d'Affaires.	Sardinia.	1853	
" "	En. Ex. and Min. Plen.	Brazil.	1857	
Medary, Samuel.	" "	Chili.	1853	
Melville, Gansevoort.	Secretary of Legation.	Great Britain.	1845	
Meyer, Brantz.	" "	Mexico.	1841	
Middleton, Arthur, Jr.	" "	Spain.	1833	
" "	" "	Spain.	1836	
*Middleton, Henry.	En. Ex. and Min. Plen.	Russia.	1820	
Miller, Horace H.	Chargé d'Affaires.	Bolivia.	1852	
Miller, William.	" "	Guatemala.	1825	
Minor, William T.	Consul General.	Havana.	1864	
*Monroe, James.	Minister Plenipotentiary.	France.	1794	Appointed, in 1803, jointly with Robert R. Livingston, to negotiate with France, and with Charles Pinckney, to negotiate with Spain.
" "	" "	Great Britain.	1803	In 1806 appointed, jointly with William Pinckney, Commissioner Plenipotentiary and Extraordinary to negotiate with Great Britain.
*Moore, Thomas P.	En. Ex. and Min. Plen.	Colombia.	1829	

Moran, Benjamin.	Assistant Secretary of Legation.	Great Britain.	1857	
Morgan, Christopher.	Consul General.	Cuba.	1863	
Morgan, George W.	Minister Resident.	Portugal.	1858	
Morgan, Thomas J.	Secretary of Legation.	Brazil.	1847	
*Morris, Edward J.	Chargé d'Affaires.	Two Sicilies.	1850	
" "	Minister Resident.	Turkey.	1861	
*Morris, Gouverneur.	Commissioner.	Great Britain.	1789	
" "	Minister Plenipotentiary.	France.	1792	
Morris, Isaac E.	Commissioner.	New Granada.	1841	
Motley, John L.	Secretary of Legation.	Russia.	1841	
" "	En. Ex. and Min. Plen.	Austria.	1861	
*Muhlenberg, Henry A.	" "	Austria.	1838	
*Murphy, Henry C.	Minister Resident.	Netherlands.	1857	
Murphy, William S.	Special and Confidential Agent.	Central Am. Confederation.	1841	
" "	Chargé d'Affaires.	Texas.	1843	
Murphy, W. W.	Consul General.	Hanseatic and Free Cities.	1861	
*Murray, William V.	Minister Resident.	Netherlands.	1797	
" "	En. Ex. and Min. Plen.	France.	1799	Appointed, jointly with Oliver Ellsworth and Patrick Henry.
Navoni, Nicholas.	Dragoman.	Turkey.	1831	
*Nelson, Hugh.	Minister Plenipotentiary.	Spain.	1823	
*Nelson, John.	Chargé d'Affaires.	Two Sicilies.	1831	
Nelson, Thomas A. R.	Commissioner.	China.	1851	
Nelson, Thomas H.	En. Ex. and Min. Plen.	Chili.	1861	
Niles, Nathaniel.	Secretary of Legation.	France.	1830	
" "	Special Agent.	Sardinia.	1838	
" "	Chargé d'Affaires.	Sardinia.	1848	
O'Brien, Smith.	Consul General.	Algiers.	1797	
*Ogle, Andrew J.	Chargé d'Affaires.	Denmark.	1852	
O'Sullivan, John L.	" "	Portugal.	1854	
" "	Minister Resident.	Portugal.	1854	
*Owen, Robert D.	Chargé d'Affaires.	Two Sicilies.	1853	
" "	Minister Resident.	Two Sicilies.	1854	

Ministers to Foreign Countries—Continued.

Name.	Office.	Place.	When appointed.	Remarks.
Page, Thomas J.	Lieutenant U. S. Navy.		1853	Authorized, jointly with R. C. Schenck and J. S. Pendleton, to negotiate with Paraguay, and in 1854 to exchange ratifications.
Palmer, Robert M.	Minister Resident.	Argentine Confederation.	1861	
Parker, Peter.	Secretary and Interpreter.	China.	1845	
" "	Commissioner.	China.	1855	
Parrott, William S.	Secretary of Legation.	Mexico.	1841	
Partridge, James R.	Minister Resident.	San Salvador.	1863	
Peden, James A.	Chargé d'Affaires.	Buenos Ayres.	1854	In 1852 appointed, with R. C. Schenck, to negotiate treaties with Uruguay and Paraguay.
" "	Minister Resident.	Buenos Ayres.	1854	
*Pendleton, J. S.	" "	Argentine Confederation.	1851	
Pennington, W. S.	Secretary of Legation.	France.	1861	
Perry, H. S.	" "	Spain.	1861	
Perry, Horatio J.	" "	Spain.	1849	
*Peyton, Bailie.	En. Ex. and Min. Plen.	Chili.	1849	
Piatt, Donn.	Secretary of Legation.	France.	1854	
*Pickens, Francis W.	En. Ex. and Min. Plen.	Russia.	1858	
Pickett, John C.	Secretary of Legation.	Colombia.	1829	In 1838 authorized to negotiate with Ecuador.
" "	Chargé d'Affaires.	Peru Bolivian Confederation.	1838	
Pike, James S.	Minister Resident.	Netherlands.	1861	
*Pinckney, Charles.	Secretary of Legation.	Russia.	1818	
" "	Minister Plenipotentiary.	Spain.	1801	
Pinckney, Charles C.	" "	France.	1796	In 1797 appointed, jointly with John Marshall and Francis Dana, and subsequently Elbridge Gerry, to negotiate with France.
" "	En. Ex. and Min. Plen.	France.	1797	
Pinckney, Thomas.	Minister Plenipotentiary.	Great Britain.	1792	

Pinckney, Thomas.	En. Ex. and Min. Plen.	Spain.	1794	
*Pinkney, William.	Commissioner Plen. and Extraordinary.	Great Britain.	1806	Appointed, jointly with James Monroe, to negotiate with Great Britain.
" "	Minister Plenipotentiary.	Great Britain.	1806	
" "	" "	Great Britain.	1808	
" "	En. Ex. and Min. Plen.	Russia.	1816	
" "	Minister Resident.	Two Sicilies.	1816	
*Poinsett, Joel R.	En. Ex. and Min. Plen.	Mexico.	1825	In 1827 appointed, jointly with John Sergeant, Envoy to the Congress at Panama.
*Polk, William H.	Chargé d'Affaires.	Two Sicilies.	1845	
Pollard, Richard.	" "	Chili.	1834	
Porter, David.	Consul General.	Algiers.	1830	
" "	Chargé d'Affaires.	Turkey.	1831	
" "	Minister Resident.	Turkey.	1839	
Potter, John F.	Consul General.	British North America.	1864	
Powers, James M.	Chargé d'Affaires.	Two Sicilies.	1844	
Preble, William P.	En. Ex. and Min. Plen.	Netherlands.	1828	
Preston, William.	" "	Spain.	1858	
*Proffit, George H.	" "	Brazil.	1843	
Pruyn, Robert H.	Minister Resident.	Japan.	1861	
*Pryor, F. Roger.	Special Agent.	Greece.	1855	
Raguet, Condy.	Chargé d'Affaires.	Brazil.	1825	
Randall, A. W.	Minister Resident.	Rome.	1861	
*Randolph, John.	En. Ex. and Min. Plen.	Russia.	1830	
Reed, William B.	" "	China.	1857	
*Rencher, Abraham.	Chargé d'Affaires.	Portugal.	1843	
Reynolds, Thomas C.	Secretary of Legation.	Spain.	1846	
Rich, William.	" "	Mexico.	1852	
Riotte, Charles N.	Minister Resident.	Costa Rica.	1861	
Rives, Francis R.	Secretary of Legation.	Great Britain.	1842	
*Rives, William C.	En. Ex. and Min. Plen.	France.	1829	
" "	" "	France.	1849	
Roberts, Edmund.	Commissioner.	Cochin China, Siam, and Muscat.	1833	

Ministers to Foreign Countries—Continued.

Name.	Office.	Place.	When appointed.	Remarks.
Robinson, Christopher.	Envoy Extraordinary and Minister Plenipotentiary.	Peru.	1861	
Robinson, Jeremy.	Special Agent.	Spain.	1833	
*Rochester, William R.	Secretary.	Panama.	1826	Secretary of the Mission to Panama.
*Rodney, Cæsar A.	Minister Plenipotentiary.	Buenos Ayres.	1823	
Rogers, H. G.	Chargé d'Affaires.	Sardinia.	1840	
*Rowan, John.	" "	Two Sicilies.	1848	
Rush, Benjamin.	Secretary of Legation.	Great Britain.	1837	
Rush, Richard.	En. Ex. and Min. Plen.	Great Britain.	1817	
" "	Special Agent.	Great Britain.	1836	
" "	En. Ex. and Min. Plen.	France.	1847	
*Russell, Jonathan.	Minister Plenipotentiary.	Sweden.	1814	Appointed, jointly with John Q. Adams, Henry Clay, and Albert Gallatin, to negotiate with Great Britain.
Rutledge, Charles.	Secretary of Legation.	Spain.	1796	
Ruyckman, George W.	" "	Chili.	1858	
Sanford, Henry S.	" "	France.	1849	
" "	Minister Resident.	Cuba.	1861	
*Saunders, Romulus M.	En. Ex. and Min. Plen.	Spain.	1846	
Savage, Charles.	Consul.	Guatemala.	1838	Authorized to negotiate with the Republic of Central America.
Sawyer, Frederic A.	Secretary of Legation.	Spain.	1848	
*Schenck, Robert C.	En. Ex. and Min. Plen.	Brazil.	1852	Authorized to negotiate with Uruguay and Paraguay.
Schroeder, Francis.	Chargé d'Affaires.	Sweden.	1849	
" "	Minister Resident.	Sweden.	1854	
Schurz, Carl.	En. Ex. and Min. Plen.	Spain.	1861	
Seaton, Gales.	Secretary of Legation.	Federal Gov't of Germany.	1849	
Seebles, J. J.	Chargé d'Affaires.	Belgium.	1853	
" "	Minister Resident.	Belgium.	1854	
*Semple, James.	Chargé d'Affaires.	New Granada.	1837	

*Sergeant, John.	En. Ex. and Min. Plen.	Panama.	1826	Appointed, jointly with Joel R. Poinsett, to the Assemblage of Nations at Panama.
*Severance, Luther.	Commissioner.	Sandwich Islands.	1853	
*Sevier, Ambrose H.	"	Mexico.	1848	
Seward, George F.	Consul General.	China.	1861	
*Seymour, Thomas H.	En. Ex. and Min. Plen.	Belgium.	1853	
Shaler, William.	Commissioner.	Algiers.	1815	Appointed, jointly with Isaac Chauncey, to negotiate a treaty.
Shannon, James.	Chargé d'Affaires.	Central America.	1832	
Shannon, Wilson.	En. Ex. and Min. Plen.	Mexico.	1844	
Sheldon, Daniel.	Secretary of Legation.	France.	1816	
Shields, Benjamin G.	Chargé d'Affaires.	Venezuela.	1845	
Short, William.	" "	France.	1790	Appointed, in 1794, jointly with William Carmichael, to negotiate with Spain.
" "	Minister Resident.	Netherlands.	1792	
" "	" "	Spain.	1794	
Shufeldt.	Consul General.	Cuba.	1861	
*Sickles, Daniel E.	Secretary of Legation.	Great Britain.	1855	
*Slidell, John.	En. Ex. and Min. Plen.	Mexico.	1841	
" "	" "	Mexico.	1845	
" "	" "	Central America.	1853	
Smith, Buckingham.	Secretary of Legation.	Spain.	1855	
Smith, Delaron.	Special Agent.	Ecuador.	1844	
Smith, John A.	Secretary of Legation.	Great Britain.	1815	
" "	" "	Spain.	1825	
" "	" "	France.	1828	
" "	" "	Russia.	1829	
Smith John C.	Minister Resident.	Bolivia.	1858	
Smith, John S.	Secretary of Legation.	Mexico.	1827	Appointed Secretary to the Joint Mission at Tacubaya.
Smith, T. B.	" "	Mexico.	1850	
*Smith, W.	Minister Plenipotentiary.	Portugal.	1797	
*Smith, William S.	Secretary of Legation.	Russia.	1812	
Somerville, William C.	Chargé d'Affaires.	Sweden.	1825	
*Soulé, Pierre.	En. Ex. and Min. Plen.	Spain.	1853	
Spence, Carroll.	Minister Resident.	Turkey.	1853	

Ministers to Foreign Countries—Continued.

Name.	Office.	Place.	When appointed.	Remarks.
Stanton, Stephen K.	Secretary of Legation.	Russia.	1848	
*Starkweather, David A.	En. Ex. and Min. Plen.	Chili.	1854	
*Steele, J. Nevitt.	Chargé d'Affaires.	Venezuela.	1850	
Steele, William H.	" "	Austria.	1849	
*Stevenson, Andrew.	En. Ex. and Min. Plen.	Great Britain.	1836	Authorized in 1838 to negotiate with Greece.
*Stiles, William H.	Chargé d'Affaires.	Austria.	1845	
Stockton, John P.	Minister Resident.	Pontifical States.	1858	
Squier, Ephraim G.	Chargé d'Affaires.	Guatemala.	1849	Accredited to San Salvador, Nicaragua, Costa Rica, and Honduras.
" "	Commissioner.	Peru.	1862	
*Sumpter, Thomas.	Secretary of Legation.	France.	1801	
" "	Minister Plenipotentiary.	Portugal.	1809	
Taylor, Bayard.	Secretary of Legation.	Russia.	1862	
Taylor, Edward T.	" "	Colombia.	1828	
Ten Eyck, Anthony.	Commissioner.	Sandwich Islands.	1845	
Thayer, W. S.	Consul General.	Egypt.	1861	
*Thompson, Waddy.	En. Ex. and Min. Plen.	Mexico.	1842	
Thornton, James B.	Chargé d'Affaires.	Peru.	1836	Authorized to negotiate a treaty with Bolivia.
*Throop, Enos T.	" "	Two Sicilies.	1838	
Tod, David.	En. Ex. and Min. Plen.	Brazil.	1847	
Todd, Charles S.	" "	Russia.	1841	
Trescot, William H.	Secretary of Legation.	Great Britain.	1852	
Trist, Nicholas P.	Special Agent.	Spain.	1833	
" "	Commissioner.	Mexico.	1847	
Trousdale, William.	En. Ex. and Min. Plen.	Brazil.	1853	
Tudor, William.	Chargé d'Affaires.	Brazil.	1827	
Turpin, Edward A.	Minister Resident.	Venezuela.	1858	
Vail, Aaron.	Secretary of Legation.	Great Britain.	1831	
" "	Chargé d'Affaires.	Great Britain.	1832	
" "	Secretary of Legation.	Great Britain.	1836	
Van Alen, John T.	Chargé d'Affaires.	Ecuador.	1849	

*Van Buren, M.	En. Ex. and Min. Plen.	Great Britain.	1831	
Van Ness, Cornelius P.	" "	Spain.	1829	
Venable, William E.	Secretary of Legation.	Brazil.	1854	
*Vroom, Peter D.	En. Ex. and Min. Plen.	Prussia.	1853	
*Walker, Robert J.	Commissioner.	China.	1853	Did not leave the United States to enter upon his mission.
Walsh, Charles S.	Secretary of Legation.	Spain.	1844	
Walsh, Robert M.	" "	Brazil.	1841	
" "	" "	Mexico.	1848	
" "	Special Envoy.	Costa Rica.	1852	
Ward, John E.	En. Ex. and Min. Plen.	China.	1858	
Warren, John E.	Secretary of Legation.	Central America.	1852	
Washburne, C. A.	Commissioner.	Paraguay.	1861	
*Watterson, Harvey M.	Special Agent.	Buenos Ayres.	1851	
Watts, Beaufort T.	Secretary of Legation.	Colombia.	1824	
" "	Chargé d'Affaires.	Colombia.	1827	
" "	Secretary of Legation.	Russia.	1828	
Webb, James Watson.	Chargé d'Affaires.	Austria.	1849	
" "	En. Ex. and Min. Plen.	Brazil.	1861	
Webster, Fletcher.	Secretary of Legation.	China.	1843	
Weller, John B.	Minister Plenipotentiary.	Mexico.	1860	
Wells, H. G.	Minister Resident.	Honduras.	1861	
West, Edward.	Chargé d'Affaires.	Peru.	1854	
Wheaton, Henry.	" "	Denmark.	1827	Authorized, in 1836, to negotiate treaties with the States of the Zollverein and the Hanoverian Union.
" "	" "	Prussia.	1835	Authorized, in 1837, to negotiate treaties and exchange ratifications with the Zollverein States.
" "	En. Ex. and Min. Plen.	Prussia.	1837	In 1843 authorized to negotiate with Mechlenberg, Oldenburg, Bavaria, Wurtemberg, Hesse-Cassel, Hesse-Darmstadt, and Baden.
Wheeler, John H.	Minister Resident.	Nicaragua.	1854	
Whidden, Benjamin F.	Commissioner.	Hayti.	1862	
White, Philo.	Chargé d'Affaires.	Ecuador.	1853	

Ministers to Foreign Countries—Continued.

Name.	Office.	Place.	When appointed.	Remarks.
Wickliffe, Robert J.	Chargé d'Affaires.	Sardinia.	1848	
Wilber, J. B.	Secretary of Legation.	France.	1857	
*Wilkins, William.	En. Ex. and Min. Plen.	Russia.	1834	
Williams, James.	Minister Resident.	Turkey.	1858	
Williams, John.	Chargé d'Affaires.	Federation of the Central States of America.	1825	
Williams, John G. A.	" "	Venezuela.	1835	
Williams, S. Wells.	Interpreter and Secretary of Legation.	China.	1855	
Wilson, C. L.	Secretary of Legation.	England.	1861	
*Wise, Henry A.	En. Ex. and Min. Plen.	Brazil.	1844	
Wise, O. Jennings.	Secretary of Legation.	Prussia.	1853	
" "	" "	France.	1855	
Wood, Bradford R.	Minister Resident.	Denmark.	1861	
Woodbury, Charles L.	Chargé d'Affaires.	Bolivia.	1854	Appointment declined.
Woodside, Jonathan F.	" "	Denmark.	1835	
Wright, Edward H.	Secretary of Legation.	Prussia.	1850	
Wright, Joseph A.	En. Ex. and Min. Res.	Prussia.	1858	
Yancey, Benjamin C.	Minister Resident.	Argentine Confederation.	1858	

THE DECLARATION OF INDEPENDENCE.

PROCEEDINGS IN THE CONGRESS OF THE UNITED COLONIES RESPECTING "A DECLARATION OF INDEPENDENCE, BY THE REPRESENTATIVES OF THE UNITED STATES OF AMERICA, IN CONGRESS ASSEMBLED."

SATURDAY, JUNE 8, 1776.

Resolved, That the resolutions respecting independency be referred to a Committee of the whole Congress.

The Congress then resolved itself into a Committee of the Whole; and, after some time, the President resumed the chair, and Mr. Harrison reported, that the Committee have taken into consideration the matter to them referred, but not having come to any resolution thereon, directed him to move for leave to sit again on Monday.

Resolved, That this Congress will, on Monday next, at 10 o'clock, resolve itself into a Committee of the Whole, to take into further consideration the resolutions referred to them.

MONDAY, JUNE 10, 1776.

Agreeable to order, the Congress resolved itself into a Committee of the Whole, to take into their further consideration the resolutions to them referred; and, after some time spent thereon, the President resumed the chair, and Mr. Harrison reported that the Committee have had under consideration the matters referred to them, and have come to a resolution thereon, which they directed him to report.

The resolution agreed to in Committee of the Whole being read,—

Resolved, That the consideration of the first resolution be postponed to Monday, the first day of July next; and in the meanwhile, that no time be lost, in case the Congress agree thereto, that a Committee be appointed to prepare a declaration to the effect of the said first resolution, which is in these words: "That these United Colonies are, and of right ought to be, free and independent States; that they are absolved from all allegiance to the British crown; and that all political connection between them and the State of Great Britain is, and ought to be, totally dissolved."

TUESDAY, JUNE 11, 1776.

Resolved, That the Committee for preparing the Declaration consist of five. The members chosen, Mr. Jefferson, Mr. John Adams, Mr. Franklin, Mr. Sherman, and Mr. R. R. Livingston.

TUESDAY, JUNE 25, 1776.

A declaration of the Deputies of Pennsylvania, met in Provincial Conference, was laid before Congress and read, expressing their willingness to concur in a vote of Congress declaring the United Colonies free and independent States.

FRIDAY, JUNE 28, 1776.

"Francis Hopkinson, one of the Delegates from New Jersey, attended and produced the credentials of their appointment," containing the following instructions:

"If you shall judge it necessary or expedient for this purpose, we empower you to join in declaring the United Colonies independent of Great Britain, entering into a confederation for union and common defence," &c.

MONDAY, JULY 1, 1776.

"A resolution of the Convention of Maryland, passed the 28th of June, was laid before Congress and read," containing the following instructions to their deputies in Congress: "That the deputies of said Colony, or any three or more of them, be authorized and empowered to concur with the other United Colonies, or a majority of them, in declaring the United Colonies free and independent States; in forming such further compact and confederation between them," &c.

The order of the day being read:

Resolved, That this Congress will resolve itself into a Committee of the Whole, to take into consideration the resolution respecting independency.

That the Declaration be referred to said Committee.

The Congress resolved itself into a Committee of the Whole. After some time the President resumed the chair, and Mr. Harrison reported that the Committee had come to a resolution, which they desired him to report, and to move for leave to sit again.

The resolution agreed to by the Committee of the Whole being read, the determination thereof was, at the request of a Colony, postponed until to-morrow.

Resolved, That this Congress will, to-morrow, resolve itself into a Committee of the Whole, to take into consideration the Declaration respecting independence.

TUESDAY, JULY 2, 1776.

The Congress resumed the consideration of the resolution reported from the Committee of the Whole, which was agreed to as follows:

RESOLVED, *That these United Colonies are, and of right ought to be, Free and Independent States; that they are absolved from all allegiance to the British crown, and that all political connection between them and the State of Great Britain is, and ought to be, totally dissolved.*

Agreeable to the order of the day, the Congress resolved itself into a Committee of the Whole; and after some time, the President resumed the chair, and Mr. Harrison reported, that the Committee have had under consideration the Declaration to them referred; but not having had time to go through the same, desired him to move for leave to sit again.

Resolved, That this Congress will, to-morrow, again resolve itself into a Committee of the Whole, to take into their further consideration the Declaration respecting independence.

WEDNESDAY, JULY 3, 1776.

Agreeable to the order of the day, the Congress resolved itself into a Committee of the Whole, to take into their further consideration the Declaration; and after some time, the President resumed the chair, and Mr. Harrison reported that the Committee, not having yet gone through it, desired leave to sit again.

Resolved, That this Congress will, to-morrow, again resolve itself into a Committee of the Whole, to take into their further consideration the Declaration of Independence.

THURSDAY, JULY 4, 1776.

Agreeable to the order of the day, the Congress resolved itself into a Committee of the Whole, to take into their further consideration the Declaration; and after some time, the President resumed the chair, and Mr. Harrison reported that the Committee had agreed to a Declaration, which they desired him to report.

The Declaration being read, was agreed to as follows:

A Declaration by the Representatives of the United States of America, in Congress assembled.

When, in the course of human events, it becomes necessary for one people to dissolve the political bands which have connected them with another, and to assume, among the powers of the earth, the separate and equal station to which the laws of nature and of nature's God entitle them, a decent respect to the opinions of mankind requires that they should declare the causes which impel them to the separation.

We hold these truths to be self-evident, that all men are created equal; that they are endowed by their Creator with certain unalienable rights; that among these are life, liberty, and the pursuit of happiness. That to secure these rights, governments are instituted among men, deriving their just powers from the consent of the governed; that whenever any form of government becomes destructive of these ends, it is the right of the people to alter or to abolish it, and to institute a new government, laying its foundation on such principles, and organizing its powers in such form, as to them shall seem most likely to effect their safety and happiness. Prudence, indeed, will dictate that governments long established, should not be changed for light and transient causes; and accordingly, all experience hath shown, that mankind are more disposed to suffer, while evils are sufferable, than to right themselves by abolishing the forms to which they are accustomed. But when a long train of abuses and usurpations, pursuing invariably the same object, evinces a design to reduce them under absolute despotism, it is their right, it is their duty, to throw off such government, and to provide new guards for their future security. Such has been the patient sufferance of these Colonies, and such is now the necessity which constrains them to alter their former systems of government. The history of the present king of Great Britain is a history of repeated injuries and usurpations, all having, in direct object, the establishment of an absolute tyranny over these States. To prove this, let facts be submitted to a candid world:

He has refused his assent to laws the most wholesome and necessary for the public good.

He has forbidden his Governors to pass laws of immediate and pressing importance, unless suspended in their operation till his assent should be obtained; and when so suspended, he has utterly neglected to attend to them.

He has refused to pass other laws for the accommodation of large districts of people, unless those people would relinquish the right of representation in the Legislature; a right inestimable to them, and formidable to tyrants only.

He has called together legislative bodies at places unusual, uncomfortable, and distant from the depository of their public records, for the sole purpose of fatiguing them into compliance with his measures.

He has dissolved representative houses repeatedly, for opposing, with manly firmness, his invasions on the rights of the people.

He has refused, for a long time after such dissolutions, to cause others to be elected; whereby the legislative powers, incapable of annihilation, have returned to the people at large for their exercise; the State remaining, in the mean time, exposed to all the danger of invasion from without, and convulsions within.

He has endeavored to prevent the population of these States: for that purpose, obstructing the laws for naturalization of foreigners; refusing to pass others to encourage their migration hither, and raising the conditions of new appropriations of lands.

He has obstructed the administration of justice, by refusing his assent to laws for establishing judiciary powers.

He has made judges dependent on his will alone, for the tenure of their offices, and the amount and payment of their salaries.

He has erected a multitude of new offices, and sent hither swarms of officers to harass our people and eat out their substance.

He has kept among us, in times of peace, standing armies, without the consent of our legislature.

He has affected to render the military independent of, and superior to, the civil power.

He has combined, with others, to subject us to a jurisdiction foreign to our constitution, and unacknowledged by our laws; giving his assent to their acts of pretended legislation:

For quartering large bodies of armed troops among us:

For protecting them, by a mock trial, from punishment, for any murders which they should commit on the inhabitants of these States:

For cutting off our trade with all parts of the world:

For imposing taxes on us without our consent:

For depriving us, in many cases, of the benefits of trial by jury:

For transporting us beyond seas to be tried for pretended offences:

For abolishing the free system of English laws in a neighboring province, establishing therein an arbitrary government, and enlarging its boundaries, so as to render it at once an example and fit instrument for introducing the same absolute rule into these Colonies:

For taking away our charters, abolishing our most valuable laws, and altering, fundamentally, the powers of our governments:

For suspending our own legislatures, and declaring themselves invested with power to legislate for us in all cases whatsoever.

He has abdicated government here, by declaring us out of his protection, and waging war against us.

He has plundered our seas, ravaged our coasts, burnt our towns, and destroyed the lives of our people.

He is, at this time, transporting large armies of foreign mercenaries to complete the works of death, desolation, and tyranny, already begun, with circumstances of cruelty and perfidy scarcely paralleled in the most barbarous ages, and totally unworthy the head of a civilized nation.

He has constrained our fellow-citizens, taken captive on the high seas, to bear arms against their country, to become the executioners of their friends and brethren, or to fall themselves by their hands.

He has excited domestic insurrections among us, and has endeavored to bring on the inhabitants of our frontiers, the merciless Indian savages, whose known rule of warfare is an undistinguished destruction, of all ages, sexes, and conditions.

In every stage of these oppressions, we have petitioned for redress in the most humble terms; our repeated petitions have been answered only by repeated injury. A prince, whose character is thus marked by every act which may define a tyrant, is unfit to be the ruler of a free people.

Nor have we been wanting in attention to our British brethren. We have warned them, from time to time, of attempts made by their legislature to extend an unwarrantable jurisdiction over us. We have reminded them of the circumstances of our emigration and settlement here. We have appealed to their native justice and magnanimity, and we have conjured them, by the ties of our common kindred, to disavow these usurpations, which would inevitably interrupt our connections and correspondence. They, too, have been deaf to the voice of justice and consanguinity. We must, therefore, acquiesce in the necessity which demands our separation, and hold them, as we hold the rest of mankind, enemies in war, in peace, friends.

We, therefore, the Representatives of the United States of America, in General Congress assembled, appealing to the Supreme Judge of the world for the rectitude of our intentions, do, in the name and by the authority of the good people of these Colonies, solemnly publish and declare, That these United Colonies are, and, of right, ought to be, *free and independent States;* that they are absolved from all allegiance to the British crown, and that all political connection between them and the State of Great Britain, is, and ought to be, totally dissolved; and that, as *free and independent States*, they have full power to levy war, conclude peace, contract alliances, establish commerce, and to do all other acts and things which *independent States* may of right do. And, for the support of this Declaration, with a firm reliance on the protection of Divine Providence, we mutually pledge to each other, our lives, our fortunes, and our sacred honor.

The foregoing Declaration was, by order of Congress, engrossed, and signed by the following members:

JOHN HANCOCK.

NEW HAMPSHIRE.

Josiah Bartlett, William Whipple, Matthew Thornton.

MASSACHUSETTS BAY.

Samuel Adams, John Adams, Robert Treat Paine, Elbridge Gerry.

RHODE ISLAND.

Stephen Hopkins, William Ellery.

CONNECTICUT.

Roger Sherman, Samuel Huntington, William Williams, Oliver Wolcott.

NEW YORK.

William Floyd, Philip Livingston, Francis Lewis, Lewis Morris.

NEW JERSEY.

Richard Stockton, John Witherspoon, Francis Hopkinson, John Hart, Abraham Clark.

PENNSYLVANIA.

Robert Morris, Benjamin Rush, Benjamin Franklin, John Morton, George Clymer, James Smith, George Taylor, James Wilson, George Ross.

DELAWARE.

Cæsar Rodney, George Read, Thomas McKean.

MARYLAND.

Samuel Chase, Charles Carroll, of Carrollton, William Paca, Thomas Stone.

VIRGINIA.

George Wythe, Richard Henry Lee, Thomas Jefferson, Benjamin Harrison, Thomas Nelson, Jr., Francis Lightfoot Lee, Carter Braxton.

NORTH CAROLINA.

William Hooper, Joseph Hewes, John Penn.

SOUTH CAROLINA.

Edward Rutledge, Thomas Heyward, Jr., Thomas Lynch, Jr., Arthur Middleton.

GEORGIA.

Button Gwinnett, Lyman Hall, George Walton.

Resolved, That copies of the Declaration be sent to the several assemblies, conventions, and committees, or councils of safety, and to the several commanding officers of the Continental troops; that it be proclaimed in each of the United States, and at the head of the army.

SIGNERS OF THE DECLARATION OF INDEPENDENCE,

IN CONGRESS ASSEMBLED, JULY 4, 1776.

The following List of Members of the Continental Congress, who signed the Declaration of Independence (although the names are included in the general list of that Congress, from 1774 to 1788), is given separately, for the purpose of showing the places and dates of their birth, and the time of their respective deaths, for convenient reference:

NAMES OF THE SIGNERS.	BORN AT	DELEGATED FROM	DIED
Adams, John, ...	Braintree, Mass., October 19, 1735	Massachusetts, .	July 4, 1826
Adams, Samuel, ...	Boston, " Sept. 27, 1722	Massachusetts, .	October 2, 1803
Bartlett, Josiah, ...	Amesbury, " in Nov. 1729	New Hampshire,	May 19, 1795
Braxton, Carter, ...	Newington, Va., Sept. 10, 1736	Virginia, . . .	October 10, 1797
Carroll, Charles, of Carrollton,	Annapolis, Md., Sept. 20, 1737	Maryland, . . .	Novem. 14, 1832
Chase, Samuel, ...	Somerset Co., Md., April 17, 1741	Maryland, . . .	June 19, 1811
Clark, Abraham, ...	Elizabethtown, N. J., Feb. 15, 1726	New Jersey, . .	September, 1794
Clymer, George, ...	Philadelphia, Penna., in 1739	Pennsylvania, .	January 23, 1813
Ellery, William, ...	Newport, R. I., Dec. 22, 1727	R. I. and Prov. Pl.	Feb'y 15, 1820
Floyd, William, ...	Suffolk Co., N. Y., Dec. 17, 1734	New York, . .	August 4, 1821
Franklin, Benjamin, ...	Boston, Mass., Jan. 17, 1706	Pennsylvania, .	April 17, 1790
Gerry, Elbridge, ...	Marblehead, Mass., July 17, 1744	Massachusetts, .	Novem. 23, 1814
Gwinnett, Button, ...	England, in 1732	Georgia, . . .	May 27, 1777
Hall, Lyman, ...	———, Conn., in 1731	Georgia, . . .	February, 1790
Hancock, John, ...	Braintree, Mass., in 1737	Massachusetts, .	October 8, 1793
Harrison, Benjamin, ...	Berkeley, Va., —	Virginia, . . .	April, 1791
Hart, John, ...	Hopewell, N J., about 1715	New Jersey, . .	—, 1780
Heyward, Thomas. Jr., . . .	St. Luke's, S. C., in 1746	South Carolina, .	March, 1809
Hewes, Joseph, ...	Kingston, N. J., in 1730	North Carolina, .	Novem. 10, 1779
Hooper, William, ...	Boston, Mass., June 17, 1742	North Carolina, .	October, 1790
Hopkins, Stephen, ...	Scituate, " March 7, 1707	R. I, and Prov. Pl.	July 13, 1785
Hopkinson, Francis, ...	Philadelphia, Penna., in 1737	New Jersey, . .	May 9, 1790
Huntington, Samuel, ...	Windham, Conn., July 3, 1732	Connecticut, . .	January 5, 1796
Jefferson, Thomas, ...	Shadwell, Va., April 13, 1743	Virginia, . . .	July 4, 1826
Lee, Francis Lightfoot, . . .	Stratford, " October 14, 1734	Virginia, . . .	April, 1797
Lee, Richard Henry, ...	Stratford, " January 20, 1732	Virginia, . . .	June 19, 1794
Lewis, Francis, ...	Landaff, Wales, in March, 1713	New York, . . .	Decem. 30, 1803
Livingston, Philip, ...	Albany, N. Y., January 15, 1716	New York, . . .	June 12, 1778
Lynch, Thomas, Jr., ...	St. George's, S. C., Aug. 5, 1749	South Carolina, .	Lost at sea, 1779
McKean, Thomas, ...	Chester Co., Pa., March 19, 1734	Delaware, . . .	June 24, 1817
Middleton, Arthur, ...	Middleton Place, S. C., in 1743	South Carolina, .	January 1, 1787
Morris, Lewis, ...	Morrisania, N. Y., in 1726	New York, . . .	January 22, 1798
Morris, Robert, ...	Lancashire, Eng., Jan. 1733-4	Pennsylvania, .	May 8, 1806
Morton, John, ...	Ridley, Penna., in 1724	Pennsylvania, .	April, 1777
Nelson, Thomas, Jr., ...	York, Va., Dec. 26, 1738	Virginia, . . .	January 4, 1789
Paca, William, ...	Wye Hill, Md., October 31, 1740	Maryland, . . .	—, 1799
Paine, Robert Treat, ...	Boston, Mass., in 1731	Massachusetts, .	May 11, 1804
Penn, John, ...	Caroline Co., Va., May 17, 1741	North Carolina, .	October 26, 1809
Read, George, ...	Cecil Co., Md., in 1734	Delaware, . . .	—, 1798
Rodney, Cæsar, ...	Dover, Del., in 1730	Delaware, . . .	—, 1783
Ross, George, ...	New Castle, Del., in 1730	Pennsylvania, .	July, 1779
Rush, Benjamin. M.D., . . .	Byberry, Penna., Dec. 24, 1745	Pennsylvania, .	April 19, 1813
Rutledge, Edward, ...	Charleston, S. C., in Nov. 1749	South Carolina, .	January 23, 1800
Sherman, Roger, ...	Newton, Mass., April 19, 1721	Connecticut, . .	July 23, 1793
Smith, James, ...	———, Ireland, —	Pennsylvania, .	July 11, 1806
Stockton, Richard, ...	Princeton, N. J., October 1, 1730	New Jersey, . .	Feb'y 28, 1781
Stone, Thomas, ...	Charles Co., Md., in 1742	Maryland, . . .	October 5, 1787
Taylor, George, ...	———, Ireland, in 1716	Pennsylvania, .	Feb'y 23, 1781
Thornton, Matthew, ...	———, Ireland, in 1714	New Hampshire,	June 24, 1803
Walton, George, ...	Frederick Co., Va., in 1740	Georgia. . . .	Feb'y 2, 1805
Whipple, William, ...	Kittery, Maine, in 1730	New Hampshire,	Novem. 28, 1785
Williams, William, ...	Lebanon, Conn., April 8, 1731	Connecticut, . .	August 2, 1811
Wilson, James, ...	Scotland, about 1742	Pennsylvania, .	August 28, 1798
Witherspoon, John, ...	Yester, Scotland, Feb 5, 1722	New Jersey, . .	Novem. 15, 1794
Wolcott, Oliver, ...	Windsor, Conn., Nov. 26, 1726	Connecticut, . .	December 1, 1797
Wythe, George, ...	Elizabeth City Co., Va., 1726	Virginia, . . .	June 8, 1806

MEMBERS OF THE CONTINENTAL CONGRESS,

FROM 1774 TO 1788.

NEW HAMPSHIRE.

	FROM	TO
Bartlett, Josiah,	1775,	'79
Blanchard, Jonathan,	1783,	'84
Folsom, Nathaniel,	1774,	'75
" "	1777,	'78
" "	1779,	'80
Foster, Abiel,	1783,	'85
Frost, George,	1777,	'79
Gilman, John Taylor,	1782,	'83
Gilman, Nicholas,	1786,	'88
Langdon, John,	1775,	'77
" "	1786,	'87
Langdon, Woodbury,	1779,	'80
Livermore, Samuel,	1780,	'83
" "	1785,	'86
Long, Pierce,	1784,	'86
Peabody, Nathaniel,	1779,	'80
Sullivan, John,	1774,	'75
" "	1780,	'81
Thornton, Matthew,	1776,	'78
Wentworth, John, Jr.,	1778,	'79
Whipple, William,	1776,	'79
White, Phillips,	1782,	'83
Wingate, Paine,	1787,	'88

MASSACHUSETTS.

	FROM	TO
Adams, John,	1774,	'78
Adams, Samuel,	1774,	'82
Cushing, Thomas,	1774,	'76
Dana, Francis,	1776,	'78
" "	1784,	'84
Dane, Nathan,	1785,	'88
Gerry, Elbridge,	1776,	'81
" "	1782,	'85
Gorham, Nathaniel,	1782,	'83
" "	1785,	'87
Hancock, John,	1775,	'80
" "	1785,	'86
Higginson, Stephen,	1782,	'83
Holten, Samuel,	1778,	'80
" "	1782,	'83
" "	1784,	'85
" "	1786,	'87
Jackson, Jonathan,	1782,	'82
King, Rufus,	1784,	'87
Lovell, James,	1776,	'82
Lowell, John,	1782,	'83
Osgood, Samuel,	1780,	'84
Otis,, Samuel A.,	1787,	'88
Paine, Robert Treat,	1774,	'78
Partridge, George,	1779,	'82
" "	1783,	'85
Sedgwick, Theodore,	1785,	'88
Sullivan, James,	1782,	'82
Thacher, George,	1787,	'88
Ward, Artemas,	1780,	'81

RHODE ISLAND.

	FROM	TO
Arnold, Jonathan,	1782,	'84
Arnold, Peleg,	1787,	'88
Collins, John,	1778,	'83
Cornell, Ezekiel,	1780,	'83
Ellery, William,	1776,	'80
" "	1783,	'85
Hazard, Jonathan,	1787,	'88
Hopkins, Stephen,	1774,	'77
" "	1778,	—
Howell, David,	1782,	'85
Manning, ——,	1785,	'86
Marchant, Henry,	1777,	'80
" "	1783,	'84
Miller, Nathan,	1785,	'86
Mowry, ——,	1781,	'81
Varnum, James M.,	1780,	'82
" "	1786,	'87
Ward, Samuel,	1774,	'76

CONNECTICUT.

	FROM	TO
Adams, Andrew,	1777,	'80
" "	1781,	'82
Cook, Joseph P.,	1784,	'88
Deane, Silas,	1774,	'76
Dyer, Eliphalet,	1774,	'79
" "	1780,	'83
Edwards, Pierpont,	1787,	'88
Ellsworth, Oliver,	1777,	'84
Hillhouse, William,	1783,	'86
Hosmer, Titus,	1775,	'76
" "	1777,	'79
Huntington, Benjamin,	1780,	'84
" "	1787,	'88
Huntington, Samuel,	1776,	'84
Johnson, William S.,	1784,	'87

	FROM	TO
Law, Richard,	1777,	'78
" "	1781,	'84
Mitchell, Stephen M.,	1783,	'84
" "	1785,	'86
" "	1787,	'88
Root, Jesse,	1778,	'83
Sherman, Roger,	1774,	'84
Spencer, Joseph,	1778,	'79
Strong, Jedediah,	1782,	'84
Sturges, Jonathan,	1785,	'87
Treadwell, John,	1785,	'86
Trumbull, Joseph,	1774,	'75
Wadsworth, James,	1783,	'84
" "	1785,	'86
Wadsworth, Jeremiah,	1787,	'88
Williams, William,	1776,	'78
" "	1783,	'84
Wolcott, Oliver,	1775,	'78
" "	1780,	'84

New York.

	FROM	TO
Alsop, John,	1774,	'76
Benson, Egbert,	1784,	'85
" "	1786,	'88
Boerum, Simon,	1774,	'77
Clinton, George,	1775,	'77
De Witt, Charles,	1783,	'85
Duane, James,	1774,	'84
Duer, William,	1777,	'78
Floyd, William,	1774,	'77
" "	1778,	'83
Gansevoort, Leonard,	1787,	'88
Hamilton, Alexander,	1782,	'83
" "	1787,	'88
Haring, John,	1774,	'75
" "	1785,	'88
Jay, John,	1774,	'77
" "	1778,	'79
Lansing, John,	1784,	'88
Lawrance, John,	1785,	'87
Lewis, Francis,	1777,	'79
Livingston, Philip,	1774,	'78
Livingston, Robert R..	1775,	'77
" "	1779,	'81
Livingston, Walter,	1784,	'85
Low, Isaac,	1774,	'75
L'Hommedieu, Ezra,	1779,	'83
" "	1787,	'88
Morris, Gouverneur,	1777,	'80
Morris, Lewis,	1775,	'77
McDougall, Alexander,	1781,	'82
" "	1784,	'85
Paine, Ephraim,	1784,	'85
Platt, Zephaniah,	1784,	'86
Schuyler, Philip,	1775,	'75
" "	1778,	'81
Scott, John Morin,	1780,	'83
Smith, Melancthon,	1785,	'88
Wisner, Henry,	1774,	'76

	FROM	TO
Yates, Abraham, Jr.,	1787,	'88
Yates, Peter W.,	1785,	'87

New Jersey.

	FROM	TO
Beatty, John,	1783,	'85
Boudinot, Elias,	1777,	'78
" "	1781,	'84
Burnett, W.,	1780,	'81
Cadwallader, Lambert,	1784,	'87
Clark, Abraham,	1776,	'82
" "	1787,	'88
Condict, Silas,	1781,	'84
Cooper, John,	1776,	'76
Crane, Stephen,	1774,	'76
Dayton, Elias,	1787,	'88
De Hart, John,	1774,	'76
Dick, Samuel,	1783,	'84
Elmer, Jonathan,	1776,	'78
" "	1781,	'84
" "	1787,	'88
Fell, John,	1778,	'80
Frelinghuysen, Frederick,	1778,	'79
" "	1782,	'83
Henderson, Thomas,	1779,	'80
Hopkinson, Francis,	1776,	'77
Hornblower, Josiah,	1785,	'86
Houston, William C.,	1779,	'82
" "	1784,	'85
Kinsey, James,	1774,	'75
Livingston, William,	1774,	'76
Neilson, John,	1778,	'79
Scheurman, J.,	1786,	'87
Scudder, Nathaniel,	1777,	'79
Sergeant, Jonathan D.,	1776,	'77
Smith, Richard,	1774,	'76
Stewart, ——,	1784,	'85
Stockton, Richard,	1776,	'77
Symmes, John C.,	1785,	'86
Witherspoon, John,	1776,	'83

Pennsylvania.

	FROM	TO
Allen, Andrew,	1775,	'76
Armstrong, John,	1778,	'80
" "	1787,	'88
Atlee, Samuel,	1778,	'82
Bayard, John,	1785,	'87
Biddle, Edward,	1774,	'76
" "	1778,	'79
Bingham, William,	1787,	'88
Clarkson, Matthew,	1785,	'86
Clingan, William,	1777,	'79
Clymer, George,	1776,	'78
" "	1780,	'83
Dickinson, John,	1774,	'76
Fitzsimmons, Thomas,	1782,	'83
Franklin, Benjamin,	1775,	'76
Galloway, Joseph,	1774,	'75
Gardner, Joseph,	1784,	'85
Hand, Edward,	1784,	'85
Henry, William,	1784,	'86

	FROM	TO
Humphreys, Charles, . . .	1774,	'76
Ingersoll, Jared, ...	1780,	'81
Irwine, ——, ...	1786,	'88
Jackson, David, ...	1785,	'86
Matlack, Timothy, . . .	1780,	'81
McClene, James, ...	1778,	'80
Meredith, ——, ...	1787,	'88
Mifflin, Thomas, ...	1774,	'76
" "	1782,	'84
Morris, Charles, ...	1783,	'84
Morris, Robert, ...	1776,	'78
Montgomery, John, . . .	1780,	'84
Morton, John, ...	1774,	'77
Muhlenberg, Frederick A., .	1778,	'80
Peters, Richard, ...	1782,	'83
Pettit, Charles, ...	1785,	'87
Read, ——, ...	1787,	'88
Reed, Joseph, ...	1777,	'78
Rhodes, Samuel, ...	1774,	'75
Roberdeau, Daniel, . . .	1777,	'79
Ross, George, ...	1774,	'77
Rush, Benjamin, ...	1776,	'77
Searle, James, ...	1778,	'80
Shippen, William, . . .	1778,	'80
Smith, James, ...	1776,	'78
Smith, Jonathan B., . . .	1777,	'78
Smith, Thomas, ...	1780,	'82
St. Clair, Arthur, ...	1785,	'87
Taylor, George, ...	1776,	'77
Willing, Thomas, ...	1775,	'76
Wilson, James, ...	1775,	'78
" "	1782,	'83
" "	1785,	'87
Wynkoop, Henry, ...	1779,	'83

DELAWARE.

	FROM	TO
Bedford, Gunning, ...	1783,	'85
" "	1786,	'87
Bedford, Gunning, Jr., . .	1785,	'86
Dickinson, John, ...	1776,	'77
" "	1779,	'80
Dickinson, Philemon, . .	1782,	'83
Evans, John, ...	1776,	'77
Kearney, Dyre, ...	1786,	'88
McComb, Eleazer, ...	1782,	'84
Mitchell, Nathaniel, . . .	1786,	'88
McKean, Thomas, . . .	1774,	'76
" " . . .	1778,	'83
Patton, John, ...	1785,	'86
Peery, William, ...	1785,	'86
Read, George, ...	1774,	'77
Rodney, Cæsar, ...	1774,	'76
" "	1777,	'78
" "	1783,	'84
Rodney, Thomas, ...	1781,	'83
" "	1785,	'87
Sykes, James, ...	1777,	'78
Tilton, James, ...	1783,	'85
Van Dyke, Nicholas, . . .	1777,	'82
Vining, John, ...	1784,	'86
Wharton, Samuel, ...	1782,	'83

MARYLAND.

	FROM	TO
Alexander, Robert, . . .	1775,	'77
Carmichael, William, . .	1778,	'80
Carroll, Charles, ...	1776,	'78
Carroll, Daniel, ...	1780,	'84
Chase, Jeremiah T., . . .	1783,	'84
Chase, Samuel, ...	1774,	'78
" "	1784,	'85
Contee, Benjamin, . . .	1787,	'88
Forbes, James, ...	1778,	'80
Forrest, Uriah, ...	1786,	'87
Goldsborough, Robert, . .	1774,	'75
Hall, John, ...	1775,	'76
" "	1783,	'84
Hanson, John, ...	1781,	'83
Harrison, William, . . .	1785,	'87
Hemsley, William, . . .	1782,	'84
Henry, John, ...	1778,	'81
" "	1784,	'87
Hindman, William, . . .	1784,	'87
Howard, John E., ...	1787,	'88
Jenifer, D., of St. Thomas, .	1778,	'82
Johnson, Thomas, ...	1775,	'77
Lee, Thomas Sim, . . .	1783,	'84
Lloyd, Edward, ...	1783,	'84
Martin, Luther, ...	1784,	'85
McHenry, James, ...	1783,	'86
Paca, William, ...	1774,	'79
Plater, George, ...	1778,	'81
Potts, Richard, ...	1781,	'82
Ramsay, Nathaniel, . . .	1785,	'87
Ridgely, Richard, ...	1785,	'86
Rogers, John, ...	1775,	'76
Ross, David, ...	1786,	'87
Rumsey, Benjamin, . . .	1776,	'78
Scott, Gustavus, ...	1784,	'85
Seney, Joshua, ...	1787,	'88
Smith, William, ...	1777,	'78
Stone, Thomas, ...	1775,	'79
" "	1784,	'85
Tilghman, Matthew, . . .	1774,	'77
Wright, Turbett, ...	1781,	'82

VIRGINIA.

	FROM	TO
Adams, Thomas, ...	1778,	'80
Banister, John, ...	1778,	'79
Bland, Richard, ...	1774,	'76
Bland, Theodoric, ...	1780,	'83
Braxton, Carter, ...	1776,	'76
Brown, John, ...	1787,	'88
Carrington, Edward, . . .	1785,	'86
Fitzhugh, ——, ...	1779,	'80
Fleming, William, . . .	1779,	'81
Grayson, William, . . .	1784,	'87
Griffin, Cyrus, ...	1778,	'81
" "	1787,	'88

	FROM	TO
Hardy, Samuel, ...	1783,	'85
Harrison, Benjamin, . . .	1774,	'78
Harvie, John, ...	1778,	'79
Henry, James, ...	1780,	'81
Henry, Patrick, ...	1774,	'76
Jefferson, Thomas, . . .	1775,	'77
" " . . .	1783,	'85
Jones, Joseph, ...	1777,	'78
" "	1780,	'83
Lee, Arthur, ...	1781,	'84
Lee, Francis Lightfoot, . .	1775,	'80
Lee, Henry, ...	1785,	'88
Lee, Richard Henry, . . .	1774,	'80
" " . . .	1784,	'87
Madison, James, Jr., . . .	1780,	'83
" " . . .	1786,	'88
Mercer, James, ...	1779,	'80
Mercer, John F., ...	1782,	'85
Monroe, James, ...	1783,	'86
Nelson, Thomas, ...	1775,	'77
" "	1779,	'80
Page, Mann, ...	1777,	'77
Pendleton, Edmund, . . .	1774,	'75
Randolph, Edmund, . . .	1779,	'82
Randolph, Peyton, . . .	1774,	'75
Smith, Merewether, . . .	1778,	'82
Washington, George, . . .	1774,	'75
Wythe, George, ...	1775,	'77

NORTH CAROLINA.

	FROM	TO
Ashe, John B., ...	1787,	'88
Bloodworth, Timothy, . .	1786,	'87
Blount, William, ...	1782,	'83
" "	1786,	'87
Burke, Thomas, ...	1777,	'81
Burton, Robert, ...	1787,	'88
Caswell, Richard, ...	1774,	'76
Cumming, William, . . .	1784,	'84
Harnett, Cornelius, . . .	1777,	'80
Hawkins, Benjamin, . . .	1781,	'84
" " . . .	1786,	'87
Hewes, Joseph, ...	1774,	'77
" "	1779,	'80
Hill, Whitmill, ...	1778,	'81
Hooper, William, ...	1774,	'77
Johnston, Samuel, . . .	1780,	'82
Jones, Allen, ...	1779,	'80
Jones, Willie, ...	1780,	'81
Nash, Abner, ...	1782,	'84
" "	1785,	'86
Penn, John, ...	1775,	'76
" "	1777,	'80
Sitgreaves, John, ...	1784,	'85
Sharpe, William, ...	1779,	'82
Spaight, Richard D., . . .	1783,	'85
Swan, John, ...	1787,	'88
Williams, John, ...	1778,	'79
Williamson, Hugh, . . .	1782,	'85
" " . . .	1787,	'88
White, Alexander, . . .	1786,	'88

SOUTH CAROLINA.

	FROM	TO
Bee, Thomas, ...	1780,	'82
Beresford, Richard, . . .	1783,	'85
Bull, John, ...	1784,	'87
Butler, Pierce, ...	1787,	'88
Drayton, William Henry, .	1778,	'79
Eveleigh, Nicholas, . . .	1781,	'82
Gadsden, Christopher, . .	1774,	'76
Gervais, John L., ...	1782,	'83
Heyward, Thomas, Jr., . .	1776,	'78
Huger, Daniel, ...	1786,	'88
Hutson, Richard, ...	1778,	'79
Izard, Ralph, ...	1782,	'83
Kean, John, ...	1785,	'87
Kinloch, Francis, ...	1780,	'81
Laurens, Henry, ...	1777,	'80
Lynch, Thomas, ...	1774,	'76
Lynch, Thomas, Jr., . . .	1776,	'77
Matthews, John, ...	1778,	'82
Middleton, Arthur, . . .	1776,	'78
" " . . .	1781,	'83
Middleton, Henry, . . .	1774,	'76
Motte, Isaac, ...	1780,	'82
Parker, John, ...	1786,	'88
Pinckney, Charles, . . .	1777,	'78
" " . . .	1784,	'87
Ramsay, David, ...	1782,	'84
" "	1785,	'86
Read, Jacob, ...	1783,	'85
Rutledge, Edward, . . .	*1774,*	*'77*
Rutledge, John, ...	1774,	'77
" "	1782,	'83
Trapier, Paul, ...	1777,	'78
Tucker, Thomas T., . . .	1787,	'88

GEORGIA.

	FROM	TO
Baldwin, Abraham, . . .	1785,	'88
Brownson, Nathan, . . .	1776,	'78
Bullock, Archibald, . . .	1775,	'76
Clay, Joseph, ...	1778,	'80
Few, William, ...	1780,	'82
" "	1785,	'88
Gibbons, William, . . .	1784,	'86
Gwinnett, Button, . . .	1776,	'77
Habersham, John, ...	1785,	'86
Hall, Lyman, ...	1775,	'79
Houston, John, ...	1775,	'77
Houston, William, . . .	1784,	'87
Howley, Richard, ...	1780,	'81
Jones, Noble Wimberly, .	1775,	'76
" " .	1781,	'83
Langworthy, Edward, . .	1777,	'79
Pierce, W., ...	1786,	'87
Telfair, Edward, ...	1777,	'79
" "	1780,	'83
Walton, George, ...	1776,	'79
" "	1780,	'81
Wood, Joseph, ...	1777,	'79
Zubly, John J., ...	1775,	'76

PRESIDENTS OF THE CONTINENTAL CONGRESS.

FROM 1774 TO 1788.

	FROM	ELECTED.
Peyton Randolph,	Virginia,	September 5, 1774.
Henry Middleton,	South Carolina,	October 22, 1774.
Peyton Randolph,	Virginia,	May 10, 1775.
John Hancock,	Massachusetts,	May 24, 1775.
Henry Laurens,	South Carolina,	November 1, 1777.
John Jay,	New York,	December 10, 1778.
Samuel Huntington,	Connecticut,	September 28, 1779.
Thomas McKean,	Delaware,	July 10, 1781.
John Hanson,	Maryland,	November 5, 1781.
Elias Boudinot,	New Jersey,	November 4, 1782.
Thomas Mifflin,	Pennsylvania,	November 3, 1783.
Richard Henry Lee,	Virginia,	November 30, 1784.
Nathaniel Gorham,	Massachusetts,	June 6, 1786.
Arthur St. Clair,	Pennsylvania,	February 2, 1787.
Cyrus Griffin,	Virginia,	January 22, 1788.

SESSIONS OF THE CONTINENTAL CONGRESS.

The sessions of the Continental Congress were commenced as follows:

September 5, 1774, also May 10, 1775, at *Philadelphia;* December 20, 1776, at *Baltimore;* March 4, 1777, at *Philadelphia;* September 27, 1777, at *Lancaster*, Pennsylvania; September 30, 1777, at *York*, Pennsylvania; July 2, 1778, at *Philadelphia;* June 30, 1783, at *Princeton*, New Jersey; November 26, 1783, at *Annapolis*, Maryland; November 1, 1784, at *Trenton*, New Jersey; January 11, 1785, at *New York*, which, from that time, continued to be the place of meeting until the adoption of the Constitution of the United States. From 1781 to 1788, Congress met annually on the first Monday in November, pursuant to the Articles of Confederation.

CONSTITUTION

OF THE

UNITED STATES OF AMERICA.

WE the People of the United States, in order to form a more perfect Union, establish justice, insure domestic tranquillity, provide for the common defence, promote the general welfare, and secure the blessings of liberty to ourselves and our posterity, do ordain and establish this CONSTITUTION for the United States of America.

ARTICLE I.

SECTION 1. All legislative powers herein granted shall be vested in a Congress of the United States, which shall consist of a Senate and House of Representatives.

SECT. 2. The House of Representatives shall be composed of members chosen every second year by the people of the several States, and the electors in each State shall have the qualifications requisite for electors of the most numerous branch of the State Legislature.

No person shall be a Representative who shall not have attained to the age of twenty-five years, and been seven years a citizen of the United States, and who shall not, when elected, be an inhabitant of that State in which he shall be chosen.

Representatives and direct taxes shall be apportioned among the several States which may be included within this Union, according to their respective numbers, which shall be determined by adding to the whole number of free persons, including those bound to service for a term of years, and excluding Indians not taxed, three-fifths of all other persons. The actual enumeration shall be made within three years after the first meeting of the Congress of the United States, and within every subsequent term of ten years, in such a manner as they shall by law direct. The number of Representatives shall not exceed one for every thirty thousand, but each State shall have at least one Representative; and until such enumeration shall be made, the State of New Hampshire shall be entitled to choose three, Massachusetts eight, Rhode Island and Providence Plantations one, Connecticut five, New York six, New Jersey four, Pennsylvania eight, Delaware one, Maryland six, Virginia ten, North Carolina five, South Carolina five, and Georgia three.

When vacancies happen in the representation from any State the executive authority thereof shall issue writs of election to fill such vacancies.

The House of Representatives shall choose their Speaker and other officers; and shall have the sole power of impeachment.

SECT. 3. The Senate of the United States shall be composed of two Senators from each State, chosen by the Legislature thereof, for six years; and each Senator shall have one vote.

Immediately after they shall be assembled in consequence of the first election, they shall be divided as equally as may be into three classes. The seats of the

Senators of the first class shall be vacated at the expiration of the second year, of the second class at the expiration of the fourth year, and of the third class at the expiration of the sixth year, so that one-third may be chosen every second year; and if vacancies happen by resignation or otherwise, during the recess of the Legislature of any State, the Executive thereof may make temporary appointments until the next meeting of the Legislature, which shall then fill such vacancies.

No person shall be a Senator who shall not have attained to the age of thirty years, and been nine years a citizen of the United States, and who shall not, when elected, be an inhabitant of that State for which he shall be chosen.

The Vice-President of the United States shall be President of the Senate, but shall have no vote, unless they be equally divided.

The Senate shall choose their other officers, and also a President *pro tempore*, in the absence of the Vice-President, or when he shall exercise the office of President of the United States.

The Senate shall have the sole power to try all impeachments. When sitting for that purpose, they shall be on oath or affirmation. When the President of the United States is tried, the Chief Justice shall preside: and no person shall be convicted without the concurrence of two-thirds of the members present.

Judgment in cases of impeachment shall not extend further than to removal from office, and disqualification to hold and enjoy any office of honor, trust, or profit under the United States; but the party convicted shall nevertheless be liable and subject to indictment, trial, judgment, and punishment, according to law.

SECT. 4. The times, places, and manner of holding elections for Senators and Representatives shall be prescribed in each State by the Legislature thereof; but the Congress may at any time by law make or alter such regulations, except as to the places of choosing Senators.

The Congress shall assemble at least once in every year, and such meeting shall be on the first Monday in December, unless they shall by law appoint a different day.

SECT 5. Each House shall be the judge of the elections, returns, and qualifications of its own members, and a majority of each shall constitute a quorum to do business; but a smaller number may adjourn from day to day, and may be authorized to compel the attendance of absent members in such manner and under such penalties as each House may provide.

Each House may determine the rules of its proceedings, punish its members for disorderly behavior, and, with the concurrence of two-thirds, expel a member.

Each House shall keep a journal of its proceedings, and from time to time publish the same, excepting such parts as may in their judgment require secrecy; and the yeas and nays of the members of either House on any question shall, at the desire of one-fifth of those present, be entered on the journal.

Neither House, during the session of Congress, shall, without the consent of the other, adjourn for more than three days, nor to any other place than that in which the two Houses shall be sitting.

SECT. 6. The Senators and Representatives shall receive a compensation for their services, to be ascertained by law, and paid out of the Treasury of the United States. They shall in all cases, except treason, felony, and breach of the peace, be privileged from arrest during their attendance at the session of their respective Houses, and in going to and returning from the same; and for any speech or debate in either House they shall not be questioned in any other place.

No Senator or Representative shall, during the time for which he was elected, be appointed to any civil office under the authority of the United States, which shall have been created, or the emoluments whereof shall have been increased during such time; and no person holding any office under the United States shall be a member of either House during his continuance in office.

SECT. 7. All bills for raising revenue shall originate in the House of Representatives; but the Senate may propose or concur with amendments as on other bills.

Every bill which shall have passed the House of Representatives and the Senate shall, before it becomes a law, be presented to the President of the United

States; if he approve he shall sign it, but if not he shall return it, with his objections, to that House in which it shall have originated, who shall enter the objections at large on their journal, and proceed to reconsider it. If after such reconsideration two-thirds of that House shall agree to pass the bill, it shall be sent, together with the objections, to the other House, by which it shall likewise be reconsidered, and if approved by two-thirds of that House, it shall become a law. But in all such cases the votes of both Houses shall be determined by yeas and nays, and the names of the persons voting for and against the bill shall be entered on the journal of each House respectively. If any bill shall not be returned by the President within ten days (Sundays excepted) after it shall have been presented to him, the same shall be a law, in like manner as if he had signed it, unless the Congress, by their adjournment, prevent its return, in which case it shall not be a law.

Every order, resolution, or vote, to which the concurrence of the Senate and House of Representatives may be necessary (except on a question of adjournment), shall be presented to the President of the United States; and before the same shall take effect, shall be approved by him, or being disapproved by him, shall be repassed by two-thirds of the Senate and House of Representatives, according to the rules and limitations prescribed in the case of a bill.

SECT. 8. The Congress shall have power

To lay and collect taxes, duties, imposts, and excises, to pay the debts and provide for the common defence and general welfare of the United States; but all duties, imposts, and excises shall be uniform throughout the United States;

To borrow money on the credit of the United States;

To regulate commerce with foreign nations, and among the several States, and with the Indian tribes;

To establish a uniform rule of naturalization, and uniform laws on the subject of bankruptcies throughout the United States;

To coin money, regulate the value thereof, and of foreign coin, and fix the standard of weights and measures;

To provide for the punishment of counterfeiting the securities and current coin of the United States;

To establish post-offices and post-roads;

To promote the progress of science and useful arts, by securing for limited times to authors and inventors the exclusive right to their respective writings and discoveries;

To constitute tribunals inferior to the Supreme Court;

To define and punish piracies and felonies committed on the high seas, and offences against the law of nations;

To declare war, grant letters of marque and reprisal, and make rules concerning captures on land and water;

To raise and support armies, but no appropriation of money to that use shall be for a longer term than two years;

To provide and maintain a navy;

To make rules for the government and regulation of the land and naval forces;

To provide for calling forth the militia to execute the laws of the Union, suppress insurrections, and repel invasions;

To provide for organizing, arming, and disciplining the militia, and for governing such part of them as may be employed in the service of the United States, reserving to the States respectively the appointment of the officers, and the authority of training the militia according to the discipline prescribed by Congress;

To exercise exclusive legislation in all cases whatsoever, over such district (not exceeding ten miles square), as may, by cession of particular States, and the acceptance of Congress, become the seat of the Government of the United States, and to exercise like authority over all places purchased by the consent of the Legislature of the State in which the same shall be, for the erection of forts, magazines, arsenals, dock-yards, and other needful buildings; and

To make all laws which shall be necessary and proper for carrying into execution the foregoing powers, and all other powers vested by this Constitution in the Government of the United States, or in any department or officer thereof.

SECT. 9. The migration or importation of such persons as any of the States now existing shall think proper to admit, shall not be prohibited by the Congress prior to the year one thousand eight hundred and eight, but a tax or duty may be imposed on such importation, not exceeding ten dollars for each person.

The privilege of the Writ of Habeas Corpus shall not be suspended, unless when in cases of rebellion or invasion the public safety may require it.

No bill of attainder or *ex post facto* law shall be passed.

No capitation or other direct tax shall be laid, unless in proportion to the census or enumeration hereinbefore directed to be taken.

No tax or duty shall be laid on articles exported from any State.

No preference shall be given by any regulation of commerce or revenue to the ports of one State over those of another; nor shall vessels bound to or from one State, be obliged to enter, clear, or pay duties in another.

No money shall be drawn from the treasury, but in consequence of appropriations made by law; and a regular statement and account of the receipts and expenditures of all public money shall be published from time to time.

No title of nobility shall be granted by the United States; and no person holding any office of profit or trust under them shall, without the consent of the Congress, accept of any present, emolument, office, or title, of any kind whatever, from any king, prince, or foreign State.

SECT. 10. No State shall enter into any treaty, alliance, or confederation; grant letters of marque and reprisal; coin money; emit bills of credit; make anything but gold and silver coin a tender in payment of debts; pass any bill of attainder, *ex post facto* law, or law impairing the obligations of contracts, or grant any title of nobility.

No State shall, without the consent of the Congress, lay any imposts or duties on imports or exports, except what may be absolutely necessary for executing its inspection laws; and the net produce of all duties and imposts, laid by any State on imports or exports, shall be for the use of the Treasury of the United States; and all such laws shall be subject to the revision and control of the Congress.

No State shall, without the consent of Congress, lay any duty on tonnage, keep troops or ships of war in time of peace, enter into any agreement or compact with another State, or with a foreign power, or engage in war, unless actually invaded, or in such imminent danger as will not admit of delay.

ARTICLE II.

SECTION 1. The Executive power shall be vested in a President of the United States of America. He shall hold his office during the term of four years, and, together with the Vice-President, chosen for the same term, be elected as follows:

Each State shall appoint, in such manner as the Legislature thereof may direct, a number of Electors, equal to the whole number of Senators and Representatives to which the State may be entitled in the Congress; but no Senator or Representative, or person holding an office of trust or profit under the United States, shall be appointed an Elector.

[* The Electors shall meet in their respective States, and vote by ballot for two persons, of whom one at least shall not be an inhabitant of the same State with themselves. And they shall make a list of all the persons voted for, and of the number of votes for each; which list they shall sign and certify, and transmit sealed to the seat of the Government of the United States, directed to the President of the Senate. The President of the Senate shall, in the presence of the Senate and House of Representatives, open all the certificates, and the votes shall then be counted. The person having the greatest number of votes shall be the President, if such number be a majority of the whole number of Electors appointed; and if there be more than one who have such majority, and have an equal number of votes, then the House of Representatives shall immediately choose by ballot one of them for President; and if no person have a majority, then from the five highest on the list the said House shall in like manner choose the President. But in choosing the President, the votes shall be taken by States, the representation from each State having one vote; a quorum for this pur-

* This clause within brackets has been superseded and annulled by the 12th amendment on page 519.

pose shall consist of a member or members from two-thirds of the States, and a majority of all the States shall be necessary to a choice. In every case, after the choice of the President, the person having the greatest number of votes of the Electors shall be the Vice-President. But if there should remain two or more who have equal votes, the Senate shall choose from them by ballot the Vice-President.]

The Congress may determine the time of choosing the Electors, and the day on which they shall give their votes; which day shall be the same throughout the United States.

No person except a natural born citizen, or a citizen of the United States at the time of the adoption of this Constitution, shall be eligible to the office of President; neither shall any person be eligible to that office who shall not have attained to the age of thirty-five years, and been fourteen years a resident within the United States.

In case of the removal of the President from office, or of his death, resignation, or inability to discharge the powers and duties of the said office, the same shall devolve on the Vice-President, and the Congress may by law provide for the case of removal, death, resignation, or inability, both of the President and Vice-President, declaring what officer shall then act as President, and such officer shall act accordingly, until the disability be removed, or a President shall be elected.

The President shall, at stated times, receive for his services a compensation, which shall neither be increased nor diminished during the period for which he shall have been elected, and he shall not receive within that period any other emolument from the United States, or any of them.

Before he enter on the execution of his office, he shall take the following oath or affirmation:

"I do solemnly swear (or affirm) that I will faithfully execute the office of President of the United States, and will, to the best of my ability, preserve, protect, and defend the Constitution of the United States."

SECT. 2. The President shall be Commander-in-chief of the Army and Navy of the United States, and of the Militia of the several States, when called into the actual service of the United States; he may require the opinion, in writing, of the principal officer in each of the Executive Departments, upon any subject relating to the duties of their respective offices, and he shall have power to grant reprieves and pardons for offences against the United States, except in cases of impeachment.

He shall have power, by and with the advice and consent of the Senate, to make treaties, provided two-thirds of the Senators present concur; and he shall nominate, and by and with the advice and consent of the Senate, shall appoint Ambassadors, other public Ministers and Consuls, Judges of the Supreme Court, and all other officers of the United States, whose appointments are not herein otherwise provided for, and which shall be established by law; but the Congress may by law vest the appointment of such inferior officers, as they think proper, in the President alone, in the Courts of law, or in the heads of Departments.

The President shall have power to fill up all vacancies that may happen during the recess of the Senate, by granting commissions which shall expire at the end of their next session.

SECT. 3. He shall from time to time give to the Congress information of the state of the Union, and recommend to their consideration such measures as he shall judge necessary and expedient; he may, on extraordinary occasions, convene both Houses, or either of them, and in case of disagreement between them, with respect to the time of adjournment, he may adjourn them to such time as he shall think proper; he shall receive Ambassadors and other public Ministers; he shall take care that the laws be faithfully executed, and shall commission all the officers of the United States.

SECT. 4. The President, Vice-President, and all civil officers of the United States, shall be removed from office on impeachment for, and conviction of, treason, bribery, or other high crimes and misdemeanors.

ARTICLE III.

SECTION 1. The Judicial power of the United States shall be vested in one

Supreme Court, and in such inferior courts as the Congress may from time to time ordain and establish. The Judges, both of the Supreme and inferior courts, shall hold their offices during good behavior, and shall, at stated times, receive for their services a compensation, which shall not be diminished during their continuance in office.

SECT. 2. The judicial power shall extend to all cases, in law and equity, arising under this Constitution, the laws of the United States, and treaties made, or which shall be made, under their authority; to all cases affecting Ambassadors, other public Ministers, and Consuls; to all cases of admiralty and maritime jurisdiction; to controversies to which the United States shall be a party; to controversies between two or more States; between a State and citizens of another State; between citizens of different States; between citizens of the same State claiming lands under grants of different States; and between a State, or the citizens thereof, and foreign States, citizens, or subjects.

In all cases affecting Ambassadors, other public Ministers, and Consuls, and those in which a State shall be party, the Supreme Court shall have original jurisdiction. In all the other cases before mentioned, the Supreme Court shall have appellate jurisdiction, both as to law and fact, with such exceptions, and under such regulations as the Congress shall make.

The trial of all crimes, except in cases of impeachment, shall be by jury; and such trial shall be held in the State where the said crimes shall have been committed; but when not committed within any State, the trial shall be at such place or places as the Congress may by law have directed.

SECT. 3. Treason against the United States shall consist only in levying war against them, or in adhering to their enemies, giving them aid and comfort. No person shall be convicted of treason unless on the testimony of two witnesses to the same overt act, or on confession in open court.

The Congress shall have power to declare the punishment of treason, but no attainder of treason shall work corruption of blood, or forfeiture, except during the life of the person attainted.

ARTICLE IV.

SECTION 1. Full faith and credit shall be given in each State to the public acts, records, and judicial proceedings of every other State. And the Congress may by general laws prescribe the manner in which such acts, records, and proceedings shall be proved, and the effect thereof.

SECT. 2. The citizens of each State shall be entitled to all privileges and immunities of citizens in the several States.

A person charged in any State with treason, felony, or other crime, who shall flee from justice, and be found in another State, shall, on demand of the Executive authority of the State from which he fled, be delivered up, to be removed to the State having jurisdiction of the crime.

No person held to service or labor in one State, under the laws thereof, escaping into another, shall, in consequence of any law or regulation therein, be discharged from such service or labor, but shall be delivered up on claim of the party to whom such service or labor may be due.

SECT. 3. New States may be admitted by the Congress into this Union; but no new State shall be formed or erected within the jurisdiction of any other State; nor any State be formed by the junction of two or more States, or parts of States, without the consent of the Legislatures of the States concerned, as well as of the Congress.

The Congress shall have power to dispose of and make all needful rules and regulations respecting the territory or other property belonging to the United States; and nothing in this Constitution shall be so construed as to prejudice any claims of the United States, or of any particular State.

SECT. 4. The United States shall guarantee to every State in this Union a republican form of government, and shall protect each of them against invasion; and on application of the Legislature, or of the Executive (when the Legislature cannot be convened), against domestic violence.

ARTICLE V.

The Congress, whenever two-thirds of both Houses shall deem it necessary, shall propose amendments to this Constitution, or on the application of the Legislatures of two-thirds of the several States, shall call a convention for proposing amendments, which, in either case, shall be valid to all intents and purposes, as part of this Constitution, when ratified by the Legislatures of three-fourths of the several States, or by conventions in three-fourths thereof, as the one or the other mode of ratification may be proposed by the Congress; *Provided*, that no amendment which may be made prior to the year one thousand eight hundred and eight, shall in any manner affect the first and fourth clauses of the ninth section of the first article; and that no State, without its consent, shall be deprived of its equal suffrage in the Senate.

ARTICLE VI.

All debts contracted and engagements entered into, before the adoption of this Constitution, shall be as valid against the United States under this Constitution, as under the Confederation.

This Constitution, and the laws of the United States which shall be made in pursuance thereof, and all treaties made, or which shall be made, under the authority of the United States, shall be the supreme law of the land; and the Judges in every State shall be bound thereby, anything in the constitution or laws of any State to the contrary notwithstanding.

The Senators and Representatives before mentioned, and the members of the several State Legislatures, and all executive and judicial officers, both of the United States and of the several States, shall be bound by oath or affirmation to support this Constitution; but no religious test shall ever be required as a qualification to any office or public trust under the United States.

ARTICLE VII.

The ratification of the Conventions of nine States shall be sufficient for the establishment of this Constitution between the States so ratifying the same.

DONE in Convention by the unanimous consent of the States present, the seventeenth day of September, in the year of our Lord one thousand seven hundred and eighty-seven, and of the Independence of the United States of America the twelfth. IN WITNESS whereof, we have hereunto subscribed our names.

GEORGE WASHINGTON,
President, and Deputy from Virginia.

NEW HAMPSHIRE.

John Langdon, Nicholas Gilman.

MASSACHUSETTS.

Nathaniel Gorham, Rufus King.

CONNECTICUT.

William S. Johnson, Roger Sherman.

NEW YORK.

Alexander Hamilton.

NEW JERSEY.

William Livingston, David Brearley,
William Paterson, Jonathan Dayton.

PENNSYLVANIA.

Benjamin Franklin, Thomas Mifflin,
Robert Morris, George Clymer,
Thomas Fitzsimmons, Jared Ingersoll,
James Wilson, Gouverneur Morris.

DELAWARE.

George Read,
John Dickinson,
Jaco. Broom,
Gunning Bedford, Jr.,
Richard Bassett.

MARYLAND.

James McHenry,
Daniel Carroll,
Daniel Jenifer, of St. Thomas.

VIRGINIA.

John Blair,
James Madison, Jr.

NORTH CAROLINA.

William Blount,
Hugh Williamson,
Richard D. Spaight.

SOUTH CAROLINA.

J. Rutledge,
Charles Pinckney,
Charles C. Pinckney,
Pierce Butler.

GEORGIA.

William Few,
Abraham Baldwin.

Attest: WILLIAM JACKSON, *Secretary.*

STATE RATIFICATIONS OF THE CONSTITUTION.

The Constitution was adopted September 17, 1787, by the Convention appointed in pursuance of the resolution of the Congress of the Confederation of February 21, 1787, and was ratified by the Conventions of the several States as follows, viz.:

By Convention of	Delaware,	December	7, 1787.
"	Pennsylvania,	December	12, 1787.
"	New Jersey,	December	18, 1787.
"	Georgia,	January	2, 1788.
"	Connecticut,	January	9, 1788.
"	Massachusetts,	February	6, 1788.
"	Maryland,	April	28, 1788.
"	South Carolina,	May	23, 1788.
"	New Hampshire,	June	21, 1788.
"	Virginia,	June	26, 1788.
"	New York,	July	26, 1788.
"	North Carolina,	November	21, 1789.
"	Rhode Island,	May	29, 1790.

ARTICLES IN ADDITION TO, AND AMENDMENT OF,

THE CONSTITUTION

OF THE

UNITED STATES OF AMERICA,

PROPOSED BY CONGRESS, AND RATIFIED BY THE LEGISLATURES OF THE SEVERAL STATES, PURSUANT TO THE FIFTH ARTICLE OF THE ORIGINAL CONSTITUTION.

ARTICLE I.

CONGRESS shall make no law respecting an establishment of religion, or prohibiting the free exercise thereof; or abridging the freedom of speech, or of the press; or the right of the people peaceably to assemble, and to petition the Government for a redress of grievances.

ARTICLE II.

A well-regulated militia being necessary to the security of a free State, the right of the people to keep and bear arms shall not be infringed.

ARTICLE III.

No soldier shall, in time of peace, be quartered in any house, without the consent of the owner, nor in time of war, but in a manner to be prescribed by law.

ARTICLE IV.

The right of the people to be secure in their persons, houses, papers, and effects, against unreasonable searches and seizures, shall not be violated, and no warrants shall issue, but upon probable cause, supported by oath or affirmation, and particularly describing the place to be searched, and the persons or things to be seized.

ARTICLE V.

No person shall be held to answer for a capital, or otherwise infamous crime, unless on a presentment or indictment of a grand jury, except in cases arising in the land or naval forces, or in the militia, when in actual service in time of war or public danger; nor shall any person be subject for the same offence to be twice put in jeopardy of life or limb; nor shall be compelled in any criminal case to be a witness against himself, nor be deprived of life, liberty, or property, without due process of law; nor shall private property be taken for public use, without just compensation.

ARTICLE VI.

In all criminal prosecutions, the accused shall enjoy the right to a speedy and public trial, by an impartial jury of the State and district wherein the crime shall have been committed, which district shall have been previously ascertained by law, and to be informed of the nature and cause of the accusation; to be confronted with the witnesses against him; to have compulsory process for obtaining witnesses in his favor, and to have the assistance of counsel for his defence.

ARTICLE VII.

In suits at common law, where the value in controversy shall exceed twenty dollars, the right of trial by jury shall be preserved, and no fact tried by a jury shall be otherwise re-examined in any court of the United States, than according to the rules of the common law.

ARTICLE VIII.

Excessive bail shall not be required, nor excessive fines imposed, nor cruel and unusual punishments inflicted.

ARTICLE IX.

The enumeration in the Constitution, of certain rights, shall not be construed to deny or disparage others retained by the people.

ARTICLE X.

The powers not delegated to the United States by the Constitution, nor prohibited by it to the States, are reserved to the States respectively, or to the people.

ARTICLE XI.

The judicial power of the United States shall not be construed to extend to any suit in law or equity, commenced or prosecuted against one of the United States by citizens of another State, or by citizens or subjects of any foreign State.

ARTICLE XII.

The Electors shall meet in their respective States, and vote by ballot for President and Vice-President, one of whom, at least, shall not be an inhabitant of the same State with themselves; they shall name in their ballots the person voted for as President, and in distinct ballots the person voted for as Vice-President, and they shall make distinct lists of all persons voted for as President, and of all persons voted for as Vice-President, and of the number of votes for each, which lists they shall sign and certify, and transmit sealed to the seat of the Government of the United States, directed to the President of the Senate. The President of the Senate shall, in presence of the Senate and House of Representatives, open all the certificates, and the votes shall then be counted; the person having the greatest number of votes for President shall be the President, if such number be a majority of the whole number of Electors appointed; and if no person have such majority, then from the persons having the highest numbers, not exceeding three on the list of those voted for as President, the House of Representatives shall choose immediately, by ballot, the President. But in choosing the President, the votes shall be taken by States, the representation from each State having one vote; a quorum for this purpose shall consist of a member or members from two-thirds of the States, and a majority of all the States shall be necessary to a choice. And if the House of Representatives shall not choose a President whenever the right of choice shall devolve upon them, before the fourth day of March next following, then the Vice-President shall act as President, as in the case of the death or other constitutional disability of the President. The person having the greatest number of votes as Vice-President, shall be the Vice-President, if such number be a majority of the whole number of Electors appointed, and if no person have a majority, then from the two highest numbers on the list, the Senate shall choose the Vice-President; a quorum for the purpose shall consist of two-thirds of the whole number of Senators, and a majority of the whole number shall be necessary to a choice. But no person constitutionally ineligible to the office of President shall be eligible to that of Vice-President of the United States.

THE FOLLOWING IS PREFIXED TO THE FIRST TEN* OF THE PRECEDING AMENDMENTS.

CONGRESS OF THE UNITED STATES.

BEGUN AND HELD AT THE CITY OF NEW YORK, ON WEDNESDAY, THE FOURTH OF MARCH, ONE THOUSAND SEVEN HUNDRED AND EIGHTY-NINE.

THE Conventions of a number of the States having, at the time of their adopting the Constitution, expressed a desire, in order to prevent misconstruction or abuse of its powers, that further declaratory and restrictive clauses should be added; and as extending the ground of public confidence in the Government will best insure the beneficent ends of its institution,—

Resolved, by the Senate and House of Representatives of the United States of America, in Congress assembled, two-thirds of both Houses concurring, That the following articles be proposed to the Legislatures of the several States, as amendments to the Constitution of the United States, all, or any of which articles, when ratified by three-fourths of the said Legislatures, to be valid to all intents and purposes, as part of the said Constitution, viz.:

Articles in addition to, and amendment of, the Constitution of the United States of America, proposed by Congress, and ratified by the Legislatures of the several States pursuant to the Fifth Article of the original Constitution.

The first ten amendments of the Constitution were ratified by the States as follows, viz.:

By New Jersey,	November 20, 1789.
" Maryland,	December 19, 1789.
" North Carolina,	December 22, 1789.
" South Carolina,	January 19, 1790.
" New Hampshire,	January 25, 1790.
" Delaware,	January 28, 1790.
" Pennsylvania,	March 10, 1790.
" New York,	March 27, 1790.
" Rhode Island,	June 15, 1790.
" Vermont,	November 3, 1791.
" Virginia,	December 15, 1791.

* It may be proper here to state that twelve articles of amendment were proposed by the First Congress, of which but ten were ratified by the States,—the first and second in order not having been ratified by the requisite number of States.

These two were as follows:

Article First.—After the first enumeration required by the First Article of the Constitution, there shall be one Representative for every thirty thousand, until the number shall amount to one hundred, after which, the proportion shall be so regulated by Congress, that there shall not be less than one hundred Representatives, nor less than one Representative for every forty thousand persons, until the number of Representatives shall amount to two hundred, after which the proportion shall be so regulated by Congress that there shall not be less than two hundred Representatives, nor more than one Representative for every fifty thousand persons.

Article Second.—No law, varying the compensation for the services of the Senators and Representatives, shall take effect until an election of Representatives shall have intervened.

THE FOLLOWING IS PREFIXED TO THE ELEVENTH OF THE PRECEDING AMENDMENTS.

THIRD CONGRESS OF THE UNITED STATES,

AT THE FIRST SESSION, BEGUN AND HELD AT THE CITY OF PHILADELPHIA, IN THE STATE OF PENNSYLVANIA, ON MONDAY, THE SECOND OF DECEMBER, ONE THOUSAND SEVEN HUNDRED AND NINETY-THREE.

Resolved, by the Senate and House of Representatives of the United States of America, in Congress assembled, two-thirds of both Houses concurring, That the following article be proposed to the Legislatures of the several States as an amendment to the Constitution of the United States; which, when ratified by three-fourths of the said Legislatures, shall be valid as part of the said Constitution, viz.:

THE FOLLOWING IS PREFIXED TO THE TWELFTH OF THE PRECEDING AMENDMENTS.

EIGHTH CONGRESS OF THE UNITED STATES,

AT THE FIRST SESSION, BEGUN AND HELD AT THE CITY OF WASHINGTON, IN THE TERRITORY OF COLUMBIA, ON MONDAY, THE SEVENTEENTH OF OCTOBER, ONE THOUSAND EIGHT HUNDRED AND THREE.

Resolved, by the Senate and House of Representatives of the United States of America, in Congress assembled, two-thirds of both Houses concurring, That in lieu of the third paragraph of the first section of the Second Article of the Constitution of the United States, the following be proposed as an amendment to the Constitution of the United States; which, when ratified by three-fourths of the Legislatures of the several States, shall be valid to all intents and purposes, as part of the said Constitution, to wit:

The ten first of the preceding amendments were proposed at the first session of the First Congress of the United States, September 25, 1789, and were finally ratified by the constitutional number of States, December 15, 1791. The eleventh amendment was proposed at the first session of the Third Congress, March 5, 1794, and was declared, in a message from the President of the United States to both houses of Congress, dated January 8, 1798, to have been adopted by the constitutional number of States. The twelfth amendment was proposed at the first session of the Eighth Congress, December 12, 1803, and was adopted by the constitutional number of States in 1804, according to a public notice thereof by the Secretary of State, dated September 25 of the same year.

ORGANIZATION OF THE EXECUTIVE DEPARTMENTS.

STATE DEPARTMENT.

THIS Department is managed by the Secretary of State, and one Assistant Secretary.

DIPLOMATIC BRANCH.

This branch has charge of all correspondence between the Department and other diplomatic agents of the United States abroad, and those of foreign powers accredited to this Government. In it all diplomatic instructions sent from the Department, and communications to Commissioners under treaties of boundaries, &c., are prepared, copied, and recorded; and all of like character received are registered and filed, their contents being first entered in an analytic table or index.

CONSULAR BRANCH.

This branch has charge of the correspondence, &c., between the Department and the Consuls and Commercial Agents of the United States. In it instructions to those officers, and answers to their despatches and to letters from other persons asking for consular agency, or relating to consular affairs, are prepared and recorded.

THE DISBURSING AGENT.

He has charge of all correspondence and other matters connected with accounts relating to any fund with the disbursement of which the Department is charged.

THE TRANSLATOR.

His duties are to furnish such translations as the Department may require. He also records the commissions of Consuls and Vice-Consuls, when not in English, upon which exequaturs are issued.

CLERK OF APPOINTMENTS AND COMMISSIONS.

He makes out and records commissions, letters of appointment, and nominations to the Senate; makes out and records exequaturs, and records, when in English, the commissions on which they are issued. Has charge of the library.

CLERK OF THE ROLLS AND ARCHIVES.

He takes charge of the rolls, or enrolled acts and resolutions of Congress, as they are received at the Department from the President; prepares the authenticated copies thereof which are called for; prepares for, and superintends their publication, and that of treaties, in the newspapers and in book form; attends to their distribution throughout the United States, and that of all documents and publications in regard to which this duty is assigned to the Department; writing and answering all letters connected therewith. Has charge of all Indian treaties, and business relating thereto.

CLERK OF TERRITORIAL BUSINESS—THE SEAL OF THE DEPARTMENT.

He has charge of the seals of the United States and of the Department, and prepares and attaches certificates to papers presented for authentication; has charge of the territorial business; immigration and registered seamen; records all letters from the Department other than the diplomatic and consular.

CLERK OF PARDONS AND PASSPORTS.

He prepares and records pardons and remissions, and registers and files the petitions and papers on which they are founded. Makes out and records passports; keeps a daily register of all letters, other than diplomatic and consular, received, and of the disposition made of them; prepares letters relating to this business.

SUPERINTENDENT OF STATISTICS.

He superintends the preparation of the "Annual Report of the Secretary of State on Foreign Commerce," as required by the Acts of 1842 and 1856.

ATTORNEY-GENERAL'S OFFICE.

The Attorney-General of the United States is at the head of this office. Its ordinary business may be classified under the following heads:

1. Official opinions on the current business of the Government, as called for by the President, by any head of Department, or by the Solicitor of the Treasury.
2. Examination of the titles of all land purchased, as the sites of arsenals, custom-houses, light-houses, and all other public works of the United States.
3. Applications for pardons in all cases of conviction in the courts of the United States.
4. Applications for appointment in all the judicial and legal business of the Government.
5. The conduct and argument of all suits in the Supreme Court of the United States in which the Government is concerned.
6. The supervision of all other suits arising in any of the Departments when referred by the head thereof to the Attorney-General.

To these ordinary heads of the business of the office has been added the direction of all appeals on land claims in California.

INTERIOR DEPARTMENT.

This Department is in charge of the Secretary of the Interior, and one Assistant Secretary, who have the supervision and management of the following branches of the public service.

The Public Lands.—The chief of this bureau is called the Commissioner of the General Land-office. The Land Bureau is charged with the survey, management, and sale of the public domain, and the issuing of titles therefor, whether derived from confirmation of grants made by former governments, by sales, donations, of grants for schools, military bounties, or public improvements, and likewise the revision of Virginia military bounty-land claims, and the issuing of scrip in lieu thereof. The Land-office, also, audits its own accounts.

Pensions.—The Commissioner is charged with the examination and adjudication of all claims arising under the various and numerous laws passed by Congress granting bounty-land or pensions for the military or naval service in the Revolutionary and subsequent wars in which the United States have been engaged.

INDIANS.—Commissioner of Indian Affairs, who has charge of all business connected with the Indian tribes.

PATENT-OFFICE.—To this bureau is committed the execution and performance of all "acts and things touching and respecting the granting and issuing of patents for new and useful discoveries, inventions, and improvements;" and the collection of statistics.

An act of Congress provided that all books, maps, charts, and other publications heretofore deposited in the Department of State, according to the laws regulating copyrights, should be removed to the Department of the Interior, which is charged with all the duties connected with matters pertaining to copyright; which duties have been assigned by the Secretary of the Interior to the Patent-office, as belonging most appropriately to this branch of the service.

AGRICULTURAL BUREAU.—In charge of a Commissioner, who has exclusive supervision of all matters connected with agriculture.

Besides the above principal branches of this Executive Department, the organic act of 1849 transferred to it from the Treasury Department the supervision of the accounts of the United States Marshals and Attorneys, and the Clerks of the United States Courts, the management of the lead and other mines of the United States, and the affairs of the Penitentiary of the United States in the District of Columbia; and from the State Department, the duty of taking and returning the Censuses of the United States, and of supervising and directing the acts of the Commissioner of Public Buildings. The Hospital for the Insane of the Army and Navy and of the District of Columbia is also under the management of this Department; in addition to which, by later laws, the Secretary of the Interior is charged with the construction of the three wagon roads leading to the Pacific coast.

Under act of February 5, 1859, "providing for keeping and distributing a public documents, all the books, documents, &c., printed or purchased by the Government," the Annals of Congress, American State Papers, American Archives, Jefferson's and Adams's works, are transferred to this Department from the State Department, Library of Congress, and elsewhere; also the Journals and Documents of the Thirty-fifth Congress. These valuable works are distributed to those who are by law entitled to receive them, and to such "colleges, public libraries, athenæums, literary and scientific institutions, boards of trade, or public associations," as shall be designated by the members of Congress.

TREASURY DEPARTMENT.

The Treasury Department is in charge of the Secretary of the Treasury, and one Assistant Secretary, and the following is a brief indication of the duties of the several bureaus.

SECRETARY'S OFFICE.

The Secretary is charged with the general supervision of the fiscal transactions of the Government, and of the execution of the laws concerning the commerce and navigation of the United States. He superintends the survey of the coast, the light-house establishment, the marine hospitals of the United States, and the construction of certain public buildings for custom-houses and other purposes.

FIRST COMPTROLLER'S OFFICE.

He prescribes the mode of keeping and rendering accounts for the civil and diplomatic service, as well as the public lands, and revises and certifies the balances arising thereon.

SECOND COMPTROLLER'S OFFICE.

He prescribes the mode of keeping and rendering the accounts of the Army and Navy, and of the Indian and Pension bureaus, of the public service, and revises and certifies the balances arising thereon.

OFFICE OF COMMISSIONER OF THE CUSTOMS.

He prescribes the mode of keeping and rendering the accounts of the customs revenue and disbursements, and for the building and repairing custom-houses, &c., and revises and certifies the balances arising thereon.

FIRST AUDITOR'S OFFICE.

He receives and adjusts the accounts of the customs revenue and disbursements, appropriations and expenditures on the account of the civil list and under private acts of Congress, and reports the balances to the Commissioner of the Customs and the First Comptroller, respectively, for their decision thereon.

SECOND AUDITOR'S OFFICE.

He receives and adjusts all accounts relating to the pay, clothing, and recruiting of the army, as well as armories, arsenals, and ordnance, and all accounts relating to the Indian Department, and reports the balances to the Second Comptroller for his decision thereon.

THIRD AUDITOR'S OFFICE.

He receives and adjusts all accounts for subsistence of the army, fortifications, Military Academy, military roads, and the Quartermaster's department, as well as for pensions, claims arising from military services previous to 1816, and for horses and other property lost in the military service, under various acts of Congress, and reports the balances to the Second Comptroller for his decision thereon.

FOURTH AUDITOR'S OFFICE.

He receives and adjusts all accounts for the service of the Navy Department, and reports the balances to the Second Comptroller for his decision thereon.

FIFTH AUDITOR'S OFFICE.

He receives and adjusts all accounts for diplomatic and similar services performed under the direction of the State Department, and reports the balances to the First Comptroller for his decision thereon.

SIXTH AUDITOR'S OFFICE.

He receives and adjusts all accounts arising from the service of the Post-office Department. His decisions are final, unless an appeal be taken in twelve months to the First Comptroller. He superintends the collection of all debts due the Post-office Department, and all penalties and forfeitures imposed on postmasters and mail contractors for failing to do their duty; he directs suits and legal proceedings, civil and criminal, and takes all such measures as may be authorized by law to enforce the prompt payment of moneys due to the department; instructing United States attorneys, marshals, and clerks in all matters relating thereto; and receives returns from each term of the United States Courts of the condition and progress of such suits and legal proceedings; has charge of all lands and other property assigned to the United States in payment of debts due the Post-office Department, and has power to sell and dispose of the same for the benefit of the United States.

TREASURER'S OFFICE.

He receives and keeps the moneys of the United States in his own office, and that of the depositories created by the Act of August 6, 1846, and pays out the same upon warrants drawn by the Secretary of the Treasury, countersigned by the First Comptroller, and upon warrants drawn by the Postmaster-General, countersigned by the Sixth Auditor, and recorded by the Register. He also holds public moneys advanced by warrant to disbursing officers, and pays out the same upon their checks.

REGISTER'S OFFICE.

He keeps the accounts of public receipts and expenditures; receives the returns and makes out the official statement of commerce and navigation of the United States; and receives from the First Comptroller and Commissioner of Customs all accounts and vouchers decided by them, and is charged by law with their safe keeping.

SOLICITOR'S OFFICE.

He superintends all civil suits commenced by the United States (*except those arising in the Post-office Department*), and instructs the United States attorneys, marshals, and clerks in all matters relating to them and their results. He receives returns from each term of the United States Courts, showing the progress and condition of such suits; has charge of all lands and other property assigned to the United States in payment of debts (*except those assigned in payment of debts due the Post-office Department*), and has power to sell and dispose of the same for the benefit of the United States.

LIGHT-HOUSE BOARD.

Secretary of the Treasury *ex-officio* President. This board directs the building and repairing of light-houses, light-vessels, buoys, and beacons, contracts for supplies of oil, &c.

UNITED STATES COAST SURVEY.

Prof. A. D. Bache, LL.D., is the Superintendent, and he is also Superintendent of Weights and Measures. All the charts of the Government emanate from this office.

INTERNAL REVENUE OFFICE.

A Commissioner, who has charge of all matters connected with the Tax Laws.

COMPTROLLER OF THE CURRENCY.

The head of this office has charge of everything connected with the issuing of money.

POST-OFFICE DEPARTMENT.

The direction and management of the Post-office Department are assigned by the Constitution and laws to the Postmaster-General. That its business may be the more conveniently arranged and prepared for his final action, it is distributed among several bureaus, as follows: The Appointment Office, in charge of the First Assistant Postmaster-General; the Contract Office, in charge of the Second Assistant Postmaster-General; the Finance Office, in charge of the Third Assistant Postmaster-General; and the Inspection Office, in charge of the Chief Clerk.

APPOINTMENT OFFICE.

To this office are assigned all questions which relate to the establishment and discontinuance of post-offices, changes of sites and names, appointment and removal of postmasters, and route and local agents, as, also, the giving of instructions to postmasters. Postmasters are furnished with marking and rating stamps and letter balances by this bureau, which is charged also with providing blanks and stationery for the use of the Department, and with the superintendence of the several agencies established for supplying postmasters with blanks. To this bureau is likewise assigned the supervision of the ocean mail steamship lines, and of the foreign and international postal arrangements.

CONTRACT OFFICE.

To this office is assigned the business of arranging the mail service of the United States, and placing the same under contract, embracing all correspondence and proceedings respecting the frequency of trips, mode of conveyance, and times of departures and arrivals on all the routes; the course of the mail between the different sections of the country, the points of mail distribution, and the regulations for the government of the domestic mail service of the United States. It prepares the advertisements for mail proposals, receives the bids, and takes charge of the annual and occasional mail lettings, and the adjustment and execution of the contracts. All applications for the establishment or alteration of mail arrangements, and the appointment of mail messengers, should be sent to this office. All claims should be submitted to it for transportation service not under contract, as the recognition of said service is first to be obtained through the Contract Office as a necessary authority for the proper credits at the Auditor's office. From this office all postmasters at the ends of routes receive the statement of mail arrangements prescribed for the respective routes. It reports weekly to the Auditor all contracts executed, and all orders affecting accounts for mail transportation; prepares the statistical exhibits of the mail service, and the reports of the mail lettings, giving a statement of each bid; also of the contracts made, the new service originated, the curtailments ordered, and the additional allowances granted within the year.

FINANCE OFFICE.

To this office are assigned the supervision and management of the financial business of the Department, not devolved by law upon the Auditor, embracing accounts with the draft offices and other depositories of the Department, the issuing of warrants and drafts in payment of balances, reported by the Auditor to be due to mail contractors and other persons, the supervision of the accounts of offices under orders to deposit their quarterly balances at designated points, and the superintendence of the rendition by postmasters of their quarterly returns of postages. It has charge of the dead-letter office, of the issuing of postage stamps and stamped envelopes for the prepayment of postage, and of the accounts connected therewith.

To the Third Assistant Postmaster-General all postmasters should direct their quarterly returns of postage; those at draft offices their letters reporting quarterly the net proceeds of their offices; and those at depositing offices their certificates of deposit; to him should also be directed the weekly and monthly returns of the depositaries of the Department, as well as all applications and receipts for postage stamps and stamped envelopes, and for dead-letters.

INSPECTION OFFICE.

To this office is assigned the duty of receiving and examining the registers of the arrivals and departures of the mails, certificates of the service of route agents, and reports of mail failures; of noting the delinquencies of contractors, and preparing cases thereon for the action of the Postmaster-General; furnishing blanks for mail registers, and reports of mail failures; providing and sending out mail-bags and mail-locks and keys, and doing all other things which may be necessary to secure a faithful and exact performance of all mail contracts.

All cases of mail depredation, of violation of law by private expresses, or by the forging or illegal use of postage stamps, are under the supervision of this office, and should be reported to it.

All communications respecting lost money, letters, mail depredations, or other violations of law, or mail-locks and keys, should be directed, "Chief Clerk, Post-office Department."

All registers of the arrivals and departures of the mails, certificates of the service of route agents, reports of mail failures, applications for blank registers, and reports of failures, and all complaints against contractors for irregular or imperfect service, should be directed, "Inspection-office, Post-office Department."

NAVY DEPARTMENT.

The Navy Department consists of the Navy Department proper, being the office of the Secretary and of five bureaus attached thereto, viz.: Bureau of Navy-yards and Docks; Bureau of Construction, Equipment, and Repair; Bureau of Provisions and Clothing; Bureau of Ordnance and Hydrography; and the Bureau of Medicine and Surgery.

The following is a statement of the duties of each of these offices.

SECRETARY'S OFFICE.

The Secretary of the Navy has charge of everything connected with the naval establishment, and the execution of all laws relating thereto is intrusted to him, under the general direction of the President of the United States, who, by the Constitution, is Commander-in-chief of the Army and Navy. All instructions to commanders of squadrons, and commanders of vessels, all orders of officers, commissions of officers both in the navy and marine corps, appointments of commissioned and warrant officers, orders for the enlistment and discharge of seamen, emanate from the Secretary's office. All the duties of the different bureaus are performed under the authority of the Secretary, and their orders are considered as emanating from him. The general superintendence of the marine corps forms, also, a part of the duties of the Secretary, and all the orders of the commandant of that corps should be approved by him.

BUREAU OF NAVY-YARDS AND DOCKS.

All the navy-yards, docks, and wharves, buildings and machinery in navy-yards, and everything immediately connected with them, are under the superintendence of this bureau. It is also charged with the management of the Naval Asylum.

BUREAU OF CONSTRUCTION, EQUIPMENT, AND REPAIR.

The office of the Engineer-in-chief of the Navy is attached to this bureau, who is assisted by three assistant engineers. This bureau has charge of the building and repairs of all vessels-of-war, purchase of materials, and the providing of all vessels with their equipments, as sails, anchors, water-tanks, &c. The Engineer-in-chief superintends the construction of all marine steam-engines for the navy, and, with the approval of the Secretary, decides upon plans for their construction.

BUREAU OF PROVISIONS AND CLOTHING.

All provisions for the use of the navy, and clothing, together with the making of contracts for furnishing the same, come under the charge of this bureau.

BUREAU OF ORDNANCE AND HYDROGRAPHY.

This bureau has charge of all ordnance and ordnance stores, the manufacture or purchase of cannon, guns, powder, shot, shells, &c., and the equipment of vessels-of-war, with everything connected therewith. It also provides them with maps, charts, chronometers, barometers, &c., together with such books as are furnished ships-of-war. "The United States Naval Observatory and Hydrographical Office," at Washington, and the Naval Academies at Annapolis and Newport, are also under the general superintendence of the chief of this bureau.

BUREAU OF MEDICINE AND SURGERY.

Everything relating to medicines and medical stores, treatment of sick and wounded, and management of hospitals, comes within the superintendence of this bureau.

WAR DEPARTMENT.

This Department is in charge of the Secretary of War, one regular Assistant and two temporary Assistant Secretaries. The following bureaus are attached to this Department:

COMMANDING GENERAL'S OFFICE.

The duties of this officer comprise the arrangement of the military forces, and the superintendence of the recruiting service; he attends to the discipline of the army; orders courts-martial; and it is his province to see that the laws and regulations of the army are enforced. This office is usually located in Washington, but wherever it may be, it is called the Headquarters of the Army.

ADJUTANT-GENERAL'S OFFICE.

In this office are kept all the records which refer to the *personnel* of the army, the rolls, &c., and where all military commissions are made out; all orders which emanate from Headquarters or the War Department proper, pass through this office; and here are received all the annual returns from the army and militia of the United States.

QUARTERMASTER-GENERAL'S OFFICE.

The objects of this bureau are to insure an efficient system of supply, and to give facility and effect to the movements and operations of the army. It also has control of the barracks, and furnishes the clothing and all transportation that may be required for the army.

PAYMASTER-GENERAL'S OFFICE.

All the disbursements in money are made to the army from this office.

COMMISSARY-GENERAL'S OFFICE.

This office is charged with the duty of purchasing and issuing all rations to the army.

SURGEON-GENERAL'S OFFICE.

All matters connected with medicine and surgery, are under the control of this office, as well as the management of the sick and wounded, and also all the hospitals.

ENGINEER'S OFFICE.

In addition to a general direction of all matters connected with the Engineer Corps of the army, this office is also charged with the care of the Military Academy at West Point.

TOPOGRAPHICAL BUREAU.

This bureau has charge of all topographical operations and surveys for military purposes, and for purposes of internal improvement, and of all maps, drawings, and documents relating to those duties.

ORDNANCE BUREAU.

This office is charged with the control of the arsenals and armories, and has the superintendence of the manufacture of the arms and cannon, and the custody of all ordnance stores.

THE

SEVERAL STATES AND TERRITORIES

OF THE

AMERICAN UNION.

THE THIRTEEN ORIGINAL STATES THAT FORMED AND CONFIRMED THE UNION, BY THE ADOPTION OF THE CONSTITUTION, ARE AS FOLLOWS:

NEW HAMPSHIRE.

First settled at Dover and Portsmouth, in 1623, by the Puritans.

Embraced under the charters of Massachusetts, and continued under the same jurisdiction until September 18, 1679, when a separate charter and government was granted. A Constitution was formed January 5, 1776, which was altered in 1784, and was further altered and amended February 13, 1792.

This State ratified the Constitution of the United States, June 21, 1788.

Area, 9280 square miles. Population in 1850, 317,976; 1860, 326,073.

MASSACHUSETTS.

First settled at Plymouth, by English Puritans from Holland, who landed December 22, 1620.

Chartered March 4, 1629; also chartered January 13, 1630; an explanatory charter granted August 20, 1726; and more completely chartered October 7, 1731. Formed a Constitution March 2, 1780, which was altered and amended November 3, 1820, and on several occasions since that time.

Ratified the Constitution of the United States, February 6, 1788.

Area, 7800 square miles. Population in 1850, 994,514; 1860, 1,231,066.

RHODE ISLAND.

First settled at Providence, in 1636, by Roger Williams.

Embraced under the charters of Massachusetts, and continued under the same jurisdiction until July 8, 1662, when a separate charter was granted, which continued in force until a Constitution was formed, September, 1842.

Ratified the Constitution of the United States, May 29, 1790.

Area, 1306 square miles. Population in 1850, 147,545; 1860, 174,621.

CONNECTICUT.

First settled at Windsor, in 1635, by Puritans.

Embraced under the charters of Massachusetts, and continued under the same jurisdiction until April 23, 1662, when a separate charter was granted, which continued in force until a Constitution was formed, September 15, 1818.

Ratified the Constitution of the United States, January 9, 1788.

Area, 4674 square miles. Population in 1850, 370,792; 1860, 460,147.

NEW YORK.

First settled on Manhattan Island in 1614.

Granted to Duke of York, March 20, 1664, April 26, 1664, and June 24, 1664. Newly patented February 9, 1674; formed a Constitution, April 20, 1777, which was amended October 27, 1801, and further amended November 10, 1821. A new Constitution was formed in 1846.

Ratified the Constitution of the United States, July 26, 1788.

Area, 46,000 square miles. Population in 1850, 3,097,394; 1860, 3,880,735.

NEW JERSEY.

First settled at Bergen, in 1620, by the Dutch.

Held under same grants as New York; separated into East and West Jersey March 3, 1677. The government surrendered to the Crown in 1702, and so continued until the formation of a Constitution, July 2, 1776.

Ratified the Constitution of the United States, December 18, 1787.

Area, 8320 square miles. Population in 1850, 489,555; 1860, 672,035.

PENNSYLVANIA.

First settled on the Delaware River, in 1682, by William Penn.

Chartered February 28, 1681; formed a Constitution September 28, 1776; amended, September 2, 1790, and in 1838, and 1857.

Ratified the Constitution of the United States, December 12, 1787.

Area, 46,000 square miles. Population in 1850, 2,311,786; 1860, 2,906,115.

DELAWARE.

First settled at Cape Henlopen, in 1627, by Swedes and Finns.

Embraced in the charter, and continued under the government of Pennsylvania until the formation of a Constitution, September 20, 1776; a new Constitution formed June 12, 1792, and amended in 1831.

Ratified the Constitution of the United States, December 7, 1787.

Area, 2120 square miles. Population in 1850, 91,532; 1860, 112,216.

MARYLAND.

First settled at St. Mary, in 1634, by Roman Catholics.

Chartered June 20, 1632; formed a Constitution August 14, 1776, which was amended in 1795 and 1799, and further amended in November, 1812, and 1851.

Ratified the Constitution of the United States, April 28, 1788.

Area, 11,124 square miles. Population in 1850, 583,034; 1860, 687,049.

VIRGINIA.

First settled at Jamestown, in 1607, by the English.

Chartered April 10, 1606, May 23, 1609, and March 12, 1612; formed a Constitution July 5, 1776; amended, January 15, 1830.

Ratified the Constitution of the United States, June 26, 1788.

Area, 38,352 square miles. Population in 1850, 1,421,661; 1860, 1,261,397.

NORTH CAROLINA.

First settled at Albemarle, in 1650, by the English.

Chartered March 20, 1663, and June 30, 1665; formed a Constitution December 18, 1776, which was amended in 1835.

Ratified the Constitution of the United States, November 21, 1789.

Area, 50,704 square miles. Population in 1850, 869,039; 1860, 992,622.

SOUTH CAROLINA.

First settled at Port Royal, in 1670, by the Huguenots.

Embraced in the charters of Carolina or North Carolina, from which it was separated in 1729; formed a Constitution March 26, 1776, which was amended March 19, 1778, and June 3, 1790.

Ratified the Constitution of the United States, May 23, 1788.

Area, 29,585 square miles. Population in 1850, 668,507; 1860, 703,708.

GEORGIA.

First settled at Savannah, in 1733, by Oglethorpe.

Chartered June 9, 1732; formed a Constitution February 5, 1777, a second in 1785, a third May 30, 1798, and amended in 1839.

Ratified the Constitution of the United States, January 2, 1788.

Area, 58,000 square miles. Population in 1850, 906,185; 1860, 1,057,386.

THE STATES ADMITTED INTO THE UNION SINCE THE ADOPTION OF THE FEDERAL CONSTITUTION ARE AS FOLLOWS:

VERMONT.

First settled at Fort Dummer in 1764.

Formed from territory of New York.

Admitted March 4, 1791.

A Constitution adopted July 9, 1793.

Area, 9056½ square miles. Population in 1850, 314,120; 1860, 315,098.

KENTUCKY.

First settled near Lexington in 1775.

Formed from territory of Virginia.

Admitted June 1, 1792.

A Constitution laid before Congress November 7, 1792.

A new Constitution adopted August 17, 1799.

Area, 37,680 square miles. Population in 1850, 982,405; 1860, 1,155,684.

TENNESSEE.

Formed from territory of North Carolina in 1790.

Adopted a Constitution February 6, 1796, and amended in 1835.

Admitted June 1, 1796.

Area, 45,600 square miles. Population in 1850, 1,002,717; 1860, 1,109,801.

OHIO.

First settled at Marietta in 1788.

Formed from Northwest Territory.

Adopted a Constitution November 1, 1802, and amended in 1851.

Admitted November 29, 1802.

Area, 39,964 square miles. Population in 1850, 1,980,329; 1860, 2,339,511.

LOUISIANA.

First settled at Iberville in 1699.

Formed from French territory.

Adopted a Constitution January 22, 1812, and amended in 1845 and 1852.

Admitted April 8, 1812.

Area, 41,255 square miles. Population in 1850, 517,762; 1860, 708,002.

INDIANA.

First settled at Vincennes in 1730.
Formed from Northwest Territory.
Adopted a Constitution June 29, 1816, and amended in 1851.
Admitted December 11, 1816.
Area, 33,809 square miles. Population in 1850, 988,416; 1860, 1,350,428.

MISSISSIPPI.

First settled at Natchez in 1716.
Formed from territory of South Carolina and Georgia.
Adopted a Constitution March 1, 1817, and amended in 1832.
Admitted December 10, 1817.
Area, 47,156 square miles. Population in 1850, 606,526; 1860, 791,305.

ILLINOIS.

First settled at Kaskaskia in 1720.
Formed from Northwest Territory.
Adopted a Constitution August 26, 1818.
Admitted December 3, 1818.
Area, 55,409 square miles. Population in 1850, 851,470; 1860, 1,711,951.

ALABAMA.

Formed from territory of South Carolina and Georgia, and for two years bore the name of Mississippi Territory.
Adopted a Constitution August 2, 1819.
Admitted December 14, 1819.
Area, 50,722 square miles. Population in 1850, 771,623; 1860, 964,201.

MAINE.

First settled at Bristol in 1624.
Formed from territory of Massachusetts.
Adopted a Constitution October 29, 1819.
Admitted March 15, 1820.
Area, 31,766 square miles. Population in 1850, 583,169; 1860, 628,279.

MISSOURI.

First settled at St. Louis in 1764.
Formed from French territory.
Adopted a Constitution July 19, 1820.
Admitted August 10, 1821.
Area, 67,380 square miles. Population in 1850, 682,044; 1860, 1,182,612.

ARKANSAS.

Formed from French territory, the Louisiana purchase.
Presented a Constitution March 1, 1836.
Admitted June 15, 1836.
Area, 52,198 square miles. Population in 1850, 209,897; 1860, 435,450.

MICHIGAN.

First settled on the Detroit River in 1650.
Formed from territory originally belonging to Virginia.
Presented a memorial for admission January 25, 1833, with a Constitution, which was revised in 1850.
Admitted January 26, 1837.
Area, 56,243 square miles. Population in 1850, 397,654; 1860, 749,013.

FLORIDA.

Discovered in 1497, and first explored by Ponce de Leon in 1512.
Formed from Spanish territory.
Presented a Constitution February 20, 1839.
Admitted March 3, 1845.
Area, 59,268 square miles. Population in 1850, 87,445; 1860, 140,425.

TEXAS.

First settled in 1792.
Was an Independent Republic.
Admitted December 29, 1845.
Area, 324,018 square miles. Population in 1850, 212,592; 1860, 604,215.

WISCONSIN.

First settled at Green Bay in 1670.
Formed from Indian territory.
Adopted a Constitution January 21, 1847.
Admitted May 29, 1848.
Area, 53,924 square miles. Population in 1850, 305,391; 1860, 775,881.

IOWA.

First settled at Galena and Dubuque.
Formed from Indian territory.
Presented a Constitution December 9, 1844.
Admitted December 28, 1846.
Area, 55,045 square miles. Population in 1850, 192,214; 1860, 674,943.

CALIFORNIA.

First settled on the Pacific slope.
Formed from Mexican territory.
Adopted a Constitution November 13, 1849.
Admitted September 9, 1850.
Area, 188,982 square miles. Population in 1850, 92 597; 1860, 380,194.

MINNESOTA.

First settled on the St. Peter's River in 1805
Formed from Indian territory.
Admitted May 11, 1858.
Area, 83,531 square miles. Population in 1850, 6077; 1860, 172,143.

OREGON.

First settled by the Spaniards.
Formed from Indian territory.
Adopted a Constitution in November, 1857.
Admitted February 12, 1859.
Area, 102,606 square miles. Population in 1850, 12,093; 1860, 52,405.

KANSAS.

Formed from Indian Territory.
Admitted December 6, 1859.
Area, 114,798 square miles. Population in 1860, 107,206.

WEST VIRGINIA.

Formed from the State of Virginia.
Admitted December 31, 1862.
Area, 23,000 square miles. Population in 1860, 393,234.

TERRITORIES OF THE UNITED STATES.

UTAH.

Organized September 9, 1850.
Area, 109,600 square miles. Population in 1850, 11,380; 1860, 188,193.

NEW MEXICO.

Organized September 9, 1850.
Area, 124,450 square miles. Population in 1850, 61,547; 1860, no census.

WASHINGTON.

Organized November 2, 1853.
Area, 71,300 square miles. Population in 1850, 1201; 1860, 11,068.

NEBRASKA.

Organized May 30, 1854.
Area, 122,007 square miles. Population in 1850, 10,716; 1863, 12,519.

COLORADO.

Organized in 1861.
Area, 106,475 square miles. Population in 1860, 70,000.

DAKOTA.

Organized in 1861.
Area, 152,500 square miles. No census.

NEVADA.

Organized in 1861.
Area, 83,500 square miles. Population in 1860, 40,000.

ARIZONA.

Organized in 1863.
Area, 130,800 square miles. No census.

IDAHO.

Organized in 1863.
Area, 310,000 square miles. No census.

DISTRICT OF COLUMBIA.

Established under the First Article of the Constitution of the United States: "Congress shall have power to exercise exclusive legislation in all cases whatsoever, over such district (not exceeding ten miles square) as may, by cession of particular States, and the acceptance of Congress, become the seat of the Government of the United States," &c. In pursuance of which provision the State of Maryland, December 23, 1788, passed "An act to cede to Congress a district of ten miles square in this State, for the seat of the Government of the United States."

And the State of Virginia, December 3, 1789, passed "An act for the cession of ten miles square, or any lesser quantity of territory within this State, to the United States in Congress assembled, for the permanent seat of the General Government."

These cessions were accepted by Congress, as required by the Constitution, and the permanent seat of government established by the "Act for establishing the temporary and permanent seat of the Government of the United States," approved July 16, 1790; and the act to amend the same, approved March 3, 1791.

The district of ten miles square was accordingly located, and its lines and boundaries particularly established by a proclamation of George Washington, President of the United States, March 30, 1791, and by the "Act concerning the District of Columbia," approved February 27, 1801, Congress assumed complete jurisdiction over the said District, as contemplated by the framers of the Constitution.

Area, 50 square miles. Population in 1850, 51,687; 1860, 75,080.

ORIGIN OF THE NAMES OF STATES.

Maine was so called as early as 1623, from Maine, in France, of which Henrietta Maria, Queen of England, was at that time proprietor.

New Hampshire was the name given to the territory conveyed by the Plymouth Company to Captain John Mason, by patent, November 7th, 1629, with reference to the patentee, who was Governor of Portsmouth, in Hampshire, England.

Vermont was so called by the inhabitants in their Declaration of Independence, January 16, 1777, from the French *verd mont*, the Green Mountains.

Massachusetts was so called from Massachusetts Bay, and that from the Massachusetts tribe of Indians, in the neighborhood of Boston. The tribe is thought to have derived its name from the Blue Hills of Milton. "I had learnt," says Roger Williams, "that the Massachusetts was so called from the Blue Hills."

Rhode Island was so called in 1664, in reference to the Island of Rhodes, in the Mediterranean.

Connecticut was so called from the Indian name of its principal river. Connecticut is a Mocheakannew word, signifying long river.

New York was so called in 1664, in reference to the Duke of York and Albany, to whom this territory was granted by the King of England.

New Jersey was so called in 1664, from the Island of Jersey, on the coast of France, the residence of the family of Sir George Carteret, to whom the territory was granted.

Pennsylvania was so called in 1681, after William Penn.

Delaware was so called in 1703, from Delaware Bay, on which it lies, and which received its name from Lord de la War, who died in this bay.

Maryland was so called in honor of Henrietta Maria, Queen of Charles I, in his patent to Lord Baltimore, June 30th, 1632.

Virginia was so called in 1584, after Elizabeth, the Virgin Queen of England.

Carolina was so called by the French in 1564, in honor of King Charles IX, of France.

Georgia was so called in 1732, in honor of King George II.

Alabama was so called in 1814, from its principal river, meaning *here we rest.*

Mississippi was so called in 1800, from its western boundary. Mississippi is said to denote the whole river, *i. e.*, the river formed by the union of many.

Louisiana was so called in honor of Louis XIV of France.

Tennessee was so called in 1796, from its principal river. The word Ten-as-se is said to signify a *curved spoon.*

Kentucky was so called in 1792, from its principal river.

Illinois was so called in 1809, from its principal river. This word is said to signify *the river of men.*

Indiana was so called in 1809, from the American Indians.

Ohio was so called in 1802, from its southern boundary.

Missouri was so called in 1821, from its principal river. Indian name.

Michigan was so called in 1805, from the lake on its border. Indian name.

Arkansas was so called in 1812, from its principal river. Indian name.

Florida was so called by Juan Ponce de Leon in 1572, because it was discovered on Easter Sunday; in Spanish, *Pascua Florida.*

Wisconsin was so called from its principal river. Indian name.

Iowa was so called from its principal river. Indian name.

Oregon was so called from its principal river. Indian name.

Minnesota is also an Indian word.

California, a Spanish word, and named from an arm of the Pacific Ocean.

Texas, a Spanish word applied to the Republic.

Kansas is an Indian name.

PROGRESS OF POPULATION IN THE UNITED STATES.

FROM 1790 TO 1860.

	Whites.	Free Colored.	Slaves.	Total.
First Census, *August* 1, 1790.				
Free States, ...	1,900,772	26,831	40,850	1,968,453
Slave States, ...	1,271,692	32,635	645,047	1,961,374
Total, ...	3,172,464	59,446	697,897	3,929,827
Second Census, *August* 1, 1800.				
Free States, ...	2,601,509	47,154	35,946	2,684,609
Slave States, ...	1,702,980	61,241	857,095	2,621,316
Total, ...	4,304,489	108,395	893,041	5,305,925
Third Census, *August* 1, 1810.				
Free States, ...	3,653,219	78,181	27,510	3,758,910
Slave States, ...	2,208,785	108,265	1,163,854	3,480,904
Total, ...	5,862,004	186,446	1,191,364	7,239,814
Fourth Census, *August* 1, 1820.				
Free States, ...	5,030,371	102,893	19,108	5,152,372
Slave States, ...	2,842,340	135,434	1,524,580	4,502,224
Total, ...	7,872,711	238,197	1,543,688	9,654,596
Fifth Census, *June* 1, 1830.				
Free States, ...	6,876,620	137,529	3,568	7,017,717
Slave States, ...	3,660,758	182,070	2,005,475	5,848,303
Total, ...	10,537,378	319,599	2,009,043	12,866,020
Sixth Census, *June* 1, 1840.				
Free States, ...	9,557,065	170,727	1,129	9,728,921
Slave States, ...	4,632,640	215,568	2,486,226	7,334,434
Total, ...	14,189,705	386,295	2,487,355	17,063,355
Seventh Census, *June* 1, 1850.				
Free States, ...	13,330,650	196,308	262	13,527,220
Slave States, ...	6,222,418	238,187	3,204,051	9,664,654
Total, ...	19,553,068	434,495	3,204,313	23,191,874

Eighth Census, *June* 1, 1860.

Total Population, ...	31,443,322
Total White Population, ...	26,973,843
Total Free Colored Population, ...	487,970
Total Free Population, ...	27,461,813
Total Slave Population, ...	3,953,760
Total Colored Population, ...	4,447,730

POPULATION OF THE SEVERAL STATES, THE RATIO OF REPRESENTATION, AND THE NUMBER OF REPRESENTATIVES ALLOWED TO EACH AT THE TIME OF THEIR ADMISSION, RESPECTIVELY.

States.	When Admitted.	Population.	Ratio of representation at time of admission.	Representatives before next apportionment.	Remarks.
New Hampshire,	Ratified Constitution, June 21, 1788	141,899	. . .	3	First Census, taken in August, 1790.
Massachusetts, .	" " Feb. 6, 1788	378,717	. . .	8	" " "
Rhode Island, .	" " May 29, 1790	69,110	. . .	1	" " "
Connecticut, . .	" " Jan. 9, 1788	238,141	. . .	5	" " "
New York, . .	" " July 26, 1788	340,120	. . .	6	" " "
New Jersey, . .	" " Dec. 18, 1787	184,139	. . .	4	" " "
Pennsylvania, .	" " Dec. 12, 1787	434,373	. . .	8	" " "
Delaware, . .	" " Dec. 7, 1787	59,096	. . .	1	" " "
Maryland, . .	" " April 28, 1788	319,728	. . .	6	" " "
Virginia, . . .	" " June 26, 1788	748,308	. . .	10	" " "
North Carolina,	" " Nov. 21, 1789	393,751	. . .	5	" " "
South Carolina, .	" " May 23, 1788	249,073	. . .	5	" " "
Georgia, . . .	" " Jan. 2, 1788	82,548	. . .	3	" " "

Vermont,	March 4, 1791	85,539	. . .	2	See Williams's History of Vermont.
Kentucky,	June 1, 1792	73,077	. . .	2	Census of 1790. No census of Territory previous to admission.
Tennessee,	June 1, 1796	77,262	33,000	1	Territorial census. See American State Papers, Mis., vol. i, p. 147.
Ohio,	Nov. 29, 1802	41,915	33,000	1	See American State Papers, Mis., vol. i, p. 325.
Louisiana,	April 8, 1812	76,556	33,000	1	Census of 1810. No census of Territory previous to admission.
Indiana,	Dec. 11, 1816	63,897	35,000	1	Territorial census. See American State Papers, Mis., vol. ii, p. 277.
Mississippi,	Dec. 10, 1817	75,512	35,000	1	Territorial census. See American State Papers, Mis., vol. ii, p. 407.
Illinois,	Dec. 3, 1818	34,620	35,000	1	Territorial census. See Niles's Register, vol. xiv, p. 359.
Alabama,	Dec. 14, 1819	144,317	35,000	1	Census of 1820.
Maine,	March 15, 1820	298,335	35,000	7	Census of 1820.
Missouri,	Aug. 10, 1821	66,586	35,000	1	Census of 1820.
Arkansas,	June 15, 1836	52,240	47,700	1	Territorial census. See Ex. Docs. H. R., vol. iv, No. 144, 1st sess. 24th Cong.
Michigan,	Jan. 26, 1837	200,000	47,700	1	Estimated population Dec. 1836. See Docs. H. R., vol. ii, No. 68, 2d sess. 24th Cong.
Florida,	March 3, 1845	54,477	70,680	1	Census of 1840. No census of Territory previous to admission.
Texas,	Dec. 29, 1845	250,000	70,680	2	See American Almanac for 1844.
Wisconsin,	May 29, 1848	210,596	70,680	2	Territorial census of 1847. See Ex. Doc. H. R., 1st sess. 30th Cong., No. 55, vol. v.
Iowa,	Dec. 28, 1846	81,920	70,680	2	Territorial census of 1844. See American Almanac for 1846.
California,	Sept. 9, 1850	107,000	70,680	2	Estimated population. See Sen. Mis. Docs., vol. i, No. 68, 1st sess. 31st Cong.
Minnesota,	May 11, 1858	150,042	93,420	2	Territorial Census. See Annual Rep. of Sec'y of the Interior, 1st sess. 35th Cong.
Oregon,	Feb. 12, 1859	52,465	. . .	1	Census of 1860.
Kansas,	Dec. 6, 1859	107,206	. . .	1	Census of 1860.
West Virginia,	Dec. 31, 1862	334,921	. . .	3	Census of 1860.

THE

STATE AND TERRITORIAL GOVERNORS,

SINCE THE ADOPTION OF THE FEDERAL CONSTITUTION.

MAINE.

	FROM	TO
William King,	1820	1822
Albion K. Parris,	1822	1827
Enoch Lincoln,	1827	1829
Jonathan G. Hunton,	1829	1831
Samuel E. Smith,	1831	1834
Robert P. Dunlap,	1834	1838
Edward Kent,	1838	1839
John Fairfield,	1839	1840
Edward Kent,	1840	1841
John Fairfield,	1841	1843
Edward Kavanagh (acting),	1843	1844
Hugh J. Anderson,	1844	1847
John W. Dana,	1847	1850
John Hubbard,	1850	1853
William G. Crosby,	1853	1855
Anson P. Morrill,	1855	1856
Samuel Wells,	1856	1857
Hannibal Hamlin,	1857	1857
Joseph H. Williams.	1857	1858
Lot M. Morrill,	1858	1859
" " (re-elected),	1859	1860
Israel Washburne, Jr.,	1860	1862
Abner Coburn,	1862	1863
Samuel Cony,	1863	1864

Salary, $1500.
Term, one year.
Seat of Government, Augusta.

NEW HAMPSHIRE.

	FROM	TO
Josiah Bartlett,	1792	1794
John Taylor Gilman,	1794	1805
John Langdon,	1805	1809
Jeremiah Smith,	1809	1810
John Langdon,	1810	1812
William Plumer,	1812	1813
John Taylor Gilman,	1813	1816
William Plumer,	1816	1819
Samuel Bell,	1819	1823
Levi Woodbury,	1823	1824
David L. Morrill,	1824	1827
Benjamin Pierce,	1827	1828
John Bell,	1828	1830
Matthew Harvey,	1830	1831
James M. Harper,	1831	1831
Samuel Dinsmoor,	1831	1834
William Badger,	1834	1836
Isaac Hill,	1836	1839
John Page,	1839	1842
Henry Hubbard,	1842	1844
John H. Steele,	1844	1846
Anthony Colby,	1846	1847
Jared W. Williams,	1847	1849
Samuel Dinsmoor,	1849	1852
Noah Martin,	1852	1854
Nathaniel B. Baker,	1854	1855
Ralph Metcalf,	1855	1856
" "	1856	1857
William Haile,	1857	1858
" " (re-elected),	1858	1859
" " "	1859	1860
Ichabod Goodwin,	1860	1861
Nathaniel S. Barry,	1862	1863
Joseph A. Gilmore,	1863	1864

Salary, $1000.
Term, one year.
Seat of Government, Concord.

VERMONT.

	FROM	TO
Moses Robinson,	1789	1790
Thomas Chittenden,	1790	1797
Isaac Tichenor,	1797	1807
Israel Smith,	1807	1808
Isaac Tichenor,	1808	1809
Jonas Galusha,	1809	1813
Martin Chittenden,	1813	1815
Jonas Galusha,	1815	1820
Richard Skinner,	1820	1823
C. P. Van Ness,	1823	1826
Ezra Butler,	1826	1828
Samuel C. Crafts,	1828	1831
William A. Palmer,	1831	1835

	FROM	TO
Silas A. Jenison,	1835	1841
Charles Paine,	1841	1843
John Mattocks,	1843	1844
William Slade,	1844	1846
Horace Eaton,	1846	1849
Charles Coolidge,	1849	1850
Charles K. Williams,	1850	1852
Erastus Fairbanks,	1852	1853
John S. Robinson,	1853	1854
Stephen Royce,	1854	1856
Ryland Fletcher,	1856	1858
Hiland Hall,	1858	1859
" " (re-elected),	1859	1860
Erastus Fairbanks,	1860	1861
Frederick Holbrook,	1861	1863
J. Gregory Smith,	1863	1864

Salary, $1000.
Term, one year.
Seat of Government, Montpelier.

MASSACHUSETTS.

	FROM	TO
John Hancock,	1789	1794
Samuel Adams,	1794	1797
Increase Sumner,	1797	1799
Moses Gill (acting),	1799	1800
Caleb Strong,	1800	1807
James Sullivan,	1807	1808
Levi Lincoln (acting),	1808	1809
Christopher Gore,	1809	1810
Elbridge Gerry,	1810	1812
Caleb Strong,	1812	1816
John Brooks,	1816	1823
William Eustis,	1823	1825
Marcus Morton (acting),	1825	1825
Levi Lincoln,	1825	1834
John Davis,	1834	1836
S. Y. Armstrong (acting),	1836	1836
Edward Everett,	1836	1840
Marcus Morton,	1840	1841
John Davis,	1841	1843
Marcus Morton,	1843	1844
George N. Briggs,	1844	1851
George S. Boutwell,	1851	1853
John H. Clifford,	1853	1854
Emory Washburn,	1854	1855
Henry J. Gardner,	1855	1858
Nathaniel P. Banks,	1858	1860
John A. Andrew,	1860	1864

Salary, $3500.
Term, one year.
Seat of Government, Boston.

RHODE ISLAND.

	FROM	TO
Arthur Fenner,	1789	1805
Henry Smith (acting),	1805	1806
Isaac Wilburn (acting),	1806	1807
James Fenner,	1807	1811
William Jones,	1811	1817
Nehemiah Knight,	1817	1821
William C. Gibbs,	1821	1824
William Findlay,	1824	1831
Lemuel H. Arnold,	1831	1832
John B. Francis,	1833	1838
William Sprague,	1838	1840
Samuel W. King,	1840	1842
James Fenner,	1842	1844
Charles Jackson,	1844	1845
Byron Diman,	1846	1847
Elisha Harris,	1847	1849
Henry B. Anthony,	1849	1851
Philip Allen,	1851	1853
F. M. Dimon,	1853	1854
William W. Hoppin,	1854	1857
Elisha Dyer,	1857	1859
Thomas G. Turner,	1859	1860
William Sprague,	1860	1863
James Y. Smith,	1863	1864

Salary, $1000.
Term, one year.
Seats of Government, Newport and Providence.

CONNECTICUT.

	FROM	TO
Samuel Huntington,	1785	1796
Oliver Wolcott,	1796	1798
Jonathan Trumbull,	1798	1809
John Treadwell,	1809	1811
Roger Griswold,	1811	1813
John Cotton Smith,	1813	1818
Oliver Wolcott,	1818	1827
Gideon Tomlinson,	1827	1831
John S. Peters,	1831	1833
Henry W. Edwards,	1833	1834
Samuel A. Foote,	1834	1835
Henry W. Edwards,	1835	1838
William W. Ellsworth,	1838	1842
Chauncey F. Cleveland,	1842	1844
Roger S. Baldwin,	1844	1846
Isaac Toucey,	1846	1847
Clark Bissell,	1847	1849
Joseph Trumbull,	1849	1850
Thomas H. Seymour,	1850	1853
C. H. Pond (acting),	1853	1854
Henry Dutton,	1854	1855
William T. Minor,	1855	1857
Alexander H. Holley,	1857	1858
William A. Buckingham,	1858	1864

Salary, $1100.
Term, one year.
Seats of Government, Hartford and New Haven, alternately.

NEW YORK.

	FROM	TO
George Clinton,	1789	1795
John Jay,	1795	1801
George Clinton,	1801	1804
Morgan Lewis,	1804	1807
Daniel D. Tompkins,	1807	1816

	FROM	TO
John Tayler,	1816	1817
De Witt Clinton,	1817	1822
Joseph C. Yates,	1822	1824
De Witt Clinton,	1824	1827
Nathaniel Pitcher,	1827	1828
Martin Van Buren,	1828	1830
Enos T. Throop,	1830	1832
William L. Marcy,	1832	1838
William H. Seward,	1838	1842
William C. Bouck,	1842	1844
Silas Wright,	1844	1846
John Young,	1846	1848
Hamilton Fish,	1848	1850
Washington Hunt,	1850	1852
Horatio Seymour,	1852	1854
Myron H. Clark,	1854	1856
John A. King,	1856	1858
Edwin D. Morgan,	1858	1862
Horatio Seymour,	1862	1864

Salary, $4000.
Term, two years.
Seat of Government, Albany.

NEW JERSEY.

	FROM	TO
William Livingston,	1789	1794
William Paterson,	1794	1794
Richard Howell,	1794	1801
Joseph Bloomfield,	1801	1812
Aaron Ogden,	1812	1813
William S. Pennington,	1813	1815
Mahlon Dickerson,	1815	1817
Isaac H. Williamson,	1817	1829
Peter D. Vroom,	1829	1832
Samuel L. Southard,	1832	1833
Elias P. Seely,	1833	1833
Peter D. Vroom,	1833	1836
Philemon Dickerson,	1836	1837
William Pennington,	1837	1843
Daniel Haines,	1843	1844
Charles C. Stratton,	1844	1848
Daniel Haines,	1848	1851
George F. Fort,	1851	1854
Rodman M. Price,	1854	1857
William A. Newell,	1857	1860
Charles S. Olden,	1860	1863
Joel Parker,	1863	1866

Salary, $1800 and fees.
Term, three years.
Seat of Government, Trenton.

PENNSYLVANIA.

	FROM	TO
Thomas Mifflin,	1790	1799
Thomas McKean,	1799	1808
Simon Snyder,	1808	1817
William Findley,	1817	1820
Joseph Heister,	1820	1823
John Andrew Shulze,	1823	1829
George Wolf,	1829	1835
Joseph Ritner,	1835	1839
David R. Porter,	1839	1845
Francis R. Shunk,	1845	1848
William F. Johnston,	1848	1852
William Bigler,	1852	1855
James Pollock,	1855	1858
William F. Packer,	1858	1861
Andrew G. Curtin,	1861	1867

Salary, $3000.
Term, three years.
Seat of Government, Harrisburg.

DELAWARE.

	FROM	TO
Joshua Clayton,	1789	1796
Gunning Bedford,	1796	1797
Daniel Rogers,	1797	1798
Richard Bassett,	1798	1801
James Sykes (acting),	1801	1802
David Hall,	1802	1805
Nathaniel Mitchell,	1805	1808
George Truett,	1808	1811
Joseph Haslett,	1811	1814
Daniel Rodney,	1814	1817
John Clarke,	1817	1820
Jacob Stout (acting),	1820	1821
John Collins,	1821	1822
Caleb Rodney (acting),	1822	1823
Joseph Haslett,	1823	1824
Samuel Paynter,	1824	1827
George Poindexter,	1827	1830
David Hazzard,	1830	1833
Caleb P. Bennett,	1833	1837
Cornelius P. Comegys,	1837	1840
William B. Cooper,	1840	1844
Thomas Stockton,	1844	1846
Joseph Maul (acting),	1846	1846
William Temple,	1846	1846
William Thorp,	1846	1851
William H. Ross,	1851	1855
Peter F. Causey,	1855	1859
William Burton,	1859	1863
William Cannon,	1863	1867

Salary, $1333⅓.
Term, four years.
Seat of Government, Dover.

MARYLAND.

	FROM	TO
John Eager Howard,	1788	1792
George Plater,	1792	1792
Thomas Sim Lee,	1792	1794
John H. Stone,	1794	1797
John Henry,	1797	1798
Benjamin Ogle,	1798	1801
John F. Mercer,	1801	1803
Robert Bowie,	1803	1805
Robert Wright,	1805	1809
Edward Lloyd,	1809	1811
Robert Bowie,	1811	1812
Levin Winder,	1812	1815
C. Ridgely,	1815	1818

	FROM	TO
C. W. Goldsborough,	1818	1819
Samuel Sprigg,	1819	1822
Samuel Stevens,	1822	1826
Joseph Kent,	1826	1829
Daniel Martin,	1829	1830
T. K. Carroll,	1830	1831
Daniel Martin,	1831	1831
George Howard (acting),	1831	1832
" "	1832	1833
James Thomas,	1833	1836
Thomas W. Veasay,	1836	1838
William Grayson,	1838	1841
Francis Thomas,	1841	1844
Thomas G. Pratt,	1844	1848
Philip F. Thomas,	1848	1851
Enoch L. Lowe,	1851	1854
Thomas W. Ligon,	1854	1858
Thomas H. Hicks,	1858	1862
Augustus W. Bradford,	1862	1866

Salary, $3600, with a furnished house.
Term, four years.
Seat of Government, Annapolis.

VIRGINIA.

	FROM	TO
Beverly Randolph,	1788	1791
Henry Lee,	1791	1794
Robert Brooke,	1794	1796
James Wood,	1796	1799
James Monroe,	1799	1802
John Page,	1802	1805
William H. Cabell,	1805	1808
John Tyler,	1808	1811
James Monroe,	1811	1811
George W. Smith,	1811	1812
James Barbour,	1812	1814
Wilson C. Nicholas,	1814	1816
James P. Preston,	1816	1819
Thomas M. Randolph,	1819	1822
James Pleasants,	1822	1825
John Tyler,	1825	1827
William B. Giles,	1827	1830
John Floyd,	1830	1834
Littleton W. Tazewell,	1834	1836
Wyndham Robertson (at'g),	1836	1837
David Campbell,	1837	1840
Thomas W. Gilmer,	1840	1841
John Rutherford,	1841	1842
John M. Gregory,	1842	1843
James McDowell,	1843	1846
William Smith,	1846	1849
John B. Floyd,	1849	1852
Joseph Johnson,	1852	1856
Henry A. Wise,	1856	1860
John Letcher,	1860	1863

Salary, $5000.
Term, three years.
Seat of Government, Richmond.

NORTH CAROLINA.

	FROM	TO
Alexander Martin,	1789	1792
Richard D. Spaight,	1792	1795
Samuel Ashe,	1795	1798
William R. Davie,	1798	1799
Benjamin Williams,	1799	1802
James Turner,	1802	1805
Nathaniel Alexander,	1805	1807
Benjamin Williams,	1807	1808
David Stone,	1808	1810
Benjamin Smith,	1810	1811
William Hawkins,	1811	1814
William Miller,	1814	1817
John Branch,	1817	1820
Jesse Franklin,	1820	1821
Gabriel Holmes,	1821	1824
Hutchins G. Burton,	1824	1827
James Iredell,	1827	1828
John Owen,	1828	1830
Montfort Stokes,	1830	1832
David L. Swain,	1832	1835
Richard D. Spaight,	1835	1837
Edward B. Dudley,	1837	1841
John M. Morehead,	1841	1845
William A. Graham,	1845	1849
Charles Manly,	1849	1851
David S. Reid,	1851	1855
Thomas Bragg,	1855	1859
John W. Ellis,	1859	1861
John B. Vance,	1861	1863

Salary, $3000, with a furnished house.
Term, two years.
Seat of Government, Raleigh.

SOUTH CAROLINA.

	FROM	TO
Charles Pinckney,	1789	1792
Arnoldus Vanderhorst,	1792	1794
William Moultrie,	1794	1796
Charles Pinckney,	1796	1798
Edward Rutledge,	1798	1800
John Drayton (acting),	1800	1800
" "	1800	1802
James B. Richardson,	1802	1804
Paul Hamilton,	1804	1806
Charles Pinckney,	1806	1808
John Drayton,	1808	1810
Henry Middleton,	1810	1812
Joseph Alston,	1812	1814
David R. Williams,	1814	1816
Andrew Pickens,	1816	1818
John Geddes,	1818	1820
Thomas Bennet,	1820	1822
John L. Wilson,	1822	1824
Richard I. Manning,	1824	1826
John Taylor,	1826	1828
Stephen D. Miller,	1828	1830
James Hamilton,	1830	1832
Robert Y. Hayne,	1832	1834
George McDuffie,	1834	1836

	FROM	TO
Pierce M. Butler,	1836	1838
Patrick Noble,	1838	1840
B. K. Hennegan (acting),	1840	1840
J. P. Richardson,	1840	1842
James H. Hammond,	1842	1844
William Aiken,	1844	1846
David Johnson,	1846	1848
W. B. Seabrook,	1848	1850
John H. Means,	1850	1852
John L. Manning,	1852	1854
James H. Adams,	1854	1856
R. F. W. Alston,	1856	1858
William H. Gist,	1858	1860
Francis W. Pickens,	1860	1862

Salary, $3500.
Term, two years.
Seat of Government, Columbia.

GEORGIA.

	FROM	TO
George Walton,	1789	1790
Edward Telfair,	1790	1793
George Matthews,	1793	1796
Jared Irwin,	1796	1798
James Jackson,	1798	1801
David Emanuel (acting),	1801	1801
Josiah Tatnall,	1801	1802
John Milledge,	1802	1806
Jared Irwin,	1806	1809
David B. Mitchell,	1809	1813
Peter Early,	1813	1815
David B. Mitchell,	1815	1817
William Rabun,	1817	1819
Matthew Talbot (acting),	1819	1819
John Clarke,	1819	1823
George M. Troup,	1823	1827
John Forsyth,	1827	1829
George R. Gilmer,	1829	1831
Wilson Lumpkin,	1831	1835
William Schley,	1835	1837
George R. Gilmer,	1837	1839
Charles J. McDonald,	1839	1843
George W. Crawford,	1843	1847
George W. B. Towns,	1847	1851
Howell Cobb,	1851	1853
Herschel V. Johnson,	1853	1857
Joseph E. Brown,	1857	1861

Salary, $3000.
Term, two years.
Seat of Government, Milledgeville.

FLORIDA.

TERRITORY.

	FROM	TO
William P. Duvall,	1822	1834
John H. Eaton,	1834	1836
Richard K. Call,	1836	1844
John Branch,	1844	1845

STATE.

	FROM	TO
William D. Moseley,	1845	1849
Thomas Brown,	1849	1853
James E. Broome,	1853	1857
Madison S. Perry,	1857	1861
John Milton,	1861	1864

Salary, $1500.
Term, four years.
Seat of Government, Tallahassee.

ALABAMA.

	FROM	TO
William W. Bibb,	1819	1820
Thomas Bibb,	1820	1821
Israel Pickens,	1821	1825
John Murphy,	1825	1829
Gabriel Moore,	1829	1831
John Gayle,	1831	1835
Clement C. Clay,	1835	1837
Arthur P. Bagby,	1837	1841
Benjamin Fitzpatrick,	1841	1845
Joshua L. Martin,	1845	1847
Reuben Chapman,	1847	1849
Henry W. Collier,	1849	1853
John A. Winston,	1853	1857
Andrew B. Moore,	1857	1861
Re-elected,	1861	1863

Salary, $2500.
Term, two years.
Seat of Government, Montgomery.

MISSISSIPPI.

TERRITORY.

	FROM	TO
Winthrop Sargent,	1798	1802
W. C. C. Claiborne,	1802	1805
Robert Williams,	1805	1809
David Holmes,	1809	1817

STATE.

	FROM	TO
David Holmes,	1817	1819
George Poindexter,	1819	1821
Walter Leake,	1821	1825
David Holmes,	1825	1827
Gerard C. Brandon,	1827	1831
Abraham M. Scott,	1831	1833
Hiram G. Runnels,	1833	1835
Charles Lynch,	1835	1837
Alexander G. McNutt,	1837	1841
Tilghman M. Tucker,	1841	1843
Albert G. Brown,	1843	1848
Joseph W. Mathews,	1848	1850
John A. Quitman,	1850	1851
John J. Guion (acting),	1851	1851
James Whitfield,	1851	1852
Henry S. Foote,	1852	1854
John J. MacRae,	1854	1858
William McWillie,	1858	1860
John J. Pettus,	1860	1862

Salary, $4000.
Term, two years.
Seat of Government, Jackson.

LOUISIANA.

TERRITORY OF ORLEANS.

	FROM	TO
William C. C. Claiborne,	1804	1812

STATE.

William C. C. Claiborne,	1812	1816
James Villare,	1816	1820
Thomas B. Robertson,	1820	1822
H. S. Thibodeaux (acting),	1822	1824
Henry Johnson,	1824	1828
Peter Derbigny,	1828	1829
A. Bauvais (acting),	1829	1830
Jacques Dupre (acting),	1830	1830
Andre B. Roman,	1830	1834
Edward D. White,	1834	1838
Andre B. Roman,	1838	1841
Alexander Warton,	1841	1845
Isaac Johnson,	1845	1850
Joseph Walker,	1850	1854
Paul O. Hebert,	1854	1858
R. C. Wickliffe,	1858	——
Thomas O. Moore,	——	1862

Salary, $4000.
Term, four years.
Seat of Government, Baton Rouge.

TEXAS.

J. Pinckney Henderson,	1846	1847
George T. Wood,	1847	1849
P. H. Bell,	1849	1853
Edward M. Pease,	1853	1857
H. G. Runnels,	1857	1859
Sam Houston,	1859	1861
F. R. Lubbeck,	1861	1863

Salary, $3000.
Term, two years.
Seat of Government, Austin.

ARKANSAS.

TERRITORY.

James Miller,	1819	1825
George Izard,	1825	1829
John Pope,	1829	1835
William S. Fulton,	1835	1836

STATE.

James S. Conway,	1836	1840
Archibald Yell,	1840	1844
Samuel Adams (acting),	1844	1844
Thomas S. Drew,	1844	1848
John S. Roane,	1848	1852
Elias N. Conway,	1852	1860
Henry M. Rector,	1860	1864

Salary, $1800.
Term, four years.
Seat of Government, Little Rock.

TENNESSEE.

	FROM	TO
John Sevier,	1796	1801
Archibald Roane,	1801	1803
John Sevier,	1803	1809
Willie Blount,	1809	1815
Joseph McMin,	1815	1821
William Carroll,	1821	1827
Samuel Houston,	1827	1829
William Carroll,	1829	1835
Newton Cannon,	1835	1839
James K. Polk,	1839	1841
James C. Jones,	1841	1845
Aaron V. Brown,	1845	1847
Neil S. Brown,	1847	1849
William Trousdale,	1849	1851
William B. Campbell,	1851	1853
Andrew Johnson,	1853	1857
Isham G. Harris,	1857	1861

Salary, $3000.
Term, two years.
Seat of Government, Nashville.

KENTUCKY.

Isaac Shelby,	1792	1796
James Garrard,	1796	1804
Christopher Greenup,	1804	1808
Charles Scott,	1808	1812
Isaac Shelby,	1812	1816
George Madison,	1816	1816
G. Slaughter (acting),	1816	1820
John Adair,	1820	1824
Joseph Desha,	1824	1828
Thomas Metcalfe,	1828	1832
John Breathitt,	1832	1834
J. T. Morehead (acting),	1834	1836
James Clark,	1836	1837
C. A. Wickliffe (acting),	1839	1840
Robert P. Letcher,	1840	1844
William Owsley,	1844	1848
John J. Crittenden,	1848	1850
John L. Helm (acting),	1850	1851
Lazarus W. Powell,	1851	1855
Charles S. Morehead,	1855	1859
Beriah Magoffin,	1859	1861
J. F. Robinson,	1861	1863
Thomas E. Bramlette,	1863	1867

Salary, $2500.
Term, four years.
Seat of Government, Frankfort.

OHIO.

TERRITORY.

Arthur St. Clair,	1788	1803

STATE.

Edward Tiffin,	1803	1808
Thomas Kirker (acting),	1808	1808
Samuel Huntington,	1808	1810

	FROM	TO
Return J. Meigs,	1810	1814
Othneil Looker (acting),	1814	1814
Thomas Worthington,	1814	1818
Ethan Allen Brown,	1818	1822
Allen Trimble (acting),	1822	1822
Jeremiah Morrow,	1822	1826
Allen Trimble,	1826	1830
Duncan McArthur,	1830	1832
Robert Lucas,	1832	1836
Joseph Vance,	1836	1838
Wilson Shannon,	1838	1840
Thomas Corwin,	1840	1842
Wilson Shannon,	1842	1844
Thomas W. Bartley (acting),	1844	1844
Mordecai Bartley,	1844	1846
William Bebb,	1846	1848
Seabury Ford,	1848	1850
Reuben Wood,	1850	1854
William Medill,	1854	1856
Salmon P. Chase,	1856	1860
William Dennison, Jr.,	1860	1862
David Todd,	1862	1864
John Brough,	1864	1866

Salary, $1800.
Term, two years.
Seat of Government, Columbus.

MICHIGAN.

TERRITORY.

	FROM	TO
William Hull,	1805	1814
Lewis Cass,	1814	1831
George B. Porter,	1831	1834
Stevens T. Mason (acting),	1834	1835
J. S. Horner (acting),	1835	1836

STATE.

	FROM	TO
Stephens T. Mason,	1836	1840
William Woodbridge,	1840	1841
J. W. Gordon (acting),	1841	1842
John S. Barry,	1842	1846
Alpheus Felch,	1846	1847
W. L. Greenley (acting),	1847	1848
Epaphroditus Ransom,	1848	1850
John S. Barry,	1850	1853
Robert McClelland,	1853	1853
A. Parsons (acting),	1853	1855
Kinsley S. Bingham,	1855	1857
" "	1857	1859
Moses Wisner,	1859	1861
Austin Blair,	1861	1863

Salary, $1000.
Term, two years.
Seat of Government, Lansing.

INDIANA.

	FROM	TO
Jonathan Jennings,	1816	1822
William Hendricks,	1822	1825
James Brown Ray,	1825	1831
Noah Noble,	1831	1837
David Wallace,	1837	1840
Samuel Bigger,	1840	1843
James Whitcomb,	1843	1848
Paris C. Dunning,*	1848	1849
Joseph A. Wright,	1849	1857
Ashbel P. Willard,	1857	Died
Henry L. Lane,	1861	1861
O. P. Morton,	1861	1865

Salary, $1500, with a furnished house.
Term, four years.
Seat of Government, Indianapolis.

ILLINOIS.

TERRITORY.

	FROM	TO
Ninian Edwards,	1809	1818

STATE.

	FROM	TO
Shadrach Bond,	1818	1822
Edward Coles,	1822	1826
Ninian Edwards,	1826	1830
John Reynolds,	1830	1834
Joseph Duncan,	1834	1838
Thomas Carlin,	1838	1842
Thomas Ford,	1842	1846
Augustus C. French,	1846	1853
Joel A. Matteson,	1853	1857
William H. Bissell,	1857	1860
Richard Yates,	1860	1865

Salary, $1500.
Term, four years.
Seat of Government, Springfield.

MISSOURI.

	FROM	TO
Alexander McNair,	1820	1824
Frederick Bates,	1824	1826
John Miller,	1826	1832
Daniel Dunklin,	1832	1836
L. W. Boggs,	1836	1840
Thomas Reynolds,	1840	1844
John C. Edwards,	1844	1848
Austin A. King,	1848	1853
Sterling Price,	1853	1857
Trusten Polk,	1857	1857
Hancock Jackson (acting),	1857	1857
R. M. Stewart,	1857	1861
Claiborne F. Jackson,	1861	
H. R. Gamble,	1861	1864

Salary, $2500, with a furnished house.
Term, four years.
Seat of Government, Jefferson City.

*** During the unexpired term of Governor Whitcomb, elected in 1848 to the United States Senate.**

IOWA.

	FROM	TO
Ansel Briggs, ...	1846	1850
Stephen Hempstead, . . .	1850	1854
James W. Grimes, . . .	1854	1858
Ralph P. Lowe, ...	1858	1860
S. J. Kirkwood, ...	1860	1862
Wm. M. Stone, ...	1862	1864

Salary, $1000.
Term, four years.
Seat of Government, Des Moines City.

WISCONSIN.

TERRITORY.

Henry Dodge, ...	1836	1841
James D. Doty, ...	1841	1844
Nathaniel P. Tallmadge, .	1844	1845
Henry Dodge, ...	1845	1848

STATE.

Nelson Dewey, ...	1848	1851
Leonard J. Farwell, . . .	1851	1853
William A. Barstow, . .	1853	1855
Coles Bashford, ...	1855	1857
Alexander W. Randall, .	1857	1861
Edward Solomon, . . .	1861	1863
James T. Lewis, ...	1863	1865

Salary, $2000.
Term, two years.
Seat of Government, Madison.

CALIFORNIA.

Peter H. Burnett, . . .	1849	1851
John McDougall (acting), .	1851	1852
John Bigler, ...	1852	1856
J. Neely Johnson, . . .	1856	1858
John B. Weller, ...	1858	1860
M. S. Latham, ...	1860	1862
John G. Downey, ...	1860	1862
Leland Stanford, ...	1861	1863
Frederick F. Low, . . .	1863	1865

Salary, $6000.
Term, two years.
Seat of Government, Sacramento.

MINNESOTA.

TERRITORY.

Alexander Ramsey, . . .	1849	1853
Willis A. Gorman, . . .	1853	1857
Samuel Medary, ...	1857	1858

STATE.

Henry H. Sibley, ...	1858	1860
Alexander Ramsey, . . .	1860	1862
Stephen Miller, ...	1863	1865

Term, two years.
Seat of Government, St. Paul.

OREGON.

TERRITORY.

James Shields, . .	Aug. 14, 1848.
Joseph Lane, . . .	Aug. 18, 1848.
John P. Gaines, . .	Sept. 9, 1850.
Joseph Lane, . . .	March 16, 1853.
John W. Davis, . .	Sept. 6, 1853.
George L. Curry, .	Oct. 24, 1854.

STATE.

John Whittaker, . .	from 1859	to 1862
A. C. Gibbs, . . .	1862	1866

Salary, $1500.
Term, four years.
Seat of Government, Salem.

KANSAS.

TERRITORY.

A. H. Reeder, . . .	June 29, 1854.
John L. Dawson, . .	July 28, 1855.
Wilson Shannon, . .	Aug. 10, 1855.
John W. Geary, . .	July 30, 1856.
R. J. Walker, . . .	March 30, 1857.
J. W. Denver, . . .	Feb. 24, 1858.
Samuel Medary, . .	Dec. 1, 1858.

STATE.

Charles Robinson, . .	Jan. 30, 1861.
Thomas Carney, .	from 1861 to 1865.

Salary, $2500.
Term, four years.

WEST VIRGINIA.

Arthur I. Boreman, from 1861 to 1865
Salary, $2000.
Term, two years.
Seat of Government, Wheeling.

TERRITORY OF NEW MEXICO.

James S. Calhoun, .	Jan. 9, 1851.
William Carr Lane, .	July 15, 1852.
Solon Borland, . .	April 18, 1853.
David Merriwether, .	May 6, 1853.
Abraham Rencher, .	Aug. 17, 1857.
Henry Connelly, ...	1861.

Salary, $2500.
Term, four years.
Seat of Government, Santa Fé.

TERRITORY OF UTAH.

Brigham Young, . .	Sept. 28, 1850.
Edward J. Steptoe, .	Dec. 21, 1854.
Alfred Cummings, .	July 11, 1857.
S. S. Hastings, ...	1861.

Salary, $2500.
Term, four years.
Seat of Government, Salt Lake City.

WASHINGTON TERRITORY.

Isaac I. Stevens, . . March 17, 1853.
J. Patton Anderson, March 15, 1857.
Fayette McMullen, . May 15, 1857.
Richard D. Gholson, ... 1861.
William Pinkney, ... 1861.
Salary, $2500.
Term, four years.
Seat of Government, Olympia.

NEBRASKA TERRITORY.

William O. Butler, . June 29, 1854.
Francis Burt, . . . Aug. 2, 1854.
Mark W. Izard, . . Dec. 20, 1854.
Wm. A. Richardson, May 30, 1857.
Samuel W. Black, ... 1861.
Oliver Landers, ... 1861.
Salary, $2500.
Term, four years.
Seat of Government, Omaha City.

TERRITORY OF COLORADO.

John Evans, ... 1861.
Salary, $2500.
Term, four years.
Seat of Government, Denver City.

TERRITORY OF DAKOTA.

William Jayne, ... 1861.
Newton Edwards, ... 1863.
Salary, $2500.
Term, four years.
Seat of Government, Yancton.

TERRITORY OF NEVADA.

James W. Nye, ... 1861.
Salary, $2500.
Term, four years.
Seat of Government, Carson City.

TERRITORY OF ARIZONA.

John N. Goodwin, ... 1863.
Salary, $2500.
Term, four years.

TERRITORY OF IDAHO.

William H. Wallace, ... 1863.
Caleb Lyon, of Lyonsdale,. . . 1864.
Salary $2500.
Term, four years.

TERRITORY OF MONTANA.

Sidney Edgerton, ... 1864.
Salary, $2500.
Term, four years.

RIGHT OF SUFFRAGE IN EACH STATE.

MAINE.

The right of suffrage is nearly universal, being granted to all male citizens of twenty-one years of age and upwards, who have resided in the State for three months next preceding the election. Paupers, persons under guardianship, and Indians not taxed, are excepted.

NEW HAMPSHIRE.

Right of suffrage granted to all males of twenty-one years of age and upwards, excepting paupers, and persons excused from paying taxes at their special request.

VERMONT.

Right of suffrage extends to all males of twenty-one years of age and upwards, who have resided one year in the State next preceding the election, and are of a quiet and peaceable behavior.

MASSACHUSETTS.

Right of suffrage extends to all males of twenty-one years of age and upwards (paupers and persons under guardianship excepted), who have resided within the Commonwealth one year, and within the town or district in which they may claim a right to vote, six months next preceding any election, and who have paid a State or county tax assessed upon them within two years next preceding such election, and also to every citizen who may be by law exempted from taxation, and who may be, in all other respects, qualified as above mentioned.

CONNECTICUT.

Must be of age, have gained a settlement in the State six months, done military duty, paid a State tax, and taken the prescribed oaths.

RHODE ISLAND.

Three months' residence, and own a freehold of one hundred and thirty-four dollars. Must have attained the age of twenty-one.

NEW YORK.

Right of suffrage extends to all males of twenty-one years of age, inhabitants of the State for the last year, and residents of the county for the last six months. A colored man must have resided in the State three years, and hold a freehold of two hundred and fifty dollars, free of all incumbrance.

NEW JERSEY.

The language of the Constitution on this point is, that all persons of full age shall have a right to vote, who are worth fifty pounds, proclamation money, clear estate in the same, and have resided in the county in which they claim to vote, for twelve months immediately preceding the election. By a special act of the Legislature, every white male inhabitant of lawful age, and who has paid a tax, is considered worth fifty pounds, and therefore entitled to vote.

PENNSYLVANIA.

A citizen of the State two years, and paid a State and county tax. Persons qualified, between the ages of twenty-one and two, may vote, although they have paid no taxes.

DELAWARE.

The right of suffrage the same as in Pennsylvania.

MARYLAND.

Must be of age, one year in the State, and six months in the county, preceding the election at which he offers to vote.

VIRGINIA.

Right of suffrage extends to every white male citizen of the Commonwealth, of the age of twenty-one years, or who has a joint interest to the amount of twenty-five dollars, and having been a housekeeper one year, and been assessed with a part of the revenue of the Commonwealth, within the preceding year, and actually paid the same.

NORTH CAROLINA.

A citizen of the State one year, who has paid taxes, may vote for members of the House of Commons, but must own fifty acres of land to vote for Senators.

SOUTH CAROLINA.

Right of suffrage is granted to every free white male citizen, of the age of twenty-one years, resident two years, a freeholder of fifty acres of land, or has paid a tax the preceding year, of three shillings sterling, towards the support of Government.

GEORGIA.

The right of suffrage extends to all citizens who have attained the age of twenty-one years, and six months' residence in the county where he offers his vote, and must have paid all taxes imposed on him.

ALABAMA.

A citizen of the United States, one year in the State, and three months' residence in the county where he offers his vote.

MISSISSIPPI.

A citizen of the United States, residence in this State one year, and in the county six months, and having done military duty or paid taxes.

LOUISIANA.

Residence in the county where he offers his vote one year, and having paid taxes within the last six months.

TENNESSEE.

A citizen of the United States, and six months' residence in the county where he offers his vote.

KENTUCKY.

The right of suffrage extends to every free male white citizen of the age of twenty-one years, who has resided in the State two years, or in the county where he votes, one year next preceding.

OHIO.

Right of suffrage extends to white male inhabitants, above twenty-one years, who have resided in the State one year immediately preceding the election, and who have paid a State or county tax.

INDIANA.

Right of suffrage is granted to all male citizens of the age of twenty-one years and upwards, who have resided in the State a year immediately preceding an election.

ILLINOIS.

Residence in the State six months, but can only vote in the county where he actually resides.

MISSOURI.

A citizen of the United States, and one year's residence in the State next preceding the election, and three months in the county.

MICHIGAN.

Twenty-one years of age, and six months' residence next preceding election.

ARKANSAS.

Same as Michigan.

FLORIDA.

Twenty-one years of age, two years in the State, and six months in the county. He must also be a militia soldier.

TEXAS.

Every white person who is a citizen of the United States, has attained the age of twenty-one years, and resided in the State one year, is a qualified voter.

IOWA.

Must have attained the age of twenty-one years, resided in the State six months, and in the county where he votes, sixty days.

WISCONSIN.

White men and certain Indians, who have attained the age of twenty-one years, and resided in the State one year.

CALIFORNIA.

White men and Mexicans, who are twenty-one years of age, and have resided in the State six months, and in the county of residence thirty days.

MINNESOTA.

Every white male person, and certain Indians of the age of twenty-one years, who have been in the United States one year, and in the State four months.

OREGON.

A native or naturalized citizen, who has attained the age of twenty-one years, and resided six months in the State.

KANSAS.

Must have attained the age of twenty-one years, and resided in the State six months preceding the election.

WEST VIRGINIA.

All white male citizens, with the usual exceptions, who have attained the age of twenty-one years, and have lived in the State one year, and thirty days in the county in which he offers his vote.

QUALIFICATIONS FOR GOVERNORS, SENATORS, AND REPRESENTATIVES IN EACH STATE.

MAINE.

Governor. A native citizen of the United States, five years a citizen of the State, and thirty years of age.—*Senators.* Five years a citizen of the United States, one year of the State, and twenty-five years of age.—*Representatives.* A citizen of the United States five years, an inhabitant of the State one year, and twenty-one years of age.

NEW HAMPSHIRE.

Governor. A citizen of the United States seven years, an estate of £500 (one-half a freehold), and thirty years of age.—*Senators.* Residence in the State seven years, a freehold estate of £200, and thirty years of age.—*Representatives.* Two years an inhabitant of the State, and an estate of £100 (one-half a freehold).

VERMONT.

Governor. A citizen of the State four years.—*Senators.* A qualified voter, and thirty years of age.—*Representatives.* Persons most noted for wisdom and virtue, and who have resided in the State two years.

MASSACHUSETTS.

Governor. A citizen of the State seven years, an estate of £1000, and of the Christian religion.—*Senators.* Five years a citizen of the State, a freehold of £300, or ratable estate of £600.—*Representatives.* A citizen of the State one year, and a freehold of £100, or ratable estate of £200.

RHODE ISLAND.

Governor. A native citizen, and a freeman.—*Senators.* A native citizen, resident of the district where he is chosen, and a freeman.

CONNECTICUT.

Governor. A voter, and thirty years of age.—*Senators.* A qualified voter.—*Representatives.* A qualified voter.

NEW YORK.

Governor. A native citizen of the United States, five years a citizen of the State, a freeholder, and thirty years of age.—*Senators.* A qualified voter, and a freeholder.—*Representatives.* No qualifications.

NEW JERSEY.

Governor. A resident of the State.—No Senate; the duties performed by the Legislative Council.—*Representatives.* A citizen of the State one year, and real or personal estate of £500, proclamation money.

PENNSYLVANIA.

Governor. A citizen of the State seven years, and thirty years of age.—*Senators.* A citizen of the State four years, and of the district where chosen the last year, and twenty-five years of age.—*Representatives.* A citizen of the State three years, and for the last year a citizen of the city or county where chosen.

DELAWARE.

Governor. A citizen of the United States twelve years, of the State the last six years, and thirty-six years of age.—*Senators.* A citizen of the State three years, a freehold of two hundred acres, or £1000, and twenty-seven years of age.—*Representatives.* A citizen of the State three years, and twenty-four years of age.

MARYLAND.

Governor. A resident of the State above five years, and twenty-five years of age.—*Senators.* A resident of the State three years, and twenty-five years of age. —*Representatives.* Resident in the county where chosen one year.

VIRGINIA.

Governor. A native citizen of the United States, citizen of the State five years, and thirty years of age; ineligible for three years after the first term.—*Senators.* A resident and freeholder in the district where chosen, and thirty years of age. —*Representatives.* A resident and freeholder in the county where chosen, and twenty-five years of age.

NORTH CAROLINA.

Governor. A resident in the State five years, freehold in the State of more than £1000, and thirty years of age.—*Senators.* A citizen of the county where chosen one year, and three hundred acres of land.—*Representatives.* A citizen of the county where chosen one year, one hundred acres of land in fee or for the term of his life.

SOUTH CAROLINA.

Governor. A citizen of the State ten years, an estate of £1500 sterling, clear of debt, and thirty years of age.—*Senators.* A citizen of the State five years, a resident of the district where chosen, and an estate of £300 sterling; or, not being a resident, an estate of £1000, and thirty years of age.—*Representatives.* A citizen of the State three years, a resident, and an estate of five hundred acres of land, ten negroes, or £150 sterling in real estate; or, not being a resident, an estate of £500 sterling.

GEORGIA.

Governor. A citizen of the United States twelve years, and of the State six years, an estate of five hundred acres of land, and other property amounting to $4000 more than debts due, and thirty years of age.—*Senators.* A citizen of the United States nine years, and of the State three years, a freehold of $500, or taxable property of $1000 more than debts due, all legal taxes paid, and twenty-five years of age.—*Representatives.* A citizen of the United States seven years, and of the State three years, a freehold of $250, or taxable property of $500 more than debts due, and all legal taxes paid.

ALABAMA.

Governor. A native citizen of the United States, and a citizen of the State four years, thirty years of age, and ineligible for more than four successive years.—*Senators.* A citizen of the United States, of the State two years, and of the district where chosen one year, and twenty-seven years of age.—*Representatives.* A citizen of the United States, of the State two years, and of the county where chosen one year, and twenty-one years of age.

MISSISSIPPI.

Governor. A citizen of the United States twenty years, and of the State five years, a freehold estate of $2000, and thirty years of age; ineligible for more than four successive years.—*Senators.* A citizen of the United States and of the State four years, the last year residing in the district where chosen, and thirty years of age.—*Representatives.* A citizen of the United States and of the State two years, the last year residing in the county where chosen, a freehold estate of $500, and twenty-one years of age.

LOUISIANA.

Governor. A citizen of the United States and of the State six years, an estate of $5000, and thirty-five years of age.—*Senators.* A citizen of the United States, of the State four years, and in the district were chosen one year, an estate of $1000, and twenty-seven years of age.—*Representatives.* A citizen of the United States, of the State two years, and of the county where chosen one year, an estate in land of $500, and twenty-one years of age.

TENNESSEE.

Governor. A citizen of the United States and of the State seven years, and thirty years of age.—*Senators.* A citizen of the United States, three years' residence in the State, and in the county where chosen one year, and thirty years of age.—*Representatives.* A citizen of the United States and of the State three years, residence in the county where chosen one year, and twenty-one years of age.

KENTUCKY.

Governor. A citizen of the United States and of the State six years, thirty-five years of age, and ineligible for more than one term in seven years.—*Senators.* A citizen of the United States, of the State six years, and of the district where chosen the last year, and thirty-five years of age.—*Representatives.* A citizen of the United States, of the State two years, and of the county where chosen the last year, and twenty-four years of age.

OHIO.

Governor. A citizen of the United States twelve years, an inhabitant of the State four years, and thirty-five years of age.—*Senators.* A citizen of the United States, and of the district where chosen two years, having paid a State and county tax, and thirty years of age.—*Representatives.* A citizen of the United States, an inhabitant of the State, and a resident in the county where chosen one year, having paid a State or county tax, and twenty-five years of age.

INDIANA.

Governor. A citizen of the United States ten years, and of the State five years, and thirty years of age.—*Senators.* A citizen of the United States, of the State two years, and of the district where chosen the last year, having paid a State or county tax, and twenty-five years of age.—*Representatives.* A citizen of the United States, and of the State and county where chosen one year, having paid a State or county tax, and twenty-one years of age.

ILLINOIS.

Governor. A citizen of the United States thirty years, and of the State two years, thirty years of age, and ineligible for two successive terms.—*Senators.* A citizen of the United States, and of the district where chosen the last year, having paid a State or county tax, and twenty-five years of age.—*Representatives.* A citizen of the United States, and an inhabitant of the State and county where chosen, having paid a State or county tax, and twenty-one years of age.

MISSOURI.

Governor. A native citizen of the United States, a resident of the State four years, and thirty-five years of age.—*Senators*. A citizen of the United States, of the State four years, and of the district where chosen one year, having paid a State or county tax, and thirty years of age.—*Representatives*. A citizen of the United States, of the State two years, and of the county where chosen one year, having paid a State or county tax, and twenty-four years of age.

MICHIGAN.

Governor. A citizen of the United States five years, and a resident of the State the last two years.—*Senators*. A citizen of the United States, and a qualified voter in the county where chosen.—*Representatives*. Same as the Senators.

ARKANSAS.

Governor. A native citizen of the United States, or a resident of the State ten years previous to the adoption of the Constitution, and four years preceding the election.—*Senators*. A citizen of the United States, a resident of the State one year, and thirty years of age.—*Representatives*. A citizen of the United States, a resident of the county where chosen, and twenty-five years of age.

FLORIDA.

Governor. Must be thirty years of age, have been a citizen of the United States for ten years, or an inhabitant of Florida at the time of the adoption of the Constitution, and a resident of the State five years preceding the day of election.—*Senators*. A citizen of the United States, a resident of the State for two years, one year a resident of the district in which he resides, and must be twenty-five years of age.—*Representatives*. Must have attained the age of twenty-one years, and in other particulars qualified as are the Senators.

TEXAS.

Governor. Must be thirty years of age, a citizen of the United States, and have been a resident of the State for three years preceding his election.—*Senators*. Must have attained the age of thirty years, be a citizen of the United States, a resident in the State for three years preceding his election, and one year in the district where he resides.—*Representatives*. Must be a citizen of the United States, have resided in the State two years, in his district one year, and have attained the age of twenty-one years.

IOWA.

Governor. Must be thirty years of age, a citizen of the United States, and a resident of the State for two years.—*Senators*. Must be twenty-five years of age, a citizen of the United States, a resident of the State for one year, and of the district where he resides at least sixty days.—*Representatives*. Must be twenty-one years of age, and in other respects possess the qualifications of Senators.

WISCONSIN.

Governor. No person except a citizen of the United States, and a qualified elector of the State, shall be eligible to this office.—*Senators and Representatives*. No person shall be eligible to the Legislature who shall not have resided in the State one year, and be a qualified elector in the district where he resides.

CALIFORNIA.

Governor. Must be twenty-five years of age, a citizen of the United States, and a resident of the State for two years.—*Senators and Representatives*. Must be qualified electors, residents of the State one year, and of their districts six months.

MINNESOTA.

Governor. Must be a citizen of the United States, twenty-five years of age, and a resident of the State for one year.—*Senators and Representatives.* Shall be qualified voters of the State, and shall have resided one year in the State, and six months in the district from which they are elected.

OREGON.

Governor. Must be a citizen of the United States, thirty years of age, and three years a resident of the State.—*Senators and Representatives.* Must be twenty-one years of age, citizens of the United States, and residents of their several districts for one year preceding their election.

KANSAS.

Governor. Must be thirty years of age, a citizen of the United States, and have resided two years in the State.—*Senators.* Must be twenty-five years of age, a citizen of the United States, and a resident of the State for one year.—*Representatives.* Must be twenty-one years of age, and possess the other qualifications of Senators.

WEST VIRGINIA.

Governor. His qualifications are not specified in the Constitution of the State.—*Senators and Representatives.* Must have been residents of the district or county where chosen for one year next preceding the election.

www.ingramcontent.com/pod-product-compliance
Lightning Source LLC
LaVergne TN
LVHW021244110826
845150LV00002B/404
* 9 7 8 1 4 2 5 5 6 1 2 1 5 *